The Blair Reader

Third Edition

EDITED BY

Laurie G. Kirszner

Philadelphia College of Pharmacy and Science

Stephen R. Mandell

Drexel University

Prentice Hall, Upper Saddle River, NJ 07458

Library of Congress Cataloging-in-Publication Data

The Blair reader / Stephen R. Mandell, Laurie G. Kirszner.—3rd ed.
   p. cm.
   Includes index.
   ISBN 0–13–080140–2
   1. College readers. 2. English language—Rhetoric. I. Mandell,
Stephen R. II. Kirszner, Laurie G.
PE1417.B54 1998
808'.0427—dc21

98-2805
CIP

Editorial Director: Charlyce Jones Owen
Acquisitions Editor: Leah Jewell
Director of Production and Manufacturing: Barbara Kittle
Senior Managing Editor: Bonnie Biller
Production Editor: Randy Pettit
Editorial Assistant: Patricia Castiglione
Manufacturing Manager: Nick Sklitsis
Prepress and Manufacturing Buyer: Mary Ann Gloriande
Marketing Director: Gina Sluss
Marketing Manager: Rob Mejia
Cover Design Director: Jayne Conte
Cover Design: Karen Salzbach
Cover Art: Juan Gris (1887–1927) Spanish, "Le Livre" ("The Book")

This book was set in 10/12 Palatino by Lithokraft II
and printed and bound by Courier-Westford.
The cover was printed by Phoenix Color Corp.

For permission to use copyrighted material, grateful acknowledgment is made
to the copyright holders listed on pages 827–832, which is considered an extension of this
copyright page.

Printed in the United States of America
10 9 8 7 6 5 4 3 2 1

ISBN 0-13-080140-2

Prentice-Hall International (UK) Limited, *London*
Prentice-Hall of Australia Pty. Limited, *Sydney*
Prentice-Hall Canada Inc., *Toronto*
Prentice-Hall Hispanoamerica, S.A., *Mexico*
Prentice-Hall of India Private Limited, *New Delhi*
Prentice-Hall of Japan, Inc., *Tokyo*
Simon & Schuster Asia Pte. Ltd., *Singapore*
Editora Prentice-Hall do Brasil, Ltda., *Rio de Janeiro*

Contents

Rhetorical Contents

Cause and Effect

Comparison and Contrast

Classification and Division

Definition

Argument and Persuasion

Topical Clusters

Belief and Doubt

Conformity and Rebellion

Self-Image

Fear and Courage

Property, Territoriality, and Space

What's in a Name?

Working

The Language of Prejudice

Mother Tongues

Stereotypes

Developing Nations

Preface

After more than twenty years of teaching composition, we have come to believe that students are most enriched and engaged if they view the reading and writing they do as a way of participating in ongoing public discussions about subjects that matter to them. This focus enables students to discover their own ideas and to see how these ideas fit into a larger discourse community, where ideas gain meaning and value. We created *The Blair Reader* to encourage students to make their own contribution to the public discussion and to help them realize that ideas take shape only in response to other ideas.

Another reason we decided to create *The Blair Reader* was that we could not find a reader that truly addressed our needs as teachers. We—like you—expect (and believe we are entitled to) compelling reading selections that engage both instructors and students in a spirited exchange. We also expect selections that reflect (and are enriched, not limited, by) the diversity of ideas that characterizes our schools and our society. We expect writers to speak in distinctive voices, to treat issues that concern us deeply, and to use language that challenges and provokes us. In addition, we expect questions that accompany readings to encourage readers to participate in the process of creating meaning—in other words, questions that ask "What does this mean *to you?*" not simply "What does this mean?" In short, we expect a book that stimulates discussion and that prompts students to discover new ideas and to see familiar ideas from new perspectives. These expectations guided us as we developed *The Blair Reader* and as we worked to enhance its usefulness in this new edition.

The Reading Selections and Their Arrangement

We began work on *The Blair Reader* determined that it would include readings that composition instructors really enjoyed teaching. To accomplish this goal, we surveyed hundreds of instructors and asked them what essays they thought were the most readable and teachable. To their selections we added our own favorites. After we assembled our table of contents, teachers from all over the country tested the readings and apparatus. The result of this effort is a reader that contains the most readable and teachable selections we could find.

To create the third edition, we followed a similar process, relying on our own experience as users of the first two editions in the classroom as well as on the thoughtful comments of the many other teachers who generously shared their reactions to the first two editions with us. The result is a text that includes 108 essays and 8 poems. The readings are arranged in ten tightly focused units: Family and Memory, Issues in Education, The Politics of Language, The Media's Message, Women and Men, The American Dream, The Way We Live Now, Medical Practice and Responsibility, Earth in the Balance, and Making Choices. These thematic groupings are diverse enough to allow many options yet focused enough for meaningful discussion and writing.

New to this edition are three features designed to increase the flexibility and usefulness of the book. The **Two Perspectives on . . .** feature presents two complementary readings that introduce students to the chapter's theme and motivate them to use their critical thinking skills. These paired readings, accompanied by a set of "Responding to Reading" questions, now appear at the beginning of every chapter. Each chapter ends with a **Focus** question that is followed by a group of essays that take a variety of different positions on a single debatable issue. For example, Chapter 2, "Issues in Education," asks "What is good teaching?" and Chapter 10, "Making Choices," asks "Are all ideas created equal?" The essays in these sections not only encourage students to add their voices to an ongoing debate but also illustrate that complex issues often elicit more than two points of view. Also new to this edition is a **Widening the Focus** feature that identifies essays in other chapters of the book that offer insight into the issues raised by the "Focus" question.

As we worked on the third edition, we added readings that would tighten the emphasis of each chapter as well as increase students' interest and involvement. Among the selections new to this edition are Neil Postman's "Virtual Students, Digital Classrooms," Bobby Fong's "Commonplaces about Teaching: Second Thoughts," Jorge Amselle's "¡Inglés, Sí!" Madeline Levine's "Media and the Adolescent," Stephanie Gutmann's "Sex and the Soldier," Susan K. Cahn's "You've Come a Long Way, Maybe." Bharati Mukherjee's "American Dreamer," Webb Hubbell's "Life in Prison," Stephen L. Carter's "Rush to Lethal Judgment," Linda Pastan's "Ethics," and Lawrence Krauss's "Equal Time for Nonsense."

These and other new readings were selected to introduce students to the ongoing ethical debates surrounding issues like divorce and the nontraditional family, communication in the information age, inequalities in education, the problems of the disabled and the homeless, stereotyping in the media, euthanasia and assisted suicide, sexism, affirmative action, the environment, animal rights, and freedom of speech. The result of our revision is a table of contents that combines time-tested favorites with provocative new pieces, thereby illustrating to students that ideas can continue to be "relevant" long after a selection was written.

Finally, the selections in *The Blair Reader,* third edition, continue to represent a wide variety of rhetorical patterns and types of discourse as well as a variety of themes, issues, and positions. In addition to essays, *The Blair Reader* contains speeches, meditations, newspaper and magazine articles, and poems. The level of diction ranges from the relaxed formality of E. B. White's "Once More to the Lake" to the biting satire of Marge Piercy's

"Barbie Doll." Every effort has been made, too, to include a diverse selection of voices, because we believe that students can best discover their own voices by becoming acquainted with the voices of others.

Resources for Students

We designed the apparatus in *The Blair Reader* to involve students and to encourage them to respond critically to what they read. Their reactions can then become the basis for more focused thinking and writing. In order to facilitate this process, we have included the following special features:

- **Introduction: Becoming a Critical Reader** explains and illustrates the process of reading and reacting critically to texts and formulating varied and original responses.

- **Student Voices**, a collection of brief, informal responses (from students' writing journals) to the unit's theme, opens each chapter.

- A brief chapter introduction, **Preparing to Read and Write,** places each chapter's broad theme in a narrower social or political context, helping students connect with the chapter's specific ideas and issues. A series of questions at the end of these chapter introductions helps students to focus their intellectual and emotional reactions to individual selections in the context of the chapter's larger issues.

- **Headnotes** that accompany each selection provide useful biographical information and often offer insight into the writer's motivation or purpose.

- **Responding to Reading** questions that follow each selection focus on thematic and rhetorical considerations. By asking students to do more than read essays simply for facts or information, these questions help them realize that reading is an interactive and intellectually stimulating process and that they have something valuable to contribute.

- **Writing** suggestions at the end of each chapter ask students to respond in writing to the ideas they have encountered. These questions encourage students to explore relationships among readings and to connect readings to their own lives.

- **A Rhetorical Table of Contents,** located in the front of the book on pages viii–xii, groups the text's readings in categories that reflect the way they arrange material: narrative, description, process, comparison and contrast, and so on.

- **Topical Clusters,** narrowly focused thematic units, (pp. xiii–xx), offer students and teachers additional options for pairing and grouping readings.

Resources for Instructors

Because we wanted *The Blair Reader* to be a rich and comprehensive resource for instructors, we developed an **Instructor's Resource Manual** to accompany the text. This manual, designed to serve as a useful and accessible classroom companion, incorporates teaching techniques drawn from our years in the classroom as well as reactions of our own students to the selections.

The **Instructor's Resource Manual,** updated for this edition by Connie Rothwell of the University of North Carolina at Charlotte, includes the following features:

- **Setting Up the Unit** begins each chapter by focusing on a rhetorical or pedagogical strategy that instructors can use in their discussion of the chapter.

- **Confronting the Issues** offers a range of activities—most of them collaborative—designed to explore some of the issues suggested by the chapter's readings.

- **For Openers,** the first prompt for each selection, is designed to initiate class discussion.

- **Teaching Strategies** for each selection provide suggestions for eliciting students' response to the reading, stimulating their discussions, and providing further information on the writer or the writing selection.

- **Collaborative Activities** present group activities through which students can develop insight and understanding by exchanging ideas with others.

- **Writer's Options** offer possibilities for exploring (in a journal entry or a longer piece of writing) personal responses, stylistic techniques, or thematic issues suggested by the selection.

- **Multimedia Resources** point to "texts" outside the scope of the anthology—movies, songs, cartoons, Internet resources, and the like—that address either the selection itself or the issues it raises.

- **Suggested Answers for "Responding to Reading"** questions provide possible responses to the questions that follow the selection.

- **Additional "Responding to Reading"** questions are supplementary questions for those instructors who want more editorial apparatus than the book includes.

- **Teaching Perspectives** prompts facilitate using the two or three readings in the chapter that have been grouped together because they provide complementary perspectives on an issue.

We encourage you to use the Instructor's Manual to complement your own proven strategies. We also encourage you to let us know your reactions to the Manual and your suggestions for making it better. We are especially interested in hearing about classroom strategies that you use successfully and reading selections that have consistently appealed to your students. In future editions of the Instructor's Resource Manual, we would like to include these suggestions along with the names of the individuals who submitted them. Just write us in care of Prentice Hall, One Lake Street, Upper Saddle River, NJ 07458.

Acknowledgments

The Blair Reader is the result of a fruitful collaboration between the two of us, between us and our students, between us and Prentice Hall, and between us and you—our colleagues who told us what you wanted in a reader.

At Prentice Hall, we want to thank our editor, Leah Jewell, and her assistant, Patricia Castiglione. We appreciate the organizational skills of Production Editor Randy Pettit, and we thank him for his patience and professionalism as he guided the book through production. We also thank our exceptional copyeditor, Margaret Ritchie, and Connie Rothwell for her creative contributions to the Instructor's Resource Manual.

As always, Mark Gallaher's editorial instincts were exactly right; as always, his contributions are much appreciated. (And, as always, he deserves his own paragraph.)

In preparing *The Blair Reader*, third edition, we benefited at every stage from the assistance and suggestions of colleagues from across the country: Kerry A. Reilly, University of New Hampshire; Jeanann Rader, Camden Community College; Mary E. Hallet, University of New Hampshire; Jeslyn Medoff, University of Massachusetts, Boston; Sue Mehlich, Pitt Community College; Anne Righton Malone, University of New Hampshire; Ted McFerrin, Collin County Community College; Bryan Polk, The Pennsylvania State University, Abington; Timothy P. Twohill, Lee College; Carolyn Allen, University of Washington; Sarah Markgraf, Bergen Community College; Beverly G. Galvan, Clark College; Charles Ross, Purdue University; Susan Kelly, Saddleback College; Suzanne I. Staszak-Silva, Hofstra University; William Keough, Fitchburg State College; Victoria Lague, Miami-Dade Community College; Andrew Tomko, Bergen Community College.

On the home front, we once again "round up the usual suspects" to thank—Mark, Adam, and Rebecca Kirszner and Demi, David, and Sarah Mandell. And, of course, we thank each other: it really has been a "beautiful friendship."

—*Laurie G. Kirszner,*
Stephen R. Mandell

INTRODUCTION:
BECOMING A
CRITICAL READER

In his autobiographical essay "The Library Card" (p. 437), Richard Wright describes his early exposure to the world of books. He says, "The plots and stories in the novels did not interest me so much as the point of view revealed. I gave myself over to each novel without reserve, without trying to criticize it; it was enough for me to see and feel something different. Reading was like a drug."

It is a rare person today for whom reading can hold this magic or inspire this awe. Most of us take the ability to read and the access to books for granted. As a student, you've probably learned to be pragmatic about your reading. In fact, "reading" most likely has come to mean reading assigned pages in a textbook. Whether the book's subject is modern American history, principles of corporate management, or quantum mechanics, you probably tend to read largely for information, expecting a book's ideas to be accessible and free of ambiguity and the book to be clearly written and logically organized.

In addition to reading textbooks, however, you also read essays and journal articles, fiction and poetry. These present special challenges because you read them not just for information but also to discover your own ideas about what the writer is saying—what the work means to you, how you react to it, why you react as you do, and how your reactions differ from the responses of other readers. And because the writers express opinions and convey impressions as well as facts, your role as a reader must be more active than it is when you read a textbook. Here, reading becomes not only a search for information, but also a search for meaning.

Reading and Meaning

Like many readers, you may assume that meaning is hidden somewhere between the lines and that if you only ask the right questions or unearth the appropriate clues, you will be able to discover exactly what the writer is getting at. But reading is not a game of hide-and-seek in which you must find ideas that have been hidden by the writer. As current reading theory demonstrates, meaning is not contained within a text; rather, it is created by the interaction between reader and text.

One way to explain this interactive process is to draw an analogy between a text—a work being read—and a word. A word is not the one natural equivalent of the thing it signifies. The word *dog,* for example, does not evoke the image of a furry, four-legged animal in all parts of the world. To speakers of Spanish, the word *perro* elicits the same mental picture *dog* does in English-speaking countries. Not only does the word *dog* have meaning only in a specific cultural context, but even within that context it evokes different images in different people. Some people may picture a collie, others a poodle, and still others a particular pet named Rex or a snarling attack dog.

Like a word, a text can have different meanings in different cultures—or even in different historical time periods. Each reader brings to the text associations that come from the cultural community in which he or she lives. These associations are determined by experience and education as well as by ethnic group, class, religion, gender, and many other factors. Each of these factors contributes to how a person views the world. Each reader also brings to the text expectations, desires, and prejudices that influence how he or she reacts to and interprets it. Thus, it is entirely possible for two readers to have very different, but equally valid, interpretations of the same text. (This does *not* mean, of course, that a text can mean whatever any individual reader wishes it to mean. To be valid, an interpretation must be supported by what actually appears in the text.)

To get an idea of the range of possible interpretations that can be suggested by a single text, consider some of the responses different readers might have to E. B. White's classic essay "Once More to the Lake" (p. 23).

In "Once More to the Lake" White tells a story about his visit with his son to a lake in Maine in the 1940s. White compares this visit with those he made as a boy with his own father. Throughout the essay, White describes the changes that have occurred since he was first there —changes that frustrate his desire to "revisit old haunts." Memories from the past flood his consciousness and lead him to remember things he did when he was a boy. At one point, after he and his son have been feeding worms to fish, he remembers doing the same thing with his father and has trouble separating the past from the present. As a result, White realizes that he will soon be just a memory in his son's mind— as his father is just a memory in his.

White had specific goals in mind in this essay. His title, "Once More to the Lake," indicates that he intended to compare his childhood and adult visits to the lake. The organization of ideas in the essay, the use of flashbacks, and the choice of particular transitional phrases reinforce this structure. In addition, descriptive details—such as the image of the tarred road that replaced the dirt road—remind readers, as well as White himself, that the years have made the lake site different from what it once was. The essay ends with the image of the son standing on the dock in cold, dripping bathing trunks and the father suddenly feeling the "chill of death."

Despite White's specific intentions, each person reading "Once More to the Lake" will respond to it somewhat differently. Young male readers might identify with the boy. If they have ever spent a vacation at a lake, they might have experienced the "peace and goodness and jollity" of the whole summer scene. Female readers might also want to share these experiences, but they might feel excluded because only males are described in the essay. Urban readers who have never been on a fishing trip might not feel the same nostalgia for the woods that White feels. To them living in the woods away from the comforts of home might seem to be an unthinkably uncomfortable ordeal. Older readers might identify with White, the adult, sympathizing with his efforts to recapture the past and seeing his son as naively innocent of the hardships of life.

Thus, although each person who reads White's essay will read the same words, each will be likely to *interpret* it differently and to see different things as important. This is because much is left open to interpretation. All essays leave blanks or gaps—missing words, phrases, or images—that readers have to fill in. In "Once More to the Lake," for example, readers must imagine what had happened in the years that separated White's last visit to the lake and the trip he took with his son.

These gaps in the text create *ambiguities*—words, phrases, descriptions, or ideas that need to be interpreted by the reader. For instance, when you read the words "One summer, along about 1904, my father rented a camp on a lake," how do you picture the camp? White's description of the setting contains a great deal of detail, but no matter how many sensory impressions he conveys, he cannot provide a complete verbal representation of the lakeside camp. He must rely on the reader's ability to visualize the setting and supply details from his or her own experience.

Readers also bring their *emotional associations* to a text. For example, how readers react to White's statement above depends, in part, on their feelings about their own fathers. If White's words bring to mind a parent who is loving, strong, and protective, they will respond favorably; if the essay calls up memories of a parent who is distant, bad-tempered, excitable, or even abusive, they may respond negatively.

Because each reader views the text from a slightly different angle, each may also see a different *focus* as central to "Once More to the Lake."

Some might see nature as the primary element in the essay and believe that White's purpose is to condemn the gradual encroachment of human beings on the environment. Others might see the passage of time as the central focus. Still others might see the initiation theme as being the most important element of the essay: each boy is brought to the wilderness by his father, and each eventually passes from childhood innocence to adulthood.

Finally, each reader may *evaluate* the essay differently. Some readers might think "Once More to the Lake" is boring because it has little action and deals with a subject in which they have no interest. Others might believe the essay is a brilliant meditation that makes an impact through its vivid description and imaginative figurative language. Still others might see the essay as a mixed bag—admitting, for example, that although White is an excellent stylist, he is also self-centered and self-indulgent. After all, they might argue, the experiences he describes are available only to those in relatively privileged segments of society and are irrelevant to others.

Reading Critically

Reading critically means interacting with a text, keeping an open mind that permits you to question the text's assumptions and to formulate and reformulate judgments about its ideas. Think of reading as a dialogue between you and the text: sometimes the author will assert himself or herself, and at other times you will dominate the conversation. Remember, though, that a critical voice is a thoughtful and responsible one, not one that shouts down the opposition. Deborah Tannen makes this distinction clear in her essay "The Triumph of the Yell" (p. 276):

> In many university classrooms, "critical thinking" means reading someone's life work, then ripping it to shreds. Though critique is surely one form of critical thinking, so are integrating ideas from disparate fields and examining the context out of which they grew. Opposition does not lead to truth when we ask only "What's wrong with this argument?" and never "What can we use from this in building a new theory, a new understanding?"

In other words, being a critical reader does not necessarily mean quarreling and contradicting; more often, it means asking questions, exploring reactions, and remaining open to new ideas.

Asking the following questions as you read will help you to become aware of the relationships between the writer's perspective and your own.

What audience does the writer address? Does the work offer clues to the writer's intended audience? For example, the strong title of Susan Estrich's essay on women's colleges, "Separate Is Better" (p. 125), not only states her position but also suggests that she is questioning her readers' preconceived notions about the value of coed versus single-sex education. The way her arguments challenge these notions indicates that she sees her readers as knowledgeable but probably not inclined to agree with her position.

What is the writer's purpose? What is the writer trying to accomplish in the essay? For example, is the writer attempting to explain, persuade, justify, evaluate, describe, debunk, entertain, preach, browbeat, threaten, or frighten? What strategies does the writer use to achieve this purpose? Does the writer, like Jane Goodall in "A Plea for the Chimps" (p. 610) or Rachel Carson in "The Obligation to Endure" (p. 669), try to move readers to action? To achieve a particular objective, does the writer use logic, emotion, or a combination of the two? Also consider whether the writer appeals to the prejudices or fears of readers, engages in name calling, or in any other way attempts to influence readers unfairly.

What kind of voice does the writer use? Does the writer seem to talk directly to readers? If so, does the writer's subjectivity get in the way, or does it help to involve readers? Does the writer's voice seem distant, even formal? Writers have many options, and each can have a different effect on readers. For example, an emotional tone like the one Martin Luther King, Jr., uses in "I Have a Dream" (p. 431), can inspire; an intimate tone, like the one Susan J. Douglas uses in "Why the Shirelles Mattered" (p. 309), can involve readers and create empathy. A straightforward, forthright voice, like those of Gloria Steinem in "Sex, Lies, and Advertising" (p. 279) and Deborah Lipstadt in "Denying the Holocaust" (p. 811), can make the writer's ideas seem reasonable and credible. An ironic tone can amuse readers or alienate them; a distant, reserved tone can inspire awe or discomfort.

What emotional response is the writer trying to evoke? In "We May Be Brothers" (p. 435) and in "Letter to President Pierce, 1855" (p. 660), Chief Seattle maintains a calm, unemotional tone even though he is describing the defeat of his people and the destruction of their land. By maintaining a dignified tone and avoiding bitterness and resentment, he succeeds in evoking sympathy and respect in his readers rather than forcing them to take a defensive stance. Other writers may attempt to evoke other emotional responses: amusement, nostalgia, curiosity, wonder over the grandeur or mystery of the world that surrounds us, even anger or fear.

What position does the writer take on the issue? Barbara Grizutti Harrison's title "Getting Away with Murder" (p. 531) clearly reveals her position on murder defendants who claim to be society's victims; Martin Luther King, Jr. conveys his position in equally unambiguous terms when, in "Letter from Birmingham Jail" (p. 749), he asserts that people have a responsibility to disobey laws they consider unjust. Keep in mind, though, that a writer's position may not always be as obvious as it is in these two examples. As you read, look carefully for statements that suggest the writer's position on a particular subject or issue—and be sure you understand how you feel about that position, particularly if it is an unusual or controversial one. Do you agree or disagree? Can you explain your reasoning? Remember, however, that a writer's support for a particular position, even if it is at odds with your own, does not automatically render the work suspect or its ideas invalid. Ideas that you might consider shocking or absurd may be readily accepted by many other readers. Unexpected, puzzling, or even repellent positions should encourage you to read carefully and thoughtfully, trying to understand the larger historical and cultural context of a writer's ideas.

How does the writer support his or her position? What kind of support is provided? Is it convincing? Does the writer use a series of individual examples, as Alleen Pace Nilsen does in "Sexism in English: A 1990s Update" (p. 214), or an extended example, as Mary Gordon does in "Mary Cassatt" (p. 374)? Does the writer use statistics, as Arthur Levine does in "The Making of a Generation" (p. 513), or does he or she rely primarily on personal experiences, as Brent Staples does in "Just Walk On By" (p. 545)? Does the writer quote experts, as Deborah Tannen does in "Marked Women" (p. 396), or present anecdotal information, as Jenny Lyn Bader does in "Larger Than Life" (p. 503)? Why does the writer choose a particular kind of support? Does he or she supply enough information to support the essay's points? Are the examples given relevant to the issues being discussed? Is the writer's reasoning valid, or do the arguments seem forced or unrealistic? Are any references in the work unfamiliar to you? If so, do they arouse your curiosity, or do they discourage you from reading further?

What beliefs, assumptions, or preconceived ideas do you have that color your responses to a work? Does the writer challenge any ideas that you accept as "natural" or "obvious"? For example, does Garrett Hardin's controversial stand in "Lifeboat Ethics: The Case against 'Aid' that Harms" (p. 764) shock you or violate your sense of fair play? Does the fact that you are against physician-assisted suicide prevent you from appreciating the perspective of Jack Kevorkian's essay "A Case of Assisted Suicide" (p. 643)?

Does your background or experience give you any special insights that enable you to understand or interpret the writer's ideas? Are the writer's experiences similar to or different from your own? Is the writer like or unlike you in terms of age, ethnic background, gender, and social class? How do the similarities and differences between you and the writer affect your reaction to the work? For example, you may be able to understand Amy Tan's "Mother Tongue" (p. 200) better than other students because you too speak one language at home and another in public. You may have a unique perspective on the problems Raymond Carver examines in "My Father's Life" (p. 53) because you too have an alcoholic parent. Or, your volunteer work at a shelter may have helped you understand the plight of the homeless as described by Lars Eighner in "On Dumpster Diving" (p. 549). Any experiences you have can help you to understand a writer's ideas and shape your response to them.

Recording Your Reactions

It is a good idea to read a work at least twice: first to get a general sense of the writer's ideas and then to think critically about these ideas. As you read critically, you interact with the text and respond in ways that will help you to develop an interpretation of it. This process of coming to understand the text will in turn prepare you to discuss the work with others and, perhaps, to write about it.

As you read and reread, record your responses; if you don't, you will forget many of your best ideas. Two activities can help you keep a record of the ideas that come to you as you read: **highlighting**—using a system of symbols and underlining to identify key ideas—and **annotating**—writing down your responses and interpretations.

When you react to what you read, don't be afraid to question or challenge the writer's ideas. As you read and make annotations, you may be bothered by or disagree with some of the writer's ideas. Jot your responses down in the margin; when you have time, you can think more about what you have written. These informal responses may be the beginning of a thought process that will lead you to an original insight—and, perhaps, to an interesting piece of writing.

Highlighting and annotating helped a student to understand the passage below, which is excerpted from Jane Goodall's essay "A Plea for the Chimps" (p. 610). As she prepared to write about Goodall's essay, the student identified the writer's key points, asked pertinent questions, made a connection with another essay, Claire McCarthy's "Dog Lab" (p. 774), and eventually reached her own conclusions. As she read, she underlined some of the passage's important words and ideas, using arrows to indicate relationships between them. She also circled the word *physiology*, to remind her to look up its meaning later on, and she wrote down questions and comments as they occurred to her.

The chimpanzee is more like us, genetically, than any other animal. It is because of similarities in physiology, in biochemistry, in the immune system, that medical science makes use of living bodies of chimpanzees in its search for cures and vaccines for a variety of human diseases.

What use?

There are also behavioral, psychological and emotional similarities between chimpanzees and humans, resemblances so striking that they raise a serious ethical question: are we justified in using an animal so close to us—an animal, moreover, that is highly endangered in its African forest home—as a human substitute in medical experimentation? *

Is there an alternative? Other animals? Computer models?

In the long run, we can hope that scientists will find ways of exploring human physiology and disease, and of testing cures and vaccines, that do not depend on the use of living animals of any sort. A number of steps in this direction have already been taken, prompted in large part by growing public awareness of the suffering that is being inflicted on millions of animals. More and more people are beginning to realize that nonhuman animals—even rats and guinea pigs—are not just unfeeling machines but are capable of enjoying their lives, and of feeling fear, pain and despair.

? Compare with "Dog Lab" (Like humans)

But until alternatives have been found, medical science will continue to use animals in the battle against human disease and suffering. And some of those animals will continue to be chimpanzees.

Is this justified? Does Goodall think it is?

Reading to Write

Much of the reading you will do as a student will be done to prepare you for writing. Writing helps you focus your ideas about various issues; in addition, the process of writing can lead you in unexpected directions, thereby enabling you to discover new insights. In fact, the most rewarding way to examine a particular text is not just to read and think about it but also to write about it. With this in mind, we have included in *The Blair Reader* a number of features that will help you as you read and prepare to write about its selections.

The readings in *The Blair Reader* are arranged in ten thematic chapters, each offering a variety of different vantage points from which to view the theme. Each chapter in the book opens with a collection of

"Student Voices," brief comments by college students about the theme the chapter explores. Next, a brief introduction, "Preparing to Read and Write," provides a context for the theme and lists questions to guide your thinking as you read the works in the chapter. These questions are designed to help you to see the reading selections from different angles and thus to sharpen your critical skills and begin to apply those skills effectively.

Each chapter's readings begin with "Two Perspectives" that offer a close-up view—often presented in personal, subjective terms—of the chapter's theme. For example, Chapter 3, "The Politics of Language," opens with Frederick Douglass's essay "Learning to Read and Write" and Malcolm X's "A Homemade Education." Both essays discuss the importance of reading and writing and illustrate how these skills can offer access to intellectual and political awareness. Each chapter ends with a "Focus" question that introduces a group of thought-provoking essays that take different positions on a complex issue. For example, Chapter 4's focus question, "Does media violence hurt?" is followed by three essays: John Grisham's "Unnatural Killers," John Leonard's "Why Blame TV?" and Madeline Levine's "Media and the Adolescent." ("Widening the Focus" suggestions identify several additional essays in other chapters in the book that also offer possible answers to the focus question.)

Following each reading selection are three questions to help you think about and respond—in discussion and perhaps in writing—to what you have read. These "Responding to Reading" questions focus on the reader's side of the interaction, encouraging you to think critically about the writer's ideas or to focus on a particular strategy a writer has used to achieve his or her purpose or, in some cases, to examine your own ideas or beliefs.

It is a good idea to keep a record of your responses to the "Responding to Reading" questions—as well as any other ideas that occur to you as you read and highlight each selection—in a **writing journal.** Your journal will not only help you maintain a record of your reactions but will also serve as a sourcebook of ideas that you can use later in your writing. (The "Student Voices" at the beginning of each chapter are entries from writing journals.)

Concluding each chapter are ten writing suggestions that expand on the ideas developed by the "Preparing to Read and Write" and "Responding to Reading" questions. Writing suggestions ask you to discuss the chapter's theme, to relate the writer's ideas to your own experiences, or to analyze connections among different works in the chapter or among selections in different chapters

As you read and write about the selections in this book, remember that you are learning ways of thinking about yourself and about the world. By considering and reconsidering the ideas of others, by rejecting easy answers and set conclusions, by considering a problem from many different angles, and by appreciating the many factors that can influence your responses, you develop critical thinking skills that you will use throughout your life. In addition, by writing about the themes discussed in this book, you participate in an ongoing conversation that has been taking place for centuries within the community of scholars and writers who care deeply about the issues that shape our world.

1

FAMILY
AND MEMORY

Student Voices

"My parents did not have very much money when I was born. I am their first child, so they were just beginning their life together when I became a part of it. They worked hard to make ends meet until they were finally able to find better jobs and make our lives more comfortable. Eventually, my sister and brother were born, and my parents were able to buy a bigger house. They have taught me that hard work does pay off.

"There were times, when I was younger, when I was ashamed of my parents. The fact that our traditions and foods were different embarrassed me at times, and I did not want to show my friends what my true life was like. Now I realize I should be proud of my parents. They have worked hard to raise their children, and now they are sending me to college. When I have grown up, I will work hard, as my parents did, so that I can be proud of myself and my family."

—Cynthia Denise Padilla

"I have only met eight or nine of my relatives. My parents have told me that many of our other relatives are dead or overseas and that I am the last of the male Jamersons left to carry on our name in this country. However, I have never met most of my relatives, and so I have little respect for or concern with my family's name or heritage or history. It is for this reason that I feel no desire to have children just to carry on the family name."

—Matthew Hunter Jamerson

"The most negative thing that ever happened to me was when my father moved out of the house. My mother took my three sisters and me out to a movie, and when we returned, my father was gone. My sisters and my mom sat there and cried for a long time, but I did nothing. I wasn't upset at him for leaving, but I was angry because of the financial situation that he left my mother in. I was young and didn't know much about money, but I knew that a single parent couldn't take care of four kids on a part-time job. What made the whole situation worse was that my father tried to avoid paying child support. This event took place when I was seven or eight, and I haven't seen or talked to my father since."

—*Charles Guittar*

"Growing up as an immigrant from India in a suburban town in New Jersey, I had a full and joyful childhood. I lived with an extended family consisting of twenty-five people, nine of them kids (seven boys and two girls). My cousins and I were inseparable, and we always hung out together. I was never lonely. I always had places to go and people to see, and I never had to go far to get help, advice, or comfort. Now that I live at school, I can still call my cousins up and talk to them for hours, but it's not the same. I miss my extended family."

—*Arti Patel*

————————— **Preparing to Read and Write** —————————

Memory preserves past events and makes them accessible to us. In this chapter, writers search their memories, trying to understand, recapture, or re-create the past, to see across the barriers imposed by time. In some cases, memories appear in sharp focus; in others, they are blurred, confused, or even partially invented. Many writers focus on themselves; others focus on their parents or other family members, struggling to close generational gaps, to replay events, to see through the eyes of others —and thus to understand their families and themselves more fully.

As you read and prepare to write about the selections in this chapter, you may consider the following questions:

- Does the writer focus on a single person, on a relationship between two people, or on family dynamics?

- Do you think the writer's perspective is *subjective* (shaped by his or her emotional responses or personal opinions) or *objective* (based mainly on observation and fact rather than on personal impressions)?

- Does the writer recount events from the perspective of an adult looking back at his or her childhood? Does the writer seem to have more insight now than when the events occurred? What has the writer learned—and how?

- Are the memories generally happy or unhappy ones?

- Are family members presented in a favorable, unfavorable, neutral, or ambivalent light?

- Does one family member seem to have a great influence over others in the family? If so, is this influence positive or negative?

- Does the writer feel close to or distant from family members? Does the writer identify with a particular family member?

- What social, political, economic, or cultural forces influence the way the family functions?

- Is the writer's purpose to observe, explore, discover, explain, rationalize, or to do something else?

- Do you identify with the writer or with another person described in the selection? What makes you identify with that person?

- Which selections have similar themes or points of view?

- Which selections seem most different in their views of past experiences? How are they different?

TWO PERSPECTIVES ON FAMILY AND MEMORY

Here, two poets reflect on family ties and the persistence of memory. Detroit-born African-American Robert Hayden (1913–1980), who taught at Fisk University and the University of Michigan and whose Complete Poems *were collected in 1985, once said that "writing poetry is one way of coming to grips with both inner and external realities"; in "Those Winter Sundays," from* Angle of Ascent *(1975), he recalls his distant father with sadness and love. Nobel Prize–winning Irish poet and critic Seamus Heaney (1939–   ), whose father and grandfather both worked the earth as farmers and turf cutters, writes about his heritage from these two men in "Digging," from his first collection of poetry,* Death of a Naturalist *(1966). Other collections include* Field Work *(1979),* Seeing Things *(1991), and* Spirit Level *(1995).*

THOSE WINTER SUNDAYS

Robert Hayden

Sundays too my father got up early
and put his clothes on in the blueblack cold,
then with cracked hands that ached
from labor in the weekday weather made
banked fires blaze. No one ever thanked him.   5

I'd wake and hear the cold splintering, breaking,
When the rooms were warm, he'd call,
and slowly I would rise and dress,
fearing the chronic angers of that house,

Speaking indifferently to him,   10
who had driven out the cold
and polished my good shoes as well.
What did I know, what did I know
of love's austere and lonely offices?

DIGGING

Seamus Heaney

Between my finger and my thumb
The squat pen rests; snug as a gun.

Under my window, a clean rasping sound
When the spade sinks into gravelly ground:
My father, digging. I look down   5

Till his straining rump among the flowerbeds
Bends low, comes up twenty years away
Stooping in rhythm through potato drills
Where he was digging.

The coarse boot nestled on the lug, the shaft   10
Against the inside knee was levered firmly.
He rooted out tall tops, buried the bright edge deep
To scatter new potatoes that we picked
Loving their cool hardness in our hands.
By God, the old man could handle a spade.   15
Just like his old man.

My grandfather cut more turf in a day
Than any other man on Toner's bog.
Once I carried him milk in a bottle
Corked sloppily with paper. He straightened up   20
To drink it, then fell to right away

Nicking and slicing neatly, heaving sods
Over his shoulder, going down and down
For the good turf. Digging.

The cold smell of potato mould, the squelch and slap   25
Of soggy peat, the curt cuts of an edge
Through living roots awaken in my head.
But I've no spade to follow men like them.

Between my finger and my thumb   30
The squat pen rests.
I'll dig with it.

Responding to Reading

1. Both speakers have vivid memories of their fathers. How are their memo-
    ries alike? How are they different?

2. Other than having "driven out the cold," what has the father in Hayden's poem done for his son? To what might the "chronic angers" (line 9) refer?

3. How would you characterize the speaker's attitude toward his father and grandfather in Heaney's poem? In what sense does he see himself as like them? Does Hayden's speaker feel a similar connection with his father?

4. What important lessons has each speaker learned? Are these lessons primarily practical or theoretical? Explain.

5. What traits, abilities, values, habits, or fears does each poem's speaker think he has inherited from his father? What have you inherited from your parents? What do you think you will pass on to your children?

6. What do you know now about your parents' responsibilities and sacrifices that you did not know when you were a child?

ONE LAST TIME

Gary Soto

Gary Soto (1952–   ) was raised in the San Joaquin valley of California, where he worked for a time as a migrant laborer. He studied geography in college but then turned to poetry, often using his childhood locale in poems about poverty and desolation among Mexican-Americans. His lean, simple prose shows his characters' struggles to rise above their difficult situations. In 1985, Soto won the American Book Award for his autobiographical prose work Living Up the Street: Narrative Recollections. *In an unpublished interview about this book, Soto says, "I would rather show and not tell about certain levels of poverty, of childhood; I made a conscious effort not to tell anything but just present the stories and let the reader come up with assumptions." His most recent books have been novels and poetry collections for children and young adults, as well as his* New and Selected Poetry *(1995). The following essay about picking grapes for a raisin company is from* Living Up the Street.

Yesterday I saw the movie *Gandhi*[1] and recognized a few of the people—not in the theater but in the film. I saw my relatives, dusty and thin as sparrows, returning from the fields with hoes balanced on their shoulders. The workers were squinting, eyes small and veined, and were using their hands to say what there was to say to those in the audience with popcorn and Cokes. I didn't have anything, though. I sat thinking of my family and their years in the fields, beginning with Grandmother who came to the United States after the Mexican revolution to settle in

---

[1] The 1982 film biography of the nonviolent revolutionary Mohandas Gandhi (known as Mahatma), which was set in part among the peasants of India. [Eds.]

Fresno where she met her husband and bore children, many of them. She worked in the fields around Fresno, picking grapes, oranges, plums, peaches, and cotton, dragging a large white sack like a sled. She worked in the packing houses, Bonner and Sun-Maid Raisin, where she stood at a conveyor belt passing her hand over streams of raisins to pluck out leaves and pebbles. For over twenty years she worked at a machine that boxed raisins until she retired at sixty-five.

Grandfather worked in the fields, as did his children. Mother also 2 found herself out there when she separated from Father for three weeks. I remember her coming home, dusty and so tired that she had to rest on the porch before she trudged inside to wash and start dinner. I didn't understand the complaints about her ankles or the small of her back, even though I had been in the grape fields watching her work. With my brother and sister I ran in and out of the rows; we enjoyed ourselves and pretended not to hear Mother scolding us to sit down and behave ourselves. A few years later, however, I caught on when I went to pick grapes rather than play in the rows.

Mother and I got up before dawn and ate quick bowls of cereal. She 3 drove in silence while I rambled on how everything was now solved, how I was going to make enough money to end our misery and even buy her a beautiful copper tea pot, the one I had shown her in Long's Drugs. When we arrived I was frisky and ready to go, self-consciously aware of my grape knife dangling at my wrist. I almost ran to the row the foreman had pointed out, but I returned to help Mother with the grape pans and jug of water. She told me to settle down and reminded me not to lose my knife. I walked at her side and listened to her explain how to cut grapes; bent down, hands on knees, I watched her demonstrate by cutting a few bunches into my pan. She stood over me as I tried it myself, tugging at a bunch of grapes that pulled loose like beads from a necklace. "Cut the stem all the way," she told me as last advice before she walked away, her shoes sinking in the loose dirt, to begin work on her own row.

I cut another bunch, then another, fighting the snap and whip of 4 vines. After ten minutes of groping for grapes, my first pan brimmed with bunches. I poured them on the paper tray, which was bordered by a wooden frame that kept the grapes from rolling off, and they spilled like jewels from a pirate's chest. The tray was only half filled, so I hurried to jump under the vines and begin groping, cutting, and tugging at the grapes again. I emptied the pan, raked the grapes with my hands to make them look like they filled the tray, and jumped back under the vine on my knees. I tried to cut faster because Mother, in the next row, was slowly moving ahead. I peeked into her row and saw five trays gleaming in the early morning. I cut, pulled hard, and stopped to gather the grapes that missed the pan; already bored, I spat on a few to wash them before tossing them like popcorn into my mouth.

So it went. Two pans equaled one tray—or six cents. By lunchtime I   5
had a trail of thirty-seven trays behind me while mother had sixty or
more. We met about halfway from our last trays, and I sat down with a
grunt, knees wet from kneeling on dropped grapes. I washed my hands
with the water from the jug, drying them on the inside of my shirt
sleeve before I opened the paper bag for the first sandwich, which I
gave to Mother. I dipped my hand in again to unwrap a sandwich without looking at it. I took a first bite and chewed it slowly for the tang of
mustard. Eating in silence I looked straight ahead at the vines, and only
when we were finished with cookies did we talk.

"Are you tired?" she asked.   6

"No, but I got a sliver from the frame," I told her. I showed her the   7
web of skin between my thumb and index finger. She wrinkled her forehead but said it was nothing.

"How many trays did you do?"   8

I looked straight ahead, not answering at first. I recounted in my   9
mind the whole morning of bend, cut, pour again and again, before
answering a feeble "thirty-seven." No elaboration, no detail. Without
looking at me she told me how she had done field work in Texas and
Michigan as a child. But I had a difficult time listening to her stories. I
played with my grape knife, stabbing it into the ground, but stopped
when Mother reminded me that I had better not lose it. I left the knife
sticking up like a small, leafless plant. She then talked about school, the
junior high I would be going to that fall, and then about Rick and Debra,
how sorry they would be that they hadn't come out to pick grapes
because they'd have no new clothes for the school year. She stopped
talking when she peeked at her watch, a bandless one she kept in her
pocket. She got up with an "Ay, Dios," and told me that we'd work until
three, leaving me cutting figures in the sand with my knife and dread-
ing the return to work.

Finally I rose and walked slowly back to where I had left off, again   10
kneeling under the vine and fixing the pan under bunches of grapes. By
that time, 11:30, the sun was over my shoulder and made me squint and
think of the pool at the Y.M.C.A. where I was a summer member. I saw
myself diving face first into the water and loving it. I saw myself gleaming like something new, at the edge of the pool. I had to daydream and
keep my mind busy because boredom was a terror almost as awful as
the work itself. My mind went dumb with stupid things, and I had to
keep it moving with dreams of baseball and would-be girlfriends. I even
sang, however softly, to keep my mind moving, my hands moving.

I worked less hurriedly and with less vision. I no longer saw that   11
copper pot sitting squat on our stove or Mother waiting for it to
whistle. The wardrobe that I imagined, crisp and bright in the closet,
numbered only one pair of jeans and two shirts because, in half a day,
six cents times thirty-seven trays was two dollars and twenty-two cents.

It became clear to me. If I worked eight hours, I might make four dollars. I'd take this, even gladly, and walk downtown to look into store windows on the mall and long for the bright madras shirts from Walter Smith or Coffee's, but settling for two imitation ones from Penney's.

That first day I laid down seventy-three trays while Mother had a 12 hundred and twenty behind her. On the back of an old envelope, she wrote out our numbers and hours. We washed at the pump behind the farm house and walked slowly to our car for the drive back to town in the afternoon heat. That evening after dinner I sat in a lawn chair listening to music from a transistor radio while Rick and David King played catch. I joined them in a game of pickle, but there was little joy in trying to avoid their tags because I couldn't get the fields out of my mind: I saw myself dropping on my knees under a vine to tug at a branch that wouldn't come off. In bed, when I closed my eyes, I saw the fields, yellow with kicked up dust, and a crooked trail of trays rotting behind me.

The next day I woke tired and started picking tired. The grapes 13 rained into the pan, slowly filling like a belly, until I had my first tray and started my second. So it went all day, and the next, and all through the following week, so that by the end of thirteen days the foreman counted out, in tens mostly, my pay of fifty-three dollars. Mother earned one hundred and forty-eight dollars. She wrote this on her envelope, with a message I didn't bother to ask her about.

The next day I walked with my friend Scott to the downtown mall 14 where we drooled over the clothes behind fancy windows, bought popcorn, and sat at a tier of outdoor fountains to talk about girls. Finally we went into Penney's for more popcorn, which we ate walking around, before we returned home without buying anything. It wasn't until a few days before school that I let my fifty-three dollars slip quietly from my hands, buying a pair of pants, two shirts, and a maroon T-shirt, the kind that was in style. At home I tried them on while Rick looked on enviously; later, the day before school started, I tried them on again wondering not so much if they were worth it as who would see me first in those clothes.

Along with my brother and sister I picked grapes until I was fifteen, 15 before giving up and saying that I'd rather wear old clothes than stoop like a Mexican. Mother thought I was being stuck-up, even stupid, because there would be no clothes for me in the fall. I told her I didn't care, but when Rick and Debra rose at five in the morning, I lay awake in bed feeling that perhaps I had made a mistake but unwilling to change my mind. That fall Mother bought me two pairs of socks, a packet of colored T-shirts, and underwear. The T-shirts would help, I thought, but who would see that I had new underwear and socks? I wore a new T-shirt on the first day of school, then an old shirt on Tuesday, then another T-shirt on Wednesday, and on Thursday an old

Nehru shirt that was embarrassingly out of style. On Friday I changed into the corduroy pants my brother had handed down to me and slipped into my last new T-shirt. I worked like a magician, blinding my classmates, who were all clothes conscious and small-time social climbers, by arranging my wardrobe to make it seem larger than it really was. But by spring I had to do something—my blue jeans were almost silver and my shoes had lost their form, puddling like black ice around my feet. That spring of my sixteenth year, Rick and I decided to take a labor bus to chop cotton. In his old Volkswagen, which was more noise than power, we drove on a Saturday morning to West Fresno—or Chinatown as some call it—parked, walked slowly toward a bus, and stood gawking at the winos, toothy blacks, Okies, *Tejanos*[2] with gold teeth, whores, Mexican families, and labor contractors shouting "Cotton" or "Beets," the work of spring.

We boarded the "Cotton" bus without looking at the contractor 16 who stood almost blocking the entrance because he didn't want winos. We boarded scared and then were more scared because two blacks in the rear were drunk and arguing loudly about what was better, a two-barrel or four-barrel Ford carburetor. We sat far from them, looking straight ahead, and only glanced briefly at the others who boarded, almost all of them broken and poorly dressed in loudly mismatched clothes. Finally when the contractor banged his palm against the side of the bus, the young man at the wheel, smiling and talking in Spanish, started the engine, idled it for a moment while he adjusted the mirrors, and started off in slow chugs. Except for the windshield there was no glass in the windows, so as soon as we were on the rural roads outside Fresno, the dust and sand began to be sucked into the bus, whipping about like irate wasps as the gravel ticked about us. We closed our eyes, clotted up our mouths that wanted to open with embarrassed laughter because we couldn't believe we were on that bus with those people and the dust attacking us for no reason.

When we arrived at a field we followed the others to a pickup 17 where we each took a hoe and marched to stand before a row. Rick and I, self-conscious and unsure, looked around at the others who leaned on their hoes or squatted in front of the rows, almost all talking in Spanish, joking, lighting cigarettes—all waiting for the foreman's whistle to begin work. Mother had explained how to chop cotton by showing us with a broom in the backyard.

"Like this," she said, her broom swishing down weeds. "Leave one 18 plant and cut four—and cut them! Don't leave them standing or the foreman will get mad."

---

[2] Texans. [Eds.]

The foreman whistled and we started up the row stealing glances at 19
other workers to see if we were doing it right. But after awhile we
worked like we knew what we were doing, neither of us hurrying or
falling behind. But slowly the clot of men, women, and kids began to
spread and loosen. Even Rick pulled away. I didn't hurry, though. I cut
smoothly and cleanly as I walked at a slow pace, in a sort of funeral
march. My eyes measured each space of cotton plants before I cut. If I
missed the plants, I swished again. I worked intently, seldom looking
up, so when I did I was amazed to see the sun, like a broken orange
coin, in the east. It looked blurry, unbelievable, like something not of
this world. I looked around in amazement, scanning the eastern horizon
that was a taut line jutted with an occasional mountain. The horizon
was beautiful, like a snapshot of the moon, in the early light of morning,
in the quiet of no cars and few people.

The foreman trudged in boots in my direction, stepping awkwardly 20
over the plants, to inspect the work. No one around me looked up. We
all worked steadily while we waited for him to leave. When he did
leave, with a feeble complaint addressed to no one in particular, we
looked up smiling under straw hats and bandanas.

By 11:00, our lunch time, my ankles were hurting from walking on 21
clods the size of hardballs. My arms ached and my face was dusted by
a wind that was perpetual, always busy whipping about. But the work
was not bad, I thought. It was better, so much better, than picking
grapes, especially with the hourly wage of a dollar twenty-five instead
of piece work. Rick and I walked sorely toward the bus where we
washed and drank water. Instead of eating in the bus or in the shade of
the bus, we kept to ourselves by walking down to the irrigation canal
that ran the length of the field, to open our lunch of sandwiches and
crackers. We laughed at the crackers, which seemed like a cruel joke
from our Mother, because we were working under the sun and the last
thing we wanted was a salty dessert. We ate them anyway and drank
more water before we returned to the field, both of us limping in exaggeration. Working side by side, we talked and laughed at our predicament because our Mother had warned us year after year that if we
didn't get on track in school we'd have to work in the fields and then
we would see. We mimicked Mother's whining voice and smirked at
her smoky view of the future in which we'd be trapped by marriage and
screaming kids. We'd eat beans and then we'd see.

Rick pulled slowly away to the rhythm of his hoe falling faster and 22
smoother. It was better that way, to work alone. I could hum made-up
songs or songs from the radio and think to myself about school and
friends. At the time I was doing badly in my classes, mainly because of
a difficult stepfather, but also because I didn't care anymore. All
through junior high and into my first year of high school there were
those who said I would never do anything, be anyone. They said I'd

work like a donkey and marry the first Mexican girl that came along. I was reminded so often, verbally and in the way I was treated at home, that I began to believe that chopping cotton might be a lifetime job for me. If not chopping cotton, then I might get lucky and find myself in a car wash or restaurant or junkyard. But it was clear; I'd work, and work hard.

I cleared my mind by humming and looking about. The sun was 23 directly above with a few soft blades of clouds against a sky that seemed bluer and more beautiful than our sky in the city. Occasionally the breeze flurried and picked up dust so that I had to cover my eyes and screw up my face. The workers were hunched, brown as the clods under our feet, and spread across the field that ran without end—fields that were owned by corporations, not families.

I hoed trying to keep my mind busy with scenes from school and 24 pretend girlfriends until finally my brain turned off and my thinking went fuzzy with boredom. I looked about, no longer mesmerized by the beauty of the landscape, no longer wondering if the winos in the fields could hold out for eight hours, no longer dreaming of the clothes I'd buy with my pay. My eyes followed my chopping as the plants, thin as their shadows, fell with each strike. I worked slowly with ankles and arms hurting, neck stiff, and eyes stinging from the dust and the sun that glanced off the field like a mirror.

By quitting time, 3:00, there was such an excruciating pain in my 25 ankles that I walked as if I were wearing snowshoes. Rick laughed at me and I laughed too, embarrassed that most of the men were walking normally and I was among the first timers who had to get used to this work. "And what about you, wino," I came back at Rick. His eyes were meshed red and his long hippie hair was flecked with dust and gnats and bits of leaves. We placed our hoes in the back of a pickup and stood in line for our pay, which was twelve fifty. I was amazed at the pay, which was the most I had ever earned in one day, and thought that I'd come back the next day, Sunday. This was too good.

Instead of joining the others in the labor bus, we jumped in the back 26 of a pickup when the driver said we'd get to town sooner and were welcome to join him. We scrambled into the truck bed to be joined by a heavy-set and laughing *Tejano* whose head was shaped like an egg, particularly so because the bandana he wore ended in a point on the top of his head. He laughed almost demonically as the pickup roared up the dirt path, a gray cape of dust rising behind us. On the highway, with the wind in our faces, we squinted at the fields as if we were looking for someone. The *Tejano* had quit laughing but was smiling broadly, occasionally chortling tunes he never finished. I was scared of him, though Rick, two years older and five inches taller, wasn't. If the *Tejano* looked at him, Rick stared back for a second or two before he looked away to the fields.

I felt like a soldier coming home from war when we rattled into 27
Chinatown. People leaning against car hoods stared, their necks following us, owl-like; prostitutes chewed gum more ferociously and showed
us their teeth; Chinese grocers stopped brooming their storefronts to
raise their cadaverous faces at us. We stopped in front of the Chi Chi
Club where Mexican music blared from the juke box and cue balls
cracked like dull ice. The *Tejano,* who was dirty as we were, stepped
awkwardly over the side rail, dusted himself off with his bandana, and
sauntered into the club.

Rick and I jumped from the back, thanked the driver who said *de* 28
nada and popped his clutch, so that the pickup jerked and coughed blue
smoke. We returned smiling to our car, happy with the money we had
made and pleased that we had, in a small way, proved ourselves to be
tough; that we worked as well as other men and earned the same pay.

We returned the next day and the next week until the season was 29
over and there was nothing to do. I told myself that I wouldn't pick
grapes that summer, saying all through June and July that it was for
Mexicans, not me. When August came around and I still had not found
a summer job, I ate my words, sharpened my knife, and joined Mother,
Rick, and Debra for one last time.

Responding to Reading

1. How does work bring Soto closer to an understanding of his family? Has
   your own work experience helped you to understand your family better?
2. In paragraph 1 Soto says he recognizes his relatives in the characters he sees
   in the film *Gandhi.* What does he mean? Do you recognize any of your own
   relatives in Soto's essay?
3. Why would Soto at age fifteen "rather wear old clothes than stoop like a
   Mexican" (15)? Does the adult Soto understand the reasons for this sentiment? What does this comment reveal about the society in which Soto
   grew up?

Once More to the Lake

E. B. White

*One of America's best-loved essayists, E. B. White (1899–1986) enjoyed
an almost idyllic childhood in Mt. Vernon, New York, graduated from college
in 1921, and embarked on a career writing for newspapers. Soon he was writing essays for the* New Yorker *and* Harper's Magazine. *White wrote the*

children's classic Charlotte's Web *(1952); in 1959, he expanded Will Strunk's grammar book, which White had used as his student, into the now classic* The Elements of Style; *and he published essays in the collections* One Man's Meat *(1944) and* Essays of E. B. White *(1977). In his nostalgic "Once More to the Lake," White revisits the lake in Maine where he vacationed as a boy with his family and explores the themes of time and change.*

One summer, along about 1904, my father rented a camp on a lake 1 in Maine and took us all there for the month of August. We all got ring-worm from some kittens and had to rub Pond's Extract on our arms and legs night and morning, and my father rolled over in a canoe with all his clothes on; but outside of that the vacation was a success and from then on none of us ever thought there was any place in the world like that lake in Maine. We returned summer after summer—always on August 1st for one month. I have since become a salt-water man, but sometimes in summer there are days when the restlessness of the tides and the fearful cold of the sea water and the incessant wind which blows across the afternoon and into the evening make me wish for the placidity of a lake in the woods. A few weeks ago this feeling got so strong I bought myself a couple of bass hooks and a spinner and returned to the lake where we used to go, for a week's fishing and to revisit old haunts.

I took along my son, who had never had any fresh water up his nose 2 and who had seen lily pads only from train windows. On the journey over to the lake I began to wonder what it would be like. I wondered how time would have marred this unique, this holy spot—the coves and streams, the hills that the sun set behind, the camps and the paths behind the camps. I was sure the tarred road would have found it out and I wondered in what other ways it would be desolated. It is strange how much you can remember about places like that once you allow your mind to return into the grooves which lead back. You remember one thing, and that suddenly reminds you of another thing. I guess I remembered clearest of all the early mornings, when the lake was cool and motionless, remembered how the bedroom smelled of the lumber it was made of and of the wet woods whose scent entered through the screen. The partitions in the camp were thin and did not extend clear to the top of the rooms, and as I was always the first up I would dress softly so as not to wake the others, and sneak out into the sweet out-doors and start out in the canoe, keeping close along the shore in the long shadows of the pines. I remembered being very careful never to rub my paddle against the gunwale for fear of disturbing the stillness of the cathedral.

The lake had never been what you would call a wild lake. There 3 were cottages sprinkled around the shores, and it was in farming coun-try although the shores of the lake were quite heavily wooded. Some of the cottages were owned by nearby farmers, and you would live at the shore and eat your meals at the farmhouse. That's what our family did. But although it wasn't wild, it was a fairly large and undisturbed lake and there were places in it which, to a child at least, seemed infinitely remote and primeval.

I was right about the tar: it led to within half a mile of the shore. But when I got back there, with my boy, and we settled into a camp near a farmhouse and into the kind of summertime I had known, I could tell that it was going to be pretty much the same as it had been before—I knew it, lying in bed the first morning, smelling the bedroom, and hearing the boy sneak quietly out and go off along the shore in a boat. I began to sustain the illusion that he was I, and therefore, by simple transposition, that I was my father. This sensation persisted, kept cropping up all the time we were there. It was not an entirely new feeling, but in this setting it grew much stronger. I seemed to be living a dual existence. I would be in the middle of some simple act, I would be picking up a bait box or laying down a table fork, or I would be saying something, and suddenly it would be not I but my father who was saying the words or making the gesture. It gave me a creepy sensation.

We went fishing the first morning. I felt the same damp moss covering the worms in the bait can, and saw the dragonfly alight on the tip of my rod as it hovered a few inches from the surface of the water. It was the arrival of this fly that convinced me beyond any doubt that everything was as it always had been, that the years were a mirage and there had been no years. The small waves were the same, chucking the rowboat under the chin as we fished at anchor, and the boat was the same boat, the same color green and the ribs broken in the same places, and under the floor-boards the same freshwater leavings and débris—the dead helgramite,[1] the wisps of moss, the rusty discarded fishhook, the dried blood from yesterday's catch. We stared silently at the tips of our rods, at the dragonflies that came and went. I lowered the tip of mine into the water, tentatively, pensively dislodging the fly, which darted two feet away, poised, darted two feet back, and came to rest again a little farther up the rod. There had been no years between the ducking of this dragonfly and the other one—the one that was part of memory. I looked at the boy, who was silently watching his fly, and it was my hands that held his rod, my eyes watching. I felt dizzy and didn't know which rod I was at the end of.

We caught two bass, hauling them in briskly as though they were mackerel, pulling them over the side of the boat in a businesslike manner without any landing net, and stunning them with a blow on the back of the head. When we got back for a swim before lunch, the lake

---

[1] The nymph of the May-fly, used as bait. [Eds.]

was exactly where we had left it, the same number of inches from the dock, and there was only the merest suggestion of a breeze. This seemed an utterly enchanted sea, this lake you could leave to its own devices for a few hours and come back to, and find that it had not stirred, this constant and trustworthy body of water. In the shallows, the dark, water-soaked sticks and twigs, smooth and old, were undulating in clusters on the bottom against the clean ribbed sand, and the track of the mussel was plain. A school of minnows swam by, each minnow with its small individual shadow, doubling the attendance, so clear and sharp in the sunlight. Some of the other campers were in swimming, along the shore, one of them with a cake of soap, and the water felt thin and clear and unsubstantial. Over the years there had been this person with the cake of soap, this cultist, and here he was. There had been no years.

Up to the farmhouse to dinner through the teeming, dusty field, 7 the road under our sneakers was only a two-track road. The middle track was missing, the one with the marks of the hooves and the splotches of dried, flaky manure. There had always been three tracks to choose from in choosing which track to walk in; now the choice was narrowed down to two. For a moment I missed terribly the middle alternative. But the way led past the tennis court, and something about the way it lay there in the sun reassured me; the tape had loosened along the backline, the alleys were green with plantains and other weeds, and the net (installed in June and removed in September) sagged in the dry noon, and the whole place steamed with midday heat and hunger and emptiness. There was a choice of pie for dessert, and one was blueberry and one was apple, and the waitresses were the same country girls, there having been no passage of time, only the illusion of it as in a dropped curtain—the waitresses were still fifteen; their hair had been washed, that was the only difference—they had been to the movies and seen the pretty girls with the clean hair.

Summertime, oh summertime, pattern of life indelible, the fade- 8 proof lake, the woods unshatterable, the pasture with the sweetfern and the juniper forever and ever, summer without end; this was the background, and the life along the shore was the design, the cottagers with their innocent and tranquil design, their tiny docks with the flagpole and the American flag floating against the white clouds in the blue sky, the little paths over the roots of the trees leading from camp to camp and the paths leading back to the outhouses and the can of lime for sprinkling, and at the souvenir counters at the store the miniature birch-bark canoes and the post cards that showed things looking a little better than they looked. This was the American family at play, escaping the city heat, wondering whether the newcomers in the camp at the head of the cove were "common" or "nice," wondering whether it was true that the people who drove up for Sunday dinner at the farmhouse were turned away because there wasn't enough chicken.

It seemed to me, as I kept remembering all this, that those times and 9
those summers had been infinitely precious and worth saving. There
had been jollity and peace and goodness. The arriving (at the beginning
of August) had been so big a business in itself, at the railway station the
farm wagon drawn up, the first smell of the pine-laden air, the first
glimpse of the smiling farmer, and the great importance of the trunks
and your father's enormous authority in such matters, and the feel of
the wagon under you for the long ten-mile haul, and at the top of the
last long hill catching the first view of the lake after eleven months of
not seeing this cherished body of water. The shouts and cries of the
other campers when they saw you, and the trunks to be unpacked, to
give up their rich burden. (Arriving was less exciting nowadays, when
you sneaked up in your car and parked it under a tree near the camp
and took out the bags and in five minutes it was all over, no fuss, no
loud wonderful fuss about trunks.)

Peace and goodness and jollity. The only thing that was wrong now, 10
really, was the sound of the place, an unfamiliar nervous sound of the
outboard motors. This was the note that jarred, the one thing that would
sometimes break the illusion and set the years moving. In those other
summertimes all motors were inboard; and when they were at a little
distance, the noise they made was a sedative, an ingredient of summer
sleep. They were one-cylinder and two-cylinder engines, and some
were make-and-break and some were jump-spark,[2] but they all made a
sleepy sound across the lake. The one-lungers throbbed and fluttered,
and the twin-cylinder ones purred and purred, and that was a quiet
sound too. But now the campers all had outboards. In the daytime, in
the hot mornings, these motors made a petulant, irritable sound; at
night, in the still evening when the afterglow lit the water, they whined
about one's ears like mosquitoes. My boy loved our rented outboard,
and his great desire was to achieve singlehanded mastery over it, and
authority, and he soon learned the trick of choking it a little (but not too
much), and the adjustment of the needle valve. Watching him I would
remember the things you could do with the old one-cylinder engine
with the heavy flywheel, how you could have it eating out of your hand
if you got really close to it spiritually. Motor boats in those days didn't
have clutches, and you would make a landing by shutting off the motor
at the proper time and coasting in with a dead rudder. But there was a
way of reversing them, if you learned the trick, by cutting the switch
and putting it on again exactly on the final dying revolution of the flywheel, so that it would kick back against compression and begin reversing. Approaching a dock in a strong following breeze, it was difficult to
slow up sufficiently by the ordinary coasting method, and if a boy felt

---

[2] Methods of ignition timing. [Eds.]

he had complete mastery over his motor, he was tempted to keep it running beyond its time and then reverse it a few feet from the dock. It took a cool nerve, because if you threw the switch a twentieth of a second too soon you would catch the flywheel when it still had speed enough to go up past center, and the boat would leap ahead, charging bull-fashion at the dock.

We had a good week at the camp. The bass were biting well and the 11 sun shone endlessly, day after day. We would be tired at night and lie down in the accumulated heat of the little bedrooms after the long hot day and the breeze would stir almost imperceptibly outside and the smell of the swamp drift in through the rusty screens. Sleep would come easily and in the morning the red squirrel would be on the roof, tapping out his gay routine. I kept remembering everything, lying in bed in the mornings—the small steamboat that had a long rounded stern like the lip of a Ubangi, and how quietly she ran on the moonlight sails, when the older boys played their mandolins and the girls sang and we ate doughnuts dipped in sugar, and how sweet the music was on the water in the shining night, and what it had felt like to think about girls then. After breakfast we would go up to the store and the things were in the same place—the minnows in a bottle, the plugs and spinners disarranged and pawed over by the youngsters from the boys' camp, the fig newtons and the Beeman's gum. Outside, the road was tarred and cars stood in front of the store. Inside, all was just as it had always been, except there was more Coca-Cola and not so much Moxie and root beer and birch beer and sarsaparilla. We would walk out with a bottle of pop apiece and sometimes the pop would backfire up our noses and hurt. We explored the streams, quietly, where the turtles slid off the sunny logs and dug their way into the soft bottom; and we lay on the town wharf and fed worms to the tame bass. Everywhere we went I had trouble making out which was I, the one walking at my side, the one walking in my pants.

One afternoon while we were there at that lake a thunderstorm 12 came up. It was like the revival of an old melodrama that I had seen long ago with childish awe. The second-act climax of the drama of the electrical disturbance over a lake in America had not changed in any important respect. This was the big scene, still the big scene. The whole thing was so familiar, the first feeling of oppression and heat and a general air around camp of not wanting to go very far away. In midafternoon (it was all the same) a curious darkening of the sky, and a lull in everything that had made life tick; and then the way the boats suddenly swung the other way at their moorings with the coming of a breeze out of the new quarter, and the premonitory rumble. Then the kettle drum, then the snare, then the bass drum and cymbals, then crackling light against the dark, and the gods grinning and licking their chops in the hills. Afterward the calm, the rain steadily rustling in the calm lake, the return of light and hope and spirits, and the campers running out in joy and relief to go swimming in the rain, their bright cries perpetuating the deathless joke about how they were getting simply drenched, and the children screaming with delight at the new sensation of bathing in the rain, and the joke about getting drenched linking the generations in a strong indestructible chain. And the comedian who waded in carrying an umbrella.

When the others went swimming my son said he was going in too. 13 He pulled his dripping trunks from the line where they had hung all through the shower, and wrung them out. Languidly, and with no thought of going in, I watched him, his hard little body, skinny and bare, saw him wince slightly as he pulled up around his vitals the small, soggy, icy garment. As he buckled the swollen belt suddenly my groin felt the chill of death.

Responding to Reading

1. How is White's "holy spot" different when he visits it with his son from how it was when he visited it with his father?
2. Is this essay primarily about a time, a place, or a relationship? Explain.
3. Why does White feel "the chill of death" (13) as he watches his son? Do you identify more with White the father or White the child? Explain.

No Name Woman

Maxine Hong Kingston

Maxine Hong Kingston (1940–) a native of California, is a nonfiction writer who has taught English in high school and at the University of Hawaii. She also contributes to Ms., *the* New Yorker, American Heritage, *and other publications. Her most recent work is the novel* Tripmaster Monkey: His Fake Book *(1989). In her autobiography,* The Woman Warrior: Memoirs of a Girlhood among Ghosts *(1976), and in* China Men *(1980), Kingston explores her Chinese ancestry. She said of* The Woman Warrior *in a 1983 interview, "One of the themes in* Warrior *was: what is it that's a story and what is it that's life? . . . Sometimes the boundaries are very clear, and sometimes they interlace and we live out stories." In the following selection from* The Woman Warrior, *Kingston tells the story of her aunt in China, who disgraced her family and suffered neglect and despair.*

"You must not tell anyone," my mother said, "what I am about to 1 tell you. In China your father had a sister who killed herself. She jumped into the family well. We say that your father has all brothers because it is as if she had never been born.

"In 1924 just a few days after our village celebrated seventeen 2 hurry-up weddings—to make sure that every young man who went 'out on the road' would responsibly come home—your father and his brothers and your grandfather and his brothers and your aunt's new husband sailed for America, the Gold Mountain. It was your grandfather's last trip. Those lucky enough to get contracts waved good-bye from the decks. They fed and guarded the stowaways and helped them off in Cuba, New York, Bali, Hawaii. 'We'll meet in California next year,' they said. All of them sent money home.

"I remember looking at your aunt one day when she and I were 3 dressing; I had not noticed before that she had such a protruding melon of a stomach. But I did not think, 'She's pregnant,' until she began to look like other pregnant women, her shirt pulling and the white tops of her black pants showing. She could not have been pregnant, you see, because her husband had been gone for years. No one said anything. We did not discuss it. In early summer she was ready to have the child, long after the time when it could have been possible.

"The village had also been counting. On the night the baby was to 4 be born the villagers raided our house. Some were crying. Like a great saw, teeth strung with lights, files of people walked zigzag across our land, tearing the rice. Their lanterns doubled in the disturbed black water, which drained away through the broken bunds. As the villagers closed in, we could see that some of them, probably men and women we knew well, wore white masks. The people with long hair hung it over their faces. Women with short hair made it stand up on end. Some had tied white bands around their foreheads, arms, and legs.

"At first they threw mud and rocks at the house. Then they threw 5 eggs and began slaughtering our stock. We could hear the animals scream their deaths—the roosters, the pigs, a last great roar from the ox. Familiar wild heads flared in our night windows; the villagers encircled us. Some of the faces stopped to peer at us, their eyes rushing like searchlights. The hands flattened against the panes, framed heads, and left red prints.

"The villagers broke in the front and the back doors at the same 6 time, even though we had not locked the doors against them. Their knives dripped with the blood of our animals. They smeared blood on the doors and walls. One woman swung a chicken, whose throat she had slit, splattering blood in red arcs about her. We stood together in the middle of our house, in the family hall with the pictures and tables of the ancestors around us, and looked straight ahead.

"At the time the house had only two wings. When the men came 7
back, we would build two more to enclose our courtyard and a third
one to begin a second courtyard. The villagers pushed through both
wings, even your grandparents' rooms, to find your aunt's, which was
also mine until the men returned. From this room a new wing for one
of the younger families would grow. They ripped up her clothes and
shoes and broke her combs, grinding them underfoot. They tore her
work from the loom. They scattered the cooking fire and rolled the new
weaving in it. We could hear them in the kitchen breaking our bowls
and banging the pots. They overturned the great waist-high earthen-
ware jugs; duck eggs, pickled fruits, vegetables burst out and mixed in
acrid torrents. The old woman from the next field swept a broom
through the air and loosed the spirits-of-the-broom over our heads.
'Pig.' 'Ghost.' 'Pig,' they sobbed and scolded while they ruined our
house.

"When they left, they took sugar and oranges to bless themselves. 8
They cut pieces from the dead animals. Some of them took bowls that
were not broken and clothes that were not torn. Afterward we swept up
the rice and sewed it back up into sacks. But the smells from the spilled
preserves lasted. Your aunt gave birth in the pigsty that night. The next
morning when I went for the water, I found her and the baby plugging
up the family well.

"Don't let your father know that I told you. He denies her. Now that 9
you have started to menstruate, what happened to her could happen to
you. Don't humiliate us. You wouldn't like to be forgotten as if you had
never been born. The villagers are watchful."

Whenever she had to warn us about life, my mother told stories that 10
ran like this one, a story to grow up on. She tested our strength to establish realities. Those in the emigrant generations who could not reassert
brute survival died young and far from home. Those of us in the first
American generations have had to figure out how the invisible world
the emigrants built around our childhoods fit in solid America.

The emigrants confused the gods by diverting their curses, mis- 11
leading them with crooked streets and false names. They must try to
confuse their offspring as well, who, I suppose, threaten them in similar
ways—always trying to get things straight, always trying to name the
unspeakable. The Chinese I know hide their names; sojourners take
new names when their lives change and guard their real names with
silence.

Chinese-Americans, when you try to understand what things in 12
you are Chinese, how do you separate what is peculiar to childhood, to
poverty, insanities, one family, your mother who marked your growing
with stories, from what is Chinese? What is Chinese tradition and what
is the movies?

If I want to learn what clothes my aunt wore, whether flashy or 13
ordinary, I would have to begin, "Remember Father's drowned-in-the-
well sister?" I cannot ask that. My mother has told me once and for all
the useful parts. She will add nothing unless powered by Necessity, a
riverbank that guides her life. She plants vegetable gardens rather than
lawns; she carries the odd-shaped tomatoes home from the fields and
eats food left for the gods.

Whenever we did frivolous things, we used up energy; we flew 14
high kites. We children came up off the ground over the melting cones
our parents brought home from work and the American movie on New
Year's Day—*Oh, You Beautiful Doll* with Betty Grable one year, and *She
Wore a Yellow Ribbon* with John Wayne another year. After the one carni-
val ride each, we paid in guilt; our tired father counted his change on
the dark walk home.

Adultery is extravagance. Could people who hatch their own chicks 15
and eat the embryos and the heads for delicacies and boil the feet in
vinegar for party food, leaving only the gravel, eating even the gizzard
lining—could such people engender a prodigal aunt? To be a woman, to
have a daughter in starvation time was a waste enough. My aunt could
not have been the lone romantic who gave up everything for sex.
Women in the old China did not choose. Some man had commanded
her to lie with him and be his secret evil. I wonder whether he masked
himself when he joined the raid on her family.

Perhaps she encountered him in the fields or on the mountain 16
where the daughters-in-law collected fuel. Or perhaps he first noticed
her in the marketplace. He was not a stranger because the village
housed no strangers. She had to have dealings with him other than sex.
Perhaps he worked an adjoining field, or he sold her the cloth for the
dress she sewed and wore. His demand must have surprised, then terrified her. She obeyed him; she always did as she was told.

When the family found a young man in the next village to be her 17
husband, she stood tractably beside the best rooster, his proxy, and
promised before they met that she would be his forever. She was lucky
that he was her age and she would be the first wife, an advantage secure
now. The night she first saw him, he had sex with her. Then he left for
America. She had almost forgotten what he looked like. When she tried
to envision him, she only saw the black and white face in the group
photograph the men had had taken before leaving.

The other man was not, after all, much different from her husband. 18
They both gave orders: she followed. "If you tell your family, I'll beat
you. I'll kill you. Be here again next week." No one talked sex, ever. And
she might have separated the rapes from the rest of living if only she did
not have to buy her oil from him or gather wood in the same forest. I
want her fear to have lasted just as long as rape lasted so that the fear

could have been contained. No drawn-out fear. But women at sex haz-
arded birth and hence lifetimes. The fear did not stop but permeated
everywhere. She told the man, "I think I'm pregnant." He organized the
raid against her.

On nights when my mother and father talked about their life back   19
home, sometimes they mentioned an "outcast table" whose business
they still seemed to be settling, their voices tight. In a commensal[1] tradition, where food is precious, the powerful older people made wrong-
doers eat alone. Instead of letting them start separate new lives like the
Japanese, who could become samurais and geishas, the Chinese family,
faces averted but eyes glowering sideways, hung on to the offenders
and fed them leftovers. My aunt must have lived in the same house as
my parents and eaten at an outcast table. My mother spoke about the
raid as if she had seen it, when she and my aunt, a daughter-in-law to a
different household, should not have been living together at all.
Daughters-in-law lived with their husbands' parents, not their own; a
synonym for marriage in Chinese is "taking a daughter-in-law." Her
husband's parents could have sold her, mortgaged her, stoned her. But
they had sent her back to her own mother and father, a mysterious act
hinting at disgraces not told me. Perhaps they had thrown her out to
deflect the avengers.

She was the only daughter; her four brothers went with her father,   20
husband, and uncles "out on the road" and for some years became
western men. When the goods were divided among the family, three of
the brothers took land, and the youngest, my father, chose an education.
After my grandparents gave their daughter away to her husband's family, they had dispensed all the adventure and all the property. They
expected her alone to keep the traditional ways, which her brothers,
now among the barbarians, could fumble without detection. The heavy,
deep-rooted women were to maintain the past against the flood, safe for
returning. But the rare urge west had fixed upon our family, and so my
aunt crossed boundaries not delineated in space.

The work of preservation demands that the feelings playing about   21
in one's guts not be turned into action. Just watch their passing like
cherry blossoms. But perhaps my aunt, my forerunner, caught in a slow
life, let dreams grow and fade and after some months or years went
toward what persisted. Fear at the enormities of the forbidden kept her
desires delicate, wire and bone. She looked at a man because she liked
the way the hair was tucked behind his ears, or she liked the question-
mark line of a long torso curving at the shoulder and straight at the hip.
For warm eyes or a soft voice or a slow walk—that's all—a few hairs, a
line, a brightness, a sound, a pace, she gave up family. She offered us up

---

[1] Eating at the same table; sharing meals as table companions. [Eds.]

for a charm that vanished with tiredness, a pigtail that didn't toss when the wind died. Why, the wrong lighting could erase the dearest thing about him.

It could very well have been, however, that my aunt did not take 22 subtle enjoyment of her friend, but, a wild woman, kept rollicking company. Imagining her free with sex doesn't fit, though. I don't know any women like that, or men either. Unless I see her life branching into mine, she gives me no ancestral help.

To sustain her being in love, she often worked at herself in the mir- 23 ror, guessing at the colors and shapes that would interest him, changing them frequently in order to hit on the right combination. She wanted him to look back.

On a farm near the sea, a woman who tended her appearance 24 reaped a reputation for eccentricity. All the married women blunt-cut their hair in flaps about their ears or pulled it back in tight buns. No nonsense. Neither style blew easily into heart-catching tangles. And at their weddings they displayed themselves in their long hair for the last time. "It brushed the backs of my knees," my mother tells me. "It was braided, and even so, it brushed the backs of my knees."

At the mirror my aunt combed individuality into her bob. A bun 25 could have been contrived to escape into black streamers blowing in the wind or in quiet wisps about her face, but only the older women in our picture album wear buns. She brushed her hair back from her forehead, tucking the flaps behind her ears. She looped a piece of thread, knotted into a circle between her index fingers and thumbs, and ran the double strand across her forehead. When she closed her fingers as if she were making a pair of shadow geese bite, the string twisted together catching the little hairs. Then she pulled the thread away from her skin, ripping the hairs out neatly, her eyes watering from the needles of pain. Opening her fingers, she cleaned the thread, then rolled it along her hairline and the tops of her eyebrows. My mother did the same to me and my sisters and herself. I used to believe that the expression "caught by the short hairs" meant a captive held with a depilatory string. It especially hurt at the temples, but my mother said we were lucky we didn't have to have our feet bound when we were seven. Sisters used to sit on their beds and cry together, she said, as their mothers or their slave removed the bandages for a few minutes each night and let the blood gush back into their veins. I hope that the man my aunt loved appreciated a smooth brow, that he wasn't just a tits-and-ass man.

Once my aunt found a freckle on her chin, at a spot that the almanac 26 said predestined her for unhappiness. She dug it out with a hot needle and washed the wound with peroxide.

More attention to her looks than these pullings of hairs and pick- 27 ings at spots would have caused gossip among the villagers. They owned work clothes and good clothes, and they wore good clothes for feasting the new seasons. But since a woman combing her hair hexes beginnings, my aunt rarely found an occasion to look her best. Women looked like great sea snails—the corded wood, babies, and laundry they carried were the whorls on their backs. The Chinese did not admire a bent back; goddesses and warriors stood straight. Still there must have been a marvelous freeing of beauty when a worker laid down her burden and stretched and arched.

Such commonplace loveliness, however, was not enough for my aunt. She dreamed of a lover for the fifteen days of New Year's, the time for families to exchange visits, money, and food. She plied her secret comb. And sure enough she cursed the year, the family, the village, and herself. 28

Even as her hair lured her imminent lover, many other men looked at her. Uncles, cousins, nephews, brothers would have looked, too, had they been home between journeys. Perhaps they had already been restraining their curiosity, and they left, fearful that their glances, like a field of nesting birds, might be startled and caught. Poverty hurt, and that was their first reason for leaving. But another, final reason for leaving the crowded house was the never-said. 29

She may have been unusually beloved, the precious only daughter, spoiled and mirror gazing because of the affection the family lavished on her. When her husband left, they welcomed the chance to take her back from the in-laws; she could live like the little daughter for just a while longer. There are stories that my grandfather was different from other people, "crazy ever since the little Jap bayoneted him in the head." He used to put his naked penis on the dinner table, laughing. And one day he brought home a baby girl, wrapped up inside his brown western-style greatcoat. He had traded one of his sons, probably my father, the youngest, for her. My grandmother made him trade back. When he finally got a daughter of his own, he doted on her. They must have all loved her, except perhaps my father, the only brother who never went back to China, having once been traded for a girl. 30

Brothers and sisters, newly men and women, had to efface their sexual color and present plain miens.[2] Disturbing hair and eyes, a smile like no other, threatened the ideal of five generations living under one roof. To focus blurs, people shouted face to face and yelled from room to room. The immigrants I know have loud voices, unmodulated to American tones even after years away from the village where they called their friendships out across the fields. I have not been able to stop my mother's screams in public libraries or over telephones. Walking erect (knees straight, toes pointed forward, not pigeon-toed, which is Chinese-feminine) and speaking in an inaudible voice, I have tried to turn myself American-feminine. Chinese communication was loud, 31

---

[2] Appearances. [Eds.]

public. Only sick people had to whisper. But at the dinner table, where the family members came nearest one another, no one could talk, not the outcasts nor any eaters. Every word that falls from the mouth is a coin lost. Silently they gave and accepted food with both hands. A preoccupied child who took his bowl with one hand got a sideways glare. A complete moment of total attention is due everyone alike. Children and lovers have no singularity here, but my aunt used a secret voice, a separate attentiveness.

She kept the man's name to herself throughout her labor and dying; 32 she did not accuse him that he be punished with her. To save her inseminator's name she gave silent birth.

He may have been somebody in her own household, but inter- 33 course with a man outside the family would have been no less abhorrent. All the village were kinsmen, and the titles shouted in loud country voices never let kinship be forgotten. Any man within visiting distance would have been neutralized as a lover—"brother," "younger brother," "older brother"—one hundred and fifteen relationship titles. Parents researched birth charts probably not so much to assure good fortune as to circumvent incest in a population that has but one hundred surnames. Everybody has eight million relatives. How useless then sexual mannerisms, how dangerous.

As if it came from an atavism[3] deeper than fear, I used to add 34 "brother" silently to boys' names. It hexed the boys, who would or would not ask me to dance, and made them less scary and as familiar and deserving of benevolence as girls.

But, of course, I hexed myself also—no dates. I should have stood 35 up, both arms waving, and shouted out across libraries, "Hey, you! Love me back." I had no idea, though, how to make attraction selective, how to control its direction and magnitude. If I made myself American-pretty so that the five or six Chinese boys in the class fell in love with me, everyone else—the Caucasian, Negro, and Japanese boys—would too. Sisterliness, dignified and honorable, made much more sense.

Attraction eludes control so stubbornly that whole societies 36 designed to organize relationships among people cannot keep order, not even when they bind people to one another from childhood and raise them together. Among the very poor and the wealthy, brothers married their adopted sisters, like doves. Our family allowed some romance, paying adult brides' prices and providing dowries so that their sons and daughters could marry strangers. Marriage promises to turn strangers into friendly relatives—a nation of siblings.

---

[3] The reappearance of a characteristic after a long absence. [Eds.]

In the village structure, spirits shimmered among the live creatures,   37
balanced and held in equilibrium by time and land. But one human
being flaring up into violence could open up a black hole, a maelstrom
that pulled in the sky. The frightened villagers, who depended on one
another to maintain the real, went to my aunt to show her a personal,
physical representation of the break she had made in the "roundness."
Misallying couples snapped off the future, which was to be embodied
in true offspring. The villagers punished her for acting as if she could
have a private life, secret and apart from them.

If my aunt had betrayed the family at a time of large grain yields   38
and peace, when many boys were born, and wings were being built on
many houses, perhaps she might have escaped such severe punishment. But the men—hungry, greedy, tired of planting in dry soil, cuck-
olded—had had to leave the village in order to send food-money home.
There were ghost plagues, bandit plagues, wars with the Japanese,
floods. My Chinese brother and sister had died of an unknown sickness.
Adultery, perhaps only a mistake during good times, became a crime
when the village needed food.

The round moon cakes and round doorways, the round tables of   39
graduated size that fit one roundness inside another, round windows
and rice bowls—these talismans had lost their power to warn this family of the law: a family must be whole, faithfully keeping the descent
line by having sons to feed the old and the dead, who in turn look after
the family. The villagers came to show my aunt and her lover-in-hiding
a broken house. The villagers were speeding up the circling of events
because she was too shortsighted to see that her infidelity had already
harmed the village, that waves of consequences would return unpre-
dictably, sometimes in disguise, as now, to hurt her. This roundness had
to be made coin-sized so that she would see its circumference: punish
her at the birth of her baby. Awaken her to the inexorable. People who
refused fatalism because they could invent small resources insisted on
culpability. Deny accidents and wrest fault from the stars.

After the villagers left, their lanterns now scattering in various   40
directions toward home, the family broke their silence and cursed her.
"Aiaa, we're going to die. Death is coming. Death is coming. Look what
you've done. You've killed us. Ghost! Dead ghost! Ghost! You've never
been born." She ran out into the fields, far enough from the house so
that she could no longer hear their voices, and pressed herself against
the earth, her own land no more. When she felt the birth coming, she
thought that she had been hurt. Her body seized together. "They've
hurt me too much," she thought. "This is gall, and it will kill me."
With forehead and knees against the earth, her body convulsed and
then relaxed. She turned on her back, lay on the ground. The black well
of sky and stars went out and out and out forever; her body and her

complexity seemed to disappear. She was one of the stars, a bright dot in blackness, without home, without a companion, in eternal cold and silence. And agoraphobia[4] rose in her, speeding higher and higher, bigger and bigger; she would not be able to contain it; there would be no end to fear.

Flayed, unprotected against space, she felt pain return, focusing her 41 body. This pain chilled her—a cold, steady kind of surface pain. Inside, spasmodically, the other pain, the pain of the child, heated her. For hours she lay on the ground, alternately body and space. Sometimes a vision of normal comfort obliterated reality: she saw the family in the evening gambling at the dinner table, the young people massaging their elders' backs. She saw them congratulating one another, high joy on the mornings the rice shoots came up. When these pictures burst, the stars drew yet further apart. Black space opened.

She got to her feet to fight better and remembered that old-fashioned 42 women gave birth in their pigsties to fool the jealous, pain-dealing gods, who do not snatch piglets. Before the next spasms could stop her, she ran to the pigsty, each step a rushing out into emptiness. She climbed over the fence and knelt in the dirt. It was good to have a fence enclosing her, a tribal person alone.

Laboring, this woman who had carried her child as a foreign 43 growth that sickened her every day, expelled it at last. She reached down to touch the hot, wet, moving mass, surely smaller than anything human, and could feel that it was human after all—fingers, toes, nails, nose. She pulled it up on to her belly, and it lay curled there, butt in the air, feet precisely tucked one under the other. She opened her loose shirt and buttoned the child inside. After resting, it squirmed and thrashed and she pushed it up to her breast. It turned its head this way and that until it found her nipple. There, it made little snuffling noises. She clenched her teeth at its preciousness, lovely as a young calf, a piglet, a little dog.

She may have gone to the pigsty as a last act of responsibility: she 44 would protect this child as she had protected its father. It would look after her soul, leaving supplies on her grave. But how would this tiny child without family find her grave when there would be no marker for her anywhere, neither in the earth nor the family hall? No one would give her a family hall name. She had taken the child with her into the wastes. At its birth the two of them had felt the same raw pain of separation, a wound that only the family pressing tight could close. A child with no descent line would not soften her life but only trail after her,

---

[4] Pathological fear of of being helpless or embarrassed in a pubic situation, characterized by avoidance of public places. [Eds.]

ghost-like, begging her to give it purpose. At dawn the villagers on their way to the fields would stand around the fence and look.

Full of milk, the little ghost slept. When it awoke, she hardened her 45 breasts against the milk that crying loosens. Toward morning she picked up the baby and walked to the well.

Carrying the baby to the well shows loving. Otherwise abandon it. 46 Turn its face into the mud. Mothers who love their children take them along. It was probably a girl; there is some hope of forgiveness for boys.

"Don't tell anyone you had an aunt. Your father does not want to 47 hear her name. She has never been born." I have believed that sex was unspeakable and words so strong and fathers so frail that "aunt" would do my father mysterious harm. I have thought that my family, having settled among immigrants who had also been their neighbors in the ancestral land, needed to clean their name, and a wrong word would incite the kinspeople even here. But there is more to this silence: they want me to participate in her punishment. And I have.

In the twenty years since I heard this story I have not asked for 48 details nor said my aunt's name; I do not know it. People who can comfort the dead can also chase after them to hurt them further—a reverse ancestor worship. The real punishment was not the raid swiftly inflicted by the villagers, but the family's deliberately forgetting her. Her betrayal so maddened them, they saw to it that she would suffer forever, even after death. Always hungry, always needing, she would have to beg food from other ghosts, snatch and steal it from those whose living descendants give them gifts. She would have to fight the ghosts massed at crossroads for the buns a few thoughtful citizens leave to decoy her away from village and home so that the ancestral spirits could feast unharassed. At peace, they could act like gods, not ghosts, their descent lines providing them with paper suits and dresses, spirit money, paper houses, paper automobiles, chicken, meat, and rice into eternity—essences delivered up in smoke and flames, steam and incense rising from each rice bowl. In an attempt to make the Chinese care for people outside the family, Chairman Mao[5] encourages us now to give our paper replicas to the spirits of outstanding soldiers and workers, no matter whose ancestors they may be. My aunt remains forever hungry. Goods are not distributed evenly among the dead.

My aunt haunts me—her ghost drawn to me because now, after 49 fifty years of neglect, I alone devote pages of paper to her, though not origamied into houses and clothes. I do not think she always means me well. I am telling on her, and she was a spite suicide, drowning herself

---

[5] Mao Zedong (1893–1976), founder and leader of the communist People's Republic of China from 1949 until his death. [Eds.]

in the drinking water. The Chinese are always very frightened of the drowned one, whose weeping ghost, wet hair hanging and skin bloated, waits silently by the water to pull down a substitute.

Responding to Reading

1.   How accurate do you imagine Kingston's "facts" are? Do you think strict accuracy is important in this essay? Why or why not?
2.   Kingston never met her aunt. Even so, in what sense is this essay about her relationship with her aunt (and with other family members, both known and unknown)?
3.   Is there a family member other than your parents who has had a profound effect on your life? In what way is this relationship like and unlike the one Kingston describes in her essay?

THE WAY TO RAINY MOUNTAIN

N. Scott Momaday

N. Scott Momaday (1934–   ) is a poet, novelist, and nonfiction writer who won the Pulitzer Prize for his novel House Made of Dawn *(1968). Critic Baine Kerr in* Southwest Review *describes this book as an attempt to "transliterate Indian culture, myth, and sensibility into an alien art form without loss." Momaday grew up on a reservation in New Mexico and now teaches at the University of Arizona. His work chronicles Native American experience and portrays Indian culture as strongly identified with the land. Recent works include* In the Presence of the Sun, *a collection of stories and poems spanning his thirty-year writing career (1992), and* The Man Made of Words: Essays, Stories, Passages *(1997). In the following selection from his collection of autobiographical essays,* The Way to Rainy Mountain *(1969), Momaday describes Kiowa culture through the stories and legends his grandmother told him.*

A single knoll rises out of the plain in Oklahoma, north and west of   1
the Wichita Range. For my people, the Kiowas, it is an old landmark, and they gave it the name Rainy Mountain. The hardest weather in the world is there. Winter brings blizzards, hot tornadic winds arise in the spring, and in summer the prairie is an anvil's edge. The grass turns brittle and brown, and it cracks beneath your feet. There are green belts along the rivers and creeks, linear groves of hickory and pecan, willow and witch hazel. At a distance in July or August the steaming foliage seems almost to writhe in fire. Great green and yellow grasshoppers are everywhere in the tall grass, popping up like corn to sting the flesh, and

tortoises crawl about on the red earth, going nowhere in the plenty of time. Loneliness is an aspect of the land. All things in the plain are isolate; there is no confusion of objects in the eye, but *one* hill or *one* tree or *one* man. To look upon that landscape in the early morning, with the sun at your back, is to lose the sense of proportion. Your imagination comes to life, and this, you think, is where Creation was begun.

I returned to Rainy Mountain in July. My grandmother had died in 2 the spring, and I wanted to be at her grave. She had lived to be very old and at last infirm. Her only living daughter was with her when she died, and I was told that in death her face was that of a child.

I like to think of her as a child. When she was born, the Kiowas were 3 living the last great moment of their history. For more than a hundred years they had controlled the open range from the Smoky Hill River to the Red, from the headwaters of the Canadian to the fork of the Arkansas and Cimarron. In alliance with the Comanches, they had ruled the whole of the southern Plains. War was their sacred business, and they were among the finest horsemen the world has ever known. But warfare for the Kiowas was preeminently a matter of disposition rather than of survival, and they never understood the grim, unrelenting advance of the U.S. Cavalry. When at last, divided and ill-provisioned, they were driven onto the Staked Plains in the cold rains of autumn, they fell into panic. In Palo Duro Canyon they abandoned their crucial stores to pillage and had nothing then but their lives. In order to save themselves, they surrendered to the soldiers at Fort Sill and were imprisoned in the old stone corral that now stands as a military museum. My grandmother was spared the humiliation of those high gray walls by eight or ten years, but she must have known from birth the affliction of defeat, the dark brooding of old warriors.

Her name was Aho, and she belonged to the last culture to evolve 4 in North America. Her forebears came down from the high country in western Montana nearly three centuries ago. They were a mountain people, a mysterious tribe of hunters whose language has never been positively classified in any major group. In the late seventeenth century they began a long migration to the south and east. It was a journey toward the dawn, and it led to a golden age. Along the way the Kiowas were befriended by the Crows, who gave them the culture and religion of the Plains. They acquired horses, and their ancient nomadic spirit was suddenly free of the ground. They acquired Tai-me, the sacred Sun Dance doll, from that moment the object and symbol of their worship, and so shared in the divinity of the sun. Not least, they acquired the sense of destiny, therefore courage and pride. When they entered upon the southern Plains they had been transformed. No longer were they slaves to the simple necessity of survival; they were a lordly and dangerous society of fighters and thieves, hunters and priests of the sun.

According to their origin myth, they entered the world through a hollow log. From one point of view, their migration was the fruit of an old prophecy, for indeed they emerged from a sunless world.

Although my grandmother lived out her long life in the shadow of 5 Rainy Mountain, the immense landscape of the continental interior lay like memory in her blood. She could tell of the Crows, whom she had never seen, and of the Black Hills, where she had never been. I wanted to see in reality what she had seen more perfectly in the mind's eye, and traveled fifteen hundred miles to begin my pilgrimage.

Yellowstone, it seemed to me, was the top of the world, a region of 6 deep lakes and dark timber, canyons and waterfalls. But, beautiful as it is, one might have the sense of confinement there. The skyline in all directions is close at hand, the high wall of the woods and deep cleavages of shade. There is a perfect freedom in the mountains, but it belongs to the eagle and the elk, the badger and the bear. The Kiowas reckoned their stature by the distance they could see, and they were bent and blind in the wilderness.

Descending eastward, the highland meadows are a stairway to the 7 plain. In July the inland slope of the Rockies is luxuriant with flax and buckwheat, stonecrop and larkspur. The earth unfolds and the limit of the land recedes. Clusters of trees, and animals grazing far in the distance, cause the vision to reach away and wonder to build upon the mind. The sun follows a longer course in the day, and the sky is immense beyond all comparison. The great billowing clouds that sail upon it are shadows that move upon the grain like water, dividing light. Farther down, in the land of the Crows and Blackfeet, the plain is yellow. Sweet clover takes hold of the hills and bends upon itself to cover and seal the soil. There the Kiowas paused on their way; they had come to the place where they must change their lives. The sun is at home on the plains. Precisely there does it have the certain character of a god. When the Kiowas came to the land of the Crows, they could see the dark lees of the hills at dawn across the Bighorn River, the profusion of light on the grain shelves, the oldest deity ranging after the solstices. Not yet would they veer southward to the caldron of the land that lay below; they must wean their blood from the northern winter and hold the mountains a while longer in their view. They bore Tai-me in procession to the east.

A dark mist lay over the Black Hills, and the land was like iron. At 8 the top of a ridge I caught sight of Devil's Tower upthrust against the gray sky as if in the birth of time the core of the earth had broken through its crust and the motion of the world was begun. There are things in nature that engender an awful quiet in the heart of man; Devil's Tower is one of them. Two centuries ago, because they could not do otherwise, the Kiowas made a legend at the base of the rock. My grandmother said:

Eight children were there at play, seven sisters and their brother. Suddenly the boy was struck dumb; he trembled and began to run upon his hands and feet. His fingers became claws, and his body was covered with fur. Directly there was a bear where the boy had been. The sisters were terrified; they ran, and the bear after them. They came to the stump of a great tree, and the tree spoke to them. It bade them climb upon it, and as they did so it began to rise into the air. The bear came to kill them, but they were just beyond its reach. It reared against the tree and scored the bark all around with its claws. The seven sisters were borne into the sky, and they became the stars of the Big Dipper.

From that moment, and so long as the legend lives, the Kiowas have kinsmen in the night sky. Whatever they were in the mountains, they could be no more. However tenuous their well-being, however much they had suffered and would suffer again, they had found a way out of the wilderness.

My grandmother had a reverence for the sun, a holy regard that 9 now is all but gone out of mankind. There was a wariness in her, and an ancient awe. She was a Christian in her later years, but she had come a long way about, and she never forgot her birthright. As a child she had been to the Sun Dances; she had taken part in those annual rites, and by them she had learned the restoration of her people in the presence of Tai-me. She was about seven when the last Kiowa Sun Dance was held in 1887 on the Washita River above Rainy Mountain Creek. The buffalo were gone. In order to consummate the ancient sacrifice— to impale the head of a buffalo bull upon the medicine tree—a delegation of old men journeyed into Texas, there to beg and barter for an animal from the Goodnight herd. She was ten when the Kiowas came together for the last time as a living Sun Dance culture. They could find no buffalo; they had to hang an old hide from the sacred tree. Before the dance could begin, a company of soldiers rode out from Fort Sill under orders to disperse the tribe. Forbidden without cause the essential act of their faith, having seen the wild herds slaughtered and left to rot upon the ground, the Kiowas backed away forever from the medicine tree. That was July 20, 1890, at the great bend of the Washita. My grandmother was there. Without bitterness, and for as long as she lived, she bore a vision of deicide.[1]

Now that I can have her only in memory, I see my grandmother in 10 the several postures that were peculiar to her: standing at the wood stove on a winter morning and turning meat in a great iron skillet; sitting at the south window, bent above her beadwork, and afterwards,

---

[1] The killing of a god. [Eds.]

when her vision failed, looking down for a long time into the fold of her hands; going out upon a cane, very slowly as she did when the weight of age came upon her; praying. I remember her most often at prayer. She made long, rambling prayers out of suffering and hope, having seen many things. I was never sure that I had the right to hear, so exclusive were they of all mere custom and company. The last time I saw her she prayed standing by the side of her bed at night, naked to the waist, the light of a kerosene lamp moving upon her dark skin. Her long, black hair, always drawn and braided in the day, lay upon her shoulders and against her breasts like a shawl. I do not speak Kiowa, and I never understood her prayers, but there was something inherently sad in the sound, some merest hesitation upon the syllables of sorrow. She began in a high and descending pitch, exhausting her breath to silence; then again and again—and always the same intensity of effort, of something that is, and is not, like urgency in the human voice. Transported so in the dancing light among the shadows of her room, she seemed beyond the reach of time. But that was illusion; I think I knew then that I should not see her again.

Houses are like sentinels in the plain, old keepers of the weather 11 watch. There, in a very little while, wood takes on the appearance of great age. All colors wear soon away in the wind and rain, and then the wood is burned gray and the grain appears and the nails turn red with rust. The windowpanes are black and opaque; you imagine there is nothing within, and indeed there are many ghosts, bones given up to the land. They stand here and there against the sky, and you approach them for a longer time than you expect. They belong in the distance; it is their domain.

Once there was a lot of sound in my grandmother's house, a lot of 12 coming and going, feasting and talk. The summers there were full of excitement and reunion. The Kiowas are a summer people; they abide the cold and keep to themselves, but when the season turns and the land becomes warm and vital they cannot hold still; an old love of going returns upon them. The aged visitors who came to my grandmother's house when I was a child were made of lean and leather, and they bore themselves upright. They wore great black hats and bright ample shirts that shook in the wind. They rubbed fat upon their hair and wound their braids with strips of colored cloth. Some of them painted their faces and carried the scars of old and cherished enmities. They were an old council of warlords, come to remind and be reminded of who they were. Their wives and daughters served them well. The women might indulge themselves; gossip was at once the mark and compensation of their servitude. They made loud and elaborate talk among themselves, full of jest and gesture, fright and false alarm. They went abroad in fringed and flowered shawls, bright beadwork and German silver. They were at home in the kitchen, and they prepared meals that were banquets.

There were frequent prayer meetings, and great nocturnal feasts. 13
When I was a child I played with my cousins outside, where the lamp-
light fell upon the ground and the singing of the old people rose up
around us and carried away into the darkness. There were a lot of good
things to eat, a lot of laughter and surprise. And afterwards, when the
quiet returned, I lay down with my grandmother and could hear the
frogs away by the river and feel the motion of the air.

Now there is funeral silence in the rooms, the endless wake of some 14
final word. The walls have closed in upon my grandmother's house.
When I returned to it in mourning, I saw for the first time in my life how
small it was. It was late at night, and there was a white moon, nearly
full. I sat for a long time on the stone steps by the kitchen door. From
there I could see out across the land; I could see the long row of trees by
the creek, the low light upon the rolling plains, and the stars of the Big
Dipper. Once I looked at the moon and caught sight of a strange thing.
A cricket had perched upon the handrail, only a few inches away from
me. My line of vision was such that the creature filled the moon like a
fossil. It had gone there, I thought, to live and die, for there, of all places,
was its small definition made whole and eternal. A warm wind rose up
and purled[2] like the longing within me.

The next morning I awoke at dawn and went out on the dirt road to 15
Rainy Mountain. It was already hot, and the grasshoppers began to fill
the air. Still, it was early in the morning, and the birds sang out of the
shadows. The long yellow grass on the mountain shone in the bright
light, and a scissortail hied above the land. There, where it ought to be,
at the end of a long and legendary way, was my grandmother's grave.
Here and there on the dark stones were ancestral names. Looking back
once, I saw the mountain and came away.

Responding to Reading

1. Momaday portrays his grandmother not only as an individual but also as a
   symbol. What larger idea do you think she stands for? Explain.
2. Does the background Momaday provides make his grandmother's life easier or harder for you to understand? What other information would help
   you understand her (and her significance to him)?
3. This essay focuses on Momaday's grandmother, not on his own relationship with her. In what sense is the essay nevertheless about the author as
   well as about his grandmother?

---

[2] Flowed; rippled. [Eds.]

BEAUTY: WHEN THE OTHER DANCER IS THE SELF

Alice Walker

Alice Walker (1944–   ) was born in Eatonton, Georgia, where her parents were sharecroppers. A writer of stories since childhood, she is today known as a poet, fiction writer, essayist, biographer, and editor. Walker often writes about the experiences of poor black women and the effects of racism and sexism. An advocate of African-American women writers, she helped revive the literary reputation of writer and folklorist Zora Neale Hurston by editing a collection of her writing, I Love Myself When I Am Laughing *(1979). Walker is also the author of five novels, including the Pulitzer Prize–winning* The Color Purple *(1982), and several collections of poetry, stories, and essays, including her most recent* Everything We Love Can Be Saved: A Writer's Activism *(1997). In the following essay from her collection* In Search of Our Mothers' Gardens *(1983), she traces the changes she experienced in her self-image after a childhood accident left her blind in one eye.*

It is a bright summer day in 1947. My father, a fat, funny man with 1 beautiful eyes and a subversive wit, is trying to decide which of his eight children he will take with him to the county fair. My mother, of course, will not go. She is knocked out from getting most of us ready: I hold my neck stiff against the pressure of her knuckles as she hastily completes the braiding and then beribboning of my hair.

My father is the driver for the rich old white lady up the road. Her 2 name is Miss Mey. She owns all the land for miles around, as well as the house in which we live. All I remember about her is that she once offered to pay my mother thirty-five cents for cleaning her house, raking up piles of her magnolia leaves, and washing her family's clothes, and that my mother—she of no money, eight children, and a chronic earache—refused it. But I do not think of this in 1947. I am two and a half years old. I want to go everywhere my daddy goes. I am excited at the prospect of riding in a car. Someone has told me fairs are fun. That there is room in the car for only three of us doesn't faze me at all. Whirling happily in my starchy frock, showing off my biscuit-polished patent-leather shoes and lavender socks, tossing my head in a way that makes my ribbons bounce, I stand, hands on hips, before my father. "Take me, Daddy," I say with assurance; "I'm the prettiest!"

Later, it does not surprise me to find myself in Miss Mey's shiny 3 black car, sharing the back seat with the other lucky ones. Does not surprise me that I thoroughly enjoy the fair. At home that night I tell the unlucky ones all I can remember about the merry-go-round, the man who eats live chickens, and the teddy bears, until they say: that's enough, baby Alice. Shut up now, and go to sleep.

It is Easter Sunday, 1950. I am dressed in a green, flocked, scalloped- 4 hem dress (handmade by my adoring sister, Ruth) that has its own smooth satin petticoat and tiny hot-pink roses tucked into each scallop. My shoes, new T-strap patent leather, again highly biscuit-polished. I am six years old and have learned one of the longest Easter speeches to be heard that day, totally unlike the speech I said when I was two: "Easter lilies/pure and white/blossom in/the morning light." When I rise to give my speech I do so on a great wave of love and pride and expectation. People in the church stop rustling their new crinolines. They seem to hold their breath. I can tell they admire my dress, but it is my spirit, bordering on sassiness (womanishness), they secretly applaud.

"That girl's a little *mess*," they whisper to each other, pleased.   5

Naturally I say my speech without stammer or pause, unlike those 6 who stutter, stammer, or, worst of all, forget. This is before the word "beautiful" exists in people's vocabulary, but "Oh, isn't she the *cutest* thing!" frequently floats my way. "And got so much sense!" they gratefully add . . . for which thoughtful addition I thank them to this day.

It was great fun being cute. But then, one day, it ended.   7

I am eight years old and a tomboy. I have a cowboy hat, cowboy 8 boots, checkered shirt and pants, all red. My playmates are my brothers, two and four years older than I. Their colors are black and green, the only difference in the way we are dressed. On Saturday nights we all go to the picture show, even my mother; Westerns are her favorite kind of movie. Back home, "on the ranch," we pretend we are Tom Mix, Hopalong Cassidy, Lash LaRue (we've even named one of our dogs Lash LaRue); we chase each other for hours rustling cattle, being out-laws, delivering damsels from distress. Then my parents decide to buy my brothers guns. These are not "real" guns. They shoot "BBs," copper pellets my brothers say will kill birds. Because I am a girl, I do not get a gun. Instantly I am relegated to the position of Indian. Now there appears a great distance between us. They shoot and shoot at every-thing with their new guns. I try to keep up with my bow and arrows.

One day while I am standing on top of our makeshift "garage"— 9 pieces of tin nailed across some poles—holding my bow and arrow and looking out toward the fields, I feel an incredible blow in my right eye. I look down just in time to see my brother lower his gun.

Both brothers rush to my side. My eye stings, and I cover it with my 10 hand. "If you tell," they say, "we will get a whipping. You don't want that to happen, do you?" I do not. "Here is a piece of wire," says the older brother, picking it up from the roof; "say you stepped on one end of it and the other flew up and hit you." The pain is beginning to start. "Yes," I say, "Yes, I will say that is what happened." If I do not say this is what happened, I know my brothers will find ways to make me wish I had. But now I will say anything that gets me to my mother.

Confronted by our parents we stick to the lie agreed upon. They 11 place me on a bench on the porch and I close my left eye while they examine the right. There is a tree growing from underneath the porch that climbs past the railing to the roof. It is the last thing my right eye sees. I watch as its trunk, its branches, and then its leaves are blotted out by the rising blood.

I am in shock. First there is intense fever, which my father tries to 12 break using lily leaves bound around my head. Then there are chills: my mother tries to get me to eat soup. Eventually, I do not know how, my parents learn what has happened. A week after the "accident" they take me to see a doctor. "Why did you wait so long to come?" he asks, looking into my eye and shaking his head. "Eyes are sympathetic," he says. "If one is blind, the other will likely become blind too."

This comment of the doctor's terrifies me. But it is really how I look 13 that bothers me most. Where the BB pellet struck there is a glob of whitish scar tissue, a hideous cataract, on my eye. Now when I stare at people—a favorite pastime, up to now—they will stare back. Not at the "cute" little girl, but at her scar. For six years I do not stare at anyone, because I do not raise my head.

Years later, in the throes of a mid-life crisis, I ask my mother and sis- 14 ter whether I changed after the "accident." "No," they say, puzzled. "What do you mean?"

What do I mean? 15

I am eight, and, for the first time, doing poorly in school, where I 16 have been something of a whiz since I was four. We have just moved to the place where the "accident" occurred. We do not know any of the people around us because this is a different county. The only time I see the friends I knew is when we go back to our old church. The new school is the former state penitentiary. It is a large stone building, cold and drafty, crammed to overflowing with boisterous, ill-disciplined children. On the third floor there is a huge circular imprint of some partition that has been torn out.

"What used to be here?" I ask a sullen girl next to me on our way 17 past it to lunch.

"The electric chair," says she. 18

At night I have nightmares about the electric chair, and about all the 19 people reputedly "fried" in it. I am afraid of the school, where all the students seem to be budding criminals.

"What's the matter with your eye?" they ask, critically.   20

When I don't answer (I cannot decide whether it was an "accident"   21
or not), they shove me, insist on a fight.

My brother, the one who created the story about the wire, comes to   22
my rescue. But then brags so much about "protecting" me, I become
sick.

After months of torture at the school, my parents decide to send me   23
back to our old community, to my old school. I live with my grandparents
and the teacher they board. But there is no room for Phoebe, my cat. By
the time my grandparents decide there *is* room, and I ask for my cat, she
cannot be found. Miss Yarborough, the boarding teacher, takes me under
her wing, and begins to teach me to play the piano. But soon she marries
an African—a "prince," she says—and is whisked away to his continent.

At my old school there is at least one teacher who loves me. She is   24
the teacher who "knew me before I was born" and bought my first
baby clothes. It is she who makes life bearable. It is her presence that
finally helps me turn on the one child at the school who continually
calls me "one-eyed bitch." One day I simply grab him by his coat and
beat him until I am satisfied. It is my teacher who tells me my mother
is ill.

My mother is lying in bed in the middle of the day, something I   25
have never seen. She is in too much pain to speak. She has an abscess in
her ear. I stand looking down on her, knowing that if she dies, I cannot
live. She is being treated with warm oils and hot bricks held against her
cheek. Finally a doctor comes. But I must go back to my grandparents'
house. The weeks pass but I am hardly aware of it. All I know is that my
mother might die, my father is not so jolly, my brothers still have their
guns, and I am the one sent away from home.

"You did not change," they say.   26

Did I imagine the anguish of never looking up?   27

I am twelve. When relatives come to visit I hide in my room. My   28
cousin Brenda, just my age, whose father works in the post office and
whose mother is a nurse, comes to find me. "Hello," she says. And then
she asks, looking at my recent school picture, which I did not want
taken, and on which the "glob," as I think of it, is clearly visible, "You
still can't see out of that eye?"

"No," I say, and flop back on the bed over my book.   29

That night, as I do almost every night, I abuse my eye. I rant   30
and rave at it, in front of the mirror. I plead with it to clear up before
morning. I tell it I hate and despise it. I do not pray for sight. I pray for
beauty.

"You did not change," they say.   31

I am fourteen and baby-sitting for my brother Bill, who lives in 32
Boston. He is my favorite brother and there is a strong bond between us.
Understanding my feelings of shame and ugliness he and his wife take
me to a local hospital, where the "glob" is removed by a doctor named
O. Henry. There is still a small bluish crater where the scar tissue was,
but the ugly white stuff is gone. Almost immediately I become a different person from the girl who does not raise her head. Or so I think. Now
that I've raised my head I win the boyfriend of my dreams. Now that
I've raised my head I have plenty of friends. Now that I've raised my
head classwork comes from my lips as faultlessly as Easter speeches
did, and I leave high school as valedictorian, most popular student, and
queen, hardly believing my luck. Ironically, the girl who was voted most
beautiful in our class (and was) was later shot twice through the chest
by a male companion, using a "real" gun, while she was pregnant. But
that's another story in itself. Or is it?

"You did not change," they say.   33

It is now thirty years since the "accident." A beautiful journalist 34
comes to visit and to interview me. She is going to write a cover story
for her magazine that focuses on my latest book. "Decide how you want
to look on the cover," she says. "Glamorous, or whatever."

Never mind "glamorous," it is the "whatever" that I hear. Suddenly 35
all I can think of is whether I will get enough sleep the night before the
photography session: if I don't, my eye will be tired and wander, as
blind eyes will.

At night in bed with my lover I think up reasons why I should not 36
appear on the cover of a magazine. "My meanest critics will say I've
sold out," I say. "My family will now realize I write scandalous books."

"But what's the real reason you don't want to do this?" he asks.   37

"Because in all probability," I say in a rush, "my eye won't be 38
straight."

"It will be straight enough," he says. Then, "Besides, I thought 39
you'd made your peace with that."

And I suddenly remember that I have.   40

I remember: 41

I am talking to my brother Jimmy, asking if he remembers anything 42
unusual about the day I was shot. He does not know I consider that day
the last time my father, with his sweet home remedy of cool lily leaves,
chose me, and that I suffered and raged inside because of this. "Well,"
he says, "all I remember is standing by the side of the highway with
Daddy, trying to flag down a car. A white man stopped, but when
Daddy said he needed somebody to take his little girl to the doctor, he
drove off."

I remember: 43

I am in the desert for the first time. I fall totally in love with it. I am 44
so overwhelmed by its beauty, I confront for the first time, consciously,

the meaning of the doctor's words years ago: "Eyes are sympathetic. If one is blind, the other will likely become blind too." I realize I have dashed about the world madly, looking at this, looking at that, storing up images against the fading of the light. *But I might have missed seeing the desert!* The shock of that possibility—and gratitude for over twenty-five years of sight—sends me literally to my knees. Poem after poem comes—which is perhaps how poets pray.

On Sight
I am so thankful I have seen
The Desert
And the creatures in the desert
And the desert Itself.

The desert has its own moon   5
Which I have seen
With my own eye.
There is no flag on it.

Trees of the desert have arms
All of which are always up   10
That is because the moon is up
The sun is up
Also the sky
The stars
Clouds   15
None with flags.

If there were flags, I doubt
the trees would point.
Would you?

But mostly, I remember this: 45

I am twenty-seven, and my baby daughter is almost three. Since her   46
birth I have worried about her discovery that her mother's eyes are different from other people's. Will she be embarrassed? I think. What will she say? Every day she watches a television program called "Big Blue Marble." It begins with a picture of the earth as it appears from the moon. It is bluish, a little battered-looking, but full of light, with whitish clouds swirling around it. Every time I see it I weep with love, as if it is a picture of Grandma's house. One day when I am putting Rebecca down for her nap, she suddenly focuses on my eye. Something inside me cringes, gets ready to try to protect myself. All children are cruel about physical differences, I know from experience, and that they don't always mean to be is another matter. I assume Rebecca will be the same.

But no-o-o-o. She studies my face intently as we stand, her inside   47
and me outside her crib. She even holds my face maternally between

her dimpled little hands. Then, looking every bit as serious and lawyer-like as her father, she says, as if it may just possibly have slipped my attention: "Mommy, there's a *world* in your eye." (As in, "Don't be alarmed, or do anything crazy.") And then, gently, but with great interest: "Mommy, where did you get that world in your eye?"

For the most part, the pain left then. (So what, if my brothers grew   48 up to buy even more powerful pellet guns for their sons and to carry real guns themselves. So what, if a young "Morehouse man"[1] once nearly fell off the steps of Trevor Arnett Library because he thought my eyes were blue.) Crying and laughing I ran to the bathroom, while Rebecca mumbled and sang herself off to sleep. Yes indeed, I realized, looking into the mirror. There was a world in my eye. And I saw that it was possible to love it: that in fact, for all it had taught me of shame and anger and inner vision, I *did* love it. Even to see it drifting out of orbit in boredom, or rolling up out of fatigue, not to mention floating back at attention in excitement (bearing witness, a friend has called it), deeply suitable to my personality, and even characteristic of me.

That night I dream I am dancing to Stevie Wonder's song "Always"   49 (the name of the song is really "As," but I hear it as "Always"). As I dance, whirling and joyous, happier than I've ever been in my life, another bright-faced dancer joins me. We dance and kiss each other and hold each other through the night. The other dancer has obviously come through all right, as I have done. She is beautiful, whole and free. And she is also me.

Responding to Reading

1. Although she is remembering past events, Walker uses present tense ("It is a bright summer day in 1947") to tell her story. Why do you think she does this? Is the present tense more effective than the past tense ("It *was* a bright summer day in 1947") would be? Explain.
2. At several points in the essay, Walker repeats the words her relatives used to reassure her: "You did not change." Why does she repeat this phrase? Were her relatives correct?
3. What circumstances or individuals does Walker blame for the childhood problems she describes? Who do you think is responsible for her misery? Would you be as forgiving as Walker seems to be?

---

[1] A student at Morehouse College, a historically black college in Atlanta, Georgia. [Eds.]

MY FATHER'S LIFE

Raymond Carver

Raymond Carver (1939–1988) was a fiction and poetry writer who grew up in a working-class family in the Pacific Northwest. Influenced by his father's storytelling, he began writing stories himself as a boy. Collections of Carver's stories include Will You Please Be Quiet, Please? *(1976),* What We Talk about When We Talk about Love *(1981),* Cathedral *(1984), and* Short Cuts *(1993). Usually about desperate people struggling for daily survival, Carver's stories often have enigmatic endings. In "My Father's Life," which originally appeared in* Esquire *in 1984, Carver tells how his father first struggled financially during the Great Depression and later suffered from psychological depression.*

My dad's name was Clevie Raymond Carver. His family called him   1
Raymond and friends called him C. R. I was named Raymond Clevie Carver Jr. I hated the "Junior" part. When I was little my dad called me Frog, which was okay. But later, like everybody else in the family, he began calling me Junior. He went on calling me this until I was thirteen or fourteen and announced that I wouldn't answer to that name any longer. So he began calling me Doc. From then until his death, on June 17, 1967, he called me Doc, or else Son.

When he died, my mother telephoned my wife with the news. I was   2
away from my family at the time, between lives, trying to enroll in the School of Library Science at the University of Iowa. When my wife answered the phone, my mother blurted out. "Raymond's dead!" For a moment, my wife thought my mother was telling her that I was dead. Then my mother made it clear *which* Raymond she was talking about and my wife said, "Thank God. I thought you meant *my* Raymond."

My dad walked, hitched rides, and rode in empty boxcars when he   3
went from Arkansas to Washington State in 1934, looking for work. I don't know whether he was pursuing a dream when he went out to Washington. I doubt it. I don't think he dreamed much. I believe he was simply looking for steady work at decent pay. Steady work was meaningful work. He picked apples for a time and then landed a construction laborer's job on the Grand Coulee Dam.[1] After he'd put aside a little money, he bought a car and drove back to Arkansas to help his folks, my grandparents, pack up for the move west. He said later that they were about to starve down there, and this wasn't meant as a figure of speech. It was during that short while in Arkansas, in a town called Leola, that my mother met my dad on the sidewalk as he came out of a tavern.

---

[1] On the Columbia River, northwest of Spokane, Washington. [Eds.]

"He was drunk," she said. "I don't know why I let him talk to me. 4
His eyes were glittery. I wish I'd had a crystal ball." They'd met once,
a year or so before, at a dance. He'd had girlfriends before her, my
mother told me. "Your dad always had a girlfriend, even after we married. He was my first and last. I never had another man. But I didn't
miss anything."

They were married by a justice of the peace on the day they left 5
for Washington, this big, tall country girl and a farmhand-turned-
construction worker. My mother spent her wedding night with my dad
and his folks, all of them camped beside the road in Arkansas.

In Omak, Washington, my dad and mother lived in a little place not 6
much bigger than a cabin. My grandparents lived next door. My dad
was still working on the dam, and later, with the huge turbines producing electricity and the water backed up for a hundred miles into
Canada, he stood in the crowd and heard Franklin D. Roosevelt when
he spoke at the construction site. "He never mentioned those guys who
died building that dam," my dad said. Some of his friends had died
there, men from Arkansas, Oklahoma, and Missouri.

He then took a job in a sawmill in Clatskanie, Oregon, a little town 7
alongside the Columbia River. I was born there, and my mother has a picture of my dad standing in front of the gate to the mill, proudly holding
me up to face the camera. My bonnet is on crooked and about to come
untied. His hat is pushed back on his forehead, and he's wearing a big
grin. Was he going in to work or just finishing his shift? It doesn't matter.
In either case, he had a job and a family. These were his salad days.

In 1941 we moved to Yakima, Washington, where my dad went to 8
work as a saw filer, a skilled trade he'd learned in Clatskanie. When war
broke out, he was given a deferment because his work was considered
necessary to the war effort. Finished lumber was in demand by the
armed services, and he kept his saws so sharp they could shave the hair
off your arm.

After my dad had moved us to Yakima, he moved his folks into the 9
same neighborhood. By the mid-1940s the rest of my dad's family—his
brother, his sister, and her husband, as well as uncles, cousins, nephews,
and most of their extended family and friends—had come out from
Arkansas. All because my dad came out first. The men went to work at
Boise Cascade, where my dad worked, and the women packed apples
in the canneries. And in just a little while, it seemed—according to my
mother—everybody was better off than my dad. "Your dad couldn't
keep money," my mother said. "Money burned a hole in his pocket. He
was always doing for others."

The first house I clearly remember living in, at 1515 South Fifteenth 10
Street, in Yakima, had an outdoor toilet. On Halloween night, or just any
night, for the hell of it, neighbor kids, kids in their early teens, would
carry our toilet away and leave it next to the road. My dad would have

to get somebody to help him bring it home. Or these kids would take the toilet and stand it in somebody else's backyard. Once they actually set it on fire. But ours wasn't the only house that had an outdoor toilet. When I was old enough to know what I was doing, I threw rocks at the other toilets when I'd see someone go inside. This was called bombing the toilets. After a while, though, everyone went to indoor plumbing until, suddenly, our toilet was the last outdoor one in the neighborhood. I remember the shame I felt when my third-grade teacher, Mr. Wise, drove me home from school one day. I asked him to stop at the house just before ours, claiming I lived there.

I can recall what happened one night when my dad came home late 11 to find that my mother had locked all the doors on him from the inside. He was drunk, and we could feel the house shudder as he rattled the door. When he'd managed to force open a window, she hit him between the eyes with a colander and knocked him out. We could see him down there on the grass. For years afterward, I used to pick up this colander— it was as heavy as a rolling pin—and imagine what it would feel like to be hit in the head with something like that.

It was during this period that I remember my dad taking me into 12 the bedroom, sitting me down on the bed, and telling me that I might have to go live with my Aunt La Von for a while. I couldn't understand what I'd done that meant I'd have to go away from home to live. But this, too—whatever prompted it—must have blown over, more or less, anyway, because we stayed together, and I didn't have to go live with her or anyone else.

I remember my mother pouring his whiskey down the sink. 13 Sometimes she'd pour it all out and sometimes, if she was afraid of getting caught, she'd only pour half of it out and then add water to the rest. I tasted some of his whiskey once myself. It was terrible stuff, and I don't see how anybody could drink it.

After a long time without one, we finally got a car, in 1949 or 1950, 14 a 1938 Ford. But it threw a rod the first week we had it, and my dad had to have the motor rebuilt.

"We drove the oldest car in town," my mother said. "We could have 15 had a Cadillac for all he spent on car repairs." One time she found someone else's tube of lipstick on the floorboard, along with a lacy handkerchief. "See this?" she said to me. "Some floozy left this in the car."

Once I saw her take a pan of warm water into the bedroom where 16 my dad was sleeping. She took his hand from under the covers and held it in the water. I stood in the doorway and watched. I wanted to know what was going on. This would make him talk in his sleep, she told me. There were things she needed to know, things she was sure he was keeping from her.

Every year or so, when I was little, we would take the North Coast 17 Limited across the Cascade Range from Yakima to Seattle and stay in the Vance Hotel and eat, I remember, at a place called the Dinner Bell Cafe. Once we went to Ivar's Acres of Clams and drank glasses of warm clam broth.

In 1956, the year I was to graduate from high school, my dad quit [18] his job at the mill in Yakima and took a job in Chester, a little sawmill town in northern California. The reasons given at the time for his taking the job had to do with a higher hourly wage and the vague promise that he might, in a few years' time, succeed to the job of head filer in this new mill. But I think, in the main, that my dad had grown restless and simply wanted to try his luck elsewhere. Things had gotten a little too predictable for him in Yakima. Also, the year before, there had been the deaths, within six months of each other, of both his parents.

But just a few days after graduation, when my mother and I were [19] packed to move to Chester, my dad penciled a letter to say he'd been sick for a while. He didn't want us to worry, he said, but he'd cut himself on a saw. Maybe he'd got a tiny sliver of steel in his blood. Anyway, something had happened and he'd had to miss work, he said. In the same mail was an unsigned postcard from somebody down there telling my mother that my dad was about to die and that he was drinking "raw whiskey."

When we arrived in Chester, my dad was living in a trailer that [20] belonged to the company. I didn't recognize him immediately. I guess for a moment I didn't want to recognize him. He was skinny and pale and looked bewildered. His pants wouldn't stay up. He didn't look like my dad. My mother began to cry. My dad put his arm around her and patted her shoulder vaguely, like he didn't know what this was all about, either. The three of us took up life together in the trailer, and we looked after him as best we could. But my dad was sick, and he couldn't get any better. I worked with him in the mill that summer and part of the fall. We'd get up in the mornings and eat eggs and toast while we listened to the radio, and then go out the door with our lunch pails. We'd pass through the gate together at eight in the morning, and I wouldn't see him again until quitting time. In November I went back to Yakima to be closer to my girlfriend, the girl I'd made up my mind I was going to marry.

He worked at the mill in Chester until the following February, when [21] he collapsed on the job and was taken to the hospital. My mother asked if I would come down there and help. I caught a bus from Yakima to Chester, intending to drive them back to Yakima. But now, in addition to being physically sick, my dad was in the midst of a nervous breakdown, though none of us knew to call it that at the time. During the entire trip back to Yakima, he didn't speak, not even when asked a direct question. ("How do you feel, Raymond?" "You okay, Dad?") He'd communicate if he communicated at all, by moving his head or by turning his palms up as if to say he didn't know or care. The only time he said anything on the trip, and for nearly a month afterward, was when I was speeding down a gravel road in Oregon and the car muffler came loose. "You were going too fast," he said.

Back in Yakima a doctor saw to it that my dad went to a psychia- 22 trist. My mother and dad had to go on relief,[2] as it was called, and the county paid for the psychiatrist. The psychiatrist asked my dad. "Who is the President?" He'd had a question put to him that he could answer. "Ike," my dad said. Nevertheless, they put him on the fifth floor of Valley Memorial Hospital and began giving him electroshock treatments. I was married by then and about to start my own family. My dad was still locked up when my wife went into this same hospital, just one floor down, to have our first baby. After she had delivered, I went upstairs to give my dad the news. They let me in through a steel door and showed me where I could find him. He was sitting on a couch with a blanket over his lap. *Hey,* I thought. *What in hell is happening to my dad?* I sat down next to him and told him he was a grandfather. He waited a minute and then he said, "I feel like a grandfather." That's all he said. He didn't smile or move. He was in a big room with a lot of other people. Then I hugged him, and he began to cry.

Somehow he got out of there. But now came the years when he 23 couldn't work and just sat around the house trying to figure what next and what he'd done wrong in his life that he'd wound up like this. My mother went from job to crummy job. Much later she referred to that time he was in the hospital, and those years just afterward, as "when Raymond was sick." The word *sick* was never the same for me again.

In 1964, through the help of a friend, he was lucky enough to be 24 hired on at a mill in Klamath, California. He moved down there by himself to see if he could hack it. He lived not far from the mill, in a one-room cabin not much different from the place he and my mother had started out living in when they went west. He scrawled letters to my mother, and if I called she'd read them aloud to me over the phone. In the letters, he said it was touch and go. Every day that he went to work, he felt like it was the most important day of his life. But every day, he told her, made the next day that much easier. He said for her to tell me he said hello. If he couldn't sleep at night, he said, he thought about me and the good times we used to have. Finally, after a couple of months, he regained some of his confidence. He could do the work and didn't think he had to worry that he'd let anybody down ever again. When he was sure, he sent for my mother.

He'd been off from work for six years and had lost everything in 25 that time—home, car, furniture, and appliances, including the big freezer that had been my mother's pride and joy. He'd lost his good

---

[2] What would today be called "public assistance" or "welfare." [Eds.]

name too—Raymond Carver was someone who couldn't pay his bills—
and his self-respect was gone. He'd even lost his virility. My mother told
my wife, "All during that time Raymond was sick we slept together in
the same bed, but we didn't have relations. He wanted to a few times,
but nothing happened. I didn't miss it, but I think he wanted to, you
know."

During those years I was trying to raise my own family and earn a   26
living. But, one thing and another, we found ourselves having to move
a lot. I couldn't keep track of what was going down in my dad's life.
But I did have a chance one Christmas to tell him I wanted to be a
writer. I might as well have told him I wanted to become a plastic surgeon. "What are you going to write about?" he wanted to know. Then,
as if to help me out, he said, "Write about stuff you know about. Write
about some of those fishing trips we took." I said I would, but I knew
I wouldn't. "Send me what you write," he said. I said I'd do that, but
then I didn't. I wasn't writing anything about fishing, and I didn't
think he'd particularly care about, or even necessarily understand,
what I was writing in those days. Besides, he wasn't a reader. Not the
sort, anyway, I imagined I was writing for.

Then he died. I was a long way off, in Iowa City, with things still to   27
say to him. I didn't have the chance to tell him goodbye, or that I
thought he was doing great at his new job. That I was proud of him for
making a comeback.

My mother said he came in from work that night and ate a big sup-   28
per. Then he sat at the table by himself and finished what was left of a
bottle of whiskey, a bottle she found hidden in the bottom of the
garbage under some coffee grounds a day or so later. Then he got up
and went to bed, where my mother joined him a little later. But in the
night she had to get up and make a bed for herself on the couch. "He
was snoring so loud I couldn't sleep," she said. The next morning when
she looked in on him, he was on his back with his mouth open, his
cheeks caved in. *Graylooking*, she said. She knew he was dead—she didn't
need a doctor to tell her that. But she called one anyway, and then she
called my wife.

Among the pictures my mother kept of my dad and herself during   29
those early days in Washington was a photograph of him standing in
front of a car, holding a beer and a stringer of fish. In the photograph he
is wearing his hat back on his forehead and has this awkward grin on
his face. I asked her for it and she gave it to me, along with some others.
I put it up on my wall, and each time we moved, I took the picture along
and put it up on another wall. I looked at it carefully from time to time,
trying to figure out some things about my dad, and maybe myself in the
process. But I couldn't. My dad just kept moving further and further
away from me and back into time. Finally, in the course of another
move, I lost the photograph. It was then that I tried to recall it, and at

the same time make an attempt to say something about my dad, and how I thought that in some important ways we might be alike. I wrote the poem when I was living in an apartment house in an urban area south of San Francisco, at a time when I found myself, like my dad, having trouble with alcohol. The poem was a way of trying to connect up with him.

Photograph of My Father in His Twenty-Second Year

October. Here in this dank, unfamiliar kitchen
I study my father's embarrassed young man's face.
Sheepish grin, he holds in one hand a string
of spiny yellow perch, in the other
a bottle of Carlsberg beer.   5

In jeans and flannel shirt, he leans
against the front fender of a 1934 Ford.
He would like to pose brave and hearty for his posterity,
wear his old hat cocked over his ear.
All his life my father wanted to be bold.   10

But the eyes give him away, and the hands
that limply offer the string of dead perch
and the bottle of beer. Father, I love you,
yet how can I say thank you, I who can't hold my liquor either
and don't even know the places to fish.   15

The poem is true in its particulars, except that my dad died in June 30 and not October, as the first word of the poem says. I wanted a word with more than one syllable to it to make it linger a little. But more than that, I wanted a month appropriate to what I felt at the time I wrote the poem—a month of short days and failing light, smoke in the air, things perishing. June was summer nights and days, graduations, my wedding anniversary, the birthday of one of my children. June wasn't a month your father died in.

After the service at the funeral home, after we had moved outside, 31 a woman I didn't know came over to me and said, "He's happier where he is now." I stared at this woman until she moved away. I still remember the little knob of a hat she was wearing. Then one of my dad's cousins—I didn't know the man's name—reached out and took my hand, "We all miss him," he said, and I knew he wasn't saying it just to be polite.

I began to weep for the first time since receiving the news. I hadn't 32 been able to before. I hadn't had the time, for one thing. Now, suddenly, I couldn't stop. I held my wife and wept while she said and did what she could do to comfort me there in the middle of that summer afternoon

I listened to people say consoling things to my mother, and I was 33 glad that my dad's family had turned up, had come to where he was. I thought I'd remember everything that was said and done that day and maybe find a way to tell it sometime. But I didn't. I forgot it all, or nearly. What I do remember is that I heard our name used a lot that afternoon, my dad's name and mine. But I knew they were talking about my dad. *Raymond,* these people kept saying in their beautiful voices out of my childhood. *Raymond.*

Responding to Reading

1. Why does Carver include details about his father's work history? His drinking? His mental illness? The photograph? Do you think these details are necessary?
2. What information is provided by the poem that follows paragraph 29 that is not provided by the essay itself? Could Carver have conveyed this information as effectively in prose?
3. What does Carver finally come to realize about his father, and about himself?

FOCUS: IS DIVORCE DESTROYING THE FAMILY?

THE PERFECT FAMILY

Alice Hoffman

Alice Hoffman (1952–   ) was born in New York City and raised on Long Island, where she attended Adelphi University, receiving her B.A. in 1973. She later received an M.F.A. from Stanford University in California. A prolific novelist, Hoffman has written a number of best-sellers, including At Risk *(1988),* Seventh Heaven *(1990),* Turtle Moon *(1992),* Practical Magic *(1995), and most recently* Here on Earth *(1997). Her work often focuses on families and the difficulties of communication, but her tales are generally optimistic, often incorporating elements of fantasy and magic. In the following essay published in the* New York Times Magazine *in 1992, Hoffman writes about her own childhood in the 1950s. Raised by a divorced working mother at a time when divorce was rare and most mothers stayed at home, Hoffman reflects on the stereotypical standards that define today's debate over family values.*

When I was growing up in the 50s, there was only one sort of 1
family, the one we watched on television every day. Right in front of us, in black and white, was everything we needed to know about family values: the neat patch of lawn, the apple tree, the mother who never once raised her voice, the three lovely children: a Princess, a Kitten, a Bud and, always, the father who knew best.[1]

People stayed married forever back then, and roses grew by the 2
front door. We had glass bottles filled with lightning bugs and brand-new swing sets in the backyard, and softball games at dusk. We had summer nights that lasted forever and well-balanced meals, three times a day, in our identical houses, on our identical streets. There was only one small bargain we had to make to exist in this world: we were never to ask questions, never to think about people who didn't have as much or who were different in any way. We ignored desperate marriages and piercing loneliness. And we were never, ever, to wonder what might be hidden from view, behind the unlocked doors, in the privacy of our neighbors' bedrooms and knotty-pine-paneled dens.

---

[1] *Father Knows Best* was a popular family comedy with a stay-at-home mother. [Eds.]

This was a bargain my own mother could not make. Having once 3 believed that her life would sort itself out to be like the television shows we watched, only real and in color, she'd been left to care for her children on her own, at a time when divorce was so uncommon I did not meet another child of divorced parents until 10 years later when I went off to college.

Back then, it almost made sense when one of my best friends was 4 not allowed to come to my house; her parents did not approve of divorce or my mother's life style. My mother, after all, had a job and boyfriend and, perhaps even more incriminating, she was the one who took the silver-colored trash cans out to the curb on Monday nights. She did so faithfully, on evenings when she had already balanced the checkbook and paid the bills and ministered to sore throats and made certain we'd had dinner; but all up and down the street everybody knew the truth: taking out the trash was clearly a job for fathers.

When I was 10, my mother began to work for the Department of 5 Social Services, a world in which the simple rules of the suburbs did not apply. She counseled young unwed mothers, girls and women who were not allowed to make their own choices, most of whom had not been allowed to finish high school or stay in their own homes, none of whom had been allowed to decide not to continue their pregnancies. Later, my mother placed most of these babies in foster care, and still later, she moved to the protective-services department, investigating charges of abuse and neglect, often having to search a child's back and legs for bruises or welts.

She would have found some on my friend, left there by her right- 6 eous father, the one who wouldn't allow her to visit our home but blackened her eye when, a few years later, he discovered that she was dating a boy he didn't approve of. But none of his neighbors had dared to report him. They would never have imagined that someone like my friend's father, whose trash cans were always tidily placed at the curb, whose lawn was always well cared for, might need watching.

To my mother, abuse was a clear-cut issue, if reported and found, 7 but neglect was more of a judgment call. It was, in effect, passing judgment on the nature of love. If my father had not sent the child support checks on time, if my mother hadn't been white and college-educated, it could have easily been us in one of those apartments she visited, where the heat didn't work on the coldest days, and the dirt was so encrusted you could mop all day and still be called a poor housekeeper, and there was often nothing more for dinner than Frosted Flakes and milk, or, if it was toward the end of the month, the cereal might be served with tap water. Would that have meant my mother loved her children any less, that we were less of a family?

My mother never once judged who was a fit mother on the basis of 8 a clean floor, or an unbalanced meal, or a boyfriend who sometimes spent the night. But back then, there were good citizens who were only too ready to set their standards for women and children, factoring out poverty or exhaustion or simply a different set of beliefs.

There are always those who are ready to deal out judgment with the ready fist of the righteous. I know this because before the age of 10 I was one of the righteous, too. I believed that mothers were meant to stay home and fathers should carry out the trash on Monday nights. I believed that parents could create a domestic life that was the next best thing to heaven, if they just tried. That is what I'd been told, that in the best of all worlds we would live identical lives in identical houses. 9

It's a simple view of the world, too simple even for childhood. Certainly, it's a vision that is much too limited for the lives we live now, when only one in 19 families is made up of a wage-earner father, a mother who doesn't work outside the home and two or more children. And even long ago, when I was growing up, we paid too high a price when we cut ourselves off from the rest of the world. We ourselves did not dare to be different. In the safety we created, we became trapped. 10

There are still places where softball games are played at dusk and roses grow by the front door. There are families with sons named Bud, with kind and generous fathers, and mothers who put up strawberry preserves every June and always have time to sing lullabies. But do these families love their children any more than the single mother who works all day? Are their lullabies any sweeter? If I felt deprived as a child, it was only when our family was measured against some notion of what we were supposed to be. The truth of it was, we lacked for little. 11

And now that I have children of my own, and am exhausted at the end of the day in which I've probably failed in a hundred different ways, I am amazed that women alone can manage. That they do, in spite of everything, is a simple fact. They rise from sleep in the middle of the night when their children call out to them. They rush for the cough syrup and cold washcloths and keep watch till dawn. These are real family values, the same ones we knew when we were children. As far as we were concerned our mother could cure a fever with a kiss. This may be the only thing we ever need to know about love. The rest, no one can judge. 12

Responding to Reading

1. What was so different about Hoffman's family? Would her family still be considered "different" in a 1990s suburb? Do suburban families still live "identical lives in identical houses" (9)? Did they ever?

2. Consider the various combinations of individuals that can constitute a family today (one example is described in the opening paragraph of Barbara Kingsolver's "Stone Soup," p. 64). How is the 1990s concept of *family* different from the 1950s definition? Despite these differences, do

you think most people's idea of the "perfect" or ideal family has changed significantly since the 1950s? How do you account for this?

3. Hoffman's mother worked for the Department of Social Services, "a world in which the simple rules of the suburbs did not apply" (5). What were the "simple rules of the suburbs"? Why didn't they apply? In what respects did the "perfect" suburban families resemble the families with whom Hoffman's mother worked? What do these similarities reveal about the 1950s suburban family?

STONE SOUP

Barbara Kingsolver

Born in Annapolis, Maryland, and raised in rural Kentucky, Barbara Kingsolver (1955–   ) received her B.A. from DePauw University and a master's degree in biology from the University of Arizona. She began her career as a technical writer and freelance journalist before turning to fiction and poetry in the 1980s. Among her works are the novels The Bean Trees *(1988),* Animal Dreams *(1990), and* Pigs in Heaven *(1993); a collection of poetry,* Another America *(1991); and* Homelands *(1989), a collection of short stories. She also wrote the nonfiction work* Holding the Line *(1989), about a 1983 mining strike spearheaded largely by Mexican-Americans in southern Arizona. "Stone Soup" is from her most recent work,* High Tide in Tucson *(1995), a collection of essays focusing on a variety of topics, including her own role as a single mother. In this essay, she discusses "nontraditional families," arguing that "[d]ivorce, remarriage, single parenthood, gay parents, and blended families" are not symptoms of some societal breakdown but simply "facts of our time."*

In the catalog of family values, where do we rank an occasion like 1 this? A curly-haired boy who wanted to run before he walked, age seven now, a soccer player scoring a winning goal. He turns to the bleachers with his fists in the air and a smile wide as a gap-toothed galaxy. His own cheering section of grown-ups and kids all leap to their feet and hug each other, delirious with love for this boy. He's Andy, my best friend's son. The cheering section includes his mother and her friends, his brother, his father and stepmother, a stepbrother and stepsister, and a grandparent. Lucky is the child with this many relatives on hand to hail a proud accomplishment. I'm there too, witnessing a family fortune. But in spite of myself, defensive words take shape in my head. I am thinking: I dare *anybody* to call this a broken home.

Families change, and remain the same. Why are our names for 2 home so slow to catch up to the truth of where we live?

When I was a child, I had two parents who loved me without cease. 3 One of them attended every excuse for attention I ever contrived, and the other made it to the ones with higher production values, like piano recitals and appendicitis. So I was a lucky child too. I played with a set of paper dolls called "The Family of Dolls," four in number, who came with the factory-assigned names of Dad, Mom, Sis, and Junior. I think you know what they looked like, at least before I loved them to death and their heads fell off.

Now I've replaced the dolls with a life. I knit my days around my 4 daughter's survival and happiness, and am proud to say her head is still on. But we aren't the Family of Dolls. Maybe you're not, either. And if not, even though you are statistically no oddity, it's probably been suggested to you in a hundred ways that yours isn't exactly a real family, but an impostor family, a harbinger of cultural ruin, a slapdash substitute— something like counterfeit money. Here at the tail end of our century, most of us are up to our ears in the noisy business of trying to support and love a thing called family. But there's a current in the air with ferocious moral force that finds its way even into political campaigns, claiming there is only one right way to do it, the Way It Has Always Been.

In the face of a thriving, particolored world, this narrow view is so 5 pickled and absurd I'm astonished that it gets airplay. And I'm astonished that it still stings.

Every parent has endured the arrogance of a child-unfriendly 6 grump sitting in judgment, explaining what those kids of ours really need (for example, "a good licking"). If we're polite, we move our crew to another bench in the park. If we're forthright (as I am in my mind, only, for the rest of the day), we fix them with a sweet imperious stare and say, "Come back and let's talk about it after you've changed a thousand diapers."

But it's harder somehow to shrug off the Family-of-Dolls Family 7 Values crew when they judge (from their safe distance) that divorced people, blended families, gay families, and single parents are failures. That our children are at risk, and the whole arrangement is messy and embarrassing. A marriage that ends is not called "finished," it's called *failed*. The children of this family may have been born to a happy union, but now they are called *the children of divorce*.

I had no idea how thoroughly these assumptions overlaid my cul- 8 ture until I went through divorce myself. I wrote to a friend: "This might be worse than being widowed. Overnight I've suffered the same losses—companionship, financial and practical support, my identity as a wife and partner, the future I'd taken for granted. I am lonely, grieving, and hard-pressed to take care of my household alone. But instead of bringing casseroles, people are acting like I had a fit and broke up the family china."

Once upon a time I held these beliefs about divorce: that everyone 9 who does it could have chosen not to do it. That it's a lazy way out of marital problems. That it selfishly puts personal happiness ahead of family integrity. Now I tremble for my ignorance. It's easy, in fortunate times, to forget about the ambush that could leave your head reeling: serious mental or physical illness, death in the family, abandonment, financial calamity, humiliation, violence, despair.

I started out like any child, intent on being the Family of Dolls. I set 10 upon young womanhood believing in most of the doctrines of my generation: I wore my skirts four inches above the knee. I had that Barbie with her zebra-striped swimsuit and a figure unlike anything found in nature. And I understood the Prince Charming Theory of Marriage, a quest for Mr. Right that ends smack dab where you find him. I did not completely understand that another whole story *begins* there, and no fairy tale prepared me for the combination of bad luck and persistent hope that would interrupt my dream and lead me to other arrangements. Like a cancer diagnosis, a dying marriage is a thing to fight, to deny, and finally, when there's no choice left, to dig in and survive. Casseroles would help. Likewise, I imagine it must be a painful reckoning in adolescence (or later on) to realize one's own true love will never look like the soft-focus fragrance ads because Prince Charming (surprise!) is a princess. Or vice versa. Or has skin the color your parents didn't want you messing with, except in the Crayola box.

It's awfully easy to hold in contempt the straw broken home, and 11 that mythical category of persons who toss away nuclear family for the sheer fun of it. Even the legal terms we use have a suggestion of caprice. I resent the phrase "irreconcilable differences," which suggests a stubborn refusal to accept a spouse's little quirks. This is specious. Every happily married couple I know has loads of irreconcilable differences. Negotiating where to set the thermostat is not the point. A nonfunctioning marriage is a slow asphyxiation. It is waking up despised each morning, listening to the pulse of your own loneliness before the radio begins to blare its raucous gospel that you're nothing if you aren't loved. It is sharing your airless house with the threat of suicide or other kinds of violence, while the ghost that whispers, "Leave here and destroy your children," has passed over every door and nailed it shut. Disassembling a marriage in these circumstances is as much *fun* as amputating your own gangrenous leg. You do it, if you can, to save a life—or two, or more.

I know of no one who really went looking to hoe the harder row, 12 especially the daunting one of single parenthood. Yet it seems to be the most American of customs to blame the burdened for their destiny. We'd like so desperately to believe in freedom and justice for all, we can hardly name that rogue bad luck, even when he's a close enough snake to bite us. In the wake of my divorce, some friends (even a few close ones) chose to vanish, rather than linger within striking distance of misfortune.

But most stuck around, bless their hearts, and if I'm any the wiser 13
for my trials, it's from having learned the worth of steadfast friendship.
And also, what not to say. The least helpful question is: "Did you want
the divorce, or didn't you?" Did I want to keep that gangrenous leg, or
not? How to explain, in a culture that venerates choice: two terrifying
options are much worse than none at all. Give me any day the quick
hand of cruel fate that will leave me scarred but blameless. As it was, I
kept thinking of that wicked third-grade joke in which some boy comes
up behind you and grabs your ear, starts in with a prolonged tug, and
asks, "Do you want this ear any longer?"

Still, the friend who holds your hand and says the wrong thing is 14
made of dearer stuff than the one who stays away. And generally,
through all of it, you live. My favorite fictional character, Kate Vaiden
(in the novel by Reynolds Price), advises: "Strength just comes in one
brand—you stand up at sunrise and meet what they send you and keep
your hair combed."

Once you've weathered the straits, you get to cross the tricky junc- 15
ture from casualty to survivor. If you're on your feet at the end of a year
or two, and have begun putting together a happy new existence, those
friends who were kind enough to feel sorry for you when you needed it
must now accept you back to the ranks of the living. If you're truly
blessed, they will dance at your second wedding. Everybody else, for
heaven's sake, should stop throwing stones.

Arguing about whether nontraditional families deserve pity or tol- 16
erance is a little like the medieval debate about left-handedness as a
mark of the devil. Divorce, remarriage, single parenthood, gay parents,
and blended families simply are. They're facts of our time. Some of the
reasons listed by sociologists for these family reconstructions are: the
idea of marriage as a romantic partnership rather than a pragmatic one;
a shift in women's expectations, from servility to self-respect and independence; and longevity (prior to antibiotics no marriage was expected
to last many decades—in Colonial days the average couple lived to be
married less than twelve years). Add to all this, our growing sense of
entitlement to happiness and safety from abuse. Most would agree
these are all good things. Yet their result—a culture in which serial
monogamy and the consequent reshaping of families are the norm—
gets diagnosed as "failing."

For many of us, once we have put ourselves Humpty-Dumpty-wise 17
back together again, the main problem with our reorganized family is
that other people think we have a problem. My daughter tells me the
only time she's uncomfortable about being the child of divorced parents
is when her friends say they feel sorry for her. It's a bizarre sympathy,
given that half the kids in her school and nation are in the same boat,

pursuing childish happiness with the same energy as their married-parent peers. When anyone asks how *she* feels about it, she spontaneously lists the benefits: our house is in the country and we have a dog, but she can go to her dad's neighborhood for the urban thrills of a pool and side-walks for roller-skating. What's more, she has three sets of grandparents!

Why is it surprising that a child would revel in a widened family 18 and the right to feel at home in more than one house? Isn't it the oppo-site that should worry us—a child with no home at all, or too few resources to feel safe? The child at risk is the one whose parents are too immature themselves to guide wisely; too diminished by poverty to nurture; too far from opportunity to offer hope. The number of children in the U.S. living in poverty at this moment is almost unfathomably large: twenty percent. There are families among us that need help all right, and by no means are they new on the landscape. The rate at which teenage girls had babies in 1957 (ninety-six per thousand) was twice what it is now. That remarkable statistic is ignored by the religious right—probably because the teen birth rate was cut in half mainly by legalized abortion. In fact, the policy gatekeepers who coined the phrase "family values" have steadfastly ignored the desperation of too-small families, and since 1979 have steadily reduced the amount of financial support available to a single parent. But, this camp's most outspoken attacks seem aimed at the notion of families getting too complex, with add-ons and extras such as a gay parent's partner, or a remarried mother's new husband and his children.

To judge a family's value by its tidy symmetry is to purchase a book 19 for its cover. There's no moral authority there. The famous family com-prised of Dad, Mom, Sis, and Junior living as an isolated economic unit is not built on historical bedrock. In *The Way We Never Were,* Stephanie Coontz writes, "Whenever people propose that we go back to the tradi-tional family, I always suggest that they pick a ballpark date for the fam-ily they have in mind." Colonial families were tidily disciplined, but their members (meaning everyone but infants) labored incessantly and died young. Then the Victorian family adopted a new division of labor, in which women's role was domestic and children were allowed time for study and play, but this was an upper-class construct supported by myriad slaves. Coontz writes, "For every nineteenth-century middle-class family that protected its wife and child within the family circle, there was an Irish or German girl scrubbing floors . . . a Welsh boy mining coal to keep the homebaked goodies warm, a black girl doing the family laundry, a black mother and child picking cotton to be made into clothes for the family, and a Jewish or an Italian daughter in a sweatshop mak-ing ladies' dresses or artificial flowers for the family to purchase."

The abolition of slavery brought slightly more democratic arrange- 20 ments, in which extended families were harnessed together in cottage industries; at the turn of the century came a steep rise in child labor in mines and sweatshops. Twenty percent of American children lived in orphanages at the time; their parents were not necessarily dead, but couldn't afford to keep them.

During the Depression and up to the end of World War II, many 21 millions of U.S. households were more multigenerational than nuclear. Women my grandmother's age were likely to live with a fluid assortment of elderly relatives, in-laws, siblings, and children. In many cases they spent virtually every waking hour working in the company of other women—a companionable scenario in which it would be easier, I imagine, to tolerate an estranged or difficult spouse. I'm reluctant to idealize a life of so much hard work and so little spousal intimacy, but its advantage may have been resilience. A family so large and varied would not easily be brought down by a single blow: it could absorb a death, long illness, an abandonment here or there, and any number of irreconcilable differences.

The Family of Dolls came along midcentury as a great American 22 experiment. A booming economy required a mobile labor force and demanded that women surrender jobs to returning soldiers. Families came to be defined by a single breadwinner. They struck out for single-family homes at an earlier age than ever before, and in unprecedented numbers they raised children in suburban isolation. The nuclear family was launched to sink or swim.

More than a few sank. Social historians corroborate that the subur- 23 ban family of the postwar economic boom, which we have recently selected as our definition of "traditional," was no panacea. Twenty-five percent of Americans were poor in the mid-1950s, and as yet there were no food stamps. Sixty percent of the elderly lived on less than $1000 a year, and most had no medical insurance. In the sequestered suburbs, alcoholism and sexual abuse of children were far more widespread than anyone imagined.

Expectations soared, and the economy sagged. It's hard to depend 24 on one other adult for everything, come what may. In the last three decades, that amorphous, adaptable structure we call "family" has been reshaped once more by economic tides. Compared with fifties families, mothers are far more likely now to be employed. We are statistically more likely to divorce, and to live in blended families or other extra-nuclear arrangements. We are also more likely to plan and space our children, and to rate our marriages as "happy." We are less likely to suffer abuse without recourse, or to stare out at our lives through a glaze of prescription tranquilizers. Our aged parents are less likely to be destitute, and we're half as likely to have a teenage daughter turn up a mother herself. All in all, I would say that if "intact" in modern family-values jargon means living quietly desperate in the bell jar, then hip-hip-hooray for "broken." A neat family model constructed to service the Baby Boom economy seems to be returning gradually to a grand, lumpy shape that human families apparently have tended toward since they first took root in the Olduvai Gorge.[1] We're social animals, deeply fond of companionship, and children love best to run in packs. If there is a *normal* for humans, at all, I expect it looks like two or three Families of Dolls, connected variously by kinship and passion, shuffled like cards and strewn over several shoeboxes.

The sooner we can let go the fairy tale of families functioning per- 25 fectly in isolation, the better we might embrace the relief of community. Even the admirable parents who've stayed married through thick and thin are very likely, at present, to incorporate other adults into their families—household help and baby-sitters if they can afford them, or neighbors and grandparents if they can't. For single parents, this support is the rock-bottom definition of family. And most parents who have split apart, however painfully, still manage to maintain family continuity for their children, creating in many cases a boisterous phenomenon that Constance Ahrons in her book *The Good Divorce* calls the "binuclear family." Call it what you will—when ex-spouses beat swords into plowshares and jump up and down at a soccer game together, it makes for happy kids.

Cinderella, look, who needs her? All those evil stepsisters? That 26 story always seemed like too much cotton-picking fuss over clothes. A childhood tale that fascinated me more was the one called "Stone Soup," and the gist of it is this: Once upon a time, a pair of beleaguered soldiers straggled home to a village empty-handed, in a land ruined by war. They were famished, but the villagers had so little they shouted evil words and slammed their doors. So the soldiers dragged out a big kettle, filled it with water, and put it on a fire to boil. They rolled a clean round stone into the pot, while the villagers peered through their curtains in amazement.

"What kind of soup is that?" they hooted. 27

"Stone soup," the soldiers replied. "Everybody can have some 28 when it's done."

"Well, thanks," one matron grumbled, coming out with a shriveled 29 carrot. "But it'd be better if you threw this in."

And so on, of course, a vegetable at a time, until the whole suspi- 30 cious village managed to feed itself grandly.

Any family is a big empty pot, save for what gets thrown in. Each 31 stew turns out different. Generosity, a resolve to turn bad luck into good, and respect for variety—these things will nourish a nation of children. Name-calling and suspicion will not. My soup contains a rock or two of hard times, and maybe yours does too. I expect it's a heck of a bouillabaise.

---

[1] Many fossils of human ancestors have been discovered at the Olduvai Gorge in Tanzania. [Eds.]

Responding to Reading

1. In paragraph 1, Kingsolver describes a family group consisting of a child's "mother and her friends, his brother, his father and stepmother, a step-brother and stepsister, and a grandparent." She continues, "I dare *anybody* to call this a broken home." Do you think most people *would* consider this a broken home? Would you?

2. What is the "Family of Dolls"? Is it the same family that Alice Hoffman (p. 61) watched on television in the 1950s? What is Kingsolver's attitude toward this kind of family? Do you think this attitude is justified, or do you think Kingsolver's status as a divorced parent colors her view?

3. Kingsolver cites examples of phrases from the language of divorce that she finds inaccurate, biased, or misleading—for example, *broken home, irreconcilable differences, failed marriage,* and *children of divorce.* (Note that Joseph Adelson uses similar "loaded" language in his essay "Splitting Up" below, referring, for instance, to "intact" families and "broken marriage.") What view of the family do these terms suggest? Do you see such language as inaccurate or biased, or do you think it accurately reflects the status of the families it describes?

SPLITTING UP

Joseph Adelson

Joseph Adelson (1925–   ) was born in New York City and received his bachelor's degree from City College there, later earning his Ph.D. in psychology at the University of California at Berkeley. Initially a member of the faculty at Berkeley, he has been a professor of psychology at the University of Michigan since 1970. The focus of much of his research and writing has been the psychology of adolescence, and his books include The Adolescent Experience *(1966) and* Inventing Adolescence *(1980). In the following essay, which was published in* Commentary *magazine in 1996, Adelson surveys the "family-values debate," looking in particular at recent research suggesting, "[W]ithout exception, when one compares children from intact families with children from one-parent families where a divorce has taken place, the data offer cause for deep alarm."*

During the whole of my childhood I knew only two youngsters 1 whose families were not intact. One was a boy in my neighborhood, quiet and almost unbearably shy, whose father had died and who was being raised by his mother. The other was my classmate for part of a year in junior high school. This boy would not talk much about himself, but we were somehow able to learn that he was being raised by his grandparents, following his own parents' divorce.

This was the only divorce I and my friends had ever heard about. 2 The boy himself was different from most of us—impulsive, hyperactive, and, though bright, unable to focus his attention on work. He became so disruptive that he was suspended from school, an event unique for that time and place. In my own family circle, his circumstances were felt to be the height of misfortune, and his fate was discussed in the most sorrowful terms. "What will happen to the poor child? What other troubles lie in wait for him?"

Within my family, indeed, broken marriage was in general viewed 3 as an alien and catastrophic event. A second cousin, who had had a hard time establishing a career, was married in his middle thirties to a woman of the same age who had been divorced. Consternation followed. A divorcee was a fallen woman, or close to it. One of my aunts even raised the question of whether the bride was really Jewish, or had simply pretended to be in order to get a new husband. In time, that marriage settled into a most ordinary one, but suspicions persisted, and for some years the hapless woman continued to be referred to as "the divorcee."

When I grew up and looked back, none of this seemed surprising to 4 me, given my family and milieu. In my neighborhood we were almost all working-class, immigrant, religious, Jewish, and those who were not were working-class, immigrant, religious, Irish or Italian Catholic. In these cultures, marriages, however wretched they might be, were permanent. A bad marriage was a sad but unalterable fact of life. You would no more think of exchanging your spouse for another than you would think of trading in your ailing cardiovascular system for a better one.

And so in later years I always assumed that the stern view of mar- 5 riage and divorce with which I was familiar as a child reflected the provincialism of my background. Americans at large, I reasoned, although they may not have approved of marital break-up, surely took it in stride and, unlike my family, did not treat it as an unspeakable tragedy. And I therefore also assumed, when I used to read about rises in rates of divorce and unmarried motherhood among Americans, that we were seeing not a dramatic nationwide acceleration but just steady increases in already well-established trends. True, more marriages were ending, and more illegitimate children were being born; but these changes marked an evolution, I thought, not a revolution.

I could not have been more mistaken. In fact, in recent decades we 6 have been witnessing *extraordinary* changes in the nature and function of the family—in marriage, child-rearing, and divorce. And these changes have not crept up on us in gradual increments: within a single generation, in some instances within a decade, we have seen doublings, triplings, and quadruplings in the incidence of very troubling behaviors. The statistics have become well-enough known, especially those concerning illegitimacy: within about a quarter-century—1970 to

1992—the proportion of children born out of wedlock increased from 11 percent to 30 percent; among blacks, the current rate is an astonishing 70 percent. Similarly, where 8 percent of white children born in the 1950's spent their childhood with one parent, for those born in 1980 the figure is 31 percent, and among black children the proportions jumped in the same period from 22 percent to 59 percent. And the figures for divorce are more arresting still: among white women marrying in the 1940's, 14 percent eventually divorced; of those married in the late 1960's and early 1970's, half are already divorced, and today there is a 60-40 chance that a marriage will end in divorce.

Commenting on these and many similar findings, Lawrence Stone, 7 the eminent historian of the family, has written:

> The scale of marital breakdown in the West since 1960 has no historical precedent, and seems unique. There has been nothing like it for the last 2,000 years, and probably longer.

Like most good historians, Stone is not given to excess, and that 8 statement is itself as startling as the findings he and others are addressing. Yet most of us, while noting the emergence of a "divorce problem," have somehow found ways to avoid confronting either its extent or its potential gravity. As the sociologist David Popenoe has pointed out, we have here an example of what Daniel P. Moynihan has called "defining deviancy down," a kind of mental trick whereby we ignore what will not fit into our wishes or assumptions by reclassifying behavior as normal that once would have been universally regarded as abnormal and undesirable.

In the case of divorce, Popenoe suggests, one reason we have 9 tended to ignore or shy away from the magnitude of the problem is that so many of us are already divorced, and we do not like to think of our individual experiences as symptomatic of a troublesome *social* phenomenon. Another reason is undoubtedly the sense that to begin thinking of divorce in this way would in any event be an exercise in futility; the practice has by now become just too deeply woven into the fabric of our social life.

Yet precisely because things have gone so far, the topic of family life 10 in general, and of divorce in particular, has actually become a little easier to discuss soberly than was the case even a few years ago. Take the derision that initially greeted Vice President Dan Quayle's 1992 venture into defending "family values." The phrase itself quickly became a *Schimpfwort*, a term of derogation and contempt, employed to signal one's distance from the sort of simpleminded sanctimony to be expected from a blockhead like Quayle. Yet as early as 1993 that judgment began to reverse itself, at least in some circles, with the appearance of Barbara DaFoe Whitehead's now-famous *Atlantic* article, "Dan Quayle Was Right," and its powerful documentation of the hazards of the fatherless home.

Today, three years later, although the "family-values debate" (to borrow the title of a seminal article by James Q. Wilson in the April 1993 *Commentary*) continues to be driven by sentiment and in some cases by theology, opinions are also more likely to be supported by evidence from history and the social sciences. Only recently, the results of research and scholarship on the subject have been drawn together in several important books and articles by authors dismayed at what has become of us. They include David Popenoe's *Life Without Father*; Maggie Gallagher's *The Abolition of Marriage*; David Blankenhorn's *Fatherless America*; and William Galston's essay in the summer 1996 *Public Interest*, "Divorce American Style." Though these works differ in the scope of their inquiry and in their style, all take a roughly similar position on what the authors see as the main culprit: a relentless, decades-long disestablishment of marriage as the central cementing institution of society and its replacement by the ideals of individual gratification and "fulfillment." 11

In one particularly useful chapter in *The Abolition of Marriage*, Maggie Gallagher examines what American courts have done to encourage conformity to those ideals. Customs and rules that grew up over centuries, she writes, have been worn away by court-imposed "rules and regulations weakening the privileged status of marriage as a child-rearing institution." As the courts have come to see marriage in the context of "equal rights," they no longer favor a married partnership over others, lest that connote an unfair preference. The push for legalizing homosexual marriage draws on this new "understanding," but it is hardly the only such effort: the New Jersey Supreme Court, for example, recently declared that ten college students who live together are the "functional equivalent" of a family. In these and other statements, as Gallagher puts it, marriage becomes simply another "close relationship situation." 12

What is worse, in Gallagher's view, the triumph of radical individualism has meant that the "fierce protectiveness once directed toward the institution of marriage" has been transferred, ironically, to divorce itself. Once considered an event to be avoided unless absolutely necessary, marital separation has come to be seen as morally neutral or even as a praiseworthy goal, even when children are present—and certainly easier to accomplish than the goal of saving an unhappy marriage. By 1985, over 80 percent of those surveyed in a sample of the general population felt that a couple should not stay together for the sake of the children; one suspects that among marriage "experts," the figure would have been closer to 100 percent. 13

Both Popenoe and Gallagher seem to feel that our country has 14
moved toward a divorce culture without fully wanting to, and without
a full recognition of its consequences, especially for children. Some of
this society-wide suspension of normal moral reflexes has been due to
the upbeat manner in which celebrity divorce and remarriage have come
to be created by the media. Some of it reflects the skill and persistence
with which the legal and mental-health professions have publicized the
virtues of no-fault divorce. The advocates of easier divorce have been
able to persuade legislators that the public desperately wants change (in
fact, until fairly late in the game, survey statistics apparently showed no
such wish). Some of it stems from the belief that children are damaged
by conflict-ridden families and would actually be better off if the source
of the conflict were removed. And social scientists have done their part
by interpreting provisions or enigmatic findings as support for a better
alternative for children in such situations: namely, a single-parent home,
free of tension.

The climate of opinion produced by this regnant ideological atmos- 15
phere still persists. Here, for instance, is the columnist Clarence Page,
asking the now-clichéd question, "Which is worse for the child, a single,
loving, and caring parent or two disgruntled parents whose tension is
palpable and sometimes violently loud . . . ?" A somewhat more sophisticated presentation of the same idea can be seen throughout current
expert writing on divorce, which typically portray a beleaguered but
"loving and caring" mother who has rescued her children from a
hate-filled and often violent marriage.

But why *should* we assume that divorce is always preceded by open 16
conflict? Some marriages die a quiet death, preceded by boredom, silent
contempt, or sheer inanition. It is not uncommon for the grown children
of such divorces to report how amazed they were when they first heard
of their parents' coming separation, since to them the family atmosphere had been quite ordinary, or no more troubled than that of other
families they knew. And why should we assume the presence of a loving, caring mother? Why not an indifferent mother, or a narcissist, or an
alcoholic? Yet such mothers, though they are to be found often enough
in the real world, rarely appear in the standard social-science literature.

On the subject of what is better or worse for children, the new stud- 17
ies, based as they are on very recent research findings, have much to tell
us. Without exception, when one compares children from intact families
with children from one-parent families where a divorce has taken place,
the data offer cause for deep alarm:

- Children in such situations are twice as likely to drop out of high
  school, and are much more likely to do poorly in reading, spelling,
  and mathematics.

- Such children are two to three times more likely to have emotional or behavior problems. They rate higher on dependency, anxiety, and aggressiveness, and lower on self-control. They rate low in peer popularity.

- They also score low in physical health and well-being.

- They show substantially higher crime rates. According to one study reported by Popenoe, "60 percent of rapists, 72 percent of adolescent murderers, and 70 percent of long-term prison inmates come from fatherless homes."

- They suffer much higher rates of both physical and sexual abuse, in the latter case most often carried out by the mother's boyfriend. Single mothers report being much more violent toward their children than do mothers in intact families.

- Finally, their problems persist. A study by Judith Wallerstein found that five, ten, and fifteen years after their parents' divorce, many children remain depressed, cannot achieve normally, and experience difficulties in love and attachment. The girls in particular are more often sexually active, likelier to contract venereal disease, to have children out of wedlock, and to enter into marriages which fail.

Almost all these studies involve American samples, but European [18] research discloses similar patterns. One impressive study in Sweden has found significant mental-health problems among adolescents who experienced family disruption. As other countries begin to approach American levels of marital break-up—and so they seem to be doing—we may expect a correlative rise in their rates of social pathology.

Of course, such studies do not—cannot—demonstrate definitive [19] causal relations. That, indeed, is the major point made by those who play down their importance. How, they ask, do we know it is the divorce itself that produces the problems, rather than the emotional turmoil which led to the divorce in the first place? How do we know it is the loss of family that leads to poor physical and emotional health, rather than the economic hardship often entailed by divorce?

Understanding when and why divorce does or does not bring seri- [20] ous psychological harm to children, or when and why sustaining a bad marriage may be more harmful than breaking up, is no easy matter. Questions like these are rather beyond the practical reach of social science. (By contrast, we do know that economic privation is responsible for some, but by no means all, of the problems attendant upon the dissolution of a marriage.) What is really troubling, however, is the collective diffidence which led us until very recently to avoid the very topic.

Whether we will now somehow overcome that diffidence remains to 21
be seen. The good news is the simultaneous appearance of works,
including those I have cited, calling attention to the unprecedented crisis
in which we find ourselves. Indeed, one can detect signs of a general
shift in the culture at large; people are not *quite* so quick as they once
were to take an optimistic view of marital separation, particularly as it
affects children. But whether this will lead to a widespread change in
behavior is, so far, doubtful. The dolorous statistics on the long-term
harmfulness of divorce are not fully accepted, even by many specialists.

And why should they be? After all, they run counter to our persis- 22
tent belief in renewal, in the limitless possibilities of the self. And they
suggest something that many Americans still show no signs of wanting
to hear: namely, that there is often a very high price to be paid for the
individualism that is so central to the American ethos.

Responding to Reading

1. Adelson observes that although "in recent decades we have been witnessing *extraordinary* changes in the nature and function of the family—in marriage, child-rearing, and divorce" (6), many of us do not seem to realize the
   seriousness of the situation. What explanations do the experts Adelson cites
   give for our inability to confront the threat to society these changes pose?
   Can you think of other explanations?
2. Do you agree with Popenoe and Gallagher (whose views are summarized
   in paragraph 14) that "our country has moved toward a divorce culture
   without fully wanting to, and without a full recognition of its consequences,
   especially for children"? In addition to those listed in paragraph 17, what
   "consequences," if any, can you identify?
3. Like Barbara Kingsolver (p. 64), Adelson discusses divorce in the context of
   "family values." How do the two writers differ in their attitudes toward
   this term? How do they differ in their general attitudes toward divorce?
   How do you account for these differences? Which attitude do you consider
   more appropriate?

Widening the Focus

- Lynda Barry, "The Sanctuary of School" (p. 86)

- Marie Winn, "Television: The Plug-in Drug" (p. 262)

- Louie Crew, "Thriving as an Outsider, Even as an Outcast, in
  Smalltown America" (p. 459)

WRITING

Family and Memory

1. What exactly is a family? Is it a group of people bound together by love? By marriage? By blood? By shared memories? By economic dependency? By habit? Is a family what Alice Hoffman remembers from 1950s television: "the neat patch of lawn, the apple tree, the mother who never once raised her voice, the three lovely children" (1)? Is it Barbara Kingsolver's "stone soup"? Or is it something else? Define *family* as it is presented in one (or several) of the essays in this chapter.

2. Leo Tolstoy's classic Russian novel *Anna Karenina* opens with the sentence "Happy families are all alike; every unhappy family is unhappy in its own way." Write an essay in which you concur with or challenge this statement, supporting your position with references to several of the readings in this chapter.

3. In a sense, memories are like snapshots, a series of disconnected candid pictures, sometimes unflattering, often out of focus, eventually fading. Writers of autobiographical memoirs often explore this parallel; for example, Raymond Carver calls the poem that appears in his essay "Photograph of My Father in His Twenty-Second Year." Using information from your own family life as well as from your reading, discuss the relationship between memories and photographs. If you like, you may incorporate a description of one or two of your own family photographs into your essay.

4. Several of the writers represented in this chapter—for example, Kingston, Momaday, and Carver—present fairly detailed biographical sketches of a family member. Using these essays as guides, write a detailed biographical sketch of a member of your family. If you can, prepare for this assignment by interviewing several family members.

5. Have you, like E. B. White, ever returned as an adult to a place that was important to you when you were a child? Write two brief descriptions, one from the point of view of your adult self and one from the point of view of your childhood self. In each description, consider both the physical appearance of the place and its significance to you. Then, expand your descriptions into an essay by writing introductory and concluding paragraphs comparing your two views.

6. In many of the selections in this chapter, central figures are portrayed as outsiders, even outcasts. Sometimes these people have chosen to isolate themselves, sometimes they have been set apart by their behavior, and sometimes they have been ostracized by the

society or by their own family. Analyze the factors that might have caused various individuals portrayed in two or three essays in this chapter to be isolated.

7. How do your parents' notions of success and failure affect you? Do you think your parents tend to expect too much of you? Too little? Explore these ideas in an essay, referring to one selection in this chapter and one in Chapter 6, "The American Dream."

8. Some writers—for example, Alice Walker and Raymond Carver— seem to have good reason to feel anger toward their parents. Are there negative events or situations in your own life for which you blame your parents? Identify several such events, and write a letter to your parents explaining why you believe your anger is justified.

9. Both Gary Soto and the speaker in Seamus Heaney's "Digging" come to understand their parents better by seeing them in the role of workers. Discuss these two men's changing attitudes toward their parents' work. If you like, you can also refer in your essay to ideas expressed by Scott Russell Sanders in "The Men We Carry in Our Minds" in Chapter 5. Or you can write an essay in which you discuss how your experience as a worker has helped you to understand or appreciate your own parents.

10. Read the poem "Photograph of My Father in His Twenty-Second Year," which follows paragraph 29 of Raymond Carver's essay. Write an essay in which you compare and contrast this poem with Robert Hayden's "Those Winter Sundays" (p. 14).

2

ISSUES
IN EDUCATION

Student Voices

"Because so much emphasis is placed on grade point averages, students may actually forget that school is a place to learn and to have fun. It should not just be an institution that prepares people to get good jobs and earn high salaries. Schools should open students up to the possibilities around them."

—*Celeste Armenti*

"Students no longer major in what they love, such as art or music. They take courses that will prepare them for what pays well, such as medicine, law, or business. Students most often become what their parents believe is good for them. Students' hopes, dreams, and aspirations have died, and now it seems that the only right thing to become is someone who will make a lot of money."

—*Linda Hoang*

"In college there are two different kinds of professors: those who care how their students do, and those who do not. Some professors just give lectures and tell students to memorize the book. Other professors give notes and have review sessions. One student has a good professor, and the other has a bad professor. Both students study for the same amount of time, but only one learns."

—*Nisha Jami*

"Coming from a small town, I never knew what living in a city was all about. Many of my friends at home will never experience living with people from many different parts of the country. They go to high school, graduate, get a job, and spend all their lives in one place. Also, many of my hometown friends are not accustomed to living together with people from many different racial and ethnic backgrounds. I consider this an important part of my education at college."

—*Kim Thompson*

"Last year when I decided to go back to school, I encountered many obstacles. Basically, I had been away from college for over five years, and during that time I had not used my mind much. But as I grew older, I began to realize what I was missing. I knew that it was about time for me to prove to myself that I could do college-level work. At first the adjustment was difficult. I went from working a fifty-hour week to working only on weekends. Eventually, however, I began to enjoy the new challenge of college material. I could feel my mind expanding and my confidence growing."

—*Robert Joiner*

PREPARING TO READ AND WRITE

It may seem odd to us today, when education is touted as a remedy for many of the social and economic problems of modern society, that a hundred years ago Mark Twain could imply that becoming educated meant paying a price: forfeiting youthful innocence and happiness. Yet that is precisely what he suggests in his essay "Reading the River," where he examines two different ways of viewing the world: one innocent and naive, the other experienced and educated; one accepting, the other questioning.

It is this view of education—as a process that radically changes a person from an unthinking, innocent child to a cognizant, questioning adult—that is largely missing from today's educational systems. In fact, more emphasis seems to be placed on increasing self-esteem and avoiding controversy than on challenging students to discover new ways of thinking and new contexts for viewing the world. As a result, classic books are censored or rewritten and ideas are presented as if they all have equal value. The result is an educational environment that has all the excitement of elevator music. Many people—educators included—seem to have forgotten that ideas *must* be unsettling if they are to make us think. What is education, after all, but a process that encourages us to think critically about the world and develop a healthy skepticism—to question, evaluate, and synthesize ideas and events?

As you read and prepare to write about the selections in this chapter, you may consider the following questions:

- How does the writer define education? Is this definition consistent with yours?

- What does the writer think the main goals of education should be? Do you agree?

- Which does the writer believe is more important, formal or informal education?

- On what aspect or aspects of education does the writer focus?

- Who does the writer believe bears primary responsibility for a student's education? The student? The school? The community? The government?

- Does the writer use personal experience to support his or her position? Or does he or she use facts and statistics or expert opinion as support? Do you find the writer's ideas convincing?

- What changes in the educational system does the writer recommend? Do you agree with the writer's recommendations?

- Are the writer's educational experiences similar to or different from yours? How do any similarities or differences affect your response to the essay?

- In what way is the essay you are reading similar to or different from other essays in this chapter?

TWO PERSPECTIVES ON EDUCATION

We lead off this chapter's readings with selections by two classic American writers, both of whom focus on how an educated understanding of the natural world can alter one's ability to see its beauty and wonder. In "Reading the River," Mark Twain (born Samuel Clemens, 1835–1910) reflects on his work as a riverboat pilot to contrast the experienced navigator's view of the Mississippi with that of an inexperienced passenger. After the Civil War ended commercial riverboat transportation in 1861, Twain turned to writing, producing humorous sketches of his travels in works like Innocents Abroad *(1869) and* Roughing It *(1872); well-known classic novels drawing on the rich material of his midwestern childhood,* The Adventures of Tom Sawyer *(1876) and* The Adventures of Huckleberry Finn *(1884); and* Life on the Mississippi *(1883), in which "Reading the River" appears. In his poem "When I Heard the Learn'd Astronomer," Walt Whitman (1819–1892) similarly contrasts the astronomer's view of the heavens with his own less scientific one. Whitman was a bold, eccentric character who wrote radical poetry that he hoped would unsettle "all the settled laws." His best-known work is the epic* Leaves of Grass *(1855); he also wrote as a journalist about the Civil War and composed essays commenting on American society and democracy.*

READING THE RIVER

Mark Twain

Now when I had mastered the language of this water and had 1 come to know every trifling feature that bordered the great river as familiarly as I knew the letters of the alphabet, I had made a valuable acquisition. But I had lost something, too. I had lost something which could never be restored to me while I lived. All the grace, the beauty, the poetry, had gone out of the majestic river! I still kept in mind a certain wonderful sunset which I witnessed when steamboating was new to me. A broad expanse of the river was turned to blood; in the middle distance the red hue brightened into gold, through which a solitary log came floating, black and conspicuous; in one place a long, slanting mark lay sparkling upon the water; in another the surface was broken by boiling, tumbling rings, that were as many-tinted as an opal; where the ruddy flush was faintest, was a smooth spot that was covered with graceful circles and radiating lines, ever so delicately traced; the shore on our left was densely wooded and the somber shadow that fell from this forest was broken in one place by a long, ruffled trail that shone like silver; and high above the forest wall a clean-stemmed dead tree waved a single leafy bough that glowed like a flame in the unobstructed splendor that was flowing from the sun. There were graceful curves, reflected images, woody heights, soft distances, and over the whole scene, far and near, the dissolving lights drifted steadily, enriching it every passing moment with new marvels of coloring.

I stood like one bewitched. I drank it in, in a speechless rapture. The world was new to me and I had never seen anything like this at home. But as I have said, a day came when I began to cease from noting the glories and the charms which the moon and the sun and the twilight wrought upon the river's face; another day came when I ceased altogether to note them. Then, if that sunset scene had been repeated, I should have looked upon it without rapture, and should have commented upon it inwardly after this fashion: "This sun means that we are going to have wind to-morrow; that floating log means that the river is rising, small thanks to it; that slanting mark on the water refers to a bluff reef which is going to kill somebody's steamboat one of these nights, if it keeps on stretching out like that; those tumbling 'boils' show a dissolving bar and a changing channel there; the lines and circles in the slick water over yonder are a warning that that troublesome place is shoaling up dangerously; that silver streak in the shadow of the forest is the 'break' from a new snag and he has located himself in the very best place he could have found to fish for steamboats; that tall dead tree, with a single living branch, is not going to last long, and then how is a body ever going to get through this blind place at night without the friendly old landmark?" 2

No, the romance and beauty were all gone from the river. All the value any feature of it had for me now was the amount of usefulness it could furnish toward compassing the safe piloting of a steamboat. Since those days, I have pitied doctors from my heart. What does the lovely flush in a beauty's cheek mean to a doctor but a "break" that ripples above some deadly disease?[1] Are not all her visible charms sown thick with what are to him the signs and symbols of hidden decay? Does he ever see her beauty at all, or doesn't he simply view her professionally and comment upon her unwholesome condition all to himself? And doesn't he sometimes wonder whether he has gained most or lost most by learning his trade? 3

---

[1] Red cheeks are one of the signs of tuberculosis. [Eds.]

WHEN I HEARD
THE LEARN'D ASTRONOMER

Walt Whitman

When I heard the learn'd astronomer,
When the proofs, the figures were ranged in columns before
me,
When I was shown the charts and diagrams, to add, divide,
and measure them,
When I sitting heard the astronomer where he lectured with
much applause in the lecture-room,
How soon unaccountable I became tired and sick,   5
Till rising and gliding out I wander'd off by myself,
In the mystical moist night-air, and from time to time,
Look'd up in perfect silence at the stars.

Responding to Reading

1. Which of the two ways of looking at nature does Twain seem to believe is
   more valuable? Do you agree?
2. Would you define Twain's view of education as optimistic or pessimistic?
   Why?
3. Whitman's poem could be divided into two 4-line segments. What kinds
   of ideas are expressed in each segment? How are the two kinds of ideas
   related?
4. What attitudes toward education are expressed in Whitman's poem? Do
   you agree with the speaker's sentiments?
5. Both Twain and Whitman use a personal experience to make a point about
   education. How else could these points be conveyed?
6. As you have become more educated, have you found yourself concentrating more on the "usefulness" of information than on its "romance and
   beauty"? Explain.

THE SANCTUARY OF SCHOOL

Lynda Barry

*Born in Richland Center, Wisconsin, Lynda Barry (1956–   ) grew up
in Seattle, Washington, as part of an extended Filipino family (her mother
was Filipino, her father an alcoholic Norwegian-Irishman). She majored in*

art at Evergreen State College—the first member of her family to go on to
higher education—and began her career as a cartoonist shortly after gradua-
tion. Known as a chronicler of adolescent angst both in her syndicated comic
strip Ernie Pook's Comeek *and in collections like* My Perfect Life *(1992)*
and The Freddie Stories *(1997), Barry has also written a widely admired*
novel about adolescence, The Good Times Are Killing Me *(1988), which*
was turned into a successful musical play. In "The Sanctuary of School,"
Barry remembers her Seattle grade school in a racially mixed neighborhood
as a nurturing safe haven from her difficult family life.

I was 7 years old the first time I snuck out of the house in the dark. 1
It was winter and my parents had been fighting all night. They were
short on money and long on relatives who kept "temporarily" moving
into our house because they had nowhere else to go.

My brother and I were used to giving up our bedroom. We slept on 2
the couch, something we actually liked because it put us that much
closer to the light of our lives, our television.

At night when everyone was asleep, we lay on our pillows watch- 3
ing it with the sound off. We watched Steve Allen's mouth moving. We
watched Johnny Carson's mouth moving. We watched movies filled
with gangsters shooting machine guns into packed rooms, dying soldiers hurling a last grenade and beautiful women crying at windows.
Then the sign-off finally came and we tried to sleep.

The morning I snuck out, I woke up filled with a panic about need- 4
ing to get to school. The sun wasn't quite up yet but my anxiety was so
fierce that I just got dressed, walked quietly across the kitchen and let
myself out the back door.

It was quiet outside. Stars were still out. Nothing moved and no one 5
was in the street. It was as if someone had turned the sound off on the
world.

I walked the alley, breaking thin ice over the puddles with my 6
shoes. I didn't know why I was walking to school in the dark. I didn't
think about it. All I knew was a feeling of panic, like the panic that
strikes kids when they realize they are lost.

That feeling eased the moment I turned the corner and saw the dark 7
outline of my school at the top of the hill. My school was made up of
about 15 nondescript portable classrooms set down on a fenced concrete
lot in a rundown Seattle neighborhood, but it had the most beautiful
view of the Cascade Mountains. You could see them from anywhere on
the playfield and you could see them from the windows of my classroom—Room 2.

I walked over to the monkey bars and hooked my arms around the 8
cold metal. I stood for a long time just looking across Rainier Valley. The
sky was beginning to whiten and I could hear a few birds.

In a perfect world my absence at home would not have gone unno- 9
ticed. I would have had two parents in a panic to locate me, instead of

two parents in a panic to locate an answer to the hard question of survival during a deep financial and emotional crisis.

But in an overcrowded and unhappy home, it's incredibly easy for 10 any child to slip away. The high levels of frustration, depression and anger in my house made my brother and me invisible. We were children with the sound turned off. And for us, as for the steadily increasing number of neglected children in this country, the only place where we could count on being noticed was at school.

"Hey there, young lady. Did you forget to go home last night?" It 11 was Mr. Gunderson, our janitor, whom we all loved. He was nice and he was funny and he was old with white hair, thick glasses and an unbelievable number of keys. I could hear them jingling as he walked across the playfield. I felt incredibly happy to see him.

He let me push his wheeled garbage can between the different 12 portables as he unlocked each room. He let me turn on the lights and raise the window shades and I saw my school slowly come to life. I saw Mrs. Holman, our school secretary, walk into the office without her orange lipstick on yet. She waved.

I saw the fifth-grade teacher Mr. Cunningham, walking under the 13 breezeway eating a hard roll. He waved.

And I saw my teacher, Mrs. Claire LeSane, walking toward us in a 14 red coat and calling my name in a very happy and surprised way, and suddenly my throat got tight and my eyes stung and I ran toward her crying. It was something that surprised us both.

It's only thinking about it now, 28 years later, that I realize I was cry- 15 ing from relief. I was with my teacher, and in a while I was going to sit at my desk, with my crayons and pencils and books and classmates all around me, and for the next six hours I was going to enjoy a thoroughly secure, warm and stable world. It was a world I absolutely relied on. Without it, I don't know where I would have gone that morning.

Mrs. LeSane asked me what was wrong and when I said "Nothing," 16 she seemingly left it at that. But she asked me if I would carry her purse for her, an honor above all honors, and she asked if I wanted to come into Room 2 early and paint.

She believed in the natural healing power of painting and drawing 17 for troubled children. In the back of her room there was always a drawing table and an easel with plenty of supplies, and sometimes during the day she would come up to you for what seemed like no good reason and quietly ask if you wanted to go to the back table and "make some pictures for Mrs. LeSane." We all had a chance at it—to sit apart from the class for a while to paint, draw and silently work out impossible problems on 11 × 17 sheets of newsprint.

Drawing came to mean everything to me. At the back table in Room 18 2, I learned to build myself a life preserver that I could carry into my home.

We all know that a good education system saves lives, but the peo- 19
ple of this country are still told that cutting the budget for public schools
is necessary, that poor salaries for teachers are all we can manage and
that art, music and all creative activities must be the first to go when
times are lean.

Before- and after-school programs are cut and we are told that pub- 20
lic schools are not made for baby-sitting children. If parents are neglect-
ful temporarily or permanently, for whatever reason, it's certainly sad,
but their unlucky children must fend for themselves. Or slip through
the cracks. Or wander in a dark night alone.

We are told in a thousand ways that not only are public schools not 21
important, but that the children who attend them, the children who
need them most, are not important either. We leave them to learn from
the blind eye of a television, or to the mercy of "a thousand points of
light"[1] that can be as far away as stars.

I was lucky. I had Mrs. LeSane. I had Mr. Gunderson. I had an abun- 22
dance of art supplies. And I had a particular brand of neglect in my
home that allowed me to slip away and get to them. But what about the
rest of the kids who weren't as lucky? What happened to them?

By the time the bell rang that morning I had finished my drawing 23
and Mrs. LeSane pinned it up on the special bulletin board she reserved
for drawings from the back table. It was the same picture I always
drew—a sun in the corner of a blue sky over a nice house with flowers
all around it.

Mrs. LeSane asked us to please stand, face the flag, place our right 24
hands over our hearts and say the Pledge of Allegiance. Children across
the country do it faithfully. I wonder now when the country will face its
children and say a pledge right back.

Responding to Reading

1. Was Barry's school like the one you remember? What kind of information
   does she not provide? How can you explain these omissions?
2. In paragraph 22, Barry asks two questions. Why doesn't she answer them?
   What do you think the answers to these questions might be?
3. Barry's essay ends on a somewhat cynical note. How effective is this conclusion? What does Barry gain or lose with this concluding strategy?

---

[1] Catchphrase for former President George Bush's plan to substitute volunteerism for government
programs. [Eds.]

GRADUATION

Maya Angelou

Maya Angelou (1928–) was born in St. Louis, where her mother lived, but was raised in Arkansas by her grandmother, who ran a general store. She began a theatrical career when she toured with Porgy and Bess *in 1954–1955. Angelou is now a poet, writer, lecturer, civil rights leader, and teacher. She read her poem "On the Pulse of Morning" at the 1993 presidential inauguration of Bill Clinton. A critic in* Southern Humanities Review *has said that "her genius as a writer is in her ability to recapture the texture of the way of life in the texture of its idioms, its idiosyncrasies, and especially its process of image-making." Angelou's many books include* Oh Pray My Wings Are Gonna Fit Me Well *(poetry, 1975) and* I Know Why the Caged Bird Sings *(autobiography, 1969); her most recent is an essay collection,* Even the Stars Look Lonesome *(1997). In "Graduation," Angelou remembers the anger and pride of graduation day at her segregated school in Stamps, Arkansas.*

The children in Stamps trembled visibly with anticipation. Some 1
adults were excited too, but to be certain the whole young population had come down with graduation epidemic. Large classes were graduating from both the grammar school and the high school. Even those who were years removed from their own day of glorious release were anxious to help with preparations as a kind of dry run. The junior students who were moving into the vacating classes' chairs were tradition-bound to show their talents for leadership and management. They strutted through the school and around the campus exerting pressure on the lower grades. Their authority was so new that occasionally if they pressed a little too hard it had to be overlooked. After all, next term was coming, and it never hurt a sixth grader to have a play sister in the eighth grade, or a tenth-year student to be able to call a twelfth grader Bubba. So all was endured in a spirit of shared understanding. But the graduating classes themselves were the nobility. Like travelers with exotic destinations on their minds, the graduates were remarkably forgetful. They came to school without their books, or tablets or even pencils. Volunteers fell over themselves to secure replacements for the missing equipment. When accepted, the willing workers might or might not be thanked, and it was of no importance to the pregraduation rites. Even teachers were respectful of the now quiet and aging seniors, and tended to speak to them, if not as equals, as beings only slightly lower than themselves. After tests were returned and grades given, the student body, which acted like an extended family, knew who did well, who excelled, and what piteous ones had failed.

Unlike the white high school, Lafayette County Training School dis- 2
tinguished itself by having neither lawn, nor hedges, nor tennis court,
nor climbing ivy. Its two buildings (main classrooms, the grade school
and home economics) were set on a dirt hill with no fence to limit either
its boundaries or those of bordering farms. There was a large expanse to
the left of the school which was used alternately as a baseball diamond
or basketball court. Rusty hoops on swaying poles represented the permanent recreational equipment, although bats and balls could be borrowed from the P.E. teacher if the borrower was qualified and if the
diamond wasn't occupied.

Over this rocky area relieved by a few shady tall persimmon trees 3
the graduating class walked. The girls often held hands and no longer
bothered to speak to the lower students. There was a sadness about
them, as if this old world was not their home and they were bound for
higher ground. The boys, on the other hand, had become more friendly,
more outgoing. A decided change from the closed attitude they projected while studying for finals. Now they seemed not ready to give up
the old school, the familiar paths and classrooms. Only a small percentage would be continuing on to college—one of the South's A & M (agricultural and mechanical) schools, which trained Negro youths to be
carpenters, farmers, handymen, masons, maids, cooks and baby nurses.
Their future rode heavily on their shoulders, and blinded them to the
collective joy that had pervaded the lives of the boys and girls in the
grammar school graduating class.

Parents who could afford it had ordered new shoes and ready-made 4
clothes for themselves from Sears and Roebuck or Montgomery Ward.
They also engaged the best seamstresses to make the floating graduating dresses and to cut down secondhand pants which would be pressed
to a military slickness for the important event.

Oh, it was important, all right. Whitefolks would attend the cere- 5
mony, and two or three would speak of God and home, and the Southern
way of life, and Mrs. Parsons, the principal's wife, would play the graduation march while the lower-grade graduates paraded down the aisles
and took their seats below the platform. The high school seniors would
wait in empty classrooms to make their dramatic entrance.

In the Store I was the person of the moment. The birthday girl. The 6
center. Bailey[1] had graduated the year before, although to do so he had
had to forfeit all pleasures to make up for his time lost in Baton Rouge.

My class was wearing butter-yellow piqué dresses, and Momma 7
launched out on mine. She smocked the yoke into tiny crisscrossing
puckers, then shirred the rest of the bodice. Her dark fingers ducked in

---

[1] Angelou's brother. The Store was run by Angelou's grandmother, whom she called Momma, and
Momma's son, Uncle Willie. [Eds.]

and out of the lemony cloth as she embroidered raised daisies around the hem. Before she considered herself finished she had added a crocheted cuff on the puff sleeves, and a pointy crocheted collar.

I was going to be lovely. A walking model of all the various styles 8 of fine hand sewing and it didn't worry me that I was only twelve years old and merely graduating from the eighth grade. Besides, many teachers in Arkansas Negro schools had only that diploma and were licensed to impart wisdom.

The days had become longer and more noticeable. The faded beige 9 of former times had been replaced with strong and sure colors. I began to see my classmates' clothes, their skin tones, and the dust that waved off pussy willows. Clouds that lazed across the sky were objects of great concern to me. Their shiftier shapes might have held a message that in my new happiness and with a little bit of time I'd soon decipher. During that period I looked at the arch of heaven so religiously my neck kept a steady ache. I had taken to smiling more often, and my jaws hurt from the unaccustomed activity. Between the two physical sore spots, I suppose I could have been uncomfortable, but that was not the case. As a member of the winning team (the graduating class of 1940) I had outdistanced unpleasant sensations by miles. I was headed for the freedom of open fields.

Youth and social approval allied themselves with me and we tram- 10 meled memories of slights and insults. The wind of our swift passage remodeled my features. Lost tears were pounded to mud and then to dust. Years of withdrawal were brushed aside and left behind, as hanging ropes of parasitic moss.

My work alone had awarded me a top place and I was going to be 11 one of the first called in the graduating ceremonies. On the classroom blackboard, as well as on the bulletin board in the auditorium, there were blue stars and white stars and red stars. No absences, no tardinesses, and my academic work was among the best of the year. I could say the preamble to the Constitution even faster than Bailey. We timed ourselves often: "WethepeopleoftheUnitedStatesinordertoformamore-perfectunion . . ." I had memorized the Presidents of the United States from Washington to Roosevelt in chronological as well as alphabetical order.

My hair pleased me too. Gradually the black mass had lengthened 12 and thickened, so that it kept at last to its braided pattern, and I didn't have to yank my scalp off when I tried to comb it.

Louise and I had rehearsed the exercises until we tired out our- 13 selves. Henry Reed was class valedictorian. He was a small, very black boy with hooded eyes, a long, broad nose and an oddly shaped head. I had admired him for years because each term he and I vied for the best grades in our class. Most often he bested me, but instead of being disappointed I was pleased that we shared top places between us. Like many Southern Black children, he lived with his grandmother, who was as strict as Momma and as kind as she knew how to be. He was courteous, respectful and soft-spoken to elders, but on the playground he chose to play the roughest games. I admired him. Anyone, I reckoned, sufficiently afraid or sufficiently dull could be polite. But to be able to operate at a top level with both adults and children was admirable.

His valedictory speech was entitled "To Be or Not to Be." The rigid 14 tenth-grade teacher had helped him write it. He'd been working on the dramatic stresses for months.

The weeks until graduation were filled with heady activities. A 15 group of small children were to be presented in a play about buttercups and daisies and bunny rabbits. They could be heard throughout the building practicing their hops and their little songs that sounded like silver bells. The older girls (nongraduates, of course) were assigned the task of making refreshments for the night's festivities. A tangy scent of ginger, cinnamon, nutmeg and chocolate wafted around the home economics building as the budding cooks made samples for themselves and their teachers.

In every corner of the workshop, axes and saws split fresh timber as 16 the woodshop boys made sets and stage scenery. Only the graduates were left out of the general bustle. We were free to sit in the library at the back of the building or look in quite detachedly, naturally, on the measures being taken for our event.

Even the minister preached on graduation the Sunday before. His 17 subject was, "Let your light so shine that men will see your good works and praise your Father, Who is in Heaven." Although the sermon was purported to be addressed to us, he used the occasion to speak to back-sliders, gamblers and general ne'er-do-wells. But since he had called our names at the beginning of the service we were mollified.

Among Negroes the tradition was to give presents to children going 18 only from one grade to another. How much more important this was when the person was graduating at the top of the class. Uncle Willie and Momma had sent away for a Mickey Mouse watch like Bailey's. Louise gave me four embroidered handkerchiefs. (I gave her crocheted doilies.) Mrs. Sneed, the minister's wife, made me an undershirt to wear for graduation, and nearly every customer gave me a nickel or maybe even a dime with the instruction "Keep on moving to higher ground," or some such encouragement.

Amazingly the great day finally dawned and I was out of bed 19 before I knew it. I threw open the back door to see it more clearly, but Momma said, "Sister, come away from that door and put your robe on."

I hoped the memory of that morning would never leave me. 20 Sunlight was itself young, and the day had none of the insistence maturity would bring it in a few hours. In my robe and barefoot in the back-yard, under cover of going to see about my new beans, I gave myself up to the gentle warmth and thanked God that no matter what evil I had done in my life He had allowed me to live to see this day. Somewhere in my fatalism I had expected to die, accidentally, and never have the chance to walk up the stairs in the auditorium and gracefully receive my hard-earned diploma. Out of God's merciful bosom I had won reprieve.

Bailey came out in his robe and gave me a box wrapped in 21 Christmas paper. He said he had saved his money for months to pay for it. It felt like a box of chocolates, but I knew Bailey wouldn't save money to buy candy when we had all we could want under our noses.

He was as proud of the gift as I. It was a soft-leather-bound copy of 22 a collection of poems by Edgar Allan Poe, or, as Bailey and I called him, "Eap." I turned to "Annabel Lee" and we walked up and down the garden rows, the cool dirt between our toes, reciting the beautifully sad lines.

Momma made a Sunday breakfast although it was only Friday. 23 After we finished the blessing, I opened my eyes to find the watch on my plate. It was a dream of a day. Everything went smoothly and to my credit. I didn't have to be reminded or scolded for anything. Near evening I was too jittery to attend to chores, so Bailey volunteered to do all before his bath.

Days before, we had made a sign for the Store, and as we turned out 24 the lights Momma hung the cardboard over the doorknob. It read clearly: CLOSED. GRADUATION.

My dress fitted perfectly and everyone said that I looked like a sun- 25 beam in it. On the hill, going toward the school, Bailey walked behind with Uncle Willie, who muttered, "Go on, Ju." He wanted him to walk ahead with us because it embarrassed him to have to walk so slowly. Bailey said he'd let the ladies walk together, and the men would bring up the rear. We all laughed, nicely.

Little children dashed by out of the dark like fireflies. Their crepe- 26 paper dresses and butterfly wings were not made for running and we heard more than one rip, dryly, and the regretful "uh uh" that followed.

The school blazed without gaiety. The windows seemed cold and 27 unfriendly from the lower hill. A sense of ill-fated timing crept over me, and if Momma hadn't reached for my hand I would have drifted back to Bailey and Uncle Willie, and possibly beyond. She made a few slow jokes about my feet getting cold, and tugged me along to the now-strange building.

Around the front steps, assurance came back. There were my fellow 28 "greats," the graduating class. Hair brushed back, legs oiled, new dresses and pressed pleats, fresh pocket handkerchiefs and little handbags, all homesewn. Oh, we were up to snuff, all right. I joined my comrades and didn't even see my family go in to find seats in the crowded auditorium.

The school band struck up a march and all classes filed in as had 29
been rehearsed. We stood in front of our seats, as assigned, and on a signal from the choir director, we sat. No sooner had this been accomplished than the band started to play the national anthem. We rose
again and sang the song, after which we recited the pledge of allegiance.
We remained standing for a brief minute before the choir director and
the principal signaled to us, rather desperately I thought, to take our
seats. The command was so unusual that our carefully rehearsed and
smooth-running machine was thrown off. For a full minute we fumbled
for our chairs and bumped into each other awkwardly. Habits change
or solidify under pressure, so in our state of nervous tension we had
been ready to follow our usual assembly pattern: the American national
anthem, then the pledge of allegiance, then the song every Black person
I knew called the Negro National Anthem. All done in the same key,
with the same passion and most often standing on the same foot.

Finding my seat at last, I was overcome with a presentiment of 30
worse things to come. Something unrehearsed, unplanned, was going
to happen, and we were going to be made to look bad. I distinctly
remember being explicit in the choice of pronoun. It was "we," the graduating class, the unit, that concerned me then.

The principal welcomed "parents and friends" and asked the 31
Baptist minister to lead us in prayer. His invocation was brief and
punchy, and for a second I thought we were getting on the high road to
right action. When the principal came back to the dais, however, his
voice had changed. Sounds always affected me profoundly and the
principal's voice was one of my favorites. During assembly it melted
and lowed weakly into the audience. It had not been in my plan to listen to him, but my curiosity was piqued and I straightened up to give
him my attention.

He was talking about Booker T. Washington, our "late great leader," 32
who said we can be as close as the fingers on the hand, etc. . . . Then he
said a few vague things about friendship and the friendship of kindly
people to those less fortunate than themselves. With that his voice
nearly faded, thin, away. Like a river diminishing to a stream and then
to a trickle. But he cleared his throat and said, "Our speaker tonight,
who is also our friend, came from Texarkana to deliver the commencement address, but due to the irregularity of the train schedule, he's
going to, as they say, 'speak and run.'" He said that we understood and
wanted the man to know that we were most grateful for the time he was
able to give us and then something about how we were willing always
to adjust to another's program, and without more ado—"I give you Mr.
Edward Donleavy."

Not one but two white men came through the door off-stage. The 33
shorter one walked to the speaker's platform, and the tall one moved to
the center seat and sat down. But that was our principal's seat, and

already occupied. The dislodged gentleman bounced around for a long breath or two before the Baptist minister gave him his chair, then with more dignity than the situation deserved, the minister walked off the stage.

Donleavy looked at the audience once (on reflection, I'm sure that 34 he wanted only to reassure himself that we were really there), adjusted his glasses and began to read from a sheaf of papers.

He was glad "to be here and to see the work going on just as it was 35 in the other schools."

At the first "Amen" from the audience I willed the offender to 36 immediate death by choking on the word. But Amens and Yes, sir's began to fall around the room like rain through a ragged umbrella.

He told us of the wonderful changes we children in Stamps had in 37 store. The Central School (naturally, the white school was Central) had already been granted improvements that would be in use in the fall. A well-known artist was coming from Little Rock to teach art to them. They were going to have the newest microscopes and chemistry equipment for their laboratory. Mr. Donleavy didn't leave us long in the dark over who made these improvements available to Central High. Nor were we to be ignored in the general betterment scheme he had in mind.

He said that he had pointed out to people at a very high level that 38 one of the first-line football tacklers at Arkansas Agricultural and Mechanical College had graduated from good old Lafayette County Training School. Here fewer Amen's were heard. Those few that did break through lay dully in the air with the heaviness of habit.

He went on to praise us. He went on to say how he had bragged 39 that "one of the best basketball players at Fisk[2] sank his first ball right here at Lafayette County Training School."

The white kids were going to have a chance to become Galileos and 40 Madame Curies and Edisons and Gauguins,[3] and our boys (the girls weren't even in on it) would try to be Jesse Owenses and Joe Louises.[4]

Owens and the Brown Bomber were great heroes in our world, but 41 what school official in the white-goddom of Little Rock had the right to decide that those two men must be our only heroes? Who decided that for Henry Reed to become a scientist he had to work like George Washington Carver, as a bootblack, to buy a lousy microscope? Bailey was obviously always going to be too small to be an athlete, so which concrete angel glued to what country seat had decided that if my brother wanted to become a lawyer he had to first pay penance for his

---

[2] Highly regarded, predominantly black university in Nashville. [Eds.]

[3] Inventors, scientists, and artists. [Eds.]

[4] The black track star and Olympic gold medalist, and the longtime world heavyweight boxing champion, known as the "Brown Bomber." [Eds.]

skin by picking cotton and hoeing corn and studying correspondence books at night for twenty years?

The man's dead words fell like bricks around the auditorium and 42 too many settled in my belly. Constrained by hard-learned manners I couldn't look behind me, but to my left and right the proud graduating class of 1940 had dropped their heads. Every girl in my row had found something new to do with her handkerchief. Some folded the tiny squares into love knots, some into triangles, but most were wadding them, then pressing them flat on their yellow laps.

On the dais, the ancient tragedy was being replayed. Professor 43 Parsons sat, a sculptor's reject, rigid. His large, heavy body seemed devoid of will or willingness, and his eyes said he was no longer with us. The other teachers examined the flag (which was draped stage right) or their notes, or the windows which opened on our now-famous playing diamond.

Graduation, the hush-hush magic time of frills and gifts and con- 44 gratulations and diplomas, was finished for me before my name was called. The accomplishment was nothing. The meticulous maps, drawn in three colors of ink, learning and spelling decasyllabic words, memorizing the whole of *The Rape of Lucrece*[5]—it was for nothing. Donleavy had exposed us.

We were maids and farmers, handymen and washerwomen, and 45 anything higher that we aspired to was farcical and presumptuous.

Then I wished that Gabriel Prosser and Nat Turner[6] had killed all 46 whitefolks in their beds and that Abraham Lincoln had been assassinated before the signing of the Emancipation Proclamation, and that Harriet Tubman[7] had been killed by that blow on her head and Christopher Columbus had drowned in the *Santa Maria*.

It was awful to be a Negro and have no control over my life. It was 47 brutal to be young and already trained to sit quietly and listen to charges brought against my color with no chance of defense. We should all be dead. I thought I should like to see us all dead, one on top of the other. A pyramid of flesh with the whitefolks on the bottom, as the broad base, then the Indians with their silly tomahawks and teepees and wigwams and treaties, the Negroes with their mops and recipes and cotton sacks and spirituals sticking out of their mouths. The Dutch children should all stumble in their wooden shoes and break their necks. The French should choke to death on the Louisiana Purchase (1803) while silkworms ate all the Chinese with their stupid pigtails. As a species, we were an abomination. All of us.

---

[5] *The Rape of Lucrece* is a long narrative poem by Shakespeare. [Eds.]

[6] Prosser and Turner both led slave rebellions. [Eds.]

[7] Harriet Tubman (1820–1913) was an African-Amencan abolitionist who became one of the most successful guides on the Underground Railroad. [Eds.]

Donleavy was running for election, and assured our parents that if 48 he won we could count on having the only colored paved playing field in that part of Arkansas. Also—he never looked up to acknowledge the grunts of acceptance—also, we were bound to get some new equipment for the home economics building and the workshop.

He finished, and since there was no need to give any more than the 49 most perfunctory thank-you's, he nodded to the men on the stage, and the tall white man who was never introduced joined him at the door. They left with the attitude that now they were off to something really important. (The graduation ceremonies at Lafayette County Training School had been a mere preliminary.)

The ugliness they left was palpable. An uninvited guest who 50 wouldn't leave. The choir was summoned and sang a modern arrangement of "Onward, Christian Soldiers," with new words pertaining to graduates seeking their place in the world. But it didn't work. Elouise, the daughter of the Baptist minister, recited "Invictus,"[8] and I could have cried at the impertinence of "I am the master of my fate, I am the captain of my soul."

My name had lost its ring of familiarity and I had to be nudged to 51 go and receive my diploma. All my preparations had fled. I neither marched up to the stage like a conquering Amazon, not did I look in the audience for Bailey's nod of approval. Marguerite Johnson,[9] I heard the name again, my honors were read, there were noises in the audience of appreciation, and I took my place on the stage as rehearsed.

I thought about colors I hated: ecru, puce, lavender, beige and 52 black.

There was shuffling and rustling around me, then Henry Reed was 53 giving his valedictory address, "To Be or Not to Be." Hadn't he heard the whitefolks? We couldn't be, so the question was a waste of time. Henry's voice came out clear and strong. I feared to look at him. Hadn't he got the message? There was no "nobler in the mind" for Negroes because the world didn't think we had minds, and they let us know it. "Outrageous fortune"? Now, that was a joke. When the ceremony was over I had to tell Henry Reed some things. That is, if I still cared. Not "rub," Henry, "erase." "Ah, there's the erase." Us.

Henry had been a good student in elocution. His voice rose on tides 54 of promise and fell on waves of warnings. The English teacher had helped him to create a sermon winging through Hamlet's soliloquy. To be a man, a doer, a builder, a leader, or to be a tool, an unfunny joke, a crusher of funky toadstools. I marveled that Henry could go through with the speech as if we had a choice.

---

[8] An inspirational poem written in 1875 by William Ernest Henley (1849–1903). Its defiant and stoic sentiments made it extremely popular with nineteenth-century readers. [Eds.]

[9] Angelou's given name. [Eds.]

I had been listening and silently rebutting each sentence with my   55
eyes closed; then there was a hush, which in an audience warns that
something unplanned is happening. I looked up and saw Henry Reed,
the conservative, the proper, the A student, turn his back to the audience
and turn to us (the proud graduating class of 1940) and sing, nearly
speaking,

"Lift ev'ry voice and sing
Till earth and heaven ring
Ring with the harmonies of Liberty . . ."

It was the poem written by James Weldon Johnson. It was the music   56
composed by J. Rosamond Johnson. It was the Negro national anthem.
Out of habit we were singing it.

Our mothers and fathers stood in the dark hall and joined the hymn   57
of encouragement. A kindergarten teacher led the small children onto
the stage and the buttercups and daisies and bunny rabbits marked time
and tried to follow:

"Stony the road we trod
Bitter the chastening rod
Felt in the days when hope, unborn, had died.
Yet with a steady beat
Have not our weary feet   5
Come to the place for which our fathers sighed?"

Each child I knew had learned that song with his ABC's and along   58
with "Jesus Loves Me This I Know." But I personally had never heard it
before. Never heard the words, despite the thousands of times I had
sung them. Never thought they had anything to do with me.

On the other hand, the words of Patrick Henry had made such an   59
impression on me that I had been able to stretch myself tall and trembling and say, "I know not what course others may take, but as for me,
give me liberty or give me death."

And now I heard, really for the first time: 60

"We have come over a way that with tears
has been watered,
We have come, treading our path through
the blood of the slaughtered."

While echoes of the song shivered in the air, Henry Reed bowed his   61
head, said "Thank you," and returned to his place in the line. The tears
that slipped down many faces were not wiped away in shame.

We were on top again. As always, again. We survived. The depths 62
had been icy and dark, but now a bright sun spoke to our souls. I was
no longer simply a member of the proud graduating class of 1940; I was
a proud member of the wonderful, beautiful Negro race.

Oh, Black known and unknown poets, how often have your auc- 63
tioned pains sustained us? Who will compute the lonely nights made
less lonely by your songs, or the empty pots made less tragic by your
tales?

If we were a people much given to revealing secrets, we might raise 64
monuments and sacrifice to the memories of our poets, but slavery
cured us of that weakness. It may be enough, however, to have it said
that we survive in exact relationship to the dedication of our poets
(include preachers, musicians and blues singers).

Responding to Reading

1. Angelou's graduation took place in 1940. What expectations did educators
   have for Angelou and her classmates? In what ways are the expectations
   different from or similar to the expectations the teachers in your high school
   had for you and your fellow students?
2. In what way does Mr. Donleavy's speech "educate" the graduates? How
   does Angelou's thinking change as she listens to him?
3. In paragraph 62, Angelou says "We were on top again." In what way were
   she and the graduates "on top"? Do you think Angelou was being overly
   optimistic in light of what she had just experienced?

SAVAGE INEQUALITIES

Jonathan Kozol

*Born in Boston into a "privileged and isolated" environment, Jonathan
Kozol (1936–   ) received his B.A. in literature from Harvard and drifted
into the civil rights movement in 1964. In 1967, he published* Death at an
Early Age: The Destruction of the Hearts and Minds of Negro School
Children in the Boston Public Schools. *Based on his experiences as a
fourth-grade teacher in an inner-city school, a position from which he was
fired for "curriculum deviation," this controversial book led to a number of
specific reforms. Since then, Kozol has divided his time between teaching and
social activism, noting "It is a simple matter of humanity to use our limited
resources in the places where they're the most needed." His books include*
Illiterate America *(1985), an excerpt from which appears on page 206;*
Rachel and Her Children *(1988), a study of homeless families; and* Savage

Inequalities (1991), an examination of the unequal resources available to suburban and inner-city public schools. His most recent book is Amazing Grace *(1995). In the following chapter from* Savage Inequalities, *Kozol looks at grade schools only a few miles apart in the Bronx, New York, where differences based on race and class could not be more apparent.*

"In a country where there is no distinction of class," Lord Acton 1 wrote of the United States 130 years ago, "a child is not born to the station of its parents, but with an indefinite claim to all the prizes that can be won by thought and labor. It is in conformity with the theory of equality . . . to give as near as possible to every youth an equal state in life." Americans, he said, "are unwilling that any should be deprived in childhood of the means of competition."

It is hard to read these words today without a sense of irony and 2 sadness. Denial of "the means of competition" is perhaps the single most consistent outcome of the education offered to poor children in the schools of our large cities; and nowhere is this pattern of denial more explicit or more absolute than in the public schools of New York City.

Average expenditures per pupil in the city of New York in 1987 3 were some $5,500. In the highest spending suburbs of New York (Great Neck or Manhasset, for example, on Long Island) funding levels rose above $11,000, with the highest districts in the state at $15,000. "Why . . . ," asks the city's Board of Education, "should our students receive less" than do "similar students" who live elsewhere? "The inequity is clear."

But the inequality to which these words refer goes even further than 4 the school board may be eager to reveal. "It is perhaps the supreme irony," says the nonprofit Community Service Society of New York, that "the same Board of Education which perceives so clearly the inequities" of funding between separate towns and cities "is perpetuating similar inequities" right in New York. And, in comment on the Board of Education's final statement—"the inequity is clear"—the CSS observes, "New York City's poorest . . . districts could adopt that eloquent statement with few changes."

New York City's public schools are subdivided into 32 school dis- 5 tricts. District 10 encompasses a large part of the Bronx but is, effectively, two separate districts. One of these districts, Riverdale, is in the northwest section of the Bronx. Home to many of the city's most sophisticated and well-educated families, its elementary schools have relatively few low-income students. The other section, to the south and east, is poor and heavily nonwhite.

The contrast between public schools in each of these two neighbor- 6 hoods is obvious to any visitor. At Public School 24 in Riverdale, the principal speaks enthusiastically of his teaching staff. At Public School 79, serving poorer children to the south, the principal says that he is forced to take the "tenth-best" teachers. "I thank God they're still breathing," he remarks of those from whom he must select his teachers.

Some years ago, District 10 received an allocation for computers. 7 The local board decided to give each elementary school an equal number of computers, even though the schools in Riverdale had smaller classes and far fewer students. When it was pointed out that schools in Riverdale, as a result, had twice the number of computers in proportion to their student populations as the schools in the poor neighborhoods, the chairman of the local board replied, "What is fair is what is determined . . . to be fair."

The superintendent of District 10, Fred Goldberg, tells the *New York* 8 *Times* that "every effort" is made "to distribute resources equitably." He speculates that some gap might exist because some of the poorer schools need to use funds earmarked for computers to buy basic supplies like pens and paper. Asked about the differences in teachers noted by the principals, he says there are no differences, then adds that next year he'll begin a program to improve the quality of teachers in the poorer schools. Questioned about differences in physical appearances between the richer and the poorer schools, he says, "I think it's demographics."[1]

Sometimes a school principal, whatever his background or his pol- 9 itics, looks into the faces of the children in his school and offers a disarming statement that cuts through official ambiguity. "These are the kids most in need," says Edward Flanery, the principal of one of the low-income schools, "and they get the worst teachers." For children of diverse needs in his overcrowded rooms, he says, "you need an outstanding teacher. And what do you get? You get the worst."

In order to find Public School 261 in District 10, a visitor is told to 10 look for a mortician's office. The funeral home, which faces Jerome Avenue in the North Bronx, is easy to identify by its green awning. The school is next door, in a former roller-skating rink. No sign identifies the building as a school. A metal awning frame without an awning supports a flagpole, but there is no flag.

In the street in front of the school there is an elevated public transit 11 line. Heavy traffic fills the street. The existence of the school is virtually concealed within this crowded city block.

In a vestibule between the outer and inner glass doors of the school 12 there is a sign with these words: "All children are capable of learning."

Beyond the inner doors a guard is seated. The lobby is long and 13 narrow. The ceiling is low. There are no windows. All the teachers that

---

[1] Marketing term tor the statistical characteristics—such as income and education—of particular population groups. [Eds.]

I see at first are middle-aged white women. The principal, who is also a white woman, tells me that the school's "capacity" is 900 but that there are 1,300 children here. The size of classes for fifth and sixth grade children in New York, she says, is "capped" at 32, but she says that class size in the school goes "up to 34." (I later see classes, however, as large as 37.) Classes for younger children, she goes on, are "capped at 25," but a school can go above this limit if it puts an extra adult in the room. Lack of space, she says, prevents the school from operating a pre-kindergarten program.

I ask the principal where her children go to school. They are 14 enrolled in private school, she says.

"Lunchtime is a challenge for us," she explains. "Limited space 15 obliges us to do it in three shifts, 450 children at a time."

Textbooks are scarce and children have to share their social studies 16 books. The principal says there is one full-time pupil counselor and another who is here two days a week: a ratio of 930 children to one counselor. The carpets are patched and sometimes taped together to conceal an open space. "I could use some new rugs," she observes.

To make up for the building's lack of windows and the crowded 17 feeling that results, the staff puts plants and fish tanks in the corridors. Some of the plants are flourishing. Two boys, released from class, are in a corridor beside a tank, their noses pressed against the glass. A school of pinkish fish inside the tank are darting back and forth. Farther down the corridor a small Hispanic girl is watering the plants.

Two first grade classes share a single room without a window, 18 divided only by a blackboard. Four kindergartens and a sixth grade class of Spanish-speaking children have been packed into a single room in which, again, there is no window. A second grade bilingual class of 37 children has its own room but again there is no window.

By eleven o'clock, the lunchroom is already packed with appetite 19 and life. The kids line up to get their meals, then eat them in ten minutes. After that, with no place they can go to play, they sit and wait until it's time to line up and go back to class.

On the second floor I visit four classes taking place within another 20 undivided space. The room has a low ceiling. File cabinets and movable blackboards give a small degree of isolation to each class. Again, there are no windows.

The library is a tiny, windowless and claustrophobic room. I count 21 approximately 700 books. Seeing no reference books, I ask a teacher if encyclopedias and other reference books are kept in classrooms.

"We don't have encyclopedias in classrooms," she replies. "That is 22 for the suburbs."

The school, I am told, has 26 computers for its 1,300 children. There 23 is one small gym and children get one period, and sometimes two, each week. Recess, however, is not possible because there is no playground.

"Head Start,"[2] the principal says, "scarcely exists in District 10. We have no space."

The school, I am told, is 90 percent black and Hispanic; the other 10 percent are Asian, white or Middle Eastern.   24

In a sixth grade social studies class the walls are bare of words or decorations. There seems to be no ventilation system, or, if one exists, it isn't working.   25

The class discusses the Nile River and the Fertile Crescent.   26

The teacher, in a droning voice: "How is it useful that these civilizations developed close to rivers?"   27

A child, in a good loud voice: "What kind of question is that?"   28

In my notes I find these words: "An uncomfortable feeling—being in a building with no windows. There are metal ducts across the room. Do they give air? I feel asphyxiated. . . ."   29

On the top floor of the school, a sixth grade of 30 children shares a room with 29 bilingual second graders. Because of the high class size there is an assistant with each teacher. This means that 59 children and four grown-ups—63 in all—must share a room that, in a suburban school, would hold no more than 20 children and one teacher. There are, at least, some outside windows in this room—it is the only room with windows in the school—and the room has a high ceiling. It is a relief to see some daylight.   30

I return to see the kindergarten classes on the ground floor and feel stifled once again by lack of air and the low ceiling. Nearly 120 children and adults are doing what they can to make the best of things: 80 children in four kindergarten classes, 30 children in the sixth grade class, and about eight grown-ups who are aides and teachers. The kindergarten children sitting on the worn rug, which is patched with tape, look up at me and turn their heads to follow me as I walk past them.   31

As I leave the school, a sixth grade teacher stops to talk. I ask her, "Is there air conditioning in warmer weather?"   32

Teachers, while inside the building, are reluctant to give answers to this kind of question. Outside, on the sidewalk, she is less constrained: "I had an awful room last year. In the winter it was 56 degrees. In the summer it was up to 90. It was sweltering."   33

I ask her, "Do the children ever comment on the building?"   34

"They don't say," she answers, "but they know."   35

I ask her if they see it as a racial message.   36

"All these children see TV," she says. "They know what suburban schools are like. Then they look around them at their school. This was a   37

---

[2] Government program for disadvantaged preschoolers. [Eds.]

roller-rink, you know. . . . They don't comment on it but you see it in their eyes. They understand."

On the following morning I visit P.S. 79, another elementary school 38 in the same district. "We work under difficult circumstances," says the principal, James Carter, who is black. "The school was built to hold one thousand students. We have 1,550. We are badly overcrowded. We need smaller classes but, to do this, we would need more space. I can't add five teachers. I would have no place to put them."

Some experts, I observe, believe that class size isn't a real issue. He 39 dismisses this abruptly. "It doesn't take a genius to discover that you learn more in a smaller class. I have to bus some 60 kindergarten children elsewhere, since I have no space for them. When they return next year, where do I put them?

"I can't set up a computer lab. I have no room. I had to put a class 40 into the library. I have no librarian. There are two gymnasiums upstairs but they cannot be used for sports. We hold more classes there. It's unfair to measure us against the suburbs. They have 17 to 20 children in a class. Average class size in this school is 30.

"The school is 29 percent black, 70 percent Hispanic. Few of these 41 kids get Head Start. There is no space in the district. Of 200 kindergarten children, 50 maybe get some kind of preschool."

I ask him how much difference preschool makes. 42

"Those who get it do appreciably better. I can't overestimate its 43 impact but, as I have said, we have no space."

The school tracks children by ability, he says. "There are five to 44 seven levels in each grade. The highest level is equivalent to 'gifted' but it's not a full-scale gifted program. We don't have the funds. We have no science room. The science teachers carry their equipment with them."

We sit and talk within the nurse's room. The window is broken. 45 There are two holes in the ceiling. About a quarter of the ceiling has been patched and covered with a plastic garbage bag.

"Ideal class size for these kids would be 15 to 20. Will these children 46 ever get what white kids in the suburbs take for granted? I don't think so. If you ask me why, I'd have to speak of race and social class. I don't think the powers that be in New York City understand, or want to understand, that if they do not give these children a sufficient education to lead healthy and productive lives, we will be their victims later on. We'll pay the price someday—in violence, in economic costs. I despair of making this appeal in any terms but these. You cannot issue an appeal to conscience in New York today. The fair-play argument won't be accepted. So you speak of violence and hope that it will scare the city into action."

While we talk, three children who look six or seven years old come 47
to the door and ask to see the nurse, who isn't in the school today. One
of the children, a Puerto Rican girl, looks haggard. "I have a pain in my
tooth," she says. The principal says, "The nurse is out. Why don't you
call your mother?" The child says, "My mother doesn't have a phone."
The principal sighs. "Then go back to your class." When she leaves, the
principal is angry. "It's amazing to me that these children ever make it
with the obstacles they face. Many *do* care and they *do* try, but there's a
feeling of despair. The parents of these children want the same things
for their children that the parents in the suburbs want. Drugs are not the
cause of this. They are the symptom. Nonetheless, they're used by people in the suburbs and rich people in Manhattan as another reason to
keep children of poor people at a distance."

I ask him, "Will white children and black children ever go to school 48
together in New York?"

"I don't see it," he replies. "I just don't think it's going to happen. 49
It's a dream. I simply do not see white folks in Riverdale agreeing to
crossbus with kids like these. A few, maybe. Very few. I don't think I'll
live to see it happen."

I ask him whether race is the decisive factor. Many experts, I 50
observe, believe that wealth is more important in determining these
inequalities.

"This," he says—and sweeps his hand around him at the room, the 51
garbage bag, the ceiling—"would not happen to white children."

In a kindergarten class the children sit cross-legged on a carpet in a 52
space between two walls of books. Their 26 faces are turned up to watch
their teacher, an elderly black woman. A little boy who sits beside me is
involved in trying to tie bows in his shoelaces. The children sing a song:
"Lift Every Voice." On the wall are these handwritten words:
"Beautiful, also, are the souls of my people."

In a very small room on the fourth floor, 52 people in two classes do 53
their best to teach and learn. Both are first grade classes. One, I am
informed, is "low ability." The other is bilingual.

"The room is barely large enough for one class," says the principal. 54

The room is 25 by 50 feet. There are 26 first graders and two adults 55
on the left, 22 others and two adults on the right. On the wall there is
the picture of a small white child, circled by a Valentine, and a
Gainsborough painting of a child in a formal dress.

"We are handicapped by scarcity," one of the teachers says. "One 56
fifth of these children may be at grade level by the year's end."

A boy who may be seven years old climbs on my lap without an 57
invitation and removes my glasses. He studies my face and runs his fingers through my hair. "You have nice hair," he says. I ask him where he
lives and he replies, "Times Square Hotel," which is a homeless shelter
in Manhattan.

I ask him how he gets here. 58

"With my father. On the train," he says. 59

"How long does it take?" 60

"It takes an hour and a half." 61

I ask him when he leaves his home. 62

"My mother wakes me up at five o'clock." 63

"When do you leave?" 64

"Six-thirty." 65

I ask him how he gets back to Times Square. 66

"My father comes to get me after school." 67

From my notes: "He rides the train three hours every day in order 68 to attend this segregated school. It would be a shorter ride to Riverdale. There are rapid shuttle-vans that make that trip in only 20 minutes. Why not let him go to school right in Manhattan, for that matter?"

At three o'clock the nurse arrives to do her recordkeeping. She tells 69 me she is here three days a week. "The public hospital we use for an emergency is called North Central. It's not a hospital that I will use if I am given any choice. Clinics in the private hospitals are far more likely to be staffed by an experienced physician."

She hesitates a bit as I take out my pen, but then goes on: "I'll give 70 you an example. A little girl I saw last week in school was trembling and shaking and could not control the motions of her arms. I was concerned and called her home. Her mother came right up to school and took her to North Central. The intern concluded that the child was upset by 'family matters'—nothing more—that there was nothing wrong with her. The mother was offended by the diagnosis. She did not appreciate his words or his assumptions. The truth is, there was nothing wrong at home. She brought the child back to school. I thought that she was ill. I told her mother, 'Go to Montefiore.' It's a private hospital, and well respected. She took my advice, thank God. It turned out that the child had a neurological disorder. She is now in treatment.

"This is the kind of thing our children face. Am I saying that the city 71 underserves this population? You can draw your own conclusions."

Out on the street, it takes a full half hour to flag down a cab. Taxi 72 drivers in New York are sometimes disconcertingly direct in what they say. When they are contemptuous of poor black people, their contempt is unadorned. When they're sympathetic and compassionate, their observations often go right to the heart of things. "Oh . . . they neglect these children," says the driver. "They leave them in the streets and slums to live and die." We stop at a light. Outside the window of the taxi, aimless men are standing in a semicircle while another man is working on his car. Old four-story buildings with their windows boarded, cracked or missing are on every side.

I ask the driver where he's from. He says Afghanistan. Turning in 73 his seat, he gestures at the street and shrugs. "If you don't, as an

American, begin to give these kids the kind of education that you give the kids of Donald Trump, you're asking for disaster."

Two months later, on a day in May, I visit an elementary school in 74 Riverdale. The dogwoods and magnolias on the lawn in front of P.S. 24 are in full blossom on the day I visit. There is a well-tended park across the street, another larger park three blocks away. To the left of the school is a playground for small children, with an innovative jungle gym, a slide and several climbing toys. Behind the school there are two playing fields for older kids. The grass around the school is neatly trimmed.

The neighborhood around the school, by no means the richest part 75 of Riverdale, is nonetheless expensive and quite beautiful. Residences in the area—some of which are large, free-standing houses, others condominiums in solid red-brick buildings—sell for prices in the region of $400,000; but some of the larger Tudor houses on the winding and tree-shaded streets close to the school can cost up to $1 million. The excellence of P.S. 24, according to the principal, adds to the value of these homes. Advertisements in the *New York Times* will frequently inform prospective buyers that a house is "in the neighborhood of P.S. 24."

The school serves 825 children in the kindergarten through sixth 76 grade. This is approximately half the student population crowded into P.S. 79, where 1,550 children fill a space intended for 1,000, and a great deal smaller than the 1,300 children packed into the former skating rink; but the principal of P.S. 24, a capable and energetic man named David Rothstein, still regards it as excessive for an elementary school.

The school is integrated in the strict sense that the middle- and 77 upper-middle-class white children here do occupy a building that contains some Asian and Hispanic and black children; but there is little integration in the classrooms since the vast majority of the Hispanic and black children are assigned to "special" classes on the basis of evaluations that have classified them "EMR"—"educable mentally retarded"— or else, in the worst of cases, "TMR"—"trainable mentally retarded."

I ask the principal if any of his students qualify for free-lunch pro- 78 grams. "About 130 do," he says. "Perhaps another 35 receive their lunches at reduced price. Most of these kids are in the special classes. They do not come from this neighborhood."

The very few nonwhite children that one sees in mainstream classes 79 tend to be Japanese or else of other Asian origins. Riverdale, I learn, has been the residence of choice for many years to members of the diplomatic corps.

The school therefore contains effectively two separate schools: one 80 of about 130 children, most of whom are poor, Hispanic, black, assigned to one of the 12 special classes; the other of some 700 mainstream students, almost all of whom are white or Asian.

There is a third track also—this one for the students who are labeled 81
"talented" or "gifted." This is termed a "pull-out" program since the
children who are so identified remain in mainstream classrooms but are
taken out for certain periods each week to be provided with intensive
and, in my opinion, excellent instruction in some areas of reasoning and
logic often known as "higher-order skills" in the contemporary jargon
of the public schools. Children identified as "gifted" are admitted to this
program in first grade and, in most cases, will remain there for six years.
Even here, however, there are two tracks of the gifted. The regular gifted
classes are provided with only one semester of this specialized instruction yearly. Those very few children, on the other hand, who are identified as showing the most promise are assigned, beginning in the third
grade, to a program that receives a full-year regimen.

In one such class, containing ten intensely verbal and impressive 82
fourth grade children, nine are white and one is Asian. The "special"
class I enter first, by way of contrast, has twelve children of whom only
one is white and none is Asian. These racial breakdowns prove to be
predictive of the schoolwide pattern.

In a classroom for the gifted on the first floor of the school, I ask a 83
child what the class is doing. "Logic and syllogisms," she replies. The
room is fitted with a planetarium. The principal says that all the elementary schools in District 10 were given the same planetariums ten
years ago but that certain schools, because of overcrowding, have been
forced to give them up. At P.S. 261, according to my notes, there was a
domelike space that had been built to hold a planetarium, but the planetarium had been removed to free up space for the small library collection. P.S. 24, in contrast, has a spacious library that holds almost 8,000
books. The windows are decorated with attractive, brightly colored curtains and look out on flowering trees. The principal says that it's inadequate, but it appears spectacular to me after the cubicle that holds a
meager 700 books within the former skating rink.

The district can't afford librarians, the principal says, but P.S. 24, 84
unlike the poorer schools of District 10, can draw on educated parent
volunteers who staff the room in shifts three days a week. A parent
organization also raises independent funds to buy materials, including
books, and will soon be running a fund-raiser to enhance the library's
collection.

In a large and sunny first grade classroom that I enter next, I see 23 85
children, all of whom are white or Asian. In another first grade, there are
22 white children and two others who are Japanese. There is a computer
in each class. Every classroom also has a modern fitted sink.

In a second grade class of 22 children, there are two black children 86
and three Asian children. Again, there is a sink and a computer. A sixth
grade social studies class has only one black child. The children have an

in-class research area that holds some up-to-date resources. A set of encyclopedias (World Book, 1985) is in a rack beside a window. The children are doing a Spanish language lesson when I enter. Foreign languages begin in sixth grade at the school, but Spanish is offered also to the kindergarten children. As in every room at P.S. 24, the window shades are clean and new, the floor is neatly tiled in gray and green, and there is not a single light bulb missing.

Walking next into a special class, I see twelve children. One is white. 87 Eleven are black. There are no Asian children. The room is half the size of mainstream classrooms. "Because of overcrowding," says the principal, "we have had to split these rooms in half." There is no computer and no sink.

I enter another special class. Of seven children, five are black, one is 88 Hispanic, one is white. A little black boy with a large head sits in the far corner and is gazing at the ceiling.

"Placement of these kids," the principal explains, "can usually be 89 traced to neurological damage."

In my notes: "How could so many of these children be brain- 90 damaged?"

Next door to the special class is a woodworking shop. "This shop is 91 only for the special classes," says the principal. The children learn to punch in time cards at the door, he says, in order to prepare them for employment.

The fourth grade gifted class, in which I spend the last part of the 92 day, is humming with excitement. "I start with these children in the first grade," says the teacher. "We pull them out of mainstream classes on the basis of their test results and other factors such as the opinion of their teachers. Out of this group, beginning in third grade, I pull out the ones who show the most potential, and they enter classes such as this one."

The curriculum they follow, she explains, "emphasizes critical 93 thinking, reasoning and logic." The planetarium, for instance, is employed not simply for the study of the universe as it exists. "Children also are designing their own galaxies," the teacher says.

A little girl sitting around a table with her classmates speaks with 94 perfect poise: "My name is Susan. We are in the fourth grade gifted program."

I ask them what they're doing and a child says, "My name is Laurie 95 and we're doing problem-solving."

A rather tall, good-natured boy who is half-standing at the table 96 tells me that his name is David. "One thing that we do," he says, "is logical thinking. Some problems, we find, have more than one good answer. We need to learn not simply to be logical in our own thinking but to show respect for someone else's logic even when an answer may be technically incorrect."

When I ask him to explain this, he goes on, "A person who gives an 97
answer that is not 'correct' may nonetheless have done some interesting
thinking that we should examine. 'Wrong' answers may be more useful
to examine than correct ones."

I ask the children if reasoning and logic are innate or if they're 98
things that you can learn.

"You know some things to start with when you enter school," Susan 99
says. "But we also learn some things that other children don't."

I ask her to explain this. 100

"We know certain things that other kids don't know because we're 101
taught them."

She has braces on her teeth. Her long brown hair falls almost to her 102
waist. Her loose white T- shirt has the word TRI-LOGIC on the front. She
tells me that Tri-Logic is her father's firm.

Laurie elaborates on the same point: "Some things you know. Some 103
kinds of logic are inside of you to start with. There are other things that
someone needs to teach you."

David expands on what the other two have said: "Everyone can 104
think and speak in logical ways unless they have a mental problem.
What this program does is bring us to a higher form of logic."

The class is writing a new "Bill of Rights." The children already 105
know the U.S. Bill of Rights and they explain its first four items to me
with precision. What they are examining today, they tell me, is the very
concept of a "right." Then they will create their own compendium of
rights according to their own analysis and definition. Along one wall of
the classroom, opposite the planetarium, are seven Apple II computers
on which children have developed rather subtle color animations that
express the themes—of greed and domination, for example—that they
also have described in writing.

"This is an upwardly mobile group," the teacher later says. "They 106
have exposure to whatever New York City has available. Their parents
may take them to the theater, to museums. . . ."

In my notes: "Six girls, four boys. Nine white, one Chinese. I am 107
glad they have this class. But what about the others? Aren't there ten
black children in the school who could enjoy this also?"

The teacher gives me a newspaper written, edited and computer- 108
printed by her sixth grade gifted class. The children, she tells me, are
provided with a link to kids in Europe for transmission of news stories.

A science story by one student asks if scientists have ever falsified 109
their research. "Gregor Mendel," the sixth grader writes, "the Austrian
monk who founded the science of genetics, published papers on his work
with peas that some experts say were statistically too good to be true.
Isaac Newton, who formulated the law of gravitation, relied on unseemly
mathematical sleight of hand in his calculations. . . . Galileo Galilei,

founder of modern scientific method, wrote about experiments that were so difficult to duplicate that colleagues doubted he had done them."

Another item in the paper, also by a sixth grade student, is less eso- 110 teric: "The Don Cossacks dance company, from Russia, is visiting the United States. The last time it toured America was 1976. . . . The Don Cossacks will be in New York City for two weeks at the Neil Simon Theater. Don't miss it!"

The tone is breezy—and so confident! That phrase—"Don't miss 111 it!"—speaks a volume about life in Riverdale.

"What makes a good school?" asks the principal when we are talk- 112 ing later on. "The building and teachers are part of it, of course. But it isn't just the building and the teacher. Our kids come from good families and the neighborhood is good. In a three-block area we have a public library, a park, a junior high. . . . Our typical sixth grader reads at eighth-grade level." In a quieter voice he says, "I see how hard my colleagues work in schools like P.S. 79. You have children in those neighborhoods who live in virtual hell. They enter school five years behind. What do they get?" Then, as he spreads his hands out on his desk, he says: "I have to ask myself why there should be an elementary school in District 10 with fifteen hundred children. Why should there be an elementary school within a skating rink? Why should the Board of Ed allow this? This is not the way that things should be."

Responding to Reading

1. Do you agree that today's educational system denies children "the means of competition" (2)? Did your education give you the ability to compete?
2. Kozol's essay focuses on schools in New York City. Should he have included examples from school districts in other parts of the country? What would be the advantages of such a strategy?
3. In paragraph 112, Kozol gives a principal's assessment of what makes a good school. Do you agree with this assessment? What, if anything, can be done to eliminate the inequities that he mentions?

COLLEGE PRESSURES

William Zinsser

William Zinsser (1922–   ) is a critic, writer, editor, and teacher who advocates clear and simple prose. He was a columnist for Look, Life, *and the* New York Times; *he taught at Yale University from 1970 to 1979; and he was the general editor of the Book-of-the-Month Club. His current work includes articles on travel and the environment in the United States. Zinsser has written nine books, including* Pop Goes America *(1963),* The Lunacy Boom *(1970), and* Writing with a Word Processor *(1983). One of his most popular books, which explains good writing to beginners, is* On Writing Well *(5th edition, 1996). Zinsser first published the following article in* Blair and Ketchum's Country Journal *(1979). In it, he defines four kinds of pressure that college students face and argues that most college students are rigidly goal-oriented young people too fearful "to imagine allowing the hand of God or chance to nudge them down some unforeseen trail."*

Dear Carlos: I desperately need a dean's excuse for my chem midterm which will begin in about 1 hour. All I can say is that I totally blew it this week. I've fallen incredibly, inconceivably behind.

Carlos: Help! I'm anxious to hear from you. I'll be in my room and won't leave it until I hear from you. Tomorrow is the last day for . . .

Carlos: I left town because I started bugging out again. I stayed up all night to finish a take-home make-up exam & am typing it to hand in on the 10th. It was due on the 5th. P.S. I'm going to the dentist. Pain is pretty bad.

Carlos: Probably by Friday I'll be able to get back to my studies. Right now I'm going to take a long walk. This whole thing has taken a lot out of me.

Carlos: I'm really up the proverbial creek. The problem is I really *bombed* the history final. Since I need that course for my major I . . .

Carlos: Here follows a tale of woe. I went home this weekend, had to help my Mom, & caught a fever so didn't have much time to study. My professor . . .

Carlos: Aargh! Trouble. Nothing original but everything's piling up at once. To be brief, my job interview . . .

Hey Carlos, good news! I've got mononucleosis.

Who are these wretched supplicants, scribbling notes so laden with anxiety, seeking such miracles of postponement and balm? They are men and women who belong to Branford College, one of the twelve residential colleges at Yale University, and the messages are just a few of the hundreds that they left for their dean, Carlos Hortas—often slipped under his door at 4 A.M.—last year. 1

But students like the ones who wrote those notes can also be found on campuses from coast to coast—especially in New England and at 2 many other private colleges across the country that have high academic standards and highly motivated students. Nobody could doubt that the notes are real. In their urgency and their gallows humor they are authentic voices of a generation that is panicky to succeed.

My own connection with the message writers is that I am master of Branford College. I live in its Gothic quadrangle and know the students well. (We have 485 of them.) I am privy to their hopes and fears—and also to their stereo music and their piercing cries in the dead of night ("Does anybody *ca-a-are?*"). If they went to Carlos to ask how to get through tomorrow, they come to me to ask how to get through the rest of their lives.

Mainly I try to remind them that the road ahead is a long one and that it will have more unexpected turns than they think. There will be plenty of time to change jobs, change careers, change whole attitudes and approaches. They don't want to hear such liberating news. They want a map—right now—that they can follow unswervingly to career security, financial security, Social Security and, presumably, a prepaid grave.

What I wish for all students is some release from the clammy grip of the future. I wish them a chance to savor each segment of their education as an experience in itself and not as a grim preparation for the next step. I wish them the right to experiment, to trip and fall, to learn that defeat is as instructive as victory and is not the end of the world.

My wish, of course, is naïve. One of the few rights that America does not proclaim is the right to fail. Achievement is the national god, venerated in our media—the million-dollar athlete, the wealthy executive—and glorified in our praise of possessions. In the presence of such a potent state religion, the young are growing up old.

I see four kinds of pressure working on college students today: economic pressure, parental pressure, peer pressure, and self-induced pressure. It is easy to look around for villains—to blame the colleges for charging too much money, the professors for assigning too much work, the parents for pushing their children too far, the students for driving themselves too hard. But there are no villains; only victims.

"In the late 1960s," one dean told me, "the typical question that I got from students was 'Why is there so much suffering in the world?' or 'How can I make a contribution?' Today it's 'Do you think it would look better for getting into law school if I did a double major in history and political science, or just majored in one of them?'" Many other deans confirmed this pattern. One said: "They're trying to find an edge—the intangible something that will look better on paper if two students are about equal."

Note the emphasis on looking better. The transcript has become a sacred document, the passport to security. How one appears on paper is more important than how one appears in person. *A* is for Admirable and *B* is for Borderline, even though, in Yale's official system of grading, *A* means "excellent" and *B* means "very good." Today, looking very good is no longer good enough, especially for students who hope to go on to law school or medical school. They know that entrance into the better schools will be an entrance into the better law firms and better medical practices where they will make a lot of money. They also know that the odds are harsh. Yale Law School, for instance, matriculates 170 students from an applicant pool of 3,700; Harvard enrolls 550 from a pool of 7,000.

It's all very well for those of us who write letters of recommenda- 10 tion for our students to stress the qualities of humanity that will make them good lawyers or doctors. And it's nice to think that admission officers are really reading our letters and looking for the extra dimension of commitment or concern. Still, it would be hard for a student not to visualize these officers shuffling so many transcripts studded with *A*s that they regard a *B* as positively shameful.

The pressure is almost as heavy on students who just want to grad- 11 uate and get a job. Long gone are the days of the "gentleman's *C*," when students journeyed through college with a certain relaxation, sampling a wide variety of courses—music, art, philosophy, classics, anthropology, poetry, religion—that would send them out as liberally educated men and women. If I were an employer I would rather employ graduates who have this range and curiosity than those who narrowly pursued safe subjects and high grades. I know countless students whose inquiring minds exhilarate me. I like to hear the play of their ideas. I don't know if they are getting *A*s or *C*s, and I don't care. I also like them as people. The country needs them, and they will find satisfying jobs. I tell them to relax. They can't.

Nor can I blame them. They live in a brutal economy. Tuition, room, 12 and board at most private colleges now comes to at least $7,000, not counting books and fees. This might seem to suggest that the colleges are getting rich. But they are equally battered by inflation. Tuition covers only 60 percent of what it costs to educate a student, and ordinarily the remainder comes from what colleges receive in endowments, grants, and gifts. Now the remainder keeps being swallowed by the cruel costs—higher every year—of just opening the doors. Heating oil is up. Insurance is up. Postage is up. Health-premium costs are up. Everything is up. Deficits are up. We are witnessing in America the creation of a brotherhood of paupers—colleges, parents, and students, joined by the common bond of debt.

Today it is not unusual for a student, even if he works part time at 13 college and full time during the summer, to accrue $5,000 in loans after four years—loans that he must start to repay within one year after graduation. Exhorted at commencement to go forth into the world, he is already behind as he goes forth. How could he not feel under pressure throughout college to prepare for this day of reckoning? I have used "he," incidentally, only for brevity. Women at Yale are under no less pressure to justify their expensive education to themselves, their parents, and society. In fact, they are probably under more pressure. For although they leave college superbly equipped to bring fresh leadership to traditionally male jobs, society hasn't yet caught up with this fact.

Along with economic pressure goes parental pressure. Inevitably, 14 the two are deeply intertwined.

I see many students taking pre-medical courses with joyless tenacity. 15 They go off to their labs as if they were going to the dentist. It saddens me because I know them in other corners of their life as cheerful people.

"Do you want to go to medical school?" I ask them.   16

"I guess so," they say, without conviction, or "Not really."   17

"Then why are you going?"   18

"Well, my parents want me to be a doctor. They're paying all this 19 money and . . ."

Poor students, poor parents. They are caught in one of the oldest 20 webs of love and duty and guilt. The parents mean well; they are trying to steer their sons and daughters toward a secure future. But the sons and daughters want to major in history or classics or philosophy—subjects with no "practical" value. Where's the payoff on the humanities? It's not easy to persuade such loving parents that the humanities do indeed pay off. The intellectual faculties developed by studying subjects like history and classics—an ability to synthesize and relate, to weigh cause and effect, to see events in perspective—are just the faculties that make creative leaders in business or almost any general field. Still, many fathers would rather put their money on courses that point toward a specific profession—courses that are pre-law, pre-medical, pre-business, or, as I sometimes heard it put, "pre-rich."

But the pressure on students is severe. They are truly torn. One part 21 of them feels obligated to fulfill their parents' expectations; after all, their parents are older and presumably wiser. Another part tells them that the expectations that are right for their parents are not right for them.

I know a student who wants to be an artist. She is very obviously an 22 artist and will be a good one—she has already had several modest local exhibits. Meanwhile she is growing as a well-rounded person and taking humanistic subjects that will enrich the inner resources out of which her art will grow. But her father is strongly opposed. He thinks that an artist is a "dumb" thing to be. The student vacillates and tries to please everybody. She keeps up with her art somewhat furtively and takes some of the "dumb" courses her father wants her to take—at least they are dumb courses for her. She is a free spirit on a campus of tense students—no small achievement in itself—and she deserves to follow her muse.

Peer pressure and self-induced pressure are also intertwined, and 23 they begin almost at the beginning of freshman year.

"I had a freshman student I'll call Linda," one dean told me, "who 24 came in and said she was under terrible pressure because her roommate,

Barbara, was much brighter and studied all the time. I couldn't tell her that Barbara had come in two hours earlier to say the same thing about Linda."

The story is almost funny—except that it's not. It's symptomatic of 25 all the pressures put together. When every student thinks every other student is working harder and doing better, the only solution is to study harder still. I see students going off to the library every night after dinner and coming back when it closes at midnight. I wish they would sometimes forget about their peers and go to a movie. I hear the clacking of typewriters in the hours before dawn. I see the tension in their eyes when exams are approaching and papers are due: *"Will I get everything done?"*

Probably they won't. They will get sick. They will get "blocked." 26 They will sleep. They will oversleep. They will bug out. *Hey Carlos, help!*

Part of the problem is that they do more than they are expected to 27 do. A professor will assign five-page papers. Several students will start writing ten-page papers to impress him. Then more students will write ten-page papers, and a few will raise the ante to fifteen. Pity the poor student who is still just doing the assignment.

"Once you have 20 or 30 percent of the student population deliber- 28 ately overexerting," one dean points out, "it's bad for everybody. When a teacher gets more and more effort from his class, the student who is doing normal work can be perceived as not doing well. The tactic works, psychologically."

Why can't the professor just cut back and not accept longer papers? 29 He can, and he probably will. But by then the term will be half over and the damage done. Grade fever is highly contagious and not easily reversed. Besides, the professor's main concern is with his course. He knows his students only in relation to the course and doesn't know that they are also overexerting in their other courses. Nor is it really his business. He didn't sign up for dealing with the student as a whole person and with all the emotional baggage the student brought along from home. That's what deans, masters, chaplains, and psychiatrists are for.

To some extent this is nothing new: a certain number of professors 30 have always been self-contained islands of scholarship and shyness, more comfortable with books than with people. But the new pauperism has widened the gap still further, for professors who actually like to spend time with students don't have as much time to spend. They also are overexerting. If they are young, they are busy trying to publish in order not to perish, hanging by their finger nails onto a shrinking profession. If they are old and tenured, they are buried under the duties of administering departments—as departmental chairmen or members of committees—that have been thinned out by the budgetary axe.

Ultimately it will be the students' own business to break the circles 31 in which they are trapped. They are too young to be prisoners of their parents' dreams and their classmates' fears. They must be jolted into believing in themselves as unique men and women who have the power to shape their own future.

"Violence is being done to the undergraduate experience," says 32 Carlos Hortas. "College should be open-ended: at the end it should open many, many roads. Instead, students are choosing their goal in advance, and their choices narrow as they go along. It's almost as if they think that the country has been codified in the type of jobs that exist— that they've got to fit into certain slots. Therefore, fit into the best-paying slot.

"They ought to take chances. Not taking chances will lead to a life 33 of colorless mediocrity. They'll be comfortable. But something in the spirit will be missing."

I have painted too drab a portrait of today's students, making them 34 seem a solemn lot. That is only half of their story; if they were so dreary I wouldn't so thoroughly enjoy their company. The other half is that they are easy to like. They are quick to laugh and to offer friendship. They are not introverts. They are unusually kind and are more considerate of one another than any student generation I have known.

Nor are they so obsessed with their studies that they avoid sports 35 and extracurricular activities. On the contrary, they juggle their crowded hours to play on a variety of teams, perform with musical and dramatic groups, and write for campus publications. But this in turn is one more cause of anxiety. There are too many choices. Academically, they have 1,300 courses to select from; outside class they have to decide how much spare time they can spare and how to spend it.

This means that they engage in fewer extracurricular pursuits than 36 their predecessors did. If they want to row on the crew and play in the symphony they will eliminate one; in the '60s they would have done both. They also tend to choose activities that are self-limiting. Drama, for instance, is flourishing in all twelve of Yale's residential colleges as it never has before. Students hurl themselves into these productions— as actors, directors, carpenters, and technicians—with a dedication to create the best possible play, knowing that the day will come when the run will end and they can get back to their studies.

They also can't afford to be the willing slave of organizations like 37 the *Yale Daily News*. Last spring at the one-hundredth anniversary banquet of that paper—whose past chairmen include such once and future kings as Potter Stewart,[1] Kingman Brewster,[2] and William F. Buckley, Jr.[3]—much was made of the fact that the editorial staff used to be small

---

[1] Potter Stewart is an associate justice of the United States Supreme Court. [Eds.]

[2] Kingman Brewster is a former president of Yale. [Eds.]

[3] William F. Buckley, Jr., is a columnist and founder of the conservative journal *The National Review*. [Eds.]

and totally committed and that "Newsies" routinely worked fifty hours a week. In effect they belonged to a club; Newsies is how they defined themselves at Yale. Today's student will write one or two articles a week, when he can, and he defines himself as a student. I've never heard the word Newsie except at the banquet.

If I have described the modern undergraduate primarily as a driven   38 creature who is largely ignoring the blithe spirit inside who keeps trying to come out and play, it's because that's where the crunch is, not only at Yale but throughout American education. It's why I think we should all be worried about the values that are nurturing a generation so fearful of risk and so goal-obsessed at such an early age.

I tell students that there is no one "right" way to get ahead—that   39 each of them is a different person, starting from a different point and bound for a different destination. I tell them that change is a tonic and that all the slots are not codified nor the frontiers closed. One of my ways of telling them is to invite men and women who have achieved success outside the academic world to come and talk informally with my students during the year. They are heads of companies or ad agencies, editors of magazines, politicians, public officials, television magnates, labor leaders, business executives, Broadway producers, artists, writers, economists, photographers, scientists, historians—a mixed bag of achievers.

I ask them to say a few words about how they got started. The stu-   40 dents assume that they started in their present profession and knew all along that it was what they wanted to do. Luckily for me, most of them got into their field by a circuitous route, to their surprise, after many detours. The students are startled. They can hardly conceive of a career that was not pre-planned. They can hardly imagine allowing the hand of God or chance to nudge them down some unforeseen trail.

Responding to Reading

1. Zinsser wrote his essay in 1979. How accurately does it portray today's college students? Do you feel the same pressures Zinsser describes?
2. Zinsser uses students who attend Yale University as his examples. How representative are these examples? Do you think students from other types of colleges face the same pressures? What pressures, for example, might a student in a community college or a large urban university face that the students in Zinsser's sample might not encounter?
3. What purpose does Zinsser think college should serve? What purpose do *you* think college should serve?

IN DEFENSE OF ELITISM

William A. Henry III

William A. Henry III (1950–1994), a reporter and critic who served for many years as the culture and theater critic for Time *magazine, also wrote stories for* Time *about American society. He was the recipient of two Pulitzer Prizes in journalism, one in 1980 for criticism and a shared prize in 1975 for reporting on desegregation in the Boston public schools. Author of* The Great One: The Life and Legend of Jackie Gleason *(1992), he also produced a PBS documentary, "Bob Fosse: Steam Heat," which received an Emmy in 1990. In his posthumously published* In Defense of Elitism *(1994), Henry argues that the United States is in decline at least in part because of Americans' increasing lack of respect for true intellectual and cultural accomplishment and, more important, because of a growing unwillingness "to assert unyieldingly that one idea, contribution, or attainment is better than another." In the following chapter from that book, Henry focuses specifically on higher education, arguing that the egalitarian attempt to make a college education available to large numbers of Americans is a costly mistake and has resulted in a serious decline in overall educational standards.*

While all the major social changes in post-war America reflect egalitarianism of some sort, no social evolution has been more willfully egalitarian than opening the academy. Half a century ago, a high school diploma was a significant credential, and college was a privilege for the few. Now high school graduation is virtually automatic for adolescents outside the ghettos and barrios, and college has become a normal way station in the average person's growing up. No longer a mark of distinction or proof of achievement, a college education is these days a mere rite of passage, a capstone to adolescent party time.

Some 63% of all American high school graduates now go on to some form of further education, according to the Department of Commerce's *Statistical Abstract of the United States,* and the bulk of those continuing students attain at least an associate's degree. Nearly 30% of high school graduates ultimately receive a four-year baccalaureate degree. A quarter or so of the population may seem, to egalitarian eyes, a small and hence elitist slice. But by world standards this is inclusiveness at its most extreme—and its most peculiarly American.

For all the socialism of British or French public policy and for all the paternalism of the Japanese, those nations restrict university training to a much smaller percentage of their young, typically 10% to 15%. Moreover, they and other First World nations tend to carry the elitism over into judgments about precisely which institution one attends. They rank their universities, colleges and technical schools along a prestige hierarchy much more rigidly gradated—and judged by standards much more widely accepted—than we Americans ever impose on our jumble of public and private institutions.

In the sharpest divergence from American values, these other coun- 4 tries tend to separate the college-bound from the quotidian masses,[1] in early adolescence, with scant hope for a second chance. For them, higher education is logically confined to those who displayed the most aptitude for lower education.

The opening of the academy's doors has imposed great economic 5 costs on the American people while delivering dubious benefits to many of the individuals supposedly being helped. The total bill for higher education is about $150 billion per year, with almost two-thirds of that spent by public institutions run with taxpayer funds. Private colleges and universities also spend the public's money. They get grants for research and the like, and they serve as a conduit for subsidized student loans—many of which are never fully repaid. President Clinton refers to this sort of spending as an investment in human capital. If that is so, it seems reasonable to ask whether the investment pays a worthwhile rate of return. At its present size, the American style of mass higher education probably ought to be judged a mistake—and one based on a giant lie.

Why do people go to college? Mostly to make money. This reality is 6 acknowledged in the mass media, which are forever running stories and charts showing how much a college degree contributes to lifetime income (with the more sophisticated publications very occasionally not-ing the counterweight costs of tuition paid and income forgone during the years of full-time study.)

But the equation between college and wealth is not so simple. 7 College graduates unquestionably do better on average economically than those who don't go at all. At the extremes, those with five or more years of college earn about triple the income of those with eight or fewer years of total schooling. Taking more typical examples, one finds that those who stop their educations after earning a four-year degree earn about 1 1/2 times as much as those who stop at the end of high school. These outcomes, however, reflect other things besides the impact of the degree itself. College graduates are winners in part because colleges attract people who are already winners—people with enough brains and drive that they would do well in almost any generation and under almost any circumstances, with or without formal credentialing.

The harder and more meaningful question is whether the mediocri- 8 ties who have also flooded into colleges in the past couple of genera-tions do better than they otherwise would have. And if they do, is it

---

[1] "Ordinary people." [Eds.]

because college actually made them better employees or because it simply gave them the requisite credential to get interviewed and hired? The U.S. Labor Department's Bureau of Labor Statistics reports that about 20% of all college graduates toil in fields not requiring a degree, and this total is projected to exceed 30% by the year 2005. For the individual, college may well be a credential without being a qualification, required without being requisite.

For American society, the big lie underlying higher education is 9 akin to Garrison Keillor's description of the children in Lake Wobegon:[2] they are all above average. In the unexamined American Dream rhetoric promoting mass higher education in the nation of my youth, the implicit vision was that one day everyone, or at least practically everyone, would be a manager or a professional. We would use the most élitist of all means, scholarship, toward the most egalitarian of ends. We would all become chiefs; hardly anyone would be left a mere Indian. On the surface, this New Jerusalem appears to have arrived. Where half a century ago the bulk of jobs were blue collar, now a majority are white or pink collar. They are performed in an office instead of on a factory floor. If they still tend to involve repetition and drudgery, at least they do not require heavy lifting.

But the wages for them are going down virtually as often as up. 10 And as a great many disappointed office workers have discovered, being better educated and better dressed at the workplace does not transform one's place in the pecking order. There are still plenty more Indians than chiefs. Lately, indeed, the chiefs are becoming even fewer. The major focus of the "downsizing" of recent years has been eliminating layers of middle management—much of it drawn from the ranks of those lured to college a generation or two ago by the idea that a degree would transform them from the mediocre to magisterial.

Yet our colleges blithely go on "educating" many more prospective 11 managers and professionals than we are likely to need. In my own field, there are typically more students majoring in journalism at any given moment than there are journalists employed at all the daily newspapers in the U.S. A few years ago, there were more students enrolled in law school than there were partners in all law firms. As trends shift, there have been periodic oversupplies of M.B.A.-wielding financial analysts, of grade school and high school teachers, of computer programmers, even of engineers. Inevitably many students of limited talent spend huge amounts of time and money pursuing some brass-ring occupation, only to see their dreams denied. As a society we consider it cruel not to give them every chance at success. It may be more cruel to let them go on fooling themselves.

---

[2] Fictional community that is the setting of Keillor's popular public radio program. [Eds.]

Just when it should be clear that we are already probably doing too 12 much to entice people into college, Bill Clinton is suggesting we do even more. In February 1994, for example, the President asserted that America needs a greater fusion between academic and vocational training in high school—not because too many mediocre people misplaced on the college track are failing to acquire marketable vocational skills, but because too many people on the vocational track are being denied courses that will secure them admission to college. Surely what Americans need is not a fusion of the two tracks but a sharper division between them, coupled with a forceful program for diverting intellectual also-rans out of the academic track and into the vocational one. That is where most of them are heading in life anyway. Why should they wait until they are older and must enroll in high-priced proprietary vocational programs of often dubious efficacy—frequently throwing away not only their own funds but federal loans in the process—because they emerged from high school heading nowhere and knowing nothing that is useful in the marketplace?

If the massive numbers of college students reflected a national 13 boom in love of learning and a prevalent yen for self-improvement, America's investment in the classroom might make sense. There are introspective qualities that can enrich any society in ways beyond the material. But one need look no further than the curricular wars to understand that most students are not looking to broaden their spiritual or intellectual horizons. Consider three basic trends, all of them implicit rejections of intellectual adventure. First, students are demanding courses that reflect and affirm their own identities in the most literal way. Rather than read a Greek dramatist of 2,000 years ago and thrill to the discovery that some ideas and emotions are universal, many insist on reading writers of their own gender or ethnicity or sexual preference, ideally writers of the present or the recent past.

The second trend, implicit in the first, is that the curriculum has 14 shifted from being what professors desire to teach to being what students desire to learn. Nowadays colleges have to hustle for students by truckling trendily. If the students want media-studies programs so they can all fantasize about becoming TV news anchors, then media studies will abound. There are in any given year some 300,000 students enrolled in undergraduate communications courses.

Of even greater significance than the solipsism of students and the 15 pusillanimity of teachers is the third trend, the sheer decline in the amount and quality of work expected in class. In an egalitarian environment the influx of mediocrities relentlessly lowers the general standards at colleges to levels the weak ones can meet. When my mother went to Trinity College in Washington in the early 1940s, at a time when it was regarded more as a finishing school for nice Catholic girls than a temple of discipline, an English major there was expected to be versed in Latin,

Anglo-Saxon and medieval French. A course in Shakespeare meant reading the plays, all 37 of them. In today's indulgent climate, a professor friend at a fancy college told me as I was writing this chapter, taking a half semester of Shakespeare compels students to read exactly four plays. "Anything more than one a week," he explained, "is considered too heavy a load."

This probably should not be thought surprising in an era when most   16 colleges, even prestigious ones, run some sort of remedial program for freshmen to learn the reading and writing skills they ought to have developed in junior high school—not to mention an era when many students vociferously object to being marked down for spelling or grammar. Indeed, all the media attention paid to curriculum battles at Stanford, Dartmouth and the like[3] obscures the even bleaker reality of American higher education. As Russell Jacoby points out in his book *Dogmatic Wisdom*, most students are enrolled at vastly less demanding institutions, where any substantial reading list would be an improvement.

My modest proposal is this: Let us reduce, over perhaps a five-year   17 span, the number of high school graduates who go on to college from nearly 60% to a still generous 33%. This will mean closing a lot of institutions. Most of them, in my view, should be community colleges, current or former state teachers' colleges and the like. These schools serve the academically marginal and would be better replaced by vocational training in high school and on-the-job training at work. Two standards should apply in judging which schools to shut down. First, what is the general academic level attained by the student body? That might be assessed in a rough-and-ready way by requiring any institution wishing to survive to give a standardized test—say, the Graduate Record Examination—to all its seniors. Those schools whose students perform below the state norm would face cutbacks or closing. Second, what community is being served? A school that serves a high percentage of disadvantaged students (this ought to be measured by family finances rather than just race or ethnicity) can make a better case for receiving tax dollars than one that subsidizes the children of the prosperous, who have private alternatives. Even ardent egalitarians should recognize the injustice of taxing people who wash dishes or mop floors for a living to pay for the below-cost public higher education of the children of lawyers so that they can go on to become lawyers too.

Some readers may find it paradoxical that a book arguing for   18 greater literacy and intellectual discipline should lead to a call for less rather than more education. Even if college students do not learn all they should, the readers' counterargument would go, surely they learn

---

[3] Universities that sparked "political correctness" controversies by proposing greater cultural diversity in course reading lists. See the essay by Dinesh D'Souza (p. 129). [Eds.]

something, and that is better than learning nothing. Maybe it is. But at what price? One hundred fifty billion dollars is awfully high for deferring the day when the idle or ungifted take individual responsibility and face up to their fate. Ultimately it is the yearning to believe that anyone can be brought up to college level that has brought colleges down to everyone's level.

Responding to Reading

1. What does Henry mean by *elitism*? Do you think his use of this term suggests his snobbishness or his insight?
2. Do you agree with Henry when he says that "the curriculum has shifted from being what professors desire to teach to being what students desire to learn" (14)? Do any of the courses at your school reflect the trend Henry describes?
3. A review of Henry's book in the *New York Times* states that his main point is that in the United States equality of opportunity has come to mean equality of outcome. What do you think this statement means? Do you agree?

SEPARATE IS BETTER

Susan Estrich

Born in suburban Boston in 1953, Susan Estrich attended Wellesley College and Harvard Law School. After clerking for Supreme Court Justice John Paul Stevens, she returned to Harvard, becoming one of the youngest tenured professors on the Law School faculty. While there, she wrote Real Rape *(1987), an examination of the social and legal issues surrounding the subject of sexual assault, which had its roots in her own earlier experience as a rape victim. She later served as the campaign manager for Michael Dukakis's 1988 presidential bid, the first woman in the country to hold such a position. Now a professor of law and political science at the University of Southern California, Estrich writes often about issues related to gender and politics. In the following essay, she presents what she sees as the benefits for female students of attending an all-women's college.*

Twenty years ago, when I attended Wellesley College, an all-women's college, coeducation fever was gripping America. Yale and Princeton had just "gone"; Dartmouth "went" next. My freshman year, we were polled on whether we thought Wellesley should join the stampede. What did I know? I said yes. But now I know I was wrong, and I'm glad my vote didn't change anything.

This year, 60 percent of the National Merit Scholarship finalists are   2
boys, because boys outscored girls on the Preliminary Scholastic
Assessment Test (P.S.A.T.), which determines eligibility for the scholarships. The test doesn't ask about sports; it does ask about math and science, though, and that's where the differences between boys and girls
are most pronounced. The American Civil Liberties Union and the
National Center for Fair and Open Testing filed a Federal civil rights
suit in February charging that the test discriminates against women.
The plaintiffs want more girls to get National Merit Scholarships. So do
I. But I want to see the girls earn them, in schools that give them a fair
chance.

I didn't win a Merit Scholarship either, although if the Fair Test   3
people had their way, I might have. My grades were near perfect. But I
didn't take the tough math and science courses. I had different priorities. I started junior high as the only girl on the math team. By high
school, I'd long since quit. Instead, I learned to twirl a baton, toss it in
the air and catch it while doing a split in the mud or the ice. The problem wasn't the P.S.A.T., but me, and my school.

Things have changed since then, but not as much as one would   4
hope. The American Association of University Women did a major
study in 1992 about how schools shortchange girls and concluded that
even though girls get better grades (except in math), they get less from
school. Teachers pay less attention to girls and give them less encouragement. Two American University researchers, Myra and David
Sadker, reached a similar conclusion after 20 years of study. Girls are the
invisible students; boys get the bulk of the teachers' time. Boys call out
eight times as often as girls do. When the boys call out, they get
answers; when the girls do, they're often admonished for speaking out.
And that's true whether the teacher is a man or a woman. Even the new
history textbooks devote only about 2 percent of their pages to women.
What is happening, says Elisabeth Griffith, a historian and headmistress
of the Madeira School in McLean, Va., is that "boys learn competence,
girls lose it."

If schools shortchange girls, why is it surprising when the tests show   5
that they're doing less well? It isn't just the P.S.A.T.'s, where 18,000 boys
generally reach the top categories and only 8,000 girls do. While the gap
has narrowed, boys also outscore girls on 11 of the 14 College Board
Achievement tests, and on the A.C.T. exams and on the S.A.T.'s. It is possible to jimmy selection standards to make sure girls win more scholarships, but equal results don't count for much if those results are forced.
Instead of declaring equality, society should be advancing it. The challenge isn't to get more scholarships for baton twirlers but to get more
baton twirlers to take up advanced mathematics.

One place that happens is in girls' schools and women's colleges.   6
Sometimes separate isn't equal; it's better. Changing the way teachers

teach in coed schools, changing the textbooks to make sure they talk about women as well as men, educating parents about raising daughters—all of these things make sense, since most girls will be educated in coed classrooms. But we've been talking about them for a decade, and the problems of gender bias stubbornly persist. In the meantime, for many girls, single-sex education is working.

In girls' schools, 80 percent of the girls take four years of science and 7 math, compared with the national average of two years in a coed environment. Elizabeth Tidball, a George Washington University researcher, found that graduates of women's colleges did better than female graduates of coed colleges in terms of test scores, graduate school admissions, number of earned doctorates, salaries and personal satisfaction. One-third of the female board members of Fortune 1,000 companies are graduates of women's colleges, even though those colleges contribute less than 4 percent of total graduates. Forty-three percent of the math doctorates and 50 percent of engineering doctorates earned by female liberal-arts college students go to graduates of Barnard, Bryn Mawr, Mount Holyoke, Smith or Wellesley—all women's colleges. Graduates of women's colleges outnumber all other female entries in Who's Who.

I stopped twirling my baton when I got to Wellesley. I'd like to say 8 that I knew I needed a women's college after all those years in the mud at football games, but it doesn't always work that way. I went to Wellesley because they gave me a generous scholarship, and because Radcliffe rejected me (the test scores, maybe). I was actually miserable a good deal of the time I was there, particularly during the long winters when the janitor was the only man around. But what I learned was worth it. I spent the better part of four years in a world in which women could do anything, because no one told us we couldn't. I even took some math courses. By senior year, somehow, I'd become an accomplished test-taker. When I got to Harvard Law School, where men vastly outnumbered women and sexism was the rule, a professor told me on the first day that women didn't do very well. I laughed and decided to prove he was wrong. That's a Wellesley education.

I'm not proposing that coed public schools be replaced with a net- 9 work of single-sex academies. But if the problem is that women don't do well in math or science, then single-sex classes, and single-sex schools, may be part of the answer.

The evidence, though scant, is promising. In Ventura, Calif., the 10 public high school has begun offering an all-girls Algebra II course. The girls, one teacher says, think so little of their ability that the teacher spends her time not only teaching math but also building self-confidence, repeatedly telling the girls that they're smart and that they can do it. The Illinois Math and Science Academy in Aurora is experimenting with a girls-only calculus-based physics class for the first semester, with the girls joining the coed class at midyear. In the girls-only class, the students report that they are jumping up to ask and answer questions instead of sitting back, hoping that the teacher doesn't call on them. One student said she was worried about the transition to a coed classroom: "We need to make sure we don't lose our newfound physics freedom." "Physics freedom" for girls—what a wonderful concept.

The biggest obstacles to such classes, or even to all-girls public 11 schools, are erected by lawyers bent on enforcing legal equality. In the 1954 case of Brown v. Board of Education, the Supreme Court declared that "separate but equal" was inherently unequal. That was certainly true in Topeka, Kan., whose school system was challenged. It was true of the black-only law school established to keep blacks out of the University of Texas law school. It is not necessarily true of the Ventura High School math class for girls or the Aurora Academy calculus-based physics class, whose futures are in jeopardy because of the knee-jerk application of Brown.

Classes like those in Ventura County or Aurora, Ill., survive consti- 12 tutional challenge by formally opening their doors to men, with a wink and a nod to keep them from coming in. Otherwise, the schools could be stripped of Federal support, and even enjoined under the Constitution by Federal court order, because they are "discriminating." Private schools may open their doors only to boys or girls under an exemption from Federal laws mandating "equality." But public schools enjoy no such freedom. The reality is that if you need a Wellesley education in America, you have to pay for it. That's the price of committing to formal equality instead of committing to real opportunity.

Boys may pay the price as well. Some educators in the African- 13 American community believe that all-boys classes may be part of the solution to the dismal failure and dropout rates of African-American boys in school. But the courts prevented the Detroit school district from establishing three public all-boys schools, effectively stopping similar projects planned in other cities. Nonetheless, all-boys classes are being held quietly in as many as two dozen schools around the country, mostly in inner cities.

Such programs may or may not succeed in the long run. Research 14 and careful study are plainly needed. But research and careful study are difficult when classes are held in near secrecy for fear of discovery by lawyers and Government officials intent on shutting them down in the name of equality.

If girls don't want to go to all-girls schools, or if parents don't want 15 to send them, that's their choice. If the experiments with girls-only math classes or boys-only classes should fail, then educators can be trusted to abandon them. But short of that, let the educators and the parents and the students decide, and leave the lawyers and judges out of it.

Responding to Reading

1. Estrich argues in favor of all-female colleges. Does she effectively apply her arguments to single-sex high schools? Could the same arguments be applied to historically black colleges? To all-male colleges?
2. Throughout her essay (for example, in paragraphs 2–4), Estrich uses both personal experiences and statistics to support her argument. How effective is each kind of support?
3. Do you agree with Estrich's position on single-sex education? Can you see any problems with her recommendations?

THE VISIGOTHS IN TWEED

Dinesh D'Souza

Born in Bombay, India, Dinesh D'Souza (1961–) came to the U.S. in 1978. He attended Dartmouth College, where from 1982 through 1983 he edited the controversial Dartmouth Review, *an independent student newspaper funded in part by William F. Buckley's highly conservative opinion magazine, the* National Review. *After graduation, D'Souza authored a biography of television evangelist Jerry Falwell and* My Dear Alex: Letters from a KGB Agent *(1987, with Gregory Fossedale), a satire of Soviet manipulation of U.S. politicians and the American press. His most recent books are* The End of Racism *(1995) and a 1997 biography of Ronald Reagan. A former policy adviser to Presidents Reagan and Bush, he is a research fellow at the American Enterprise Institute. In 1991, he published the widely read* Illiberal Education: The Politics of Race and Sex on Campus, *a scathing attack on what D'Souza calls higher education's "attempted brainwashing [of students] that deprecates Western learning and exalts a neo-Marxist ideology promoted in the name of multiculturalism." The following essay, which originally appeared in the business magazine* Forbes, *is adapted from that book and presents D'Souza's central thesis.*

"I am a male WASP who attended and succeeded at Choate (prep-   1 aratory) School, Yale College, Yale Law School, and Princeton Graduate School. Slowly but surely, however, my life-long habit of looking, listening, feeling, and thinking as honestly as possible has led me to see that white, male-dominated, western European culture is the most destructive phenomenon in the known history of the planet.

"[This Western culture] is deeply hateful of life and committed to   2 death; therefore, it is moving rapidly toward the destruction of itself and most other life forms on earth. And truly it deserves to die. . . . We have to face our own individual and collective responsibility for what is happening—our greed, brutality, indifference, militarism, racism, sexism, blindness. . . . Meanwhile, everything we have put into motion continues to endanger us more every day."

This bizarre outpouring, so reminiscent of the "confessions" from 3 victims of Stalin's show trials,[1] appeared in a letter to *Mother Jones* magazine and was written by a graduate of some of our finest schools. But the truth is that the speaker's anguish came not from any balanced assessment but as a consequence of exposure to the propaganda of the new barbarians who have captured the humanities, law, and social science departments of so many of our universities. It should come as no surprise that many sensitive young Americans reject the system that has nurtured them. At Duke University, according to the *Wall Street Journal*, professor Frank Lentricchia in his English course shows the movie *The Godfather* to teach his students that organized crime is "a metaphor for American business as usual."

Yes, a student can still get an excellent education—among the best 4 in the world—in computer technology and the hard sciences at American universities. But liberal arts students, including those attending Ivy League schools, are very likely to be exposed to an attempted brainwashing that deprecates Western learning and exalts a neo-Marxist ideology promoted in the name of multiculturalism. Even students who choose hard sciences must often take required courses in the humanities, where they are almost certain to be inundated with an anti-Western, anticapitalist view of the world.

Each year American society invests $160 billion in higher educa- 5 tion, more per student than any nation in the world except Denmark. A full 45 percent of this money comes from the federal, state, and local governments. No one can say we are starving higher education. But what are we getting for our money, at least so far as the liberal arts are concerned?

A fair question? It might seem so, but in university circles it is con- 6 sidered impolite because it presumes that higher education must be accountable to the society that supports it. Many academics think of universities as intellectual enclaves, insulated from the vulgar capitalism of the larger culture.

Yet, since the academics constantly ask for more money, it seems 7 hardly unreasonable to ask what they are doing with it. Honest answers are rarely forthcoming. The general public sometimes gets a whiff of what is going on—as when Stanford alters its core curriculum in the classics of Western civilization—but it knows very little of the systematic and comprehensive change sweeping higher education.

---

[1] During his brutal assumption of totalitarian control over the Soviet Union in the 1930s, Joseph Stalin purged many of his enemies in mock trials where they were forced to confess their "crimes" before they were executed. [Eds.]

An academic and cultural revolution has overtaken most of our 8
3,535 colleges and universities. It's a revolution to which most Americans have paid little attention. It is a revolution imposed upon the
students by a university elite, not one voted upon or even discussed by
the society at large. It amounts, according to University of Wisconsin-
Madison Chancellor Donna Shalala, to "a basic transformation of American higher education in the name of multiculturalism and diversity."

The central thrust of this "basic transformation" involves replacing 9
traditional core curricula—consisting of the great works of Western culture—with curricula flavored by minority, female, and Third World
authors.

Here's a sample of the viewpoint represented by the new curricu- 10
lum. Becky Thompson, a sociology and women's studies professor, in a
teaching manual distributed by the American Sociological Association,
writes: "I begin my course with the basic feminist principle that in a
racist, classist, and sexist society we have all swallowed oppressive
ways of being, whether intentionally or not. Specifically, this means that
it is not open to debate whether a white student is racist or a male student is sexist. He/she simply is."

Professors at several colleges who have resisted these regnant dog- 11
mas about race and gender have found themselves the object of denunciation and even university sanctions. Donald Kagan, dean of Yale
College, says: "I was a student during the days of Joseph McCarthy,[2]
and there is less freedom now than there was then."

As in the McCarthy period, a particular group of activists has 12
cowed the authorities and bent them to its will. After activists forcibly
occupied his office, President Lattie Coor of the University of Vermont
explained how he came to sign a sixteen-point agreement establishing,
among other things, minority faculty hiring quotas. "When it became
clear that the minority students with whom I had been discussing these
issues wished to pursue negotiations *in the context of occupied offices* . . . I
agreed to enter negotiations." As frequently happens in such cases,
Coor's "negotiations" ended in a rapid capitulation by the university
authorities.

At Harvard, historian Stephan Thernstrom was harangued by stu- 13
dent activists and accused of insensitivity and bigotry. What was his
crime? His course included a reading from the journals of slave owners,
and his textbook gave a reasonable definition of affirmative action as
"preferential treatment" for minorities. At the University of Michigan,
renowned demographer Reynolds Farley was assailed in the college

---

[2] The notorious U.S. senator of the late 1940s and early 1950s who instigated a search for suspected
Communists and others with "un-American" leanings in government, academia, and the enter-
tainment industry, ruining many careers. McCarthy was eventually censured by the U.S. Senate.
[Eds.]

press for criticizing the excesses of Marcus Garvey and Malcolm X; yet the administration did not publicly come to his defense.

University leaders argue that the revolution suggested by these 14 examples is necessary because young Americans must be taught to live in and govern a multiracial and multicultural society. Immigration from Asia and Latin America, combined with relatively high minority birth rates, is changing the complexion of America. Consequently, in the words of University of Michigan President James Duderstadt, universities must "create a model of how a more diverse and pluralistic community can work for our society."

No controversy, of course, about benign goals such as pluralism or 15 diversity, but there is plenty of controversy about how these goals are being pursued. Although there is no longer a Western core curriculum at Mount Holyoke or Dartmouth, students at those schools must take a course in non-Western or Third World culture. Berkeley and the University of Wisconsin now insist that every undergraduate enroll in ethnic studies, making this virtually the only compulsory course at those schools.

If American students were truly exposed to the richest elements of 16 other cultures, this could be a broadening and useful experience. A study of Chinese philosophers such as Confucius or Mencius would enrich students' understanding of how different peoples order their lives, thus giving a greater sense of purpose to their own. Most likely, a taste of Indian poetry such as Rabindranath Tagore's *Gitanjali* would increase the interest of materially minded young people in the domain of the spirit. An introduction to Middle Eastern history would prepare the leaders of tomorrow to deal with the mounting challenge of Islamic culture. It would profit students to study the rise of capitalism in the Far East.

But the claims of the academic multiculturalists are largely phony. 17 They pay little attention to the Asian or Latin American classics. Rather, the non-Western or multicultural curriculum reflects a different agenda. At Stanford, for example, Homer, Plato, Dante, Machiavelli, and Locke[3] are increasingly scarce. But often their replacements are not non-Western classics. Instead the students are offered exotic topics such as popular religion and healing in Peru, Rastafarian poetry, and Andean music.

What do students learn about the world from the books they are 18 required to read under the new multicultural rubric? At Stanford one of the non-Western works assigned is *I, Rigoberta Menchú,* subtitled "An Indian Woman in Guatemala."

The book is hardly a non-Western classic. Published in 1983, *I,* 19 *Rigoberta Menchú* is the story of a young woman who is said to be a representative voice of the indigenous peasantry. Representative of

---

[3] European writers and philosophers from ancient times through the 17th century. [Eds.]

Guatemalan Indian culture? In fact, Rigoberta met the Venezuelan feminist to whom she narrates this story at a socialist conference in Paris, where, presumably, very few of the Third World's poor travel. Moreover, Rigoberta's political consciousness includes the adoption of such politically correct causes as feminism, homosexual rights, socialism, and Marxism. By the middle of the book she is discoursing on "bourgeois youths" and "Molotov cocktails," not the usual terminology of Indian peasants. One chapter is titled "Rigoberta Renounces Marriage and Motherhood," a norm that her tribe could not have adopted and survived.

If Rigoberta does not represent the convictions and aspirations of 20 Guatemalan peasants, what is the source of her importance and appeal? The answer is that Rigoberta seems to provide independent Third World corroboration for Western left-wing passions and prejudices. She is a mouthpiece for a sophisticated neo-Marxist critique of Western society, all the more powerful because it seems to issue not from some embittered American academic but from a Third World native. For professors nourished on the political activism of the late 1960s and early 1970s, texts such as *I, Rigoberta Menchú* offer a welcome opportunity to attack capitalism and Western society in general in the name of teaching students about the developing world.

We learn in the introduction of *I, Rigoberta Menchú* that Rigoberta is 21 a quadruple victim. As a person of color, she has suffered racism. As a woman, she has endured sexism. She lives in South America, which is— of course—a victim of North American colonialism. She is also an Indian, victimized by Latino culture within Latin America.[4]

One of the most widely used textbooks in so-called multicultural 22 courses is *Multi-Cultural Literacy*, published by Graywolf Press in St. Paul, Minnesota. The book ignores the *The Tale of Genji*, the Upanishads and Vedas, the Koran and Islamic commentaries. It also ignores such brilliant contemporary authors as Jorge Luis Borges, V.S. Naipaul, Octavio Paz, Naguib Mahfouz, and Wole Soyinka. Instead it offers thirteen essays of protest, including Michele Wallace's autobiographical "Invisibility Blues" and Paula Gunn Allen's "Who Is Your Mother? The Red Roots of White Feminism."

One student I spoke with at Duke University said he would not 23 study *Paradise Lost* because John Milton was a Eurocentric white male sexist. At the University of Michigan, a young black woman who had converted to Islam refused to believe that the prophet Muhammad owned slaves and practiced polygamy. She said she had taken courses on cultural diversity and the courses hadn't taught her that.

---

[4] Menchú was awarded the Nobel Peace Prize in 1992, shortly after this article was published. [Eds.]

One of the highlights of this debate on the American campus was a   24
passionate statement delivered a few years ago by Stanford undergraduate William King, president of the Black Student Union, who argued
the benefits of the new multicultural curriculum before the faculty senate of the university. Under the old system, he said, "I was never
taught . . . the fact that Socrates, Herodotus, Pythagoras, and Solon studied in Egypt and acknowledged that much of their knowledge of astron-
omy, geometry, medicine, and building came from the African
civilization in and around Egypt. [I was never taught] that the Hippocratic oath acknowledges the Greeks' 'father of medicine,' Imhotep, a
black Egyptian pharaoh whom they called Aesculapius . . . I was never
informed when it was found that the 'very dark and wooly haired'
Moors in Spain preserved, expanded, and reintroduced the classical
knowledge that the Greeks had collected, which led to the 'renaissance.' . . . I read the Bible without knowing Saint Augustine looked
black like me, that the Ten Commandments were almost direct copies
from the 147 Negative Confessions of Egyptian initiates. . . . I didn't
learn Toussaint L'Ouverture's defeat of Napoleon in Haiti directly influenced the French Revolution, or that the Iroquois Indians in America
had a representative democracy which served as a model for the
American system."

This statement drew wild applause and was widely quoted. The   25
only trouble is that much of it is untrue. There is no evidence that
Socrates, Pythagoras, Herodotus, and Solon studied in Egypt, although
Herodotus may have traveled there. Saint Augustine was born in North
Africa, but his skin color is unknown, and in any case he could not have
been mentioned in the Bible; he was born over 350 years after Christ.
Viewing King's speech at my request, Bernard Lewis, an expert on
Islamic and Middle Eastern culture at Princeton, described it as "a few
scraps of truth amidst a great deal of nonsense."

Why does multicultural education, in practice, gravitate toward   26
such myths and half-truths? To find out why, it is necessary to explore
the complex web of connections that the academic revolution generates
among admissions policies, life on campus, and the curriculum.

American universities typically begin with the premise that in a   27
democratic and increasingly diverse society the composition of their
classes should reflect the ethnic distribution of the general population.
Many schools officially seek "proportional representation," in which the
percentage of applicants admitted from various racial groups roughly
approximates the ratio of those groups in society at large.

Thus universities routinely admit black, Hispanic, and American   28
Indian candidates over better-qualified white and Asian American applicants. As a result of zealously pursued affirmative action programs,
many selective colleges admit minority students who find it extremely
difficult to meet demanding academic standards and to compete with

the rest of the class. This fact is reflected in the dropout rates of blacks and Hispanics, which are more than 50 percent higher than those of whites and Asians. At Berkeley a study of students admitted on a preferential basis between 1978 and 1982 concluded that nearly 70 percent failed to graduate within five years.

For affirmative action students who stay on campus, a common 29 strategy of dealing with the pressures of university life is to enroll in a distinctive minority organization. Among such organizations at Cornell University are Lesbian, Gay & Bisexual Coalition; La Association Latina; National Society of Black Engineers; Society of Minority Hoteliers; Black Students United; and Simba Washanga.

Although the university brochures at Cornell and elsewhere con- 30 tinue to praise integration and close interaction among students from different backgrounds, the policies practiced at these schools actually encourage segregation. Stanford, for example, has "ethnic theme houses" such as the African house called Ujaama. And President Donald Kennedy has said that one of his educational objectives is to "support and strengthen ethnic theme houses." Such houses make it easier for some minority students to feel comfortable but help to create a kind of academic apartheid.

The University of Pennsylvania has funded a black yearbook, even 31 though only 6 percent of the student body is black and all other groups appeared in the general yearbook. Vassar, Dartmouth, and the University of Illinois have allowed separate graduation activities and ceremonies for minority students. California State University at Sacramento has just established an official "college within a college" for blacks.

Overt racism is relatively rare at most campuses, yet minorities are 32 told that bigotry operates in subtle forms such as baleful looks, uncorrected stereotypes, and "institutional racism"—defined as the underrepresentation of blacks and Hispanics among university trustees, administrators, and faculty.

Other groups such as feminists and homosexuals typically get into 33 the game, claiming their own varieties of victim status. As Harvard political scientist Harvey Mansfield bluntly puts it, "White students must admit their guilt so that minority students do not have to admit their incapacity."

Even though universities regularly accede to the political demands 34 of victim groups, their appeasement gestures do not help black and Hispanic students get a genuine liberal arts education. They do the opposite, giving the apologists of the new academic orthodoxy a convenient excuse when students admitted on a preferential basis fail to meet academic standards. At this point student activists and administrators often blame the curriculum. They argue that it reflects a "white male perspective" that systematically depreciates the views and achievements of other cultures, minorities, women, and homosexuals.

With this argument, many minority students can now explain why 35 they had such a hard time with Milton in the English department, Publius in political science, and Heisenberg in physics. Those men reflected white male aesthetics, philosophy, and science. Obviously, non-white students would fare much better if the university created more black or Latino or Third World courses, the argument goes. This epiphany leads to a spate of demands: Abolish the Western classics, establish new departments such as Afro-American Studies and Women's Studies, hire minority faculty to offer distinctive black and Hispanic "perspectives."

Multicultural or non-Western education on campus frequently 36 glamorizes Third World cultures and omits inconvenient facts about them. In fact, several non-Western cultures are caste-based or tribal, and often disregard norms of racial equality. In many of them feminism is virtually nonexistent, as indicated by such practices as dowries, widow-burning, and genital mutilation; and homosexuality is some-times regarded as a crime or mental disorder requiring punishment. These nasty aspects of the non-Western cultures are rarely mentioned in the new courses. Indeed, Bernard Lewis of Princeton argues that while slavery and the subjugation of women have been practiced by all known civilizations, the West at least has an active and effective move-ment for the abolition of such evils.

Who is behind this academic revolution, this contrived multicultur- 37 alism? The new curriculum directly serves the purposes of a newly ascendant generation of young professors weaned in the protest culture of the late 1960s and early 1970s. In a frank comment, Jay Parini, who teaches English at Middlebury College, writes, "After the Vietnam War, a lot of us didn't just crawl back into our library cubicles. We stepped into academic positions. . . . Now we have tenure, and the work of reshaping the university has begun in earnest."

The goal that Parini and others like him pursue is the transforma- 38 tion of the college classroom from a place of learning to a laboratory of indoctrination for social change. Not long ago most colleges required that students learn the basics of the physical sciences and mathematics, the rudiments of economics and finance, and the fundamental princi-ples of American history and government. Studies by the National Endowment for the Humanities show that this coherence has disap-peared from the curriculum. As a result, most universities are now graduating students who are scientifically and culturally impoverished, if not illiterate.

At the University of Pennsylvania, Houston Baker, one of the most 39 prominent black academics in the country, denounces reading and writ-ing as oppressive technologies and celebrates such examples of oral cul-ture as the rap group N.W.A. (Niggers With Attitude). One of the group's songs is about the desirability of killing policemen. Alison Jaggar, who teaches women's studies at the University of Colorado, denounces the traditional nuclear family as a "cornerstone of women's oppression" and anticipates scientific advances enabling men to carry fetuses in their bodies so that child-bearing responsibilities can be shared between the sexes. Duke professor Eve Sedgwick's scholarship is devoted to unmasking what she terms the heterosexual bias in Western culture, a project that she pursues through papers such as "Jane Austen and the Masturbating Girl" and "How To Bring Your Kids Up Gay."

Confronted by racial tension and Balkanization on campus, university leaders usually announce that, because of a resurgence of bigotry, "more needs to be done." They press for redoubled preferential recruitment of minority students and faculty, funding for a new Third World or Afro-American center, mandatory sensitivity education for whites, and so on. The more the university leaders give in to the demands of minority activists, the more they encourage the very racism they are supposed to be fighting. Surveys indicate that most young people today hold fairly liberal attitudes toward race, evident in their strong support for the civil rights agenda and for interracial dating. However, these liberal attitudes are sorely tried by the demands of the new orthodoxy: many undergraduates are beginning to rebel against what they perceive as a culture of preferential treatment and double standards actively fostered by university policies. 40

Can there be a successful rolling back of this revolution, or at least of its excesses? One piece of good news is that blatant forms of racial preference are having an increasingly tough time in the courts, and this has implications for university admissions policies. The Department of Education is more vigilant than it used to be in investigating charges of discrimination against whites and Asian Americans. With help from Washington director Morton Halperin, the American Civil Liberties Union has taken a strong stand against campus censorship. Popular magazines such as *Newsweek* and *New York* have poked fun at "politically correct" speech. At Tufts University, undergraduates embarrassed the administration into backing down on censorship by putting up taped boundaries designating areas of the university to be "free speech zones," "limited speech zones," and "Twilight Zones." 41

Even some scholars on the political left are now speaking out against such dogmatism and excess. Eugene Genovese, a Marxist historian and one of the nation's most respected scholars of slavery, argues that "too often we find that education has given way to indoctrination. Good scholars are intimidated into silence, and the only diversity that obtains is a diversity of radical positions." More and more professors from across the political spectrum are resisting the politicization and lowering of standards. At Duke, for example, sixty professors, led by political scientist James David Barber, a liberal Democrat, have repudiated the extremism of the victims' revolution. To that end they have joined the National 42

Association of Scholars, a Princeton, New Jersey-based group devoted to fairness, excellence, and rational debate in universities.

But these scholars need help. Resistance on campus to the academic 43 revolution is outgunned and sorely needs outside reinforcements. Parents, alumni, corporations, foundations, and state legislators are generally not aware that they can be very effective in promoting reform. The best way to encourage reform is to communicate in no uncertain terms to university leadership and, if necessary, to use financial incentives to assure your voice is heard. University leaders do their best to keep outsiders from meddling or even finding out what exactly is going on behind the tall gates, but there is little doubt that they would pay keen attention to the views of the donors on whom they depend. By threatening to suspend donations if universities continue harmful policies, friends of liberal learning can do a lot. In the case of state-funded schools, citizens and parents can pressure elected representatives to ask questions and demand more accountability from the taxpayer-supported academics.

The illiberal revolution can be reversed only if the people who foot 44 the bills stop being passive observers. Don't just write a check to your alma mater; that's an abrogation of responsibility. Keep abreast of what is going on and don't be afraid to raise your voice and even to close your wallet in protest. Our Western, free-market culture need not provide the rope to hang itself.

Responding to Reading

1. What does D'Souza mean when he says, "An academic and cultural revolution has overtaken most of our 3,535 colleges and universities" (8)? Do you agree? Is there any evidence of such a revolution at your school?

2. On the whole, do you find D'Souza's arguments convincing or unconvincing? With which points in this essay do you agree? With which do you disagree?

3. In paragraph 3, D'Souza compares the "bizarre outpouring" of a white male WASP to the "'confessions' from victims of Stalin's show trials" in the 1930s. What does he mean? What, if anything, does D'Souza accomplish with such a comparison?

FOCUS: WHAT IS GOOD TEACHING?

VIRTUAL STUDENTS, DIGITAL CLASSROOM

Neil Postman

Neil Postman, currently chairman of the Department of Culture and Communication at New York University, has been writing about issues of education and technology for over thirty years. His interest in education began when he worked as an elementary and secondary schoolteacher in the New York City public schools in the 1960s. Growing out of that experience, his first important book, Teaching as a Subversive Activity *(1969, 1979), sparked considerable controversy over its call for radical educational reform. Among Postman's more than twenty subsequent books are* Crazy Talk, Stupid Talk *(1976);* Amusing Ourselves to Death *(1985), a scathing critique of television;* The Disappearance of Childhood *(1992);* Technopoly *(1993), focusing on the impact of technology on personal freedom; and* The End of Education *(1995). In the following essay, adapted from* The End of Education *and originally published in* The Nation, *Postman questions the notion current among many education specialists that new information technologies should revolutionize our schools.*

If one has a trusting relationship with one's students (let us say, graduate students), it is not altogether gauche to ask them if they believe in God (with a capital G). I have done this three or four times and most students say they do. Their answer is preliminary to the next question: If someone you love were desperately ill, and you had to choose between praying to God for his or her recovery or administering an antibiotic (as prescribed by a competent physician), which would you choose?

Most say the question is silly since the alternatives are not mutually exclusive. Of course. But suppose they were—which would you choose? God helps those who help themselves, some say in choosing the antibiotic, therefore getting the best of two possible belief systems. But if pushed to the wall (e.g., God does not always help those who help themselves; God helps those who pray and who believe), most choose the antibiotic, after noting that the question is asinine and proves nothing. Of course, the question was not asked, in the first place, to prove anything but to begin a discussion of the nature of belief. And I do not fail to inform the students, by the way, that there has recently emerged evidence of a "scientific" nature that when sick people are prayed for they do better than those who aren't.

As the discussion proceeds, important distinctions are made among 3 the different meanings of "belief," but at some point it becomes far from asinine to speak of the god of Technology—in the sense that people believe technology works, that they rely on it, that it makes promises, that they are bereft when denied access to it, that they are delighted when they are in its presence, that for most people it works in mysterious ways, that they condemn people who speak against it, that they stand in awe of it and that, in the "born again" mode, they will alter their life-styles, their schedules, their habits, and their relationships to accommodate it. If this be not a form of religious belief, what is?

In all strands of American cultural life, you can find so many exam- 4 ples of technological adoration that it is possible to write a book about it. And I would if it had not already been done so well. But nowhere do you find more enthusiasm for the god of Technology than among educators. In fact, there are those, like Lewis Perelman, who argue (for example, in his book, *School's Out*) that modern information technologies have rendered schools entirely irrelevant since there is now much more information available outside the classroom than inside it. This is by no means considered an outlandish idea. Dr. Diane Ravitch, former Assistant Secretary of Education, envisions, with considerable relish, the challenge that technology presents to the tradition that "children (and adults) should be educated in a specific place, for a certain number of hours, and a certain number of days during the week and year." In other words, that children should be educated in school. Imagining the possibilities of an information superhighway offering perhaps a thousand channels, Dr. Ravitch assures us that:

> in this new world of pedagogical plenty, children and adults will be able to dial up a program on their home television to learn whatever they want to know, at their own convenience. If Little Eva cannot sleep, she can learn algebra instead. At her home-learning station, she will tune in to a series of interesting problems that are presented in an interactive medium, much like video games. . . .
>
> Young John may decide that he wants to learn the history of modern Japan, which he can do by dialing up the greatest authorities and teachers on the subject, who will not only use dazzling graphs and illustrations, but will narrate a historical video that excites his curiosity and imagination.

In this vision there is, it seems to me, a confident and typical sense 5 of unreality. Little Eva can't sleep, so she decides to learn a little algebra? Where does Little Eva come from? Mars? If not, it is more likely she will tune in to a good movie. Young John decides that he wants to learn the history of modern Japan? How did young John come to this point? How is it that he never visited a library up to now? Or is it that he, too, couldn't sleep and decided that a little modern Japanese history was just what he needed?

What Ravitch is talking about here is not a new technology but a ₆ new species of child, one who, in any case, no one has seen up to now. Of course, new technologies do make new kinds of people, which leads to a second objection to Ravitch's conception of the future. There is a kind of forthright determinism about the imagined world described in it. The technology is here or will be; we must use it because it is there; we will become the kind of people the technology requires us to be, and whether we like it or not, we will remake our institutions to accommodate technology. All of this must happen because it is good for us, but in any case, we have no choice. This point of view is present in very nearly every statement about the future relationship of learning to technology. And, as in Ravitch's scenario, there is always a cheery, gee-whiz tone to the prophecies. Here is one produced by the National Academy of Sciences, written by Hugh McIntosh.

School for children of the Information Age will be vastly different than it was for Mom and Dad.

Interested in biology? Design your own life forms with computer simulation.

Having trouble with a science project? Teleconference about it with a research scientist.

Bored with the real world? Go into a virtual physics lab and rewrite the laws of gravity.

These are the kinds of hands-on learning experiences schools could be providing right now. The technologies that make them possible are already here, and today's youngsters, regardless of economic status, know how to use them. They spend hours with them every week—not in the classroom, but in their own homes and in video game centers at every shopping mall.

It is always interesting to attend to the examples of learning, and ₇ the motivations that ignite them, in the songs of love that technophiles perform for us. It is for example, not easy to imagine research scientists all over the world teleconferencing with thousands of students who are having difficulty with their science projects. I can't help thinking that most research scientists would put a stop to this rather quickly. But I find it especially revealing that in the scenario above we have an example of a technological solution to a psychological problem that would seem to be exceedingly serious. We are presented with a student who is "bored with the real world." What does it mean to say someone is bored with the real world, especially one so young? Can a journey into virtual reality cure such a problem? And if it can, will our troubled youngster want to return to the real world? Confronted with a student who is bored with the real world, I don't think we can solve the problem so easily by making available a virtual reality physics lab.

The role that new technology should play in schools or anywhere 8 else is something that needs to be discussed without the hyperactive fantasies of cheerleaders. In particular, the computer and its associated technologies are awesome additions to a culture, and are quite capable of altering the psychic, not to mention the sleeping, habits of our young. But like all important technologies of the past, they are Faustian bargains,[1] giving and taking away, sometimes in equal measure, sometimes more in one way than the other. It is strange—indeed, shocking—that with the twenty-first century so close, we can still talk of new technologies as if they were unmixed blessings—gifts, as it were, from the gods. Don't we all know what the combustion engine has done for us and against us? What television is doing for us and against us? At the very least, what we need to discuss about Little Eva, Young John, and McIntosh's trio is what they will lose, and what we will lose, if they enter a world in which computer technology is their chief source of motivation, authority, and, apparently, psychological sustenance. Will they become, as Joseph Weizenbaum warns, more impressed by calculation than human judgment? Will speed of response become, more than ever, a defining duality of intelligence? If, indeed, the idea of a school will be dramatically altered, what kinds of learning will be neglected, perhaps made impossible? Is virtual reality a new form of therapy? If it is, what are its dangers?

These are serious matters, and they need to be discussed by those 9 who know something about children from the planet Earth, and whose vision of children's needs, and the needs of society, go beyond thinking of school mainly as a place for the convenient distribution of information. Schools are not now and have never been largely about getting information to children. That has been on the schools' agenda, of course, but has always been way down on the list. For technological utopians, the computer vaults information access to the top. This reshuffling of priorities comes at a most inopportune time. The goal of giving people greater access to more information faster, more conveniently, and in more diverse forms was the main technological thrust of the nineteenth century. Some folks haven't noticed it but that problem was largely solved, so that for almost a hundred years there has been more information available to the young outside the school than inside. That fact did not make the schools obsolete, nor does it now make them obsolete. Yes, it is true that Little Eva, the insomniac from Mars, could turn on an

---

[1] That is, bargains with the devil. [Eds.]

algebra lesson, thanks to the computer, in the wee hours of the morning. She could also, if she wished, read a book or magazine, watch television, turn on the radio or listen to music. All of this she could have done before the computer. The computer does not solve any problem she has but does exacerbate one. For Little Eva's problem is not how to get access to a well-structured algebra lesson but what to do with all the information available to her during the day, as well as during sleepless nights. Perhaps this is why she couldn't sleep in the first place. Little Eva, like the rest of us, is overwhelmed by information. She lives in a culture that has 260,000 billboards, 17,000 newspapers, 12,000 periodicals, 27,000 video outlets for renting tapes, 400 million television sets, and well over 500 million radios, not including those in automobiles. There are 40,000 new book titles published every year, and each day 41 million photographs are taken. And thanks to the computer, more than 60 billion pieces of advertising junk come into our mailboxes every year. Everything from telegraphy and photography in the nineteenth century to the silicon chip in the twentieth has amplified the din of information intruding on Little Eva's consciousness. From millions of sources all over the globe, through every possible channel and medium—light waves, air waves, ticker tape, computer banks, telephone wires, television cables, satellites, and printing presses—information pours in. Behind it in every imaginable form of storage—on paper, on video, on audiotape, on disks, film, and silicon chips—is an even greater volume of information waiting to be retrieved. In the face of this we might ask, What can schools do for Little Eva besides making still more information available? If there is nothing, then new technologies will indeed make schools obsolete. But in fact, there is plenty.

One thing that comes to mind is that schools can provide her with 10 a serious form of technology education. Something quite different from instruction in using computers to process information, which, it strikes me, is a trivial thing to do, for two reasons. In the first place, approximately 35 million people have already learned how to use computers without the benefit of school instruction. If the schools do nothing, most of the population will know how to use computers in the next ten years, just as most of the population learns how to drive a car without school instruction. In the second place, what we needed to know about cars— as we need to know about computers, television, and other important technologies—is not how to use them but how they use *us*. In the case of cars, what we needed to think about in the early twentieth century was not how to drive them but what they would do to our air, our landscape, our social relations, our family life, and our cities. Suppose in 1946 we had started to address similar questions about television: What will be its effects on our political institutions, our psychic habits, our children, our religious conceptions, our economy? Would we be better positioned today to control TV's massive assault on American culture?

I am talking here about making technology itself an object of inquiry so that Little Eva and Young John are more interested in asking questions about the computer than getting answers from it.

I am not arguing against using computers in school. I am arguing 11 against our sleepwalking attitudes toward it, against allowing it to distract us from important things, against making a god of it. This is what Theodore Roszak warned against in *The Cult of Information:* "Like all cults," he wrote, "this one also has the intention of enlisting mindless allegiance and acquiescence. People who have no clear idea of what they mean by information or why they should want so much of it are nonetheless prepared to believe that we live in an Information Age, which makes every computer around us what the relics of the True Cross were in the Age of Faith: emblems of salvation." To this, I would add the sage observation of Alan Kay of Apple Computer. Kay is widely associated with the invention of the personal computer, and certainly has an interest in schools using them. Nonetheless, he has repeatedly said that any problems the schools cannot solve without computers, they cannot solve with them. What are some of those problems? There is, for example, the traditional task of teaching children how to behave in groups. One might even say that schools have never been essentially about individualized learning. It is true, of course, that groups do not learn, individuals do. But the idea of a school is that individuals must learn in a setting in which individual needs are subordinated to group interests. Unlike other media of mass communication, which celebrate individual response and are experienced in private, the classroom is intended to tame the ego, to connect the individual with others, to demonstrate the value and necessity of group cohesion. At present, most scenarios describing the uses of computers have children solving problems alone; Little Eva, Young John, and the others are doing just that. The presence of other children may, indeed, be an annoyance.

Like the printing press before it, the computer has a powerful bias 12 toward amplifying personal autonomy and individual problem-solving. That is why educators must guard against computer technology's undermining some of the important reasons for having the young assemble (to quote Ravitch) "in a specific place, for a certain number of hours, and a certain number of days during the week and year."

Although Ravitch is not exactly against what she calls "state 13 schools," she imagines them as something of a relic of a pretechnological age. She believes that the new technologies will offer all children equal access to information. Conjuring up a hypothetical Little Mary who is presumably from a poorer home than Little Eva, Ravitch imagines that Mary will have the same opportunities as Eva "to learn any subject, and to learn it from the same master teachers as children in the richest neighborhood." For all of its liberalizing spirit, this scenario makes some important omissions. One is that though new technologies may be a solution to the learning of "subjects," they work against the learning of what are called "social values," including an understanding of democratic processes. If one reads the first chapter of Robert Fulghum's *All I Really Need to Know I Learned in Kindergarten*, one will find an elegant summary of a few things Ravitch's scenario has left out. They include learning the following lessons: Share everything, play fair, don't hit people, put things back where you found them, clean up your own mess, wash your hands before you eat, and, of course, flush. The only thing wrong with Fulghum's book is that no one has learned all these things at kindergarten's end. We have ample evidence that it takes many years of teaching these values in school before they have been accepted and internalized. That is why it won't do for children to learn in "settings of their own choosing." That is also why schools require children to be in a certain place at a certain time and to follow certain rules, like raising their hands when they wish to speak, not talking when others are talking, not chewing gum, not leaving until the bell rings, exhibiting patience toward slower learners, etc. This process is called making civilized people. The god of Technology does not appear interested in this function of schools. At least, it does not come up much when technology's virtues are enumerated.

The god of Technology may also have a trick or two up its sleeve 14 about something else. It is often asserted that new technologies will equalize learning opportunities for the rich and poor. It is devoutly to be wished for, but I doubt it will happen. In the first place, it is generally understood by those who have studied the history of technology that technological change always produces winners and losers. There are many reasons for this, among them economic differences. Even in the case of the automobile, which is a commodity most people can buy (although not all), there are wide differences between the rich and poor in the quality of what is available to them. It would be quite astonishing if computer technology equalized all learning opportunities, irrespective of economic differences. One may be delighted that Little Eva's parents could afford the technology and software to make it possible for her to learn algebra at midnight. But Little Mary's parents may not be able to, may not even know such things are available. And if we say that the school could make the technology available to Little Mary (at least during the day), there may [be] something else Little Mary is lacking.

It turns out, for example, that Little Mary may be having sleepless 15 nights as frequently as Little Eva but not because she wants to get a leg up on her algebra. Maybe because she doesn't know who her father is, or, if she does, where he is. Maybe we can understand why McIntosh's kid is bored with the real world. Or is the child confused about it? Or terrified? Are there educators who seriously believe that these problems can be addressed by new technologies?

I do not say, of course, that schools can solve the problems of 16
poverty, alienation, and family disintegration, but schools can *respond* to
them. And they can do this because there are people in them, because
these people are concerned with more than algebra lessons or modern
Japanese history, and because these people can identify not only one's
level of competence in math but one's level of rage and confusion and
depression. I am talking here about children as they really come to us,
not children who are invented to show us how computers may enrich
their lives. Of course, I suppose it is possible that there are children who,
waking at night, want to study algebra or who are so interested in their
world that they yearn to know about Japan. If there be such children,
and one hopes there are, they do not require expensive computers to
satisfy their hunger for learning. They are on their way, with or without
computers. Unless, of course, they do not care about others or have no
friends, or little respect for democracy or are filled with suspicion about
those who are not like them. When we have machines that know how
to do something about these problems, that is the time to rid ourselves
of the expensive burden of schools or to reduce the function of teachers
to "coaches" in the uses of machines (as Ravitch envisions). Until then,
we must be more modest about this god of Technology and certainly not
pin our hopes on it.

We must also, I suppose, be empathetic toward those who search 17
with good intentions for technological panaceas. I am a teacher myself
and know how hard it is to contribute to the making of a civilized person. Can we blame those who want to find an easy way, through the
agency of technology? Perhaps not. After all, it is an old quest. As early
as 1918, H. L. Mencken (although completely devoid of empathy) wrote,
"There is no sure-cure so idiotic that some superintendent of schools
will not swallow it. The aim seems to be to reduce the whole teaching
process to a sort of automatic reaction, to discover some master formula
that will not only take the place of competence and resourcefulness in
the teacher but that will also create an artificial receptivity in the child."

Mencken was not necessarily speaking of technological panaceas 18
but he may well have been. In the early 1920s a teacher wrote the following poem:

Mr. Edison says
That the radio will supplant the teacher.
Already one may learn languages by means of Victrola records.
The moving picture will visualize
What the radio fails to get across.
Teachers will be relegated to the backwoods,
With fire-horses,
And long-haired women;
Or, perhaps shown in museums.

Education will become a matter
Of pressing the button.
Perhaps I can get a position at the switchboard.

I do not go as far back as the radio and Victrola, but I am old enough   19
to remember when 16-millimeter film was to be the sure-cure. Then
closed-circuit television. Then 8-millimeter film. Then teacher-proof
textbooks. Now computers.

I know a false god when I see one.   20

Responding to Reading

1. What role does Postman think that new technologies should play in
   schools? Why does he call the new technologies a mixed blessing? What
   does he see as their advantages? Their disadvantages?
2. What does Postman mean when he says that schools should provide students with "a serious form of technology education" (10)? What form
   would this education take? With what issues would it deal? What does
   Postman mean in paragraph 11 when he warns against making the computer a god?
3. Both Mark Edmundson (p. 158) and Postman discuss the effects of new
   technologies on students. Overall, would you consider their assessments
   optimistic or pessimistic? What challenges does each writer think the new
   technologies pose for educators? For students?

COMMONPLACES ABOUT TEACHING: SECOND THOUGHTS

Bobby Fong

Members of almost any profession share certain assumptions about how
best to do their job. In the following essay, college professor Bobby Fong con-
siders six assumptions shared by many teachers today: (1) that students who
don't participate in class discussion are uninvolved in learning; (2) that
grades are a necessary evil; (3) that discussion is better for learning than lec-
ture is; (4) that teachers and students can be fellow learners; (5) that the goal
of education should be the acquisition of skills, not the memorization of infor-
mation; and (6) that instruction should be geared to the experiences and per-
spectives students bring to college. In arguing that these assumptions are
overly simplified, Fong concludes that teaching is a complicated process,
"idiosyncratic, resistant to generalization," and that it must be "thought-
fully tailored to the particular situations" in which teachers find themselves.
Fong was a professor at Berea College in Kentucky when this essay was pub-
lished in Change *magazine in 1987.*

Going to conferences provides opportunity to reflect on my own 1
routine, to re-examine the assumptions that drive my scholarship and
pedagogy.

The 1987 American Association of Higher Education annual meet- 2
ing, "Taking Teaching Seriously," was an occasion for such reflection,
but not in the usual way. From some sessions I came away thinking that
teaching had been more praised than examined, that slogans had substituted for more subtle study of how students learn and how we ought
to approach our teaching.

The source of my discomfort was the recurrence of a set of com- 3
monplaces about teaching. Call them clichés, generalizations, maxims,
what you will, they served as a verbal shorthand meant to call forth
reflexive agreement. They were voiced without elaboration, as received
wisdom too obvious to need defense.

Many of us listeners, however, withheld our assent because these 4
commonplaces seemed false to our own classroom experiences. Let me
raise six of them and tell why they troubled me.

The silent student is an uninvolved learner.

When I began teaching at Berea College, colleagues warned me of 5
"The Great Stone Face," the impassive silence that would greet my
attempts to foster class discussion. The students did prove to be less vol-
uble than classmates and students I had known on the East and West
coasts. I too would have construed my students' silence as a sign of their
lack of preparation or their lack of confidence except for one thing: As a
student, I too had been a "Great Stone Face."

There's a presumption that the students excitedly waving their 6
hands are somehow more involved in learning than the ones who hang
back from discussion. The usual suggestion is to call on the silent ones,
help them learn that their contributions are valued in class, and encourage them to take part in educating themselves rather than sitting and
waiting for others to provide the answers. Good advice—as far as it
goes—but it neglects to ask why students are silent and whether silent
students are really as uninvolved in learning as we think.

Research on learning styles has helped us see that our classroom 7
practices are culturally bound. The value we put on students' actively
contributing to their education by talking in class may reflect the egalitarian assumptions of our society, the notions of individual initiative
and democratic citizenship. In this context, silence is taken to be a mark
of apathy, an inability or unwillingness to participate, a dereliction of
civic duty. Silence is a stigma.

My students from Appalachia,[1] as well as my personal experience, 8
convince me that this can be a cultural misreading. Silence in oriental

---

[1] A largely poor, rural region of the Eastern United States. [Eds.]

culture is a sign of deference and respect. Elders speak from accumulated wisdom. In order to gain from the wisdom, the young must learn to listen. Many of my mountain students are from families where words are carefully weighed, where speaking is a craft. Their silence arises from a respect for language and a consequent reluctance to engage, unrehearsed, in public conversation. In both cases, silence stems, not from apathy, but from cultural folkways that make silence, before elders or more accomplished speakers, a virtue.

This kind of silence is also not uninvolved. Walter Ong suggests 9 that civilizations, in moving from orality to literacy, often lose some of their capacity for aural memory, the ability to retain information by hearing it as opposed to reading it. This is accompanied, I think, by a loss of respect for the skill of listening, a skill that involves being silent. Learning by listening entails anticipatory attention, the capacity to foresee what will be a speaker's next point, the direction in which a presentation can be expected to flow. The students who listen well aren't only keeping up with what is being said by an instructor or classmates, they're already anticipating what the next points might be. By the same token, a particular pleasure of anticipation comes at those moments when the argument swerves onto a track that is wholly appropriate, wholly logical, but wholly unexpected. Like a triple rhyme in a poem composed of couplets, the foiled expectation is the very source of joy, surprise, and learning.

Many of the silent students prove to be the highest-achieving stu- 10 dents in my classes. Their silence is active, and their nods as I speak betoken not only that they understand my latest point, but that they were already there waiting for me to arrive. As teachers, we think nothing of sitting through a two-hour conference or seminar presentation that, if worthy of the time, will be a mental aerobics session including the same kind of anticipatory attention and gamesmanship of expectations I've claimed for silent students.

Whatever their cultural background, students do need to learn the 11 folkways of the academy and the workplace, and that includes speaking in groups. Initiation into interactive learning, however, demands that I first respect their silence: they are not "dumb," neither unintelligent nor lacking verbal facility, nor are they apathetic.

They can be encouraged, however, to see speaking as another 12 avenue to learning. One might begin, then, not with unstructured discussion, but with short oral reports and discussions based on exercises prepared before class. Silent students can speak—and well—if they have had time to consider their remarks and have had prior notice that they will be expected to contribute.

I have also found that even after four years of such encouragement, 13 some of my brightest students still appear shy of speech. The mainstream culture's liking for ready quips and shoot-from-the-hip volubility makes us tend to denigrate these students. But I've come to beware of the smooth sententiousness that can hide a fundamental vacuousness of thought. When "Great Stone Faces" speak, they often speak from a rich, ruminative silence.

Grades are a necessary evil.

Yes, the most-asked question in a classroom is, "Will it be on the 14 exam?" Reflexively, teachers resent this query for being extraneous to learning. One should not go to college to accumulate good grades by passing exams. At the same time, grades serve as a prod or whip (choose your weapon) whereby students are coerced into mastering the material. Such coercion leaves a bad taste, however, for teachers dislike playing the heavies of the academy, wielding the club (another weapon) of authority to enforce what should be the dulcet pleasures of learning.

Let me suggest that grades are neither evil nor necessary. Given our 15 present system of education, they are essential to most students, not as prods to learning, but as the most tangible form, perhaps in many cases the only form, of feedback students get from teachers. The grade on a paper or exam may be the students' only way of knowing whether, in the teacher's estimation, they have learned the subject, and how well. It's the only way they have of gauging their own performance.

It's unrealistic to claim that students should know how well they're 16 learning independent of teacher feedback. Few of us are supremely confident of the quality of our own work. We send an article to a journal, hopeful that the referees will like it, but never certain that the article will be accepted until it is. We believe in our performance as teachers and scholars, but who has not approached tenure with some trepidation? We think we're good, but somewhere we need that assessment corroborated by others.

How much more so for apprentice learners who are still becoming 17 acquainted with the criteria for rigor, quality, and thoroughness in a discipline. They think their work passes muster, but does it? The grade is their confirmation. In this context, the question, "Will it be on the exam?" can be understood to mean, "I think this is an important point, isn't it?" Exams, and the grades that go with them, validate their judgment. Grades used in this sense are not evil.

At the same time, grades are certainly not the best kind of feedback. 18 They can indicate a level of achievement, but they can't in themselves explain what is lacking or how to improve. Conferences and written comments on a regular basis are superior means of accomplishing these ends. A few schools have successfully used written and oral evaluation in lieu of grades. Such institutions testify that grades are not absolutely necessary to promoting learning.

Nevertheless, grades persist. They are the coin of the realm, a suc- 19 cinct, well-understood and widely accepted means of indicating achievement. Words can be slippery, as anyone can attest who has had to weigh the vagaries of a letter of recommendation. Many of us use a conference or a written comment to encourage and redirect. Unfortunately, these attempts at positive reinforcement can obscure the hard reality that a piece of work is not adequate. The grade is cold and summary, but also unequivocal.

To adopt a legal metaphor, grades are the judgment, written evaluations the opinion. In the long term, the reasoning behind a judgment may prove more important than in whose favor the case is decided, but for the litigant before the bar, the judgment, in the short term, is everything. A responsible judge grants a fair verdict that is explained and defended in a written opinion; a decision without an opinion remains insufficient. So should we as teachers seek to provide feedback in forms other than grades. Still, our students and the educational system in which we labor ask us to render judgment, to validate learning by grades. Grades are ritual, but they remain potent symbols in our world. 20

In the abstract, grades are not strictly necessary to education, but they are expeditious and pervasive in the way we educate in America, and their presence is part of the very expectation of our students. As a convention for indicating achievement, they are not evil, and we do our students a disservice by dismissing their concern with grades as irrelevant to learning. 21

Discussion is preferable to lecture.

The quality of discussion can be an invaluable indicator of how well students are understanding the material. Discussion requires them to make public their learning, to claim ownership and responsibility for their education. Not to use discussion in a class is to cut off a source of continuous information on student progress. Like a pilot refusing to use radar in a fog, the instructor of a discussionless class flies blind, relying only on occasional glimpses through exams and papers to determine whether his students are on course or not. 22

This acknowledged, let it also be said that the lecture is a useful teaching tool. Comparisons between discussion and lecture formats tend to be invidious. First, they wrongly imply that the modes are mutually exclusive. Experience shows that both can be used to advantage in a course or an individual class meeting. For example, studies have demonstrated that an audience's attention begins to flag after twenty minutes of exposition, and so a teacher can use the lecture for one-third of an hour session and shift to other activities for the remainder of the time. 23

Second, the tendency is to compare bad lectures with good discussions: "The professor pulled out a sheaf of yellowed notes and began to drone . . ." versus "a lively discussion ensued about who would make a better president of the United States—the Erasmian prince or the 24

Machiavellian prince." Of course the discussion appears the more attractive. But a just comparison must at least pit excellence against excellence. It would be equally unfair to contrast the memory of a scintillating presentation against a rambling discussion in which participants with nothing to say took their time saying it.

Third, comparison of the two formats matches apples and oranges, 25 for discussion and lecture do different things. Lectures may be low on feedback value, but at their best they display three particular virtues.

For one, a well-conceived lecture is a reflection on the reading, not 26 simply a recapitulation. The speaker is responsible for providing context and perspective, for highlighting points of interest, for drawing out implications. I disagree with B. F. Skinner's opinion that what can be presented in a lecture is better read in a book. The sentences of a book are like the trees in a forest, where the novice woodsman can easily get lost. The lecturer, by summarizing, stressing, and suggesting, can throw a forest into topographical relief, indicating vividly some paths by which the forest can be traversed. Novices gain by exploring byways for themselves, but the confidence to go exploring is strengthened by the knowledge of where the main roads lie.

For another, a large part of learning is by emulation, modeling our- 27 selves after the style of mentors whose examples prove especially congenial and appropriate for our own. Good lecturers are patterns for how to formulate an issue and how to think through a complex sequence of connections. They demonstrate how to weigh evidence, consider alternatives, and build toward a conclusion. The best are characterized by cogency of thought, eloquence of expression, and civility of spirit. A lecturer enters into dialogue with his material and with himself. One of my most delightful memories is of a professor arguing with himself over how a line of Shakespeare ought to scan. His willingness to critique his own initial statement, his rehearsal of the arguments in favor of each reading, and his final revision of what he had said but moments before exemplify for me the active intelligence of a scholar who measures his own words and corrects himself as he finds himself wanting.

Finally, some lectures at their best are performances. A lecturer 28 controls the pace of an hour, effectively using modulation, gesture, and silences to provide a palpable emotional energy to the subject at hand. I remember Walter Jackson Bate intoning epigrams from Samuel Johnson's essays, his weathered face flinching with the agonies of earned experience that Johnson paid for his wisdom. I remember Alan Heimert in sonorous bass speaking of Puritan jeremiads, staring at the back of the room as Jonathan Edwards stared at the bellrope at the rear of the church while he preached "Sinners at the Hands of an Angry God." As teachers we would do well to remember that the lecture and sermon were once considered art forms, as sources of entertainment and edification as well as of learning.

The real question is not which mode is preferable, discussion or lec- 29
ture, but which is appropriate to the goals a teacher has set from session
to session, given the subject and the student, given the constraints of
time and class size. Both modes are valuable instruments of instruction
when competently handled.

Teachers are fellow-learners with their students.

Our students do teach us. I have received poetry analyses and short 30
stories at which I've marvelled, "I never thought of that," and "I could
never have written this!" I'm a better instructor, and I hope a better person, for the students whose lives touched mine. At the same time, I am
skeptical of a false egalitarianism that suggests teachers and students
meet on equal terms.

The structure of our educational institutions, for one, doesn't allow 31
for it. We are asked, in preparing a course, to specify what texts we will
assign, to submit a syllabus for the class to follow, to note the criteria by
which the students will be graded. There's considerable freedom for
variation from class session to session and from term to term, but the
fact remains that we set the agenda in advance of the first class and
grade our students—judge their achievements—after the last. Even
armed with teacher evaluation forms, our students have no comparable
check to the powers and prerogatives our educational system has
entrusted to us.

But what if the system were transformed? Would there be more 32
opportunity for students to build courses in conjunction with instructors? Of course, and such situations exist. At the same time, the relations
would still not be equal. We remain instructors, regardless of the system, because we have accumulated a body of knowledge and skills,
through time spent in a discipline if nothing else, of which students
want to avail themselves. We may suggest rather than demand, offer
alternatives rather than dictate direction, encourage rather than grade,
but the occasion by which we and students interact is still founded on
our being certified in a way in which they are not. To ignore this reality
is to be disingenuous.

The fellow-learner image grew up in opposition to that of the infal- 33
lible authority, the teacher who claimed to know everything. Students
were neophytes, receptacles into which learning was poured. The
teacher was uplifted, but only by denigrating the agency of the student.
By contrast, however, the fellow-learner image suggests to many students an irresponsible abrogation of authority, an evasion of the obligation to teach. As a student once complained about her professor, "That
he learns from me is fine, but I took his course to learn from him."

The middle way between aggrandized and abrogated authority may 34
be exemplified by the master-apprentice relation in the arts. A master
potter has much to teach students regarding materials and techniques.

Students, however, are not passive recipients of her knowledge, for they have to integrate what is taught with their own individual needs and interests. It is no great compliment to the potter if she simply produces clones of herself. There is great satisfaction, on the other hand, if a student develops successfully in ways very different from the master, or even surpasses the master in the use of particular materials and techniques. The expertise of the master is not denied; neither are the personal vision and potential of the student.

In none of this is there any presumption that student and teacher 35 are equal in what they bring to the potter's wheel or the classroom. Within a teaching situation, an instructor may learn from the students, may learn with the students, but not the same things or in the same way as the students. There isn't equality of input or of result. In cases when such equality exists, instruction, that is teaching and learning in any academic sense, does not.

Students need to acquire skills, not memorize information.

In opposing rote memorization, many thoughtful teachers have 36 stressed mastery of skills rather than the body of knowledge in a discipline. Students do need introduction to the processes whereby knowledge is found or created. The heart of literary education is not the survey of a canon, but learning how to read critically.

Chemistry is not a cookbook of formulae, but the complex skills of 37 observation, experimentation, and analysis. Knowledge is not static, and students must learn how to learn, to master ways of knowing and doing, in order to stay attuned to the shifts in knowledge and to use it effectively in the years after college. Nevertheless, this emphasis on skills can be overdone, for the division between the processes and products of knowing is finally artificial and untenable.

How one learns is inextricably bound up in what one knows. Skills 38 can't develop independently of an underlying body of knowledge. As a teaching assistant at UCLA, I once tried to make a point about the construction of an especially felicitous sentence. A student suddenly interjected, "Excuse me, Mr. Fong, that word you're using, what's a 'verb'? " The student had used verbs most of her life, but her capacity to examine language was hindered by her lack of knowledge about grammar. She could not understand what options existed for that sentence until she mastered the vocabulary necessary to speak about the act of writing.

Disciplines are founded on grammars, bodies of definitions, rules 39 and principles that form the conceptual bedrock of a subject. In literature, "Rabelaisian humor" and "Longinus' theory of the sublime"[2] are ways of characterizing the nature and effects of what we read. They are

---

[2] Specialized concepts in literary study. [Eds.]

not themselves techniques or processes, but they are conceptualizations that serve as categories to facilitate literary analysis. On a different level, the terms "classic" and "romantic" have multiple and even conflicting meanings; the complex ideas associated with them continue to change. Nonetheless, students of Western literature and intellectual history, of music and architecture, must have some understanding of their origins, and the ways in which these words have been used, in order to make sense of their studies. These terms are embedded in the very framework of the disciplines.

E. D. Hirch's recent *Cultural Literacy* is already notorious for its 40 appendix of what a literate American in 1987 should know. The list has been criticized, parodied, trivialized, and, most unfortunately, taken to represent the gist of the book. This fuss obscures a central point that Hirsch supports with extensive reference to current psychological research: Beyond the rudimentary deciphering of letters and words, the skill of reading must be embedded in knowledge of the subject matter. We don't merely read—we read about something. And we thus need frameworks of information about the subject at hand in order to understand and interpret what we read. In a similar vein, John McPeck has asserted that critical thinking depends on what one is thinking about. To be a critical thinker in chemistry means that one must have some knowledge of chemistry. To think critically about a poem means having some knowledge about the conventions of poems. For both men, the mature exercise of a skill depends on the critical mass of knowledge that underlies it. Pedagogically, this means that teaching a competency involves teaching knowledge.

Moreover, the provisional nature of current knowledge is no reason 41 not to teach it. Each academic discipline, with its characteristic vocabulary, methods, and body of learning, represents a community of knowledge. Students joining that community need to be oriented to the current topics of conversation. Some students will participate in changing the direction of the conversation, contributing new perspectives and insights to it; others will be content simply to listen. For all, however, current knowledge serves as both the point of initiation and a point of departure.

Proficiency and knowledge are intertwined. In the classroom, both 42 must be explicitly taught. Accumulating information doesn't guarantee that one can make use of it, but we also should not underestimate how much knowledge is necessary before one can competently exercise a skill.

Instruction must be geared to student backgrounds and aspirations.

When higher education was readily available only to the privileged 43 few, it might have been possible to describe a generic culture of college, a common body of socio-economic assumptions and standards of instruction. But America's commitment to educational equity means serving students who bring experiences and agendas that are more diverse than ever before. Instruction must be tailored to the needs and hopes of these students: A new clientele of working-class students, for example, may require new developmental programs to address gaps in their prior preparation. Nor can we cling to an unchanging culture of college: preachments about "knowledge for its own sake" ring hollow to students intent on acquiring professional credentials that will lead to better lives for themselves, their children, and their parents. Their concern about careers is not simply narrow vocationalism; it may also express filial love and discipline, values that demand respect, not denigration.

The response, again, must be to begin with students where they are. 44 Education means bridging the distance between the academy and their own worlds through advising and counseling, through co-curricular organizations and activities, and, above all, through programs of instruction that acknowledge the legitimacy of their backgrounds and aspirations. This is in healthy contrast to the days when the academy presumed that only its values had currency. Senior colleagues at Berea remember an earlier time when Bach precluded bluegrass, Appalachian culture was patronized as noble primitivism, and mountain accents were to be expunged because they sounded ignorant. Then it was the college that certified what "real life" was, and those elements of one's personal past that did not fit were best left behind.

Colleges, with good reason, are now more reluctant to act as 45 arbiters of what students ought to be. I have misgivings, however, that we now err in the extent to which we privilege the experiences and perspectives that students bring to college and consequently neglect the ways in which college can change students.

On the most basic level, take the way that we privilege vocational 46 goals. I don't dispute the need for professional programs in undergraduate education, but I believe it a mistake to assume that most incoming freshmen have chosen a major or future profession in any systematic or informed fashion. This mistake is compounded by vocational tracks that require students to declare a major during (or before!) their freshman year. I don't take lightly the conviction with which students tell me how they've wanted to be teachers or nurses or social workers all their lives, and how general education and distribution requirements only distract them from their chosen fields. My college roommates and I felt the same way: Let us get on with our pre-med and business and philosophy and religion and history majors. As it turned out, the history major is today a businessman, the religion major a lawyer, the philosophy major a medical doctor, the business major a minister, and the pre-med an English professor. We were forced by distribution requirements and encouraged by teachers to examine worlds outside our initial obsessions. Liberal education provided a context out of which we could make more informed choices. A college must hold to an appropriate balance between acknowledging the professional interests of their students and structuring a required range of general studies that promises some time to play with possibilities before the commitment is made to a particular discipline or profession.

Then there is the way in which ethnic and cultural backgrounds are 47 taken as givens. In respecting the origins of our students, we sometimes exempt their pasts from criticism or change. The log cabin up a hollow may testify to mountaineer self-sufficiency and independence, but the menfolk may also work a nearby mine whose runoff poisons their own drinking water. It does no good to romanticize the scene in the course of asserting the virtues of Appalachian culture. Culture is also not static, and ethnic realities are deeply affected by economic class and social mobility, two things closely tied to college education and the vocational possibilities that follow upon it. Yet in courses and co-curricular life, colleges promulgate images of Black, Hispanic, or Appalachian culture that validate students' pasts but limit visions of what students can and should do in their lives.

Berea was once accused of educating the mountains out of its stu- 48 dents; now we sometimes make students feel guilty because their horizons, widened by their education, seem incompatible with life in the mountains. One student I knew was torn between graduate study in philosophy and pursuing a teaching certificate so that he could be of service back home. He loved philosophy, but as he said, "Boyle County has little need for a metaphysician." I myself was the child of newly arrived immigrants whose world in America was Chinatown. My son was born in rural Kentucky to a professor and a lawyer. My mother, myself, and my son all have claim to being Chinese Americans, but each in very different ways. Neither Chinese nor American culture can mean the same thing to all three of us.

So instruction must take the backgrounds and aspirations of stu- 49 dents into account, but education must also move students beyond their backgrounds and change their aspirations. What students learn will transform them, sometimes in ways distressing to their families and themselves. The college can offer students new experiences and possibilities that bear no resemblance to anything they had before known. Prior experience may be of no help. College becomes a foreign country, and they are strangers in a strange land. Instructors can bridge cultures, but it would be a disservice to domesticate the strangeness, like tour guides scrounging for hamburgers in Paris for homesick Americans.

Teachers begin with what students bring to college, but our instruc- 50 tion cannot be limited to connecting with those prior experiences. Educating into possibility means challenging students to lose themselves in the unknown and to make the new and strange familiar by living with them over time.

In qualifying these six commonplaces, I realize how difficult it is for 51 any maxim to encompass teaching in all its diversity. Certainly the inverse of each of these commonplaces would be no more true, or false, than the commonplaces themselves. Teachers must mediate the dictates of laudable but divergent general principles in pursuit of an imaginative integration involving a thousand particulars of culture, student, subject, and instructor. Teaching is thus idiosyncratic, resistant to generalization.

I have benefitted most from opportunities to hear individual 52 instructors discourse in detail about their work, where I could analogize from their experience to mine. Much of my own discussion here has necessarily been anecdotal, its lessons shaped by my own work in a particular discipline at a particular college. We do not teach in the abstract: Commonplaces such as those I've discussed cannot substitute for solutions thoughtfully tailored to the particular pedagogical situations in which we find ourselves.

Responding to Reading

1. What is a *commonplace*? How do you think commonplaces become accepted as fact? List several commonplaces about teaching that Fong does not discuss in his essay.
2. In paragraph 49, Fong says that although education must consider students' cultural backgrounds, it must move them "beyond their backgrounds and change their aspirations." What does Fong mean by this statement? In what way has your education changed your aspirations?
3. Let's see how innovative Mark Edmundson's below and Neil Postman's (p. 139) ideas actually are. Using Fong's list of educational commonplaces as your guide, read Edmundson's and Postman's essays and identify as many commonplaces as you can. After you have finished, draw your own conclusions about the originality of Edmundson's and Postman's ideas.

On the Uses of a Liberal Education:
Lite Entertainment
for Bored College Students

Mark Edmundson

Mark Edmundson (1952–) grew up in Medford, Massachusetts. He received his B.A. from Bennington College and his Ph.D from Yale, and he currently teaches at the University of Virginia. He is also a contributing editor for Harper's *magazine. Edmundson has written on Freud and on literary theory, and his works include* Literature against Philosophy:

A Defense of Poetry *(1995) and* Nightmare on Main Street: Angels, Sadomasochism, and the Culture of Gothic *(1997), a study of Gothic imagery in the 1990s. The following essay, which he says he wrote to "cause trouble of a useful sort," was published in* Harper's *in 1997. In it, Edmundson criticizes the "consumer culture" of higher education.*

Today is evaluation day in my Freud[1] class, and everything has changed. The class meets twice a week, late in the afternoon, and the clientele, about fifty undergraduates, tends to drag in and slump, looking disconsolate and a little lost, waiting for a jump start. To get the discussion moving, they usually require a joke, an anecdote, an off-the-wall question—When you were a kid, were your Halloween getups ego costumes, id costumes, or superego costumes? That sort of thing. But today, as soon as I flourish the forms, a buzz rises in the room. Today they write their assessments of the course, their assessments of *me*, and they are without a doubt wide-awake. "What is your evaluation of the instructor?" asks question number eight, entreating them to circle a number between five (excellent) and one (poor, poor). Whatever interpretive subtlety they've acquired during the term is now out the window. Edmundson: one to five, stand and shoot.

And they do. As I retreat through the door—I never stay around for this phase of the ritual—I look over my shoulder and see them toiling away like the devil's auditors. They're pitched into high writing gear, even the ones who struggle to squeeze out their journal entries word by word, stoked on a procedure they have by now supremely mastered. They're playing the informed consumer, letting the provider know where he's come through and where he's not quite up to snuff.

But why am I so distressed, bolting like a refugee out of my own classroom, where I usually hold easy sway? Chances are the evaluations will be much like what they've been in the past—they'll be just fine. It's likely that I'll be commended for being "interesting" (and I am commended, many times over), that I'll be cited for my relaxed and tolerant ways (that happens, too), that my sense of humor and capacity to connect the arcana of the subject matter with current culture will come in for some praise (yup). I've been hassled this term, finishing a manuscript, and so haven't given their journals the attention I should have, and for that I'm called—quite civilly, though—to account. Overall, I get off pretty well.

Yet I have to admit that I do not much like the image of myself that emerges from these forms, the image of knowledgeable, humorous detachment and bland tolerance. I do not like the forms themselves, with their number ratings, reminiscent of the sheets circulated after the

---

[1] Austrian psychiatrist Sigmund Freud (1856–1939); he posited that the human personality was divided into the ego, the id, and the superego. [Eds.]

TV pilot has just played to its sample audience in Burbank. Most of all I dislike the attitude of calm consumer expertise that pervades the responses. I'm disturbed by the serene belief that my function—and, more important, Freud's, or Shakespeare's, or Blake's[2] is to divert, entertain, and interest. Observes one respondent, not at all unrepresentative: "Edmundson has done a fantastic job of presenting this difficult, important & controversial material in an enjoyable and approachable way."

Thanks but no thanks. I don't teach to amuse, to divert, or even, for   5 that matter, to be merely interesting. When someone says she "enjoyed" the course—and that word crops up again and again in my evaluations—somewhere at the edge of my immediate complacency I feel encroaching self-dislike. That is not at all what I had in mind. The off-the-wall questions and the sidebar jokes are meant as lead-ins to stronger stuff—in the case of the Freud course, to a complexly tragic view of life. But the affability and the one-liners often seem to be all that land with the students; their journals and evaluations leave me little doubt.

I want some of them to say that they've been changed by the course.   6 I want them to measure themselves against what they've read. It's said that some time ago a Columbia University instructor used to issue a harsh two-part question. One: What book did you most dislike in the course? Two: What intellectual or characterological flaws in you does that dislike point to? The hand that framed that question was surely heavy. But at least it compels one to see intellectual work as a confrontation between two people, student and author, where the stakes matter. Those Columbia students were being asked to relate the quality of an *encounter*, not rate the action as though it had unfolded on the big screen.

Why are my students describing the Oedipus complex and the   7 death drive[3] as being interesting and enjoyable to contemplate? And why am I coming across as an urbane, mildly ironic, endlessly affable guide to this intellectual territory, operating without intensity, generous, funny, and loose?

Because that's what works. On evaluation day, I reap the rewards of   8 my partial compliance with the culture of my students and, too, with the culture of the university as it now operates. It's a culture that's gotten little exploration. Current critics tend to think that liberal-arts education is in crisis because universities have been invaded by professors with peculiar ideas: deconstruction, Lacanianism, feminism, queer theory. They believe that genius and tradition are out and that P.C., multiculturalism, and identity politics are in because of an invasion by tribes of tenured radicals, the late millennial equivalents of the Visigoth hordes that cracked Rome's walls.

---

[2] English poet William Blake (1757–1827). [Eds.]
[3] Important Freudian concepts. [Eds.]

But mulling over my evaluations and then trying to take a hard, 9
extended look at campus life both here at the University of Virginia and
around the country eventually led me to some different conclusions. To
me, liberal-arts education is as ineffective as it is now not chiefly
because there are a lot of strange theories in the air. (Used well, those
theories *can* be illuminating.) Rather, it's that university culture, like
American culture writ large, is, to put it crudely, ever more devoted to
consumption and entertainment, to the using and using up of goods
and images. For someone growing up in America now, there are few
available alternatives to the cool consumer worldview. My students
didn't ask for that view, much less create it, but they bring a consumer
weltanschauung[4] to school, where it exerts a powerful, and largely
unacknowledged, influence. If we want to understand current universities, with their multiple woes, we might try leaving the realms of expert
debate and fine ideas and turning to the classrooms and campuses,
where a new kind of weather is gathering.

From time to time I bump into a colleague in the corridor and we 10
have what I've come to think of as a Joon Lee fest. Joon Lee is one of the
best students I've taught. He's endlessly curious, has read a small
library's worth, seen every movie, and knows all about showbiz and
entertainment. For a class of mine he wrote an essay using Nietzsche's
Apollo and Dionysus[5] to analyze the pop group The Supremes. A trite,
cultural-studies bonbon? Not at all. He said striking things about conceptions of race in America and about how they shape our ideas of
beauty. When I talk with one of his other teachers, we run on about the
general splendors of his work and presence. But what inevitably follows
a JL fest is a mournful reprise about the divide that separates him and a
few other remarkable students from their contemporaries. It's not that
some aren't nearly as bright—in terms of intellectual ability, my students are all that I could ask for. Instead, it's that Joon Lee has decided
to follow his interests and let them make him into a singular and rather
eccentric man; in his charming way, he doesn't mind being at odds with
most anyone.

It's his capacity for enthusiasm that sets Joon apart from what I've 11
come to think of as the reigning generational style. Whether the students are sorority/fraternity types, grunge aficionados, piercer/tattoo-
ers, black or white, rich or middle class (alas, I teach almost no students
from truly poor backgrounds), they are, nearly across the board, very,
very self-contained. On good days they display a light, appealing glow;

---

[4] German term referring to one's conception of the world. [Eds.]

[5] German philosopher Friedrich Nietzsche (1844–1900) used the opposing images of the Greek gods
Apollo and Dionysus to classify artistic creators. [Eds.]

on bad days, shuffling disgruntlement. But there's little fire, little passion to be found.

This point came home to me a few weeks ago when I was wandering across the university grounds. There, beneath a classically cast portico, were two students, male and female, having a rip-roaring argument. They were incensed, bellowing at each other, headstrong, confident, and wild. It struck me how rarely I see this kind of full-out feeling in students anymore. Strong emotional display is forbidden. When conflicts arise, it's generally understood that one of the parties will say something sarcastically propitiating ("whatever" often does it) and slouch away.

How did my students reach this peculiar state in which all passion seems to be spent? I think that many of them have imbibed their sense of self from consumer culture in general and from the tube in particular. They're the progeny of 100 cable channels and omnipresent Blockbuster outlets. TV, Marshall McLuhan famously said, is a cool medium. Those who play best on it are low key and nonassertive; they blend in. Enthusiasm, à la Joon Lee, quickly looks absurd. The form of character that's most appealing on TV is calmly self-interested though never greedy, attuned to the conventions, and ironic, ludicrous timing is preferred to sudden self-assertion. The TV medium is inhospitable to inspiration, improvisation, failures, slipups. All must run perfectly.

Naturally, a cool youth culture is a marketing bonanza for producers of the right products, who do all they can to enlarge that culture and keep it grinding. The Internet, TV, and magazines now teem with what I call persona ads, ads for Nikes and Reeboks and Jeeps and Blazers that don't so much endorse the capacities of the product per se as show you what sort of person you will be once you've acquired it. The Jeep ad that features hip, outdoorsy kids whipping a Frisbee from mountaintop to mountaintop isn't so much about what Jeeps can do as it is about the kind of people who own them. Buy a Jeep and be one with them. The ad is of little consequence in itself, but expand its message exponentially and you have the central thrust of current consumer culture—buy in order to be.

Most of my students seem desperate to blend in, to look right, not to make a spectacle of themselves. (Do I have to tell you that those two students having the argument under the portico turned out to be acting in a role-playing game?) The specter of the uncool creates a subtle tyranny. It's apparently an easy standard to subscribe to, this Letterman-like, Tarantino-like cool, but once committed to it, you discover that matters are rather different. You're inhibited, except on ordained occasions, from showing emotion, stifled from trying to achieve anything original. You're made to feel that even the slightest departure from the reigning code will get you genially ostracized. This is a culture tensely committed to a laid-back norm.

Am I coming off like something of a crank here? Maybe. Oscar 16
Wilde,[6] who is almost never wrong, suggested that it is perilous to
promiscuously contradict people who are much younger than yourself.
Point taken. But one of the lessons that consumer hype tries to insinu-
ate is that we must never rebel against the new, never even question it.
If it's new—a new need, a new product, a new show, a new style, a new
generation—it must be good. So maybe, even at the risk of winning the
withered, brown laurels of crankdom, it pays to resist newness-worship
and cast a colder eye.

Praise for my students? I have some of that too. What my students 17
are, at their best, is decent. They are potent believers in equality. They
help out at the soup kitchen and volunteer to tutor poor kids to get a
stripe on their résumés, sure. But they also want other people to have a
fair shot. And in their commitment to fairness they are discerning; there
you see them at their intellectual best. If I were on trial and innocent, I'd
want them on the jury.

What they will not generally do, though, is indict the current sys- 18
tem. They won't talk about how the exigencies of capitalism lead to a
reserve army of the unemployed and nearly inevitable misery. That
would be getting too loud, too brash. For the pervading view is the cool
consumer perspective, where passion and strong admiration are forbidden. "To stand in awe of nothing, Numicus, is perhaps the one and only
thing that can make a man happy and keep him so," says Horace[7] in the
Epistles, and I fear that his lines ought to hang as a motto over the university in this era of high consumer capitalism.

It's easy to mount one's high horse and blame the students for this 19
state of affairs. But they didn't create the present culture of consumption. (It was largely my own generation, that of the Sixties, that let the
counterculture search for pleasure devolve into a quest for commodities.) And they weren't the ones responsible, when they were six and
seven and eight years old, for unplugging the TV set from time to time
or for hauling off and kicking a hole through it. It's my generation of
parents who sheltered these students, kept them away from the hard
knocks of everyday life, making them cautious and overfragile, who
demanded that their teachers, from grade school on, flatter them endlessly so that the kids are shocked if their college profs don't reflexively
suck up to them.

Of course, the current generational style isn't simply derived from 20
culture and environment. It's also about dollars. Students worry that
taking too many chances with their educations will sabotage their
future prospects. They're aware of the fact that a drop that looks more

---

6 Oscar Wilde (1854–1900) was an Irish writer known for his intellectual wit and clever way of
phrasing human truths. [Eds.]
7 Ancient Roman poet. [Eds.]

and more like one wall of the Grand Canyon separates the top economic tenth from the rest of the population. There's a sentiment currently abroad that if you step aside for a moment, to write, to travel, to fall too hard in love, you might lose position permanently. We may be on a conveyor belt, but it's worse down there on the filth-strewn floor. So don't sound off, don't blow your chance.

But wait. I teach at the famously conservative University of Virginia.   21
Can I extend my view from Charlottesville to encompass the whole country, a whole generation of college students? I can only say that I hear comparable stories about classroom life from colleagues everywhere in America. When I visit other schools to lecture, I see a similar scene unfolding. There are, of course, terrific students everywhere. And they're all the better for the way they've had to strive against the existing conformity. At some of the small liberal-arts colleges, the tradition of strong engagement persists. But overall, the students strike me as being sweet and sad, hovering in a nearly suspended animation.

Too often now the pedagogical challenge is to make a lot from a lit-   22
tle. Teaching Wordsworth's[8] "Tintern Abbey," you ask for comments. No one responds. So you call on Stephen. Stephen: "The sound, this poem really flows." You: "Stephen seems interested in the music of the poem. We might extend his comment to ask if the poem's music coheres with its argument. Are they consistent? Or is there an emotional pain submerged here that's contrary to the poem's appealing melody?" All right, it's not usually that bad. But close. One friend describes it as rebound teaching: they proffer a weightless comment, you hit it back for all you're worth, then it comes dribbling out again. Occasionally a professor will try to explain away this intellectual timidity by describing the students as perpetrators of postmodern irony, a highly sophisticated mode. Everything's a slick counterfeit, a simulacrum, so by no means should any phenomenon be taken seriously. But the students don't have the urbane, Oscar Wilde–type demeanor that should go with this view. Oscar was cheerful, funny, confident, strange. (Wilde, mortally ill, living in a Paris flophouse: "My wallpaper and I are fighting a duel to the death. One or the other of us has to go.") This generation's style is considerate, easy to please, and a touch depressed.

Granted, you might say, the kids come to school immersed in a con-   23
sumer mentality—they're good Americans, after all—but then the university and the professors do everything in their power to fight that dreary mind-set in the interest of higher ideals, right? So it should be. But let us look at what is actually coming to pass.

Over the past few years, the physical layout of my university has   24
been changing. To put it a little indecorously, the place is looking more

---

[8] William Wordsworth (1770–1850), English romantic poet. [Eds.]

and more like a retirement spread for the young. Our funds go to construction, into new dorms, into renovating the student union. We have a new aquatics center and ever-improving gyms, stocked with StairMasters and Nautilus machines. Engraved on the wall in the gleaming aquatics building is a line by our founder, Thomas Jefferson, declaring that everyone ought to get about two hours' exercise a day. Clearly even the author of the Declaration of Independence endorses the turning of his university into a sports-and-fitness emporium.

But such improvements shouldn't be surprising. Universities need 25 to attract the best (that is, the smartest *and* the richest) students in order to survive in an ever more competitive market. Schools want kids whose parents can pay the full freight, not the ones who need scholarships or want to bargain down the tuition costs. If the marketing surveys say that the kids require sports centers, then, trustees willing, they shall have them. In fact, as I began looking around, I came to see that more and more of what's going on in the university is customer driven. The consumer pressures that beset me on evaluation day are only a part of an overall trend.

From the start, the contemporary university's relationship with 26 students has a solicitous, nearly servile tone. As soon as someone enters his junior year in high school, and especially if he's living in a prosperous zip code, the informational material—the advertising— comes flooding in. Pictures, testimonials, videocassettes, and CD ROMs (some bidden, some not) arrive at the door from colleges across the country, all trying to capture the student and his tuition cash. The freshman-to-be sees photos of well-appointed dorm rooms; of elaborate phys-ed facilities; of fine dining rooms; of expertly kept sports fields; of orchestras and drama troupes; of students working alone (no overbearing grown-ups in range), peering with high seriousness into computers and microscopes; or of students arrayed outdoors in attractive conversational garlands.

Occasionally—but only occasionally, for we usually photograph 27 rather badly; in appearance we tend at best to be styleless—there's a professor teaching a class. (The college catalogues I received, by my request only, in the late Sixties were austere affairs full of professors' credentials and course descriptions; it was clear on whose terms the enterprise was going to unfold.) A college financial officer recently put matters to me in concise, if slightly melodramatic, terms: "Colleges don't have admissions offices anymore, they have marketing departments." Is it surprising that someone who has been approached with photos and tapes, bells and whistles, might come in thinking that the Freud and Shakespeare she had signed up to study were also going to be agreeable treats?

How did we reach this point? In part the answer is a matter of demo- 28 graphics and (surprise) of money. Aided by the G.I. bill, the college-going population in America dramatically increased after the Second

World War. Then came the baby boomers, and to accommodate them, schools continued to grow. Universities expand easily enough, but with tenure locking faculty in for lifetime jobs, and with the general reluctance of administrators to eliminate their own slots, it's not easy for a university to contract. So after the baby boomers had passed through—like a fat meal digested by a boa constrictor—the colleges turned to energetic promotional strategies to fill the empty chairs. And suddenly college became a buyer's market. What students and their parents wanted had to be taken more and more into account. That usually meant creating more comfortable, less challenging environments, places where almost no one failed, everything was enjoyable, and everyone was nice.

Just as universities must compete with one another for students, so must the individual departments. At a time of rank economic anxiety, the English and history majors have to contend for students against the more success-insuring branches, such as the sciences and the commerce school. In 1968, more than 21 percent of all the bachelor's degrees conferred in America were in the humanities; by 1993, that number had fallen to about 13 percent. The humanities now must struggle to attract students, many of whose parents devoutly wish they would study something else. 29

One of the ways we've tried to stay attractive is by loosening up. We grade much more softly than our colleagues in science. In English, we don't give many Ds, or Cs for that matter. (The rigors of Chem 101 create almost as many English majors per year as do the splendors of Shakespeare.) A professor at Stanford recently explained grade inflation in the humanities by observing that the undergraduates were getting smarter every year; the higher grades simply recorded how much better they were than their predecessors. Sure. 30

Along with softening the grades, many humanities departments have relaxed major requirements. There are some good reasons for introducing more choice into curricula and requiring fewer standard courses. But the move, like many others in the university now, jibes with a tendency to serve—and not challenge—the students. Students can also float in and out of classes during the first two weeks of each term without making any commitment. The common name for this time span—shopping period—speaks volumes about the consumer mentality that's now in play. Usually, too, the kids can drop courses up until the last month with only an innocuous "W" on their transcripts. Does a course look too challenging? No problem. Take it pass-fail. A happy consumer is, by definition, one with multiple options, one who can always have what he wants. And since a course is something the students and their parents have bought and paid for, why can't they do with it pretty much as they please? 31

A sure result of the university's widening elective leeway is to give students more power over their teachers. Those who don't like you can 32 simply avoid you. If the clientele dislikes you en masse, you can be left without students, period. My first term teaching I walked into my introduction to poetry course and found it inhabited by one student, the gloriously named Bambi Lynn Dean. Bambi and I chatted amiably awhile, but for all that she and the pleasure of her name could offer, I was fast on the way to meltdown. It was all a mistake, luckily, a problem with the scheduling book. Everyone was waiting for me next door. But in a dozen years of teaching I haven't forgotten that feeling of being ignominiously marooned. For it happens to others, and not always because of scheduling glitches. I've seen older colleagues go through hot embarrassment at not having enough students sign up for their courses: they graded too hard, demanded too much, had beliefs too far out of keeping with the existing disposition. It takes only a few such instances to draw other members of the professoriat further into line.

And if what's called tenure reform—which generally just means the 33 abolition of tenure—is broadly enacted, professors will be yet more vulnerable to the whims of their customer-students. Teach what pulls the kids in, or walk. What about entire departments that don't deliver? If the kids say no to Latin and Greek, is it time to dissolve classics? Such questions are being entertained more and more seriously by university administrators.

How does one prosper with the present clientele? Many of the most 34 successful professors now are the ones who have "decentered" their classrooms. There's a new emphasis on group projects and on computer-generated exchanges among the students. What they seem to want most is to talk to one another. A classroom now is frequently an "environment," a place highly conducive to the exchange of existing ideas, the students' ideas. Listening to one another, students sometimes change their opinions. But what they generally can't do is acquire a new vocabulary, a new perspective, that will cast issues in a fresh light.

The Socratic method[9]—the animated, sometimes impolite give-and- 35 take between student and teacher—seems too jagged for current sensibilities. Students frequently come to my office to tell me how intimidated they feel in class; the thought of being embarrassed in front of the group fills them with dread. I remember a student telling me how humiliating it was to be corrected by the teacher, by me. So I asked the logical question: "Should I let a major factual error go by so as to save discomfort?" The student—a good student, smart and earnest—said that was a tough question. He'd need to think about it.

Disturbing? Sure. But I wonder, are we really getting students ready 36 for Socratic exchange with professors when we push them off into vast lecture rooms, two and three hundred to a class, sometimes face them

---

[9] Based on the dialogues written by the ancient Greek philosopher Plato, the Socratic method involves rigorous questioning by both sides in a philosophical debate. [Eds.]

with only grad students until their third year, and signal in our myriad professorial ways that we often have much better things to do than sit in our offices and talk with them? How bad will the student-faculty ratios have to become, how teeming the lecture courses, before we hear students righteously complaining, as they did thirty years ago, about the impersonality of their schools, about their decline into knowledge factories? "This is a firm," said Mario Savio at Berkeley during the Free Speech protests of the Sixties, "and if the Board of Regents are the board of directors, . . . then . . . the faculty are a bunch of employees and we're the raw material. But we're a bunch of raw material that don't mean . . . to be made into any product."

Teachers who really do confront students, who provide significant   37 challenges to what they believe, can be very successful, granted. But sometimes such professors generate more than a little trouble for themselves. A controversial teacher can send students hurrying to the deans and the counselors, claiming to have been offended ("Offensive" is the preferred term of repugnance today, just as "enjoyable" is the summit of praise.) Colleges have brought in hordes of counselors and deans to make sure that everything is smooth, serene, unflustered, that everyone has a good time. To the counselor, to the dean, and to the university legal squad, that which is normal, healthy, and prudent is best.

An air of caution and deference is everywhere. When my students   38 come to talk with me in my office, they often exhibit a Franciscan humility.[10] "Do you have a moment?" "I know you're busy. I won't take up much of your time." Their presences tend to be very light; they almost never change the temperature of the room. The dress is nondescript: clothes are in earth tones; shoes are practical—cross-trainers, hiking boots, work shoes, Dr. Martens, with now and then a stylish pair of raised-sole boots on one of the young women. Many, male and female both, peep from beneath the bills of monogrammed baseball caps. Quite a few wear sports, or even corporate, logos, sometimes on one piece of clothing but occasionally (and disconcertingly) on more. The walk is slow, speech is careful, sweet, a bit weary, and without strong inflection. (After the first lively week of the term, most seem far in debt to sleep.) They are almost unfailingly polite. They don't want to offend me; I could hurt them, savage their grades.

Naturally, there are exceptions, kids I chat animatedly with, who   39 offer a joke, or go on about this or that new CD (almost never a book, no). But most of the traffic is genially sleepwalking. I have to admit that I'm a touch wary, too. I tend to hold back. An unguarded remark, a joke that's taken to be off-color, or simply an uncomprehended comment

---

[10] That is, humility worthy of St. Francis, the 13th-century founder of the Franciscan order of priests, who was devoted to absolute poverty. [Eds.]

can lead to difficulties. I keep it literal. They scare me a little, these kind and melancholy students, who themselves seem rather frightened of their own lives.

Before they arrive, we ply the students with luscious ads, guaran- 40 teeing them a cross between summer camp and lotusland. When they get here, flattery and nonstop entertainment are available, if that's what they want. And when they leave? How do we send our students out into the world? More and more, our administrators call the booking agents and line up one or another celebrity to usher the graduates into the millennium. This past spring, Kermit the Frog won himself an honorary degree at Southampton College on Long Island; Bruce Willis and Yogi Berra took credentials away at Montclair State; Arnold Schwarzenegger scored at the University of Wisconsin–Superior. At Wellesley, Oprah Winfrey gave the commencement address. (*Wellesley*—one of the most rigorous academic colleges in the nation.) At the University of Vermont, Whoopi Goldberg laid down the word. But why should a worthy administrator contract the likes of Susan Sontag, Christopher Hitchens, or Robert Hughes[11]—someone who might actually say something, something disturbing, something "offensive"—when he can get what the parents and kids apparently want and what the newspapers will softly commend—more lite entertainment, more TV?

Is it a surprise, then, that this generation of students—steeped in 41 consumer culture before going off to school, treated as potent customers by the university well before their date of arrival, then pandered to from day one until the morning of the final kiss-off from Kermit or one of his kin—are inclined to see the books they read as a string of entertainments to be placidly enjoyed or languidly cast down? Given the way universities are now administered (which is more and more to say, given the way that they are currently marketed), is it a shock that the kids don't come to school hot to learn, unable to bear their own ignorance? For some measure of self-dislike, or self-discontent—which is much different than simple depression—seems to me to be a prerequisite for getting an education that matters. My students, alas, usually lack the confidence to acknowledge what would be their most precious asset for learning: their ignorance.

Not long ago, I asked my Freud class a question that, however 42 hoary, never fails to solicit intriguing responses: Who are your heroes? Whom do you admire? After one remarkable answer, featuring T. S. Eliot[12] as hero, a series of generic replies rolled in, one gray wave after the next: my father, my best friend, a doctor who lives in our town, my

---

[11] Prominent contemporary intellectuals. [Eds.]

[12] American-British poet and critic T. S. Eliot (1888–1965) had a profound influence on 20th-century literature. [Eds.]

high school history teacher. Virtually all the heroes were people my students had known personally, people who had done something local, specific, and practical, and had done it for them. They were good people, unselfish people, these heroes, but most of all they were people who had delivered the goods.

My students' answers didn't exhibit any philosophical resistance to 43 the idea of greatness. It's not that they had been primed by their professors with complex arguments to combat genius. For the truth is that these students don't need debunking theories. Long before college, skepticism became their habitual mode. They are the progeny of Bart Simpson and David Letterman, and the hyper-cool ethos of the box. It's inane to say that theorizing professors have created them, as many conservative critics like to do. Rather, they have substantially created a university environment in which facile skepticism can thrive without being substantially contested.

Skeptical approaches have *potential* value. If you have no all- 44 encompassing religious faith, no faith in historical destiny, the future of the West, or anything comparably grand, you need to acquire your vision of the world somewhere. If it's from literature, then the various visions literature offers have to be inquired into skeptically. Surely it matters that women are denigrated in Milton and in Pope,[13] that some novelistic voices assume an overbearing godlike authority, that the poor are, in this or that writer, inevitably cast as clowns. You can't buy all of literature wholesale if it's going to help draw your patterns of belief.

But demystifying theories are now overused, applied mechanically. 45 It's all logocentrism, patriarchy, ideology. And in this the student environment—laid-back, skeptical, knowing—is, I believe, central. Full-out debunking is what plays with this clientele. Some have been doing it nearly as long as, if more crudely than, their deconstructionist teachers. In the context of the contemporary university, and cool consumer culture, a useful intellectual skepticism has become exaggerated into a fundamentalist caricature of itself. The teachers have buckled to their students' views.

At its best, multiculturalism can be attractive as well-deployed 46 theory. What could be more valuable than encountering the best work of far-flung cultures and becoming a citizen of the world? But in the current consumer environment, where flattery plays so well, the urge to encounter the other can devolve into the urge to find others who embody and celebrate the right ethnic origins. So we put aside the African novelist Chinua Achebe's abrasive, troubling *Things Fall Apart* and gravitate toward hymns on Africa, cradle of all civilizations.

What about the phenomenon called political correctness? Raising 47 the standard of civility and tolerance in the university has been—who

---

[13] British poets John Milton (1608–1674) and Alexander Pope (1688–1744). [Eds.]

can deny it?—a very good thing. Yet this admirable impulse has expanded to the point where one is enjoined to speak well—and only well—of women, blacks, gays, the disabled, in fact of virtually everyone. And we can owe this expansion in many ways to the student culture. Students now do not wish to be criticized, not in any form. (The culture of consumption never criticizes them, at least not *overtly*.) In the current university, the movement for urbane tolerance has devolved into an imperative against critical reaction, turning much of the intellectual life into a dreary Sargasso Sea. At a certain point, professors stopped being usefully sensitive and became more like careful retailers who have it as a cardinal point of doctrine never to piss the customers off.

To some professors, the solution lies in the movement called cul- 48 tural studies. What students need, they believe, is to form a critical perspective on pop culture. It's a fine idea, no doubt. Students should be able to run a critical commentary against the stream of consumer stimulations in which they're immersed. But cultural-studies programs rarely work, because no matter what you propose by way of analysis, things tend to bolt downhill toward an uncritical discussion of students' tastes, into what they like and don't like. If you want to do a Frankfurt School–style analysis of *Braveheart,* you can be pretty sure that by mid-class Adorno and Horkheimer[14] will be consigned to the junk heap of history and you'll be collectively weighing the charms of Mel Gibson. One sometimes wonders if cultural studies hasn't prospered because, under the guise of serious intellectual analysis, it gives the customers what they most want—easy pleasure, more TV. Cultural studies becomes nothing better than what its detractors claim it is—Madonna studies—when students kick loose from the critical perspective and groove to the product, and that, in my experience teaching film and pop culture, happens plenty.

On the issue of genius, as on multiculturalism and political correct- 49 ness, we professors of the humanities have, I think, also failed to press back against our students' consumer tastes. Here we tend to nurse a pair of—to put it charitably—disparate views. In one mode, we're inclined to a programmatic debunking criticism. We call the concept of genius into question. But in our professional lives per se, we aren't usually disposed against the idea of distinguished achievement. We argue animatedly about the caliber of potential colleagues. We support a star system, in which some professors are far better paid, teach less, and under better conditions than the rest. In our own profession we are creating a system that is the mirror image of the one we're dismantling in the curriculum. Ask a professor what she thinks of the work of Stephen Greenblatt, a

---

[14] The Frankfurt School refers to a group of German philosophers who developed a Marxist-influenced method of "critical studies." Theodor Adorno (1903–1969) and Max Horkheimer (1895–1973) were among its influential members. [Eds.]

leading critic of Shakespeare, and you'll hear it for an hour. Ask her what her views are on Shakespeare's genius and she's likely to begin questioning the term along with the whole "discourse of evaluation." This dual sensibility may be intellectually incoherent. But in its awareness of what plays with students, it's conducive to good classroom evaluations and, in its awareness of where and how the professional bread is buttered, to self-advancement as well.

My overall point is this: It's not that a leftwing professorial coup has 50 taken over the university. It's that at American universities, left-liberal politics have collided with the ethos of consumerism. The consumer ethos is winning.

Then how do those who at least occasionally promote genius and 51 high literary ideals look to current students? How do we appear, those of us who take teaching to be something of a performance art and who imagine that if you give yourself over completely to your subject you'll be rewarded with insight beyond what you individually command?

I'm reminded of an old piece of newsreel footage I saw once. The 52 speaker (perhaps it was Lenin, maybe Trotsky)[15] was haranguing a large crowd. He was expostulating, arm waving, carrying on. Whether it was flawed technology or the man himself, I'm not sure, but the orator looked like an intricate mechanical device that had sprung into fast-forward. To my students, who mistrust enthusiasm in every form, that's me when I start riffing about Freud or Blake. But more and more, as my evaluations showed, I've been replacing enthusiasm and intellectual animation with stand-up routines, keeping it all at arm's length, praising under the cover of irony.

It's too bad that the idea of genius has been denigrated so far, 53 because it actually offers a live alternative to the demoralizing culture of hip in which most of my students are mired. By embracing the works and lives of extraordinary people, you can adapt new ideals to revise those that came courtesy of your parents, your neighborhood, your clan—or the tube. The aim of a good liberal-arts education was once, to adapt an observation by the scholar Walter Jackson Bate, to see that "we need not be the passive victims of what we deterministically call 'circumstances' (social, cultural, or reductively psychological-personal), but that by linking ourselves through what Keats calls an 'immortal free-masonry' with the great we can become freer—freer to be ourselves, to be what we most want and value."

But genius isn't just a personal standard; genius can also have polit- 54 ical effect. To me, one of the best things about democratic thinking is the

---

[15] Vladimir Lenin (1870–1924) and Leon Trotsky (1879–1940) were leaders of the 1917 Russian revolution; Lenin was the first leader of the USSR. [Eds.]

conviction that genius can spring up anywhere. Walt Whitman[16] is born into the working class and thirty-six years later we have a poetic image of America that gives a passionate dimension to the legalistic brilliance of the Constitution. A democracy needs to constantly develop, and to do so it requires the most powerful visionary minds to interpret the present and to propose possible shapes for the future. By continuing to notice and praise genius, we create a culture in which the kind of poetic gamble that Whitman made—a gamble in which failure would have entailed rank humiliation, depression, maybe suicide—still takes place. By rebelling against established ways of seeing and saying things, genius helps us to apprehend how malleable the present is and how promising and fraught with danger is the future. If we teachers do not endorse genius and self-overcoming, can we be surprised when our students find their ideal images in TV's latest persona ads?

A world uninterested in genius is a despondent place, whose sad   55
denizens drift from coffee bar to Prozac dispensary, unfired by ideals, by the glowing image of the self that one might become. As Northrop Frye says in a beautiful and now dramatically unfashionable sentence "The artist who uses the same energy and genius that Homer and Isaiah[17] had will find that he not only lives in the same palace of art as Homer and Isaiah, but lives in it at the same time." We ought not to deny the existence of such a place simply because we, or those we care for, find the demands it makes intimidating, the rent too high.

What happens if we keep trudging along this bleak course? What   56
happens if our most intelligent students never learn to strive to overcome what they are? What if genius, and the imitation of genius, become silly, outmoded ideas? What you're likely to get are more and more one-dimensional men and women. These will be people who live for easy pleasures, for comfort and prosperity, who think of money first, then second, and third, who hug the status quo; people who believe in God as a sort of insurance policy (cover your bets); people who are never surprised. They will be people so pleased with themselves (when they're not in despair of the general pointlessness of their lives) that they cannot imagine humanity could do better. They'll think it their highest duty to clone themselves as frequently as possible. They'll claim to be happy, and they'll live a long time.

It is probably time now to offer a spate of inspiring solutions. Here   57
ought to come a list of reforms, with due notations about a core curriculum and various requirements. What the traditionalists who offer

---

[16] American poet Walt Whitman (1819–1892), whose *Leaves of Grass* sang the praises of democracy and the universal spirit. See "When I Heard the Learn'd Astronomer," p. 86. [Eds.]

[17] The former is the ancient Greek poet to whom the great epics the *Iliad* and the *Odyssey* are attributed; the latter is the Hebrew writer to whom the biblical book of Isaiah is attributed. [Eds.]

such solutions miss is that no matter what our current students are given to read, many of them will simply translate it into melodrama, with flat characters and predictable morals. (The unabated capitalist culture that conservative critics so often endorse has put students in a position to do little else.) One can't simply wave a curricular wand and reverse acculturation.

Perhaps it would be a good idea to try firing the counselors and 58 sending half the deans back into their classrooms, dismantling the football team and making the stadium into a playground for local kids, emptying the fraternities, and boarding up the student-activities office. Such measures would convey the message that American colleges are not northern outposts of Club Med. A willingness on the part of the faculty to defy student conviction and affront them occasionally—to be usefully offensive—also might not be a bad thing. We professors talk a lot about subversion, which generally means subverting the views of people who never hear us talk or read our work. But to subvert the views of our students, our customers, that would be something else again.

Ultimately, though, it is up to individuals—and individual students 59 in particular—to make their own way against the current sludgy tide. There's still the library, still the museum, there's still the occasional teacher who lives to find things greater than herself to admire. There are still fellow students who have not been cowed. Universities are inefficient, cluttered, archaic places, with many unguarded corners where one can open a book or gaze out onto the larger world and construe it freely. Those who do as much, trusting themselves against the weight of current opinion, will have contributed something to bringing this sad dispensation to an end. As for myself, I'm canning my low-key one-liners; when the kids' TV-based tastes come to the fore, I'll aim and shoot. And when it's time to praise genius, I'll try to do it in the right style, full-out, with faith that finer artistic spirits (maybe not Homer and Isaiah quite, but close, close), still alive somewhere in the ether, will help me out when my invention flags, the students doze, or the dean mutters into the phone. I'm getting back to a more exuberant style; I'll be expostulating and arm waving straight into the millennium, yes I will.

Responding to Reading

1. According to Edmundson, his students have reached the "state in which all passion seems to be spent" (13). In what ways has America's consumer culture affected them? How have the media—particularly television and the Internet—shaped their sense of self?
2. "Over the past few years," says Edmundson, "the physical layout of my university has been changing" (24). In what ways has it been changing? How do these changes reflect (and reinforce) the consumer mentality

that Edmundson sees in his students? How does Edmundson explain this phenomenon?

3. What does Edmundson think instructors and the university should do to correct the problems he sees? Do you think he is being fair when he says in his conclusion that ultimately it is up to individuals—especially individual students—to solve the problems he has pointed out?

Widening the Focus

- Deborah Tannen, "The Triumph of the Yell" (p. 276)

- Marie Winn, "The Plug-in Drug" (p. 262)

- Lawrence Krauss, "Equal Time for Nonsense" (p. 808)

—————————— WRITING ——————————

Issues in Education

1. Both Lynda Barry and Maya Angelou describe personal experiences related to their education. Write an essay in which you describe a positive or negative experience you had with your education. Be specific, and make sure you include plenty of vivid descriptive details.

2. At the end of his essay, Jonathan Kozol describes a program for "talented" or "gifted" students. What would be the advantages and disadvantages of such a program in the kind of school he describes? Do you think children should be grouped according to their abilities? Answer these questions in an essay.

3. What purpose do you think college should serve? Write an essay in which you explain your views, including specific references to essays in this chapter by Zinsser, Edmundson, and others as well as examples from your own experience.

4. Both Maya Angelou in "Graduation" and Jonathan Kozol in "Savage Inequalities" look at ways in which in which race affects the educational experience. In what ways do your high school and college experiences support or contradict their views?

5. After reading Mark Edmundson's essay "On the Uses of a Liberal Education," develop a picture of the student whom Edmundson describes. Then, write a letter to Edmundson in which you discuss whether his characterization of students is accurate or inaccurate, pointing out where he hits and misses the mark.

6. Write an essay in which you describe a teacher who had a significant effect (positive or negative) on you. In what ways was this teacher like and unlike the teachers mentioned in the selections by Lynda Barry, Jonathan Kozol, and Mark Edmundson?

7. Both Mark Twain in "Reading the River" and Walt Whitman in "When I Heard the Learn'd Astronomer" seem to value innocence. Bobby Fong, however, goes to great lengths to challenge his students' uninformed views. Write an essay in which you compare either Twain's or Whitman's ideas about education with Fong's. Be sure you use specific examples from each work to support your ideas.

8. In his essay "In Defense of Elitism," William A. Henry III argues that too many unqualified students go to college. To remedy this situation, he proposes limiting the number of high school students who are allowed to attend college. Referring to "Savage Inequalities" by Jonathan Kozol, argue for or against Henry's proposal.

9. A Review of Dinesh D'Souza's book *Illiberal Education: The Politics of Race and Sex on Campus* in *Time* magazine said that students on most

campuses are untouched by the academic debates that take place around multiculturalism and political correctness. Do you agree? What debates are taking place on your campus? In what ways are they like or unlike the debates D'Souza describes in "The Visigoths in Tweed"?

10. Write an essay in which you develop a definition of good teaching. As you write, consider the relationship of the teacher to the class, the standards teachers should use to evaluate students, and what students should gain from their educational experience. Make sure you refer to the ideas of Neil Postman, Mark Edmundson, and Bobby Fong in your essay.

3

THE POLITICS
OF LANGUAGE

Student Voices

"I think a person learns language at home and at school. If a person is well educated and comes from a family that speaks well, then that person will speak well too. If the person comes from a bad school or from a family in which the language is not spoken well, then that person will have trouble. My parents come from Vietnam and do not speak English well. . . . All through school I have had difficulty speaking and writing correct English."

—Din Ngoc Dang

"I basically speak in slang. I enjoy being different, and language is one way to separate myself from others. I regularly use words like *chill, sweet, right on,* and *excellent.* People know who's talking when they hear these words. The language I use not only catches their attention, but it also makes it easier for me to express myself. To me, language is just one of many ways to set myself apart."

—Todd Snellenburg

"Words can be sexist or racist. I personally am offended when I hear a male refer to women as *chicks* or *babes.* We are not *chicks* or *babes.* We are *women* or *females.* Racist remarks also offend me. I once heard a young child, a fourth grader, shout a racist term out of a school bus window at an old man working in his garden. There is no way to stop sexist or racist remarks. To do so, we would have to limit free speech, and this would be a violation of our constitutional rights. I suppose this means that we must all put up with offensive terms so we can preserve our right to express ourselves freely."

—Megan Seely

"When I first heard the question "Should any limits be placed on free speech?" I thought the sky was falling down. How could anyone question the great American dream of freedom of speech? Later, however, I saw neofascists on television preaching racism, hate, and the superiority of a 'higher race.' Is this what freedom of speech means? I don't think that remarks such as these should be allowed on television. Maybe there should be some limitations on what people can say. Maybe American society has entered a stage where limiting hate speech could help protect human rights."

—*Gennadiy Levit*

PREPARING TO READ AND WRITE

During the years he spent in prison, political activist Malcolm X became increasingly frustrated by his inability to express himself in writing, so he began the tedious and often frustrating task of copying words from the dictionary—page by page. The eventual result was that for the first time, he could pick up a book and read it with understanding. "Anyone who has read a great deal," he says, "can imagine the new world that opened." In addition, by becoming a serious reader, Malcolm X was able to develop the ideas about race, politics, and economics that he would present so forcefully after he was released from prison.

In our society, language is constantly manipulated for political ends. This fact should come as no surprise if we consider the potential power of words. Often the power of a word comes not from its dictionary definitions, or *denotations,* but from its *connotations,* the associations that surround it. Often these connotations are subtle, giving language the power to confuse and even to harm. For example, whether a doctor who performs an abortion is "terminating a pregnancy" or "murdering a preborn child" is not just a matter of semantics. It is also a political issue, one that has provoked not only debate but violence. This potential for disagreement, and possibly danger, makes careful word choice very important.

As you read and prepare to write about the selections in this chapter, you may consider the following questions:

- Does the selection deal primarily with written or spoken language?

- Does the writer place more emphasis on the denotations or the connotations of words?

- Does the writer make any distinctions between language applied to males and to females? Do you consider such distinctions valid?

- Does the writer discuss language in the context of a particular culture? Does he or she see language as a unifying or a divisive factor?

- In what ways would the writer like to change or reshape language? What do you see as the possible advantages or disadvantages of these changes?

- Does the writer believe that people are shaped by language or that language is shaped by people?

- Does the writer see language as having a particular social or political function? In what sense?

- Does the writer see language as empowering?

- Does the writer make assumptions about people's status on the basis of their use of language? Do these assumptions seem justified?

- Does the writer make a convincing case for the importance of language?

- Is the writer's focus primarily on language's ability to help or its power to harm?

- In what ways are your ideas about the power of words similar to or different from the writer's?

- How is the essay like and unlike other essays in this chapter?

TWO PERSPECTIVES ON
THE POLITICS OF LANGUAGE

Here two African-American writers, separated by a century, describe the empowering nature of literacy. Frederick Douglass (1818–1895)–editor, author, lecturer, U.S. minister to Haiti–was born a slave in agricultural Maryland and later served a family in Baltimore. In the city, he had opportunities for personal improvement—and the luck to escape to the North in 1838, where he became active in the abolitionist movement. In 1845 Douglass wrote his most famous work, Narrative of the Life of Frederick Douglass. *In the following excerpt from his* Narrative, *Douglass writes of outwitting his owners in order to become literate and find "the pathway from slavery to freedom." Writer, lecturer, and political activist Malcolm X (1925–1965) was born Malcolm Little in Omaha, Nebraska. His father, a Baptist minister, supported the back-to-Africa movement of the 1920s. This support led to threats by the Ku Klux Klan, and eventually Malcolm's father was murdered; his mother was committed to a mental institution. Malcolm X quit high school, preferring the street world of criminals and drug addicts. While in prison from 1946 to 1952, he read books and studied the Black Muslim religion, finally becoming an articulate advocate of black separatism. Malcolm X later split with Elijah Muhammad, the Black Muslim leader. For his defection, he was assassinated. "A Homemade Education," about how he taught himself to read in prison, is from Malcolm X's autobiography, which was written with Alex Haley and published in 1965.*

LEARNING TO READ AND WRITE

Frederick Douglass

I lived in Master Hugh's family about seven years. During this time, 1 I succeeded in learning to read and write. In accomplishing this, I was compelled to resort to various stratagems. I had no regular teacher. My mistress, who had kindly commenced to instruct me, had, in compliance with the advice and direction of her husband, not only ceased to instruct, but had set her face against my being instructed by any one else. It is due, however, to my mistress to say of her, that she did not adopt this course of treatment immediately. She at first lacked the depravity indispensable to shutting me up in mental darkness. It was at least necessary for her to have some training in the exercise of irresponsible power, to make her equal to the task of treating me as though I were a brute.

My mistress was, as I have said, a kind and tender-hearted woman; 2
and in the simplicity of her soul she commenced, when I first went to
live with her, to treat me as she supposed one human being ought to
treat another. In entering upon the duties of a slaveholder, she did not
seem to perceive that I sustained to her the relation of a mere chattel,[1]
and that for her to treat me as a human being was not only wrong, but
dangerously so. Slavery proved as injurious to her as it did to me. When
I went there, she was a pious, warm, and tender-hearted woman. There
was no sorrow or suffering for which she had not a tear. She had bread
for the hungry, clothes for the naked, and comfort for every mourner
that came within her reach. Slavery soon proved its ability to divest her
of these heavenly qualities. Under its influence, the tender heart became
stone, and the lamblike disposition gave way to one of tigerlike fierce-
ness. The first step in her downward course was in her ceasing to
instruct me. She now commenced to practise her husband's precepts.
She finally became even more violent in her opposition than her husband himself. She was not satisfied with simply doing as well as he had
commanded; she seemed anxious to do better. Nothing seemed to make
her more angry than to see me with a newspaper. She seemed to think
that here lay the danger. I have had her rush at me with a face made all
up of fury, and snatch from me a newspaper, in a manner that fully
revealed her apprehension. She was an apt woman; and a little experience soon demonstrated, to her satisfaction, that education and slavery
were incompatible with each other.

From this time I was most narrowly watched. If I was in a separate 3
room any considerable length of time, I was sure to be suspected of having a book, and was at once called to give an account of myself. All this,
however, was too late. The first step had been taken. Mistress, in teaching me the alphabet, had given me the *inch,* and no precaution could
prevent me from taking the *ell.*

The plan which I adopted, and the one by which I was most suc- 4
cessful, was that of making friends of all the little white boys whom I
met in the street. As many of these as I could, I converted into teachers.
With their kindly aid, obtained at different times and in different places,
I finally succeeded in learning to read. When I was sent on errands, I
always took my book with me, and by going one part of my errand
quickly, I found time to get a lesson before my return. I used also to carry
bread with me, enough of which was always in the house, and to which
I was always welcome; for I was much better off in this regard than
many of the poor white children in our neighborhood. This bread I used
to bestow upon the hungry little urchins, who, in return, would give me
that more valuable bread of knowledge. I am strongly tempted to give

---

[1] Property. [Eds.]

the names of two or three of those little boys, as a testimonial of the gratitude and affection I bear them; but prudence forbids;—not that it would injure me, but it might embarrass them; for it is almost an unpardonable offence to teach slaves to read in this Christian country. It is enough to say of the dear little fellows, that they lived on Philpot Street, very near Durgin and Bailey's ship-yard. I used to talk this matter of slavery over with them. I would sometimes say to them, I wished I could be as free as they would be when they got to be men. "You will be free as soon as you are twenty-one, *but I am a slave for life!* Have not I as good a right to be free as you have?" These words used to trouble them; they would express for me the liveliest sympathy, and console me with the hope that something would occur by which I might be free.

I was now about twelve years old, and the thought of being *a slave* 5 *for life* began to bear heavily upon my heart. Just about this time, I got hold of a book entitled "The Columbian Orator."[2] Every opportunity I got, I used to read this book. Among much of other interesting matter, I found in it a dialogue between a master and his slave. The slave was represented as having run away from his master three times. The dialogue represented the conversation which took place between them, when the slave was retaken the third time. In this dialogue, the whole argument in behalf of slavery was brought forward by the master, all of which was disposed of by the slave. The slave was made to say some very smart as well as impressive things in reply to his master—things which had the desired though unexpected effect; for the conversation resulted in the voluntary emancipation of the slave on the part of the master.

In the same book, I met with one of Sheridan's might speeches on 6 and in behalf of Catholic emancipation.[3] These were choice documents to me. I read them over and over again with unabated interest. They gave tongue to interesting thoughts of my own soul, which had frequently flashed through my mind, and died away for want of utterance. The moral which I gained from the dialogue was the power of truth over the conscience of even a slaveholder. What I got from Sheridan was a bold denunciation of slavery, and a powerful vindication of human rights. The reading of these documents enabled me to utter my thoughts, and to meet the arguments brought forward to sustain slavery; but while they relieved me of one difficulty, they brought on another even more painful than the one of which I was relieved. The more I read, the more I was led to abhor and detest my enslavers. I could regard them in no other light than a band of successful robbers,

---

[2] A popular textbook that taught the principles of effective public speaking. [Eds.]

[3] Richard Brinsley Sheridan (1751–1816), British playwright and statesman who made speeches supporting the right of English Catholics to vote. Full emancipation was not granted to Catholics until 1829. [Eds.]

who had left their homes, and gone to Africa, and stolen us from our homes, and in a strange land reduced us to slavery. I loathed them as being the meanest as well as the most wicked of men. As I read and contemplated the subject, behold! that very discontentment which Master Hugh had predicted would follow my learning to read had already come, to torment and sting my soul to unutterable anguish. As I writhed under it, I would at times feel that learning to read had been a curse rather than a blessing. It had given me a view of my wretched condition, without the remedy. It opened my eyes to the horrible pit, but to no ladder upon which to get out. In moments of agony, I envied my fellow-slaves for their stupidity. I have often wished myself a beast. I preferred the condition of the meanest reptile to my own. Any thing, no matter what, to get rid of thinking! It was the everlasting thinking of my condition that tormented me. There was no getting rid of it. It was pressed upon me by every object within sight or hearing, animate or inanimate. The silver trump of freedom had roused my soul to eternal wakefulness. Freedom now appeared, to disappear no more forever. It was heard in every sound, and seen in every thing. It was ever present to torment me with a sense of my wretched condition. I saw nothing without seeing it, I heard nothing without hearing it, and felt nothing without feeling it. It looked from every star, it smiled in every calm, breathed in every wind, and moved in every storm.

I often found myself regretting my own existence, and wishing 7 myself dead; and but for the hope of being free, I have no doubt but that I should have killed myself, or done something for which I should have been killed. While in this state of mind, I was eager to hear any one speak of slavery. I was a ready listener. Every little while, I could hear something about the abolitionists. It was some time before I found what the word meant. It was always used in such connections as to make it an interesting word to me. If a slave ran away and succeeded in getting clear, or if a slave killed his master, set fire to a barn, or did any thing very wrong in the mind of a slaveholder, it was spoken of as the fruit of *abolition*. Hearing the word in this connection very often, I set about learning what it meant. The dictionary afforded me little or no help. I found it was "the act of abolishing"; but then I did not know what was to be abolished. Here I was perplexed. I did not dare to ask any one about its meaning, for I was satisfied that it was something they wanted me to know very little about. After a patient waiting, I got one of our city papers, containing an account of the number of petitions from the north, praying for the abolition of slavery in the District of Columbia, and of the slave trade between the States. From this time I understood the words *abolition* and *abolitionist*, and always drew near when that word was spoken, expecting to hear something of importance to myself and fellow-slaves. The light broke in upon me by degrees. I went one day down on the wharf of Mr. Waters; and seeing two Irishmen unloading a scow of stone, I went, unasked, and helped them. When we had finished, one of them came to me and asked me if I were a slave. I told him I was. He asked, "Are ye a slave for life?" I told him that I was. The good Irishman seemed to be deeply affected by the statement. He said to the other that it was a pity so fine a little fellow as myself should be a slave for life. He said it was a shame to hold me. They both advised me to run away to the north; that I should find friends there, and that I should be free. I pretended not to be interested in what they said, and treated them as if I did not understand them; for I feared they might be treacherous. White men have been known to encourage slaves to escape, and then, to get the reward, catch them and return them to their masters. I was afraid that these seemingly good men might use me so; but I nevertheless remembered their advice, and from that time I resolved to run away. I looked forward to a time at which it would be safe for me to escape. I was too young to think of doing so immediately; besides, I wished to learn how to write, as I might have occasion to write my own pass. I consoled myself with the hope that I should one day find a good chance. Meanwhile, I would learn to write.

The idea as to how I might learn to write was suggested to me by 8 being in Durgin and Bailey's ship-yard, and frequently seeing the ship carpenters, after hewing, and getting a piece of timber ready for use, write on the timber the name of that part of the ship for which it was intended. When a piece of timber was intended for the larboard side, it would be marked thus—"L." When a piece was for the starboard side, it would be marked thus—"S." A piece for the larboard side forward, would be marked thus—"L. F." When a piece was for starboard side forward, it would be marked thus—"S. F." For larboard aft, it would be marked thus—"L.A." For starboard aft, it would be marked thus— "S. A." I soon learned the names of these letters, and for what they were intended when placed upon a piece of timber in the shipyard. I immediately commenced copying them, and in a short time was able to make the four letters named. After that, when I met with any boy who I knew could write, I would tell him I could write as well as he. The next word would be, "I don't believe you. Let me see you try it." I would then make the letters which I had been so fortunate as to learn, and ask him to beat that. In this way I got a good many lessons in writing, which it is quite possible I should never have gotten in any other way. During this time, my copy-book was the board fence, brick wall, and pavement; my pen and ink was a lump of chalk. With these, I learned mainly how to write. I then commenced and continued copying the Italics in Webster's Spelling Book, until I could make them all without looking on the book. By this time, my little Master Thomas had gone to school, and learned how to write, and had written over a number of copy-books. These had been brought home, and shown to some of our near neighbors, and then laid aside. My mistress used to go to class meeting at the

Wilk Street meetinghouse every Monday afternoon, and leave me to take care of the house. When left thus, I used to spend the time in writing in the spaces left in Master Thomas's copy-book, copying what he had written. I continued to do this until I could write a hand very similar to that of Master Thomas. Thus, after a long, tedious effort for years, I finally succeeded in learning how to write.

A HOMEMADE EDUCATION

Malcolm X

It was because of my letters that I happened to stumble upon starting to acquire some kind of a homemade education.

I became increasingly frustrated at not being able to express what I wanted to convey in letters that I wrote, especially those to Mr. Elijah Muhammad. In the street, I had been the most articulate hustler out there—I had commanded attention when I said something. But now, trying to write simple English, I not only wasn't articulate, I wasn't even functional. How would I sound writing in slang, the way I would *say* it, something such as, "Look, daddy, let me pull your coat about a cat, Elijah Muhammad—"

Many who today hear me somewhere in person, or on television, or those who read something I've said, will think I went to school far beyond the eighth grade. This impression is due entirely to my prison studies.

It had really begun back in the Charlestown Prison, when Bimbi[1] first made me feel envy of his stock of knowledge. Bimbi had always taken charge of any conversations he was in, and I had tried to emulate him. But every book I picked up had few sentences which didn't contain anywhere from one to nearly all of the words that might as well have been in Chinese. When I just skipped those words, of course, I really ended up with little idea of what the book said. So I had come to the Norfolk Prison Colony still going through only book-reading motions. Pretty soon, I would have quit even these motions, unless I had received the motivation that I did.

I saw that the best thing I could do was get hold of a dictionary—to study, to learn some words. I was lucky enough to reason also that I should try to improve my penmanship. It was sad. I couldn't even write in a straight line. It was both ideas together that moved me to request a dictionary along with some tablets and pencils from the Norfolk Prison Colony school.

---

[1] A fellow inmate. [Eds.]

I spent two days just riffling uncertainly through the dictionary's ₆ pages. I'd never realized so many words existed! I didn't know *which* words I needed to learn. Finally, just to start some kind of action, I began copying.

In my slow, painstaking, ragged handwriting, I copied into my ₇ tablet everything printed on that first page, down to the punctuation marks.

I believe it took me a day. Then, aloud, I read back, to myself, every- ₈ thing I'd written on the tablet. Over and over, aloud, to myself, I read my own handwriting.

I woke up the next morning, thinking about those words— ₉ immensely proud to realize that not only had I written so much at one time, but I'd written words that I never knew were in the world. Moreover, with a little effort, I also could remember what many of these words meant. I reviewed the words whose meanings I didn't remember. Funny thing, from the dictionary first page right now, that "aardvark" springs to my mind. The dictionary had a picture of it, a long-tailed, long-eared, burrowing African mammal, which lives off termites caught by sticking out its tongue as an anteater does for ants.

I was so fascinated that I went on—I copied the dictionary's next ₁₀ page. And the same experience came when I studied that. With every succeeding page, I also learned of people and places and events from history. Actually the dictionary is like a miniature encyclopedia. Finally the dictionary's A section had filled a whole tablet—and I went on into the B's. That was the way I started copying what eventually became the entire dictionary. It went a lot faster after so much practice helped me to pick up handwriting speed. Between what I wrote in my tablet, and writing letters, during the rest of my time in prison I would guess I wrote a million words.

I suppose it was inevitable that as my word-base broadened, I could ₁₁ for the first time pick up a book and read and now begin to understand what the book was saying. Anyone who has read a great deal can imagine the new world that opened. Let me tell you something: from then until I left that prison, in every free moment I had, if I was not reading in the library, I was reading on my bunk. You couldn't have gotten me out of books with a wedge. Between Mr. Muhammad's teachings, my correspondence, my visitors—usually Ella and Reginald[2]—and my reading of books, months passed without my even thinking about being imprisoned. In fact, up to then, I never had been so truly free in my life.

The Norfolk Prison Colony's library was in the school building. A ₁₂ variety of classes was taught there by instructors who came from such places as Harvard and Boston universities. The weekly debates between

---

[2] Ella was Malcolm's half sister, and Reginald was his brother. [Eds.]

inmate teams were also held in the school building. You would be astonished to know how worked up convict debaters and audiences would get over subjects like "Should Babies Be Fed Milk?"

Available on the prison library's shelves were books on just about 13 every general subject. Much of the big private collection that Parkhurst[3] had willed to the prison was still in crates and boxes in the back of the library—thousands of old books. Some of them looked ancient: covers faded; old-time parchment-looking binding. Parkhurst, I've mentioned, seemed to have been principally interested in history and religion. He had the money and the special interest to have a lot of books that you wouldn't have in general circulation. Any college library would have been lucky to get that collection.

As you can imagine, especially in a prison where there was heavy 14 emphasis on rehabilitation, an inmate was smiled upon if he demonstrated an unusually intense interest in books. There was a sizable number of well-read inmates, especially the popular debaters. Some were said by many to be practically walking encyclopedias. They were almost celebrities. No university would ask any student to devour literature as I did when this new world opened to me, of being able to read and *understand*.

I read more in my room than in the library itself. An inmate who 15 was known to read a lot could check out more than the permitted maximum number of books. I preferred reading in the total isolation of my own room.

When I had progressed to really serious reading, every night at 16 about ten P.M. I would be outraged with the "lights out." It always seemed to catch me right in the middle of something engrossing.

Fortunately, right outside my door was a corridor light that cast a 17 glow into my room. The glow was enough to read by, once my eyes adjusted to it. So when "lights out" came, I would sit on the floor where I could continue reading in that glow.

At one-hour intervals the night guards paced past every room. Each 18 time I heard the approaching footsteps, I jumped into bed and feigned sleep. And as soon as the guard passed, I got back out of bed onto the floor area of that light-glow, where I would read for another fifty-eight minutes—until the guard approached again. That went on until three or four every morning. Three or four hours of sleep a night was enough for me. Often in the years in the streets I had slept less than that.

The teachings of Mr. Muhammad stressed how history had been 19 "whitened"—when white men had written history books, the black man simply had been left out. Mr. Muhammad couldn't have said anything

---

[3] A philanthropist. [Eds.]

that would have struck me much harder. I had never forgotten how when my class, me and all of those whites, had studied seventh-grade United States history back in Mason,[4] the history of the Negro had been covered in one paragraph, and the teacher had gotten a big laugh with his joke, "Negroes' feet are so big that when they walk, they leave a hole in the ground."

This is one reason why Mr. Muhammad's teachings spread so 20 swiftly all over the United States, among *all* Negroes, whether or not they became followers of Mr. Muhammad. The teachings ring true—to every Negro. You can hardly show me a black adult in America—or a white one, for that matter—who knows from the history books anything like the truth about the black man's role. In my own case, once I heard of the "glorious history of the black man," I took special pains to hunt in the library for books that would inform me on details about black history.

I can remember accurately the very first set of books that really 21 impressed me. I have since bought that set of books and I have it at home for my children to read as they grow up. It's called *Wonders of the World*. It's full of pictures of archeological finds, statues that depict, usually, non-European people.

I found books like Will Durant's *Story of Civilization*. I read H. G. 22 Wells' *Outline of History*. *Souls of Black Folk* by W. E. B. Du Bois gave me a glimpse into the black people's history before they came to this country. Carter G. Woodson's *Negro History* opened my eyes about black empires before the black slave was brought to the United States, and the early Negro struggles for freedom.

J. A. Rogers' three volumes of *Sex and Race* told about race-mixing 23 before Christ's time; about Aesop being a black man who told fables; about Egypt's Pharaohs; about the great Coptic Christian Empires; about Ethiopia, the earth's oldest continuous black civilization, as China is the oldest continuous civilization.

Mr. Muhammad's teaching about how the white man had been cre- 24 ated led me to *Findings in Genetics* by Gregor Mendel.[5] (The dictionary's G section was where I had learned what "genetics" meant.) I really studied this book by the Austrian monk. Reading it over and over, especially certain sections, helped me to understand that if you started with a black man, a white man could be produced; but starting with a white man, you never could produce a black man—because the white chromosome is recessive. And since no one disputes that there was but one Original Man, the conclusion is clear.

---

[4] The junior high school that Malcolm X attended. [Eds.]

[5] Austrian monk (1822–1884) acknowledged as the father of modern genetics. [Eds.]

During the last year or so, in the *New York Times*, Arnold Toynbee[6]   25
used the word "bleached" in describing the white man. (His words were:
"White [i.e. bleached] human beings of North European origin. . . .")
Toynbee also referred to the European geographic area as only a
peninsula of Asia. He said there is no such thing as Europe. And if you
look at the globe, you will see for yourself that America is only an extension of Asia. (But at the same time Toynbee is among those who have
helped to bleach history. He has written that Africa was the only continent that produced no history. He won't write that again. Every day
now, the truth is coming to light.)

I never will forget how shocked I was when I began reading about   26
slavery's total horror. It made such an impact upon me that it later
became one of my favorite subjects when I became a minister of Mr.
Muhammad's. The world's most monstrous crime, the sin and the
blood on the white man's hands, are almost impossible to believe.
Books like the one by Frederick Olmstead[7] opened my eyes to the horrors suffered when the slave was landed in the United States. The
European woman, Fannie Kimball, who had married a Southern white
slaveowner, described how human beings were degraded. Of course I
read *Uncle Tom's Cabin*. In fact, I believe that's the only novel I have ever
read since I started serious reading.

Parkhurst's collection also contained some bound pamphlets of the   27
Abolitionist Anti-Slavery Society of New England. I read descriptions of
atrocities, saw those illustrations of black slave women tied up and
flogged with whips; of black mothers watching their babies being
dragged off, never to be seen by their mothers again; of dogs after
slaves, and of the fugitive slave catchers, evil white men with whips and
clubs and chains and guns. I read about the slave preacher Nat Turner,
who put the fear of God into the white slavemaster. Nat Turner wasn't
going around preaching pie-in-the-sky and "nonviolent" freedom for
the black man. There in Virginia one night in 1831, Nat and seven other
slaves started out at his master's home and through the night they went
from one plantation "big house" to the next, killing, until by the next
morning 57 white people were dead and Nat had about 70 slaves following him. White people, terrified for their lives, fled from their
homes, locked themselves up in public buildings, hid in the woods, and
some even left the state. A small army of soldiers took two months to
catch and hang Nat Turner. Somewhere I have read where Nat Turner's
example is said to have inspired John Brown to invade Virginia and

---

[6] English historian (1889–1975). [Eds.]

[7] American landscape architect and writer (1822–1903) who first achieved fame for his accounts of
the South in the early 1850s. [Eds.]

attack Harper's Ferry nearly thirty years later, with thirteen white men and five Negroes.

I read Herodotus, "the father of History," or, rather, I read about him. 28 And I read the histories of various nations, which opened my eyes gradually, then wider and wider, to how the whole world's white men had indeed acted like devils, pillaging and raping and bleeding and draining the whole world's non-white people. I remember, for instance, books such as Will Durant's *The Story of Oriental Civilization*, and Mahatma Gandhi's accounts of the struggle to drive the British out of India.

Book after book showed me how the white man had brought upon 29 the world's black, brown, red, and yellow peoples every variety of the sufferings of exploitation. I saw how since the sixteenth century, the so-called "Christian trader" white man began to ply the seas in his lust for Asian and African empires, and plunder, and power. I read, I saw, how the white man never has gone among the non-white peoples bearing the Cross in the true manner and spirit of Christ's teachings—meek, humble, and Christlike.

I perceived, as I read, how the collective white man had been actu- 30 ally nothing but a piratical opportunist who used Faustian machinations to make his own Christianity his initial wedge in criminal conquests. First, always "religiously," he branded "heathen" and "pagan" labels upon ancient non-white cultures and civilizations. The stage thus set, he then turned upon his non-white victims his weapons of war.

I read how, entering India—half a *billion* deeply religious brown 31 people—the British white man, by 1759, through promises, trickery and manipulations, controlled much of India through Great Britain's East India Company. The parasitical British administration kept tentacling out to half of the subcontinent. In 1857, some of the desperate people of India finally mutinied—and, excepting the African slave trade, nowhere has history recorded any more unnecessary bestial and ruthless human carnage than the British suppression of the nonwhite Indian people.

Over 115 million African blacks—close to the 1930s population of 32 the United States—were murdered or enslaved during the slave trade. And I read how when the slave market was glutted, the cannibalistic white powers of Europe next carved up, as their colonies, the richest areas of the black continent. And Europe's chancelleries for the next century played a chess game of naked exploitation and power from Cape Horn to Cairo.

Ten guards and the warden couldn't have torn me out of those 33 books. Not even Elijah Muhammad could have been more eloquent than those books were in providing indisputable proof that the collective white man had acted like a devil in virtually every contact he had with the world's collective non-white man. I listen today to the radio, and watch television, and read the headlines about the collective white man's fear and tension concerning China. When the white man professes ignorance about why the Chinese hate him so, my mind can't help flashing back to what I read, there in prison, about how the blood forebears of this same white man raped China at a time when China was trusting and helpless. Those original white "Christian traders" sent into China millions of pounds of opium. By 1839, so many of the Chinese were addicts that China's desperate government destroyed twenty thousand chests of opium. The first Opium War was promptly declared by the white man. Imagine! Declaring war upon someone who objects to being narcotized! The Chinese were severely beaten, with Chinese-invented gunpowder.

The Treaty of Nanking made China pay the British white man for $_{34}$ the destroyed opium: forced open China's major ports to British trade; forced China to abandon Hong Kong; fixed China's import tariffs so low that cheap British articles soon flooded in, maiming China's industrial development.

After a second Opium War, the Tientsin Treaties legalized the rav- $_{35}$ aging opium trade, legalized a British-French-American control of China's customs. China tried delaying that Treaty's ratification; Peking was looted and burned

"Kill the foreign white devils" was the 1901 Chinese war cry in the $_{36}$ Boxer Rebellion. Losing again, this time the Chinese were driven from Peking's choicest areas. The vicious, arrogant white man put up the famous signs, "Chinese and dogs not allowed."

Red China after World War II closed its doors to the Western white $_{37}$ world. Massive Chinese agricultural, scientific, and industrial efforts are described in a book that *Life* magazine recently published. Some observers inside Red China have reported that the world never has known such a hate-white campaign as is now going on in this non-white country where, present birthrates continuing, in fifty more years Chinese will be half the earth's population. And it seems that some Chinese chickens will soon come home to roost, with China's recent successful nuclear tests.

Let us face reality. We can see in the United Nations a new world $_{38}$ order being shaped, along color lines—an alliance among the nonwhite nations. America's U.N. Ambassador Adlai Stevenson complained not long ago that in the United Nations "a skin game" was being played. He was right. He was facing reality. A "skin game" *is* being played. But Ambassador Stevenson sounded like Jesse James accusing the marshal of carrying a gun. Because who in the world's history ever has played a worse "skin game" than the white man?

Mr. Muhammad, to whom I was writing daily, had no idea of what $_{39}$ a new world had opened up to me through my efforts to document his teachings in books.

When I discovered philosophy, I tried to touch all the landmarks of 40
philosophical development. Gradually, I read most of the old philosophers, Occidental and Oriental. The Oriental philosophers were the ones
I came to prefer; finally, my impression was that most Occidental philosophy had largely been borrowed from the Oriental thinkers. Socrates,
for instance, traveled in Egypt. Some sources even say that Socrates was
initiated into some of the Egyptian mysteries. Obviously Socrates got
some of his wisdom among the East's wise men.

I have often reflected upon the new vistas that reading opened to 41
me. I knew right there in prison that reading had changed forever the
course of my life. As I see it today, the ability to read awoke inside me
some long dormant craving to be mentally alive. I certainly wasn't seeking any degree, the way a college confers a status symbol upon its students. My homemade education gave me, with every additional book
that I read, a little bit more sensitivity to the deafness, dumbness, and
blindness that was afflicting the black race in America. Not long ago, an
English writer telephoned me from London, asking questions. One was,
"What's your alma mater?" I told him, "Books." You will never catch
me with a free fifteen minutes in which I'm not studying something I
feel might be able to help the black man.

Yesterday I spoke in London, and both ways on the plane across 42
the Atlantic I was studying a document about how the United Nations
proposes to insure the human rights of the oppressed minorities of the
world. The American black man is the world's most shameful case of
minority oppression. What makes the black man think of himself as
only an internal United States issue is just a catch-phrase, two words,
"civil rights." How is the black man going to get "civil rights" before
first he wins his *human* rights? If the American black man will start
thinking about his *human* rights, and then start thinking of himself as
part of one of the world's great peoples, he will see he has a case for the
United Nations.

I can't think of a better case! Four hundred years of black blood and 43
sweat invested here in America, and the white man still has the black
man begging for what every immigrant fresh off the ship can take for
granted the minute he walks down the gangplank.

But I'm digressing. I told the Englishman that my alma mater was 44
books, a good library. Every time I catch a plane, I have with me a book
that I want to read—and that's a lot of books these days. If I weren't out
here every day battling the white man, I could spend the rest of my life
reading, just satisfying my curiosity—because you can hardly mention
anything I'm not curious about. I don't think anybody ever got more out
of going to prison than I did. In fact, prison enabled me to study far
more intensively than I would have if my life had gone differently and I
had attended some college. I imagine that one of the biggest troubles

with colleges is there are too many distractions, too much panty-raiding, fraternities, and boola-boola and all of that. Where else but in a prison could I have attacked my ignorance by being able to study intensely sometimes as much as fifteen hours a day?

Responding to Reading

1. Douglass escaped from slavery in 1838 and became a leading figure in the antislavery movement. How did reading and writing help him develop his ideas about slavery? In what way did language empower him?
2. What were Malcolm X's reasons for wanting to increase his skill in reading and writing? With what else did his "homemade" education provide him?
3. In what ways were Douglass's and Malcolm X's methods of learning to read and write similar? In what ways were they different?
4. Do you think education and slavery are incompatible? What about education and prison? Why do you think slaveholders did not want slaves to read and write? Why didn't prison officials encourage Malcolm X to pursue an education?
5. Both Douglass and Malcolm X taught themselves to read and write. What are the drawbacks of this way of learning? Does either man acknowledge these drawbacks?
6. What comment do you think Douglass's essay makes on the conditions of African-Americans in the 1850s? What comment does Malcolm X's essay make on the conditions of African-Americans in the 1950s? Do you think these essays still have relevance? Explain.

FROM OUTSIDE, IN

Barbara Mellix

In "From Outside, In" South Carolina–born Barbara Mellix, an acade-mic who holds a master's degree in creative writing, describes the conflicts raised in her childhood between the black English she spoke within her family and the Standard English she was expected to master to communi-cate with the "others"; her essay originally appeared in the Georgia Review *in 1987.*

Two years ago, when I started writing this paper, trying to bring   1 order out of chaos, my ten-year-old daughter was suffering from an acute attack of boredom. She drifted in and out of the room complaining that she had nothing to do, no one to "be with" because none of her friends were at home. Patiently I explained that I was working on something special and needed peace and quiet, and I suggested that she paint, read, or work with her computer. None of these interested her. Finally, she pulled up a chair to my desk and watched me, now and then heaving long, loud sighs. After two or three minutes (nine or ten sighs), I lost my patience. "Looka here, Allie," I said, "you too old for this kinda carryin' on. I done told you this is important. You wronger than dirt to be in here haggin' me like this and you know it. Now git on outta here and leave me off before I put my foot all the way down."

I was at home, alone with my family, and my daughter understood 2 that this way of speaking was appropriate in that context. She knew, as a matter of fact, that it was almost inevitable; when I get angry at home, I speak some of my finest, most cherished black English. Had I been speaking to my daughter in this manner in certain other environments, she would have been shocked and probably worried that I had taken leave of my sense of propriety.

Like my children, I grew up speaking what I considered two dis- 3 tinctly different languages—black English and standard English (or as I thought of them then, the ordinary everyday speech of "country" coloreds and "proper" English)—and in the process of acquiring these languages, I developed an understanding of when, where, and how to use them. But unlike my children, I grew up in a world that was primarily black. My friends, neighbors, minister, teachers—almost everybody I associated with every day—were black. And we spoke to one another in our own special language: *That sho is a pretty dress you got on. If she don' soon leave me off I'm gon tell her head a mess. I was so mad I could'a pissed a blue nail. He all the time trying to low-rate somebody. Ain't that just about the nastiest thing you ever set ears on?*

Then there were the "others," the "proper" blacks, transplanted rel- 4 atives and one-time friends who came home from the city for weddings, funerals, and vacations. And the whites. To these we spoke standard English. "Ain't?" my mother would yell at me when I used the term in the presence of "others." "You *know* better than that." And I would hang my head in shame and say the "proper" word.

I remember one summer sitting in my grandmother's house in 5 Greeleyville, South Carolina, when it was full of the chatter of city relatives who were home on vacation. My parents sat quietly, only now and then volunteering a comment or answering a question. My mother's face took on a strained expression when she spoke. I could see that she was being careful to say just the right words in just the right way. Her voice sounded thick, muffled. And when she finished speaking, she would lapse into silence, her proper smile on her face. My father was more articulate, more aggressive. He spoke quickly, his words sharp and clear. But he held his proud head higher, a signal that he, too, was uncomfortable. My sisters and brothers and I stared at our aunts, uncles, and cousins, speaking only when prompted. Even then, we hesitated, formed our sentences in our minds, then spoke softly, shyly.

My parents looked small and anxious during those occasions, and I 6 waited impatiently for our leave-taking when we would mock our relatives the moment we were out of their hearing. "Reeely," we would say to one another, flexing our wrists and rolling our eyes, "how dooo you stan' this heat? Chile, it just too hy*ooo*-mid for words." Our relatives had made us feel "country," and this was our way of regaining pride in ourselves while getting a little revenge in the bargain. The words bubbled in our throats and rolled across our tongues, a balming.

As a child I felt this same doubleness in uptown Greeleyville where 7 the whites lived. "Ain't that a pretty dress you're wearing!" Toby, the town policeman, said to me one day when I was fifteen. "Thank you very much," I replied, my voice barely audible in my own ears. The words felt wrong in my mouth, rigid, foreign. It was not that I had never spoken that phrase before—it was common in black English, too—but I was extremely conscious that this was an occasion for proper English. I had taken out my English and put it on as I did my church clothes, and I felt as if I were wearing my Sunday best in the middle of the week. It did not matter that Toby had not spoken grammatically correct English. He was white and could speak as he wished. I had something to prove. Toby did not.

Speaking standard English to whites was our way of demonstrating 8 that we knew their language and could use it. Speaking it to standard-English-speaking blacks was our way of showing them that we, as well as they, could "put on airs." But when we spoke standard English, we acknowledged (to ourselves and to others—but primarily to ourselves) that our customary way of speaking was inferior. We felt foolish, embarrassed, somehow diminished because we were ashamed to be our real selves. We were reserved, shy in the presence of those who owned and/or spoke *the* language.

My parents never set aside time to drill us in standard English. 9 Their forms of instruction were less formal. When my father was feeling particularly expansive, he would regale us with tales of his exploits in the outside world. In almost flawless English, complete with dialogue and flavored with gestures and embellishment, he told us about his attempt to get a haircut at a white barbershop; his refusal to acknowledge one of the town merchants until the man addressed him as "Mister"; the time he refused to step off the sidewalk uptown to let some whites pass; his airplane trip to New York City (to visit a sick relative) during which the stewardesses and porters—recognizing that he was a "gentleman"—addressed him as "Sir." I did not realize then—nor, I think, did my father—that he was teaching us, among other things, standard English and the relationship between language and power.

My mother's approach was different. Often, when one of us said, 10 "I'm gon wash off my feet," she would say, "And what will you walk on if you wash them off?" Everyone would laugh at the victim of my mother's "proper" mood. But it was different when one of us children was in a proper mood. "You think you are so superior," I said to my oldest sister one day when we were arguing and she was winning. "Superior!" my sister mocked. "You mean I am acting 'biggidy'?" My sisters and brothers sniggered, then joined in teasing me. Finally, my mother said, "Leave your sister alone. There's nothing wrong with using proper English." There was a half-smile on her face. I had gotten "up-pity," had "put on airs" for no good reason. I was at home, alone with the family, and I hadn't been prompted by one of my mother's proper moods. But there was also a proud light in my mother's eyes; her children were learning English very well.

Not until years later, as a college student, did I begin to understand 11 our ambivalence toward English, our scorn of it, our need to master it, to own and be owned by it—an ambivalence that extended to the public-school classroom. In our school, where there were no whites, my teachers taught standard English but used black English to do it. When my grammar-school teachers wanted us to write, for example, they usually said something like, "I want y'all to write five sentences that make a statement. Anybody git done before the rest can color." It was probably almost those exact words that led me to write these sentences in 1953 when I was in the second grade:

The white clouds are pretty.

There are only 15 people in our room.

We will go to gym.

We have a new poster.

We may go out doors.

Second grade came after "Little First" and "Big First," so by then I 12 knew the implied rules that accompanied all writing assignments. Writing was an occasion for proper English. I was not to write in the way we spoke to one another: The white clouds pretty; There ain't but 15 people in our room; We going to gym. We got a new poster; We can go out in the yard. Rather I was to use the language of "others": clouds *are, there are*, we *will*, we *have*, we *may*.

My sentences were short, rigid, perfunctory, like the letters my 13 mother wrote to relatives:

Dear Papa,
How are you? How is Mattie? Fine I hope. We are fine. We will
come to see you Sunday. Cousin Ned will give us a ride.

>Love,
>Daughter

The language was not ours. It was something from outside us, 14
something we used for special occasions.

But my coloring on the other side of that second-grade paper is 15
different. I drew three hearts and a sun. The sun has a smiling face that
radiates and envelops everything it touches. And although the sun and
its world are enclosed in a circle, the colors I used—red, blue, green,
purple, orange, yellow, black—indicate that I was less restricted with
drawing and coloring than I was with writing standard English. My
valentines were not just red. My sun was not just a yellow ball in the
sky.

By the time I reached the twelfth grade, speaking and writing stan- 16
dard English had taken on new importance. Each year, about half of the
newly graduated seniors of our school moved to large cities—particularly in the North—to live with relatives and find work. Our English
teacher constantly corrected our grammar: "Not 'ain't,' but 'isn't.'" We
seldom wrote papers, and even those few were usually plot summaries
of short stories. When our teacher returned the papers, she usually lectured on the importance of using standard English: "I *am; you are;* he,
she, or it *is,*" she would say, writing on the chalkboard as she spoke.
"How you gon git a job talking about 'I is,' or 'I isn't' or 'I ain't?'"

In Pittsburgh, where I moved after graduation, I watched my aunt 17
and uncle—who had always spoken standard English when in
Greeleyville—switch from black English to standard English to a mixture of the two, according to where they were or who they were with.
At home and with certain close relatives, friends, and neighbors, they
spoke black English. With those less close, they spoke a mixture. In public and with strangers, they generally spoke standard English.

In time, I learned to speak standard English with ease and to switch 18
smoothly from black to standard or a mixture, and back again. But no
matter where I was, no matter what the situation or occasion, I continued to write as I had in school:

Dear Mommie,
How are you? How is everybody else? Fine I hope. I am fine. So
are Aunt and Uncle. Tell everyone I said hello. I will write again
soon.

>Love,
>Barbara

Responding to Reading

1. In what sense is Mellix's essay as much about class and race as it is about language?
2. Throughout her essay, Mellix seems ambivalent about speaking Standard English. With what does she associate Standard English? With what does she associate black English? Do you agree with her assumptions?
3. What does Mellix think she has gained by adopting Standard English? What does she think she has lost? Was there any way she could have avoided this loss?

MOTHER TONGUE

Amy Tan

Amy Tan (1952–) was born in Oakland, California, to parents who had emigrated from China only a few years earlier. (Her given name is actually An-mei, which means "blessing from America.") After receiving degrees from San Francisco State University (including a master's degree in linguistics), she became a business writer, composing speeches for corporate executives. A workaholic, Tan began writing stories as a means of personal therapy, and these eventually became the phenomenally successful The Joy Luck Club *(1987), a novel about Chinese-born mothers and their American-born daughters that was later made into a widely praised film. Tan's other books include two more novels,* The Kitchen God's Wife *(1991) and* The Hundred Secret Senses *(1995), and two illustrated children's books,* The Moon Lady *(1992) and* The Chinese Siamese Cat *(1994). In the following essay, which was originally delivered as a speech, Tan considers her relationship with her own mother, concentrating on the different "Englishes" they use to communicate with each other and with the world.*

I am not a scholar of English or literature. I cannot give you much more than personal opinions on the English language and its variations in this country or others.

I am a writer. And by that definition, I am someone who has always loved language. I am fascinated by language in daily life. I spend a great deal of my time thinking about the power of language—the way it can evoke an emotion, a visual image, a complex idea, or a simple truth. Language is the tool of my trade. And I use them all—all the Englishes I grew up with.

Recently, I was made keenly aware of the different Englishes I do use. I was giving a talk to a large group of people, the same talk I had already given to half a dozen other groups. The nature of the talk was about my writing, my life, and my book, *The Joy Luck Club.* The talk was going along well enough, until I remembered one major difference that made the whole talk sound wrong. My mother was in the room. And it was perhaps the first time she had heard me give a lengthy speech, using the kind of English I have never used with her. I was saying things like, "The intersection of memory upon imagination" and "There is an aspect of my fiction that relates to thus-and-thus"—a speech filled with carefully wrought grammatical phrases, burdened, it suddenly seemed to me, with nominalized forms, past perfect tenses, conditional phrases, all the forms of standard English that I had learned in school and through books, the forms of English I did not use at home with my mother.

Just last week, I was walking down the street with my mother, and 4 I again found myself conscious of the English I was using, and the English I do use with her. We were talking about the price of new and used furniture and I heard myself saying this: "Not waste money that way." My husband was with us as well, and he didn't notice any switch in my English. And then I realized why. It's because over the twenty years we've been together I've often used that same kind of English with him, and sometimes he even uses it with me. It has become our language of intimacy, a different sort of English that relates to family talk, the language I grew up with.

So you'll have some idea of what this family talk I heard sounds 5 like, I'll quote what my mother said during a recent conversation which I videotaped and then transcribed. During this conversation, my mother was talking about a political gangster in Shanghai who had the same last name as her family's, Du, and how the gangster in his early years wanted to be adopted by her family, which was rich by comparison. Later, the gangster became more powerful, far richer than my mother's family, and one day showed up at my mother's wedding to pay his respects. Here's what she said in part:

"Du Yusong having business like fruit stand. Like off the street 6 kind. He is Du like Du Zong—but not Tsung-ming Island people. The local people call putong, the river east side, he belong to that side local people. The man want to ask Du Zong father take him in like become own family. Du Zong father wasn't look down on him, but didn't take seriously, until that man big like become a mafia. Now important person, very hard to inviting him. Chinese way, came only to show respect, don't stay for dinner. Respect for making big celebration, he shows up. Mean gives lots of respect. Chinese custom. Chinese social life that way. If too important won't have to stay too long. He come to my wedding. I didn't see, I heard it. I gone to boy's side, they have YMCA dinner. Chinese age I was nineteen."

You should know that my mother's expressive command of English 7 belies how much she actually understands. She reads the Forbes report, listens to *Wall Street Week*, converses daily with her stockbroker, reads all of Shirley MacLaine's[1] books with ease—all kinds of things I can't begin to understand. Yet some of my friends tell me they understand 50 percent of what my mother says. Some say they understand 80 to 90 percent. Some say they understand none of it, as if she were speaking pure Chinese. But to me, my mother's English is perfectly clear, perfectly natural. It's my mother tongue. Her language, as I hear it, is vivid, direct, full of observation and imagery. That was the language that helped shape the way I saw things, expressed things, made sense of the world.

Lately, I've been giving more thought to the kind of English my 8 mother speaks. Like others, I have described it to people as "broken" or "fractured" English. But I wince when I say that. It has always bothered me that I can think of no way to describe it other than "broken," as if it were damaged and needed to be fixed, as if it lacked a certain wholeness and soundness. I've heard other terms used, "limited English," for example. But they seem just as bad, as if everything is limited, including people's perceptions of the limited English speaker.

I know this for a fact, because when I was growing up, my mother's 9 "limited" English limited *my* perception of her. I was ashamed of her English. I believed that her English reflected the quality of what she had to say. That is, because she expressed them imperfectly her thoughts were imperfect. And I had plenty of empirical evidence to support me: the fact that people in department stores, at banks, and at restaurants did not take her seriously, did not give her good service, pretended not to understand her, or even acted as if they did not hear her.

My mother has long realized the limitations of her English as well. 10 When I was fifteen, she used to have me call people on the phone to pretend I was she. In this guise, I was forced to ask for information or even to complain and yell at people who had been rude to her. One time it was a call to her stockbroker in New York. She had cashed out her small portfolio and it just so happened we were going to go to New York the next week, our very first trip outside California. I had to get on the phone and say in an adolescent voice that was not very convincing, "This is Mrs. Tan."

And my mother was standing in the back whispering loudly, "Why 11 he don't send me check, already two weeks late. So mad he lie to me, losing me money."

---

[1] Actress known for her autobiographical books, in which she traces her many past lives. [Eds.]

And then I said in perfect English, "Yes, I'm getting rather con- 12 cerned. You had agreed to send the check two weeks ago, but it hasn't arrived."

Then she began to talk more loudly. "What he want, I come to New 13 York tell him front of his boss, you cheating me?" And I was trying to calm her down, make her be quiet, while telling the stockbroker, "I can't tolerate any more excuses. If I don't receive the check immediately, I am going to have to speak to your manager when I'm in New York next week." And sure enough, the following week there we were in front of this astonished stockbroker, and I was sitting there red-faced and quiet, and my mother, the real Mrs. Tan, was shouting at his boss in her impeccable broken English.

We used a similar routine just five days ago, for a situation that was 14 far less humorous. My mother had gone to the hospital for an appointment, to find out about a benign brain tumor a CAT scan had revealed a month ago. She said she had spoken very good English, her best English, no mistakes. Still, she said, the hospital did not apologize when they said they had lost the CAT scan and she had come for nothing. She said they did not seem to have any sympathy when she told them she was anxious to know the exact diagnosis, since her husband and son had both died of brain tumors. She said they would not give her any more information until the next time and she would have to make another appointment for that. So she said she would not leave until the doctor called her daughter. She wouldn't budge. And when the doctor finally called her daughter, me, who spoke in perfect English—lo and behold—we had assurances the CAT scan would be found, promises that a conference call on Monday would be held, and apologies for any suffering my mother had gone through for a most regrettable mistake.

I think my mother's English almost had an effect on limiting my 15 possibilities in life as well. Sociologists and linguists probably will tell you that a person's developing language skills are more influenced by peers. But I do think that the language spoken in the family, especially in immigrant families which are more insular, plays a large role in shaping the language of the child. And I believe that it affected my results on achievement tests, IQ tests, and the SAT. While my English skills were never judged as poor, compared to math, English could not be considered my strong suit. In grade school I did moderately well, getting perhaps B's, sometimes B-pluses, in English and scoring perhaps in the sixtieth or seventieth percentile on achievement tests. But those scores were not good enough to override the opinion that my true abilities lay in math and science, because in those areas I achieved A's and scored in the ninetieth percentile or higher.

This was understandable. Math is precise; there is only one correct 16 answer. Whereas, for me at least, the answers on English tests were always a judgment call, a matter of opinion and personal experience. Those tests were constructed around items like fill-in-the-blank sentence completion, such as, "Even though Tom was   , Mary thought he was   ." And the correct answer always seemed to be the most bland combinations of thoughts, for example, "Even though Tom was shy, Mary thought he was charming," with the grammatical structure "even though" limiting the correct answer to some sort of semantic opposites, so you wouldn't get answers like, "Even though Tom was foolish, Mary thought he was ridiculous." Well, according to my mother, there were very few limitations as to what Tom could have been and what Mary might have thought of him. So I never did well on tests like that.

The same was true with word analogies, pairs of words in which   17 you were supposed to find some sort of logical, semantic relationship—for example, "*Sunset* is to *nightfall* as is to   ." And here you would be presented with a list of four possible pairs, one of which showed the same kind of relationship: *red* is to s*toplight, bus* is to *arrival, chills* is to *fever, yawn* is to *boring.* Well, I could never think that way. I knew what the tests were asking, but I could not block out of my mind the images already created by the first pair, "*sunset* is to *nightfall*"—and I would see a burst of colors against a darkening sky, the moon rising, the lowering of a curtain of stars. And all the other pairs of words—red, bus, stoplight, boring—just threw up a mass of confusing images, making it impossible for me to sort out something as logical as saying: "A sunset precedes nightfall" is the same as "a chill precedes a fever." The only way I would have gotten that answer right would have been to imagine an associative situation, for example, my being disobedient and staying out past sunset, catching a chill at night, which turns into feverish pneumonia as punishment, which indeed did happen to me.

I have been thinking about all this lately, about my mother's   18 English, about achievement tests. Because lately I've been asked, as a writer, why there are not more Asian Americans represented in American literature. Why are there few Asian Americans enrolled in creative writing programs? Why do so many Chinese students go into engineering? Well, these are broad sociological questions I can't begin to answer. But I have noticed in surveys—in fact, just last week—that Asian students, as a whole, always do significantly better on math achievement tests than in English. And this makes me think that there are other Asian-American students whose English spoken in the home might also be described as "broken" or "limited." And perhaps they also have teachers who are steering them away from writing and into math and science, which is what happened to me.

Fortunately, I happen to be rebellious in nature and enjoy the chal-   19 lenge of disproving assumptions made about me. I became an English major my first year in college, after being enrolled as pre-med. I started writing nonfiction as a freelancer the week after I was told by my former boss that writing was my worst skill and I should hone my talents toward account management.

But it wasn't until 1985 that I finally began to write fiction. And ₂₀ at first I wrote using what I thought to be wittily crafted sentences, sentences that would finally prove I had mastery over the English language. Here's an example from the first draft of a story that later made its way into *The Joy Luck Club*, but without this line: "That was my mental quandary in its nascent state." A terrible line, which I can barely pronounce.

Fortunately, for reasons I won't get into today, I later decided I ₂₁ should envision a reader for the stories I would write. And the reader I decided upon was my mother, because these were stories about mothers. So with this reader in mind—and in fact she did read my early drafts— I began to write stories using all the Englishes I grew up with: the English I spoke to my mother, which for lack of a better term might be described as "simple"; the English she used with me, which for lack of a better term might be described as "broken"; my translation of her Chinese, which could certainly be described as "watered down"; and what I imagined to be her translation of her Chinese if she could speak in perfect English, her internal language, and for that I sought to preserve the essence, but neither an English nor a Chinese structure. I wanted to capture what language ability tests can never reveal: her intent, her passion, her imagery, the rhythms of her speech and the nature of her thoughts.

Apart from what any critic had to say about my writing, I knew I ₂₂ had succeeded where it counted when my mother finished reading my book and gave me her verdict: "So easy to read."

Responding to Reading

1. Why does Tan begin her essay with the disclaimer "I am not a scholar of English or literature. I cannot give you much more than personal opinions" (1)? Does this opening add to her credibility or detract from it? Explain.
2. Tan implies that some languages are more expressive than others. Do you agree? Are there some ideas you can express in one language that are difficult or impossible to express in another? Give examples if you can.
3. Do you agree with Tan's statement in paragraph 15 that the kind of English spoken at home can have an effect on a student's performance on IQ tests and the SAT? Do you think the English you speak at home has had a positive or a negative effect on your command of English?

THE HUMAN COST
OF AN ILLITERATE SOCIETY

Jonathan Kozol

For over thirty years, Jonathan Kozol (see also p. 100) has written com-passionately about many of the social problems confronting the United States, particularly those that affect the poor and the disadvantaged. In the following excerpt from his 1985 book Illiterate America, *Kozol exposes the problems facing the sixty million Americans who are unable to read well enough to function in society and argues that their plight has important implications for the literate among us as well.*

PRECAUTIONS. READ BEFORE USING.
Poison: Contains sodium hydroxide (caustic soda-lye).
Corrosive: Causes severe eye and skin damage, may cause blindness.
Harmful or fatal if swallowed.
If swallowed, give large quantities of milk or water.
Do not induce vomiting.
Important: Keep water out of can at all times to prevent contents from violently erupting . . .

—warning on a can of Drano

Questions of literacy, in Socrates' belief, must at length be judged as 1 matters of morality. Socrates could not have had in mind the moral com-promise peculiar to a nation like our own. Some of our Founding Fathers did, however, have this question in their minds. One of the wis-est of those Founding Fathers (one who may not have been most com-passionate but surely was more prescient than some of his peers) recognized the special dangers that illiteracy would pose to basic equity in the political construction that he helped to shape.

"A people who mean to be their own governors," James Madison 2 wrote, "must arm themselves with the power knowledge gives. A pop-ular government without popular information or the means of acquir-ing it, is but a prologue to a farce or a tragedy, or perhaps both."

Tragedy looms larger than farce in the United States today. Illiterate 3 citizens seldom vote. Those who do are forced to cast a vote of ques-tionable worth. They cannot make informed decisions based on serious print information. Sometimes they can be alerted to their interests by aggressive voter education. More frequently, they vote for a face, a smile, or a style, not for a mind or character or body of beliefs.

The number of illiterate adults exceeds by 16 million the entire vote 4 cast for the winner in the 1980 presidential contest. If even one third of all illiterates could vote, and read enough and do sufficient math to vote in their self-interest, Ronald Reagan would not likely have been chosen president. There is, of course, no way to know for sure. We do know this: Democracy is a mendacious[1] term when used by those who are prepared to countenance the forced exclusion of one third of our electorate. So long as 60 million people are denied significant participation, the government is neither of, nor for, nor by, the people. It is a government, at best, of those two thirds whose wealth, skin color, or parental privilege allows them opportunity to profit from the provocation and instruction of the written word.

The undermining of democracy in the United States is one 5 "expense" that sensitive Americans can easily deplore because it represents a contradiction that endangers citizens of all political positions. The human price is not so obvious at first.

Since I first immersed myself within this work I have often had the 6 following dream: I find that I am in a railroad station or a large department store within a city that is utterly unknown to me and where I cannot understand the printed words. None of the signs or symbols is familiar. Everything looks strange: like mirror writing of some kind. Gradually I understand that I am in the Soviet Union. All the letters on the walls around me are Cyrillic. I look for my pocket dictionary but I find that it has been mislaid. Where have I left it? Then I recall that I forgot to bring it with me when I packed my bags in Boston. I struggle to remember the name of my hotel. I try to ask somebody for directions. One person stops and looks at me in a peculiar way. I lose the nerve to ask. At last I reach into my wallet for an ID card. The card is missing. Have I lost it? Then I remember that my card was confiscated for some reason, many years before. Around this point, I wake up in a panic.

This panic is not so different from the misery that millions of adult 7 illiterates experience each day within the course of their routine existence in the U.S.A.

Illiterates cannot read the menu in a restaurant. 8

They cannot read the cost of items on the menu in the *window* of the 9 restaurant before they enter.

Illiterates cannot read the letters that their children bring home 10 from their teachers. They cannot study school department circulars that tell them of the courses that their children must be taking if they hope to pass the SAT exams. They cannot help with homework. They cannot write a letter to the teacher. They are afraid to visit in the classroom. They do not want to humiliate their child or themselves.

---

[1] Basely dishonest. [Eds.]

Illiterates cannot read instructions on a bottle of prescription medi-   11
cine. They cannot find out when a medicine is past the year of safe consumption; nor can they read of allergenic risks, warnings to diabetics, or
the potential sedative effect of certain kinds of nonprescription pills.
They cannot observe preventive health care admonitions. They cannot
read about "the seven warning signs of cancer" or the indications of
blood-sugar fluctuations or the risks of eating certain foods that aggra-
vate the likelihood of cardiac arrest.

Illiterates live, in more than literal ways, an uninsured existence.   12
They cannot understand the written details on a health insurance form.
They cannot read the waivers that they sign preceding surgical procedures. Several women I have known in Boston have entered a slum
hospital with the intention of obtaining a tubal ligation and have
emerged a few days later after having been subjected to a hysterectomy.[2] Unaware of their rights, incognizant of jargon, intimidated by the
unfamiliar air of fear and atmosphere of ether that so many of us find
oppressive in the confines even of the most attractive and expensive
medical facilities, they have signed their names to documents they
could not read and which nobody, in the hectic situation that prevails so
often in those overcrowded hospitals that serve the urban poor, had
even bothered to explain.

Childbirth might seem to be the last inalienable right of any female   13
citizen within a civilized society. Illiterate mothers, as we shall see,
already have been cheated of the power to protect their progeny against
the likelihood of demolition in deficient public schools and, as a result,
against the verbal servitude within which they themselves exist. Surgical
denial of the right to bear that child in the first place represents an ultimate denial, an unspeakable metaphor, a final darkness that denies even
the twilight gleamings of our own humanity. What greater violation of
our biological, our biblical, our spiritual humanity could possibly exist
than that which takes place nightly, perhaps hourly these days, within
such over-burdened and benighted institutions as the Boston City
Hospital? Illiteracy has many costs; few are so irreversible as this.

Even the roof above one's head, the gas or other fuel for heating that   14
protects the residents of northern city slums against the threat of illness
in the winter months become uncertain guarantees. Illiterates cannot
read the lease that they must sign to live in an apartment which, too
often, they cannot afford. They cannot manage check accounts and
therefore seldom pay for anything by mail. Hours and entire days of difficult travel (and the cost of bus or other public transit) must be added
to the real cost of whatever they consume. Loss of interest on the check

---

[2] A hysterectomy, the removal of the uterus, is a much more radical procedure than a tubal ligation,
a method of sterilization that is a common form of birth control. [Eds.]

accounts they do not have, and could not manage if they did, must be regarded as another of the excess costs paid by the citizen who is excluded from the common instruments of commerce in a numerate society.

"I couldn't understand the bills," a woman in Washington, D.C., 15 reports, "and then I couldn't write the checks to pay them. We signed things we didn't know what they were."

Illiterates cannot read the notices that they receive from welfare 16 offices or from the IRS. They must depend on word-of-mouth instruction from the welfare worker—or from other persons whom they have good reason to mistrust. They do not know what rights they have, what deadlines and requirements they face, what options they might choose to exercise. They are half-citizens. Their rights exist in print but not in fact.

Illiterates cannot look up numbers in a telephone directory. Even if 17 they can find the names of friends, few possess the sorting skills to make use of the yellow pages; categories are bewildering and trade names are beyond decoding capabilities for millions of nonreaders. Even the emergency numbers listed on the first page of the phone book—"Ambulance," "Police," and "Fire"—are too frequently beyond the recognition of nonreaders.

Many illiterates cannot read the admonition on a pack of cigarettes. 18 Neither the Surgeon General's warning nor its reproduction on the package can alert them to the risks. Although most people learn by word of mouth that smoking is related to a number of grave physical disorders, they do not get the chance to read the detailed stories which can document this danger with the vividness that turns concern into determination to resist. They can see the handsome cowboy or the slim Virginia lady lighting up a filter cigarette; they cannot heed the words that tell them that this product is (not "may be") dangerous to their health. Sixty million men and women are condemned to be the unalerted, high-risk candidates for cancer.

Illiterates do not buy "no-name" products in the supermarkets. 19 They must depend on photographs or the familiar logos that are printed on the packages of brand-name groceries. The poorest people, therefore, are denied the benefits of the least costly products.

Illiterates depend almost entirely upon label recognition. Many 20 labels, however, are not easy to distinguish. Dozens of different kinds of Campbell's soup appear identical to the nonreader. The purchaser who cannot read and does not dare to ask for help, out of the fear of being stigmatized (a fear which is unfortunately realistic), frequently comes home with something which she never wanted and her family never tasted.

Illiterates cannot read instructions on a pack of frozen food. 21 Packages sometimes provide an illustration to explain the cooking preparations; but illustrations are of little help to someone who must "boil water, drop the food—*within* its plastic wrapper—in the boiling water, wait for it to simmer, instantly remove."

Even when labels are seemingly clear, they may be easily mistaken. 22 A woman in Detroit brought home a gallon of Crisco for her children's dinner. She thought that she had bought the chicken that was pictured on the label. She had enough Crisco now to last a year—but no more money to go back and buy the food for dinner.

Recipes provided on the packages of certain staples sometimes 23 tempt a semiliterate person to prepare a meal her children have not tasted. The longing to vary the uniform and often starchy content of low-budget meals provided to the family that relies on food stamps commonly leads to ruinous results. Scarce funds have been wasted and the food must be thrown out. The same applies to distribution of food-surplus produce in emergency conditions. Government induce-ments to poor people to "explore the ways" in which to make a tasty meal from tasteless noodles, surplus cheese, and powdered milk are useless to nonreaders. Intended as benevolent advice, such recommen-dations mock reality and foster deeper feelings of resentment and of inability to cope. (Those, on the other hand, who cautiously refrain from "innovative" recipes in preparation of their children's meals must suf-fer the opprobrium of "laziness," "lack of imagination. . . .")

Illiterates cannot travel freely. When they attempt to do so, they 24 encounter risks that few of us can dream of. They cannot read traffic signs and, while they often learn to recognize and to decipher symbols, they cannot manage street names which they haven't seen before. The same is true for bus and subway stops. While ingenuity can sometimes help a man or woman to discern directions from familiar landmarks, buildings, cemeteries, churches, and the like, most illiterates are virtu-ally immobilized. They seldom wander past the streets and neighbor-hoods they know. Geographical paralysis becomes a bitter metaphor for their entire existence. They are immobilized in almost every sense we can imagine. They can't move up. They can't move out. They cannot see beyond. Illiterates may take an oral test for drivers' permits in most sec-tions of America. It is a questionable concession. Where will they go? How will they get there? How will they get home? Could it be that some of us might like it better if they stayed where they belong?

Travel is only one of many instances of circumscribed existence. 25 Choice, in almost all its facets, is diminished in the life of an illiterate adult. Even the printed TV schedule, which provides most people with the luxury of preselection, does not belong within the arsenal of options in illiterate existence. One consequence is that the viewer watches only what appears at moments when he happens to have time to turn the switch. Another consequence, a lot more common, is that the TV set remains in operation night and day. Whatever the program offered at the hour when he walks into the room will be the nutriment that he accepts and swallows. Thus, to passivity, is added frequency—indeed, almost uninterrupted continuity. Freedom to select is no more possible here than in the choice of home or surgery or food.

"You don't choose," said one illiterate woman. "You take your 26 wishes from somebody else." Whether in perusal of a menu, selection of highways, purchase of groceries, or determination of affordable enjoyment, illiterate Americans must trust somebody else: a friend, a relative, a stranger on the street, a grocery clerk, a TV copywriter.

"All of our mail we get, it's hard for her to read. Settin' down and 27 writing a letter, she can't do it. Like if we get a bill . . . we take it over to my sister-in-law . . . My sister-in-law reads it."

Billing agencies harass poor people for the payment of the bills for 28 purchases that might have taken place six months before. Utility companies offer an agreement for a staggered payment schedule on a bill past due. "You have to trust them," one man said. Precisely for this reason, you end up by trusting no one and suspecting everyone of possible deceit. A submerged sense of distrust becomes the corollary to a constant need to trust. "They are cheating me . . . I have been tricked . . . I do not know . . ."

Not knowing: This is a familiar theme. Not knowing the right word 29 for the right thing at the right time is one form of subjugation. Not knowing the world that lies concealed behind those words is a more terrifying feeling. The longitude and latitude of one's existence are beyond all easy apprehension. Even the hard, cold stars within the firmament above one's head begin to mock the possibilities for self-location. Where am I? Where did I come from? Where will I go?

"I've lost a lot of jobs," one man explains. "Today, even if you're a 30 janitor, there's still reading and writing . . . They leave a note saying, 'Go to room so-and-so . . .' You can't do it. You can't read it. You don't know."

"The hardest thing about it is that I've been places where I didn't 31 know where I was. You don't know where you are . . . You're lost."

"Like I said: I have two kids. What do I do if one of my kids starts 32 choking? I go running to the phone . . . I can't look up the hospital phone number. That's if we're at home. Out on the street, I can't read the sign. I get to a pay phone. 'Okay, tell us where you are. We'll send an ambulance.' I look at the street sign. Right there, I can't tell you what it says. I'd have to spell it out, letter for letter. By that time, one of my kids would be dead . . . These are the kinds of fears you go with, every single day . . ."

"Reading directions, I suffer with. I work with chemicals . . . That's 33 scary to begin with . . ."

"You sit down. They throw the menu in front of you. Where do you ³⁴ go from there? Nine times out of ten you say, 'Go ahead. Pick out something for the both of us.' I've eaten some weird things, let me tell you!"

Menus. Chemicals. A child choking while his mother searches for a ³⁵ word she does not know to find assistance that will come too late. Another mother speaks about the inability to help her kids to read: "I can't read to them. Of course that's leaving them out of something they should have. Oh, it matters. You *believe* it matters! I ordered all these books. The kids belong to a book club. Donny wanted me to read a book to him. I told Donny: 'I can't read,' He said: 'Mommy, you sit down. I'll read it to you.' I tried it one day, reading from the pictures. Donny looked at me. He said, 'Mommy, that's not right.' He's only five. He knew I couldn't read . . ."

A landlord tells a woman that her lease allows him to evict her if her ³⁶ baby cries and causes inconvenience to her neighbors. The consequence of challenging his words conveys a danger which appears, unlikely as it seems, even more alarming than the danger of eviction. Once she admits that she can't read, in the desire to maneuver for the time in which to call a friend, she will have defined herself in terms of an explicit impotence that she cannot endure. Capitulation in this case is preferable to self-humiliation. Resisting the definition of oneself in terms of what one cannot do, what others take for granted, represents a need so great that other imperatives (even one so urgent as the need to keep one's home in winter's cold) evaporate and fall away in face of fear. Even the loss of home and shelter, in this case, is not so terrifying as the loss of self.

"I come out of school. I was sixteen. They had their meetings. The ³⁷ directors meet. They said that I was wasting their school paper. I was wasting pencils . . ."

Another illiterate, looking back, believes she was not worthy of her ³⁸ teacher's time. She believes that it was wrong of her to take up space within her school. She believes that it was right to leave in order that somebody more deserving could receive her place.

Children choke. Their mother chokes another way: on more than ³⁹ chicken bones.

People eat what others order, know what others tell them, struggle ⁴⁰ not to see themselves as they believe the world perceives them. A man in California speaks about his own loss of identity, of self-location, definition:

"I stood at the bottom of the ramp. My car had broke down on the ⁴¹ freeway. There was a phone. I asked for the police. They was nice. They said to tell them where I was. I looked up at the signs. There was one that I had seen before. I read it to them: ONE WAY STREET. They thought it was a joke. I told them I couldn't read. There was other signs above the ramp. They told me to try. I looked around for somebody to help. All the cars was going by real fast. I couldn't make them understand that I was lost. The cop was nice. He told me: 'Try once more.' I did my best. I couldn't read. I only knew the sign above my head. The cop was trying to be nice. He knew that I was trapped. 'I can't send out a car to you if you can't tell me where you are.' I felt afraid. I nearly cried. I'm forty-eight years old. I only said: 'I'm on a one-way street . . .'"

The legal problems and the courtroom complications that confront 42 illiterate adults have been discussed above. The anguish that may underlie such matters was brought home to me this year while I was working on this book. I have spoken, in the introduction, of a sudden phone call from one of my former students, now in prison for a criminal offense. Stephen is not a boy today. He is twenty-eight years old. He called to ask me to assist him in his trial, which comes up next fall. He will be on trial for murder. He has just knifed and killed a man who first enticed him to his home, then cheated him, and then insulted him—as "an illiterate subhuman."

Stephen now faces twenty years to life. Stephen's mother was illit- 43 erate. His grandparents were illiterate as well. What parental curse did not destroy was killed off finally by the schools. Silent violence is repaid with interest. It will cost us $25,000 yearly to maintain this broken soul in prison. But what is the price that has been paid by Stephen's victim? What is the price that will be paid by Stephen?

Perhaps we might slow down a moment here and look at the reali- 44 ties described above. This is the nation that we live in. This is a society that most of us did not create but which our President and other leaders have been willing to sustain by virtue of malign neglect. Do we possess the character and courage to address a problem which so many nations, poorer than our own, have found it natural to correct?

The answers to these questions represent a reasonable test of our 45 belief in the democracy to which we have been asked in public school to swear allegiance.

Responding to Reading

1. According to Kozol, how does illiteracy undermine democracy in the United States? Do you agree with him? What do think can be done to lessen the problem of illiteracy?

2. Do you think Kozol accurately describes the difficulties illiterates face in their daily lives, or does he seem to be exaggerating? If you think he is exaggerating, what motive might he have?

3. Kozol concludes his essay by asking whether we as a nation have "the character and the courage to address" illiteracy (44). He does not, how-ever, offer any concrete suggestions for doing so. Can you offer any suggestions?

SEXISM IN ENGLISH: A 1990s UPDATE

Alleen Pace Nilsen

*Alleen Pace Nilsen (1936–   ) is an educator and essayist who has con-
tributed to many journals and has taught English at Arizona State
University and other schools. In 1967, Nilsen lived in Afghanistan, where
for two years she observed the subordinate position of women in that society.
When she returned to the United States, she began to study American
English for its cultural biases toward men and women. She says of that project, "As I worked my way through the dictionary, I concentrated on the way
that particular usages, metaphors, slang terms, and definitions reveal society's attitude towards males and females." Currently interested in what
teenagers read, Nilsen has coauthored* Literature for Today's Young
Adults *(5th edition, 1995). The following essay is an updated version of
some of Nilsen's findings from her dictionary study.*

Twenty years ago I embarked on a study of the sexism inherent in   1
American English. I had just returned to Ann Arbor, Michigan, after living for two years (1967–69) in Kabul, Afghanistan, where I had begun to
look critically at the role society assigned to women. The Afghan version of the *chaderi*[1] prescribed for Moslem women was particularly confining. Afghan jokes and folklore were blatantly sexist, such as this
proverb: "If you see an old man, sit down and take a lesson; if you see
an old woman, throw a stone."

But it wasn't only the native culture that made me question   2
women's roles, it was also the American community.

Most of the American women were like myself—wives and moth-   3
ers whose husbands were either career diplomats, employees of USAID
[U. S. Agency for International Development], or college professors who
had been recruited to work on various contract teams. We were suddenly bereft of our traditional roles: some of us became alcoholics, others got very good at bridge, while still others searched desperately for
ways to contribute either to our families or to the Afghans. The local
economy provided few jobs for women and certainly none for foreigners; we were isolated from former friends and the social goals we had
grown up with.

When I returned in the fall of 1969 to the University of Michigan in   4
Ann Arbor, I was surprised to find that many other women were also
questioning the expectations they had grown up with. In the spring of
1970, a women's conference was announced. I hired a babysitter and

---

[1] A *chador* is a heavily draped cloth covering the entire head and body. [Eds.]

attended, but I returned home more troubled than ever. The militancy of these women frightened me. Since I wasn't ready for a revolution, I decided I would have my own feminist movement. I would study the English language and see what it could tell me about sexism. I started reading a desk dictionary and making notecards on every entry that seemed to tell something about male and female. I soon had a dog-eared dictionary, along with a collection of notecards filling two shoe boxes.

Ironically, I started reading the dictionary because I wanted to avoid 5 getting involved in social issues, but what happened was that my note-cards brought me right back to looking at society. Language and society are as intertwined as a chicken and an egg. The language a culture uses is telltale evidence of the values and beliefs of that culture. And because there is a lag in how fast a language changes—new words can easily be introduced, but it takes a long time for old words and usages to disappear—a careful look at English will reveal the attitudes that our ancestors held and that we as a culture are therefore predisposed to hold. My notecards revealed three main points. Friends have offered the opinion that I didn't need to read the dictionary to learn such obvious facts. Nevertheless, it was interesting to have linguistic evidence of sociological observations.

Women Are Sexy; Men Are Successful

First, in American culture a woman is valued for the attractiveness 6 and sexiness of her body, while a man is valued for his physical strength and accomplishments. A woman is sexy. A man is successful.

A persuasive piece of evidence supporting this view is the 7 eponyms—words that have come from someone's name—found in English. I had a two-and-a-half-inch stack of cards taken from men's names but less than a half-inch stack from women's names, and most of those came from Greek mythology. In the words that came into American English since we separated from Britain, there are many eponyms based on the names of famous American men: *Bartlett pear, boysenberry, diesel engine, Franklin stove, Ferris wheel, Gatling gun, mason jar, sideburns, sousaphone, Schick test,* and *Winchester rifle.* The only common eponyms taken from American women's names are *Alice blue* (after Alice Roosevelt Longworth), *bloomers* (after Amelia Jenks Bloomer), and *Mae West jacket* (after the buxom actress). Two out of the three feminine eponyms relate closely to a woman's physical anatomy, while the masculine eponyms (except for *sideburns* after General Burnsides) have nothing to do with the namesake's body but, instead, honor the man for an accomplishment of some kind.

Although in Greek mythology women played a bigger role than 8 they did in the biblical stories of the Judeo-Christian cultures and so the names of goddesses are accepted parts of the language in such place names as *Pomona* from the goddess of fruit and *Athens* from Athena and in such common words as *cereal* from Ceres, *psychology* from Psyche, and *arachnoid* from Arachne, the same tendency to think of women in relation to sexuality is seen in the eponyms *aphrodisiac* from Aphrodite, the Greek name for the goddess of love and beauty, and *venereal disease* from Venus, the Roman name for Aphrodite.

Another interesting word from Greek mythology is *Amazon*. 9 According to Greek folk etymology, the *a* means "without" as in *atypical* or *amoral*, while *mazon* comes from *mazos* meaning "breast" as still seen in *mastectomy*. In the Greek legend, Amazon women cut off their right breasts so that they could better shoot their bows. Apparently, the storytellers had a feeling that for women to play the active, "masculine" role the Amazons adopted for themselves, they had to trade in part of their femininity.

This preoccupation with women's breasts is not limited to ancient 10 stories. As a volunteer for the University of Wisconsin's *Dictionary of American Regional English (DARE)*, I read a western trapper's diary from the 1930s. I was to make notes of any unusual usages or language patterns. My most interesting finding was that the trapper referred to a range of mountains as *The Teats*, a metaphor based on the similarity between the shapes of mountains and women's breasts. Because today we use the French wording, *The Grand Tetons*, the metaphor isn't as obvious, but I wrote to mapmakers and found the following listings: *Nippletop* and *Little Nipple Top* near Mount Marcy in the Adirondacks; *Nipple Mountain* in Archuleta County, Colorado; *Nipple Peak* in Coke County, Texas; *Nipple Butte* in Pennington, South Dakota; *Squaw Peak* in Placer County, California (and many other locations); *Maiden's Peak* and *Squaw Tit* (they're the same mountain) in the Cascade Range in Oregon; *Mary's Nipple* near Salt Lake City, Utah; and *Jane Russell Peaks* near Stark, New Hampshire.

Except for the movie star Jane Russell, the women being referred to 11 are anonymous—it's only a sexual part of their body that is mentioned. When topographical features are named after men, it's probably not going to be to draw attention to a sexual part of their bodies but instead to honor individuals for an accomplishment. For example, no one thinks of a part of the male body when hearing a reference to Pike's Peak, Colorado, or Jackson Hole, Wyoming.

Going back to what I learned from my dictionary cards, I was surprised to realize how many pairs of words we have in which the feminine word has acquired sexual connotations while the masculine word retains a serious businesslike aura. For example, a *callboy* is the person who calls actors when it is time for them to go on stage, but a *callgirl* is a prostitute. Compare *sir* and *madam*. *Sir* is a term of respect, while *madam* has acquired the specialized meaning of a brothel manager. Something similar has happened to *master* and *mistress*. Would you rather have a painting by an *old master* or an *old mistress?*

It's because the word *woman* had sexual connotations, as in "She's his woman," that people began avoiding its use, hence such terminology as *ladies' room, lady of the house,* and *girls' school* or *school for young ladies*. Feminists, who ask that people use the term *woman* rather than *girl* or *lady,* are rejecting the idea that *woman* is primarily a sexual term. They have been at least partially successful in that today *woman* is commonly used to communicate gender without intending implications about sexuality. 13

I found two hundred pairs of words with masculine and feminine forms, e.g., *heir-heiress, hero-heroine, steward-stewardess, usher-usherette*. In nearly all such pairs, the masculine word is considered the base, with some kind of a feminine suffix being added. The masculine form is the one from which compounds are made, e.g., from *king-queen* comes *kingdom* but not *queendom,* from *sportsman-sportslady* comes *sportsmanship* but not *sportsladyship*. There is one—and only one—semantic area in which the masculine word is not the base or more powerful word. This is in the area dealing with sex and marriage. When someone refers to a *virgin,* a listener will probably think of a female, unless the speaker specifies *male* or uses a masculine pronoun. The same is true for *prostitute*. 14

In relation to marriage, there is much linguistic evidence showing that weddings are more important to women than to men. A woman cherishes the wedding and is considered a bride for a whole year, but a man is referred to as a groom only on the day of the wedding. The word *bride* appears in *bridal attendant, bridal gown, bridesmaid, bridal shower,* and even *bridegroom. Groom* comes from the Middle English *groom,* meaning "man," and in the sense is seldom used outside of the wedding. With most pairs of male/female words, people habitually put the masculine word first, *Mr. and Mrs., his and hers, boys and girls, men and women, kings and queens, brothers and sisters, guys and dolls,* and *host and hostess,* but it is the *bride and groom* who are talked about, not the *groom and bride.* 15

The importance of marriage to a woman is also shown by the fact that when a marriage ends in death, the woman gets the title of *widow.* A man gets the derived title of *widower*. This term is not used in other phrases or contexts, but *widow* is seen in *widowhood, widow's peak,* and *widow's walk. A widow* in a card game is an extra hand of cards, while in typesetting it is an extra line of type. 16

How changing cultural ideas bring changes to language is clearly visible in this semantic area. The feminist movement has caused the differences between the sexes to be downplayed, and since I did my dictionary study two decades ago, the word *singles* has largely replaced such sex specific and value-laden terms as *bachelor, old maid, spinster,* 17 *divorcee, widow,* and *widower.* And in 1970, I wrote that when a man is called *a professional* he is thought to be a doctor or a lawyer, but when people hear a woman referred to as a professional, they are likely to think of a prostitute. That's not as true today because so many women have become doctors and lawyers that it's no longer incongruous to think of women in those professional roles

Another change that has taken place is in wedding announcements. 18 They used to be sent out from the bride's parents and did not even give the name of the groom's parents. Today, most couples choose to list either all or none of the parents' names. Also it is now much more likely that both the bride and groom's picture will be in the newspaper, while a decade ago only the bride's picture was published on the "Women's" or the "Society" page. Even the traditional wording of the wedding ceremony is being changed. Many officials now pronounce the couple "husband and wife" instead of the old "man and wife," and they ask the bride if she promises "to love, honor, and cherish," instead of "to love, honor, and obey."

Women Are Passive; Men Are Active

The wording of the wedding ceremony also relates to the second 19 point that my cards showed, which is that women are expected to play a passive or weak role while men play an active or strong role. In the traditional ceremony, the official asks, "Who gives the bride away?" and the father answers, "I do." Some fathers answer, "Her mother and I do," but that doesn't solve the problem inherent in the question. The idea that a bride is something to be handed over from one man to another bothers people because it goes back to the days when a man's servants, his children, and his wife were all considered to be his property. They were known by his name because they belonged to him, and he was responsible for their actions and their debts.

The grammar used in talking or writing about weddings as well as 20 other sexual relationships shows the expectation of men playing the active role. Men *wed* women while women *become* brides of men. A man *possesses* a woman; he *deflowers* her; he *performs*; he *scores*; he *takes away* her virginity. Although a woman can *seduce* a man, she cannot offer him her virginity. When talking about virginity, the only way to make the woman the actor in the sentence is to say that "She lost her virginity," but people lose things by accident rather than by purposeful actions, and so she's only the grammatical, not the real-life, actor.

The reason that women tried to bring the term *Ms.* into the language to replace *Miss* and *Mrs.* relates to this point. Married women resent being identified only under their husband's names. For example, when Susan Glascoe did something newsworthy, she would be identified in the newspaper only as Mrs. John Glascoe. The dictionary cards showed what appeared to be an attitude on the part of the editors that it was almost indecent to let a respectable woman's name march unaccompanied across the pages of a dictionary. Women were listed with male names whether or not the male contributed to the woman's reason for being in the dictionary or in his own right was as famous as the woman. For example, Charlotte Bronte was identified as Mrs. Arthur B. Nicholls, Amelia Earhart as Mrs. George Palmer Putnam, Helen Hayes as Mrs. Charles MacArthur, Jenny Lind as Mme. Otto Goldschmit, Cornelia Otis Skinner as the daughter of Otis, Harriet Beecher Stowe as the sister of Henry Ward Beecher, and Edith Sitwell as the sister of Osbert and Sacheverell.[2] A very small number of women got into the dictionary without the benefit of a masculine escort. They were rebels and crusaders: temperance leaders Frances Elizabeth Caroline Willard and Carry Nation, women's rights leaders Carrie Chapman Catt and Elizabeth Cady Stanton, birth control educator Margaret Sanger, religious leader Mary Baker Eddy, and slaves Harriet Tubman and Phillis Wheatley.

Etiquette books used to teach that if a woman had *Mrs.* in front of her name, then the husband's name should follow because *Mrs.* is an abbreviated form of *Mistress* and a woman couldn't be a mistress of herself. As with many arguments about "correct" language usage, this isn't very logical because *Miss* is also an abbreviation of *Mistress*. Feminists hoped to simplify matters by introducing *Ms.* as an alternative to both *Mrs.* and *Miss,* but what happened is that *Ms.* largely replaced *Miss,* to become a catch-all business title for women. Many married women still prefer the title *Mrs.,* and some resent being addressed with the term *Ms.* As one frustrated newspaper reporter complained, "Before I can write about a woman, I have to know not only her marital status but also her political philosophy." The result of such complications may contribute to the demise of titles, which are already being ignored by many computer programmers who find it more efficient to simply use names, for example in a business letter: "Dear Joan Garcia," instead of "Dear Mrs. Joan Garcia," "Dear Ms. Garcia," or "Dear Mrs. Louis Garcia." 22

The titles given to royalty provide an example of how males can be disadvantaged by the assumption that they are always to play the more powerful role. In British royalty, when a male holds a title, his wife is automatically given the feminine equivalent. But the reverse is not true. 23

---

[2] Charlotte Brontë (1816–1855), author of *Jane Eyre;* Amelia Earhart (1898–1937), first woman to fly over the Atlantic; Helen Hayes (1900–1993), actress; Jenny Lind (1820–1887), Swedish soprano known at the "Swedish nightingale"; Cornelia Otis Skinner (1901–1979), actress and writer; Harriet Beecher Stowe (1811–1896), author of *Uncle Tom's Cabin;* and Edith Sitwell (1877–1964), English poet and critic. [Eds.]

For example, a *count* is a high political officer with a *countess* being his wife. The same is true for a *duke* and a *duchess* and a *king* and a *queen*. But when a female holds the royal title, the man she marries does not automatically acquire the matching title. For example, Queen Elizabeth's husband has the title of *prince* rather than *king*, but if Prince Charles should become king while he is still married to Lady or Princess Diana,[3] she will be known as the queen. The reasoning appears to be that since masculine words are stronger, they are reserved for true heirs and withheld from males coming into the royal family by marriage. If Prince Phillip were called *King Phillip*, it would be much easier for British subjects to forget where the true power lies.

The names that people give their children show the hopes and 24 dreams they have for them, and when we look at the differences between male and female names in a culture, we can see the cumulative expectations of that culture. In our culture girls often have names taken from small, aesthetically pleasing items, e.g., *Ruby, Jewel,* and *Pearl. Esther* and *Stella* mean '"star," *Ada* means "ornament," and *Vanessa* means "butterfly." Boys are more likely to be given names with meanings of power and strength, e.g., *Neil* means "champion," *Martin* is from Mars, the God of War, *Raymond* means "wise protection," *Harold* means "chief of the army," *Ira* means "vigilant," *Rex* means "king," and *Richard* means "strong king."

We see similar differences in food metaphors. Food is a passive sub- 25 stance just sitting there waiting to be eaten. Many people have recognized this and so no longer feel comfortable describing women as "delectable morsels." However, when I was a teenager, it was considered a compliment to refer to a girl (we didn't call anyone a *woman* until she was middle-aged) as a *cute tomato, a peach, a dish, a cookie, honey, sugar,* or *sweetie-pie.* When being affectionate, women will occasionally call a man *honey* or *sweetie,* but in general, food metaphors are used much less often with men than with women. If a man is called *a fruit,* his masculinity is being questioned. But it's perfectly acceptable to use a food metaphor if the food is heavier and more substantive than that used for women. For example pin-up pictures of women have long been known as *cheesecake,* but when Burt Reynolds posed for a nude centerfold the picture was immediately dubbed *beefcake,* cf., *a hunk of meat.* That such sexual references to men have come into the language is another reflection of how society is beginning to lessen the difference between their attitudes toward men and women.

Something similar to the *fruit* metaphor happens with references to 26 plants. We insult a man by calling him a *pansy,* but it wasn't considered particularly insulting to talk about a girl being a *wallflower,* a *clinging*

---

[3] Princess Diana died in 1997. [Eds.]

vine, or a *shrinking violet,* or to give girls such names as *Ivy, Rose, Lily, Iris, Daisy, Camellia, Heather,* and *Flora.* A plant metaphor can be used with a man if the plant is big and strong, for example, Andrew Jackson's nickname of *Old Hickory.* Also, the phrases *blooming idiots* and *budding geniuses* can be used with either sex, but notice how they are based on the most active thing a plant can do, which is to bloom or bud.

Animal metaphors also illustrate the different expectations for 27 males and females. Men are referred to as *studs, bucks,* and *wolves* while women are referred to with such metaphors as *kitten, bunny, beaver, bird, chick,* and *lamb.* In the 1950s we said that boys went *tomcatting,* but today it's just *catting around* and both boys and girls do it. When the term *foxy,* meaning that someone was sexy, first became popular it was used only for girls, but now someone of either sex can be described as *a fox.* Some animal metaphors that are used predominantly with men have negative connotations based on the size and/or strength of the animals, e.g., *beast, bullheaded, jackass, rat, loanshark,* and *vulture.* Negative metaphors used with women are based on smaller animals, e.g. *social butterfly, mousy, catty,* and *vixen.* The feminine terms connote action, but not the same kind of large scale action as with the masculine terms.

Women Are Connected with Negative Connotations; Men with Positive Connotations

The final point that my notecards illustrated was how many posi- 28 tive connotations are associated with the concept of masculine, while there are either trivial or negative connotations connected with the corresponding feminine concept. An example from the animal metaphors makes a good illustration. The word *shrew* taken from the name of a small but especially vicious animal was defined in my dictionary as "an ill-tempered scolding woman," but the word *shrewd* taken from the same root was defined as "marked by clever, discerning awareness" and was illustrated with the phrase "a shrewd businessman."

Early in life, children are conditioned to the superiority of the 29 masculine role. As child psychologists point out, little girls have much more freedom to experiment with sex roles than do little boys. If a little girl acts like a *tomboy,* most parents have mixed feelings, being at least partially proud. But if their little boy acts like a *sissy* (derived from *sister*), they call a psychologist. It's perfectly acceptable for a little girl to sleep in the crib that was purchased for her brother, to wear his hand-me-down jeans and shirts, and to ride the bicycle that he has outgrown. But few parents would put a boy baby in a white and gold crib decorated with frills and lace, and virtually no parents would have their little boys wear his sister's hand-me-down dresses, nor would they have their son ride a girl's pink bicycle with a flower-bedecked basket. The proper names given to girls and boys show this same attitude. Girls can have "boy" names—*Cris, Craig, Jo, Kelly, Shawn, Teri, Toni,* and *Sam*—but it doesn't work the other way around. A couple of generations ago, *Beverly, Frances, Hazel, Marion,* and *Shirley* were common boys' names. As parents gave these names to more and more girls, they fell into disuse for males, and some older men who have these names prefer to go by their initials or by such abbreviated forms as *Haze* or *Shirl.*

When a little girl is told to *be a lady,* she is being told to sit with her   30
knees together and to be quiet and dainty. But when a little boy is told to *be a man* he is being told to be noble, strong, and virtuous—to have all the qualities that the speaker looks on as desirable. The concept of manliness has such positive connotations that it used to be a compliment to call someone a *he-man,* to say that he was doubly a man. Today many people are more ambivalent about this term and respond to it much as they do to the word *macho.* But calling someone a *manly man* or a *virile man* is nearly always meant as a compliment. *Virile* comes from the Indo-European *vir* meaning "man," which is also the basis for *virtuous.* Contrast the positive connotations of both *virile* and *virtuous* with the negative connotations of *hysterical.* The Greeks took this latter word from their name for uterus (as still seen in *hysterectomy*). They thought that women were the only ones who experienced uncontrolled emotional outbursts, and so the condition must have something to do with a part of the body that only women have.

Differences in the connotations between positive male and negative   31
female connotations can be seen in several pairs of words that differ denotatively only in the matter of sex. *Bachelor* as compared to *spinster* or *old maid* has such positive connotations that women try to adopt them by using the term *bachelor-girl* or *bachelorette. Old maid* is so negative that it's the basis for metaphors: pretentious and fussy old men are called *old maids,* as are the leftover kernels of unpopped popcorn, and the last card in a popular children's game.

Patron and *matron* (Middle English for *father* and *mother*) have such   32
different levels of prestige that women try to borrow the more positive masculine connotations with the word *patroness,* literally "female father." Such a peculiar term came about because of the high prestige attached to *patron* in such phrases as *a patron of the arts* or *a patron saint. Matron* is more apt to be used in talking about a woman in charge of a jail or a public restroom.

When men are doing jobs that women often do, we apparently try   33
to pay the men extra by giving them fancy titles, for example, a male cook is more likely to be called a *chef* while a male seamstress will get the title of *tailor.* The armed forces have a special problem in that they recruit under such slogans as "The Marine Corps builds men!" and

"Join the Army! Become a Man." Once the recruits are enlisted, they find themselves doing much of the work that has been traditionally thought of as "women's work." The solution to getting the work done and not insulting anyone's masculinity was to change the titles as shown below:

waitress	orderly
nurse	medic or corpsman
secretary	clerk-typist
assistant	adjutant
dishwasher or kitchen helper	KP (kitchen police)

Compare *brave* and *squaw*. Early settlers in America truly admired 34 Indian men and hence named them with a word that carried connotations of youth, vigor, and courage. But they used the Algonquin's name for "woman" and over the years it developed almost opposite connotations to those of *brave*. *Wizard* and *witch* contrast almost as much. The masculine *wizard* implies skill and wisdom combined with magic, while the feminine *witch* implies evil intentions combined with magic. Part of the unattractiveness of both *witch* and *squaw* is that they have been used so often to refer to old women, something with which our culture is particularly uncomfortable, just as the Afghans were. Imagine my surprise when I ran across the phrases *grandfatherly advice* and *old wives' tales* and realized that the underlying implication is the same as the Afghan proverb about old men being worth listening to while old women talk only foolishness.

Other terms that show how negatively we view old women as com- 35 pared to young women are *old nag* as compared to *filly, old crow* or *old bat* as compared to *bird,* and of being *catty* as compared to being *kittenish.* There is no matching set of metaphors for men. The chicken metaphor tells the whole story of a woman's life. In her youth she is a *chick.* Then she marries and begins *feathering her nest.* Soon she begins feeling *cooped up,* so she goes to *hen parties* where she *cackles* with her friends. Then she has her *brood,* begins to *henpeck* her husband, and finally turns into an *old biddy.*

I embarked on my study of the dictionary not with the intention of 36 prescribing language change but simply to see what the language would tell me about sexism. Nevertheless I have been both surprised and pleased as I've watched the changes that have occurred over the past two decades. I'm one of those linguists who believes that new language customs will cause a new generation of speakers to grow up with different expectations. This is why I'm happy about people's efforts to use inclusive language, to say *he or she* or *they* when speaking about individuals whose names they do not know. I'm glad that leading publishers have developed guidelines to help writers use language that is fair to both sexes, and I'm glad that most newspapers and magazines list women by their own names instead of only by their husbands' names and that educated and thoughtful people no longer begin their business letters with "Dear Sir" or "Gentlemen," but instead use a memo form or begin with such salutations as "Dear Colleagues," "Dear Reader," or "Dear Committee Members." I'm also glad that such words as *poetess, authoress, conductress,* and *aviatrix* now sound quaint and old-fashioned and that *chairman* is giving way to *chair* or *head, mailman* to *mail carrier, clergyman* to *clergy,* and *stewardess* to *flight attendant.* I was also pleased when the National Oceanic and Atmospheric Administration bowed to feminist complaints and in the late 1970s began to alternate men's and women's names for hurricanes. However, I wasn't so pleased to discover that the change did not immediately erase sexist thoughts from everyone's mind, as shown by a headline about Hurricane David in a 1979 New York tabloid, "David Rapes Virgin Islands." More recently a similar metaphor appeared in a headline in the *Arizona Republic* about Hurricane Charlie, "Charlie Quits Carolinas, Flirts with Virginia."

What these incidents show is that sexism is not something existing 37 independently in American English or in the particular dictionary that I happened to read. Rather, it exists in people's minds. Language is like an X-ray in providing visible evidence of invisible thoughts. The best thing about people being interested in and discussing sexist language is that as they make conscious decisions about what pronouns they will use, what jokes they will tell or laugh at, how they will write their names, or how they will begin their letters, they are forced to think about the underlying issue of sexism. This is good because as a problem that begins in people's assumptions and expectations, it's a problem that will be solved only when a great many people have given it a great deal of thought.

Responding to Reading

1. What point is Nilsen making about the culture in which she lives? Does your experience support her conclusions?
2. Does Nilsen use enough examples to support her claims? What others can you think of? In what way do her examples—and your own—illustrate the power of language to define the way people think?
3. Many of the connotations of the words Nilsen discusses are hundreds of years old and are also found in languages other than English. Given the widespread and long-standing linguistic bias against women, do you think attempts by Nilsen and others to change this situation succeed?

POLITICS AND THE ENGLISH LANGUAGE

George Orwell

Eric Blair (1903–1950) was an Englishman, born in Bengal, India, who took the pen name George Orwell. He attended school in England and then joined the Indian Imperial Police in Burma, where he came to question the British methods of colonialism. (See his essay "Shooting an Elephant," p. 724). An enemy of totalitarianism in any form and a spokesman for the oppressed, Orwell criticized totalitarian regimes in his bitterly satirical novels Animal Farm *(1945) and* 1984 *(1949). The following essay was written during the period between these two novels' publications, at the end of World War II when jingoistic praise for "our democratic institutions" and blindly passionate defenses of Marxist ideology were the two common extremes of public political discourse. Orwell's plea for clear thinking and writing at a time when "[p]olitical language . . . is designed to make lies sound truthful and murder respectable, and to give an appearance of solidity to pure wind" is as relevant today as when it was written.*

Most people who bother with the matter at all would admit that the 1 English language is in a bad way, but it is generally assumed that we cannot by conscious action do anything about it. Our civilization is decadent and our language—so the argument runs—must inevitably share in the general collapse. It follows that any struggle against the abuse of language is a sentimental archaism, like preferring candles to electric light or hansom cabs to airplanes. Underneath this lies the half-conscious belief that language is a natural growth and not an instrument which we shape for our own purposes.

Now, it is clear that the decline of a language must ultimately have 2 political and economic causes: it is not due simply to the bad influence of this or that individual writer. But an effect can become a cause, reinforcing the original cause and producing the same effect in an intensified form, and so on indefinitely. A man may take to drink because he feels himself to be a failure, and then fail all the more completely because he drinks. It is rather the same thing that is happening to the English language. It becomes ugly and inaccurate because our thoughts are foolish, but the slovenliness of our language makes it easier for us to have foolish thoughts. The point is that the process is reversible. Modern English, especially written English, is full of bad habits which spread by imitation and which can be avoided if one is willing to take the necessary trouble. If one gets rid of these habits one can think more clearly, and to think clearly is a necessary first step towards political regeneration: so that the fight against bad English is not frivolous and is not the exclusive concern of professional writers. I will come back to this presently, and I hope that by that time the meaning of what I have said here will have become clearer. Meanwhile, here are five specimens of the English language as it is now habitually written.

These five passages have not been picked out because they are espe- 3 cially bad—I could have quoted far worse if I had chosen—but because they illustrate various of the mental vices from which we now suffer. They are a little below the average, but are fairly representative samples. I number them so that I can refer back to them when necessary:

> "(1) I am not, indeed, sure whether it is not true to say that the Milton who once seemed not unlike a seventeenth-century Shelley had not become, out of an experience ever more bitter in each year, more alien (*sic*) to the founder of that Jesuit sect which nothing could induce him to tolerate."
>
> Professor Harold Laski (Essay in *Freedom of Expression*).

> "(2) Above all, we cannot play ducks and drakes with a native battery of idioms which prescribes such egregious collocations of vocables as the Basic *put up with* for *tolerate* or *put at a loss* for *bewilder*."
>
> Professor Lancelot Hogben (*Interglossa*).

> "(3) On the one side we have the free personality: by definition it is not neurotic, for it has neither conflict nor dream. Its desires, such as they are, are transparent, for they are just what institutional approval keeps in the forefront of consciousness; another institutional pattern would alter their number and intensity; there is little in them that is natural, irreducible, or culturally dangerous. But *on the other side*, the social bond itself is nothing but the mutual reflection of these self-secure integrities. Recall the definition of love. Is not this the very picture of a small academic? Where is there a place in this hall of mirrors for either personality or fraternity?"
>
> Essay on psychology in *Politics* (New York).

> "(4) All the 'best people' from the gentlemen's clubs, and all the frantic fascist captains, united in common hatred of Socialism and bestial horror of the rising tide of the mass revolutionary movement, have turned to acts of provocation, to foul incendiarism, to medieval legends of poisoned wells, to legalize their own destruction of proletarian organizations, and rouse the agitated petty-bourgeoisie to chauvinistic fervor on behalf of the fight against the revolutionary way out of the crisis."
>
> Communist pamphlet.

> "(5) If a new spirit *is* to be infused into this old country, there is one thorny and contentious reform which must be tackled, and that is the humanization and galvanization of the B.B.C. Timidity here will

bespeak cancer and atrophy of the soul. The heart of Britain may be sound and of strong beat, for instance, but the British lion's roar at present is like that of Bottom in Shakespeare's *Midsummer Night's Dream*— as gentle as any sucking dove. A virile new Britain cannot continue indefinitely to be traduced in the eyes or rather ears, of the world by the effete languors of Langham Place, brazenly masquerading as 'standard English.' When the Voice of Britain is heard at nine o'clock, better far and infinitely less ludicrous to hear aitches honestly dropped than the present priggish, inflated, inhibited, school-ma'amish arch braying of blameless bashful mewing maidens!"

Letter in Tribune.

Each of these passages has faults of its own, but, quite apart from   4 avoidable ugliness, two qualities are common to all of them. The first is staleness of imagery: the other is lack of precision. The writer either has a meaning and cannot express it, or he inadvertently says something else, or he is almost indifferent as to whether his words mean anything or not. This mixture of vagueness and sheer incompetence is the most marked characteristic of modern English prose, and especially of any kind of political writing. As soon as certain topics are raised, the concrete melts into the abstract and no one seems able to think of turns of speech that are not hackneyed: prose consists less and less of *words* chosen for the sake of their meaning, and more and more of *phrases* tacked together like the sections of a prefabricated hen-house. I list below, with notes and examples, various of the tricks by means of which the work of prose-construction is habitually dodged:

Dying Metaphors

A newly invented metaphor assists thought by evoking a visual   5 image, while on the other hand a metaphor which is technically "dead" (e.g. *iron resolution*) has in effect reverted to being an ordinary word and can generally be used without loss of vividness. But in between these two classes there is a huge dump of worn-out metaphors which have lost all evocative power and are merely used because they save people the trouble of inventing phrases for themselves. Examples are: *Ring the changes on, take up the cudgels for, toe the line, ride roughshod over, stand shoulder to shoulder with, play into the hands of, no axe to grind, grist to the mill, fishing in troubled waters, on the order of the day, Achilles' heel, swan song, hotbed.* Many of these are used without knowledge of their meaning (what is a "rift,"[1] for instance?), and incompatible metaphors are frequently mixed, a sure sign that the writer is not interested in what he is

---

[1] Originally *rift* referred to a geological fault or fissure. Now it is commonly used to indicate a breach or estrangement. [Eds.]

saying. Some metaphors now current have been twisted out of their original meaning without those who use them even being aware of the fact. For example, *toe the line* is sometimes written *tow the line*. Another example is the *hammer and the anvil*, now always used with the implication that the anvil gets the worst or it. In real life it is always the anvil that breaks the hammer, never the other way about: a writer who stopped to think what he was saying would be aware of this, and would avoid perverting the original phrase.

Operators or Verbal False Limbs

These save the trouble of picking out appropriate verbs and nouns, 6 and at the same time pad each sentence with extra syllables which give it an appearance of symmetry. Characteristic phrases are: *render inoperative, militate against, make contact with, be subjected to, give rise to, give grounds for, have the effect of, play a leading part (role) in, make itself felt, take effect, exhibit a tendency to, serve the purpose of, etc., etc.* The keynote is the elimination of simple verbs. Instead of being a single word, such as *break, stop, spoil, mend, kill,* a verb becomes a *phrase,* made up of a noun or adjective tacked on to some general-purposes verb such as *prove, serve, form, play, render.* In addition, the passive voice is wherever possible used in preference to the active, and noun constructions are used instead of gerunds (*by examination of* instead of *by examining*). The range of verbs is further cut down by means of the *-ize* and *de-* formation, and the banal statements are given an appearance of profundity by means of the *not un-* formation. Simple conjunctions and prepositions are replaced by such phrases as *with respect to, having regard to, the fact that, by dint of, in view of, in the interests of, on the hypothesis that;* and the ends of sentences are saved from anticlimax by such resounding commonplaces as *greatly to be desired, cannot be left out of account, a development to be expected in the near future, deserving of serious consideration, brought to a satisfactory conclusion,* and so on and so forth.

Pretentious Diction

Words like *phenomenon, element, individual* (as noun), *objective, cate-* 7 *gorical, effective, virtual, basic, primary, promote, constitute, exhibit, exploit, utilize, eliminate, liquidate,* are used to dress up simple statements and give an air of scientific impartiality to biased judgments. Adjectives like *epoch-making, epic, historic, unforgettable, triumphant, age-old, inevitable, inexorable, veritable,* are used to dignify the sordid processes of international politics, while writing that aims at glorifying war usually takes on an archaic color, its characteristic words being: *realm, throne, chariot, mailed fist, trident, sword, shield, buckler, banner, jackboot, clarion.* Foreign words and expressions such as *cul de sac, ancien régime, deus ex machina, mutatis mutandis, status quo, gleichschaltung, weltanschauung,* are used to give an air of culture and elegance. Except for the useful abbreviations *i.e., e.g.,* and *etc.,* there is no real need for any of the hundreds of foreign phrases now current in English. Bad writers, and especially scientific, political and sociological writers, are nearly always haunted by the notion that Latin or Greek words are grander than Saxon ones, and unnecessary words like *expedite, ameliorate, predict, extraneous, deracinated, clandestine, subaqueous* and hundreds of others constantly gain ground from their Anglo-Saxon opposite numbers.[2] The jargon peculiar to Marxist writing (*hyena, hangman, cannibal, petty bourgeois, these gentry, lacquey, flunkey, mad dog, White Guard,* etc.) consists largely of words and phrases translated from Russian, German or French; but the normal way of coining a new word is to use a Latin or Greek root with the appropriate affix and, where necessary, the *-ize* formation. It is often easier to make up words of this kind (*deregionalize, impermissible, extra-marital, nonfragmentatory* and so forth) than to think up the English words that will cover one's meaning. The result, in general, is an increase in slovenliness and vagueness.

Meaningless Words

In certain kinds of writing, particularly in art criticism and literary   8
criticism, it is normal to come across long passages which are almost completely lacking in meaning.[3] Words like *romantic, plastic, values, human, dead, sentimental, natural, vitality,* as used in art criticism, are strictly meaningless in the sense that they not only do not point to any discoverable object, but are hardly ever expected to do so by the reader. When one critic writes, "The outstanding feature of Mr. X's work is its living quality," while another writes, "The immediately striking thing about Mr. X's work is its peculiar deadness," the reader accepts this as a simple difference of opinion. If words like *black* and *white* were involved, instead of the jargon words *dead* and *living,* he would see at once that language was being used in an improper way. Many political words are similarly abused. The word *Fascism* has now no meaning

---

[2] An interesting illustration of this is the way in which the English flower names which were in use till very recently are being ousted by Greek ones, *snapdragon* becoming *antirrhinum, forget-me-not* becoming *myosotis,* etc. It is hard to see any practical reason for this change in fashion: it is probably due to an instinctive turning-away from the more homely word and a vague feeling that the Greek word is scientific.

[3] Example: "Comfort's catholicity of perception and image, strangely Whitmanesque in range, almost the exact opposite in aesthetic compulsion, continues to evoke that trembling atmospheric accumulative hinting at a cruel, an inexorably serene timelessness. . . . Wrey Gardiner scores by aiming at simple bull's-eyes with precision. Only they are not so simple, and through this contended sadness—runs more than the surface bittersweet of resignation" (*Poetry Quarterly*).

except in so far as it signifies "something not desirable." The words *democracy, socialism, freedom, patriotic, realistic, justice,* have each of them several different meanings which cannot be reconciled with one another. In the case of a word like *democracy,* not only is there no agreed definition, but the attempt to make one is resisted from all sides. It is almost universally felt that when we call a country democratic we are praising it: consequently the defenders of every kind of regime claim that it is a democracy, and fear that they might have to stop using the word if it were tied down to any one meaning. Words of this kind are often used in a consciously dishonest way. That is, the person who uses them has his own private definition, but allows his hearer to think he means something quite different. Statements like *Marshal Pétain was a true patriot, The Soviet Press is the freest in the world, The Catholic Church is opposed to persecution,* are almost always made with intent to deceive. Other words used in variable meanings, in most cases more or less dishonestly, are: *class, totalitarian, science, progressive, reactionary, bourgeois, equality.*

Now that I have made this catalogue of swindles and perversions, 9 let me give another example of the kind of writing that they lead to. This time it must of its nature be an imaginary one. I am going to translate a passage of good English into modern English of the worst sort. Here is a well-known verse from *Ecclesiastes:*

> "I returned and saw under the sun, that the race is not to the swift, nor the battle to the strong, neither yet bread to the wise, nor yet riches to men of understanding, nor yet favor to men of skill; but time and chance happeneth to them all."

Here it is in modern English: 10

> "Objective consideration of contemporary phenomena compels the conclusion that success or failure in competitive activities exhibits no tendency to be commensurate with innate capacity, but that a considerable element of the unpredictable must invariably be taken into account."

This is a parody, but not a very gross one. Exhibit (3), above, for 11 instance, contains several patches of the same kind of English. It will be seen that I have not made a full translation. The beginning and ending of the sentence follow the original meaning fairly closely, but in the middle the concrete illustrations—race, battle, bread—dissolve into the vague phrase "success or failure in competitive activities." This had to be so, because no modern writer of the kind I am discussing—no one capable of using phrases like "objective consideration of contemporary phenomena"—would ever tabulate his thoughts in that precise and detailed way. The whole tendency of modern prose is away from concreteness. Now analyze these two sentences a little more closely. The first contains forty-nine words but only sixty syllables, and all its words are those of everyday life. The second contains thirty-eight words of ninety syllables: eighteen of its words are from Latin roots, and one from Greek. The first sentence contains six vivid images, and only one phrase ("time and chance") that could be called vague. The second contains not a single fresh, arresting phrase, and in spite of its ninety syllables it gives only a shortened version of the meaning contained in the first. Yet without a doubt it is the second kind of sentence that is gaining ground in modern English. I do not want to exaggerate. This kind of writing is not yet universal, and outcrops of simplicity will occur here and there in the worst-written page. Still, if you or I were told to write a few lines on the uncertainty of human fortunes, we should probably come much nearer to my imaginary sentence than to the one from *Ecclesiastes*.

As I have tried to show, modern writing at its worst does not consist in picking out words for the sake of their meaning and inventing images in order to make the meaning clearer. It consists in gumming together long strips of words which have already been set in order by someone else, and making the results presentable by sheer humbug. The attraction of this way of writing is that it is easy. It is easier—even quicker, once you have the habit—to say *In my opinion it is a not unjustifiable assumption that* than to say *I think*. If you use ready-made phrases, you not only don't have to hunt about for words; you also don't have to bother with the rhythms of your sentences, since these phrases are generally so arranged as to be more or less euphonious. When you are composing in a hurry—when you are dictating to a stenographer, for instance, or making a public speech—it is natural to fall into a pretentious, Latinized style. Tags like *a consideration which we should do well to bear in mind* or *a conclusion to which all of us would readily assent* will save many a sentence from coming down with a bump. By using stale metaphors, similes and idioms, you save much mental effort, at the cost of leaving your meaning vague, not only for your reader but for yourself. This is the significance of mixed metaphors. The sole aim of a metaphor is to call up a visual image. When these images clash—as in *The Fascist octopus has sung its swan song, the jackboot is thrown into the melting pot*— it can be taken as certain that the writer is not seeing a mental image of the objects he is naming; in other words he is not really thinking. Look again at the examples I gave at the beginning of this essay. Professor Laski (1) uses five negatives in fifty-three words. One of these is superfluous, making nonsense of the whole passage, and in addition there is the slip *alien* for *akin*, making further nonsense, and several avoidable pieces of clumsiness which increase the general vagueness. Professor Hogben (2) plays ducks and drakes with a battery which is able to write prescriptions, and, while disapproving of the everyday phrase *put up*

12

with, is unwilling to look *egregious* up in the dictionary and see what it means. (3), if one takes an uncharitable attitude towards it, is simply meaningless: probably one could work out its intended meaning by reading the whole of the article in which it occurs. In (4), the writer knows more or less what he wants to say, but an accumulation of stale phrases chokes him like tea leaves blocking a sink. In (5), words and meaning have almost parted company. People who write in this manner usually have a general emotional meaning—they dislike one thing and want to express solidarity with another—but they are not interested in the detail of what they are saying. A scrupulous writer, in every sentence that he writes, will ask himself at least four questions, thus: What am I trying to say? What words will express it? What image or idiom will make it clearer? Is this image fresh enough to have an effect? And he will probably ask himself two more: Could I put it more shortly? Have I said anything that is avoidably ugly? But you are not obliged to go to all this trouble. You can shirk it by simply throwing your mind open and letting the ready-made phrases come crowding in. They will construct your sentences for you—even think your thoughts for you, to a certain extent—and at need they will perform the important service of partially concealing your meaning even from yourself. It is at this point that the special connection between politics and the debasement of language becomes clear.

In our time it is broadly true that political writing is bad writing. 13 Where it is not true, it will generally be found that the writer is some kind of rebel, expressing his private opinions and not a "party line." Orthodoxy, of whatever color, seems to demand a lifeless, imitative style. The political dialects to be found in pamphlets, leading articles, manifestos, White Papers and the speeches of under-secretaries do, of course, vary from party to party, but they are all alike in that one almost never finds in them a fresh, vivid, home-made turn of speech. When one watches some tired hack on the platform mechanically repeating the familiar phrases—*bestial atrocities, iron heel, bloodstained tyranny, free peoples of the world, stand shoulder to shoulder*—one often has a curious feeling that one is not watching a live human being but some kind of dummy: a feeling which suddenly becomes stronger at moments when the light catches the speaker's spectacles and turns them into blank discs which seem to have no eyes behind them. And this is not altogether fanciful. A speaker who uses that kind of phraseology has gone some distance towards turning himself into a machine. The appropriate noises are coming out of his larynx, but his brain is not involved as it would be if he were choosing his words for himself. If the speech he is making is one that he is accustomed to make over and over again, he may be almost unconscious of what he is saying, as one is when one utters the responses in church. And this reduced state of consciousness, if not indispensable, is at any rate favorable to political conformity.

In our time, political speech and writing are largely the defence of 14 the indefensible. Things like the continuance of British rule in India, the Russian purges and deportations, the dropping of the atom bombs on Japan, can indeed be defended, but only by arguments which are too brutal for most people to face, and which do not square with the professed aims of political parties Thus political language has to consist largely of euphemism, question-begging and sheer cloudy vagueness. Defenceless villages are bombarded from the air, the inhabitants driven out into the countryside, the cattle machine-gunned, the huts set on fire with incendiary bullets: this is called *pacification*. Millions of peasants are robbed of their farms and sent trudging along the roads with no more than they can carry: this is called *transfer of population* or *rectification of frontiers*. People are imprisoned for years without trial, or shot in the back of the neck or sent to die of scurvy in Arctic lumber camps: this is called *elimination of unreliable elements*. Such phraseology is needed if one wants to name things without calling up mental pictures of them. Consider for instance some comfortable English professor defending Russian totalitarianism. He cannot say outright, "I believe in killing off your opponents when you can get good results by doing so." Probably, therefore, he will say something like this:

"While freely conceding that the Soviet régime exhibits certain fea- 15 tures which the humanitarian may be inclined to deplore, we must, I think, agree that a certain curtailment of the right to political opposition is an unavoidable concomitant of transitional periods, and that the rigors which the Russian people have been called upon to undergo have been amply justified in the sphere of concrete achievement."

The inflated style is itself a kind of euphemism. A mass of Latin 16 words falls upon the facts like soft snow, blurring the outlines and covering up all the details. The great enemy of clear language is insincerity. When there is a gap between one's real and one's declared aims, one turns as it were instinctively to long words and exhausted idioms, like a cuttlefish squirting out ink. In our age there is no such thing as "keeping out of politics." All issues are political issues, and politics itself is a mass of lies, evasions, folly, hatred and schizophrenia. When the general atmosphere is bad, language must suffer. I should expect to find—this is a guess which I have not sufficient knowledge to verify—that the German, Russian and Italian languages have all deteriorated in the last ten to fifteen years, as a result of dictatorship.

But if thought corrupts language, language can also corrupt 17 thought. A bad usage can spread by tradition and imitation, even among people who should and do know better. The debased language that I have been discussing is in some ways very convenient. Phrases like *a not unjustifiable assumption, leaves much to be desired, would serve no good purpose, a consideration which we should do well to bear in mind,* are a continuous temptation, a packet of aspirins always at one's elbow. Look back through this essay, and for certain you will find that I have again and again committed the very faults I am protesting against. By this morning's post I have received a pamphlet dealing with conditions in Germany. The author tells me that he "felt impelled" to write it. I open it at random, and here is almost the first sentence that I see: "(The Allies) have an opportunity not only of achieving a radical transformation of Germany's social and political structure in such a way as to avoid a nationalistic reaction in Germany itself, but at the same time of laying the foundations of a cooperative and unified Europe." You see, he "feels impelled" to write—feels, presumably, that he has something new to say—and yet his words, like cavalry horses answering the bugle, group themselves automatically into the familiar dreary pattern. This invasion of one's mind by ready-made phrases (*lay the foundations, achieve a radical transformation*) can only be prevented if one is constantly on guard against them, and every such phrase anesthetizes a portion of one's brain.

I said earlier that the decadence of our language is probably curable. Those who deny this would argue, if they produced an argument at all, that language merely reflects existing social conditions, and that we cannot influence its development by any direct tinkering with words and constructions. So far as the general tone or spirit of a language goes, this may be true, but it is not true in detail. Silly words and expressions have often disappeared, not through any evolutionary process but owing to the conscious action of a minority. Two recent examples were *explore every avenue* and *leave no stone unturned*, which were killed by the jeers of a few journalists. There is a long list of flyblown metaphors which could similarly be got rid of if enough people would interest themselves in the job; and it should also be possible to laugh the *not un-* formation out of existence,[4] to reduce the amount of Latin and Greek in the average sentence, to drive out foreign phrases and strayed scientific words, and, in general, to make pretentiousness unfashionable. But all these are minor points. The defence of the English language implies more than this, and perhaps it is best to start by saying what it does *not* imply.

To begin with it has nothing to do with archaism, with the salvaging of obsolete words and turns of speech, or with the setting up of a "standard English" which must never be departed from. On the contrary, it is especially concerned with the scrapping of every word or idiom which has outworn its usefulness. It has nothing to do with correct grammar and syntax, which are of no importance so long as one makes one's meaning clear, or with the avoidance of Americanisms, or with having what is called a "good prose style." On the other hand it is not

18

19

---

[4] One can cure oneself of the *not un-* formation by memorizing this sentence: *A not unblack dog was chasing a not unsmall rabbit across a not ungreen field.*

concerned with fake simplicity and the attempt to make written English colloquial. Nor does it even imply in every case preferring the Saxon word to the Latin one, though it does imply using the fewest and shortest words that will cover one's meaning. What is above all needed is to let the meaning choose the word and not the other way about. In prose, the worst thing one can do with words is to surrender to them. When you think of a concrete object, you think wordlessly, and then, if you want to describe the thing you have been visualizing you probably hunt about till you find the exact words that seem to fit. When you think of something abstract you are more inclined to use words from the start, and unless you make a conscious effort to prevent it, the existing dialect will come rushing in and do the job for you, at the expense of blurring or even changing your meaning. Probably it is better to put off using words as long as possible and get one's meaning as clear as one can through pictures or sensations. Afterwards one can choose—not simply accept—the phrases that will best cover the meaning, and then switch round and decide what impression one's words are likely to make on another person. This last effort of the mind cuts out all stale or mixed images, all prefabricated phrases, needless repetitions, and humbug and vagueness generally. But one can often be in doubt about the effect of a word or a phrase, and one needs rules that one can rely on when instinct fails. I think the following rules will cover most cases:

(i) Never use a metaphor, simile or other figure of speech which you are used to seeing in print.
(ii) Never use a long word where a short one will do.
(iii) If it is possible to cut a word out, always cut it out.
(iv) Never use the passive where you can use the active.
(v) Never use a foreign phrase, a scientific word, or a jargon word if you can think of an everyday English equivalent.
(vi) Break any of these rules sooner than say anything outright barbarous.

These rules sound elementary, and so they are, but they demand a 20 deep change of attitude in anyone who has grown used to writing in the style now fashionable. One could keep all of them and still write bad English, but one could not write the kind of stuff that I quoted in those five specimens at the beginning of this article.

I have not here been considering the literary use of language, but 21 merely language as an instrument for expressing and not for concealing or preventing thought. Stuart Chase[5] and others have come near to claiming that all abstract words are meaningless, and have used this as

---

[5] Author known for his advocacy of clear writing and clear thinking. [Eds.]

a pretext for advocating a kind of political quietism. Since you don't know what Fascism is, how can you struggle against Fascism? One need not swallow such absurdities as this, but one ought to recognize that the present political chaos is connected with the decay of language, and that one can probably bring about some improvement by starting at the verbal end. If you simplify your English, you are freed from the worst follies of orthodoxy. You cannot speak any of the necessary dialects, and when you make a stupid remark its stupidity will be obvious, even to yourself. Political language—and with variations this is true of all political parties, from Conservatives to Anarchists—is designed to make lies sound truthful and murder respectable, and to give an appearance of solidity to pure wind. One cannot change this all in a moment, but one can at least change one's own habits, and from time to time one can even, if one jeers loudly enough, send some worn-out and useless phrase, some *jackboot, Achilles' heel, hotbed, melting pot, acid test, veritable inferno* or other lump of verbal refuse—into the dustbin where it belongs.

Responding to Reading

1. According to Orwell, what is the relationship between politics and the English language? Do you think he overstates his case?
2. What does Orwell mean in paragraph 14 when he says, "In our time, political speech and writing are largely the defence of the indefensible"? Do you believe his statement applies to current times as well? Look through some newspapers, and find several present-day examples of political language that support your conclusion.
3. Locate some examples of dying metaphors used in the popular press. Do you agree with Orwell that they undermine clear thought and expression? Why or why not?

FOCUS: SHOULD ALL AMERICANS SPEAK ENGLISH?

AGAINST A CONFUSION OF TONGUES

William A. Henry III

William A. Henry III (see also p. 120) wrote frequently on American society and culture, often from a conservative perspective, until his untimely death in 1994. In the following essay, originally published in Time *magazine in 1983, Henry argues that bilingual and bicultural education is divisive and disruptive because it poses the threat that large segments of American society will never learn to speak English.*

In the store windows of Los Angeles, gathering place of the world's aspiring peoples, the signs today ought to read, "English spoken here." Supermarket price tags are often written in Korean, restaurant menus in Chinese, employment-office signs in Spanish. In the new city of dreams, where gold can be earned if not found on the sidewalk, there are laborers and businessmen who have lived five, ten, twenty years in America without learning to speak English. English is not the common denominator for many of these new Americans. Disturbingly, some of them insist it need not be.

America's image of itself as a melting pot, enriched by every culture yet subsuming all of them, dates back far beyond the huddled yearning masses at the Baja California border and Ellis Island, beyond the passage in steerage of victims of the potato famine and the high-minded Teutonic settlements in the nascent Midwest. Just months after the Revolution was won, in 1782, French-American Writer Michel-Guillaume-Jean de Crevecoeur said of his adopted land: "Individuals of all nations are melted into a new race of men." Americans embittered by the wars of Europe knew that fusing diversity into unity was more than a poetic ideal, it was a practical necessity. In 1820 future Congressman Edward Everett warned, "From the days of the Tower of Babel, confusion of tongues has ever been one of the most active causes of political misunderstanding."

The successive waves of immigrants did not readily embrace the new culture, even when intimidated by the xenophobia of the know-nothing era or two World Wars. Says Historian James Banks: "Each nationality group tried desperately to remake North America in the image of its native land." When the question arose of making the U.S. multilingual or multicultural in public affairs, however, Congress stood firm. In the 1790s, 1840s and 1860s, the lawmakers voted down pleas to print Government documents in German. Predominantly French-speaking Louisiana sought statehood in 1812; the state constitution that it submitted for approval specified that its official language would be English. A century later, New Mexico was welcomed into the union, but only after an influx of settlers from the North and East had made English, not Spanish, the majority tongue.

Occasional concentrations of immigrants were able to win local 4 recognition of their language and thereby enforce an early form of affirmative action: by 1899 nearly 18,000 pupils in Cincinnati divided their school time between courses given in German and in English, thus providing employment for 186 German-speaking teachers. In 1917 San Francisco taught German in eight primary schools, Italian in six, French in four and Spanish in two. Yet when most cities consented to teach immigrant children in their native Chinese or Polish or Yiddish or Gujarati, the clearly stated goal was to transform the students as quickly as possible into speakers of English and full participants in society.

Now, however, a new bilingualism and biculturalism is being pro- 5 mulgated that would deliberately fragment the nation into separate, unassimilated groups. The movement seems to take much of its ideology from the black separatism of the 1960s but derives its political force from the unprecedented raw numbers—15 million or more—of a group linked to a single tongue, Spanish. The new metaphor is not the melting pot but the salad bowl, with each element distinct. The biculturalists seek to use public services, particularly schools, not to Americanize the young but to heighten their consciousness of belonging to another heritage. Contends Tomas A. Arciniega, vice president for academic affairs at California State University at Fresno: "The promotion of cultural differences has to be recognized as a valid and legitimate educational goal." Miguel Gonzalez-Pando, director of the Center for Latino Education of Florida International University in Miami, says: "I speak Spanish at home, my social relations are mostly in Spanish, and I am raising my daughter as a Cuban American. It is a question of freedom of choice." In Gonzalez-Pando's city, where Hispanics outnumber whites, the anti-assimilationist theory has become accepted practice: Miami's youth can take twelve years of bilingual public schooling with no pretense made that the program is transitional toward anything. The potential for separatism is greater in Los Angeles. Philip Hawley, president of the Carter Hawley Hale retail store chain, cautions: "This is the only area in the U.S. that over the next 50 years could have a polarization into two distinct cultures, of the kind that brought about the Quebec situation in Canada." Professor Rodolfo Acuna of California State University at Northridge concurs. Says Acuna: "Talk of secession may come when there are shrinking economic resources and rising expectations among have-not Hispanics."

Already the separatists who resist accepting English have won laws and court cases mandating provision of social services, some government instructions, even election ballots in Spanish. The legitimizing effect of these decisions can be seen in the proliferation of billboards, roadside signs and other public communications posted in Spanish. Acknowledged Professor Ramón Ruiz of the University of California at San Diego: "The separatism question is with us already." The most portentous evidence is in the classrooms. Like its political cousins, equal opportunity and social justice, bilingual education is a catchall term that means what the speaker wishes it to mean.

There are at least four ways for schools to teach students who speak another language at home:

1) Total immersion in English, which relies on the proven ability of children to master new languages. Advocates of bilingual education argue that this approach disorients children and sometimes impedes their progress in other subjects, because those who have already mastered several grades' worth of material in their first language may be compelled to take English-language classes with much younger or slower students.

2) Short-term bilingual education, which may offer a full curriculum but is directed toward moving students into English-language classes as rapidly as possible. In a report last month by a Twentieth Century Fund task force, members who were disillusioned with the performance of elaborate bilingual programs urged diversion of federal funds to the teaching of English. The panel held: "Schoolchildren will never swim in the American mainstream unless they are fluent in English."

3) Dual curriculum, which permits students to spend several years making the transition. This is the method urged by many moderate Hispanic, Chinese and other ethnic minority leaders. Says Historian Ruiz: "The direct approach destroys children's feelings of security. Bilingual education eases them from something they know to something they do not."

4) Language and cultural maintenance, which seeks to enhance students' mastery of their first language while also teaching them English. In Hispanic communities, the language training is often accompanied by courses in ethnic heritage. Argues Miami Attorney Manuel Diaz, a vice chairman of the Spanish American League Against Discrimination: "Cultural diversity makes this country strong. It is not a disease."

The rhetoric of supporters of bilingualism suggests that theirs may   8
be a political solution to an educational problem. Indeed, some of them
acknowledge that they view bilingual programs as a source of jobs for
Hispanic administrators, teachers and aides. In cities with large minority enrollments, says a Chicago school principal who requested
anonymity, "those of us who consider bilingual education ineffective
are afraid that if we say so we will lose our jobs." Lawrence Uzzell, president of Learn Inc., a Washington-based research foundation, contends
that Hispanic educational activists are cynically protecting their own
careers. Says Uzzell: "The more the Hispanic child grows up isolated,
the easier it is for politicians to manipulate him as part of an ethnic voting bloc."

The signal political success for bilingualism has been won at the   9
U.S. Department of Education. After the Supreme Court ruled in 1974
that Chinese-speaking students were entitled to some instruction in a
language they could understand, the DOE issued "informal" rules that
now bind more than 400 school districts. Immersion in English, even
rapid transition to English, does not satisfy the DOE; the rules compel
school systems to offer a full curriculum to any group of 20 or more students who share a foreign language. The DOE rules have survived three
presidencies, although Jesse Soriano, director of the Reagan Administration's $138 million bilingual program, concedes, "This is money that
could be spent more effectively." About half of students from
Spanish-speaking homes drop out before the end of high school; of the
ones who remain, 30% eventually score two or more years below their
age group on standardized tests. But it is hard to demonstrate the value
of any bilingual approach in aiding those students. In 1982 Iris Rotberg
reported in the Harvard Education Review: "Research findings have
shown that bilingual programs are neither better nor worse than other
instructional methods." Indeed, the DOE's review found that of all
methods for teaching bilingual students English and mathematics, only
total immersion in English clearly worked.

One major problem in assessing the worth of bilingual programs is   10
that they often employ teachers who are less than competent in either
English or Spanish, or in the specific subjects they teach. In a 1976 test
of 136 teachers and aides in bilingual programs in New Mexico, only 13
could read and write Spanish at third-grade level. Says former Boston
School Superintendent Robert Wood: "Many bilingual teachers do not
have a command of English, and after three years of instruction under
them, children also emerge without a command of English." Another
complicating factor is the inability of researchers to determine whether
the problems of Hispanic students stem more from language difficulty
or from their economic class. Many Hispanic children who are unable to
speak English have parents with little education who hold unskilled
jobs; in school performance, these students are much like poor blacks

and whites. Notes Harvard's Nathan Glazer: "If these students do poorly in English, they may be doing poorly in a foreign language."

Even if the educational value of bilingual programs were beyond 11 dispute, there would remain questions about their psychic value to children. Among the sharpest critics of bilingualism is author Richard Rodriguez, who holds a Berkeley Ph.D. in literature and grew up in a Spanish-speaking, working-class household; in his autobiography *Hunger of Memory*, Rodriguez argues that the separation from his family that a Hispanic child feels on becoming fluent in English is necessary to develop a sense of belonging to American society. Writes Rodriguez: "Bilingualists do not seem to realize that there are two ways a person is individualized. While one suffers a diminished sense of private individuality by becoming assimilated into public society, such assimilation makes possible the achievement of public individuality." By Rodriguez's reasoning, the discomfort of giving up the language of home is far less significant than the isolation of being unable to speak the language of the larger world.

The dubious value of bilingualism to students is only part of 12 America's valid concern about how to absorb the Hispanic minority. The U.S., despite its exceptional diversity, has been spared most of the ethnic tensions that beset even such industrialized nations as Belgium and Spain. The rise of a large group, detached from the main population by language and custom, could affect the social stability of the country. Hispanic leaders, moreover, acknowledge that their constituents have been less inclined to become assimilated than previous foreign-language communities, in part because many of them anticipated that after earning and saving, they would return to Puerto Rico, Mexico, South America or Cuba. Says Historian Doyce Nunis of the University of Southern California: "For the first time in American experience, a large immigrant group may be electing to bypass the processes of acculturation." Miami Mayor Maurice Ferre, a Puerto Rican, claims that in his city a resident can go from birth through school and working life to death without ever having to speak English. But most Hispanic intellectuals claim that their communities, like other immigrant groups before them, cling together only to combat discrimination.

The disruptive potential of bilingualism and biculturalism is still 13 worrisome: millions of voters cut off from the main sources of information, millions of potential draftees inculcated with dual ethnic loyalties, millions of would-be employees ill at ease in the language of their workmates. Former Senator S. I. Hayakawa of California was laughed at for proposing a constitutional amendment to make English the official language of the U.S. It was a gesture of little practical consequence but great symbolic significance: many Americans mistakenly feel there is something racist, or oppressive, in expecting newcomers to share the nation's language and folkways.

Beyond practical politics and economics, separation belittles the 14
all-embracing culture that America has embodied for the world. Says
Writer Irving Howe, a scholar of literature and the Jewish immigrant
experience: "The province, the ethnic nest, remains the point from
which everything begins, but it must be transcended." That transcen-
dence does not mean disappearance. It is possible to eat a Mexican
meal, dance a Polish polka, sing in a Rumanian choir, preserve one's
ethnicity however one wishes, and still share fully in the English-speaking
common society.   15

Just as American language, food and popular culture reflect the past
groups who landed in the U.S. so future American culture will reflect
the Hispanics, Asians and many other groups who are replanting their
roots. As Author Rodriguez observes after his journey into the mainstream, "Culture survives whether you want it to or not."

Responding to Reading

1. In what way does the image of the "melting pot" (2) help Henry to make
   his point about assimilation? What image could you use to help those who
   want to preserve their ethnic identities support their position?
2. Henry calls those who favor bilingualism "separatists" and "anti-assimila-
   tionists." Is he being fair when he uses these terms? Does he overstate his
   case in paragraph 5 when he outlines the position of those who favor
   biligualism?
3. Both Henry and Jorge Amselle (p. 253) criticize federal bilingual-education
   policy. Do both writers make the same points? What kind of information
   does each writer use to support his position? Which writer do you think
   makes the more convincing case? Explain.

SHOULD ENGLISH BE THE LAW?

Robert D. King

*Robert D. King (1936–   ) was born in Hattiesburg, Mississippi.
He received his B.S. and M.S. degrees in mathematics from the Georgia
Institute of Technology and later earned an M.A. and a Ph.D in linguistics
from the University of Wisconsin. He is currently a professor of linguistics
at the University of Texas at Austin, where he also holds the Audre and
Bernard Rappaport chair in Jewish Studies. His scholarly works include*
Historical Linguistics and Generative Grammar *(1969) and* Nehru and
the Language Politics of India *(1997). The following essay for a general
audience originally appeared in the* Atlantic Monthly *in 1997. In it, King*

surveys the "English Only" movement and uses the examples of Switzerland and India, countries whose linguistic diversity has never threatened national unity, to argue that we Americans should "relax and luxuriate in our linguistic richness and traditional tolerance of language differences."

We have known race riots, draft riots, labor violence, secession, anti-war protests, and a whiskey rebellion, but one kind of trouble we've never had: a language riot. Language riot? It sounds like a joke. The very idea of language as a political force—as something that might threaten to split a country wide apart—is alien to our way of thinking and to our cultural traditions.

This may be changing. On August 1 of last year the U.S. House of Representatives approved a bill that would make English the official language of the United States. The vote was 259 to 169, with 223 Republicans and thirty-six Democrats voting in favor and eight Republicans, 160 Democrats, and one independent voting against. The debate was intense, acrid, and partisan. On March 25 of last year the Supreme Court agreed to review a case involving an Arizona law that would require public employees to conduct government business only in English. Arizona is one of several states that have passed "Official English" or "English Only" laws. The appeal to the Supreme Court followed a 6-to-5 ruling, in October of 1995, by a federal appeals court striking down the Arizona law. These events suggest how divisive a public issue language could become in America—even if it has until now scarcely been taken seriously.

Traditionally, the American way has been to make English the national language—but to do so quietly, locally, without fuss. The Constitution is silent on language: the Founding Fathers had no need to legislate that English be the official language of the country. It has always been taken for granted that English *is* the national language, and that one must learn English in order to make it in America.

To say that language has never been a major force in American history or politics, however, is not to say that politicians have always resisted linguistic jingoism. In 1753 Benjamin Franklin voiced his concern that German immigrants were not learning English: "Those [Germans] who come hither are generally the most ignorant Stupid Sort of their own Nation. . . . they will soon so outnumber us, that all the advantages we have will not, in My Opinion, be able to preserve our language, and even our government will become precarious." Theodore Roosevelt articulated the unspoken American linguistic-melting-pot theory when he boomed, "We have room for but one language here, and that is the English language, for we intend to see that the crucible turns our people out as Americans, of American nationality, and not as dwellers in a polyglot boarding house." And: "We must have but one flag. We must also have but one language. That must be the language of the Declaration of Independence, of Washington's Farewell address, of Lincoln's Gettysburg speech and second inaugural."

Official English

TR's linguistic tub-thumping long typified the tradition of American politics. That tradition began to change in the wake of the anything-goes attitudes and the celebration of cultural differences arising in the 1960s. A 1975 amendment to the Voting Rights Act of 1965 mandated the "bilingual ballot" under certain circumstances, notably when the voters of selected language groups reached five percent or more of a voting district. Bilingual education became a byword of educational thinking during the 1960s. By the 1970s linguists had demonstrated convincingly—at least to other academics—that black English (today called African-American vernacular English or Ebonics) was not "bad" English but a different kind of authentic English with its own rules. Predictably, there have been scattered demands that black English be included in bilingual-education programs.

It was against this background that the movement to make English the official language of the country arose. In 1981 Senator S. I. Hayakawa, long a leading critic of bilingual education and bilingual ballots, introduced in the U.S. Senate a constitutional amendment that not only would have made English the official language, but would have prohibited federal and state laws and regulations requiring the use of other languages. His English Language Amendment died in the Ninety-seventh Congress.

In 1983 the organization called U.S. English was founded by Hayakawa and John Tanton, a Michigan ophthalmologist. The primary purpose of the organization was to promote English as the official language of the United States. (The best background readings on America's "neolinguisticism" are the books *Hold Your Tongue*, by James Crawford, and *Language Loyalties*, edited by Crawford, both published in 1992.) Official English initiatives were passed by California in 1986, by Arkansas, Mississippi, North Carolina, North Dakota, and South Carolina in 1987, by Colorado, Florida, and Arizona in 1988, and by Alabama in 1990. The majorities voting for these initiatives were generally not insubstantial: California's, for example, passed by 73 percent.

It was probably inevitable that the Official English (or English Only—the two names are used almost interchangeably) movement would acquire a conservative, almost reactionary undertone in the 1990s. Official English is politically very incorrect. But its cofounder John Tanton brought with him strong liberal credentials. He had been active in the Sierra Club and Planned Parenthood, and in the 1970s served as the national president of Zero Population Growth. Early advisers of U.S. English resist ideological pigeonholing: they included Walter Annenberg, Jacques Barzun, Bruno Bettelheim, Alistair Cooke, Denton Cooley, Walter Cronkite, Angier Biddle Duke, George Gilder, Sidney Hook, Norman Podhoretz, Arnold Schwarzenegger, and Karl Shapiro.[1] In 1987 U.S. English installed as its president Linda Chávez, a Hispanic who had been prominent in the Reagan Administration. A year later she resigned her position, citing "repugnant" and "anti-Hispanic" overtones in an internal memorandum written by Tanton. Tanton, too, resigned, and Walter Cronkite, describing the affair as "embarrassing," left the advisory board. One board member, Norman Cousins, defected in 1986, alluding to the "negative symbolic significance" of California's Official English initiative, Proposition 63. The current chairman of the board and CEO of U.S. English is Mauro E. Mujica, who claims that the organization has 650,000 members.

The popular wisdom is that conservatives are pro and liberals con. 9 True, conservatives such as George Will and William F. Buckley Jr. have written columns supporting Official English. But would anyone characterize as conservatives the present and past U.S. English board members Alistair Cooke, Walter Cronkite, and Norman Cousins? One of the strongest opponents of bilingual education is the Mexican-American writer Richard Rodríguez, best known for his eloquent autobiography, *Hunger of Memory* (1982). There is a strain of American liberalism that defines itself in nostalgic devotion to the melting pot.

For several years relevant bills awaited consideration in the U.S. 10 House of Representatives. The Emerson Bill (H.R. 123), passed by the House last August, specifies English as the official language of government, and requires that the government "preserve and enhance" the official status of English. Exceptions are made for the teaching of foreign languages; for actions necessary for public health, international relations, foreign trade, and the protection of the rights of criminal defendants; and for the use of "terms of art" from languages other than English. It would, for example, stop the Internal Revenue Service from sending out income-tax forms and instructions in languages other than English, but it would not ban the use of foreign languages in census materials or documents dealing with national security. *"E Pluribus Unum"* can still appear on American money. U.S. English supports the bill.

What are the chances that some version of Official English will 11 become federal law? Any language bill will face tough odds in the Senate, because some western senators have opposed English Only measures in the past for various reasons, among them a desire by Republicans not to alienate the growing number of Hispanic Republicans, most of whom are uncomfortable with mandated monolingualism. Texas Governor George W. Bush, too, has forthrightly said that he would oppose any English

---

[1] A diverse group of writers, academics, and media figures. [Eds.]

Only proposals in his state. Several of the Republican candidates for President in 1996 (an interesting exception is Phil Gramm) endorsed versions of Official English, as has Newt Gingrich. While governor of Arkansas, Bill Clinton signed into law an English Only bill. As President, he has described his earlier action as a mistake.

Many issues intersect in the controversy over Official English: immigration (above all), the rights of minorities (Spanish-speaking minorities in particular), the pros and cons of bilingual education tolerance, how best to educate the children of immigrants, and the place of cultural diversity in school curricula and in American society in general. The question that lies at the root of most of the uneasiness is this: Is America threatened by the preservation of languages other than English? Will America, if it continues on its traditional path of benign linguistic neglect, go the way of Belgium, Canada, and Sri Lanka—three countries among many whose unity is gravely imperiled by language and ethnic conflicts?

Language and Nationality

Language and nationalism were not always so intimately intertwined. Never in the heyday of rule by sovereign was it a condition of employment that the King be able to speak the language of his subjects. George I spoke no English and spent much of his time away from England, attempting to use the power of his kingship to shore up his German possessions. In the Middle Ages nationalism was not even part of the picture: one owed loyalty to a lord, a prince, a ruler, a family, a tribe, a church, a piece of land, but not to a nation and least of all to a nation as a language unit. The capital city of the Austrian Hapsburg empire was Vienna, its ruler a monarch with effective control of peoples of the most varied and incompatible ethnicities, and languages, throughout Central and Eastern Europe. The official language, and the lingua franca as well, was German. While it stood—and it stood for hundreds of years—the empire was an anachronistic relic of what for most of human history had been the normal relationship between country and language: none.

The marriage of language and nationalism goes back at least to Romanticism and specifically to Rousseau,[2] who argued in his *Essay on the Origin of Languages* that language must develop before politics is possible and that language originally distinguished nations from one another. A little-remembered aim of the French Revolution—itself the legacy of Rousseau—was to impose a national language on France,

---

[2] Jean-Jacques Rousseau (1712–1788), Swiss-French philosopher, novelist, and political theorist, who argued that humans in their natural state are good, but are corrupted by society. [Eds.]

where regional languages such as Provençal, Breton, and Basque were still strong competitors against standard French, the French of the Ile de France. As late as 1789, when the Revolution began, half the population of the south of France, which spoke Provençal, did not understand French. A century earlier the playwright Racine said that he had had to resort to Spanish and Italian to make himself understood in the southern French town of Uzès. After the Revolution nationhood itself became aligned with language.

In 1846 Jacob Grimm, one of the Brothers Grimm of fairy-tale fame 15 but better known in the linguistic establishment as a forerunner of modern comparative and historical linguists, said that "a nation is the totality of people who speak the same language." After midcentury, language was invoked more than any other single criterion to define nationality. Language as a political force helped to bring about the unification of Italy and of Germany and the secession of Norway from its union with Sweden in 1905. Arnold Toynbee observed—unhappily—soon after the First World War that "the growing consciousness of Nationality had attached itself neither to traditional frontiers nor to new geographical associations but almost exclusively to mother tongues."

The crowning triumph of the new desideratum was the Treaty of 16 Versailles, in 1919, when the allied victors of the First World War began redrawing the map of Central and Eastern Europe according to nationality as best they could. The magic word was "self-determination," and none of Woodrow Wilson's Fourteen Points[3] mentioned the word "language" at all. Self-determination was thought of as being related to "nationality," which today we would be more likely to call "ethnicity"; but language was simpler to identify than nationality or ethnicity. When it came to drawing the boundary lines of various countries—Czechoslovakia, Yugoslavia, Romania, Hungary, Albania, Bulgaria, Poland—it was principally language that guided the draftsman's hand. (The main exceptions were Alsace-Lorraine, South Tyrol, and the German-speaking parts of Bohemia and Moravia.) Almost by default language became the defining characteristic of nationality.

And so it remains today. In much of the world, ethnic unity and cul- 17 tural identification are routinely defined by language. To be Arab is to speak Arabic. Bengali identity is based on language in spite of the division of Bengali-speakers between Hindu India and Muslim Bangladesh. When eastern Pakistan seceded from greater Pakistan in 1971, it named itself Bangladesh: *desa* means "country;" the *bangla* means not the Bengali people or the Bengali territory but the Bengali language.

---

[3] President Woodrow Wilson formulated a fourteen-point European peace plan at the close of World War I; presented to Congress in 1918, it included a number of recommendations for redrawing the map of Europe. [Eds.]

Scratch most nationalist movements and you find a linguistic griev-   18
ance. The demands for independence of the Baltic states (Latvia,
Lithuania, and Estonia) were intimately bound up with fears for the loss
of their respective languages and cultures in a sea of Russianness. In
Belgium the war between French and Flemish threatens an already
weakly fused country. The present atmosphere of Belgium is dark and
anxious, costive; the metaphor of divorce is a staple of private and public discourse. The lines of terrorism in Sri Lanka are drawn between
Tamil Hindus and Sinhalese Buddhists—and also between the Tamil
and Sinhalese languages. Worship of the French language fortifies the
movement for an independent Quebec. Whether a united Canada will
survive into the twenty-first century is a question too close to call. Much
of the anxiety about language in the United States is probably fueled by
the "Quebec problem": unlike Belgium, which is a small European
country, or Sri Lanka, which is halfway around the world, Canada is our
close neighbor.

Language is a convenient surrogate for nonlinguistic claims that are   19
often awkward to articulate, for they amount to a demand for more
political and economic power. Militant Sikhs in India call for a state of
their own: Khalistan ("Land of the Pure" in Punjabi). They frequently
couch this as a demand for a linguistic state, which has a certain simplicity about it, a clarity of motive—justice, even, because states in India
are normally linguistic states. But the Sikh demands blend religion, economics, language, and retribution for sins both punished and unpun-
ished in a country where old sins cast long shadows.

Language is an explosive issue in the countries of the former Soviet   20
Union. The language conflict in Estonia has been especially bitter. Ethnic
Russians make up almost a third of Estonia's population, and most of
them do not speak or read Estonian, although Russians have lived in
Estonia for more than a generation. Estonia has passed legislation
requiring knowledge of the Estonian language as a condition of citizenship. Nationalist groups in independent Lithuania sought restrictions on
the use of Polish—again, old sins, long shadows.

In 1995 protests erupted in Moldova, formerly the Moldavian   21
Soviet Socialist Republic, over language and the teaching of Moldovan
history. Was Moldovan history a part of Romanian history or of Soviet
history? Was Moldova's language Romanian? Moldovan—earlier called
Moldavian—*is* Romanian, just as American English and British English
are both English. But in the days of the Moldavian SSR, Moscow
insisted that the two languages were different, and in a piece of linguistic nonsense required Moldavian to be written in the Cyrillic alphabet to
strengthen the case that it was not Romanian.

The official language of Yugoslavia was Serbo-Croatian, which was   22
never so much a language as a political accommodation. The Serbian

and Croatian languages are mutually intelligible. Serbian is written in the Cyrillic alphabet, is identified with the Eastern Orthodox branch of the Catholic Church, and borrows its high-culture words from the east—from Russian and Old Church Slavic. Croatian is written in the Roman alphabet, is identified with Roman Catholicism, and borrows its high-culture words from the west—from German, for example, and Latin. One of the first things the newly autonomous Republic of Serbia did, in 1991, was to pass a law decreeing Serbian in the Cyrillic alphabet the official language of the country. With Croatia divorced from Serbia, the Croatian and Serbian languages are diverging more and more. Serbo-Croatian has now passed into history, a language-museum relic from the brief period when Serbs and Croats called themselves Yugoslavs and pretended to like each other.

Slovakia, relieved now of the need to accommodate to Czech cos- 23 mopolitan sensibilities, has passed a law making Slovak its official language. (Czech is to Slovak pretty much as Croatian is to Serbian.) Doctors in state hospitals must speak to patients in Slovak, even if another language would aid diagnosis and treatment. Some 600,000 Slovaks—more than 10 percent of the population—are ethnically Hungarian. Even staff meetings in Hungarian-language schools must be in Slovak. (The government dropped a stipulation that church weddings be conducted in Slovak after heavy opposition from the Roman Catholic Church.) Language inspectors are told to weed out "all sins perpetrated on the regular Slovak language." Tensions between Slovaks and Hungarians, who had been getting along, have begun to arise.

The twentieth century is ending as it began—with trouble in the 24 Balkans and with nationalist tensions flaring up in other parts of the globe. (Toward the end of his life Bismarck predicted that "some damn fool thing in the Balkans" would ignite the next war.) Language isn't always part of the problem. But it usually is.

Unique Otherness

Is there no hope for language tolerance? Some countries manage to 25 maintain their unity in the face of multilingualism. Examples are Finland, with a Swedish minority, and a number of African and Southeast Asian countries. Two others could not be more unlike as countries go: Switzerland and India.

German, French, Italian, and Romansh are the languages of 26 Switzerland. The first three can be and are used for official purposes; all four are designated "national" languages. Switzerland is politically almost hyperstable. It has language problems (Romansh is losing ground), but they are not major, and they are never allowed to threaten national unity.

Contrary to public perception, India gets along pretty well with a   27
host of different languages. The Indian constitution officially recognizes
nineteen languages, English among them. Hindi is specified in the constitution as the national language of India, but that is a pious post-
colonial fiction: outside the Hindi-speaking northern heartland of India,
people don't want to learn it. English functions more nearly than Hindi
as India's lingua franca.

From 1947, when India obtained its independence from the British,   28
until the 1960s blood ran in the streets and people died because of language. Hindi absolutists wanted to force Hindi on the entire country,
which would have split India between north and south and opened up
other fracture lines as well. For as long as possible Jawaharlal Nehru,
independent India's first Prime Minister, resisted nationalist demands
to redraw the capricious state boundaries of British India according to
language. By the time he capitulated, the country had gained a precious
decade to prove its viability as a union.

Why is it that India preserves its unity with not just two languages   29
to contend with, as Belgium, Canada, and Sri Lanka have, but nineteen?
The answer is that India, like Switzerland, has a strong national identity.
The two countries share something big and almost mystical that holds
each together in a union transcending language. That something I call
"unique otherness."

The Swiss have what the political scientist Karl Deutsch called   30
"learned habits, preferences, symbols, memories, and patterns of land-
holding": customs, cultural traditions, and political institutions that
bind them closer to one another than to people of France, Germany, or
Italy living just across the border and speaking the same language.
There is Switzerland's traditional neutrality, its system of universal military training (the "citizen army"), its consensual allegiance to a strong
Swiss franc—and fondue, yodeling, skiing, and mountains. Set against
all this, the fact that Switzerland has four languages doesn't even
approach the threshold of becoming a threat.

As for India, what Vincent Smith, in the *Oxford History of India*, calls   31
its "deep underlying fundamental unity" resides in institutions and
beliefs such as caste, cow worship, sacred places, and much more.
Consider *dharma*, *karma*, and *maya*, the three root convictions of
Hinduism; India's historical epics; Gandhi; *ahimsa* (nonviolence); vege-
tarianism; a distinctive cuisine and way of eating; marriage customs; a
shared past; and what the Indologist Ainslie Embree calls "Brahmanical
ideology."[4] In other words, "We are Indian; we are different."

Belgium and Canada have never managed to forge a stable   32
national identity; Czechoslovakia and Yugoslavia never did either.

---

[4] *Brahman* refers to a Hindu of the highest caste. [Eds.]

Unique otherness immunizes countries against linguistic destabilization. Even Switzerland and especially India have problems; in any country with as many different languages as India has, language will never *not* be a problem. However, it is one thing to have a major illness with a bleak prognosis; it is another to have a condition that is irritating and occasionally painful but not life-threatening.

History teaches a plain lesson about language and governments: 33 there is almost nothing the government of a free country can do to change language usage and practice significantly, to force its citizens to use certain languages in preference to others, and to discourage people from speaking a language they wish to continue to speak (The rebirth of Hebrew in Palestine and Israel's successful mandate that Hebrew be spoken and written by Israelis is a unique event in the annals of language history.) Quebec has since the 1970s passed an array of laws giving French a virtual monopoly in the province. One consequence—unintended, one wishes to believe—of these laws is that last year kosher products imported for Passover were kept off the shelves, because the packages were not labeled in French. Wise governments keep their hands off language to the extent that it is politically possible to do so.

We like to believe that to pass a law is to change behavior; but pass- 34 ing laws about language, in a free society, almost never changes attitudes or behavior. Gaelic (Irish) is living out a slow, inexorable decline in Ireland despite enormous government support of every possible kind since Ireland gained its independence from Britain. The Welsh language, in contrast, is alive today in Wales in spite of heavy discrimination during its history. Three out of four people in the northern and western counties of Gwynedd and Dyfed speak Welsh.

I said earlier that language is a convenient surrogate for other 35 national problems. Official English obviously has a lot to do with concern about immigration, perhaps especially Hispanic immigration. America may be threatened by immigration; I don't know. But America is not threatened by language.

The usual arguments made by academics against Official English 36 are commonsensical. Who needs a law when, according to the 1990 census, 94 percent of American residents speak English anyway? (Mauro E. Mujica, the chairman of U.S. English, cites a higher figure: 97 percent.) Not many of today's immigrants will see their first language survive into the second generation. This is in fact the common lament of first-generation immigrants: their children are not learning their language and are losing the culture of their parents. Spanish is hardly a threat to English, in spite of isolated (and easily visible) cases such as Miami, New York City, and pockets of the Southwest and southern California. The everyday language of south Texas is Spanish, and yet south Texas is not about to secede from America.

But empirical, calm arguments don't engage the real issue: lan- 37
guage is a symbol, an icon. Nobody who favors a constitutional ban
against flag burning will ever be persuaded by the argument that the
flag is, after all, just a "piece of cloth." A draft card in the 1960s, was
never merely a piece of paper. Neither is a marriage license.

Language, as one linguist has said, is "not primarily a means of 38
communication but a means of communion." Romanticism exalted language, made it mystical, sublime—a bond of national identity. At the
same time, Romanticism created a monster: it made of language a
means for destroying a country.

America has that unique otherness of which I spoke. In spite of all 39
our racial divisions and economic unfairness, we have the frontier tradition, respect for the individual, and opportunity; we have our love
affair with the automobile; we have in our history a civil war that freed
the slaves and was fought with valor; and we have sports, hot dogs,
hamburgers, and milk shakes—things big and small, noble and petty,
important and trifling. "We are Americans; we are different."

If I'm wrong, then the great American experiment will fail—not 40
because of language but because it no longer means anything to be an
American; because we have forfeited that "willingness of the heart" that
F. Scott Fitzgerald[5] wrote was America; because we are no longer joined
by Lincoln's "mystic chords of memory."

We are not even close to the danger point. I suggest that we relax 41
and luxuriate in our linguistic richness and our traditional tolerance of
language differences. Language does not threaten American unity.
Benign neglect is a good policy for any country when it comes to language, and it's a good policy for America.

Responding to Reading

1. According to King, what are the dangers of trying to maintain a bilingual
   society? What examples does he present to support his position? Does he
   offer enough examples?
2. What countries does King mention to support his argument that a multilingual society can maintain its unity? In what ways are these countries
   like the United States? In what ways are they different? Is King's argument
   convincing?
3. King says, "America may be threatened by immigration. . . . But America is
   not threatened by language" (35). Later, he says that "the great American
   experiment will fail—not because of language but because it no longer
   means anything to be an American." (40). How do you think Jorge Amselle
   (p. 253) would respond to these statements?

---

[5] Twentieth-century American writer. [Eds.]

¡INGLÉS, SÍ!

Jorge Amselle

Jorge Amselle (1969–) was born in Washington, D.C., to Nicaraguan immigrant parents. He spoke little English when he first started school, but he learned the language as part of his cultural assimilation. In 1992, he received a degree in economics from the University of Maryland and began to work for a variety of research organizations in the Washington area. Since 1994, he has been communications director for the Center for Equal Opportunity, an organization that lobbies against affirmative action programs. His writing has appeared in the Wall Street Journal, *the* Washington Times, *the* National Review, *and the* Weekly Standard, *among other periodicals. In the following essay, which appeared in the* National Review, *Amselle argues that most Hispanic parents are opposed to extensive bilingual education and want their children to learn English as quickly as possible.*

As the new school year gets under way, over one million Hispanic 1 children are beginning their classroom experience in the United States in Spanish rather than English. For nearly thirty years professional Hispanic activists and bilingual-education proponents have been telling us that this is what Hispanic parents want, and that it is in the best interests of Hispanic children.

But every poll conducted of language-minority parents has shown 2 that what they want for their children is English. The Center for Equal Opportunity recently commissioned a national survey of six hundred Hispanic parents—the first of its kind in more than eight years. This survey found that more than 80 per cent of Hispanic parents want their children taught in English and not in Spanish. And 63 per cent want their children to be taught English as quickly as possible—whereas bilingual-education theory calls for children to be taught academic content courses in their native language for five to seven years.

While the education establishment is resisting the deconstruction of 3 bilingual education, some progress is being made. In response to parents' protests, New York City is ending the automatic testing of children with Spanish names for placement in bilingual programs. The main problem with this approach was that students were being misidentified as needing bilingual education when their problem was that they had not been taught to read in any language. Hispanic children who scored below the 40th percentile in a standardized English exam, which by definition is 40 per cent of all the students taking the test, were automatically placed in Spanish-language programs, even if they did not speak Spanish.

In Los Angeles, over 100 Latino parents picketed their local school 4 for almost two weeks to protest the lack of English instruction. These parents had a legal right to request all-English instruction for their children, but their rights were nullified by the hurdles placed before them by school administrators.

The boycott ended only when the school promised to provide 5 classes in English. The school also promised to halt the practice of requiring parents to attend parent-teacher conferences before allowing children out of the bilingual program. Parent-teacher conferences are often used to bully, intimidate, and shame parents into leaving their children in bilingual programs they know don't work.

Indeed, bilingual education is working so poorly in California that 6 the State Board of Education is backing off from forcing school districts to use native-language instruction. The California Teachers Association has also joined the stampede away from bilingual education. Its newsletter states that the emphasis on using children's native language has "crippled the Spanish-speaking child's educational development."

Despite the mounting evidence, there are researchers and organiza- 7 tions, like Virginia Collier of George Mason University and the National Association for Bilingual Education (NABE), that continue to praise this failed educational technique. Professor Collier's study is often cited as proof that bilingual education works. However, her study has yet to be completed, let alone subjected to peer review.

In a monograph published by the New Jersey Teachers of English to 8 Speakers of Other Languages-Bilingual Education (NJTESOL-BE), Professor Collier shares some of her less publicized insights. "We must encourage language-minority parents to speak the first language at home, not to speak English. The worse advice [teachers] can give parents is to speak only English at home," she writes. She even suggests that teaching children only in English is child abuse. She writes: "To deny a child the only means of communicating with his parents or to denigrate an adolescent for expressing her emotions through first language is tantamount to physical violence toward that student."

NABE readily admits that bilingual education is failing at least 9 some students, calling these cases "abhorrent aberration[s]." However, NABE ignores the fact that the few bilingual-education programs that work do so only because they are more English-intensive than what NABE advocates.

In fact, the vast majority of the research in favor of bilingual educa- 10 tion is desperately flawed. Professor Christine Rossell of Boston University has conducted an extensive review of over 300 bilingual-education studies. She found that only 60 measured reading ability in a methodologically acceptable way; of these, 78 per cent found bilingual education to be no better or actually worse than doing nothing. For math scores, 91 per cent of the 34 scientifically valid studies showed bilingual education to be no better than doing nothing.

In spite of this evidence, Latino parents who oppose bilingual edu- 11
cation often find themselves fighting a lonely battle. In fact, in both Los
Angeles and New York City anti-bilingual-education parents' groups
are being assisted by the religious organizations, not by traditional
Hispanic advocacy groups. The reason is that traditional Hispanic organizations long ago sold out the interests of Latino parents to the bilingual education establishment. Now, whenever parents complain about
a system that fails to teach their children English, their representatives
not only ignore their pleas for help, but actually oppose them.

Some Members of Congress as well as many state legislators are 12
seeking far-reaching reforms of bilingual education. Unfortunately,
because Congress ignored an opportunity to reform federal bilingual-
education policy as part of the Official English legislation passed
recently by the House, Hispanic children and parents will have to suffer through another year of bilingual education.

Responding to Reading

1. Amselle begins his essay by saying that there is a split between "what
   Hispanic parents want" and what "professional Hispanic activists and
   bilingual-education proponents" want (1). What evidence does he present
   to support this statement? Should he have offered more evidence? A different kind of evidence?
2. If, as Amselle contends, there is mounting evidence that bilingual education programs do not work, why does the federal government still
   require schools to use this method of teaching? Do you find his explanation plausible?
3. In "Should English Be the Law?" (p. 242), Robert D. King refutes a number
   of familiar arguments against bilingual education. Which of Amselle's
   points does King address? How convincing are these refutations?

Widening the Focus

- Jonathan Kozol, "Savage Inequalities" (p. 100)

- Bharati Mukherjee, "American Dreamer" (p. 445)

—————————————— **WRITING** ——————————————

The Politics of Language

1. Both Malcolm X and Frederick Douglass discuss how they undertook a program of self-education. Write an essay in which you discuss how their efforts were similar and different. Make certain you discuss what they learned about themselves and about their respective societies by learning to read and write.

2. How does people's spoken and written language affect your response to them? Considering friends as well as public figures, write an essay in which you define and illustrate the criteria by which you evaluate the communication skills of others.

3. Write an editorial for your local newspaper in which you argue for or against a constitutional amendment making English the official language of the United States. In your essay refer to William A. Henry III's "Against a Confusion of Tongues," Robert D. King's "Should English Be the Law?" and Jorge Amselle's "¡Inglés, Sí!"

4. In "Mother Tongue," Amy Tan discusses the different Englishes she grew up with: "simple English" (the English she spoke to her mother), "broken English" (the English her mother spoke), and "watered-down English" (the English translation of her mother's Chinese). Write an essay in which you compare Tan's concept of different Englishes with Barbara Mellix's use of different kinds of English in "From Outside, In."

5. Both Barbara Mellix in "From Outside, In" and Amy Tan in "Mother Tongue" talk about how education can change one's use of language. Write an essay discussing the effect that education has had on your own spoken and written language. What do you think you have gained and lost as your language has changed?

6. Which of your daily activities would you be unable to carry out if, like the people Jonathan Kozol describes in "The Human Cost of an Illiterate Society," you could neither read nor write? Write an article for your local newspaper in which you report on a typical day. For example, begin by having breakfast and then walking, driving, or taking public transportation to class. Make sure you refer to specific tasks you could not do. In addition, explain some strategies you would use to hide the fact you couldn't read or write.

7. In paragraph 21 of his essay, Orwell says, "Political language . . . is designed to make lies sound truthful and murder respectable, and to give an appearance of solidarity to pure wind." Write an essay in which you agree or disagree with this statement. Support your position with examples you find in newspapers and magazines, on TV or on the Internet.

8. When people speak, they usually send class signals; that is, the higher their social class, the more correctly they speak. Write an essay in which you compare the class signals sent by characters in two TV sitcoms.

8. In "Sexism in English: A 1990s Update" Alleen Pace Nilsen says, "The feminist movement has caused the differences between the sexes to be downplayed" in languagew (17). Is this true of advertising? Find advertisements in several newspapers and magazines, and analyze their use of language, particularly their use of gender-specific words. Then, write an essay in which you agree or disagree with Pace's contention. If you wish, you may also refer to "Sex, Lies, and Advertising" by Gloria Steinem (p. 000).

9. Recently, there has been a great deal of debate about the benefits and drawbacks of a multilingual society. Supporters say that a multilingual society allows people to preserve their own cultures and thus fosters pride. Detractors say that a multilingual society reinforces differences and ultimately tears a country apart. What do you see as the benefits and drawbacks of a multilingual society? As a country, what would we gain if we encouraged multilingualism? What would we lose? Use any of the essays in this chapter to support your position.

4

THE MEDIA'S MESSAGE

Student Voices

"I was born in 1975. I spent most of my formative years in front of the television watching cartoons and kids' shows. I learned just about everything I needed to know from TV, and if something important happened, there would be a break in the programming to tell me. My experience tells me that my generation is just waiting for that program break to let them know what to do next. And if the TV is going to tell us what's going on, there's no reason to go out and find out on our own."

—*Stephen Berger*

"The mass media create stereotypes and set impossible standards. Movies, television, and radio also have a tendency to sensationalize immoral acts and bad habits. Because the media give a limited, inaccurate view of the world, they should not be treated as a reliable source of information."

—*Megan A. Seely*

"When I was young, the movies definitely had an effect on me. I found role models in them. I was a kid who liked to be adventurous, who wanted to fly like Superman or be a pilot or a Jedi knight in *Star Wars*. My dreams of being a hero made life exciting to me."

—*Dave Zimecki*

"Movies are not a good source of role models or heroes. It appears that the majority of today's films focus on violence and crime. Since we live in a nation where crime is the cause of many social problems, I do not think that portraying criminals and violent characters as heroes is good for children. By doing this, the film industry tells the audience that violent people are admirable and that their values should be embraced. I feel there should be more positive role models in movies and on

258

television so that young people can actually have someone to look up to who represents positive values."

—*Celeste Armenti*

"Television and radio have changed the music scene. Alternative music seems to be becoming mainstream because people are having it shoved in their faces on MTV. It seems there is no underground. The punk generation in the past (not that I'm a huge fan) had a purpose. It was for outcasts who were rebelling against a commercial society. But now the media push punk as a cool thing, so punks are showing up all over. How can music rebel against society when everything is accepted?"

—*D. Scot Ackertman*

"My main source of news is the newspaper, which I try to buy every day. The only problem with this is that I only read the sports page. I start from the back and read all the sports and then flip through the other pages. I sometimes stop at the comics. The other stuff doesn't interest me."

—*Charles Guittar*

─────────── **PREPARING TO READ AND WRITE** ───────────

The popular media—newspapers and magazines, radio, television, and movies—have been around for a long time, but in recent years, they have come to have a particularly powerful and significant impact on our lives. Cable television has brought us literally hundreds of stations—along with sitcom reruns that endlessly recycle our childhood (or our parents' childhood). Satellites have brought immediacy: the Vietnam War was the first televised war, but we had to wait for the evening news to see it; during the Persian Gulf War, CNN brought us news as it happened. Talk radio has become so powerful that it may actually be shaping government policy. Other innovations have also appeared: film special effects that have the power to mystify or terrify, newspapers that seem to have more color and graphics than words, and, on television, tabloid journalism, home shopping, infomercials, and music videos. In addition, the Internet has made available a world of information—and with it, the ability to communicate easily with millions of people all over the planet.

Many more innovations have come to our world. Fiber-optic cables have begun to redefine our relationship with the media, enabling us to bank, shop, and participate in public opinion polls—all without ever leaving our homes. With this explosion of technology, however, come questions: How will we cope with the flood of information this new technology brings? What use will we make of it? Who will have access to it? Who will control it? How we answer these and other questions will determine whether the new technology will bring people of the world together or whether it will produce a world of isolated individuals mindlessly surfing through hundreds of channels and thousands of web sites. After all, as the writers in this chapter remind us, that quantity and variety do not necessarily equal quality.

As you read and prepare to write about the selections in this chapter, you may consider the following questions:

- Does the selection focus on one particular medium or on the media in general?

- Does the writer see the media as a positive, negative, or neutral force? Why?

- If the writer sees negative effects, where does he or she place blame? Do you agree?

- Does the writer make any recommendations for change? Do these recommendations seem reasonable?

- Is the writer focusing on the media's effect on society or on the media's effect on his or her own life?

- Does the writer discuss personal observations or experiences? If so, are they similar to or different from your own?

- When was the selection written? Has the situation the writer describes changed since then?

- Which writers' positions on the impact of the media (or on the media's shortcomings) are most alike? Most different? Most like your own?

TWO PERSPECTIVES ON THE MEDIA'S MESSAGE

The first two essays in this chapter look at television and its impact on young viewers. Marie Winn's "Television: The Plug-In Drug," a chapter from her book The Plug-In Drug: Television, Children, and the Family *(1977), is a highly critical examination of the effects of television on family life and parent-child relationships, which Winn sees as almost wholly negative. The author of children's books as well as several other critiques of television, Winn (1936–   ), an avid bird watcher, has most recently published* Red-Tails in Love: A Wildlife Drama in Central Park *(1998). Charles McGrath (1954–   ), some twenty years younger than Winn, offers an opposing perspective on children and television. An editor of the* New York Times Book Review, *McGrath affectionately recalls the cartoons and other children's programming he grew up watching in the 1950s and 1960s, and in "Giving Saturday Morning Some Slack," he argues that television cartoons today are not essentially different from those of earlier years, that they offer important "downtime" for children, and that the solution is not fewer cartoons but better cartoons.*

TELEVISION: THE PLUG-IN DRUG

Marie Winn

A quarter of a century after the introduction of television into 1 American society, a period that has seen the medium become so deeply ingrained in American life that in at least one state the television set has attained the rank of a legal necessity, safe from repossession in case of debt along with clothes, cooking utensils, and the like, television viewing has become an inevitable and ordinary part of daily life. Only in the early years of television did writers and commentators have sufficient perspective to separate the activity of watching television from the actual content it offers the viewer. In those early days writers frequently discussed the effects of television on family life. However, a curious myopia afflicted those early observers: almost without exception they regarded television as a favorable, beneficial, indeed, wondrous influence upon the family.

"Television is going to be a real asset in every home where there are 2 children," predicts a writer in 1949.

"Television will take over your way of living and change your chil- 3
dren's habits, but this change can be a wonderful improvement," claims
another commentator.

"No survey's needed, of course, to establish that television has 4
brought the family together in one room," writes the *New York Times*
television critic in 1949.

Each of the early articles about television is invariably accompanied 5
by a photograph or illustration showing a family cozily sitting together
before the television set, Sis on Mom's lap, Buddy perched on the arm
of Dad's chair, Dad with his arm around Mom's shoulder. Who could
have guessed that twenty or so years later Mom would be watching a
drama in the kitchen, the kids would be looking at cartoons in their
room, while Dad would be taking in the ball game in the living room?

Of course television sets were enormously expensive in those early 6
days. The idea that by 1975 more than 60 percent of American families
would own two or more sets was preposterous. The splintering of the
multiple-set family was something the early writers could not foresee.
Nor did anyone imagine the numbers of hours children would eventually devote to television, the common use of television by parents as a
child pacifier, the changes television would effect upon child-rearing
methods, the increasing domination of family schedules by children's
viewing requirements—in short, the *power* of the new medium to dominate family life.

After the first years, as children's consumption of the new medium 7
increased, together with parental concern about the possible effects of
so much television viewing, a steady refrain helped to soothe and reassure anxious parents. "Television always enters a pattern of influences
that already exist: the home, the peer group, the school, the church and
culture generally," write the authors of an early and influential study of
television's effects on children. In other words, if the child's home life is
all right, parents need not worry about the effects of all that television
watching.

But television does not merely influence the child; it deeply influ- 8
ences that "pattern of influences" that is meant to ameliorate its effects.
Home and family life has changed in important ways since the advent
of television. The peer group has become television-oriented, and much
of the time children spend together is occupied by television viewing.
Culture generally has been transformed by television. Therefore it is
improper to assign to television the subsidiary role its many apologists
(too often members of the television industry) insist it plays. Television
is not merely one of a number of important influences upon today's
child. Through the changes it has made in family life, television emerges
as *the* important influence in children's lives today.

Television's contribution to family life has been an equivocal one. 9 For while it has, indeed, kept the members of the family from dispersing, it has not served to bring them *together*. By its domination of the time families spend together, it destroys the special quality that distinguishes one family from another, a quality that depends to a great extent on what a family *does*, what special rituals, games, recurrent jokes, familiar songs, and shared activities it accumulates.

"Like the sorcerer of old," writes Urie Bronfenbrenner, "the televi- 10 sion set casts its magic spell, freezing speech and action, turning the living into silent statues so long as the enchantment lasts. The primary danger of the television screen lies not so much in the behavior it produces—although there is danger there—as in the behavior it prevents: the talks, the games, the family festivities and arguments through which much of the child's learning takes place and through which his character is formed. Turning on the television set can turn off the process that transforms children into people."

Yet parents have accepted a television-dominated family life so 11 completely that they cannot see how the medium is involved in whatever problems they might be having. A first-grade teacher reports:

"I have one child in the group who's an only child. I wanted to find 12 out more about her family life because this little girl was quite isolated from the group, didn't make friends, so I talked to her mother. Well, they don't have time to do anything in the evening, the mother said. The parents come home after picking up the child at the babysitter's. Then the mother fixes dinner while the child watches TV. Then they have dinner and the child goes to bed. I said to this mother. 'Well, couldn't she help you fix dinner? That would be a nice time for the two of you to talk,' and the mother said, 'Oh, but I'd hate to have her miss "Zoom."[1] It's such a good program!'"

Even when families make efforts to control television, too often its 13 very presence counterbalances the positive features of family life. A writer and mother of two boys aged 3 and 7 described her family's television schedule in an article in the *New York Times:*

> We were in the midst of a full-scale War. Every day was a new battle and every program was a major skirmish. We agreed it was a bad scene all around and were ready to enter diplomatic negotiations. . . . In principle we have agreed on 2 1/2 hours of TV a day, "Sesame Street," "Electric Company" (with dinner gobbled up in between) and two half-hour shows between 7 and 8:30 which enables the grownups to eat in peace and prevents the two boys from destroying one another. Their pre-bedtime choice is dreadful, because, as Josh recently

---

[1] An educational program broadcast on PBS. [Eds.]

admitted, "There's nothing much on I really like." So . . . it's "What's My Line" or "To Tell the Truth"[2] . . . Clearly there is a need for first-rate children's shows at this time. . . .

Consider the "family life" described here: Presumably the father 14 comes home from work during the "Sesame Street"–"Electric Company" stint. The children are either watching television, gobbling their dinner, or both. While the parents eat their dinner in peaceful privacy, the children watch another hour of television. Then there is only a half-hour left before bedtime, just enough time for baths, getting pajamas on, brushing teeth, and so on. The children's evening is regimented with an almost military precision. They watch their favorite programs, and when there is "nothing much on I really like," they watch whatever else is on—because *watching* is the important thing. Their mother does not see anything amiss with watching programs just for the sake of watching; she only wishes there were some first-rate children's shows on at those times.

Without conjuring up memories of the Victorian era with family 15 games and long, leisurely meals, and large families, the question arises: isn't there a better family life available than this dismal, mechanized arrangement of children watching television for however long is allowed them, evening after evening?

Of course, families today still do *special* things together at times: go 16 camping in the summer, go to the zoo on a nice Saturday, take various trips and expeditions. But their *ordinary* daily life together is diminished—that sitting around at the dinner table, that spontaneous taking up of an activity, those little games invented by children on the spur of the moment when there is nothing else to do, the scribbling, the chatting, and even the quarreling, all the things that form the fabric of a family, that define a childhood. Instead, the children have their regular schedule of television programs and bedtime, and the parents have their peaceful dinner together.

The author of the article in the *Times* notes that "keeping a family 17 sane means mediating between the needs of both children and adults." But surely the needs of adults are being better met than the needs of the children, who are effectively shunted away and rendered untroublesome, while their parents enjoy a life as undemanding as that of any childless couple. In reality, it is those very demands that young children make upon a family that lead to growth, and it is the way parents accede to those demands that builds the relationships upon which the future of the family depends. If the family does not accumulate its backlog of shared experiences, shared *everyday* experiences that occur and

---

[2] Long-running game shows. [Eds.]

recur and change and develop, then it is not likely to survive as anything other than a caretaking institution.

Family Rituals

Ritual is defined by sociologists as "that part of family life that the   18
family likes about itself, is proud of and wants formally to continue."
Another text notes that "the development of a ritual by a family is an
index of the common interest of its members in the family as a group."

What has happened to family rituals, those regular, dependable,   19
recurrent happenings that gave members of a family a feeling of *belonging* to a home rather than living in it merely for the sake of convenience,
those experiences that act as the adhesive of family unity far more than
any material advantages?

Mealtime rituals, going-to-bed rituals, illness rituals, holiday rituals, how many of these have survived the inroads of the television set?   20

A young woman who grew up near Chicago reminisces about   21
her childhood and gives an idea of the effects of television upon family rituals:

"As a child I had millions of relatives around—my parents both   22
come from relatively large families. My father had nine brothers and sisters. And so every holiday there was this great swoop-down of aunts,
uncles, and millions of cousins. I just remember how wonderful it used
to be. These thousands of cousins would come and everyone would
play and ultimately, after dinner, all the women would be in the front of
the house, drinking coffee and talking, all the men would be in the back
of the house, drinking and smoking, and all the kids would be all over
the place, playing hide and seek. Christmas time was particularly nice
because everyone always brought all their toys and games. Our house
had a couple of rooms with go-through closets, so there was always kids
running in a great circle route. I remember it was just wonderful.

"And then all of a sudden one year I remember becoming suddenly   23
aware of how different everything had become. The kids were no longer
playing Monopoly or Clue or the other games we used to play together.
It was because we had a television set which had been turned on for a
football game. All of that socializing that had gone on previously had
ended. Now everyone was sitting in front of the television set, on a holiday, at a family party! I remember being stunned by how awful that
was. Somehow the television had become more attractive."

As families have come to spend more and more of their time   24
together engaged in the single activity of television watching, those rituals and pastimes that once gave family life its special quality have
become more and more uncommon. Not since prehistoric times when
cave families hunted, gathered, ate, and slept, with little time remaining

to accumulate a culture of any significance, have families been reduced to such a sameness.

Real People

It is not only the activities that a family might engage in together 25 that are diminished by the powerful presence of television in the home. The relationships of the family members to each other are also affected, in both obvious and subtle ways. The hours that the young child spends in a one-way relationship with television people, an involvement that allows for no communication or interaction, surely affect his relationships with real-life people.

Studies show the importance of eye-to-eye contact, for instance, in 26 real-life relationships, and indicate that the nature of a person's eye-contact patterns, whether he looks another squarely in the eye or looks to the side or shifts his gaze from side to side, may play a significant role in his success or failure in human relationships. But no eye contact is possible in the child-television relationship, although in certain children's programs people purport to speak directly to the child and the camera fosters this illusion by focusing directly upon the person being filmed. (Mr. Rogers is an example, telling the child "I like you, you're special," etc.) How might such a distortion of real-life relationships affect a child's development of trust, of openness, of an ability to relate well to other *real* people?

Bruno Bettelheim writes: 27

> Children who have been taught, or conditioned, to listen passively most of the day to the warm verbal communications coming from the TV screen, to the deep emotional appeal of the so-called TV personality, are often unable to respond to real persons because they arouse so much less feeling than the skilled actor. Worse, they lose the ability to learn from reality because life experiences are much more complicated than the ones they see on the screen. . . .

A teacher makes a similar observation about her personal viewing 28 experiences:

"I have trouble mobilizing myself and dealing with real people after 29 watching a few hours of television. It's just hard to make that transition from watching television to a real relationship. I suppose it's because there was no effort necessary while I was watching, and dealing with real people always requires a bit of effort. Imagine, then, how much harder it might be to do the same thing for a small child, particularly one who watches a lot of television every day."

But more obviously damaging to family relationships is the elimi- 30 nation of opportunities to talk, and perhaps more important, to argue, to air grievances, between parents and children and brothers and sisters. Families frequently use television to avoid confronting their problems, problems that will not go away if they are ignored but will only fester and become less easily resolvable as time goes on.

A mother reports: 31

"I find myself, with three children, wanting to turn on the TV set 32 when they're fighting. I really have to struggle not to do it because I feel that's telling them this is the solution to the quarrel—but it's so tempting that I often do it."

A family therapist discusses the use of television as an avoidance 33 mechanism:

"In a family I know the father comes home from work and turns on 34 the television set. The children come and watch with him and the wife serves them their meal in front of the set. He then goes and takes a shower, or works on the car or something. She then goes and has her own dinner in front of the television set. It's a symptom of a deeper-rooted problem, sure. But it would help them all to get rid of the set. It would be far easier to work on what the symptom really means without the television. The television simply encourages a double avoidance of each other. They'd find out more quickly what was going on if they weren't able to hide behind the TV. Things wouldn't necessarily be better, of course, but they wouldn't be anesthetized."

The decreased opportunities for simple conversation between par- 35 ents and children in the television-centered home may help explain an observation made by an emergency room nurse at a Boston hospital. She reports that parents just seem to sit there these days when they come in with a sick or seriously injured child, although talking to the child would distract and comfort him. "They don't seem to know *how* to talk to their own children at any length," the nurse observes. Similarly, a television critic writes in the *New York Times:* "I had just a day ago taken my son to the emergency ward of a hospital for stitches above his left eye, and the occasion seemed no more real to me than Maalot or 54th Street, south-central Los Angeles. There was distance and numbness and an inability to turn off the total institution. I didn't behave at all; I just watched. . . ."

A number of research studies substantiate the assumption that tele- 36 vision interferes with family activities and the formation of family relationships. One survey shows that 78 percent of the respondents indicated no conversation taking place during viewing except at specified times such as commercials. The study notes: "The television atmosphere in most households is one of quiet absorption on the part of family members who are present. The nature of the family social life during a program could be described as 'parallel' rather than interactive, and the set does seem to dominate family life when it is on." Thirty-six percent of the respondents in another study indicated that television viewing was the only family activity participated in during the week.

In a summary of research findings on television's effect on family 37 interactions James Gabardino states: "The early findings suggest that television had a disruptive effect upon interaction and thus presumably human development. . . . It is not unreasonable to ask: 'Is the fact that the average American family during the 1950s came to include two parents, two children and a television set somehow related to the psychosocial characteristics of the young adults of the 1970s?'"

Undermining the Family

In its effect on family relationships, in its facilitation of parental 38 withdrawal from an active role in the socialization of their children, and in its replacement of family rituals and special events, television has played an important role in the disintegration of the American family. But of course it has not been the only contributing factor, perhaps not even the most important one. The steadily rising divorce rate, the increase in the number of working mothers, the decline of the extended family, the breakdown of neighborhoods and communities, the growing isolation of the nuclear family—all have seriously affected the family.

As Urie Bronfenbrenner suggests, the sources of family breakdown 39 do not come from the family itself, but from the circumstances in which the family finds itself and the way of life imposed upon it by those circumstances. "When those circumstances and the way of life they generate undermine relationships of trust and emotional security between family members, when they make it difficult for parents to care for, educate and enjoy their children, when there is no support or recognition from the outside world for one's role as a parent and when time spent with one's family means frustration of career, personal fulfillment and peace of mind, then the development of the child is adversely affected," he writes.

But while the roots of alienation go deep into the fabric of American 40 social history, television's presence in the home fertilizes them, encourages their wild and unchecked growth. Perhaps it is true that America's commitment to the television experience masks a spiritual vacuum, an empty and barren way of life, a desert of materialism. But it is television's dominant role in the family that anesthetizes the family into accepting its unhappy state and prevents it from struggling to better its condition, to improve its relationships, and to regain some of the richness it once possessed.

Others have noted the role of mass media in perpetuating an unsat- 41
isfactory *status quo*. Leisure-time activity, writes Irving Howe, "must
provide relief from work monotony without making the return to work
too unbearable; it must provide amusement without insight and pleasure without disturbance—as distinct from art which gives pleasure
through disturbance. Mass culture is thus oriented towards a central
aspect of industrial society: the depersonalization of the individual."
Similarly, Jacques Ellul rejects the idea that television is a legitimate
means of educating the citizen: "Education . . . takes place only incidentally. The clouding of his consciousness is paramount. . . ."

And so the American family muddles on, dimly aware that some- 42
thing is amiss but distracted from an understanding of its plight by an
endless stream of television images. As family ties grow weaker and
vaguer, as children's lives become more separate from their parents', as
parents' educational role in their children's lives is taken over by television and schools, family life becomes increasingly more unsatisfying for
both parents and children. All that seems to be left is Love, an abstraction that family members *know* is necessary but find great difficulty giving each other because the traditional opportunities for expressing love
within the family have been reduced or destroyed.

For contemporary parents, love toward each other has increasingly 43
come to mean successful sexual relations, as witnessed by the proliferation of sex manuals and sex therapists. The opportunities for manifesting other forms of love through mutual support, understanding,
nurturing, even, to use an unpopular word, *serving* each other, are less
and less available as mothers and fathers seek their independent destinies outside the family.

As for love of children, this love is increasingly expressed through 44
supplying material comforts, amusements, and educational opportunities. Parents show their love for their children by sending them to good
schools and camps, by providing them with good food and good doctors,
by buying them toys, books, games, and a television set of their very own.
Parents will even go further and express their love by attending PTA
meetings to improve their children's schools, or by joining groups that
are acting to improve the quality of their children's television programs.

But this is love at a remove, and is rarely understood by children. 45
The more direct forms of parental love require time and patience,
steady, dependable, ungrudgingly given time actually spent *with* a
child, reading to him, comforting him, playing, joking, and working
with him. But even if a parent were eager and willing to demonstrate
that sort of direct love to his children today, the opportunities are diminished. What with school and Little League and piano lessons and, of
course, the inevitable television programs, a day seems to offer just
enough time for a good-night kiss.

GIVING SATURDAY MORNING SOME SLACK

Charles McGrath

Remember Saturday morning? The expectancy, the blissfulness, the 1
sense of utter freedom? The most sublime moment was the first—the
instant when, unprodded by either alarm clock or parental summons,
you emerged into consciousness and experienced an almost physical
sense of release, a floating up from the mattress, as you realized that you
didn't have to go to school. And the rest of the day—of the whole weekend—then seemed to spead out limitlessly from the edge of the bed-
covers, a blank and beckoning horizon.

You could do absolutely anything you chose. You could turn over, 2
tunnel under the pillow and go back to sleep. You could just lie there for
a while, woolgathering and listening to Dad's snores rumble from
down the hall. You could get up and play with your slot cars or your
electric train. You could check on the gerbils, in hopes that they might
be mating again. You could build a model plane, snuffling in deep,
head-jolting whiffs of Testor's glue. You could even read—that was not
unheard of back then.

But what you chose to do, of course, was watch TV. You sprang up 3
and, still in your pj's, went to the kitchen and fixed yourself a bowl of
Froot Loops or Lucky Charms, which in violation of the first com-
mandment of the household—no food in the living room!—you carried
boldly over the forbidden threshold and set on top of the Magnavox.
You turned on your favorite show and then curled up on the sofa or
stretched out on the carpet in front, and with any luck you remained
there, motionless, for hours. If, as the critics used to complain, TV is a
drug, then no opium den was ever sweeter. On a good Saturday morning, one when Mom wasn't too cranky, you got to stay in your pajamas
until noon.

In those days, of course, television was largely unregulated. No one, 4
not even Mom, was paying much attention to what or how much we
watched. In recent years, children's programming has been endlessly
scrutinized, and thanks in large part to parental lobbying groups, it has
come under more vigilant Federal controls. The newest set of regulations was supposed to go into effect this fall, requiring that stations
devote at least three hours a week—most of them on Saturday, presumably—to educational programming for children under 16. So far, compliance has been spotty at best. Like those that preceded them, the new
regulations are vague and unenforceable. No one can agree on what
constitutes educational television, and the burden of policing falls not
on the Government but on viewers, who are expected to keep tabs on
their local stations. The stations claim, not unreasonably, that their

hands are tied by the networks, which these days supply almost all the programming. The networks, meanwhile, have for the most part done little more than tinker with the existing shows and declare that they fit the bill. Disney's "101 Dalmatians," for example, turns out to teach friendship and responsibility, and "N.B.A. Inside Stuff," professional basketball's show for children, is said to impart "life lessons."

This is actually not as dumb as it sounds. *All* TV imparts life lessons 5 of a sort—if only lessons in how greedy or manipulative or boring television producers can be. And what we take away from the experience of watching television is more than what the programmers have put there. Watching television, even if you watch it alone, is also a social experience, and it's often a ritual. Part of the magic of the old Saturday-morning drill had almost nothing to do with content, or with anything that could be regulated. The magic was in the safeness and the sameness—the reassuring security—of the ritual itself.

What you watched, if you grew up in the 50's or early 60's, was not 6 the parade of otherworldly characters that nowadays lurches forth— robots and superheroes mostly, so poorly animated that their dialogue and their expressionless mouths are forever out of sync and that Captain America, for example, walks as stiffly as if he had just had a hip replacement. In those days, what you watched, most likely, was a Saturday-morning program that originated at your local station. It featured an adult figure, either clownish or avuncular, depending on local custom, and perhaps a puppet or two or a dimwitted visitor, whose job it was to fill with patter the intervals between the showing of vintage cartoons, doled out as sparingly as if they were some rare elixir—which indeed they were.

In Boston, where I grew up, we had "Boomtown," with Rex Trailer, 7 a handsome singing cowboy, and his faithful, if none-too-bright, side-kick, the sombreroed and serape-clad Pablo. (I was astonished to discover once, when my father took me to one of Rex's "personal appearances," that Pablo was not really Mexican and that he also had extremely bad breath.) The show began with a film clip of Rex galloping to the studio on his handsome palomino, Goldrush—galloping from where was never entirely clear; New Hampshire, perhaps—but the rest, except for the cartoons, was broadcast live. Rex did rope tricks and was occasionally persuaded to take out his guitar, or his "git-fiddle," as he called it, and sing. (One of his tunes, I seem to recall, had a chorus that consisted of the word "hoofbeats," repeated over and over.) Once in a while a visitor dropped by to talk about fire safety or disease prevention.

It was all a little boring and overearnest, and in retrospect it's amaz- 8 ing that "Boomtown" lasted as long as it did, from 1956 to 1976. (Pablo died years ago, but Rex, I was happy to learn recently while trolling through the Internet, has prospered in the new business of video résumés.) Yet the very dullness and predictability was an essential and soothing part of Saturday morning; it slowed time down, after a fashion, and helped stretch out those precious hours into a drowsy prelunch eternity—a kind of Keatsian daze in which the antics of Popeye and Bluto and Elmer and Woody never staled, no matter how many times we'd seen them before.

Had we known it, we never would have watched, but "Boomtown" 9 was, by today's standards at least, highly "educational." And oddly enough, this show and others like it were in part done in through the efforts of Action for Children's Television and other lobbying groups dedicated to reforming children's programming and reducing its dependency on commercials.

Still, today's Saturday-morning fare, though much maligned, is in a 10 number of essential ways no worse than what we watched as kids. Some of it, in fact, is little altered: the whole inspired Looney Tunes gang (Bugs, Porky, Daffy, Sylvester, Tweety et al.) still turn up; the Lucky Charms leprechaun, ageless and ever-twinkly, still boasts about how many marshmallows his product contains; Franken Berry, Count Chocula, Cocoa Puffs—they're still being hawked, too, the latter newly enhanced with an infusion of Hershey's chocolate. Barbie's still around, of course, and so are those various creatures—dolls, ponies, mermaids, trolls—with long manes in need of curling and brushing. Dolls that urinate have not gone out of fashion, and neither have weapons-laden space vehicles (batteries not included).

There are even some cartoons on now that are better and more 11 sophisticated than anything we ever watched: the darkly ironic "Ren and Stimpy," for example, or "Men in Black" (where the cheesiness of the animation actually contributes to the humor) or, my favorite, the improbable "Pinky and the Brain," about a pair of lab mice that, as the result of an accident at Acme Labs, have been transformed into, on the one hand, an airhead rodent with a high-pitched North London accent and, on the other, a macrocephalic mad-scientist mouse with plans to take over the world. These shows, like the better prime-time cartoons—"The Simpsons" and "King of the Hill"—successfully talk to kids and adults both. They sometimes seem to operate on two simultaneous planes of reference, in fact, and they pay children the great compliment of not dumbing everything down for them. Or maybe they merely recognize that children know more than we think, or wish, they did.

But where the Saturday-morning TV of today differs enormously 12 from the TV most of us watched is in the virtual absence (except in shows like "Captain Kangaroo," for very young children) of adult figures—of the Rexes and Pablos, those benign gatekeepers, or emissaries from the real world, who while seeming to share our delight in cartoons, our near reverence for them, also reminded us of the importance of brushing our teeth and crossing at crosswalks. Grown-ups turn up on Saturday morning now as either idiots, like the crazed geek who does comic spots on "Disney's 1 Saturday Morning," or meanies, like the crotchety, incompetent teachers and principals on the cartoons "Recess" and "Pepper Ann."

Saturday-morning TV, moreover, is nothing like as sweetly langu- 13
ourous as it used to be. Where a show like "Boomtown" used to come on at 6:30 or 7 and stay on the air for several hours, the new programs come, one after the other, at half-hour intervals, further punctuated by promos and advertisements for shows coming up later, and most of these shows leap on the screen with MTV-like logo sequences and rock-inspired theme songs and then lurch from commercial to commercial in short, hyperactive bursts. Many of the newer shows—"The X-Men" and "The New Adventures of Voltron," for example—are inspired by comic books, and with their lantern-jawed, steroidal heroes, stilted dialogue and creaky plots, they employ an aggressive, hard-edged freeze-frame style in which there is seldom a quiet or reflective moment. The violence in these shows, of which there's a fair amount, isn't realistic, exactly—the bad guys tend to be rendered unconscious rather than outright killed or maimed—but neither is it as surreally goofy as the violence in a Road Runner or Tweety and Sylvester episode, say, where bombs and missiles and explosives of every kind go off with thrilling frequency, blowing cats and coyotes sky high and wreaking amazing, if temporary, disfigurement (popping eyeballs, missing digits, smoking ears, anvil-shaped heads) without causing any harm at all.

In the end, the effect of the new, hyper Saturday-morning style, 14
whether deliberate or not, is to make time pass faster and to do away with the old sensation of endlessness, of moments hardly ticking by. As an experiment, on a recent Saturday I watched children's TV for five hours straight, from 7 to noon. (Don't try this at home, parents, without medical supervision.) I was bored much of the time, yet when I closed my eyes and tried to doze, I was invariably jarred awake by some new sound effect or other. But I was astonished by how quickly the hours flew. It was Saturday afternoon before I knew it.

The kids may not mind, however, or even notice, for how many of 15
them get to enjoy the full five-hour orgy anymore? We wake them up before dawn for the long drive to the hockey rink, and then there's band practice, ballet lessons, the math tutor and, if there's time, that play date we penciled in a few weeks ago and that we can confirm now on the car phone on the way to the orthodontist.

Many kids today, if they watch Saturday-morning TV at all, watch 16
it the way grown-ups watch "Today" or "Good Morning America"—on

the run, in snatches, while hastily swallowing a vitamin pill. And on those mornings, increasingly rare, when we parents yield to temptation—when, in response to that gentle tugging on our foot or to the tiny hand clamped over our nose, we say, "Mommy and Daddy are tired right now, why don't you turn on TV for a little while?"—we are afterward undone with guilt, certain that we have cost them at least 20 points on the SAT's. For grown-ups as well as children, Saturday morning is quickly becoming a thing of the past, just another slot in the overfull datebook of our lives.

In the grand scheme of things, this may not be the worst fate that 17 has befallen our civilization, but it's regrettable nonetheless. We all of us need some down time, and children especially. There is actually something to be said for doing nothing and for learning how to be bored. There is even more to be said for escapism, for stepping out of time. And this is where children's TV has truly let us down: not in its shameless huckstering or in its shying away from "educational content," whatever that is. The problem is that the sustained quality of the daydreaming it offers is so seldom worth waking up for. Children's TV doesn't need fewer cartoons; it needs better cartoons, better drawn and with better characters. It needs narrative, which is not the same as an action plot. It needs modulation and variety. And it needs, every now and then, the voice of an adult—if for no other reason than to gently remind children that they can't stay in their pajamas forever.

Responding to Reading

1. Winn says, "Home and family life has changed in important ways since the advent of television" (8). How, according to Winn, has family life changed? How do you think your own family life would change if you were suddenly deprived of all access to television?

2. Do you agree with Winn that television is an evil, addictive drug that has destroyed cherished family rituals, undermined family relationships, and "[anesthesized] the family into accepting its unhappy state and [prevented] it from struggling to better its condition, to improve its relationships, and to regain some of the richness it once possessed" (40)? How might Winn react to Charles McGrath's idea that watching TV can itself become a ritual? How might she react to his statement, "If . . . TV is a drug, then no opium den was ever sweeter" (3)?

3. In paragraph 5, McGrath says, "*All* TV imparts life lessons of a sort—if only lessons in how greedy or manipulative or boring television producers can be. And what we take away from the experience of watching television is more than what the programmers have put there." Do you agree? What lessons do you think television teaches its viewers?

4. How, according to McGrath, is the Saturday morning television of the 1950s like and unlike that of today? Given the similarities and differences he identifies, do you agree that the effect of Saturday morning television on children can still be seen as largely positive?

5. McGrath says, "Watching television, even if you watch it alone, is also a social experience . . ." (5). What does he mean? Does this statement support or contradict Winn's view of television?
6. Marie Winn believes it is television that is undermining family life. What does McGrath see as responsible for the breakdown in the family? In what sense does he see television as a solution to the problems he identifies?

THE TRIUMPH OF THE YELL

Deborah Tannen

A professor of linguistics at Georgetown University in Washington, D.C., Deborah Tannen (1945–) has written both scholarly and popular books examining the problems people encounter communicating across cultural and gender lines. Her three bestsellers—That's Not What I Meant: How Conversational Style Makes or Breaks Your Relationships *(1987),* You Just Don't Understand: Women and Men in Conversation *(1990), and* Talking from 9 to 5 *(1994)—have given her readers a new perspective on how communication style affects how a message is perceived. A frequent guest on television news and talk shows, Tannen successfully translates complex linguistic theory into language nonlinguists can readily comprehend. She developed her "humanistic approach to linguistic analysis," she says, to help people everywhere understand and improve human communication. In the following essay focusing on public discourse, which is the subject of her most recent book,* For the Sake of Argument *(1998), Tannen suggests that the media in the United States encourage public debate to degenerate into simple-minded, mean-spirited verbal fighting because "the spectacles that result when extremes clash are thought to get higher ratings or larger readership."*

I put the question to a journalist who had written a vitriolic attack on a leading feminist researcher: "Why do you need to make others wrong for you to be right?" Her response: "It's an argument!"

That's the problem. More and more these days, journalists, politicians and academics treat public discourse as an argument—not in the sense of *making* an argument, but in the sense of *having* one, of having a fight.

When people have arguments in private life, they're not trying to understand what the other person is saying. They're listening for weaknesses in logic to leap on, points they can distort to make the other look bad. We all do this when we're angry, but is it the best model for public intellectual interchange? This breakdown of the boundary between public and private is contributing to what I have come to think of as a culture of critique.

Fights have winners and losers. If you're fighting to win, the temp- 4
tation is great to deny facts that support your opponent's views and
present only those facts that support your own.

At worst, there's a temptation to lie. We accept this style of arguing 5
because we believe we can tell when someone is lying. But we can't.
Paul Ekman, a psychologist at the University of California at San Francisco, has found that even when people are very sure they can tell
whether or not someone is dissembling, their judgments are as likely as
not to be wrong.

If public discourse is a fight, every issue must have two sides—no 6
more, no less. And it's crucial to show "the other side," even if one has
to scour the margins of science or the fringes of lunacy to find it.

The culture of critique is based on the belief that opposition leads to 7
truth: when both sides argue, the truth will emerge. And because people are presumed to enjoy watching a fight, the most extreme views are
presented, since they make the best show. But it is a myth that opposition leads to truth when truth does not reside on one side or the other
but is rather a crystal of many sides. Truth is more likely to be found in
the complex middle than in the simplified extremes, but the spectacles
that result when extremes clash are thought to get higher ratings or
larger readership.

Because the culture of critique encourages people to attack and 8
often misrepresent others, those others must waste their creativity and
time correcting the misrepresentations and defending themselves.
Serious scholars have had to spend years of their lives writing books
proving that the Holocaust happened, because a few fanatics who
claim it didn't have been given a public forum. Those who provide the
platform know that what these people say is, simply put, not true, but
rationalize the dissemination of lies as showing "the other side." The
determination to find another side can spread disinformation rather
than lead to truth.

The culture of critique has given rise to the journalistic practice of 9
confronting prominent people with criticism couched as others' views.
Meanwhile, the interviewer has planted an accusation in readers' or
viewers' minds. The theory seems to be that when provoked, people are
spurred to eloquence and self-revelation. Perhaps some are. But others
are unable to say what they know because they are hurt, and begin to
sputter when their sense of fairness is outraged. In those cases, opposition is not the path to truth.

When people in power know that what they say will be scrutinized 10
for weaknesses and probably distorted, they become more guarded. As
an acquaintance recently explained about himself, public figures who
once gave long, free-wheeling press conferences now limit themselves
to reading brief statements. When less information gets communicated,
opposition does not lead to truth.

Opposition also limits information when only those who are adept 11
at verbal sparring take part in public discourse, and those who cannot
handle it, or do not like it, decline to participate. This winnowing
process is evident in graduate schools, where many talented students
drop out because what they expected to be a community of intellectual
inquiry turned out to be a ritual game of attack and counterattack.

One such casualty graduated from a small liberal arts college, 12
where she "luxuriated in the endless discussions." At the urging of her
professors, she decided to make academia her profession. But she
changed her mind after a year in an art history program at a major university. She felt she had fallen into a "den of wolves." "I wasn't cut out
for academia," she concluded. But does academia have to be so combative that it cuts people like her out?

In many university classrooms, "critical thinking" means reading 13
someone's life work, then ripping it to shreds. Though critique is surely
one form of critical thinking, so are integrating ideas from disparate
fields and examining the context out of which they grew. Opposition
does not lead to truth when we ask only "What's wrong with this argument?" and never "What can we use from this in building a new theory,
and a new understanding?"

Several years ago I was on a television talk show with a representa- 14
tive of the men's movement. I didn't foresee any problem, since there is
nothing in my work that is anti-male. But in the room where guests
gather before the show I found a man wearing a shirt and tie and a
floor-length skirt, with waist-length red hair. He politely introduced
himself and told me he liked my book. Then he added: "When I get out
there, I'm going to attack you. But don't take it personally. That's why
they invite me on, so that's what I'm going to do."

When the show began, I spoke only a sentence or two before this 15
man nearly jumped out of his chair, threw his arms before him in gestures of anger and began shrieking—first attacking me, but soon moving on to rail against women. The most disturbing thing about his
hysterical ranting was what it sparked in the studio audience: they too
became vicious, attacking not me (I hadn't had a chance to say anything) and not him (who wants to tangle with someone who will scream
at you?) but the other guests: unsuspecting women who had agreed to
come on the show to talk about their problems communicating with
their spouses.

This is the most dangerous aspect of modeling intellectual inter- 16
change as a fight: it contributes to an atmosphere of animosity that
spreads like a fever. In a society where people express their anger by
shooting, the result of demonizing those with whom we disagree can be
truly demonic.

I am not suggesting that journalists stop asking tough questions nec- 17
essary to get at the facts, even if those questions may appear challenging.

And of course it is the responsibility of the media to represent serious opposition when it exists, and of intellectuals everywhere to explore potential weaknesses in others' arguments. But when opposition becomes the overwhelming avenue of inquiry, when the lust for opposition exalts extreme views and obscures complexity, when our eagerness to find weaknesses blinds us to strengths, when the atmosphere of animosity precludes respect and poisons our relations with one another, then the culture of critique is stifling us. If we could move beyond it, we would move closer to the truth.

Responding to Reading

1. Tannen has no quarrel with our tendency to argue in our private lives. Why, then, does she think this tendency, fostered by what she calls the "culture of critique," is a negative, even dangerous, force in "public intellectual interchange" (3)? Do you agree with her?

2. Tannen says, "If public discourse is a fight, every issue must have two sides—no more, no less" (6). Why does she see this as a problem? Give some examples of issues that you believe have more than two sides. Can you think of any issues that have only one side?

3. In paragraphs 11–12 Tannen explains how the "culture of critique" has spread to graduate schools, where it has created "a ritual game of attack and counterattack" (11). Why do you think graduate schools foster this combative behavior? Do you see it in operation in your own undergraduate classes?

SEX, LIES, AND ADVERTISING

Gloria Steinem

Feminist writer, editor, speaker, and political activist Gloria Steinem (1934–) was born in Toledo, Ohio. After graduation from Smith College, she became active in the women's movement as an organizer and speaker, worked as a journalist, and founded Ms. *magazine in 1971. Steinem came to national prominence with her essay "I Was a Playboy Bunny," a humorous and sarcastic exposé of the harassment she suffered on the job. Her most recent books are* Revolution from Within: A Book of Self-Esteem *(1992),* Moving Beyond Words *(1993), and* On Self-Esteem *(1995). Of social change, she has said, "When one member of a group changes, it shifts the balance for everyone, and when one group changes, it changes the balance of society." In the following essay, first published in* Ms. *in 1990, Steinem describes the difficulties a serious women's magazine like* Ms. *has in attracting advertisers and asserts that advertisers often control a magazine's content.*

About three years ago, as *glasnost*[1] was beginning and *Ms.* seemed ₁
to be ending, I was invited to a press lunch for a Soviet official. He entertained us with anecdotes about new problems of democracy in his
country. Local Communist leaders were being criticized in their media
for the first time, he explained, and they were angry.

"So I'll have to ask my American friends," he finished pointedly, ₂
"how more *subtly* to control the press." In the silence that followed, I
said, "Advertising."

The reporters laughed, but later, one of them took me aside: How ₃
dare I suggest that freedom of the press was limited? How dare I imply
that his newsweekly could be influenced by ads?

I explained that I was thinking of advertising's media-wide influ- ₄
ence on most of what we read. Even newsmagazines use "soft" cover
stories to sell ads, confuse readers with "advertorials," and occasionally
self-censor on subjects known to be a problem with big advertisers.

But, I also explained, I was thinking especially of women's mag- ₅
azines. There, it isn't just a little content that's devoted to attracting ads,
it's almost all of it. That's why advertisers, not readers, have always
been the problem for *Ms.* As the only women's magazine that didn't
supply what the ad world euphemistically describes as "supportive editorial atmosphere" or "complementary copy" (for instance, articles that
praise food/fashion/beauty subjects to "support" and "complement"
food/fashion/beauty ads), *Ms.* could never attract enough advertising
to break even.

"Oh, *women's* magazines," the journalist said with contempt. "Every- ₆
body knows they're catalogs—but who cares? They have nothing to do
with journalism."

I can't tell you how many times I've had this argument in 25 years ₇
of working for many kinds of publications. Except as money-making
machines—"cash cows" as they are so elegantly called in the trade—
women's magazines are rarely taken seriously. Though changes being
made by women have been called more far-reaching than the industrial
revolution—and though many editors try hard to reflect some of them
in the few pages left to them after all the ad-related subjects have been
covered—the magazines serving the female half of this country are still
far below the journalistic and ethical standards of news and general
interest publications. Most depressing of all, this doesn't even rate an
exposé.

If *Time* and *Newsweek* had to lavish praise on cars in general and ₈
credit General Motors in particular to get GM ads, there would be a

---

[1] A policy of greater openness and freedom instituted by the Soviet Union's Communist government in the late 1980s. [Eds.]

scandal—maybe a criminal investigation. When women's magazines from *Seventeen* to *Lear's* praise beauty products in general and credit Revlon in particular to get ads, it's just business as usual.

1

When *Ms.* began, we didn't consider *not* taking ads. The most 9 important reason was keeping the price of a feminist magazine low enough for most women to afford. But the second and almost equal reason was providing a forum where women and advertisers could talk to each other and improve advertising itself. After all, it was (and still is) as potent a source of information in this country as news or TV and movie dramas.

We decided to proceed in two stages. First, we would convince 10 makers of "people products" used by both men and women but advertised mostly to men—cars, credit cards, insurance, sound equipment, financial services, and the like—that their ads should be placed in a women's magazine. Since they were accustomed to the division between editorial and advertising in news and general interest magazines, this would allow our editorial content to be free and diverse. Second, we would add the best ads for whatever traditional "women's products" (clothes, shampoo, fragrance, food, and so on) that surveys showed *Ms.* readers used. But we would ask them to come in *without* the usual quid pro quo of "complementary copy."

We knew the second step might be harder. Food advertisers have 11 always demanded that women's magazines publish recipes and articles on entertaining (preferably ones that name their products) in return for their ads; clothing advertisers expect to be surrounded by fashion spreads (especially ones that credit their designers); and shampoo, fragrance, and beauty products in general usually insist on positive editorial coverage of beauty subjects, plus photo credits besides. That's why women's magazines look the way they do. But if we could break this link between ads and editorial content, then we wanted good ads for "women's products," too.

By playing their part in this unprecedented mix of *all* the things our 12 readers need and use, advertisers also would be rewarded: Ads for products like cars and mutual funds would find a new growth market; the best ads for women's products would no longer be lost in oceans of ads for the same category; and both would have access to a laboratory of smart and caring readers whose response would help create effective ads for other media as well.

I thought then that our main problem would be the imagery in ads 13 themselves. Car-makers were still draping blondes in evening gowns over the hoods like ornaments. Authority figures were almost always male, even in ads for products that only women used. Sadistic, he-man campaigns even won industry praise. For instance, *Advertising Age* had hailed the infamous Silva Thin cigarette theme, "How to Get a Woman's Attention: Ignore Her," as "brilliant." Even in medical journals, tranquilizer ads showed depressed housewives standing beside piles of dirty dishes and promised to get them back to work.

Obviously, *Ms.* would have to avoid such ads and seek out the best 14 ones—but this didn't seem impossible. *The New Yorker* had been selecting ads for aesthetic reasons for years, a practice that only seemed to make advertisers more eager to be in its pages. *Ebony* and *Essence* were asking for ads with positive black images, and though their struggle was hard, they weren't being called unreasonable.

Clearly, what *Ms.* needed was a very special publisher and ad sales 15 staff. I could think of only one woman with experience on the business side of magazines—Patricia Carbine, who recently had become a vice president of *McCall's* as well as its editor in chief—and the reason I knew her name was a good omen. She had been managing editor at *Look* (really *the* editor, but its owner refused to put a female name at the top of his masthead) when I was writing a column there. After I did an early interview with Cesar Chavez, then just emerging as a leader of migrant labor, and the publisher turned it down because he was worried about ads from Sunkist, Pat was the one who intervened. As I learned later, she had told the publisher she would resign if the interview wasn't published. Mainly because *Look* couldn't afford to lose Pat, it *was* published (and the ads from Sunkist never arrived).

Though I barely knew this woman, she had done two things I 16 always remembered: put her job on the line in a way that editors often talk about but rarely do, and been so loyal to her colleagues that she never told me or anyone outside *Look* that she had done so.

Fortunately, Pat did agree to leave *McCall's* and take a huge cut in 17 salary to become publisher of *Ms.* She became responsible for training and inspiring generations of young women who joined the *Ms.* ad sales force, many of whom went on to become "firsts" at the top of publishing. When *Ms.* first started, however, there were so few women with experience selling space that Pat and I made the rounds of ad agencies ourselves. Later, the fact that *Ms.* was asking companies to do business in a different way meant our saleswomen had to make many times the usual number of calls—first to convince agencies and then client companies besides—and to present endless amounts of research. I was often asked to do a final ad presentation, or see some higher decision-maker, or speak to women employees so executives could see the interest of women they worked with. That's why I spent more time persuading advertisers than editing or writing for *Ms.* and why I ended up with an unsentimental education in the seamy underside of publishing that few writers see (and even fewer magazines can publish).

Let me take you with us through some experiences, just as they 18
happened:

• Cheered on by early support from Volkswagen and one or two 19
other car companies, we scrape together time and money to put on a
major reception in Detroit. We know U.S. car-makers firmly believe that
women choose the upholstery, not the car, but we are armed with statistics and reader mail to prove the contrary: A car is an important purchase for women, one that symbolizes mobility and freedom.

But almost nobody comes. We are left with many pounds of shrimp 20
on the table, and quite a lot of egg on our face. We blame ourselves for
not guessing that there would be a baseball pennant play-off on the
same day, but executives go out of their way to explain they wouldn't
have come anyway. Thus begins ten years of knocking on hostile doors,
presenting endless documentation, and hiring a full-time saleswoman
in Detroit; all necessary before *Ms.* gets any real results.

This long saga has a semihappy ending: foreign and, later, domes- 21
tic car-makers eventually provided *Ms.* with enough advertising to
make cars one of our top sources of ad revenue. Slowly, Detroit began
to take the women's market seriously enough to put car ads in other
women's magazines, too, thus freeing a few pages from the hothouse of
fashion-beauty-food ads.

But long after figures showed a third, even a half, of many car mod- 22
els being bought by women, U.S. makers continued to be uncomfortable
addressing women. Unlike foreign car-makers, Detroit never quite
learned the secret of creating intelligent ads that exclude no one, and
then placing them in women's magazines to overcome past exclusion.
(*Ms.* readers were so grateful for a routine Honda ad featuring rack and
pinion steering, for instance, that they sent fan mail.) Even now, Detroit
continues to ask, "Should we make special ads for women?" Perhaps
that's why some foreign cars still have a disproportionate share of the
U.S. women's market.

• In the *Ms.* Gazette, we do a brief report on a congressional hear- 23
ing into chemicals used in hair dyes that are absorbed through the skin
and may be carcinogenic. Newspapers report this too, but Clairol, a
Bristol-Myers subsidiary that makes dozens of products—a few of
which have just begun to advertise in *Ms.*—is outraged. Not at newspapers or news magazines, just at us. It's bad enough that *Ms.* is the
only women's magazine refusing to provide the usual "complementary" articles and beauty photos, but to criticize one of their categories—
that is going too far.

We offer to publish a letter from Clairol telling its side of the story. 24
In an excess of solicitousness, we even put this letter in the Gazette, not
in Letters to the Editors where it belongs. Nonetheless—and in spite of
surveys that show *Ms.* readers are active women who use more of
almost everything Clairol makes than do the readers of any other

women's magazine—*Ms.* gets almost none of these ads for the rest of its natural life.

Meanwhile, Clairol changes its hair-coloring formula, apparently in response to the hearings we reported. 25

• Our saleswomen set out early to attract ads for consumer elec- 26 tronics: sound equipment, calculators, computers, VCRs, and the like. We know that our readers are determined to be included in the technological revolution. We know from reader surveys that *Ms.* readers are buying this stuff in numbers as high as those of magazines like *Playboy,* or "men 18 to 34," the prime targets of the consumer electronics industry. Moreover, unlike traditional women's products that our readers buy but don't need to read articles about, these are subjects they want covered in our pages. There actually *is* a supportive editorial atmosphere.

"But women don't understand technology," say executives at the 27 end of ad presentations. "Maybe not," we respond, "but neither do men—and we all buy it."

"If women *do* buy it," say the decision-makers, "they're asking their 28 husbands and boyfriends what to buy first." We produce letters from *Ms.* readers saying how turned off they are when salesmen say things like "Let me know when your husband can come in."

After several years of this, we get a few ads for compact sound sys- 29 tems. Some of them come from JVC, whose vice president, Harry Elias, is trying to convince his Japanese bosses that there is something called a women's market. At his invitation, I find myself speaking at huge trade shows in Chicago and Las Vegas, trying to persuade JVC dealers that showrooms don't have to be locker rooms where women are made to feel unwelcome. But as it turns out, the shows themselves are part of the problem. In Las Vegas, the only women around the technology displays are seminude models serving champagne. In Chicago, the big attraction is Marilyn Chambers, who followed Linda Lovelace of *Deep Throat* fame as Chuck Traynor's captive and/or employee. VCRs are being demonstrated with her porn videos.

In the end, we get ads for a car stereo now and then, but no VCRs; 30 some IBM personal computers, but no Apple or Japanese ones. We notice that office magazines like *Working Woman* and *Savvy* don't benefit as much as they should from office equipment ads either. In the electronics world, women and technology seem mutually exclusive. It remains a decade behind even Detroit.

• Because we get letters from little girls who love toy trains, and 31 who ask our help in changing ads and box-top photos that feature little boys only, we try to get toy-train ads from Lionel. It turns out that Lionel executives *have* been concerned about little girls. They made a pink train, and were surprised when it didn't sell.

Lionel bows to consumer pressure with a photograph of a boy *and* 32
a girl—but only on some of their boxes. They fear that, if trains are
associated with girls, they will be devalued in the minds of boys.
Needless to say, *Ms.* gets no train ads, and little girls remain a mostly
unexplored market. By 1986, Lionel is put up for sale.

But for different reasons, we haven't had much luck with other 33
kinds of toys either. In spite of many articles on child-rearing; an annual
listing of nonsexist, multiracial toys by Letty Cottin Pogrebin; Stories for
Free Children, a regular feature also edited by Letty; and other prize-
winning features for or about children, we get virtually no toy ads.
Generations of *Ms.* saleswomen explain to toy manufacturers that a
larger proportion of *Ms.* readers have preschool children than do the
readers of other women's magazines, but this industry can't believe
feminists have or care about children.

• When *Ms.* begins, the staff decides not to accept ads for femi- 34
nine hygiene sprays or cigarettes: they are damaging and carry no
appropriate health warnings. Though we don't think we should tell our
readers what to do, we do think we should provide facts so they can
decide for themselves. Since the antismoking lobby has been pressing
for health warnings on cigarette ads, we decide to take them only as
they comply.

Philip Morris is among the first to do so. One of its brands, Virginia 35
Slims, is also sponsoring women's tennis and the first national polls of
women's opinions. On the other hand, the Virginia Slims theme,
"You've come a long way, baby," has more than a "baby" problem. It
makes smoking a symbol of progress for women.

We explain to Philip Morris that this slogan won't do well in our 36
pages, but they are convinced its success with some women means it
will work with *all* women. Finally, we agree to publish an ad for a
Virginia Slims calendar as a test. The letters from readers are critical—
and smart. For instance: Would you show a black man picking cotton,
the same man in a Cardin suit, and symbolize the antislavery and civil
rights movements by smoking? Of course not. But instead of honoring
the test results, the Philip Morris people seem angry to be proven
wrong. They take away ads for *all* their many brands.

This costs *Ms.* about $250,000 the first year. After five years, we can 37
no longer keep track. Occasionally, a new set of executives listens to *Ms.*
saleswomen, but because we won't take Virginia Slims, not one Philip
Morris product returns to our pages for the next 16 years.

Gradually, we also realize our naiveté in thinking we *could* decide 38
against taking cigarette ads. They became a disproportionate support of
magazines the moment they were banned on television, and few magazines could compete and survive without them; certainly not *Ms.*,
which lacks so many other categories. By the time statistics in the 1980s

showed that women's rate of lung cancer was approaching men's, the
necessity of taking cigarette ads has become a kind of prison.

• General Mills, Pillsbury, Carnation, Del Monte, Dole, Kraft,   39
Stouffer, Hormel, Nabisco: You name the food giant, we try it. But no
matter how desirable the *Ms.* readership, our lack of recipes is lethal.

We explain to them that placing food ads *only* next to recipes associ-   40
ates food with work. For many women, it is a negative that works *against*
the ads. Why not place food ads in diverse media without recipes (thus
reaching more men, who are now a third of the shoppers in supermarkets anyway), and leave the recipes to specialty magazines like *Gourmet*
(a third of whose readers are also men)?

These arguments elicit interest, but except for an occasional ad for a   41
convenience food, instant coffee, diet drinks, yogurt, or such extras as
avocados and almonds, this mainstay of the publishing industry stays
closed to us. Period.

• Traditionally, wines and liquors didn't advertise to women: Men   42
were thought to make the brand decisions, even if women did the buying.
But after endless presentations, we begin to make a dent in this category.
Thanks to the unconventional Michel Roux of Carillon Importers (distrib-
utors of Grand Marnier, Absolut Vodka, and others), who assumes that
food and drink have no gender, some ads are leaving their men's club.

Beermakers are still selling masculinity. It takes *Ms.* fully eight years   43
to get its first beer ad (Michelob). In general, however, liquor ads are less
stereotyped in their imagery—and far less controlling of the editorial
content around them—than are women's products. But given the
underrepresentation of other categories, these very facts tend to create a
disproportionate number of alcohol ads in the pages of *Ms.* This in turn
dismays readers worried about women and alcoholism.

• We hear in 1980 that women in the Soviet Union have been pro-   44
ducing feminist *samizdat* (underground, self-published books) and cir-
culating them throughout the country. As punishment, four of the
leaders have been exiled. Though we are operating on our usual shoe-
string, we solicit individual contributions to send Robin Morgan to
interview these women in Vienna.

The result is an exclusive cover story that includes the first news of   45
a populist peace movement against the Afghanistan occupation, a pre-
diction of *glasnost* to come, and a grassroots, intimate view of Soviet
women's lives. From the popular press to women's studies courses, the
response is great. The story wins a Front Page award.

Nonetheless, this journalistic coup undoes years of efforts to get an   46
ad schedule from Revlon. Why? Because the Soviet women on our
cover *are not wearing makeup.*

• Four years of research and presentations go into convincing air-   47
lines that women now make travel choices and business trips. United,
the first airline to advertise in *Ms.*, is so impressed with the response

from our readers that one of its executives appears in a film for our ad presentations. As usual, good ads get great results.

But we have problems unrelated to such results. For instance: 48 Because American Airlines flight attendants include among their labor demands the stipulation that they could choose to have their last names preceded by "Ms." on their name tags—in a long-delayed revolt against the standard, "I am your pilot, Captain Rothgart, and this is your flight attendant, Cindy Sue"—American officials seem to hold the magazine responsible. We get no ads.

There is still a different problem at Eastern. A vice president cancels 49 subscriptions for thousands of copies on Eastern flights. Why? Because he is offended by ads for lesbian poetry journals in the *Ms.* Classified. A "family airline," as he explains to me coldly on the phone, has to "draw the line somewhere."

It's obvious that *Ms.* can't exclude lesbians and serve women. 50 We've been trying to make that point ever since our first issue included an article by and about lesbians, and both Suzanne Levine, our managing editor, and I were lectured by such heavy hitters as Ed Kosner, then editor of *Newsweek* (and now of *New York Magazine*), who insisted that *Ms.* should "position" itself *against* lesbians. But our advertisers have paid to reach a guaranteed number of readers, and soliciting new subscriptions to compensate for Eastern would cost $150,000, plus rebating money in the meantime.

Like almost everything ad-related, this presents an elaborate orga- 51 nizing problem. After days of searching for sympathetic members of the Eastern board, Frank Thomas, president of the Ford Foundation, kindly offers to call Roswell Gilpatrick, a director of Eastern. I talk with Mr. Gilpatrick, who calls Frank Borman, then the president of Eastern. Frank Borman calls me to say that his airline is not in the business of censoring magazines: *Ms.* will be returned to Eastern flights.

• Women's access to insurance and credit is vital, but with the 52 exception of Equitable and a few other ad pioneers, such financial services address men. For almost a decade after the Equal Credit Opportunity Act passes in 1974, we try to convince American Express that women are a growth market—but nothing works.

Finally, a former professor of Russian named Jerry Welsh becomes 53 head of marketing. He assumes that women should be cardholders, and persuades his colleagues to feature women in a campaign. Thanks to this 1980s series, the growth rate for female cardholders surpasses that for men.

For this article, I asked Jerry Welsh if he would explain why Amer- 54 ican Express waited so long. "Sure," he said, "they were afraid of having a 'pink' card."

• Women of color read *Ms.* in disproportionate numbers. This is a 55 source of pride to *Ms.* staffers, who are also more racially representative than the editors of other women's magazines. But this reality is obscured by ads filled with enough white women to make a reader snowblind.

Pat Carbine remembers mostly "astonishment" when she requested 56 African American, Hispanic, Asian, and other diverse images. Marcia Ann Gillespie, a *Ms.* editor who was previously the editor in chief of *Essence*, witnesses ad bias a second time: Having tried for *Essence* to get white advertisers to use black images (Revlon did so eventually, but L'Oréal, Lauder, Chanel, and other companies never did), she sees similar problems getting integrated ads for an integrated magazine. Indeed, the ad world often creates black and Hispanic ads only for black and Hispanic media. In an exact parallel of the fear that marketing a product to women will endanger its appeal to men, the response is usually, "But your [white] readers won't identify."

In fact, those we are able to get—for instance, a Max Factor ad made 57 for *Essence* that Linda Wachner gives us after she becomes president— are praised by white readers, too. But there are pathetically few such images.

• By the end of 1986, production and mailing costs have risen 58 astronomically, ad income is flat, and competition for ads is stiffer than ever. The 60/40 preponderance of edit over ads that we promised to readers becomes 50/50; children's stories, most poetry, and some fiction are casualties of less space; in order to get variety into limited pages, the length (and sometimes the depth) of articles suffers; and, though we do refuse most of the ads that would look like a parody in our pages, we get so worn down that some slip through. Still, readers perform miracles. Though we haven't been able to afford a subscription mailing in two years, they maintain our guaranteed circulation of 450,000.

Nonetheless, media reports on *Ms.* often insist that our unprof- 59 itability must be due to reader disinterest. The myth that advertisers simply follow readers is very strong. Not one reporter notes that other comparable magazines our size (say, *Vanity Fair* or *The Atlantic*) have been losing more money in one year than *Ms.* has lost in 16 years. No matter how much never-to-be-recovered cash is poured into starting a magazine or keeping one going, appearances seem to be all that matter. (Which is why we haven't been able to explain our fragile state in public. Nothing causes ad flight like the smell of nonsuccess.)

My healthy response is anger. My not-so-healthy response is constant 60 worry. Also an obsession with finding one more rescue. There is hardly a night when I don't wake up with sweaty palms and pounding heart, scared that we won't be able to pay the printer or the post office; scared most of all that closing our doors will hurt the women's movement.

Out of chutzpah and desperation, I arrange a lunch with Leonard 61 Lauder, president of Estée Lauder. With the exception of Clinique (the brainchild of Carol Phillips), none of Lauder's hundreds of products has been advertised in *Ms*. A year's schedule of ads for just three or four of them could save us. Indeed, as the scion of a family-owned company whose ad practices are followed by the beauty industry, he is one of the few men who could liberate many pages in all women's magazines just by changing his mind about "complementary copy."

Over a lunch that costs more than we can pay for some articles, I 62 explain the need for his leadership. I also lay out the record of *Ms*.: more literary and journalistic prizes won, more new issues introduced into the mainstream, new writers discovered, and impact on society than any other magazine; more articles that became books, stories that became movies, ideas that became television series, and newly advertised products that became profitable; and, most important for him, a place for his ads to reach women who aren't reachable through any other women's magazine. Indeed, if there is one constant characteristic of the ever-changing *Ms*. readership, it is their impact as leaders. Whether it's waiting until later to have first babies, or pioneering PABA as sun protection in cosmetics, *whatever* they are doing today, a third to a half of American women will be doing three to five years from now. It's never failed.

But, he says, *Ms*. readers are not *our* women. They're not interested 63 in things like fragrance and blush-on. If they were, *Ms*. would write articles about them.

On the contrary, I explain, surveys show they are more likely to buy 64 such things than the readers of, say, *Cosmopolitan* or *Vogue*. They're good customers because they're out in the world enough to need several sets of everything: home, work, purse, travel, gym, and so on. They just don't need to read articles about these things. Would he ask a men's magazine to publish monthly columns on how to shave before he advertised Aramis products (his line for men)?

He concedes that beauty features are often concocted more for 65 advertisers than readers. But *Ms*. isn't appropriate for his ads anyway, he explains. Why? Because Estée Lauder is selling "a kept-woman mentality."

I can't quite believe this. Sixty percent of the users of his products 66 are salaried, and generally resemble *Ms*. readers. Besides, his company has the appeal of having been started by a creative and hardworking woman, his mother, Estée Lauder.

That doesn't matter, he says. He knows his customers, and they 67 would *like* to be kept women. That's why he will never advertise in *Ms*.

In November 1987, by vote of the Ms. Foundation for Education 68 and Communication (*Ms*.'s owner and publisher, the media subsidiary of the Ms. Foundation for Women), *Ms*. was sold to a company whose officers, Australian feminists Sandra Yates and Anne Summers, raised the investment money in their country that *Ms*. couldn't find in its own. They also started *Sassy* for teenage women.

In their two-year tenure, circulation was raised to 550,000 by invest- 69
ment in circulation mailings, and, to the dismay of some readers, editorial features on clothes and new products made a more traditional bid
for ads. Nonetheless, ad pages fell below previous levels. In addition,
Sassy, whose fresh voice and sexual frankness were an unprecedented
success with young readers, was targeted by two mothers from Indiana
who began, as one of them put it, "calling every Christian organization
I could think of." In response to this controversy, several crucial advertisers pulled out.

Such links between ads and editorial content was a problem in 70
Australia, too, but to a lesser degree. "Our readers pay two times more
for their magazines," Anne explained, "so advertisers have less power
to threaten a magazine's viability."

"I was shocked," said Sandra Yates with characteristic directness. 71
"In Australia, we think you have freedom of the press—but you don't."

Since Anne and Sandra had not met their budget's projections for 72
ad revenue, their investors forced a sale. In October 1989, *Ms.* and *Sassy*
were bought by Dale Lang, owner of *Working Mother, Working Woman,*
and one of the few independent publishing companies left among the
conglomerates. In response to a request from the original *Ms.* staff—as
well as to reader letters urging that *Ms.* continue, plus his own belief
that *Ms.* would benefit his other magazines by blazing a trail—he
agreed to try the ad-free, reader-supported *Ms.* . . . and to give us complete editorial control.

2

In response to the workplace revolution of the 1970s, traditional 73
women's magazines—that is, "trade books" for women working at
home—were joined by *Savvy, Working Woman,* and other trade books
for women working in offices. But by keeping the fashion/beauty/
entertaining articles necessary to get traditional ads and then adding
career articles besides, they inadvertently produced the antifeminist
stereotype of Super Woman. The male-imitative, dress-for-success
woman carrying a briefcase became the media image of a woman
worker, even though a blue-collar woman's salary was often higher
than her glorified secretarial sister's, and though women at a real briefcase level are statistically rare. Needless to say, these dress-for-success
women were also thin, white, and beautiful.

In recent years, advertisers' control over the editorial content of 74
women's magazines has become so institutionalized that it is written
into "insertion orders" or dictated to ad salespeople as official policy.
The following are recent typical orders to women's magazines:

- Dow's Cleaning Products stipulates that ads for its Vivid and 75
Spray 'n Wash products should be adjacent to "children or fashion editorial"; ads for Bathroom Cleaner should be next to "home furnish-
ing/family" features; and so on for other brands. "If a magazine fails for
half the brands or more," the Dow order warns, "it will be omitted from
further consideration."

- Bristol-Myers, the parent of Clairol, Windex, Drano, Bufferin, 76
and much more, stipulates that ads be placed next to "a full page of
compatible editorial."

- S. C. Johnson & Son, makers of Johnson Wax, lawn and laundry 77
products, insect sprays, hair sprays, and so on, orders that its ads
*"should not be opposite extremely controversial features or material antitheti-
cal to the nature/copy of the advertised product."* (Italics theirs.)

- Maidenform, manufacturer of bras and other apparel, leaves 78
a blank for the particular product and states: "The creative concept of
the ——— campaign, and the very nature of the product itself appeal to
the positive emotions of the reader/consumer. Therefore, it is imperative that all editorial adjacencies reflect that same positive tone. The editorial must not be negative in content or lend itself contrary to the
——— product imagery/message (e.g., *editorial relating to illness, disillu-
sionment, large size fashion, etc.*)." (Italics mine.)

- The De Beers diamond company, a big seller of engagement 79
rings, prohibits magazines from placing its ads with "adjacencies to
hard news or anti- love/romance themed editorial."

- Procter & Gamble, one of this country's most powerful and 80
diversified advertisers, stands out in the memory of Anne Summers
and Sandra Yates (no mean feat in this context): Its products were not
to be placed in *any* issue that included *any* material on gun control,
abortion, the occult, cults, or the disparagement of religion. Caution
was also demanded in any issue covering sex or drugs, even for educational purposes.

Those are the most obvious chains around women's magazines. 81
There are also rules so clear they needn't be written down: for instance,
an overall "look" compatible with beauty and fashion ads. Even "real"
nonmodel women photographed for a woman's magazine are usually
made up, dressed in credited clothes, and retouched out of all reality.
When editors do include articles on less-than-cheerful subjects (for
instance, domestic violence), they tend to keep them short and unillus-
trated. The point is to be "upbeat." Just as women in the street are
asked, "Why don't you smile, honey?" women's magazines acquire an
institutional smile.

Within the text itself, praise for advertisers' products has become so 82
ritualized that fields like "beauty writing" have been invented. One of
its frequent practitioners explained seriously that "It's a difficult art.
How many new adjectives can you find? How much greater can you

make a lipstick sound? The FDA[2] restricts what companies can say on labels, but we create illusion. And ad agencies are on the phone all the time pushing you to get their product in. A lot of them keep the business based on how many editorial clippings they produce every month. The worst are products," like Lauder's as the writer confirmed, "with their own name involved. It's all ego."

Often, editorial becomes one giant ad. Last November, for instance, 83 *Lear's* featured an elegant woman executive on the cover. On the contents page, we learned she was wearing Guerlain makeup and Samsara, a new fragrance by Guerlain. Inside were full-page ads for Samsara and Guerlain antiwrinkle cream. In the cover profile, we learned that this executive was responsible for launching Samsara and is Guerlain's director of public relations. When the *Columbia Journalism Review* did one of the few articles to include women's magazines in coverage of the influence of ads, editor Frances Lear was quoted as defending her magazine because "this kind of thing is done all the time."

Often, advertisers also plunge odd-shaped ads into the text, no mat- 84 ter what the cost to the readers. At *Woman's Day*, a magazine originally founded by a supermarket chain, editor in chief Ellen Levine said, "The day the copy had to rag around a chicken leg was not a happy one."

Advertisers are also adamant about where in a magazine their ads 85 appear. When Revlon was not placed as the first beauty ad in one Hearst magazine, for instance, Revlon pulled its ads from *all* Hearst magazines. Ruth Whitney, editor in chief of *Glamour*, attributes some of these demands to "ad agencies wanting to prove to a client that they've squeezed the last drop of blood out of a magazine." She also is, she says, "sick and tired of hearing that women's magazines are controlled by cigarette ads." Relatively speaking, she's right. To be as censoring as are many advertisers for women's products, tobacco companies would have to demand articles in praise of smoking and expect glamorous photos of beautiful women smoking their brands.

I don't mean to imply that the editors I quote here share my objec- 86 tions to ads: Most assume that women's magazines have to be the way they are. But it's also true that only former editors can be completely honest. "Most of the pressure came in the form of direct product mentions," explains Sey Chassler, who was editor in chief of *Redbook* from the sixties to the eighties. "We got threats from the big guys, the Revlons, blackmail threats. They wouldn't run ads unless we credited them.

"But it's not fair to single out the beauty advertisers because these 87 pressures came from everybody. Advertisers want to know two things: What are you going to charge me? What *else* are you going to do for me? It's a holdup. For instance, management felt that fiction took up too much space. They couldn't put any advertising in that. For the last ten

---

[2] The federal Food and Drug Administration. [Eds.]

years, the number of fiction entries into the National Magazine Awards has declined.

"And pressures are getting worse. More magazines are more bottom- 88 line oriented because they have been taken over by companies with no interest in publishing.

"I also think advertisers do this to women's magazines especially," 89 he concluded, "because of the general disrespect they have for women."

Even media experts who don't give a damn about women's maga- 90 zines are alarmed by the spread of this ad-edit linkage. In a climate *The Wall Street Journal* describes as an unacknowledged Depression for media, women's products are increasingly able to take their low standards wherever they go. For instance: Newsweeklies publish uncritical stories on fashion and fitness. *The New York Times Magazine* recently ran an article on "firming creams," complete with mentions of advertisers. *Vanity Fair* published a profile of one major advertiser, Ralph Lauren, illustrated by the same photographer who does his ads, and turned the lifestyle of another, Calvin Klein, into a cover story. Even the outrageous *Spy* has toned down since it began to go after fashion ads.

And just to make us really worry, films and books, the last media 91 that go directly to the public without having to attract ads first, are in danger, too. Producers are beginning to depend on payments for displaying products in movies, and books are now being commissioned by companies like Federal Express.

But the truth is that women's products—like women's magazines— 92 have never been the subjects of much serious reporting anyway. News and general interest publications, including the "style" or "living" sections of newspapers, write about food and clothing as cooking and fashion, and almost never evaluate such products by brand name. Though chemical additives, pesticides, and animal fats are major health risks in the United States, and clothes, shoddy or not, absorb more consumer dollars than cars, this lack of information is serious. So is ignoring the contents of beauty products that are absorbed into our bodies through our skins, and that have profit margins so big they would make a loan shark blush.

3

What could women's magazines be like if they were as free as books? 93 as realistic as newspapers? as creative as films? as diverse as women's lives? We don't know.

But we'll only find out if we take women's magazines seriously. If 94 readers were to act in a concerted way to change traditional practices of *all* women's magazines and the marketing of *all* women's products, we could do it. After all, they are operating on our consumer dollars; money that we now control. You and I could:

- write to editors and publishers (with copies to advertisers) that we're willing to pay *more* for magazines with editorial independence, but will *not* continue to pay for those that are just editorial extensions of ads;

- write to advertisers (with copies to editors and publishers) that we want fiction, political reporting, consumer reporting—whatever is, or is not, supported by their ads;

- put as much energy into breaking advertising's control over content as into changing the images in ads, or protesting ads for harmful products like cigarettes;

- support only those women's magazines and products that take *us* seriously as readers and consumers.

- Those of us in the magazine world can also use the carrot- 95 and-stick technique. For instance: Pointing out that, if magazines were a regulated medium like television, the demands of advertisers would be against FCC[3] rules. Payola and extortion could be punished. As it is, there are probably illegalities. A magazine's postal rates are determined by the ratio of ad to edit pages, and the former costs more than the latter. So much for the stick.

The carrot means appealing to enlightened self-interest. For 96 instance: There are many studies showing that the greatest factor in determining an ad's effectiveness is the credibility of its surroundings. The "higher the rating of editorial believability," concluded a 1987 survey by the *Journal of Advertising Research*, "the higher the rating of the advertising." Thus, an impenetrable wall between edit and ads would also be in the best interest of advertisers.

Unfortunately, few agencies or clients hear such arguments. Editors 97 often maintain the false purity of refusing to talk to them at all. Instead, they see ad salespeople who know little about editorial, are trained in business as usual, and are usually paid by commission. Editors might also band together to take on controversy. That happened once when all the major women's magazines did articles in the same month on the Equal Rights Amendment. It could happen again.

It's almost three years away from life between the grindstones of 98 advertising pressures and readers' needs. I'm just beginning to realize how edges got smoothed down—in spite of all our resistance.

---

[3] The Federal Communications Commission. [Eds.]

I remember feeling put upon when I changed "Porsche" to "car" in   99
a piece about Nazi imagery in German pornography by Andrea
Dworkin—feeling sure Andrea would understand that Volkswagen, the
distributor of Porsche and one of our few supportive advertisers, asked
only to be far away from Nazi subjects. It's taken me all this time to realize that Andrea was the one with a right to feel put upon.

Even as I write this, I get a call from a writer for *Elle*, who is doing   100
a whole article on where women part their hair. Why, she wants to
know, do I part mine in the middle?

It's all so familiar. A writer trying to make something of a nothing   101
assignment; an editor laboring to think of new ways to attract ads; readers assuming that other women must want this ridiculous stuff; more
women suffering for lack of information, insight, creativity, and laughter that could be on these same pages.

I ask you: Can't we do better than this?   102

Responding to Reading

1. In paragraph 4, Steinem observes, "Even news magazines use 'soft' cover
   stories to sell ads, confuse readers with 'advertorials,' and occasionally
   self-censor on subjects known to be a problem with big advertisers." Do
   you believe such practices are ethical? Does the fact that they are so widespread make them more acceptable to you?
2. Why, according to Steinem, are women's magazines particularly vulnerable
   to advertisers' demands? Do you agree with her statement in paragraph 8:
   "If *Time* and *Newsweek* had to lavish praise on cars in general and credit
   General Motors in particular to get GM ads, there would be a scandal—
   maybe a criminal investigation. When women's magazines . . . praise
   beauty products in general and credit Revlon in particular to get ads, it's
   just business as usual"?
3. Do you think Steinem may be overstating her case? If so, what might be
   motivating her?

HOOKED

Stanley Crouch

*Stanley Crouch (1945–   ) was born in Los Angeles. Essentially self-
educated, he is a jazz critic, musician-composer, poet, and social commentator
whose essays have appeared, among other places, in the* Soho Weekly News,
the Village Voice, *and the* New Republic, *where he is a contributing editor.
His well-received poetry collection,* Ain't No Ambulances for No Niggahs
Tonight, *was published in 1972, and in 1990, he published* Notes of a

Hanging Judge: Essays and Reviews 1979 to 1989. His subjects in this volume ranged from feminism to black power to boxing to the films of Spike Lee. The All-American Skin Game, or the Decoy of Race *was published in 1995. A former black nationalist, Crouch now criticizes the movement's excesses and advocates personal responsibility and reasoned debate. Called by one critic "provocative and perceptive," Crouch's opinions reflect the independence of his thinking. The following 1995 essay, which was anthologized as one of the best essays of that year, examines the phenomenon of Michael Jackson and how it "helps us face what has happened to our society as issues cut across all false fire walls of race, class, gender, religion."*

It used to be that if one didn't hurry up and say something about a 1
show business event, the boat train was gone, splashing egg in the face of the slowpoke commentator. Today's commercial questions center around how long a product built to superstardom can maintain a position at the top of the huckster's calculated wave. Then those questions break down into how much print and electronic media space it can attract. The final issue is whether or not the product can become a marlin pulling the ship of public gullibility on and on until—Lord have mercy on us!—it ends up on the deck, not a real fish but a motorized piece of plastic counterfeit sporting a serious price tag. Its falseness doesn't matter, because so many of us, the hook actually in our own mouths, have been trained to ceaselessly admire and drool over the special effects of the marketplace. We resent anyone interrupting our freedom to pay for being duped. We wear our hooks with pride.

That is why the Michael Jackson phenomenon helps us face what 2
has happened to our society as issues cut across all false fire walls of race, class, gender, religion. At thirty-six, Jackson represents both the hard facts of open opportunity and the swollen vision of self-worth that have evolved in our narcissistic culture. A now bone-colored big, big fish in the media, Jackson with every move foams up cultural essences that are at the nub of our perpetually embattled democratic grandeur and our equally persistent childishness. He is an entertainer whom we have watched rise from an itty-bitty cute kid to a man remade quite remarkably by modern surgical techniques, all the while maintaining his emotional position in the yellow submarine of adolescent sensibility. That is why his work, at its core, is a summation of the inflated failure that now dominates our popular arts, where the value of youth is hysterically championed at the expense of a mature sense of life. This exploits the insecurities of young people by telling them, over and over, that never growing up is the best defense against an oppressive world where fun isn't given its proper due. That kind of exploitation made Jackson the King of Pop.

Even so, none of this came about by natural means. It was all con- 3
nected to the gold-rush entertainment possibilities of a country such as ours, where there are so many people that consistently hooking no more

than 1 percent of the public wallet guarantees millions. That is exactly 3
what went down. As a boy and part of the Jackson Five, he was pushed
into the world of show business by his father Joe's ambition, which perfectly coincided with the slick Motown packaging of Berry Gordy and
the high wind of teenage bad taste that accounts for so many blips on
the sales screen. But Jackson eventually went further than anyone could
have imagined.

He broke out of the Jackson Five and became a single, flipping and 4
flopping his way into the air of international celebrity. Along the way, his
looks changed. The tumbleweed afro of the past was replaced by a dark,
gooey mop. His skin went from brown to beige to bone. The wide-angle
nose went on a starvation diet that achieved ultra-slimness and an
upward Peter Pan turn worthy of a self-willed Disney cartoon. Then the
chin came clean with a cleft. The former child star was ready for another
degree of prime time. As his videos and concert performances show,
Jackson extended his stardom by adding to his repertoire all the basic
trends of his idiom, white or black, and the slogans that pass for ideas.
Always a mediocre singer given to progressively unimaginative phrasing and overstatement, Jackson delivers a shallow version of gospel,
some maudlin rhythm and blues, uses the false bravado of hard rock
inflection, postures as a love child reciting the pieties necessary for world
peace, stoops to the vulgar gestures that are a priggish shorthand for
lower-class rage, alludes to the spanking that paddles under the brand
name of sadomasochism and executes a few leftover Jackson Five dance
steps that serve as quicksilver interludes within a choreographed syn-
thesis of cheerleading moves, navy signaling without flags and aerobic
exercises. His album *Thriller* sold more than 40 million units worldwide,
24 million in the United States, which meant that 236 million Americans
didn't buy it.

Michael Jackson became more than a whale of a success. He also 5
developed into something of an entertainment blob, swallowing up
whatever he came in contact with or whatever took him further into
the mythology of pop aristocracy, where small but glimmering talents
are elevated with a hysteria that bespeaks the swill of bad faith our culture has been guzzling since Woodstock. An eccentric jellyfish on the
surface but truly a canny businessman, Jackson snatched up the Beatles
catalogue when it was there for the buying, startling Paul McCartney
and angering Ringo Starr. He was more on top than ever.

Then, after years of seeming a goody blue suede shoes, Jackson was 6
sucked into a whirlpool of controversy by a child molestation scandal in
which he was accused of slurping a twelve-year-old boy in unmention-
able places. The response was dramatic: Jackson canceled a tour that
was in progress, claiming addiction to painkillers. He disappeared. He
reappeared. He went on television complaining that the police examined his weewee. He lost endorsements. He settled out of court for a

large but unrevealed amount. Not one to stay outside the limelight, Jackson suddenly married a Lisa Marie who was the daughter of Elvis Presley, that Tarzan of rock 'n' roll, he who swung to ever-larger bank accounts on the vines of pop Negro rhythms and redneck sentimentality. It brought two entertainment kingdoms of swamp water together, Neverland flowing into Graceland.

At every point, the King of Pop was greatly helped by the arrival and evolution of promotional aids like *Entertainment Tonight*, MTV, VH-1, and channel E! These television shows and cable stations are dedicated to nothing but the marketing of products, few serious questions asked. Hype and genuflection are their trade. For the good ship of show business, pop stars, directors, choreographers and technicians are interviewed, promotional videos are shown, films of films being made, videos of the making of videos, all tagged by the glistening barnacles of a forced enthusiasm American entertainment used to lampoon at every chance. 7

Such things, along with the regular avenues of promotion, guarantee that we will have Michael Jackson and his latest recording, *HIStory*, pushed in our ears and faces for quite a while. In fact, Sony Entertainment has already spent $30 million on a promotional campaign planned to continue through two Christmas seasons. 8

Yet this kind of attention and success doesn't reduce the all-American tendencies to self-inflated melodrama and even more self-righteous bitching. While Jackson's millions allow him to build fantasy kingdoms, he also usurps the mantle of wealthy nut that Howard Hughes[1] once wore with such unflagging madness. Like Hughes, Jackson also suffers from the distinct paranoia that those who must face legions of jealousy sometimes orchestrate into endless symphonies of plots and subplots, ranging from the press to the government. The alienation that comes with vast success builds upon the familiar theme of the poor little rich kid and becomes the basis for innumerable expressions of complaint. 9

This paranoia has not been missed, even in the world of rock criticism, where posterior-licking and fantasies of aesthetic value are assiduously taught. Though there was some understandable alarm expressed when Jackson's gargantuan poormouthing and his lyrics were examined in the double CD of *HIStory*, and while some rock critics even noted the fascist imagery of the video, what all of them missed was the problem at the very center of pop music, which is the function of its incantational rhythms. 10

Incantation always has two audience possibilities in our culture: one is the collective fused into a throbbing vitality through the repeating 11

---

[1] Hughes (1905–1976) was a flamboyant American entrepreneur and film producer whose numerous eccentricities in later life included never clipping his fingernails. [Eds.]

groove of a syncopated dance beat, the other is the transformation of individuals into a mindless mass of putty in the hands of a band or a central figure. The distinction is important, because the vital collective is the highest achievement of dance-oriented rhythm. Essential to that vitality is the expression of adult emotion. While blues might also have simple musical elements similar to those pop has derived from it, blues is fundamentally a music that fights self-pity and even holds it up to ridicule, the singer scorning all self-deceptive attempts at ducking responsibility for at least part of the bad state of affairs.

In jazz, for another example, the rhythmic phenomenon of swing is 12 posed as an antidote to the sentimentality of the popular song, with the improvisation allowing for collective inventions that insert emotional irony and complexity into the music. The evolution of pop music is quite different because, far more often than not, the rhythm is used to *reinforce* the sentimentality of the material. Those pop rhythms now arrive in a form that has largely submitted to the mechanical, often using electronic programmed "drums" for static pulsations that never interact with the rest of the music, a supreme example of the very alienation it so successfully foments.

It is because of the subordination of everything to the beat that the 13 lyrics so often go by, barely noticed. When they are noticed, especially when expressing the choked up, immature resentment of a demanding adult world, the words become either anthems of estrangement or bludgeons against some vision of corrupt and hypocritical authority. But, as with fascism, the authority of a mass "conspiracy"—of bankers, lawyers, politicians, educators, law enforcement and so on—is rejected through obeisance to a figure of gargantuan certitude. That is where the big beat of pop and the big idol of the rock star meet in the fascist garden of dance-oriented totalitarianism.

Michael Jackson has been evolving in this direction over the last few 14 years, one video after another showing either the world or his opposition melting into mass chorus lines overwhelmed by his magical leadership. We see this most clearly in the video for "HIStory," where Jackson marches in front of legions of troops, children scream that they love him, and a huge statue of the King of Pop, one as ugly as any Hitler, Stalin, or Mao would have appreciated, is unveiled. We understand in clear terms the assertion that Hitler was the first rock star because of the way his rallies used technology to create hypnotic rituals of enormously magnified passion.

The Indian poet and philosopher Tagore once observed that the 15 invention of the pen knife leaped past the centuries of evolution that resulted in the claw, but that we often find ourselves in a world where those with the pen-knife mentalities of adolescents command weapons of destruction that they aren't mature enough to handle. When we make embittered little boys into idols by genuflecting before a briny charisma that has negligible adult application, we shouldn't be surprised when they decide they should lead the world into a resurrection of an Eden, through which they will walk in the cool of the day, omnipotent as the jealous God of the Old Testament.

Responding to Reading

1. How, according to Crouch, does "the Michael Jackson phenomenon [help] us face what has happened to our society" (2)? What negative messages does Crouch believe the King of Pop's fame conveys to young people? Do you agree with Crouch, or do you believe Jackson's fame conveys a positive message?

2. Explain Crouch's title. Do you find it effective? Why or why not? What other titles might be more effective?

3. Beginning in paragraph 10, Crouch discusses what he calls "the problem at the very center of pop music," which he identifies as "the function of its incantational rhythms." According to Crouch, incantation has the power to "[transform] individuals into a mindless mass of putty in the hands of a band or a central figure" (11). He goes on to develop an analogy between Jackson's music and political totalitarianism. Is this analogy convincing? Is it logical? Is it fair?

THE MOVIE THAT CHANGED MY LIFE

Terry McMillan

Novelist Terry McMillan (1951–) was born in Port Huron, Michigan, and developed her interest in writing after taking a job shelving books at a local library. When she was seventeen, she set out on her own for the West Coast, later receiving a degree in journalism from the University of California at Berkeley. Soon afterward, she moved to New York City, where she worked as a word processor and joined the Harlem Writer's Guild, a workshop for mostly African-American writers. Her first novel, Mama *(1987), written during this time, was a critical and popular success. It was followed by* Disappearing Acts *(1989) and the bestseller* Waiting to Exhale *(1992), a story of the romantic complications besetting four contemporary African-American women friends. Her most recent novel is* How Stella Got Her Groove Back *(1996). She has also edited* Breaking the Ice: An Anthology of Contemporary African-American Fiction *(1990) and has taught at the universities of Wyoming and Arizona. In the following essay, from a 1991 anthology edited by David Rosenberg for which a number of writers were asked to remember a movie important to their lives, McMillan describes both her positive and negative reactions to MGM's classic* The Wizard of Oz *as a reflection of mainstream American values and culture.*

I grew up in a small industrial town in the thumb of Michigan: Port 1
Huron. We had barely gotten used to the idea of color TV. I can guess
how old I was when I first saw *The Wizard of Oz* on TV because I remember the house we lived in when I was still in elementary school. It was
a huge, drafty house that had a fireplace we never once lit. We lived on
two acres of land, and at the edge of the backyard was the woods, which
I always thought of as a forest. We had weeping willow trees, plum and
pear trees, and blackberry bushes. We could not see into our neighbors'
homes. Railroad tracks were part of our front yard, and the house shook
when a train passed—twice, sometimes three times a day. You couldn't
hear the TV at all when it zoomed by, and I was often afraid that if it
ever flew off the tracks, it would land on the sun porch, where we all
watched TV. I often left the room during this time, but my younger sisters and brother thought I was just scared. I think I was in the third
grade around this time.

It was a raggedy house which really should've been condemned, 2
but we fixed it up and kept it clean. We had our German shepherd,
Prince, who slept under the rickety steps to the side porch that were on
the verge of collapsing but never did. I remember performing a ritual
whenever *Oz* was coming on. I either baked cookies or cinnamon rolls
or popped popcorn while all five of us waited for Dorothy to spin from
black and white on that dreary farm in Kansas to the luminous land of
color of Oz.

My house was chaotic, especially with four sisters and brothers and 3
a mother who worked at a factory, and if I'm remembering correctly, my
father was there for the first few years of the *Oz* (until he got tuberculosis and had to live in a sanitarium for a year). I do recall the noise and
the fighting of my parents (not to mention my other relatives and neighbors). Violence was plentiful, and I wanted to go wherever Dorothy was
going where she would not find trouble. To put it bluntly, I wanted to
escape because I needed an escape.

I didn't know any happy people. Everyone I knew was either angry 4
or not satisfied. The only time they seemed to laugh was when they were
drunk, and even that was short-lived. Most of the grown-ups I was in
contact with lived their lives as if it had all been a mistake, an accident,
and they were paying dearly for it. It seemed as if they were always at
someone else's mercy—women at the mercy of men (this prevailed in
my hometown) and children at the mercy of frustrated parents. All I
knew was that most of the grown-ups felt trapped, as if they were stuck
in this town and no road would lead out. So many of them felt a sense of
accomplishment just getting up in the morning and making it through
another day. I overheard many a grown-up conversation, and they were
never life-affirming: "Chile, if the Lord'll just give me the strength to
make it through another week . . ."; "I just don't know how I'ma handle
this, I can't take no more. . . ." I rarely knew what they were talking

about, but even a fool could hear that it was some kind of drudgery. When I was a child, it became apparent to me that these grown-ups had no power over their lives, or, if they did, they were always at a loss as to how to exercise it. I did not want to grow up and have to depend on someone else for my happiness or be miserable or have to settle for whatever I was dished out—if I could help it. That much I knew already.

I remember being confused a lot. I could never understand why no 5 one had any energy to do anything that would make them feel good, besides drinking. Being happy was a transient and very temporary thing which was almost always offset by some kind of bullshit. I would, of course, learn much later in my own adult life that these things are called obstacles, barriers—or again, bullshit. When I started writing, I began referring to them as "knots." But life wasn't one long knot. It seemed to me it just required stamina and common sense and the wherewithal to know when a knot was before you and you had to dig deeper than you had in order to figure out how to untie it. It could be hard, but it was simple.

The initial thing I remember striking me about *Oz* was how nasty 6 Dorothy's Auntie Em talked to her and everybody on the farm. I was used to that authoritative tone of voice because my mother talked to us the same way. She never asked you to do anything; she gave you a command and never said "please," and, once you finished it, rarely said "thank you." The tone of her voice was always hostile, and Auntie Em sounded just like my mother—bossy and domineering. They both ran the show, it seemed, and I think that because my mother was raising five children almost single-handedly, I must have had some inkling that being a woman didn't mean you had to be helpless. Auntie Em's husband was a wimp, and for once the tables were turned: he took orders from her! My mother and Auntie Em were proof to me that if you wanted to get things done you had to delegate authority and keep everyone apprised of the rules of the game as well as the consequences. In my house it was punishment—you were severely grounded. What little freedom we had was snatched away. As a child, I often felt helpless, powerless, because I had no control over my situation and couldn't tell my mother when I thought (or knew) she was wrong or being totally unfair, or when her behavior was inappropriate. I hated this feeling to no end, but what was worse was not being able to do anything about it except keep my mouth shut.

So I completely identified when no one had time to listen to 7 Dorothy. That dog's safety was important to her, but no one seemed to think that what Dorothy was saying could possibly be as urgent as the situation at hand. The bottom line was, it was urgent to her. When I was younger, I rarely had the opportunity to finish a sentence before my mother would cut me off or complete it for me, or, worse, give me something to do. She used to piss me off, and nowadays I catch myself—stop myself—from doing the same thing to my seven-year-old. Back then, it was as if what I had to say wasn't important or didn't warrant her undivided attention. So when Dorothy's Auntie Em dismisses her and tells her to find somewhere where she'll stay out of trouble, and little Dorothy starts thinking about if there in fact is such a place—one that is trouble free—I was right there with her, because I wanted to know, too.

I also didn't know or care that Judy Garland was supposed to have 8 been a child star, but when she sang "Somewhere Over the Rainbow," I *was* impressed. Impressed more by the song than by who was singing it. I mean, she wasn't exactly Aretha Franklin or the Marvelettes or the Supremes, which was the only vocal music I was used to. As kids, we often laughed at white people singing on TV because their songs were always so corny and they just didn't sound anything like the soulful music we had in our house. Sometimes we would mimic people like Doris Day and Fred Astaire and laugh like crazy because they were always so damn happy while they sang and danced. We would also watch square-dancing when we wanted a real laugh and try to look under the women's dresses. What I hated more than anything was when in the middle of a movie the white people always had to start singing and dancing to get their point across. Later, I would hate it when black people would do the same thing—even though it was obvious to us that at least they had more rhythm and, most of the time, more range vocally.

We did skip through the house singing "We're off to see the 9 Wizard," but other than that, most of the songs in this movie are a blank, probably because I blanked them out. Where I lived, when you had something to say to someone, you didn't sing it, you told them, so the cumulative effect of the songs wore thin.

I was afraid for Dorothy when she decided to run away, but at the 10 same time I was glad. I couldn't much blame her—I mean, what kind of life did she have, from what I'd seen so far? She lived on an ugly farm out in the middle of nowhere with all these old people who did nothing but chores, chores, and more chores. Who did she have to play with besides that dog? And even though I lived in a house full of people, I knew how lonely Dorothy felt, or at least how isolated she must have felt. First of all, I was the oldest, and my sisters and brother were ignorant and silly creatures who often bored me because they couldn't hold a decent conversation. I couldn't ask them questions, like: Why are we living in this dump? When is Mama going to get some more money? Why can't we go on vacations like other people? Like white people? Why does our car always break down? Why are we poor? Why doesn't Mama ever laugh? Why do we have to live in Port Huron? Isn't there someplace better than this we can go live? I remember thinking this kind of stuff in kindergarten, to be honest, because times were hard, but I'd saved twenty-five cents in my piggy bank for hotdog-and-chocolate- milk day at school, and on the morning I went to get it, my piggy bank was empty. My mother gave me some lame excuse as to why she had to spend it, but all I was thinking was that I would have to sit there (again) and watch the other children slurp their chocolate milk, and I could see the ketchup and mustard oozing out of the hot-dog bun that I wouldn't get to taste. I walked to school, and with the exception of walking to my father's funeral when I was sixteen, this was the longest walk of my entire life. My plaid dress was starched and my socks were white, my hair was braided and not a strand out of place, but I wanted to know why I had to feel this kind of humiliation when in fact I had saved the money for this very purpose. Why? By the time I got to school, I'd wiped my nose and dried my eyes and vowed not to let anyone know that I was even moved by this. It was no one's business why I couldn't eat my hot dog and chocolate milk, but the irony of it was that my teacher, Mrs. Johnson, must have sensed what had happened, and she bought my hot dog and chocolate milk for me that day. I can still remember feeling how unfair things can be, but how they somehow always turn out good. I guess seeing so much negativity had already started to turn me into an optimist.

I was a very busy child, because I was the oldest and had to see to 11 it that my sisters and brother had their baths and did their homework; I combed my sisters' hair, and by fourth grade I had cooked my first Thanksgiving dinner. It was my responsibility to keep the house spotless so that when my mother came home from work it would pass her inspection, so I spent many an afternoon and Saturday morning mopping and waxing floors, cleaning ovens and refrigerators, grocery shopping, and by the time I was thirteen, I was paying bills for my mother and felt like an adult. I was also tired of it, sick of all the responsibility. So yes, I rooted for Dorothy, when she and Toto were vamoosing, only I wanted to know: Where in the hell was she going? Where would I go if I were to run away? I had no idea because there was nowhere to go. What I did know was that one day I would go somewhere—which is why I think I watched so much TV. I was always on the lookout for Paradise, and I think I found it a few years later on "Adventures in Paradise," with Gardner McKay, and on "77 Sunset Strip."[1] Palm trees and blue water and islands made quite an impression on a little girl from a flat, dull little depressing town in Michigan.

Professor Marvel really pissed me off, and I didn't believe for a 12 minute that that crystal ball was real, even before he started asking Dorothy all those questions, but I knew this man was going to be important, I just couldn't figure out how. Dorothy was so gullible, I thought, and I knew this word because my mother used to always drill it in us that you should "never believe everything somebody tells you." So after

---

[1] These were 1950s television shows set in Hawaii and Southern California. [Eds.]

Professor Marvel convinced Dorothy that her Auntie Em might be in trouble, and Dorothy scoops up Toto and runs back home, I was totally disappointed, because now I wasn't going to have an adventure. I was thinking I might actually learn how to escape drudgery by watching Dorothy do it successfully, but before she even gave herself the chance to discover for herself that she could make it, she was on her way back home. "Dummy!" we all yelled on the sun porch. "Dodo brain!"

The storm. The tornado. Of course, now the entire set of this film 13 looks so phony it's ridiculous, but back then I knew the wind was a tornado because in Michigan we had the same kind of trapdoor underground shelter that Auntie Em had on the farm. I knew Dorothy was going to be locked out once Auntie Em and the workers locked the door, and I also knew she wasn't going to be heard when she knocked on it. This was drama at its best, even though I didn't know what drama was at the time.

In the house she goes, and I was frightened for her. I knew that 14 house was going to blow away, so when little Dorothy gets banged in the head by a window that flew out of its casement, I remember all of us screaming. We watched everybody fly by the window, including the wicked neighbor who turns out to be the Wicked Witch of the West, and I'm sure I probably substituted my mother for Auntie Em and fantasized that all of my siblings would fly away, too. They all got on my nerves because I could never find a quiet place in my house—no such thing as peace—and I was always being disturbed.

It wasn't so much that I had so much I wanted to do by myself, but 15 I already knew that silence was a rare commodity, and when I managed to snatch a few minutes of it, I could daydream, pretend to be someone else somewhere else—and this was fun. But I couldn't do it if someone was bugging me. On days when my mother was at work, I would often send the kids outside to play and lock them out, just so I could have the house to myself for at least fifteen minutes. I loved pretending that none of them existed for a while, although after I finished with my fantasy world, it was reassuring to see them all there. I think I was grounded.

When Dorothy's house began to spin and spin and spin, I was curi- 16 ous as to where it was going to land. And to be honest, I didn't know little Dorothy was actually dreaming until she woke up and opened the door and everything was in color! It looked like Paradise to me. The foliage was almost an iridescent green, the water bluer than I'd ever seen in any of the lakes in Michigan. Of course, once I realized she was in fact dreaming, it occurred to me that this very well might be the only way to escape. To dream up another world. Create your own.

I had no clue that Dorothy was going to find trouble, though, even 17 in her dreams. Hell, if I had dreamed up something like another world, it would've been a perfect one. I wouldn't have put myself in such a precarious situation. I'd have been able to go straight to the Wizard, no strings attached. First of all, that she walked was stupid to me; I would've asked one of those Munchkins for a ride. And I never bought into the idea of those slippers, but once I bought the whole idea, I accepted the fact that the girl was definitely lost and just wanted to get home. Personally, all I kept thinking was, if she could get rid of that Wicked Witch of the West, the Land of Oz wasn't such a bad place to be stuck in. It beat the farm in Kansas.

At the time, I truly wished I could spin away from my family and 18 home and land someplace as beautiful and surreal as Oz—if only for a little while. All I wanted was to get a chance to see another side of the world, to be able to make comparisons, and then decide if it was worth coming back home.

What was really strange to me, after the Good Witch of the North 19 tells Dorothy to just stay on the Yellow Brick Road to get to the Emerald City and find the Wizard so she can get home, was when Dorothy meets the Scarecrow, the Tin Man, and the Lion—all of whom were missing something I'd never even given any thought to. A brain? What did having one really mean? What would not having one mean? I had one, didn't I, because I did well in school. But because the Scarecrow couldn't make up his mind, thought of himself as a failure, it dawned on me that having a brain meant you had choices, you could make decisions and, as a result, make things happen. Yes, I thought, I had one, and I was going to use it. One day. And the Tin Man, who didn't have a heart. Not having one meant you were literally dead to me, and I never once thought of it as being the house of emotions (didn't know what emotions were), where feelings of jealousy, devotion, and sentiment lived. I'd never thought of what else a heart was good for except keeping you alive. But I did have feelings, because they were often hurt, and I was envious of the white girls at my school who wore mohair sweaters and box-pleat skirts, who went skiing and tobogganing and yachting and spent summers in Quebec. Why didn't white girls have to straighten their hair? Why didn't their parents beat each other up? Why were they always so goddamn happy?

And courage. Oh, that was a big one. What did having it and not 20 having it mean? I found out that it meant having guts and being afraid but doing whatever it was you set out to do anyway. Without courage, you couldn't do much of anything. I liked courage and assumed I would acquire it somehow. As a matter of fact, one day my mother *told* me to get her a cup of coffee, and even though my heart was pounding and I was afraid, I said to her pointblank, "Could you please say please?" She looked up at me out of the corner of her eye and said, "What?" So I repeated myself, feeling more powerful because she hadn't slapped me across the room already, and then something came over her and she looked at me and said, "Please." I smiled all the way to the kitchen, and from that point forward, I managed to get away with this kind of behavior until I left home when I was seventeen. My sisters and brother—to this day—don't know how I stand up to my mother, but I know. I decided not to be afraid or intimidated by her, and I wanted her to treat me like a friend, like a human being, instead of her slave.

I do believe that Oz also taught me much about friendship. I mean, 21 the Tin Man, the Lion, and the Scarecrow hung in there for Dorothy, stuck their "necks" out and made sure she was protected, even risked their own "lives" for her. They told each other the truth. They trusted each other. All four of them had each other's best interests in mind. I believe it may have been a while before I actually felt this kind of sincerity in a friend, but really good friends aren't easy to come by, and when you find one, you hold on to them.

Okay. So Dorothy goes through hell before she gets back to Kansas. 22 But the bottom line was, she made it. And what I remember feeling when she clicked those heels was that you have to have faith and be a believer, for real, or nothing will ever materialize. Simple as that. And not only in life but even in your dreams there's always going to be adversity, obstacles, knots, or some kind of bullshit you're going to have to deal with in order to get on with your life. Dorothy had a good heart and it was in the right place, which is why I supposed she won out over the evil witch. I've learned that one, too. That good *always* overcomes evil; maybe not immediately, but in the long run, it does. So I think I vowed when I was little to try to be a good person. An honest person. To care about others and not just myself. Not to be a selfish person, because my heart would be of no service if I used it only for myself. And I had to have the courage to see other people and myself as not being perfect (yes, I had a heart and a brain, but some other things would turn up missing, later), and I would have to learn to untie every knot that I encountered—some self-imposed, some not—in my life, and to believe that if I did the right things, I would never stray too far from my Yellow Brick Road.

I'm almost certain that I saw *Oz* annually for at least five or six 23 years, but I don't remember how old I was when I stopped watching it. I do know that by the time my parents were divorced (I was thirteen), I couldn't sit through it again. I was a mature teen-ager and had finally reached the point where Dorothy got on my nerves. Singing, dancing, and skipping damn near everywhere was so corny and utterly sentimental that even the Yellow Brick Road became sickening. I already knew what she was in for, and sometimes I rewrote the story in my head. I kept asking myself, what if she had just run away and kept going, maybe she would've ended up in Los Angeles with a promising singing career. What if it had turned out that she hadn't been dreaming, and the Wizard had given her an offer she couldn't refuse—say, for instance, he had asked her to stay on in the Emerald City, that she could visit the farm whenever she wanted to, but, get a clue, Dorothy, the

Emerald City is what's happening; she could make new city friends and get a hobby and a boyfriend and free rent and never have to do chores . . .

I had to watch *The Wizard of Oz* again in order to write this, and my 24 six-and-a-half-year-old son, Solomon, joined me. At first he kept asking me if something was wrong with the TV because it wasn't in color, but as he watched, he became mesmerized by the story. He usually squirms or slides to the floor and under a table or just leaves the room if something on TV bores him, which it usually does, except if he's watching Nickelodeon, a high-quality cable kiddie channel. His favorite shows, which he watches with real consistency, and, I think, actually goes through withdrawal if he can't see them for whatever reason, are "Inspector Gadget," "Looney Tunes," and "Mr. Ed." "Make the Grade," which is sort of a junior-high version of "Jeopardy," gives him some kind of thrill, even though he rarely knows any of the answers. And "Garfield" is a must on Saturday morning. There is hardly anything on TV that he watches that has any real, or at least plausible, drama to it, but you can't miss what you've never had.

The Wicked Witch intimidated the boy no end, and he was afraid of 25 her. The Wizard was also a problem. So I explained—no, I just told him pointblank—"Don't worry she'll get it in the end, Solomon, because she's bad. And the Wizard's a fake and he's trying to sound like a tough guy, but he's a wus." That offered him some consolation, and even when the Witch melted he kind of looked at me with those *Home Alone* eyes and asked, "But where did she go, Mommy?" "She's history," I said. "Melted. Gone. Into the ground. Remember, this is pretend. It's not real. Real people don't melt. This is only TV," I said. And then he got that look in his eyes as if he'd remembered something.

Of course he had a nightmare that night and of course there was a 26 witch in it, because I had actually left the sofa a few times during this last viewing to smoke a few cigarettes (the memory bank is a powerful place—I still remembered many details), put the dishes in the dishwasher, make a few phone calls, water the plants. Solomon sang "We're off to see the Wizard" for the next few days because he said that was his favorite part, next to the Munchkins (who also showed up in his nightmare).

So, to tell the truth, I really didn't watch the whole movie again. I 27 just couldn't. Probably because about thirty or so years ago little Dorothy had made a lasting impression on me, and this viewing felt like overkill. You only have to tell me, show me, once in order for me to get it. But even still, the movie itself taught me a few things that I still find challenging. That it's okay to be an idealist, that you have to imagine something better and go for it. That you have to believe in *something*, and it's best to start with yourself and take it from there. At least give it a try. As corny as it may sound, sometimes I am afraid of what's around the corner, or what's not around the corner. But I look anyway. I believe that writing is one of my "corners"—an intersection, really; and when I'm confused or reluctant to look back, deeper, or ahead, I create my own Emerald Cities and force myself to take longer looks, because it is one sure way that I'm able to see.

Of course, I've fallen, tumbled, and been thrown over all kinds of 28 bumps on my road, but it still looks yellow, although every once in a while there's still a loose brick. For the most part, though, it seems paved. Perhaps because that's the way I want to see it.

Responding to Reading

1. How was McMillan's life in Port Huron like Dorothy's life in Kansas? How was it different? Why did Dorothy's escape to Oz have such great appeal to McMillan?
2. McMillan strongly identifies with Dorothy, yet she also feels impatient with her—even let down by her, by the film's ending. Why? Do you think McMillan's reactions are understandable?
3. How, according to McMillan, did *The Wizard of Oz* change her life? Can you identify any changes that McMillan does not mention?

WHY THE SHIRELLES MATTERED

Susan J. Douglas

Media and American culture expert Susan J. Douglas (1950–   ) received her B.A. from Hampshire College and her M.A. from Amherst. A member of the faculty of the Department of Communication at the University of Michigan, she serves as media critic for the Progressive *and has contributed articles to the* Village Voice, TV Guide *and the* Journal of American History. *Her first book,* Inventing American Broadcasting 1899–1922 *(1987), focused on the history of radio. In* Where the Girls Are: Growing Up Female with the Mass Media *(1994), she looks at images of women in movies, television, and popular music from the 1950s to the 1970s. While the perspective of the book is feminist and Douglas points to many negative images, she sees a number of positive images as well. Among these, as the following chapter from* Where the Girls Are *suggests, are the hit recordings of the various "girl groups" that came to prominence in the 1960s.*

Ok—here's a test. Get a bunch of women in their thirties and forties 1 and put them in a room with a stereo. Turn up the volume to the "incurs temporary deafness" level and play "Will You Love Me Tomorrow" and see how many know the words—all the words—by heart. If the answer is 100 percent, these are bona fide American baby boomers. Any less, and the group has been infiltrated by impostors, pod people, Venusians. But even more interesting is the fact that non-baby boomers, women both older and younger than my generation, adore this music too, and cling to the lyrics like a life raft.

Why is it that, over thirty years after this song was number one in 2 the country, it still evokes in us such passion, such longing, such euphoria, and such an irresistible desire to sing very loudly off key and not care who hears us? And it's not just this song, it's girl group music in general, from "He's So Fine" to "Nowhere to Run" to "Sweet Talkin' Guy." Today, the "oldies" station is one of the most successful FM formats going, in no small part because when these songs come on the radio, baby boomers get that faraway, knowing, contented look on their faces that prompts them to scream along with the lyrics while running red lights on the way home from work. None of this is silly—there's a good reason why, even on our deathbeds, we'll still know the words to "Leader of the Pack."

First of all, girl group music was really about us—girls. When rock 3 'n' roll swiveled onto the national scene in the mid-1950s and united a generation in opposition to their parents, it was music performed by rebellious and sexually provocative young men. Elvis Presley was, of course, rock 'n' roll's most famous and insistently masculine star—in 1956, five of the nine top singles of the year were by Elvis. At the same time, there would be weeks, even months, when no woman or female group had a hit among the top fifteen records. When women in the fifties did have hits, they were about the moon, weddings, some harmless dreamboat, like Annette's[1] "Tall Paul," or maybe about kissing. But they were never, ever about doing the wild thing.

Then, in December 1960, the Shirelles hit number one with "Will 4 You Love Me Tomorrow"; it was the first time a girl group, and one composed of four black teenagers, had cracked the number one slot. And these girls were not singing about doggies in windows or old Cape Cod. No, the subject matter here was a little different. They were singing about whether or not to go all the way and wondering whether the boyfriend, so seemingly full of heartfelt, earnest love in the night, would prove to be an opportunistic, manipulative, lying cad after he got his way, or whether he would, indeed, still be filled with love in the morning. Should the girl believe everything she'd heard about going all the way and boys losing respect for girls who did? Or should she believe the boy in her arms who was hugging and kissing her (and doing who knows what else) and generally making her feel real good?

Even though this song was about sex, it didn't rely on the musical 5 instrument so frequently used to connote sex in male rockers' songs, the

---

[1] Annette Funicello, a former Mouseketeer, was one of the top teenage stars of the late 1950s and early 1960s. [Eds.]

saxophone. Saxes were banished, as were electric guitars; instead, an entire string section of an orchestra provided the counterpoint to Shirley Owens's haunting, earthy, and provocative lead vocals. The producer, Luther Dixon, who had previously worked with Perry Como and Pat Boone,[2] even overlaid the drumbeats with violins, so it sounded as if the strings gave the song its insistent, pulsing rhythm. While Owens's alto voice vibrated with teen girl angst and desire, grounding the song in fleshly reality, violin arpeggios fluttered through like birds, and it was on their wings that our erotic desires took flight and gained a more acceptable spiritual dimension. It was this brilliant juxtaposition of the sentimentality of the violins and the sensuality of the voice that made the song so perfect, because it was simultaneously lush and spare, conformist and daring, euphemistic yet dead-on honest. The tens of millions of girls singing along could be starry-eyed and innocent, but they could also be sophisticated and knowing. They could be safe and sing about love, or dangerous and sing about sex. "Will You Love Me Tomorrow" was about a traditional female topic, love, but it was also about female longing and desire, including sexual desire. And, most important, it was about having a choice. For these girls, the decision to have sex was now a choice, and *this* was new. This was, in fact, revolutionary. Girl group music gave expression to our struggles with the possibilities and dangers of the Sexual Revolution.

What were you to do if you were a teenage girl in the early and 6 mid-1960s, your hormones catapulting you between desire and paranoia, elation and despair, horniness and terror? You didn't know which instincts to act on and which ones to suppress. You also weren't sure whom to listen to since, by the age of fourteen, you'd decided that neither your mother nor your father knew anything except how to say no and perhaps the lyrics to a few Andy Williams[3] songs. For answers— real answers—many of us turned to the record players, radios, and jukeboxes of America. And what we heard were the voices of teenage girls singing about—and dignifying—our most basic concern: how to act around boys when so much seemed up for grabs. What were you to do to survive all those raging hormones? Why, dance, of course.

There's been a lot of talk, academic analysis, and the like about how 7 Elvis Presley and rock 'n' roll made rebelliousness acceptable for boys. But what about the girls? Did girl group music help *us* become rebels? Before you say "no way" and cite "I Will Follow Him," "Chapel of Love," and "I Wanna Be Bobby's Girl" to substantiate your point, hear me out. Girl group music has been denied its rightful place in history by a host of male music critics who've either ignored it or trashed it. Typical is this pronouncement, by one of the contributors to *The Rolling*

---

[2] Well-known "crooners." [Eds.]
[3] Another famous "crooner." [Eds.]

Stone History of Rock & Roll: "The female group of the early 1960s served to drive the concept of art completely away from rock 'n' roll. . . . I feel this genre represents the low point in the history of rock 'n' roll." Nothing could be more wrong-headed, or more ignorant of the role this music played in girls' lives. It would be ideal if this [essay] were accompanied by a customized CD replaying all these fabulous songs for you. Since that's not possible, I do urge you to listen to this music again, and to hear all the warring impulses, desires, and voices it contained. . . .

The most important thing about this music, the reason it spoke to 8 us so powerfully, was that it gave voice to all the warring selves inside us struggling, blindly and with a crushing sense of insecurity, to forge something resembling a coherent identity. Even though the girl groups were produced and managed by men, it was in their music that the contradictory messages about female sexuality and rebelliousness were most poignantly and authentically expressed. In the early 1960s, pop music became the one area of popular culture in which adolescent female voices could be clearly heard. They sang about the pull between the need to conform and the often overwhelming desire to rebel, about the tension between restraint and freedom, and about the rewards— and costs—of prevailing gender roles. They sang, in other words, about getting mixed messages and about being ambivalent in the face of the upheaval in sex roles. That loss of self, the fusing of yourself with another, larger-than-life persona that girls felt as they sang along was at least as powerful as what they felt in a darkened movie theater. And singing along with one another, we shared common emotions and physical reactions to the music.

This music was, simultaneously, deeply personal and highly public, 9 fusing our neurotic, quivering inner selves with the neurotic, quivering inner selves of others in an effort to find strength and confidence in numbers. We listened to this music in the darkness of our bedrooms, driving around in our parents' cars on the beach, making out with some boy, and we danced to it—usually with other girls—in the soda shops, basements, and gymnasiums of America. This music burrowed into the everyday psychodramas of our adolescence, forever intertwined with our most private, exhilarating, and embarrassing memories. This music exerted such a powerful influence on us, one that we may barely have recognized, because of this process of identification. By superimposing our own dramas, from our own lives, onto each song, each of us could assume an active role in shaping the song's meaning. Songs that were hits around the country had very particular associations and meanings for each listener, and although they were mass-produced they were individually interpreted. The songs were ours—but they were also everyone else's. We were all alone, but we weren't really alone at all. In this music, we found solidarity as girls.

Some girl group songs, like "I Will Follow Him," allowed us to   10
assume the familiar persona *Cinderella* had trained us for, the selfless
masochist whose identity came only from being some appendage to a
man. As we sang along with Dionne Warwick's "Walk On By," we were
indeed abject martyrs to love, luxuriating in our own self-pity. But other
songs addressed our more feisty and impatient side, the side unwilling
to sit around and wait for the boy to make the first move. In "tell him"
songs like "Easier Said Than Done," "Wishin' and Hopin'," and, of
course, "Tell Him," girls were advised to abandon the time-wasting and
possibly boy-losing stance of passively waiting for *him* to make the first
move. We were warned that passivity might cost us our man, and we
were urged to act immediately and unequivocally, before some more daring girl got there first. Girls were urged to take up a previously male prerogative—to be active agents of their own love lives and to go out and
court the boy. Regardless of how girls actually behaved—and I know
from personal experience that what was derisively called "boy chasing"
was on the rise—now there were lyrics in girls' heads that said, "Don't be
passive, it will cost you."

Was being cautious too safe? Was being daring too risky? Girl group   11
music acknowledged—even celebrated—our confusion and ambivalence. Some of us wanted to be good girls, and some of us wanted to be
bad. But most of us wanted to get away with being both, and girl group
music let us try on and act out a host of identities, from traditional, obedient girlfriend to brassy, independent rebel, and lots in between. We
could even do this in the same song, for often the lead singer represented one point of view and the backup singers another, so the very
wars raging in our own heads about how to behave, what pose to strike,
were enacted in one two-minute hit single. . . .

Girl group songs were, by turns, boastful, rebellious, and self-   12
abnegating, and through them girls could assume different personas,
some of them strong and empowering and others masochistic and
defeating. As girls listened to their radios and record players, they could
be martyrs to love ("Please Mr. Postman"), sexual aggressors
("Beechwood 4-5789"), fearsome Amazons protecting their men ("Don't
Mess with Bill" and "Don't Say Nothin' Bad About My Baby"), devoted,
selfless girlfriends ("My Guy," "I Will Follow Him"), taunting, competitive brats ("Judy's Turn to Cry," "My Boyfriend's Back"), sexual sophisticates ("It's in His Kiss"), and, occasionally, prefeminists ("Don't Make
Me Over" and "You Don't Own Me"). The Shirelles themselves, in hit
after hit, assumed different stances, from the faithful romantic ("Soldier
Boy," "Dedicated to the One I Love") to knowing adviser ("Mama
Said," "Foolish Little Girl") to sexual slave ("Baby, It's You"). The songs
were about escaping from yet acquiescing to the demands of a male-
dominated society, in which men called the shots but girls could still try

to give them a run for their money. Girls in these songs enjoyed being looked at with desire, but they also enjoyed looking with desire themselves. The singers were totally confident; they were abjectly insecure. Some songs said do and others said don't. Sometimes the voice was of an assertive, no-nonsense girl out to get the guy or showing off her boyfriend to her friends. At other times, the voice was that of the passive object, yearning patiently to be discovered and loved. Often the girl tried to get into the boy's head and imagined the boy regarding her as the object of his desire. Our pathetic struggles and anxieties about popularity were glamorized and dignified in these songs.

In girl group music, girls talked to each other confidentially, primarily about boys and sex. The songs took our angst-filled conversations, put them to music, and gave them a good beat. Some songs, like "He's So Fine" (doo lang, doo lang, doo lang), picked out a cute boy from the crowd and plotted how he would be hooked. In this song the choice was clearly hers, not his. Songs also re-created images of a clot of girls standing around in their mohair sweaters assessing the male talent and, well, looking over boys the way boys had always looked over girls. Other songs, like "Playboy" or "Too Many Fish in the Sea," warned girls about two-timing Romeo types who didn't deserve the time of day, and the sassy, defiant singers advised girls to tell boys who didn't treat them right to take a hike. Opening with a direct address to their sisters— "Look here, girls, take this advice"—the Marvelettes passed on what sounded like age-old female wisdom: "My mother once told me something/And every word is true/Don't waste your time on a fella/Who doesn't love you." Urging the listener to "stand tall," the lead singer asserted, "I don't want nobody that don't want me/Ain't gonna love nobody that don't love me." 13

The absolute necessity of female collusion in the face of thoughtless or mystifying behavior by boys bound these songs together, and bound the listeners to the singers in a knowing sorority. They knew things about boys and love that they shared with each other, and this shared knowledge—smarter, more deeply intuitive, more worldly wise than any male locker room talk—provided a powerful bonding between girls, a kind of bonding boys didn't have. And while boys were often identified as the love object, they were also identified as the enemy. So while some of the identities we assumed as we sang along were those of the traditional, passive, obedient, lovesick girl, each of us could also be a sassy, assertive, defiant girl who intended to have more control over her life—or at least her love life. In numerous advice songs, from "Mama Said" to "You Can't Hurry Love," the message that girls knew a thing or two, and that they would share that knowledge with one another to beat the odds in a man's world, circulated confidently. 14

Other songs fantasized about beating a different set of odds—the seeming inevitability, for white, middle-class girls, of being married off 15 to some boring, respectable guy with no sense of danger or adventure, someone like David Nelson or one of Fred MacMurray's three sons.[4] Here we come to the rebel category—"Leader of the Pack," "Uptown," "He's a Rebel," "Give Him a Great Big Kiss," and "He's Sure the Boy I Love." Academic zeros, on unemployment, clad in leather jackets, sporting dirty fingernails, and blasting around on motorcycles, the boy heroes in these songs were every suburban parent's nightmare, the boys they loved to hate. By allying herself romantically and morally with the rebel hero, the girl singer and listener proclaimed her independence from society's predictable expectations about her inevitable domestication. There is a role reversal here, too—the girls are gathered in a group, sharing information about their boyfriends, virtually eyeing them up and down, while the rebel heroes simply remain the passive objects of their gaze and their talk. And the girls who sang these songs, like the Shangri-Las, dressed the part of the defiant bad girl who stuck her tongue out at parental and middle-class authority. The Ronettes, whose beehives scraped the ceiling and whose eyeliner was thicker than King Tut's, wore spiked heels and skintight dresses with slits up the side as they begged some boy to "Be My Baby." They combined fashion rebellion with in-your-face sexual insurrection.

In "Will You Love Me Tomorrow," Shirley Owens asked herself, 16 Should she or shouldn't she? Of course, the question quickly became Should I or shouldn't I? The answer wasn't clear, and we heard plenty of songs in which girls found themselves smack in the grip of sexual desire. Sexuality emerged as an eternal ache, a kind of irresistible, unquenchable tension. But in the early 1960s, sex and sexual desire were still scary for many girls. The way many of these songs were produced—orchestrated with violins instead of with electric guitars or saxophones—muted the sexual explicitness and made it more romantic, more spiritual, more safe. "And Then He Kissed Me" alluded to some kind of new kiss tried on the singer by her boyfriend, one she really liked and wanted to have a lot more of. In "Heat Wave, " Martha Reeves sang at the top of her lungs about being swept up in a sexual fever that just wouldn't break, and the whispering, bedroom-voiced lead in "I'm Ready" confessed that she didn't really know quite what she was supposed to do but that she was sure ready to learn—right now. Claudine Clark desperately begged her mother to let her go off to the source of the "Party Lights," where one helluva party was happening, and she sounded like someone who had been in Alcatraz[5] for twenty years and would simply explode if she didn't get out.

The contradictions of being a teenage girl in the early and mid-1960s 17 also percolated from the conflict between the lyrics of the song and the

---

[4] Squeaky-clean sitcom characters. [Eds.]
[5] San Francisco maximum-security federal prison, now closed. [Eds.]

beat of the music. Girl group music had emerged at the same time as all these new dance crazes that redefined how boys and girls did—or, more accurately, did not—dance with each other. Chubby Checker's 1960 hit "The Twist" revolutionized teenage dancing, because it meant that boys and girls didn't have to hold hands anymore, boys didn't have to lead and girls didn't have to follow, so girls had a lot more autonomy and control as they danced. Plus, dancing was one of the things girls usually did much better than boys. As the twist gave way to the locomotion, the Bristol stomp, the mashed potatoes, the pony, the monkey, the slop, the jerk, and the frug, the dances urged us to loosen up our chests and our butts, and learn how to shimmy, grind, and thrust. This was something my friends and I did with gleeful abandon.

Many of us felt most free and exhilarated while we were dancing, 18 so bouncing around to a song like "Chains" or "Nowhere to Run" put us smack-dab between feelings of liberation and enslavement, between a faith in free will and a surrender to destiny. Both songs describe prisoners of love, and if you simply saw the lyrics without hearing the music, you'd think they were a psychotherapist's notes from a session with a deeply paranoid young woman trapped in a sadomasochistic relationship. Yet with "Chains," sung by the Cookies, girls were primed for dancing from the very beginning by the hand clapping, snare drums, and saxophones, so that the music worked in stark contrast to the lyrics, which claimed that the girl couldn't break free from her chains of love. Then, in a break from the chorus, the lead singer acknowledged, "I wanna tell you pretty baby/Your lips look sweet/I'd like to kiss them/But I can't break away from all of these chains." At least two personas emerge here, coexisting in the same teenager. One is the girl who loves the bittersweet condition of being hopelessly consumed by love. The other is the girl who, despite her chains, has a roving and appreciative eye for other boys. The conflict between the sense of entrapment in the lyrics and the utter liberation of the beat is inescapable. The tension is too delicious for words. . . .

While a few girl groups and individual singers were white—the 19 Angels, the Shangri-Las, Dusty Springfield—most successful girl groups were black. Unlike the voices of Patti Page or Doris Day, which seemed as innocent of sexual or emotional angst as a Chatty Cathy doll,[6] the vibrating voices of black teenagers, often trained in the gospel traditions of their churches, suggested a perfect fusion of naivete and knowingness. And with the rise of the civil rights movement, which by 1962 and 1963 dominated the national news, black voices conveyed both a moral authority and a spirited hope for the future. These were the voices of exclusion, of hope for something better, of longing. They

---

[6] One of the first pull-the-string talking dolls. [Eds.]

were not, like Annette or the Lennon Sisters,[7] the voices of sexual repression, of social complacency, or of homogenized commercialism.

From the Jazz Age to rap music, African American culture has always kicked white culture upside the head for being so pathologically repressed; one consequence, for black women, is that too often they have been stereotyped as more sexually active and responsive than their white-bread sisters. Because of these stereotypes, it was easier, more acceptable, to the music industry and no doubt to white culture at large that black girls, instead of white ones, be the first teens to give voice to girls' changing attitudes toward sex. But since the sexuality of black people has always been deeply threatening to white folks, black characters in popular culture also have been desexualized, the earth-mother mammy being a classic example. The black teens in girl groups, then, while they sounded orgiastic at times, had to look feminine, innocent, and as white as possible. Berry Gordy, the head of Motown, knew this instinctively, and made his girl groups take charm school lessons and learn how to get into and out of cars, carry their handbags, and match their shoes to their dresses. They were trapped, and in the glare of the spotlight, no less, between the old and new definitions of femininity. But under their crinolined skirts and satin cocktail dresses, they were also smuggling into middle-class America a taste of sexual liberation. So white girls like me owe a cultural debt to these black girls for straddling these contradictions, and for helping create a teen girl culture that said, "Let loose, break free, don't take no shit."

The Shirelles paved the way for the decade's most successful girl group, the Supremes, who had sixteen records in the national top ten between 1964 and 1969. But of utmost importance was the role Diana Ross played in making African American beauty enviable to white girls. As slim as a rail with those cavernous armpits, gorgeous smile, and enormous, perfectly made-up eyes, Diana Ross is the first black woman I remember desperately wanting to look like, even if some of her gowns were a bit too Vegas. I couldn't identify with her completely, not because she was black, but because when I was fourteen, she seemed so glamorous and sophisticated. Ross has taken a lot of heat in recent years as the selfish bitch who wanted all the fame and glory for herself, so it's easy to forget her importance as a cultural icon in the 1960s. But the Supremes—who seemed to be both girls and women, sexy yet respectable, and a blend of black and white culture—made it perfectly normal for white girls to idolize and want to emulate their black sisters. . . .

While girl group music celebrated love, marriage, female masochism, and passivity, it also urged girls to make the first move, to rebel against their parents and middle-class conventions, and to dump boys

---

[7] Teenage group that appeared on the musically conservative *Lawrence Welk Show*. [Eds.]

who didn't treat them right. Most of all, girl group music—precisely because these were groups, not just individual singers—insisted that it was critically important for girls to band together, talking about men, singing about men, trying to figure them out.

What we have here is a pop culture harbinger in which girl groups, 23 however innocent and commercial, anticipate women's groups, and girl talk anticipates a future kind of women's talk. The consciousness-raising groups of the late sixties and early seventies came naturally to many young women because we'd had a lot of practice. We'd been talking about boys, about loving them and hating them, about how good they often made us feel and how bad they often treated us, for ten years. The Shirelles mattered because they captured so well our confusion in the face of changing sexual mores. And as the confusion of real life intersected with the contradictions in popular culture, girls were prepared to start wondering, sooner or later, why sexual freedoms didn't lead to other freedoms as well.

Girl group music gave us an unprecedented opportunity to try on 24 different, often conflicting, personas. For it wasn't just that we could be, as we sang along first with the Dixie Cups and then the Shangri-Las, traditional passive girls one minute and more active, rebellious, even somewhat prefeminist girls the next. Contradiction was embedded in almost all the stances a girl tried on, and some version, no matter how thwarted, of prefeminism, constituted many of them. We couldn't sustain this tension forever, especially when one voice said, "Hey, hon, you're equal" and the other voice said, "Oh no, you're not."

The Shirelles and the other girl groups mattered because they helped 25 cultivate inside us a desire to rebel. The main purpose of pop music is to make us feel a kind of euphoria that convinces us that we can transcend the shackles of conventional life and rise above the hordes of others who do get trapped. It is the euphoria of commercialism, designed to get us to buy. But this music did more than that; it generated another kind of euphoria as well. For when tens of millions of young girls started feeling, at the same time, that they, as a generation, would not be trapped, there was planted the tiniest seed of a social movement.

Few symbols more dramatically capture the way young women in 26 the early 1960s were pinioned between entrapment and freedom than one of the most bizarre icons of the period, the go-go girl dancing in a cage. While African American performers like the Dixie Cups or Mary Wells sang on *Shindig* or *Hullabaloo*, white girls in white go-go boots pranced and shimmied in their cages in the background. Autonomous yet objectified, free to dance by herself on her own terms yet highly choreographed in her little prison, seemingly indifferent to others yet trapped in a voyeuristic gaze, the go-go girl seems, in retrospect, one of the sicker, yet more apt, metaphors for the teen female condition during this era. It's not surprising that when four irreverent, androgynous, and irresistible young men[8] came over from England and incited a collective jailbreak, millions of these teens took them up on it. For we had begun to see some new kinds of girls in the mass media—some perky, some bohemian, some androgynous—who convinced us that a little anarchy was exactly what we, and American gender roles, needed.

Responding to Reading

1. According to Douglas, exactly why did the Shirelles (and "girl groups" in general) matter to the women of her generation? What music artists "matter" in the same way to you? Why?

2. Douglas cannot assume that all her readers will be familiar with the many groups and songs she discusses. In what ways does she try to accommodate those who are not? Does she succeed?

3. The style of this essay is very informal. For example, Douglas uses contractions, the pronouns *we* and *us,* and colloquial expressions like "a bunch of women" (1). Identify other examples of conversational style in the essay. Do you think this informal style reduces Douglas's credibility in any way? Does it have any advantages?

WE TALK, YOU LISTEN

Vine Deloria, Jr.

A Standing Rock Sioux born in South Dakota, Vine Deloria, Jr. (1933–) holds a B.S. from Iowa State University, a master's of theology from Rock Island Lutheran School, and a law degree from the University of Colorado. He was executive director of the National Congress of American Indians from 1964 to 1967, and his early books—including Custer Died for Your Sins: An Indian Manifesto *(1969) and* Behind the Trail of Broken Treaties: An American Indian Declaration of Independence *(1974)— made him a leader in the "Red Power" movement of the 1970s. His most recent book is* Red Earth, White Lies: Native Americans and the Myth of Scientific Fact *(1995). A professor of history, law, and religious studies at the University of Colorado, Deloria has argued for the establishment of new treaties between Native American tribes and the U.S. government "to ensure the survival of the tribes, their lands, and their ways of life." In the following essay from* We Talk, You Listen: New Tribes, New Turf *(1970), Deloria looks at media stereotypes of Native Americans and other minorities as well as at university ethnic studies programs.*

---

[8] The Beatles. [Eds.]

One reason that Indian people have not been heard from until 1
recently is that we have been completely covered up by movie Indians.
Western movies have been such favorites that they have dominated the
public's conception of what Indians are. It is not all bad when one thinks
about the handsome Jay Silverheels bailing the Lone Ranger out of a
jam, or Ed Ames rescuing Daniel Boone with some clever Indian trick.
But the other mythologies that have wafted skyward because of the
movies have blocked out any idea that there might be real Indians with
real problems.

Other minority groups have fought tenaciously against stereotyping, 2
and generally they have been successful. Italians quickly quashed the
image of them as mobsters that television projected in *The Untouchables.*
Blacks have been successful in getting a more realistic picture of the black
man in a contemporary setting because they have had standout performers like Bill Cosby and Sidney Poitier to represent them.

Since stereotyping was highlighted by motion pictures, it would 3
probably be well to review the images of minority groups projected in
the movies in order to understand how the situation looks at present.
Perhaps the first aspect of stereotyping was the tendency to exclude
people on the basis of their inability to handle the English language. Not
only were racial minorities excluded, but immigrants arriving on these
shores were soon whipped into shape by ridicule of their English.

Traditional stereotypes pictured the black as a happy watermelon- 4
eating darky whose sole contribution to American society was his indiscriminate substitution of the "d" sound for "th." Thus a black always
said "dis" and "dat," as in "lift dat bale." The "d" sound carried over
and was used by white gangsters to indicate disfavor with their situation, as in "dis is de end, ya rat." The important thing was to indicate
that blacks were like lisping children not yet competent to undertake
the rigors of economic opportunities and voting.

Mexicans were generally portrayed as shiftless and padded out for 5
siesta, without any redeeming qualities whatsoever. Where the black
had been handicapped by his use of the "d," the Mexican suffered from
the use of the double "e." This marked them off as a group worth watching. Mexicans, according to the stereotype, always said "theenk,"
"peenk," and later "feenk." Many advertisements today still continue
this stereotype, thinking that it is cute and cuddly.

These groups were much better off than Indians were. Indians were 6
always devoid of any English whatsoever. They were only allowed to
speak when an important message had to be transmitted on the screen.
For example, "many pony soldiers die" was meant to indicate that
Indians were going to attack the peaceful settlers who happened to have
broken their three hundredth treaty moments before. Other than that
Indian linguistic ability was limited to "ugh" and "kemo sabe" (which
means honky in some obscure Indian language).

The next step was to acknowledge that there was a great American 7
dream to which any child could aspire. (It was almost like the train in
the night that Richard Nixon heard as a child anticipating the dream
fairy.) The great American dream was projected in the early World War
II movies. The last reel was devoted to a stirring proclamation that we
were going to win the war and it showed factories producing airplanes,
people building ships, and men marching in uniform to the transports.
There was a quick pan of a black face before the scene shifted to scenes
of orchards, rivers, Mount Rushmore, and the Liberty Bell as we found
out what we were fighting for.

The new images expressed a profound inability to understand why 8
minority groups couldn't "make it" when everybody knew that America was all about freedom and equality. By projecting an image of everyone working hard to win the war, the doctrine was spread that America
was just one big happy family and that there really weren't any differences so long as we had to win the war.

It was a rare war movie in the 1940s that actually showed a black or 9
a Mexican as a bona fide fighting man. When they did appear it was in
the role of cooks or orderlies serving whites. In most cases this was a
fairly accurate statement of their situation, particularly with respect to
the Navy.

World War II movies were entirely different for Indians. Each pla- 10
toon of red-blooded white American boys was equipped with its own
set of Indians. When the platoon got into trouble and was surrounded,
its communications cut off except for one slender line to regimental
headquarters, and that line tapped by myriads of Germans, Japanese, or
Italians, the stage was set for the dramatic episode of the Indians.

John Wayne, Randolph Scott, Sonny Tufts, or Tyrone Power would 11
smile broadly as he played his ace, which until this time had been hidden from view. From nowhere, a Navaho, Comanche, Cherokee, or
Sioux would appear, take the telephone, and in some short and
inscrutable phraseology communicate such a plenitude of knowledge to
his fellow tribesman (fortunately situated at the general's right hand)
that fighting units thousands of miles away would instantly perceive
the situation and rescue the platoon. The Indian would disappear as
mysteriously as he had come, only to reappear the next week in a different battle to perform his esoteric rites. Anyone watching war movies
during the '40s would have been convinced that without Indian telephone operators the war would have been lost irretrievably, in spite of
John Wayne.

Indians were America's secret weapon against the forces of evil. The 12
typing spoke of a primitive gimmick, and it was the strangeness of
Indians that made them visible, not their humanity. With the Korean
War era and movies made during the middle '50s, other minority
groups began to appear and Indians were pushed into the background.

This era was the heyday of the "All-American Platoon." It was the ultimate conception of intergroup relations. The "All-American Platoon" was a "one each": one black, one Mexican, one Indian, one farm boy from Iowa, one Southerner who hated blacks, one boy from Brooklyn, one Polish boy from the urban slums of the Midwest, one Jewish intellectual, and one college boy. Every possible stereotype was included and it resulted in a portrayal of Indians as another species of human being for the first time in moving pictures.

The platoon was always commanded by a veteran of grizzled coun- 13 tenance who had been at every battle in which the United States had ever engaged. The whole story consisted in killing off the members of the platoon until only the veteran and the college boy were left. The Southerner and the black would die in each other's arms singing "Dixie." The Jewish intellectual and the Indian formed some kind of attachment and were curiously the last ones killed. When the smoke cleared, the college boy, with a prestige wound in the shoulder, returned to his girl, and the veteran reconciled with his wife and checked out another platoon in anticipation of taking the same hill in the next movie.

While other groups have managed to make great strides since those 14 days, Indians have remained the primitive unknown quantity. Dialogue has reverted back to the monosyllabic grunt and even pictures that attempt to present the Indian side of the story depend upon unintelligible noises to present their message. The only exception to this rule is a line famed for its durability over the years. If you fall asleep during the Late Show and suddenly awaken to the words "go in peace, my son," it is either an Indian chief bidding his son good bye as the boy heads for college or a Roman Catholic priest forgiving Paul Newman or Steve McQueen for killing a hundred men in the preceding reel.

Anyone raising questions about the image of minority groups as 15 portrayed in television and the movies is automatically suspect as an un-American and subversive influence on the minds of the young. The historical, linguistic, and cultural differences are neatly blocked out by the fad of portraying members of minority groups in roles which formerly were reserved for whites. Thus Burt Reynolds played a Mohawk detective busy solving the crime problem in New York City. Diahann Carroll played a well-to-do black widow with small child in a television series that was obviously patterned after the unique single-headed white family.

In recent years the documentary has arisen to present the story of 16 Indian people and a number of series on Black America have been produced. Indian documentaries are singularly the same. A reporter and television crew hasten to either the Navaho or Pine Ridge reservation, quickly shoot reels on poverty conditions, and return East blithely thinking that they have captured the essence of Indian life. In spite of the best intentions, the eternal yearning to present an exciting story of a strange people overcomes, and the endless cycle of poverty-oriented films continues.

This type of approach continually categorizes the Indian as an 17 incompetent boob who can't seem to get along and who is hopelessly mired in a poverty of his own making. Hidden beneath these documentaries is the message that Indians really *want* to live this way. No one has yet filmed the incredible progress that is being made by the Makah tribe, the Quinaults, Red Lake Chippewas, Gila River Pima-Waricopas, and others. Documentaries project the feeling that reservations should be eliminated because the conditions are so bad. There is no effort to present the bright side of Indian life.

With the rise of ethnic studies programs and courses in minority- 18 group history, the situation has become worse. People who support these programs assume that by communicating the best aspects of a group they have somehow solved the major problems of that group in its relations with the rest of society. By emphasizing that black is beautiful or that Indians have contributed the names of rivers to the road map, many people feel that they have done justice to the group concerned.

One theory of interpretation of Indian history that has arisen in the 19 past several years is that all of the Indian war chiefs were patriots defending their lands. This is the "patriot chief" interpretation of history. Fundamentally it is a good theory in that it places a more equal balance to interpreting certain Indian wars as wars of resistance. It gets away from the tendency, seen earlier in this century, to classify all Indian warriors as renegades. But there is a tendency to overlook the obvious renegades: Indians who were treacherous and would have been renegades had there been no whites to fight. The patriot chiefs interpretation also conveniently overlooks the fact that every significant leader of the previous century was eventually done in by his own people in one way or another. Sitting Bull was killed by Indian police working for the government. Geronimo was captured by an army led by Apache scouts who sided with the United States.

If the weak points of each minority group's history are to be covered 20 over by a sweetness-and-light interpretation based on what we would like to think happened rather than what did happen, we doom ourselves to decades of further racial strife. Most of the study programs today emphasize the goodness that is inherent in the different minority communities, instead of trying to present a balanced story. There are basically two schools of interpretation running through all of these efforts as the demand for black, red, and brown pride dominates the programs.

One theory derives from the "All-American Platoon" concept of a 21 decade ago. Under this theory members of the respective racial minority groups had an important role in the great events of American history. Crispus Attucks, a black, almost single-handedly started the Revolutionary War, while Eli Parker, the Seneca Indian general, won the Civil

War and would have concluded it sooner had not there been so many stupid whites abroad in those days. This is the "cameo" theory of history. It takes a basic "manifest destiny" white interpretation of history and lovingly plugs a few feathers, woolly heads, and sombreros into the famous events of American history. No one tries to explain what an Indian is who was helping the whites destroy his own people, since we are now all Americans and have these great events in common.

The absurdity of the cameo school of ethnic pride is self-apparent. 22 Little Mexican children are taught that there were some good Mexicans at the Alamo. They can therefore be happy that Mexicans have been involved in the significant events of Texas history. Little is said about the Mexicans on the other side at the Alamo. The result is a denial of a substantial Mexican heritage by creating the feeling that "we all did it together." If this trend continues I would not be surprised to discover that Columbus had a Cherokee on board when he set sail from Spain in search of the Indies.

The cameo school smothers any differences that existed historically 23 by presenting a history in which all groups have participated through representatives. Regardless of Crispus Attucks's valiant behavior during the Revolution, it is doubtful that he envisioned another century of slavery for blacks as a cause worth defending.

The other basic school of interpretation is a projection backward of 24 the material blessings of the white middle class. It seeks to identify where all the material wealth originated and finds that each minority group *contributed* something. It can therefore be called the contribution school. Under this conception we should all love Indians because they contributed corn, squash, potatoes, tobacco, coffee, rubber, and other agricultural products. In like manner, blacks and Mexicans are credited with Carver's work on the peanut, blood transfusion, and tacos and tamales.

The ludicrous implication of the contribution school visualizes the 25 minority groups clamoring to enter American society, lined up with an abundance of foods and fancies, presenting them to whites in a never ending stream of generosity. If the different minority groups were given an overriding two-percent royalty on their contributions, the same way whites have managed to give themselves royalties for their inventions, this school would have a more realistic impact on minority groups.

The danger with both of these types of ethnic studies theories is that 26 they present an unrealistic account of the role of minority groups in American history. Certainly there is more to the story of the American Indian than providing cocoa and popcorn for Columbus's landing party. When the clashes of history are smoothed over in favor of a mushy togetherness feeling, then people begin to wonder what has happened in the recent past that has created the conditions of today. It has been the feeling of younger people that contemporary problems have arisen because community leadership has been consistently betraying them. Older statesmen are called Uncle Toms, and the entire fabric of accumulated wisdom and experience of the older generation of minority groups is destroyed. . . .

Under present conceptions of ethnic studies there can be no lasting 27 benefit either to minority groups or to society at large. The pride that can be built into children and youth by acknowledgment of the validity of their group certainly cannot be built by simply transferring symbols and interpretations arising in white culture history into an Indian, black, or Mexican setting. The result will be to make the minority groups bear the white man's burden by using his symbols and stereotypes as if they were their own.

There must be a drive within each minority group to understand its 28 own uniqueness. This can only be done by examining what experiences were relevant to the group, not what experiences of white America the group wishes itself to be represented in. As an example, the discovery of gold in California was a significant event in the experience of white America. The discovery itself was irrelevant to the western Indian tribes, but the migrations caused by the discovery of gold were vitally important. The two histories can dovetail around this topic but ultimately each interpretation must depend upon its orientation to the group involved.

What has been important and continues to be important is the 29 Constitution of the United States and its continual adaptation to contemporary situations. With the Constitution as a framework and reference point, it would appear that a number of conflicting interpretations of the experience of America could be validly given. While they might conflict at every point as each group defines to its own satisfaction what its experience has meant, recognition that within the Constitutional framework we are engaged in a living process of intergroup relationships would mean that no one group could define the meaning of American society to the exclusion of any other.

Self-awareness of each group must define a series of histories about 30 the American experience. Manifest destiny has dominated thinking in the past because it has had an abstract quality that appeared to interpret experiences accurately. Nearly every racial and ethnic group has had to bow down before this conception of history and conform to an understanding of the world that it did not ultimately believe. Martin Luther King, Jr., spoke to his people on the basis of self-awareness the night before he died. He told them that they as a people would reach the promised land. Without the same sense of destiny, minority groups will simply be adopting the outmoded forms of stereotyping by which whites have deluded themselves for centuries.

We can survive as a society if we reject the conquest-oriented inter- 31
pretation of the Constitution. While some Indian nationalists want the
whole country back, a guarantee of adequate protection of existing
treaty rights would provide a meaningful compromise. The Constitution should provide a sense of balance between groups as it has between
conflicting desires of individuals.

As each group defines the ideas and doctrines necessary to main- 32
tain its own sense of dignity and identity, similarities in goals can be
drawn that will have relevance beyond immediate group aspirations.
Stereotyping will change radically because the ideological basis for portraying the members of any group will depend on that group's values.
Plots in books and movies will have to show life as it is seen from within
the group. Society will become broader and more cosmopolitan as innovative themes are presented to it. The universal sense of inhumanity
will take on an aspect of concreteness. From the variety of cultural
behavior patterns we can devise a new understanding of humanity.

The problem of stereotyping is not so much a racial problem as it is 33
a problem of limited knowledge and perspective. Even though minority groups have suffered in the past by ridiculous characterizations of
themselves by white society, they must not fall into the same trap by
simply reversing the process that has stereotyped them. Minority
groups must thrust through the rhetorical blockade by creating within
themselves a sense of "peoplehood." This ultimately means the creation
of a new history and not mere amendments to the historical interpretations of white America.

Responding to Reading

1. In paragraphs 1–17, Deloria focuses on media stereotypes; in paragraphs
   18–33 his focus is on ethnic studies programs. What connection does he
   make between these two subjects?
2. Deloria's essay was first published in 1970. Based on what you see today,
   do you think the media's treatment of African-Americans and Latinos has
   changed significantly since then? Has its treatment of Native Americans
   also changed? Or do you think Native Americans remain "the primitive
   unknown quantity" (14) Deloria believed they were in 1970?
3. Despite his thoughtful critique of the media's tendency to stereotype ethnic
   minorities, Deloria's essay does not mention Asians, even in his description
   of the "All-American Platoon"—which, he says, included "every possible
   stereotype" (12). How do you explain this omission? Are other important
   groups omitted?

WHERE THE BOYS ARE

Steven Stark

Steven Stark (1952–   ), a graduate of Harvard and the Yale Law School and a former aide to President Jimmy Carter, writes frequently about popular culture and contemporary political and social issues. He has worked for the Wall Street Journal, Boston Magazine, *the* Boston Phoenix, *and the* Boston Globe, *and he is a featured contributor to the* Atlantic Monthly *and many other publications, as well as a regular commentator on National Public Radio and CNN's "Showbiz Today." In 1997, he published* Glued to the Set: The 60 Television Shows and Events That Made Us Who We Are Today. *In the following essay, which originally appeared in the* Atlantic Monthly *in 1994, Stark looks at what he considers a disturbing tendency of contemporary media to celebrate uncritically "the early-teen male sensibility."*

Over the past several years American pop culture has spawned a   1
wide range of wildly popular offerings that appear remarkably similar in sensibility. Although at first glance little appears to link the infamous syndicated-radio talk-meisters Howard Stern and Don Imus with the movies *Jurassic Park* and *Field of Dreams,* the comedy of David Letterman and Jerry Seinfeld, the cartoon series *Beavis and Butt-head* and *The Simpsons,* and journalism's *The McLaughlin Group,* they in fact share a motif: though for the most part aimed at adults, these are all offerings that strongly echo the world of boys in early adolescence, ages eleven to fifteen. The unspoken premise of much of American pop culture today is that a large group of men would like nothing better than to go back to their junior high school locker rooms and stay there.

There is nothing new, of course, about men acting like boys, as any-   2
one who has read *The Odyssey* or *Don Quixote*[1] knows. But something different is going on today: never before have so many seemed to produce so much that is so popular to evoke what is, after all, a brief and awkward stage of life. What's more, the trend spans the range of popular culture. Take talk radio: One of its most popular approaches today is to offer the listener a world of close-knit boyish pals. The style of Stern and Imus is that of the narcissistic class cutup in seventh grade: both sit in a playhouse-like radio studio with a bunch of guys and horse around for hours talking about sex or sports, along with political and show-biz gossip, all the while laughing at the gang's consciously loutish, subversive jokes. To the extent that women participate, they are often treated to a barrage of sexual and scatological humor. It's no wonder the audience for both shows is predominantly male.

---

[1] Classic tales of adventurous quests. [Eds.]

Late Show With David Letterman and *Seinfeld* similarly echo the ethos ₃ of young teenage boys. Late-night television has always been a chiefly male world, but until recently it wasn't a boy's world. One of Letterman's contributions to late-night entertainment has been to take its humor out of the nightclub-act tradition—replete with all of Johnny Carson's jokes about drinking or adult sex—and place it firmly in that prankish, subversive, back-of-the-classroom seventh-grade realm that has become so culturally prominent. Although Letterman rarely greets women guests with filthy jokes (you can't do that on network television), he often treats them with the exaggerated deference and shyness typical of fourteen-year-old boys.

Like a group of fourteen-year-olds, the men on *Seinfeld* seem not to ₄ hold regular jobs, the better to devote time to "the gang." One woman, Elaine, is allowed to tag along with the boys, much like those younger sisters who are permitted to hang out with their brothers. It's not simply that everyone in Seinfeld's gang is unmarried and pushing forty-something. It's that given their personas, it's difficult to imagine any of them having a real relationship with any woman but his mother. (Note how much more often parents of adult children appear here than on other shows.) Compare this situation comedy with the one that was roughly its cultural predecessor, *Cheers*, which appeared in the same time slot. On that show, too, the men didn't spend much time at work, but they did hang out in a traditional domain of adults (the tavern), and the hero, Sam Malone, spent many of his waking hours chasing women. Seinfeld is better known for sitting in a diner eating french fries with his pals. One of the show's most celebrated "risqué" episodes was about—what else?—masturbation.

And so it goes in various ways, as the early-teen male sensibility is ₅ celebrated in everything from *Wayne's World* (the adventures of two adolescent goofballs) to *The Simpsons* (starring the proud underachiever Bart) to *Beavis and Butt-head* (MTV's notorious early-adolescent icons). The heavy-metal sound of bands with names like Danzig, Gwar, and Genitorturers is in vogue now, and with its constant evocation of sexism, violence, and hostility for hostility's sake, that rock genre has always reeked of the adolescent experience more than others have.

Like many recent cinema hits, ranging from the Indiana Jones series ₆ to most Arnold Schwarzenegger offerings, last year's blockbuster film *Jurassic Park* was largely a traditional teenage "boys' movie"—heavy on adventure and violence, light on romance and relationships. Psychologists have observed that the culture-wide trend toward "pumped-up" male heroes—Schwarzenegger, Sylvester Stallone, and half the guys at your local health club—is a pre-teen male fantasy brought to life. Even popular "adult" movies, such as *City Slickers* and *Big*, often revolve around the premise that once a man has passed through puberty, it's pretty much all downhill.

The cult of baseball can be seen as an intensely nostalgic return to 7
early adolescence for many Americans. The rite of Rotisserie League
baseball—an activity in which men spend hours every week poring over
sheets of statistics, as they did when they were young—is part of this
phenomenon, as are the wearing of baseball hats and the collecting of
autographs and baseball cards by men of all ages. So, too, are baseball-
movie parables like the quasi-religious *Field of Dreams*, in which male
adolescence, the pastoral life, and baseball are linked in a way that
would make both Jean Jacques Rousseau and Casey Stengel proud. In
these visions of utopia, of course, women are again peripheral—except,
perhaps, when baking cookies or waving in maternal fashion from the
front porch as Dad and Son play catch. In the 1955 America that is usually the baseball lover's Paradise Lost, there are no Astroturf, no new sta-
diums, and no western teams to challenge the prominence of New York
and the eastern urban society it represents. That America is not only a
man's world but also, by and large, a white man's world.

Today's early-adolescent attitude is certainly on display throughout 8
the news media. It's not simply that in a tabloid age many publications
have adopted a kind of sneering, sophomoric attitude toward public
affairs, or that shows such as *Crossfire* and *The McLaughlin Group*—with
their mostly male screaming casts—resemble nothing so much as a
junior high social-studies debate (in which the girls were always
shouted down by the boys regardless of what they had to say). It's that
today's journalism is obsessed with the kinds of things that tend to pre-
occupy thirteen-year-old boys: sports, sex, crime, and narcissism—that
is, itself. Also in journalism as currently practiced, reporters often set
themselves up as passive observers of events and then spend much of
their time identifying with those who exercise real power—a point of
view that is reminiscent of the way a young teenager views his parents.
Moreover, if today's journalism has a driving principle, that principle
centers on an obsession with hypocrisy. Journalism is about many
things, but these days it is often about revealing that public figures are
phonies. Covering Bill Clinton, or Prince Charles, or Michael Jackson,
reporters frame their stories by saying implicitly, "These people aren't
what they say they are. Look, they lied to you." Although there is a cultural role for balloon deflators, journalism has brought this characteristic attitude of the early adolescent to the adult world and elevated it to
the status of cultural religion. That's why much of journalism today is
really a form of institutionalized early adolescence.

Because the press tends to set the agenda for our culture, these sen- 9
timents have enormous ramifications. Whether in the form of the
media's obsession with violence or its preoccupation with polls and
popularity, the fantasy life of the adolescent male ends up defining
much of our political reality. Political coverage tends to focus on gaffes,

girlfriends, and youthful indiscretions while far more important, "adult" issues go underreported.

The press has also seen to it that the cardinal sin in American poli- 10 tics today is not to run up a deficit or lose an important court case but to change one's mind: like a fourteen-year-old, the press always takes a switch as evidence of hypocrisy. Thus George Bush was skewered by the media in 1990 for flip-flopping on the issue of taxes, and Bill Clinton was attacked unmercifully last year for going back on his promise of a tax cut for the middle class. Maybe both men had misled the voters during their campaigns, but a less iconoclastic press corps might have concluded that both men changed their minds for unselfish policy reasons. While an adolescent often looks at a change in direction and sees deceit, an adult realizes that life is usually more complex than that. Mature leaders recognize their mistakes and often adjust accordingly—though not without peril in today's climate.

Admittedly, too much can be made of all this. Entertainment has 11 always evoked certain stages of life in ways that appeal to the masses: think of *The Wizard of Oz* and *Rebel Without a Cause*. The fourteen-year-old sensibility is certainly not the only one celebrated in a culture that includes *The Golden Girls, Murphy Brown,* and Barney the dinosaur. And it's true that other eras in America have celebrated youth in various forms, from Shirley Temple to the Brady Bunch. But it's hard to make the case that the male early-adolescent mind-set was as pervasive or influential in those eras as it is in this one.

There are, of course, antecedents in our cultural life for this venera- 12 tion of male early adolescence. The western often celebrated the young cowboy or outlaw like Billy the Kid, who, surrounded by his loyal gang in a world without commitment to women, broke the rules. In his recent book, *American Manhood,* E. Anthony Rotundo shows how American culture came to celebrate the misbehavior of boys as a way of idolizing the traits of childishness without idolizing children. In *Love and Death in the American Novel* (1960) Leslie Fiedler traces the evolution of the "bad boy" in American fiction from its roots in late-nineteenth-century best-sellers like *Peck's Bad Boy* and *The Story of a Bad Boy.* He also describes American fiction's traditional preoccupation with "The Good Bad Boy" —from Huckleberry Finn to Holden Caulfield to the characters in Jack Kerouac's *On the Road.* Fiedler wrote, "The Good Bad Boy is, of course, America's vision of itself, crude and unruly in his beginnings, but endowed by his creator with an instinctive sense of what is right."

Thirty-four years ago Fiedler wrote that from the Puritan- 13 influenced Hawthorne and Melville on, Americans had been drawn to tales of boys and neutered women as a way of avoiding the subject of sex. In a tabloid era of penis-mutilation trials, prime-time network nudity, condom ads, and endless talk-show discussions of sexual fetishes, however, it's hard to continue to make his case. Still, if early-adolescent boys are notable for their inclinations to look at dirty pictures and talk about sex, they aren't quite ready to do something about it responsibly with a woman. That propensity to be in the world of sex but not really of it is certainly a sign of the times.

What's more, even if men aren't trying to avoid sex today, a retreat 14 into teenhood may be a convenient way to avoid the opposite sex. As Susan Faludi and other writers have noted, the women's movement—perhaps the greatest social change of our time—has triggered something of a well-documented backlash. One result may be the creation of this boyish countermovement that looks with nostalgic longing on perhaps the last period in life when it's socially acceptable for males to exclude women, if not deride them.

The reasons for the cultural ubiquity of male early adolescence have 15 little to do with puritanism. Many psychologists consider that stage of life, when one is acutely aware of being powerless, to be the time when individuals are most subversive of the society at large. That idea also fits a wider cultural mood, always somewhat prevalent in America, that exalts the outsider. Such an anti-establishment mood, rooted in powerlessness, is particularly strong today, and the proof is not simply in the Ross Perot phenomenon. Whether the subject is how the tabloid press now eagerly tears down public figures or the pervasiveness of gossip masquerading as news (to demonstrate how the famous are no better than anyone else) or the rise of anti-establishment talk radio and comedy clubs where the humor grows more derisive by the day, America is full of the defiant, oppositional anger that often characterizes the early adolescent.

That anger is also an asset for TV programmers in the cable era. 16 Television, of course, tends to encourage a kind of passivity that isn't ultimately much different from the angry powerlessness early teens tend to feel: Beavis and Butt-head have become cultural symbols precisely because a nation of couch potatoes feels like a nation of fifteen-year-olds. Moreover, in an age of multiple offerings and channel surfing, what tends to draw these passive audiences is the irately outrageous and exhibitionistic—the Howard Sterns, not the Arthur Godfreys.[2] It also doesn't hurt that adolescents tend to be what advertisers call "good consumers" —narcissistic, with a fair amount of disposable income, and with no one but themselves to spend it on. A culture that is obsessed with this stage of life is arguably in a better frame of mind to buy—to run up the limit on Dad's (or Uncle Sam's) credit card—than one that worships, say, thrifty middle age.

---

[2] Host of a long-running radio (and, later, television) variety show in the 1950s and 1960s who projected a kindly, uncle-like image. [Eds.]

In a country whose citizens have always had tendencies that   17
remind observers of those of a fourteen-year-old boy, it would be wrong
to lay all the blame for society's vulgarity and violence, its exhibitionist
inclinations, its fear of powerful women, its failure to grow up and take
care of its real children, and its ambivalence about paternal authority at
the feet of Howard Stern, John McLaughlin, and Jerry Seinfeld. But they
have helped, and many of us have willingly obliged. After all, as Fiedler
reminded us, boys will be boys.

Responding to Reading

1. In paragraph 1, Stark says that many popular films and television and radio
    programs, though aimed at adults, "strongly echo the world of boys in
    early adolescence, ages eleven to fifteen." Do you think he is correct?
2. Can you think of movies and television shows that explore the female sen-
    sibility? Exactly how are they different from those Stark cites?
3. Stark sees not only television and films but journalism, too, as "obsessed
    with the kinds of things that tend to preoccupy thirteen-year-old boys:
    sports, sex, crime, and narcissism—that is, itself" (8). In fact, he sees much
    of today's journalism as "a form of institutionalized early adolescence" (8).
    Do you agree? What does he see as some of the negative results of this
    "retreat into teenhood" (14)? Can you think of others?

TESTIFYING: TELEVISION

Wendy Kaminer

*Cultural critic Wendy Kaminer (1953–   ) received a bachelor's degree
from Smith College and a law degree from Boston University Law School.
She practiced law in New York City from 1977 to 1984, both for the Legal
Aid Society and for the Office of the Mayor, and later taught English at Tufts
University. She is currently a fellow at Radcliffe College, a contributing edi-
tor to the* Atlantic Monthly, *and a commentator on National Public Radio's*
Morning Edition, *as well as the president of the National Coalition against
Censorship. In addition to numerous articles in periodicals ranging from*
Dissent *to* Mirabella, *she has published five books, most recently* True Love
Waits: Essays and Criticism *(1996) and* It's All the Rage: Crime and
Culture *(1995). Her subjects include feminism, politics, culture, and law,
and she is particularly interested in ideas of individual accountability and the
politics of victimhood. In* I'm Dysfunctional, You're Dysfunctional: The
Recovery Movement and Other Self-Help Fashions *(1992), she takes on
the various self-help movements. "Testifying: Television," a chapter from that
book, focuses on television tell-all talk shows and the culture of lurid self-
revelation and "recovery."*

Recovering substance abuser Kitty Dukakis once called a press con- 1
ference to announce her descent into alcoholism and request respect for
her privacy. It was shortly after her husband's defeat in the 1988 presidential race, when she was less newsworthy than the pearls adorning
Barbara Bush's neck. I marveled only briefly at the spectacle of a
woman seeking privacy in a press conference and public confession of
an addiction. Some people, especially famous and formerly famous
ones, seem to enjoy their privacy only in public. *Now You Know*, Kitty
Dukakis called her book, in case you cared.

Still, millions of readers who don't care about Dukakis and all the 2
other recovering personalities who write books are curious, I guess.
Confessional autobiographies by second-string celebrities are publish-
ing staples (and where would the talk shows be without them?). Ali
MacGraw exposes her sex addiction and the lurid details of her mar-
riage to Steve McQueen. Suzanne Somers chronicles her life as an
ACOA [Adult Child of an Alcoholic]. Former first children Michael
Reagan and Patti Davis reveal their histories of abuse.

"I truly hope my book will help others to heal," the celebrity diarists 3
are likely to say. Or they assure us that writing their books was therapeutic (and if they pay me to read them, I will). But the celebrities don't
really have to explain the decision to go public. In our culture of recovery we take their confessions for granted. Talking about yourself is "part
of the process." Suggesting to someone that she is talking too much
about herself is a form of abuse. If you can't feign interest in someone
else's story, you're supposed to maintain respectful or, better yet,
stunned silence. In recovery, where everyone gets to claim that she's
survived some holocaust of family life, everyone gets to testify.

The tradition of testifying in court, church, or the marketplace for 4
justice, God, or the public good is a venerable one that I would not
impugn. But it is also a tradition I'd rather not debase by confusing testifying with advertisements for yourself or simple plays for sympathy
and attention. The recovery movement combines the testimonial tradition that serves a greater good, like justice, with the therapeutic tradition in which talking about yourself is its own reward. It also borrows
liberally from the revivalist tradition of testifying to save your soul and
maybe others: in recovery, even the most trivial testimony is sanctified.

I'm not impugning therapy or religion either, but I wish that peo- 5
ple would keep them off the streets. Religion has, of course, a complicated, controversial history of public uses and abuses, which are
beyond the scope of this [essay]. But therapy was conceived as a private transaction between doctors and patients (experts and clients) or
between groups of patients, clients, seekers of psychic well-being.
Testimony was public. By blurring the distinction between confession
and testimony, recovery transforms therapy into a public process too.
People even do it on TV.

Most of us do love to talk about ourselves, although I've always 6
regarded it as a slightly illicit pleasure or one you pay for by the hour.
Etiquette books dating back over a century gently admonish readers to
cultivate the art of listening, assuming that, unmannered in their natural
states, most people are braggarts and bores. Success primers have
always stressed that listening skills will help you get ahead: Listen raptly
to someone in power who loves talking about himself in order to impress
him with your perspicacity. Listening is a useful form of flattery, Dale
Carnegie[1] advised, sharing with men what women have always known.
Flirting is a way of listening. (Feminism is women talking.)

For women who were socialized to listen, uncritically, talking too 7
much about themselves may feel like an act of rebellion. Maybe Kitty
Dukakis felt liberated by her book. Personal development passes for politics, and what might once have been called whining is now exalted as a
process of asserting selfhood; self-absorption is regarded as a form of
self-expression, as if creative acts involved no interactions with the
world. Feminists did say that the personal was political, but they meant
that private relations between the sexes reflected public divisions of
power, that putatively private events, like wife beating, were public concerns. They didn't mean that getting to know yourself was sufficient
political action. Consciousness raising was supposed to inspire activism.
Feminism is women talking, but it is not women only talking and not
women talking only about themselves.

Talk shows and the elevation of gossip to intellectual discourse are, 8
after all, postfeminist, postmodern phenomena. In academia, where
gossip is now text, poststructural scholars scour history for the private,
particular experiences of ordinary "unempowered" people; and like
denizens of daytime TV, they also talk a lot about themselves, decon-
structing their own class, racial, or ethnic biases in perverse assertions
of solidarity with what are presumed to be other entirely subjective
selves. On talk shows, ordinary people, subject of tomorrow's scholars,
find their voice. Men and mostly women distinguished only by various
and weird infidelities or histories of drug abuse and overeating get
equal time with movie actors, soap stars, and the occasional hair stylist.
Now everyone can hope for sixty minutes of fame, minus some time for
commercials.

I never really wonder anymore why people want to talk about them- 9
selves for nearly an hour in front of millions of strangers. They find it
"affirming"; like trees that fall in the forest, they're not sure that they exist
when no one's watching. I've accepted that as postmodern human
nature. I do wonder at the eagerness and pride with which they reveal,
on national television, what I can't help thinking of as intimacies—sexual

---

[1] Author of one of the first successful series of self-improvement books. [Eds.]

and digestive disorders; personal conflicts with parents, children, spouses, lovers, bosses, and best friends. I wonder even more at the intensity with which the audience listens.

Why aren't they bored? It may be that listening is simply the price 10 they pay for their turn to grab the mike and have their say, offering criticism or advice, just like the experts. But they seem genuinely intrigued by the essentially unremarkable details of other people's lives and other people's feelings. Something in us likes soap operas, I know, but watching the talks is not like watching "Dallas" or "Days of Our Lives." The guests aren't particularly articulate, except on "Geraldo" sometimes, where they seem to be well coached; they rarely finish their sentences, which trail off in vague colloquialisms, you know what I mean? Most guests aren't witty or perceptive or even telegenic. They aren't artful. They are the people you'd ignore if you saw them on line at the supermarket instead of on TV.

I'm not sure how we got to the point of finding anyone else's con- 11 fessions, obsessions, or advertisements for herself entertaining. I'm not sure why watching other people's home movies became fun; the appeal of "America's Funniest Home Videos" eludes me. But it's clear that the popularity of "real people" television—talk shows and home videos— has little to do with compassion and the desire to connect. If an average person on the subway turns to you, like the ancient mariner, and starts telling you her tale, you turn away or nod and hope she stops, not just because you fear she might be crazy. If she tells her tale on camera, you might listen. Watching strangers on television, even responding to them from a studio audience, we're disengaged—voyeurs collaborating with exhibitionists in rituals of sham community. Never have so many known so much about people for whom they cared so little.

A woman appears on "Oprah Winfrey" to tell the nation that she 12 hates herself for being ugly. Oprah and the expert talk to her about self-esteem and the woman basks, I think, in their attention. The spectacle is painful and pathetic, and watching it, I feel diminished.

Oprah, I suspect, regards her show as a kind of public service. The 13 self-proclaimed ugly woman is appearing on a segment about our obsession with good looks. We live in a society that values pretty people over plain, Oprah explains; and maybe she is exploring a legitimate public issue, by exploiting a private pathology.

Daytime TV, however, is proudly pathological. On "Geraldo" a 14 recovering sex addict shares a story of incest—she was raped by her father and stepfather; her husband and children are seated next to her on the stage. This is family therapy. (The family that reveals together congeals together.) Her daughter talks about being a lesbian. Two sex addiction experts—a man and a woman, "professional and personal partners"—explain and offer commentary on sex and love addictions.

"It's not a matter of frequency," they say in response to questions about how often sex addicts have sex. Anonymous addicts call in with their own tales, boring and lurid: "I do specifically use sex to make myself feel better," one caller confesses. Who doesn't?

Geraldo, his experts, and the members of his audience address the   15 problem of promiscuity with the gravity of network anchors discussing a sub-Saharan famine. If I were a recovering person, I might say that they're addicted to melodrama. In fact, Geraldo does a show on people "addicted to excitement—drama, danger, and self destruction"—people who create crises for themselves. He offers us a self-evaluation tool— eleven questions "to determine whether you're a soap opera queen." Do you get mad at other drivers on the road? Do you talk about your problems with a lot of other people? Questions like these make addicts of us all, as experts must hope. Labeling impatience in traffic a symptom of disease creates a market for the cure; and Joy Davidson, the expert/ author who identifed the "soap opera syndrome" for us is here on "Geraldo," peddling her book.

The audience is intrigued. People stand up to testify to their own   16 experiences with drama and excitement addictions. With the concern of any patient describing her symptoms, one woman says that she often disagrees with her husband for no good reason. Someone else confesses to being a worrier.

No one suggests to Davidson that calling the mundane concerns   17 and frustrations of daily life symptoms of the disease of overdramatizing is, well, overdramatizing. In the language of recovery, we might say that Davidson is an enabler, encouraging her readers to indulge in their melodrama addictions, or we might say that she too is a practicing melodrama addict. One man does point out that there are "people in the ghetto" who don't have to fabricate their crises. But if Davidson gets the point, she successfully eludes it. Yes, she admits, the crises in the ghetto are real, but what matters is the way you deal with them. As Norman Vincent Peale[2] might say, people in crisis have only to develop a happiness habit.

Meanwhile, on daytime TV, middle-class Americans are busy prac-   18 ticing their worry habits, swapping stories of disease and controversial eccentricities. Here is a sampling of "Oprah": Apart from the usual assortment of guests who eat, drink, shop, worry, or have sex too much, there are fathers who sleep with their sons' girlfriends (or try to), sisters who sleep with their sisters' boyfriends, women who sleep with their best friends' sons, women who sleep with their husbands' bosses (to help their husbands get ahead), men who hire only pretty women, and men and women who date only interracially. Estranged couples share

---

[2] Minister, lecturer, and writer (1898–1993), whose best-selling series of books beginning with *The Power of Positive Thinking* (1952) made him one of the first self-help authors. [Eds.]

their grievances while an expert provides on-air counseling: "Why are you so afraid to let your anger out at her?" he asks a husband. "Why don't you let him speak for himself," he chides the wife. Couples glare at each other, sometimes the women cry, and the expert keeps advising them to get in touch with their feelings and build up their self-esteem. The chance to sit in on someone else's therapy session is part of the appeal of daytime TV. When Donahue[3] interviews the children of prostitutes, he has an expert on hand to tell them how they feel.

The number of viewers who are helped by these shows is impossi- 19 ble to know, but it's clear that they're a boon to several industries—publishing, therapy, and, of course, recovery. Commercials often tie in to the shows. A segment on food addiction is sponsored by weight-loss programs: "It's not what you're eating. It's what's eating you," the ads assure anxious overeaters. Shows on drug and alcohol abuse are sponsored by treatment centers, set in sylvan glades. Standing by lakes, leaning on trees, the pitchmen are soft and just a little somber—elegiac; they might be selling funeral plots instead of a recovery lifestyle and enhanced self-esteem.

On almost every show, someone is bound to get around to self- 20 esteem; most forms of misconduct are said to be indicative of low self-esteem. On every other show, someone talks about addiction. The audiences usually speak fluent recovery. You can talk about your inner child or your grief work on "Oprah" and no one will ask you what you mean. "I follow a twelve-step program that helps me deal with the disease concept, the addiction [to overeating]," a man in the audience announces, and people nod. No one asks, "What's a twelve-step program?" or "What do you mean by addiction?" Oprah testifies too: "I'm still addicted [to food]. I'll never be free."

On stage, a panel of recovering food addicts, all women, is vowing 21 never to diet again. "We have to allow ourselves to love ourselves," they say, and Oprah agrees. "I'm never going to weigh another piece of chicken." Tired of "seeking control," these women want to accept their weight, not constantly struggle to lose it, and I wish them luck. Beauty may lack moral value, but it's useful, and what has been labeled beastly—obesity or really bad skin—is a painful liability, as the women on "Oprah" make clear. They've apparently spent much of their lives embarrassed by their bodies; now, in recovery, they talk about the "shame" of fatness. They find some self-esteem in victimhood. They aren't gluttons but "victims of a disease process." Being fat is not their fault. Recovering from obesity "is not about self-control," one woman says, voicing the ethos of recovery that dispenses with will. "It's about self-love."

---

[3] Among the first to host a day-time talk show focusing on the personal problems of "average" people, Donahue was on the air from 1967 to 1996. [Eds.]

But the next day, when Oprah does a show on troubled marriages, 22 some sort of therapist, Dr. Ron, advises a woman who is self-conscious about her small breasts to have implants. He berates her unfaithful husband for not supporting her in this quest for a better body, for her own good, for the sake of her self-esteem, and to help save their marriage: her poor self-image was one of the reasons he strayed. That a woman with small breasts can't be expected to improve her self-esteem without implants is apparently evident to Dr. Ron and everyone else on the show. No one questions his wisdom, not even learning-to-love-herself Oprah, recovering dieter.

I digress, but so do Geraldo, Donahue, and Oprah. Talking about 23 these shows, I find it hard to be entirely coherent, and coherence would not do justice to the kaleidoscope of complaints, opinions, prejudices, revelations, and celebrations they comprise: Geraldo discusses celibacy with a panel of virgins and Helen Gurley Brown. "There are no medical risks associated with virginity," a doctor assures us. Adopted children and their biological parents as well as siblings separated from birth for over twenty years meet, for the first time, on "Geraldo" ("Reunions of the Heart: Finding a Lost Love," the show is called). "Welcome long-lost brother Brian," Geraldo commands, to wild applause, as Brian emerges from backstage, and in a TV minute people are hugging and sobbing on camera as they did years ago on "This Is Your Life." I want someone in the audience to ask them why they're not having their reunions in private, but I already know the answer. "We want to share the love and joy of this moment," they'd say. "We want to inspire other people from broken families not to give up the search." I suspect that the audience knows these answers too. Clapping and crying (even Geraldo is teary), reached for and touched, they offer support and validation: "It's a real blessing to see how you've all been healed of your hurts," one woman in the audience declares. Geraldo makes a plea for open adoption, grappling with an issue, I guess.

Occasionally, I admit, the shows are instructive in ways they intend, 24 not just as portraits of popular culture. Donahue's segment on grandparents who are raising the children of their drug-addicted children manages to be dignified and sad. He talks to obese children without overdramatizing their struggles or exploiting them. (Donahue is good with kids.) Oprah seems likable and shrewd in the midst of her silliest shows, and, once in a while, the testimony illuminates an issue: date rape or racially segregated proms.

This is the new journalism—issues packaged in anecdotes that may 25 or may not be true. As an occasional, alternative approach to news and analysis, it is affecting; as the predominant approach, it is not just trite but stupefying. If all issues are personalized, we lose our capacity to entertain ideas, to generalize from our own or someone else's experiences, to think abstractly. We substitute sentimentality for thought.

TV talk shows certainly didn't invent the new journalism and are   26
hardly the only abusers of it. But they are emblematic of the widespread
preference for feelings over ideas that is celebrated by recovery and
other personal development movements. It is no coincidence that the
two trends—talk shows and recovery—have fueled each other. The
shows often seem like orchestrated support groups; the groups seem
like rehearsals for the shows.

Accusing talk shows of not providing critical analysis of issues is,   27
I know, like accusing "Ozzie and Harriet"[2] of idealizing the nuclear
family. "He wrestles with the obvious," a friend once said of an especially boring pundit, and I don't mean to wrestle with TV. I just wanna
testify too.

Once, I appeared on the "Oprah Winfrey" show. I was one of six   28
alleged experts participating in what was billed as a "debate" on codependency. Joining me onstage were two against-codependency allies
and three for-codependency opponents. (The two sides were driven in
separate limousines and kept in separate rooms before the show.) Oprah
was more or less pro-codependency too—someone said she had just
returned from one of John Bradshaw's retreats—and the audience
seemed filled with evangelical twelve steppers.

"Just jump in. Don't wait to be called on," one of Oprah's people   29
told us when she prepped us for the show. "You mean you want us to
interrupt each other?" I asked; the woman nodded. "You want us to be
really rude and step on each other's lines?" She nodded again. "You
want us to act as if we're at a large, unruly family dinner on Thanksgiving?" She smiled and said, "You got it!"

I had a good time on "Oprah." Being chauffeured around in a limo   30
and housed in a first-class hotel, I felt like Cinderella, especially when I
got home. I liked being on national television, almost as much as my
mother liked watching me. I also like unruly family dinners, but I'd
never call what goes on over the turkey a debate.

The trouble with talk shows is that they claim to do so much more   31
than entertain; they claim to inform and explain. They dominate the
mass marketplace and help make it one that is inimical to ideas.

That's probably not a startling revelation, but appearing on a talk   32
show, you are hit hard with the truth of it. Being on "Oprah" was still a
shock, although not a surprise. I watch a fair amount of talk shows and
understand the importance of speaking in sound bites, although I don't
always succeed in doing so. I know that talk show "debates" are not
usually coherent; they don't usually follow any pattern of statement

---

[2] Quintessential 1950s family comedy. [Eds.]

and response. They don't make sense. The host is less a moderator than a traffic cop. People don't talk to each other; they don't even talk at each other. They talk at the camera. So I wasn't surprised when Oprah's assistant told us to "just jump in." I expected the show to be chaotic (the experience exceeded the expectation). What I did not expect, and should have, was the audience's utter lack of interest in argument; they wanted only to exchange testimony.

I had nothing to say to the studio audience—and talked at the cam- 33 era too—because I had no personal experience with addiction and recovery to convey. The most popular "expert" on our panel was the most melodramatic: Lois, a recovering codependent from Texas, declared repeatedly, in response to nothing in particular, "Mah parents died of this disease!" ("What disease?" we asked, in vain.) "Recovery saved mah life!" Once or twice she added cryptically, "Ah was not supposed to be born! Ah was a mistake!" as the audience applauded.

On daytime talk shows a "debate" generally consists of a parade of 34 people onstage or in the audience stating strong personal preferences with frequent references to some searing personal experience. "Does too!" "Does not!" people say, debating whether the recovery movement helps us. "I'm a recovering person and I just want to say that this movement saved my life," members of the audience on "Oprah" declared. "I would be dead today if it weren't for this movement!"

You can't argue with a testimonial. You can only counter it with a 35 testimonial of your own. ("Does too!" "Does not!") Testimony has no value as argument. You can't even be sure of its value as testimony. Is it true? What do people mean when they say that they are addicted? Addicted to what, at what cost? What do people mean when they say they've been abused? Are they talking about emotional or physical abuse? Was it real or imagined? Were they beaten by their parents or ignored? "What are you all recovering from?" one man in the back row of Oprah's audience asked repeatedly and in vain as self-proclaimed recovering persons testified.

But if you can't evaluate or argue with testimony, you can say that 36 it's beside the point. How one hundred people in a studio audience feel about codependency doesn't tell us very much about its impact on the culture, or even its general success and failure rate with individuals. Testimony often precludes analysis. What was striking to me about the audience on "Oprah" was its collective inability or unwillingness to think about recovery in any terms other than the way it made them feel. To the extent that they commented on it as a cultural phenomenon at all, they simply universalized their own experiences: "It worked for me. So it will work for everyone else."

Testifying, as a substitute for thinking, is contagious. You even 37 find it in the halls of academe. Teaching college freshmen, I quickly discovered that my students were interested only in issues that were dramatized—in fiction, memoirs, or popular journalism. Raised on "Donahue" and docudramas, they found mere discussions of ideas "too dry and academic." You can't even be academic in academia anymore. Instead of theory, they sought testimony.

Among graduate students and professors too, subjectivity has been 38 in fashion for several years. The diversification of student populations and concern for multiculturalism have made respect for subjective experiences and points of view political imperatives. Fashions in literary and legal theory and historical research focus on knowledge as a matter of perspective, disdaining the "pretense" of objectivity. Scholars get to talk about themselves. Theory is nothing but testimony.

I'm not suggesting that the dead white males who once held sway 39 and set standards had The Answer or that a multiplicity of perspectives in matters of politics and theory isn't welcome. Nor am I suggesting that analysis should somehow be divorced from experience. I'm only suggesting the obvious—that analysis and experience need to be balanced. There are degrees of objectivity worth trying to acquire.

It should be needless to say that individual preferences are not 40 always the best measures of what is generally good. A tax provision that saves you money may still be generally unfair. Of course, the recovery movement is not analogous to the tax code. It is not imposed on us. It is not a public policy that demands deliberation and debate. I don't want to gloss over the difference between public acts and private experiments with personality development. Indeed, I want to highlight it.

A self-referential evaluation of a self-help movement is probably 41 inevitable and, to some extent, appropriate. A self-referential evaluation of public policies can be disastrous. What is disturbing about watching the talk shows is recognizing in discussions of private problems a solipsism that carries over into discussions of public issues. What you see on "Oprah" is what you see in the political arena. We choose our elected officials and formulate policies on the basis of how they make us feel about ourselves. (Jimmy Carter's biggest mistake was in depressing us.) We even evaluate wars according to their effect on our self-esteem: Vietnam was a downer. The Persian Gulf War, like a good self-help program, cured us of our "Vietnam syndrome" and "gave us back our pride," as General Motors hopes to do with Chevrolets. Norman Schwarzkopf and Colin Powell satisfied our need for heroes, everyone said. The networks stroked us with video montages of handsome young soldiers, leaning on tanks, staring off into the desert, wanting to "get the job done" and go home. By conservative estimates, 150,000 people were killed outright in the war; the number who will die from disease, deprivation, and environmental damage may be incalculable. Whether or not the war was necessary, whether or not the victory was real, we should consider it a great success because it gave us parades and a proud Fourth of July. The culture of recovery is insidious: now the moral measure of a war is how it makes us feel about ourselves.

"Try and put aside your own experiences in recovery and the way 42 it makes you feel," I suggested to the audience on "Oprah." "Think about what the fascination with addiction means to us as a culture. Think about the political implications of advising people to surrender their will and submit to a higher power." People in the audience looked at me blankly. Later, in the limo, one of my copanelists (against codependency) shook his head at me and smiled and said, "That was a PBS comment."

Some two months later I showed my "Oprah" tape to a group of 43 college friends, over a bottle of wine. None of them is involved in the recovery movement or familiar with its programs or jargon. Listening to six panelists and a studio audience compete for air time, in eight-minute segments between commercials, none of them thought the "Oprah" show made any sense. Like the man in the audience who asked, "What are you all recovering from?" they didn't have a clue. "You have to think with your hearts and not your heads," a for-codependency expert exhorted us at the end of the show, as the credits rolled.

Responding to Reading

1. According to Kaminer, what is the difference between "confessing" and "testifying"? What danger does she see in "blurring the distinction between confession and testimony" (5)?
2. In paragraph 11, Kaminer says, "Never have so many known so much about people for whom they cared so little." Why do you suppose so many people are willing "to talk about themselves for nearly an hour in front of millions of strangers" (9)? Why do you think so many viewers of talk shows find them so compelling?
3. "The trouble with talk shows," Kaminer says, "is that they claim to do so much more than entertain; they claim to inform and explain" (31). In paragraph 24 she concedes that talk shows can sometimes be "'instructive'; for the most part, though, she is highly critical of these programs, saying, among other things, that they encourage viewers to "substitute sentimentality for thought" (25). Do you think Kaminer is being too hard on talk shows? Do you think she is taking them too seriously? Explain.

FOCUS: DOES MEDIA VIOLENCE HURT?

UNNATURAL KILLERS

John Grisham

*Best-selling novelist John Grisham (1955–   ) was born in Jonesboro, Arkansas, and graduated from Mississippi State University. After earning his law degree from the University of Mississippi in 1981, he worked as an attorney until 1990, also serving three terms in the Mississippi state legislature. Although his first novel (*A Time to Kill*)—written while he was still practicing law—was not an immediate success, with* The Firm *(1991) Grisham began a string of blockbusters that so far remains unbroken:* The Pelican Brief *(1992),* The Client *(1993),* The Chamber *(1994),* The Rainmaker *(1995),* The Runaway Jury *(1996),* The Partner *(1997), and* The Street Lawyer *(1998). While most of his books have also been turned into highly successful films, Grisham's relationship with Hollywood is not without strain. Following the senseless murder of a Mississippi friend by a teenage couple apparently influenced by the film* Natural Born Killers, *Grisham filed a highly publicized lawsuit against the director, Oliver Stone, and the studio that released the film, seeking damages for wrongful death. In the following essay written in 1996 for the* Oxford American, *Grisham describes the couple's killing spree and argues that lawsuits such as his are the only way to bring Hollywood violence under control.*

The town of Hernando, Mississippi has five thousand people, more 1 or less, and is the seat of government for DeSoto County. It is peaceful and quiet, with an old courthouse in the center of the square. Memphis is only fifteen minutes away, to the north, straight up Interstate 55. To the west is Tunica County, now booming with casino fever and drawing thousands of tourists.

For ten years I was a lawyer in Southaven, a suburb to the north, 2 and the Hernando courthouse was my hangout. I tried many cases in the main courtroom. I drank coffee with the courthouse regulars, ate in the small cafes around the square, visited my clients in the nearby jail.

It was in the courthouse that I first met Mr. Bill Savage. I didn't 3 know much about him back then, just that he was soft-spoken, exceedingly polite, always ready with a smile and a warm greeting. In 1983, when I first announced my intentions to seek an office in the state legislature, Mr. Savage stopped me in the second-floor rotunda of the courthouse and offered me his encouragement and good wishes.

A few months later, on election night as the votes were tallied and 4 the results announced to a rowdy throng camped on the courthouse lawn, it became apparent that I would win my race. Mr. Savage found me and expressed his congratulations. "The people have trusted you," he said. "Don't let them down."

He was active in local affairs, a devout Christian and solid citizen 5 who believed in public service and was always ready to volunteer. For thirty years, he worked as the manager of a cotton gin two miles outside Hernando on a highway that is heavily used by gamblers anxious to get to the casinos in Tunica.

Around five p.m., on March 7, 1995, someone entered Bill Savage's 6 office next to the gin, shot him twice in the head at point-blank range, and took his wallet, which contained a few credit cards and two hundred dollars.

There were no witnesses. No one heard gunshots. His body was 7 discovered later by an insurance salesman making a routine call.

The crime scene yielded few clues. There were no signs of a strug- 8 gle. Other than the bullets found in the body, there was little physical evidence. And since Bill Savage was not the kind of person to create ill will or maintain enemies, investigators had nowhere to start. They formed the opinion that he was murdered by outsiders who'd stopped by for a fast score, then hit the road again, probably toward the casinos.

It had to be a simple robbery. Why else would anybody want to 9 murder Bill Savage?

The townspeople of Hernando were stunned. Life in the shadows 10 of Memphis had numbed many of them to the idea of random violence, but here was one of their own, a man known to all, a man who, as he went about his daily affairs, minding his own business, was killed in his office just two miles from the courthouse.

The next day, in Ponchatoula, Louisiana, three hundred miles south, 11 and again just off Interstate 55, Patsy Byers was working the late shift at a convenience store. She was thirty-five years old, a happily married mother of three, including an eighteen-year-old who was about to graduate from high school. Patsy had never worked outside the home, but had taken the job to earn a few extra dollars to help with the bills.

Around midnight, a young woman entered the convenience store 12 and walked to a rack where she grabbed three chocolate bars. As she approached the checkout counter, Patsy Byers noticed the candy, but she didn't notice the .38. The young woman thrust it forward, pulled the trigger, and shot Patsy in the throat.

The bullet instantly severed Patsy's spinal cord, and she fell to the 13 floor bleeding. The young woman screamed and fled the store, leaving Patsy paralyzed under the cash register.

The girl returned. She'd forgotten the part about the robbery. When 14 she saw Patsy she said, "Oh, you're not dead yet." Patsy began to plead, "Don't kill me," she kept saying to the girl who stepped over her and tried in vain to open the cash register. She asked Patsy how to open it.

Patsy explained it as best she could. The girl fled with $105 in cash, 15 leaving Patsy, once again, to die.

But Patsy did not die, though she will be a quadriplegic for the rest 16 of her life.

The shooting and robbery was captured on the store's surveillance 17 camera, and the video was soon broadcast on the local news. Several full facial shots of the girl were shown.

The girl, however, vanished. Weeks, and then months, passed with- 18 out the slightest hint to her identity making itself known.

Authorities in Louisiana had no knowledge of the murder of Bill 19 Savage, and authorities in Mississippi had no knowledge of the shoot- ing of Patsy Byers, and neither state had reason to suspect the two shootings were committed by the same people.

The crimes, it was clear, were not committed by sophisticated crim- 20 inals. Soon two youths began bragging about their exploits. And then an anonymous informant whispered to officials in Louisiana that a cer- tain young woman in Oklahoma was involved in the shooting of Patsy Byers.

The young woman was Sarah Edmondson, age nineteen, the 21 daughter of a state court judge in Muskogee, Oklahoma. Her uncle is the Attorney General of Oklahoma. Her grandfather once served as Congressman, and her great uncle was Governor and then later a U.S. Senator. Sarah Edmondson was arrested on June 2, 1995, at her parents' home, and suddenly the pieces fell into place.

Sarah and her boyfriend, Benjamin Darras, age eighteen, had 22 drifted south in early March. The reason for the journey has not been made clear. One version has them headed for Florida so that Ben could finally see the ocean. Another has them aiming at New Orleans and Mardi Gras. And a third is that they wanted to see the Grateful Dead concert in Memphis, but, not surprisingly, got the dates mixed-up.

At any rate, they stumbled through Hernando on March 7, and 23 stayed just long enough, Sarah says, to kill and rob Bill Savage. Then they raced deeper south until they ran out of money. They decided to pull another heist. This is when Patsy Byers met them.

Though Sarah and Ben have different socioeconomic backgrounds, 24 they made a suitable match. Sarah, a member of one of Oklahoma's most prominent political families, began using drugs and alcohol at the age of thirteen. At fourteen she was locked up for psychiatric treatment. She has admitted to a history of serious drug abuse. She managed to finish high school, with honors, but then dropped out of college.

Ben's family is far less prominent. His father was an alcoholic who 25 divorced Ben's mother twice, then later committed suicide. Ben too has a history of drug abuse and psychiatric treatment. He dropped out of high school. Somewhere along the way he met Sarah, and for awhile they lived the great American romance—the young, troubled, mindless drifters surviving on love.

Once they were arrested, lawyers got involved, and the love affair 26 came to a rapid end. Sarah blames Ben for the killing of Bill Savage. Ben blames Sarah for the shooting of Patsy Byers. Sarah has better lawyers, and it appears she will also attempt to blame Ben for somehow controlling her in such a manner that she had no choice but to rob the store and shoot Patsy Byers. Ben, evidently, will have none of this. It looks as if he will claim his beloved Sarah went into the store only to rob it, that he had no idea whatsoever that she planned to shoot anyone, that, as he waited outside in the getaway car, he was horrified when he heard a gunshot. And so on.

It should be noted here that neither Ben nor Sarah have yet been 27 tried for any of these crimes. They have not been found guilty of anything, yet. But as the judicial wheels begin to turn, deals are being negotiated and cut. Pacts are being made.

Sarah's lawyers managed to reach an immunity agreement with 28 the State of Mississippi in the Savage case. Evidently, she will testify against Ben, and in return will not be prosecuted. Her troubles will be confined to Louisiana, and if convicted for the attempted murder of Patsy Byers and the robbing of the store, Sarah could face life in prison. If Ben is found guilty of murdering and robbing Bill Savage, he will most likely face death by lethal injection at the state penitentiary in Parchman, Mississippi. Juries in Hernando are notorious for quick death verdicts.

On January 24, 1996, during a preliminary hearing in Louisiana, 29 Sarah testified, under oath, about the events leading up to both crimes. It is from this reported testimony that the public first heard the appalling details of both crimes.

According to Sarah, she and Ben decided to travel to Memphis to 30 see the Grateful Dead. They packed canned food and blankets, and left the morning of March 6. Sarah also packed her father's .38, just in case Ben happened to attack her for some reason. Shortly before leaving Oklahoma, they watched the Oliver Stone movie *Natural Born Killers*.

For those fortunate enough to have missed *Natural Born Killers*, it is 31 a repulsive story of two mindless young lovers, Mickey (Woody Harrelson) and Mallory (Juliette Lewis), who blaze their way across the

Southwest, killing everything in their path while becoming famous. According to the script, they indiscriminately kill fifty-two people before they are caught. It seems like many more. Then they manage to kill at least fifty more as they escape from prison. They free themselves, have children, and are last seen happily rambling down the highway in a Winnebago.

Ben loved *Natural Born Killers,* and as they drove to Memphis he spoke openly of killing people, randomly, just like Mickey spoke to Mallory. He mentioned the idea of seizing upon a remote farmhouse, murdering all its occupants, then moving on to the next slaughter. Just like Mickey and Mallory.   32

We do not know, as of yet, what role Sarah played in these discussions. It is, of course, her testimony we're forced to rely upon, and she claims to have been opposed to Ben's hallucinations.   33

They left Memphis after learning the concert was still a few days away, and headed south. Between Memphis and Hernando, Ben again talked of finding an isolated farmhouse and killing a bunch of people. Sarah said it sounded like he was fantasizing from the movie. They left Interstate 55, drove through Hernando and onto the highway leading to the cotton gin where Bill Savage was working in his office.   34

Ben was quite anxious to kill someone, she says.   35

He professed a sudden hatred for farmers. This was the place where they would kill, he said, and told Sarah to stop the car a short distance away so he could test-fire the gun. It worked. They then drove to the gin, parked next to Bill Savage's small office. Ben told her to act "angelic," and then they went inside.   36

Ben asked Bill Savage for directions to Interstate 55. Sarah says that Mr. Savage knew they were up to something. As he gave directions, he walked around the desk toward Ben, at which point Ben removed the .38 and shot Mr. Savage in the head. "He threw up his hands and made a horrible sound," she testified. There was a brief struggle between the two men, a struggle that ended when Ben shot Mr. Savage for the second time.   37

Sarah claims to have been so shocked by Ben's actions that she started to run outside, then, after a quick second thought, decided to stand by her man. Together they rummaged through Mr. Savage's pockets and took his wallet.   38

Back in the car, Ben removed the credit cards from the wallet, threw the driver's license out the window, and found two one-hundred-dollar bills. According to Sarah, "Ben mocked the noise the man made when Ben shot him. Ben was laughing about what happened and said the feeling of killing was powerful."   39

You see, the Mickey character in *Natural Born Killers* felt much the same way. He sneered and laughed a lot when he killed people, and then he sneered and laughed some more after he killed them. He felt   40 powerful. Murder for Mickey was the ultimate thrill. It was glorious. Murder was a mystical experience, nothing to be ashamed of and certainly nothing to be remorseful about. In fact, remorse was a sign of weakness. Mickey was, after all, a self-described "natural born killer." And Mickey encouraged Mallory to kill.

Ben encouraged Sarah. [41]

After the murder of Mr. Savage, he and Sarah drove to New Orleans, [42] where they roamed the streets of the French Quarter. Ben repeatedly assured Sarah that he felt no aftershocks from committing the murder. He felt fine. Just like Mickey. He pressed her repeatedly to kill someone herself. "It's your turn," he kept saying. And, "We're partners."

Sarah, as might be expected, claims she was completely repulsed by [43] Ben's demands that she slay the next person. She claims that she considered killing herself as an alternative to surrendering to Ben's demands that she shed blood.

But Sarah did not kill herself. Instead, she and Ben drove to [44] Ponchatoula for their ill-fated meeting with Patsy Byers.

According to Sarah, she did not want to rob the store, and she certainly didn't wish to shoot anyone. But they were out of money, and, [45] just like Mickey and Mallory, robbery was the most convenient way to survive. Ben selected the store, and, through some yet-to-be-determined variety of coercion, forced her out of the car and into the store, with the gun. It was, after all, her turn to kill.

In *Natural Born Killers*, we are expected to believe that Mickey and [46] Mallory are tormented by demons, and that they are forced to commit many of their heinous murders, not because they are brainless young idiots, but because evil forces propel them. They both suffered through horrible, dysfunctional childhoods, their parents were abusive, etc. Demons have them in their clutches, and haunt them, and stalk them, and make them slaughter fifty-two people.

This demonic theme, so as not to be missed by even the simplest [47] viewer, recurs, it seems, every five minutes in the movie.

Guess what Sarah Edmondson saw when she approached the [48] checkout stand and looked at Patsy Byers? She didn't see a thirty-five-year-old woman next to the cash register. No.

She saw a "demon." And so she shot it. [49]

Then she ran from the store. Ben, waiting in the car, asked where the [50] money was. Sarah said she forgot to take the money. Ben insisted she return to the store and rob the cash register.

We can trust the judicial systems of both Mississippi and Louisiana [51] to effectively deal with the aftermath of the Sarah and Ben romance. Absent a fluke, Sarah will spend the rest of her life behind bars in a miserable prison and Ben will be sent to death row at Parchman, where he'll endure an indescribable hell before facing execution. Their families will never be the same. And their families deserve compassion.

The wife and children and countless friends of Bill Savage have 52 already begun the healing process, though the loss is beyond measure.

Patsy Byers is a quadriplegic for life, confined to a wheelchair, faced 53 with enormous medical bills, unable to hug her children or do any one of a million things she did before she met Sarah Edmondson. She's already filed a civil suit against the Edmondson family, but her prospects of a meaningful physical recovery are dim.

A question remains: Are there other players in this tragic episode? 54 Can fault be shared?

I think so. 55

Troubled as they were, Ben and Sarah had no history of violence. 56 Their crime spree was totally out of character. They were confused, disturbed, shiftless, mindless—the adjectives can be heaped on with shovels—but they had never hurt anyone before.

Before, that is, they saw a movie. A horrific movie that glamorized 57 casual mayhem and bloodlust. A movie made with the intent of glorifying random murder.

Oliver Stone has said that *Natural Born Killers* was meant to be a 58 satire on our culture's appetite for violence and the media's craving for it. But Oliver Stone always takes the high ground in defending his dreadful movies. A satire is supposed to make fun of whatever it is attacking. But there is no humor in *Natural Born Killers*. It is a relentlessly bloody story designed to shock us and to further numb us to the senselessness of reckless murder. The film wasn't made with the intent of stimulating morally depraved young people to commit similar crimes, but such a result can hardly be a surprise.

Oliver Stone is saying that murder is cool and fun, murder is a high, 59 a rush, murder is a drug to be used at will. The more you kill, the cooler you are. You can be famous and become a media darling with your face on magazine covers. You can get by with it. You will not be punished.

It is inconceivable to expect either Stone or the studio executives to 60 take responsibility for the aftereffects of their movie. Hollywood has never done so; instead, it hides behind its standard pious First Amendment arguments, and it pontificates about the necessities of artistic freedom of expression. Its apologists can go on, ad nauseam, about how meaningful even the most pathetic film is to social reform.

It's no surprise that *Natural Born Killers* has inspired several young 61 people to commit murder. Sadly, Ben and Sarah aren't the only kids now locked away and charged with murder in copycat crimes. Since the release of the movie, at least several cases have been reported in which random killings were executed by troubled young people who claim they were all under the influence, to some degree, of Mickey and Mallory.

Any word from Oliver Stone?   62
Of course not.   63
I'm sure he would disclaim all responsibility. And he'd preach a bit 64
about how important the film is as a commentary on the media's insa-
tiable appetite for violence. If pressed, he'd probably say that there are
a lot of crazies out there, and he can't be held responsible for what they
might do. He's an *artist* and he can't be bothered with the effects of what
he produces.

I can think of only two ways to curb the excessive violence of a film 65
like *Natural Born Killers*. Both involve large sums of money—the only
medium understood by Hollywood.
The first way would be a general boycott of similar films. If people 66
refused to purchase tickets to watch such an orgy of violence as *Natural
Born Killers*, then similar movies wouldn't be made. Hollywood is pious,
but only to a point. It will defend its crassest movies on the grounds that
they are necessary for social introspection, or that they need to test the
limits of artistic expression, or that they can ignore the bounds of
decency as long as these movies label themselves as satire. This all works
fine if the box office is busy. But let the red ink flow and Hollywood suddenly has a keen interest in rediscovering what's mainstream.
Unfortunately, boycotts don't seem to work. The viewing public is 67
a large, eclectic body, and there are usually enough curious filmgoers to
sustain a controversial work.
So, forget boycotts.   68
The second and last hope of imposing some sense of responsibility on 69
Hollywood, will come through another great American tradition, the
lawsuit. Think of a movie as a product, something created and brought to
market, not too dissimilar from breast implants, Honda three-wheelers,
and Ford Pintos. Though the law has yet to declare movies to be products, it is only one small step away. If something goes wrong with the
product, whether by design or defect, and injury ensues, then its makers are held responsible.
A case can be made that there exists a direct causal link between the 70
movie *Natural Born Killers* and the death of Bill Savage. Viewed another
way, the question should be: Would Ben have shot innocent people *but
for* the movie? Nothing in his troubled past indicates violent propensi-
ties. But once he saw the movie, he fantasized about killing, and his fantasies finally drove them to their crimes.
The notion of holding filmmakers and studios legally responsible 71
for their products has always been met with guffaws from the industry.
But the laughing will soon stop. It will take only one large verdict 72
against the likes of Oliver Stone, and his production company, and perhaps the screenwriter, and the studio itself, and then the party will be
over. The verdict will come from the heartland, far away from Southern

California, in some small courtroom with no cameras. A jury will finally say enough is enough; that the demons placed in Sarah Edmondson's mind were not solely of her making.

Once a precedent is set, the litigation will become contagious, and 73 the money will become enormous. Hollywood will suddenly discover a desire to rein itself in.

The landscape of American jurisprudence is littered with the 74 remains of large, powerful corporations which once thought themselves bulletproof and immune from responsibility for their actions. Sadly, Hollywood will have to be forced to shed some of its own blood before it learns to police itself.

Even sadder, the families of Bill Savage and Patsy Byers can only 75 mourn and try to pick up the pieces, and wonder why such a wretched film was allowed to be made.

Responding to Reading

1. Grisham opens his essay by providing background, including an explanation of his relationship to murder victim Bill Savage. Is this background information necessary? In what way does it help Grisham make his point?
2. Is this essay an attack on one film, *Natural Born Killers,* and its director, Oliver Stone? A critique of Hollywood's values? A call to action designed to encourage readers to hold studios legally responsible for their films? What do you see as Grisham's primary purpose in writing this essay?
3. In paragraph 70, Grisham says, "A case can be made that there exists a direct causal link between the movie *Natural Born Killers* and the death of Bill Savage." Do you agree? Does Grisham make such a case? Explain your conclusions.

WHY BLAME TV?

John Leonard

John Leonard (1939–   ) was born in Washington, D.C., and attended Harvard University and the University of California at Berkeley. A long-time staff writer for the New York Times *and now a cultural critic for a number of different periodicals—as well as television critic for* New York *magazine—he has published a number of books, beginning with* The Naked Martini *in 1964. His most recent are* The Last Innocent White Man in America *(1993) and* Smoke and Mirrors: Violence, Television, and Other American Cultures *(1996). "Why Blame TV?" which originally appeared in 1993 in the liberal periodical the* Nation, *is Leonard's response to legislation proposed by Congress that year that would have severely limited the amount of violence broadcast by television networks, particularly during children's viewing hours. Leonard takes the position that television has little if any negative effect on its audience and that, in fact, television offers a surprising amount of beneficial programming.*

Like a warrior-king of Sumer, daubed with sesame oil, gorged on 1 goat, hefting up his sword and drum, Senator Ernest Hollings looked down November 23 from a ziggurat to intone, all over the op-ed page of the *New York Times:* "If the TV and cable industries have no sense of shame, we must take it upon ourselves to stop licensing their violence-saturated programming."

Hollings, of course, is co-sponsor in the Senate, with Daniel 2 Inouye, of a ban on any act of violence on television before, say, midnight. Never mind whether this is constitutional, or what it would do to the local news. Never mind, either, that in Los Angeles last August, in the International Ballroom of the Beverly Hilton, in front of 600 industry executives, the talking heads—a professor here, a producer there, a child psychologist and a network veep for program standards—couldn't even agree on a definition of violence. (Is it only violent if it hurts or kills?) And they disagreed on which was worse, a "happy" violence that sugarcoats aggressive behavior or a "graphic" violence that at least suggests consequences. (How, anyway, does television manage somehow simultaneously to *desensitize* and to *incite?*) Nor were they really sure what goes on in the dreamy heads of our children as they crouch in the dark to commune with the tube while their parents, if they have any, aren't around. (*Road Runner?* Beep-beep.) Nor does the infamous scarlet V "parent advisory" warning even apply to cartoons, afternoon soaps, or Somalias.

Never mind, because everybody agrees that watching television 3 causes anti-social behavior, especially among the children of the poor; that there seems to be more violent programming on the air now than there ever was before; that *Beavis and Butt-head* inspired an Ohio 5-year-old to burn down the family trailer; that in the blue druidic light of television we will have spawned generations of toadstools and triffids.

In fact, there is less violence on network television than there used 4 to be; because of ratings, it's mostly sitcoms. The worst stuff is the Hollywood splatterflicks; they're found on premium cable, which means the poor are less likely to be watching. Everywhere else on cable, not counting the court channel or home shopping and not even to think about blood sports and Pat Buchanan, the fare is innocent to the point of stupefaction (Disney, Discovery, Family, Nickelodeon). That Ohio trailer wasn't even wired for cable, so the littlest firebird must have got his MTV elsewhere in the dangerous neighborhood. (And kids have been playing with matches since, at least, Prometheus. I recall burning down my very own bedroom when I was 5 years old. The fire department had to tell my mother that the evidence pointed to me.) Since the '60s, according to statistics cited by Douglas Davis in *The Five Myths of*

Television Power, more Americans than ever before are going out to eat in restaurants, see films, plays, and baseball games, visit museums, travel abroad, jog, even *read.* Watching television, everybody does *something else* at the same time. While our children are playing with their Adobe Illustrators and Domark Virtual Reality Toolkits, the rest of us eat, knit, smoke, dream, read magazines, sign checks, feel sorry for ourselves, think about Hillary, and plot shrewd career moves or revenge.

Actually watching television, unless it's C-Span, is usually more 5 interesting than the proceedings of Congress. Or what we read in hysterical books like Jerry Mander's *Four Arguments for the Elimination of Television,* or George Gilder's *Life After Television,* or Marie Winn's *The Plug-In Drug,* or Neil Postman's *Amusing Ourselves to Death,* or Bill McKibben's *The Age of Missing Information.*[1] Or what we'll hear at panel discussions on censorship, where right-wingers worry about sex and left-wingers worry about violence. Or just lolling around an academic deepthink-tank, trading mantras like "violence profiles" (George Gerbner), "processed culture" (Richard Hoggart), "narcoleptic joys" (Michael Sorkin), and "glass teat" (Harlan Ellison).

Of *course* something happens to us when we watch television; net- 6 works couldn't sell their millions of pairs of eyes to advertising agencies, nor would ad agencies buy more than $21 billion worth of commercial time each year, if speech (and sound, and motion) didn't somehow modify action. But what happens is far from clear and won't be much clarified by lab studies, however longitudinal, of habits and behaviors isolated from the larger feedback loop of a culture full of gaudy contradictions. The only country in the world that watches more television than we do is Japan, and you should see its snuff movies and pornographic comic books; but the Japanese are pikers compared with us when we compute per capita rates of rape and murder. Some critics in India tried to blame the recent rise in communal violence there on a state-run television series dramatizing the *Mahabharata,*[2] but not long ago they were blaming Salman Rushdie,[3] as in Bangladesh they have decided to blame the writer Taslima Nasrin. No Turk I know of attributes skinhead violence to German TV.[4] It's foolish to pretend that all behavior is mimetic, and that our only model is Spock or Brokaw. Or Mork and Mindy. Why, after so many years of *M*A*S*H,* weekly in prime time and nightly in reruns, aren't all of us out there hugging trees and morphing dolphins? Why, with so many sitcoms, aren't all of us comedians?

---

[1] Books critical of the effects of television. See p. 262 for an excerpt from *The Plug-In Drug.* [Eds.]

[2] Epic Sanskrit poem describing the exploits of ancient kings and heroes. [Eds.]

[3] Indian-born novelist long in hiding because of a death sentence imposed by Islamic extremists, who deemed his novel *The Satanic Verses* sacrilegious. [Eds.]

[4] Turkish-born immigrants in Germany have been victims of violent attacks by neo-Nazi groups. [Eds.]

But nobody normal watches television the way congressmen, acad-   7
emics, symposiasts, and Bill McKibbens do. We are less thrilling. For
instance:

On March 3, 1993, a Wednesday, midway through the nine-week   8
run of *Homicide* on NBC, in an episode written by Tom Fontana and
directed by Martin Campbell, Baltimore detectives Bayliss (Kyle Secor)
and Pembleton (Andre Braugher) had 12 hours to wring a confession
out of "Arab" Tucker (Moses Gunn) for the strangulation and disem-
boweling of an 11-year-old girl. In the dirty light and appalling intimacy
of a single claustrophobic room, with a whoosh of wind sound like
some dread blowing in from empty Gobi spaces, among maps, library
books, diaries, junk food, pornographic crime-scene photographs, and a
single black overflowing ashtray, these three men seemed as nervous as
the hand-held cameras—as if their black coffee were full of jumping
beans, amphetamines, and spiders; as if God himself were jerking them
around.

Well, you may think the culture doesn't really need another cop   9
show. And, personally, I'd prefer a weekly series in which social problems are solved through creative nonviolence, after a Quaker meeting,
by a collective of vegetarian carpenters. But in a single hour, for which
Tom Fontana eventually won an Emmy, I learned more about the behavior of fearful men in small rooms than from any number of better-known
movies, plays, and novels on the topic by the likes of Don DeLillo, Mary
McCarthy, Alberto Moravia, Heinrich Böll, and Doris Lessing.[5]

This, of course, was an accident, as it usually is when those of us   10
who watch television like normal people are startled in our expectations. We leave home expecting, for a lot of money, to be exalted, and
almost never are. But staying put, slumped in an agnosticism about
sentience itself, suspecting that our cable box is just another bad-faith
credit card enabling us to multiply our opportunities for disappointment, we are ambushed in our lethargy. And not so much by "event"
television, like Ingmar Bergman's *Scenes from a Marriage,* originally a
six-hour miniseries for Swedish television; or Marcel Ophuls' *The
Sorrow and the Pity,* originally conceived for French television; or Rainer
Werner Fassbinder's *Berlin Alexanderplatz,* commissioned by German
television; or *The Singing Detective;* or *The Jewel in the Crown.*[6] On the
contrary, we've stayed home on certain nights to watch television,
the way on other nights we'll go out to a neighborhood restaurant, as
if on Mondays we ordered in for laughs, as on Fridays we'd rather eat
Italian. We go to television—message center, mission control, Big
Neighbor, electronic Elmer's glue-all—to look at Oscars, Super Bowls,

---

[5] Highly regarded modern writers. [Eds.]
[6] The first three of these are films by important European directors; the last two are popular and
critically acclaimed British miniseries aired on PBS. [Eds.]

moon shots, Watergates, Pearlygates, ayatollahs, dead Kings, dead Kennedys; and also, perhaps, to experience some "virtual" community as a nation. But we also go because we are hungry, angry, lonely, or tired, and television is always there for us, a 24-hour user-friendly magic box grinding out narrative, novelty, and distraction, news and laughs, snippets of high culture, remedial seriousness and vulgar celebrity, an incitement and a sedative, a place to celebrate and a place to mourn, a circus and a wishing well.

And suddenly Napoleon shows up, like a popsicle, on *Northern* 11 *Exposure*, while Chris on the radio is reading Proust. Or Roseanne is about lesbianism instead of bowling. Or *Picket Fences* has moved on, from serial bathers and elephant abuse to euthanasia and gay-bashing.

Kurt Vonnegut on Showtime! David ("Masturbation") Mamet on 12 TNT! Norman Mailer wrote the TV screenplay for *The Executioner's Song*, and Gore Vidal gave us *Lincoln* with Mary Tyler Moore as Mary Todd. In just the past five years, if I hadn't been watching television, I'd have missed *Tanner '88*, when Robert Altman and Garry Trudeau ran Michael Murphy for president of the United States; *My Name Is Bill W.*, with James Woods as the founding father of Alcoholics Anonymous; *The Final Days*, with Theodore Bikel as Henry Kissinger; *No Place Like Home*, where there wasn't one for Christine Lahti and Jeff Daniels, as there hadn't been for Jane Fonda in *The Dollmaker* and Mare Winningham in *God Bless the Child*; *Eyes on the Prize*, a home movie in two parts about America's second civil war; *The Last Best Year*, with Mary Tyler Moore and Bernadette Peters learning to live with their gay sons and HIV; *Separate but Equal*, with Sidney Poitier as Thurgood Marshall; and *High Crimes and Misdemeanors*, the Bill Moyers special on Irangate and the scandal of our intelligence agencies; Graham Greene, John Updike, Philip Roth, Gloria Naylor, Arthur Miller, and George Eliot, plus Paul Simon and Stephen Sondheim. Not to mention—guiltiest of all our secrets—those hoots without which any popular culture would be as tedious as a John Cage or an Anaïs Nin, like Elizabeth Taylor in *Sweet Bird of Youth* and the Redgrave sisters in a remake of *Whatever Happened to Baby Jane?*

What all this television has in common is narrative. Even network 13 news—which used to be better than most newspapers before the bean counters started closing down overseas bureaus and the red camera lights went out all over Europe and Asia and Africa—is in the story-telling business. And so far no one in Congress has suggested banning narrative.

Because I watch all those despised network TV movies, I know 14 more about racism, ecology, homelessness, gun control, child abuse, gender confusion, date rape, and AIDS than is dreamt of by, say, Katie Roiphe, the Joyce Maynard of Generation X, or than Hollywood has ever bothered to tell me, especially about AIDS. Imagine, Jonathan

Demme's *Philadelphia* opened in theaters around the country well after at least a dozen TV movies on AIDS that I can remember without troubling my hard disk. And I've learned something else, too:

We were a violent culture before television, from Wounded Knee to   15 the lynching bee, and we'll be one after all our children have disappeared by video game into the pixels of cyberspace. Before television, we blamed public schools for what went wrong with the Little People back when classrooms weren't overcrowded in buildings that weren't falling down in neighborhoods that didn't resemble Beirut, and whose fault is that? *The A-Team?* We can't control guns, or drugs, and each year two million American women are assaulted by their male partners, who are usually in an alcoholic rage, and whose fault is that? *Miami Vice?* The gangs that menace our streets aren't home watching Cinemax, and neither are the sociopaths who make bonfires, in our parks, from our homeless, of whom there are at least a million, a supply-side migratory tide of the deindustrialized and dispossessed, of angry beggars, refugee children, and catatonic nomads, none of them traumatized by *Twin Peaks.* So cut Medicare, kick around the Brady Bill, and animadvert Amy Fisher movies. But children who are loved and protected long enough to grow up to have homes and respect and lucky enough to have jobs don't riot in the streets. Ours is a tantrum culture that measures everyone by his or her ability to produce wealth, and morally condemns anybody who fails to prosper, and now blames Burbank for its angry incoherence. Why not recessive genes, angry gods, lousy weather? The mafia, the zodiac, the *Protocols of the Elders of Zion?* Probability theory, demonic possession, Original Sin? George Steinbrenner? Sunspots?

Responding to Reading

1. Leonard claims that "there is less violence on network television than there used to be" and that, other than on premium cable, "the fare is innocent to the point of stupefaction" (4). Do your observations support or challenge his conclusions?

2. Leonard says, "We were a violent culture before television, from Wounded Knee to the lynching bee" (15). Does this fact justify the inclusion of so much violence on TV? Could you argue that the acts of group violence Leonard mentions are different from the many individual acts of violence we see today? Do you believe television is in any way responsible for *individual* acts of violence? Explain.

3. In defending television, Leonard says that "children who are loved and protected long enough to grow up to have homes and respect and lucky enough to have jobs don't riot in the streets" (15). What point is he making? Is his argument a logical one? How would John Grisham (p. 343) reply to Leonard?

MEDIA AND THE ADOLESCENT

Madeline Levine

Child psychologist Madeline Levine (1947–   ) has taught graduate courses at the University of California Medical Center in San Francisco and serves as a consultant to a number of schools in the Bay Area. A private practitioner who has focused on parenting issues since 1980, Levine is also a frequent lecturer on media violence and childhood and adolescent development. In the following section from her book Viewing Violence: How Media Violence Affects Your Child's and Adolescent's Development *(1996), Levine argues that while "no one movie or television program, no matter how violent, is likely to be damaging to reasonably healthy adolescents," the fact that "violence is the rule rather than the exception" in many popular movies and on television does have a negative effect—especially on adolescent boys, who can come to see "intimidation and abuse of power as ways to navigate the world."*

"I wouldn't mind thinking I was somebody."
—Mike in *Breaking Away*

This simple statement, spoken by an adolescent who feels his future 1 options are limited, illustrates the longing and hopefulness of all teenagers. If, at the end of adolescence, teenagers feel like they are "somebody," then the developmental tasks of adolescence have been successfully resolved. These young people will carry into adulthood an enduring sense of self. Those adolescents who enter adulthood feeling like "nobody," however, are at risk for leading lives that are nonproductive, unsatisfying, and frequently antisocial.

While this is not [an essay] about the sociology of adolescence, it is 2 impossible to write about teenagers while ignoring the crisis that American youth are experiencing. The role of media and their effects on adolescents can be understood only if we realize that our teenagers are confronting unprecedented social problems. While the reasons for these problems are complex and not likely to be easily solved, the media's contribution to the problems of teenage violence, pregnancy, drug and alcohol abuse, and hopelessness are well documented and substantial.

It would be preposterous to claim that all these social ills are 3 caused by the media. But to ignore the role of the media in contributing to these dreadful statistics is to ignore one of the most potent influences in the lives of teenagers. Children who watch *Sesame Street* can increase their cognitive skills; those who watch *Mister Rogers* have been shown to exhibit more compassionate behavior. Adults have learned to buckle up, quit smoking, and begin exercising, largely from massive public health campaigns presented through the media. Advertisers spend millions of dollars each year to "educate" us about the virtues of their various soaps, detergents, and deodorants, knowing that a successful ad campaign can change the way we think and what we buy. So certainly adolescents, with their thirst for information and taste for experimentation, are also likely to learn from the media. Don Roberts, chair of the Department of Communication at Stanford University, aptly summarized the hard reality of media influence on adolescents: "The issue is not whether mass media affect adolescent perceptions, beliefs, behaviors. Rather, it is one of society's judging how many adolescents need to be put at risk, in what way, before various corrective actions are viewed as necessary and justified."

Adolescents turn to the media for many different reasons. They are   4
plagued by concerns about identity, are actively seeking information about the adult world they will soon enter, and need significant amounts of time to "do nothing" in order to work on their internal preoccupations. The media provide relief, information, and distraction. Are the media honestly meeting these needs or are they in large measure exploiting a vulnerable market?

The media have glamorized the portrayal of guns so completely   5
that adolescents brought into emergency rooms with gunshot wounds are amazed to find that they are in pain. Guns have become as ubiquitous a symbol of adult power as packs of cigarettes were in previous decades. It is the throwaway lines of casual violence like "Make my day" and "Are you feeling lucky, punk?" that have become part of the common lexicon. There is not a single studio head in this country who is not aware of the exploding homicide rate for adolescents. These captains of industry have all been shown the connection between media portrayals of violence and real-world violence. Their continued dismissal of these facts is criminal.

Teenagers, for the most part, do not need protection from the reali-   6
ties of life. On the contrary, they need as much information and education as possible. *Dead Poets Society* deals with suicide, *Boyz N the Hood* deals with homicide, *Schindler's List* documents genocide. Responsible movies such as these do not hesitate to confront and explore the kinds of difficult topics that interest adolescents. But they provide a historical context, emphasize complexity, explore alternatives, and show teenagers the consequences of actions that may limit or even destroy future opportunities. They are important movies for teenagers to see.

Of course, one of the purposes of media is to provide distraction, a   7
way of "kicking back" and forgetting about one's problems. We all need "downtime." Action movies are exciting and engrossing and as a result allow us to turn our attention away from our own difficulties. This is a perfectly reasonable function of entertainment. Horror movies can also serve a psychological function for adolescents. They are a rite of passage

that allows teenagers, at a safe distance, to "dare" to be unafraid and willing to confront demons. They hold the same attraction that fairy tales hold for younger children. They are preparation for going out into a world that contains many frightening unknowns. They also help adolescent males, the major consumers of action and horror movies, to lessen the psychological grip of mother by proving that they are "man enough" to manage on their own.

Evil has its attractions—from fire-breathing dragons and evil step- 8 mothers to serial killers; people at all ages are interested in the darker aspects of humanity. This is because we all carry within ourselves thoughts and fantasies that are cruel and violent. It is naive and dangerous to deny the duality of human nature. But it is the socializing agents of society—family, school, religious institutions, and mass media—that are charged with the responsibility of helping children and adolescents understand and control their aggressive impulses.

At the risk of being repetitious, I will say again that no one movie 9 or television program, no matter how violent, is likely to be damaging to reasonably healthy adolescents. The problem lies in the fact that violence is the rule rather than the exception. While boys do benefit from the man-as-dragon-slayer story, it is only one of many stories they need to hear. They also need man-as-father, man-as-nurturer, man-as-healer, and man-as-peacemaker stories if they are to enter adulthood truly equipped for the varied responsibilities they will find there. Unfortunately, outstanding television programs such as *My So-Called Life*, which dealt with serious and common adolescent problems, are often short-lived on network television. Teenagers have become so habituated to extreme violence that they lack the patience and insight needed to appreciate even marginally more demanding programs.

In spite of the industry's claim that it is only giving the public what 10 they want, research shows that it is action, not violence, that appeals to audiences. The surprise summer hit of 1994, *Speed,* with Keanu Reeves, while not an intellectually demanding movie, managed to be thrilling while maintaining a minimal body count. *Apollo 13* was a gripping and fascinating history lesson, loudly applauded by the group of teenagers sitting next to me in the theater. *Crimson Tide* provided a good dose of action and suspense and still managed to pose questions particularly appealing to adolescents: Where does one's greatest responsibility lie? What constitutes betrayal? How to decide between one's conscience and the dictates of society? All of these movies were popular with adolescents, and they're good examples of the fact that audiences can be entertained and even riveted without being soaked in blood. Entertainment executives might consider these types of action movies as absorbing, responsible and profitable alternatives to movies featuring gratuitous violence.

Attachment

. . . One of the extraordinary events taking place [during adoles- 11 cence] is the teenager's discovery of love and sex. While emotional reliance on parents is diminishing, the adolescent is finding new support and nurturance in intimate relationships with peers. These relationships can be sexual or not, heterosexual or homosexual. They become part of the process by which the adolescent comes to define his or her identity. Erik Erikson[1] describes this stage with great insight:

> This initiates the stage of "falling in love," which is by no means entirely, or even primarily, a sexual matter—except where the mores demand it. To a considerable extent adolescent love is an attempt to arrive at a definition of one's identity by projecting one's diffused ego image on another and by seeing it thus reflected and gradually clarified. This is why so much of young love is conversation.

It is unfortunate that the media choose to ignore this reality of ado- 12 lescent development. Conversation, discussion, and endless thinking are large components of adolescent life that are virtually ignored in favor of sexual adventure. While sexual issues are critical as never before, and will be discussed at length later in this [essay], let's focus for a moment on the equally compelling emotional aspect of adolescent love. As parents, we know that it can be hard to remember parts of our adolescence, but we all remember our first broken heart. The emotional investment that teenagers make in each other is perhaps unparalleled. Although couples break up frequently and seem to treat each other with apparent indifference, the truth is that these foundered relationships can be excruciatingly painful to the adolescent.

One of the reasons *My So-Called Life* was so well liked by many ado- 13 lescents was that it acknowledged the primacy of adolescent emotional connection, not just sexual activity. The producers of that program made a sound decision by having their fifteen-year-old central character, Angela, remain a virgin. This device allowed the show to circumvent many of the mandatory sexual escapades of television characters and instead focus on psychological development. While sex certainly came up as a subject, it was mainly talked about, not acted upon. Characters were given the opportunity to plumb some of the conflict and ambivalence characteristic of adolescents.

---

[1] American psychoanalyst (1902–1990) and important contributor to contemporary theories of human development. [Eds.]

Teenagers and Sex in the Media

The basis of all successful human relationships is respect and affec- 14
tion. Teenagers should be encouraged to see programs and movies that
acknowledge that fact. It is unfortunate that teenagers frequently feel
pushed into sexual activity before they have a firm grasp on the emotional underpinnings of human connection. The media have failed to
show that real human connection comes out of emotional intimacy, not
just sexual intimacy. Overall, the media portray sex as glamorous, spontaneous, and, most dangerously, risk free.

Learning about sex is different for teens than any other kind of 15
social learning because the information comes not through participation
and observation but from each other—and much of it turns out to be
false. Teenagers watch each other skateboard and then try it themselves.
Even such things as "how to talk to girls" are things that teenage boys
watch in a variety of contexts (how dad talks to mom, how big brother
talks to his girlfriend) and then gradually participate in at the level they
find comfortable. Sex, however, is not something that teenagers learn
through observation. The actual act of intercourse is rarely a public
event.

When it comes to disseminating sexual information, parents, 16
schools, and religious institutions vary greatly in their willingness and
comfort level. Parental denial plays a large part in limiting access to sexual information as teenagers have sex at younger and younger ages.
This trend has potentially devastating implications for our society, for it
is well documented that younger teenagers are less likely to be well
informed about birth control and disease prevention and are more
likely to engage in unprotected sex than older teens.

Since adolescence is a time of lessened parental control, greater 17
access to media, and few competing sources of information about sex, it
is no surprise that the media play a very important role in the sexual
socialization of teenagers. Unfortunately, little of what teenagers see
about sex in the media is thoughtful or respectful. Instead, teenagers are
exposed to a sexual world heavy on violence and other assertions of
power and low on love and commitment. MTV has immersed adolescents in a world where sexual activity is primarily the province of hor-
monally flooded males with little concern for their female partners.
Consequences of sexual activity are virtually nonexistent and the few
mentions of contraception that exist are often paired with emotional
indifference. Snoop Doggy Dog may have a "pocketful of rubbers" for
the "bitches in the living room," but he has nothing meaningful to teach
adolescents about the joys and responsibilities of love.

The media have been grossly negligent in their portrayals of sex and 18
its consequences. Approximately 85 percent of all sexual relationships on

television are between unmarried or uncommitted couples. The media are content to stick with the subject of "screwing around" rather than struggle with the far more complex issue of human intimacy. Watching television and movies, one would think that sex stops at the altar.

While preparing [my book *Viewing Violence*], I watched many 19 dozens of the most popular teenage movies, and I never saw a reasoned and intelligent discussion of birth control. According to most stories told by the media, intercourse and pregnancy are unrelated. Can we measure the percentage of the million babies born to teenagers each year who in some measure owe their existence to such repeated irresponsible portrayals of teenage sex? Probably not. Like violence, teenage pregnancy is the endpoint of many individual and social factors. But there is absolutely no doubt that the media portrayals, *on the whole*, have been derelict in informing teenagers about the consequences of sexual activity.

Aggression as a style of dealing with conflict is something that is 20 learned early in childhood and learned well. It is in fact quite difficult to modify aggression once it is the preferred way of handling problems. By adolescence, most children have a reasonably consistent way of handling interpersonal conflict. It is unlikely that media violence can turn a previously cooperative and peaceful child into a mid-adolescent criminal. That kind of damage is probably done earlier in life by any number of social and individual factors.

Although crimes are being committed by younger and younger 21 individuals, it is still adolescence that contains a disproportionate number of both perpetrators and victims. With very few exceptions, seven-year-olds don't rape and murder; seventeen-year olds do. In her powerful book *Boys Will Be Boys*, Myriam Miedzian looks at the many factors in our society that contribute to boys developing a sense of self that relies heavily on aggressive posturing: "Many of the values of the masculine mystique, such as toughness, dominance, repression of empathy, extreme competitiveness, play a major role in criminal and domestic violence and underlie the thinking and policy decisions of many of our political leaders." The book forces the realization that it is usually not "aggression" that is being studied, but male aggression. The vast majority of crimes are committed by men, and so we need to pay particular attention to the messages that both parents and the media send to boys.

The media have failed to provide teenage boys with role models 22 that are worthy of imitation. Conversely, why is it that males seem particularly attracted to media messages that stress intimidation and the abuse of power as ways to navigate the world? Boys are far more affected by male role models than by female role models, while girls are equally affected by both. Women in the media are typically portrayed as being less aggressive and more socially conscious than men. Perhaps it is the acceptance of female role models that confers a protective factor on girls, making them less vulnerable to the aggressive, macho images that suffuse popular culture. Boys desperately need a wider range of male models, some of whom incorporate the more traditional female values of cooperation and sensitivity. It would be of great benefit for adolescent boys to see male characters who are attractive without being violent. Unfortunately male characters who are presented as gentle are frequently also portrayed as defective or crazy as in *Edward Scissorhands* or *Don Juan Demarco.*

It is a peculiarity of our culture that exposure to sexual material is 23 considered more damaging to children than exposure to violence. The Puritan aversion to sex still evident in our culture results in some truly extraordinary contradictions. In 1995, *NYPD Blue* caused a stir by breaking the nudity code on television. For the first time a major television program allowed one of its stars to bare his buttocks. No matter that we had seen decades of shootings, knifings, rapes, and mutilations. Jimmy Smits was shown bare-assed. Personally, I would rather have my children see someone's butt hanging out than his brains hanging out. Call me a romantic.

We have decided, against all scientific evidence, that it is sex, not 24 violence, that we need to shield our youth from. Tom Cruise saying "fuck" twice in *Rain Man* is in no way the equivalent of John Travolta blowing someone's brains out in *Pulp Fiction* (both R-rated movies). The effects of these two movies on children are considerably different, and that difference is not adequately acknowledged under the current rating system. While there is a value to ratings that reflect what the hypothetical "average American parent" would consider appropriate for his or her child, there is also value in considering what research has to tell us about what is damaging to children and teens. The rating system would be far more useful to parents if it acknowledged different developmental stages and gave additional information about why films received their particular rating.

Total Recall, Terminator, Die Hard, and *Robocop* all feature gratuitous 25 violence and often combine sexual and aggressive messages. Is it true that the sexual content is what is most damaging? After all, adolescent boys, heavy consumers of media violence, are having their first sexual experiences and are formulating attitudes toward women that they will carry for a lifetime. Edward Donnerstein, one of this country's leading authorities on pornography and a member of Surgeon General C. Everett Koop's Task Force on Pornography, has spent decades studying the effects of pornography and violence. In 1987, Donnerstein and his colleagues published *The Question of Pornography: Research Findings and Policy Implications.* They write in their preface:

It is perhaps ironic, but we did not write this book because of our concern about the prevalence of sexually explicit materials in American society. Rather, we were concerned that so much attention was being paid to the possibly damaging consequences of exposure to pornography, that more pervasive and more troubling combinations of sex and aggression in the media were being ignored. We contend that the violence against women in some types of R-rated films shown in neighborhood theaters and on cable TV far exceeds that portrayed in even the most graphic pornography.

One of the chapters in the book, entitled "Is It the Sex or Is It the 26 Violence?," attempts to bring decades of scientific research to bear on answering this question. Typical of many studies cited, a series of studies by Donnerstein and colleagues shows that it is violence, or a combination of sex and violence, but not sex alone, that tends to encourage callous attitudes toward women. For example, in one of the experiments, a group of college-age males were shown one of three edited versions of the same movie. In the sexually aggressive version, the woman was tied up, threatened with a gun, and raped. In the aggression-only version, the sex was deleted; and in the sex-only version, the aggression was deleted.

After viewing the movie, the men were asked to complete ques- 27 tionnaires measuring their attitudes toward rape, their willingness to use force against women, and their willingness to rape if not caught. In the sex-only group, only 11 percent of the men indicated some likelihood that they would commit rape. In the sex and violence group, 25 percent indicated some likelihood, and *in the violence-only group, fully 50 percent of the men indicated some likelihood that they would rape a woman.* The researchers conclude the chapter by saying, "We risk the possibility that many members of our society, particularly young viewers, will evolve into less sensitive and responsive individuals as a result, at least partly, of repeated exposure to violent media, particularly sexually violent media. Such a possibility should be alarming, if not to law makers, at least to policy makers responsible for rating motion pictures and thus to limiting young people's access to sexually violent depictions."

Knowing as much as we do about the effects of sexually violent 28 entertainment, we must, as parents, respond. At the very least, we must work to ensure that our teenage boys understand that such attitudes and behavior are reprehensible. Mothers need to command respect from their sons, and fathers need to be involved in lessening the impact of degrading messages by discussing the realities of love, sex, and aggression with their sons. The high levels of sexual abuse in our society suggest that sexual violence is not committed by a few deviant men. Rather, it is a common and too frequently acceptable way of exercising control over women.

Responding to Reading

1. Consider these three statements by Levine:

   • "Evil has its attractions . . . ; people at all ages are interested in the darker aspects of humanity" (8).

   • "It is a peculiarity of our culture that exposure to sexual material is considered more damaging to children than exposure to violence" (23).

   • "In spite of the industry's claim that it is only giving the public what they want, research shows that it is action, not violence, that appeals to audiences" (10).

   Whom (or what) does each statement seem to blame for media violence? Where do you think the greatest blame should be placed?

2. In paragraph 9, Levine states emphatically that "no one movie or television program, no matter how violent, is likely to be damaging to reasonably healthy adolescents." Does this statement contradict John Grisham's (p. 343) claim that *Natural Born Killers* was the direct cause of Ben and Sarah's shooting spree? Explain your reasoning.

3. In Levine's view, what is the real problem inherent in media violence and its effect on adolescents? What possible solutions does she see? Does your assessment of the situation differ from hers?

Widening the Focus

• Sharon Olds, "Rite of Passage" (p. 373)

• Stanton L. Wormley, Jr., "Fighting Back" (p. 381)

• Barbara Grizutti Harrison, "Getting Away with Murder" (p. 531)

• Barbara Ehrenreich, "The Myth of Man as Hunter" (p. 707)

WRITING

The Media's Message

1. Was there for you, as there was for McMillan, a movie that changed your life—opening a new world, introducing you to new ideas, or giving you new insight into your own life? Write a fan letter to the movie's director. (Or write a letter of praise to a recording artist or a television producer).

2. Deborah Tannen comments, "If public discourse is a fight, . . . it's crucial to show 'the other side,' even if one has to scour the margins of science or the fringes of lunacy to find it" (6). She warns, however, "The determination to find another side can spread disinformation rather than lead to truth" (8). Apply these ideas and others in Tannen's essay to the situation Deborah Lipstadt describes in "Denying the Holocaust" in Chapter 10 (p. 811).

3. Does media violence hurt? If so, whom does it hurt most? Use the essays by Grisham, Leonard, and Levine as well as your own observations to support your conclusion.

4. What do you think the impact of various media (including the Internet) will be in the years to come? What trends do you see emerging that you believe will change the way you think or the way you live? What will the media's message be in the twenty-first century? Write an essay in which you speculate about future trends and their impact. (If you like, you may consider information presented in the essays by Pico Iyer, Gregory J. E. Rawlins, or Ted Gup in Chapter 7.)

5. Reconsider the charges leveled at the media by one or more writers in this chapter—for example, Deloria or Grisham—but apply them to the commercial messages that make most magazines and television programs possible. Are magazine ads and television commercials more or less guilty of the sins with which this chapter's writers charge the media? Read (or reread) Gloria Steinem's "Sex, Lies, and Advertising" (p. 279) before you begin.

6. Keep a daily log of the programs you listen to on the radio and watch on television, the movies you see, and the newspapers and magazines you read. After one week, review what you chose to read, listen to, and watch, and consider why you chose what you did and how these different kinds of media informed, provoked, or entertained you. Chart your habits, including the time you spent and what you selected, and write a report evaluating the impact of various media on you.

7. Do the media present an accurate image of your gender, race, religion, or ethnic group? In what ways, if any, is the image unrealistic?

In what ways, if any, is it demeaning? You may refer to the selections in this chapter by Stark, Deloria, or Douglas, but you should focus on specific examples from your own observations. If possible, include recommendations for improving the image of the group you discuss. What can be done to challenge—or change—simplistic or negative images?

8. Should the government continue to support public television and radio? What, if anything, do public radio and television provide that commercial programming does not offer?

9. Steven Stark says, "Whether in the form of the media's obsession with violence or its preoccupation with polls and popularity, the fantasy life of the adolescent male ends up defining much of our political reality" (9). Apply this statement to the observations made by Deborah Tannen about politicians, journalists, and academics. Does Stark's theory help to explain the traits and behavior Tannen discusses?

10. What kind of "family values" are promoted on television? Would you say that these media are largely "profamily" or "antifamily"? Using the essays in this chapter by Winn, McGrath, and Kaminer for background, choose several films and television programs that support your position. Then, write an essay that takes a strong stand. (Consult the essays by Alice Hoffman and Joseph Adelson in Chapter 1 if necessary for an explanation of the concept of family values.)

5

WOMEN AND MEN

Student Voices

"Being a woman in the work force can be difficult. Many women are discriminated against, sexually harassed, or just not taken seriously. Today, a woman needs to be self-confident and self-assured. She must know that she can go out and do her job well."

—Kim Cerino

"I don't see any real difficulty being a woman. I don't hate my body or feel weak because of my gender. Still, it does disturb me that the male-female ratio at my school isn't equal and that there are fewer female than male engineering students.

"Certainly there are difficulties being female. You have to have a thick skin. Some men have a hard time with certain assertions or demonstrations of will. Many of these attitudes seem to be going out with my father's generation, however."

—Elizabeth Zaffarano

"The entire gender issue confuses me. I know that I'll probably get many women upset by writing this, but it's my opinion. Women are constantly fighting for equal rights, but then they try to use their gender as an excuse not to do certain things or to change things in their favor."

—John Buchinsky

"There has definitely been a change in female-male roles since my parents' generation. Females of my generation have a difficult time because they look at their futures differently from the way they did forty years ago. A female is supposed to be not only the ultimate homemaker but also an independent, ambitious member of the working world. Even with all the talk of liberation, most males still only do one thing—earn a living. Sometimes I get really upset thinking about the situation."

—Jennifer Liebl

"During these times of political correctness, it's hard to be a white male. White men are made out to be evil beings who are responsible for all the evils of the world. I am not saying that there are not bad men who have done horrible things. What I am saying is that there are a lot of men who are loving and kind, and I wish we would get some credit for this."

—Stephen Berger

"Men have traditionally been the breadwinners of the family. They gained a sense of pride when they were able to take care of their family. They displayed very little emotion even though they had a lot of emotion inside. Women stayed home to care for their children. The difficulty of women's work was frequently overlooked.

"The feminist movement has helped women improve their status. There are now many more opportunities for women to succeed than there were before. Men continue to hold the majority of senior-level positions, however. There still hasn't been a female president, but there may be one soon."

—Jennifer Falk

─────────────── **Preparing to Read and Write** ───────────────

Attitudes about gender have changed dramatically over the past thirty years, and they continue to change. For some, these changes have resulted in confusion and anger as well as liberation. One reason for this confusion is that people can no longer rely on fixed roles to tell them how to behave in public and how to function within their families. Still, many men and women—uncomfortable with the demands of confining gender roles and unhappy with the expectations those roles create— yearn for even less rigidity, for an escape from stereotypes into a society where roles are not defined solely by gender.

Unfortunately, many people still tend to see men and women in terms of outdated and unrealistic stereotypes: Men are strong, tough, and brave, and women are weak, passive, and in need of protection. Men understand mathematics and science and have a natural aptitude for mechanical tasks. They also have the drive, the aggressiveness, the competitive edge, and the power to succeed. They are never sentimental and never cry. Women are better at small, repetitive tasks and shy away from taking bold, decisive actions. They enjoy, and are good at, domestic activities, and they have a natural aptitude for nurturing. They may like their jobs, but they will leave them to devote themselves to husband and children.

As we read the preceding list of stereotypes, some of us may react neutrally (or even favorably), while others may react with annoyance; how we react tells us something about our society and something about ourselves. But as a number of writers in this section point out, stereotypes are not just inaccurate; they also limit the way people think, the roles they chose to assume, and, ultimately, the positions they occupy in society.

As you read and prepare to write about the selections in this chapter, you may consider the following questions:

- Is the writer male or female? Are you able to determine the author's gender without reading the author's name or the headnote? Does the writer's gender really matter?

- Is the writer's focus on males, on females, or on both sexes?

- When was the selection written? Does the date of publication affect its content?

- Does the selection seem fair? Balanced?

- Does the writer discuss gender as a sexual, political, economic, or social issue?

- What does the writer suggest are the specific advantages or disadvantages of being male? Of being female?

- Does the writer support the status quo, or does he or she suggest that change is necessary? Possible? Inevitable?

- Does the writer recommend specific changes? What are they?

- Is your interpretation of the issue the same as the interpretation presented in the selection?

- Does the writer express the view that men and women are fundamentally different? If so, does he or she suggest that these differences can (or should) be overcome, or at least lessened?

- Does the writer see gender differences as the result of environment or of heredity?

- Does the selection challenge any of your ideas about male-female roles?

- In what ways is the essay like other essays in this chapter?

TWO PERSPECTIVES
ON WOMEN AND MEN

Following are two poems that focus in different ways on gender roles and images in contemporary culture. In "Barbie Doll," Marge Piercy (1936–   ) takes an ironic look at the influence of that controversial cultural icon. The poem appeared in Circles on the Water *(1988), a collection in which, Piercy writes, she hopes "that readers will find poems that speak to and for them." The author of more than thirteen novels and twelve collections of poetry, Piercy has long been active in the women's movement. Her recent works include* City of Darkness, City of Light *(1996), a novel, and* What Are Big Girls Made Of? *(1997). In "Rite of Passage," Sharon Olds (1942–   ) focuses on the behavior of a group of young boys at a birthday party, behavior that seems to foreshadow their adult roles. A graduate of Stanford and Columbia universities, Olds currently teaches at New York University. Her collections include* Waiting for My Life *(1981), in which "Rites of Passage" appears;* The Gold Cell *(1987); and* The Wellspring *(1996). In her poetry, Olds often dwells on family and relationships, particularly relationships among parents and children, using plain language that reveals surprising emotional depths. According to one critic, "out of private revelations she makes poems of universal truth of sex, death, fear, and love."*

BARBIE DOLL

Marge Piercy

This girlchild was born as usual
and presented dolls that did pee-pee
and miniature GE stoves and irons
and wee lipsticks the color of cherry candy.
Then in the magic of puberty, a classmate said: 5
You have a great big nose and fat legs.

She was healthy, tested intelligent,
possessed strong arms and back,
abundant sexual drive and manual dexterity.
She went to and fro apologizing.   10
Everyone saw a fat nose on thick legs.

She was advised to play coy,
exhorted to come on hearty,
exercise, diet, smile and wheedle.
Her good nature wore out   15
like a fan belt.
So she cut off her nose and her legs
and offered them up.

In the casket displayed on satin she lay
with the undertaker's cosmetics painted on,   20
a turned-up putty nose,
dressed in a pink and white nightie.
Doesn't she look pretty? everyone said.
Consummation at last.
To every woman a happy ending.   25

RITE OF PASSAGE

Sharon Olds

As the guests arrive at my son's party
they gather in the living room—
short men, men in first grade
with smooth jaws and chins.
Hands in pockets, they stand around   5
jostling, jockeying for place, small fights
breaking out and calming. One says to another
How old are you? Six. I'm seven. So?
They eye each other, seeing themselves
tiny in the other's pupils. They clear their   10
throats a lot, a room of small bankers,
they fold their arms and frown. *I could beat you
up*, a seven says to a six,
the dark cake, round and heavy as a
turret, behind them on the table. My son,   15
freckles like specks of nutmeg on his cheeks,
chest narrow as the balsa keel[1] of a
model boat, long hands
cool and thin as the day they guided him
out of me, speaks up as a host   20
for the sake of the group.

---

[1] The long, narrow bottom of a wooden ship. [Eds.]

We could easily kill a two-year-old,
he says in his clear voice. The other
men agree, they clear their throats
like Generals, they relax and get down to   25
playing war, celebrating my son's life.

Responding to Reading

1. Is Piercy exaggerating the negative impact of Barbie dolls and similar toys on girls? If so, why? Can you think of a similar toy that might define "maleness" for boys?
2. What is a "rite of passage"? Why do you think Olds gives her poem the title she does?
3. Why does Olds refer to the children at her son's birthday party as "men"?
4. Both these poems focus on the gender roles with which children are presented as they are growing up. What comment does each make about being male or female in contemporary American society? Do you agree with these assessments?
5. In what ways are the speakers' views similar? In what ways are their views different?
6. Both poems end on a cynical note. How effective are these conclusions? What does each poet gain or lose with this concluding strategy?

MARY CASSATT

Mary Gordon

Novelist and critic Mary Gordon (1940–) was born in Far Rockaway, New York, and educated at Barnard and Syracuse Universities. Her first novel, Final Payments *(1978), was an immediate critical and popular success and was followed by the equally successful* The Company of Women *(1980),* Men and Angels *(1985), and* The Rest of Life *(1993). Her most recent books are a memoir,* Shadow Man *(1996), and a novel,* Spending *(1998). She lives and writes in upstate New York. In the following selection from her 1991 collection of essays,* Good Boys and Dead Girls, *Gordon considers the life and career of American impressionist painter Mary Cassatt (1845–1926), who "exemplified the paradoxes of the woman artist."*

When Mary Cassatt's father was told of her decision to become a   1
painter, he said: "I would rather see you dead." When Edgar Degas saw a show of Cassatt's etchings, his response was: "I am not willing to admit that a woman can draw that well." When she returned to Philadelphia after twenty-eight years abroad, having achieved renown

as an Impressionist painter and the esteem of Degas, Huysmans, Pissarro, and Berthe Morisot, the *Philadelphia Ledger* reported: "Mary Cassatt, sister of Mr. Cassatt, president of the Pennsylvania Railroad, returned from Europe yesterday. She has been studying painting in France and owns the smallest Pekingese dog in the world."

Mary Cassatt exemplified the paradoxes of the woman artist. Cut 2 off from the experiences that are considered the entitlement of her male counterpart, she has access to a private world a man can only guess at. She has, therefore, a kind of information he is necessarily deprived of. If she has almost impossible good fortune—means, self-confidence, heroic energy and dedication, the instinct to avoid the seductions of ordinary domestic life, which so easily become a substitute for creative work— she may pull off a miracle: she will combine the skill and surety that she has stolen from the world of men with the vision she brings from the world of women.

Mary Cassatt pulled off such a miracle. But if her story is particu- 3 larly female, it is also American. She typifies one kind of independent American spinster who keeps reappearing in our history in forms as various as Margaret Fuller and Katharine Hepburn. There is an astringency in such women, a fierce discipline, a fearlessness, a love of work. But they are not inhuman. At home in the world, they embrace it with a kind of aristocratic greed that knows nothing of excess. Balance, proportion, an instinct for the distant and the formal, an exuberance, a vividness, a clarity of line: the genius of Mary Cassatt includes all these elements. The details of the combination are best put down to grace; the outlines may have been her birthright.

She was one of those wealthy Americans whose parents took the 4 children abroad for their education and medical care. The James family comes to mind and, given her father's attitude toward her career, it is remarkable that Cassatt didn't share the fate of Alice James.[1] But she had a remarkable mother, intelligent, encouraging of her children. When her daughter wanted to study in Paris, and her husband disapproved, Mrs. Cassatt arranged to accompany Mary as her chaperone.

From her beginnings as an art student, Cassatt was determined to 5 follow the highest standards of craftsmanship. She went first to Paris, then to Italy, where she studied in Parma with Raimondi and spent many hours climbing up scaffolding (to the surprise of the natives) to study the work of Correggio and Parmigianino. Next, she was curious to visit Spain to look at the Spanish masters and to make use of the picturesque landscape and models. Finally, she returned to Paris, where she was to make her home, and worked with Degas, her sometime friend and difficult mentor. There has always been speculation as to

---

[1] Alice James, a woman of Cassatt's generation and social rank, sublimated her own intellectual and artistic talents to those of her brothers, the novelist Henry and the philosopher William. [Eds.]

whether or not they were lovers; her burning their correspondence gave the rumor credence. But I believe that they were not; she was, I think, too protective of her talent to make herself so vulnerable to Degas as a lover would have to be. But I suppose I don't believe it because I cherish, instead, the notion that a man and a woman can be colleagues and friends without causing an excuse for raised eyebrows. Most important, I want to believe they were not lovers because if they were, the trustworthiness of his extreme praise grows dilute.

She lived her life until late middle age among her family. Her 6 beloved sister, Lydia, one of her most cherished models, had always lived as a semi-invalid and died early, in Mary's flat, of Bright's disease. Mary was closely involved with her brothers and their children. Her bond with her mother was profound: when Mrs. Cassatt died, in 1895, Mary's work began to decline. At the severing of her last close familial tie, when her surviving brother died as a result of an illness he contracted when traveling with her to Egypt, she broke down entirely. "How we try for happiness, poor things, and how we don't find it. The best cure is hard work—if only one has the health for it," she said, and lived that way.

Not surprisingly, perhaps, Cassatt's reputation has suffered because 7 of the prejudice against her subject matter. Mothers and children: what could be of lower prestige, more vulnerable to the charge of sentimentality. Yet if one looks at the work of Mary Cassatt, one sees how triumphantly she avoids the pitfalls of sentimentality because of the astringent rigor of her eye and craft. The Cassatt iconography dashes in an instant the notion of the comfortable, easily natural fit of the maternal embrace. Again and again in her work, the child's posture embodies the ambivalence of his or her dependence. In *The Family*, the mother and child exist in positions of unease; the strong diagonals created by their postures of opposition give the pictures their tense strength, a strength that renders sentimental sweetness impossible. In *Ellen Mary Cassatt in a White Coat* and *Girl in the Blue Arm Chair*, the children seem imprisoned and dwarfed by the trappings of respectable life. The lines of Ellen's coat, which create such a powerful framing device, entrap the round and living child. The sulky little girl in the armchair seems about to be swallowed up by the massive cylinders of drawing room furniture and the strong curves of emptiness that are the floor. In *The Bath*, the little girl has all the unformed charming awkwardness of a young child: the straight limbs, the loose stomach. But these are not the stuff of Gerber babies— even of the children of Millais. In this picture, the center of interest is not the relationship between the mother and the child but the strong vertical and diagonal stripes of the mother's dress, whose opposition shapes the picture with an insistence that is almost abstract.

Cassatt changed the iconography of the depiction of mothers and 8 children. Hers do not look out into and meet the viewer's eye; neither supplicating nor seductive, they are absorbed in their own inner thoughts. Minds are at work here, a concentration unbroken by an awareness of themselves as objects to be gazed at by the world.

The brilliance of Cassatt's colors, the clarity and solidity of her 9 forms, are the result of her love and knowledge of the masters of European painting. She had a second career as adviser to great collectors: she believed passionately that America must, for the sake of its artists, possess masterpieces, and she paid no attention to the outrage of her European friends, who felt their treasures were being sacked by barbarians. A young man visiting her in her old age noted her closed mind regarding the movement of the moderns. She thought American painters should stay home and not become "café loafers in Paris. Why should they come to Europe?" she demanded. "When I was young it was different. . . . Our Museums had not great paintings for the students to study. Now that has been corrected and something must be done to save our young over here."

One can hear the voice of the old, irascible, still splendid aunt in 10 that comment and see the gesture of her stick toward the Left Bank.[2] Cassatt was blinded by cataracts; the last years of her life were spent in a fog. She became ardent on the subjects of suffragism, socialism, and spiritualism; the horror of the First World War made her passionate in her conviction that mankind itself must change. She died at her country estate near Grasse, honored by the French, recipient of the Légion d'honneur, but unappreciated in America, rescued only recently from misunderstanding, really, by feminist art critics. They allowed us to begin to see her for what she is: a master of line and color whose great achievement was to take the "feminine" themes of mothers, children, women with their thoughts alone, to endow them with grandeur without withholding from them the tenderness that fits so easily alongside the rigor of her art.

Responding to Reading

1. Gordon says Cassatt "exemplified the paradoxes of the woman artist" (2). What do you suppose she means? Do you think these paradoxes exist today? Explain.

2. As Gordon points out, Cassatt was wealthy. Do you believe she would have been able to accomplish what she did if she had been middle-class or poor? Does the fact that she was wealthy make you less sympathetic to her?

3. In paragraph 3, Gordon says Cassatt's story is "particularly female, [but] it is also American." In what sense is her story "particularly female"? In what sense is it American?

---

[2] Paris neighborhood populated by artists, students, and bohemians. [Eds.]

THE MEN WE CARRY IN OUR MINDS

Scott Russell Sanders

Scott Russell Sanders (1945–   ) was born in Memphis, Tennessee, and received his B.A. from Brown University and his Ph.D. from Cambridge University in England. A professor of English at Indiana University, he is the author of novels, children's books, science fiction stories, and collections of personal essays, including The Paradise of Bombs *(1988),* Secrets of the Universe: Scenes from the Journey Home *(1991), and* Staying Put: Making a Home in a Restless World *(1993). An ardent environmentalist, Sanders has said, "If my writing does not help my neighbors to live more alertly, pleasurably, or wisely, then it is worth little." In "The Men We Carry in Our Minds," he recalls how he—a poor rural boy at an elite Ivy League college—first encountered women who railed at the "joys and privileges of men," privileges that did not apply to the working-class men of his experience.*

When I was a boy, the men I knew labored with their bodies. They 1
were marginal farmers, just scraping by, or welders, steelworkers, carpenters; they swept floors, dug ditches, mined coal, or drove trucks, their forearms ropy with muscle; they trained horses, stoked furnaces, built tires, stood on assembly lines wrestling parts onto cars and refrigerators. They got up before light, worked all day long whatever the weather, and when they came home at night they looked as though somebody had been whipping them. In the evenings and on weekends they worked on their own places, tilling gardens that were lumpy with clay, fixing broken-down cars, hammering on houses that were always too drafty, too leaky, too small.

The bodies of the men I knew were twisted and maimed in ways vis- 2
ible and invisible. The nails of their hands were black and split, the hands tattooed with scars. Some had lost fingers. Heavy lifting had given many of them finicky backs and guts weak from hernias. Racing against conveyor belts had given them ulcers. Their ankles and knees ached from years of standing on concrete. Anyone who had worked for long around machines was hard of hearing. They squinted, and the skin of their faces was creased like the leather of old work gloves. There were times, studying them, when I dreaded growing up. Most of them coughed, from dust or cigarettes, and most of them drank cheap wine or whiskey, so their eyes looked bloodshot and bruised. The fathers of my friends always seemed older than the mothers. Men wore out sooner. Only women lived into old age.

As a boy I also knew another sort of men, who did not sweat and 3
break down like mules. They were soldiers, and so far as I could tell they scarcely worked at all. During my early school years we lived on a

military base, an arsenal in Ohio, and every day I saw GIs in the guard-shacks, on the stoops of barracks, at the wheels of olive drab Chevrolets. The chief fact of their lives was boredom. Long after I left the Arsenal I came to recognize the sour smell the soldiers gave off as that of souls in limbo. They were all waiting—for wars, for transfers, for leaves, for pro-motions, for the end of their hitch—like so many braves waiting for the hunt to begin. Unlike the warriors of older tribes, however, they would have no say about when the battle would start or how it would be waged. Their waiting was broken only when they practiced for war. They fired guns at targets, drove tanks across the churned-up fields of the military reservation, set off bombs in the wrecks of old fighter planes. I knew this was all play. But I also felt certain that when the hour for killing arrived, they would kill. When the real shooting started, many of them would die. This was what soldiers were *for,* just as a ham-mer was for driving nails.

Warriors and toilers: those seemed, in my boyhood vision, to be the 4 chief destinies for men. They weren't the only destinies, as I learned from having a few male teachers, from reading books, and from watching tele-vision. But the men on television—the politicians, the astronauts, the generals, the savvy lawyers, the philosophical doctors, the bosses who gave orders to both soldiers and laborers—seemed as removed and unreal to me as the figures in tapestries. I could no more imagine grow-ing up to become one of these cool, potent creatures than I could imag-ine becoming a prince.

A nearer and more hopeful example was that of my father, who had 5 escaped from a red-dirt farm to a tire factory, and from the assembly line to the front office. Eventually he dressed in a white shirt and tie. He car-ried himself as if he had been born to work with his mind. But his body, remembering the earlier years of slogging work, began to give out on him in his fifties, and it quit on him entirely before he turned sixty-five. Even such a partial escape from man's fate as he had accomplished did not seem possible for most of the boys I knew. They joined the Army, stood in line for jobs in the smoky plants, helped build highways. They were bound to work as their fathers had worked, killing themselves or preparing to kill others.

A scholarship enabled me not only to attend college, a rare enough 6 feat in my circle, but even to study in a university meant for the children of the rich. Here I met for the first time young men who had assumed from birth that they would lead lives of comfort and power. And for the first time I met women who told me that men were guilty of having kept all the joys and privileges of the earth for themselves. I was baffled. What privileges? What joys? I thought about the maimed, dismal lives of most of the men back home. What had they stolen from their wives and daughters? The right to go five days a week, twelve months a year, for thirty or forty years to a steel mill or a coal mine? The right to drop bombs and die in war? The right to feel every leak in the roof, every gap in the fence, every cough in the engine, as a wound they must mend? The right to feel, when the lay-off comes or the plant shuts down, not only afraid but ashamed?

I was slow to understand the deep grievances of women. This was 7 because, as a boy, I had envied them. Before college, the only people I had ever known who were interested in art or music or literature, the only ones who read books, the only ones who ever seemed to enjoy a sense of ease and grace were the mothers and daughters. Like the men-folk, they fretted about money, they scrimped and made-do. But, when the pay stopped coming in, they were not the ones who had failed. Nor did they have to go to war, and that seemed to me a blessed fact. By comparison with the narrow, ironclad days of fathers, there was an expansiveness, I thought, in the days of mothers. They went to see neighbors, to shop in town, to run errands at school, at the library, at church. No doubt, had I looked harder at their lives, I would have envied them less. It was not my fate to become a woman, so it was eas-ier for me to see the graces. Few of them held jobs outside the home, and those who did filled thankless roles as clerks and waitresses. I didn't see, then, what a prison a house could be, since houses seemed to me brighter, handsomer places than any factory. I did not realize—because such things were never spoken of—how often women suffered from men's bullying. I did learn about the wretchedness of abandoned wives, single mothers, widows; but I also learned about the wretchedness of lone men. Even then I could see how exhausting it was for a mother to cater all day to the needs of young children. But if I had been asked, as a boy, to choose between tending a baby and tending a machine, I think I would have chosen the baby. (Having now tended both, I know I would choose the baby.)

So I was baffled when the women at college accused me and my sex 8 of having cornered the world's pleasures. I think something like my baf-flement has been felt by other boys (and by girls as well) who grew up in dirt-poor farm country, in mining country, in black ghettos, in Hispanic barrios, in the shadows of factories, in Third World nations—any place where the fate of men is as grim and bleak as the fate of women. Toilers and warriors. I realize now how ancient these identities are, how deep the tug they exert on men, the undertow of a thousand generations. The miseries I saw, as a boy, in the lives of nearly all men I continue to see in the lives of many—the body-breaking toil, the tedium, the call to be tough, the humiliating powerlessness, the battle for a living and for territory.

When the women I met at college thought about the joys and priv- 9 ileges of men, they did not carry in their minds the sort of men I had known in my childhood. They thought of their fathers, who were bankers, physicians, architects, stockbrokers, the big wheels of the big cities. These fathers rode the train to work or drove cars that cost more than any of my childhood houses. They were attended from morning to night by female helpers, wives and nurses and secretaries. They were never laid off, never short of cash at month's end, never lined up for welfare. These fathers made decisions that mattered. They ran the world.

The daughters of such men wanted to share in this power, this   10
glory. So did I. They yearned for a say over their future, for jobs worthy of their abilities, for the right to live at peace, unmolested, whole. Yes, I thought, yes yes. The difference between me and these daughters was that they saw me, because of my sex, as destined from birth to become like their fathers, and therefore as an enemy to their desires. But I knew better. I wasn't an enemy, in fact or in feeling. I was an ally. If I had known, then, how to tell them so, would they have believed me? Would they now?

Responding to Reading

1. What do the men Sanders carries in his mind have in common? How have they helped shape his attitude toward gender? Do you know men like Sanders's father? Do you know men (or women) who have "made decisions that mattered" (9)?

2. Do you agree with Sanders that women believe all men have greater access to power than they themselves do? Do you agree that women who believe this are mistaken?

3. In his conclusion, Sanders says that contrary to what they themselves believed, he was an "ally" of women who wanted to better themselves (10). What does he mean by this statement? Do you think the women about whom he is talking would see him as an ally?

FIGHTING BACK

Stanton L. Wormley, Jr.

Stanton L. Wormley, Jr. (1951–   ), who holds a B.A. in Spanish from Howard University and a master's in forensic science from George Washington University, has held various administrative positions at Howard and at the University of Southern Maine in Portland. Now a free-lance writer based in Maine, Wormley has published technical writing pieces, video scripts for industrial training films, science articles, and three articles in American Negro Biography *about a Washington, D.C., family.*

In addition, he has published a number of articles about shooting and firearms, subjects on which he says he plans to concentrate in the future. In the following essay, Wormley talks about the lessons to be learned from fighting back—and from not fighting back—especially for members of minority groups who feel "disenfranchised and often victimized by discrimination and poverty."

In the spring of 1970, I was an 18-year-old army private at Fort 1 Jackson, S.C. I had been in the Army for less than six months and was still making the difficult transition from life as an only child in an upper-middle-class black family. One rite of passage was particularly intense: on a cool April night, a drunken white soldier whom I barely knew attacked me as I lay sleeping.

My recollection of the incident is, in some details, still hazy. Like the 2 seven other men in the squad bay, I was asleep in my bunk. I half-remember some vigorous off-key singing, the ceiling light going on and someone roughly shaking my foot. I sat up, drowsily irritated at being disturbed. Everything happened very quickly then: a voice began shouting, an arm tightened around my neck and a fist pounded the top of my head. I was still somewhat asleep and confused. Why was this happening to me? It didn't occur to me to fight. I simply covered my head as best I could. There was a hubbub, arms reaching in to separate us and then the sight of the man above me, struggling against the others holding him back, his face red with fury. By then I was fully awake, and I saw the strained tendons in the man's neck, the wormlike vein pulsing at his temple, the spittle that sprayed as he screamed obscenities at me. I wasn't hurt, at least not physically, and all I could do was stare, bewildered. I never did discover what had provoked him.

Afterward, I was angrily confronted by a young black streetwise 3 soldier named Morris. He eyed me with unconcealed contempt. "What the hell's wrong with you, man?" he demanded. "Why didn't you fight back? I would've killed that mother." I had no answer for him. How could I have made him understand the sheltered world of my childhood, in which violence was deplored and careful deliberation encouraged. I was brought up to *think,* not just react.

Nevertheless, that question—*Why didn't I fight back?*—haunted me 4 long after the incident had been forgotten by everyone else. Was I less of a man for not having beaten my attacker to a bloody pulp? Morris—and undoubtedly others—certainly thought so. And so, perhaps, would the majority of American men. The ability and the will to fight back are integral parts of our society's conception of manhood. It goes beyond mere self-defense, I think, for there is a subtle but significant difference between self-defense and fighting back. Self-defense is essentially passive; it involves no rancor, pride or ego. Running away from danger is what martial-arts instructors sometimes recommend as the appropriate response, the best self-defense strategy. Fighting back, on the other hand, is active and defiant. It involves the adoption of an attitude that one's retribution is morally justified—or even, at times, morally obligatory.

And we American men buy that attitude—especially those of us 5 who are members of minority groups. For us, largely disenfranchised and often victimized by discrimination and poverty, fighting back is a statement of individual potency and self-determination. It is the very antithesis of victimization: it is a sign of empowerment. The symbolic consequences of fighting back—or failing to do so—reflect upon the group as a whole. To Morris, I had disgraced the entire black American population.

I suppose that there are still situations in which immediate, violent 6 retaliation is necessary. Sometimes it seems that fighting back is the only way to command respect in the world. Women are now learning that unfortunate lesson, as did blacks and other minorities in recent decades. I can't help feeling, however, that when one gains the ability to fight back one loses something as well. What that something is, I can't easily define: a degree of compassion, perhaps, or tolerance or empathy. It is a quality I hope is possessed by the men in Washington and Moscow who have the power to dispense the ultimate retribution.

Once in a great while, past events are repeated, granting people a 7 chance either to redeem themselves or to relive their mistakes. Two years ago, in a small roadside diner in Virginia, a man—again white, again drunk—chanced to make a derogatory remark to me. I was sitting with my back to him and ignored it. Thinking I had not heard him, he drew close to repeat his taunt, grabbing my shoulder. I suppose I could have moved away, shaken his hand off or complained to the manager. But the accumulated frustrations of years of ignoring such remarks—plus the memory of the incident at Fort Jackson—dictated otherwise. Before I knew what was happening, I was up out of my chair. I hit the man hard in the stomach and he sank to one knee with a moan. Grasping his collar, I almost hit again, but it was obvious that he had had enough. He looked up at me, gasping, his face contorted with pain and fear. The man was perhaps 50, of average size, with a fleshy, florid face surmounted by close-cropped gray bristle. I noted that he had bad teeth, a fact that gave me a moment of spiteful satisfaction. Suddenly sober, he stammered something unintelligible—it might have been an apology—and I let him go.

As I walked away, I was filled with a feeling of exultation. I had not 8 stopped to wonder why; I had not been checked by compassion or sympathy. I had retaliated and it had felt good. But later, my exhilaration passed, leaving a strange sensation of hollowness. I felt vaguely embarrassed, even ashamed. In my mind I was still confident I had acted rightly, but my heart was no longer sure. I remembered my fury, and the quiet way the people in the diner had watched me stalk angrily away. I remembered, too, the abject grimace on the man's face, partly from the pain of the blow and partly in anticipation of a second; and I realized that there was a trace of sadness in the knowledge that I, too, had learned to fight back.

Responding to Reading

1. What preconceptions about African-American men does Wormley expect his readers to have? How can you tell? In what way does he address these preconceptions in his essay?

2. In many ways Wormley's initial situation is similar to that of a woman: when first attacked, his instinctive response is to protect himself; it simply does not occur to him to fight back. Later he says that "when one gains the ability to fight back one loses something as well" (6). Do you think most women would agree with him? Do you agree?

3. Is the fact that Wormley is African-American of any special significance in this essay? Is the fact that he is an only child? That he was eighteen at the time of the incident he describes? That he comes from an upper-middle-class family? Does any of this information influence your expectations about how Wormley might respond to a physical challenge? If so, how?

WHY I WANT A WIFE

Judy Brady

Judy Brady (1937–   ) studied painting in college and wanted to pursue painting as a career. Instead, she has said, she was discouraged from an art career in higher education by her male teachers, and so she married and had a family. First a housewife, Brady began to write articles on social issues and became involved in the feminist movement. In recent years, she has edited several books about women and cancer. Her popular essay "Why I Want a Wife" appeared in the preview issue of Ms. *in 1972.*

I belong to that classification of people known as wives. I am A 1 Wife. And, not altogether incidentally, I am a mother.

Not too long ago a male friend of mine appeared on the scene fresh 2 from a recent divorce. He had one child, who is, of course, with his ex-wife. He is looking for another wife. As I thought about him while I was ironing one evening, it suddenly occurred to me that I, too, would like to have a wife. Why do I want a wife?

I would like to go back to school so that I can become economically 3 independent, support myself, and, if need be, support those dependent upon me. I want a wife who will work and send me to school. And while I am going to school I want a wife to take care of my children. I want a wife to keep track of the children's doctor and dentist appointments. And to keep track of mine, too. I want a wife to make sure my children eat properly and are kept clean. I want a wife who will wash the children's clothes and keep them mended. I want a wife who is a good nurturant attendant to my children, who arranges for their schooling, makes sure that they have an adequate social life with their peers, takes them to the park, the zoo, etc. I want a wife who takes care of the children when they are sick, a wife who arranges to be around when the children need special care, because, of course, I cannot miss classes at school. My wife must arrange to lose time at work and not lose the job. It may mean a small cut in my wife's income from time to time, but I guess I can tolerate that. Needless to say, my wife will arrange and pay for the care of the children while my wife is working.

I want a wife who will take care of *my* physical needs. I want a wife 4 who will keep my house clean. A wife who will pick up after me. I want a wife who will keep my clothes clean, ironed, mended, replaced when need be, and who will see to it that my personal things are kept in their proper place so that I can find what I need the minute I need it. I want a wife who cooks the meals, a wife who is a *good* cook. I want a wife who will plan the menus, do the necessary grocery shopping, prepare the meals, serve them pleasantly, and then do the cleaning up while I do my studying. I want a wife who will care for me when I am sick and sympathize with my pain and loss of time from school. I want a wife to go along when our family takes a vacation so that someone can continue to care for me and my children when I need a rest and change of scene.

I want a wife who will not bother me with rambling complaints 5 about a wife's duties. But I want a wife who will listen to me when I feel the need to explain a rather difficult point I have come across in my course of studies. And I want a wife who will type my papers for me when I have written them.

I want a wife who will take care of the details of my social life. When 6 my wife and I are invited out by friends, I want a wife who will take care of the babysitting arrangements. When I meet people at school that I like and want to entertain, I want a wife who will have the house clean, will prepare a special meal, serve it to me and my friends, and not interrupt when I talk about the things that interest me and my friends. I want a wife who will have arranged that the children are fed and ready for bed before my guests arrive so that the children do not bother us. I want a wife who takes care of the needs of my guests so that they feel comfortable, who makes sure that they have an ashtray, that they are passed the hors d'oeuvres, that they are offered a second helping of the food, that their wine glasses are replenished when necessary, that their coffee is

served to them as they like it. And I want a wife who knows that sometimes I need a night out by myself.

I want a wife who is sensitive to my sexual needs, a wife who makes 7
love passionately and eagerly when I feel like it, a wife who makes sure
that I am satisfied. And, of course, I want a wife who will not demand
sexual attention when I am not in the mood for it. I want a wife who
assumes the complete responsibility for birth control, because I do not
want more children. I want a wife who will remain sexually faithful to
me so that I do not have to clutter up my intellectual life with jealousies.
And I want a wife who understands that *my* sexual needs may entail
more than strict adherence to monogamy. I must, after all, be able to
relate to people as fully as possible.

If, by chance, I find another person more suitable as a wife than the 8
wife I already have, I want the liberty to replace my present wife with
another one. Naturally, I will expect a fresh, new life; my wife will take
the children and be solely responsible for them so that I am left free.

When I am through with school and have a job, I want my wife to 9
quit working and remain at home so that my wife can more fully and
completely take care of a wife's duties.

My God, who *wouldn't* want a wife?   10

Responding to Reading

1. What is your definition of a wife? How closely does it conform to Brady's
   definition? Do you know any women who meet Brady's criteria?
2. This essay, written over twenty years ago, has been anthologized many
   times. To what do you attribute its continued popularity? In what ways is
   the essay dated? In what ways is it still relevant?
3. Brady wrote her essay to address a stereotype and set of social conventions
   that she thought were harmful to women. Could you make the case that
   Brady's characterization of a "wife" is harmful both to women and to
   feminism?

SEX AND THE SOLDIER

Stephanie Gutmann

*Stephanie Gutmann (1960–   ) was born in Chicago, Illinois, and holds
a B.A. from Roosevelt University there and an M.S. from the Columbia
University School of Journalism. She has been on the staffs of the
Wilkes-Barre (Pennsylvania)* Times Leader, *the* Los Angeles Times, *and
the* New York Post, *serving as a features writer, entertainment critic, and*

reporter. She has also written for the New York Times, Playboy, Cosmopolitan, *and the* Washington Post, *among others. In the following essay, which first appeared in the* New Republic *in 1997, Gutmann takes a critical look at current attempts to integrate women recruits into the U.S. military forces.*

February 4, 1997, and an all-too-familiar looking headline—"TOP 1 ENLISTED MAN IN THE ARMY STANDS ACCUSED OF SEX ASSAULT"—occupies a prime corner of the front page of *The New York Times*. Just a few weeks earlier, the papers had been reporting charges of inappropriate hazing of female cadets at the Citadel. And just a few months before that, several female recruits at the Army's Aberdeen Proving Ground had accused drill instructors of rape and sexual harassment, unleashing a torrent of similar accusations from female soldiers around the country. In this latest case, as in so many of the others, blame will be difficult to affix. Once more it will come down to "he said, she said." Once more there will be op-eds, hand-wringing and counselors; once more the Army will have to deploy its investigatory troops. This, just as the Army digs out from Aberdeen—where there are still over 200 criminal charges to investigate, and a hot-line brings in new complaints every day.

What no one is publicly saying (but what everyone in the military 2 knows) is that incidents like these are bound to recur. In a military that is dedicated to the full integration of women, and to papering over the implications of that integration as best it can, sex and sexual difference will continue to be a disruptive force. And regulating sex will become an ever more important military sideline, one whose full costs in money, labor and morale we will not really know until the forces are called on to do what they are assembled to do: fight.

The military's sex problems begin with the simple anatomical dif- 3 ferences between men and women. Racial integration, to which the integration of women is ceaselessly compared, took the military about a century to achieve (quite successfully in the end) and that involved differences that are only skin deep. An effective fighting force depends on a steady supply of known quantities; it needs "units" made up of interchangeable elements called soldiers. Once one got over skin color, racial integration was still about integrating the same body.

But what happens when you try to absorb a population that is not, 4 in unit terms, interchangeable? What happens when you try to integrate into a cohesive whole two populations with radically different bodies? In the elemental, unremittingly physical world of the soldier, sex differences—masked by technology in the civilian world—stand out in high relief. Consider the female soldier not in political terms, but in the real, inescapable terms of physical structure. She is, on average, about five inches shorter than the male soldier, has half the upper body strength, lower aerobic capacity and 37 percent less muscle mass. She has a lighter skeleton, which may mean, for instance, that she won't be able to "pull G forces" as reliably in a fighter plane. She cannot pee standing up, a problem that may seem trivial, but whose impact on long marches was the subject of an entire Army research study; under investigation was a device called the "Freshette Complete System," which would allow women to pee standing up in places where foliage doesn't supply ample cover. She tends, particularly if she is under the age of 30 (as are 60 percent of military personnel) to get pregnant.

One would expect that such a sweeping social experiment (and one 5 so expensive—just refitting the *U.S.S. Eisenhower* to accommodate 400 new female sailors cost $1 million, for example) would hit some rough patches. But don't expect to hear about them from the military brass. Afflicted by a kind of "Vietnam syndrome" about the possibility of winning an ideological battle against the civilians who increasingly influence military policy, the brass now seem mostly concerned with trying to prove how well, as one officer put it, they "get it" where women are concerned. This week, when Army Chief of Staff General Dennis J. Reimer said he thought the service should re-examine whether the advantages of jointly training men and women outweigh the drawbacks, it was something of a bombshell. In general, the military has maintained a virtual silence about problems with the new influx of female soldiers, and, in the ranks, negative comments about integration are considered "career killers." Those who don't "get it" talk about it in the barracks and on the Internet, which has become a haven for military samizdat[1] about sex and other dicey matters. As one soldier wrote in a typical online exchange, "examples of these latest 'revelations' [about sex between subordinates and their immediate superiors] are known to nearly everyone who has served. But we were never allowed to discuss . . . our concerns openly because it would raise issues about the efficacy of mixing girls and boys and that was politically incorrect, a career-ending taboo."

In general, the military's response to the problems of gender inte- 6 gration has been to recruit more women. The more women, the more feminized the culture, the fewer problems with sex, goes the thinking. (One corollary of this may be the recent decline in male enlistment. In focus groups, young men tend to cite, among other reasons for not joining up, fear of purges like the one after Tailhook and the increased presence of females in the ranks.)

The big recruitment drive has brought the percentage of women in 7 the force to 14 percent, which may not seem like much but is up from 2 percent at the close of the Vietnam War. Women now make up 20 percent of new recruits—compared to 12 percent a decade ago. And the

---

[1] A clandestine network for thoughts and ideas.

effort to recruit still more women is relentless. In 1991, when the Marines replaced their slogan "A FEW GOOD MEN" with "THE FEW, THE PROUD, THE MARINES," the idea was to sound more female-friendly. Nowadays, much of a military recruiter's time is consumed with trying to cajole women to enlist. And in practice, unfortunately, this often means adapting—which is to say, lowering—standards without exactly admitting to doing so.

The goal for a young Marine recruiter named C. J. Chivers, for 8 example, became just "'Get 'em on the plane.' If there were any problems, boot camp could sort it out." Chivers, whose stint as a recruiter lasted from 1992–94, adds that "invariably we would fill up the white male quotas almost immediately. So it became any woman that came in there that met the minimums, we gotta hire. What that did was take all the subjectivity out of it, an enormous part of the evaluation process. I couldn't say 'I got a bad vibe' the way I could with a guy." A recruiter also had to work hard to maintain what Chivers calls an "informal double standard" on strength differences: "Invariably the guys went down to Officer Candidate School with a near-perfect physical score while the women just cleared the minimum"—even using what military brass call "gender-normed" test results and "dual," i.e. lower, standards: for example, in the Marines, fitness for women is tested with a flexed arm hang instead of pull-ups, half the number of sit-ups and a slower run.

Women have also been lured into the service with the promise of a 9 more important role. Since 1994 more than 80,000 new jobs have been opened in positions that were formerly off-limits. Rescinding the combat exclusion law and the risk rule has allowed women to qualify to fly combat planes and to serve on combat ships. Women are still not allowed to serve on submarines, but *Navy Times* reports that "a review underway to examine future submarine designs may include a study on including women crew members."

And ever since the Gulf war, when women served in combat sup- 10 port roles, the possibility of taking that last step—of knocking down barriers to the infantry—has been very much in the air. Ground combat, considered the most potentially brutal, the most physically demanding and certainly the grubbiest form of combat, is seen as a crucial piece of turf by the Old Guard and plenty of the young old guard, too. Opponents of integrating ground combat tend to argue that mixed-sex units won't achieve the right kind of "cohesion," that women on the whole aren't strong enough to, say, effectively lob grenades or load tanks, and that there is, at bottom, something repugnant about a male officer ordering women barely out of their teens into harm's way. The opposing argument has been pointedly made by N.O.W.[2] President Patricia Ireland, who maintains that exclusion promotes the view that

---

[2] The National Organization for Women, a feminist organization. [Eds.]

women are weak, inferior and in need of protection. (With Patricia Schroeder,[3] the great pro-combat warrior, in retirement, the next pro-combat push may come from a commission appointed by Army Secretary Togo D. West Jr. after the rape charges surfaced at Aberdeen. The commission's official mandate is to look at causes of sexual harassment, but the many pro-women-in-combat appointees are expected to argue the familiar exclusion-equals-lower-status-equals-harassment line when they make their recommendations.)

To understand why gender integration became such an unquestionable in the military culture, we have to return to 1992, the year of the Clarence Thomas hearings, the trial of Mike Tyson, "They Just Don't Get It"—and the Tailhook investigations.[4] Tailhook was officially declared a symptom of a larger problem—not an isolated event involving at most about six men—when investigators were ordered to scrutinize the "cultural" context. Through the prism of Tailhook and of sexual harassment, the culture that had long prepared men for battle suddenly looked, as then-acting Navy Secretary J. Daniel Howard put it, "diseased and decaying." "What happened at Tailhook," he told reporters, "was not just a problem with the integration of men and women in our ranks. It was just as much a problem with the toleration of Stone Age attitudes about warriors returning from the sea. . . ." 11

Somewhere in the committees and hearings charged with studying this "cultural problem" a remedy swam into focus: men harassed women because they did not see them as equals. If women were brought in in great numbers, "the warrior culture" would be diluted. After Tailhook, the military made recruitment of women a top priority; barriers toppled, policies changed, promotions were spirited through the pipelines. 12

The new thinking also held that, if you got to them early enough, all kinds of "sexist attitudes" could be nipped in the bud. And early enough meant starting with boot camp. Enter Gender Integrated Basic Training. In 1992 the Navy began training all new female recruits at one of three integrated boot camps—a way, as Captain Kathleen Bruyere put it, to give recruits "a chance to make mistakes, say stupid things, and tell them we don't do that here." At Bruyere's camp in Orlando, Florida, recruits did "everything but sleep together in the same compartment"—including physical training and bunk and dress inspections. They also spent a good deal of time watching films about sexual 13

---

[3] A former U.S. representative from Colorado. [Eds.]

[4] During his confirmation hearings, Supreme Court justice Thomas was accused of sexual harassment, but the all-male committee presiding over the hearings dismissed the charges (leading to the slogan "They [men] just don't get it"). Former heavyweight champion Mike Tyson was convicted of rape. The Tailhook scandal came to light when the media were provided with videotapes of female personnel being harassed during a convention of U.S. naval officers. [Eds.]

harassment, while questionnaires like the one that stated "The Navy is a man's world. True? or False?" gave the new troops ample opportunity to "say stupid things."

By the end of 1993, and into 1994, the Army followed suit with its 14 own gender-integrated training. The Army may have been slower on the uptake because it had already experimented with the process in the early '80s and found that when the sexes, say, ran obstacle courses together, the women tended to have a high injury rate from trying to keep up, and the men complained that they weren't challenged.

To avoid dealing with the problems posed by differences in physi- 15 cal strength between men and women, the proponents of sexual integration have increasingly favored a movement to "re-evaluate" the way soldiers are trained. As Barbara Pope, then assistant secretary of the Navy for manpower and reserve affairs, put it in the early '90s, "We are in the process of weeding out the white male as norm. We're about changing the culture." And so, in some boot camps, the fundamental character of training is changing. Fort Jackson, the camp where gender-integrated training was thought to have failed in the early '80s, began to evaluate "soldierization skills" by putting more emphasis on skills like "map-making and first aid" at which female recruits excel. The result has been a kind of feel-good feminization of boot camp culture, with the old (male) ethos of competition and survival giving at least partial way to a new (female) spirit of cooperation and esteem-building.

At the instigation of a Navy weekly called *Soundings,* a group of 16 middle-aged officers revisited their old basic training camp last fall to see how "the kinder, gentler Navy" was doing things. The oldsters were greeted by a commander—one Captain Cornelia de Groot Whitehead—who used her opening briefing to inform them that 40 percent of new recruits have at some time been victims of serious physical or sexual abuse, while 26 percent have contemplated suicide. Accordingly, de Groot Whitehead said, "We've decided we needed to do something different." The tourists from the "Old Navy" were bemused to learn that the infamous obstacle course of yore had been renamed the "confidence course" and moved indoors to comprise "an indoor labyrinth of pipes to crawl through, monkey bars to swing from, ladders to climb up and balance beams to sidestep over."

And at Fort Jackson, South Carolina—where, in 1995, boys and 17 girls shared barracks—an *Army Times* reporter recently found that grunts no longer have to do pushups to a count. Instead, they are asked to perform "a timed exercise in which soldiers do the best they can in a set period." One drill instructor has solved the male/female strength discrepancy problem by putting young recruits in "ability groups" for their morning run. "You're not competing with the rest of the company," Colonel Byron D. Greene, the director of Plans, Training and

Mobilization, told *Army Times*. "You are competing against yourself and your own abilities."

But life—especially military life—does not ignore physical differ- 18 ences. When young soldiers leave training, they are assigned jobs (called Military Occupational Specialities or MOSs), and the physical requirements of these jobs are not nearly as forgiving as a "New Army" drill instructor. A typical Army MOS, the kind of combat support MOS a young woman might request, could involve lots of lifting and loading, of shell casings, for instance. Pat Schroeder can say what she likes, but "a shell casing," groused an Army physiologist, "is always gonna weigh ninety pounds. There's nothing we can do about that."

Female soldiers themselves know this. A 1987 Army Research 19 Institute survey found that women are more likely than men to report that insufficient upper body strength interferes with their job performance. Twenty-six percent of female light wheel vehicle mechanics, for example, said they found it "very difficult" to do their job, as opposed to 9 percent of the men in that specialty who were polled.

And, according to Army physiologist Everett Harman, "[Command 20 Reports] have indicated that many soldiers are not physically capable of meeting the demands of their military occupational specialities. Unfortunately women fall disproportionately into this category." Attrition is particularly high, Harman said, in "heavy" (requiring 100-pound lifting) and "very heavy" (over 100 pounds) MOSs like Food Service Specialist, Motor Transport Operator and Unit Supply Specialist. Retraining and reassigning a soldier has been estimated to cost about $16,000, but advising a female soldier that she may have trouble with an MOS she is considering is, sources say, one of those "career-killing" statements that bureaucratically wise officers have learned to avoid.

There have been two attempts made in the past fifteen years to 21 establish "gender-neutral" strength standards and a qualifying pre-test for each MOS, but as *Army Times* reported, "on both occasions, the requirements were eventually abandoned when studies showed most women couldn't meet the standards proposed for nearly 70 percent of the Army specialties." In 1995, a group of military researchers were set to try again, but this time the project didn't even reach the partial implementation stage because funding was denied. Funding was also recently denied to Harman, who had applied for a grant to do a second study of "remedial strength training for women," after his first had shown promising results. Harman believes the brass do not like his approach because it admits that female soldiers are not strong enough to perform basic military tasks, which is contrary to the military's line. "At the highest level, I think they feel that if we show that women can get stronger, then the onus would be on the women to get stronger," he says, "while it is the jobs that should be made easier."

But can the jobs be made easier? Can weapons get lighter (as some   22
advisers are urging)—without reducing lethality? Proponents of the
change-the-equipment-not-the-people view point to the highly automated Air Force. But the Air Force is not the Army, and it is not the
Marines. "If you have a plane sitting on the runway and you have to
load it with supplies—bombs, whatever, you can have machines that
drive out there, that raise the stuff on a little elevator," Harman points
out. "But out in the woods and fields a lot has to get done by hand. Even
in the kitchen there are big pots weighing about 100 pounds or so. It
would take a tremendous amount of research to make certain jobs
lighter, because you're talking about re-engineering the whole thing.
Carrying a tool box, changing a truck tire; there are certain jobs, for
instance, where you have to carry a toolbox that might weigh a few
hundred pounds and put it up on the wing of a plane."

Online, where military folk often say impolitic things, there is a   23
sense of foreboding about the danger of ignoring the strength issue:
"Nothing is more demoralizing," wrote one Marine, "than to have to
turn your formation around to go pick up the females. This is only training. I can even put the females on remedial training and they still hold
up my formations. I would hate to see how many Marines I would lose
if we were in combat and had to be somewhere fast."

There is one respect, though, in which the stubborn physical reali-   24
ties of integrating women cannot be easily denied—and that is their
capacity for childbearing. A recent article in *Stars and Stripes* reported
that a woman had to be evacuated for pregnancy approximately every
three days in the Bosnian theater from December 20, 1995, when the
deployment began, until July 19, 1996. Army public relations people in
Bosnia don't dispute that claim, but they also say pregnancy is no particular problem for the Army, "no different than appendicitis."

It is clearly not a problem anymore in a career sense. All branches   25
and some of the service academies have softened policies on pregnancies and made it clear that their official stance is now completely accepting. Unfurling one such policy in February, 1995, Navy Secretary John
H. Dalton told reporters that "Navy leadership recognize that pregnancy is a natural event that can occur in the lives of Navy service-
women . . . and is not a presumption of medical incapacity." The Army
has followed suit, stating that "Pregnancy does not normally adversely
affect the career of a soldier."

In fact, pregnancy is now so "non-adverse" that soldiers say it's   26
sometimes used to get out of "hell tours" like Bosnia, to go home. "I
know other females that have done things . . . probably to get out of
going somewhere," Specialist Carrie Lambertus told *Army Times*. "It
happens all the time."

A woman who turns up pregnant in Bosnia is shipped in short 27
order to the U.S. or Germany. Then, according to an Army spokesman,
"female soldiers have the option of either staying on active duty or
applying for release [with an honorable discharge] from active duty."
Those who decide to stay in the military get six weeks maternity leave.
The new Navy policy also provides for help in locating a runaway dad
and in establishing paternity.

In the Navy, pregnancy rates run about 8 percent of the force at any 28
given time. A pregnant woman is allowed to stay onboard ship up to
her fifth month; then she gets reassigned to shore duty to avoid the
heavy lifting that is a sailor's lot, not to mention the hazardous chemicals in engine rooms. Of the 400 women on the first gender-integrated
warship, the *U.S.S. Eisenhower*, twenty-four were "non-deployable"
due to pregnancy at the start of a Persian Gulf tour and another fifteen
were evacuated once on the water. On the *U.S.S. Acadia*—dubbed "the
Love Boat" by the press—thirty-six out of a total 360 female sailors
aboard had to be evacuated during a Gulf tour.

And no matter how determinedly the military defines pregnancy as 29
a non-issue, the facts of pregnancy cannot be altered. A pregnant soldier
is—or soon will be—a non-deployable soldier. A General Accounting
Office study of soldiers called up to go to the Persian Gulf showed that
women were four times more nondeployable than men—because of the
pregnancy and recovery numbers. As Lambertus puts it, "If you're in a
platoon where they're moving equipment or digging, setting up tents,
[pregnant soldiers] are not going to be doing anything, except maybe sitting there and answering the phone all day. That really does cause some
resentment." If her commanders had wanted to make sure the unit was
truly deployable "they'll have to reclassify me and send me somewhere
else, which would take more money, more time. So actually, it would be
cheaper for them just to wait and keep me [here]."

Then there is the matter of how one gets pregnant in the first 30
place—the matter of what happens when you take men and women,
aged on average 18 to 25, away from what are generally small-town
homes, ship them to exotic ports of call, house them in the
catacomb-like berthing areas of ships, in coed tents or in crowded barracks and then subject them to loneliness, boredom and high stress. The
fantasy of civilian activists like Pat Schroeder is that the result will look
something like the bustling, efficient bridge of the *Starship Enterprise*.
The reality is apt to look more like "a big high school"—which is the
way a sailor named Elizabeth Rugh described her ship, the newly integrated *U.S.S. Samuel Gompers*.

Troops in Bosnia and Herzegovina (there were 1,500 female troops 31
in the first deployment) generally live in coed tents with eight to ten
people. Ranks are mixed, privates bedded down next to superiors.

Troops are not allowed to drink alcohol or eat in restaurants, but they *are* allowed to have sex—as long as they are single and not doing it with a subordinate (or superior) in their chain of command. In a solemn statement provided to *Stars and Stripes*, Army spokesman Captain Ken Clifton wrote that "the Army does not prohibit heterosexual relations among consenting single soldiers . . . but it does not provide facilities for sexual relations."

Lack of official facilities does not seem to be a great obstacle. 32 "Where there's a will there's a way!" Captain Chris Scholl told *Stars and Stripes.* Favorite locations, he said, include the backs of Humvees parked on a deserted air strip, tents, latrines, even underground bunkers—if you can hack standing up to your ankles in icy water. "It's going on all over the place," said Scholl. "They've locked us down so what else is there to do?"

And there is, of course, the problem of nonconsensual sex. A 33 Defense Department spokesman says "there is no way to get a good number" on the frequency of rapes and sexual assaults in the armed forces, because each service keeps its own numbers and defines things slightly differently. Still, it is clear that the Aberdeen case was not an isolated incident. The Army recorded twenty-four incidents it categorized as "sexual assaults" involving U.S. soldiers in the Gulf war; these cases range from that of a 24-year-old specialist who had been on overnight guard duty in the desert with a male soldier and awoke to find him fondling her under the blanket they had shared for warmth to that of a 21-year-old private who was raped at knifepoint by a sergeant.

The making of a soldier is a rough, hands-on, invasive process—a 34 preparation for what may be a very rough end. "[T]he training, the discipline, the daily humiliations, the privileges of 'brutish' sergeants, the living en masse like schools of fish," wrote James Jones in his essay "The Evolution of a Soldier," "are all directed toward breaking down the sense of sanctity of the physical person, and toward hardening the awareness that a soldier is the chattel (hopefully the proud chattel but a chattel all the same) of the society he serves."

Soldiers abuse each other—in training, in command, in hazing ritu- 35 als. It is a self-regulating mechanism; finding the weak links, then shaming them or bullying them to come up to par, is one way a unit ensures, or tries to ensure, its own survival, since on the battlefield one's life depends on one's buddies' performance.

Meanwhile, the brass attempt to operate on both tracks, to honor 36 the standards of both the civilian and the military world. They know they must encourage "cohesion" in their mixed-gender units, but they know, too, that they must avoid the wrong kind of cohesion—the kind that could stimulate jealousies, lovers' spats and . . . babies. So they end up sending a rather scrambled message, something like "Women are different but they're not different"; "We have the same expectations for women but you cannot treat them the same."

"Cry havoc and let slip the dogs of war," roared Shakespeare's Marc 37 Antony. Something tells me he wasn't talking about 19-year-old girls. "Let the dogs loose," read a piece of locker-room samizdat (observed by writer Kathy Dobie) at a coed basic training program in Florida. Men ache to unleash their dogs of war. Women generally have to be exhorted or trained to—then, good students and employees that they are, they can probably manage a semblance of dogginess at least for a while. But do we really want them to? Can a man of say, 35, be trained not to stay his hand when he needs to send a 20-year-old girl onto a mortar-strafed field? Can the impulse which, still, impels men to try to protect women be overridden? Do we want it to be? Won't sex always gum up the works? Would we really prefer if it didn't?

Responding to Reading

1. According to Gutmann, why will women never be successfully integrated into the armed forces? What evidence does she offer to support her position? How convincing a case does she make?
2. At what points does Gutmann address the arguments against her position? Should she have included additional opposing arguments? How effective are her responses to these opposing arguments?
3. Is there an intermediate position that Gutmann does not consider? For example, could women perform some kinds of combat duties but not others? Should she have discussed such a compromise position? Why or why not?

MARKED WOMEN

Deborah Tannen

Language researcher Deborah Tannen is widely known for her best-selling books on the problems people have communicating across gender and cultural lines (see p. 276). The following essay, written in 1993, is something of a departure from her usual work. Here she focuses not on different communication styles, but rather on the striking contrast she finds between the neutral way men in our culture are able to present themselves to the world and the more message-laden way women must generally do so.

Some years ago I was at a small working conference of four women 1 and eight men. Instead of concentrating on the discussion I found myself looking at the three other women at the table, thinking how each had a different style and how each style was coherent.

One woman had dark brown hair in a classic style, a cross between 2 Cleopatra and Plain Jane. The severity of her straight hair was softened by wavy bangs and ends that turned under. Because she was beautiful, the effect was more Cleopatra than plain.

The second woman was older, full of dignity and composure. Her 3 hair was cut in a fashionable style that left her with only one eye, thanks to a side part that let a curtain of hair fall across half her face. As she looked down to read her prepared paper, the hair robbed her of bifocal vision and created a barrier between her and the listeners.

The third woman's hair was wild, a frosted blond avalanche falling 4 over and beyond her shoulders. When she spoke she frequently tossed her head, calling attention to her hair and away from her lecture.

Then there was makeup. The first woman wore facial cover that 5 made her skin smooth and pale, a black line under each eye and mascara that darkened already dark lashes. The second wore only a light gloss on her lips and a hint of shadow on her eyes. The third had blue bands under her eyes, dark blue shadow, mascara, bright red lipstick and rouge; her fingernails flashed red.

I considered the clothes each woman had worn during the three 6 days of the conference: In the first case, man-tailored suits in primary colors with solid-color blouses. In the second, casual but stylish black T-shirts, a floppy collarless jacket and baggy slacks or a skirt in neutral colors. The third wore a sexy jump suit; tight sleeveless jersey and tight yellow slacks; a dress with gaping armholes and an indulged tendency to fall off one shoulder.

Shoes? No. 1 wore string sandals with medium heels; No. 2, sensi- 7 ble, comfortable walking shoes; No. 3, pumps with spike heels. You can fill in the jewelry, scarves, shawls, sweaters—or lack of them.

As I amused myself finding coherence in these styles, I suddenly 8 wondered why I was scrutinizing only the women. I scanned the eight men at the table. And then I knew why I wasn't studying them. The men's styles were unmarked.

The term "marked" is a staple of linguistic theory. It refers to the 9 way language alters the base meaning of a word by adding a linguistic particle that has no meaning on its own. The unmarked form of a word carries the meaning that goes without saying—what you think of when you're not thinking anything special.

The unmarked tense of verbs in English is the present—for example, 10 *visit*. To indicate past, you mark the verb by adding *ed* to yield *visited*. For future, you add a word: *will visit*. Nouns are presumed to be singular until marked for plural, typically by adding *s* or *es*, so *visit* becomes *visits* and *dish* becomes *dishes*.

The unmarked forms of most English words also convey "male." 11
Being male is the unmarked case. Endings like *ess* and *ette* mark words
as "female." Unfortunately, they also tend to mark them for frivolous-
ness. Would you feel safe entrusting your life to a doctorette? Alfre
Woodard, who was an Oscar nominee for best supporting actress, says
she identifies herself as an actor because "actresses worry about eyelashes and cellulite, and women who are actors worry about the characters we are playing." Gender markers pick up extra meanings that
reflect common associations with the female gender: not quite serious,
often sexual.

Each of the women at the conference had to make decisions about 12
hair, clothing, makeup and accessories, and each decision carried meaning. Every style available to us was marked. The men in our group had
made decisions, too, but the range from which they chose was incom-
parably narrower. Men can choose styles that are marked, but they
don't have to, and in this group none did. Unlike the women, they had
the option of being unmarked.

Take the men's hair styles. There was no marine crew cut or oily 13
longish hair falling into eyes, no asymmetrical, two-tiered construction
to swirl over a bald top. One man was unabashedly bald; the others
had hair of standard length, parted on one side, in natural shades of
brown or gray or graying. Their hair obstructed no views, left little to
toss or push back or run fingers through and, consequently, needed
and attracted no attention. A few men had beards. In a business setting,
beards might be marked. In this academic gathering, they weren't.

There could have been a cowboy shirt with string tie or a three- 14
piece suit or a necklaced hippie in jeans. But there wasn't. All eight men
wore brown or blue slacks and nondescript shirts of light colors. No
man wore sandals or boots; their shoes were dark, closed, comfortable
and flat. In short, unmarked.

Although no man wore makeup, you couldn't say the men didn't 15
wear makeup in the sense that you could say a woman didn't wear
makeup. For men, no makeup is unmarked.

I asked myself what style we women could have adopted that 16
would have been unmarked, like the men's. The answer was none.
There is no unmarked woman.

There is no woman's hair style that can be called standard, that says 17
nothing about her. The range of women's hair styles is staggering, but a
woman whose hair has no particular style is perceived as not caring
about how she looks, which can disqualify her for many positions, and
will subtly diminish her as a person in the eyes of some.

Women must choose between attractive shoes and comfortable 18
shoes. When our group made an unexpected trek, the woman who
wore flat, laced shoes arrived first. Last to arrive was the woman in
spike heels, shoes in hand and a handful of men around her.

If a woman's clothing is tight or revealing (in other words, sexy), it 19
sends a message—an intended one of wanting to be attractive, but also a
possibly unintended one of availability. If her clothes are not sexy, that too
sends a message, lent meaning by the knowledge that they could have
been. There are thousands of cosmetic products from which women can
choose and myriad ways of applying them. Yet no makeup at all is anything but unmarked. Some men see it as a hostile refusal to please them.

Women can't even fill out a form without telling stories about them- 20
selves. Most forms give four titles to choose from. "Mr." carries no
meaning other than that the respondent is male. But a woman who
checks "Mrs." or "Miss" communicates not only whether she has been
married but also whether she has conservative tastes in forms of
address—and probably other conservative values as well. Checking
"Ms." declines to let on about marriage (checking "Mr." declines nothing since nothing was asked), but it also marks her as either liberated or
rebellious, depending on the observer's attitudes and assumptions.

I sometimes try to duck these variously marked choices by giving 21
my title as "Dr."—and in so doing risk marking myself as either uppity
(hence sarcastic responses like *"Excuse me!"*) or an overachiever (hence
reactions or congratulatory surprise like "Good for you!").

All married women's surnames are marked. If a woman takes her 22
husband's name, she announces to the world that she is married and
has traditional values. To some it will indicate that she is less herself,
more identified by her husband's identity. If she does not take her husband's name, this too is marked, seen as worthy of comment: she has
done something; she has "kept her own name." A man is never said to
have "kept his own name" because it never occurs to anyone that he
might have given it up. For him using his own name is unmarked.

A married woman who wants to have her cake and eat it too may 23
use her surname plus his, with or without a hyphen. But this too
announces her marital status and often results in a tongue-tying string.
In a list (Harvey O'Donovan, Jonathan Feldman, Stephanie Woodbury
McGillicutty), the woman's multiple name stands out. It is marked.

I have never been inclined toward biological explanations of gender 24
differences in language, but I was intrigued to see Ralph Fasold bring
biological phenomena to bear on the question of linguistic marking in
his book "The Sociolinguistics of Language." Fasold stresses that language and culture are particularly unfair in treating women as the
marked case because biologically it is the male that is marked. While
two X chromosomes make a female, two Y chromosomes make nothing.
Like the linguistic markers *s, es* or *ess*, the Y chromosome doesn't
"mean" anything unless it is attached to a root form—an X chromosome.

Developing this idea elsewhere, Fasold points out that girls are
born with fully female bodies, while boys are born with modified

female bodies. He invites men who doubt this to lift up their shirts and contemplate why they have nipples.

In his book, Fasold notes "a wide range of facts which demonstrates 26 that female is the unmarked sex." For example, he observes that there are a few species that produce only females, like the whiptail lizard. Thanks to parthenogenesis, they have no trouble having as many daughters as they like. There are no species, however, that produce only males. This is no surprise, since any such species would become extinct in its first generation.

Fasold is also intrigued by species that produce individuals not 27 involved in reproduction, like honeybees and leaf-cutter ants. Reproduction is handled by the queen and a relatively few males; the workers are sterile females. "Since they do not reproduce," Fasold says, "there is no reason for them to be one sex or the other, so they default, so to speak, to female."

Fasold ends his discussion of these matters by pointing out that if 28 language reflected biology, grammar books would direct us to use "she" to include males and females and "he" only for specifically male refer-ents. But they don't. They tell us that "he" means "he or she," and that "she" is used only if the referent is specifically female. This use of "he" as the sex-indefinite pronoun is an innovation introduced into English by grammarians in the 18th and 19th centuries, according to Peter Mühlhäusler and Rom Harré in "Pronouns and People." From at least about 1500, the correct sex-indefinite pronoun was "they," as it still is in casual spoken English. In other words, the female was declared by grammarians to be the marked case.

Writing this article may mark me not as a writer, not as a linguist, 29 not as an analyst of human behavior, but as a feminist—which will have positive or negative, but in any case powerful, connotations for readers. Yet I doubt that anyone reading Ralph Fasold's book would put that label on him.

I discovered the markedness inherent in the very topic of gender 30 after writing a book on differences in conversational style based on geo-graphical region, ethnicity, class, age and gender. When I was inter-viewed, the vast majority of journalists wanted to talk about the differences between women and men. While I thought I was simply describing what I observed—something I had learned to do as a researcher—merely mentioning women and men marked me as a fem-inist for some.

When I wrote a book devoted to gender differences, in ways of 31 speaking, I sent the manuscript to five male colleagues, asking them to alert me to any interpretation, phrasing or wording that might seem unfairly negative toward men. Even so, when the book came out, I encountered responses like that of the television talk show host who, after interviewing me, turned to the audience and asked if they thought I was male-bashing.

Leaping upon a poor fellow who affably nodded in agreement, she 32 made him stand and asked, "Did what she said accurately describe you?" "Oh, yes," he answered. "That's me exactly." "And what she said about women—does that sound like your wife?" "Oh yes," he responded. "That's her exactly." "Then why do you think she's male-bashing?" He answered, with disarming honesty, "Because she's a woman and she's saying things about men."

To say anything about women and men without marking oneself as 33 either feminist or anti-feminist, male-basher or apologist for men seems as impossible for a woman as trying to get dressed in the morning without inviting interpretations of her character.

Sitting at the conference table musing on these matters, I felt sad to 34 think that we women didn't have the freedom to be unmarked that the men sitting next to us had. Some days you just want to get dressed and go about your business. But if you're a woman, you can't, because there is no unmarked woman.

Responding to Reading

1. Tannen notes that men "can choose styles that are marked, but they don't have to" (12); however, she believes that women do not have the "option of being unmarked." What does she mean? If possible, give some examples of women's styles that you believe are unmarked. (Note that in paragraph 16, Tannen says there are no such styles.)
2. In paragraph 33, Tannen says, "To say anything about women and men without marking oneself as either feminist or anti-feminist, male-basher or apologist for men seems as impossible for a woman as trying to get dressed in the morning without inviting interpretations of her character." Do you agree?
3. In paragraphs 24–28 Tannen discusses Ralph Fasold's book *The Sociolinguistics of Language*. Why does she include this material? Could she have made her point as effectively without it?

FOCUS: IS THE PLAYING FIELD LEVEL?

TITLE IX: IT'S TIME TO LIVE UP TO THE LETTER OF THE LAW

Donna Lopiano

Title IX of the Education Amendments Act, passed by Congress in 1972, requires that "[n]o person in the United States shall, on the basis of sex, be denied the benefits of, or be subjected to discrimination under any educational programs or activities receiving federal financial assistance." When applied to academic athletic programs, this controversial legislation has been interpreted by the courts to mean that high schools and colleges must offer roughly the same number of varsity sports for female and male students and that spending must be allocated equally in relation to the numbers of female and male participants. Although participation in and financial support for women's intercollegiate sports has grown enormously since the passage of Title IX, men's sports in general still receive considerably more funding. A number of schools have faced lawsuits by women athletes denied access to sporting opportunities, including a suit filed against Brown University by a female gymnast after Brown, because of budget cuts, eliminated funding for two men's teams and two women's teams, including gymnastics. In 1997, the case reached the Supreme Court, which let stand a lower court's ruling against Brown. In the following essay, Donna Lopiano—former director of women's athletics at the University of Texas and currently executive director of the Women's Sports Foundation—applauds that decision and its ramifications.

Lopiano (b. 1947), who holds degrees from Southern Connecticut State University and the University of Southern California, was denied a place on her local Little League when she was eleven and has been fighting for equal opportunity for women in sports ever since.

The U.S. Court of Appeals for the First Circuit has upheld a district-court decision finding Brown University and its athletics program in violation of Title IX of the Education Amendments of 1972. 1

Brown argued that it should be permitted to offer fewer athletic opportunities for women because men are more interested in sports than women are. A lawsuit was filed soon after Brown eliminated varsity-level teams for women in gymnastics and volleyball. 2

To comply with Title IX, Brown has threatened to drop men's 3
"minor" sports (such as wrestling or gymnastics) and to blame it all on
Title IX and women's sports. Sour grapes? Sure sounds like it. Let's not
forget that the Brown lawsuit began after Brown had spent $250,000 to
buy out the football coach's contract and then dropped two men's and
two women's sports to balance the budget. Worse yet, Brown then spent
well over half a million dollars litigating the Title IX case, a sum that
could have brought the university's sports program into compliance
with the statute. What is going on here? This just doesn't make any sense.

The Brown decision is consistent with other court decisions. In 4
other cases in which institutions have dropped a women's sports program—despite the fact that women on campus were clearly underrepresented in athletics—the courts have sided with the female plaintiffs.
Colleges and universities need to recognize that women will continue
going to court to enforce the law. So isn't it time that institutions stop
wasting money in legal fees and get on with the job of expanding
opportunities for women athletes?

June 23, 1997, will mark the 25th anniversary of the passage of Title 5
IX, the federal law prohibiting sex discrimination by educational institutions receiving federal money. Yet most colleges and universities still
do not comply with the law. Has progress been made? Definitely. The
glass is not as empty as it was in 1972, when women were receiving less
than 1 per cent of all athletic-scholarship dollars and still buying their
own uniforms and equipment. But the glass is only half full. At the college level, across all divisions of the National Collegiate Athletic
Association, twice as many men as women participate in sports. (The
proportions are the same at the high-school level.) Women are still
receiving $179-million less than men in college athletic scholarships
each year. (Men receive $356-million annually.) And women's sports
budgets are far short of the budgets for men's sports.

Let us remember that sports are not just fun and games. At the col- 6
lege level, athletic scholarships and admissions preferences for athletes
translate into access to education. At the junior-high and high-school
levels, participation in sports makes a huge impact on girls' lives: It is
associated with pluses such as better grades and graduation rates,
increased confidence and self-esteem, and reduced risk of breast cancer,
osteoporosis, and heart disease later in life. It is no accident that 80 percent of the executive women in Fortune 500 companies identify themselves as having been "tomboys" and say that they played sports when
they were young.

So why are so many high schools, colleges, and universities still 7
fighting the law? In 1972, almost 100 per cent of the money in college
athletics went to support athletic programs for men. The money wasn't
there, and still isn't there, to give women equal athletic opportunities

unless male athletes and coaches are willing to accept a smaller piece of the financial pie, and unless all athletes take a cut in traditional levels of support. Therein lies the problem. On every campus, one or two men's sports—usually football and basketball—traditionally have received a disproportionate share of the athletics budget (30 to 60 per cent) and are powerful enough to reject any effort to reduce their "standard of living." College presidents (and high-school principals) take the easy way out by cutting men's "minor" sports and blaming it on the women—pitting victims against victims.

Some supporters of men's teams say they are concerned that decisions like that in the Brown case will lead institutions to cut athletics opportunities for men. This issue is beside the point. The real point is that institutions need to stop hiding behind the threat of cutting men's teams and start increasing opportunities for women. Historically, institutions made progress in the 1970s in opening up athletics opportunities for women. But then they slowed down their efforts, and they got caught. When you commit a traffic violation, you can try to make excuses, but that rarely works. Or you can change your driving habits. 8

Can an institution keep sports opportunities for men intact while increasing opportunities for women? Yes, but only by avoiding easy choices and taking some less-than-popular steps. 9

Cutting the level of men's participation needs to be a last choice. Before any college or university does that, every one of its sports should cut back on excessive expenditures. Doing so may mean eliminating a spring-break trip or one or two regular-season games. Maybe uniforms should be bought every other year or every three years. The point is that all sports—including the powerhouses like football and basketball—need to find ways to tighten their belts without cutting back on student participation. 10

We also need to start at the opposite end of the continuum by asking if we can generate more revenues. Colleges and universities need to put more effort into raising money for women's sports; they need to promote those sports, so that women's teams generate bigger gate receipts. They put the time and effort into raising money for men's sports; now put the same time and effort into women's sports. 11

Colleges and universities also should remember that expanding opportunities for women is not only right; over the long term, it is in their best financial interest to do so. Quite simply, colleges and universities risk further costly lawsuits if they don't "do the right thing." Even if institutions manage to avoid lawsuits, they may not be able to avoid negative publicity. As of October 1, 1996, institutions of higher education are required to publish annually their expenditures on men's and women's sports under a new federal law, the Gender Equity in Athletics Disclosure Act. Public embarrassment can be a strong force that creates change. 12

Remember, the 20-year-olds of the 1970s are the first generation of 13
mothers and fathers who grew up fully believing that their daughters
were going to have equal opportunities in sports. These 40-year-olds of
the 1990s are now being asked to support their institutions of higher
learning in a big way. How will they feel if their daughters are not
receiving the same opportunities as their sons? Moms and dads of
female athletes are paying taxes and tuition. They want equal treatment
for their children.

The smart colleges and universities will quickly take the high 14
ground. Institutions need to promise to achieve rates of male and
female participation in athletics that are in proportion to the enrollment
of male and female students. If they develop a plan that will achieve
such results within five years, no one is likely to sue.

The bottom line is the need for strong ethical leadership by college 15
and university presidents. They need to admit that sports are as important to our daughters as to our sons. They need to ask their alumni and
alumnae to step up to the donation plate to help keep athletic opportunities for men while, at the same time, adding opportunities for women.
They need to require Title IX self-evaluation studies that would show
them just what their athletics directors are—or are not—doing to
increase opportunities for women. They need to require their athletics
directors to submit written plans with reasonable timetables to insure
compliance with Title IX. Finally, they need to monitor those plans to
see that progress is being made. Otherwise, they—like Brown—may
end up in court.

While the Brown University decision can be viewed as a victory for 16
women's sports, that victory will be hollow if other college presidents
and educational institutions fail to do the right thing for our daughters
who play sports.

Responding to Reading

1. According to Lopiano, why is participation in athletics so important in
   girls' lives? If this is the case, why are so many high schools and colleges
   failing to comply with Title IX?
2. What objections do supporters of men's teams have to Title IX? How
   does Lopiano address these objections? How effective are her
   counterarguments?
3. In "You've Come a Long Way, Maybe" (p. 408), Susan K. Cahn presents the
   history of women's sports in the United States since the 1960s. Is her analysis of the current situation consistent with Lopiano's analysis? In what ways
   are they similar? In what ways are they different?

THE NUMBERS DON'T ADD UP

Maureen E. Mahoney

The following essay deals with the thorny issue of how gender equity is to be perceived under the terms of Title IX (see the headnote to the previous essay, by Donna Lopiano). Should the goal be that 50 percent of a school's resources be spent on women's sports and 50 percent on men's sports? Or should a school's resources be allocated in terms of the relative number of women and men who participate in varsity sports? Like Lopiano, Maureen Mahoney writes about a lawsuit filed against Brown University by a female gymnast after Brown eliminated funding for the women's gymnastics team. However, Mahoney—one of Brown's attorneys in the case—takes the opposite stance from Lopiano. In this editorial, originally published in 1997 in Sports Illustrated, *she argues that despite the Supreme Court's refusal to side with the university, Brown's action was justified because neither sex received preferential treatment.*

Everyone agrees that Title IX was supposed to end the reign of athletic directors who thought women had no place on their fields or in their arenas. But a Title IX class-action suit filed in 1992, Cohen v. Brown University, raised a different issue: Does a fair-minded university where half the students are women have an obligation to try to fill its varsity rosters with equal numbers of men and women even if far more men than women want to participate? 1

Brown was at the forefront of the women's athletic movement when it established 14 women's varsity teams shortly after it became coed in 1971. Women now constitute 53% of the Brown student body, but Brown doesn't want to count heads and set aside 53% of its varsity positions for women because it believes that equal opportunity can be afforded through a broad array of teams that reflect the relative interests and abilities of both sexes. 2

In 1991, when Brown needed to make university-wide budget cuts, it changed the source of funding for two men's teams and two women's teams (37 varsity spots for men, 23 for women) so that neither sex would receive preferential treatment. But Amy Cohen, a gymnast, and the other plaintiffs said Title IX means ladies first: Schools must fund all viable women's sports or continually expand opportunities for women until gender parity is achieved on the varsity level. The case isn't over yet, but so far the courts have sided with the plaintiffs. 3

The federal trial and appeals courts ruled that Brown was not in compliance with the cut-and-dried formula the courts adopted for measuring equality under Title IX: A school must structure teams so that the percentage of male and female varsity athletes mirrors (or is moving 4 toward mirroring) the gender ratio of the student body, or it must fund every viable varsity sport that its female students want to play. The appellate court told Brown to find the necessary sources for all sports women want to play, including fencing, skiing and water polo, or eliminate as many as 213 varsity slots for men. Last week the Supreme Court chose not to review this issue yet.

Is that a victory for women, for equal opportunity? I don't think so. 5 Shortly after I began representing Brown in this case, a radio commentator asked me how I would feel, as a woman, if Brown won and set back the movement for "gender equity." In the eyes of the commentator, also a woman, Cohen v. Brown was subtitled Women v. Men, and I was giving aid and comfort to the enemy. I am the mother of a 12-year-old daughter who loves sports, but I also have a 14-year-old son. In my eyes Brown's approach captures the essence of gender equity: The school has welcomed women with open arms, and it has relied upon the good faith and common sense of its faculty and administrators—not mathematical formulas—to offer programs that nurture the talents and interests of our sons and daughters.

Title IX should not be read to prohibit a varsity program that is 60% 6 male at a university where half the students are women for the same reason that we do not prohibit a collegiate dance program that is 90% female or an engineering program that is 70% male. Who would advocate a rule requiring colleges that receive applications from 100 qualified dancers— 75 women, 25 men—to set aside 25 spaces for men and 25 spaces for women to ensure gender balance in a program with room for 50 dancers? Is it fair to structure that dance program so that it affords qualified men a far greater chance of participating and guarantees that many more qualified women will be excluded? That's not equal opportunity; that's preferential treatment—which Title IX expressly says is not required.

So now we get to the heart of Brown's position in Cohen v. Brown: 7 Are there substantially more men than women who have the desire and ability to compete on the varsity level? Because if there are, accomplished male athletes should not have to duke it out among themselves to get the slots that are left after all the women have been accommodated. The court didn't require that question to be answered. It said we should just presume that "women, given the opportunity, will naturally participate in athletics in numbers equal to men." That may be true someday, but is it true now? How do we square that presumption with the fact that the men in Brown's intramural program—which has no limits on participation—outnumber the women by 8 to 1, or with evidence that approximately 60% of students around the country who want to play varsity sports are men? And why do we think that it is so important to ensure that half the athletes are women when we don't seem to care that far less than half the dancers are men?

My bottom line is this: Women don't have to have 50% of the var- 8
sity positions to succeed as athletes. They need equal opportunity, and
you don't get that from a numerical formula. It comes from equality-
minded athletic directors who try their best to respond to the interests
and abilities of all the students, and it comes from universities like
Brown that display the courage to defend their principles and autonomy, even at the risk of being accused of defending men in the gender-
equity battle. And someday equal opportunity will come from judges
who will recognize that Congress wanted athletic directors to be guided
by the rules of fair play.

Responding to Reading

1. Mahoney begins her essay by discussing the history of Title IX at Brown
   University. What is the purpose of this historical overview? How does it
   help Mahoney make her point about Title IX?
2. Why does Mahoney think that the courts' decision upholding the male-
   female gender ratio in sports is not a victory for women? Do you agree with
   her when she says that "Brown's approach captures the essence of gender
   equity" (5)?
3. In paragraph 8, Mahoney says, "Women don't have to have 50% of the varsity positions to succeed as athletes." In the same paragraph, she goes on to
   say that "Congress wanted athletic directors to be guided by the rules of fair
   play." Would Donna Lopiano (p. 402) agree? Would Susan Cahn (p. 408)?
   Explain.

YOU'VE COME A LONG WAY, MAYBE:
A "REVOLUTION" IN WOMEN'S SPORTS?

Susan K. Cahn

In the preface to her book Coming on Strong: Gender and Sexuality
in 20th Century Women's Sports *(1994), Susan K. Cahn writes, "As a
sports-minded teenager of the 1970s, I marveled at the courage and skill of the
pioneer female athletes of my generation. Prompted by new federal legislation
against sex discrimination and, more generally, by feminist demands for
female access to traditionally male realms of society, the sports world seemed
to undergo a rapid, almost instant transformation. . . . As one of the grateful
beneficiaries of these changes, I eagerly joined my high school basketball team
and thrilled at my good fortune—the chance to be involved in what I assumed
was the first-ever interscholastic sporting opportunity for girls." Later, as a
graduate student at the University of Minnesota, she grew curious about the
tradition of women's athletics in the United States, researching which "specific time periods, classes, or cultures supported women's athletics before the
1970s" and wondering, "If women had participated in the past, why had sports*

remained such a bastion of male activity and identity?" Coming on Strong, *which began as her Ph.D. dissertation, considers these issues from a historical perspective. In its final chapter, reprinted here, Cahn looks at the triumphs and continued challenges of women's sports from the 1960s to the present.*

In the late 1960s and early 1970s, women's sport entered a dramat- 1 ically new era, a period of tremendous gains and even higher hopes for women athletes. Participation in high school girls' sport increased more than 500 percent between the late 1960s and the early 1980s. At the college level the figures showed an increase of between 300 percent and 500 percent. In international amateur sport, female Olympians attained unprecedented popularity, beginning with sprinter Wilma Rudolph in 1960 and continuing with gymnasts Olga Korbut and Nadia Comaneci in the 1970s. Women's professional sport experienced a similar boom, led by tennis but with significant breakthroughs in golf and team sports as well. The feminist movement of the late 1960s and 1970s, in conjunction with the fitness boom of the 1970s and 1980s, had sparked renewed interest in women's sport nationwide. Barriers that had remained unbreakable for most of the century seemed to be rapidly tumbling, creating a new era of excitement and genuine possibility in women's athletics.

Amid the swirl of change, in November 1983 women's sport advo- 2 cates from around the country assembled for a groundbreaking gathering called "The New Agenda Conference." Subtitled "A Blueprint for the Future of Women's Sports," it reflected the efforts of women's sport leaders to develop strategies and momentum that would allow them to solidify recent gains and set an even brighter course for women's athletics in the coming decades.

Yet the impetus for the conference came not from an envisioned 3 future but rather from immediate setbacks. In what many women viewed as a crushing defeat, the leaders of men's intercollegiate athletics had just completed a successful takeover bid for the right to govern women's collegiate sport, running roughshod over the existing female-headed governing body of women's athletics. Fearing a loss of female autonomy and power in the sports world, concerned women called a national conference where they hoped to take stock of the situation, and from this assessment generate a practical yet visionary plan for the future.

The New Agenda Conference met in Washington, D.C., exactly sixty 4 years and seven months after the first national conference on women's sport had gathered in the same city to found the Women's Division of the NAAF. In 1923, in response to what they understood as hostile attempts by male sport leaders to take over women's athletic activities and impose a dangerous and undemocratic model of sport derived from male athletic culture, women physical educators and recreation leaders had organized to push forward their own new agenda.

Six decades later the issues remained startlingly similar. Angry at 5 being steamrolled by a powerful men's organization, women leaders of the 1980s argued that male-dominated collegiate sport was marred by crass commercialism, corruption, and win-at-all-costs attitudes. They reiterated the well-worn claim that only female leadership could provide an alternative model of women's sport that avoided these pitfalls. And like their predecessors they plotted a strategy for change that combined academic research on female athletes, active promotion of women's sports, and political confrontation with obdurate male sport leaders.

The similarities between the 1923 and 1983 conferences are in one 6 sense predictable, but in another puzzling. Given the long history of men's control of sporting institutions and a pattern of opportunistic involvement in women's sport, it is not surprising that when women's athletics grew in popularity over the 1970s, male-controlled organizations exhibited a sudden interest in managing women's collegiate sport. Contemporary women leaders are grappling with a problem that plagued earlier physical educators: how to press for full inclusion in athletics without being subsumed into a preexisting model of sport viewed by many as fundamentally sexist, elitist, and exploitative.

What is more surprising is that the issues have changed so little 7 when women's athletics have apparently undergone so momentous a change. The transformation begun in the late 1960s has permanently altered the face of athletic culture and provided unprecedented opportunities for the millions of girls and women who have taken up sport in recent years. Yet just beneath the surface strong currents of resistance continue to frustrate women's efforts to achieve full participation and self-determination in athletics. The effect has been successfully to limit the impact of change on established athletic institutions, on each woman's personal sense of possibility, and on the surrounding culture. As in the past the conflict sparked by women's pursuit of athletic access and excellence tells two stories—one about the dynamic interplay of gender and power within the world of sport and the other about the complicated synergy between women's sport and gender relations in the wider society.

The roots of the sea change in women's sports during the 1970s lay 8 in a series of more cautious but important steps taken in the late 1950s and 1960s. After Ohio State University sponsored the first intercollegiate women's golf championship in 1941, the event became an annual one, and by the mid-1950s its backers had succeeded in turning the stubborn disapproval of leading physical educators into a limited endorsement. However, with the exception of golf, leaders of the field remained only minimally receptive to competitive intercollegiate sport. It took the maturation of a younger generation to push for more far-reaching changes, beginning with the founding of the Commission on Intercollegiate

Athletics for Women (CIAW) in 1966 to govern and promote major intercollegiate tournaments for women. This group was the direct predecessor of the Association for Intercollegiate Athletics for Women (AIAW), which after its founding in 1971 became the sole sponsor and chief advocate of women's intercollegiate sports during the 1970s.

As an eager young generation of athletes and instructors succeeded 9 in gradually liberalizing the long-standing ban on female varsity competition, their efforts received unanticipated support from forces outside the insular world of women's physical education. The pace of change quickened dramatically when women's sport became swept up in the larger winds of social change that characterized American society of the 1960s and 1970s. By the early 1970s a language of equality, opportunity, and rights fostered by the black civil rights movement, the American Indian and Chicano movements, and the women's and gay liberation movements circulated widely among American citizens who demonstrated a renewed sensitivity to issues of fairness and discrimination. Women in sport could now approach the issue of athletic resources and opportunity from an explicitly political perspective. They were aided by organized feminism. Groups dedicated to women's liberation were increasingly using the courts, the legislature, and organized pressure tactics to address gender discrimination in work, education, and the law.

Beyond formal politics the 1960s and 1970s were also marked by a 10 cultural revolution, expressed most boldly by members of the counterculture and by activists in a "sexual revolution" that advocated a more permissive and experimental approach to sexual expression. Although sport remained peripheral to these developments, the counterculture's emphasis on physical freedom, bodily pleasure, and leisure offered an indirect source of encouragement for women to take up sport and fitness activities as a form of pleasurable recreation. Trends within mainstream commercial culture tendered women another form of inducement. The television era made sports more widely accessible and popular than ever. And in an ever-expanding consumer economy, sport and recreational activities became tied to a multibillion dollar sporting industry that depended on persuading more and more Americans to take up one or more sports and buy the requisite clothing, services, and equipment.

Currents of political reform, women's activism, and cultural innova- 11 tion fostered a renewed excitement about women's sport and an awareness of its feminist implications, an atmosphere much like that of the post–World War I era. This time, however, the disputed concept of a woman's right to athletic enjoyment became, for the first time, codified in law. When Congress passed the Educational Act of 1972, the legislation included a section addressing the issue of sex discrimination. Title IX of the act stated: "No person in the United States shall, on the basis of sex, be excluded from participation in, be denied the benefits of, or be subjected to discrimination under any educational programs or activities receiving federal financial assistance." Without even mentioning the word "athletics," Title IX ushered in what many believed to be a "revolution" in women's sport. Although it would take years to sort out the law's exact meaning, it indicated that women and men would have to receive equal treatment in both high school and college athletics.

Strictly interpreted, the law might require momentous changes in   12 school sport. Even a relatively lenient interpretation, while not mandating absolute equality, would require that schools offer approximately the same number of sports for women and men, and that athletic department funding be allocated to women's and men's programs in roughly equivalent proportions to the ratio of female to male athletes active in varsity sports. These requirements would begin to redress the egregious inequities discovered in nearly every college athletic budget. At a typical midwestern university in the Big Ten Conference, men's athletics received thirteen hundred dollars for every dollar spent on the women's program. A mid-Atlantic university allocated nineteen hundred dollars for women's sport while granting men's athletics over two million dollars. On the West Coast, Washington State University appropriated less than 1 percent of its two-million-dollar athletic budget for women's sports.

Such extreme disparities characterized women's sport outside the   13 schools as well. In 1970 Billie Jean King became the first professional woman tennis player to exceed the one-hundred-thousand-dollar mark in annual winnings. However, the top male winner of 1970, Rod Laver, raked in nearly three times that amount while winning only one-third as many tournaments as King won. Professional golf presented a similar story. The top female winner of 1972, Kathy Whitworth, played in twenty-nine tournaments and earned $65,000 while the top male pro Jack Nicklaus, earned more than $320,000 in only nineteen tournaments. Pay inequities found their corollary in wildly imbalanced media coverage. Between August 1972 and September 1973, of NBC's 366 hours of televised live sports a mere 1 hour of coverage went to women. CBS devoted ten hours of its 260 hours of athletic coverage to women's events. Altogether, with regard to publicity, funding, coaching, and playing opportunities, the inequities were so glaring that former Olympic sprinter Doris Brown commented that the prospect of being "second-class citizens" seemed to her to be a great leap forward: "Second-class citizenship sounds good when you are accustomed to being regarded as fifth class."

While Title IX would have no official impact beyond federally   14 funded educational institutions, its clearly stated stance against discrimination advanced a principle of equality which women's sport advocates would attempt to apply throughout amateur and professional sport. Even before the passage of Title IX supporters had already begun to pressure athletic officials to remedy the pervasive gender inequities in sport. Lawyers had filed numerous law suits on behalf of female high school athletes seeking access to boys' sports teams in the absence of school teams for girls. Within the Olympic movement steady pressure from women's sport leaders had increased women's representation between 1952 and 1976 from 10 percent to 20.6 percent of Olympic competitors.

In professional sport Billie Jean King led a 1970 boycott to protest 15 pay inequities on the pro tennis tour. Over the next three years she helped launch a separate women's pro circuit sponsored by Virginia Slims, successfully pressured the United States Lawn Tennis Association into equalizing prize money in the U.S. Open, and organized the Women's Tennis Association to represent women on the tour. In September 1973 King won what appeared to be the ultimate victory against sexism in sport when she defeated the fifty-five-year-old former tennis star and self-proclaimed "male chauvinist pig," Bobby Riggs. An estimated forty-eight million television viewers joined more than thirty thousand spectators at the Houston Astrodome to watch a high stakes match that was as much circus as sporting event. After entering the arena on a red-draped divan carried by four men dressed as ancient slaves, King met Riggs—who had rolled onto the scene in a ricksha pulled by five scantily clad women he dubbed "Bobby's bosom buddies"—at center court and proceeded to handily defeat both her opponent and the odds makers, who had not imagined that a woman at the top of her career could defeat an aging male tennis hustler.

King promptly cashed in on her popularity through endorsement 16 earnings, part of which she gave back to women's sports by financing *WomenSports* magazine, a monthly publication for and about women athletes that debuted in 1974. That same year she joined with former Olympic swimmer Donna de Varona and other insiders in the sports world in founding the Women's Sports Foundation, an advocacy group that has worked to advance women's opportunities and challenge sexism at all levels of sport.

Although as an athletic superstar King wielded resources and clout 17 unavailable to other advocates of women's sport, she was in no way a lone activist. Rather, she used her position to gain publicity and inroads for a much broader grass-roots movement of women who were determined to break down long-standing barriers to women's access to sport and physical development. Few of these activists laid explicit claim to the word *feminist* or attempted to forge connections with the larger, more politically oriented feminist movement. Nevertheless, women's efforts to attain the right to fully participate in sport, to enhance their strength and coordination, and to compete without psychological or institutional restrictions were consistent with a broad range of feminist activities designed to win for women the right to control and enjoy their own bodies. In this sense, whether they claimed it or not, women's sports advocates shared an agenda and an activist spirit with self-defined feminists involved in reproductive rights campaigns, anti-rape organizing, women's health clinics, women's self-defense classes, lesbian feminist activism, and self-help efforts that encouraged women to explore their own sexuality.

Infused with the spirit of a broader feminist movement and inspired 18 by their own early successes, women who played, organized, and wrote about women's sports shared a tremendous excitement and sense of possibility. Perceiving that advancements in women's athletics were directly linked to the improvements in women's condition and the dismantling of sexism within American society, many believed that they were involved in revolutionizing women's lives. A *Ms.* magazine article from 1973, titled "Closing the Muscle Gap," celebrated women's athletic achievements and linked them directly to a revolutionary change in gender relations: "By developing her power to the fullest, any woman, from Olympic star to the weekend tennis player, can be a match for any man she chooses to take on. More importantly, she will inherit the essential source of human self-confidence—pride in and control over a finely tuned body. That alone would be a revolution." Leanne Schreiber, the editor of *WomenSports*, advanced a similar claim, arguing that the systematic discouragement of female physicality served historically to "divorce" women's identities from their bodies. Women, she claimed, "have been divorced from the most basic sense of power and the most basic source of power," experiencing as a result "a very primary disconnection with the world." Sport promised to reconnect women with their bodies and their power.

The sense of revolutionary change spread beyond the confines of 19 feminist sport reformers, capturing the attention of the mainstream sport and news media. In 1973 *Sports Illustrated* published a three-part series on sexism in sport that acknowledged the pressing need for change by presenting an unambiguously feminist indictment of the male-dominated sports world. Five years later *Time* magazine made women's sports its cover story. The article, titled "Comes the Revolution," noted that the female athlete, "whether aged six, sixty or beyond, . . . is running, jumping, hitting and throwing as U.S. women have never done before." The author concluded: "The revolution in women's athletics is at full, running tide, bringing with it a sea change—not just in activities, but in attitudes as well." The article captured the widely shared sentiment that advances in women's sports represented both the personal and collective empowerment of women; confident and strong in their individual bodies, women in a group were mounting an effective challenge to men's athletic monopoly and privileged status in society.

The strong sense of promise that characterized women's sport in the 20 1970s seemed to be borne out as the decade advanced. By the end of the seventies, the number of women competing in intercollegiate sport had doubled, many of them assisted by athletic scholarships. Participation rates had risen even more dramatically at the high school level. Even team sports, which historically had attracted the least support and the greatest scorn, appeared to be on their way toward full acceptance. Women's basketball, the most popular collegiate sport, received approval as an Olympic sport in 1976, along with women's team handball and, four years later, women's field hockey. At the professional level a women's pro softball league began play in 1976. Although it folded in 1979, that same year saw the launching of the professional Women's Basketball League, which operated for three seasons before going under.[1] The failure to establish a long-running professional team sports venture did not dampen the confident tone that characterized women's sports during most of the 1970s. Advocates saw setbacks such as these as temporary obstacles on a path of irreversible and rapid progress. A hopeful mood prevailed, generating what one report described as an "overall impression of inevitability."

Behind the scenes, however, sports activists were beginning to comprehend the depth and power of the resistance to women's demands for athletic equity. The opposition took several forms. It included a well-organized and financed campaign to reverse Title IX, foot-dragging on the part of officials charged with implementing or enforcing the law and the sports media, which occasionally ridiculed and consistently neglected women's sports.

The strongest opposition to Title IX came from the National Collegiate Athletic Association (NCAA), the governing agency for men's intercollegiate sport. NCAA executive director Walter Byers forcefully denounced the legislation, announcing that Title IX would spell the "possible doom of intercollegiate sports." Behind this ominous claim lay the belief that men's programs would suffer irreparable damage if forced to endure budget cuts, scholarship reductions, and the loss of other resources that would go toward the support of women's athletics. Under Byers's leadership, the NCAA financed a major lobbying effort aimed at the Department of Health, Education and Welfare (HEW)[2] and Congress. It pressured HEW to excuse athletic departments from compliance regulations, or more generally to interpret the law as applying only to specific programs funded by federal moneys

---

[1] The Women's National Basketball Association, an offshoot of the NBA, played its first season in 1997 to crowds much greater than expected. [Eds.]

[2] Now two different agencies, the Department of Education and the Department of Health and Human Services.

rather than to every program within a federally supported institution. In Congress the NCAA lobbied for the Tower Amendment of 1974, legislation that specifically exempted athletic departments from Title IX requirements.

These efforts failed in the long run, but the intense pressure did 23 succeed in delaying federal action. Officials at HEW did not issue enforcement regulations until 1975, after which schools were given until 1978 to comply. As of 1979, seven years after the act's passage and amid continued shrill cries from male athletic leaders that Title IX presented a crisis "of unprecedented magnitude," not one school had been fined as much as a single dollar for failure to redress gender inequities in school athletics.

Women found their advances blocked on other fronts as well. Some 24 high school athletic administrators matched college officials in their reluctance to comply with Title IX. Jack Short, the director of physical education for the state of Georgia, spoke out against funding girls' interscholastic sport, stating, "I don't think the physical education program on any level should be directed toward making an athlete of a girl." Potential commercial sponsors of professional sport showed a similar reluctance to support women's teams. Despite the significant advances made in women's tennis, the financial base for the women's professional golf tour remained precarious and any attempt to establish professional team sports met with corporate demands that the league promote a "sexy" feminine image. Finally, except for the hoopla surrounding single events like the King-Riggs match, the media continued to neglect women's sports. Both television and print media coverage remained minimal.

When journalists did focus on women, they discovered (or some- 25 times revealed their own) lingering cultural suspicions about the validity of women's sport and the femininity of women athletes. The press sometimes intimated that beneath these misgivings lay a more fundamental fear—a concern that the new female athleticism signaled a profound challenge to traditional gender relations. In September 1976 *Time* ran a cover story, called "Sex and Tennis: The New Battleground." Both title and text employed military metaphors of sexual "battles" and "warfare" to describe the tennis craze sweeping America. The image of sport as a battleground in the "war between the sexes" was a recurring one, suggesting that many observers understood women's athletic demands for equality as part of a deeper societal rift over the distribution of power and the definition of masculinity and femininity. Looking back on the changes of the 1970s, a writer for the *New York Times* posed the question forthrightly when he wondered, "How good are women, and how do they compare with men? . . . And incidentally, does any of this have a bearing on the battle between the sexes?"

The rhetorical battle between the sexes became a real one in the 26
early 1980s when the NCAA made its bid to assume leadership of
women's intercollegiate athletics. By the end of the 1970s, the NCAA
realized that the federal government intended to enforce Title IX and
that, consequently, college athletic departments would have to increase
their support for women's sports substantially. It was at this point, in
1980, that NCAA leaders decided to offer collegiate championships in a
variety of women's sports, even though the AIAW already coordinated
750 state, regional, and national championships for its 970 member
institutions. AIAW leaders interpreted the NCAA's offer as an opportunistic, aggressive takeover attempt. The NCAA defended the move as
being consistent with its "obligations" under Title IX: If it sponsored
men's championships, it must also sponsor women's.

While most women's athletic leaders urged schools to maintain 27
their allegiance to the AIAW, the NCAA offered colleges something that
the AIAW could not—money and television exposure. The NCAA
promised teams that it would pay travel expenses to championship
tournaments and would, in the near future, add women's events to the
multi-million-dollar television package the NCAA had arranged with
major networks. The AIAW, with a total budget of only two million dollars, could not hope to match the NCAA's financial incentives. Women
leaders urged schools to consider whether the financial gains were worth
the loss of self-governance under NCAA control. The NCAA countered
by offering women 16 percent representation on the NCAA Council and
18–24 percent on other important governance committees.

Most schools judged the incentives too attractive to turn down. 28
When the NCAA sponsored its first set of women's championships in
the 1981–82 school year, the vast majority of women's programs
switched their affiliation to the NCAA. The AIAW faded quickly from
the scene, closing down operations in 1982 and conceding final defeat
in 1984 when it lost an antitrust suit against the NCAA, a last-ditch
effort to use the courts to halt the takeover.

The antitrust ruling was followed by another, even graver legal set- 29
back in 1984. In the early 1980s, under the direction of the Reagan administration, HEW officials had already slackened the pace and rigor of Title
IX enforcement. But in 1984 a Supreme Court ruling completely reversed
the existing interpretation of the law. In *Grove City College* v. *Bell*, the
Court ruled that Title IX applied only to those programs receiving direct
federal funds and had no bearing on nonfederally funded programs,
even if the sponsoring school received federal support.

In the aftermath of the Grove City ruling, women's sport advocates 30
faced the possibility that more than a decade of anticipated and actual
gains might be eradicated. They nervously watched HEW drop more
than eight hundred Title IX complaint investigations and compliance

reviews. However, the projected disaster did not materialize, prevented in part by subsequent congressional action. Passage of the Civil Rights Restoration Act of 1988 restored the original interpretation of Title IX, once again mandating that schools eliminate gender discrimination in all programs, including athletics.

The tug-of-war between women's sport advocates and the courts, 31 and between the AIAW and the NCAA, was indicative of more general developments in women's sports in the 1980s. The ready enthusiasm and belief in "inevitable" progress that characterized the 1970s was tempered by a new cautiousness and political savvy acquired through years of struggle. The situation in women's sport mirrored that in other feminist-inspired efforts of the 1980s. Women's advocacy groups continued to make headway, often by organizing within, and exerting pressure on, existing institutions. At the same time feminist activists had to weather an antifeminist backlash waged by conservatives of the New Right and supported by a conservative political administration. These crosscurrents were especially strong in the arena of sport. Women continued to work for greater access to and control of sport, while conservatives within sport organizations, media, and corporations dug in their heels trying to preserve sport as they knew it—a profitable industry that, with few exceptions, was governed by men in the interests of men's athletics.

These contending forces produced a complicated outcome. In 32 response to the question of how much has really changed since the early 1960s, and with what implications for women's lives and American gender relations, no simple answer suffices. Women's sport has undergone a genuine and dramatic transformation; girls growing up today have a sense of possibility and entitlement that few girls or women in generations past ever experienced. They can choose from school sports, Little League baseball, youth soccer, and a variety of other activities, some mixed and some for girls only. For this reason talk of discrimination, inequality, and male dominance in sport may seem foreign and oddly irrelevant to them. But not far beneath the surface they will find more disturbing signs of institutional and ideological resistance to women in athletics. Men still receive resources far superior to women's, leaving female athletes little choice but to compete in male-controlled sporting organizations, which are in turn influenced by corporations whose decisions are based on profits, not fairness.

These constraints reveal the limited nature of the changes in athletic 33 culture. The limits, in turn, tell us something about how sport continues to be a bulwark of "old-fashioned" male privilege and at the same time has become instrumental in the development of new, more subtle forms of male domination. A brief exploration of how critical issues from earlier decades have been played out in recent years will suggest both the significance of—and the limits to—the remarkable changes in late-twentieth-century American sport.

Two central concerns guided the work of early generations of 34
women's sport advocates through most of this century: how to involve
more young women in physical activity and how, at the same time, to
preserve the leadership of women. Ironically, while physical educators
saw these developments as inseparable, in recent decades they seem to
be at odds. The most dramatic, yet paradoxical, set of changes in
women's sport centers on the tremendous increase in participation and
the simultaneous decline of female leadership.

In earlier decades the bulk of female sporting involvement took 35
place in school intramural programs and in community-based recreational sports. While these avenues continue to offer an important athletic resource for women, the dynamic center of women's sport has
moved to highly competitive high school and college varsity sports, in
which both the sheer numbers and the rate of female participation sky-
rocketed between 1970 and 1990. At the high school level the number of
girls in interscholastic sport climbed from three hundred thousand in
1971 to more than two million in 1992. This number includes the hundreds of female athletes who now wrestle or play ice hockey, baseball,
or football on previously all-male teams. In intercollegiate sport,
women have increased their numbers from 16,000 in the early 1970s to
more than 160,000 by the late 1980s. Currently women make up 34 percent of intercollegiate athletes and receive approximately one-third of
college athletic scholarships. Schools that averaged 2.5 women's varsity
teams before Title IX now average more than 7.

The increases are equally impressive in nonelite sports, where 36
women make up the majority of new participants in leading fitness and
athletic activities like jogging, swimming, and cycling. Women have
benefited from new programs that seek to make athletics accessible to
people of all ages and ability levels. They participate avidly in masters
events organized for older athletes and in sports organized for the physically and mentally disabled, such as wheelchair basketball or the
Special Olympics.

Yet as impressive as the numbers appear, women have not come 37
close to parity with men. In high schools and colleges women constitute just over half the student body, yet they make up only slightly more
than one-third of varsity athletes, and they receive far less than that in
resources. College athletic departments allocate twice as much scholarship money to men than to women and budget three times more in
operating funds and five times more in recruiting expenses for men
than for women. Despite the rhetoric of progress, after twenty years of
Title IX an NCAA committee found that only one of 646 schools actually
met its standard for gender equity. Similarly, a study of high school
sports reported that despite the advances of the past two decades, girls
continue to receive inferior facilities, uniforms, practice schedules, and
promotional support. As both high schools and colleges undergo severe

budget cuts in a weak economic climate, the strain on resources will increase and women's programs will have to fight to maintain even current levels of support.

These problems pale in comparison to the astounding decline in 38 female leadership which has occurred in the past two decades. As a result of Title IX the vast majority of schools merged their separate women's and men's athletic departments. In almost every case, they named men as department heads and appointed men to most of the administrative positions. Similarly, as the status of women's sports rose and salary levels moved closer to parity with men's, more and more men grew interested in coaching women's sports. As a result women have experienced a severe decline in both coaching and administrative positions.

Before the passage of Title IX, more than 90 percent of women's col- 39 lege teams were coached by women. Today more than 50 percent of these positions go to men, while women receive fewer than 1 percent of the coaching jobs for men's teams. The decline has been even more extensive in athletic administration, in which women used to hold virtually all positions relevant to women's athletics. Today only 17 percent of women's programs are headed by women, and women fill less than 31 percent of all administrative positions in women's college sport. More than 25 percent of women's athletic programs contain *no* female administrators.

The simultaneous increase in participation and decrease in leader- 40 ship suggests that women have struck an unintended bargain, trading control over sport for greater access to sporting opportunities and resources. The tension between pursuing equal opportunities within an existing system and maintaining a realm of autonomous leadership is not a new one; the bargain struck in the 1970s and 1980s is precisely the trade-off women physical educators warned against in the 1920s and 1930s. The resulting situation, which one contemporary sport advocate described as "perspiration without representation," has allowed a greater number of women to develop athletic skills with fewer restrictions than ever before, but at the same time has meant that women have less ability to influence athletic institutions and chart the course for the future. . . .

Responding to Reading

1. According to Cahn, what problems are inherent in the male model of sports? Why do women's sports activists think that only female leadership can prevent the problems that dominate male collegiate sports?
2. How much does Cahn believe has really changed in women's sports since the 1960s? What effect does she think Title IX has had on the current crop of female collegiate athletes? What does she see as the problems in the present situation?

3. In her book *Coming on Strong,* Cahn says that the entry of women into highly competitive sports challenges the idea that sports are just for men. In other words, the more women participate in sports, the freer they are to be athletic without jeopardizing their status as women. How do you think Donna Lopiano (p. 402) would respond to this observation?

Widening the Focus

- Alice Walker, "Beauty: When the Other Dancer Is the Self" (p. 46)
- Susan Estrich, "Separate Is Better" (p. 125)
- Susan J. Douglas, "Why the Shirelles Mattered" (p. 309)
- Brenda Peterson, "Growing Up Game" (p. 701)

WRITING

Women and Men

1. In her well-known work *A Room of One's Own,* novelist and critic Virginia Woolf observes that "any woman born with a great gift in the sixteenth century would certainly have gone crazed, shot herself, or ended her days in some lonely cottage outside the village, half witch, half wizard, feared and mocked at." Write an essay in which you discuss whether or not this statement applies to gifted women of your own generation and of your parents' generation. You may consider the essays by Mary Gordon and Stephanie Gutmann and Marge Piercy's poem "Barbie Doll" as you plan your paper.

2. List all the stereotypes of women—and of men—identified in the selections you read in this chapter. Then, write an essay in which you identify those that have had the most negative effects on your life and explain why. Do you consider these stereotypes to be just annoying, or actually dangerous? You may, if you wish, read the essays by Susan J. Douglas (p. 309) and Steven Stark (p. 327).

3. Several essays in this chapter deal with women trying to succeed in areas that have traditionally been exclusively male—namely, war and sports. Write an essay in which you discuss whether gender equality in these areas is necessary or desirable. Refer specifically to Stephanie Gutmann's "Sex and the Soldier" as well as to one or more of the three essays in the "Focus" section of this chapter.

4. In "Marked Women," Deborah Tannen discusses the nonverbal messages women send through their appearance. Discuss this idea as it applies to Marge Piercy's poem "Barbie Doll" and to Judith Ortiz Cofer's "The Myth of the Latin Woman" in Chapter 6 (p. 452) and Laura Fraser's "Losing It" in Chapter 7 (p. 524).

5. Write a letter to Judy Brady in which you develop further (or challenge) her characterization of a wife. Support your assertions with specific references to women you know as well as to Alice Hoffman's "The Perfect Family" (p. 61).

6. Critics have argued that activists in women's sports have trouble agreeing on what they really want. Write an essay in which you discuss the points on which Donna Lopiano, Susan K. Cahn, and Maureen E. Mahoney agree.

7. Several of the selections in this chapter—for example, "The Men We Carry in Our Minds," "Sex and the Soldier," and "Why I Want a Wife"—draw distinctions, implicitly or explicitly, between "men's work" and "women's work." Write an essay in which you consider the extent to which such distinctions exist today and how they have affected your professional goals.

8. In her essay "Marked Women," Deborah Tannen draws a distinction between the terms *marked* and *unmarked*. Study the men and women around you, and determine if your observations support Tannen's point that unlike women, men have "the option of being unmarked" (12). Write an essay in which you agree or disagree with Tannen's assertion. In your essay, refer to Tannen's essay as well as to your own observations. (Make sure you define the terms *marked* and *unmarked* in your introduction.)

9. Stanton L. Wormley, Jr., Scott Russell Sanders, and Sharon Olds express definite ideas about what it means to be male. Write an essay in which you define *maleness*. Refer to Wormley's "Fighting Back," Sanders's "The Men We Carry in Our Minds," and Olds's "Rite of Passage" in this chapter (or, if you like, you may consider George Orwell's "Shooting an Elephant" in Chapter 10).

10. Do you think success means the same thing for men and for women? Do you believe it should? Use the readings in this chapter by Mary Gordon and Stanton L. Wormley, Jr., as well as your own observations to support your thesis.

6

THE AMERICAN DREAM

Student Voices

"The American dream to my Chinese-American family is more a vision than a dream. It is a vision of being financially prosperous, attaining a good future through a college education. Although my family has been lucky, others were less fortunate. During the early years of Chinese immigration into this country, they were denied citizenship and sometimes denied entrance into certain states; they were denied access to certain occupations and even admission into the U.S. armed forces; they were also harassed by whites and even by the government itself; and they experienced segregation in schools and housing. Still, they had the vision."

—*Jeff Hui*

"I have learned a lot from my grandparents, who came from Scotland, and I am fascinated with the ancient tales of my ancestors and nation. I have attended the Highland Games and found that I am related to what was once the greatest clan in Scotland, ruling the island for most of the 1400s. I do find pride in my heritage, and it is intriguing to investigate what my ancestors have done, but this is just a hobby for me, not a way of life."

—*Matt McDonald*

"My mother's parents arrived in this country from Ireland in hope of becoming what they thought of as 'American.' They did not come here to maintain their Irish culture, but to take on another culture and start their new lives in a positive way. They obviously succeeded in their goal because I have grown into a true American girl."

—*Beth Wright*

"I like to think of America not as a melting pot, but as a double boiler. On the bottom level you have the family, where tradition and heritage play a vital role. On this level cultures are separate. On the top level, the melting occurs. This is the social system, where heritage and tradition must sometimes be sacrificed. On this level individuality is sacrificed, but the overall product strengthens our nation."

—*Russell Jayne*

"In defining who I am, I must first consider where I come from. This place, just northwest of Philadelphia, is the small town of Easton, which is also the home of Larry Holmes, the former heavyweight boxing champion of the world. Like my family, Easton is on the rebound after difficult economic hardships associated with the geographic area in general, including the strip mining of the western suburbs and, most of all, the demise of Bethlehem Steel.

"Easton is a melting pot, home to numerous immigrants from Europe and the Middle East. In the town, as in my family, it is no longer assumed that children will grow up to be laborers. As children, we were challenged to look up to the Hill where Lafayette College stands. The Hill remains a source of inspiration for me, reminding me to not accept what is given, but to challenge and excel in order to give."

—*Michael Karam*

"The American Dream once involved having a family with 2.5 children and a small house with a white picket fence. Now that dream has turned into a nightmare for many. People who once struggled to achieve lofty goals are now disillusioned. They have given up on their dreams. Many people don't dare to dream because they can see no way out of their situation. Many will never have a chance at the old dream. But I believe a new dream can take its place. The new dream may not be as lofty as the old one, but it's still a dream."

—*Jeff Morris*

"The American Dream is not only for Americans."

—*Ashley Shaner*

Preparing to Read and Write

The American Dream—of political and religious freedom, equal access to education, equal opportunity in the workplace, and ultimately, success and wealth—is often elusive, but it still continues to attract many who have heard its call. In the process of working toward the dream, some individuals and groups struggle to overcome their status as newcomers, while others who have been "Americans" for many years try to overcome their status as outsiders—to fit in, to belong, to be accepted. As they work toward their goals, however, some must make painful decisions, for full participation in American society all too often means assimilating, giving up language, custom, and culture to become more like others. Thus, although the American Dream may ultimately mean winning something, it can also mean losing a vital part of oneself.

Many of the selections in this chapter are written from the point of view of outsiders looking in. All these writers want to be accepted; all believe that the American Dream's reward is worth the struggle. Still, while some eagerly anticipate (or even demand) full acceptance as "Americans," with all the rights and responsibilities that this entails, others are more cautious, afraid of the personal or cultural price they will have to pay for full acceptance into the American mainstream.

As you read and prepare to write about the selections in this chapter, you may consider the following questions:

- What does the American Dream mean to the writer?

- Is the essay a personal narrative? An analysis of a problem facing a group? Both of these?

- Has the writer been able to achieve the American Dream? If so, how? If not, why not?

- What are the greatest obstacles that stand between the writer (or the group he or she writes about) and the American Dream? Would you characterize these obstacles as primarily cultural, social, political, racial, economic, religious, or educational?

- Who has the easiest access to the American Dream? For whom is access most difficult? Why?

- Is the writer looking at the United States from the point of view of an insider or an outsider?

- Does the writer want to change his or her status? To change the status of others? What steps, if any, does he or she take to do so? What additional steps could he or she take?

- What is the writer's attitude toward his or her own group? Toward a group of which he or she is not (or cannot be) a part?

- Does the writer speak as an individual or as a representative of a particular group?

- Which writers' views of the American Dream are most similar? Most different? Most like your own?

TWO PERSPECTIVES ON THE AMERICAN DREAM

Following are two of the most famous documents in American history. The first is the Declaration of Independence, which was drafted by founding father Thomas Jefferson (1743–1826) and amended by the Continental Congress in 1776 as an announcement to the world that the American colonists were rejecting the tyrannical rule of the British crown, sparking the Revolutionary War. The opening of the second paragraph expresses the fundamental American ideal that "all men are created equal," which is deeply ironic in light of the fact that Jefferson himself and other signers were slaveholders at the time. (Jefferson's original draft included a strong statement against slavery, but the Congress deleted this passage.) The second selection is the famous "I Have a Dream" speech, which Martin Luther King, Jr. (see also p. 431), delivered from the steps of the Lincoln Memorial during the 1963 civil rights march on Washington. One of the greatest orators of the century, King offers a stirring indictment of the lack of equality shared by black Americans almost two hundred years after the Declaration was written but also looks hopefully, almost joyfully, to a future when "all of God's children" will be free.

THE DECLARATION OF INDEPENDENCE

Thomas Jefferson

In Congress, July 4, 1776: The Unanimous Declaration of the Thirteen United States of America

When in the Course of human events it becomes necessary for one people to dissolve the political bands which have connected them with another, and to assume among the powers of the earth, the separate and equal station to which the Laws of Nature and of Nature's God entitle them, a decent respect to the opinions of mankind requires that they should declare the causes which impel them to the separation.

We hold these truths to be self-evident, that all men are created equal, that they are endowed by their Creator with certain unalienable Rights, that among these are Life, Liberty and the pursuit of Happiness. That to secure these rights, Governments are instituted among Men, deriving their just powers from the consent of the governed. That whenever any Form of Government becomes destructive of these ends, it is the Right of the People to alter or to abolish it, and to institute new Government, laying its foundation on such principles and organizing its powers in such form, as to them shall seem most likely to effect their Safety and Happiness. Prudence, indeed, will dictate that Governments long established should not be changed for light and transient causes; and accordingly all experience hath shewn, that mankind are more disposed to suffer, while evils are sufferable, than to right themselves by abolishing the forms to which they are accustomed. But when a long train of abuses and usurpations, pursuing invariably the same Object, evinces a design to reduce them under absolute Despotism, it is their right, it is their duty, to throw off such Government, and to provide new Guards for their future security. Such has been the patient sufferance of these Colonies; and such is now the necessity which constrains them to alter their former Systems of Governors. The history of the present King of Great Britain is a history of repeated injuries and usurpations, all having in direct object the establishment of an absolute Tyranny over these States. To prove this, let Facts be submitted to a candid world.

3   He has refused his Assent to Laws, the most wholesome and necessary for the public good.

4   He has forbidden his Governors to pass laws of immediate and pressing importance, unless suspended in their operation till his Assent should be obtained; and when so suspended, he has utterly neglected to attend to them.

5   He has refused to pass other Laws for the accommodation of large districts of people, unless those people would relinquish the right of Representation in the Legislature, a right inestimable to them and formidable to tyrants only.

6   He has called together legislative bodies at places unusual, uncomfortable, and distant from the depository of their Public Records, for the sole purpose of fatiguing them into compliance with his measures.

7   He has dissolved Representative Houses repeatedly, for opposing with manly firmness his invasions on the rights of the people.

8   He has refused for a long time, after such dissolutions, to cause others to be elected; whereby the Legislative Powers, incapable of Annihilation, have returned to the People at large for their exercise; the State remaining in the mean time exposed to all the dangers of invasion from without, and convulsions within.

9   He has endeavored to prevent the population of these States; for that purpose obstructing the Laws for Naturalization of Foreigners; refusing to pass others to encourage their migration hither, and raising the conditions of new Appropriations of Lands.

10   He has obstructed the Administration of Justice, by refusing his Assent to Laws for establishing Judiciary Powers.

11   He has made Judges dependent on his Will alone, for the tenure of their offices, and the amount and payment of their salaries.

He has erected a multitude of New Offices, and sent hither swarms 12 of Officers to harass our people, and eat out their substance.

He has kept among us, in times of peace, Standing Armies without 13 the Consent of our legislatures.

He has affected to render the Military independent of and superior 14 to the Civil Power.

He has combined with others to subject us to a jurisdiction foreign 15 to our constitution, and unacknowledged by our laws; giving his Assent to their Acts of pretended Legislation: For quartering large bodies of armed troops among us: For protecting them, by a mock Trial, from punishment for any Murders which they should commit on the Inhabitants of these States: For cutting off our Trade with all parts of the world: For imposing Taxes on us without our Consent: For depriving us in many cases, of the benefits of Trial by Jury; For transporting us beyond Seas to be tried for pretended offenses: For abolishing the free System of English Laws in a neighboring Province, establishing therein an Arbitrary government, and enlarging its Boundaries so as to render it at once an example and fit instrument for introducing the same absolute rule into these Colonies: For taking away our Charters, abolishing our most valuable Laws and altering fundamentally the Forms of our Governments: For suspending our own Legislatures, and declaring themselves invested with power to legislate for us in all cases whatsoever.

He has abdicated Government here, by declaring us out of his 16 Protection and waging War against us.

He has plundered our seas, ravaged our Coasts, burnt our towns, 17 and destroyed the lives of our people.

He is at this time transporting large Armies of foreign Mercenaries 18 to complete the works of death, desolation and tyranny, already begun with circumstances of Cruelty & Perfidy scarcely paralleled in the most barbarous ages, and totally unworthy the Head of a civilized nation.

He has constrained our fellow Citizens taken Captive on the high 19 Seas to bear Arms against their Country, to become the executioners of their friends and Brethren, or to fall themselves by their Hands.

He has excited domestic insurrections amongst us, and has endeav- 20 ored to bring on the inhabitants of our frontiers, the merciless Indian Savages, whose known rule of warfare, is an undistinguished destruction of all ages, sexes, and conditions.

In every stage of these Oppressions We have Petitioned for Redress 21 in the most humble terms: Our repeated Petitions have been answered only by repeated injury. A Prince, whose character is thus marked by every act which may define a Tyrant, is unfit to be the ruler of a free people.

Nor have We been wanting in attention to our British brethren. We 22 have warned them from time to time of attempts by their legislature to extend an unwarrantable jurisdiction over us. We have reminded them of the circumstances of our emigration and settlement here. We have appealed to their native justice and magnanimity, and we have conjured them by the ties of our common kindred to disavow these usurpations, which would inevitably interrupt our connections and correspondence. They too have been deaf to the voice of justice and of consanguinity. We must, therefore, acquiesce in the necessity, which denounces our Separation, and hold them, as we hold the rest of mankind, Enemies in War, in Peace Friends.

We, THEREFORE, the Representatives of the UNITED STATES OF   23 AMERICA, in General Congress, Assembled, appealing to the Supreme Judge of the world for the rectitude of our intentions, do, in the Name, and by Authority of the good People of these Colonies, solemnly publish and declare, That these United Colonies are, and of Right ought to be FREE AND INDEPENDENT STATES; that they are Absolved from all Allegiance to the British Crown, and that all political connection between them and the State of Great Britain, is and ought to be totally dissolved; and that as Free and Independent States, they have full Power to levy War, conclude Peace, contract Alliances, establish Commerce, and to do all other Acts and Things which Independent States may of right do. And for the support of this Declaration, with a firm reliance on the protection of Divine Providence, we mutually pledge to each other our Lives, our Fortunes, and our sacred Honor.

I HAVE A DREAM

Martin Luther King, Jr.

I am happy to join with you today in what will go down in history   1 as the greatest demonstration for freedom in the history of our nation.

Fivescore years ago, a great American, in whose symbolic shadow   2 we stand today, signed the Emancipation Proclamation. This momentous decree came as a great beacon light of hope to millions of Negro slaves who had been seared in the flames of withering injustice. It came as a joyous daybreak to end the long night of their captivity.

But one hundred years later, the Negro still is not free; one hundred   3 years later, the life of the Negro is still sadly crippled by the manacles of segregation and the chains of discrimination; one hundred years later, the Negro lives on a lonely island of poverty in the midst of a vast ocean of material prosperity; one hundred years later, the Negro is still languishing in the corners of American society and finds himself in exile in his own land.

So we've come here today to dramatize a shameful condition. In a   4 sense we've come to our nation's capital to cash a check. When the architects of our republic wrote the magnificent words of the Constitution and the Declaration of Independence, they were signing a promissory note to which every American was to fall heir. This note was the promise that all men, yes, black men as well as white men, would be guaranteed the unalienable rights of life, liberty, and the pursuit of happiness.

It is obvious today that America has defaulted on this promissory 5 note in so far as her citizens of color are concerned. Instead of honoring this sacred obligation, America has given the Negro people a bad check; a check which has come back marked "insufficient funds." We refuse to believe that there are insufficient funds in the great vaults of opportunity of this nation. And so we've come to cash this check, a check that will give us upon demand the riches of freedom and the security of justice.

We have also come to this hallowed spot to remind America of the 6 fierce urgency of now. This is no time to engage in the luxury of cooling off or to take the tranquilizing drug of gradualism. Now is the time to make real the promises of democracy; now is the time to rise from the dark and desolate valley of segregation to the sunlit path of racial justice; now is the time to lift our nation from the quicksands of racial injustice to the solid rock of brotherhood; now is the time to make justice a reality for all God's children. It would be fatal for the nation to overlook the urgency of the moment. This sweltering summer of the Negro's legitimate discontent will not pass until there is an invigorating autumn of freedom and equality.

Nineteen sixty-three is not an end, but a beginning. And those who 7 hope that the Negro needed to blow off steam and will now be content, will have a rude awakening if the nation returns to business as usual.

There will be neither rest nor tranquility in America until the Negro 8 is granted his citizenship rights. The whirlwinds of revolt will continue to shake the foundations of our nation until the bright day of justice emerges.

But there is something that I must say to my people who stand on 9 the warm threshold which leads into the palace of justice. In the process of gaining our rightful place we must not be guilty of wrongful deeds.

Let us not seek to satisfy our thirst for freedom by drinking from the 10 cup of bitterness and hatred. We must forever conduct our struggle on the high plane of dignity and discipline. We must not allow our creative protest to degenerate into physical violence. Again and again we must rise to the majestic heights of meeting physical force with soul force.

The marvelous new militancy which has engulfed the Negro com- 11 munity must not lead us to a distrust of all white people, for many of our white brothers, as evidenced by their presence here today, have come to realize that their destiny is tied up with our destiny and they have come to realize that their freedom is inextricably bound to our freedom. This offense we share mounted to storm the battlements of injustice must be carried forth by a biracial army. We cannot walk alone.

And as we walk, we must make the pledge that we shall always 12 march ahead. We cannot turn back. There are those who are asking the devotees of civil rights, "When will you be satisfied?" We can never be satisfied as long as the Negro is the victim of the unspeakable horrors of police brutality.

We can never be satisfied as long as our bodies, heavy with fatigue 13 of travel, cannot gain lodging in the motels of the highways and the hotels of the cities. We cannot be satisfied as long as the Negro's basic mobility is from a smaller ghetto to a larger one.

We can never be satisfied as long as our children are stripped of 14 their selfhood and robbed of their dignity by signs stating "for whites only." We cannot be satisfied as long as a Negro in Mississippi cannot vote and a Negro in New York believes he has nothing for which to vote. No, we are not satisfied, and we will not be satisfied until justice rolls down like waters and righteousness like a mighty stream.

I am not unmindful that some of you have come here out of exces- 15 sive trials and tribulation. Some of you have come fresh from narrow jail cells. Some of you have come from areas where your quest for free- dom left you battered by the storms of persecution and staggered by the winds of police brutality. You have been the veterans of creative suffering. Continue to work with the faith that unearned suffering is redemptive.

Go back to Mississippi; go back to Alabama; go back to South 16 Carolina; go back to Georgia; go back to Louisiana; go back to the slums and ghettos of the northern cities, knowing that somehow this situation can, and will be changed. Let us not wallow in the valley of despair.

So I say to you, my friends, that even though we must face the dif- 17 ficulties of today and tomorrow, I still have a dream. It is a dream deeply rooted in the American dream that one day this nation will rise up and live out the true meaning of its creed—we hold these truths to be self-evident, that all men are created equal.

I have a dream that one day on the red hills of Georgia, sons of for- 18 mer slaves and sons of former slave-owners will be able to sit down together at the table of brotherhood.

I have a dream that one day, even the state of Mississippi, a state 19 sweltering with the heat of injustice, sweltering with the heat of oppres- sion, will be transformed into an oasis of freedom and justice.

I have a dream my four little children will one day live in a nation 20 where they will not be judged by the color of their skin but by the con- tent of their character. I have a dream today!

I have a dream that one day, down in Alabama, with its vicious 21 racists, with its governor having his lips dripping with the words of interposition and nullification, that one day, right there in Alabama, little black boys and black girls will be able to join hands with little white boys and white girls as sisters and brothers. I have a dream today!

I have a dream that one day every valley shall be exalted, every hill 22 and mountain shall be made low, the rough places shall be made plain, and the crooked places shall be made straight and the glory of the Lord will be revealed and all flesh shall see it together.

This is our hope. This is the faith that I go back to the South with.   23

With this faith we will be able to hew out of the mountain of despair 24 a stone of hope. With this faith we will be able to transform the jangling discords of our nation into a beautiful symphony of brotherhood.

With this faith we will be able to work together, to pray together, to 25 struggle together, to go to jail together, to stand up for freedom together, knowing that we will be free one day. This will be the day when all of God's children will be able to sing with new meaning— "my country 'tis of thee; sweet land of liberty; of thee I sing; land where my fathers died, land of the pilgrim's pride; from every mountain side, let freedom ring"—and if America is to be a great nation, this must become true.

So let freedom ring from the prodigious hilltops of New 26 Hampshire.

Let freedom ring from the mighty mountains of New York.   27

Let freedom ring from the heightening Alleghenies of Pennsylvania. 28

Let freedom ring from the snow-capped Rockies of Colorado.   29

Let freedom ring from the curvaceous slopes of California.   30

But not only that.   31

Let freedom ring from Stone Mountain of Georgia.   32

Let freedom ring from Lookout Mountain of Tennessee.   33

Let freedom ring from every hill and molehill of Mississippi, from 34 every mountainside, let freedom ring.

And when we allow freedom to ring, when we let it ring from every 35 village and hamlet, from every state and city, we will be able to speed up that day when all of God's children—black men and white men, Jews and Gentiles, Catholics and Protestants—will be able to join hands and to sing in the words of the old Negro spiritual, "Free at last, free at last; thank God Almighty, we are free at last."

Responding to Reading

1. The Declaration of Independence was written in the eighteenth century, a time when logic and reason were thought to be the supreme achievements of human beings. Do you think this document is as reasonable as it seems to be on the surface, or does it also include appeals to the emotions? Explain your position.
2. Do you think it is fair, as some have done, to accuse the framers of the Declaration of Independence of being racist? Sexist?

3. What exactly is King's dream? Do you believe it has come true in any sense?
4. Speaking as a representative of his fellow African-American citizens, King tells his audience that African-Americans find themselves "in exile in [their] own land" (3). Do you believe this is still true of African-Americans? Of members of other minority groups? Which groups? Why?
5. Jefferson wrote in the eighteenth century; King, in the twentieth. Jefferson wrote as an insider, a man of privilege; King, as an outsider. What do their dreams have in common? How does each man intend to achieve his dream?
6. What does the American Dream mean to Jefferson? To King? What does it mean to you?

WE MAY BE BROTHERS

Chief Seattle

> *Son of a Suquamish chief and a Duwamish chief's daughter, Sealth (1786?–1866) became in 1810 chief of the Suquamish, Duwamish, and other saltwater tribes occupying the area around Puget Sound in what is now the state of Washington. A skilled diplomat and orator, he helped maintain peace between his followers and the white settlers who began arriving in the area around 1851. (Unable to pronounce his name in the original Salish tongue, the whites changed its pronunciation to "Seattle," eventually naming their new town after him.) In 1854, during treaty negotiations with the U.S. territorial governor, the chief delivered a moving speech in which he described the inevitable displacement of his people by the better-armed, more technologically advanced newcomers. This speech was not in fact transcribed until some thirty years later, and then by a white onlooker who wrote in the flowery English popular at the time; as a result, it is impossible to say how closely what we reprint here corresponds to Seattle's exact words. The message, however, is a timeless one about the relationship between human beings and the earth.*

Yonder sky that has wept tears of compassion upon my people for centuries untold, and which to us appears changeless and eternal, may change. Today is fair. Tomorrow it may be overcast with clouds. My words are like the stars that never change. Whatever Seattle says the great chief at Washington can rely upon with as much certainty as he can upon the return of the sun or the seasons. The White Chief says that Big Chief at Washington sends us greetings of friendship and goodwill. That is kind of him for we know he has little need of our friendship in return. His people are many. They are like the grass that covers vast prairies. My people are few. They resemble the scattering trees of a storm-swept plain. . . . I will not dwell on, nor mourn over, our untimely decay, nor reproach our paleface brothers with hastening it, as we too may have been somewhat to blame. . . .

Your God is not our God. Your God loves your people and hates 2 mine. He folds his strong and protecting arms lovingly about the paleface and leads him by the hand as a father leads his infant son—but He has forsaken His red children—if they really are His. Our God, the Great Spirit, seems also to have forsaken us. Your God makes your people strong every day. Soon they will fill the land. Our people are ebbing away like a rapidly receding tide that will never return. The white man's God cannot love our people or He would protect them. They seem to be orphans who can look nowhere for help. How then can we be brothers? . . . We are two distinct races with separate origins and separate destinies. There is little in common between us.

To us the ashes of our ancestors are sacred and their resting place is 3 hallowed ground. You wander far from the graves of your ancestors and seemingly without regret. Your religion was written upon tables of stone by the iron finger of your God so that you could not forget. The Red Man could never comprehend nor remember it. Our religion is the traditions of our ancestors—the dreams of our old men, given them in solemn hours of night by the Great Spirit; and the visions of our sachems; and it is written in the hearts of our people.

Your dead cease to love you and the land of their nativity as soon as 4 they pass the portals of the tomb and wander way beyond the stars. They are soon forgotten and never return. Our dead never forget the beautiful world that gave them being.

Day and night cannot dwell together. The Red Man has ever fled 5 the approach of the White Man, as the morning mist flees before the morning sun. However, your proposition seems fair and I think that my people will accept it and will retire to the reservation you offer them. Then we will dwell apart in peace. . . . It matters little where we pass the remnant of our days. They will not be many. A few more moons; a few more winters—and not one of the descendants of the mighty hosts that once moved over this broad land or lived in happy homes, protected by the Great Spirit, will remain to mourn over the graves of a people once more powerful and hopeful than yours. But why should I mourn at the untimely fate of my people? Tribe follows tribe, and nation follows nation, like the waves of the sea. It is the order of nature, and regret is useless. Your time of decay may be distant, but it will surely come, for even the White Man whose God walked and talked with him as friend with friend cannot be exempt from the common destiny. We may be brothers after all. We will see. . . .

Every part of this soil is sacred in the estimation of my people. 6 Every hillside, every valley, every plain and grove, has been hallowed by some sad or happy event in days long vanished. The very dust upon which you now stand responds more lovingly to their footsteps than to yours, because it is rich with the blood of our ancestors and our bare feet are conscious of the sympathetic touch. Even the little children who lived here and rejoiced here for a brief season will love these somber solitudes and at eventide they greet shadowy returning spirits. And when the last Red Man shall have perished, and the memory of my tribe shall have become a myth among the White Men, these shores will swarm with the invisible dead of my tribe, and when your children's children think themselves alone in the field, the store, the shop, upon the highway, or in the silence of the pathless woods, they will not be alone. At night when the streets of your cities and villages are silent and you think them deserted, they will throng with the returning hosts that once filled and still love this beautiful land. The White Man will never be alone.

Let him be just and deal kindly with my people, for the dead are not 7 powerless. Dead, did I say? There is no death, only a change of worlds.

Responding to Reading

1. The point is made in paragraph 2 that Native Americans and whites are "two distinct races with separate origins and separate destinies." What differences are then identified? Are there any similarities?
2. Is the speech's tone primarily hopeful, resigned, conciliatory, angry, or bitter? What dreams, if any, does the speech suggest for Chief Seattle's people?
3. Paragraph 5 offers the observation, "We may be brothers after all. We will see." What do you suppose Chief Seattle means? Do you agree?

THE LIBRARY CARD

Richard Wright

Born on a plantation near Natchez, Mississippi, Richard Wright (1908–1960) spent much of his childhood in an orphanage or with various relatives. He moved to Chicago in 1934 and worked at a number of unskilled jobs before joining the Federal Writer's Project. Wright's politics became radical at this time, and he wrote poetry for leftist publications. In 1938, he published his first book, Uncle Tom's Children: Four Novellas; *in 1940, his novel* Native Son *made him famous. After World War II, Wright lived as an expatriate in Paris, where he wrote his autobiography,* Black Boy (1945), *a book that celebrates African-American resilience and courage much as nineteenth-century slave narratives do. In this excerpt from* Black Boy, *Wright tells how he took advantage of an opportunity to feed his hunger for an intellectual life.*

One morning I arrived early at work and went into the bank lobby 1
where the Negro porter was mopping. I stood at a counter and picked
up the Memphis *Commercial Appeal* and began my free reading of the
press. I came finally to the editorial page and saw an article dealing with
one H. L. Mencken.[1] I knew by hearsay that he was the editor of the
American Mercury, but aside from that I knew nothing about him. The
article was a furious denunciation of Mencken, concluding with one hot,
short sentence: Mencken is a fool.

I wondered what on earth this Mencken had done to call down upon 2
him the scorn of the South. The only people I had ever heard denounced
in the South were Negroes, and this man was not a Negro. Then what
ideas did Mencken hold that made a newspaper like the *Commercial
Appeal* castigate him publicly? Undoubtedly he must be advocating
ideas that the South did not like. Were there, then, people other than
Negroes who criticized the South? I knew that during the Civil War the
South had hated northern whites, but I had not encountered such hate
during my life. Knowing no more of Mencken than I did at that moment,
I felt a vague sympathy for him. Had not the South, which had assigned
me the role of a non-man, cast at him its hardest words?

Now, how could I find out about this Mencken? There was a huge 3
library near the riverfront, but I knew that Negroes were not allowed to
patronize its shelves any more than they were the parks and play-
grounds of the city. I had gone into the library several times to get books
for the white men on the job. Which of them would now help me to get
books? And how could I read them without causing concern to the
white men with whom I worked? I had so far been successful in hiding
my thoughts and feelings from them, but I knew that I would create
hostility if I went about this business of reading in a clumsy way.

I weighed the personalities of the men on the job. There was Don, a 4
Jew; but I distrusted him. His position was not much better than mine
and I knew that he was uneasy and insecure; he had always treated me
in an offhand, bantering way that barely concealed his contempt. I was
afraid to ask him to help me to get books; his frantic desire to demonstrate a racial solidarity with the whites against Negroes might make
him betray me.

Then how about the boss? No, he was a Baptist and I had the sus- 5
picion that he would not be quite able to comprehend why a black boy
would want to read Mencken. There were other white men on the job
whose attitudes showed clearly that they were Kluxers or sympathizers,
and they were out of the question.

---

[1] Henry Louis Mencken (1880–1956), journalist, critic, and essayist, who was known for his pointed, outspoken, and satirical comments about the blunders and imperfections of democracy and the
cultural awkwardness of Americans. [Eds.]

There remained only one man whose attitude did not fit into an 6
anti-Negro category, for I had heard the white men refer to him as a
"Pope lover." He was an Irish Catholic and was hated by the white
Southerners. I knew that he read books, because I had got him volumes
from the library several times. Since he, too, was an object of hatred, I
felt that he might refuse me but would hardly betray me. I hesitated,
weighing and balancing the imponderable realities.

One morning I paused before the Catholic fellow's desk. 7

"I want to ask you a favor," I whispered to him. 8

"What is it?" 9

"I want to read. I can't get books from the library. I wonder if you'd 10
let me use your card?"

He looked at me suspiciously. 11

"My card is full most of the time," he said. 12

"I see," I said and waited, posing my question silently. 13

"You're not trying to get me into trouble, are you, boy?" he asked, 14
staring at me.

"Oh, no, sir." 15

"What book do you want?" 16

"A book by H. L. Mencken." 17

"Which one?" 18

"I don't know. Has he written more than one?" 19

"He has written several." 20

"I didn't know that." 21

"What makes you want to read Mencken?" 22

"Oh, I just saw his name in the newspaper," I said. 23

"It's good of you to want to read," he said. "But you ought to read 24
the right things."

I said nothing. Would he want to supervise my reading? 25

"Let me think," he said. "I'll figure out something." 26

I turned from him and he called me back. He stared at me quizzically. 27

"Richard, don't mention this to the other white men," he said. 28

"I understand," I said. "I won't say a word." 29

A few days later he called me to him. 30

"I've got a card in my wife's name," he said. "Here's mine." 31

"Thank you, sir." 32

"Do you think you can manage it?" 33

"I'll manage fine," I said. 34

"If they suspect you, you'll get in trouble," he said. 35

"I'll write the same kind of notes to the library that you wrote when 36
you sent me for books," I told him. "I'll sign your name."

He laughed. 37

"Go ahead. Let me see what you get," he said. 38

That afternoon I addressed myself to forging a note. Now, what 39
were the names of books written by H. L. Mencken? I did not know any

of them. I finally wrote what I thought would be a foolproof note: *Dear Madam: Will you please let this nigger boy*—I used the word "nigger" to make the librarian feel that I could not possibly be the author of the note—*have some books by H. L. Mencken?* I forged the white man's name.

I entered the library as I had always done when on errands for   40
whites, but I felt that I would somehow slip up and betray myself. I doffed my hat, stood a respectful distance from the desk, looked as unbookish as possible, and waited for the white patrons to be taken care of. When the desk was clear of people, I still waited. The white librarian looked at me.

"What do you want, boy?"   41

As though I did not possess the power of speech, I stepped forward   42
and simply handed her the forged note, not parting my lips.

"What books by Mencken does he want?" she asked.   43

"I don't know, ma'am," I said, avoiding her eyes.   44

"Who gave you this card?"   45

"Mr. Falk," I said.   46

"Where is he?"   47

"He's at work, at the M—— Optical Company," I said. "I've been in   48
here for him before."

"I remember," the woman said. "But he never wrote notes like this."   49

Oh, God, she's suspicious. Perhaps she would not let me have the   50
books? If she had turned her back at that moment, I would have ducked out the door and never gone back. Then I thought of a bold idea.

"You can call him up, ma'am," I said, my heart pounding.   51

"You're not using these books, are you?" she asked pointedly.   52

"Oh, no, ma'am. I can't read."   53

"I don't know what he wants by Mencken," she said under her   54
breath.

I knew now that I had won; she was thinking of other things and   55
the race question had gone out of her mind. She went to the shelves. Once or twice she looked over her shoulder at me, as though she was still doubtful. Finally she came forward with two books in her hand.

"I'm sending him two books," she said. "But tell Mr. Falk to come   56
in next time, or send me the names of the books he wants. I don't know what he wants to read."

I said nothing. She stamped the card and handed me the books. Not   57
daring to glance at them, I went out of the library, fearing that the woman would call me back for further questioning. A block away from the library I opened one of the books and read a title: *A Book of Prefaces.* I was nearing my nineteenth birthday and I did not know how to pronounce the word "preface." I thumbed the pages and saw strange words and strange names. I shook my head, disappointed. I looked at the other book; it was called *Prejudices.* I knew what that word meant; I had heard it all my life. And right off I was on guard against Mencken's

books. Why would a man want to call a book *Prejudices?* The word was so stained with all my memories of racial hate that I could not conceive of anybody using it for a title. Perhaps I had made a mistake about Mencken? A man who had prejudices must be wrong.

When I showed the books to Mr. Falk, he looked at me and 58 frowned.

"That librarian might telephone you," I warned him. 59

"That's all right," he said. "But when you're through reading those 60 books, I want you to tell me what you get out of them."

That night in my rented room, while letting the hot water run over 61 my can of pork and beans in the sink, I opened *A Book of Prefaces* and began to read. I was jarred and shocked by the style, the clear, clean, sweeping sentences. Why did he write like that? And how did one write like that? I pictured the man as a raging demon, slashing with his pen, consumed with hate, denouncing everything American, extolling everything European or German, laughing at the weaknesses of people, mocking God, authority. What was this? I stood up, trying to realize what reality lay behind the meaning of the words. . . . Yes, this man was fighting, fighting with words. He was using words as a weapon, using them as one would use a club. Could words be weapons? Well, yes, for here they were. Then, maybe, perhaps, I could use them as a weapon? No. It frightened me. I read on and what amazed me was not what he said, but how on earth anybody had the courage to say it.

Occasionally I glanced up to reassure myself that I was alone in the 62 room. Who were these men about whom Mencken was talking so passionately? Who was Anatole France? Joseph Conrad? Sinclair Lewis, Sherwood Anderson, Dostoevski, George Moore, Gustave Flaubert, Maupassant, Tolstoy, Frank Harris, Mark Twain, Thomas Hardy, Arnold Bennett, Stephen Crane, Zola, Norris, Gorky, Bergson, Ibsen, Balzac, Bernard Shaw, Dumas, Poe, Thomas Mann, O. Henry, Dreiser, H. G. Wells, Gogol, T. S. Eliot, Gide, Baudelaire, Edgar Lee Masters, Stendhal, Turgenev, Huneker, Nietzsche, and scores of others? Were these men real? Did they exist or had they existed? And how did one pronounce their names?

I ran across many words whose meanings I did not know, and I 63 either looked them up in a dictionary or, before I had a chance to do that, encountered the word in a context that made its meaning clear. But what strange world was this? I concluded the book with the conviction that I had somehow overlooked something terribly important in life. I had once tried to write, had once reveled in feeling, had let my crude imagination roam, but the impulse to dream had been slowly beaten out of me by experience. Now it surged up again and I hungered for books, new ways of looking and seeing. It was not a matter of believing or disbelieving what I read, but of feeling something new, of being affected by something that made the look of the world different.

As dawn broke I ate my pork and beans, feeling dopey, sleepy. I 64
went to work, but the mood of the book would not die; it lingered, coloring everything I saw, heard, did. I now felt that I knew what the white
men were feeling. Merely because I had read a book that had spoken of
how they lived and thought, I identified myself with that book. I felt
vaguely guilty. Would I, filled with bookish notions, act in a manner
that would make the whites dislike me?

I forged more notes and my trips to the library became frequent. 65
Reading grew into a passion. My first serious novel was Sinclair Lewis's
Main Street.[2] It made me see my boss, Mr. Gerald, and identify him as
an American type. I would smile when I saw him lugging his golf bags
into the office. I had always felt a vast distance separating me from the
boss, and now I felt closer to him, though still distant. I felt now that I
knew him, that I could feel the very limits of his narrow life. And this
had happened because I had read a novel about a mythical man called
George F. Babbitt.[3]

The plots and stories in the novels did not interest me so much as 66
the point of view revealed. I gave myself over to each novel without
reserve, without trying to criticize it; it was enough for me to see and
feel something different. And for me, everything was something different. Reading was like a drug, a dope. The novels created moods in
which I lived for days. But I could not conquer my sense of guilt, my
feeling that the white men around me knew that I was changing, that I
had begun to regard them differently.

Whenever I brought a book to the job, I wrapped it in newspaper— 67
a habit that was to persist for years in other cities and under other circumstances. But some of the white men pried into my packages when I
was absent and they questioned me.

"Boy, what are you reading those books for?"   68

"Oh, I don't know, sir."   69

"That's deep stuff you're reading, boy."   70

"I'm just killing time, sir."   71

"You'll addle your brains if you don't watch out."   72

I read Dreiser's *Jennie Gerhardt* and *Sister Carrie*[4] and they revived 73
in me a vivid sense of my mother's suffering; I was overwhelmed. I
grew silent, wondering about the life around me. It would have been
impossible for me to have told anyone what I derived from these novels, for it was nothing less than a sense of life itself. All my life had

---

[2] *Main Street*, published in 1920, examines the smugness, intolerance, and lack of imagination that
characterize small-town Amencan life. [Eds.]

[3] The central character in Sinclair Lewis's *Babbit* (1922), who believed in the virtues of home, the
Republican Party, and middle-class conventions. To Wright, Babbitt symbolizes the mindless complacency of white middle-class America. [Eds.]

[4] Both *Jennie Gerhardt* (1911) and *Sister Carrie* (1900) tell the stories of working women who struggle
against poverty and social injustice. [Eds.]

shaped me for the realism, the naturalism of the modern novel, and I could not read enough of them.

Steeped in new moods and ideas, I bought a ream of paper and 74 tried to write; but nothing would come, or what did come was flat beyond telling. I discovered that more than desire and feeling were necessary to write and I dropped the idea. Yet I still wondered how it was possible to know people sufficiently to write about them. Could I ever learn about life and people? To me, with my vast ignorance, my Jim Crow station in life, it seemed a task impossible of achievement. I now knew what being a Negro meant. I could endure the hunger. I had learned to live with hate. But to feel that there were feelings denied me, that the very breath of life itself was beyond my reach, that more than anything else hurt, wounded me. I had a new hunger.

In buoying me up, reading also cast me down, made me see what 75 was possible, what I had missed. My tension returned, new, terrible, bitter, surging, almost too great to be contained. I no longer *felt* that the world about me was hostile, killing; I *knew* it. A million times I asked myself what I could do to save myself, and there were no answers. I seemed forever condemned, ringed by walls.

I did not discuss my reading with Mr. Falk, who had lent me his 76 library card; it would have meant talking about myself and that would have been too painful. I smiled each day, fighting desperately to maintain my old behavior, to keep my disposition seemingly sunny. But some of the white men discerned that I had begun to brood.

"Wake up there, boy!" Mr. Olin said one day. 77

"Sir!" I answered for the lack of a better word. 78

"You act like you've stolen something," he said. 79

I laughed in the way I knew he expected me to laugh, but I resolved 80 to be more conscious of myself, to watch my every act, to guard and hide the new knowledge that was dawning within me.

If I went north, would it be possible for me to build a new life then? 81 But how could a man build a life upon vague, unformed yearnings? I wanted to write and I did not even know the English language. I bought English grammars and found them dull. I felt that I was getting a better sense of the language from novels than from grammars. I read hard, discarding a writer as soon as I felt that I had grasped his point of view. At night the printed page stood before my eyes in sleep.

Mrs. Moss, my landlady, asked me one Sunday morning: "Son, 82 what is this you keep on reading?"

"Oh, nothing. Just novels." 83

"What you get out of 'em?" 84

"I'm just killing time," I said. 85

"I hope you know your own mind," she said in a tone which 86 implied that she doubted if I had a mind.

I knew of no Negroes who read the books I liked and I wondered if 87 any Negroes ever thought of them. I knew that there were Negro doctors, lawyers, newspapermen, but I never saw any of them. When I read a Negro newspaper I never caught the faintest echo of my preoccupation in its pages. I felt trapped and occasionally, for a few days, I would stop reading. But a vague hunger would come over me for books, books that opened up new avenues of feeling and seeing, and again I would forge another note to the white librarian. Again I would read and wonder as only the naïve and unlettered can read and wonder, feeling that I carried a secret, criminal burden about with me each day.

That winter my mother and brother came and we set up house- 88 keeping, buying furniture on the installment plan, being cheated and yet knowing no way to avoid it. I began to eat warm food and to my surprise found that regular meals enabled me to read faster. I may have lived through many illnesses and survived them, never suspecting that I was ill. My brother obtained a job and we began to save toward the trip north, plotting our time, setting tentative dates for departure. I told none of the white men on the job that I was planning to go north; I knew that the moment they felt I was thinking of the North they would change toward me. It would have made them feel that I did not like the life I was living, and because my life was completely conditioned by what they said or did, it would have been tantamount to challenging them.

I could calculate my chances for life in the South as a Negro fairly 89 clearly now.

I could fight the southern whites by organizing with other Negroes, 90 as my grandfather had done. But I knew that I could never win that way; there were many whites and there were but few blacks. They were strong and we were weak. Outright black rebellion could never win. If I fought openly I would die and I did not want to die. News of lynchings were frequent.

I could submit and live the life of a genial slave, but that was impos- 91 sible. All of my life had shaped me to live by my own feelings and thoughts. I could make up to Bess and marry her and inherit the house. But that, too, would be the life of a slave; if I did that, I would crush to death something within me, and I would hate myself as much as I knew the whites already hated those who had submitted. Neither could I ever willingly present myself to be kicked, as Shorty had done. I would rather have died than do that.

I could drain off my restlessness by fighting with Shorty and 92 Harrison. I had seen many Negroes solve the problem of being black by transferring their hatred of themselves to others with a black skin and fighting them. I would have to be cold to do that, and I was not cold and I could never be.

I could, of course, forget what I had read, thrust the whites out of 93
my mind, forget them; and find release from anxiety and longing in sex
and alcohol. But the memory of how my father had conducted himself
made that course repugnant. If I did not want others to violate my life,
how could I voluntarily violate it myself?

I had no hope whatever of being a professional man. Not only had 94
I been so conditioned that I did not desire it, but the fulfillment of such
an ambition was beyond my capabilities. Well-to-do Negroes lived in a
world that was almost as alien to me as the world inhabited by whites.

What, then, was there? I held my life in my mind, in my conscious- 95
ness each day, feeling at times that I would stumble and drop it, spill it
forever. My reading had created a vast sense of distance between me
and the world in which I lived and tried to make a living, and that sense
of distance was increasing each day. My days and nights were one long,
quiet, continuously contained dream of terror, tension, and anxiety. I
wondered how long I could bear it.

Responding to Reading

1. Do you think access to books brought Wright closer to achieving the
   American Dream? What new obstacles did books introduce?
2. In paragraph 74, Wright mentions his "Jim Crow station in life." The term
   Jim Crow, derived from a character in a minstrel show, refers to laws enacted in Southern states that legalized racial segregation. What is Wright's
   "station in life"? In what ways does he adapt his behavior to accommodate
   this Jim Crow image? In what ways does he defy this stereotype?
3. After World War II, Wright left the United States to live in Paris. Given what
   you have read in this essay, does his decision surprise you? Do you think
   he made the right choice?

AMERICAN DREAMER

Bharati Mukherjee

*Novelist and short-story writer Bharati Mukherjee (1940–   ) was born
in Calcutta, India, and attended the university there. In 1961, she came to
the United States to attend the University of Iowa, where she received an
M.F.A. degree in creative writing. In 1963, she married a fellow student, an
American of Canadian parentage, thus gaining U.S. citizenship. She and her
husband lived in Canada for fourteen years, where she taught at McGill*

University. A U.S. resident since then, she is currently on the faculty at Skidmore College. Much of Mukherjee's fiction deals with the conflicts faced by Indian immigrants in North America as they attempt to embrace a new culture that does not always embrace them in return. Among her novels are Tiger's Daughter *(1972) and* Wife *(1975), both set in Canada, and* Jasmine *(1989) and* The Holder of the World *(1993), set in the United States. Her short-story collection* The Middleman and Other Stories *(1988) won the National Book Critics Circle Award. An avowed assimilationist, Mukherjee has written, "My books have often been read as unapologetic (and in some quarters overenthusiastic) texts for cultural and psychological 'mongrelization.' It's a word I celebrate." In the following essay written in 1997, she celebrates her "American dream" of diverse cultures coming together "as a constantly reforming, transmogrifying 'we.'"*

The United States exists as a sovereign Nation. "America," in con- 1 trast, exists as a myth of democracy and equal opportunity to live by, or as an ideal goal to reach.

I am a naturalized U.S. citizen, which means that, unlike native-born 2 citizens, I had to prove to the U.S. government that I merited citizenship. What I didn't have to disclose was that I desired "America," which to me is the stage for the drama of self-transformation.

I was born in Calcutta and first came to the United States—to Iowa 3 City, to be precise—on a summer evening in 1961. I flew into a small airport surrounded by cornfields and pastures, ready to carry out the two commands my father had written out for me the night before I left Calcutta: Spend two years studying creative writing at the Iowa Writers' Workshop, then come back home and marry the bridegroom he selected for me from our caste and class.

In traditional Hindu families like ours, men provided and women 4 were provided for. My father was a patriarch and I a pliant daughter. The neighborhood I'd grown up in was homogeneously Hindu, Bengali-speaking, and middle-class. I didn't expect myself to ever disobey or disappoint my father by setting my own goals and taking charge of my future.

When I landed in Iowa 35 years ago, I found myself in a society in 5 which almost everyone was Christian, white, and moderately well-off. In the women's dormitory I lived in my first year, apart from six international graduate students (all of us were from Asia and considered "exotic"), the only non-Christian was Jewish, and the only nonwhite an African-American from Georgia. I didn't anticipate then, that over the next 35 years, the Iowa population would become so diverse that it would have 6,931 children from non-English-speaking homes registered as students in its schools, nor that Iowans would be in the grip of a cultural crisis in which resentment against immigrants, particularly refugees from Vietnam, Sudan, and Bosnia, as well as unskilled

Spanish-speaking workers, would become politicized enough to cause the Immigration and Naturalization Service to open an "enforcement" office in Cedar Rapids in October for the tracking and deporting of undocumented aliens.

In Calcutta in the '50s, I heard no talk of "identity crisis"—communal or individual. The concept itself—of a person not knowing who he or she is—was unimaginable in our hierarchical, classification-obsessed society. One's identity was fixed, derived from religion, caste, patrimony, and mother tongue. A Hindu Indian's last name announced his or her forefathers' caste and place of origin. A Mukherjee could *only* be a Brahmin from Bengal. Hindu tradition forbade intercaste, interlanguage, interethnic marriages. Bengali tradition even discouraged emigration: To remove oneself from Bengal was to dilute true culture.

Until the age of 8, I lived in a house crowded with 40 or 50 relatives. My identity was viscerally connected with ancestral soil and genealogy. I was who I was because I was Dr. Sudhir Lal Mukherjee's daughter, because I was a Hindu Brahmin, because I was Bengali-speaking, and because my *desh*—the Bengali word for homeland—was an East Bengal village called Faridpur.

The University of Iowa classroom was my first experience of coeducation. And after not too long, I fell in love with a fellow student named Clark Blaise, an American of Canadian origin, and impulsively married him during a lunch break in a lawyer's office above a coffee shop.

That act cut me off forever from the rules and ways of upper-middle-class life in Bengal, and hurled me into a New World life of scary improvisations and heady explorations. Until my lunch-break wedding, I had seen myself as an Indian foreign student who intended to return to India to live. The five-minute ceremony in the lawyer's office suddenly changed me into a transient with conflicting loyalties to two very different cultures.

The first 10 years into marriage, years spent mostly in my husband's native Canada, I thought of myself as an expatriate Bengali permanently stranded in North America because of destiny or desire. My first novel, *The Tiger's Daughter*, embodies the loneliness I felt but could not acknowledge, even to myself, as I negotiated the no man's land between the country of my past and the continent of my present. Shaped by memory, textured with nostalgia for a class and culture I had abandoned, this novel quite naturally became an expression of the expatriate consciousness.

It took me a decade of painful introspection to put nostalgia in perspective and to make the transition from expatriate to immigrant. After a 14-year stay in Canada, I forced my husband and our two sons to relocate to the United States. But the transition from foreign student to

U.S. citizen, from detached onlooker to committed immigrant, has not been easy.

The years in Canada were particularly harsh. Canada is a country 12 that officially, and proudly, resists cultural fusion. For all its rhetoric about a cultural "mosaic," Canada refuses to renovate its national self-image to include its changing complexion. It is a New World country with Old World concepts of a fixed, exclusivist national identity. Canadian official rhetoric designated me as one of the "visible minority" who, even though I spoke the Canadian languages of English and French, was straining "the absorptive capacity" of Canada. Canadians of color were routinely treated as "not real" Canadians. One example: In 1985 a terrorist bomb, planted in an Air-India jet on Canadian soil, blew up after leaving Montreal, killing 329 passengers, most of whom were Canadians of Indian origin. The prime minister of Canada at the time, Brian Mulroney, phoned the prime minister of India to offer Canada's condolences for India's loss.

Those years of race-related harassments in Canada politicized me 13 and deepened my love of the ideals embedded in the American Bill of Rights. I don't forget that the architects of the Constitution and the Bill of Rights were white males and slaveholders. But through their declaration, they provided us with the enthusiasm for human rights, and the initial framework from which other empowerments could be conceived and enfranchised communities expanded.

I am a naturalized U.S. citizen and I take my American citizenship 14 very seriously. I am not an economic refugee, nor am I a seeker of political asylum. I am a voluntary immigrant. I became a citizen by choice, not by simple accident of birth.

Yet these days, questions such as who is an American and what is 15 American culture are being posed with belligerence, and being answered with violence. Scapegoating of immigrants has once again become the politicians' easy remedy for all that ails the nation. Hate speeches fill auditoriums for demagogues willing to profit from stirring up racial animosity. An April Gallup poll indicated that half of Americans would like to bar almost all legal immigration for the next five years.

The United States, like every sovereign nation, has a right to for- 16 mulate its immigration policies. But in this decade of continual, large-scale diasporas, it is imperative that we come to some agreement about who "we" are, and what our goals are for the nation, now that our community includes people of many races, ethnicities, languages, and religions.

The debate about American culture and American identity has to 17 date been monopolized largely by Eurocentrists and ethnocentrists whose rhetoric has been flamboyantly divisive, pitting a phantom "us" against a demonized "them."

All countries view themselves by their ideals. Indians idealize the 18 cultural continuum, the inherent value system of India, and are properly incensed when foreigners see nothing but poverty, intolerance, strife, and injustice. Americans see themselves as the embodiments of liberty, openness, and individualism, even as the world judges them for drugs, crime, violence, bigotry, militarism, and homelessness. I was in Singapore in 1994 when the American teenager Michael Fay was sentenced to caning for having spraypainted some cars. While I saw Fay's actions as those of an individual, and his sentence as too harsh, the overwhelming local sentiment was that vandalism was an "American" crime, and that flogging Fay would deter Singapore youths from becoming "Americanized."

Conversely, in 1994, in Tavares, Florida, the Lake County School 19 Board announced its policy (since overturned) requiring middle school teachers to instruct their students that American culture, by which the board meant European-American culture, is inherently "superior to other foreign or historic cultures." The policy's misguided implication was that culture in the United States has not been affected by the American Indian, African-American, Latin-American, and Asian-American segments of the population. The sinister implication was that our national identity is so fragile that it can absorb diverse and immigrant cultures only by recontextualizing them as deficient.

Our nation is unique in human history in that the founding idea of 20 "America" was in opposition to the tenet that a nation is a collection of like-looking, like-speaking, like-worshiping people. The primary criterion for nationhood in Europe is homogeneity of culture, race, and religion—which has contributed to blood-soaked balkanization[1] in the former Yugoslavia and the former Soviet Union.

America's pioneering European ancestors gave up the easy homo- 21 geneity of their native countries for a new version of utopia. Now, in the 1990s, we have the exciting chance to follow that tradition and assist in the making of a new American culture that differs from both the enforced assimilation of a "melting pot" and the Canadian model of a multicultural "mosaic."

The multicultural mosaic implies a contiguity of fixed, self- 22 sufficient, utterly distinct cultures. Multiculturalism, as it has been practiced in the United States in the past 10 years, implies the existence of a central culture, ringed by peripheral cultures. The fallout of official multiculturalism is the establishment of one culture as the norm and the rest as aberrations. At the same time, the multiculturalist emphasis on race- and ethnicity-based group identity leads to a lack of respect for

---

[1] A breakdown into smaller, often hostile, units. [Eds.]

individual differences within each group, and to vilification of those individuals who place the good of the nation above the interests of their particular racial or ethnic communities.

We must be alert to the dangers of an "us" vs. "them" mentality. In 23 California, this mentality is manifesting itself as increased violence between minority, ethnic communities. The attack on Korean-American merchants in South Central Los Angeles in the wake of the Rodney King beating trial is only one recent example of the tragic side effects of this mentality. On the national level, the politicization of ethnic identities has encouraged the scapegoating of legal immigrants, who are blamed for economic and social problems brought about by flawed domestic and foreign policies.

We need to discourage the retention of cultural memory if the aim of 24 that retention is cultural balkanization. We must think of American culture and nationhood as a constantly reforming, transmogrifying "we."

In this age of diasporas,[2] one's biological identity may not be one's 25 only identity. Erosions and accretions come with the act of emigration. The experience of cutting myself off from a biological homeland and settling in an adopted homeland that is not always welcoming to its dark-complexioned citizens has tested me as a person, and made me the writer I am today.

I choose to describe myself on my own terms, as an American, 26 rather than as an Asian-American. Why is it that hyphenation is imposed only on nonwhite Americans? Rejecting hyphenation is my refusal to categorize the cultural landscape into a center and its peripheries; it is to demand that the American nation deliver the promises of its dream and its Constitution to all its citizens equally.

My rejection of hyphenation has been misrepresented as race 27 treachery by some India-born academics on U.S. campuses who have appointed themselves guardians of the "purity" of ethnic cultures. Many of them, though they reside permanently in the United States and participate in its economy, consistently denounce American ideals and institutions. They direct their rage at me because, by becoming a U.S. citizen and exercising my voting rights, I have invested in the present and not the past; because I have committed myself to help shape the future of my adopted homeland, and because I celebrate racial and cultural mongrelization.

What excites me is that as a nation we have not only the chance to 28 retain those values we treasure from our original cultures but also the chance to acknowledge that the outer forms of those values are likely to

---

[2] Migrations. [Eds.]

change. Among Indian immigrants, I see a great deal of guilt about the inability to hang on to what they commonly term "pure culture." Parents express rage or despair at their U.S.-born children's forgetting of, or indifference to, some aspects of Indian culture. Of those parents I would ask: What is it we have lost if our children are acculturating into the culture in which we are living? Is it so terrible that our children are discovering or are inventing homelands for themselves?

Some first-generation Indo-Americans, embittered by racism and by 29
unofficial "glass ceilings," construct a phantom identity, more-Indian-than-Indians-in-India, as a defense against marginalization. I ask: Why don't you get actively involved in fighting discrimination? Make your voice heard. Choose the forum most appropriate for you. If you are a citizen, let your vote count. Reinvest your energy and resources into revitalizing your city's disadvantaged residents and neighborhoods. Know your constitutional rights, and when they are violated, use the agencies of redress the Constitution makes available to you. Expect change, and when it comes, deal with it!

As a writer, my literary agenda begins by acknowledging that 30
America has transformed me. It does not end until I show that I (along with the hundreds of thousands of immigrants like me) am minute by minute transforming America. The transformation is a two-way process: It affects both the individual and the national-cultural identity.

Others who write stories of migration often talk of arrival at a new 31
place as a loss, the loss of communal memory and the erosion of an original culture. I want to talk of arrival as gain.

Responding to Reading

1. As a self-described "transient with conflicting loyalties to two very different cultures" (9), the newly married Mukherjee found herself in the midst of an "identity crisis." Has she been able to resolve this crisis? If so, how? Do you think it is possible for a native-born American to suffer a similar identity crisis?

2. In what sense has Mukherjee's immigration been a loss? In what sense has it been a gain? Is she speaking primarily for herself in this essay, or does she mean to speak for immigrants in general? How can you tell?

3. In paragraph 18, Mukherjee says, "Americans see themselves as the embodiments of liberty, openness, and individualism, even as the world judges them for drugs, crime, violence, bigotry, militarism, and homelessness." What is your reaction to this statement? Do you think it is true? Do you think it is fair?

THE MYTH OF THE LATIN WOMAN: I JUST MET A GIRL NAMED MARIA

Judith Ortiz Cofer

Born in Puerto Rico and raised in Paterson, New Jersey, Judith Ortiz Cofer (1952–) is an award-winning poet and novelist as well as an essayist. Her books include the novel The Line of the Sun *(1989);* Silent Dancing *(1990), a collection of biographical essays; and* The Latin Deli: Prose and Poetry *(1993). A teacher of creative writing at the University of Georgia, she has said that she began writing because "as a native speaker of Spanish, I first perceived of language, especially the English language, as a barrier, a challenge to be met with the same kind of closed-eyed bravado that prompted me to jump into the deep end of the pool before taking my first swimming lesson." In the following essay from* The Latin Deli, *Cofer describes the stereotypes she has confronted as a Latina.*

On a bus trip to London from Oxford University where I was earn-   1
ing some graduate credits one summer, a young man, obviously fresh from a pub, spotted me and as if struck by inspiration went down on his knees in the aisle. With both hands over his heart he broke into an Irish tenor's rendition of "Maria" from *West Side Story*.[1] My politely amused fellow passengers gave his lovely voice the round of gentle applause it deserved. Though I was not quite as amused, I managed my version of an English smile: no show of teeth, no extreme contortions of the facial muscles—I was at this time of my life practicing reserve and cool. Oh, that British control, how I coveted it. But "Maria" had followed me to London, reminding me of a prime fact of my life: you can leave the island, master the English language, and travel as far as you can, but if you are a Latina, especially one like me who so obviously belongs to Rita Moreno's[2] gene pool, the island travels with you.

This is sometimes a very good thing—it may win you that extra   2
minute of someone's attention. But with some people, the same things can make *you* an island—not a tropical paradise but an Alcatraz, a place nobody wants to visit. As a Puerto Rican girl living in the United States[3] and wanting like most children to "belong," I resented the stereotype that my Hispanic appearance called forth from many people I met.

Growing up in a large urban center in New Jersey during the 1960s,   3
I suffered from what I think of as "cultural schizophrenia." Our life was

---

[1] A popular Broadway musical, loosely based on *Romeo and Juliet*, about two rival street gangs, one Anglo and one Puerto Rican, in New York City.

[2] Puerto Rico–born actress who won an Oscar for her role in the 1960 movie version of *West Side Story*. [Eds.]

[3] Although it is an island, Puerto Rico is part of the U.S. (it is a self-governing commonwealth).

designed by my parents as a microcosm of their *casas*[4] on the island. We spoke in Spanish, ate Puerto Rican food bought at the *bodega*,[5] and practiced strict Catholicism at a church that allotted us a one-hour slot each week for mass, performed in Spanish by a Chinese priest trained as a missionary for Latin America.

As a girl I was kept under strict surveillance by my parents, since 4 my virtue and modesty were, by their cultural equation, the same as their honor. As a teenager I was lectured constantly on how to behave as a proper *senorita*. But it was a conflicting message I received, since the Puerto Rican mothers also encouraged their daughters to look and act like women and to dress in clothes our Anglo friends and their mothers found too "mature" and flashy. The difference was, and is, cultural; yet I often felt humiliated when I appeared at an American friend's party wearing a dress more suitable to a semi-formal than to a playroom birthday celebration. At Puerto Rican festivities, neither the music nor the colors we wore could be too loud.

I remember Career Day in our high school, when teachers told us to 5 come dressed as if for a job interview. It quickly became obvious that to the Puerto Rican girls "dressing up" meant wearing their mother's ornate jewelry and clothing, more appropriate (by mainstream standards) for the company Christmas party than as daily office attire. That morning I had agonized in front of my closet, trying to figure out what a "career girl" would wear. I knew how to dress for school (at the Catholic school I attended, we all wore uniforms), I knew how to dress for Sunday mass, and I knew what dresses to wear for parties at my relatives' homes. Though I do not recall the precise details of my Career Day outfit, it must have been a composite of these choices. But I remember a comment my friend (an Italian American) made in later years that coalesced my impressions of that day. She said that at the business school she was attending, the Puerto Rican girls always stood out for wearing "everything at once." She meant, of course, too much jewelry, too many accessories. On that day at school we were simply made the negative models by the nuns, who were themselves not credible fashion experts to any of us. But it was painfully obvious to me that to the others, in their tailored skirts and silk blouses, we must have seemed "hopeless" and "vulgar." Though I now know that most adolescents feel out of step much of the time, I also know that for the Puerto Rican girls of my generation that sense was intensified. The way our teachers and classmates looked at us that day in school was just a taste of the cultural clash that awaited us in the real world, where prospective employers and men on the street would often misinterpret our tight skirts and jingling bracelets as a "come-on."

---

[4] Homes. [Eds.]
[5] Small grocery store. [Eds.]

Mixed cultural signals have perpetuated certain stereotypes—for 6 example, that of the Hispanic woman as the "hot tamale" or sexual fire-brand. It is a one-dimensional view that the media have found easy to promote. In their special vocabulary, advertisers have designated "sizzling" and "smoldering" as the adjectives of choice for describing not only the foods but also the women of Latin America. From conversations in my house I recall hearing about the harassment that Puerto Rican women endured in factories where the "boss-men" talked to them as if sexual innuendo was all they understood, and worse, often gave them the choice of submitting to their advances or being fired.

It is custom, however, not chromosomes, that leads us to choose 7 scarlet over pale pink. As young girls, it was our mothers who influenced our decisions about clothes and colors—mothers who had grown up on a tropical island where the natural environment was a riot of primary colors, where showing your skin was one way to keep cool as well as to look sexy. Most important of all, on the island, women perhaps felt freer to dress and move more provocatively since, in most cases, they were protected by the traditions, mores, and laws of a Spanish/Catholic system of morality and machismo whose main rule was: *You may look at my sister, but if you touch her I will kill you.* The extended family and church structure could provide a young woman with a circle of safety in her small pueblo on the island; if a man "wronged" a girl, everyone would close in to save her family honor.

My mother has told me about dressing in her best party clothes on 8 Saturday nights and going to the town's plaza to promenade with her girlfriends in front of the boys they liked. The males were thus given an opportunity to admire the women and to express their admiration in the form of *piropos*: erotically charged street poems they composed on the spot. (I have myself been subjected to a few *piropos* while visiting the island, and they can be outrageous, although custom dictates that they must never cross into obscenity.) This ritual, as I understand it, also entails a show of studied indifference on the woman's part; if she is "decent," she must not acknowledge the man's impassioned words. So I do understand how things can be lost in translation. When a Puerto Rican girl dressed in her idea of what is attractive meets a man from the mainstream culture who has been trained to react to certain types of clothing as a sexual signal, a clash is likely to take place. I remember the boy who took me to my first formal dance leaning over to plant a sloppy, over-eager kiss painfully on my mouth; when I didn't respond with sufficient passion, he remarked resentfully: "I thought you Latin girls were supposed to mature early," as if I were expected to *ripen* like a fruit or vegetable, not just grow into womanhood like other girls.

It is surprising to my professional friends that even today some 9 people, including those who should know better, still put others "in their place." It happened to me most recently during a stay at a classy

metropolitan hotel favored by young professional couples for weddings. Late one evening after the theater, as I walked toward my room
with a colleague (a woman with whom I was coordinating an arts program), a middle-aged man in a tuxedo, with a young girl in satin and
lace on his arm, stepped directly into our path. With his champagne
glass extended toward me, he exclaimed "Evita!"[6]

Our way blocked, my companion and I listened as the man half-   10
recited, half-bellowed "Don't Cry for Me, Argentina." When he finished, the young girl said: "How about a round of applause for my
daddy?" We complied, hoping this would bring the silly spectacle to a
close. I was becoming aware that our little group was attracting the
attention of the other guests. "Daddy" must have perceived this too,
and he once more barred the way as we tried to walk past him. He
began to shout-sing a ditty to the tune of "La Bamba"—except the lyrics
were about a girl named Maria whose exploits rhymed with her name
and gonorrhea. The girl kept saying "Oh, Daddy" and looking at me
with pleading eyes. She wanted me to laugh along with the others. My
companion and I stood silently waiting for the man to end his offensive
song. When he finished, I looked not at him but at his daughter. I
advised her calmly never to ask her father what he had done in the
army. Then I walked between them and to my room. My friend compli-
mented me on my cool handling of the situation, but I confessed that I
had really wanted to push the jerk into the swimming pool. This same
man—probably a corporate executive, well-educated, even worldly by
most standards—would not have been likely to regale an Anglo woman
with a dirty song in public. He might have checked his impulse by
assuming that she could be somebody's wife or mother, or at least *somebody* who might take offense. But, to him, I was just an Evita or a Maria:
merely a character in his cartoon-populated universe.

Another facet of the myth of the Latin woman in the United States is   11
the menial, the domestic—Maria the housemaid or countergirl. It's true
that work as domestics, as waitresses, and in factories is all that's available to women with little English and few skills. But the myth of the
Hispanic menial—the funny maid, mispronouncing words and cooking
up a spicy storm in a shiny California kitchen—has been perpetuated by
the media in the same way that "Mammy" from *Gone with the Wind*
became America's idea of the black woman for generations. Since I do
not wear my diplomas around my neck for all to see, I have on occasion
been sent to that "kitchen" where some think I obviously belong.

One incident has stayed with me, though I recognize it as a minor   12
offense. My first public poetry reading took place in Miami, at a restaurant where a luncheon was being held before the event. I was nervous

---

[6] A Broadway musical, later made into a movie, about Eva Duarte de Perón, the former first lady
of Argentina. [Eds.]

and excited as I walked in with notebook in hand. An older woman motioned me to her table, and thinking (foolish me) that she wanted me to autograph a copy of my newly published slender volume of verse, I went over. She ordered a cup of coffee from me, assuming that I was the waitress. (Easy enough to mistake my poems for menus, I suppose.) I know it wasn't an intentional act of cruelty. Yet of all the good things that happened later, I remember that scene most clearly, because it reminded me of what I had to overcome before anyone would take me seriously. In retrospect I understand that my anger gave my reading fire. In fact, I have almost always taken any doubt in my abilities as a challenge, the result most often being the satisfaction of winning a convert, of seeing the cold, appraising eyes warm to my words, the body language change, the smile that indicates I have opened some avenue for communication. So that day as I read, I looked directly at that woman. Her lowered eyes told me she was embarrassed at her faux pas, and when I willed her to look up at me, she graciously allowed me to punish her with my full attention. We shook hands at the end of the reading and I never saw her again. She has probably forgotten the entire incident, but maybe not.

Yet I am one of the lucky ones. There are thousands of Latinas 13 without the privilege of an education or the entrees into society that I have. For them life is a constant struggle against the misconceptions perpetuated by the myth of the Latina. My goal is to try to replace the old stereotypes with a much more interesting set of realities. Every time I give a reading, I hope the stories I tell, the dreams and fears I examine in my work, can achieve some universal truth that will get my audience past the particulars of my skin color, my accent, or my clothes.

I once wrote a poem in which I called all Latinas "God's brown 14 daughters." This poem is really a prayer of sorts, offered upward, but also, through the human-to-human channel of art, outward. It is a prayer for communication and for respect. In it, Latin women pray "in Spanish to an Anglo God/with a Jewish heritage," and they are "fervently hoping/that if not omnipotent,/at least He be bilingual."

Responding to Reading

1. What exactly is the "myth of the Latin woman"? According to Cofer, what has perpetuated this stereotype? Do you see this myth as simply demeaning, or as potentially dangerous?

2. In paragraph 1, Cofer says, "you can leave [Puerto Rico], master the English language, and travel as far as you can, but if you are a Latina, . . . the island travels with you." What does she mean? Do you think this is true of people from other ethnic groups as well?

3. Throughout this essay, Cofer speaks of the "cultural schizophrenia" (3) she felt, describing the "conflicting messages" (4), the "cultural clash" (5), and the "mixed cultural signals" (6) she received from the two worlds she inhabited. Is there any indication in the essay that she still feels torn between her two cultures? Explain.

LIMITED SEATING ON BROADWAY

John Hockenberry

John Hockenberry (1956–) is a news reporter who has covered stories ranging from the eruption of Mount St. Helens to the Persian Gulf War as a correspondent for National Public Radio. He is also a wheelchair-bound paraplegic, paralyzed since the age of nineteen as the result of an automobile accident when he was a student at the University of Chicago. Eventually a music major at the University of Oregon, Hockenberry began his journalistic career at an NPR affiliate in Eugene. In 1992 he joined ABC television's newsmagazine Day One, *becoming the first—and only—network reporter to appear in a wheelchair. He now reports for NBC's* Dateline. *A fierce advocate of strict enforcement of laws that protect the disabled, Hockenberry has said, "For the struggles I've gone through to mean something, I have to be an activist." His book* Moving Violations: War Zones, Wheelchairs, and Declarations of Independence *(1995) chronicles some of his battles. In the following opinion piece, written for the* New York Times *op-ed page in 1992, Hockenberry describes his outrage at being denied access to a Broadway theater. He later sued the theater, and under the terms of the settlement, its owners installed a lift to allow wheelchair access.*

The show at the Virginia Theater, "Jelly's Last Jam," is in previews, 1 and even though tickets are $60 for orchestra seats (the only option for patrons in wheelchairs), the price was a minor impediment to the prospect of an evening of Jelly Roll Morton's jazz.

The art community in New York City has a reputation for being 2 progressive. It is the forum and agent for challenging America's hardened perceptions about race, politics, class, gender, religion and, more recently, AIDS and homophobia. In particular, the theater world likes to think of itself as a seeker of such challenges and is proudest when a play or musical becomes a vehicle for change.

I thought of this two Saturdays ago as I sat at the top of some stairs 3 in the Virginia Theater waiting to be helped into my seat. Because the Virginia, like virtually all Broadway theaters, refuses to take orders for wheelchair tickets over the phone, except for purchases well in advance, I had to make a special trip to the box office the day before to buy my ticket.

At the box office, I was told that a ticket was available but that I 4 would have to sit far from my friend. I was told the house manager would seat me when I arrived. Here again, minor hassles well worth bearing on the way to an evening of good theater.

But that didn't happen. Two minutes before curtain time the house 5 manager emerged from a white door with a copy of the theater's "Policy for Disabled Patrons." He abruptly told me to leave the theater. I was shocked and asked why. He asked if I could walk, something I thought was fairly clear when I had bought the ticket the day before. He mentioned stairs for the first time and noted that since I could not walk and had not brought my own crew with me that it was impossible to seat me. I said that there was no problem and that I would show him how to get me up the stairs with the help of the usher standing next to him.

He said in a loud voice audible to everyone around us: "Sir, we are 6 not allowed to touch you. Our staff is not allowed to do that." I reminded him that my friend had already taken her seat at the suggestion of the usher and would react with some alarm if she saw my seat empty after the show began. "I'm sorry, sir, you'll have to leave," was his only response.

Having had many close calls with the inaccessible infrastructure of 7 the world, I still could not believe I would not be able to see the show. I recalled an incident some years before at the Hakawati Theater in East Jerusalem when four fellow patrons and the playwright, all strangers, helped me up 12 stairs to see a puppet show. They demanded that I be carried even when I was doubtful.

The theatergoers at the Virginia eyed me with the detached, craven 8 interest that New Yorkers reserve for the white chalk outline of a corpse at a crime scene. "You are a fire hazard, sir," the manager insisted. Only moments before I had been a component of his cash flow. I grabbed his collar and told him what he could do with his Policy for Disabled Patrons. I was easily overpowered and ushered, the only ushering I would experience that night, to the 52d Street sidewalk.

I sat powerless and humiliated; all dressed up, nowhere to go. Of 9 course, the Virginia Theater staff probably thought differently. They might recall a rude, angry man trying to get rules bent in his favor. But outside, it seemed as if I was the only one who thought that a few stairs shouldn't stand in the way of seeing a play. Certainly there was no one to complain to about the lack of ramps. There was no meaning to the incident at all.

The Virginia Theater was not my first such encounter with New 10 York City's art community. Some months ago on 10th Avenue I tried to empty a bottle of urine I had carried for 40 blocks. In the absence of any public restroom I rolled into a dirty parking lot to pour out the jar in a discreet corner. Two attendants with all the righteousness of crusaders grabbed me and threw me out of my chair and onto the sidewalk as people walked by.

Not long after the event I learned that a proposal for handicapped-accessible public restrooms on city streets was opposed by the Public Art Commission, which had determined that the structures would be too ugly. (Uglier even than public defecation, and heaven knows the arts community knows best about that.)   11

Artists might shrink from taking blame for the insensitive acts of architects, producers and theater owners. But as society's voice of protest, are artists to be excused for ignoring discrimination that hasn't yet made it to Broadway?   12

Maybe if I was an artist who daringly confronted whole flights of stairs in front of a paying audience and who carried around bottles of urine just to make a point about society I might keep from wetting my pants and, better yet, get to see "Jelly's Last Jam." But then that wouldn't be honest. Art and theater are nothing if not honest.   13

Responding to Reading

1. Hockenberry is clearly angry in this piece. For whom does he reserve his greatest anger? Why? Do you share his anger?
2. What specific changes does Hockenberry feel must be made before he and other disabled people can participate fully in American society? Do you believe the changes he wants are reasonable? Possible? Do you believe he has a basic right to expect, or even demand, such accommodations?
3. Hockenberry is a well-educated white male with a prestigious job, and he is willing and able to pay $60 for a theater ticket. Could you argue that, despite his physical disability, he has achieved the American Dream? Or do you believe part of the dream has nonetheless eluded him?

THRIVING AS AN OUTSIDER, EVEN AS AN OUTCAST, IN SMALLTOWN AMERICA

Louie Crew

A founder of Integrity, the national organization of gay and lesbian Episcopalians, Alabama native Louie Crew (1936–) has long been an active participant in the gay rights and civil rights movements, seeing in both the common goal of overcoming oppression and intolerance. Educated at Baylor University, Auburn University, and the University of Alabama,

Crew is a teacher, lecturer, and writer, as well as a social and religious reformer. His books include The Gay Academic *(1978) and* The Book of Revelations: Lesbian and Gay Episcopalians Tell Their Own Stories *(1991). In the following essay (1981) he recalls the four years he and his African-American companion spent as residents of a small, conservative town in Georgia, living openly as a gay couple. Their methods of survival, he suggests, "should interest anyone who values the role of the dissident in our democracy."*

From 1973 to 1979, my spouse and I lived in Fort Valley, a town of 1 12,000 people, the seat of Peach County, sixty miles northeast of Plains, right in the geographic center of Georgia. I taught English at a local black college and my spouse was variously a nurse, hairdresser, choreographer for the college majorettes, caterer, and fashion designer.

The two of us have often been asked how we survived as a gay, 2 racially integrated couple living openly in that small town. We are still perhaps too close to the Georgia experience and very much caught up in our similar struggles in central Wisconsin to offer a definite explanation, but our tentative conjectures should interest anyone who values the role of the dissident in our democracy.

Survive we did. We even throve before our departure. Profession- 3 ally, my colleagues and the Regents of the University System of Georgia awarded me tenure, and the Chamber of Commerce awarded my spouse a career medal in cosmetology. Socially, we had friends from the full range of the economic classes in the community. We had attended six farewell parties in our honor before we called a halt to further fetes, especially several planned at too great a sacrifice by some of the poorest folks in the town. Furthermore, I had been away only four months when the college brought me back to address an assembly of Georgia judges, majors, police chiefs, and wardens. We are still called two to three times a week by scores of people seeking my spouse's advice on fashion, cooking, or the like.

It was not always so. In 1974 my spouse and I were denied housing 4 which we had "secured" earlier before the realtor saw my spouse's color. HUD documented that the realtor thought that "the black man looked like a criminal." Once the town was up in arms when a bishop accused the two of us of causing a tornado which had hit the town early in 1975, an accusation which appeared on the front page of the newspaper. "This is the voice of God. The town of Fort Valley is harboring Sodomists. Would one expect God to keep silent when homosexuals are tolerated? We remember what He did to Sodom and Gomorrah" (*The Macon Herald*, March 20, 1975: 1). A year later my Episcopal vestry[1] asked me to leave the parish, and my own bishop summoned me for

---

[1] Elected board that administers affairs in an Episcopal parish. [Eds.]

discipline for releasing to the national press correspondence related to the vestry's back-room maneuvers. Prompted in part by such officials, the local citizens for years routinely heckled us in public, sometimes threw rocks at our apartment, trained their children to spit on us from their bicycles if we dared to jog, and badgered us with hate calls on an average of six to eight times a week.

One such episode offers a partial clue to the cause of our survival. 5 It was late summer, 1975 or 1976. I was on my motorcycle to post mail at the street-side box just before the one daily pickup at 6:00 P.M. About fifty yards away, fully audible to about seventy pedestrians milling about the court house and other public buildings, a group of police officers, all men, began shouting at me from the steps of their headquarters: "Louise! Faggot! Queer!"

Anyone who has ever tried to ease a motorcycle from a still position 6 without revving the engine knows that the feat is impossible: try as I did to avoid the suggestion, I sounded as if I were riding off in a huff. About half-way up the street, I thought to myself, "I'd rather rot in jail than feel the way I do now." I turned around, drove back—the policemen still shouting and laughing—and parked in the lot of the station. When I walked to the steps, only the lone black policeman remained.

"Did you speak to me?" I asked him.   7

"No, sir," he replied emphatically.   8

Inside I badgered the desk sergeant to tell her chief to call me as 9 soon as she could locate him, and I indicated that I would press charges if necessary to prevent a recurrence. I explained that the police misconduct was an open invitation to more violent hoodlums to act out the officers' fantasies with impunity in the dark. Later, I persuaded a black city commissioner and a white one, the latter our grocer and the former our mortician, to threaten the culprits with suspension if ever such misconduct occurred again.

Over a year later, late one Friday after his payday, a black friend of 10 my spouse knocked at our door to offer a share of his Scotch to celebrate his raise—or so he said. Thus primed, he asked me, "You don't recognize me, do you?"

"No," I admitted.   11

"I'm the lone black policeman that day you were heckled. I came by 12 really because I thought you two might want to know what happened inside when Louie stormed up to the sergeant."

"Yes," we said.   13

"Well, all the guys were crouching behind the partition to keep you 14 from seeing that they were listening. Their eyes bulged when you threatened to bring in the F.B.I. and such. Then when you left, one spoke for all when he said, 'But sissies aren't supposed to do things like that!'"

Ironically, I believe that a major reason for our thriving on our own 15 terms of candor about our relationship has been our commitment to resist the intimidation heaped upon us. For too long lesbians and gay males have unwillingly encouraged abuses against ourselves by serving advance notice to any bullies, be they the barnyard-playground variety, or the Bible-wielding pulpiteers, that we would whimper or run into hiding when confronted with even the threat of exposure. It is easy to confuse sensible nonviolence with cowardly nonresistance.

In my view, violent resistance would be counter-productive, espe-   16
cially for lesbians and gays who are outnumbered 10 to 1 by heterosexuals, according to Kinsey's statistics. Yet our personal experience suggests that special kinds of creative nonviolent resistance are a major source of hope if lesbians and gay males are going to reverse the physical and mental intimidation which is our daily portion in this culture.

Resistance to oppression can be random and spontaneous, as   17
was my decision to return to confront the police hecklers, or organized and sustained, as more typically has been the resistance by which my spouse and I have survived. I believe that only organized and sustained resistance offers much hope for long-range change in any community. The random act is too soon forgotten or too easily romanticized.

Once we had committed ourselves to one another, my spouse and I   18
never gave much thought for ourselves to the traditional device most gays have used for survival, the notorious "closet" in which one hides one's identity from all but a select group of friends. In the first place, a black man and a white man integrating a Georgia small town simply cannot be inconspicuous. More importantly, the joint checking account and other equitable economies fundamental to the quality of our marriage are public, not private acts. Our denial of the obvious would have secured closet space only for our suffocation; we would have lied, "We are ashamed and live in secret."

All of our resistance stems from our sense of our own worth, our   19
conviction that we and our kind do not deserve the suffering which heterosexuals continue to encourage or condone for sexual outcasts. Dr. Martin Luther King used to say, "Those who go to the back of the bus, deserve the back of the bus."

Our survival on our own terms has depended very much on our   20
knowing and respecting many of the rules of the system which we resist. We are not simply dissenters, but conscientious ones.

For example, we are both very hard workers. As a controversial per-   21
son, I know that my professionalism comes under far more scrutiny than that of others. I learned early in my career that I could secure space for my differences by handling routine matters carefully. If one stays on good terms with secretaries, meets all deadlines, and willingly does one's fair share of the busy work of institutions, one is usually already well on the way towards earning collegial space, if not collegial support. In Georgia, I routinely volunteered to be secretary for most committees

on which I served, thereby having enormous influence in the final form of the groups' deliberations without monopolizing the forum as most other molders of policy do. My spouse's many talents and sensibilities made him an invaluable advisor and confidante to scores of people in the community. Of course, living as we did in a hairdresser's salon, we knew a great deal more about the rest of the public than that public knew about us.

My spouse and I are fortunate in the fact that we like the enormous amount of work which we do. We are not mere opportunists working hard only as a gimmick to exploit the public for lesbian and gay issues. Both of us worked intensely at our professional assignments long before we were acknowledged dissidents with new excessive pressures to excel. We feel that now we must, however unfairly, be twice as effective as our competitors just to remain employed at all. 22

Our survival has also depended very much on our thorough knowledge of the system, often knowledge more thorough than that of those who would use the system against us. For example, when my bishop summoned me for discipline, I was able to show him that his own canons give him no authority to discipline a lay person except by excommunication. In fact, so hierarchical have the canons of his diocese become, that the only laity who exist worthy of their mention are the few lay persons on vestries. 23

Especially helpful has been our knowledge of communication procedures. For example, when an area minister attacked lesbians and gays on a TV talk show, I requested equal time; so well received was my response that for two more years I was a regular panelist on the talk show, thereby reaching most residents of the entire middle Georgia area as a known gay person, yet one speaking not just to sexual issues, but to a full range of religious and social topics. 24

When I was occasionally denied access to media, as in the parish or diocese or as on campus when gossip flared, I knew the value of candid explanations thoughtfully prepared, xeroxed, and circulated to enough folks to assure that the gossips would have access to the truthful version. For example, the vestry, which acted in secret, was caught by surprise when I sent copies of their hateful letter to most other parishioners, together with a copy of a psalm which I wrote protesting their turning the House of Prayer into a Court House. I also was able to explain that I continued to attend, not in defiance of their withdrawn invitation, but in obedience to the much higher invitation issued to us all by the real head of the Church. In January, 1979, in the first open meeting of the parish since the vestry's letter of unwelcome three years earlier, the entire parish voted to censure the vestry for that action and to extend to me the full welcome which the vestry had tried to deny. Only three voted against censure, all three of them a minority of the vestry being censured. 25

My spouse and I have been very conscious of the risks of our con- 26
victions. We have viewed our credentials—my doctorate and his professional licenses—not as badges of comfortable respectability, but as
assets to be invested in social change. Dr. King did not sit crying in the
Albany jail, "Why don't these folk respect me? How did this happen?
What am I doing here?" When my spouse and I have been denied jobs
for which we were the most qualified applicants, we have not naively
asked how such things could be, nor have we dwelt overly long on self-
pity, for we have known in advance the prices we might have to pay,
even if to lose our lives. Our realism about danger and risk has helped
us to preserve our sanity when everyone about us has seemed insane. I
remember the joy which my spouse shared with me over the fact that he
had just been fired for his efforts to organize other black nurses to
protest their being treated as orderlies by the white managers of a local
hospital.

Never, however, have we affirmed the injustices. Finally, we simply 27
cannot be surprised by any evil and are thus less likely to be intimidated
by it. Hence, we find ourselves heirs to a special hybrid of courage, a
form of courage too often ignored by the heterosexual majority, but
widely manifest among sexual outcasts, not the courage of bravado on
battlegrounds or sportsfields, but the delicate courage of the lone person who patiently waits out the stupidity of the herd, the cagey courage
that has operated many an underground railway station.

Our survival in smalltown America has been helped least, I suspect, 28
by our annoying insistence that potential friends receive us not only in
our own right, but also as members of the larger lesbian/gay and black
communities of which we are a part. Too many whites and heterosexuals are prepared to single us out as "good queers" or "good niggers,"
offering us thereby the "rewards" of their friendship only at too great a
cost to our integrity. My priest did not whip up the vestry against me
the first year we lived openly together. He was perfectly happy to have
one of his "clever queers" to dress his wife's hair and the other to help
him write his annual report. We became scandalous only when the two
of us began to organize the national group of lesbian and gay-male
Episcopalians, known as INTEGRITY; then we were no longer just
quaint. We threatened his image of himself as the arbiter of community
morality, especially as he faced scores of queries from brother priests
elsewhere.

Many lesbians and gay males are tamed by dependencies upon 29
carefully selected heterosexual friends with whom they have shared
their secret, often never realizing that in themselves alone, they could
provide far more affirmation and discover far more strength than is
being cultivated by the terms of these "friendships." Lesbians and gay
males have always been taught to survive on the heterosexuals' terms,

rarely on one's own terms, and almost never on the terms of a community shared with other lesbians and gay males.

Heterosexuals are often thus the losers. The heterosexual acquaintances close to us early on when we were less visible who dropped us later as our notoriety spread were in most cases folks of demonstrably much less character strength than those heterosexuals who remained our friends even as we asserted our difference with thoughtful independence. 30

My spouse and I have never been exclusive nor aspired to move to any ghetto. In December 1978, on the night the Macon rabbi and I had successfully organized the area's Jews and gays to protest a concert by Anita Bryant,[2] I returned home to watch the videotape of the march on the late news in the company of eight house guests invited by my spouse for a surprise party, not one of them gay (for some strange reason nine out of ten folks are not), not one of them obligated to be at the earlier march and not one of them uneasy, as most of our acquaintances would have been a few years earlier before we had undertaken this reeducation together. 31

Folks who work for social change need to be very careful to allow room for it to happen, not to allow realistic appraisals of risks to prevent their cultivation of the very change which they germinate. 32

Our survival has been helped in no small way by our candor and clarity in response to rumor and gossip, which are among our biggest enemies. On my campus in Georgia, I voluntarily spoke about sexual issues to an average of fifty classes per year outside my discipline. Initially, those encounters sharpened my wits for tougher national forums, but long after I no longer needed these occasions personally for rehearsal, I continued to accept the invitations, thereby reaching a vast majority of the citizens of the small town where we continued to live. I used to enjoy the humor of sharing with such groups facts which would make my day-to-day life more pleasant. For example, I routinely noted that when a male student is shocked at my simple public, "Hello," he would look both ways to see who might have seen him being friendly with the gay professor. By doing this he is telling me and all other knowledgeable folks far more new information about his own body chemistry than he is finding out about mine. More informed male students would reply, "Hello" when greeted. With this method I disarmed the hatefulness of one of their more debilitating weapons of ostracism. 33

All personal references in public discussions inevitably invade one's privacy, but I have usually found the invasion a small price to pay 34

---

[2] Former beauty queen who, during the late 1970s and early 1980s, attempted to bolster a faltering singing career by becoming a visible opponent of gay rights. [Eds.]

for the opportunity to educate the public to the fact that the issues which most concern sexual outcasts are not genital, as the casters-out have so lewdly imagined, but issues of justice and simple fairness.

Resistance is ultimately an art which no one masters to perfection. 35 Early in my struggles, I said to a gay colleague living openly in rural Nebraska, "We must stamp on every snake." Wisely he counseled, "Only if you want to get foot poisoning." I often wish I had more of the wisdom mentioned in *Ecclesiastes,* the ability to judge accurately, "The time to speak and the time to refrain from speaking." Much of the time I think it wise to pass public hecklers without acknowledging their taunts, especially when they are cowardly hiding in a crowd. When I have faced bullies head-on, I have tried to do so patiently, disarming them by my own control of the situation. Of course, I am not guaranteed that their violence can thus be aborted every time.

Two major sources of our survival are essentially very private—one, 36 the intense care and love my spouse and I share, and the other, our strong faith in God as Unbounding Love. To these we prefer to make our secular witness, more by what we do than by what we say.

I am not a masochist. I would never choose the hard lot of the sex- 37 ual outcast in smalltown America. Had I the choice to change myself but not the world, I would return as a white male heterosexual city-slicker millionaire, not because whites, males, heterosexuals, city-slickers, and millionaires are better, but because they have it easier.

Yet everyone faces a different choice: Accept the world the way you 38 find it, or change it. For year after year I dissented, right in my own neighborhood.

America preserves an ideal of freedom, although it denies freedom 39 in scores of instances. My eighth-grade civics teacher in Alabama did not mention the price I would have to pay for the freedom of speech she taught me to value. I know now that the docile and ignorant dislike you fiercely when you speak truth they prefer not to hear. But I had a good civics class, one that showed me how to change our government. I rejoice.

Sometimes I think a society's critics must appreciate the society far 40 more than others, for the critics typically take very seriously the society's idle promises and forgotten dreams. When I occasionally see them, I certainly don't find many of my heterosexual eighth-grade classmates probing much farther than the issues of our common Form 1040 headaches and the issues as delivered by the evening news. Their lives seem often far duller than ours and the main adventures in pioneering they experience come vicariously, through television, the movies, and for a few, through books. In defining me as a criminal, my society may well have hidden a major blessing in its curse by forcing me out of lethargy into an on-going, rigorous questioning of the entire process.

Not only do I teach *The Adventures of Huckleberry Finn*,[3] my spouse and I have in an important sense had the chance to be Huck and Jim fleeing a different form of slavery and injustice in a very real present.

Responding to Reading

1. In this essay's title, Crew describes himself as "an outsider, even . . . an outcast." In what ways were he and his companion excluded from mainstream society? Do you think they were wise to move to a small town, or do you feel they should have taken up residence in a place that might have been more hospitable? Explain your views.
2. Which do you suppose the town objected to more, the idea of a gay couple or the idea of a racially integrated couple? Explain.
3. Again and again Crew uses the word *survival*. How do you think he would define this word? What specific tactics did Crew and his companion use to ensure that they survived in "smalltown America"? How was this "survival" different from the title's "thriving"?

HOW IT FEELS TO BE COLORED ME

Zora Neale Hurston

Folklorist and writer Zora Neale Hurston (1901–1969) grew up in Eatonville, Florida, the first incorporated African-American community in the United States, and Hurston herself was the first African-American woman admitted to Barnard College in New York City. There she developed an interest in anthropology, and she studied with Columbia University's famous anthropologist, Franz Boas. Mules and Men (1935) is her book of folklore about voodoo among southern blacks. During the Harlem Renaissance of the 1920s and 1930s, Hurston wrote stories celebrating the hope and joy of African-American life, music, and stories. Her most notable novel is Their Eyes Were Watching God *(1937). The essay below, which features Hurston's strong personal voice, is from the collection* I Love Myself When I Am Laughing *(1979), edited by Alice Walker.*

I am colored but I offer nothing in the way of extenuating circum-   1
stances except the fact that I am the only Negro in the United States whose grandfather on the mother's side was *not* an Indian chief.

---

[3] Mark Twain tale (1884) of the exploits of a young white boy and a slave on the Mississippi River. [Eds.]

I remember the very day that I became colored. Up to my thir- 2
teenth year I lived in the little Negro town of Eatonville, Florida. It is
exclusively a colored town. The only white people I knew passed
through the town going to or coming from Orlando. The native whites
rode dusty horses, the Northern tourists chugged down the sandy village road in automobiles. The town knew the Southerners and never
stopped cane chewing[1] when they passed. But the Northerners were
something else again. They were peered at cautiously from behind curtains by the timid. The more venturesome would come out on the
porch to watch them go past and got just as much pleasure out of the
tourists as the tourists got out of the village.

The front porch might seem a daring place for the rest of the town, 3
but it was a gallery seat for me. My favorite place was atop the
gate-post. Proscenium[2] box for a born first-nighter. Not only did I enjoy
the show, but I didn't mind the actors knowing that I liked it. I usually
spoke to them in passing. I'd wave at them and when they returned my
salute, I would say something like this: "Howdy-do-well-I-thank-you-
where-you-goin'?" Usually automobile or the horse paused at this, and
after a queer exchange of compliments, I would probably "go a piece of
the way" with them, as we say in farthest Florida. If one of my family
happened to come to the front in time to see me, of course negotiations
would be rudely broken off. But even so, it is clear that I was the first
"welcome-to-our-state" Floridian, and I hope the Miami Chamber of
Commerce will please take notice.

During this period, white people differed from colored to me only 4
in that they rode through town and never lived there. They liked to hear
me "speak pieces" and sing and wanted to see me dance the parse-mela,
and gave me generously of their small silver for doing these things,
which seemed strange to me for I wanted to do them so much that I
needed bribing to stop. Only they didn't know it. The colored people
gave no dimes. They deplored any joyful tendencies in me, but I was
their Zora nevertheless. I belonged to them, to the nearby hotels, to the
county—everybody's Zora.

But changes came in the family when I was thirteen, and I was sent 5
to school in Jacksonville. I left Eatonville, the town of the oleanders,[3] as
Zora. When I disembarked from the river-boat at Jacksonville, she was
no more. It seemed that I had suffered a sea change. I was not Zora of
Orange County any more, I was now a little colored girl. I found it out

---

[1] Chewing sugar cane. [Eds.]

[2] In the ancient Greek theater, the stage; in the moodern theater, the area between the curtain and
the orchestra. [Eds.]

[3] Tropical flowers. [Eds.]

in certain ways. In my heart as well as in the mirror, became a fast brown—warranted not to rub nor run.

But I am not tragically colored. There is no great sorrow dammed 6
up in my soul, nor lurking behind my eyes. I do not mind at all. I do not belong to the sobbing school of Negrohood who hold that nature somehow has given them a lowdown dirty deal and whose feelings are all hurt about it. Even in the helter-skelter skirmish that is my life, I have seen that the world is to the strong regardless of a little pigmentation more or less. No, I do not weep at the world—I am too busy sharpening my oyster knife.[4]

Someone is always at my elbow reminding me that I am the grand- 7
daughter of slaves. It fails to register depression with me. Slavery is sixty years in the past. The operation was successful and the patient is doing well, thank you. The terrible struggle[5] that made me an American out of a potential slave said "On the line!" The Reconstruction[6] said "Get set!"; and the generation before said "Go!" I am off to a flying start and I must not halt in the stretch to look behind and weep. Slavery is the price I paid for civilization, and the choice was not with me. It is a bully adventure and worth all that I have paid through my ancestors for it. No one on earth ever had a greater chance for glory. The world to be won and nothing to be lost. It is thrilling to think—to know that for any act of mine, I shall get twice as much praise or twice as much blame. It is quite exciting to hold the center of the national stage, with the spectators not knowing whether to laugh or to weep.

The position of my white neighbor is much more difficult. No brown 8
specter pulls up a chair beside me when I sit down to eat. No dark ghost thrusts its leg against mine in bed. The game of keeping what one has is never so exciting as the game of getting.

I do not always feel colored. Even now I often achieve the uncon- 9
scious Zora of Eatonville before the Hegira.[7] I feel most colored when I am thrown against a sharp white background.

For instance at Barnard. "Beside the waters of the Hudson" I feel 10
my race. Among the thousand white persons, I am a dark rock surged upon, and overswept, but through it all, I remain myself. When covered by the waters, I am; and the ebb but reveals me again.

Sometimes it is the other way around. A white person is set down 11
in our midst, but the contrast is just as sharp for me. For instance, when I sit in the drafty basement that is The New World Cabaret with a white

---

[4] Reference is to the expression "The world is my oyster." [Eds.]
[5] The Civil War. [Eds.]
[6] The period immediately following the Civil War. [Eds.]
[7] The flight of Muhammad from Mecca in A.D. 622; here, an escape from a dangerous situation. [Eds.]

person, my color comes. We enter chatting about any little nothing that we have in common and are seated by the jazz waiters. In the abrupt way that jazz orchestras have, this one plunges into a number. It loses no time in circumlocutions, but gets right down to business. It constricts the thorax and splits the heart with its tempo and narcotic harmonies. This orchestra grows rambunctious, rears on its hind legs and attacks the tonal veil with primitive fury, rending it, clawing it until it breaks through to the jungle beyond. I follow those heathen—follow them exultingly. I dance wildly inside myself; I yell within, I whoop; I shake my assegai[8] above my head, I hurl it true to the mark *yeeeeooww!* I am in the jungle and living in the jungle way. My face is painted red and yellow and my body is painted blue. My pulse is throbbing like a war drum. I want to slaughter something—give paid, give death to what, I do not know. But the piece ends. The men of the orchestra wipe their lips and rest their fingers. I creep back slowly to the veneer we call civilization with the last tone and find the white friend sitting motionless in his seat, smoking calmly.

"Good music they have here," he remarks, drumming the table with his fingertips.   12

Music. The great blobs of purpose and red emotion have not touched him. He has only heard what I felt. He is far away and I see him but dimly across the ocean and the continent that have fallen between us. He is so pale with his whiteness then and I am so colored.   13

At certain times I have no race, I am *me*. When I set my hat at a certain angle and saunter down Seventh Avenue, Harlem City, feeling as snooty as the lions in front of the Forty-Second Street Library, for instance. So far as my feelings are concerned, Peggy Hopkins Joyce[9] on the Boule Mich with her gorgeous raiment, stately carriage, knees knocking together in a most aristocratic manner, has nothing on me. The cosmic Zora emerges. I belong to no race nor time. I am the eternal feminine with its string of beads.   14

I have no separate feeling about being an American citizen and colored. I am merely a fragment of the Great Soul that surges within the boundaries. My country, right or wrong.   15

Sometimes, I feel discriminated against, but it does not make me angry. It merely astonishes me. How *can* any deny themselves the pleasure of my company? It's beyond me.   16

But in the main, I feel like a brown bag of miscellany propped against a wall. Against a wall in company with other bags, white, red and yellow. Pour out the contents, and there is discovered a jumble of   17

---

[8] South African hunting spear. [Eds.]

[9] American known for setting trends in beauty and fashion in the 1920s. The Boule Mich (also Boul' Mich), short for *Boulevard St. Michel,* is a street on Paris's Left Bank. [Eds.]

small things priceless and worthless. A first-water diamond, an empty spool, bits of broken glass, lengths of string, a key to a door long since crumbled away, a rusty knife-blade, old shoes saved for a road that never was and never will be, a nail bent under the weight of things too heavy for any nail, a dried flower or two still a little fragrant. In your hand is the brown bag. On the ground before you is the jumble it held—so much like the jumble in the bags, could they be emptied, that all might be dumped in a single heap and the bags refilled without altering the contents of any greatly. A bit of colored glass more or less would not matter. Perhaps that is how the Great Stuffer of Bags filled them in the first place—who knows?

Responding to Reading

1. How, according to Hurston, does it feel to be "colored"? How do her feelings about her color change as she grows older? Why do they change?
2. In what sense does Hurston see herself as fundamentally different from the whites she encounters? Does she see this difference as a problem? Does her reaction surprise you?
3. When Hurston says, "At certain times I have no race, I am *me*" (14), does she mean she feels assimilated into the larger society, or does she mean something else? Do you think it is possible to be only yourself and not a member of any particular racial or ethnic group? Explain.

FOCUS: DO WE NEED AFFIRMATIVE ACTION?

SINS OF ADMISSION

Dinesh D'Souza

In the following essay, originally published in the New Republic *in 1991, Dinesh D'Souza (see p. 129) argues against university admissions programs that are based on the concept of "proportional representation" because they wind up discriminating against more qualified white and Asian applicants.*

When Michael Williams, head of the civil rights division of the 1 Department of Education, sought to prevent American universities from granting minority-only scholarships, he blundered across the trip-wire of affirmative action, the issue that is central to understanding racial tensions on campus and the furor over politically correct speech and the curriculum.

Nearly all American universities currently seek to achieve an eth- 2 nically diverse student body in order to prepare young people to live in an increasingly multiracial and multicultural society. Diversity is usually pursued through "proportional representation," a policy that attempts to shape each university class to approximate the proportion of blacks, Hispanics, whites, Asian Americans, and other groups in the general population. At the University of California, Berkeley, where such race balancing is official policy, an admissions report argues that proportional representation is the only just allocation of privileges for a state school in a democratic society, and moreover, "a broad diversity of backgrounds, values, and viewpoints is an integral part of a stimulating intellectual and cultural environment in which students educate one another."

The lofty goals of proportional representation are frustrated, how- 3 ever, by the fact that different racial groups perform very differently on academic indicators used by admissions officials, such as grades and standardized test scores. For example, on a scale of 400 to 1600, white and Asian-American students on average score nearly 200 points higher than black students on the Scholastic Aptitude Test (SAT). Consequently, the only way for colleges to achieve ethnic proportionalism is to downplay or abandon merit criteria, and to accept students from typically underrepresented groups, such as blacks, Hispanics, and American Indians, over better-qualified students from among whites and Asian Americans.

At Ivy League colleges, for instance, where the median high school ₄ grade average of applicants approaches 4.0 and SAT scores are around 1300, many black, Hispanic, and American Indian students are granted admission with grade scores below 3.0 and SATs lower than 1000. Each year state schools such as Berkeley and the University of Virginia turn away hundreds of white and Asian American applicants with straight As and impressive extracurriculars, while accepting students from underrepresented groups with poor to mediocre academic and other credentials. John Bunzel, former president of San Jose State University, argues that since the pool of qualified minority students is small, selective colleges "soon realize they have to make big academic allowances" if they are going to meet affirmative action targets.

Although universities strenuously deny the existence of quota ceil- ₅ ings for Asians, it is mathematically impossible to raise the percentage of students from under-represented groups without simultaneously reducing the percentage of students from overrepresented groups. Former Berkeley chancellor Ira Heyman has admitted and apologized for his university's discriminatory treatment of Asians, and this year the Department of Education found the University of California, Los Angeles, guilty of illegal anti-Asian policies. Stanford, Brown, and Yale are among the dozen or so prestigious institutions under close scrutiny by Asian groups.

For Asian Americans, the cruel irony is that preferential admissions ₆ policies, which are set up to atone for discrimination, seem to have institutionalized and legitimized discrimination against a minority group that is itself the victim of continuing prejudice in America. Moreover, for Asians, minority quotas that were intended as instruments of inclusion have become instruments of exclusion.

The second major consequence of proportional representation is not ₇ an overall increase in the number of blacks and other preferred minorities in American universities, but rather the *misplacement* of such students throughout higher education. In other words, a student who might be qualified for admission to a community college now finds himself at the University of Wisconsin. The student whose grades and extracurriculars are good enough for Wisconsin is offered admission to Bowdoin or Berkeley. The student who meets Bowdoin's or Berkeley's more demanding standards is accepted through affirmative action to

Yale or Princeton. Somewhat cynically, one Ivy League official terms this phenomenon "the Peter Principle of university admissions."[1]

Aware of the fact that many affirmative action students are simply   8 not competitive with their peers, many colleges offer special programs in remedial reading, composition, and basic mathematics to enable disadvantaged students to keep pace. But enrollment in such programs is generally poor: students who are already experiencing difficulties with their regular course load often do not have the time or energy to take on additional classes. Consequently, the dropout rate of affirmative action students is extremely high. Figures from the Department of Education show that blacks and Hispanics are twice as likely as whites and Asians to drop out for academic reasons. A recent study of 1980 high school graduates who entered four-year colleges found that only 26 percent of black and Hispanic students had graduated by 1986.

Even taking into account other factors for leaving college, such as   9 financial hardship, the data leave little doubt that preferential admissions seriously exacerbate what universities euphemistically term "the retention problem." An internal report that Berkeley won't release to the public shows that, of students admitted through affirmative action who enrolled in 1982, only 22 percent of Hispanics and 18 percent of blacks had graduated by 1987. Blacks and Hispanics not admitted through preferential programs graduated at the rates of 42 and 55 percent respectively.

Although most universities do everything they can to conceal the   10 data about preferential admissions and dropout rates, administrators will acknowledge the fact that a large number of minority students who stay in college experience severe academic difficulties. These classroom pressures, compounded by the social dislocation that many black and Hispanic students feel in the new campus environment, are at the root of the serious racial troubles on the American campus.

It is precisely these pressures that thwart the high expectations of   11 affirmative action students, who have been repeatedly assured by college recruiters that standards have not been abridged to let them in, that they belong at the university, indeed, that they provide a special perspective that the school could not hope to obtain elsewhere. Bewildered at the realities of college life, many minority students seek support and solace from others like them, especially older students who have traveled the unfamiliar paths. Thus begins the process of minority separatism and self-segregation on campus, which is now fairly advanced

---

[1] The "Peter Principle," a term coined by Lawrence J. Peter (1919–1990), states that "in a hierarchy every employee tends to rise to the level of his incompetence." [Eds.]

and which has come as such a surprise to universities whose catalogs celebrate integration and the close interaction of diverse ethnic groups.

Distinctive minority organizations, such as Afro-American societies   12
and Hispanic student organizations, provide needed camaraderie, but they do not provide academic assistance to disadvantaged students. Instead, they offer an attractive explanation: classroom difficulties of minorities are attributed not to insufficient academic preparation, but to the pervasive atmosphere of bigotry on campus. In particular, both the curriculum and testing systems are said to embody a white male ethos that is inaccessible to minorities.

Through the political agitation of minority organizations, many   13
black and Hispanic students seek to recover a confident identity and sense of place on campuses where they otherwise feel alienated and even inadequate. Consequently, minority activists at several universities now have elaborate campaigns to identify and extirpate bigotry, such as racism hotlines and mandatory consciousness-raising sessions directed at white students. In addition, activists demand that "institutional racism" be remedied through greater representation of blacks and Hispanics among administrators and faculty. The logical extreme of this trend is a bill that Assemblyman Tom Hayden has introduced in the California legislature that mandates not just proportional admissions but equal pass rates for racial groups in state universities.

Both survey data and interviews with students published in *The*   14
Chronicle of Higher Education over the past few years show that many white students who are generally sympathetic to the minority cause become weary and irritated by the extent of preferential treatment and double standards involving minority groups on campus. Indeed, racial incidents frequently suggest such embitterment; at the University of Michigan, for example, the affirmative action office has been sent a slew of posters, letters, poems—many racist—objecting specifically to special treatment for blacks and deriding the competence of minority students at the university. An increasing number of students are coming to believe what undergraduate Jake Shapiro recently told the "MacNeil/ Lehrer News Hour": "The reason why we have racial tensions at Rutgers is they have a very strong minority recruitment program, and this means that many of my friends from my hometown were not accepted even though they are more qualified."

Other students have complained that universities routinely recog-   15
nize and subsidize minority separatist organizations, black and Hispanic fraternities, and even racially segregated residence quarters while they would never permit a club or fraternity to restrict membership to whites. A couple of American campuses have witnessed the disturbing rise of white student unions in bellicose resistance to perceived minority favoritism on campus.

A new generation of university leaders, weaned on the protest pol- 16
itics of the 1960s, such as Nannerl Keohane of Wellesley, James
Freedman of Dartmouth, and Donna Shalala of the University of
Wisconsin-Madison, are quite happy to attribute all opposition to resurgent bigotry. Some of this may be true, but as thoughtful university
leaders and observers are now starting to recognize, administration
policies may also be playing a tragic, counter-productive role. A redou-
bling of those policies, which is the usual response to racial tension, is
not likely to solve the problem and might make it worse.

If universities wish to eliminate race as a factor in their students' 17
decision-making, they might consider eliminating it as a factor in their
own. It may be time for college leaders to consider basing affirmative
action programs on socioeconomic disadvantage rather than ethnicity.
This strategy would help reach those disadvantaged blacks who desperately need the education our colleges provide, but without the deleterious effects of racial head-counting. And it would set a color-blind
standard of civilized behavior, which inspired the civil rights movement
in the first place.

Responding to Reading

1. What negative consequences of "proportional representation" does
   D'Souza identify? Do you think he is fair to attribute all these problems to
   affirmative action, or do you believe some of the problems have other
   causes? For example, is he too quick to dismiss the role "resurgent bigotry"
   (16) may play?
2. D'Souza holds conservative views about education (see the headnote
   accompanying his essay "The Visigoths in Tweed" on page 129). Does his
   political orientation diminish his credibility in your eyes? Should it?
3. In his conclusion (paragraph 17), D'Souza proposes "basing affirmative
   action programs on socioeconomic disadvantage rather than ethnicity."
   Would Shelby Steele (p. 476) agree with D'Souza's proposal? Why or why
   not?

A NEGATIVE VOTE ON AFFIRMATIVE ACTION

Shelby Steele

*Shelby Steele (1945–), professor of English at San Jose State
University, writes thoughtfully about African-Americans and his own experience growing up as the son of a white mother and a black father. He produced the film documentary* Seven Days in Bensonhurst *(1990), about the
murder of Yusef Hawkins, an African-American youth who was chased and*

beaten by a group of whites. He has also published a collection of essays called
The Content of Our Character: A New Vision of Race in America
(1990), which won the National Book Critics Circle Award. Of his work,
Steele has remarked, "Some people say I shine a harsh light on difficult social
problems. But I never shine a light on anything I haven't experienced or
write about fears I don't see in myself first." In this essay from 1990, Steele
argues that the liabilities of affirmative action programs outweigh their ben-
efits for blacks.

In a few short years, when my two children will be applying to col- 1
lege, the affirmative-action policies by which most universities offer
black students some form of preferential treatment will present me
with a dilemma. I am a middle-class black, a college professor, far from
wealthy, but also well removed from the kind of deprivation that
would qualify my children for the label "disadvantaged." Both of them
have endured racial insensitivity from whites. They have been called
names, have suffered slights and have experienced first hand the peculiar malevolence that racism brings out of people. Yet they have never
experienced racial discrimination, have never been stopped by their
race on any path they have chosen to follow. Still, their society now
tells them that if they will only designate themselves as black on their
college applications, they will probably do better in the college lottery
than if they conceal this fact. I think there is something of a Faustian
bargain[1] in this.

Of course many blacks and a considerable number of whites would 2
say that I was sanctimoniously making affirmative action into a test of
character. They would say that this small preference is the meagerest rec-
ompense for centuries of unrelieved oppression. And to these arguments
other very obvious facts must be added. In America, many marginally
competent or flatly incompetent whites are hired every day—some
because their white skin suits the conscious or unconscious racial preference of their employers. The white children of alumni are often grand-
fathered into elite universities in what can only be seen as a residual
benefit of historic white privilege. Worse, white incompetence is always
an individual matter, but for blacks it is often confirmation of ugly
stereotypes. Given that unfairness cuts both ways, doesn't it only balance the scales of history, doesn't this repay, in a small way, the systematic denial under which my children's grandfather lived out his days?

In theory, affirmative action certainly has all the moral symmetry 3
that fairness requires. It is reformist and corrective, even repentent and
redemptive. And I would never sneer at these good intentions. Born in
the late 1940's in Chicago, I started my education (a charitable term, in

---

[1] That is, a bargain with the devil. [Eds.]

this case) in a segregated school, and suffered all the indignities that come to blacks in a segregated society. My father, born in the South, made it only to the third grade before the white man's fields took permanent priority over his formal education. And though he educated himself into an advanced reader with an almost professorial authority, he could only drive a truck for a living, and never earned more than $90 a week in his entire life. So yes, it is crucial to my sense of citizenship, to my ability to identify with the spirit and the interests of America, to know that this country, however imperfectly, recognizes its past sins and wishes to correct them.

Yet good intentions can blind us to the effects they generate when 4 implemented. In our society affirmative action is, among other things, a testament to white good will and to black power, and in the midst of these heavy investments its effects can be hard to see. But after 20 years of implementation I think that affirmative action has shown itself to be more bad than good and that blacks—whom I will focus on in this essay—now stand to lose more from it than they gain.

In talking with affirmative-action administrators and with blacks 5 and whites in general, I found that supporters of affirmative action focus on its good intentions and detractors emphasize its negative effects. It was virtually impossible to find people outside either camp. The closest I came was a white male manager at a large computer company who said, "I think it amounts to reverse discrimination, but I'll put up with a little of that for a little more diversity." But this only makes him a half-hearted supporter of affirmative action. I think many people who don't really like affirmative action support it to one degree or another anyway.

I believe they do this because of what happened to white and black 6 Americans in the crucible of the 1960's, when whites were confronted with their racial guilt and blacks tasted their first real power. In that stormy time white absolution and black power coalesced into virtual mandates for society. Affirmative action became a meeting ground for those mandates in the law. At first, this meant insuring equal opportunity. The 1964 civil-rights bill was passed on the understanding that equal opportunity would not mean racial preference. But in the late 60's and early 70's, affirmative action underwent a remarkable escalation of its mission from simple anti-discrimination enforcement to social engineering by means of quotas, goals, timetables, set-asides and other forms of preferential treatment.

Legally, this was achieved through a series of executive orders and 7 Equal Employment Opportunity Commission guidelines that allowed racial imbalances in the workplace to stand as proof of racial discrimination. Once it could be assumed that discrimination explained racial imbalances, it became easy to justify group remedies to presumed discrimination rather than the normal case-by-case redress.

Even though blacks had made great advances during the 60's with- 8
out quotas, the white mandate to achieve a new racial innocence and the
black mandate to gain power, which came to a head in the very late 60's,
could no longer be satisfied by anything less than racial preferences. I
don't think these mandates, in themselves, were wrong, because whites
clearly needed to do better by blacks and blacks needed more real
power in society. But as they came together in affirmative action, their
effect was to distort our understanding of racial discrimination. By
making black the color of preference, these mandates have reburdened
society with the very marriage of color and preference (in reverse) that
we set out to eradicate.

When affirmative action grew into social engineering, diversity 9
became a golden word. Diversity is a term that applies democratic principles to races and cultures rather than to citizens, despite the fact that
there is nothing to indicate that real diversity is the same thing as proportionate representation. Too often the result of this, on campuses for
example, has been a democracy of colors rather than of people, an artificial diversity that gives the appearance of an educational parity
between black and white students that has not yet been achieved in reality. Here again, racial preferences allow society to leapfrog over the difficult problem of developing blacks to parity with whites and into a
cosmetic diversity that covers the blemish of disparity—a full six years
after admission, only 26 to 28 percent of blacks graduate from college.

Racial representation is not the same thing as racial development. 10
Representation can be manufactured; development is always hard
earned. But it is the music of innocence and power that we hear in affirmative action that causes us to cling to it and to its distracting emphasis on representation. The fact is that after 20 years of racial preferences
the gap between median incomes of black and white families is greater
than it was in the 1970's. None of this is to say that blacks don't need
policies that insure our right to equal opportunity, but what we need
more of is the development that will let us take advantage of society's
efforts to include us.

I think one of the most troubling effects of racial preferences for 11
blacks is a kind of demoralization. Under affirmative action, the quality
that earns us preferential treatment is an implied inferiority. However
this inferiority is explained—and it is easily enough explained by the
myriad deprivations that grew out of our oppression—it is still inferiority. There are explanations and then there is the fact. And the fact must
be borne by the individual as a condition apart from the explanation,
apart even from the fact that others like himself also bear this condition.
In integrated situations in which blacks must compete with whites who
may be better prepared, these explanations may quickly wear thin and
expose the individual to racial as well as personal self-doubt. (Of course
whites also feel doubt, but only personally, not racially.)

What this means in practical terms is that when blacks deliver them- 12
selves into integrated situations they encounter a nasty little reflex in
whites, a mindless, atavistic reflex that responds to the color black with
negative stereotypes, such as intellectual ineptness. I think this reflex
embarrasses most whites today and thus it is usually quickly repressed.
On an equally atavistic level, the black will be aware of the reflex his
color triggers and will feel a stab of horror at seeing himself reflected in
this way. He, too, will do a quick repression, but a lifetime of such stabbings is what constitutes his inner realm of racial doubt. Even when the
black sees no implication of inferiority in racial preferences, he knows
that whites do, so that—consciously or unconsciously—the result is virtually the same. The effect of preferential treatment—the lowering of
normal standards to increase black representation—puts blacks at war
with an expanded realm of debilitating doubt, so that the doubt itself
becomes an unrecognized preoccupation that undermines their ability to
perform, especially in integrated situations.

I believe another liability of affirmative action comes from the fact 13
that it indirectly encourages blacks to exploit their own past victimization. Like implied inferiority, victimization is what justifies preference,
so that to receive the benefits of preferential treatment one must, to
some extent, become invested in the view of one's self as a victim. In this
way, affirmative action nurtures a victim-focused identity in blacks and
sends us the message that there is more power in our past suffering than
in our present achievements.

When power itself grows out of suffering, blacks are encouraged 14
to expand the boundaries of what qualifies as racial oppression, a situation that can lead us to paint our victimization in vivid colors even
as we receive the benefits of preference. The same corporations and
institutions that give us preference are also seen as our oppressors. At
Stanford University, minority-group students—who receive at least
the same financial aid as whites with the same need—recently took
over the president's office demanding, among other things, more financial aid.

But I think one of the worst prices that blacks pay for preference has 15
to do with an illusion. I saw this illusion at work recently in the mother
of a middle-class black student who was going off to his first semester
of college: "They owe us this, so don't think for a minute that you don't
belong there." This is the logic by which many blacks, and some whites,
justify affirmative action—it is something "owed," a form of reparation.
But this logic overlooks a much harder and less digestible reality, that it
is impossible to repay blacks living today for the historic suffering of the
race. If all blacks were given a million dollars tomorrow it would not
amount to a dime on the dollar for three centuries of oppression, nor
would it dissolve the residues of that oppression that we still carry

today. The concept of historic reparation grows out of man's need to impose on the world a degree of justice that simply does not exist. Suffering can be endured and overcome, it cannot be repaid. To think otherwise is to prolong the suffering.

Several blacks I spoke with said they were still in favor of affirma- 16
tive action because of the "subtle" discrimination blacks were subject to once they were on the job. One photojournalist said, "They have ways of ignoring you." A black female television producer said: "You can't file a lawsuit when your boss doesn't invite you to the insider meetings without ruining your career. So we still need affirmative action." Others mentioned the infamous "glass ceiling" through which blacks can see the top positions of authority but never reach them. But I don't think racial preferences are a protection against this subtle discrimination; I think they contribute to it.

In any workplace, racial preferences will always create two-tiered 17
populations composed of preferreds and unpreferred. In the case of blacks and whites, for instance, racial preferences imply that whites are superior just as they imply that blacks are inferior. They not only reinforce America's oldest racial myth but, for blacks, they have the effect of stigmatizing the already stigmatized.

I think that much of the "subtle" discrimination that blacks talk 18
about is often (not always) discrimination against the stigma of questionable competence that affirmative action marks blacks with. In this sense, preferences make scapegoats of the very people they seek to help. And it may be that at a certain level employers impose a glass ceiling, but this may not be against the race so much as against the race's reputation for having advanced by color as much as by competence. This ceiling is the point at which corporations shift the emphasis from color to competency and stop playing the affirmative-action game. Here preference backfires for blacks and becomes a taint that holds them back. Of course one could argue that this taint, which is after all in the minds of whites, becomes nothing more than an excuse to discriminate against blacks. And certainly the result is the same in either case—blacks don't get past the glass ceiling But this argument does not get around the fact that racial preferences now taint this color with a new theme of suspicion that makes blacks even more vulnerable to discrimination. In this crucial yet gray area of perceived competence, preferences make whites look better than they are and blacks worse, while doing nothing whatever to stop the very real discrimination that blacks may encounter. I don't wish to justify the glass ceiling here, but only suggest the very subtle ways that affirmative action revives rather than extinguishes the old rationalizations for racial discrimination.

I believe affirmative action is problematic in our society because we 19
have demanded that it create parity between the races rather than

insure equal opportunity. Preferential treatment does not teach skills, or educate, or instill motivation. It only passes out entitlement by color, a situation that in my profession has created an unrealistically high demand for black professors. The social engineer's assumption is that this high demand will inspire more blacks to earn Ph.D's and join the profession. In fact, the number of blacks earning Ph.D's has declined in recent years. Ph.D's must be developed from preschool on. They require family and community support. They must acquire an entire system of values that enables them to work hard while delaying gratification.

It now seems clear that the Supreme Court, in a series of recent 20 decisions, is moving away from racial preferences. It has disallowed preferences except in instances of "identified discrimination," eroded the precedent that statistical racial imbalances are prima facie evidence of discrimination, and, in effect, granted white males the right to challenge consent decrees that use preference to achieve racial balances in the workplace. Referring to this and other Supreme Court decisions, one civil-rights leader said, "Night has fallen . . . as far as civil rights are concerned." But I am not so sure. The effect of these decisions is to protect the constitutional rights of everyone, rather than to take rights away from blacks. Night has fallen on racial preferences, not on the fundamental rights of black Americans. The reason for this shift, I believe, is that the white mandate for absolution from past racial sins has weakened considerably in the 1980's. Whites are now less willing to endure unfairness to themselves in order to grant special entitlements to blacks, even when those entitlements are justified in the name of past suffering. Yet the black mandate for more power in society has remained unchanged. And I think part of the anxiety many blacks feel over these decisions has to do with the loss of black power that they may signal.

But the power we've lost by these decisions is really only the power 21 that grows out of our victimization. This is not a very substantial or reliable power, and it is important that we know this so we can focus more exclusively on the kind of development that will bring enduring power. There is talk now that Congress may pass new legislation to compensate for these new limits on affirmative action. If this happens, I hope the focus will be on development and anti-discrimination, rather than entitlement, on achieving racial parity rather than jerry-building racial diversity.

But if not preferences, what? The impulse to discriminate *is* subtle 22 and cannot be ferreted out unless its many guises are made clear to people. I think we need social policies that are committed to two goals: the educational and economic development of disadvantaged people regardless of race and the eradication from our society—through close monitoring and severe sanctions—of racial, ethnic or gender discrimination. Preferences will not get us to either of these goals, because they tend to benefit those who are not disadvantaged— middle-class white women and middle-class blacks—and attack one form of discrimination with another. Preferences are inexpensive and carry the glamour of good intentions—change the numbers and the good deed is done. To be against them is to be unkind. But I think the unkindest cut is to bestow on children like my own an undeserved advantage while neglecting the development of those disadvantaged children in the poorer sections of my city who will most likely never be in a position to benefit from a preference. Give my children fairness; give disadvantaged children a better shot at development— better elementary and secondary schools, job training, safer neighborhoods, better financial assistance for college and so on. A smaller percentage of black high school graduates go to college today than 15 years ago; more black males are in prison, jail or in some other way under the control of the criminal-justice system than in college. This despite racial preferences.

The mandates of black power and white absolution out of which ²³ preferences emerged were not wrong in themselves. What was wrong was that both races focused more on the goals of those mandates than on the means to the goals. Blacks can have no real power without taking responsibility for their own educational and economic development. Whites can have no racial innocence without earning it by eradicating discrimination and helping the disadvantaged to develop. Because we ignored the means, the goals have not been reached and the real work remains to be done.

Responding to Reading

1. Why does Steele object to affirmative action? What problems does he believe this policy has created? What solutions does he recommend?
2. This essay was published in 1990; Dinesh D'Souza's essay (p. 472) appeared in 1991; and Charles R. Lawrence III and Mari Matsuda's (p. 484), in 1997. Does any information provided in the two more recent essays undercut Steele's arguments? Does any of this information support his claims?
3. In paragraph 5, Steele observes that "supporters of affirmative action focus on its good intentions and detractors emphasize its negative effects." Does this generalization apply as well to the other three essays on affirmative action in this section? Does it apply to Steele? Does this "either/or" approach oversimplify the problem?

THE TELLTALE HEART:
APOLOGY, REPARATION, AND REDRESS

Charles R. Lawrence III and Mari Matsuda

Charles R. Lawrence (1943–   ) and Mari Matsuda (1956–   ) are professors at Georgetown University Law School. Their book We Won't Go Back: Making the Case for Affirmative Action *(1997) argues that affirmative action programs are still necessary to provide educational and professional opportunities for members of groups that have historically been limited by discrimination. It includes not only the authors' own reasoning but also testimony from people who have experienced discrimination and benefited from affirmative action. In the following chapter from the book, Lawrence and Matsuda suggest that affirmative action as reparation for past injustice can bring "balance to all our lives—not just the material balance of integration, but the emotional and spiritual balance of healthy souls."*

> I tremble for my country, when I reflect that God is just.
> —*Thomas Jefferson*

> They shall build up the ancient ruins,
> they shall raise up the former devastations;
> they shall repair the ruined cities,
> the devastations of many generations.
> —*Isaiah 61:4*

One sunny day, on the island of Yap, in part of the Pacific island 1
group of Micronesia, I was running a course designed to teach the common law of torts to Micronesian judges. I posed a hypothetical designed to illustrate the master rule of fault-based liability in tort. "What if," I asked, "a little boy runs out from behind the high brush, into the road, and is hit by a car? The driver was driving carefully and could not have stopped in time to avoid the accident. The child is killed instantly."

This was the easy case, the first of a series of hypotheticals designed 2
to show that once fault is unclear, liability becomes unclear. To the judges, however, it was not an easy case. It was a false case. No one could respond to it justly without more facts.

One of the judges, enjoying the Socratic method[1] and intending to 3
teach me a thing or two, asked for more facts. How many sons, he asked, in the family of the driver? How many sons in the family of the injured child? How did the family of the injured child learn of the injury? How soon, and from whom?

---

[1] Educational method that involves the use of probing questions. [Eds.]

"Okay," I said, "I give up. You tell me how you would decide the 4 case."

What the judges learned that day was the peculiar habit, in Western 5 law, of limiting the relevant facts. All an American jurist would want to know is whether the driver was at fault in the accident; there would be no liability if the driver was exercising ordinary care.

What I learned from the judges that day is that there is a universe 6 of relevant questions to ask after an accident if one lives on a tiny, isolated island, and if it is an absolute imperative to live in peace.

Fault is irrelevant, the judges explained. If your driving hurts some- 7 one, you should make sure you go immediately to the family to tell of the tragedy and of your grief. They should not hear the news first from someone else. Your remorse must meet the test of sincerity. Your kin should come quickly with food and gifts to show their intent to make amends. If you are lucky, you will have a son to work the taro fields of the family who lost a son. Your son will work for them all of his days, as part of your apology, and the apology, sanctified by elders and sacred ritual, must find a gracious welcome in the wounded family. If they allow their loss to overcome them, such that your sincere apology is received insincerely, they will lose status in the community.

This system of repairing great loss is not about account keeping. It 8 is part of the sacred, in a culture that does not separate the sacred from the secular. The longstanding customs that govern reactions to the tragedy of an automobile accident guarantee the spiritual wholeness of all citizens. When either side—what we would call in Western law the plaintiff or the defendant—fails to comport itself according to custom, the well-being of the entire community is in jeopardy.

If the judges' system works in the idealized way they described, it 9 achieves something the American legal system does not: both the plaintiff and the defendant walk away at peace.

In another part of the Pacific, Native Hawaiians speak matter-of- 10 factly about the payback for human failings. Traditional Hawaiians place value in the concept of *pono*, the state of being that is peace, repose, goodness. Upsetting *pono*, disrupting the rhythms of the land and its people, is a wrong—not only to fellow human beings, but to the cosmology. The price is illness, misfortune, cataclysm. When the volcano erupts, taking out roads and villages, the Hawaiians look around for someone who acted against *pono*—perhaps the developer who bulldozed old burial grounds, or the politician who acted out of greed, or a family whose feud was left to fester.

In the Judeo-Christian tradition, the Lord says, "Vengeance is mine." 11 There is a wisdom beyond human comprehension that determines what pain to exact for human transgression. Few cultures exist that do not have some notion of judgment. Actions have consequences. This is a law of physics we transmute to a law of our lives.

Those cultures which make active use of apology rituals are often 12 the ones that acknowledge the importance of community cohesion. Apology rituals, within societies that depend on the clan or village to provide a social safety net, are essential for survival. A dispute resolution mechanism that results in one party's walking home happy and the other's walking away from the village forever is an utter failure. To make the community whole, to erase the bad feelings of the past, to come jointly once again to the table, is imperative. In the Jalé villages of New Guinea, for instance, elders require feuding clan members to come together to feast on pig, each tearing the best morsel from the bone to place in the mouth of the former foe. This is what makes the elders smile. An apology in such communities leads to a gain, not a loss, in status.

This approach contrasts with the modern Western view that an 13 apology diminishes status. Typically, in American society, when someone confesses an error or wrongdoing, he is seen as weak and vanquished, disempowered and vulnerable. Ask an American lawyer what to do at the scene of an accident, whether a car crash or a nuclear meltdown, and the first rule is "Don't apologize."

In America we have no comparable clan, no network of kin and 14 near kin with whom we must maintain peace, with whom we must ceremoniously share our food even when we don't want to. The failure to know that the globe is our village, that every act of disregard for the planet and its inhabitants sets in motion disruptions of the good, is the curse of modernism. It is what makes us unable to see affirmative action as bringing balance to all our lives—not just the material balance of integration, but the emotional and spiritual balance of healthy souls.

The case for affirmative action includes notions of reparation, recti- 15 fication, and redress: the deliberate effort to identify and make amends for past wrong. Reparation is not all there is to affirmative action. It is neither the most compelling nor the most persuasive reason for it, but it is a reason worth considering, for there are costs in the refusal, ever, to apologize.

As the fiftieth anniversary of the end of the Second World War 16 approached, refusal to apologize became a leitmotif. The Smithsonian canceled the Enola Gay exhibit because some felt it focused too much on the horror and not enough on the military rationale for dropping the atomic bomb. Meanwhile, the Japanese government was persistently embarrassed by the claims of its victims: brave women in Korea and the Philippines who came forward to tell how they were raped, imprisoned, tortured, and forced into prostitution, as well as POW survivors of death marches and horrific abuse. No one in a position of power in either country could say he was sorry for the lives lost and damaged in the horror of war, or suggest publicly that some of the loss was unnecessary, wrong, or evil.

Whatever the record of history will bear, and I believe it will show 17 that the bombing of Hiroshima was racist, as were the many atrocities committed by the Japanese army, there is a social code that stands in the way of even asking the factual questions that might lead to the need for an apology. We don't need to look back at American military action, this code tells us. The war is over, the cause was just, we will only hurt ourselves, our prestige, and the honor of those who sacrificed all by asking, Was there anything we could have done differently, more justly, with more care?

What does it do, to a nation and the world, to refuse to look back? 18 When someone else, someday, is making the decision about dropping the bomb on me, I want him to face a record of history that judges the United States wrong for what happened to civilians in 1945. When someone, someday, is preparing new internment camps for citizens rounded up without habeas corpus,[2] I want him to know the judgment of both courts and Congress: the World War II internment of Japanese Americans was unconstitutional. This historical memory, the careful judgment made on the record of history, is the only inoculation we have against future harm. This is not endless, useless guilt; it is judgment with utility. It takes past harm as the teaching that will shelter future citizens.

The way to imprint that teaching is through reparation. To the 19 extent that at least part of the justification for affirmative action is reparation, affirmative action rests on a notion that is alien to modern jurisprudence. Oliver Wendell Holmes—seen by some as the architect of modern American legal thought—saw as his life's greatest work his distillation of the common law into its basic principles. At the core of his conceptualized system of justice was the notion of objectively determined, fault-based liability: if a person does something that is unreasonable under society's objective rules of behavior, that person is at fault and must pay compensation to the victim.

Reparation, affirmative action, and the remediation of past injustice 20 look like nothing Holmes envisioned. Rather than defying societal norms, the perpetrators of racial and gender injustice acted precisely in accordance with those norms. They had no particular victim in mind, nor a comprehensive plan, for example, to perpetrate the genocide of Native Americans. It was just something that happened on their way to achieving a destiny made manifest by their casual belief in superiority and entitlement.

---

[2] Legal term referring to the formal writ required to arrest a person. [Eds.]

The standard liberal legal ideology, which focuses on individual 21
fault, clashes with the ideology supporting reparation. A standard legal
claim pits an individual victim against a perpetrator of recent wrong-
doing, whereas a claim in reparation pits victim group members against
perpetrator descendants and current beneficiaries of past injustice.

A reparations claim lacks the logic and efficiency paramount in the 22
Holmesean world view. It is out of control. In reparations, the lines
delineating liability are fuzzy, the exact identities of parties in action are
unknowable, and the costs are potentially bankrupting. Under a regime
of reparations, no individual actor could calculate in advance the parameters of potential liability.

The logic of reparation lies beyond the logic of the law, raising pre- 23
dictable objections. First, critics claim that reparations are politically
untenable: divisive, obsessive, distracting from real issues. Second, they
argue that the historical basis of the claim is invalid: either the past
harm did not occur, or it was somehow justifiable. Third, the imprecise
outlines of both the victim and the perpetrator class render reparation
claims fatally imprecise. Fourth, the passage of time renders connection
between the original wrong and present effects of that wrong vague and
unprovable. Fifth, damages for past wrong are impossible to calculate
and to distribute fairly. Finally, to the extent that reparation is aimed
toward a group rather than an individual, it raises the ethical objection
of disregard of the individual.

We reject these arguments. Correcting past wrongs, such as dis- 24
crimination, through programs like affirmative action is divisive
because it just might work. It may open the doors of opportunity and
break down barriers to power sharing. It is, indeed, less divisive to let
power and privilege stay where they are. The uneasy peace gained from
silence in the face of oppression is a known quantity, one that even the
disenfranchised sometimes choose over the unknown.

Every movement for progressive social change is called "too divi- 25
sive," which often translates as "Keep the status quo."[3] The objection
that reparations set up a hierarchy of suffering, however, merits a
thoughtful response. We are leery of proclamations that some wrongs
are worse than others or that some people are particularly privileged in
their pain. Experienced seekers of justice usually conclude that ranking
oppressions is a useless exercise. At the same time, asserting the pure
equality of pain deprecates human experience. In our own lives we
know that some losses are greater than others, some pain easily surmounted, other pain a lifetime's burden. In an account of justice that
takes history seriously, we do need to say, with caution, that there are

---

[3] Latin for "the existing state of affairs." [Eds.]

losses of such magnitude that we, as Americans, need to recognize them as our particular obligation to address.

In the United States, a key question is whether a certain historical 26 wrong bears any relation to our ongoing culture of subordination. The enslavement of African Americans and the genocide of Native Americans are parts of American history that gave rise to particular forms of current American racism. This is not the same as saying that only members of these two groups are the victims of racism, nor is it the same as making the moral evaluation that what happened in these cases was the worst thing ever experienced by any group of human beings. Rather, these events loom large in the origin of our constitutional order, our economic development, and our shared culture. The slave ships brought to the United States an institution that indelibly shaped our understanding of race. Similarly, the massacres of Native Americans required a rationalization and a psychology of denial that mark American colonialism. White supremacy, sometimes expressed explicitly, and just as often denied vehemently, is the legacy of these events.

The record of broken bodies is on the ground we tread; the narra- 27 tive traditions of native people and of African Americans tell us that something extraordinary happened on this land, in a time close to ours. Some 90 percent of the estimated hundred million American Indians who lived at the time of European contact were decimated, in what one author called "a demographic disaster [that] has no equal in history." That number is significant enough to call extraordinary, and to suggest an extraordinary care as we consider our responsibilities to American Indians today.

Edgar Allan Poe, an American who lived in the time of slavery, 28 understood the dark side. He wrote of a man who murdered his tormentor and hid the victim's heart under the floorboards. The investigators arrived, and the murderer proceeded with his calm rendition of a coverup. Somewhere in the background he heard a noise and realized the heart was beating. Surely the constables heard it, he thought as he escalated his professions of innocence. Unable to bear the noise, he ripped open the floorboards and revealed his guilt to the astonished onlookers.

Like the telltale heart beating beneath the floorboards in Poe's 29 story, the weeping at the 1890 Wounded Knee[4] massacre and the moans of the Middle Passage[5] make a persistent pounding when we speak of

---

[4] Almost two hundred unarmed Sioux men, women, and children were shot by U.S. Cavalry troops at Wounded Knee, South Dakota. [Eds.]

[5] The "Middle Passage" refers to the triangular route of African slave trade, from ports in Europe, to the African coast, to the Americas, and back. [Eds.]

liberty and equality and the greatness of our America. The casual superiority of a rich and free nation is something we maintain only by speaking loudly, drowning out the sounds that grow ever larger as our frantic efforts to deny and explain escalate. What Myrdal[6] called the American dilemma, what Du Bois[7] called the color line, and what present commentators call the race relations problem are all part of our national culture. Until we speak the truth about it, we cannot know the truth about our own condition.

Keeping the telltale heart under the floorboards is a preoccupation 30 of the postrevisionist historians who argue that dredging up past wrongs is false history. When Pete Wilson[8] announced his soon-to-fail bid for the presidency of the United States, he chose as a central theme the evil of negative history. We've got to stop talking about slavery and Native Americans and emphasize what is good about America, he said. This echoes the view of professional historians, like Lynne Cheney and Arthur Schlesinger. Why all this talk about victims? Why not admit the greatness of the United States? Why this compulsion to look for the bad?

Other detractors of reparation try to deny or justify past harm. The 31 argument that no harm occurred presents factual claims that are refuted elsewhere. We note, however, that a denial of the harm is often not a factual claim at all, but a form of assault designed to perpetuate the harm itself.

Unlike the claim that no wrong occurred, various attempts at justi- 32 fication try to explain or deflect the wrong. A common explanation for slavery, for example, is that within the culture of that era, the inferiority of Africans was taken for granted. To condemn acts from the vantage point of the present is "ahistoric" or "anachronistic." It is precisely because there were many people in the time of slavery who knew it was wrong that we are able to judge it as wrong today. The truth about slavery was made plain by the enslaved Africans themselves, who in narratives and song left a contemporaneous text of condemnation. This truth was not held exclusively by the enslaved; the international antislavery movement brought together many, educated and uneducated, rich and poor, black and white, who studied the evils of slavery and condemned the institution in its time. It is not only from our present vantage point, but also in wise eyes of the past, including Thomas Jefferson's, that slavery is unmitigated evil.

---

[6] Swedish economist and sociologist Gunnar Myrdal (1898–1987) wrote *The American Dilemma* (1944, 1962), a detailed study of race relations in the United States which concluded that racial problems are inextricably entwined with the democratic functioning of American society. [Eds.]

[7] W. E. B. Du Bois (1868–1963) was an early civil rights leader who demanded both economic and political equality for blacks. [Eds.]

[8] Republican California governor from 1990 to 1998. [Eds.]

Similarly, when feminists condemn the sexism of past political lead- 33 ers and social institutions, we are warned that we are using the distort- ing lens of the present. This argument ignores the many noted women and some men who have condemned patriarchy for over a hundred years, as well as the anonymous women of generations earlier who sang their versions of the blues, telling us that "hard is the fortune of all womankind."

In the end, however, the argument over whether what happened in 34 American history was justified or explainable, given past realities, does not answer the call for reparation. Whether the wrong was somehow "understandable in context" does not mean it was just, and justice requires attention to harm regardless of the parameters of blame.

Regardless of past transgressions, some argue, present remedies are 35 impossible because of imprecision. If the *res*, the thing, is stolen and the thief caught, the law returns it to the rightful owner. This is the para- digm of what the law does, and among the oldest writs are those for the return of the *res*. What if the thing that is stolen, however, is not a *res*, but rather freedom, sovereignty, dignity? What if there is no clearly identifiable thief and no single owner, but multitudes who benefit and multitudes who suffer because of some historic wrong? Lack of preci- sion in the law weakens a claim. Those who come before the law are expected to make a coherent case against a fixed defendant: Who did this to you? How were you harmed? What was the price of your loss? If the answer to any of these is "I cannot say with certainty," then the claimant is not worthy in the eyes of the law.

In today's world, in the interests of justice, we make some excep- 36 tions to this demand for precision. When poisonous pollution enters the river from sources unknown, for instance, affecting millions of downstream users and planting in some communities the seeds of can- cer that will become evident only years in the future, a so-called Superfund problem arises. The solution may be to tax all producers of the poison and create a fund for possible future harms. Though the details about perpetrator and victim are not known, there is often a sense that the law should respond in some way to the disaster, typically through legislation.

Similarly, in the world of antitrust and commercial law, it some- 37 times happens that a great way to make money is to bilk a million peo- ple out of a dollar apiece. The victims may never know of their loss, and identifying all who were cheated and proving their loss is a logistical impossibility. Class action suits or class remedies are possible solutions. If everyone who used a teller machine at Cheatum Savings was illegally deprived of a dollar in one year, for example, a court might require a dollar discount on fees to everyone who banks there the next year. Not everyone who benefits from the discount is someone who lost out during the period of cheating, but the fit is close enough, and the inability to identify the victims with precision is not a reason to let Cheatum off the hook. We allow this imprecision in order to uphold standards of the marketplace that are seen as critical to consumer confidence. Obsession with precision puts the demands of arithmetic before the demands of justice, ignoring the more central goals of stability and fairness.

Along with imprecision, there is the problem of time. According to 38 American jurisprudence, as time passes, regardless of right or wrong, claims are put to rest. For an ordinary negligence claim, states typically set the limit at two to six years. After that, it is too late for a plaintiff to bring a claim. The time bar, or statute of limitations, is said to promote settled expectations and business planning; we need to know the outer limits of our liability so that we can go on with the business of commerce.

If seven years is too long ago for a civil law suit, what are we to 39 make of a hundred years? In most nations a hundred years is not so long ago. A theory of reparation focuses on the magnitude of harm done and its continuing effects, weighed against the passage of time. When the evidence of continuing effect is strong, the passage of time is not a reason to waive the wrong. While dwelling on the past is not always a good thing, in some cases forgiving and forgetting are impossible, particularly if the old wrongs continue to give rise to new harms.

Reflective adults ponder and regret the mistakes of their lives and 40 recall the traumas done to them. Victims of childhood abuse or neglect may well spend hours trying to understand how their past shapes their present attitudes, relations, and personality. A common survival strategy for the most egregious abuse is to forget or diminish what happened. There is no real forgetting, however. The anxiety, flashback, depression, and other symptoms of repressed trauma remain. The body remembers, calling out with a range of illnesses and behaviors the words we cannot say: something terrible happened to me, and I am in pain. A person stuck in the past, reciting a list of grievances over and over without resolution, is not whole; but neither is the person who cannot see the past, who does not know she is sad today because she was raised yesterday by someone who saw no joy in life.

"Forgive and forget" is too simple a solution for the complex harms 41 human beings inflict on one another. The abused child must remember, confront, and express anger before any forgiveness is mentally healthy. On a larger scale, national healing, something politicians seek in platitudinous addresses, will not come cheap. The forgiveness that is close to godliness is a deep forgiveness, the one that comes when the work is done, the past confronted, the pain acknowledged and expressed. This task is not about feeling guilty, pointing fingers, extracting vengeance. It is about liberation. . . .

No one wants to confront that which hurts the most; no one wants 42 to open up the carefully cabined places of forgetting; but some wise souls learn that hiding from what is hard gives no shelter. The past, whether personal or geopolitical, is ours, and acknowledging our origins is what enables us to make our lives better than what the past alone might have predicted.

What is the price of peace? The story of the Native Hawaiians is 43 illustrative. Native Hawaiians have long protested the loss of their sovereign nation, their lands, and much of their culture as a result of the U.S.–backed takeover of Hawaii in 1893. One of the specific claims relates to native lands, ceded to the State of Hawaii by the United States government, and held in trust for Native Hawaiians. The state, the Native Hawaiians claim, is in breach of the terms of that trust. They would like to sue the state to force it to use the ceded lands, as required by law, for the benefit of Native Hawaiians. There is one problem, however. State law does not give Hawaiians the right of legal action. They cannot sue in state court.

For years, the Hawaiians have lobbied the state legislature for 44 a "right to sue" bill, which would allow their claims to come to court. In opposing the bill, the state has argued that if it is sued, it will go bankrupt. If the Hawaiians could sue, they could very well win, and the actual damages, for years of misdirection of benefits that were intended for Hawaiians, could surpass the revenues and assets of the state.

Making up for past wrong, in short, should not happen, according 45 to the state, because it would cost too much. This argument against reparation trumps all the others. Instead of saying it didn't happen or it was too long ago, it says if the harm caused is too large, there is no remedy. The argument is somewhat disingenuous. The practical reality is that no litigant will ever collect full damages if they will bankrupt the state. At some point, the political process will have to allow for compromise. When Japanese Americans sought redress for their internment during World War II, for example, most recognized that no monetary amount could compensate them for what they lost: careers, education, land, businesses, hand-built farm houses, loved ones lost to poor medical care, a lifetime's possessions left behind for the junkman, the comfort of familiar streets and faces gone—so much, tangible and intangible, that was irreplaceable. Most significant of all, though, was the loss of rights and the shattering of expectations about freedom and citizenship. A million dollars would not have made whole what each person lost. No one asked for a million dollars. What they asked for, and got, was an amount large enough to constitute a genuine apology but small enough to pass through the legislative process. Reparations exact not a pound of flesh, but, rather, sixteen ounces of mutual sorrow over loss.

Reparation, to the extent that it recognizes group harm and group   46
responsibility, rings of collectivism, something feared by Red baiters and
derogated by those classical philosophers who ground their ethics in the
individual. Although the criticism of dehumanizing individualism is
implicit throughout this book, we do not reject the belief that each
human being is sacred, unique, and entitled to individual recognition
before the law. A simple choice that puts either individuals or groups
first is not enough to resolve the reparations debate, for groups are made
up of individuals. Any philosophy giving primacy either to individual
rights or to the group must confront that fact of human life. The relations
of individuals to groups and groups to other groups are something we
cannot avoid in defining what is just.

Reparation, like affirmative action, is for everyone. The direct ben-   47
eficiaries, as deserving as they may be, are not the center of reparation.
All of the objections to reparation come down to one thing: the failure
to see individual interest as tied inextricably to community interest.
Making peace with the past, so that we can live and work together in a
peaceful future, is what will ultimately save all individuals. The person
free to invent himself or herself and walk unfettered, the person whose
individual choices are paramount in the political philosophies of the
modern age, that individual is revealed only when the legacy of past
oppressions is wiped away.

Reparation is only one part of affirmative action. . . . Affirmative   48
action is required in order to institute equality today. Nonetheless, part
of the justification for affirmative action is and should be the correction
of past injustice.

When affirmative action is defined strictly as a remedy for past injus-   49
tice, it is easy to attack. Some argue that a focus on the past detracts from
the issues or problems of the present; people become mired in past grievances and are sapped of the will to struggle around current injustice.
Some, like the majority of the present Supreme Court, are skeptical of
claims that past wrongs, such as the enslavement of African Americans,
are connected to present disadvantage. The unstated message is "Get
over it; it was a long time ago." Others feel that if past wrongdoing is the
basis for affirmative action, then only African Americans, and not other
minorities, should benefit from affirmative action. This leads to a no-win
game of comparing oppressions—whose suffering was the most egregious, whose claim for compensation the most compelling—and it over-
simplifies the goals of affirmative action into a settling of accounts: "Let's
find the true historical wrong, the clear victim, the price of their pain,
and then fix it up with a direct payment."

This notion of affirmative action as simple payback for past wrong   50
misunderstands the social function of history in our lives. We are made
by our past; we can't live, breathe, act, or invent apart from it.

Confronting and knowing our collective history is important because it is what shapes present circumstances; we are racist today because we were racist yesterday. The forms and the dynamics of that racism will change over time, but the root is connected to the branch in a way that is present in the here and now.

Of course, the fight for affirmative action of the 1960s and beyond 51 was not a fight merely for acknowledgment of past wrong; it was a passionate struggle to improve present conditions, to gain jobs, education, and political participation today.

Acknowledging this doesn't remove the element of reparation from 52 affirmative action, however. There is a past-based part of the original demand: this country must know and acknowledge past wrong if it is to progress on the road to justice. We cannot end racism without knowing where it came from and how it works in our culture. In this sense, the inability to say "We were wrong, we are sorry, we will right this wrong" means that we are stuck in time. If we refuse to confront the past, we become bound to it and cannot move forward.

What this means for affirmative action, and for progressive politics in 53 general, is that we have to do two things at once. We should . . . live in the present, focusing on present need and expanding affirmative action programs to reach all people who, for whatever reason, are excluded from education, jobs, and participation in the democratic process. At the same time, we can recognize our particular responsibility for correcting the past wrongs in our history. It was right for this nation to issue a formal apology to the thousands of Japanese Americans who were incarcerated in America's concentration camps. The healing of the Japanese Americans required this, as did our self-perception as a good and free country. There are apologies we have not made; atrocities carried out in our name that continue to debase our most sacred symbols of democracy. We must confront our horrors and pledge that they will not happen again.

As this . . . was written, the Truth Commission, charged with find- 54 ing out what happened to the thousands of South Africans who were victims of atrocities during the struggle to end apartheid, began its work in South Africa, that nation determined to remember and move forward from a bloody past. One by one the witnesses came before the commissioners. The tortured whispered their survivors' stories; the parents wept describing their murdered children; some of the murderers wept, too, holding out their killing hands as an entire nation watched.

There is no more powerful process a nation can undertake. The 55 commissioners had to halt the proceedings at times when neither they nor the witnesses could bear to continue. Counselors were called on to help the commissioners confront their own traumas at hearing one story after another of human suffering.

Nothing that happens before the Truth Commission can restore a   56
peaceful heart to grieving parents, nor absolve the eternal guilt of the
torturer. Nothing will happen except confrontation with truth, and out
of that beginning the new South Africa will start its healing.

The living struggle to give meaning to the loss of the dead; the   57
grieving heart seeks reasons. The freedom fighters of South Africa knew
they risked all for their people's liberation. They did not know, when
they joined their cause, that they were bringing an additional gift to the
larger world. In its search to uncover the past and thereby move forward to healing, South Africa is setting an example while the world
watches. No nation, great or small, past or present, has undertaken this
level of collective confrontation with its own evil as part of a peaceful
transition to a free and equal society.

May they find their peace, and, someday, may we find ours.   58

Responding to Reading

1. Lawrence and Matsuda defend affirmative action because they believe it is
   needed to make amends for past injustices—that is, to offer "apology, reparation, and redress." Shelby Steele (p. 000), who acknowledges affirmative
   action as "reformist and corrective, even repentant and redemptive" (3),
   nevertheless opposes it. Would he be swayed by Lawrence and Matsuda's
   arguments in favor of the importance of "apology rituals" (12), or would he
   consider such arguments irrelevant? What is your reaction to Lawrence and
   Matsuda's application of "reparation, rectification, and redress" (15) to
   affirmative action?

2. Reread paragraphs 28–29, in which Lawrence and Matsuda draw an analogy between Poe's "telltale heart" and the sad and shameful secrets in U.S.
   history. Do you find this analogy convincing? Why or why not? What other
   events do you think have created a similar kind of "persistent pounding"?
   Do you believe it is possible to make amends for such events? Explain.

3. In recent years, the U.S. government has issued apologies for past
   "mistakes"—for example, the Tuskegee syphilis experiments and the institution of slavery. In addition, the government has paid reparations to the
   Japanese-Americans interned during World War II. How do you think
   Lawrence and Matsuda feel about these practices? How do you suppose
   each of the other writers in this section feels?

Widening the Focus

- Maya Angelou, "Graduation" (p. 90)

- Jonathan Kozol, "Savage Inequalities" (p. 100)

- Frederick Douglass, "Learning to Read and Write" (p. 182)

WRITING

The American Dream

1. Write an essay in which you support the idea that the strength of the United States comes from its ability to assimilate many different groups. In your essay, discuss specific contributions your own ethnic group and others have made to American society.

2. To what extent can a person's estrangement from mainstream society be the very force that drives his or her life? Consider Zora Neale Hurston and any other writer whose separateness is a source of strength or power.

3. Both Cofer and Mukherjee identify strongly with a culture that is not part of the mainstream. Compare and contrast their views about assimilation into the dominant culture. Then, consider whether your own ethnic group can—or should—assimilate.

4. Some of the writers in this chapter—for example, Crew and Hockenberry—explicitly or implicitly connect their personal struggles to achieve the American Dream with the struggles of the American civil rights movement. Do you think this parallel between the struggles of African-Americans for equality and the difficulties faced by other individuals or groups is fair, or even legitimate? Write a letter supporting your view to the writer of one of the essays in this chapter.

5. In paragraph 22 of her essay "American Dreamer," Bharati Mukherjee discusses the limitations of the "multicultural mosaic" metaphor; later in her essay, she explains why she rejects hyphenation, preferring to see herself "as an American rather than as an Asian-American" (26). Choose several of the writers in this chapter and consider how they would react to Mukherjee's position.

6. The essays by Dinesh D'Souza, Shelby Steele, and Charles R. Lawrence III and Mari Matsuda present a variety of viewpoints on the topic of affirmative action. Use the information in one or more of these essays to help you write an essay in which you consider how Richard Wright's life would have been different if he had had the benefits of an affirmative action program. (If you like, you may write instead about Maya Angelou—see page 90—or any other member of a minority group whose work appears in this text.) Be sure to consider the possible negative effects of such a program.

7. Write an essay in which you argue that the United States is still a land of opportunity. Support this position with references to reading selections in this chapter and elsewhere in this book. Be sure to explain what you mean by *opportunity*.

8. Some writers respond to their exclusion from mainstream society with anger and protest, others with resignation and acceptance. Considering several different writers and situations, write an essay in which you contrast these two kinds of responses. Does each response make sense? Why or why not?

9. What do you see as the greatest obstacle to full access to the American Dream? For example, is success most likely to depend on gender, race, language, social class, ethnicity, family, ability, education, income, or sexual orientation? Support your thesis with your own experiences or with references to selections in this chapter.

10. In paragraph 39 of "Thriving as an Outsider, Even as an Outcast, in Smalltown America," Louie Crew states, "America preserves an ideal of freedom, although it denies freedom in scores of instances." Use three or four of this chapter's essays to support this thesis—or to argue that it is not valid.

7

THE WAY WE LIVE NOW

Student Voices

"I see myself as part of the Why Bother? generation."

—*Stephen Berger*

"Whenever you look for me, I'm in chill mode. I enjoy almost everything I do. When I don't enjoy something, I just get it over with and never have to think of it again.

"My whole goal in life today is having fun. When I wake up in the morning, which is the worst part of the day, I imagine I'm going to have an excellent day. How I live may be immature, but I think it is beneficial and different. People admire my lifestyle. Friends try to mimic it. It's one I have planned out for a while. I hope to be in chill mode for the rest of my life."

—*Todd Snellenburg*

"We live in a world of violence. Violence surrounds us every day of our lives. We are told that violence doesn't solve problems and that violence is wrong. Even though this is instilled in us, we see that violence is used to entertain us from childhood to adulthood."

—*Teren Brown*

"We have problems now that our parents did not have—for example, drugs, teenage pregnancy, and gang violence. The old-fashioned family values of the past that kept families together seem to be diminishing. Where these values have gone, I am not certain. Maybe this society of fast money and quick fixes is to blame. Who knows?"

—*William Fulton*

"Basically, I think our generation doesn't want to be in the mainstream. I think people today are free thinkers. They do what they want to do. Kids want to be part of a group, but today there are so many different types of groups out there that almost nothing is mainstream."

—*Pat DiStefano*

"Our own city, once a city of clean streets and friendly people, now is a dirty, cold place where fear is felt more often than happiness. Neighbors who once looked out for one another now look the other way. Streets lined with well-kept brick rowhomes are now overgrown, broken down, grafitti-covered eyesores."

—*Jeff Morris*

"My parents grew up in a time in which things were simpler. For example, people in my generation started doing things a lot earlier than my parents did. The things they were doing in college, I did in junior high."

—*Robin Michel*

"When I was growing up, my parents told me to try everything at least once. However, when I started trying things on my own, they would tell me not to."

—*Marko D'Avignon*

"My generation is a scary one. We are the target generation for AIDS and, according to some, are at an all-time moral low. Despite actions taken to inform and educate us, I know that even my best friends are still behaving carelessly and not being sexually responsible. Everyone's thinking, 'It won't happen to me.'"

—*Natalie Chepelevich*

PREPARING TO READ AND WRITE

There was a time in the United States when, seemingly united by common habits, values, and goals, we thought we could define our nation and ourselves. In the 1940s, for example, World War II united us against common enemies and gave us a sense of purpose. In the 1950s, we worked together to expand the American economy and build the suburbs, all the while searching for the "good life." Beginning in the 1960s, however, the facade of a unified, homogeneous population, with all its citizens heading in the same direction, began to crack. Eventually, it splintered into hundreds of pieces. Now, on the brink of a new millennium, contemporary life in the United States is diverse, dynamic, and extremely difficult to characterize. In fact, because we all have different experiences, it might be said that each of us lives in a different society— different even from that of our family members or close friends. Of course, we also have a good deal in common. We share concerns about issues like violence, racism, and homelessness; we are confused and curious (and, sometimes, exhilarated) about how the world is changing; and we have hopes, dreams, and heroes to inspire us.

Each of the writers whose essays are collected in this chapter has a different way of looking at the world. Some look ahead; others look back. Some are optimistic; others are pessimistic. Perhaps your own view of present-day society is like one of theirs; more likely, you see the world from a different angle, one that is unlike the one any of them describes.

As you read the selections in this chapter and prepare to write about them, you may consider the following questions:

- Does the writer present a primarily positive or negative picture of society?

- Is the writer looking forward or backward?

- On what issue or issues does the writer focus?

- Would you say the writer's primary objective is to understand an issue and its effect, to inform readers, or to change readers' minds?

- Does the writer have a personal stake in the issue? If so, does your awareness of this involvement weaken or strengthen the selection's impact on you?

- If the selection identifies a problem, does it focus on finding solutions, speculating about long-term effects, or warning about consequences?

- Does the writer focus on the need for change—for example, in basic attitudes, in habits, or in the law? Is the writer optimistic or pessimistic about the possibility of change?

- Are you emotionally connected to the issue under discussion, or are you relatively detached from it?

- What areas of common concern do the writers explore? How are their views alike? How are they different? In what ways are they like and unlike your own?

- How are the writers' hopes and dreams for the future alike? How are they different? In what ways are they like and unlike your own?

TWO PERSEPCTIVES
ON THE WAY WE LIVE NOW

The following two essays focus on the influences that have shaped the current generation of young people in their late teens and twenties. In "Larger than Life," which originally appeared in the collection Next: Young Americans Writers on the New Generation *(1994), Jenny Lyn Bader (1969–) argues that because her generation has lost faith in the idea of conventional heroes, it is now required "to steer a course between naïveté and nihilism, to reshape vintage stories, to create stories of spirit without apologies." An editor and a contributor to the* New York Times, *Bader is also co-author of* The Male-Female/Female-Male Dictionary *(1996). The second essay originally appeared in 1993 in* Change, *the publication of the American Association for Higher Education. In it, Arthur Levine (1948–) reports, based on interviews with focus groups conducted during the 1992–1993 academic year, what undergraduates at twenty-eight U.S. colleges see as the five social and political events that have most influenced their generation. Currently president of Teachers College at Columbia University, Levine won the American Council of Education book-of-the-year award for* Reform of Undergraduate Education *(1973) and is well known for his many other books and articles focusing on higher education.*

LARGER THAN LIFE

Jenny Lyn Bader

When my grandmother was young, she would sometimes spot 1 the emperor Franz Josef riding down the cobbled roads of the Austro-Hungarian Empire.

She came of age so long ago that the few surviving photographs are 2 colored cream and chestnut. Early on, she saw cars replace horses and carriages. When she got older, she marveled at the first televisions. Near the end of her life, she grew accustomed to remote control and could spot prime ministers on color TV. By the time she died, the world was freshly populated by gadgetry and myth. Her generation bore witness to the rise of new machinery created by visionaries. My generation has seen machinery break down and visionaries come under fire.

As children, we enjoyed collecting visionaries, the way we collected 3 toys or baseball cards. When I was a kid, I first met Patrick Henry and Eleanor Roosevelt, Abraham Lincoln and Albert Einstein. They could always be summoned by the imagination and so were never late for play dates. I thought heroes figured in any decent childhood. I knew their stats.

Nathan Hale. Nelson Mandela. Heroes have guts.   4

Michelangelo. Shakespeare. Heroes have imagination.   5

They fight. Alexander the Great. Joan of Arc.   6

They fight for what they believe in. Susan B. Anthony. Martin 7 Luther King.

Heroes overcome massive obstacles. Beethoven, while deaf, still 8 managed to carry an unforgettable tune. Homer, while blind, never failed to give an excellent description. Helen Keller, both deaf and blind, still spoke to the world. FDR, despite his polio, became president. Moses, despite his speech impediment, held productive discussions with God.

They inspire three-hour movies. They make us weepy. They do the 9 right thing while enduring attractive amounts of suffering. They tend to be self-employed. They are often killed off. They sense the future. They lead lives that make us question our own. They are our ideals, but not our friends.

They don't have to be real. Some of them live in books and legends. 10 They don't have to be famous. There are lower-profile heroes who get resurrected by ambitious biographers. There are collective heroes: fire-fighters and astronauts, unsung homemakers, persecuted peoples. There are those whose names we can't remember, only their deeds: "you know, that woman who swam the English Channel," "the guy who died run-ning the first marathon," "the student who threw himself in front of the tank at Tiananmen Square." There are those whose names we'll never find out: the anonymous benefactor, the masked man, the undercover agent, the inventor of the wheel, the unknown soldier. The one who did the thing so gutsy and terrific that no one will ever know what it was.

Unlike icons (Marilyn, Elvis) heroes are not only sexy but noble, 11 too. Unlike idols (Gretzky, Streisand), who vary from fan to fan, they are almost universally beloved. Unlike icons and idols, heroes lack irony. And unlike icons and idols, heroes are no longer in style.

As centuries end, so do visions of faith—maybe because the faithful 12 get nervous as the double zeroes approach and question what they've been worshiping. Kings and queens got roughed up at the end of the eighteenth century; God took a beating at the end of the nineteenth; and as the twentieth century draws to a close, outstanding human beings are the casualties of the moment. In the 1970s and 1980s, Americans started feeling queasy about heroism. Those of us born in the sixties found ourselves on the cusp of that change. A sweep of new beliefs, pri-orities, and headlines has conspired to take our pantheon away from us.

Members of my generation believed in heroes when they were 13 younger but now find themselves grasping for them. Even the word *hero* sounds awkward. I find myself embarrassed to ask people who their heroes are, because the word just doesn't trip off the tongue. My

friend Katrin sounded irritated when I asked for hers. She said, "Oh,
Jesus . . . Do people still have heroes?"

We don't. Certainly not in the traditional sense of adoring perfect 14
people. Frequently not at all. "I'm sort of intrigued by the fact that I
don't have heroes right off the top of my head," said a colleague, Peter.
"Can I get back to you?"

Some of us are more upset about this than others. It's easy to tell 15
which of us miss the heroic age. We are moved by schmaltzy political
speeches, we warm up to stories of pets saving their owners, we even
get misty-eyed watching the Olympics. We mope when model citizens
fail us. My college roommate, Linda, remembers a seventh-grade class
called "Heroes and She-roes." The first assignment was to write about
a personal hero or she-ro. "I came home," Linda told me, "and cried and
cried because I didn't have one. . . . Carter had screwed up in Iran and
given the malaise speech. Gerald Ford was a nothing and Nixon was
evil. My parents told me to write about Jane Fonda the political activist
and I just kept crying."

Not everyone feels sentimental about it. A twentyish émigré raised 16
in the former Soviet Union told me: "It's kind of anticlimactic to look for
heroes when you've been brought up in a culture that insists on so
many heroes. . . . What do you want me to say? Lenin? Trotsky?" Even
though I grew up in the relatively propaganda-free United States, I
understood. The America of my childhood insisted on heroes, too.

Of all the myths I happily ate for breakfast, the most powerful one 17
was our story of revolution. I sang about it as early as kindergarten and
read about it long after. The story goes, a few guys in wigs skipped town
on some grumpy church leaders and spurned a loopy king to branch
out on their own. The children who hear the story realize they don't
have to believe in oldfangled clergy or a rusty crown—but they had better believe in those guys with the wigs.

I sure did. I loved a set of books known as the "Meet" series: *Meet* 18
*George Washington, Meet Andrew Jackson, Meet the Men Who Sailed the
Seas,* and many more. I remember one picture of an inspired Thomas
Jefferson, his auburn ponytail tied in a black ribbon, penning words
with a feather as a battle of banners and cannon fire raged behind him.

A favorite "Meet" book starred Christopher Columbus. His resis- 19
tance to the flat-earth society of his day was engrossing, especially to a
kid like me who had trouble trying new foods let alone seeking new
land masses. I identified with his yearning for a new world and his difficulty with finding investors. Standing up to the king and queen of
Spain was like convincing your parents to let you do stuff they thought
was idiotic. Now, my allowance was only thirty-five cents a week, but
that didn't mean I wasn't going to ask for three ships at some later date.

This is pretty embarrassing: I adored those guys. The ones in the 20
white powder and ponytails, the voluptuous hats, the little breeches and

cuffs. They were funny-looking, but lovable. They did outrageous things without asking for permission. They invented the pursuit of happiness.

I had a special fondness for Ben Franklin, statesman and eccentric inventor. Inventions, like heroes, made me feel as though I lived in a dull era. If I'd grown up at the end of the nineteenth century, I could have spoken on early telephones. A few decades later, I could have heard the new sounds of radio. In the sixties, I could have watched black-and-white TVs graduate to color.

Instead, I saw my colorful heroes demoted to black and white. Mostly white. By the time I finished high school, it was no longer hip to look up to the paternalistic dead white males who launched our country, kept slaves and mistresses, and massacred native peoples. Suddenly they weren't visionaries but oppressors, or worse—objects. Samuel Adams became a beer, John Hancock became a building, and the rest of the guys in wigs were knocked off one by one, in a whodunit that couldn't be explained away by the fact of growing up.

The flag-waving of my youth, epitomized by America's bicentennial, was a more loving homage than I know today. The year 1976 rolled in while Washington was still reeling from Saigon, but the irony was lost on me and my second-grade classmates. The idea of losing seemed miles away. We celebrated July fourth with wide eyes and patriotic parties. Grown-ups had yet to tell themselves (so why should they tell us?) that the young nation on its birthday had suffered a tragic defeat.

Historians soon filled us in about that loss, and of others. Discovering America was nothing compared to discovering the flaws of its discoverers, now cast as imperialist sleaze, racist and sexist and genocidal. All things heroic—human potential, spiritual fervor, moral resplendence—soon became suspect. With the possible exception of bodybuilding, epic qualities went out of fashion. Some will remember 1992 as the year Superman died. Literally, the writers and illustrators at *D.C. Comics* decided the guy was too old to keep leaping buildings and rescuing an aging damsel in distress. When rumors circulated that he would be resurrected, readers protested via calls to radio shows, letters to editors, and complaints to stores that they were in no mood for such an event.

A monster named Doomsday killed Superman, overcoming him not with Kryptonite but with brute force. Who killed the others? I blame improved modes of character assassination, media hype artists, and scholars. The experts told me that Columbus had destroyed cultures and ravaged the environment. They also broke the news that the cowboys had brazenly taken land that wasn't theirs. In a way, I'm glad I didn't know that earlier; dressing up as a cowgirl for Halloween wouldn't have felt right. In a more urgent way, I wish I had known it then so I wouldn't have had to learn it later.

Just fifteen years after America's bicentennial came Columbus's quincentennial, when several towns canceled their annual parades in protest of his sins. Soon other festivities started to feel funny. When my aunt served corn pudding last Thanksgiving, my cousin took a spoonful, then said dryly that the dish was made in honor of the Indians who taught us to use corn before we eliminated them. Uncomfortable chuckles followed. Actually, neither "we" nor my personal ancestors had come to America in time to kill any Native Americans. Yet the holiday put us in the same boat with the pilgrims and anchored us in the white man's domain.

I am fascinated by how we become "we" and "they." It's as if siding with the establishment is the Alka-Seltzer that helps us stomach the past. To swallow history lessons, we turn into "we": one nation under God of proud but remorseful Indian killers. We also identify with people who look like us. For example, white northerners studying the Civil War identify both with white slaveholders and with northern abolitionists, aligning with both race and place. Transsexuals empathize with men and women. Immigrants identify with their homeland and their adopted country. Historians proposing a black Athena and a black Jesus have inspired more of such bonding. 27

I'll admit that these empathies can be empowering. I always understood the idea of feeling stranded by unlikely role models but never emotionally grasped it until I watched Penny Marshall's movie *A League of Their Own*. For the first time, I appreciated why so many women complain that sports bore them. I had enjoyed baseball before but never as intensely as I enjoyed the games in that film. The players were people like me. Lori Petty, petite, chirpy, wearing a skirt, commanded the pitcher's mound with such aplomb that I was moved. There's something to be said for identifying with people who remind us of ourselves, though Thomas Jefferson and Lori Petty look more like each other than either of them looks like me. I'll never know if I would've read the "Meet" books with more zeal if they'd described our founding mothers. I liked them as they were. 28

Despite the thrill of dames batting something on the big screen besides their eyelashes, the fixation on look-alike idols is disturbing for those who get left out. In the movie *White Men Can't Jump*, Wesley Snipes tells Woody Harrelson not to listen to Jimi Hendrix, because "White people can't hear Jimi." Does this joke imply that black people can't hear Mozart? That I can admire Geena Davis's batting but never appreciate Carlton Fisk? Besides dividing us from one another, these emotional allegiances divide us from potential heroes too, causing us to empathize with, say, General Custer and his last stand instead of with Sitting Bull and the victorious Sioux. 29

Rejecting heroes for having the wrong ethnic credentials or sex organs says less about our multicultural vision than our lack of imagination. By focusing on what we are instead of who we can become, by typecasting and miscasting our ideals—that's how we become "we" and "they." If heroes are those we'd like to emulate, it does make sense 30 that they resemble us. But the focus on physical resemblance seems limited and racist.

Heroes should be judged on their deeds, and there are those with 31 plenty in common heroically but not much in terms of ethnicity, nationality, or gender. Just look at Harriet Tubman and Moses; George Washington and Simón Bolívar; Mahatma Gandhi and Martin Luther King; Murasaki and Milton; Cicero and Ann Richards. Real paragons transcend nationality. It didn't matter to me that Robin Hood was English—as long as he did good, he was as American as a barbecue. It didn't matter to Queen Isabella that Columbus was Italian as long as he sailed for Spain and sprinkled her flags about. The British epic warrior Beowulf was actually Swedish. Both the German hero Etzel and the Scandinavian hero Atli were really Attila, king of the Huns. With all this borrowing going on, we shouldn't have to check the passports of our luminaries; the idea that we can be like them not literally but spiritually is what's uplifting in the first place.

The idea that we can never be like them has led to what I call jeal- 32 ousy journalism. You know, we're not remotely heroic so let's tear down anyone who is. It's become hard to remember which papers are tabloids. Tell-all articles promise us the "real story"—implying that greatness can't be real. The safe thing about *Meet George Washington* was that you couldn't actually meet him. Today's stories and pictures bring us closer. And actually meeting your heroes isn't the best idea. Who wants to learn that a favorite saint is really just an egomaniac with a publicist?

Media maestros have not only knocked public figures off their 33 pedestals, they've also lowered heroism standards by idealizing just about everyone. Oprah, Geraldo, and the rest turn their guests into heroes of the afternoon because they overcame abusive roommates, childhood disfigurement, deranged spouses, multiple genitalia, cheerleading practice, or zany sexual predilections. In under an hour, a studio audience can hear their epic sagas told.

While TV and magazine producers helped lead heroes to their 34 graves, the academic community gave the final push. Just as my peers and I made our way through college, curriculum reformers were promoting "P.C." agendas at the expense of humanistic absolutes. Scholars invented their own tabloidism, investigating and maligning both dead professors and trusty historical figures. Even literary theory helped, when deconstructionists made it trendy to look for questions instead of answers, for circular logic instead of linear sense, for defects, contradictions, and the ironic instead of meaning, absolutes, and the heroic.

It was the generations that preceded ours who killed off our heroes. 35 And like everyone who crucified a superstar, these people thought they were doing a good thing. The professors and journalists consciously moved in a positive direction—toward greater tolerance, openness, and realism—eliminating our inspirations in the process. The death of an era of hero worship was not the result of the cynical, clinical materialism too often identified with my generation. It was the side effect of a complicated cultural surgery, of an operation that may have been necessary and that many prescribed.

So with the best of intentions, these storytellers destroyed bedtime 36 stories. Which is too bad for the kids, because stories make great teachers. Children glean by example. You can't tell a child "Be ingenious," or "Do productive things." You can tell them, "This Paul Revere person jumped on a horse at midnight, rode wildly through the dark, figured out where the mean British troops were coming to attack the warm, fuzzy, sweet, great-looking colonists, and sent messages by code, igniting our fight for freedom," and they'll get the idea. America's rugged values come gift wrapped in the frontier tales of Paul Bunyan, Daniel Boone, Davy Crockett—fables of independence and natural resources. Kids understand that Johnny Appleseed or Laura Ingalls Wilder would never need a Cuisinart. Pioneer and prairie stories convey the fun of roughing it, showing kids how to be self-reliant, or at least less spoiled.

Children catch on to the idea of imitating qualities, not literal feats. 37 After returning his storybook to the shelf, little Billy doesn't look around for a dragon to slay. Far-off stories capture the imagination in an abstract but compelling way, different from, say, the more immediate action-adventure flick. After watching a James Bond film festival, I might fantasize about killing the five people in front of me on line at the supermarket, while legends are remote enough that Columbus might inspire one to be original, but not necessarily to study Portuguese or enlist in the navy. In tales about conquerors and cavaliers, I first flirted with the idea of ideas.

Even Saturday-morning cartoons served me as parables, when I 38 woke up early enough to watch the classy Superfriends do good deeds. Sure, the gender ratio between Wonder Woman and the gaggle of men in capes seemed unfair, but I was rapt. I wonder whether I glued myself to my television and my high expectations with too much trust, and helped to set my own heroes up for a fall.

Some heroes have literally been sentenced to death by their own fol- 39 lowers. *Batman* subscribers, for example, were responsible for getting rid of Batman's sidekick, Robin. At the end of one issue, the Joker threatened to kill the Boy Wonder, and readers could decide whether Robin lived or died by calling one of two "900" numbers. The public voted overwhelmingly for his murder. I understand the impulse of those who dialed for death. At a certain point, eternal invincibility grows as dull and predictable as wearing a yellow cape and red tights every day of the year. It's not human. We get fed up.

My generation helped to kill off heroism as teenagers, with our lan- 40 guage. We used heroic words that once described brave deeds—*excellent, amazing, awesome*—to describe a good slice of pizza or a sunny day.

In our everyday speech, *bad* meant good. *Hot* meant cool. In the sarcastic slang of street gangs in Los Angeles, *hero* currently means traitor, specifically someone who snitches on a graffiti artist.

Even those of us who lived by them helped shatter our own myths, 41 which wasn't all negative. We discovered that even the superhero meets his match. Every Achilles needs a podiatrist. Every rhapsodically handsome leader has a mistress or a moment of moral ambiguity. We injected a dose of reality into our expectations. We even saw a viable presidential candidate under a heap of slung mud, a few imperfections, an alleged tryst or two.

We're used to trysts in a way our elders aren't. Our parents and 42 grandparents behave as if they miss the good old days when adulterers wore letter sweaters. They feign shock at the extramarital exploits of Thomas Jefferson, Frank Sinatra, JFK, Princess Di. Their hero worship is a romance that falters when beloved knights end up unfaithful to their own spouses. People my age aren't amazed by betrayal. We are suspicious of shining armor. Even so, tabloid sales escalate when a Lancelot gives in to temptation—maybe because the jerk who cheats on you somehow becomes more attractive. Other generations have gossiped many of our heroes into philanderers. The presumptuous hero who breaks your heart is the most compelling reason not to get involved in the first place.

Seeing your legends discredited is like ending a romance with 43 someone you loved but ultimately didn't like. However much you longed to trust that person, it just makes more sense not to. Why pine away for an aloof godlet who proves unstable, erratic, and a rotten lover besides? It's sad to give up fantasies but mature to trade them in for healthier relationships grounded in reality.

We require a new pantheon[1]: a set of heroes upon whom we can 44 rely, who will not desert us when the winds change, and whom we will not desert. It's unsettling, if not down-right depressing, to go through life embarrassed about the identity of one's childhood idols.

Maybe we should stick to role models instead. Heroes have 45 become quaint, as old-fashioned as gas-guzzlers—and as unwieldy, requiring too much investment and energy. Role models are more like compact cars, less glam and roomy but easier to handle. They take up less parking space in the imagination. Role models have a certain degree of consciousness about their job. The cast members of "Beverly Hills 90210," for example, have acknowledged that they serve as role models for adolescents, and their characters behave accordingly: they refrain from committing major crimes; they overcome inclinations toward substance abuse; they see through adult hypocrisy; and any

---

[1] Literally, a temple dedicated to all the Greek gods, but also the gods themselves; sometimes refers to a group of illustrious people. [Eds.]

misdemeanors they do perpetrate are punished. For moral mediators we could do better, but at least the prime-time writing staff is aware of the burden of having teen groupies.

Heroes don't have the luxury of staff writers or the opportunity to endorse designer jeans. Hercules can't go on "Nightline" and pledge to stop taking steroids. Prometheus can't get a presidential pardon. Columbus won't have a chance to weep to Barbara Walters that he didn't mean to endanger leatherback turtles or monk seals or the tribes of the Lucayas. Elizabeth I never wrote a best-seller about how she did it her way. ⁴⁶

Role models can go on talk shows, or even host them. Role models may live next door. While a hero might be a courageous head of state, a saint, a leader of armies, a role model might be someone who put in a three-day presidential bid, your local minister, your boss. They don't need their planes to go down in flames to earn respect. Role models have a job, accomplishment, or hairstyle worth emulating. ⁴⁷

Rather than encompassing the vast kit and caboodle of ideals, role models can perform a little neat division of labor. One could wish to give orders like Norman Schwarzkopf but perform psychoanalysis like Lucy Van Pelt, to chair a round-table meeting as well as King Arthur but negotiate as well as Queen Esther, to eat like Orson Welles but look like Helen of Troy, and so forth. It was General Schwarzkopf, the most tangible military hero for anyone my age, who vied instead for role-model status by claiming on the cover of his book: *It Doesn't Take a Hero.* With this title he modestly implies that anyone with some smarts and élan could strategize and storm as well as he has. ⁴⁸

Role models are admirable individuals who haven't given up their lives or livelihoods and may even have a few hang-ups. They don't have to be prone to excessive self-sacrifice. They don't go on hunger strikes; they diet. They are therefore more likely than heroes to be free for lunch, and they are oftener still alive. ⁴⁹

Heroism is a living thing for many of my contemporaries. In my informal poll, I not only heard sob stories about the decline of heroes, I also discovered something surprising: the ascent of parents. While the founding fathers may be passé, actual mothers, fathers, grands, and great-grands are undeniably "in." An overwhelming number of those I polled named their household forebears as those they most admired. By choosing their own relatives as ideals, people in their twenties have replaced impersonal heroes with the most personal role models of all. Members of my purportedly lost generation have not only realized that it's time to stop believing in Santa Claus, they have chosen to believe instead in their families—the actual tooth fairy, the real Mr. and Mrs. Claus. They have stopped needing the folks from the North Pole, the guys with the wigs, the studs and studettes in tights and capes. ⁵⁰

In a way it bodes well that Superman and the rest could be killed 51
or reported missing. They were needed to quash the most villainous
folks of all: insane communists bearing nuclear weapons, heinous war
criminals, monsters named Doomsday. The good news about Superman bleeding to death was that Doomsday died in the struggle.

If the good guys are gone, so is the world that divides down the 52
middle into good guys and bad guys. A world without heroes is a rigorous, demanding place, where things don't boil down to black and
white but are rich with shades of gray; where faith in lofty, dead per-
sonages can be replaced by faith in ourselves and one another; where
we must summon the strength to imagine a five-dimensional future in
colors not yet invented. My generation grew up to see our world shift,
so it's up to us to steer a course between naïveté and nihilism, to reshape
vintage stories, to create stories of spirit without apologies.

I've heard a few. There was one about the woman who taught 53
Shakespeare to inner-city fourth graders in Chicago who were previously thought to be retarded or hopeless. There was the college
groundskeeper and night watchman, a black man with a seventh-grade
education, who became a contracts expert, wrote poetry and memoirs,
and invested his salary so wisely that he bequeathed 450 acres of moun-
tainous parkland to the university when he died. There was the motor-
cyclist who slid under an eighteen-wheeler at full speed, survived his
physical therapy only to wind up in a plane crash, recovered, and as a
disfigured quadriplegic started a business, got happily married, and ran
for public office; his campaign button bore a caption that said "Send me
to Congress and I won't be just another pretty face. . . ."

When asked for her heroes, a colleague of mine spoke of her great- 54
grandmother, a woman whose husband left her with three kids in
Galicia, near Poland, and went to the United States. He meant to send
for her, but the First World War broke out. When she made it to
America, her husband soon died, and she supported her family; at one
point she even ran a nightclub. According to the great-granddaughter,
"When she was ninety she would tell me she was going to volunteer at
the hospital. I would ask how and she'd say, 'Oh, I just go over there to
read to the old folks.' The 'old folks' were probably seventy. She was a
great lady."

My grandmother saved her family, too, in the next great war. She 55
did not live to see the age of the fax, but she did see something remarkable in her time, more remarkable even than the emperor riding down
the street: she saw him walking down the street. I used to ask her, "Did
you really see the emperor Franz Josef walking down the street?"

She would say, "Ya. Walking down the street." I would laugh, and 56
though she'd repeat it to amuse me, she did not see what was so funny.
To me, the emperor was someone you met in history books, not on the
streets of Vienna. He was larger than life, a surprising pedestrian. He

was probably just getting some air, but he was also laying the groundwork for my nostalgia of that time when it would be natural for him to take an evening stroll, when those who were larger than life roamed cobblestones.

Today, life is larger.   57

THE MAKING OF A GENERATION

Arthur Levine

Every college generation is defined by the social events of its age. 1 The momentous occurrences of an era—from wars and economics to politics and inventions—give meaning to the lives of the individuals who live through them. They also serve to knit those individuals together by creating a collective memory and a common historic or generational identity.

In 1979, I went to 26 college and university campuses, selected to 2 represent the diversity of American higher education, and asked students what social or political events most influenced their generation. I told them that the children who came of age in the decade after World War I might have answered the Great Depression. The bombing of Pearl Harbor, World War II, or perhaps the death of Franklin Roosevelt might have stood out for those born a few years later. For my generation, born after World War II, the key event was the assassination of John F. Kennedy. We remember where we were when we heard the news. The whole world seemingly changed in its aftermath.

The Me Generation

I asked what stood out for that generation of undergraduates on the 3 eve of the 1980s. They said Vietnam and Watergate. These events had defined their world. Few could remember a time in their lives when there had been no war, and Watergate seemed a confirmation about the way the world worked in business, government, and all sectors of society. On Watergate, students' comments echoed one another:

> *"Government doesn't give a damn."*
> *"All politicians are crooks."*
> *"Nixon was like all of us, only he got caught."*
> *"It happens all the time."*
> *"I don't trust government as far as I can throw the Capitol building."*
> *"Nixon was a victim, that's all."*
> *"The whole thing was out of proportion."*

For three out of four students, the effects of Watergate and Vietnam 4
had been distinctly negative, causing undergraduates to turn away from
politics, politicians, and government. Most said they had no heroes.

Trust in all social institutions had declined among college students. 5
A plurality of undergraduates described the major social institutions of
society—Congress, corporations, labor unions, and the rest—as dishonest and immoral. They expressed a belief that there was nothing left to
hold onto: "Everything is bad."

In response, the students had turned inward, and the refuge they 6
had chosen was "me." They described the mood on campus this way:

"People only care about me, me, me."
"We're just interested in staying alive."
"We're part of the me generation."
"Concerns today are not about social issues, but about me."
"People are looking out for number one."
"The me generation is not concerned with the good of society, but with
what's good for themselves."

Ninety-one percent of the undergraduates interviewed were opti- 7
mistic about their personal futures, but only 41 percent expressed hope
about our collective future together. Student interests focused increasingly on being well-off financially. At the same time they had become
more and more vocationally oriented, seeking careers in the platinum
professions—law, medicine, and business. They had adopted what
might be called a Titanic ethic: a sense that they were riding on a
doomed ship called the United States or the world, and as long as it
remained afloat, they would go first class.

The Current Generation

The findings of the 1979 study were so telling that I decided to 8
repeat it this academic year. Once again I, along with several colleagues,
visited a diverse selection of colleges and universities across the country. We followed the same approach as the original study, meeting with
intentionally heterogeneous groups consisting of 8 to 10 students on
each campus. The number of institutions was raised to 28 to reflect the
changing character of higher education since 1979. (This was part of a
larger study including a survey of 10,000 undergraduates, a survey of
300 chief student affairs officers, and interviews with undergraduate
student body presidents, newspaper editors, vice presidents and deans
of students, and others.) Again we asked the undergraduate groups
what social and political events had most influenced their generation.
They gave five common answers.

Challenger. The most frequent answer was the *Challenger* explosion. 9
Once a student mentioned it, members of the group commonly nodded
in affirmation or said "yes." It was the equivalent of the Kennedy assassination for this generation. The students all knew where they had been
when they heard the news. Many had watched it on television in school.
Those who had not, saw it "on the news over and over and over again."
Some had been scheduled to have teacher-astronaut Christa McAuliffe
teach them from space. For a number it was the first time they had ever
seen an adult, their own teacher, break down and cry. It was a first brush
with death for quite a few.

That students answered the *Challenger* explosion surprised me. 10
When I thought about the responses students might give to my question, the Shuttle disaster was not on the list. My generation had witnessed other fatalities in the space program, and while the *Challenger*
explosion was a very sad occurrence, it did not seem to me to be a defining moment for the nation.

I asked them why they had selected the *Challenger.* Beyond the fact 11
that it was the first shared generational tragedy, students talked of a
shattering of both their idealism and their sense of safety:

"I always thought NASA was perfect."
"There were smashed dreams because of it."
"My hopes were in it. There was an Asian, a black, and a woman."
"Thought America invincible."
"Burst my bubble."
"It was something good and then it blew up."
"NASA fell off its pedestal."

Students also said the *Challenger* explosion had marked a "wake-up
call" or "reality check" for them and the nation. For some it was "a sign
of a lot of things wrong" with the United States, such as in manufacturing, and for others it highlighted the decline of America due to its inability to compete economically and technologically. As one student put it,
until then "I thought we were the best; we're really only second class."

End of the Cold War. The fall of communism was a second event stu- 12
dents cited. They spoke in terms of "pride," "hope," "drama," "energy,"
and "a closer world." The symbol that stood out for them was the razing
of the Berlin Wall.

Today's undergraduates are the last Cold War generation. They had 13
studied Russia in school as an evil power to be feared. Although none
of the 18-to-24-year-old undergraduates had seen Khrushchev bang his
shoe at the U.N. or lived through the Cuban Missile Crisis, and only a
small minority had engaged in duck-and-cover exercises in school, most
had seen films like *The Day After,* which warned of the danger of a
nuclear war. As a group, the students interviewed had been scared of

the Soviet Union and afraid of the prospect of nuclear holocaust. In this sense the fall of communism was an extremely positive event.

However, the students were quite somber about the results. They 14 regularly talked of the instability of Central and Eastern Europe, but in recent months, their focus shifted to U.S. involvement in a potential Vietnam-like ground war in Bosnia. They noted almost as frequently the danger of a now uncontrolled Soviet nuclear arsenal. They often worried whether the world was, in retrospect, a better place because of the demise of communism. One student put it this way: "For my generation, every silver lining brings a cloud."

Persian Gulf War. The third event students mentioned was the 1991 15 Gulf War, which they described as "our first war"—"Every generation has a war; this was ours." Like the *Challenger* explosion, they had watched it on television. TVs in student lounges, which were usually tuned to soap operas, had stayed fixed on the war. With the rise of CNN, students joked that friends would drop by and say, "You want to watch the war for a while?," and off they would go.

Despite fear of a draft and another potential Vietnam, students said 16 the Gulf War had pulled them together. Many knew people who had been called up to serve in the Gulf. On their campuses, demonstrations against the war had tended to be tiny or absent in comparison to those in favor. The initial student reaction was pride: "We're still number one"; and "We can get things done." This seemed to be generally true among both liberal and conservative undergraduates. Students talked of flags and yellow ribbons appearing in profusion on many campuses.

By the 1992–93 academic year, undergraduate reactions had 17 changed, with students becoming much more critical:

"It's still a mess."
"We didn't finish the job."
"We botched another one."
"No reason to be there."
"Only a political show."
"Bush just wanted to be a hero."
"People were risking their lives and then had to return and not get jobs."
"We were in there to keep our oil prices down."
"Did it for economic interest only."

Few students were willing to speak out in favor of the Gulf War in spring of 1993 or to offer non-economic rationales for it. In conversation after conversation, students disavowed the U.S. role as world peace officer. They rejected the notion that when "anything goes wrong, we have to straighten it out."

AIDS. A fourth event the students cited was the AIDS epidemic. 18 AIDS has been a fact of life for this generation as long as sexuality has been a possibility for them. Many reported lectures, pamphlets, films, and condom demonstrations in school. They commonly lamented, "I hear about it all the time"; "I'm tired of it."

But more than being tired, the students were often angry. They fre- 19 quently compared their situation with that of the baby boomers, complaining, "When the boomers had sex, they got laid. When we have sex, we get AIDS." One student said it this way: "Free love is more expensive [now]."

Nonetheless, even though undergraduates resented a sword dan- 20 gling over their heads, they acted as if it were not there. Though most said they knew what constituted safe sex, only a minority said they practiced it consistently. Students interviewed felt AIDS could not happen to them. They felt immortal. Very few knew anyone who had been diagnosed as HIV positive. Women undergraduates regularly expressed a greater fear of rape and pregnancy than AIDS.

Rodney King. The final event students mentioned was the verdict in 21 the Rodney King beating trial and the riots that followed. Minorities—African-Americans, Hispanics, and Asian-Americans—cited it most frequently, but by no means exclusively. Students expressed polar opinions; some had been appalled by the verdict, and others repulsed by the subsequent violence. The only commonality was the strong negative reaction:

> *"I lost faith in the judicial system."*
> *"I lost faith in the police."*
> *"I lost confidence in people."*
> *"It was a lesson in how to buy off a jury."*
> *"Everything is politics."*
> *"I used to believe the civil rights movement made a difference."*
> *"Racism lives."*
> *"Laws were created, but minds were not changed."*
> *"Another shock to the system."*
> *"Rioting inexcusable."*
> *"Lawless."*
> *"Verdict really disturbed me."*
> *"I was glad. It's the only way to get people to see."*
> *"It reminded me that society treats me differently."*
> *"Police jobs are stressful."*

What Do These Events Mean?

What stands out about the five events the students cited is first how 22 recent they were. Most of today's freshmen were born in 1975—after John F. Kennedy's death, the end of the Great Society, the assassinations of Martin Luther King, Jr., and Robert Kennedy, the moon landing, the Watergate break-in and Richard Nixon's resignation, and the end of the war in Vietnam. They were a year old when Jimmy Carter was elected president, four when the hostages were taken in Iran, five when Ronald Reagan entered the White House, ten when Gorbachev came to power, and thirteen when George Bush became president. More than 40 percent have never heard of Hubert Humphrey, Ralph Nader, or Barry Goldwater.

As a consequence, the events that stand out to their parents and fac-   23
ulty have little meaning to current undergraduates. Those events do not stir the same anger, elation, frustration, or vivid emotions in students that they do in older adults. They are at best history to contemporary undergraduates.

Today's students really know only two presidents of the United   24
States, Ronald Reagan and George Bush. They have lived through three wars, Granada, Panama, and Iraq. The longest war in their lives lasted six weeks. They are living through a period of profound demographic, economic, global, and technological change.

In addition to being recent, the five events the students cited were   25
at least in part negative. They described three—the *Challenger* explosion, AIDS, and the Rodney King affair—in wholly negative terms, and their initial optimism about the fall of communism and the Gulf War has faded significantly. In general, students thought they were living in a deeply troubled nation in which intractable problems were multiplying and solutions were growing more distant:

> "Our experience is of flaws, problems, decline. We're not number one in anything. Our generation grew up with that."
> "The world seems to be falling apart."
> "We don't have anything that stable to hold onto."

The students interviewed shared a sense that their "generation   26
would be called on to fix everything." As a group, they rejected the likelihood of broadscale solutions. For them the five events they cited showed that such solutions are unlikely to occur and unlikely to work. They also dismissed the possibility that answers would come from government. They saw Congress as bankrupt, but held out hope for the Clinton presidency in its earliest days.

An Increased, If Guarded, Optimism

Yet the students I interviewed expressed some optimism about the   27
future. Again, more than nine out of 10 were optimistic about their personal fates, but the level of optimism about our collective future shot up

to 55 percent. This is in large measure because students have shifted their focus. While they were rather negative about the future of the country, they were remarkably optimistic about the future of their communities. Today's students emphasize the local in their thinking and their action.

Heroes are back too. More than three out of four students had 28 heroes, but those heroes were local—Mom and Dad, my teacher, my neighbor, the person leading the community clean-up campaign.

Participation in service activities increased dramatically as well. 29 Prior to coming to college about half of all current undergraduates had been engaged in some form of community service. Such programs are booming on college campuses today as well, particularly in the area of environmentalism, a common interest among today's undergraduates. Even on some campuses in which political action was low or absent, recycling bins have appeared at the behest of students.

Nonetheless, fear and anger were a part of the conversation with 30 every student group I interviewed. Current undergraduates were afraid of being unable to find jobs, of living in an economy in which they will do less well than their parents, of facing a mounting national debt, of having to contend with environmental disasters, and much, much more. They felt put upon, cheated, and robbed of the opportunity that had been given to previous generations. They especially resented the baby boomers for their advantages. They criticized the students of the 1980s for their "me-ism."

For most of the students interviewed the real struggle was choosing 31 between making money and performing good deeds. Six out of eight undergraduates said it was essential or very important to be very well-off financially, but five out of eight said it was essential or very important to have a career that would make a meaningful social contribution. The big issue facing students I interviewed was how to choose. Most didn't want to be Donald Trump, but the prospect of Mother Teresa was not all that appealing either. Above all, this is a generation torn between doing good and doing well.

Responding to Reading

1. What kinds of heroes does Bader say people of her generation—she was born in the late 1960s—have? What kinds of heroes does Levine say the students he studied—born in 1975—have? How are they alike? How are they different?

2. Are the five key political and social events Levine mentions the ones that have had the greatest impact on your life? Are there others you consider more significant? How do you account for any differences between your choices and those of the students Levine surveyed?

3. In paragraphs 29–31, Bader touches on a sensitive issue: the idea that one's heroes must be representatives of one's own gender, race, ethnic group, and nationality. Do you agree that this is important? Do you have heroes from backgrounds unlike your own?

4. Levine's conclusions reflect students' general optimism. Are you optimistic about your future? About the future of your community, your nation, and your world? What events do you see that encourage (or discourage) you?

5. The last words in Bader's essay are, "Today, life is larger." What does she mean? Do you think she is correct? Would Levine agree with her?

6. In his conclusion, Levine characterizes the generation he profiles as one "torn between doing good and doing well." Do you think that "doing good" and "doing well" are mutually exclusive?

ELEGY FOR THE HOBBY

Randy Cohen

Randy Cohen (1948–   ) was born in Charleston, South Carolina, and received his M.F.A in music from the California Institute of Music in Los Angeles. Turning from composition to writing, he wrote for David Letterman's Late Show *for seven years and served as head writer for the startup of* The Rosie O'Donnell Show *in 1996. His book* Death of a Flying Man, *a collection of essays and stories, was published in 1996. He is currently working on a screenplay and writing and performing monologues for WNYC, New York public radio. In "Elegy for the Hobby," which was published in the* New York Times Magazine *in 1997, Cohen looks at changes in American life by considering how many fewer people have hobbies today than in times past.*

In his 1963 novel, "Jubb," the English writer Keith Waterhouse epit-   1
omizes the hobbyist as suburban nerd. Jubb—male, 36, married—is a rent collector in a town 30 miles from London. He is trying to start a photography club because, as he explains to a teenage boy constructing a model aircraft carrier: "If you read Hobbies Digest at all, you'll find that many people make a second hobby of photographing their handi-work." Jubb's interest in photography is less than wholesome. On the novel's opening page, he says, "Sometimes I spend the whole day going up and down the Piccadilly Line, looking at girls."

In a constant state of sexual yearning, Jubb wears eyeglasses and   2
has gum disease. He collects old boys' magazines. He is a hobbyist.

I don't have a hobby. No one I know does. In Manhattan, where I   3
live, my friends and I are too busy with worthy urban pursuits. We're

consuming culture and being consumed by work. (And we're chatting on the phone.) It may also be that we lack the nerve for anything as unglamorous as a hobby. We are deterred by the taint of Jubb.

But, you may object, I have a hobby: I take a cooking class. I bowl. 4 These are not really hobbies, though, not in the Jubbian sense. True hobbies require single-mindedness. They provide a strong counterbalance to work. They are a marital aid, a mechanism for spouse avoidance. They involve the accumulation of equipment and lore; that is, irredeemably specific information. This gives the hobbyist a pleasing sense of progress—or pseudoprogress, because hobbies are conservative. Here is the prime law of hobbies: Absorbing but Not Transforming. They fill the mind without altering it.

I used to have a hobby, but I gave it up. In college and for a few 5 years after, I played Go, the Japanese board game. I read Go books. I had Go friends to whom I never spoke except to say, "Your move." Go is an elegant game, complex and absorbing. When I stared at the board, considering my move, I thought of nothing else. When I looked up, an hour had passed. Go is played on a 19-by-19 grid, a geometry that organized my world. I'd walk into a classroom, look at the desks and think, "If that one were placed one row over, its position would be stronger."

Eventually I gave up the game. It wasted time. It wasn't useful. To 6 be an adult, I thought, was to be urbane, ambitious. And if at the time I lacked a passionate attachment to any particular work, I didn't want to advertise the fact by conspicuously playing board games. And after work? No, I'm afraid. The decline of hobbies parallels the decline of leisure: there's just no time. We don't bring home model cars; we bring home file folders.

There was a time when work was only the first activity among 7 equals. In an essay called "Leeds Trams," the playwright Alan Bennett describes how his father, "a good amateur violinist," struggled to learn the double bass: "He sounds as if he's sawing (which he also does, actually, as one of his other hobbies is fretwork)." One of his *other* hobbies. Bennet's father was a butcher by trade, work to which he seriously applied himself. But like his friends and neighbors, he enjoyed a variety of activities. He had hobbies.

But 1947 is not 1997. My friends and I have forsworn the hobby 8 shop for the gym, the movies, the museum; we pursue fitness and culture. We go to be transformed, to see the world fresh. But we also go for a more dubious reason: to keep up. People won't ask about your hobby, but they will ask if you've seen this year's Best Foreign Language Film, "Kolya." If you want to participate in the cultural conversation, you've got to do the homework.

Most nights, in any case, we are not at the opera; we are at home. The 9 decline of hobbies, like that of so many forms of American sociability, can in part be ascribed to television. Dad's not in his basement workshop;

he's sitting on the couch. The prime law of hobbies—absorbing but not transforming—manifests itself in TV's formal necessities. Real drama demands transformation: the protagonist (and the audience) is different at the end of the story than at the beginning. The sitcom, TV's dominant form, requires an amiable stasis: the natural order is presented, gently ruffled and 30 minutes later restored. No one can change because next week the same characters must interact in the same way. Furthermore, TV stimulates that other hobby replacement, recreational shopping. The modest accomplishment of putting coins in an album is replaced by the pseudoaccomplishment of buying something, as advertised on TV.

On my bookshelf is a set of 1960 World Book Encyclopedias, the set   10
I grew up with. Volume "H" devotes six and a half pages to the entry on hobbies. The 1995 Grolier Multimedia Encyclopedia, a CD-ROM bundled with the Macintosh my daughter and I use, has no listing for hobby. In the shift between these two encyclopedias, we can see the shift in the cultural meaning of hobbies.

The World Book essay begins, "HOBBY can be almost anything a   11
person likes to do in his spare time." (Spare time? Already we're in unfamiliar territory.) Theodore M. O'Leary, the author, goes on to describe four general classes of "all the hundreds of widely popular hobbies"— collections, handicrafts, the arts, games and sports. He helps his readers navigate this sea of leisure in a section called "How to Choose a Hobby." His guiding principle—hobbies balance jobs:

> A person who works indoors all day may be wise to choose an   12
> outdoor hobby. If he works alone, he may find the most pleasure in a group hobby, such as choral singing. A man who works on an assembly line, where he is constantly part of a group, may prefer to relax alone with a stamp collection.

So balanced. So convivial. So humane. It's like Margaret Mead   13
describing a Samoan village.[1] Considering the hobbyist's practical limitations, O'Leary strikes an almost Confucian tone: "A man would be foolish to collect antique automobiles if he lived in an apartment and had no place to put them. He would be wiser to start a coin collection." Wiser indeed. The photographs illustrating the essay depict a family-centered world where white people of all ages gather around common interests. A woman in dark lipstick and a provocatively tight sweater makes leaf prints. A pipe-smoking man builds a model ship.

Though the 1995 Grolier Multimedia Encyclopedia includes no   14
separate listing under "Hobby," a word search yields 28 hits, including

---

[1] Anthropologist Margaret Mead (1901–1978) did considerable fieldwork in the Pacific Islands, including Samoa. [Eds.]

basketry, bird-watching, paper folding, philately, Rockwood ware, terrarium, toy theaters and tropical fish.

One topic ignored by Grolier but much discussed in the 1960 World   15
Book is the hobby as a defense against madness. One article quotes Sir
William Osler, "a famous Canadian doctor," as saying that no man
could really be "happy or safe" without a hobby. The danger Dr. Osler
saw was in the unoccupied mind turned against itself. He may have
been borrowing from another famous doctor, speaking some two centuries before. On Friday, March 22, 1776, riding in a coach from Henley
to Birmingham, Boswell asked Dr. Johnson's[2] counsel on coping with
"hypochondria"—what we would call depression. Johnson's advice—
get a hobby:

> When you have a place in the country, lay out twenty pounds a   16
> year upon a laboratory. It will be an amusement to you. . . . Take a
> course of chemistry or a course of rope-dancing, or a course of anything to which you are inclined at the time. Contrive to have as many
> retreats for your mind as you can, as many things to which it can fly
> from itself.

Boswell, being Boswell, delighted in the attentions of the great man,   17
but contemplated another sort of hobby: "There was a liberal philosophy in this advice which pleased me much. I *thought* of a course of concubinage, but was afraid to mention it." He meant taking up sex as a
hobby.

Of course in modern American life, we don't need sex or hobbies;   18
we can have Prozac instead.

Or the Internet. In the last few years, the World Wide Web has   19
become a promising refuge for would-be hobbyists—both an absorbing
pastime in itself and the gateway to the sites of other pursuits. The
hacker of today is portrayed much like the hobbyist of yesterday: geeky,
socially inept and sexually frustrated—Jubb with a Pentium processor.
Look up "Hobby" on any of the popular search engines—Yahoo, Lycos,
Alta Vista, Infoseek—and you'll be flooded with entries. The search
engine Excite creates 26 subcategories, including pastimes familiar from
the 1960 World Book (models and miniatures) and some new ones
(guns, pets and smoking).

Browsing the subtopics, I encountered an entirely new hybrid   20
hobby, garden railroading, an activity popular enough for a doctrinal
rift. On its Web site, Aristo-Craft Trains notes, "There are two schools of
thought on garden railroading; one is to have a garden with trains running through it and the other is to replicate the landscape typical of

---

[2] James Boswell (1740–1795) wrote *The Life of Samuel Johnson,* a classic biography of the leading literary scholar and critic of his time (1709–1784). [Eds.]

full-size trains." These two ideologies—the whimsical and the authentic, the bucolic and the industrial, fiction and nonfiction—are expressed through two magazines, Garden Railways and Finescale Railroader, formerly Outdoor Railroader. I'd like to think that the editorial staffs refuse to speak. (Gardening itself, incidentally, remains a popular hobby, but to a purist its taxonomy is tricky. When an activity requires a shovel, free time and a country home, in my opinion it is not a hobby; it is social climbing with manure.)

To say that true hobbies lack glamour is another way of saying that 21 they are unratified by talk shows and fashion magazines, uncolonized by advertising. A hobby is pursued simply because it is enjoyable. Could such pastimes be a defense against madness? Maybe. A defense against neurosis, certainly. I miss the particular calm of having an absorbing interest, something that makes an hour pass without my noticing it.

A few weeks ago my daughter, Sophie, age 9, and I went downtown 22 to a hobby shop on West 22d Street. She bought a model kit for a one-twentieth-scale Pontiac Firebird. I hope she'll let me help.

Responding to Reading

1. According to Cohen, what purpose do hobbies serve? Can you think of others? What do all hobbies have in common? Why don't people like Cohen and his friends have hobbies?
2. In paragraph 4, Cohen states what he calls the "prime law of hobbies: Absorbing but Not Transforming. They fill the mind without altering it." Using some typical hobbies as examples, explain what he means. Given this definition, can reading be a hobby? Explain.
3. In paragraph 9 and elsewhere, Cohen talks about the decline of the hobby. In paragraph 19, however, he suggests that "the World Wide Web has become a promising refuge for would-be hobbyists—both an absorbing pastime in itself and the gateway to the sites of other pursuits." Do you agree? Do you think the hobby is in decline or alive and well? What do you think the state of the hobby reveals about present-day society?

LOSING IT

Laura Fraser

Laura Fraser (1961–) is a freelance writer specializing in wellness issues and a contributing editor for Health *magazine. In her book* Losing It *(1997), a survey of Americans' obsession with thinness, she takes a critical look at media images, diet plans and programs, and the multi-million-dollar diet industry in general. In the following essay, part of that book's preface, she describes her own battles with weight and self-esteem, her eventual acceptance of her body, and the extent to which weight is a source of consuming concern for many women.*

Late one afternoon after school, I was sitting in a brown padded chair in a dimly lit office. Across the room, a psychologist with domino-sized sideburns was speaking softly. "Wouldn't you like to be thin, Laurie?" he asked me. "You'd be a pretty girl, you know, if you lost some of that weight."

I had just turned thirteen. I was going through that awful period when it seemed as if everyone was focusing on my body when all I wanted was to be invisible. But like most other girls, I couldn't hide my changing body and forget about it. Nor could I skip out on what seemed to be America's favorite rite of female passage: Dieting.

Actually, I'd been practicing this feminine ritual ever since I started counting calories in kindergarten; I can't remember a time when I wasn't on a diet. But at thirteen, when my already chubby body was growing more curves, it was time to get serious. It was getting more and more clear to me that becoming a woman—at least an attractive and successful woman—meant being able to lose weight. Nothing else seemed to matter more.

My parents sent me to this psychologist—I've repressed his name—to figure out why I was overeating. I had always been chubby, near the top of the growth charts since the age of two, but my parents were worried that my eating and weight were getting out of hand. They had tried everything they could think of to keep me from getting fat: They served low-calorie meals, banished peanut butter and potato chips from the house, encouraged me to be active, and kept a watchful eye on my weight. They did the best they could, but somehow their strategy backfired.

Years later, I could explain to them why it did. Children whose parents worry about their weight and control how much they eat, according to studies, tend to be fatter than kids whose parents are more relaxed. That's because kids who are put on diets don't learn to eat when they're hungry and stop when they're full, as normal kids do, but learn instead to eat according to someone else's rules. Often they break those rules, out of rebellion, as I did, sneaking into the kitchen pantry for handfuls of Cap'n Crunch, and eating huge bowls of ice cream or potato chips at friends' houses, where the cupboards were stocked with forbidden foods.

For kids like me, the pleasure in eating was the taste of independence, but the aftertaste was one of shame. We got called "fat face" in preschool and were told by our dance teachers, at the age of five, that ballerinas never have such big tummies. In grade school, we were mocked in gym class, where we couldn't climb the ropes or run very fast. By junior high, the boys had ruled us out as potential love interests. And so we ate some more, to console ourselves, and what might have been only a slight tendency toward pudginess turned into real fat.

In the mid 1970s, though—at the time I was sitting in that psychol-   7
ogist's office—no one dreamed that putting kids on diets would end up making them fatter. My parents thought, sensibly, that a psychologist would not only put me on a diet but also help me sort out the feelings that led me to overeat. And so I went every week, while the shrink—who, it turned out, never asked me much about my feelings at all—charted my progress on yet another thousand-calorie-a-day diet. I was supposed to weigh myself twice a day and walk a mile every morning, using an early power-walking technique that I knew would greatly amuse the neighborhood kids. I didn't do the jog-walk, for fear of humiliation; I'd already been called a "whale" once on the way to school and didn't want to risk attracting attention to myself. When the psychologist's diet, like every other diet I had tried, didn't work, I simply lied, made up the numbers, and felt guilty.

Did I want to be thin and pretty? the psychologist had asked. Of   8
course I did, more than almost anything. I had all kinds of fantasies about life as a thin teenager. I'd be popular at school, especially with the guys, who would ask me to dances and stop being so quick to announce that they wanted to be "just friends." I would feel smug next to the cheerleaders, knowing I could be one of them if I wanted to, but I'd rather not. I'd get chosen for teams, and run the fifty-yard dash as fast as the kid in gym class who made fun of me for being slow. I would eat like a normal person, wear colorful clothes (I always dressed in dark brown to look thinner), and make my parents happy. The desire to be thin, and the knowledge that I was falling short, was the soundtrack to my childhood, always playing somewhere in the background.

"Yes," I whispered to the psychologist. "I want to be skinny."   9

He nodded approvingly, and told me we were going to try some-   10
thing different that day. My parents said he practiced something called "behavior modification," which I gathered had to do with changing people's eating habits. I'd heard that these behavior modification shrinks gave people little shocks when they ate something wrong, the way you might experiment on rats in a maze. I was scared, imagining that this psychologist, whom I didn't like or trust, would hook me up to an electric machine and give me some sort of shock treatment for being fat. I told myself to be brave: It would be worth it to lose weight.

Instead, to my great relief, he said we'd try hypnosis. Before we   11
began, he asked me to tell him all the "bad" foods I liked to eat. I knew which ones he was talking about, because at the time I believed there were only two food groups: "good" and "bad." Good food included cottage cheese, D-Zerta Jell-O, and celery sticks. Bad food meant just about

anything else. Whatever tasted good seemed to be fattening and made you feel bad about yourself for eating it. So I gave the shrink a really good list of bad food: Sugar Babies, hot tamales, cookie dough, long john doughnuts, Hostess fruit pies, and pizza. He sank into his avocado green executive chair, tapped his fingers together, and thought for a while. Then he told me to lean back and get comfortable.

He led me through a series of deep relaxation exercises, instructing 12 me to breathe deeply, to clench and release the muscles up and down my body, and to imagine my thoughts floating out the window. In no time at all I was surfing the clouds. Then the psychologist began telling me elaborate stories about the foods I'd listed. He started by describing the factory where the candy was made, where workers spat, dripped sweat, and blew their noses into large vats of syrupy concoctions. Rats climbed in and out of the cookie dough, leaving behind chocolate chip–sized turds. The long johns weren't really filled with cream, but were stuffed with rancid Crisco. It was Charlie and the Chocolate Factory in hell. My stomach was beginning to turn.

Then came the pièce de résistance: the pizza. The psychologist told 13 me to imagine picking up a piece of hot, juicy, deep-dish pizza, covered with thick mozzarella that stretched away from my fingers in long, greasy strings. I took a big bite of the pizza, sank my teeth into a piece of sausage, and hit on something hard. I worked and worked at chewing the tough clump of meat, but it wouldn't give. I stuck my fingers into my mouth and pulled out a large, bony mass of gristle. Sticking out of the gristle were big tufts of slippery pig's hair.

"Pig," the psychologist intoned in his professionally soothing voice. 14 "Pig, pig. Isn't that disgusting?" Later it would occur to me that hair probably doesn't grow on gristle. But at the time I was too grossed out to think clearly. Pig, I kept thinking to myself. That's what I was: A big, fat pig. After what seemed like hours, the fifty minutes were up, and the psychologist told me I was gradually going to become aware of my surroundings again, feel myself sitting in the chair, and finally open my eyes.

"How did you feel?" he asked eagerly. "Did you feel like throwing up?" 15

I nodded yes. I felt sick to my stomach. I felt terribly ashamed of myself. Fortunately, some tough part of my thirteen-year-old self felt 16 like leaving and never coming back again. I suppose the psychologist's technique, which is called aversion therapy, was, to some degree, a success. I never did eat sausage again. I felt like a pig. And I would learn to throw up "bad" food.

And so my career as a dieter began in earnest. When I look back at 17 photos of myself from that age, I'm surprised: I was plump, but hardly fat. Yet at the time it felt as if no one in the world was as fat as I was. Now it seems to me that if everyone hadn't paid so much attention to my weight, it wouldn't have been such a problem. I might have been a little heavy, since I come from sturdy stock on both sides of the family, but I probably wouldn't have been driven to overeat compulsively. I'll never be sure. All I know is that when I finally ended my dieting career a few years ago—prematurely, since most women continue well into retirement—I found that left alone, with some exercise, my weight stabilized somewhere above the cultural ideal, but not fat.

My dieting career wasn't unusual; worse than some, and far better 18 than others. I went on five-hundred-calorie-a-day diets and attended Weight Watchers meetings after school. I learned to make "pancakes" out of a piece of crumbled-up bread blended with powdered milk, liquid sweetener, egg white, water, and artificial maple flavoring. I forever ruined my reputation as a cook in my family by feeding them "Fish Delish" one evening, a Weight Watchers recipe concocted from, as I recall, catfish, canned red cabbage, and mandarin oranges packed in saccharin-laced syrup. I weighed and measured my food, kept detailed lists of how much I ate, and stepped on the scale every day. Whatever diet I went on—and there were many—the results were always the same: I gained the weight back, and felt more and more like a failure. I binged on Sundays and promised to be good again on Monday. I hated my body and ate to feel better. By the end of high school, at five feet six inches tall, I weighed 175 pounds. Desperate to lose weight by college, I starved myself and learned to throw up what I ate.

Bulimia was uncommon then, or at least rarely admitted. There was 19 no such word yet—no eating disorders therapists, no support groups, and certainly no celebrities like Jane Fonda, Princess Diana, or Paula Abdul who had struggled with the problem publicly and somehow salvaged their pride. I first learned about the practice, I believe, in an Ann Landers column. A reader wrote in asking if eating and then vomiting up the food was a good way to lose weight. After consulting one of her medical experts, Ann said she didn't think it was such a great idea, and cautioned that you might not get rid of all the calories since some would be absorbed too quickly.

I put the newspaper down and went to the bathroom to tickle my 20 throat. It took me about a year to learn to vomit neatly, no hands, using only my stomach muscles. By that time, my weight had dropped to 130 pounds, and everyone congratulated me on my fabulous willpower and my newly thin body. Still unhappy with my weight, I became addicted to the feeling of control and the physical after-buzz that came with vomiting. I flushed away my feelings and self-respect several times a day, completely numb.

In some ways, I was fortunate that my dieting and weight obsession 21 took such a drastic turn, because it forced me to reckon with the problem. I had to change: At some point I realized that bulimia had taken over my life, and I wanted it back again. I couldn't keep wasting my time and energy in an endless, secret ritual of self-destruction. I had to stop throwing up in order to grow up. It took me years to recover, to go back to the beginning and learn how to eat like a child again, a kid who was never told that foods were "bad" or "good," and who learned to satisfy herself. It took me even longer to feel comfortable and cheerful in a body that was, without vomiting, about twenty pounds heavier than the ideal.

The more I pulled myself out of my own eating disorder, the more   22
I became aware of how many other women were struggling with the same pressures to be thin. I noticed those women whose feet were pointed the wrong way in bathroom stalls, flushing more than once; I realized there are many, many more women who don't have a full-blown eating disorder, but whose lives are nevertheless consumed by dieting and worries about their weight. They live with a low-grade preoccupation that continually erodes their self-esteem, and it just seems normal to them. Surprisingly, it didn't seem to matter much whether those women were actually fat. Women I thought looked normal, attractive, and healthy would confess their eating sins to me and complain about how they felt so huge. Almost no woman I knew, fat or thin, felt satisfied with her appetites or comfortable in her own skin.

These weight preoccupations take many forms. Some women count   23
the fat grams in every morsel of food they eat and tally them up against the minutes they'll have to spend on the StairMaster. Others weigh themselves each morning, bargain with themselves over what they can eat for lunch, and wonder whether their colleagues or lovers will notice that extra half pound. Some worry that being thirty pounds heavier than a ridiculously thin ideal means they'll die early of heart disease, diabetes, or cancer; they resolve once again to try something drastic— no matter how unhealthy—to lose that weight. Others diet in front of their families and friends but eat cookies in secret, comforting themselves; later, they feel bad, and bemoan their self-indulgence and weakness. Almost all of us live under the false illusion that if we just controlled ourselves, ate and exercised exactly the right amount, we could become an ideal size. In the meantime, we stand before our mirrors in scrutiny, pinching our flesh, allowing our talents, achievements, and beauty to diminish before our size.

Many people have observed that women in the United States, in the   24
last century and particularly in the last two decades, are living hectic lives, holding down two jobs: the traditional one of being a sexually desirable mother and wife, and the newer one of working to make a living. The truth is that we hold down three jobs, and the third is, in part, an expression of the uneasiness we feel about the tension between the other two. The third job is being thin.

Most of us are convinced it's an important job. For one thing, our   25
efforts to control our weight give us the illusion that we have control

over at least one part of our chaotic lives. And it's the most visible part: Being thin sends a visual message to the world that a woman is competent at her other two jobs. She works hard at being attractive, and is therefore good at her traditional job of being a desirable sexual object, romantic partner, and consumer. By being lean, she also conveys the idea that she's disciplined, efficient, and in control of herself, which makes her an ideal employee in today's competitive work world. But the pursuit of thinness—which, unless you're born with the genes of a jeans model, is time-consuming, stressful, and psychologically debilitating—really prevents women from being successful at either job. It keeps us from having real control over our own bodies, and our own lives.

Very few American women I know are like some Italian friends of 26 mine, who take passionate interest in what they cook and eat. They drizzle olive oil on vegetables with abandon, relish every bite of their meals, and eat dessert or not as they please. Eating, for them, is a sensual experience, not a fearful one. They never feel guilty afterward. Food isn't "good" or "bad" depending on the calories or fat grams it contains, but according to how fresh it is and how lovingly prepared. My Italian friends don't binge when they're upset, because food doesn't have the power to overwhelm or hurt them. When they're finished eating, they're satisfied, and they don't think much about food until the next meal; it's only one part of their full lives. They don't worry about their weight and somehow they don't gain any.

Surely there are Italian women who have imported the American 27 bad habit of believing that food, fat, and their own bodies are the enemy. There may even be Italian women who are afraid of olive oil. But it's American women, and white American women in particular—because women of color, who already deviate from the blonde ideal, tend to have more respect for differences in size—who are especially obsessed with their weight. American men are increasingly worried about their weight, too, certainly, but the effects on women are much more penetrating and severe.

I was luckier in my diet career than many women. I was too young 28 to have been given amphetamines, as many women were a decade earlier, with devastating consequences to their health. I was never fat enough to suffer the pain and discrimination that the truly obese endure. I never went on a liquid diet, shedding pounds rapidly only to see them boomerang back again. I didn't get my stomach stapled, my jaw wired, or my intestines shortened. I didn't suffer a stroke after taking over-the-counter diet pills, or die after ingesting herbal weight-loss remedies, as some women have. I wasn't like a very bright and talented college friend of mine, whose bulimia has consumed her life ever since, keeping her in miserable jobs, floating in and out of eating disorders treatment centers, lost and depressed.

I was more fortunate than that. I not only recovered from a serious 29
eating disorder and weight obsession, I developed a healthy, positive,
and downright pleasurable attitude about eating and my own body. But
my awareness of the time and energy I lost, and of what so many other
women continue to lose, haunted me.

Responding to Reading

1. In paragraph 2, Frazer identifies dieting as "America's favorite rite of
   female passage." Why do you think dieting is perceived largely as a *female*
   rite of passage?
2. Frazer says, "The desire to be thin, and the knowledge that I was falling
   short, was the soundtrack to my childhood, always playing somewhere in
   the background" (8). What does she mean? From where are these "messages" coming? TV? Movies? Other sources? What other messages are on
   the soundtrack that plays in the backgrounds of children's and adolescents'
   lives? Are these largely positive or negative messages? Explain.
3. In paragraph 17, Frazer talks of her "career as a dieter"; in paragraph 24,
   she describes "being thin" as a job. In what sense is dieting like a job? In
   what sense is it like a career? Is there a difference?

GETTING AWAY WITH MURDER

Barbara Grizutti Harrison

A frequent contributor to periodicals such as Harper's *and the* New
Republic *and author of a monthly column for* Mademoiselle, *Barbara
Grizutti Harrison (1934–   ) has been noted for her hard-edged journalism,
which she often combines with autobiography. For example, her most famous
book,* Visions of Glory: A History and Memory of Jehovah's Witnesses
*(1978), is a critical but even-handed examination of the religious group, which
Harrison joined at age nine and was a member of for eleven years. A native of
Brooklyn, New York, Harrison has written a novel,* Foreign Bodies *(1984),
as well as a number of travel books and essay collections. Her most recent book
is* An Accidental Autobiography *(1996). A social critic with strong opinions, Harrison has said of contemporary society, "People may not be more selfish than they were before, but they're less ashamed of being selfish." In the
following essay, which appeared in the magazine* Mirabella *in 1994,
Harrison focuses her critical attention on another vexing issue: the increasing
number of claims by those who commit crimes that they are themselves "victims" who don't deserve punishment.*

There's a whole lot of blubbering going on these days; and there's a whole lot of support—even hysterical admiration—for the blubberers.

The rich Menendez brothers, Lyle and Erik, bust into their family's den and fire off sixteen rounds from two 12-gauge shotguns at their parents, who are eating ice cream and strawberries and watching the tube. On the stand, the boys, who are in fact men, offer teary accounts of years of childhood sexual abuse—no corroboration, just awfully convenient allegations. Claiming self-defense, they are rewarded with deadlocked juries[1] and with groupies. Erik's attorney calls the killers "adorable," never mind that the blood and guts of Mom and Pop Menendez had to be scraped off the walls.

In Gainesville, Florida, one Danny Harold Rolling was convicted of having murdered four women and one man, all college students between seventeen and twenty-three years old. After killing one woman as she slept, he stabbed her roommate five times, saying, "Take the pain, bitch. Take the pain." He then stopped for a snack—a banana and an apple—before posing the bodies in "lewd positions." In the courtroom, Rolling was permitted to sing the little love ditties he had composed to a smitten female tabloid TV journalist. Rolling's defense attorney informed the jury that Danny Harold Rolling came from a dysfunctional family.

So what.

Attorney William Kunstler is using what is being called the "black rage" defense on behalf of Colin Ferguson, who shot twenty-five unsuspecting people on a Long Island Rail Road commuter train, killing six and wounding nineteen. Ferguson was driven to a shooting rage because he'd been relegated to second-class citizenship, Kunstler says, and because he had a "pre-existing mental illness." (Maybe the attorney invokes Ferguson's "mental illness" in case any of us remembers that Martin Luther King, Jr., and Fannie Lou Hamer were also victims of racism—as a consequence of which they became prophets and saints.) Tell me this: would *anybody* whose elevator went all the way to the top floor randomly shoot twenty-five dozing citizens?[2]

In *Race Matters*, Cornel West, a professor of religion and director of Afro-American studies at Princeton and the grandson of a Baptist minister, sensibly requires us to acknowledge "the lingering effect of black history—a history inseparable from though not reducible to victimization." But, he writes, to say that "More and more black people [are] vulnerable to daily lives endured with little sense of self and fragile existential moorings . . . is not the same as asserting that individual

---

[1] Both men were eventually found guilty and are now serving prison terms.

[2] Ferguson, who eventually decided to defend himself, was convicted of multiple counts of murder in 1995. [Eds.]

black people are not responsible for their actions—black murderers and rapists should go to jail."

Why is it not possible to say both that any murder is an insane act 7 *and* that any murderer should pay for his crime?

I began obsessively to question our ability to hold these two 8 thoughts in our heads simultaneously in the late 1970s, when a Yale graduate named Richard Herrin killed his girlfriend, twenty-year-old Bonnie Garland, with a claw hammer in her own bed, in her own house, in which her parents and brother and sister were sleeping: "Her head split open like a watermelon," Herrin said. For good measure he'd smashed her larynx and hammered her breast and throttled her. Herrin's lawyer, Jack Litman—the same sweetie pie who defended Robert Chambers, the "preppie murderer"—argued that his client was suffering from "overwhelming stress" and from "transient situational reaction," whatever that is. He managed to convince a malleable jury that Herrin was crazy enough to be excused from maximum responsibility but not so crazy as to be locked up forever: Herrin was found not guilty of murder in the second degree, guilty of manslaughter. His lawyer argued that Herrin's childhood had been traumatic: he'd been abandoned by his father and obliged to work for his stepfather in a flea market, he'd suffered from childhood eczema (otherwise known as a rash) and was a late bed wetter. So when Bonnie told him she wanted to date other guys, he snapped. Or, as Herrin himself put it, he killed Bonnie Garland because he was "out of touch with [his] feelings." And he got away with murder.

If every killer is "disturbed," is no killing a crime? 9

I want to go back for a moment to those Menendezes and to what 10 *Newsweek*'s smart Meg Greenfield said about the alleged systematic abuse they endured: "Can anyone doubt that if such abuse did occur and that if the parents, while they lived, had been convincingly charged with it, they would have, in their turn, suggested that they had been abused as children themselves?"

She has it right. 11

Walter Goodman, the *New York Times*'s TV critic, offers us this daz- 12 zling TV vignette, which would be ever so funny if it were not ever so true: a woman called Adrienne comes on a television talk show to speak of having been forced to have oral sex with her father when she was eight. A man called Michael talks of having had oral sex with his older sister when he was seven. "But wait. Here comes Adrienne's father, with roses, and he reveals that he was homosexually raped when he was five. And here comes Michael's sister, with a doll and the announcement. 'I'm a victim, too.'"

How far back can we go? If you were victimized by your father who 13 was in turn victimized by his father who was . . . see what I mean? That road leads to Adam and Eve. That road leads to a signpost: if everyone is to blame, no one is to blame.

In a book called *What You Can Change and What You Can't*, Martin 14
E. P. Seligman, Ph.D., professor of clinical psychology at the University of Pennsylvania, says that in studies claiming to demonstrate the effect of major childhood traumas on adult personality "the influence is barely detectable. . . . Bad childhood events, contrary to the credo, do not mandate adult troubles—far from it. There is no justification, according to these studies, for blaming your adult depression, anxiety, bad marriage, drug use, sexual problems, unemployment, beating up your children, alcoholism, or anger on what happened to you as a child." In the current love-the-victim/hug-the-inner-child climate, Seligman is not likely to be given much talk-TV time.

But wait! Seligman says the studies were "methodologically inade- 15
quate anyway. They failed, in their enthusiasm for human plasticity, to control for genes."

For *genes!* Genes are big now. 16

Writing in *Time*, columnist Dennis Overbye says: "Scientists say 17
they are on the verge of pinning down genetic and biochemical abnormalities that predispose their bearers to violence. An article in the journal *Science* last summer carried the headline EVIDENCE FOUND FOR A POSSIBLE 'AGGRESSION' GENE."

I say a predisposition (unproven) is not a life sentence or a doom. I 18
say we all know we can compensate for our weaknesses and even—if they threaten other people—for our strengths. You are not permitted to murder people. Period. No matter what the ideological flavor of the day—environmental or genetic—you are not allowed, and that's that.

A ruthless Freudian determinism is yielding to a banal biological 19
determinism: if your mommy and daddy didn't do it, your genes did. There is no room left for freedom or for grace; no room, for example, for the arrival of the accidental person or event that changes, converts, transforms and lifts us. (Did you know that the man who wrote "Amazing Grace" was a slave trader—until he, who "was blind," saw, with life-changing light, the foul error of his ways?)

We have relentlessly and stupidly separated the individual and the 20
community; in effect, we have said that what is good for one is not necessarily good for all, and vice versa. I do not believe this. It is a gross and coarse polarization. We are all individuals within a community. We are accountable to that community, which requires, if it is to retain sanity, retribution. *Forgive yourself*, the talkshow gurus say—that's what one priest said to Bonnie Garland's killer. But accountability has to precede forgiveness for it not to be a rotten farce.

I can remember when we believed in Judgment Day—a day not 21
arranged by the Almighty to allow us to "get in touch with our feelings."

Cornel West argues, and I agree, for a return to spiritual values, 22
community values, for—conservatives don't have a lock on this—family values. These words make people nervous; they're afraid their liberty will be threatened. I say: how free are we now? How free are Jose and Kitty Menendez? How free are the man and the women killed in their youth by a self-romanticizing singing serial killer? Do you think Bonnie Garland's younger sister will ever feel free?

Suppose I'm wrong. Perhaps God is an invention; perhaps it's naive 23
to believe in free will. Albert Camus, who was quite sure there is no God and not at all sure that we are capable of exercising free will, had this formula: *act* as if you had free will. And, as my father used to say: don't let those suckers on the radio—or on the television—get to you.

The O. J. Simpson story broke as this issue was going to press. I do not 24
know whether Mr. Simpson is guilty of double murder as charged, but—in keeping with the times—he was certainly positioning himself as victim when he, who made it a practice to beat his wife, wrote: "At times I have felt like a battered husband or boyfriend," standing truth on its head.

Responding to Reading

1. Harrison does not attempt to be an objective journalist in this essay. In paragraph 1, for example, she refers to those who claim victim status as "blubberers," and in paragraph 5, she suggests that Colin Ferguson is a man whose "elevator [doesn't go] all the way to the top floor." Find other examples of such casual, even irreverent, language in the essay. Do you think such language diminishes the strength of Harrison's arguments, or do you believe it gives her essay a refreshing honesty? Explain your position.
2. Do you believe the "dysfunctional family," "black rage," or "disadvantaged background" defense is ever a valid one? Under what circumstances, if any, should a murderer's background absolve him or her or mitigate guilt?
3. In paragraph 20, Harrison says that "accountability has to precede forgiveness for it not to be a rotten farce." What does she mean? Do you agree with her?

LIFE IN PRISON

Webb Hubbell

A long-time friend of Bill Clinton and Hillary Rodham Clinton, Webb Hubbell (b. 1948–) was appointed Associate Attorney General during the first Clinton term. He resigned in 1994 amid allegations that he had embezzled hundreds of thousands of dollars from clients and partners of the Rose Law Firm in Little Rock, Arkansas (where Mrs. Clinton had once been a partner). After pleading guilty, he served a twenty-one-month jail term beginning in August 1995, first in the Cumberland Federal Correctional Institute in Maryland and later at a halfway house in Washington. He continues to be dogged by accusations that he received special favors from the White House after his resignation and that he has not been forthcoming with information pertaining to the Whitewater investigation. He is currently researching alternative sentencing proposals for a Washington think tank. In the following essay, written for George magazine shortly after he completed his prison sentence, Hubbell describes life in prison as an "insider" and proposes reforms he believes would reduce the rate of criminal recidivism.

When General William Sherman marched to the sea through 1 Georgia during the Civil War, he burned everything in his path, including the city of Atlanta. Last year, I found myself in Atlanta, not in a vibrant part of Olympic City but in a five-by-seven-foot jail cell, scared and hardly in a mood for contemplating history's lessons. But as the damp, cold cell became my reality and I tried to sleep amid the night noises of an inner-city jail, I thought about the ironies of fate that had brought me in chains to the city of flames.

Sherman's strategy shortened the war, but it left a wound that took 2 more than 100 years to heal. As a boy growing up in Memphis, Montgomery, and Little Rock, I witnessed how much of the South, subjected to the harsh policies of Reconstruction, had taken out its anger on blacks. We saw discrimination in housing, schools, transportation, and at lunch counters. We lived unequal and separate lives. The racial epithets and jokes I heard at school every day were only the symptoms of decades of resentment. Today, we are again a nation at war with our own citizens. In the past two decades, we have been fighting a War on Drugs and a War on Crime—battles not nearly as decisive as the one Sherman waged, of course, but we have ignited the same flames of bitterness and hatred. This time, 100 years may not be long enough to extinguish the fire.

As Arkansas's chief justice and then as associate attorney general of 3 the United States, I never dreamed I would be locked behind bars. I had always been on the other side of the fence. Yet there I was, guilty of mail and tax fraud, serving a 21-month sentence in federal prison that began on August 7, 1995. In a strange way, I was prepared for the humbling experience imprisonment is bound to be. I had anticipated the humiliation of strip searches and the depersonalization, shame, and discomfort of being shackled and handcuffed while walking through a federal courthouse or through the halls of Congress when I was called upon to testify in the Whitewater hearings. I committed a serious crime, and I caused serious harm to my friends and family. I went through a long period of denial, convinced that things could be worked out, that surely I would never get to the point of pleading guilty and actually going to prison. I was overwhelmed by guilt. Something inside me knew that I needed a period of self-examination—a chance for introspection. I decided to treat each difficult moment as one more opportunity to strip myself of yet another layer of pride and so get to the core of my heart and soul.

What I did not anticipate was being enlightened in a profound way. 4 Suddenly, I was seeing the impact of orders I had given and reports I had read from an inmate's perspective. In 1993, for example, when a rumor had circulated that all Cuban prisoners were going to be deported, I had approved a standard lockdown of all federal inmates to prevent violent incidents. The prisoners were to be confined to their cells—no recreation, no TV, no movement—until the rumor could be proven wrong. Two years later, I personally experienced a lockdown the week after Congress failed to address the disparity in federal sentencing guidelines for possession of crack versus cocaine. (Today, one has to possess 100 times as much powder cocaine as crack to trigger the same mandatory penalties.) I saw the fear of violence in the faces of guards and inmates alike—the tension and disruption. I listened with keen interest as they talked about the rioting, stabbings, and fires that had erupted during the Cuban lockdown I had ordered. Although a lockdown is meant to stem violence, more often it inspires inmates to start fires in their cells, create weapons, and go on strikes in protest.

At Justice, I used to read reports that certain high-profile prisoners 5 had been sent to segregated housing for their own protection, which sounded smart and compassionate to me. In prison, I learned that segregated housing means being "sent to the hole"—locked in a small cell 23 hours a day, with minimal access to a phone or reading and writing materials. No one wants to be sent to the hole.

Before I went to prison, I never thought twice about directing that 6 an inmate be transferred to another facility or sent to a local county jail to testify in a case. Yet, as an inmate in 1995, I personally experienced a routine transfer to another facility. Such a procedure can easily become what prisoners call "diesel therapy"—weeks of spending nights in county jails and days shackled on buses or on "Con Air."

As associate attorney general, I listened to debates about changing 7 the federal sentencing guidelines and heard people say, "Webb, we can't do that. We can't be perceived as being soft on crime." Although I thought I was fair and had all the insight necessary, it took families and the faces of real people for me to understand the consequences. It had never occurred to me that so many well-intentioned, educated, and serious soldiers in this war against crime were repeating the same mistakes that were the mark of Reconstruction. Not until I was forced by my own crimes to do what I so often counsel my children to do—walk in the other person's shoes—did I begin to see that our seemingly well-reasoned, short-term solutions to crime and punishment are a disaster.

The statistics I had read during my career in the justice system 8 should have signaled an alarm to my southern soul—forged as it was by the destructive legacy of racism. Since 1980, our nation's prison population has almost quadrupled. We have built more federal prisons in the past 16 years than were constructed in the rest of our century. At Justice, we faced an intense demand to create new prison bed space. The issue dominated every budget session, and we constantly found the money for new construction by borrowing from other programs. This demand for prison space was not driven by an acceleration in the nation's crime rate, which has been stable overall and declining for certain types of crime since the 1970s. The prison-space crisis was created by the simple fact that we are incarcerating more nonviolent offenders—and for longer sentences. In 1994, 92 percent of federal prisoners were incarcerated for committing nonviolent crimes, costing taxpayers more than $23,000 per year per inmate.

The U.S. incarcerates its citizens at five times the rate of Canada and 9 seven times that of most European democracies, even though our overall crime rates are similar. For some crimes, the victim rates are actually lower in the U.S. For example, assault with force claims 2.2 percent of the American population as victims per year, compared with 2.8 for Australia. For robbery, 1.7 percent of Americans are victimized annually; in Spain, it's 2.9 percent.

Yet I was as short-sighted as the rest. Political wisdom has long dic- 10 tated that the only solution to stopping crime and drug use is harsher sentences. By not listening to my southern soul, I put political expediency ahead of conscience—always a sure path to ruin and chaos.

One of the ironies of being in prison is that the thing you lose is the 11 very thing you gain. I'm talking about time. Time in prison is different than it is in the outside world. In the outside world, time is a flash flood, a whirling blur of forces and temptations, choices and consequences. In prison, time stops. You suddenly have time to face who you are. The prison that I was assigned to had no outer walls to barricade me in, but I couldn't escape from myself or my fellow inmates. Privacy was a precious commodity. I learned to sneak away on Sunday mornings, sit in the ball-field bleachers, and lose myself in the lush choral programs of the nearby college radio station. I learned to wear headphones when I slept to drown out the cacophony, and I woke up in the middle of the night so I could read without the noise. The most treasured jobs in prison are the ones that either grant privacy during the day or keep a man so busy that time will pass more quickly.

Still, from the 6 A.M. wake-up call, most of the day is spent talking 12 to other inmates—while you work, eat your meals, during recreation, or while you're just sitting in the dorm or cell. Everyone wants to discuss their case, their family problems, their dreams for the future, and, most of all, their frustrations. We all shared one thing: loneliness and a boundless longing for family and friends. So we talked. As I listened to story after story and learned to glean truth from fiction, I began to see a criminal justice system that was broken.

What really surprised me was that our prisons had become nothing 13 more than warehouses. I met inmates who desperately wanted to use their time to get an education, to learn to read and write, or to obtain a skill so when they finally got out, they might break the grip of the criminal cycle and begin to live clean, productive lives. Dedicated professionals within the Bureau of Prisons (BOP) wanted to help, but they were not given the opportunity or were so frustrated by what they saw that they had given up. There were virtually no educational or training programs, or any attempt to allow an inmate to improve himself.

I will never forget a 19-year-old man who had been in and out of 14 correctional facilities since he was 13. One day, he pulled me aside and asked me to help him address a Christmas card to his mother. He had been in federal prison for more than a year and a half, and he couldn't even address an envelope. Although his lack of education can't be blamed on the prison system, his prison time could have been put to much more productive use, for his sake and society's.

From the reports of other inmates and from firsthand experience, I 15 discovered that there is severe overcrowding and dismal, dangerous conditions in our state and local facilities. I saw 30 people in a cell built to house eight and people taking turns sleeping to avoid lying on urine-soaked floors. Prison overcrowding creates an atmosphere of distrust and a tendency toward violence. Anyone in such a situation might resort to force, threats, or betrayal. The most hardened prisoner may explode at an insignificant event that involves neither cruelty nor pain but is perceived as an insult. As we dehumanize prisoners, we leave them with no will to behave like citizens. The more we pile on such insults as chain gangs and stun belts—shame in the name of punishment and control—the less chance there is for the restorative process of confession, penance, and forgiveness.

I saw too many inmates who reminded me of the canary in a story 16 told by a Baptist preacher in Little Rock. The bird was accidentally sucked into the vacuum cleaner, then washed and dried with a blow-dryer. When the owner asked what happened, he was told, "He's been sucked in, washed up, and blown over. Now he just sits there, staring, with neither joy nor song." Our prisons are filled with men without hope—no chance for joy or song.

Everyone in prison ultimately receives a nickname. The man 17 who dubbed me Big Easy is a 30-year-old college-educated African-American who had owned several successful night clubs in Pennsylvania. His wife is a physician. He is a loving father to his two children.

When I met him, he had already served more than four years in prison. He had refused to allow the FBI to set up a drug sting operation in one of his clubs, so he became another target of their investigation and was eventually convicted of using part of his business loans to pay off his wife's medical school loans. During his last year in prison, he helped me see our justice system through the eyes of a young black man.

Before his arrest, he kept his head clean shaven and drove a Jaguar. 18 He was routinely pulled over by police, searched, and questioned simply because of the color of his skin. After his indictment, he was advised by his lawyers to plead guilty because they believed he would have no chance with the western Pennsylvania jury picked for his case. He said to me, "The judge was white, the jury was white—they would all figure I was a drug dealer. Big Easy, you're the only white man I have ever called a friend."

Several days after the Million Man March in 1995, he said to me, 19 "Big Easy, don't you understand? Black men are being targeted. This country is engaging in genocide of black males." He wasn't being paranoid; he knew the statistics that create such strong feelings in his community. Almost one-third of young black males between the ages of 20 and 29 are in prison or on some form of probation. In certain major cities, the numbers are even higher. Blacks make up 12 percent of the nation's population and 13 percent of its drug users. Yet for drug possession, African-Americans constitute 35 percent of the arrests, 55 percent of the convictions, and 74 percent of the incarcerations. Since 1980, the percentage of minorities in federal prisons has increased from 33 percent to 64 percent, and the number of minority inmates has grown from 8,000 to 65,000. Blacks make up 89 percent of the prisoners who have been sentenced for federal crack-cocaine crimes, while the majority of crack users are white.

I do not believe this disparity is a conscious plan on anyone's part. 20 There is not a racist bone in either President Clinton's or Attorney General Janet Reno's body; I know them both too well. Nor do I believe that previous administrations targeted only African-American males. I know of many dedicated people at Justice and in law enforcement who would resign immediately if they thought they were engaging in what many citizens in the African-American community call genocide or ethnic cleansing—ugly, frightening words.

I have come to believe, however, that regardless of intentions, our 21 crime policies do indeed target minorities. The statistics make an overwhelming prima facie[1] case for discrimination. More important than my own newfound convictions are those of thousands of prisoners who believe they are targeted by a racist system determined to diminish and

---

[1] Legal term for "at first view." [Eds.]

ultimately extinguish them. Their perceptions are becoming their unquestioned reality, and the effect of this reality may one day overwhelm us all.

This belief also grows outside prison, as the families and friends of young African-Americans see their husbands, brothers, and sons heading to jail at an alarming rate. It is no surprise that more and more prosecutors are facing black jurors who say, "I just will not send another child to prison." The African-American community believes there is no dialogue. [22]

In the '60s and early '70s, we knew that we were not winning the war in Vietnam, and our failure to rethink our involvement almost tore this country apart. We are making the same mistake, refusing to address divisive, ineffective policies. Once again, we plant the seeds of disobedience and civil unrest and put into peril the ability of a significant number of our citizens to believe in the legal system. [23]

Some scholars and politicians have justified the disparate impact of our criminal justice system by saying that blacks are more likely than whites to commit crime. This was my reaction when I first confronted these statistics. I was quick to look for explanations in poverty and the effects of centuries of discrimination. But I was taken aback to learn that the proportion of serious, violent crimes committed by blacks has been level for more than a decade. [24]

Again, I do not believe that our leaders in the '80s intended to target only African-American males. They were trying to stem the tide of a growing drug problem. But as with many policies enacted to target crime, we failed to analyze the long-term consequences. [25]

These policies were exacerbated by racism at all levels: More blacks are arrested, they face a predominantly white justice system, and poverty affects the quality of their legal representation. I also believe that the government and police agencies targeting drug crimes have successfully infiltrated, through their informants, the minority drug community while they have either chosen to ignore or have not successfully infiltrated the white drug population. All of these issues need to be addressed. But our criminal justice policy is a good place to start. [26]

Racial injustice—the perception or reality, whatever your point of view—impedes the potentially restorative aspects of prison. An inmate who can accept his past guilt is far down the path toward rehabilitation. In contrast, an inmate who believes he has been racially targeted for persecution is more likely to embrace bitterness and hopelessness than engage in the self-examination necessary to come out of prison with the right attitude. I saw too many inmates use this sense of persecution to avoid admitting they had done anything wrong. Add to this the lack of education or job training, and the circle of futility becomes complete. [27]

If there is one area of agreement developing on both sides of prison 28
walls, it is that the way we sentence people in the federal courts is a failure. In 1987, Congress implemented an experiment called the federal
sentencing guidelines. Congress hoped that setting up a rigid structure
of specific sentences for specific crimes would bring certainty and
equality. Among the goals enumerated by Congress were just punishment, deterrence, incapacitation, and rehabilitation. But judges, probation officers, wardens, and especially inmates know that the experiment
is not meeting those goals. In a recent survey of federal judges, 70 to 80
percent favor major changes in the guidelines. In fact, rehabilitation
seems no longer to be a goal of imprisonment. The most lasting accomplishment of the guidelines experiment has been to mete out long, harsh
sentences to nonviolent offenders.

Time and again, I encountered inmates who had been imprisoned 29
for long periods when they should have been in their communities supporting their families, paying taxes, paying restitution to their victims,
doing community service, and the like. I saw firsthand how the sentencing guidelines have shifted power to prosecutors who are hungry
for convictions. These lawyers can offer felons their only chance for
leniency from the sentencing guidelines by asking judges to grant
"downward departures"—less time in jail—to criminals who help the
prosecution's case by turning informant. Oftentimes, the kingpin or
ringleader gets the lightest sentence—because at the end of an investigation, he or she comes in with good lawyers and makes a deal—while
the underling, who hasn't talked in fear for his or her life, gets more
time behind bars.

One prisoner I knew escaped the coal mines of West Virginia by 30
selling cocaine to lawyers and doctors. When one of these lawyers got
caught, he was only too happy to escape prison by "giving up" his
source. My friend is now serving close to ten years. This man is bright,
articulate, and engaging. He wants to go straight but has few skills and
readily admits that he will violate the law again if the only alternative
is returning to poverty. Upon release, he will face the stigma of being a
felon, with no education, job skills, or support system to get him on his
feet.

It is not just the poor, the unskilled, or the uneducated who leave 31
prison with a lasting stigma and no viable means of re-engaging with
society. Ask the savings and loan president who now sacks groceries, the
corporate executive busing tables in a Mexican restaurant, or the bank
president who is still working at a dry cleaners after being out of prison
for more than a year. We seem to have forgotten the concepts of forgiveness and of paying one's debt to society. For example, President Clinton
recently announced an initiative to weed out health care fraud. Its cornerstone is to prohibit former felons from becoming health care pro-
viders for Medicare and Medicaid. Will people coming out of prison

after serving time for committing nonviolent crimes such as tax evasion or drug possession really be prevented from becoming doctors, nurses, technicians, or physical therapists? There is absolutely no logical link that says a teen picked up for drug possession will grow up to be an adult who overbills Medicare patients. Offenders can and do change.

Yet our leaders usually get tough on crime by further punishing 32 those who are trying to turn their lives around. Do we really intend to create a permanent underclass? If our leaders do, they should be aware that more than one million people come out of our prisons and jails annually. That's equivalent to the entire population of Dallas exiting detention every year.

Are there solutions to this destructive process? Yes. We must admit 33 our mistakes and change course. Are there signs of hope? Yes. In Arizona, the Medical Marijuana Initiative, which legalized the drug for medicinal use, has gained a great deal of attention. What is hardly noticed is that the initiative—passed directly by the citizens—also prohibits incarcerating people convicted of first- or second-time possession charges, offering medical and rehabilitative treatment instead. The people can't trust politicians to have the courage to change sentencing guidelines, so they have to vote for the reform themselves.

The U.S. has always prided itself on being progressive and humane. 34 In keeping with this tradition, Congress mandated the U.S. Sentencing Commission in 1984 to incorporate new understanding about human behavior into the criminal justice system. The Coalition for Federal Sentencing Reform was recently founded in Alexandria, Virginia, to ensure that goal is met. After the group presents its own report on the effects of sentencing guidelines, it wants Congress to review the experiment.

We must put more money into education and job training in pris- 35 ons; in the long run, it will save money. The only creative effort evident at the Cumberland facility where I was held was the Drug and Alcohol abuse program. Eligible inmates who successfully complete the program may get their sentences reduced by up to one year. It was tough, well planned, and I expect it will be extremely successful. Last year, Congress, again fearful of being labeled soft on crime, introduced legislation to eliminate this program. Thank God, the bill failed.

We should offer similar incentives for completion of the high school 36 GED, college equivalency, and job training programs. Alternatives to incarceration, such as community sentences for nonviolent offenders, have been shown to work. Such sentences are often more challenging than employment in prison, cost substantially less, and allow families to remain intact. Nonviolent offenders, while they are on home confinement or living in halfway houses, could clean up streets and parks. Doctors convicted of nonviolent crimes could be treating poor patients instead of sitting in a cell. Lawyers could be serving the elderly or the disadvantaged instead of writing petitions in prison libraries. At Cumberland, five inmates were allowed to work in the community under the supervision of local volunteers. They repaired abandoned housing that was then rented to the elderly. The community benefited, no one was at risk, and the inmates received an enormous sense of accomplishment and of giving something back.

Prison helped me. During those long days and nights, I was forced 37 to confront my crimes, my mistakes, and my weaknesses. I was fortunate in that I have a strong family and a loving wife who stayed with me. I also have a good education and the belief that I have a future. My situation was unique. I constantly received mail and phone calls from friends and enjoyed their frequent visits. I was lucky enough to have people who still cared about me and my family and who allowed me to vent my feelings throughout the many days of intense loneliness and frustration.

Most men and women who enter prison lose their families, have no 38 education, and, thanks to harsh, long sentences for nonviolent crimes, cannot envision a future. They receive no mail, no visits, and they have no one to call. Time crawls in an atmosphere of little hope. If they were given an education and skills, given a sentence that gives them some hope for the future and perhaps allowed them to remain connected to their families, then the restorative aspects of penance might have a chance to work. Congress is now considering proposals to extend mandatory sentencing to 14-year-olds. This is heading in the wrong direction. Those children will be lost forever.

For me, the most difficult part of prison was being separated from 39 my wife and children. The destruction of the family is an everyday consequence for prisoners. Marriages dissolve, children are abandoned, and this cycle only broadens the crime problem. Every visit received was followed by a period of anxiety that my wife and friends would make it home safely. I knew that if anyone close to me was injured or became ill and had to be hospitalized, I couldn't be with them. Many inmates whose parents, brothers, or sisters died while they were in prison were tormented because they couldn't even attend the funeral. Some even severed all emotional ties with home rather than confront their loneliness and pain. Home confinement, home monitoring, and halfway houses place similar restraints on movement as does prison, but they provide greater opportunities for marriages and families to stay intact while resulting in substantial savings to taxpayers.

The bottom line is that we have to stop the rhetoric and simply 40 become more humane. I agree that criminals should be punished. But if we must fight a war against our own citizens, let us use surgical strikes, not nuclear weapons. And let us offer offenders compassion, forgiveness, and the chance for true freedom. If we begin to steer a new course, we will reduce the chance of creating a permanent class of untouchables who are bitter and vengeful. Let's not make the same mistakes we made during Reconstruction. We have a foreign policy that promotes the rebuilding and restoration of our former enemies. We should not have a domestic policy that essentially crushes a class of our own citizens under an iron boot.

While I was incarcerated, I had many discussions about how I would have done my job at Justice differently. A young man who worked with me in the kitchen said before my release, "Big Easy, don't forget us." I answered something like, "Of course I won't. I'll write, I'll keep in touch." And he said, "No, you don't understand. Don't forget us! Tell them what you saw and heard, and maybe if you tell them, they'll listen." I promised I would not forget.

Responding to Reading

1. What did Hubbell learn in prison? Do you think these lessons are permanent ones? Does he ever admit his guilt? Does he show remorse? Do you think he has really changed?
2. Is this essay primarily about Hubbell's prison experience and its enlightening effect on him, or about the problems facing the modern prison system? What do you think his purpose in writing this essay was? How can you tell?
3. In paragraph 21, Hubbell says, "I have come to believe . . . that regardless of intentions, our crime policies do indeed target minorities." Why does he believe this to be the case? Are his arguments convincing? If he is correct, how do you think this inequity in policy affects members of minority groups? The African-American prison population? Our society as a whole?

JUST WALK ON BY

Brent Staples

Brent Staples (1951–) is an editor and writer who studied behavioral science and psychology, taught, and then turned to journalism, writing for the Chicago Sun-Times *and the* New York Times, *on whose editorial board he currently serves. He has also contributed essays to* Harper's *and* Ms. *His memoir,* Parallel Time *(1994), was sparked by his brother's murder in a dispute over a cocaine deal and describes Staples's own internal struggles in crossing back and forth between the black and the white worlds. In the following essay, which originally appeared in* Ms. *in 1986, Staples talks personally about white people's images of black men and how he deals with them.*

My first victim was a woman—white, well dressed, probably in her   1
early twenties. I came upon her late one evening on a deserted street in
Hyde Park, a relatively affluent neighborhood in an otherwise mean,
impoverished section of Chicago. As I swung onto the avenue behind
her, there seemed to be a discreet, uninflammatory distance between us.
Not so. She cast back a worried glance. To her, the youngish black
man—a broad six feet two inches with a beard and billowing hair, both
hands shoved into the pockets of a bulky military jacket—seemed men-
acingly close. After a few more quick glimpses, she picked up her pace
and was soon running in earnest. Within seconds she disappeared into
a cross street.

That was more than a decade ago. I was 22 years old, a graduate stu-   2
dent newly arrived at the University of Chicago. It was in the echo of
that terrified woman's footfalls that I first began to know the unwieldy
inheritance I'd come into—the ability to alter public space in ugly ways.
It was clear that she thought herself the quarry of a mugger, a rapist, or
worse. Suffering a bout of insomnia, however, I was stalking sleep, not
defenseless wayfarers. As a softy who is scarcely able to take a knife to a
raw chicken—let alone hold it to a person's throat—I was surprised,
embarrassed, and dismayed all at once. Her flight made me feel like an
accomplice in tyranny. It also made it clear that I was indistinguishable
from the muggers who occasionally seeped into the area from the surrounding ghetto. That first encounter, and those that followed, signified
that a vast, unnerving gulf lay between nighttime pedestrians—particularly women—and me. And I soon gathered that being perceived as dangerous is a hazard in itself. I only needed to turn a corner into a dicey
situation, or crowd some frightened, armed person in a foyer somewhere, or make an errant move after being pulled over by a policeman.
Where fear and weapons meet—and they often do in urban America—
there is always the possibility of death.

In that first year, my first away from my hometown, I was to   3
become thoroughly familiar with the language of fear. At dark, shadowy intersections in Chicago, I could cross in front of a car stopped at a
traffic light and elicit the *thunk, thunk, thunk, thunk* of the driver—black,
white, male, or female—hammering down the door locks. On less traveled streets after dark, I grew accustomed to but never comfortable with
people who crossed to the other side of the street rather than pass me.
Then there were the standard unpleasantries with police, doormen,
bouncers, cab drivers, and others whose business it is to screen out troublesome individuals *before* there is any nastiness.

I moved to New York nearly two years ago and I have remained an   4
avid night walker. In central Manhattan, the near-constant crowd cover
minimizes tense one-on-one street encounters. Elsewhere—visiting
friends in SoHo, where sidewalks are narrow and tightly spaced buildings shut out the sky—things can get very taut indeed.

Black men have a firm place in New York mugging literature. 5
Norman Podhoretz in his famed (or infamous) 1963 essay, "My Negro
Problem—And Ours," recalls growing up in terror of black males; they
"were tougher than we were, more ruthless," he writes—and as an
adult on the Upper West Side of Manhattan, he continues, he cannot
constrain his nervousness when he meets black men on certain streets.
Similarly, a decade later, the essayist and novelist Edward Hoagland
extols a New York where once "Negro bitterness bore down mainly on
other Negroes." Where some see mere panhandlers, Hoagland sees "a
mugger who is clearly screwing up his nerve to do more than just *ask*
for money." But Hoagland has "the New Yorker's quickhunch posture
for broken-field maneuvering," and the bad guy swerves away.

I often witness that "hunch posture," from women after dark on 6
the warrenlike streets of Brooklyn where I live. They seem to set their
faces on neutral and, with their purse straps strung across their chests
bandolier style, they forge ahead as though bracing themselves against
being tackled. I understand, of course, that the danger they perceive is
not a hallucination. Women are particularly vulnerable to street violence, and young black males are drastically overrepresented among
the perpetrators of that violence. Yet these truths are no solace against
the kind of alienation that comes of being ever the suspect, against
being set apart, a fearsome entity with whom pedestrians avoid making eye contact.

It is not altogether clear to me how I reached the ripe old age of 22 7
without being conscious of the lethality nighttime pedestrians attributed to me. Perhaps it was because in Chester, Pennsylvania, the small,
angry industrial town where I came of age in the 1960s, I was scarcely
noticeable against a backdrop of gang warfare, street knifings, and murders. I grew up one of the good boys, had perhaps a half-dozen fist
fights. In retrospect, my shyness of combat has clear sources.

Many things go into the making of a young thug. One of those 8
things is the consummation of the male romance with the power to
intimidate. An infant discovers that random flailings send the baby bottle flying out of the crib and crashing to the floor. Delighted, the joyful
babe repeats those motions again and again, seeking to duplicate the
feat. Just so, I recall the points at which some of my boyhood friends
were finally seduced by the perception of themselves as tough guys.
When a mark cowered and surrendered his money without resistance,
myth and reality merged—and paid off. It is, after all, only manly to
embrace the power to frighten and intimidate. We, as men, are not supposed to give an inch of our lane on the highway; we are to seize the
fighter's edge in work and in play and even in love; we are to be valiant
in the face of hostile forces.

Unfortunately, poor and powerless young men seem to take all this 9
nonsense literally. As a boy, I saw countless tough guys locked away; I

have since buried several, too. They were babies, really—a teenage cousin, a brother of 22, a childhood friend in his mid-twenties—all gone down in episodes of bravado played out in the streets. I came to doubt the virtues of intimidation early on. I chose, perhaps even unconsciously, to remain a shadow—timid, but a survivor.

The fearsomeness mistakenly attributed to me in public places often has a perilous flavor. The most frightening of these confusions occurred in the late 1970s and early 1980s when I worked as a journalist in Chicago. One day, rushing into the office of a magazine I was writing for with a deadline story in hand, I was mistaken for a burglar. The office manager called security and, with an ad hoc posse, pursued me through the labyrinthine halls, nearly to my editor's door. I had no way of proving who I was. I could only move briskly toward the company of someone who knew me.

Another time I was on assignment for a local paper and killing time before an interview. I entered a jewelry store on the city's affluent Near North Side. The proprietor excused herself and returned with an enormous red Doberman pinscher straining at the end of a leash. She stood, the dog extended toward me, silent to my questions, her eyes bulging nearly out of her head. I took a cursory look around, nodded, and bade her good night. Relatively speaking, however, I never fared as badly as another black male journalist. He went to nearby Waukegan, Illinois, a couple of summers ago to work on a story about a murderer who was born there. Mistaking the reporter for the killer, police hauled him from his car at gunpoint and but for his press credentials would probably have tried to book him. Such episodes are not uncommon. Black men trade tales like this all the time.

In "My Negro Problem—And Ours," Podhoretz writes that the hatred he feels for blacks makes itself known to him through a variety of avenues—one being his discomfort with that "special brand of paranoid touchiness" to which he says blacks are prone. No doubt he is speaking here of black men. In time, I learned to smother the rage I felt at so often being taken for a criminal. Not to do so would surely have led to madness—via that special "paranoid touchiness" that so annoyed Podhoretz at the time he wrote the essay.

I began to take precautions to make myself less threatening. I move about with care, particularly late in the evening. I give a wide berth to nervous people on subway platforms during the wee hours, particularly when I have exchanged business clothes for jeans. If I happen to be entering a building behind some people who appear skittish, I may walk by, letting them clear the lobby before I return, so as not to seem to be following them. I have been calm and extremely congenial on those rare occasions when I've been pulled over by the police.

And on late-evening constitutionals along streets less traveled by, I employ what has proved to be an excellent tension-reducing measure:

I whistle melodies from Beethoven and Vivaldi and the more popular classical composers. Even steely New Yorkers hunching toward night-time destinations seem to relax, and occasionally they even join in the tune. Virtually everybody seems to sense that a mugger wouldn't be warbling bright, sunny selections from Vivaldi's *Four Seasons*. It is my equivalent of the cowbell that hikers wear when they know they are in bear country.

Responding to Reading

1. Staples speaks quite matter-of-factly of the fear he inspires. Does your experience support his assumption that black men have the "ability to alter public space (2)"? Why or why not? Do you believe white men also have this ability? Explain.
2. In paragraph 13, Staples suggests some strategies that he believes make him "less threatening." What else, if anything, do you think he could do? Do you believe he *should* adopt such strategies? Explain your position.
3. Although Staples says he arouses fear in others, he also admits that he himself feels fearful. Why? Do you think he has reason to be fearful?

ON DUMPSTER DIVING

Lars Eighner

> *When Lars Eighner (1948–   ) was eighteen years old, his mother threw him out of her house because she found out he was gay. Then a student at the University of Texas at Austin, Eighner began a series of part-time and dead-end jobs that ended in 1988 when he was fired from his position at an Austin mental hospital and soon after evicted from his apartment. At that point he headed for Los Angeles, spending three years homeless on the streets, shuttling between California and Texas with Lizbeth, his Labrador retriever. During his travels, he began to keep a journal, and these entries, along with letters he wrote to a friend, resulted in the remarkable document* Travels with Lizbeth: Three Years on the Road and on the Streets *(1993), portions of which had been published previously in several different magazines and journals. In the following chapter from that book, originally published in the* Threepenny Review *in 1991, Eighner takes readers on a graphic yet lyrical voyage through the process of scavenging Dumpsters for food and other necessities.*

This chapter was composed while the author was homeless. The present tense has been preserved.

Long before I began Dumpster diving I was impressed with 1
Dumpsters, enough so that I wrote the Merriam-Webster research service to discover what I could about the word *Dumpster*. I learned from
them that it is a proprietary word belonging to the Dempsey Dumpster
company. Since then I have dutifully capitalized the word, although it
was lowercased in almost all the citations Merriam-Webster photo-
copied for me. Dempsey's word is too apt. I have never heard these
things called anything but Dumpsters. I do not know anyone who
knows the generic name for these objects. From time to time I have
heard a wino or hobo give some corrupted credit to the original and call
them Dipsy Dumpsters.

I began Dumpster diving about a year before I became homeless.   2

I prefer the word *scavenging* and use the word *scrounging* when I   3
mean to be obscure. I have heard people, evidently meaning to be
polite, use the word *foraging*, but I prefer to reserve that word for gathering nuts and berries and such which I do also according to the season
and the opportunity. *Dumpster diving* seems to me to be a little too cute
and, in my case, inaccurate because I lack the athletic ability to lower
myself into the Dumpsters as the true divers do, much to their increased
profit.

I like the frankness of the word *scavenging*, which I can hardly think   4
of without picturing a big black snail on an aquarium wall. I live from
the refuse of others. I am a scavenger. I think it a sound and honorable
niche, although if I could I would naturally prefer to live the comfortable consumer life, perhaps—and only perhaps—as a slightly less
wasteful consumer, owing to what I have learned as a scavenger.

While Lizbeth and I were still living in the shack on Avenue B as   5
my savings ran out, I put almost all my sporadic income into rent. The
necessities of daily life I began to extract from Dumpsters. Yes, we
ate from them. Except for jeans, all my clothes came from Dumpsters.
Boom boxes, candles, bedding, toilet paper, a virgin male love doll,
medicine, books, a typewriter, dishes, furnishings, and change, sometimes amounting to many dollars—I acquired many things from the
Dumpsters.

I have learned much as a scavenger. I mean to put some of what I   6
have learned down here, beginning with the practical art of Dumpster
diving and proceeding to the abstract.

What is safe to eat?   7

After all, the finding of objects is becoming something of an urban   8
art. Even respectable employed people will sometimes find something
tempting sticking out of a Dumpster or standing beside one. Quite a
number of people, not all of them of the bohemian type, are willing to
brag that they found this or that piece in the trash. But eating from
Dumpsters is what separates the dilettanti from the professionals.

Eating safely from the Dumpsters involves three principles: using the senses and common sense to evaluate the conditions of the found materials, knowing the Dumpsters of a given area and checking them regularly, and seeking always to answer the question "Why was this discarded?"

Perhaps everyone who has a kitchen and a regular supply of gro- 9 ceries has, at one time or another, made a sandwich and eaten half of it before discovering mold on the bread or got a mouthful of milk before realizing the milk had turned. Nothing of the sort is likely to happen to a Dumpster diver because he is constantly reminded that most food is discarded for a reason. Yet a lot of perfectly good food can be found in Dumpsters.

Canned goods, for example, turn up fairly often in the Dumpsters I 10 frequent. All except the most phobic people would be willing to eat from a can, even if it came from a Dumpster. Canned goods are among the safest of foods to be found in Dumpsters but are not utterly foolproof.

Although very rare with modern canning methods, botulism is 11 a possibility. Most other forms of food poisoning seldom do lasting harm to a healthy person, but botulism is most certainly fatal and often the first symptom is death. Except for carbonated beverages, all canned goods should contain a slight vacuum and suck air when first punctured. Bulging, rusty, and dented cans and cans that spew when punctured should be avoided, especially when the contents are not very acidic or syrupy.

Heat can break down the botulin, but this requires much more 12 cooking than most people do to canned goods. To the extent that botulism occurs at all, of course, it can occur in cans on pantry shelves as well as in cans from Dumpsters. Need I say that home-canned goods are simply too risky to be recommended.

From time to time one of my companions, aware of the source of my 13 provisions, will ask, "Do you think these crackers are really safe to eat?" For some reason it is most often the crackers they ask about.

This question has always made me angry. Of course I would not 14 offer my companion anything I had doubts about. But more than that, I wonder why he cannot evaluate the condition of the crackers for himself. I have no special knowledge and I have been wrong before. Since he knows where the food comes from, it seems to me he ought to assume some of the responsibility for deciding what he will put in his mouth. For myself I have few qualms about dry foods such as crackers, cookies, cereal, chips, and pasta if they are free of visible contaminants and still dry and crisp. Most often such things are found in the original packaging, which is not so much a positive sign as it is the absence of a negative one.

Raw fruits and vegetables with intact skins seem perfectly safe to 15 me, excluding of course the obviously rotten. Many are discarded for minor imperfections that can be pared away. Leafy vegetables, grapes, cauliflower, broccoli, and similar things may be contaminated by liquids and may be impractical to wash.

Candy, especially hard candy, is usually safe if it has not drawn 16 ants. Chocolate is often discarded only because it has become discolored as the cocoa butter de-emulsified. Candying, after all, is one method of food preservation because pathogens do not like very sugary substances.

All of these foods might be found in any Dumpster and can be eval- 17 uated with some confidence largely on the basis of appearance. Beyond these are foods that cannot be correctly evaluated without additional information.

I began scavenging by pulling pizzas out of the Dumpster behind a 18 pizza delivery shop. In general, prepared food requires caution, but in this case I knew when the shop closed and went to the Dumpster as soon as the last of the help left.

Such shops often get prank orders; both the orders and the products 19 made to fill them are called *bogus*. Because help seldom stays long at these places, pizzas are often made with the wrong topping, refused on delivery for being cold, or baked incorrectly. The products to be discarded are boxed up because inventory is kept by counting boxes: A boxed pizza can be written off; an unboxed pizza does not exist.

I never placed a bogus order to increase the supply of pizzas and I 20 believe no one else was scavenging in this Dumpster. But the people in the shop became suspicious and began to retain their garbage in the shop overnight. While it lasted I had a steady supply of fresh, sometimes warm pizza. Because I knew the Dumpster I knew the source of the pizza, and because I visited the Dumpster regularly I knew what was fresh and what was yesterday's.

The area I frequent is inhabited by many affluent college students. 21 I am not here by chance; the Dumpsters in this area are very rich. Students throw out many good things, including food. In particular they tend to throw everything out when they move at the end of a semester, before and after breaks, and around midterm, when many of them despair of college. So I find it advantageous to keep an eye on the academic calendar.

Students throw food away around breaks because they do not know 22 whether it has spoiled or will spoil before they return. A typical discard is a half jar of peanut butter. In fact, nonorganic peanut butter does not require refrigeration and is unlikely to spoil in any reasonable time. The student does not know that, and since it is Daddy's money, the student decides not to take a chance. Opened containers require caution and some attention to the question "Why was this discarded?" But in the case of discards from student apartments, the answer may be that the item was thrown out through carelessness, ignorance, or wastefulness. This can sometimes be deduced when the item is found with many others, including some that are obviously perfectly good.

Some students, and others, approach defrosting a freezer by chuck- 23 ing out the whole lot. Not only do the circumstances of such a find tell the story, but also the mass of frozen goods stays cold for a long time and items may be found still frozen or freshly thawed.

Yogurt, cheese, and sour cream are items that are often thrown out 24 while they are still good. Occasionally I find a cheese with a spot of mold, which of course I just pare off, and because it is obvious why such a cheese was discarded, I treat it with less suspicion than an apparently perfect cheese found in similar circumstances. Yogurt is often discarded, still sealed, only because the expiration date on the carton had passed. This is one of my favorite finds because yogurt will keep for several days, even in warm weather.

Students throw out canned goods and staples at the end of semes- 25 ters and when they give up college at midterm. Drugs, pornography, spirits, and the like are often discarded when parents are expected— Dad's day, for example. And spirits also turn up after big party week- ends, presumably discarded by the newly reformed. Wine and spirits, of course, keep perfectly well even once opened, but the same cannot be said of beer.

My test for carbonated soft drinks is whether they still fizz vigor- 26 ously. Many juices or other beverages are too acidic or too syrupy to cause much concern, provided they are not visibly contaminated. I have discovered nasty molds in vegetable juices, even when the product was found under its original seal; I recommend that such products be decanted slowly into a clear glass. Liquids always require some care. One hot day I found a large jug of Pat O'Brien's Hurricane mix. The jug had been opened, but it was still ice cold. I drank three large glasses before it became apparent to me that someone had added the rum to the mix, and not a little rum. I never tasted the rum, and by the time I began to feel the effects I had already ingested a very large quantity of the bev- erage. Some divers would have considered this a boon, but being sud- denly intoxicated in a public place in the early afternoon is not my idea of a good time.

I have heard of people maliciously contaminating discarded food 27 and even handouts, but mostly I have heard of this from people with vivid imaginations who have had no experience with Dumpsters them- selves. Just before the pizza shop stopped discarding its garbage at night, jalapeños began showing up on most of the discarded pizzas. If indeed this was meant to discourage me it was a wasted effort because I am native Texan.

For myself, I avoid game, poultry, pork, and egg-based foods, 28 whether I find them raw or cooked. I seldom have the means to cook what I find, but when I do I avail myself of plentiful supplies of beef, which is often in very good condition. I suppose fish becomes disagreeable before it becomes dangerous. Lizbeth is happy to have any such thing that is past its prime and, in fact, does not recognize fish as food until it is quite strong.

Home leftovers, as opposed to surpluses from restaurants, are very 29 often bad. Evidently, especially among students, there is a common type of personality that carefully wraps up even the smallest leftover and shoves it into the back of the refrigerator for six months or so before discarding it. Characteristic of this type are the reused jars and margarine tubs to which the remains are committed. I avoid ethnic foods I am unfamiliar with. If I do not know what it is supposed to look like when it is good, I cannot be certain I will be able to tell if it is bad.

No matter how careful I am I still get dysentery at least once a 30 month, oftener in warm weather. I do not want to paint too romantic a picture. Dumpster diving has serious drawbacks as a way of life.

I learned to scavenge gradually, on my own. Since then I have initi- 31 ated several companions into the trade. I have learned that there is a predictable series of stages a person goes through in learning to scavenge.

At first the new scavenger is filled with disgust and self-loathing. 32 He is ashamed of being seen and may lurk around, trying to duck behind things, or he may try to dive at night. (In fact, most people instinctively look away from a scavenger. By skulking around, the novice calls attention to himself and arouses suspicion. Diving at night is ineffective and needlessly messy.)

Every grain of rice seems to be a maggot. Everything seems to stink. 33 He can wipe the egg yolk off the found can, but he cannot erase from his mind the stigma of eating garbage.

That stage passes with experience. The scavenger finds a pair of 34 running shoes that fit and look and smell brand-new. He finds a pocket calculator in perfect working order. He finds pristine ice cream, still frozen, more than he can eat or keep. He begins to understand: People throw away perfectly good stuff, a lot of perfectly good stuff.

At this stage, Dumpster shyness begins to dissipate. The diver, after 35 all, has the last laugh. He is finding all manner of good things that are his for the taking. Those who disparage his profession are the fools, not he.

He may begin to hang on to some perfectly good things for which 36 he has neither a use nor a market. Then he begins to take note of the things that are not perfectly good but are nearly so. He mates a Walkman with broken earphones and one that is missing a battery cover. He picks up things that he can repair.

At this stage he may become lost and never recover. Dumpsters are 37 full of things of some potential value to someone and also of things that never have much intrinsic value but are interesting. All the Dumpster divers I have known come to the point of trying to acquire everything they touch. Why not take it, they reason, since it is all free? This is, of course, hopeless. Most divers come to realize that they must restrict themselves to items of relatively immediate utility. But in some cases the diver simply cannot control himself. I have met several of these pack-rat types. Their ideas of the values of various pieces of junk verge on the psychotic. Every bit of glass may be a diamond, they think, and all that glistens, gold.

I tend to gain weight when I am scavenging. Partly this is because I 38 always find far more pizza and doughnuts than water-packed tuna, nonfat yogurt, and fresh vegetables. Also I have not developed much faith in the reliability of Dumpsters as a food source, although it has been proven to me many times. I tend to eat as if I have no idea where my next meal is coming from. But mostly I just hate to see food go to waste and so I eat much more than I should. Something like this drives the obsession to collect junk.

As for collecting objects, I usually restrict myself to collecting one 39 kind of small object at a time, such as pocket calculators, sunglasses, or campaign buttons. To live on the street I must anticipate my needs to a certain extent: I must pick up and save warm bedding I find in August because it will not be found in Dumpsters in November. As I have no access to health care, I often hoard essential drugs, such as antibiotics and antihistamines. (This course can be recommended only to those with some grounding in pharmacology. Antibiotics, for example, even when indicated are worse than useless if taken in insufficient amounts.) But even if I had a home with extensive storage space, I could not save everything that might be valuable in some contingency.

I have proprietary feelings about my Dumpsters. As I have men- 40 tioned, it is no accident that I scavenge from ones where good finds are common. But my limited experience with Dumpsters in other areas suggests to me that even in poorer areas, Dumpsters, if attended with sufficient diligence, can be made to yield a livelihood. The rich students discard perfectly good kiwifruit; poorer people discard perfectly good apples. Slacks and Polo shirts are found in the one place; jeans and T-shirts in the other. The population of competitors rather than the affluence of the dumpers most affects the feasibility of survival by scavenging. The large number of competitors is what puts me off the idea of trying to scavenge in places like Los Angeles.

Curiously, I do not mind my direct competition, other scavengers, 41 so much as I hate the can scroungers.

People scrounge cans because they have to have a little cash. I have 42 tried scrounging cans with an able-bodied companion. Afoot a can scrounger simply cannot make more than a few dollars a day. One can extract the necessities of life from the Dumpsters directly with far less effort than would be required to accumulate the equivalent value in cans. (These observations may not hold in places with container redemption laws.)

Can scroungers, then, are people who must have small amounts of 43 cash. These are drug addicts and winos, mostly the latter because the amounts of cash are so small. Spirits and drugs do, like all other commodities, turn up in Dumpsters and the scavenger will from time to time have a half bottle of a rather good wine with his dinner. But the wino cannot survive on these occasional finds; he must have his daily dose to stave off the DTs. All the cans he can carry will buy about three bottles of Wild Irish Rose.

I do not begrudge them the cans, but can scroungers tend to tear up 44 the Dumpsters, mixing the contents and littering the area. They become so specialized that they can see only cans. They earn my contempt by passing up change, canned goods, and readily hockable items.

There are precious few courtesies among scavengers. But it is com- 45 mon practice to set aside surplus items: pairs of shoes, clothing, canned goods, and such. A true scavenger hates to see good stuff go to waste, and what he cannot use he leaves in good condition in plain sight.

Can scroungers lay waste to everything in their path and will stir 46 one of a pair of good shoes to the bottom of a Dumpster, to be lost or ruined in the muck. Can scroungers will even go through individual garbage cans, something I have never seen a scavenger do.

Individual garbage cans are set out on the public easement only on 47 garbage days. On other days going through them requires trespassing close to a dwelling. Going through individual garbage cans without scattering litter is almost impossible. Litter is likely to reduce the public's tolerance of scavenging. Individual cans are simply not as productive as Dumpsters; people in houses and duplexes do not move so often and for some reason do not tend to discard as much useful material. Moreover, the time required to go through one garbage can that serves one household is not much less than the time required to go through a Dumpster that contains the refuse of twenty apartments.

But my strongest reservation about going through individual 48 garbage cans is that this seems to me a very personal kind of invasion to which I would object if I were a householder. Although many things in Dumpsters are obviously meant never to come to light, a Dumpster is somehow less personal.

I avoid trying to draw conclusions about the people who dump in 49 the Dumpsters I frequent. I think it would be unethical to do so, although I know many people will find the idea of scavenger ethics too funny for words.

Dumpsters contain bank statements, correspondence, and other 50 documents, just as anyone might expect. But there are also less obvious sources of information. Pill bottles, for example. The labels bear the name of the patient, the name of the doctor, and the name of the drug. AIDS drugs and antipsychotic medicines, to name but two groups, are specific and are seldom prescribed for any other disorders. The plastic compacts for birth-control pills usually have complete label information.

Despite all of this sensitive information, I have had only one apartment resident object to my going through the Dumpster. In that case it turned out the resident was a university athlete who was taking bets and who was afraid I would turn up his wager slips.   51

Occasionally a find tells a story. I once found a small paper bag containing some unused condoms, several partial tubes of flavored sexual lubricants, a partially used compact of birth-control pills, and the torn pieces of a picture of a young man. Clearly she was through with him and planning to give up sex altogether.   52

Dumpster things are often sad—abandoned teddy bears, shredded wedding books, despaired-of sales kits. I find many pets lying in state in Dumpsters. Although I hope to get off the streets so that Lizbeth can have a long and comfortable old age, I know this hope is not very realistic. So I suppose when her time comes she too will go into a Dumpster. I will have no better place for her. And after all, it is fitting, since for most of her life her livelihood has come from the Dumpster. When she finds something I think is safe that has been spilled from a Dumpster, I let her have it. She already knows the route around the best ones. I like to think that if she survives me she will have a chance of evading the dog catcher and of finding her sustenance on the route.   53

Silly vanities also come to rest in the Dumpsters. I am a rather accomplished needleworker. I get a lot of material from the Dumpsters. Evidently sorority girls, hoping to impress someone, perhaps themselves, with their mastery of a womanly art, buy a lot of embroider-by-number kits, work a few stitches horribly, and eventually discard the whole mess. I pull out their stitches, turn the canvas over, and work an original design. Do not think I refrain from chuckling as I make gifts from these kits.   54

I find diaries and journals. I have often thought of compiling a book of literary found objects. And perhaps I will one day. But what I find is hopelessly commonplace and bad without being, even unconsciously, camp. College students also discard their papers. I am horrified to discover the kind of paper that now merits an A in an undergraduate course. I am grateful, however, for the number of good books and magazines the students throw out.   55

In the area I know best I have never discovered vermin in the Dumpsters, but there are two kinds of kitty surprise. One is alley cats whom I meet as they leap, claws first, out of Dumpsters. This is especially thrilling when I have Lizbeth in tow. The other kind of kitty surprise is a plastic garbage bag filled with some ponderous, amorphous mass. This always proves to be used cat litter.   56

City bees harvest doughnut glaze and this makes the Dumpster at 57 the doughnut shop more interesting. My faith in the instinctive wisdom of animals is always shaken whenever I see Lizbeth attempt to catch a bee in her mouth, which she does whenever bees are present. Evidently some birds find Dumpsters profitable, for birdie surprise is almost as common as kitty surprise of the first kind. In hunting season all kinds of small game turn up in Dumpsters, some of it, sadly, not entirely dead. Curiously, summer and winter, maggots are uncommon.

The worst of the living and near-living hazards of the Dumpsters 58 are the fire ants. The food they claim is not much of a loss, but they are vicious and aggressive. It is very easy to brush against some surface of the Dumpster and pick up half a dozen or more fire ants, usually in some sensitive area such as the underarm. One advantage of bringing Lizbeth along as I make Dumpster rounds is that, for obvious reasons, she is very alert to ground-based fire ants. When Lizbeth recognizes a fire-ant infestation around our feet, she does the Dance of the Zillion Fire Ants. I have learned not to ignore this warning from Lizbeth, whether I perceive the tiny ants or not, but to remove ourselves at Lizbeth's first pas de bourrée.[1] All the more so because the ants are the worst in the summer months when I wear flip-flops if I have them. (Perhaps someone will misunderstand this. Lizbeth does the Dance of the Zillion Fire Ants when she recognizes more fire ants than she cares to eat, not when she is being bitten. Since I have learned to react promptly, she does not get bitten at all. It is the isolated patrol of fire ants that falls in Lizbeth's range that deserves pity. She finds them quite tasty.)

By far the best way to go through a Dumpster is to lower yourself 59 into it. Most of the good stuff tends to settle at the bottom because it is usually weightier than the rubbish. My more athletic companions have often demonstrated to me that they can extract much good material from a Dumpster I have already been over.

To those psychologically or physically unprepared to enter a 60 Dumpster, I recommend a stout stick, preferably with some barb or hook at one end. The hook can be used to grab plastic garbage bags. When I find canned goods or other objects loose at the bottom of a Dumpster, I lower a bag into it, roll the desired object into the bag, and then hoist the bag out—a procedure more easily described than executed. Much Dumpster diving is a matter of experience for which nothing will do except practice.

Dumpster diving is outdoor work, often surprisingly pleasant. It is 61 not entirely predictable; things of interest turn up every day and some days there are finds of great value. I am always very pleased when I can

---

[1] A short walking or running step in ballet. [Eds.]

turn up exactly the thing I most wanted to find. Yet in spite of the element of chance, scavenging more than most other pursuits tends to yield returns in some proportion to the effort and intelligence brought to bear. It is very sweet to turn up a few dollars in change from a Dumpster that has just been gone over by a wino.

The land is now covered with cities. The cities are full of Dumpsters. 62 If a member of the canine race is ever able to know what it is doing, then Lizbeth knows that when we go around to the Dumpsters, we are hunting. I think of scavenging as a modern form of self-reliance. In any event, after having survived nearly ten years of government service, where everything is geared to the lowest common denominator, I find it refreshing to have work that rewards initiative and effort. Certainly I would be happy to have a sinecure again, but I am no longer heartbroken that I left one.

I find from the experience of scavenging two rather deep lessons. 63 The first is to take what you can use and let the rest go by. I have come to think that there is no value in the abstract. A thing I cannot use or make useful, perhaps by trading, has no value however rare or fine it may be. I mean useful in a broad sense—some art I would find useful and some otherwise.

I was shocked to realize that some things are not worth acquiring, 64 but now I think it is so. Some material things are white elephants that eat up the possessor's substance. The second lesson is the transience of material being. This has not quite converted me to a dualist,[2] but it has made some headway in that direction. I do not suppose that ideas are immortal, but certainly mental things are longer lived than other material things.

Once I was the sort of person who invests objects with sentimental 65 value. Now I no longer have those objects, but I have the sentiments yet.

Many times in our travels I have lost everything but the clothes I 66 was wearing and Lizbeth. The things I find in Dumpsters, the love letters and rag dolls of so many lives, remind me of this lesson. Now I hardly pick up a thing without envisioning the time I will cast it aside. This I think is a healthy state of mind. Almost everything I have now has already been cast out at least once, proving that what I own is valueless to someone.

Anyway, I find my desire to grab for the gaudy bauble has been 67 largely sated. I think this is an attitude I share with the very wealthy— we both know there is plenty more where what we have came from. Between us are the rat-race millions who nightly scavenge the cable channels looking for they know not what.

I am sorry for them. 68

---

[2] One who believes that material things also exist as spiritual ideals or abstractions. [Eds.]

Responding to Reading

1. In paragraph 6, Eighner explains, "I have learned much as a scavenger. I mean to put some of what I have learned down here, beginning with the practical art of Dumpster diving and proceeding to the abstract." Do you think Eighner's purpose goes beyond educating his readers? What other purpose do you think he might have?

2. What surprised you most about Eighner's essay? Did any information embarrass you? Repulse you? Make you feel guilty? Arouse your sympathy? Arouse your pity? Explain your response. Do you think Eighner intended you to feel the way you do?

3. Does Eighner's essay succeed in putting a human face on an abstract problem? Or does the fact that he was able to write and publish a book about his situation lead you to see him as an atypical example rather than as a representative of all homeless people? Does he change the way you feel about the homeless?

FOCUS: WHERE IS TECHNOLOGY TAKING US?

THE GLOBAL VILLAGE[1] FINALLY ARRIVES

Pico Iyer

Born in England to parents who had emigrated from India, Pico Iyer (1957–) attended Oxford University and Harvard. During the 1980s, he was a correspondent for Time *magazine, focusing on international affairs, and he continues to contribute essays and reviews to that magazine as well as to the* Partisan Review, *the* Village Voice, *and the (London)* Times Literary Supplement. *His books include* Video Nights in Kathmandu and Other Reports from the Not-So-Far-East *(1988), a humorous look at encounters between Eastern and Western cultures;* Cuba and the Night *(1995), a novel; and* Tropical Classical: Essays from Several Directions *(1997). In the following essay, which was written for* Time *in 1993, Iyer suggests that the blending of international cultures he observes at home in Southern California is becoming the paradigm for the entire world.*

This is the typical day of a relatively typical soul in today's diversi- 1 fied world. I wake up to the sound of my Japanese clock radio, put on a T-shirt sent me by an uncle in Nigeria and walk out into the street, past German cars, to my office. Around me are English-language students from Korea, Switzerland and Argentina—all on this Spanish-named road in this Mediterranean-style town. On TV, I find, the news is in Mandarin; today's baseball game is being broadcast in Korean. For lunch I can walk to a sushi bar, a tandoori palace, a Thai café or the newest burrito joint (run by an old Japanese lady). Who am I, I some- times wonder, the son of Indian parents and a British citizen who spends much of his time in Japan (and is therefore—what else?—an American permanent resident)? And where am I?

I am, as it happens, in Southern California, in a quiet, relatively 2 uninternational town, but I could as easily be in Vancouver or Sydney or London or Hong Kong. All the world's a rainbow coalition, more and more; the whole planet, you might say, is going global. When I fly to

---

[1] The term *global village* was coined in 1967 by Canadian cultural critic Marshall McLuhan to describe an increasingly interdependent world, linked by electronic technology. [Eds.]

Toronto, or Paris, or Singapore, I disembark in a world as hyphenated as the one I left. More and more of the globe looks like America, but an America that is itself looking more and more like the rest of the globe. Los Angeles famously teaches 82 different languages in its schools. In this respect, the city seems only to bear out the old adage that what is in California today is in America tomorrow, and next week around the globe.

In ways that were hardly conceivable even a generation ago, the 3 new world order is a version of the New World writ large: a wide-open frontier of polyglot terms and postnational trends. A common multiculturalism links us all—call it Planet Hollywood, Planet Reebok or the United Colors of Benetton. *Taxi* and *hotel* and *disco* are universal terms now, but so too are *karaoke* and *yoga* and *pizza*. For the gourmet alone, there is *tiramisù* at the Burger King in Kyoto, echt[2] angel-hair pasta in Saigon and enchiladas on every menu in Nepal.

But deeper than mere goods, it is souls that are mingling. In 4 Brussels, a center of the new "unified Europe," 1 new baby in every 4 is Arab. Whole parts of the Paraguayan capital of Asunción are largely Korean. And when the prostitutes of Melbourne distributed some pro-condom pamphlets, one of the languages they used was Macedonian.[3] Even Japan, which prides itself on its centuries-old socially engineered uniculture, swarms with Iranian illegals, Western executives, Pakistani laborers and Filipina hostesses.

The global village is defined, as we know, by an international youth 5 culture that takes its cues from American pop culture. Kids in Perth and Prague and New Delhi are all tuning in to *Santa Barbara* on TV, and wriggling into 501 jeans, while singing along to Madonna's latest in English. CNN (which has grown 70-fold in 13 years) now reaches more than 140 countries; an American football championship pits London against Barcelona. As fast as the world comes to America, America goes round the world—but it is an America that is itself multi-tongued and many hued, an America of Amy Tan and Janet Jackson and movies with dialogue in Lakota.[4]

For far more than goods and artifacts, the one great influence being 6 broadcast around the world in greater numbers and at greater speed than ever before is people. What were once clear divisions are now tangles of crossed lines: there are 40,000 "Canadians" resident in Hong Kong, many of whose first language is Cantonese. And with people come customs: while new immigrants from Taiwan and Vietnam and India—some of the so-called Asian Calvinists—import all-American values of hard work and family closeness and entrepreneurial energy to

---

[2] Real, authentic. [Eds.]
[3] Melbourne is in Autralia, Macedonia in eastern Europe. [Eds.]
[4] Native American language used in the movie *Dances with Wolves*. [Eds.]

America, America is sending its values of upward mobility and individualism and melting-pot hopefulness to Taipei and Saigon and Bombay.

Values, in fact, travel at the speed of fax; by now, almost half the 7 world's Mormons live outside the U.S. A diversity of one culture quickly becomes a diversity of many: the "typical American" who goes to Japan today may be a third-generation Japanese American, or the son of a Japanese woman married to a California serviceman, or the offspring of a Salvadoran father and an Italian mother from San Francisco. When he goes out with a Japanese women, more than two cultures are brought into play.

None of this, of course, is new: Chinese silks were all the rage in 8 Rome centuries ago, and Alexandria before the time of Christ was a paradigm of the modern universal city. Not even American eclecticism is new: many a small town has long known Chinese restaurants, Indian doctors and Lebanese grocers. But now all these cultures are crossing at the speed of light. And the rising diversity of the planet is something more than mere cosmopolitanism: it is a fundamental recoloring of the very complexion of societies. Cities like Paris, or Hong Kong, have always had a soigné, international air and served as magnets for exiles and émigrés, but now smaller places are multinational too. Marseilles speaks French with a distinctly North African twang. Islamic fundamentalism has one of its strongholds in Bradford, England. It is the sleepy coastal towns of Queensland, Australia, that print their menus in Japanese.

The dangers this internationalism presents are evident: not for 9 nothing did the Tower of Babel collapse. As national borders fall, tribal alliances, and new manmade divisions, rise up, and the world learns every day terrible new meanings of the word Balkanization.[5] And while some places are wired for international transmission, others (think of Iran or North Korea or Burma) remain as isolated as ever, widening the gap between the haves and the have-nots, or what Alvin Toffler has called the "fast" and the "slow" worlds. Tokyo has more telephones than the whole continent of Africa.

Nonetheless, whether we like it or not, the "transnational" future is 10 upon us: as Kenichi Ohmae, the international economist, suggests with his talk of a "borderless economy," capitalism's allegiances are to products, not places. "Capital is now global," Robert Reich, the Secretary of Labor, has said, pointing out that when an Iowan buys a Pontiac from General Motors, 60% of his money goes to South Korea, Japan, West Germany, Taiwan, Singapore, Britain and Barbados. Culturally we are being re-formed daily by the cadences of world music and world fiction: where the great Canadian writers of an older generation had names like Frye and Davies and Laurence, now they are called Ondaatje and Mistry and Skvorecky.

---

[5] Breaking up of a region into smaller, often hostile groups. [Eds.]

As space shrinks, moreover, time accelerates. This hip-hop mish-   11
mash is spreading overnight. When my parents were in college, there
were all of seven foreigners living in Tibet, a country the size of Western
Europe, and in its entire history the country had seen fewer than 2,000
Westerners. Now a Danish student in Lhasa is scarcely more surprising
than a Tibetan in Copenhagen. Already a city like Miami is beyond the
wildest dreams of 1968; how much more so will its face in 2018 defy our
predictions of today?

It would be easy, seeing all this, to say that the world is moving   12
toward the *Raza Cósmica* (Cosmic Race), predicted by the Mexican
thinker José Vasconcelos in the '20s—a glorious blend of mongrels and
mestizos.[6] It may be more relevant to suppose that more and more of
the world may come to resemble Hong Kong, a stateless special economic zone full of expats[7] and exiles linked by the lingua franca[8] of
English and the global marketplace. Some urbanists already see the
world as a grid of 30 or so highly advanced city-regions, or technopoles,
all plugged into the same international circuit.

The world will not become America. Anyone who has been to a   13
baseball game in Osaka, or a Pizza Hut in Moscow, knows instantly that
she is not in Kansas. But America may still, if only symbolically, be a
model for the world. *E Pluribus Unum*, after all, is on the dollar bill. As
Federico Mayor Zaragoza, the director-general of UNESCO, has said,
"America's main role in the new world order is not as a military superpower, but as a multicultural superpower."

The traditional metaphor for this is that of a mosaic. But Richard   14
Rodriguez, the Mexican-American essayist who is a psalmist for our
new hybrid forms, points out that the interaction is more fluid than that,
more human, subject to daily revision. "I am Chinese," he says,
"because I live in San Francisco, a Chinese city. I became Irish in America. I became Portuguese in America." And even as he announces this
new truth, Portuguese women are becoming American, and Irishmen
are becoming Portuguese, and Sydney (or is it Toronto?) is thinking to
compare itself with the "Chinese city" we know as San Francisco.

Responding to Reading

1. Do you see any evidence in your community of the exchange of languages,
    goods, values, and people Iyer describes? Do you see it at your school? Give
    specific examples. How has technology made this exchange possible? Do

---

[6] People of mixed race. [Eds.]

[7] Expatriates (that is, those from other countries).

[8] A common language used for the purposes of commerce among people who generally speak different languages. [Eds.]

you think Ted Gup (p. 567) and Gregory J. E. Rawlins (p. 565) consider the global village to be as inclusive as Iyer does? Explain.
2. Do you believe the global village Iyer describes has brought with it an increased understanding and knowledge (or tolerance) of other cultures and nations? If so, how? If not, why not?
3. In paragraph 9, Iyer touches on some of the possible negative effects of the global village. Can you think of others? For example, what *personal* price, if any, do we pay for the increasingly multicultural and multinational nature of our world?

PREGNANT WITH POSSIBILITY

Gregory J. E. Rawlins

Gregory J. E. Rawlins (1958–) received his bachelor's degree in mathematics from the University of the West Indies and his doctorate in computer science from the University of Waterloo. Currently a professor of computer science at Indiana University, he is the author of numerous scholarly articles, as well as the textbooks Foundations of Genetic Algorithms *(1991) and* Compared to What? An Introduction to the Analysis of Algorithms *(1992). A popular speaker on issues of electronic publishing, Rawlins has also published two books on technology for a general audience:* Moths to the Flame: The Seductions of Computer Technology (1996) *and* Slaves of the Machine: The Quickening of Computer Technology *(1997). The following selection from* Moths to the Flame *argues that computer technology has the grim potential to increase the divisions among the world's citizens in terms of money and power relationships.*

Only connect! That was the whole of her sermon. Only connect the prose and the passion, and both will be exalted, and human love will be seen at its highest.

—E. M. Forster, *Howards End*

Today's computer technology is rapidly turning us into three completely new races: the superpoor, the rich, and the superrich. The superpoor are perhaps eight thousand in every ten thousand of us. The rich —me and you—make up most of the remaining two thousand, while the superrich are perhaps the last two of every ten thousand. Roughly speaking, the decisions of two superrich people control what almost two thousand of us do, and our decisions, in turn, control what the remaining eight thousand do. These groups are really like races since the group you're born into often determines which group your children will be born into.

Only the rich and superrich have the opportunity, education, and resources to own and use computer technology. It's hard to get excited about computers when you're busy starving to death; or living in a tense matrix of drugs and crime and fear; or being forced to prostitute yourself for food and shelter; or being repressed by your own government.

A boy in Bangladesh, a girl in Somalia, or—perhaps saddest of all— many ghetto children in the world's richest countries, might never be able to step onto the world stage that is the net. Working their way among the destroyed buildings and equally destroyed social structures of their environment, they are permanently disenfranchised from the world many of us take for granted. Computers alone cannot erode that mountain of destitution.

Today, we number nearly six thousand million people, but we have only five hundred million telephones—one for each twelve of us. Half of us have never placed a single telephone call in our lives. There are already well over a hundred million computers, and over sixteen million more are added each year—with the number rising rapidly. In a decade or two, five hundred million of us may be connected to a computer network. That connection might eventually make the difference between being an information-starved peon and a global villager.

It is often said that computers will destroy ancient power centers and enfranchise greater masses of people. It is true that in America over a third of all households already have computers. Yet that proportion jumps to well over half for homes with university graduates and to three quarters for homes with incomes above seventy-five thousand dollars. If that pattern is repeated in the world as a whole, computers might merely ensure that the ancient pyramid of power extends into a thin sharp spike, with a tiny few determining the fate of the millions.

By the time that happens, however, there should be a few hundred million people active on the net. (Just think, a global electronic community of a hundred million gossipers.) Perhaps among them will be enough people both connected to the rest of us and compassionate enough to speak for the dispossessed. Perhaps.

Every new communication medium is special. But the net is extra special, because we, the users, are the ones making it, not some faceless corporation. It's growing as fast as it is because it merges two hugely endowed technologies: computers and communications. But it's also growing rapidly because the more people who get on it, the more valuable access to it becomes. Like telephones and fax machines, tennis clubs and bars, the net becomes more attractive as more of us join it. So it's likely that everyone who can afford to will be on the net in fairly short order.

We're gregarious, gossipy creatures, continually talking to each other to find out what others think—or what we should think. Out of that reliance we build community, whether in a pub, at the laundromat, or on the net. Without that communication, that bonding, human society would cease to be. But the net presents numerous dangers too. The search for communion could easily turn into a flight from community. Don't like your neighbors? No problem; turn off, tune in, and drop into a whole other world of people you never have to actually touch. Further, as its demographics broaden and it goes commercial, the net's content will inevitably become more splintered, more trivialized, and perhaps more acrimonious. That's the way of things.

Computers won't bring about a better world—perhaps nothing can 9 do that. But they certainly can change the world: in some ways for the better; in others, for the worse. That's the nature of today's new technology. By changing things in fundamental ways right before our eyes, it lets us see more clearly who we really are by showing us what we truly value. Sometimes, perhaps far more often than necessary, what we see is an ugly side of human nature.

Still, the net today is a glorious experiment. Considering that no 10 one planned it and no one controls it, it shows us that we can make very complex systems work despite our many flaws. As it quickly commercializes, and changes drastically, we should work to preserve some of its more democratic and humane characteristics. Because that's something to be proud of.

Only connect. 11

Responding to Reading

1. Why does Rawlins open and close his essay with a reference to E. M. Forster's phrase "Only connect"? What does this phrase mean? How might it apply to Pico Iyer's essay (p. 561)?

2. In the opening paragraphs of his essay, Rawlins discusses the gap (technological as well as economic) between "the superpoor, the rich, and the superrich" (1). He concludes, "Computers alone cannot erode [the] mountain of destitution" poor people confront (3). Do you think the fact that they do not have access to the technology so many others take for granted could actually make poor people's lives *worse?* Explain.

3. Would you describe Rawlins's attitude as essentially optimistic or pessimistic? On what issues would he and Ted Gup (p. 567) agree? On what issues would he and Iyer agree?

THE END OF SERENDIPITY

Ted Gup

Born in Lima, Ohio, Ted Gup (1950–   ) attended Brandeis University and Trinity College in Dublin, Ireland. He also holds a law degree from Case Western Reserve University. He was a staff writer at the Washington Post *for ten years and, later, a correspondent for* Time *magazine. Currently a professor in the College of Journalism at the University of Maryland and at*

Georgetown University, Gup has published articles and essays on a variety of topics in Gentleman's Quarterly, Sports Illustrated, *the* Smithsonian, *and* National Geographic, *among others. The following essay appeared in the* Chronicle of Higher Education *in 1997. In it, Gup suggests that in terms of gaining access to information, the information superhighway may have "shortened the time between departure and arrival, but gone is all scenery in between."*

When I was a young boy, my parents bought me a set of *The World* 1 *Book Encyclopedia.* The 22 burgundy-and-gold volumes lined the shelves above my bed. On any given day or night I would reach for a book and lose myself for hours in its endless pages of maps, photographs, and text. Even when I had a purpose in mind—say, for instance, a homework assignment on salamanders—I would invariably find myself reading instead of Salem and its witch hunts or of Salamis, where the Greeks routed the Persians in the fifth century B.C. Like all encyclopedias of the day, it was arranged alphabetically, based on sound and without regard to subject. As a child, I saw it as a system wondrously whimsical and exquisitely inefficient. Perfect for exploration. The "S" volume alone could lead me down 10,000 unconnected highways.

The world my two young sons inherit is a very different place. That 2 same encyclopedia now comes on CD-ROM. Simply drop the platinum disk into the A-drive and type in a key word. In a flash the subject appears on the screen. The search is perfected in a single keystroke—no flipping of pages, no risk of distraction, no unintended consequences. And therein lies the loss.

My boys belong to an age vastly more efficient in its pursuit of 3 information but oblivious to the pleasures and rewards of serendipity. From Silicon Valley to M.I.T., the best minds are dedicated to refining our search for answers. Noble though their intentions may be, they are inadvertently smothering the opportunity to find what may well be the more important answers—the ones to questions that have not yet even occurred to us. I wish, then, to write on behalf of random epiphanies and the virtues of accidental discovery—before they, too, go the way of my old Remington manual[1].

My boys are scarcely aware that they are part of a grand experiment 4 in which the computer, the Internet, and the World-Wide Web are redefining literacy and reshaping the architecture of how they learn. These innovations are ushering in a world that, at least to my tastes, is entirely too purposeful—as devoid of romance us an arranged marriage. Increasingly, we hone our capacity to target the information that we seek. More ominous still, we weed out that which we deem extraneous.

---

[1] A manual—that is, non-electric—typewriter. [Eds.]

In a world of information overload, this ability to filter what reaches us has been hailed as an unqualified good. I respectfully disagree.

Consider, for example, those of my sons' generation who are learn- 5 ing to read the newspaper on a computer screen. They do not hold in their hands a cumbersome front page but instead see a neat menu that has sliced and diced the news into user-friendly categories. They need not read stories but merely scan topical headings—sports, finance, entertainment. The risk that they or any readers will inadvertently be drawn into a story afield from their peculiar interests, or succumb to some picture or headline, grows ever more remote. The users define their needs while the computer, like an overly eager waiter, stands ready to deliver, be it the latest basketball scores, updates of a personal stock portfolio, or tomorrow's weather. In my youth, information was a smorgasbord. Walking past so irresistible an array of dishes, I found it impossible not to fill my plate. Today, everything is à la carte.

There are moral consequences to being able to tailor the information 6 that reaches us. Like other journalists, I have spent much of my life writing stories that I knew, even as I worked on them, would not be welcomed by my readers. Accounts of war, of hardship or want seldom are. But those stories found their way first into readers' hands and then into their minds. They were read sometimes reluctantly, sometimes with resentment, and, most often, simply because they appeared on the printed page. Doubtless the photo of a starving child or a string of refugees stretching above the morning's shredded wheat and orange juice may be viewed as an unsightly intrusion, but it is hard to ignore.

In cyberspace, such intrusions will become less frequent. There will 7 be fewer and fewer uninvited guests. Nothing will come unless summoned. Unless the mouse clicks on the story, the account will not materialize. And who will click on the story headlined "Rwandans Flee," "Inner-City Children Struggle," or even "Endangered Butterflies Fight for Survival"? If the mouse is a key, it is also a padlock to keep the world out.

Those already on the margins of our consciousness—the homeless, 8 the weak, the disenfranchised—are being pushed right off the page, exiled into cyberspace and the ever-expanding domain of the irrelevant. Already the phrase "That's not on my screen" has found its way into common parlance. In the end, self-interest may be the most virulent form of censorship, inimical to compassion and our sense of community. It is the ultimate V-chip, this power to sanitize reality, to bar unpleasantries. "Technology," the Swiss playwright Max Frisch once observed, is "the knack of so arranging the world that we don't have to experience it."

It would be ironic if the computer, this great device of interconnec- 9 tivity, should engender a world of isolationists. Yet increasingly we use its powers to read about ourselves and to feed our own parochial self-interests. Instead of a global village, we risk a race of cyber-hermits. And the World-Wide Web, the promised badge to that which is beyond ourselves, may be yet another moat to protect the self-absorbed.

A friend of mine recently joined Microsoft. He was struck by the 10 youthfulness of those around him and the absolute faith they had that every question had an answer, every problem a solution. It is the defining character of the Microsoft Culture, its celebration of answers. Within that church, there are few Luthers[2] to challenge its orthodoxy. So much energy is spent to produce the right answers that little time is left to ponder the correctness of the questions.

I find it amusing that Bill Gates, shrewd investor that he is, has 11 emerged as one of the world's premier art collectors, acquiring the notebooks of Leonardo da Vinci, the consummate figure of the Renaissance. I wonder: Does he identify with that genius, or, perhaps recognizing the peril in which that humanistic traditon is now placed, is he simply attempting to corner the market on its artifacts?

This is not a revolution but an evolution. In ancient caves can be 12 found flakes of flint left by early humans, evidence of the first impulse to put a point on our tools, to refine them. The computer, with its search engines, is simply an extension of that primal urge. From the Olduvai Gorge[3] to Silicon Valley, we have always been obsessed with bringing our tools to a perfect point. But where knowledge of the world is concerned, I suspect there is some virtue to possessing a blunter instrument. Sometimes a miss produces more than a hit.

Ironically, we continue to call entrées to cyberspace "Web browers," 13 but increasingly they are used not to browse but to home in on a narrow slice of the universe. We invoke mystery with corporate names such as "Oracle," but we measure progress in purely quantitative terms—gigabits and megahertz, capacity and speed. Our search engines carry names such as "Yahoo" and "Excite," but what they deliver is ever more predictable. The parameters of the universe shrink, defined by key words and Boolean filters, sieves that—with each improvement in search engines—increasingly succeed in siphoning off anything less than responsive to our inquiries. The more precise the response, the more the process is hailed as a success.

What has been billed as the information superhighway has, like all 14 superhighways, come with a price. We have shortened the time between departure and arrival, but gone is all scenery in between,

---

[2] The reference is to Martin Luther (1483–1546), the religious reformer who broke with the Catholic Church. [Eds.]

[3] Site in Tanzania where the fossilized remains of many protohumans have been discovered. [Eds.]

reduced to a Pentium blur. We settle for information at the expense of understanding and mistake retrieval for exploration. The vastness of the Internet's potential threatens to shrink into yet another utility. As the technology matures, the adolescent exuberance of surfing the Web yields to the drudgery of yet another commute.

One need not be a Luddite[4] or technophobe to sound a cautionary word in the midst of euphoria over technology. I have a fantasy that one day I will produce a computer virus and introduce it into my own desktop, so that when my sons put in their key word—say, "salamander"—the screen will erupt in a brilliant but random array of maps and illustrations and text that will divert them from their task. This I will do so that they may know the sheer joy of finding what they have not sought. I might even wish for this virus to spread from computer to computer. And I would name this virus for that which ought not to be lost—serendipity.

Responding to Reading

1. According to Gup, how is browsing on the Internet different from browsing through a print encyclopedia? What does he feel has been lost? Do you think he is right?
2. Explain the "moral consequences" Gup discusses in paragraphs 6 through 8. Do you think he is an alarmist, or do you agree that our ability to block unpleasant "intrusions" and "uninvited guests"(7) has potentially serious social implications?
3. In paragraph 9, Gup observes that more and more often, we seem to be using the powers of the computer "to read about ourselves and to feed our own parochial self-interests. " He continues, "Instead of a global village, we risk a race of cyber-hermits." Do you agree? Would Pico Iyer (p. 561)?

Widening the Focus

- Jonathan Kozol, "Savage Inequalities" (p. 100).
- Neil Postman, "Virtual Students, Digital Classrooms" (p. 139)
- Robert Frost, "The Road Not Taken" (p. 718)

---

[4] Name given to groups of laborers who rioted in 1811 and 1816 in parts of England, destroying knitting machines—a new technology—which they believed were responsible for unemployment; more generally, a term for one who opposes new technology. [Eds].

--- **WRITING** ---

The Way We Live Now

1. Who are your heroes? Are they real or fictional? Are they famous? Are they living? Applying the criteria suggested by Jenny Lyn Bader in "Larger Than Life" as well as some criteria of your own to the figures you select, explain why they qualify as heroes.

2. Some of this chapter's essays, such as those by Lars Eighner, Webb Hubbell, and Brent Staples, discuss serious social problems; others, like those by Randy Cohen and Laura Fraser, address what might be called "lifestyle issues." Choose one issue from either category, and discuss its impact on your life and the lives of people you know. (If you like, you may focus on an issue that is not discussed in this chapter's readings.)

3. Identify several "signs of the times," familiar images that you believe typify the way we live now, and write an essay explaining what they tell you about your world.

4. In "Pregnant with Possibility," Gregory J. E. Rawlins expresses concern about the gap between the "superpoor" and the rest of society, a gap that is being exacerbated by the expansion of computer technology. How do you think the dramatic technological changes the nation is experiencing will affect those who live in poverty? Do you see the "savage inequalities" between rich and poor, identified by Jonathan Kozol in his essay in Chapter 2 (p. 100) as inevitably widening? Explain what needs to be done to resolve any problems you identify.

5. Several of the selections in this chapter suggest that some of modern-day society's problems are caused (or at least aggravated) by the media, which expose private lives and turn personal problems into economic commodities. Do you believe the media make social problems worse—or even create social problems? Support your conclusion with examples from essays in this chapter and in Chapter 4 as well as from your own experiences.

6. In "The Making of a Generation," Arthur Levine says, "Every . . . generation is defined by the social events of its age," (1). Identify several pivotal social and political events—local or national—that have had an impact on you and others your age, and explain how these events define your generation.

7. Pico Iyer, Gregory J. E. Rawlins, and Ted Gup regard the future with varying degrees of optimism. What do you predict for our society's future? In light of these predictions, are you optimistic or pessimistic about what lies ahead?

8. Ted Gup believes that many of us use computers "to read about ourselves and to feed our own parochial self-interests" (9); this narrowing of focus from the global to the personal also concerns Wendy Kaminer, whose essay about television talk shows appears in Chapter 4 (p. 000). Kaminer writes, "If all issues are personalized, we lose our capacity to entertain ideas, to generalize from our own or someone else's experiences, to think abstractly" (25). Write an essay in which you explore the tendency that troubles Gup and Kaminer.

9. Do you believe the American family is deteriorating? Are the ties that connect family members weakening? If so, what contemporary social forces do you hold responsible for this decline? If not, how do you explain its continued strength? Consider your own extended family as well as the essays in this chapter or in Chapter 1.

10. As selections like "Just Walk on By" and "Getting Away with Murder" reveal, we live in an increasingly violent society. Logically, then, we should be becoming more and more accustomed to violence. Do your own observations and experiences suggest that we *are* becoming accustomed to violence? If so, what dangers do you see in this attitude? Explain your views in a letter to a local or national government official.

8

MEDICAL PRACTICE AND RESPONSIBILITY

Student Voices

"I In my opinion, there should be very few legal restrictions on what work a scientist should be able to do. However, I do feel that morality and common sense should play a major part in deciding what and how medical research is done.

"I believe people should suffer as little as possible if they have a terminal illness. If a person decides that pain and suffering is unbearable, that person should be able to end his or her life. It should be the person's decision, not someone else's."

—*Todd Lemon*

"Death is a word that frightens me. I prefer not to think of it."

—*Renee Higgins*

"My grandmother tells me that if she ever gets too feeble to take care of herself, I should take her behind the barn and shoot her. She doesn't think it is fair to keep people alive when their time has come. I don't think most of my friends would agree with her. I suppose their attitudes are based on the fear of death we have in this culture. Since we view death as a permanent separation from those we love, we try our best to prevent it. We also look with awe upon those who we think can save us. I think this fear has made us think of doctors as some sort of gods."

—*Elizabeth Zaffarano*

"AIDS is unfortunately here with us, and we must deal with it. This disease affects everybody either directly or indirectly. For this reason, we must all take the responsibility to learn about this disease, to help slow it down, and someday to stop the virus completely."

—*Dave Zimecki*

"I think AIDS is a problem that will always be with us. This means AIDS will get worse and become so widespread that millions will die from it. Sometimes I try to be positive about the disease, but I can't. Maybe it's because I'm a biology major, but I only see a nightmare that will not end any time soon."

—*Jennifer Liebl*

————————— Preparing to Read and Write —————————

Because medical science has made such great advances, it is easy to forget that until the 1930s, doctors could do little more than diagnose most diseases. With the discovery of sulfa drugs and penicillin, the situation changed, and physicians were actually able to cure diseases that had decimated human populations for centuries. Since the mid-1970s, medical science has made tremendous advances toward understanding basic biological processes and prolonging human life. Recently, however, new diseases or new forms of old diseases have threatened to wipe out these gains. For example, AIDS, a disease almost unheard of twenty years ago, afflicts millions of people worldwide, and tuberculosis in new drug-resistant forms (ironically, caused in part by the medications used to *cure* tuberculosis) is making a deadly comeback in American cities. Thus, scientists could once again face the uncomfortable fact that in the near future, epidemics might be as common as they were a hundred years ago.

Like our gains against disease, our advances in medical technology have proved to be a mixed blessing. Although doctors are armed with an array of high-tech equipment, they must face problems this technology has created. For example, how far should doctors go to preserve human life? At what point, if any, does a life become not worth saving? Once this point has been reached, should the patient be allowed to end his or her life? The writers in this chapter struggle with these and other questions. In some cases, they simply define the issues and acknowledge their difficulty. In other cases, they offer answers that at best are tentative or incomplete. Still, writers—along with doctors, ethicists, and theologians—continue to search for answers.

As you read and prepare to write about the selections in this chapter, you may consider the following questions:

- Is the writer a physician? A scientist? A layperson? Does the writer's background make you more or less receptive to his or her ideas?

- On what issue does the writer focus?

- What position does the writer take on the issue? Do you agree or disagree with this position?

- Is the writer's emphasis on the theory or on the practice of medicine?

- What preconceptions do you have about the issue? Does the selection reinforce or contradict your preconceptions?

- What background in science or medicine does the writer assume readers have?

- Is the writer optimistic or pessimistic about the future of medicine? About the future in general?

- Is the writer's purpose to educate? To make readers think about a provocative idea? To persuade them? To warn them?

- In what ways is the selection similar to or different from others in this chapter?

TWO PERSPECTIVES ON MEDICAL PRACTICE AND RESPONSIBILITY

In the following essays, two young doctors write about surprising encounters with unexpected pathologies. "My Own Country," the first chapter of Abraham Verghese's 1994 book of the same name, recounts the case of the first AIDS patient treated in Johnson City, Tennessee. East Indian by birth, Verghese (1956–) studied medicine in Madras before coming to the United States in 1980. He had dealt with many AIDS cases while training in New York and Boston but didn't expect to find a similar epidemic when he joined the staff of a hospital in rural Tennessee. He has said of his experiences, "You are suddenly dealing with people your own age whose plight makes you reflect on your ideas about sex, about social issues, and, of course, about your own mortality." In the second essay, American-trained pediatrician Perri Klass (1958–) recalls her experiences working in a prestigious hospital in India, where patients suffered from ailments that are common there but that she found unfamiliar, even mystifying. A graduate of Harvard Medical School, Klass contributes articles to many popular magazines and has published novels and short stories—including Other Women's Children *(1990)—as well as a book about her first year as a medical student,* A Not Entirely Benign Procedure *(1987), from which "India" is taken.*

MY OWN COUNTRY

Abraham Verghese

Summer, 1985. A young man is driving down from New York to visit his parents in Johnson City, Tennessee.

I can hear the radio playing. I can picture his parents waiting, his mother cooking his favorite food, his father pacing. I see the young man in my mind, despite the years that have passed; I can see him driving home along a route that he knows well and that I have traveled many times. He started before dawn. By the time it gets hot, he has reached Pennsylvania. Three hundred or so miles from home, he begins to feel his chest tighten.

He rolls up the windows. Soon, chills shake his body. He turns the heater on full blast; it is hard for him to keep his foot on the accelerator or his hands on the wheel.

By the time he reaches Virginia, the chills give way to a profuse sweat. Now he is burning up and he turns on the air conditioner, but the perspiration still soaks through his shirt and drips off his brow. His lungs feel heavy as if laden with buckshot. His breath is labored, weighted by fear and perhaps by the knowledge of the burden he is bringing to his parents. Maybe he thinks about taking the next exit off Interstate 81 and seeking help. But he knows that no one can help him, and the dread of finding himself sick and alone keeps him going. That and the desire for home.

I know this stretch of highway that cuts through the Virginia moun- 5 tains; I know how the road rises, sheer rock on one side, how in places the kudzu takes over and seems to hold up a hillside, and how, in the early afternoon, the sun glares directly into the windshield. He would have seen hay rolled into tidy bundles, lined up on the edges of fields. And tobacco plants and sagging sheds with their rusted, corrugated-tin roofs and shutterless side-openings. It would have all been familiar, this country. His own country.

In the early evening of August 11, 1985, he was rolled into the emer- 6 gency room (ER) of the Johnson City Medical Center—the "Miracle Center," as we referred to it when we were interns. Puffing like an over-heated steam engine, he was squeezing in forty-five breaths a minute. Or so Claire Bellamy, the nurse, told me later. It had shocked her to see a thirty-two-year-old man in such severe respiratory distress.

He sat bolt upright on the stretcher, his arms propped behind him 7 like struts that braced his heaving chest. His blond hair was wet and stuck to his forehead; his skin, Claire recalled, was gun-metal gray, his lips and nail beds blue.

She had slapped an oxygen mask on him and hollered for someone 8 to pull the duty physician away from the wound he was suturing. A genuine emergency was at hand, something she realized, even as it overtook her, she was not fully comprehending. She knew what it was not: it was *not* severe asthma, status asthmaticus; it was *not* a heart attack. She could not stop to take it all in. Everything was happening too quickly.

With every breath he sucked in, his nostrils flared. The strap mus- 9 cles of his neck stood out like cables. He pursed his lips when he exhaled, as if he was loath to let the oxygen go, hanging on to it as long as he could.

Electrodes placed on his chest and hooked to a monitor showed his 10 heart fluttering at a desperate 160 beats per minute.

On his chest X ray, the lungs that should have been dark as the night 11 were instead whited out by a veritable snowstorm.

My friend Ray, a pulmonary physician, was immediately sum- 12 moned. While Ray listened to his chest, the phlebotomist drew blood for serum electrolytes and red and white blood cell counts. The respiratory therapist punctured the radial artery at the wrist to measure blood oxygen levels. Claire started an intravenous line. And the young man slumped on the stretcher. He stopped breathing.

Claire punched the "Code Blue" button on the cubicle wall and an 13
operator's voice sounded through the six-story hospital building:
"Code Blue, emergency room!"

The code team—an intern, a senior resident, two intensive care unit 14
nurses, a respiratory therapist, a pharmacist—thundered down the
hallway.

Patients in their rooms watching TV sat up in their beds; visitors 15
froze in place in the corridors.

More doctors arrived; some came in street clothes, having heard 16
the call as they headed for the parking lot. Others came in scrub suits.
Ray was "running" the code; he called for boluses of bicarbonate and
epinephrine, for a second intravenous line to be secured, and for Claire
to increase the vigor but slow down the rate of her chest compressions.

The code team took their positions. The beefy intern with Nautilus 17
shoulders took off his jacket and climbed onto a step stool. He moved
in just as Claire stepped back, picking up the rhythm of chest compression without missing a beat, calling the cadence out loud. With locked
elbows, one palm over the back of the other, he squished the heart
between breastbone and spine, trying to squirt enough blood out of it to
supply the brain.

The ER physician unbuttoned the young man's pants and cut away 18
the underwear, now soiled with urine. His fingers reached for the
groin, feeling for the femoral artery to assess the adequacy of the chest
compressions.

A "crash cart" stocked with ampules of every variety, its defibrilla- 19
tor paddles charged and ready, stood at the foot of the bed as the pharmacist recorded each medication given and the exact time it was
administered.

The clock above the stretcher had been automatically zeroed when 20
the Code Blue was called. A code nurse called out the elapsed time at
thirty-second intervals. The resident and another nurse from the code
team probed with a needle for a vein to establish the second "line."

Ray "bagged" the patient with a tight-fitting mask and hand-held 21
squeeze bag as the respiratory therapist readied an endotracheal tube
and laryngoscope.

At a signal from Ray, the players froze in midair while he bent the 22
young man's head back over the edge of the stretcher. Ray slid the laryngoscope in between tongue and palate and heaved up with his left hand,
pulling the base of the tongue up and forward until the leaf-shaped
epiglottis appeared.

Behind it, the light at the tip of the laryngoscope showed glimpses of 23
the voice box and the vocal cords. With his right hand, Ray fed the endotracheal tube alongside the laryngoscope, down the back of the throat,
past the epiglottis, and past the vocal cords—this part done almost
blindly and with a prayer—and into the trachea. Then he connected the

squeeze bag to the end of the endotracheal tube and watched the chest rise as he pumped air into the lungs. He nodded, giving the signal for the action to resume.

Now Ray listened with his stethoscope over both sides of the chest 24 as the respiratory therapist bagged the limp young man. He listened for the muffled *whoosh* of air, listened to see if it was equally loud over both lungs.

He heard sounds only over the right lung. The tube had gone down 25 the right main bronchus, a straighter shot than the left.

He pulled the tube back an inch, listened again, and heard air enter- 26 ing both sides. The tube was sitting above the carina, above the point where the trachea bifurcates. He called for another chest X ray; a radiopaque marker at the end of the tube would confirm its exact position.

With a syringe he inflated the balloon cuff at the end of the endo- 27 tracheal tube that would keep it snugly in the trachea. Claire wound tape around the tube and plastered it down across the young man's cheeks and behind his neck.

The blue in the young man's skin began to wash out and a faint 28 pink appeared in his cheeks. The EKG machine which had spewed paper into a curly mound on the floor, now showed the original rapid heart rhythm restored.

At this point the young man was alive again, but just barely. The 29 Code Blue had been a success.

In no time, the young man was moved to the intensive care unit 30 (ICU) and hooked up via the endotracheal tube to a machine that looked like a top-loading washer, gauges and dials covering its flat surface. Its bellows took over the work of his tired diaphragm.

He came awake an hour later to the suffocating and gagging sensa- 31 tion of the endotracheal tube lodged in his throat. Even as the respirator tried to pump oxygen into his lungs, he bucked and resisted it, tried to cough out the tube. One can only imagine his terror at this awakening: naked, blazing light shining in his eyes, tubes in his mouth, tubes up his nose, tubes in his penis, transfixed by needles and probes stuck into his arms.

He must have wondered if this was hell. 32

The Miracle Center ICU nurses who were experienced—at least in 33 theory—with this sort of fright and dislocation, reassured him in loud tones. Because of the tube passing between his vocal cords and because his hands were tied to prevent his snatching at the tube (an automatic gesture in this setting), he could not communicate at all. With every passing second, his terror escalated. His heart rate rose quickly.

He was immediately sedated with a bolus of morphine injected into 34 one of his lines. He was paralyzed with a curarelike agent, a cousin of the paste used on arrow-tips by indigenous tribes in the Amazon. As the drug shot through his circulation and reached the billions of junctions where nerve met and directed muscle, it blocked all signals and he lay utterly still and flaccid.

The respirator sent breaths into him with rhythmic precision at the 35 rate dialed in by Ray, even throwing in a mechanical sigh—a breath larger than usual—to recruit and keep patent the air sacs in the base of the lung.

The young man's parents now arrived at the hospital and were 36 escorted up to their son's bedside. They had been waiting for him at home. Now they stood, I was told, in utter disbelief, trying to see their son through the forest of intravenous poles and the thicket of tubing and wires that covered him, asking again and again *what* had happened. And *why?*

By the next day the pneumonia had progressed. His lungs were 37 even stiffer, making the respirator work overtime to drive oxygen into him. Ray performed a bronchoscopy, sliding a fiberoptic device into the endotracheal tube. Through the bronchoscope he could see the glossy red lining of the trachea and the bronchi. All looked normal. He directed the bronchoscope as far out as it would go, then passed a biopsy forceps through it and took a blind bite of the air sacs of the lung.

Under the microscope, the honeycomblike air spaces of the lung 38 were congealed with a syrupy outpouring of inflammatory fluid and cells. Embedded in this matrix were thousands upon thousands of tiny, darkly staining, flying-saucerlike discs that the pathologist identified as *Pneumocystis carinii.*

The young man had no predisposing illness like leukemia or cancer 39 that would explain this fulminant pneumonia caused by an innocuous organism.

His immune system *had* to be abnormal.   40

It was clear, though no one had yet seen a case, that he was Johnson 41 City's first case of the acquired immune deficiency syndrome—AIDS.

Word spread like wildfire through the hospital. All those involved 42 in his care in the ER and ICU agonized over their exposure.

The intern remembered his palms pressed against the clammy 43 breast as he performed closed-chest massage.

Claire remembered starting the intravenous line and having blood 44 trickle out and touch her ungloved skin.

The respiratory therapist recalled the fine spray that landed on his 45 face as he suctioned the tracheal tube.

The emergency room physician recalled the sweat and the wet 46 underwear his fingers encountered as he sought out the femoral artery.

Even those who had not touched the young man—the pharmacist, 47 the orderlies, the transport personnel—were alarmed.

Ray worried too; he had been exposed as much as anyone. In the 48 days to follow, he was stopped again and again in the corridor by people quizzing him about the danger, about their exposure. Ray even felt some anger directed at him. As if he, who had done everything right and diagnosed the case in short order, could have prevented this or warned them.

An ICU nurse told me that the young man's room took on a special 49 aura. In the way a grisly murder or the viewing of an apparition can transform an otherwise ordinary abode, so cubicle 7C was forever transformed. Doctors and others in the ICU peeked through the glass, watching the inert body of the young man. His father was seated beside him. The hometown boy was now regarded as an alien, the father an object of pity.

Ray told me how the parents took the news. The mother froze, star- 50 ing at Ray's lips as if he was speaking a foreign language. The father turned away, only the sound of his footsteps breaking the silence as he walked out into the corridor and on out into the parking lot, unable to stay in the building where that word had been uttered.

Much later, the father asked, "But *how* did he get it? How could he 51 have gotten this?"

Ray pointed out that he had had no time to get a history: perhaps 52 they could give him some information. Had their son been healthy in the past year and in the days preceding the trip? Lord, yes! (The father did all the answering.) Did he ever use intravenous drugs? Lord, no! And to their knowledge had he ever had a blood transfusion?

No.   53

Was he married?   54

No.   55

Did he live alone? No, he had a friend in New York.   56

A male friend? Yes . . . they had never met him.   57

"Oh Lord! Is that what you're saying? Is that how he got it? Is my 58 son a queer?"

Ray just stood there, unable to respond to the father's words.   59

The father turned to his wife and said, "Mother, do you hear this? 60 Do you hear this?"

She gazed at the floor, nodding slowly, confirming finally what she 61 had always known.

The mother never left the ICU or her son's side. And in a day or so, 62 the father also rallied around his son, spending long hours with him, holding his hand, talking to him. Behind the glass one could watch as the father bent over his son, his lips moving soundlessly.

He balked when his son's buddies flew down from New York. He 63 was angry, on the verge of a violent outburst. This was all too much. This nightmare, these city boys, this new world that had suddenly engulfed his family.

Ray tried to mediate. But only when it seemed his boy's death was 64 inevitable did the father relent and allow the New Yorkers near him. He guarded the space around his son, marshaling his protection.

The two visitors were men with closely cut hair. One had a pierced 65
ear, purple suede boots, tight jeans and what the ICU ward clerk, Jennie,
described to me as a "New York attitude—know what I mean?"

Jennie said the other friend, clearly the patient's lover, was dressed 66
more conservatively and was in his early forties. She thought he was "a
computer person." She remembers the tears that trickled continuously
down his cheeks and the handkerchief squeezed in his hand. Jennie
thought the mother wanted to talk to her son's lover. He, in turn,
needed badly to talk to anyone. But in the presence of the father there
was no chance for them to speak.

Three weeks after his arrival, the young man died. 67

The New Yorkers left before the funeral. 68

The respirator was unhooked and rolled back to the respiratory 69
therapy department. A heated debate ensued as to what to do with it.
There were, of course, published and simple recommendations for dis-
infecting it. But that was not the point. The machine that had sustained
the young man had come to symbolize AIDS in Johnson City.

Some favored burying the respirator, deep-sixing it in the swampy 70
land at the back of the hospital. Others were for incinerating it. As a
compromise, the machine was opened up, its innards gutted and most
replaceable parts changed. It was then gas disinfected several times.
Even so, it was a long time before it was put back into circulation.

About two months after the young man died, I returned to Johnson 71
City. I had previously worked there as an intern and resident in internal medicine and I was now coming back after completing my training
in infectious diseases in Boston. People who knew me from my resi-
dency days stopped me and told me the sad story of this young man's
homecoming.

But it was not always recounted as a sad story. "Did you hear what 72
happened to Ray?" a doctor asked me. He proceeded to tell me how a
young man had dropped into the emergency room looking like he had
pneumonia but turning out to be "a homo from New York with AIDS."
The humor resided in what had happened to the unsuspecting Ray, the
pie-in-your-face nature of the patient's diagnosis.

Some of the veteran ICU nurses, perhaps because this case broke 73
through their I've-seen-it-all-and-more-honey attitudes, astonished me
with their indignation. In their opinion, this "homo-sex-shual" with
AIDS clearly had no right to expect to be taken care of in our state-of-
the-art, computerized ICU.

When I heard the story, the shock waves in the hospital had already 74
subsided. Everyone thought it had been a freak accident, a one-time
thing in Johnson City. This was a small town in the country, a town of
clean-living, good country people. AIDS was clearly a big city problem.
It was something that happened in other kinds of lives.

INDIA

Perri Klass

The people look different. The examining room is crowded with chil- 1
dren and their parents, gathered hopefully around the doctor's desk,
jockeying for position. Everyone seems to believe, if the doctor gets
close to *my* child everything will be okay. Several Indian medical students are also present, leaning forward to hear their professor's explanations as they watch one particular child walk across the far end of the
room. I stand on my toes, straining to see over the intervening heads so
I, too, can watch this patient walk. I can see her face, intent, bright dark
eyes, lips pinched in concentration. She's about ten years old. I can see
her sleek black head, the two long black braids pinned up in circles over
her ears in the style we used to call doughnuts. All she's wearing is a
long loose shirt, so her legs can be seen, as with great difficulty she wob-
bles across the floor. At the professor's direction, she sits down on the
floor and then tries to get up again; she needs to use her arms to push
her body up.

I'm confused. This patient looks like a child with absolutely classic 2
muscular dystrophy, but muscular dystrophy is a genetic disease carried
on the X chromosome, like hemophilia. It therefore almost never occurs
in girls. Can this be one of those one-in-a-trillion cases? Or is it a more
unusual form of muscle disease, one that isn't sex-linked in inheritance?

Finally the child succeeds in getting up on her feet, and her parents 3
come forward to help her dress. They pull her over near to where I'm
standing, and as they're helping with the clothing, the long shirt slides
up over the child's hips. No, this isn't one of those one-in-a-trillion
cases. I've been watching a ten-year-old boy with muscular dystrophy;
he comes from a Sikh family, and Sikh males don't cut their hair. Adults
wear turbans, but young boys often have their hair braided and pinned
up in those two knots.

Recently I spent some time in India, working in the pediatric 4
department of an important New Delhi hospital. I wanted to learn
about medicine outside the United States, to work in a pediatric clinic
in the Third World, and I suppose I also wanted to test my own medical
education, to find out whether my newly acquired skills are in fact
transferable to any place where there are human beings, with human
bodies, subject to their range of ills and evils.

But it wasn't just a question of my medical knowledge. In India, I 5
found that my cultural limitations often prevented me from thinking
clearly about patients. Everyone looked different, and I was unable to
pick up any clues from their appearance, their manner of speech, their
clothing. This is a family of Afghan refugees. This family is from the

south of India. This child is from a very poor family. This child has a Nepalese name. All the clues I use at home to help me evaluate patients, clues ranging from what neighborhood they live in to what ethnic origin their names suggest, were hidden from me in India.

The people don't just look different on the outside, of course. It 6
might be more accurate to say *the population is different.* The gene pool, for example: there are some genetic diseases that are much more common here than there, cystic fibrosis, say, which you have to keep in mind when evaluating patients in Boston, but which would be a show-offy and highly unlikely diagnosis-out-of-a-book for a medical student to suggest in New Delhi (I know—in my innocence I suggested it).

And all of this, in the end, really reflects human diversity, though 7
admittedly it's reflected in the strange warped mirror of the medical profession; it's hard to exult in the variety of human genetic defects, or even in the variety of human culture, when you're looking at it as a tool for examining a sick child. Still, I can accept the various implications of a world full of different people, different populations.

The diseases are different. The patient is a seven-year-old boy whose 8
father says that over the past week and a half he has become more tired, less active, and lately he doesn't seem to understand everything going on around him. Courteously, the senior doctor turns to me, asks what my assessment is. He asks this in a tone that suggests that the diagnosis is obvious, and as a guest I'm invited to pronounce it. The diagnosis, whatever it is, is certainly not obvious to me. I can think of a couple of infections that might look like this, but no single answer. The senior doctor sees my difficulty and offers a maxim, one that I've heard many times back in Boston. Gently, slightly reprovingly, he tells me, "Common things occur commonly. There are many possibilities, of course, but I think it is safe to say that this is almost certainly tuberculous meningitis."

Tuberculous meningitis? Common things occur commonly? 9
Somewhere in my brain (and somewhere in my lecture notes) "the complications of tuberculosis" are filed away, and yes, I suppose it can affect the central nervous system, just as I can vaguely remember that it can affect the stomach and the skeletal system. . . . To tell the truth, I've never even seen a case of straightforward tuberculosis of the lung in a small child, let alone what I would have thought of as a rare complication.

And hell, it's worse than that. I've done a fair amount of pediatrics 10
back in Boston, but there are an awful lot of things I've never seen. When I was invited in New Delhi to give an opinion on a child's rash, I came up with quite a creative list of tropical diseases, because guess what? I had never seen a child with measles before. In the United States, children are vaccinated against measles, mumps, and rubella at the age of one year. There are occasional outbreaks of measles among college

students, but the disease is now very rare in small children. ("Love this Harvard medical student. Can't recognize tuberculous meningitis. Can't recognize measles or mumps. What the hell do they teach them over there in pediatrics?")

And this, of course, is one of the main medical student reasons for 11 going to study abroad, the chance to see diseases you wouldn't see at home. The pathology, we call it, as in "I got to see some amazing pathology while I was in India." It's embarrassing to find yourself suddenly ignorant, but it's interesting to learn all about a new range of diagnoses, symptoms, treatments, all things you might have learned from a textbook and then immediately forgotten as totally outside your own experience.

The difficult thing is that these differences don't in any way, how- 12 ever tortured, reflect the glory of human variation. They reflect instead the sad partitioning of the species, because they're almost all preventable diseases, and their prevalence is a product of poverty, of lack of vaccinations, of malnutrition and poor sanitation. And therefore, though it's all very educational for the medical student (and I'm by now more or less used to parasitizing my education off of human suffering), this isn't a difference to be accepted without outrage.

The expectations are different. The child is a seven-month-old girl with 13 diarrhea. She has been losing weight for a couple of weeks, she won't eat or drink, she just lies there in her grandmother's arms. The grandmother explains: one of her other grandchildren has just died from very severe diarrhea, and this little girl's older brother died last year, not of diarrhea but of a chest infection. . . . I look at the grandmother's face, at the faces of the baby's mother and father, who are standing on either side of the chair where the grandmother is sitting with the baby. All these people believe in the possibility of death, the chance that the child will not live to grow up. They've all seen many children die. These parents lost a boy last year, and they know that they may lose their daughter.

The four have traveled for almost sixteen hours to come to this hos- 14 pital, because after the son died last year, they no longer have faith in the village doctor. They're hopeful, they offer their sick baby to this famous hospital. They're prepared to stay in Delhi while she's hospitalized, the mother will sleep in the child's crib with her, the father and grandmother may well sleep on the hospital grounds. They've brought food, cooking pots, warm shawls because it's January and it gets cold at night. They're tough, and they're hopeful, but they believe in the possibility of death.

Back home, in Boston, I've heard bewildered, grieving parents say, 15 essentially, "Who would have believed that in the 1980s a child could just die like that?" Even parents with terminally ill children, children who spend months or years getting sicker and sicker, sometimes have great difficulty accepting that all the art and machinery of modern medicine are completely helpless. They expect every child to live to grow up.

In India, it isn't that parents are necessarily resigned, and certainly 16 not that they love their children less. They may not want to accept the dangers, but poor people, people living in poor villages or in urban slums, know the possibility is there. If anything, they may be even more terrified than American parents, just because perhaps they're picturing the death of some other loved child, imagining this living child going the way of that dead one.

I don't know. This is a gap I can't cross. I can laugh at my own 17 inability to interpret the signals of a different culture, and I can read and ask questions and slowly begin to learn a little about the people I'm trying to help care for. I can blush at my ignorance of diseases uncommon in my home territory, study up in textbooks, and deplore inequalities that allow preventable diseases to ravage some unfortunate population while others are protected. But I can't draw my lesson from this grandmother, these parents, this sick little girl. I can't imagine their awareness, their accommodations of what they know. I can't understand how they live with it. I can't accept their acceptance. My medical training has taken place in a world where all children are supposed to grow up, and the exceptions to this rule are rare horrible diseases, disastrous accidents. That is the attitude, the expectation I demand from patients. I'm left most disturbed not by the fact of children dying, not by the different diseases from which they die, or the differences in the medical care they receive, but by the way their parents look at me, at my profession. Perhaps it is only in this that I allow myself to take it all personally.

Responding to Reading

1. Why do you think Verghese describes the examination and treatment of the patient in such detail? What does he hope to accomplish with such a detailed and graphic presentation?
2. How did Verghese's medical team react in 1985 when they heard the patient was gay and had AIDS? Do you think they would react the same way today? Explain.
3. Klass observes that in India, *"The people look different"* (1), *"the diseases are different"* (8), and *"the expectations are different"* (13). Exactly how are they different? How do you account for the differences?
4. How are Klass's and Verghese's attitudes toward their patients alike? How are they different? Do their attitudes change? Do they ever get used to what they see?

5. Both Verghese and Klass had to deal with people's attitudes about death. How did these attitudes make it difficult for them to treat disease?
6. Do Verghese and Klass expect you to identify with the doctors, with the patients, or with both? Explain.

IMELDA

Richard Selzer

A surgeon as well as an accomplished writer, Richard Selzer (1928–   ) was born in Troy, New York, where his father had a family medical practice until his death when Selzer was twelve. Following in his father's footsteps, he attended Albany Medical College and Yale Medical School, later serving on the faculty there as a professor of surgery. Influenced by his artistic mother, Selzer also took an early interest in literature but didn't himself begin writing for publication until he was in his forties. Since then he has published essays and stories in a variety of magazines and journals, and his collections include Mortal Lessons *(1977),* Letters to a Young Doctor *(1982), and* Imagine a Woman *(1991). His latest book is a memoir,* Raising the Dead: A Doctor's Encounter with His Own Mortality *(1994). Of his two professions, Selzer has written, "The surgeon sutures together the tissues of the body to make whole what is sick or injured; the writer sews words into sentences to fashion a new version of human experience." Selzer's work often focuses on the complex relationship between doctor and patient; in the following essay, he recalls a surgeon he worked under in medical school whose compassionate gesture toward a young patient has remained with Selzer all his life.*

I heard the other day that Hugh Franciscus had died. I knew him once. He was the Chief of Plastic Surgery when I was a medical student at Albany Medical College. Dr. Franciscus was the archetype of the professor of surgery—tall, vigorous, muscular, as precise in his technique as he was impeccable in his dress. Each day a clean lab coat monkishly starched, that sort of thing. I doubt that he ever read books. One book only, that of the human body, took the place of all others. He never raised his eyes from it. He read it like a printed page as though he knew that in the calligraphy there just beneath the skin were all the secrets of the world. Long before it became visible to anyone else, he could detect the first sign of granulation at the base of a wound, the first blue line of new epithelium at the periphery that would tell him that a wound would heal, or the barest hint of necrosis that presaged failure. This gave him the appearance of a prophet. "This skin graft will take," he would say, and you must believe beyond all cyanosis, exudation and inflammation that it would.

He had enemies, of course, who said he was arrogant, that he exalted 2 activity for its own sake. Perhaps. But perhaps it was no more than the honesty of one who knows his own worth. Just look at a scalpel, after all. What a feeling of sovereignty, megalomania even, when you know that it is you and you alone who will make certain use of it. It was said, too, that he was a ladies' man. I don't know about that. It was all rumor. Besides, I think he had other things in mind than mere living. Hugh Franciscus was a zealous hunter. Every fall during the season he drove upstate to hunt deer. There was a glass-front case in his office where he showed his guns. How could he shoot a deer? we asked. But he knew better. To us medical students he was someone heroic, someone made up of several gods, beheld at a distance, and always from a lesser height. If he had grown accustomed to his miracles, we had not. He had no close friends on the staff. There was something a little sad in that. As though once long ago he had been flayed by friendship and now the slightest breeze would hurt. Confidences resulted in dishonor. Perhaps the person in whom one confided would scorn him, betray. Even though he spent his days among those less fortunate, weaker than he—the sick, after all—Franciscus seemed aware of an air of personal harshness in his environment to which he reacted by keeping his own counsel, by a certain remoteness. It was what gave him the appearance of being haughty. With the patients he was forthright. All the facts laid out, every question anticipated and answered with specific information. He delivered good news and bad with the same dispassion.

I was a third-year student, just turned onto the wards for the first 3 time, and clerking on Surgery. Everything—the operating room, the morgue, the emergency room, the patients, professors, even the nurses—was terrifying. One picked one's way among the mines and booby traps of the hospital, hoping only to avoid the hemorrhage and perforation of disgrace. The opportunity for humiliation was everywhere.

It all began on Ward Rounds. Dr. Franciscus was demonstrating a 4 cross-leg flap graft he had constructed to cover a large fleshy defect in the leg of a merchant seaman who had injured himself in a fall. The man was from Spain and spoke no English. There had been a comminuted fracture of the femur, much soft tissue damage, necrosis. After weeks of debridement and dressings, the wound had been made ready for grafting. Now the patient was in his fifth postoperative day. What we saw was a thick web of pale blue flesh arising from the man's left thigh, and which had been sutured to the open wound on the right thigh. When the surgeon pressed the pedicle with his finger, it blanched; when he let up, there was a slow return of the violaceous color.

"The circulation is good," Franciscus announced. "It will get bet- 5 ter." In several weeks, we were told, he would divide the tube of flesh at its site of origin, and tailor it to fit the defect to which, by then, it would have grown more solidly. All at once, the webbed man in the bed reached out, and gripping Franciscus by the arm, began to speak rapidly, pointing to his groin and hip. Franciscus stepped back at once to disengage his arm from the patient's grasp.

"Anyone here know Spanish? I didn't get a word of that."   6

"The cast is digging into him up above," I said. "The edges of the   7
plaster are rough. When he moves, they hurt."

Without acknowledging my assistance, Dr. Franciscus took a plas-   8
ter shears from the dressing cart and with several large snips cut away the rough edges of the cast.

"*Gracias, gracias.*" The man in the bed smiled. But Franciscus had   9
already moved on to the next bed. He seemed to me a man of immense strength and ability, yet without affection for the patients. He did not want to be touched by them. It was less kindness that he showed them than a reassurance that he would never give up, that he would bend every effort. If anyone could, he would solve the problems of their flesh.

Ward Rounds had disbanded and I was halfway down the corridor   10
when I heard Dr. Franciscus's voice behind me.

"You speak Spanish." It seemed a command.   11

"I lived in Spain for two years," I told him.   12

"I'm taking a surgical team to Honduras next week to operate on   13
the natives down there. I do it every year for three weeks, somewhere. This year, Honduras. I can arrange the time away from your duties here if you'd like to come along. You will act as interpreter. I'll show you how to use the clinical camera. What you'd see would make it worthwhile."

So it was that, a week later, the envy of my classmates, I joined the   14
mobile surgical unit—surgeons, anesthetists, nurses and equipment—aboard a Military Air Transport plane to spend three weeks performing plastic surgery on people who had been previously selected by an advance team. Honduras. I don't suppose I shall ever see it again. Nor do I especially want to. From the plane it seemed a country made of clay—burnt umber, raw sienna, dry. It had a deadweight quality, as though the ground had no buoyancy, no air sacs through which a breeze might wander. Our destination was Comayagua, a town in the Central Highlands. The town itself was situated on the edge of one of the flat-lands that were linked in a network between the granite mountains. Above, all was brown, with only an occasional Spanish cedar tree; below, patches of luxuriant tropical growth. It was a day's bus ride from the airport. For hours, the town kept appearing and disappearing with the convolutions of the road. At last, there it lay before us, panting and exhausted at the bottom of the mountain.

That was all I was to see of the countryside. From then on, there was   15
only the derelict hospital of Comayagua, with the smell of spoiling bananas and the accumulated odors of everyone who had been sick

there for the last hundred years. Of the two, I much preferred the frank smell of the sick. The heat of the place was incendiary. So hot that, as we stepped from the bus, our own words did not carry through the air, but hung limply at our lips and chins. Just in front of the hospital was a thirsty courtyard where mobs of waiting people squatted or lay in the meager shade, and where, on dry days, a fine dust rose through which untethered goats shouldered. Against the walls of this courtyard, gaunt, dejected men stood, their faces, like their country, preternaturally solemn, leaden. Here no one looked up at the sky. Every head was bent beneath a wide-brimmed straw hat. In the days that followed, from the doorway of the dispensary, I would watch the brown mountains sliding about, drinking the hospital into their shadow as the afternoon grew later and later, flattening us by their very altitude.

The people were mestizos, of mixed Spanish and Indian blood. 16
They had flat, broad, dumb museum feet. At first they seemed to me indistinguishable the one from the other, without animation. All the vitality, the hidden sexuality, was in their black hair. Soon I was to know them by the fissures with which each face was graven. But, even so, compared to us, they were masked, shut away. My job was to follow Dr. Franciscus around, photograph the patients before and after surgery, interpret and generally act as aide-de-camp. It was exhilarating. Within days I had decided that I was not just useful, but essential. Despite that we spent all day in each other's company, there were no overtures of friendship from Dr. Franciscus. He knew my place, and I knew it, too. In the afternoon he examined the patients scheduled for the next day's surgery. I would call out a name from the doorway to the examining room. In the courtyard someone would rise. I would usher the patient in, and nudge him to the examining table where Franciscus stood, always, I thought, on the verge of irritability. I would read aloud the case history, then wait while he carried out his examination. While I took the "before" photographs, Dr. Franciscus would dictate into a tape recorder:

"Ulcerating basal cell carcinoma of the right orbit—six by eight cen- 17
timeters—involving the right eye and extending into the floor of the orbit. Operative plan: wide excision with enucleation of the eye. Later, bone and skin grafting." The next morning we would be in the operating room where the procedure would be carried out.

We were more than two weeks into our tour of duty—a few days to 18
go—when it happened. Earlier in the day I had caught sight of her through the window of the dispensary. A thin, dark Indian girl about fourteen years old. A figurine, orange-brown, terra-cotta, and still attached to the unshaped clay from which she had been carved. An older, sun-weathered woman stood behind and somewhat to the left of the girl. The mother was short and dumpy. She wore a broad-brimmed hat with a high crown, and a shapeless dress like a cassock. The girl had

long, loose black hair. There were tiny gold hoops in her ears. The dress she wore could have been her mother's. Far too big, it hung from her thin shoulders at some risk of slipping down her arms. Even with her in it, the dress was empty, something hanging on the back of a door. Her breasts made only the smallest imprint in the cloth, her hips none at all. All the while, she pressed to her mouth a filthy, pink, balled-up rag as though to stanch a flow or buttress against pain. I knew that what she had come to show us, what we were there to see, was hidden beneath that pink cloth. As I watched, the woman handed down to her a gourd from which the girl drank, lapping like a dog. She was the last patient of the day. They had been waiting in the courtyard for hours.

"Imelda Valdez," I called out. Slowly she rose to her feet, the cloth   19
never leaving her mouth, and followed her mother to the examining-room door. I shooed them in.

"You sit up there on the table," I told her. "Mother, you stand over   20
there, please." I read from the chart:

"This is a fourteen-year-old girl with a complete, unilateral, left-   21
sided cleft lip and cleft palate. No other diseases or congenital defects. Laboratory tests, chest X ray—negative."

"Tell her to take the rag away," said Dr. Franciscus. I did, and the   22
girl shrank back, pressing the cloth all the more firmly.

"Listen, this is silly," said Franciscus. "Tell her I've got to see it.   23
Either she behaves, or send her away."

"Please give me the cloth," I said to the girl as gently as possible.   24
She did not. She could not. Just then, Franciscus reached up and, taking the hand that held the rag, pulled it away with a hard jerk. For an instant the girl's head followed the cloth as it left her face, one arm still upflung against showing. Against all hope, she would hide herself. A moment later, she relaxed and sat still. She seemed to me then like an animal that looks outward at the infinite, at death, without fear, with recognition only.

Set as it was in the center of the girl's face, the defect was utterly   25
hideous—a nude rubbery insect that had fastened there. The upper lip was widely split all the way to the nose. One white tooth perched upon the protruding upper jaw projecting through the hole. Some of the bone seemed to have been gnawed away as well. Above the thing, clear almond eyes and long black hair reflected the light. Below, a slender neck where the pulse trilled visibly. Under our gaze the girl's eyes fell to her lap where her hands lay palms upward, half open. She was a beautiful bird with a crushed beak. And tense with the expectation of more shame.

"Open your mouth," said the surgeon. I translated. She did so, and   26
the surgeon tipped back her head to see inside.

"The palate, too. Complete," he said. There was a long silence. At   27
last he spoke.

"What is your name?" The margins of the wound melted until she 28 herself was being sucked into it.

"Imelda." The syllables leaked through the hole with a slosh and a 29 whistle.

"Tomorrow," said the surgeon, "I will fix your lip. *Mañana.*" 30

It seemed to me that Hugh Franciscus, in spite of his years of expe- 31 rience, in spite of all the dreadful things he had seen, must have been awed by the sight of this girl. I could see it flit across his face for an instant. Perhaps it was her small act of concealment, that he had had to demand that she show him the lip, that he had had to force her to show it to him. Perhaps it was her resistance that intensified the disfigure-ment. Had she brought her mouth to him willingly, without shame, she would have been for him neither more nor less than any other patient.

He measured the defect with calipers, studied it from different 32 angles, turning her head with a finger at her chin.

"How can it ever be put back together?" I asked. 33

"Take her picture," he said. And to her, "Look straight ahead." 34 Through the eye of the camera she seemed more pitiful than ever, her humiliation more complete.

"Wait!" The surgeon stopped me. I lowered the camera. A strand of 35 her hair had fallen across her face and found its way to her mouth, becoming stuck there by saliva. He removed the hair and secured it behind her ear.

"Go ahead," he ordered. There was the click of the camera. The girl 36 winced.

"Take three more, just in case." 37

When the girl and her mother had left, he took paper and pen and 38 with a few lines drew a remarkable likeness of the girl's face.

"Look," he said. "If this dot is A, and this one B, this, C, and this, D, 39 the incisions are made A to B, then C to D. CD must equal AB. It is all equilateral triangles." All well and good, but then came X and Y and rotation flaps and the rest.

"Do you see?" he asked. 40

"It is confusing," I told him. 41

"It is simply a matter of dropping the upper lip into a normal posi- 42 tion, then crossing the gap with two triangular flaps. It is geometry," he said.

"Yes," I said. "Geometry." And relinquished all hope of becoming a 43 plastic surgeon.

In the operating room the next morning the anesthesia had already 44 been administered when we arrived from Ward Rounds. The tube emerging from the girl's mouth was pressed against her lower lip to be kept out of the field of surgery. Already, a nurse was scrubbing the face which swam in a reddish-brown lather. The tiny gold earrings were included in the scrub. Now and then, one of them gave a brave flash. The face was washed for the last time, and dried. Green towels were placed over the face to hide everything but the mouth and nose. The drapes were applied.

"Calipers!" The surgeon measured, locating the peak of the dis- 45 torted Cupid's bow.

"Marking pen!" He placed the first blue dot at the apex of the bow. 46 The nasal sills were dotted; next, the inferior philtral dimple, the vermilion line. The *A* flap and the *B* flap were outlined. On he worked, peppering the lip and nose, making sense of chaos, realizing the lip that lay waiting in that deep essential pink, that only he could see. The last dot and line were placed. He was ready.

"Scalpel!" He held the knife above the girl's mouth. 47

"O.K. to go ahead?" he asked the anesthetist. 48

"Yes." 49

He lowered the knife. 50

"No! Wait!" The anesthetist's voice was tense, staccato. "Hold it!" 51

The surgeon's hand was motionless. 52

"What's the matter?" 53

"Something's wrong. I'm not sure. God, she's hot as a pistol. 54 Blood pressure is way up. Pulse one eighty. Get a rectal temperature." A nurse fumbled beneath the drapes. We waited. The nurse retrieved the thermometer.

"One hundred seven . . . no . . . eight." There was disbelief in her 55 voice.

"Malignant hyperthermia," said the anesthetist. "Ice! Ice! Get lots of 56 ice!" I raced out the door, accosted the first nurse I saw.

"Ice!" I shouted. *"Hielo!*[1] Quickly! *Hielo!"* The woman's expression 57 was blank. I ran to another. *"Hielo! Hielo!* For the love of God, ice."

"Hielo?" She shrugged. *"Nada."*[2] I ran back to the operating room. 58

"There isn't any ice." I reported. Dr. Franciscus had ripped off his 59 rubber gloves and was feeling the skin of the girl's abdomen. Above the mask his eyes were the eyes of a horse in battle.

"The EKG is wild . . ." 60

"I can't get a pulse . . ." 61

"What the hell . . ." 62

The surgeon reached for the girl's groin. No femoral pulse. 63

"EKG flat. My God! She's dead!" 64

"She can't be." 65

"She is." 66

---

[1] Ice. [Eds.]
[2] Nothing. [Eds.]

The surgeon's fingers pressed the groin where there was no pulse to 6567
be felt, only his own pulse hammering at the girl's flesh to be let in.

It was noon, four hours later, when we left the operating room. It 68
was a day so hot and humid I felt steamed open like an envelope. The
woman was sitting on a bench in the courtyard in her dress like a cassock. In one hand she held the piece of cloth the girl had used to conceal
her mouth. As we watched, she folded it once neatly, and then again,
smoothing it, cleaning the cloth which might have been the head of the
girl in her lap that she stroked and consoled.

"I'll do the talking here," he said. He would tell her himself, in 69
whatever Spanish he could find. Only if she did not understand was I
to speak for him. I watched him brace himself, set his shoulders. How
could he tell her? I wondered. What? But I knew he would tell her
everything, exactly as it had happened. As much for himself as for her,
he needed to explain. But suppose she screamed, fell to the ground,
attacked him, even? All that hope of love . . . gone. Even in his discomfort I knew that he was teaching me. The way to do it was professionally. Now he was standing above her. When the woman saw that he did
not speak, she lifted her eyes and saw what he held crammed in his
mouth to tell her. She knew, and rose to her feet.

"*Señora*," he began, "I am sorry." All at once he seemed to me 70
shorter than he was, scarcely taller than she. There was a place at the
crown of his head where the hair had grown thin. His lips were stones.
He could hardly move them. The voice dry, dusty.

"No one could have known. Some bad reaction to the medicine for 71
sleeping. It poisoned her. High fever. She did not wake up." The last, a
whisper. The woman studied his lips as though she were deaf. He tried,
but could not control a twitching at the corner of his mouth. He raised
a thumb and forefinger to press something back into his eyes.

"*Muerte*,"[3] the woman announced to herself. Her eyes were human, 72
deadly.

"*Sí, muerte.*" At that moment he was like someone cast, still alive, 73
as an effigy for his own tomb. He closed his eyes. Nor did he open
them until he felt the touch of the woman's hand on his arm, a touch
from which he did not withdraw. Then he looked and saw the grief cor-
roding her face, breaking it down, melting the features so that eyes,
nose, mouth ran together in a distortion, like the girl's. For a long time
they stood in silence. It seemed to me that minutes passed. At last her
face cleared, the features rearranged themselves. She spoke, the words
coming slowly to make certain that he understood her. She would go
home now. The next day her sons would come for the girl, to take her

---

[3] Dead. [Eds.]

home for burial. The doctor must not be sad. God has decided. And she was happy now that the harelip had been fixed so that her daughter might go to Heaven without it. Her bare feet retreating were the felted pads of a great bereft animal.

The next morning I did not go to the wards, but stood at the gate 74 leading from the courtyard to the road outside. Two young men in striped ponchos lifted the girl's body wrapped in a straw mat onto the back of a wooden cart. A donkey waited. I had been drawn to this place as one is drawn, inexplicably, to certain scenes of desolation—executions, battlefields. All at once, the woman looked up and saw me. She had taken off her hat. The heavy-hanging coil of her hair made her head seem larger, darker, noble. I pressed some money into her hand.

"For flowers," I said. "A priest." Her cheeks shook as though min- 75 utes ago a stone had been dropped into her navel and the ripples were just now reaching her head. I regretted having come to that place.

"Sí, sí," The woman said. Her own face was stitched with flies. "The 76 doctor is one of the angels. He has finished the work of God. My daughter is beautiful."

What could she mean! The lip had not been fixed. The girl had died 77 before he would have done it.

"Only a fine line that God will erase in time," she said. 78

I reached into the cart and lifted a corner of the mat in which the girl 79 had been rolled. Where the cleft had been there was now a fresh line of tiny sutures. The Cupid's bow was delicately shaped, the vermilion border aligned. The flattened nostril had now the same rounded shape as the other one. I let the mat fall over the face of the dead girl, but not before I had seen the touching place where the finest black hairs sprang from the temple.

"Adiós, adiós. . . ." And the cart creaked away to the sound of 80 hooves, a tinkling bell.

There are events in a doctor's life that seem to mark the boundary 81 between youth and age, seeing and perceiving. Like certain dreams, they illuminate a whole lifetime of past behavior. After such an event, a doctor is not the same as he was before. It had seemed to me then to have been the act of someone demented, or at least insanely arrogant. An attempt to reorder events. Her death had come to him out of order. It should have come after the lip had been repaired, not before. He could have told the mother that, no, the lip had not been fixed. But he did not. He said nothing. It had been an act of omission, one of those strange lapses to which all of us are subject and which we live to regret. It must have been then, at that moment, that the knowledge of what he would do appeared to him. The words of the mother had not consoled him; they had hunted him down. He had not done it for her. The dire necessity was his. He would not accept that Imelda had died before he could repair her lip. People who do such things break free from society.

They follow their own lonely path. They have a secret which they can never reveal. I must never let on that I knew.

How often I have imagined it. Ten o'clock at night. The hospital of [82] Comayagua is all but dark. Here and there lanterns tilt and skitter up and down the corridors. One of these lamps breaks free from the others and descends the stone steps to the underground room that is the morgue of the hospital. This room wears the expression as if it had waited all night for someone to come. No silence so deep as this place with its cargo of newly dead. Only the slow drip of water over stone. The door closes gassily and clicks shut. The lock is turned. There are four tables, each with a body encased in a paper shroud. There is no mistaking her. She is the smallest. The surgeon takes a knife from his pocket and slits open the paper shroud, that part in which the girl's head is enclosed. The wound seems to be living on long after she has died. Waves of heat emanate from it, blurring his vision. All at once, he turns to peer over his shoulder. He sees nothing, only a wooden crucifix on the wall.

He removes a package of instruments from a satchel and arranges [83] them on a tray. Scalpel, scissors, forceps, needle holder. Sutures and gauze sponges are produced. Stealthy, hunched, engaged, he begins. The dots of blue dye are still there upon her mouth. He raises the scalpel, pauses. A second glance into the darkness. From the wall a small lizard watches and accepts. The first cut is made. A sluggish flow of dark blood appears. He wipes it away with a sponge. No new blood comes to take its place. Again and again he cuts, connecting each of the blue dots until the whole of the zigzag slice is made, first on one side of the cleft, then on the other. Now the edges of the cleft are lined with fresh tissue. He sets down the scalpel and takes up scissors and forceps, undermining the little flaps until each triangle is attached only at one side. He rotates each flap into its new position. He must be certain that they can be swung without tension. They can. He is ready to suture. He fits the tiny curved needle into the jaws of the needle holder. Each suture is placed precisely the same number of millimeters from the cut edge, and the same distance apart. He ties each knot down until the edges are apposed. Not too tightly. These are the most meticulous sutures of his life. He cuts each thread close to the knot. It goes well. The vermilion border with its white skin roll is exactly aligned. One more stitch and the Cupid's bow appears as if by magic. The man's face shines with moisture. Now the nostril is incised around the margin, released, and sutured into a round shape to match its mate. He wipes the blood from the face of the girl with gauze the he has dipped in water. Crumbs of light are scattered on the girl's face. The shroud is folded once more about her. The instruments are handed into the satchel. In a moment the morgue is dark and a lone lantern ascends the stairs and is extinguished.

Six weeks later I was in the darkened amphitheater of the Medical 84
School. Tiers of seats rose in a semicircle above the small stage where
Hugh Franciscus stood presenting the case material he had encountered
in Honduras. It was the highlight of the year. The hall was filled. The
night before he had arranged the slides in the order in which they were
to be shown. I was at the controls of the slide projector.

"Next slide!" he would order from time to time in that military 85
voice which had called forth blind obedience from generations of medical students, interns, residents and patients.

"This is a fifty-seven-year-old man with a severe burn contracture 86
of the neck. You will notice the rigid webbing that has fused the chin to
the presternal tissues. No motion of the head on the torso is possible. . . . Next slide!"

"Click," went the projector. 87

"Here he is after the excision of the scar tissue and with the head in 88
full extension for the first time. The defect was then covered. . . . Next
slide!"

"Click." 89

". . . with full-thickness drums of skin taken from the abdomen with 90
the Padgett dermatome. Next slide!"

"Click." 91

And suddenly there she was, extracted from the shadows, sus- 92
pended above and beyond all of us like a resurrection. There was the
oval face, the long black hair unbraided, the tiny gold hoops in her ears.
And that luminous gnawed mouth. The whole of her life seemed to
have been summed up in this photograph. A long silence followed that
was the surgeon's alone to break. Almost at once, like the anesthetist in
the operating room in Comayagua, I knew that something was wrong.
It was not that the man would not speak as that he could not. The audience of doctors, nurses and students seemed to have been infected by
the black, limitless silence. My own pulse doubled. It was hard to
breathe. Why did he not call out for the next slide? Why did he not save
himself? Why had he not removed this slide from the ones to be shown?
All at once I knew that he had used his camera on her again. I could see
the long black shadows of her hair flowing into the darker shadows of
the morgue. The sudden blinding flash . . . The next slide would be the
one taken in the morgue. He would be exposed.

In the dim light reflected from the slide, I saw him gazing up at her, 93
seeing not the colored photograph, I thought, but the negative of it
where the ghost of the girl was. For me, the amphitheater had become
Honduras. I saw again that courtyard littered with patients. I could see
the dust in the beam of light from the projector. It was then that I knew
that she was his measure of perfection and pain—the one lost, the other
gained. He, too, had heard the click of the camera, had seen her wince
and felt his mercy enlarge. At last he spoke.

"Imelda." It was the one word he had heard her say. At the sound 94 of his voice I removed the next slide from the projector. "Click" . . . and she was gone. "Click" again, and in her place the man with the orbital cancer. For a long moment Franciscus looked up in my direction, on his face an expression that I have given up trying to interpret. Gratitude? Sorrow? It made me think of the gaze of the girl when at last she understood that she must hand over to him the evidence of her body.

"This is a sixty-two-year-old man with a basal cell carcinoma of the 95 temple eroding into the bony orbit . . ." he began as though nothing had happened.

At the end of the hour, even before the lights went on, there was 96 loud applause. I hurried to find him among the departing crowd. I could not. Some weeks went by before I caught sight of him. He seemed vaguely convalescent, as though a fever had taken its toll before burning out.

Hugh Franciscus continued to teach for fifteen years, although he 97 operated a good deal less, then gave it up entirely. It was as though he had grown tired of blood, of always having to be involved with blood, of having to draw it, spill it, wipe it away, stanch it. He was a quieter, softer man, I heard, the ferocity diminished. There were no more expeditions to Honduras or anywhere else.

I, too, have not been entirely free of her. Now and then, in the years 98 that have passed, I see that donkey-cart cortège, or his face bent over hers in the morgue. I would like to have told him what I now know, that his unrealistic act was one of goodness, one of those small, persevering acts done, perhaps, to ward off madness. Like lighting a lamp, boiling water for tea, washing a shirt. But, of course, it's too late now.

Responding to Reading

1. What motivated Dr. Franciscus to repair Imelda's lip after she had died? Do you think he did the right thing?
2. What were Dr. Franciscus's good qualities? What were his shortcomings as a physician? Overall, does Selzer consider him a good doctor? Do you?
3. What does Selzer learn from the story of Imelda? What does he mean when he says, "I too, have not been entirely free of her" (98)? Do you think the true subject of the essay is Imelda, Dr. Franciscus, or Richard Selzer? Explain.

THE BLACK DEATH

Barbara Tuchman

Historical writer and journalist Barbara Tuchman (1912–1989) won Pulitzer Prizes for two of her books: The Guns of August *(1962) and* Stillwell and the American Experience in China, 1911–1945 *(1971). Known for both her literary approach and her factual accuracy, Tuchman once described herself as "a writer whose subject is history." Some of her many works are* The Proud Tower: A Portrait of the World before the War, 1890–1914 *(1966), A* Distant Mirror: The Calamitous Fourteenth Century *(1978), and a collection of essays,* Practicing History *(1981). Tuchman was awarded the American Academy of Arts and Sciences gold medal for history in 1978. In the following excerpt from* A Distant Mirror, *she graphically describes the Black Death (or bubonic plague) without sentimentality or melodrama, using a variety of different sources to document this plague's horrifying effects.*

In October 1347, two months after the fall of Calais, Genoese trad- 1
ing ships put into the harbor of Messina in Sicily with dead and dying men at the oars. The ships had come from the Black Sea port of Caffa (now Feodosiya) in the Crimea, where the Genoese maintained a trading post. The diseased sailors showed strange black swellings about the size of an egg or an apple in the armpits and groin. The swellings oozed blood and pus and were followed by spreading boils and black blotches on the skin from internal bleeding. The sick suffered severe pain and died quickly within five days of the first symptoms. As the disease spread, other symptoms of continuous fever and spitting of blood appeared instead of the swellings or buboes. These victims coughed and sweated heavily and died even more quickly, within three days or less, sometimes in 24 hours. In both types everything that issued from the body—breath, sweat, blood from the buboes and lungs, bloody urine, and blood-blackened excrement—smelled foul. Depression and despair accompanied the physical symptoms, and before the end "death is seen seated on the face."

The disease was bubonic plague, present in two forms: one that 2
infected the bloodstream, causing the buboes and internal bleeding, and was spread by contact; and a second, more virulent pneumonic type that infected the lungs and was spread by respiratory infection. The presence of both at once caused the high mortality and speed of contagion. So lethal was the disease that cases were known of persons going to bed well and dying before they woke, of doctors catching the illness at a bedside and dying before the patient. So rapidly did it spread from

one to another that to a French physician, Simon de Covino, it seemed as if one sick person "could infect the whole world." The malignity of the pestilence appeared more terrible because its victims knew no prevention and no remedy.

The physical suffering of the disease and its aspect of evil mystery ₃ were expressed in a strange Welsh lament which saw "death coming into our midst like black smoke, a plague which cuts off the young, a footless phantom which has no mercy for fair countenance. Woe is me of the shilling in the armpit! It is seething, terrible . . . a head that gives pain and causes a loud cry . . . a painful angry knob. . . . Great is its seething like a burning cinder . . . a grievous thing of ashy color." Its eruption is ugly like the "seeds of black peas, broken fragments of brittle sea-coal . . . the early ornaments of black death, cinders of the peelings of the cockle weed, a mixed multitude, a black plague like halfpence, like berries. . . ."

Rumors of a terrible plague supposedly arising in China and ₄ spreading through Tartary (Central Asia) to India and Persia, Mesopotamia, Syria, Egypt, and all of Asia Minor had reached Europe in 1346. They told of a death so devastating that all of India was said to be depopulated, whole territories covered by dead bodies, other areas with no one left alive. As added up by Pope Clement VI at Avignon, the total of reported dead reached 23,840,000. In the absence of a concept of contagion, no serious alarm was felt in Europe until the trading ships brought their black burden of pestilence into Messina while other infected ships from the Levant carried it to Genoa and Venice.

By January 1348 it penetrated France via Marseille, and North Africa ₅ via Tunis. Shipborne along coasts and navigable rivers, it spread westward from Marseille through the ports of Languedoc to Spain and northward up the Rhône to Avignon, where it arrived in March. It reached Narbonne, Montpellier, Carcassonne, and Toulouse between February and May, and at the same time in Italy spread to Rome and Florence and their hinterlands. Between June and August it reached Bordeaux, Lyon, and Paris, spread to Burgundy and Normandy, and crossed the Channel from Normandy into southern England. From Italy during the same summer it crossed the Alps into Switzerland and reached eastward to Hungary.

In a given area the plague accomplished its kill within four to six ₆ months and then faded, except in the larger cities, where, rooting into the close-quartered population, it abated during the winter, only to reappear in spring and rage for another six months.

In 1349 it resumed in Paris, spread to Picardy, Flanders, and the ₇ Low Countries, and from England to Scotland and Ireland as well as to Norway, where a ghost ship with a cargo of wool and a dead crew drifted offshore until it ran aground near Bergen. From there the plague passed into Sweden, Denmark, Prussia, Iceland, and as far as

Greenland. Leaving a strange pocket of immunity in Bohemia, and
Russia unattacked until 1351, it had passed from most of Europe by
mid-1350. Although the mortality rate was erratic, ranging from one
fifth in some places to nine tenths or almost total elimination in others,
the overall estimate of modern demographers has settled—for the area
extending from India to Iceland—around the same figure expressed in
Froissart's casual words: "a third of the world died." His estimate, the
common one at the time, was not an inspired guess but a borrowing of
St. John's figure for mortality from plague in Revelation, the favorite
guide to human affairs of the Middle Ages.

A third of Europe would have meant about 20 million deaths. No   8
one knows in truth how many died. Contemporary reports were an
awed impression, not an accurate count. In crowded Avignon, it was
said, 400 died daily; 7,000 houses emptied by death were shut up; a single graveyard received 11,000 corpses in six weeks; half the city's inhabitants reportedly died, including 9 cardinals or one third of the total,
and 70 lesser prelates. Watching the endlessly passing death carts,
chroniclers let normal exaggeration take wings and put the Avignon
death toll at 62,000 and even at 120,000, although the city's total population was probably less than 50,000.

When graveyards filled up, bodies at Avignon were thrown into the   9
Rhône until mass burial pits were dug for dumping the corpses. In
London in such pits corpses piled up in layers until they overflowed.
Everywhere reports speak of the sick dying too fast for the living to
bury. Corpses were dragged out of homes and left in front of doorways.
Morning light revealed new piles of bodies. In Florence the dead were
gathered up by the Compagnia della Misericordia—founded in 1244 to
care for the sick—whose members wore red robes and hoods masking
the face except for the eyes. When their efforts failed, the dead lay
putrid in the streets for days at a time. When no coffins were to be had,
the bodies were laid on boards, two or three at once, to be carried to
graveyards or common pits. Families dumped their own relatives into
the pits, or buried them so hastily and thinly "that dogs dragged them
forth and devoured their bodies."

Amid accumulating death and fear of contagion, people died with-   10
out last rites and were buried without prayers, a prospect that terrified
the last hours of the stricken. A bishop in England gave permission to
laymen to make confession to each other as was done by the Apostles,
"or if no man is present then even to a woman," and if no priest could
be found to administer extreme unction, "then faith must suffice."
Clement VI found it necessary to grant remissions of sin to all who died
of the plague because so many were unattended by priests. "And no
bells tolled," wrote a chronicler of Siena, "and nobody wept no matter
what his loss because almost everyone expected death. . . . And people
said and believed, 'this is the end of the world.'"

In Paris, where the plague lasted through 1349, the reported death 11
rate was 800 a day, in Pisa 500, in Vienna 500 to 600. The total dead in
Paris numbered 50,000 or half the population. Florence, weakened by
the famine of 1347, lost three to four fifths of its citizens, Venice two
thirds, Hamburg and Bremen, though smaller in size, about the same
proportion. Cities, as centers of transportation, were more likely to be
affected than villages, although once a village was infected, its death
rate was equally high. At Givry, a prosperous village in Burgundy of
1,200 to 1,500 people, the parish register records 615 deaths in the space
of fourteen weeks, compared to an average of thirty deaths a year in the
previous decade. In three villages of Cambridgeshire, manorial records
show a death rate of 47 percent, 57 percent, and in one case 70 percent.
When the last survivors, too few to carry on, moved away, a deserted
village sank back into the wilderness and disappeared from the map
altogether, leaving only a grass-covered ghostly outline to show where
mortals once had lived.

In enclosed places such as monasteries and prisons, the infection of 12
one person usually meant that of all, as happened in the Franciscan
convents of Carcassonne and Marseille, where every inmate without
exception died. Of the 140 Dominicans at Montpellier only seven survived. Petrarch's[1] brother Gherardo, member of a Carthusian monas-
tery, buried the prior and 34 fellow monks one by one, sometimes three
a day, until he was left alone with his dog and fled to look for a place
that would take him in. Watching every comrade die, men in such
places could not but wonder whether the strange peril that filled the
air had not been sent to exterminate the human race. In Kilkenny,
Ireland, Brother John Clyn of the Friars Minor, another monk left alone
among dead men, kept a record of what had happened lest "things
which should be remembered perish with time and vanish from
the memory of those who come after us." Sensing "the whole world, as
it were, placed within the grasp of the Evil One," and waiting for death
to visit him too, he wrote, "I leave parchment to continue this work,
if perchance any man survive and any of the race of Adam escape
this pestilence and carry on the work which I have begun." Brother
John, as noted by another hand, died of the pestilence, but he foiled
oblivion.

The largest cities of Europe, with populations of about 100,000, 13
were Paris and Florence, Venice and Genoa. At the next level, with more
than 50,000, were Ghent and Bruges in Flanders, Milan, Bologna, Rome,
Naples, and Palermo, and Cologne. London hovered below 50,000, the
only city in England except York with more than 10,000. At the level of
20,000 to 50,000 were Bordeaux, Toulouse, Montpellier, Marseille, and

---

[1] Italian poet (1304–1374). [Eds.]

Lyon in France, Barcelona, Seville, and Toledo in Spain, Siena, Pisa, and other secondary cities in Italy, and the Hanseatic[2] trading cities of the Empire. The plague raged through them all, killing anywhere from one third to two thirds of their inhabitants. Italy, with a total population of 10 to 11 million, probably suffered the heaviest toll. Following the Florentine bankruptcies, the crop failures and workers' riots of 1346–47, the revolt of Cola di Rienzi that plunged Rome into anarchy, the plague came as the peak of successive calamities. As if the world were indeed in the grasp of the Evil One, its first appearance on the European mainland in January 1348 coincided with a fearsome earthquake that carved a path of wreckage from Naples up to Venice. Houses collapsed, church towers toppled, villages were crushed, and the destruction reached as far as Germany and Greece. Emotional response, dulled by horrors, underwent a kind of atrophy epitomized by the chronicler who wrote, "And in these days was burying without sorrowe and wedding without friendschippe."

In Siena, where more than half of the inhabitants died of the plague, 14 work was abandoned on the great cathedral, planned to be the largest in the world, and never resumed, owing to loss of workers and master masons and "the melancholy and grief" of the survivors. The cathedral's truncated transept still stands in permanent witness to the sweep of death's scythe. Agnolo di Tura, a chronicler of Siena, recorded the fear of contagion that froze every other instinct. "Father abandoned child, wife husband, one brother another," he wrote, "for this plague seemed to strike through the breath and sight. And so they died. And no one could be found to bury the dead for money or friendship. . . . And I, Agnolo di Tura, called the Fat, buried my five children with my own hands, and so did many others likewise."

There were many to echo his account of inhumanity and few to bal- 15 ance it, for the plague was not the kind of calamity that inspired mutual help. Its loathsomeness and deadliness did not herd people together in mutual distress, but only prompted their desire to escape each other. "Magistrates and notaries refused to come and make the wills of the dying," reported a Franciscan friar of Piazza in Sicily; what was worse, "even the priests did not come to hear their confessions." A clerk of the Archbishop of Canterbury reported the same of English priests who "turned away from the care of their benefices from fear of death." Cases of parents deserting children and children their parents were reported across Europe from Scotland to Russia. The calamity chilled the hearts of men, wrote Boccaccio[3] in his famous account of the plague in Florence that serves as introduction to the *Decameron*. "One man

---

[2] A league of medieval German market towns. [Eds.]

[3] Italian writer (1313–1375) whose *Decameron* is a collection of one hundred stories told by a group of plague survivors who flee to a country estate to escape contagion. [Eds.]

shunned another . . . kinsfolk held aloof, brother was forsaken by brother, oftentimes husband by wife; nay, what is more, and scarcely to be believed, fathers and mothers were found to abandon their own children to their fate, untended, unvisited as if they had been strangers." Exaggeration and literary pessimism were common in the 14th century, but the Pope's physician, Guy de Chauliac, was a sober, careful observer who reported the same phenomenon: "A father did not visit his son, nor the son his father. Charity was dead."

Yet not entirely. In Paris, according to the chronicler Jean de Venette, the nuns of the Hôtel Dieu or municipal hospital, "having no fear of death, tended the sick with all sweetness and humility." New nuns repeatedly took the places of those who died, until the majority "many times renewed by death now rest in peace with Christ as we may piously believe." 16

When the plague entered northern France in July 1348, it settled first in Normandy and, checked by winter, gave Picardy a deceptive interim until the next summer. Either in mourning or warning, black flags were flown from church towers of the worst-stricken villages of Normandy. "And in that time," wrote a monk of the abbey of Fourcarment, "the mortality was so great among the people of Normandy that those of Picardy mocked them." The same unneighborly reaction was reported of the Scots, separated by a winter's immunity from the English. Delighted to hear of the disease that was scourging the "southrons," they gathered forces for an invasion, "laughing at their enemies." Before they could move, the savage mortality fell upon them too, scattering some in death and the rest in panic to spread the infection as they fled. 17

In Picardy in the summer of 1349 the pestilence penetrated the castle of Coucy to kill Enguerrand's[4] mother, Catherine, and her new husband. Whether her nine-year-old son escaped by chance or was perhaps living elsewhere with one of his guardians is unrecorded. In nearby Amiens, tannery workers, responding quickly to losses in the labor force, combined to bargain for higher wages. In another place villagers were seen dancing to drums and trumpets, and on being asked the reason, answered that, seeing their neighbors die day by day while their village remained immune, they believed that they could keep the plague from entering "by the jollity that is in us. That is why we dance." Further north in Tournai on the border of Flanders, Gilles li Muisis, Abbot of St. Martin's, kept one of the epidemic's most vivid accounts. The passing bells rang all day and all night, he recorded, because sextons were anxious to obtain their fees while they could. Filled with the sound of mourning, the city became oppressed by fear, so that the authorities forbade the tolling of bells and the wearing of black and restricted funeral 18

---

[4] Throughout *A Distant Mirror*, the book from which this excerpt is taken, Tuchman traces the impact of events on the life a French nobleman named Enguerrand de Coucy. [Eds.]

services to two mourners. The silencing of funeral bells and of criers' announcements of deaths was ordained by most cities. Siena imposed a fine on the wearing of mourning clothes by all except widows.

Flight was the chief recourse of those who could afford it or arrange 19 it. The rich fled to their country places like Boccaccio's young patricians of Florence, who settled in a pastoral palace "removed on every side from the road" with "wells of cool water and vaults of rare wines." The urban poor died in their burrows, "and only the stench of their bodies informed neighbors of their death." That the poor were more heavily afflicted than the rich was clearly remarked at the time, in the north as in the south. A Scottish chronicler, John of Fordun, stated flatly that the pest "attacked especially the meaner sort and common people—seldom the magnates." Simon de Covino of Montpellier made the same observation. He ascribed it to the misery and want and hard lives that made the poor more susceptible, which was half the truth. Close contact and lack of sanitation was the unrecognized other half. It was noticed too that the young died in greater proportion than the old; Simon de Covino compared the disappearance of youth to the withering of flowers in the fields.

In the countryside peasants dropped dead on the roads, in the fields, 20 in their houses. Survivors in growing helplessness fell into apathy, leaving ripe wheat uncut and livestock untended. Oxen and asses, sheep and goats, pigs and chickens ran wild and they too, according to local reports, succumbed to the pest. English sheep, bearers of the precious wool, died throughout the country. The chronicler Henry Knighton, canon of Leicester Abbey, reported 5,000 dead in one field alone, "their bodies so corrupted by the plague that neither beast nor bird would touch them," and spreading an appalling stench. In the Austrian Alps wolves came down to prey upon sheep and then, "as if alarmed by some invisible warning, turned and fled back into the wilderness." In remote Dalmatia bolder wolves descended upon a plague-stricken city and attacked human survivors. For want of herdsmen, cattle strayed from place to place and died in hedgerows and ditches. Dogs and cats fell like the rest.

The dearth of labor held a fearful prospect because the 14th century lived close to the annual harvest both for food and for next year's seed. 21 "So few servants and laborers were left," wrote Knighton, "that no one knew where to turn for help." The sense of a vanishing future created a kind of dementia of despair. A Bavarian chronicler of Neuberg on the Danube recorded that "Men and women . . . wandered around as if mad" and let their cattle stray "because no one had any inclination to concern themselves about the future." Fields went uncultivated, spring seed unsown. Second growth with nature's awful energy crept back over cleared land, dikes crumbled, salt water reinvaded and soured the lowlands. With so few hands remaining to restore the work of centuries, people felt, in Walsingham's words, that "the world could never again regain its former prosperity."

Though the death rate was higher among the anonymous poor, the 22
known and the great died too. King Alfonso XI of Castile was the only
reigning monarch killed by the pest, but his neighbor King Pedro of
Aragon lost his wife, Queen Leonora, his daughter Marie, and a niece in
the space of six months. John Cantacuzene, Emperor of Byzantium, lost
his son. In France the lame Queen Jeanne and her daughter-in-law
Bonne de Luxemburg, wife of the Dauphin, both died in 1349 in the
same phase that took the life of Enguerrand's mother. Jeanne, Queen of
Navarre, daughter of Louis X, was another victim. Edward III's second
daughter, Joanna, who was on her way to marry Pedro, the heir of
Castile, died in Bordeaux. Women appear to have been more vulnerable
than men, perhaps because, being more housebound, they were more
exposed to fleas. Boccaccio's mistress Fiammetta, illegitimate daughter
of the King of Naples, died, as did Laura, the beloved—whether real or
fictional—of Petrarch. Reaching out to us in the future, Petrarch cried,
"Oh happy posterity who will not experience such abysmal woe and
will look upon our testimony as a fable."

In Florence Giovanni Villani, the great historian of his time, died at 23
68 in the midst of an unfinished sentence: ". . . *e dure questo pistolenza fino
a* . . . (in the midst of this pestilence there came to an end . . .)." Siena's
master painters, the brothers Ambrogio and Pietro Lorenzetti, whose
names never appear after 1348, presumably perished in the plague, as
did Andrea Pisano, architect and sculptor of Florence. William of
Ockham and the English mystic Richard Rolle of Hampole both disappear from mention after 1349. Francisco Datini, merchant of Prato, lost
both his parents and two siblings. Curious sweeps of mortality afflicted
certain bodies of merchants in London. All eight wardens of the
Company of Cutters, all six wardens of the Hatters, and four wardens
of the Goldsmiths died before July 1350. Sir John Pulteney, master
draper and four times Mayor of London, was a victim, likewise Sir John
Montgomery, Governor of Calais.

Among the clergy and doctors the mortality was naturally high 24
because of the nature of their professions. Out of 24 physicians in Venice,
20 were said to have lost their lives in the plague, although, according to
another account, some were believed to have fled or to have shut themselves up in their houses. At Montpellier, site of the leading medieval
medical school, the physician Simon de Covino reported that, despite the
great number of doctors, "hardly one of them escaped." In Avignon, Guy
de Chauliac confessed that he performed his medical visits only because
he dared not stay away for fear of infamy, but "I was in continual fear."
He claimed to have contracted the disease but to have cured himself by
his own treatment; if so, he was one of the few who recovered.

Clerical mortality varied with rank. Although the one-third toll of 25
cardinals reflects the same proportion as the whole, this was probably
due to their concentration in Avignon. In England, in strange and

almost sinister procession, the Archbishop of Canterbury, John Stratford, died in August 1348, his appointed successor died in May 1349, and the next appointee three months later, all three within a year. Despite such weird vagaries, prelates in general managed to sustain a higher survival rate than the lesser clergy. Among bishops the deaths have been estimated at about one in twenty. The loss of priests, even if many avoided their fearful duty of attending the dying, was about the same as among the population as a whole.

Government officials, whose loss contributed to the general chaos, 26 found, on the whole, no special shelter. In Siena four of the nine members of the governing oligarchy died, in France one third of the royal notaries, in Bristol 15 out of the 52 members of the Town Council or almost one third. Tax-collecting obviously suffered, with the result that Philip VI was unable to collect more than a fraction of the subsidy granted him by the Estates in the winter of 1347–48.

Lawlessness and debauchery accompanied the plague as they had 27 during the great plague of Athens of 430 B.C., when according to Thucydides,[5] men grew bold in the indulgence of pleasure: "For seeing how the rich died in a moment and those who had nothing immediately inherited their property, they reflected that life and riches were alike transitory and they resolved to enjoy themselves while they could." Human behavior is timeless. When St. John had his vision of plague in Revelation, he knew from some experience or race memory that those who survived "repented not of the work of their hands. . . . Neither repented they of their murders, nor of their sorceries, nor of their fornication, nor of their thefts."

Responding to Reading

1. Many passages of Tuchman's essay include graphic, unpleasant descriptions of the plague victims' symptoms. Is this kind of descriptive detail— for example, "the dead lay putrid in the streets" (9)—necessary? Why do you think Tuchman includes it? How do you react to this kind of detail?
2. Which kinds of supporting detail do you find most compelling in Tuchman's essay: statistics, quotations from contemporary sources, anecdotes, victims' names, or summaries of historical sources? What do you think Tuchman would gain by adding other kinds of support, such as artists' re-creations of the scenes, quotations from modern-day historians, analysis by modern-day medical professionals, or a case study of one family?
3. This essay about the dead and dying is remarkably free of sentimentality. Where might another writer have become sentimental, even melodramatic? How do you think you would respond to a more emotional treatment?

---

[5] Ancient Greek historian. [Eds.]

A PLEA FOR THE CHIMPS

Jane Goodall

English-born Jane Goodall (1934–   ) has spent most of her adult life studying the behavior of wild chimpanzees in the jungles of Tanzania. Shortly after graduating high school, she visited Kenya, where she met naturalist and paleontologist Louis Leakey. Impressed by her love of wildlife and despite her lack of formal training, Leakey arranged for her to conduct a six-month field study of chimpanzees on a Tanzanian reserve, a project which has stretched to almost four decades. Goodall has described her fascinating observations in a number of popular books, including In the Shadow of Man *(1971; revised 1988),* The Chimpanzees of Gombe: Patterns of Behavior *(1986), and* Through a Window: My Thirty Years with the Chimpanzees of Gombe *(1990). As she has said, "Animals are like us. They feel pain like we do. We want people to understand that every chimp is an individual, with the same kinds of intellectual abilities." In the following 1987 article, Goodall makes the case for more humane treatment of chimpanzees used for medical research.*

The chimpanzee is more like us, genetically, than any other animal. 1 It is because of similarities in physiology, in biochemistry, in the immune system, that medical science makes use of the living bodies of chimpanzees in its search for cures and vaccines for a variety of human diseases.

There are also behavioral, psychological and emotional similarities 2 between chimpanzees and humans, resemblances so striking that they raise a serious ethical question: are we justified in using an animal so close to us—an animal, moreover, that is highly endangered in its African forest home—as a human substitute in medical experimentation?

In the long run, we can hope that scientists will find ways of explor- 3 ing human physiology and disease, and of testing cures and vaccines, that do not depend on the use of living animals of any sort. A number of steps in this direction already have been taken, prompted in large part by a growing public awareness of the suffering that is being inflicted on millions of animals. More and more people are beginning to realize that nonhuman animals—even rats and guinea pigs—are not just unfeeling machines but are capable of enjoying their lives, and of feeling fear, pain and despair.

But until alternatives have been found, medical science will con- 4 tinue to use animals in the battle against human disease and suffering. And some of those animals will continue to be chimpanzees.

Because they share with us 99 percent of their genetic material, 5 chimpanzees can be infected with some human diseases that do not infect other animals. They are currently being used in research on the nature of hepatitis non-A non-B, for example, and they continue to play a major role in the development of vaccines against hepatitis B.

Many biomedical laboratories are looking to the chimpanzee to help them in the race to find a vaccine against acquired immune deficiency syndrome. Chimpanzees are not good models for AIDS research; although the AIDS virus stays alive and replicates within the chimpanzee's bloodstream, no chimp has yet come down with the disease itself. Nevertheless, many of the scientists involved argue that only by using chimpanzees can potential vaccines be safely tested. 6

Given the scientists' professed need for animals in research, let us turn aside from the sensitive ethical issue of whether chimpanzees *should* be used in medical research, and consider a more immediate issue: how are we treating the chimpanzees that are actually being used? 7

Just after Christmas I watched, with shock, anger and anguish, a videotape—made by an animal-rights group during a raid—revealing the conditions in a large biomedical research laboratory, under contract to the National Institutes of Health, in which various primates, including chimpanzees, are maintained. In late March, I was given permission to visit the facility. 8

It was a visit I shall never forget. Room after room was lined with small, bare cages, stacked one above the other, in which monkeys circled round and round and chimpanzees sat huddled, far gone in depression and despair. 9

Young chimpanzees, 3 or 4 years old, were crammed, two together, into tiny cages measuring 22 inches by 22 inches and only 24 inches high. They could hardly turn around. Not yet part of any experiment, they had been confined in these cages for more than three months. 10

The chimps had each other for comfort, but they would not remain together for long. Once they are infected, probably with hepatitis, they will be separated and placed in another cage. And there they will remain, living in conditions of severe sensory deprivation, for the next several years. During that time, they will become insane. 11

A juvenile female rocked from side to side, sealed off from the outside world behind the glass doors of her metal isolation chamber. She was in semidarkness. All she could hear was the incessant roar of air rushing through vents into her prison. 12

In order to demonstrate the "good" relationship the lab's caretaker had with this chimpanzee, one of the scientists told him to lift her from the cage. The caretaker opened the door. She sat, unmoving. He reached in. She did not greet him—nor did he greet her. As if drugged, she allowed him to take her out. She sat motionless in his arms. He did not speak to her, she did not look at him. He touched her lips briefly. She did not respond. He returned her to her cage. She sat again on the bars of the floor. The door closed. 13

I shall be haunted forever by her eyes, and by the eyes of the other 14
infant chimpanzees I saw that day. Have you ever looked into the eyes
of a person who, stressed beyond endurance, has given up, succumbed
utterly to the crippling helplessness of despair? I once saw a little
African boy, whose whole family had been killed during the fighting in
Burundi. He too looked out at the world, unseeing, from dull, blank
eyes.

Though this particular laboratory may be one of the worst, from 15
what I have learned, most of the other biomedical animal-research facilities are not much better. Yet only when one has some understanding of
the true nature of the chimpanzee can the cruelty of these captive conditions be fully understood.

Chimpanzees are very social by nature. Bonds between individuals, 16
particularly between family members and close friends, can be affectionate, supportive, and can endure throughout their lives. The accidental separation of two friendly individuals may cause them intense
distress. Indeed, the death of a mother may be such a psychological
blow to her child that even if the child is 5 years old and no longer
dependent on its mother's milk, it may pine away and die.

It is impossible to overemphasize the importance of friendly physi- 17
cal contact for the well-being of the chimpanzee. Again and again one
can watch a frightened or tense individual relax if she is patted, kissed
or embraced reassuringly by a companion. Social grooming, which provides hours of close contact, is undoubtedly the single most important
social activity.

Chimpanzees in their natural habitat are active for much of the day. 18
They travel extensively within their territory, which can be as large as
50 square kilometers for a community of about 50 individuals. If they
hear other chimpanzees calling as they move through the forest, or
anticipate arriving at a good food source, they typically break into
excited charging displays, racing along the ground, hurling sticks and
rocks and shaking the vegetation. Youngsters, particularly, are full of
energy, and spend long hours playing with one another or by themselves, leaping through the branches and gamboling along the ground.
Adults sometimes join these games. Bunches of fruit, twigs and rocks
may be used as toys.

Chimpanzees enjoy comfort. They construct sleeping platforms each 19
night, using a multitude of leafy twigs to make their beds soft. Often, too,
they make little "pillows" on which to rest during a midday siesta.

Chimps are highly intelligent. They display cognitive abilities that 20
were, until recently, thought to be unique to humans. They are capable
of cross-model transfer of information—that is, they can identify by
touch an object they previously have only seen, and vice versa. They are
capable of reasoned thought, generalization, abstraction and symbolic

representation. They have some concept of self. They have excellent memories and can, to some extent, plan for the future. They show a capacity for intentional communication that depends, in part, on their ability to understand the motives of the individuals with whom they are communicating.

Chimpanzees are capable of empathy and altruistic behavior. They 21 show emotions that are undoubtedly similar, if not identical, to human emotions—joy, pleasure, contentment, anxiety, fear and rage. They even have a sense of humor.

The chimpanzee child and the human child are alike in many ways; 22 in their capacity for endless romping and fun; their curiosity; their ability to learn by observation, imitation and practice; and, above all, in their need for reassurance and love. When young chimpanzees are brought up in a human home and treated like human children, they learn to eat at table, to help themselves to snacks from the refrigerator, to sort and put away cutlery, to brush their teeth, to play with dolls, to switch on the television and select a program that interests them and watch it.

Young chimpanzees can easily learn over 200 signs of the American 23 language of the deaf and use these signs to communicate meaningfully with humans and with one another. One youngster, in the laboratory of Dr. Roger S. Fouts, a psychologist at Central Washington University, has picked up 68 signs from four older signing chimpanzee companions, with no human teaching. The chimp uses the signs in communication with other chimpanzees and with humans.

The chimpanzee facilities in most biomedical research laboratories 24 allow for the expression of almost none of these activities and behaviors. They provide little—if anything—more than the warmth, food and water, and veterinary care required to sustain life. The psychological and emotional needs of these creatures are rarely catered to, and often not even acknowledged.

In most labs the chimpanzees are housed individually, one chimp to 25 a cage, unless they are part of a breeding program. The standard size of each cage is about 25 feet square and about 6 feet high. In one facility, a cage described in the catalogue as "large," designed for a chimpanzee of up to 25 kilograms (55 pounds), measures 2 feet 6 inches by 3 feet 8 inches, with a height of 5 feet 4 inches. Federal requirements for cage size are dependent on body size; infant chimpanzees, who are the most active, are often imprisoned in the smallest cages.

In most labs, the chimpanzees cannot even lie with their arms and 26 legs outstretched. They are not let out to exercise. There is seldom anything for them to do other than eat, and then only when food is brought. The caretakers are usually too busy to pay much attention to individual chimpanzees. The cages are bleak and sterile, with bars above, bars below, bars on every side. There is no comfort in them, no bedding. The chimps, infected with human diseases, will often feel sick and miserable.

What of the human beings who administer these facilities—the 27 caretakers, veterinarians and scientists who work at them? If they are decent, compassionate people, how can they condone, or even tolerate, the kind of conditions I have described?

They are, I believe, victims of a system that was set up long before 28 the cognitive abilities and emotional needs of chimpanzees were understood. Newly employed staff members, equipped with a normal measure of compassion, may well be sickened by what they see. And, in fact, many of them do quit their jobs, unable to endure the suffering they see inflicted on the animals yet feeling powerless to help.

But others stay on and gradually come to accept the cruelty, believ- 29 ing (or forcing themselves to believe) that it is an inevitable part of the struggle to reduce human suffering. Some become hard and callous in the process, in Shakespeare's words, "all pity choked with custom of fell deeds."

A handful of compassionate and dedicated caretakers and veteri- 30 narians are fighting to improve the lots of the animals in their care. Vets are often in a particularly difficult position, for if they stand firm and try to uphold high standards of humane care, they will not always be welcome in the lab.

Many of the scientists believe that a bleak, sterile and restricting 31 environment is necessary for their research. The cages must be small, the scientists maintain, because otherwise it is too difficult to treat the chimpanzees—to inject them, to draw their blood or to anesthetize them. Moreover, they are less likely to hurt themselves in small cages.

The cages must also be barren, with no bedding or toys, say the sci- 32 entists. This way, the chimpanzees are less likely to pick up diseases or parasites. Also, if things are lying about, the cages are harder to clean.

And the chimpanzees must be kept in isolation, the scientists believe, 33 to avoid the risk of cross-infection, particularly in hepatitis research.

Finally, of course, bigger cages, social groups and elaborate fur- 34 nishings require more space, more caretakers—and more money. Perhaps, then, if we are to believe these researchers, it is not possible to improve conditions for chimpanzees imprisoned in biomedical research laboratories.

I believe not only that it is possible, but that improvements are 35 absolutely necessary. If we do not do something to help these creatures, we make a mockery of the whole concept of justice.

Perhaps the most important way we can improve the quality of life 36 for the laboratory chimps is to increase the number of carefully trained caretakers. These people should be selected for their understanding of animal behavior and their compassion and respect for, and dedication to, their charges. Each caretaker, having established a relationship of trust with the chimpanzees in his care, should be allowed to spend time with the animals over and above that required for cleaning the cages and providing the animals with food and water.

It has been shown that a chimpanzee who has a good relationship 37 with his caretaker will cooperate calmly during experimental procedures, rather than react with fear or anger. At the Dutch Primate Research Center, at Rijswijk, for example, some chimpanzees have been trained to leave their group cage on command and move into small, single cages for treatment. At the Stanford Primate Center in California, a number of chimpanzees were taught to extend their arms for the drawing of blood. In return they were given a food reward.

Much can be done to alleviate the pain and stress felt by younger 38 chimpanzees during experimental procedures. A youngster, for example, can be treated when in the presence of a trusted human friend. Experiments have shown that young chimps react with high levels of distress if subjected to mild electric shocks when alone, but show almost no fear or pain when held by a sympathetic caretaker.

What about cage size? Here we should emulate the animal protec- 39 tion regulations that already exist in Switzerland. These laws stipulate that a cage must be, at minimum, about 20 meters square and 3 meters high for pairs of chimpanzees.

The chimpanzees should never be housed alone unless this is an 40 essential part of the experimental procedure. For chimps in solitary confinement, particularly youngsters, three to four hours of friendly interaction with a caretaker should be mandatory. A chimp taking part in hepatitis research, in which the risk of cross-infection is, I am told, great, can be provided with a companion of a compatible species if it doesn't infringe on existing regulations—a rhesus monkey, for example, which cannot catch or pass on the disease.

For healthy chimpanzees there should be little risk of infection from 41 bedding and toys. Stress and depression, however, can have deleterious effects on their health. It is known that clinically depressed humans are more prone to a variety of physiological disorders, and heightened stress can interfere with immune function. Given the chimpanzee's similarities to humans, it is not surprising that the chimp in a typical laboratory, alone in his bleak cage, is an easy prey to infections and parasites.

Thus, the chimpanzees also should be provided with a rich and 42 stimulating environment. Climbing apparatus should be obligatory. There should be many objects for them to play with or otherwise manipulate. A variety of simple devices designed to alleviate boredom could be produced quite cheaply. Unexpected food items will elicit great pleasure. If a few simple buttons in each cage were connected to a computer terminal, it would be possible for the chimpanzees to feel they at least have some control over their world—if one button produced a grape when pressed, another a drink, or another a video picture. (The Canadian Council of Animal Care recommends the provision of television for primates in solitary confinement, or other means of enriching their environment.)

Without doubt, it will be considerably more costly to maintain 43 chimpanzees in the manner I have outlined. Should we begrudge them the extra dollars? We take from them their freedom, their health and often their lives. Surely, the least we can do is try to provide them with some of the things that could make their imprisonment more bearable.

There are hopeful signs. I was immensely grateful to officials of the 44 National Institutes of Health for allowing me to visit the primate facility, enabling me to see the conditions there and judge them for myself. And I was even more grateful for the fact that they gave me a great deal of time for serious discussions of the problem. Doors were opened and a dialogue begun. All who were present at the meetings agreed that, in light of present knowledge, it is indeed necessary to give chimpanzees a better deal in the labs.

Plans are now under way for a major conference to discuss ways 45 and means of bringing about such change. Sponsored by the N.I.H. and organized by Roger Fouts (who toured the lab with me) and myself, this conference—which will be held in mid-December at the Jane Goodall Institute in Tucson, Ariz.—will bring together for the first time administrators, scientists and animal technicians from various primate facilities around the country and from overseas. The conference will, we hope, lead to the formulation of new, humane standards for the maintenance of chimpanzees in the laboratory.

I have had the privilege of working among wild, free chimpanzees 46 for more than 26 years. I have gained a deep understanding of chimpanzee nature. Chimpanzees have given me so much in my life. The least I can do is to speak out for the hundreds of chimpanzees who, right now, sit hunched, miserable and without hope, staring out with dead eyes from their metal prisons. They cannot speak for themselves.

Responding to Reading

1. Goodall says in paragraph 7 that she doesn't want to discuss the issue of whether chimpanzees should be used in medical research. Does she successfully sidestep this issue in her essay, or does she indirectly address it? Explain.
2. What arguments against Goodall's proposals could scientists who use chimpanzees in experiments make? Does Goodall address any of these arguments in her essay? Should she have?
3. Some proponents of animal rights say that animals should not be used in experiments where human beings would not be used. Do you agree? Do you think Goodall would agree with this position?

MY WORLD NOW

Anna Mae Halgrim Seaver

The following essay originally appeared as a "My Turn" column in Newsweek *magazine in June 1994. Anna Mae Halgrim Seaver (1919–1994) had recently died at the nursing home where she had been confined for some time, and her son discovered these notes in her room after her death.*

This is my world now; it's all I have left. You see, I'm old. And, I'm 1 not as healthy as I used to be. I'm not necessarily happy with it but I accept it. Occasionally, a member of my family will stop in to see me. He or she will bring me some flowers or a little present, maybe a set of slippers—I've got 8 pair. We'll visit for awhile and then they will return to the outside world and I'll be alone again.

Oh, there are other people here in the nursing home. Residents, 2 we're called. The majority are about my age. I'm 84. Many are in wheelchairs. The lucky ones are passing through—a broken hip, a diseased heart, something has brought them here for rehabilitation. When they're well they'll be going home.

Most of us are aware of our plight—some are not. Varying stages of 3 Alzheimer's have robbed several of their mental capacities. We listen to endlessly repeated stories and questions. We meet them anew daily, hourly or more often. We smile and nod gracefully each time we hear a retelling. They seldom listen to my stories, so I've stopped trying.

The help here is basically pretty good, although there's a large 4 turnover. Just when I get comfortable with someone he or she moves on to another job. I understand that. This is not the best job to have.

I don't much like some of the physical things that happen to us. I 5 don't care much for a diaper. I seem to have lost the control acquired so diligently as a child. The difference is that I'm aware and embarrassed but I can't do anything about it. I've had 3 children and I know it isn't pleasant to clean another's diaper. My husband used to wear a gas mask when he changed the kids. I wish I had one now.

Why do you think the staff insists on talking baby talk when speak- 6 ing to me? I understand English. I have a degree in music and am a certified teacher. Now I hear a lot of words that end in "y." Is this how my kids felt? My hearing aid works fine. There is little need for anyone to position their face directly in front of mine and raise their voice with those "y" words. Sometimes it takes longer for a meaning to sink in; sometimes my mind wanders when I am bored. But there's no need to shout.

I tried once or twice to make my feelings known. I even shouted 7 once. That gained me a reputation of being "crotchety." Imagine me, crotchety. My children never heard me raise my voice. I surprised myself. After I've asked for help more than a dozen times and received nothing more than a dozen condescending smiles and a "Yes, deary, I'm working on it," something begins to break. That time I wanted to be taken to a bathroom.

I'd love to go out for a meal, to travel again. I'd love to go to my 8 own church, sing with my own choir. I'd love to visit my friends. Most of them are gone now or else they are in different "homes" of their children's choosing. I'd love to play a good game of bridge but no one here seems to concentrate very well.

My children put me here for my own good. They said they would 9 be able to visit me frequently. But they have their own lives to lead. That sounds normal. I don't want to be a burden. They know that. But I would like to see them more. One of them is here in town. He visits as much as he can.

Something else I've learned to accept is loss of privacy. Quite often 10 I'll close my door when my roommate—imagine having a roommate at my age—is in the TV room. I do appreciate some time to myself and believe that I have earned at least that courtesy. As I sit thinking or writing, one of the aides invariably opens the door unannounced and walks in as if I'm not there. Sometimes she even opens my drawers and begins rummaging around. Am I invisible? Have I lost my right to respect and dignity? What would happen if the roles were reversed? I am still a human being. I would like to be treated as one.

The meals are not what I would choose for myself. We get variety 11 but we don't get a choice. I am one of the fortunate ones who can still handle utensils. I remember eating off such cheap utensils in the Great Depression. I worked hard so I would not have to ever use them again. But here I am.

Did you ever sit in a wheelchair over an extended period of time? 12 It's not comfortable. The seat squeezes you into the middle and applies constant pressure on your hips. The armrests are too narrow and my arms slip off. I am luckier than some. Others are strapped into their chairs and abandoned in front of the TV. Captive prisoners of daytime television; soap operas, talk shows and commercials.

One of the residents died today. He was a loner who, at one time, 13 started a business and developed a multimillion-dollar company. His children moved him here when he could no longer control his bowels. He didn't talk to most of us. He often snapped at the aides as though they were his employees. But he just gave up; willed his own demise. The staff has made up his room and another man has moved in.

A typical day. Awakened by the woman in the next bed wheezing— 14 a former chain smoker with asthma. Call an aide to wash me and place me in my wheelchair to wait for breakfast. Only 67 minutes until breakfast. I'll wait. Breakfast in the dining area. Most of the residents are in wheelchairs. Others use canes or walkers. Some sit and wonder what they are waiting for. First meal of the day. Only 3 hours and 26 minutes until lunch. Maybe I'll sit around and wait for it. What is today? One day blends into the next until day and date mean nothing.

Let's watch a little TV. Oprah and Phil and Geraldo and who cares   15 if some transvestite is having trouble picking a color-coordinated wardrobe from his husband's girlfriend's mother's collection. Lunch. Can't wait. Dried something with puréed peas and coconut pudding. No wonder I'm losing weight.

Back to my semiprivate room for a little semiprivacy or a nap. I do   16 need my beauty rest, company may come today. What is today, again? The afternoon drags into early evening. This used to be my favorite time of the day. Things would wind down. I would kick off my shoes. Put my feet up on the coffee table. Pop open a bottle of Chablis and enjoy the fruits of my day's labor with my husband. He's gone. So is my health. *This* is my world.

Responding to Reading

1. Seaver's son compiled this essay from notes left in his mother's room after her death. Perhaps for this reason, it seems to jump from one subject to another. Are there any advantages to this somewhat choppy structure? Would a smoother, more unified structure have been more effective?

2. What picture of life in a nursing home does Seaver present? How does she characterize the people who live there?

3. In paragraph 9 Seaver says "My children put me here for my own good. . . . But they have their own lives to lead. . . . I don't want to be a burden." Do you think Seaver means what she says? How do you imagine Seaver's son reacted when he read these statements? What do you think he hoped to accomplish by publishing her notes?

ON THE FEAR OF DEATH

Elisabeth Kübler-Ross

Born in Zurich, Switzerland, psychologist and physician Elisabeth Kübler-Ross (1917–) has made a distinguished career of her interest in dying patients and their families. She established a pioneering interdisciplinary seminar in the care of the terminally ill when she taught at the University of Chicago, and for many years, she headed a center for terminal patients in rural Virginia. Her first book on the subject was On Death and Dying *(1969), and she has also written* Death: The Final State *(1974), On*

Childhood and Death *(1985), and* AIDS: The Ultimate Challenge *(1987). In recent years she has turned her attention to what happens after death, the subject of* On Life after Death *(1991). Her most recent book is* The Wheel of Life: A Memoir of Living and Dying *(1997). In the following excerpt from* On Death and Dying, *Kübler-Ross argues that we should confront death directly to reduce our fear of it.*

Let me not pray to be sheltered from dangers but to be fearless in facing them.
Let me not beg for the stilling of my pain but for the heart to conquer it.
Let me not look for allies in life's battlefield but to my own strength.
Let me not crave in anxious fear to be saved but hope for the patience to win my freedom.
Grant me that I may not be a coward, feeling your mercy in my success alone; but let me find the grasp of your hand in my failure.

Rabindranath Tagore, *Fruit-Gathering*

Epidemics have taken a great toll of lives in past generations. Death 1 in infancy and early childhood was frequent and there were few families who didn't lose a member of the family at an early age. Medicine has changed greatly in the last decades. Widespread vaccinations have practically eradicated many illnesses, at least in western Europe and the United States. The use of chemotherapy, especially the antibiotics, has contributed to an ever decreasing number of fatalities in infectious diseases. Better child care and education have effected a low morbidity and mortality among children. The many diseases that have taken an impressive toll among the young and middle-aged have been conquered. The number of old people is on the rise, and with this fact come the number of people with malignancies and chronic diseases associated more with old age.

Pediatricians have less work with acute and life-threatening situa- 2 tions as they have an ever increasing number of patients with psychosomatic disturbances and adjustment and behavior problems. Physicians have more people in their waiting rooms with emotional problems than they have ever had before, but they also have more elderly patients who not only try to live with their decreased physical abilities and limitations but who also face loneliness and isolation with all its pains and anguish. The majority of these people are not seen by a psychiatrist. Their needs have to be elicited and gratified by other professional people, for instance, chaplains and social workers. It is for them that I am trying to outline the changes that have taken place in the last few decades, changes that are ultimately responsible for the increased fear of death, the rising number of emotional problems, and the greater need for understanding of and coping with the problems of death and dying.

When we look back in time and study old cultures and people, we ₃ are impressed that death has always been distasteful to man and will probably always be. From a psychiatrist's point of view this is very understandable and can perhaps best be explained by our basic knowledge that, in our unconscious, death is never possible in regard to ourselves. It is inconceivable for our unconscious to imagine an actual ending of our own life here on earth, and if this life of ours had to end, the ending is always attributed to a malicious intervention from the outside by someone else. In simple terms, in our unconscious mind we can only be killed; it is inconceivable to die of a natural cause or of old age. Therefore death in itself is associated with a bad act, a frightening happening, something that in itself calls for retribution and punishment.

One is wise to remember these fundamental facts as they are essen- ₄ tial in understanding some of the most important, otherwise unintelligible communications of our patients.

The second fact that we have to comprehend is that in our uncon- ₅ scious mind we cannot distinguish between a wish and a deed. We are all aware of some of our illogical dreams in which two completely opposite statements can exist side by side—very acceptable in our dreams but unthinkable and illogical in our wakening state. Just as our unconscious mind cannot differentiate between the wish to kill somebody in anger and the act of having done so, the young child is unable to make this distinction. The child who angrily wishes his mother to drop dead for not having gratified his needs will be traumatized greatly by the actual death of his mother—even if this event is not linked closely in time with his destructive wishes. He will always take part or the whole blame for the loss of his mother. He will always say to himself—rarely to others—"I did it, I am responsible, I was bad, therefore Mommy left me." It is well to remember that the child will react in the same manner if he loses a parent by divorce, separation, or desertion. Death is often seen by a child as an impermanent thing and has therefore little distinction from a divorce in which he may have an opportunity to see a parent again.

Many a parent will remember remarks of their children such as, "I ₆ will bury my doggy now and next spring when the flowers come up again, he will get up." Maybe it was the same wish that motivated the ancient Egyptians to supply their dead with food and goods to keep them happy and the old American Indians to bury their relatives with their belongings.

When we grow older and begin to realize that our omnipotence is ₇ really not so omnipotent, that our strongest wishes are not powerful enough to make the impossible possible, the fear that we have contributed to the death of a loved one diminishes—and with it the guilt. The fear remains diminished, however, only so long as it is not challenged too strongly. Its vestiges can be seen daily in hospital corridors and in people associated with the bereaved.

A husband and wife may have been fighting for years, but when the 8
partner dies, the survivor will pull his hair, whine and cry louder and
beat his chest in regret, fear and anguish, and will hence fear his own
death more than before, still believing in the law of talion—an eye for
an eye, a tooth for a tooth—"I am responsible for her death, I will have
to die a pitiful death in retribution."

Maybe this knowledge will help us understand many of the old cus- 9
toms and rituals which have lasted over the centuries and whose purpose is to diminish the anger of the gods or the people as the case may
be, thus decreasing the anticipated punishment. I am thinking of the
ashes, the torn clothes, the veil, the *Klage Weiber*[1] of the old days—they
are all means to ask you to take pity on them, the mourners, and are
expressions of sorrow, grief, and shame. If someone grieves, beats his
chest, tears his hair, or refuses to eat, it is an attempt at self-punishment
to avoid or reduce the anticipated punishment for the blame that he
takes on the death of a loved one.

This grief, shame, and guilt are not very far removed from feelings 10
of anger and rage. The process of grief always includes some qualities
of anger. Since none of us likes to admit anger at a deceased person,
these emotions are often disguised or repressed and prolong the period
of grief or show up in other ways. It is well to remember that it is not up
to us to judge such feelings as bad or shameful but to understand their
true meaning and origin as something very human. In order to illustrate
this I will again use the example of the child—and the child in us. The
five-year-old who loses his mother is both blaming himself for her disappearance and being angry at her for having deserted him and for no
longer gratifying his needs. The dead person then turns into something
the child loves and wants very much but also hates with equal intensity
for this severe deprivation.

The ancient Hebrews regarded the body of a dead person as some- 11
thing unclean and not to be touched. The early American Indians talked
about the evil spirits and shot arrows in the air to drive the spirits away.
Many other cultures have rituals to take care of the "bad" dead person,
and they all originate in this feeling of anger which still exists in all of
us, though we dislike admitting it. The tradition of the tombstone may
originate in this wish to keep the bad spirits deep down in the ground,
and the pebbles that many mourners put on the grave are left-over symbols of the same wish. Though we call the firing of guns at military

---

[1] Wailing wives. [Eds.]

funerals a last salute, it is the same symbolic ritual as the Indian used when he shot his spears and arrows into the skies.

I give these examples to emphasize that man has not basically 12 changed. Death is still a fearful, frightening happening, and the fear of death is a universal fear even if we think we have mastered it on many levels.

What has changed is our way of coping and dealing with death and 13 dying and our dying patients.

Having been raised in a country in Europe where science is not so 14 advanced, where modern techniques have just started to find their way into medicine, and where people still live as they did in this country half a century ago, I may have had an opportunity to study a part of the evolution of mankind in a shorter period.

I remember as a child the death of a farmer. He fell from a tree and 15 was not expected to live. He asked simply to die at home, a wish that was granted without questioning. He called his daughters into the bedroom and spoke with each one of them alone for a few moments. He arranged his affairs quietly, though he was in great pain, and distributed his belongings and his land, none of which was to be split until his wife should follow him in death. He also asked each of his children to share in the work, duties, and tasks that he had carried on until the time of the accident. He asked his friends to visit him once more, to bid good-bye to them. Although I was a small child at the time, he did not exclude me or my siblings. We were allowed to share in the preparations of the family just as we were permitted to grieve with them until he died. When he did die, he was left at home, in his own beloved home which he had built, and among his friends and neighbors who went to take a last look at him where he lay in the midst of flowers in the place he had lived in and loved so much. In that country today there is still no make-believe slumber room, no embalming, no false makeup to pretend sleep. Only the signs of very disfiguring illnesses are covered up with bandages and only infectious cases are removed from the home prior to the burial.

Why do I describe such "old-fashioned" customs? I think they are 16 an indication of our acceptance of a fatal outcome, and they help the dying patient as well as his family to accept the loss of a loved one. If a patient is allowed to terminate his life in the familiar and beloved environment, it requires less adjustment for him. His own family knows him well enough to replace a sedative with a glass of his favorite wine; or the smell of a home-cooked soup may give him the appetite to sip a few spoons of fluid which, I think, is still more enjoyable than an infusion. I will not minimize the need for sedatives and infusions and realize full well from my own experience as a country doctor that they are sometimes life-saving and often unavoidable. But I also know that patience and familiar people and foods could replace many a bottle of intravenous fluids given for the simple reason that it fulfills the physiological need without involving too many people and/or individual nursing care.

The fact that children are allowed to stay at home where a fatality 17 has stricken and are included in the talk, discussions, and fears gives them the feeling that they are not alone in the grief and gives them the comfort of shared responsibility and shared mourning. It prepares them gradually and helps them view death as part of life, an experience which may help them grow and mature.

This is in great contrast to a society in which death is viewed as 18 taboo, discussion of it is regarded as morbid, and children are excluded with the presumption and pretext that it would be "too much" for them. They are then sent off to relatives, often accompanied with some unconvincing lies of "Mother has gone on a long trip" or other unbelievable stories. The child senses that something is wrong, and his distrust in adults will only multiply if other relatives add new variations of the story, avoid his questions or suspicions, shower him with gifts as a meager substitute for a loss he is not permitted to deal with. Sooner or later the child will become aware of the changed family situation and, depending on the age and personality of the child, will have an unresolved grief and regard this incident as a frightening, mysterious, in any case very traumatic experience with untrustworthy grownups, which he has no way to cope with.

It is equally unwise to tell a little child who lost her brother that God 19 loved little boys so much that he took little Johnny to heaven. When this little girl grew up to be a woman she never solved her anger at God, which resulted in a psychotic depression when she lost her own little son three decades later.

We would think that our great emancipation, our knowledge of sci- 20 ence and of man, has given us better ways and means to prepare ourselves and our families for this inevitable happening. Instead the days are gone when a man was allowed to die in peace and dignity in his own home.

The more we are making advancements in science, the more we 21 seem to fear and deny the reality of death. How is this possible?

We use euphemisms, we make the dead look as if they were asleep, 22 we ship the children off to protect them from the anxiety and turmoil around the house if the patient is fortunate enough to die at home, we don't allow children to visit their dying parents in the hospitals, we have long and controversial discussions about whether patients should be told the truth—a question that rarely arises when the dying person is tended by the family physician who has known him from delivery to death and who knows the weaknesses and strengths of each member of the family.

I think there are many reasons for this flight away from facing death 23 calmly. One of the most important facts is that dying nowadays is more gruesome in many ways, namely, more lonely, mechanical, and dehumanized; at times it is even difficult to determine technically when the time of death has occurred.

Dying becomes lonely and impersonal because the patient is often 24
taken out of his familiar environment and rushed to an emergency room. Whoever has been very sick and has required rest and comfort especially may recall his experience of being put on a stretcher and enduring the noise of the ambulance siren and hectic rush until the hospital gates open. Only those who have lived through this may appreciate the discomfort and cold necessity of such transportation which is only the beginning of a long order—hard to endure when you are well, difficult to express in words when noise, light, pumps, and voices are all too much to put up with. It may well be that we might consider more the patient under the sheets and blankets and perhaps stop our well-meant efficiency and rush in order to hold the patient's hand, to smile, or to listen to a question. I include the trip to the hospital as the first episode in dying, as it is for many. I am putting it exaggeratedly in contrast to the sick man who is left at home—not to say that lives should not be saved if they can be saved by a hospitalization but to keep the focus on the patient's experience, his needs and his reactions.

When a patient is severely ill, he is often treated like a person with 25
no right to an opinion. It is often someone else who makes the decision if and when and where a patient should be hospitalized. It would take so little to remember that the sick person too has feelings, has wishes and opinions, and has—most important of all—the right to be heard.

Well, our presumed patient has now reached the emergency room. 26
He will be surrounded by busy nurses, orderlies, interns, residents, a lab technician perhaps who will take some blood, an electrocardiogram technician who takes the cardiogram. He may be moved to X ray and he will overhear opinions of his condition and discussions and questions to members of the family. He slowly but surely is beginning to be treated like a thing. He is no longer a person. Decisions are made often without his opinion. If he tries to rebel he will be sedated and after hours of waiting and wondering whether he has the strength, he will be wheeled into the operating room or intensive treatment unit and become an object of great concern and great financial investment.

He may cry for rest, peace, and dignity, but he will get infusions, 27
transfusions, a heart machine, or tracheotomy[2] if necessary. He may want one single person to stop for one single minute so that he can ask one single question—but he will get a dozen people around the clock, all busily preoccupied with his heart rate, pulse, electrocardiogram or pulmonary functions, his secretions or excretions but not with him as a human being. He may wish to fight it all but it is going to be a useless

---

[2] An incision into the trachea in the neck to allow the insertion of a breathing tube. [Eds.]

fight since all this is done in the fight for his life, and if they can save his life they can consider the person afterwards. Those who consider the person first may lose precious time to save his life! At least this seems to be the rationale or justification behind all this—or is it? Is the reason for this increasingly mechanical, depersonalized approach our own defensiveness? Is this approach our own way to cope with and repress the anxieties that a terminally or critically ill patient evokes in us? Is our concentration on equipment, on blood pressure, our desperate attempt to deny the impending death which is so frightening and discomforting to us that we displace all our knowledge onto machines, since they are less close to us than the suffering face of another human being which would remind us once more of our lack of omnipotence, our own limits and failures, and last but not least perhaps our own mortality?

Maybe the question has to be raised: Are we becoming less human 28 or more human? . . . It is clear that whatever the answer may be, the patient is suffering more—not physically, perhaps, but emotionally. And his needs have not changed over the centuries, only our ability to gratify them.

Responding to Reading

1. Despite advances in medical science over the centuries, Kübler-Ross says, death remains "a fearful, frightening happening, and the fear of death is a universal fear even if we think we have mastered it on many levels" (12). Do you think she is correct?
2. To what extent do you agree with Kübler-Ross that we should confront the reality of death directly—for example, by being honest with children, keeping terminally ill patients at home, and allowing dying patients to determine their own treatment? What arguments are there against each of her suggestions?
3. Instead of quoting medical authorities, Kübler-Ross supports her points with anecdotes. Do you find this support convincing? Would hard scientific data be more convincing? Explain.

What Nurses Stand For

Suzanne Gordon

Suzanne Gordon (1945–   ) was born in New York City and received her B.A. from Cornell University and her M.A. from Johns Hopkins. A freelance writer and editor, she writes frequently about social issues and health care. She is coeditor of Caregiving: Readings in Knowledge, Practice, Ethics, and

Politics (1996), and her book Life Support: Three Nurses on the Front Lines *was published in 1997. The following excerpt from* Life Support *appeared in the* Atlantic Monthly; *in it, Gordon explains that nurses play a far greater role in medical caregiving is far greater than most people realize.*

At four o'clock on a Friday afternoon the hematology-oncology 1 clinic at Boston's Beth Israel Hospital is quiet. Paddy Connelly and Frances Kiel, two of the eleven nurses who work in the unit, sit at the nurses' station—an island consisting of two long desks equipped with phones, which ring constantly, and computers. They are encircled by thirteen blue-leather reclining chairs, in which patients may spend only a brief time, for a short chemotherapy infusion, or an entire afternoon, to receive more complicated chemotherapy or blood products. At one of the chairs Nancy Rumplik is starting to administer chemotherapy to a man in his mid-fifties who has colon cancer.

Rumplik is forty-two and has been a nurse on the unit for seven 2 years. She stands next to the wan-looking man and begins to hang the intravenous [IV] drugs that will treat his cancer. As the solution drips through the tubing and into his vein, she sits by his side, watching to make sure that he has no adverse reaction.

Today she is acting as triage nurse—the person responsible for 3 patients who walk in without an appointment, for patients who call with a problem but can't reach their primary nurse, for the smooth functioning of the unit, and, of course, for responding to any emergencies. Rumplik's eyes thus constantly sweep the room to check on the other patients. She focuses for a moment on a heavy-set African-American woman in her mid-forties, dressed in a pair of navy slacks and a brightly colored shirt, who is sitting in the opposite corner. Her sister, who is younger and heavier, is by her side. The patient seems fine, so Rumplik returns her attention to the man next to her. Several minutes later she looks up again, checks the woman, and stiffens. There is now a look of anxiety on the woman's face. Rumplik, leaning forward in her chair, stares at her.

"What's she getting?" she mouths to Kiel.   4

Looking at the patient's chart, Frances Kiel names a drug that has 5 been known to cause severe allergic reactions. In that brief moment, as the two nurses confer, the woman suddenly clasps her chest. Her look of anxiety turns to terror. Her mouth opens and shuts in silent panic. Rumplik leaps up from her chair, as do Kiel and Connelly, and sprints across the room.

"I can't breathe," the woman sputters when Rumplik is at her side. 6 Her eyes bulging, she grasps Rumplik's hand tightly; her eyes roll back as her head slips to the side. Realizing that the patient is having an anaphylactic reaction (her airway is swelling and closing), Rumplik immediately turns a small spigot on the IV tubing to shut off the drip. At the same instant Kiel calls a physician and the emergency-response team. By this time the woman is struggling for breath.

Kiel slips an oxygen mask over the woman's head and wraps a 7 blood-pressure cuff around her arm. Connelly administers an antihistamine to stop the allergic reaction, and cortisone to decrease the inflammation blocking her airway. The physician, an oncology fellow, arrives within minutes. He assesses the situation and then notices the woman's sister standing paralyzed, watching the scene. "Get out of here!" he commands sharply. The woman moves away as if she had been slapped.

Just as the emergency team arrives, the woman's breathing returns 8 to normal and the look of terror fades from her face. Taking Rumplik's hand again, she looks up and says, "I couldn't breathe. I just couldn't breathe." Rumplik gently explains that she has had an allergic reaction to a drug and reassures her that it has stopped.

After a few minutes, when the physician is certain that the patient 9 is stable, he and the emergency-response team walk out of the treatment area, but the nurses continue to comfort the shaken woman. Rumplik then crosses the room to talk with her male patient, who is ashen-faced at this reminder of the potentially lethal effects of the medication that he and others are receiving. Responding to his unspoken fears, Rumplik says quietly, "It's frightening to see something like that. But it's under control."

He nods silently, closes his eyes, and leans his head back against the 10 chair. Rumplik goes over to the desk where Connelly and Kiel are breathing a joint sigh of relief. One of the nurses comments on the physician's treatment of the patient's sister. "Did you hear him? He just told her to get out."

Wincing with distress, Rumplik looks around for the sister. She goes 11 into the waiting room, where the woman is sitting in a corner, looking bereft and frightened. Rumplik sits down next to her, explains what happened, and suggests that the patient could probably benefit from some overnight company. Then she adds, "I'm sorry the doctor talked to you like that. You know, it's a very anxious time for all of us."

At this gesture of respect and recognition the woman, who has 12 every strike—race, class, and sex—against her when dealing with elite white professionals in this downtown hospital, smiles solemnly. "I understand. Thank you."

Nancy Rumplik returns to her patient.   13

"I Am Ready to Die"

It is 6:00 P.M. Today Jeannie Chaisson, a clinical nurse specialist, 14 arrived at her general medical unit at seven in the morning and cared for patients until three-thirty in the afternoon. At home now, she makes herself a pot of coffee and sits down in the living room, cradling her cup. Just as she is shedding the strain of the day, the phone rings.

It's the husband of one of Chaisson's patients—a sixty-three-year-old 15 woman suffering from terminal multiple myeloma, a cancer of the bone marrow. When Chaisson left the hospital, she knew the family was in crisis. Having endured the cancer for several years, the woman is exhausted from the pain, from the effects of the disease and failed treatments, and from the pain medication on which she has become increasingly dependent. Chaisson knows she is ready to let death take her. But her husband and daughter are not.

Now the crisis that was brewing has exploded. Chaisson's caller is 16 breathless, frantic with anxiety, as he relays his wife's pleas. She wants to die. She is prepared to die. She says the pain is too much. "You've got to do something," he implores Chaisson. "Keep her going—stop her from doing this."

Chaisson knows that it is indeed time for her to do something—but, 17 sadly, not what the anguished husband wishes. "Be calm," she tells him. "Please hold on. We'll all talk together. I'm coming right in." Leaving a note for her family, she gets into her car and drives back to the hospital.

When Chaisson walks into the patient's room, she is not surprised 18 by what she finds. Seated next to the bed is the visibly distraught husband. Behind him the patient's twenty-five-year-old daughter paces in front of a picture window with a view across Boston. The patient is lying in a state somewhere between consciousness and coma, shrunken by pain and devoured by the cancer's progress. Chaisson has seen scenes like this many times before in her fifteen-year career as a nurse.

As she looks at the woman, she can understand why her husband 19 and her daughter are so resistant. They remember her as she first appeared to Chaisson, three years ago—a bright, feisty sixty-year-old woman, her nails tapered and polished, her hair sleekly sculpted into a perfect silver pouf. Chaisson remembers the day, during the first of many admissions to the unit, when she asked the woman if she wanted her hair washed.

The woman replied in astonishment, "I do not wash my hair. I have 20 it done. Once a week."

Now her hair is unkempt, glued to her face with sweat. Her nails 21 are no longer polished. Their main work these days is to dig into her flesh when the pain becomes too acute. The disease has slowly bored into her bones. Simply to stand is painful and could even be an invitation to a fracture. Her pelvis is disintegrating. The nurses have inserted an indwelling catheter, because having a bedpan slipped underneath her causes agony, but she has developed a urinary-tract infection. Because removing the catheter will make the infection easier to treat, doctors suggest this course of action. Yet if the catheter is removed, the pain will be intolerable each time she has to urinate.

When the residents and interns argued that failure to treat the infec- 22
tion could mean the patient would die, Chaisson responded, "She's
dying anyway. It's her disease that is killing her, not a urinary tract
infection." They relented.

Now the family must confront this reality.   23

Chaisson goes to the woman's bed and gently wakes her. Smiling at 24
her nurse, the woman tries to muster the energy to explain to her husband and her daughter that the pain is too great and she can no longer
attain that delicate balance, so crucial to dying patients, between fighting off pain and remaining alert for at least some of the day. Only when
she is practically comatose from drugs can she find relief.

"I am ready to die," she whispers weakly.   25

Her husband and daughter contradict her—there is still hope.   26

Jeannie Chaisson stands silent during this exchange and then inter- 27
venes, asking them to try to take in what their loved one is telling them.
Then she repeats the basic facts about the disease and its course. "At this
point there is no treatment for the disease," she explains, "but there is
treatment for the pain, to make the patient comfortable and ease her suffering." Chaisson spends another hour sitting with them, answering
their questions and allowing them to feel supported. Finally the family
is able to heed the patient's wishes—leave the catheter in and do not
resuscitate her if she suffers a cardiac arrest. Give her enough morphine
to stop the pain. Let her go.

The woman visibly relaxes, lies back, and closes her eyes. Chaisson 28
approaches the husband and the daughter, with whom she has worked
for so long, and hugs them both. Then she goes out to talk to the medical team.

Before leaving for home, Chaisson again visits her patient. The hus- 29
band and the daughter have gone for a cup of coffee. The woman is
quiet. Chaisson sits down at the side of her bed and takes her hand. The
woman opens her eyes. Too exhausted to say a word, she merely
squeezes the nurse's hand in gratitude. For the past three years
Chaisson has helped her to fight her disease and live as long as possible. Now she is here to help her die.

The Endangered RN

When we hear the word "hospital," technology and scientific inven- 30
tion spring to mind: mechanical ventilators, dialysis machines, intravenous pumps, biomedical research, surgery, medication. These, many
believe, are the life supports in our health-care system. This technology
keeps people alive, and helps to cure and heal them.

In fact there are other, equally important life supports in our health 31
care system: the 2.2 million nurses who make up the largest profession

in health care, the profession with the highest percentage of women, and the second largest profession after teaching. These women and men weave a tapestry of care, knowledge, and trust that is critical to patients' survival.

Nancy Rumplik and Jeannie Chaisson have between them more than a quarter century's experience caring for the sick. They work in an acute-care hospital, one of Harvard Medical School's teaching hospitals. Beth Israel not only is known for the quality of its patient care but also is world-renowned for the quality of its nursing staff and its institutional commitment to nursing. 32

The for-profit, market-driven health care that is sweeping the nation is threatening this valuable group of professionals. To gain an advantage in the competitive new health-care marketplace, hospitals all over the country are trying to cut their costs. One popular strategy is to lay off nurses and replace them with lower-paid, less-skilled workers. 33

American hospitals already use 20 percent fewer nurses than their counterparts in other industrialized countries. Nursing does provide attractive middle-income salaries. In 1992 staff nurses earned, on average, $33,000 a year. Clinical nurse specialists, who have advanced education and specialize in a particular field, earned an average of $41,000, and nurse practitioners, who generally have a master's degree and provide primary-care services, earned just under $44,000. Yet RN salaries and benefits altogether represent only about 16 percent of total hospital costs. 34

Nevertheless, nurses are a major target of hospital "restructuring" plans, which in some cases have called for a reduction of 20 to 50 percent in registered nursing staff. 35

The process of job elimination, deskilling, and downgrading seriously erodes opportunities for stable middle-class employment in nursing as in other industries. However, as the late David Gordon documented in his book *Fat and Mean: The Corporate Squeeze of Working Americans and the Myth of Managerial "Downsizing,"* reduced "head counts" among production or service workers don't necessarily mean that higher-level jobs (and the pay and perquisites associated with them) are being chopped as well. In fact, Gordon argued, many headline-grabbing exercises in corporate cost-cutting leave executive compensation untouched, along with other forms of managerial "bloat." 36

Even in this era of managed-care limits on physicians' compensation, nurses' pay is relatively quite modest. And the managers of care themselves—particularly hospital administrators and health-maintenance-organization executives—are doing so well that even doctors look underpaid by comparison. 37

According to the business magazine *Modern Healthcare*'s 1996 physician-compensation report, the average salary in family practice is $128,096, in internal medicine $135,755, in oncology $164,621, in 38 anesthesiology $193,242, and in general surgery $199,342. Some specialists earn more than a million dollars a year.

A survey conducted in 1995 by *Hospitals & Health Networks*, the 39 magazine of the American Hospital Association, found that the average total cash compensation for hospital CEOs was $188,500. In large hospitals the figure went up to $280,900, and in for-profit chains far higher. In 1995, at age forty-three, Richard Scott, the CEO of Columbia/ Healthcare Corporation, received a salary of $2,093,844. He controlled shares in Columbia/HCA worth $359.5 million.

In 1994 compensation for the CEOs of the seven largest for-profit 40 HMOs averaged $7 million. Even those in the not-for-profit sector of insurance earn startling sums: in 1995 John Burry Jr., the chairman and CEO of Ohio Blue Cross and Blue Shield, was paid $1.6 million.

According to a report in *Modern Healthcare*, a proposed merger with 41 the for-profit Columbia/HCA would have paid him $3 million "for a decade-long no-compete contract. . . . [and] up to $7 million for two consulting agreements."

At the other end of the new health-care salary spread are "unli- 42 censed assistive personnel" (UAPs), who are now being used instead of nurses. They usually have little background in health care and only rudimentary training. Yet UAPs may insert catheters, read EKGs, suction tracheotomy tubes, change sterile dressings, and perform other traditional nursing functions. To keep patients from becoming unduly alarmed about—or even aware of—this development, some hospitals now prohibit nurses from wearing any badges that identify them as RNs. Thus everyone at the bedside is some kind of generic "patient-care technician"—regardless of how much or how little training and experience she or he has.

In some health-care facilities other nonprofessional staff—janitors, 43 housekeepers, security guards, and aides—are also being "cross-trained" and transformed into "multi-skilled" workers who can be assigned to nursing duties. One such employee was so concerned about the impact of this on patient care that he recently wrote a letter to Timothy McCall, M.D., a critic of multi-skilling, after reading a magazine article the latter had written on the subject.

> I am an employee of a 95-bed, long-term care facility. My position is that of a security guard. Ninety-five percent of my job consists of maintenance, housekeeping, admitting persons into clinical lab to pick-up & leave specimens. Now a class, 45 minutes, is being given so employees can feed, give bedpans & move patients. My expertise is in law enforcement & security, 25 years. I am not trained or licensed in patient care, maintenance, lab work, etc. . . . This scares me. Having untrained, unlicensed people performing jobs, in my opinion, is dangerous.

Training of RN replacements is indeed almost never regulated by 44
state licensing boards. There are no minimum requirements governing
the amount of training that aides or cross-trained workers must have
before they can be redeployed to do various types of nursing work.
Training periods can range from a few hours to six weeks. One 1994
study cited in a 1996 report by the Institute of Medicine on nursing
staffing found that

> 99 percent of the hospitals in California reported less than 120
> hours of on-the-job training for newly hired ancillary nursing person-
> nel. Only 20 percent of the hospitals required a high school diploma.
> The majority of hospitals (59 percent) provided less than 20 hours of
> classroom instruction and 88 percent provided 40 hours or less of
> instruction time.

Because the rapidly accelerating UAP trend is so new, its impact on 45
patient care has not yet been fully documented. However, in a series of
major studies over the past twenty years researchers have directly
linked higher numbers and greater qualifications of registered nurses
on hospital units to lower mortality rates and decreased lengths of hospital stay. Reducing the number of expert nurses in the hospital, the
community, and homes endangers patients' lives and wastes scarce
resources. Choosing to save money by reducing nursing care aggravates
the impersonality of a medical system that tends to turn human beings
into their diseases and the doctors who care for them into sophisticated
clinical machines. When they're sick, patients do not ask only what pills
they should take or what operations they should have. They are preoccupied with questions such as Why me? Why now? Nurses are there
through this day-by-day, minute-by-minute attack on the soul. They
know that for the patient not only a sick or infirm body but also a life, a
family, a community, a society, needs to heal.

Media Stereotypes

Although nurses help us to live and die, in the public depiction of 46
health care patients seem to emerge from hospitals without ever having
benefited from their assistance. Whether patients are treated in an emergency room in a few short hours or on a critical-care unit for months on
end, we seem to assume that physicians are responsible for all the successes—and failures—in our medical system. In fact, we seem to believe
that they are responsible not only for all of the curing but also for much
of the caring.

Nurses remain shadowy figures moving mysteriously in the back- 47
ground. In television series they often appear as comic figures. On TV's
short-lived *Nightingales*, on the sitcom *Nurses*, and on the medical

drama *Chicago Hope* nurses are far too busy pining after doctors or racing off to aerobics classes to care for patients.

ER gives nurses more prominence than many other hospital shows,   48
but doctors on *ER* are constantly barking out commands to perform the
simplest duties—get a blood pressure, call the OR—to experienced
emergency-room nurses. In reality the nurses would have thought of all
this before the doctor arrived. In an emergency room as busy and
sophisticated as the one on *ER*, the first clinician a patient sees is a triage
nurse, who assesses the patient and dictates what he needs, who will
see him, and when. Experienced nurses will direct less-experienced residents (and have sometimes done so on *ER*), suggesting a medication, a
test, consultation with a specialist, or transfer to the operating room.
The great irony of *ER* is that Carol Hathaway, the nurse in charge, is
generally relegated to comforting a child or following a physician's
orders rather than, as would occur in real life, helping to direct the staff
in saving lives.

Not only do doctors dominate on television but they are the focus   49
of most hard-news health-care coverage. Reporters rarely cover innovations in nursing, use nurses as sources, or report on nursing research.
The health-care experts whom reporters or politicians consult are
invariably physicians, representatives of physician organizations, or
policy specialists who tend to look at health care through the prism of
economics. "Who Counts in News Coverage of Health Care?," a 1990
study by the Women, Press & Politics Project, in Cambridge,
Massachusetts, of health-care coverage in *The New York Times*, the *Los
Angeles Times*, and *The Washington Post*, found that out of 908 quotations
that appeared in three months' worth of health-care stories, nurses were
the sources for ten.

The revolution in health care has become big news. Occasionally   50
reporters will turn their attention to layoffs in nursing, but the story is
rarely framed as an important public-health issue. Rather, it is generally
depicted as a labor-management conflict. Nursing unions are battling
with management. Nurses say this; hospital administrators claim that.
Whom can you believe?

Worse still, this important issue may be couched in the stereotypes   51
of nursing or of women's work in general. A typical example appeared
on *NBC Nightly News* in September of 1994. The show ran a story that
involved a discussion of the serious problems, including deaths, resulting from replacing nurses with unlicensed aides. The anchor introduced
it as "a new and controversial way of administering TLC."[1] Imagine
how the issue would be characterized if 20 to 50 percent of staff physicians were eliminated in thousands of American hospitals. Would it not

---

[1] That is, "tender, loving care." [Eds.]

be front-page news, a major public-health catastrophe? Patients all over the country would be terrified to enter hospitals. Yet we learn about the equivalent in nursing with only a minimum of concern. If laying off thousands of nurses results only in the loss of a little TLC, what difference does it make if an aide replaces a nurse?

Nursing is not simply a matter of TLC. It's a matter of life and 52 death. In hospitals, which employ 66 percent of America's nurses, nurses monitor a patient's condition before, during, and after high-tech medical procedures. They adjust medication, manage pain and the side effects of treatment, and instantly intervene if a life-threatening change occurs in a patient's condition.

In our high-tech medical system nurses care for the body and the 53 soul. No matter how sensitive, caring, and attentive physicians are, nurses are often closer to the patient's needs and wishes. That's not because they are inherently more caring but because they spend far more time with patients and are likely to know them better. This time and knowledge allows them to save lives. Nurses also help people to adjust to the lives they must live after they have recovered. And when death can no longer be delayed, nurses help patients confront their own mortality with at least some measure of grace and dignity.

The Stigma of Sickness

There is another reason that nurses' work so often goes unrecog- 54 nized. Even some of the patients who have benefited the most from nurses' critical care are unable to credit its importance publicly. Because nurses observe and cushion what the physician and writer Oliver Sacks has called human beings' falling "radically into sickness," they are a reminder of the pain, fear, vulnerability, and loss of control that adults find difficult to tolerate and thus to discuss. A man who has had a successful heart bypass will boast of his surgeon's accomplishments to friends at a dinner party. A woman who has survived a bone-marrow transplant will extol her oncologist's triumph in the war against cancer to her friends and relatives. But what nurses did for those two patients will rarely be mentioned. It was a nurse who bathed the cardiac patient and comforted him while he struggled with the terror of possible death. It was a nurse who held the plastic dish under the cancer patient's lips as she was wracked with nausea, and who wiped a bottom raw from diarrhea. As Claire Fagin and Donna Diers have explained in an eloquent essay titled "Nursing as Metaphor," nurses stand for intimacy. They are our secret sharers. Even though they are lifelines during illness, when control is restored the residue of our anxiety and mortality clings to them like dust, and we flee the memory.

At one moment a nurse like Nancy Rumplik or Jeannie Chaisson 55 may be involved in a sophisticated clinical procedure that demands expert judgment and advanced training in the latest technology. The next moment she may do what many people consider trivial or menial work, such as emptying a bedpan, giving a sponge bath, administering medication, or feeding or walking a patient.

The fact that nurses' work incorporates many so-called menial tasks 56 that don't demand total attention is not a reason to replace nurses with less-skilled workers. This hands-on care allows nurses to explore patients' physical condition *and* to register their anxiety and fear. It allows them to save lives *and* to ascertain when it's appropriate to help patients die. It is only in watching nurses weave the tapestry of care that we grasp its integrity and its meaning for a society that too easily forgets the value of things that are beyond price.

Responding to Reading

1. Gordon begins her essay with two long narratives. What does each of these stories illustrate? How do they help Gordon make her point about nurses? How is this section of the essay different from the rest of the essay?
2. What new positions have for-profit health care corporations created to save money? (For example, what are "unlicensed assistive personnel," or UAPs, and "multiskilled" workers?) According to Gordon, how are the actions of these corporations compromising health care in the United States?
3. According to Gordon, why does the work of nurses so often go unnoticed? In what way do the media contribute to this situation? In what way do people's attitudes toward "nurses' work" add to the problem (54)?

FOCUS: WHOSE LIFE IS IT ANYWAY?

THE ETHICS OF EUTHANASIA

Lawrence J. Schneiderman

Born in New York City, Lawrence J. Schneiderman (1932–   ) received his M.D. from Harvard Medical School in 1957 and has been on the staffs of Boston City Hospital, the National Institutes of Health, and Stanford University School of Medicine. Since 1970, he has been a professor at the University of California-San Diego School of Medicine, where he is direc-tor of the program in medical ethics. In addition to his contributions to med-ical journals, Schneiderman is the author of Wrong Medicine: Doctors, Patients, and Futile Treatments *(1995). In the following essay, which orig-inally appeared in the* Humanist *in 1990, he considers the complex question "What will become of a society that permits—indeed promotes—death as a social good?"*

Should physicians be permitted to offer death among their thera- 1
peutic options? Should they be licensed to kill—not inadvertently or negligently but willfully, openly, and compassionately? This, on the most superficial level, is the euthanasia debate.

In California, a petition to put this matter before the voters failed to 2
gain sufficient signatures. Perhaps this was because too many of those life-affirming hedonists cringed at the thought of signing their own death warrants, or—more likely in this land where almost everything has a price—because the sponsoring Hemlock Society[1] did not hire enough solicitors.

In any case, euthanasia is being performed. 3

As a medical ethicist, when I give talks on this subject to physicians, 4
I always ask: "How many of you have ever hastened death to alleviate the suffering of your patients?" Many hands are raised—uneasily; I can offer them no legal immunity. Of all the humane acts physicians per-form, euthanasia is the one we do most furtively.

But this is an old story. In 1537, while serving in the army of 5
Francis I, the troubled surgeon Ambroise Paré confided in his diary:

---

[1] Organization devoted to the individual's right to suicide. [Eds.]

We thronged into the city and passed over the dead bodies and some that were not yet dead, hearing them cry under the feet of our horses, which made a great pity in my heart, and truly I repented that I had gone forth from Paris to see so pitiful a spectacle. Being in the city, I entered a stable, thinking to lodge my horse and that of my man, where I found four dead soldiers and three who were propped against the wall, their faces wholly disfigured, and they neither saw, nor heard, nor spoke, and their clothes yet flaming from the gun powder, which had burnt them. Beholding them with pity there came an old soldier who asked me if there was any means of curing them. I told him no. At once he approached them and cut their throats gently and without anger. Seeing this great cruelty I said to him that he was an evil man. He answered me that he prayed God that when he should be in such a case, he might find someone that would do the same for him, to the end that he might not languish miserably.

Today, the euthanasia debate takes place under the shadow of Nazi   6
doctors who appropriated the term to describe the "special treatment" given first to the physically and mentally handicapped, then to the weak and elderly, and, finally, to Jews, gypsies, and other "undesirables" as part of the Final Solution—all in the name of social hygiene. In that monstrous orgy of evil, numbers replaced names, bodies replaced souls; all were hauled by the trainload to work or to death, then converted to ashes or merely dumped in such profusion that the very earth bubbled. That was no *euthanasia*—no easy, pleasant death. That was ugly, debasing death.

But we are different, are we not? Not like *them*. And yet, and   7
yet . . . didn't we American physicians commit atrocities of our own, such as allowing untreated blacks to succumb to the "natural course" of syphilis; misleading Spanish-speaking women into thinking they were obtaining contraceptives, when in fact they were receiving inactive dummy tablets to distinguish drug side-effects, resulting in unwanted pregnancies; and injecting cancer cells into unwitting elderly patients? All for the sake of medical progress . . . we can only look back and shake our heads.

Worthy colleagues—with whom I respectfully disagree—are so   8
fearful of the "Naziness" in us all that they oppose withholding life-sustaining treatment from *anyone:* the malformed newborn with no hope of survival, the permanently unconscious patient, the terminal cancer patient who begs to be allowed to die. Who would be next? they argue. The physically and mentally handicapped? The weak and the elderly? And then? And then? This, of course, is the familiar "slippery slope" argument. Start with one exception and you inevitably skid down the moral slope of ever more exceptions. This also is the euthanasia debate, on a deeper level. What will become of a society that permits—indeed promotes—death as a social good?

An ethics consultation is where we ponder such questions at the 9
bedside of a patient who perhaps is hopelessly ill. Not infrequently,
back in the doctor's conference room, a harried resident will burst out:
"What good is it for us to keep him alive anyway?" I don't regard this as a
callous question for the simple reason that it is phrased intimately and
in the singular: Why do *we* keep *him* alive? In contrast, you'd be surprised how often decent people who possess the most humane and
compassionate sensibilities demand: "Why do *they* keep *them* alive?"
That question, in my view, is morally indistinguishable from: "Why do
they let *them* die?"

For, you see, the first question arises from *this* patient, this special 10
case, *here.* The second question arises from a state of mind—*those* people. *There.* It is a state of mind that provides a dehumanizing abstraction
appealing to both extremes of the political spectrum, and it has been
applied to both ends of life. It can lead to the demand that *all* handicapped newborns be kept alive without regard to their specific agonies
and that life-prolonging treatment be denied to *all* the elderly beyond a
certain age.

What is so special about the special case? For those of us in medi- 11
cine, it exerts a palpable moral power; the special case is our daily news,
our gossip, a shaping force in our culture. Case studies and case reports
are basic teaching tools. *Case* (from *casus,* "happening," "accident") in
its original meaning refers to a unique person in unique circumstances.
Physicians are molded by their particular autobiography of cases, by
their own singular distressing experiences. My first physical diagnosis
teacher said, "Make sure you examine the neck veins. Always. Once I
missed a patient with congestive heart failure because I neglected to do
so." Since then, I have heard many such honest confessions—covertly,
for in the litigious world of contemporary medicine, it is almost treachery to reveal that this is how we learn best, by being wrong. To help my
compulsively driven and terrified students get on with their duties, I
tell them that, if it is true you learn from your mistakes, someday I will
know everything.

And we do learn from our special cases, one by one—sometimes 12
badly and incompletely, but each time the lesson is so painful that ultimately we do learn. For example, as a medical student, I was monitoring
the blood pressure of a man dying of acute pulmonary edema and
myocardial infarction.[2] The end of a gala evening for him. Next to me
was the man's wife—coiffed and elegantly gowned, cradling his head
and crooning her love while the man blanched into death. It was a good
death, since his physician, who was controlling the intravenous infusion
on the other side of the bed, had made sure that the man was heavily
sedated with morphine. It was a lesson I took with me to my internship,

---

[2] In layperson's terms, a severe heart attack. [Eds.]

when I treated my first patient with terminal cancer of the bowel. She was tough, this woman, crusty, white-haired, and quite prepared to die. The searing looks she leveled at me made me very much aware of my youth, my health, my innocence.

Alas, she was right about my innocence. I had not yet learned 13 everything there was to know about morphine. Pumping in large doses to control her pain, I failed to deal with its paralytic effects on the intestine. As a result, her last day was a horror of acute intestinal obstruction. I shall never forget the curses she hurled at me between squalls of sewage. I doubt there was a soul in the world who knew or cared that she died, but, of course, she was for me immemorial, a special case. Am I forgiven now that countless others have received the blessing of her curses?—for you can be sure that I never fail to teach the importance of keeping the bowels open when caring for a cancer patient. Am I forgiven? I do not know.

Yet, you can see how easy it is to corrupt this experience, to slide 14 from the special case to a state of mind based upon dehumanizing abstractions. For it was a failure in mechanics that led to the poor woman's suffering, and it is merely with the hope of better attending to such mechanics that we have developed the powerful technology that now pervades medicine. Now we can better manage not only the bowels but also the hearts, livers, kidneys, lungs, and all combinations thereof. How do we know we manage them better? We do randomized, double-blind, prospective experimental trials in which patients are aggregated into treatment groups, outcomes are analyzed, and their differences compared by statistics—another state of mind (a related word, in fact), another set of abstractions. Bearing the weight of these massive studies like armies of pharaonic slaves, we plod step by step up federally funded pyramids of therapeutic progress. Read any good medical journal: It is filled with multiauthored, multi-institutional papers. Modern medicine; how dehumanizing, we are told.

And lo and behold, we are repelled into an opposite state of mind, 15 a sentimental longing to escape such cold-blooded modernity. We applaud the hit play *Whose Life Is It Anyway?*, which ends with the quadriplegic hero rejecting life-sustaining technology and going home to die. As the lights come up, we are left to assume that offstage he will effervesce nobly, wittily, free of hunger, thirst, and embarrassing bodily products—fulfilling Milan Kundera's[3] definition of *kitsch*.

But the facts are not so vaporous, and the truth is not so clean- 16 shaven. For the truth is: Death is not an artist many of us admire. This artist's work is often messy. Pretending otherwise is sentimentality—a state of mind that we define as reaching sentiments too cheaply and easily. Of course, there is also the opposite state of mind, the reaction to

---

[3] Czech novelist and essayist. *Kitsch* is anything that appeals to popular or middlebrow taste. [Eds.]

sentimentality: cynicism, which can also be arrived at too cheaply and easily. Both of these states of mind are false. It is against both of these states of mind that the special case protests.

This, I submit, is what the euthanasia debate is about: theoretical 17 and statistical abstractions versus the anguishing, messy particulars of the special case. In illness, we are made exquisitely aware of what it means to be ourselves, no other, alone—this is happening to me. Those of us still healthy, if we are compassionate, acknowledge and even honor the unbreachable solitude of those who are ill. It joins us in a *community* of human feeling—notice that I do not use the word *state*. Because it is truly human, such a community—unlike the totalitarian state (of politics or of mind)—is as varied and unpredictable as the beings within it. And so, the argument goes, if we honor our fellow human beings—their variety, each and every life—it follows that we must honor how each person chooses to live that life, so long as it causes no harm to others. We must also honor—if fate so grants—whatever coda[4] each person sees fit to put on that life. In euthanasia, as in abortion, this issue of choice gets lost in the rhetorical smoke. No one is really *pro*-abortion. Similarly, no one claims to *like* euthanasia. Proponents merely want to have these options available in desperate circumstances.

But what will happen then? my worthy colleagues ask. Will things 18 fall apart? Is Nazi Germany our malign destiny? Or could it be, rather, that peaceable kingdom, the Netherlands, where an estimated five to ten thousand patients are administered euthanasia on request (and illegally) every year? Explicitly defined violations simply are not prosecuted. The physician is permitted to administer painless death only when a fully informed, rational patient voluntarily and repeatedly requests it in a medical situation that is considered intolerable and hopeless and unresponsive to any other means of medical relief. As a further safeguard, two physicians must concur with a patient's request. At no time are social goals considered. Each patient is treated as a special case, and in each case the act is voluntary.

But is it necessary to kill? my worthy colleagues argue, dubious that 19 a person in such extremity is capable of any voluntary act and drawing a distinction between "active" and "passive" euthanasia. Can't we simply allow such a case to die? Such a distinction, in my view, makes no sense, now that medicine has become so powerful that almost *any* life can be prolonged, however briefly. And once a decision is made that death is preferable to existence, *any* choice—whether giving or withholding treatment, whether it be surgery or antibiotics or narcotics—is an act toward or against that end. So, the only relevant moral questions

---

[4] Concluding section of a musical or dramatic work. [Eds.]

become *why* (the motive) and *how* (the method). One can have the cruelest motive and employ the kindest method; for example, slipping Gramps an overdose of sleeping medicine to get rid of him and get at his money. Or, one can have the kindest motive and employ the cruelest method: letting him "languish miserably" (in the words of Paré) out of a loving reluctance to hasten his death. Neither of these acts is as morally defensible, in my opinion, as the bloody dagger-thrust performed "gently and without anger" by that old unknown soldier.

And so, while the cautious Dutch carry on, several states—including California, once again—are preparing euthanasia initiatives.[5] And the difficult questions will have to be faced. Can we be both merciful and just in matters of medically administered death? How? Do we keep the laws the way they are and grant no exceptions, thus publicly condemning (while at the same time insidiously perpetuating) unsupervised euthanasia? Or should we change the laws? And if we do so, can we craft them in such a way so as not to destroy hallowed and fragile values? Should we explicitly define and sanction certain acts of humane suicide assisted by physicians? Should we allow patients direct legal access to the necessary drugs? Or should we not attempt to change the laws but only openly acknowledge (as in the Netherlands) certain permissible violations—thus cautioning physicians to weigh each act as one they may have to defend in criminal court? The approach we take will reveal much about ourselves as a society. Are our moral cousins the Nazis or the Dutch? Can we keep our anguish fresh each time we contemplate the end of a fellow human being? Or will our anguish grow stale, allowing us to slide down the slope from "easy death" to "useful death," heaping *them* into nameless, faceless piles, saying there go *they*, not *I*, and discovering too late—as others have before—that if yesterday *they* were the retarded, the handicapped, the Jews, the blacks; and if today *they* are the elderly, the AIDS patient; then tomorrow *they* will be ourselves, wondering where all the others are—common waste requiring special treatment rather than special cases sharing a common fate.

Responding to Reading

1. Should physicians be able to "offer death among their therapeutic options" (1)? Or should doctors maintain life at all costs? How do you respond to the "slippery slope" argument (8) offered by opponents of euthanasia?
2. What does Schneiderman mean when he says, "This, I submit, is what the euthanasia debate is about: theoretical and statistical abstractions versus the anguishing, messy particulars of the special case" (17)? Do you agree that this is indeed "what the debate is all about"?

---

[5] In late 1997, doctor-assisted suicide became legal in Oregon. [Eds.]

3. Both Schneiderman and Jack Kevorkian (below) are physicians, but they take different positions on euthanasia. How would Schneiderman react to Kevorkian's statement that he "acted openly, ethically, legally with complete and uncompromising honesty" (14) when he assisted in a suicide?

A CASE OF ASSISTED SUICIDE

Jack Kevorkian

Popularly known as "Dr. Death," Jack Kevorkian (1928–   ) has had a long interest in death and dying, which some critics trace to the fact that most of his Armenian family was annihilated by German soldiers during World War II. Trained in pathology at the University of Michigan, he was one of the earliest advocates of executing criminals by lethal injection, a practice which is followed in many states today. He has also argued in favor of using condemned criminals in medical experiments that will eventually kill them. Kevorkian's greatest notoriety, however, stems from his publicly acknowledged assistance in the suicides of over one hundred people with terminal or debilitatingly painful illnesses, actions for which he has been charged with murder four times in Michigan courts, resulting in three mistrials and one acquittal. In the following chapter from his book Prescription Medicide: The Goodness of Planned Death *(1991), Kevorkian describes in detail the first suicide in which he assisted using his "Mercitron," the device he invented for this purpose.*

Amid the flurry of telephone calls in the fall of 1989 was one from a man in Portland, Oregon, who learned of my campaign from an item in *Newsweek* (November 13, 1989). Ron Adkins's rich, baritone, matter-of-fact voice was tinged with a bit of expectant anxiety as he calmly explained the tragic situation of his beloved wife. Janet Adkins was a remarkable, accomplished, active woman—wife, mother, grandmother, revered friend, teacher, musician, mountain climber, and outdoorsperson—who, for some time, had noticed (as did her husband) subtle and gradually progressive impairment of her memory. The shock of hearing the diagnosis of Alzheimer's disease four months earlier was magnified by the abrupt and somewhat callous way her doctor announced it. The intelligent woman knew what the diagnosis portended, and at that instant decided she would not live to experience the horror of such a death.

Knowing that Janet was a courageous fighter, Ron and their three sons pleaded with her to reconsider and at least give a promising new therapy regimen a try. Ron explained to me that Janet was eligible to take part in an experimental trial using the newly developed drug Tacrine® or THA at the University of Washington in Seattle. I concurred that Janet should enroll in the program because any candidate for the Mercitron must have exhausted every potentially beneficial medical intervention, no matter how remotely promising.

I heard nothing more from the Adkinses until April 1990. Ron called 3 again, after Janet and he saw me and my device on a nationally televised talk show. Janet had entered the experimental program in January, but it had been stopped early because the new drug was ineffective. In fact, her condition got worse; and she was more determined than ever to end her life. Even though from a physical standpoint Janet was not imminently terminal, there seemed little doubt that mentally she was— and, after all, it is one's mental status that determines the essence of one's existence. I asked Ron to forward to me copies of Janet's clinical records, and they corroborated what Ron had said.

I then telephoned Janet's doctor in Seattle. He opposed her planned 4 action and the concept of assisted suicide in general. It was his firm opinion that Janet would remain mentally competent for at least a year (but from Ron's narrative I concluded that her doctor's opinion was wrong and that time was of the essence). Because Janet's condition was deteriorating and there was nothing else that might help arrest it, I decided to accept her as the first candidate—a qualified, justifiable candidate if not "ideal"—and well aware of the vulnerability to criticism of picayune and overly emotional critics.

A major obstacle was finding a place to do it. Because I consider 5 medicide to be necessary, ethical, and legal, there should be nothing furtive about it. Another reason to pursue the practice above-board is to avert the harassment or vindictiveness of litigation. Consequently, when searching for a suitable site I always explained that I planned to assist a suffering patient to commit suicide. That posed no problem for helping a Michigan resident in his or her own residence. But it was a different matter for an out-of-state guest who must rent temporary quarters.

And I soon found out how difficult a matter it could be. My own 6 apartment could not be used because of lease constraints, and the same was true of my sister's apartment. I inquired at countless motels, funeral homes, churches of various denominations, rental office buildings, clinics, doctors' offices for lease, and even considered the futile hope of renting an emergency life-support ambulance. Many owners, proprietors, and landlords were quite sympathetic but fearful and envisioned the negative public reaction that could seriously damage and even destroy their business enterprises. In short, they deemed it bad for public relations. More dismaying yet was the refusal of people who are known supporters and active campaigners for euthanasia to allow Janet and me the use of their homes.

Finally, a friend agreed to avail us of his modest home in Detroit; 7 I immediately contacted Ron to finalize plans. My initial proposal was to carry out the procedure at the end of May 1990, but Ron and Janet preferred to avoid the surge of travel associated with the Memorial Day weekend. The date was postponed to Monday, June 4th.

In the meantime, my friend was warned by a doctor, in whom he 8 confided, not to make his home available for such a purpose. Soon thereafter the offer was quickly withdrawn. With the date set and airline tickets having been purchased by Janet, Ron, and a close friend of Janet's, I had to scamper to find another site. The device required an electrical outlet, which limited the possibilities.

I had made a Herculean effort to provide a desirable, clinical set- 9 ting. Literally and sadly, there was "no room at the inn." Now, having been refused everywhere I applied, the *only alternative* remaining was my 1968 camper and a suitable campground.

As expected, the owners of a commercial site refused permission, 10 even though they were sympathetic to the proposed scheme. They then suggested the solution by recommending that I rent space at a public camping site not too far away. The setting was pleasant and idyllic.

As with many other aspects of this extraordinary event, I was aware 11 of the harsh criticism that would be leveled at the use of a "rusty old van." In the first place, the twenty-two-year-old body may have been rusting on the outside, but its interior was very clean, orderly, and comfortable. I have slept in it often and not felt degraded. But carping critics missed the point: the essence and significance of the event are far more important than the splendor of the site where it takes place. If critics are thus deluded into denouncing the exit from existence under these circumstances, then why not the same delusional denunciation of entrance into existence when a baby is, of necessity, born in an old taxicab? On the contrary, the latter identical scenario seems to arouse only feelings of sentimental reverence and quaint joy.

But the dishonesty doesn't stop there. I have been repeatedly criti- 12 cized for having assisted a patient after a short personal acquaintance of two days. Overlooked or ignored is my open avowal to be the first practitioner in this country of a new and as yet officially unrecognized specialty. Because of shameful stonewalling by her own doctors, Janet was forced to refer herself to me. And acting as a unique specialist, of necessity self-proclaimed, solitary, and independent, I was obligated to scrutinize Janet's clinical records and to consult with her personal doctor. The latter's uncooperative attitude (tacitly excused by otherwise harsh critics) impaired but did not thwart fulfillment of my duties to a suffering patient and to my profession.

It is absurd even to imply, let alone to protest outright, that a med- 13 ical specialist's competence and ethical behavior are contingent upon some sort of time interval, imposed arbitrarily or by fiat. When a doctor refers a patient for surgery, in many cases the surgical specialist performs his *ultimate* duty after personal acquaintance with the patient from a mere hour or two of prior consultation (in contrast to my having spent at least twelve hours in personal contact with Janet). In a few instances the surgeon operates on a patient seen for the first time on the operating table—and anesthetized to unconsciousness.

Moreover, in sharp contrast to the timorous, secretive, and even 14 deceitful intention and actions of other medical euthanasists on whom our so-called bioethicists now shower praise, I acted openly, ethically, legally, with complete and uncompromising honesty, and—even more important—I remained in personal attendance during the second most meaningful medical event in a patient's earthly existence. Were he alive today, it's not hard to guess what Hippocrates[1] would say about all this.

My two sisters, Margo and Flora, and I met with Ron, Janet, and 15 Janet's close friend Carroll Rehmke in their motel room on Saturday afternoon, 2 June 1990. After getting acquainted through a few minutes of conversation, the purpose of the trip was thoroughly discussed. I had already prepared authorization forms signifying Janet's intent, determination, and freedom of choice, which she readily agreed to sign. Here again, while she was resolute in her decision, and absolutely mentally competent, her impaired memory was apparent when she needed her husband's assistance in forming the cursive letter "A." She could print the letter but not write it, and the consent forms required that her signature be written. So her husband showed her on another piece of paper how to form the cursive "A," and Janet complied. At this time, Ron and Carroll also signed a statement attesting to Janet's mental competence. Following this signing session, I had Flora videotape my interview with Janet and Ron. The forty-five-minute taping reinforced my own conviction that Janet was mentally competent but that her memory had failed badly. However, the degree of memory failure led me to surmise that within four to six months she would be too incompetent to qualify as a candidate. It should be pointed out that in medical terms loss of memory does not automatically signify mental incompetence. Any rational critic would concede that a mentally sound individual can be afflicted with even total amnesia.

Around 5:30 P.M. that same day all six of us had dinner at a well- 16 known local restaurant. Seated around the same table for many hours, our conversation covered many subjects, including the telling of jokes. Without appearing too obvious, I constantly observed Janet's behavior and assessed her moods as well as the content and quality of her thoughts. There was absolutely no doubt that her mentality was intact and that she was not the least depressed over her impending death. On the contrary, the only detectable anxiety or disquieting demeanor was among the rest of us to a greater or lesser degree. Even in response to

---

[1] Ancient Greek physician, called the father of medicine, who gave his name to the Hippocratic oath taken by all medical doctors. [Eds.]

jokes, Janet's appropriately timed and modulated laughter indicated clear and coherent comprehension. The only uneasiness or distress she exhibited was due to her embarrassment at being unable to recall aspects of the topic under discussion at the time. And that is to be expected of intelligent, sensitive, and diligent individuals.

We left the restaurant at 12:30 A.M. Sunday. Janet and Ron enjoyed 17 their last full day by themselves.

At 8:30 A.M. the next day, Monday, 4 June 1990, I drove into a rented 18 space at Groveland Park in north Oakland County, Michigan. At the same time, my sisters drove to the motel to fetch Janet, who had composed (and submitted to my sister) a brief and clear note reiterating her genuine desire to end her life and exonerating all others in this desire and the actual event. For the last time, Janet took tearful leave of her grieving husband and Carroll, both of whom were inconsolable. It was Janet's wish that they not accompany her to the park.

The day began cold, damp, and overcast. I took a lot of time in set- 19 ting up the Mercitron and giving it a few test runs. In turning to get a pair of pliers in the cramped space within the van, I accidentally knocked over the container of thiopental solution, losing a little over half of it. I was fairly sure that the remainder was enough to induce and maintain adequate unconsciousness, but I chose not to take the risk. I drove the forty-five miles home and got some more.

In the meantime, at about 9:30 A.M. my sisters and Janet had arrived 20 at the park. They were dismayed to learn of the accidental spill and opted to accompany me on the extra round trip, which required two and one-half hours. We reentered the park at approximately noontime. Janet remained in the car with Margo while Flora helped me with minor tasks in the van as I very carefully prepared and tested the Mercitron. Everything was ready by about 2:00 P.M., and Janet was summoned.

She entered the van alone through the open sliding side door and 21 lay fully clothed on the built-in bed covered with freshly laundered sheets. Her head rested comfortably on a clean pillow. The windows were covered with new draperies. With Janet's permission I cut small holes in her nylon stockings at the ankles, attached ECG electrodes to her ankles and wrists, and covered her body with a light blanket. Our conversation was minimal. In accordance with Janet's wish, Flora read to her a brief note from her friend Carroll, followed by a reading of the Lord's prayer. I then repeated my earlier instructions to Janet about how the device was to be activated, and asked her to go through the motions. In contrast to my sister and me, Janet was calm and outwardly relaxed.

I used a syringe with attached needle to pierce a vein near the 22 frontal elbow area of her left arm. Unfortunately, her veins were delicate and fragile; even slight movement of the restrained arm caused the needle to penetrate through the wall of the vein resulting in leakage. Two more attempts also failed, as did a fourth attempt on the right side.

Finally an adequate puncture was obtained on the right arm. (It was reassuring to me to learn later that doctors in Seattle had had similar difficulty with her veins.)

The moment had come. With a nod from Janet I turned on the ECG 23 and said, "Now." Janet hit the Mercitron's switch with the outer edge of her palm. In about ten seconds her eyelids began to flicker and droop. She looked up at me and said, "Thank you, thank you." I replied at once as her eyelids closed, "Have a nice trip." She was unconscious and perfectly still except for two widely spaced and mild coughs several minutes later. Agonal complexes in the ECG tracing indicated death due to complete cessation of blood circulation in six minutes.

It was 2:30 P.M. Suddenly—for the first time that cold, dank day— 24 warm sunshine bathed the park.

Responding to Reading

1. Throughout his essay, Kevorkian uses euphemisms ("procedure," "assisted suicide," "medicide," and the name "Mercitron," for example) and makes snide remarks—"so called bioethicists" in paragraph 14, for example. In what way do these uses of language affect his credibility?
2. In paragraph 12, Kevorkian accuses his critics of intellectual dishonesty. Are there any points in this essay where you think Kevorkian is being less than honest with readers? With himself?
3. Where does Kevorkian address the arguments against his position? Do these arguments answer any of Lawrence J. Schneiderman's questions about euthanasia (p. 637)? How effectively does Kevorkian address these questions?

RUSH TO LETHAL JUDGMENT

Stephen L. Carter

Stephen L. Carter (1954–   ) attended Stanford University and the Yale Law School, and he is currently William Nelson Cromwell Professor of Law at Yale. Both a legal scholar and a wide-ranging social critic, Carter is the author of Reflections of an Affirmative Action Baby *(1991), a memoir of how he himself benefited from affirmative action but in which he also critiques such policies;* The Culture of Disbelief: How American Law and Politics Trivialize Religious Devotion *(1993);* The Confirmation Mess: Cleaning Up the Federal Appointments Process *(1994); and* Integrity *(1996), a series of essays in which he reflects on issues of personal responsibility and morality. He is currently at work on a second collection of essays to be titled* Civility. *In "Rush to Lethal Judgment," which originally appeared in the* New York Times Magazine, *Carter criticizes two 1996 appellate court rulings affirming a terminally ill patient's right to physician-assisted suicide, arguing that, by extension, anyone—ill or not—could demand that right.*

Many years ago, a psychiatrist who was treating someone I loved 1 asked me to remember that she had the right to kill herself if she wanted to. Sometimes, he said softly, the decision to commit suicide is the decision of a rational mind, a reasonable if tragic answer to the question of whether life is worth continuing.

When he said "right," he did not, of course, mean constitutional 2 right; he meant moral right, a part of human dignity. As long as her mind was sound, she had the right as an autonomous individual to decide whether to continue living. Her responsibilities to her loved ones and her community might have carried weight in the moral calculus, but the final decision had to be hers alone.

Although I saw the logic of his position then and see it now, the law 3 has traditionally offered a rather different understanding. Suicide was a felony under England's common-law regime, and was illegal everywhere in the United States into this century. Some cynics have identified the age-old prohibition on suicide as a matter of royal selfishness—at common law, if you committed a felony, your worldly goods went to the crown—but the better answer is that the laws reflected a strong belief that the lives of individuals belonged not to themselves alone but to the communities in which they lived and to the God who gave them breath.

Nowadays, we have a broader notion of individual autonomy. Our 4 laws increasingly reflect the belief that our lives do belong to us alone. Some anti-suicide statutes are still on the books, but today the societal distaste for suicide is registered through the civil, not the criminal, law: people who try suicide but do not succeed may be involuntarily hospitalized to determine whether they are continuing threats to themselves. So although we certainly try to prevent suicide, we no longer punish it.

There is one exception: most jurisdictions continue to treat the person 5 who directly assists someone else's suicide as a felon. That is the basis, for example, of Michigan's prosecutions of the notorious "suicide doctor," Jack Kevorkian, who, as of this writing, has been involved in more than 30 suicides.[1] Many a family harbors its secret story of indirect assistance—leaving the bottle of sleeping pills within reach of the dying relative, for example—but the reason for the secrecy in part has been the traditional view that assistance of any kind is at least immoral and often illegal.

In recent months, however, two Federal appellate courts have 6 held that terminally ill patients have a constitutional right to seek the

---

[1] Now over one hundred. [Eds.]

assistance of physicians in ending their lives. With the entire dispute plainly on its way to the Supreme Court[2] anyway, opponents and supporters of what has come to be called the "right to die" are even now battling their way through the implications. The moral questions raised by assisted suicide are weighty, but our ability as a society to deal with them has been seriously weakened by the judicial rush to enshrine one side's moral answer in the framework of constitutional rights.

The two cases presented the same basic question, but the courts dealt 7 with it in very different ways. In March, the Court of Appeals for the Ninth Circuit, based in San Francisco, decided the case of Compassion in Dying v. State of Washington, resting the right to assisted suicide for the terminally ill on the due process clause of the 14th Amendment, the same provision in which the courts have located the abortion right. The right to choose how to end one's own life, the court explained, was a direct descendant of the right to choose whether to bear a child, and, as with abortion, the state must have a very strong reason before it may interfere.

Then, less than a month later, the Second Circuit struck down New 8 York's assisted-suicide ban in the case of Quill v. Vacco. The Second Circuit rejected the due process argument, pointing out that the United States Supreme Court has limited that approach to cases in which the state is interfering with a fundamental liberty "deeply rooted in this Nation's history and tradition," like the freedom to marry or procreate. The right to obtain assistance in suicide, the court sensibly concluded, does not fit this definition. But the Quill court found a rationale of its own: the right to assisted suicide is supported, said the judges, by another part of the 14th Amendment—the equal protection clause. Why? Because New York allows mentally competent terminally ill patients on life support to direct the removal of the supporting apparatus, even when the removal will hasten or directly cause their deaths, but prohibits those who do not need life support from obtaining drugs to hasten or directly cause their deaths. So the state is discriminating, in the court's terms, by allowing some of the terminally ill, but not others, to die quickly.

The logic of Quill, although more attractive than that of Com- 9 passion in Dying, seems terribly forced, not least because the state allows many other distinctions among the terminally ill—for example, wealthier patients often have access to experimental drugs and therapies that others do not. These distinctions may not always seem sensible or fair but they hardly rise to the level of constitutional concern.

---

[2] Carter's essay was published in 1996. In June of 1997, the U.S. Supreme Court ruled unanimously against a constitutional right to assisted suicide; however, in November of that same year voters in Oregon passed a final ballot measure supporting physician-assisted suicide in that state, and in March of 1998, terminally patients there first received such assistance. [Eds.]

And there is a larger analytical problem with both decisions. If the 10 right to choose suicide with the help of a physician is of constitutional dimension, it is difficult to discern how it can be limited to those who are terminally ill. Terminal illness is not a legal category—it is a medical category, and one that even doctors sometimes have trouble defining. Some of us who teach constitutional law—the old-fashioned types, I suppose—still tell our students that constitutional rights arise by virtue of citizenship, not circumstance. This implies that each of us (each who is a competent adult, at least) possesses an identical set of rights. So if there is indeed a constitutional right to suicide, assisted or not, it must attach to all citizens.

If the right to pursue assistance in suicide attaches to all citizens, 11 then the Constitution is at present being violated by all the state laws permitting the involuntary hospitalization of individuals who try suicide. Instead of locking them up, we should be asking them if they would like assistance in their task. In fact, the Second Circuit has matters precisely backward: if everybody except the terminally ill were allowed to seek the assistance of physicians in suicide, the equal protection claim might have merit. If, on the other hand, the terminally ill are allowed to seek suicide, the court's concern for equality might suggest that everybody should be allowed to do it, lest the state discriminate between two groups who want to die, those who desire to commit suicide because they are terminally ill and those who desire to commit suicide because they are dreadfully unhappy.

Except in emergencies, a court decision is the worst way to resolve 12 a moral dilemma. Constitutional rights, as they mature, have a nagging habit of bursting from the analytical confinements in which they are spawned. When the Supreme Court struck down organized classroom prayer in 1962, nobody other than a few opponents of the rulings, dismissed as cranks, envisioned a future in which courts would order traditional religious language and symbols stripped from official buildings and state seals. And did the justices who voted to legalize abortion in 1973 really imagine that two decades later, the United States would be home to 1.5 million abortions a year?

In the case of the right to assisted suicide, the risks are many. For 13 example, it is far from obvious that the right can be limited to adults. The abortion right isn't. The Supreme Court has ruled that pregnant minors must be allowed to demonstrate to a judge that they are mature enough to make up their own minds about abortion. It does not take much of a stretch to imagine a judge concluding that a young person mature enough to decide that a child should not come into the world is also mature enough to decide that her (or his) own life is not worth living.

And there are other, more ominous difficulties. Some worried med- 14 ical ethicists have predicted that a right to assisted suicide might lead exhausted families to encourage terminally ill relatives to kill themselves. Moreover, women are more likely than men to try suicide, but men succeed much more often than women. With the help of health care workers, women, too, might begin to succeed at a high rate. Is this form of gender equality what we are looking for?

But the biggest problem with the idea of a constitutional right to 15 assisted suicide is that the courts (if the decisions stand) are preempting a moral debate that is, for most Americans, just beginning. To criticize the constitutional foundation for the recent decisions is not at all to suggest that the policy questions are easy ones. There are strong, thoughtful voices—and plausible moral arguments—on both sides of the assisted-suicide debate, as there are in the larger euthanasia debate. The questions are vital ones: Do our mortal lives belong to us alone or do they belong to the communities or families in which we are embedded? Will this new right give the dying a greater sense of control over their circumstances, or will it weaken our respect for life?

These are, as I said, weighty questions, and the policy arguments on 16 either side are the stuff of which public political and moral debates are made. And a thoughtful, well-reasoned debate over assisted suicide is precisely what we as a nation need; we do not need judicial intervention to put a decisive end to a conversation that we as a people have scarcely begun. Because the arguments on both sides carry such strong moral plausibility—and because the claim of constitutional right is anything but compelling—the questions should be answered through popular debate and perhaps legislation, not through legal briefs and litigation. In an ideal world, the Supreme Court would swiftly overturn Quill and Compassion in Dying, allowing the rest of us the space and time for the moral reflection that the issue demands.

Responding to Reading

1. What does Carter mean when he says, "The moral questions raised by assisted suicide are weighty, but our ability as a society to deal with them has been seriously weakened by the judicial rush to enshrine one side's moral answer in the framework of constitutional rights" (6)?

2. Carter argues against making the "right to die" a constitutional right by identifying the problems that would occur if such a right were granted. What are these problems? According to Carter, how should society handle the issue of assisted suicide?

3. Carter criticizes two Supreme Court decisions: *Compassion in Dying v. State of Washington* and *Quill v. Vacco*. How would Jack Kevorkian (p. 643) respond to these decisions? Is Carter sidestepping the moral issue by focusing on the Constitution?

Widening the Focus

────────────── **WRITING** ──────────────

Medical Practice and Responsibility

1. In a 1993 editorial in *Forbes* magazine, publisher Malcolm S. Forbes, Jr., called Dr. Jack Kevorkian a "serial killer" who should be "tried for murder—or at least manslaughter." Write an essay in which you side with either Forbes or Kevorkian, referring to the other essays in the Focus section to support your position.

2. Write an essay in which you describe your ideal doctor. Refer specifically to readings in this chapter as you develop your description.

3. Assume you are either an animal rights activist or a person who believes that animal experimentation is necessary. Write an editorial for your local newspaper in which you present your case, citing information in Jane Goodall's essay. If you like, you may also refer to Claire McCarthy's "Dog Lab" in Chapter 10 (p. 774).

4. Write an essay in which you compare your own ideas about disease with the ideas of Perri Klass's Indian patients. In what ways are your ideas similar to theirs? In what ways are they different? What do you conclude from this comparison?

5. In "What Nurses Stand For," Suzanne Gordon says that the public's lack of concern about the layoffs of nurses "may be couched in the stereotypes of nursing or of women's work in general" (51). Interview several of your friends and family members about their attitudes toward nurses. Find out whether they see them as highly trained professionals or as people who do menial tasks. Then, write an essay in which you discuss your findings.

6. Abraham Verghese in "My Own Country," Perri Klass in "India," and Richard Selzer in "Imelda" all consider the limitations of medical science. Choose a medical problem and discuss how it presents challenges for both medical personnel and the general public. If you like, you may refer to the essays by Verghese, Klass, and Selzer.

7. Identify a medical advance that has changed either your own life or the life of someone you know. Write an essay in which you discuss how this development has affected you or the person you know—and, possibly, society as a whole.

8. Assume you are the new director of Anna Mae Halgrim Seaver's nursing home. Write a memo in which you outline changes that would make life in the nursing home better for its residents. In your memo, respond specifically to the points Seaver mentions in her essay.

9. Some people have compared the current AIDS epidemic to the bubonic plague that Barbara Tuchman describes in "The Black Death." Write an essay in which you compare the two diseases. In what ways are they the same, and in what ways are they different?

For example, are our attitudes toward AIDS different from those of the people who lived in the fourteenth century toward the bubonic plague? In addition to Tuchman's essay, you may also refer to Abraham Verghese's "My Own Country."

10. Do you think a person has a right to die? Is this right guaranteed by the Constitution? Under what circumstances? In what way? Who, if anyone, should "assist" the patient? Write an essay in which you discuss these issues. Include information from Lawrence J. Schneiderman's "The Ethics of Euthanasia," Stephen L. Carter's "Rush to Lethal Judgment," and Jack Kevorkian's "A Case of Assisted Suicide."

9

EARTH IN THE BALANCE

Student Voices

"I think there is a definite problem between human beings and nature. Human beings need the resources of nature in order to live, but we must use them in moderation. If we would just take the time to consider how important nature is to our survival, we would try harder to maintain the proper balance between us and nature."

—*Eric Forte*

"There are many opportunities to make the earth a cleaner and better place. Most damage to the earth's surface comes from industrial waste. For years industries have been dumping their waste into the earth's waterways, thinking that it would wash out to sea and disappear. The truth, however, is that many of our lakes and waterways have become so polluted that they are unable to support life.

"Today we're starting to try to clean up the mess we have made. Laws have been passed to prohibit dumping in the oceans or in waterways. Landfills are being engineered to make them less likely to leak. And paper, aluminum, glass, and some plastics are being recycled."

—*Lauren Adair*

"One of the simplest ways a person can help save the environment is by recycling. Still, I don't think recycling will have much of an impact until industry uses recycled products on a much larger scale."

—*Robert Barr*

"When people overpopulate a piece of land, they destroy the resources they depend on—trees for shade and wood, land for grazing and farming, and animals for food. In addition, when their farm animals overgraze, they eat the grass down to its roots and kill the plants they need to survive."

—*Elisha Mark*

"The destruction of the earth is unavoidable. People will not make the changes or pay the price to save the planet. Some day they will look back and think how beautiful the earth was and how long it could have lasted if they only had cared more. But then it will be too late."

—*Jeff Morris*

"People need to care for the earth. It's not ours to damage. We belong to the earth just as those before us did and just as those after us will. Each individual effort is one step toward preserving the earth. For example, I have stopped eating meat. I don't really think it will make a difference, but it's my way of showing I care."

—*Renee Higgins*

—————————— PREPARING TO READ AND WRITE ——————————

Over a hundred years ago essayist Henry David Thoreau, already sensing the dangers of industrialism and expansionism, decided to move into the woods next to Walden Pond to reestablish his connections with nature. To one degree or another, *Walden*, Thoreau's account of his retreat, has influenced many of the writers in this section. Like Thoreau, they are concerned with examining the complex relationship between human beings and the environment; most believe that by ignoring this relationship, human beings cause the disappearance of scores of species each year, destroy thousands of acres of rain forest, and, ultimately, risk the extinction of all life on earth.

Today, we live in a technological culture, yet nature, with all its majesty, endures. By such phenomena as grass pushing up through cracks in the pavement or dead animals littering the roads, nature reminds us that another, larger world exists outside our limited human sphere. Of course, the price we pay for living in society is our estrangement from the natural environment. We are not estranged in the literal sense of the word, for we are surrounded by the trees in our parks, the animals we keep as pets or in zoos, and the gardens we maintain in our yards. Still, the nature with which we have become familiar has become so domesticated that we have ceased to see it as alien or exotic.

Despite the gulf that seems to separate many contemporary men and women from nature, one thing remains clear: nature continues to affect us in subtle and mysterious ways. As Chief Seattle says in "Letter to President Pierce, 1855," humankind cannot break its contact with nature, for "whatever happens to the beasts also happens to man. All things are connected. Whatever befalls the earth befalls the sons of the earth." In many ways, we are dependent upon our natural environment, and we have a responsibility—perhaps even a duty—to preserve it.

As you read and prepare to write about the selections in this chapter, you may consider the following questions:

- What is the writer's attitude toward nature?

- Is nature seen as hostile or friendly?

- Does the writer present an objective or subjective description of nature?

- Do you think the writer is being realistic or idealistic? Reasonable or unreasonable? Practical or romantic?

- What relationship does the writer think people have with nature? What relationship does he or she think people *ought* to have with nature?

- What does the writer see as the consequences of being separated from nature?

- What effect does interaction with nature have on the writer?

- What preconceived ideas does the writer think people have about nature? Does the writer reinforce or challenge these ideas?

- What effect does the writer think civilization has on nature? Do you agree with the writer?

- In what ways is the essay similar to or different from other essays in this chapter?

TWO PERSPECTIVES ON EARTH IN THE BALANCE

Written more than a century apart, the following two statements make a surprisingly similar point about the effects of human "progress" on the environment. The first selection is an 1855 letter to U.S. President Franklin Pierce from Native American Chief Seattle (see p. 660), who served as a mediator between his tribes and the first white settlers in the area around Puget Sound; in it, Seattle warns the conquering white nation, "Continue to contaminate your bed, and you will one night suffocate in your own waste." Following this is an excerpt from Earth in the Balance *(1992), Al Gore's (b. 1948) best-selling examination of a wide range of environmental problems. In his chapter entitled "The Wasteland," Gore looks specifically at the extent to which we are, as Chief Seattle predicted, suffocating in our own waste. A graduate of Harvard and both the School of Religion and the School of Law at Vanderbilt, Gore was an investigative reporter at the Nashville* Tennessean *before following in his father's footsteps and entering politics. He served Tennessee as a member of the U.S. House of Representatives (1977–1985) and Senator (1985–1993), before assuming the vice presidency. He is also the author of* Common Sense Government *(1995). Much of* Earth in the Balance *is based on research he conducted in the course of his work on congressional subcommittees.*

LETTER TO PRESIDENT PIERCE, 1855

Chief Seattle

We know that the white man does not understand our ways. One   1
portion of the land is the same to him as the next, for he is a stranger who comes in the night and takes from the land whatever he needs. The earth is not his brother, but his enemy, and when he has conquered it, he moves on. He leaves his fathers' graves, and his children's birthright is forgotten. The sight of your cities pains the eyes of the red man. But perhaps it is because the red man is a savage and does not understand.

There is no quiet place in the white man's cities. No place to hear   2
the leaves of spring or the rustle of insect's wings. But perhaps because I am a savage and do not understand, the clatter only seems to insult the ears. The Indian prefers the soft sound of the wind darting over the face of the pond, the smell of the wind itself cleansed by a mid-day rain, or scented with the piñon pine. The air is precious to the red man. For all

things share the same breath—the beasts, the trees, the man. Like a man dying for many days, he is numb to the stench.

What is man without the beasts? If all the beasts were gone, men 3 would die from great loneliness of spirit, for whatever happens to the beasts also happens to man. All things are connected. Whatever befalls the earth befalls the sons of the earth.

It matters little where we pass the rest of our days; they are not 4 many. A few more hours, a few more winters, and none of the children of the great tribes that once lived on this earth, or that roamed in small bands in the woods, will be left to mourn the graves of a people once as powerful and hopeful as yours.

The whites, too, shall pass—perhaps sooner than other tribes. 5 Continue to contaminate your bed, and you will one night suffocate in your own waste. When the buffalo are all slaughtered, the wild horses all tamed, the secret corners of the forest heavy with the scent of many men, and the view of the ripe hills blotted by talking wires,[1] where is the thicket? Gone. Where is the eagle? Gone. And what is it to say goodby to the swift and the hunt, the end of living and the beginning of survival? We might understand if we knew what it was that the white man dreams, what he describes to his children on the long winter nights, what visions he burns into their minds, so they will wish for tomorrow. But we are savages. The white man's dreams are hidden from us.

THE WASTELAND

Al Gore

One of the clearest signs that our relationship to the global environ- 1 ment is in severe crisis is the floodtide of garbage spilling out of our cities and factories. What some have called the "throwaway society" has been based on the assumptions that endless resources will allow us to produce an endless supply of goods and that bottomless receptacles (i.e., landfills and ocean dumping sites) will allow us to dispose of an endless stream of waste. But now we are beginning to drown in that stream. Having relied for too long on the old strategy of "out of sight, out of mind," we are now running out of ways to dispose of our waste in a manner that keeps it out of either sight or mind.

In an earlier era, when the human population and the quantities of 2 waste generated were much smaller and when highly toxic forms of waste were uncommon, it was possible to believe that the world's

---

[1] Telegraph wires. [Eds.]

absorption of our waste meant that we need not think about it again. Now, however, all that has changed. Suddenly, we are disconcerted—even offended—when the huge quantities of waste we thought we had thrown away suddenly demand our attention as landfills overflow, incinerators foul the air, and neighboring communities and states attempt to dump their overflow problems on us.

The American people have, in recent years, become embroiled in   3 debates about the relative merits of various waste disposal schemes, from dumping it in the ocean to burying it in a landfill to burning it or taking it elsewhere, anywhere, as long as it is somewhere else. Now, however, we must confront a strategic threat to our capacity to dispose of—or even recycle—the enormous quantities of waste now being produced. Simply put, the way we think about waste is leading to the production of so much of it that no method for handling it can escape being completely overwhelmed. There is only one way out: we have to change our production processes and dramatically reduce the amount of waste we create in the first place and ensure that we consider thoroughly, ahead of time, just how we intend to recycle or isolate that which unavoidably remains. But first we have to think clearly about the complexities of the predicament.

Waste is a multifaceted problem. We think of waste as whatever is   4 useless, or unprofitable according to our transitory methods of calculating value, or sufficiently degraded so that the cost of reclamation seems higher than the cost of disposal. But anything produced in excess—nuclear weapons, for example, or junk mail—also represents waste. And in modern civilization, we have come to think of almost any natural resource as "going to waste" if we have failed to develop it, which usually means exploiting it for commercial use. Ironically, however, when we do transform natural resources into something useful, we create waste twice—once when we generate waste as part of the production process and a second time when we tire of the thing itself and throw it away.

Perhaps the most visible evidence of the waste crisis is the problem   5 of how to dispose of our mountains of municipal solid waste, which is being generated at the rate of more than five pounds a day for every citizen of this country, or approximately one ton per person per year. But two other kinds of waste pose equally difficult challenges. The first is the physically dangerous and politically volatile material known as hazardous waste, which accompanied the chemical revolution of the 1930s and which the United States now produces in roughly the same quantities as municipal solid waste. (This is a conservative estimate, one that would double if we counted all the hazardous waste that is currently exempted from regulation for a variety of administrative and political reasons.) Second, one ton of industrial solid waste is created each week for every man, woman, and child—and this does not even count the gaseous waste steadily being vented into the atmosphere. (For example, each person in the United States also produces an average of twenty tons of CO_2[1] each year.) Incredibly, taking into account all three of these conservatively defined categories of waste, every person in the United States produces *more than twice his or her weight in waste every day.*

It's easy to discount the importance of such a statistic, but we can 6 no longer consider ourselves completely separate from the waste we help to produce at work or the waste that is generated in the process of supplying us with the things we buy and use.

Our cavalier attitude toward this problem is an indication of how 7 hard it will be to solve. Even the words we use to describe our behavior reveal the pattern of self-deception. Take, for example, the word *consumption*, which implies an almost mechanical efficiency, suggesting that all traces of whatever we consume magically vanish after we use it. In fact, when we consume something, it doesn't go away at all. Rather, it is transformed into two very different kinds of things: something "useful" and the stuff left over, which we call "waste." Moreover, anything we think of as useful becomes waste as soon as we are finished with it, so our perception of the things we consume must be considered when deciding what is and isn't waste. Until recently, none of these issues has seemed terribly important; indeed, a high rate of consumption has often been cited as a distinguishing characteristic of an advanced society. Now, however, this attitude can no longer be considered in any way healthy, desirable, or acceptable.

The waste crisis is integrally related to the crisis of industrial civi- 8 lization as a whole. Just as our internal combustion engines have automated the process by which our lungs transform oxygen into carbon dioxide (CO_2), our industrial apparatus has vastly magnified the process by which our digestive system transforms raw material (food) into human energy and growth—and waste. Viewed as an extension of our own consumption process, our civilization now ingests enormous quantities of trees, coal, oil, minerals, and thousands of substances taken from their places of discovery, then transforms them into "products" of every shape, kind, and description—and into vast mountain ranges of waste.

The chemical revolution has burst upon the world with awesome 9 speed. Our annual production of organic chemicals soared from 1 million tons in 1930 to 7 million tons in 1950, 63 million in 1970, and half a billion in 1990. At the current rate, world chemical production is now doubling in volume every seven to eight years. The amount of chemical waste dumped into landfills, lakes, rivers, and oceans is staggering. In the United States alone, there are an estimated 650,000 commercial and

---

[1] Carbon dioxide. [Eds.]

industrial sources of hazardous waste; the Environmental Protection Agency (EPA) believes that 99 percent of this waste comes from only 2 percent of the sources, and an estimated 64 percent of all hazardous waste is managed at only ten regulated facilities. Two thirds of all hazardous waste comes from chemical manufacturing and almost one quarter from the production of metals and machinery. The remaining 11 percent is divided between petroleum refining (3 percent) and a hundred other smaller categories. According to the United Nations Environment Programme, more than 7 million chemicals have now been discovered or created by humankind, and several thousand new ones are added each year. Of the 80,000 now in common use in significant quantities, most are produced in a manner that also creates chemical waste, much of it hazardous. While many kinds of hazardous chemical waste can be managed fairly easily, other kinds can be extremely dangerous to large numbers of people in even minute quantities. Unfortunately, there is such a wide range of waste labeled "hazardous" that the public is often misled about what is really dangerous and what is not. Most troubling of all, many of the new chemical waste compounds are never tested for their potential toxicity.

In addition, we now produce significant quantities of heavy metal 10 contaminants, like lead and mercury, and medical waste, including infectious waste. Nuclear waste, of course, is the most dangerous of all, since it is highly toxic and remains so for thousands of years. Indeed, the most serious waste problems appear to be those created by federal facilities involved in nuclear weapons production. These problems may have received less attention in the past because most federal facilities are somewhat isolated from their communities. In contrast, the public has become outraged by the dumping of hazardous waste into landfills, because numerous studies and disastrous events have shown that the practice is simply not safe. Basically, the technology for disposing of waste hasn't caught up with the technology of producing it.

Few communities want to serve as a dumping ground for toxic 11 waste; studies have noted the disproportionate number of landfills and hazardous waste facilities in poor and minority areas. For example, a major study, *Toxic Wastes and Race in the United States*, by the United Church of Christ, came to the following conclusion:

> Race proved to be the most significant among variables tested in association with the location of commercial hazardous waste facilities. This represented a consistent national pattern. Communities with the greatest number of commercial hazardous waste facilities had the highest composition of racial and ethnic residents. In communities with two or more facilities or one of the nation's five largest landfills, the average minority percentage of the population was more than three times that of communities without facilities (38% vs. 12%).

It's practically an American tradition: waste has long been dumped   12
on the cheapest, least desirable land in areas surrounded by less fortunate citizens. But the volume of hazardous waste being generated is
now so enormous that it is being transported all over the country by
haulers who are taking it wherever they can. A few years ago, some
were actually dumping it on the roads themselves, opening a faucet
underneath the truck and letting the waste slowly drain out as they
crossed the countryside. In other cases, hazardous waste was being
turned over to unethical haulers controlled by organized crime who
dumped the waste on the side of the road in rural areas or into rivers in
the middle of the night. There is some evidence that we have made
progress in addressing these parts of the problem.

However, the danger we face as a result of improper waste hauling   13
is nothing compared to what happens in most older cities in America
every time it rains heavily: huge quantities of raw, untreated sewage are
dumped directly into the nearest river, creek, or lake. Since the so-called
storm water sewers in these cities were built to connect to the sewer system (before the combined pipes reach the processing plant), the total
volume of water during a hard rain is such that the processing plant
would be overwhelmed if it didn't simply open the gates, forget about
treating the raw sewage, and just dump it directly into the nearest large
body of water. This practice is being allowed to continue indefinitely
because local officials throughout the country have convinced Congress
that the cost of separating the sewers that carry human waste from the
sewers that carry rainwater would be greater than the cost of continuing to poison the rivers and oceans. But no effort has been made to calculate the cost of the growing contamination. Could it be because
Congress, and indeed this generation of voters, seem to feel that this
practice is acceptable because the cost of handling the waste properly
will be borne by us, and much of the cost for fouling the environment
can be shunted off on our children and their children?

Though federal law purports to prohibit the dumping of municipal   14
sewage and industrial waste into the oceans by 1991, it is obvious that
the increasing volumes being generated and the enormous cost of the
steps required to prevent ocean dumping will make that deadline
laughably irrelevant. Currently, our coastal waters receive 2.3 trillion
gallons of municipal effluent and 4.9 billion gallons of industrial waste-
water each year, most of which fails to pass muster under the law. Nor
are we the only nation guilty of this practice. Germany's river system
carries huge quantities of waste toward the sea each day. Most rivers
throughout Asia and Europe, Africa and Latin America, are treated as
open sewers, especially for industrial waste and sewage. And, the first
major tragedy involving chemical waste in the water was in Japan in the
1950s, at Minimata. International cooperative efforts have focused on

regional ocean pollution problems, such as the Mediterranean, the North Sea, and the Caribbean.

The disposal of hazardous waste has received a good deal of atten- 15 tion in recent years, though there is still much to be done. For one thing, how do we know which waste is truly hazardous and which isn't? We produce more industrial waste than any other kind, but do we really know enough about it? Most industrial waste is disposed of on sites owned by the generator, often next to the facility that creates the waste. The landfills and dumps used by industry are therefore often far from public view and—especially because these companies create jobs—their waste is usually noticed only when it escapes from the site by means of underground water flow or dispersal by the winds.

Much more difficult to hide are the landfills used for municipal 16 solid waste. Many of us grew up assuming that although every town and city needed a dump, there would always be a hole wide enough and deep enough to take care of all our trash. But like so many other assumptions about the earth's infinite capacity to absorb the impact of human civilization, this one too was wrong. Which brings us to the second major change concerning our production of waste: the volume of garbage is now so high that we are running out of places to put it. Out of 20,000 landfills in the United States in 1979, more than 15,000 have since reached their permanent capacity and closed. Although the problem is most acute in older cities, especially in the Northeast, virtually every metropolitan area is either facing or will soon face the urgent need to find new landfills or dispose of their garbage by some other means.

Those landfills still in operation feature mountains of garbage that 17 are reaching heroic proportions: Fresh Kills Landfill on Staten Island, for instance, receives 44 million pounds of New York City garbage every single day. According to a study by a *Newsday* investigative team, it will soon become "the highest point on the Eastern Seaboard south of Maine." It will soon legally require a Federal Aviation Administration permit as a threat to aircraft.

Dr. W. L. Rathje, a professor of anthropology at the University of 18 Arizona and perhaps the leading "garbologist" in the world, testified to the epic scale of these modern landfills before one of my subcommittee hearings: "When I was a graduate student, I was told that the largest monument ever built by a New World civilization was the Temple of the Sun, constructed in Mexico around the time of Christ and occupying thirty million cubic feet of space. Durham Road Landfill near San Francisco is two mounds compiled since 1977 solely out of cover dirt and the municipal solid waste from three California cities. I can still remember my shock when my students calculated that each mound was seventy million cubic feet in volume, a total of nearly five Sun

Temples. Landfills are clearly the largest garbage middens (i.e., refuse heaps) in the history of the world."

What is in these mountains? Various forms of paper, mostly news- 19 papers and packaging, take up approximately half the space. Another 20 percent or so is made up of yard waste, construction wood, and assorted organic waste, especially food. (Rathje found that 15 percent of all the solid food purchased by Americans ends up in landfills.) An unbelievable conglomeration of odds and ends accounts for the rest, with almost 10 percent made up of plastic, including the so-called biodegradable plastic. (Starch is added to the plastic compound as an appetizer for microorganisms, who will theoretically disassemble the plastic as they consume the starch.) Rathje dryly noted that he was skeptical of such claims: "In our landfill refuse from decades past we have uncovered corncobs with all their kernels still intact. If microorganisms won't eat corn-on-the-cob, I doubt whether they will dig cornstarch out of plastics."

But much organic waste does ultimately decompose, in the pro- 20 cess generating a great deal of methane,[2] which poses a threat of explosions and underground fires in older dumps that do not have proper venting or control. More significant, it contributes to the increased amount of methane entering the atmosphere. As we now know, rising levels of methane are one reason that the greenhouse effect has become so dangerous.

As existing landfills close, cities throughout the United States are 21 desperately searching for new ones. And they are not easy to find. In fact, in my home state of Tennessee, to take one example, the single hottest political issue in the majority of our ninety-five counties is where to locate a new landfill or incinerator. Since these problems have customarily been addressed at the local level, they have not been defined as national issues, even though they generate more political controversy nationwide than many other issues. Now, however, the accumulation of waste has gotten so out of hand that cities and states have begun shipping large quantities across state lines. The Congressional Research Service has estimated that more than 12 million tons of municipal solid waste were shipped across state lines in 1989. Although some of this volume is due to the fact that some major cities are next to a state line and some is due to formal interstate compacts for regional disposal facilities (which can be among the more responsible alternatives), there is an enormous growth in shipments by private haulers to landowners in poorer areas of the country who are ready to make a dollar by having garbage dumped on their property.

---

[2] A flammable gas. [Eds.]

I remember the day that citizens from the small Tennessee town of   22
Mitchellville (pop. 500) called me to complain about four smelly boxcars
dripping with garbage from New York City that had been sitting in the
hot sun for a week on a railroad siding in their town. "What worries
me," said one resident to a reporter from the *Nashville Banner*, "is that so
many germs are carried through the air, viruses and this type of thing.
When that wind is blowing that stuff all over town, them little germs are
not saying, 'Now, we can't leave this boxcar, you know we've got to stay
here.'" Mitchellville's vice mayor, Bill Rogers, said, "A lot of the time
you can see water, or some kind of liquid, dripping out the bottom of
the cars, and some of them contain pure New York garbage." As it
turned out, the mayor had agreed to let the hauling company, Tuckasee
Inc., bring trash from New York, New Jersey, and Pennsylvania to a
landfill thirty-five miles from the railroad siding for a fee of $5 per box-
car, which looked like a good deal for a city whose annual budget is less
than $50,000.

Small communities like Mitchellville throughout the Southeast and   23
Midwest are being deluged with shipments of garbage from the
Northeast. Rural areas of the western United States are receiving
garbage from large cities on the Pacific coast. No wonder that bands of
vigilantes have formed to patrol the highways and backroads in areas
besieged by trucks of garbage from larger population centers. One of
my favorite spoofs on *Saturday Night Live* was a mock commercial for a
product called the Yard-a-Pult, a scaled-down model of a medieval cat-
apult, just large enough for the backyard patio, suitable for the launching of garbage bags into your neighbor's property. No need for
recycling, incineration, or landfills. The Yard-a-Pult is the ultimate in
"out of sight, out of mind" convenience. Unfortunately, the fiction is disturbingly like the reality of our policy for dealing with waste.

Sometimes truth is even stranger than fiction. One of the most   24
bizarre and disturbing consequences of this considerable shipment of
waste is the appearance of a new environmental threat called backhaul-
ing. Truckers take loads of chemical waste and garbage in one direction
and food and bulk liquids (like fruit juice) in the opposite direction—in
the same containers. In a lengthy report, the *Seattle Post-Intelligencer*
found hundreds of examples of food being carried in containers that
had been filled with hazardous waste on the first leg of the journey.
Although the trucks were typically washed between loads, the drivers
(at some threat to their jobs) described lax inspections, totally inadequate washouts, and the use of liquid deodorizers, themselves dangerous, to mask left-over chemical smells. In 1990, Senators Jim Exon, Slade
Gorton, and I joined with Congressman Bill Clinger to pass legislation
prohibiting this practice.

But no legislation, by itself, can stop the underlying problem.   25
When one means of disposal is prohibited, the practice continues

underground or a new method is found. And what used to be considered unthinkable becomes commonplace because of the incredible pressure from the mounting volumes of waste.

Responding to Reading

1. What relationship does Chief Seattle say Native Americans have to the land? In what way does this relationship differ from other American's? Do you think Chief Seattle's assessment of nature is accurate?
2. At the end of his letter, Chief Seattle says, "But we are savages. The white man's dreams are hidden from us" (5). Why does he call himself a savage? Do you think he wants to be taken literally?
3. What does Gore mean when he says that America is a "throwaway society" (1)? Do you agree? Has the situation improved since Gore published his book in 1992?
4. Does the method of waste disposal in the area in which you live support or refute Gore's argument?
5. How do you think Chief Seattle would react to Gore's essay? Would he be encouraged or discouraged? Explain.
6. Are you optimistic or pessimistic about people's ability to live in harmony with the environment? Which selection, Chief Seattle's or Gore's, more closely reflects your views? Why?

THE OBLIGATION TO ENDURE

Rachel Carson

Naturalist and environmentalist Rachel Carson (1907–1964) was a specialist in marine biology. She won the National Book Award for The Sea around Us *(1951), which, like her other books, appeals to scientists and laypeople alike. While working as an aquatic biologist for the U.S. Fish and Wildlife Service, Carson became concerned about ecological hazards and wrote* Silent Spring *(1962), in which she warned readers about the indiscriminate use of pesticides. This book influenced President John F. Kennedy to begin investigations into this and other environmental problems. In the selection from* Silent Spring *that follows, Carson urges us to question the use of chemical pesticides.*

The history of life on earth has been a history of interaction between 1 living things and their surroundings. To a large extent, the physical form and the habits of the earth's vegetation and its animal life have been molded by the environment. Considering the whole span of earthly time, the opposite effect, in which life actually modifies its surroundings, has been relatively slight. Only within the moment of time represented by the present century has one species—man—acquired significant power to alter the nature of his world.

During the past quarter century this power has not only increased to one of disturbing magnitude but it has changed in character. The most alarming of all man's assaults upon the environment is the contamination of air, earth, rivers, and sea with dangerous and even lethal materials. This pollution is for the most part irrecoverable; the chain of evil it initiates not only in the world that must support life but in living tissues is for the most part irreversible. In this now universal contamination of the environment, chemicals are the sinister and little-recognized partners of radiation in changing the very nature of the world—the very nature of its life. Strontium 90, released through nuclear explosions into the air, comes to earth in rain or drifts down in fallout, lodges in soil, enters into the grass or corn or wheat grown there, and in time takes up its abode in the bones of a human being, there to remain until his death. Similarly, chemicals sprayed on croplands or forests or gardens lie long in soil, entering into living organisms, passing from one to another in a chain of poisoning and death. Or they pass mysteriously by underground streams until they emerge and, through the alchemy of air and sunlight, combine into new forms that kill vegetation, sicken cattle, and work unknown harm on those who drink from once pure wells. As Albert Schweitzer[1] has said, "Man can hardly even recognize the devils of his own creation."

It took hundreds of millions of years to produce the life that now inhabits the earth—eons of time in which that developing and evolving and diversifying life reached a state of adjustment and balance with its surroundings. The environment, rigorously shaping and directing the life it supported, contained elements that were hostile as well as supporting. Certain rocks gave out dangerous radiation; even within the light of the sun, from which all life draws its energy, there were short-wave radiations with power to injure. Given time—time not in years but in millennia—life adjusts, and a balance has been reached. For time is the essential ingredient; but in the modern world there is no time.

The rapidity of change and the speed with which new situations are created follow the impetuous and heedless pace of man rather than the deliberate pace of nature. Radiation is no longer merely the background radiation of rocks, the bombardment of cosmic rays, the ultraviolet of the sun that have existed before there was any life on earth; radiation is now the unnatural creation of man's tampering with the atom. The

---

[1] Prominent theologian (1875–1965) honored for his work as a scientist, humanitarian, musician, and religious thinker. In 1952, he was awarded the Nobel Peace Prize. [Eds.]

chemicals to which life is asked to make its adjustment are no longer merely the calcium and silica and copper and all the rest of the minerals washed out of the rocks and carried in rivers to the sea; they are the synthetic creations of man's inventive mind, brewed in his laboratories, and having no counterparts in nature.

To adjust to these chemicals would require time on the scale that is 5 nature's; it would require not merely the years of a man's life but the life of generations. And even this, were it by some miracle possible, would be futile, for the new chemicals come from our laboratories in an endless stream; almost five hundred annually find their way into actual use in the United States alone. The figure is staggering and its implications are not easily grasped—500 new chemicals to which the bodies of men and animals are required somehow to adapt each year, chemically totally outside the limits of biologic experience.

Among them are many that are used in man's war against nature. 6 Since the mid-1940s over 200 basic chemicals have been created for use in killing insects, weeds, rodents, and other organisms described in the modern vernacular as "pests"; and they are sold under several thousand different brand names.

These sprays, dusts, and aerosols are now applied almost universally to farms, gardens, forests, and homes—nonselective chemicals that have the power to kill every insect, the "good" and the "bad," to still the songs of birds and the leaping of fish in the streams, to coat the leaves with a deadly film, and to linger on in soil—all this though the intended target may be only a few weeds or insects. Can anyone believe it is possible to lay down such a barrage of poisons on the surface of the earth without making it unfit for all life? They should not be called "insecticides," but "biocides."

The whole process of spraying seems caught up in an endless spiral. Since DDT was released for civilian use, a process of escalation has been going on in which ever more toxic materials must be found. This has happened because insects, in a triumphant vindication of Darwin's principle of the survival of the fittest, have evolved super races immune to the particular insecticide used, hence a deadlier one has always to be developed—and then a deadlier one than that. It has happened also because, for reasons to be described later, destructive insects often undergo a "flare-back" or resurgence, after spraying, in numbers greater than before. Thus the chemical war is never won, and all life is caught in its violent crossfire.

Along with the possibility of the extinction of mankind by nuclear 9 war, the central problem of our age has therefore become the contamination of man's total environment with such substances of incredible potential for harm—substances that accumulate in the tissues of plants and animals and even penetrate the germ cells to shatter or alter the very material of heredity upon which the shape of the future depends.

Some would-be architects of our future look toward a time when it 10 will be possible to alter the human germ plasm by design. But we may easily be doing so now by inadvertence, for many chemicals, like radiation, bring about gene mutations. It is ironic to think that man might determine his own future by something so seemingly trivial as the choice of an insect spray.

All this has been risked—for what? Future historians may well be 11 amazed by our distorted sense of proportion. How could intelligent beings seek to control a few unwanted species by a method that contaminated the entire environment and brought the threat of disease and death even to their own kind? Yet this is precisely what we have done. We have done it, moreover, for reasons that collapse the moment we examine them. We are told that the enormous and expanding use of pesticides is necessary to maintain farm production. Yet is our real problem not one of *overproduction?* Our farms, despite measures to remove acreages from production and to pay farmers *not* to produce, have yielded such a staggering excess of crops that the American taxpayer in 1962 paid out more than one billion dollars a year as the total carrying cost of the surplus-food storage program. And is the situation helped when one branch of the Agriculture Department tries to reduce production while another states, as it did in 1958, "It is believed generally that reduction of crop acreages under provisions of the Soil Bank will stimulate interest in use of chemicals to obtain maximum production on the land retained in crops."

All this is not to say there is no insect problem and no need of con- 12 trol. I am saying, rather, that control must be geared to realities, not to mythical situations, and that the methods employed must be such that they do not destroy us along with the insects.

The problem whose attempted solution has brought such a train of 13 disaster in its wake is an accomplishment of our modern way of life. Long before the age of man, insects inhabited the earth—a group of extraordinarily varied and adaptable beings. Over the course of time since man's advent, a small percentage of the more than half a million species of insects have come into conflict with human welfare in two principal ways: as competitors for the food supply and as carriers of human disease.

Disease-carrying insects become important where human beings 14 are crowded together, especially under conditions where sanitation is poor, as in time of natural disaster or war or in situations of extreme poverty and deprivation. Then control of some sort becomes necessary. It is a sobering fact, however, as we shall presently see, that the method of massive chemical control has had only limited success, and also threatens to worsen the very conditions it is intended to curb.

Under primitive agricultural conditions the farmer had few insect 15 problems. These arose with the intensification of agriculture—the devotion of immense acreages to a single crop. Such a system set the stage for explosive increases in specific insect populations. Single-crop farming does not take advantage of the principles by which nature works; it is agriculture as an engineer might conceive it to be. Nature has introduced great variety into the landscape, but man has displayed a passion for simplifying it. Thus he undoes the built-in checks and balances by which nature holds the species within bounds. One important natural check is a limit on the amount of suitable habitat for each species. Obviously then, an insect that lives on wheat can build up its population to much higher levels on a farm devoted to wheat than on one in which wheat is intermingled with other crops to which the insect is not adapted.

The same thing happens in other situations. A generation or more 16 ago, the towns of large areas of the United States lined their streets with the noble elm tree. Now the beauty they hopefully created is threatened with complete destruction as disease sweeps through the elms, carried by a beetle that would have only limited chance to build up large populations and to spread from tree to tree if the elms were only occasional trees in a richly diversified planting.

Another factor in the modern insect problem is one that must be 17 viewed against a background of geologic and human history: the spreading of thousands of different kinds of organisms from their native homes to invade new territories. This worldwide migration has been studied and graphically described by the British ecologist Charles Elton in his recent book *The Ecology of Invasions*. During the Cretaceous Period, some hundred million years ago, flooding seas cut many land bridges between continents and living things found themselves confined in what Elton calls "colossal separate nature reserves." There, isolated from others of their kind, they developed many new species. When some of the land masses were joined again, about 15 million years ago, these species began to move out into new territories—a movement that is not only still in progress but is now receiving considerable assistance from man.

The importation of plants is the primary agent in the modern 18 spread of species, for animals have almost invariably gone along with the plants, quarantine being a comparatively recent and not completely effective innovation. The United States Office of Plant Introduction alone has introduced almost 200,000 species and varieties of plants from all over the world. Nearly half of the 180 or so major insect enemies of plants in the United States are accidental imports from abroad, and most of them have come as hitchhikers on plants.

In new territory, out of reach of the restraining hand of the natural 19 enemies that kept down its numbers in its native land, an invading plant or animal is able to become enormously abundant. Thus it is no accident that our most troublesome insects are introduced species.

These invasions, both the naturally occurring and those dependent 20 on human assistance, are likely to continue indefinitely. Quarantine and massive chemical campaigns are only extremely expensive ways of buying time. We are faced, according to Dr. Elton, "with a life-and-death need not just to find new technological means of suppressing this plant or that animal"; instead we need the basic knowledge of animal populations and their relations to their surroundings that will "promote an even balance and damp down the explosive power of outbreaks and new invasions."

Much of the necessary knowledge is now available but we do not 21 use it. We train ecologists in our universities and even employ them in our governmental agencies but we seldom take their advice. We allow the chemical death rain to fall as though there were no alternative, whereas in fact there are many, and our ingenuity could soon discover many more if given opportunity.

Have we fallen into a mesmerized state that makes us accept as 22 inevitable that which is inferior or detrimental, as though having lost the will or the vision to demand that which is good? Such thinking, in the words of the ecologist Paul Shepard, "idealizes life with only its head out of water, inches above the limits of toleration of the corruption of its own environment. . . . Why should we tolerate a diet of weak poisons, a home in insipid surroundings, a circle of acquaintances who are not quite our enemies, the noise of motors with just enough relief to prevent insanity? Who would want to live in a world which is just not quite fatal?"

Yet such a world is pressed upon us. The crusade to create a chem- 23 ically sterile, insect-free world seems to have engendered a fanatic zeal on the part of many specialists and most of the so-called control agencies. On every hand there is evidence that those engaged in spraying operations exercise a ruthless power. "The regulatory entomologists[2] . . . function as prosecutor, judge and jury, tax assessor and collector and sheriff to enforce their own orders," said Connecticut entomologist Neely Turner. The most flagrant abuses go unchecked in both state and federal agencies.

It is not my contention that chemical insecticides must never be 24 used. I do contend that we have put poisonous and biologically potent chemicals indiscriminately into the hands of persons largely or wholly ignorant of their potentials for harm. We have subjected enormous numbers of people to contact with these poisons, without their consent and often without their knowledge. If the Bill of Rights contains no guarantee that a citizen shall be secure against lethal poisons distributed either by private individuals or by public officials, it is surely only because our forefathers, despite their considerable wisdom and foresight, could conceive of no such problem.

---

[2] Scientists who study insects. [Eds.]

I contend, furthermore, that we have allowed these chemicals to be 25
used with little or no advance investigation of their effect on soil, water,
wildlife, and man himself. Future generations are unlikely to condone
our lack of prudent concern for the integrity of the natural world that
supports all life.

There is still very limited awareness of the nature of the threat. This 26
is an era of specialists, each of whom sees his own problem and is
unaware of or intolerant of the larger frame into which it fits. It is also
an era dominated by industry, in which the right to make a dollar at
whatever cost is seldom challenged. When the public protests, confronted with some obvious evidence of damaging results of pesticide
applications, it is fed little tranquilizing pills of half truth. We urgently
need an end to these false assurances, to the sugar coating of unpalat-
able facts. It is the public that is being asked to assume the risks that the
insect controllers calculate. The public must decide whether it wishes to
continue on the present road, and it can do so only when in full possession of the facts. In the words of Jean Rostand, "The obligation to
endure gives us the right to know."

Responding to Reading

1. After this essay was written, DDT was banned. Recently, however, some
   scientists have suggested that because some insects have developed resistance to safer insecticides, spraying of DDT should be reinstituted on a limited basis. How would Carson respond to this suggestion? Do you think
   health considerations and the need for food outweigh the environmental
   hazards of spraying DDT?
2. In paragraph 9 of her essay, Carson says that along with the possibility of
   nuclear extinction, "the central problem of our age has . . . become the contamination of man's total environment." Is she exaggerating? Do you think
   her assessment is accurate?
3. Should Carson have devoted more time to describing "the interaction
   between living things and their surroundings" (1)—For example, by showing what we have lost and what we have to lose? What in particular could
   she have described?

RECYCLING: NO PANACEA

William Rathje and Cullen Murphy

*Anthropologist William Rathje (1945–) was born in South Bend,
Indiana, and graduated from the University of Arizona, later receiving his
doctorate from Harvard. Since 1971, he has taught at the University of*

Arizona, where he directs the Garbage Project; students working with the project analyze public landfills as though they were archaeological digs, quantifying the contents as a way of evaluating the kinds of waste generated by Americans and of providing solutions for reducing this waste. Cullen Murphy (1952–   ) was born in New Rochelle, New York, and received his B.A. from Amherst College. He is the managing editor of the Atlantic Monthly, *and for many years, he has also written the text for the "Prince Valiant" comic strip (his father is the artist). A collection of his essays,* Just Curious, *was published in 1995. Rathje and Cullen joined forces to write* Rubbish! The Archaeology of Garbage *(1992), based on Rathje's work with the Garbage Project. The book, according to one critic, "put[s] important garbage issues in perspective; it demolishes myths that hamper our ability to act sensibly; as a nice bonus, it entertains as it goes about its business." In the following section from* Rubbish! *the authors argue that many environmentally conscious Americans put far too much faith in recycling as a cure for our environmental woes.*

Recycling is a necessary component of a sound solid-waste- 1 management program. Properly conceived and executed, a recycling program can make good economic sense, can help save natural resources, can help reduce pollution, and can divert some tributaries of the solid-waste stream away from landfills. These are all essential goals. There is no reason, however, for recycling to become an individual or social obsession. Indeed, when recycling does become an obsession in a society, it is sometimes a sign that important aspects of that society have gone seriously awry; as they have, for example, in the Soviet Union, where the scarcity of even the most basic consumer goods has driven the populace to the most desperate frenzies of recycling imaginable. Still, without becoming obsessed by recycling there are useful, pragmatic steps that Americans can and should take to bolster the recycling enterprise—in particular by fostering demand for recycled materials. These steps include buying consumer goods that have truly been made from recycled materials (beware of misleading claims on the packaging) and buying consumer goods that, once discarded, will have the most resale value for the recyclers. . . .

In the meantime it must be remembered that while recycling is one 2 valuable way of coping with America's—or any society's—solid waste, it is by no means a panacea. Yes, from a narrow, technical perspective almost anything that one might find in municipal solid waste *could* be thought of as being somehow recyclable or reusable; the problem is finding significant outlets for such recycled or reused products that also make economic, political, environmental, and psychological sense.

For one thing, it is not farfetched to think that recycling may one day 3 be met with antagonism by its erstwhile middle-class allies. Despite the virtuous public image that recycling possesses when considered in the abstract, in the real world recycling could find its reputation tarnished.

There have already been reports, for example, of inroads into the recycling business by organized crime. On a more mundane level, garbage-sorting centers and recycling centers, like any public-works projects, are increasingly becoming objects of NIMBY-type opposition.[1] Most recycling centers and plants are nothing more than enclosed spaces where presorted cans, bottles, and newspapers are temporarily stored or, at worst, where mixed recyclables passing by on conveyer belts are separated by human hands. They do not belch noxious fumes. The work being done inside them may very well be God's. But, BUT, they bear the unholy taint of garbage. And don't forget all those trucks coming and going all day long. As the collection and sorting of garbage for recycling become a growing and regular part of our lives, so will protests against conducting these activities anyplace nearby.

The large-scale composting of municipal solid waste is touted by 4 many as one way of recycling the 5 to 20 percent of household garbage that consists of yard waste and food waste. (The yard-waste volume varies considerably by region.) But composting also confronts NIMBY problems, and environmental concerns of other kinds as well. Composting is an ancient practice—there is evidence that composting pits were in use at Knossos, in Crete, some four thousand years ago— and in theory composting seems compelling and attractive. Yard waste has been banned from landfills in more than ten states precisely in order to encourage small-scale composting at home, and a number of companies now sell small plastic "green cones" for this purpose. Large-scale composting of municipal solid waste is something of a different proposition. The enormous volume of rich humus that results from large-scale composting has a variety of commercial uses, and the Europeans began resorting to a significant amount of composting years ago. But composting is expensive. Composting yards are also big, and they can smell; siting them may not prove to be as difficult as siting landfills, but doing so will still take a lot of work. Moreover, if precautions are not taken to prevent certain kinds of biodegradable garbage from joining the compost piles, the compost can become tainted with hazardous elements, such as the heavy metals in inks and pigments. Yard waste may contain traces of pesticides and herbicides. Composting is only just getting under way in the United States, and there are as yet fewer than a hundred composting plants planned or in operation, most of them small. A lot of thought is being given by composting proponents to ways of dampening potential opposition (such as making sure that the composting piles are physically enclosed, to contain "fugitive odors"). But this industry, if such it becomes, is starting out with some handicaps.

Recycling of other kinds exacts an environmental price. The reuse 5 of paper, for example, involves processes that generate a considerable

---

[1] NIMBY is an acronym for "not in my back yard." [Eds.]

amount of hazardous waste. In order to recycle newspapers, magazines, and, indeed, any printed paper, the paper must first be de-inked. At the end of the de-inking process one is left with essentially two products: on the one hand, de-inked fiber that will be turned into new paper; and on the other, a large quantity of toxic sludge. The recycling of iron and steel, of aluminum, and of plastics, for their part, also result in the production of various kinds of toxic waste and in air emissions that may be hazardous. A 1988 U.S. Office of Technology Assessment report on solid waste observed bluntly of recycling that "it is usually not clear whether secondary manufacturing produces less pollution per ton of material processed than primary manufacturing."

Another vexing reality that communities must confront is that recy- 6 cling can be expensive. A myth was once abroad that recycling was not only an environmentally sound garbage-disposal option but also a potential money-maker or at least money-saver. That this was going to be the case was at least implicitly the notion that lay behind the various "zero-net-cost" recycling schemes many communities adopted. The idea here is that when a city (for example) considers bids from independent recyclers for handling its recycling program, the amount the city finally agrees to pay per ton must be no greater than the cheapest available disposal method other than recycling (which is usually landfilling, the high cost of which in some places is what makes recycling attractive to begin with). The assumption, of course, was that the recycling agency would earn enough from sales of recyclables to more than offset the difference, if any, between city fees and the actual cost of operations. This frequently has turned out not to be the case for private recyclers of household-level commodities, and the same economic realities that bedevil them, of course, also bedevil recycling programs operated by communities themselves. From the start, recyclers have been beset by slumps in commodities prices. The cost of collection programs is high to begin with—think of the capital investment required for new kinds of trucks. There have also been unexpected problems. One major glitch collection programs have faced: the inability of many consumers to sort their recyclables properly prior to pickup, resulting in "contaminated" deliveries that may be rejected by buyers or must be sold for reduced prices. Most cities have had to set up costly labor-intensive or mechanical sorting operations to sort once more the garbage that households have already sorted.

The problem of improper sorting by households is pervasive. The 7 Garbage Project last year sampled the sorting behavior of twenty randomly selected households in a middle-income neighborhood in Tucson. Under the rules of the local curbside recycling program, residents were to separate out all recyclables and place them in a special blue bag. The rest of the garbage was to go into the traditional garbage can. What is and is not recyclable depends, of course, on what the community has decided to recycle, and all participants in the recycling program were given clear definitions of what should and should not go into the blue bag. The results of the Garbage Project's survey of the contents of the twenty blue bags and the garbage cans that went with them were not really unexpected. Taken together, the discards in the blue bags weighed 318 pounds, but fifty of those pounds were taken up by nonrecyclables. Every household made mistakes, either by contaminating the recyclable bag or throwing recyclables into the garbage cans. Indeed, fully half of all the aluminum cans thrown away were found not in the recyclable bag but in the garbage can.

This is why materials-recovery facilities (MRFs) are needed. Once 8 again the American consumer has proved capable of dashing the fondest of hopes. The inevitable consequence of this and other developments is that, far from being a gold mine, recycling will be a procedure—a worthwhile procedure—for which communities must pay considerable sums, often unexpectedly, perhaps consoling themselves with the recognition that resources have been conserved and that some garbage has been kept out of landfills and incinerators.

A further reality that will become apparent with time is that some 9 significant elements of the solid-waste stream that are without question recyclable will prove resistant, for a variety of reasons, to all attempts to recycle them. Rubber tires have so far proved to be a case in point. Tires are every landfill manager's nightmare. They possess a peculiar property: Bury them in a landfill and over time they will slowly rise and eventually emerge onto the surface, as if all the raisins in a loaf of bread had ascended to the top. (One explanation given for this phenomenon is that landfill compactors initially compress the hollow, newly arrived tires, but that over time the tires expand back into the original shape; the act of expansion gradually takes them upwards because the garbage above them is always less compact than the garbage below. An alternative explanation—which also explains how rocks rise to the surface of a pasture—attributes the phenomenon to temperature fluctuations that cause the tire to expand and contract, with small particles drifting into the tiny void that forms under the tire after each contraction; slowly but surely the tire works its way to the surface.) Periodically landfill operators skim the landfill surface with a special vehicle that picks up the latest crop; this is the source of those large tire islands that one sees alongside most landfills, and that every so often ignite uncontrollably and blacken the skies for weeks. In theory, tires would seem an ideal candidate for recycling. There are lots of them—200 million are thrown away every year. They are relatively homogeneous. They even, as we have seen, eerily separate themselves from all the other garbage. And yet nothing that has yet been tried—not using them to make road surfaces or airport runways, not burning them (along with coal) as fuel, not using them for artificial reefs—has made anyone terribly excited (or made anyone much money).

Finally, to repeat, recycling can be a surpassingly fragile enterprise. 10 There are many variables, and their configuration from place to place must dictate strategy and tactics. Some kinds of recycling, such as of aluminum cans, probably make sense everywhere. Other kinds, such as of newsprint, may not. Homogeneity of materials may be a necessity when it comes to recycling, but homogeneity of policy across geographical boundaries ought not to be the watchword with respect to how much of what kinds of garbage America's communities should be recycling. The key is to maintain a tautness between supply and demand, a task that is not always easy and, frankly, not always possible. It may become increasingly difficult as the many collection programs that have been enacted into law begin to take hold, and the volume of recyclables on the market suddenly doubles or triples. What may seem like "success" in the eyes of those who run local recycling programs—an outpouring of public cooperation, an Everest of sorted trash—can at times spell failure for the system as a whole, dooming truckloads of recyclables to be dumped into landfills (as some are even now), driving local programs bankrupt, and, depending on the degree of overabundance of this or that, and its effect on prices, even threatening the health of scrap dealers. Too many communities around the country are now reading headlines like this one from a Boston-area newspaper, *The Enterprise* (Brockton): "RECYCLING WORKING TOO WELL; Industry Can't Handle Glut of Materials." Too many are now reading headlines like this one from *The New York Times:* "Our Towns: When Recycling Means Too Much of a Good Thing." Or this one from *Waste Age:* "Recyclers Brace for Office Paper Oversupply." It would be an ironic consequence indeed if recycling were undermined by the best of intentions.

The messages to recycling activists: Pay attention to these market 11 factors. Make sure that people in local communities understand the sometimes fickle dynamics of the recycling process. And make sure they understand that recycling has not happened until the loop has been closed.

Responding to Reading

1. What mistaken ideas do Rathje and Murphy assume their readers have about recycling? Where in their essay do they address these misconceptions? What do they gain by discussing them at this point? Do people you know actually have these ideas?
2. Rathje and Murphy say that recycling may one day "be met with antagonism by its erstwhile middle-class allies"(3). Why? What can people do to avoid this possibility?

3. What do Rathje and Murphy mean when they say that "recycling has not happened until the loop has been closed" (11)?

THE PLEASURES OF EATING

Wendell Berry

Writer and environmentalist Wendell Berry (1934–) was born in Henry County, Kentucky, and received his B.A. and M.A. degrees from the University of Kentucky in Lexington. Formerly a professor of English there, he now runs a farm near Port Royal, Kentucky. Berry is a prolific author. His works include the novels Nathan Coulter *(1960, 1985),* The Memory of Jack *(1974),* Remembering *(1988), and* Watch with Me *(1994); the poetry collections* The Broken Ground *(1964),* The Country of Marriage *(1973),* Collected Poems 1957–1982 *(1987), and* Entries *(1994); and the essay collections* The Long-Legged House *(1976),* Standing by Words *(1983), and* Another Turn of the Crank *(1995). His* Unsettling of America: Culture and Agriculture *(1977) is considered one of the key texts of the environmental movement, and much of his writing focuses on the need for humans to live harmoniously with the earth's natural rhythms. Novelist Larry Woiwode has said Berry's central message is that "all land is a gift, and all of it is good, if we only had the eye to see that." In the following essay from* What Are People For? *(1990), Berry asks readers to develop a better understanding of the food they eat and how it is produced.*

Many times, after I have finished a lecture on the decline of 1 American farming and rural life, someone in the audience has asked, "What can city people do?"

"Eat responsibly," I have usually answered. Of course, I have tried 2 to explain what I meant by that, but afterwards I have invariably felt that there was more to be said than I had been able to say. Now I would like to attempt a better explanation.

I begin with the proposition that eating is an agricultural act. 3 Eating ends the annual drama of the food economy that begins with planting and birth. Most eaters, however, are no longer aware that this is true. They think of food as an agricultural product, perhaps, but they do not think of themselves as participants in agriculture. They think of themselves as "consumers." If they think beyond that, they recognize that they are passive consumers. They buy what they want—or what they have been persuaded to want—within the limits of what they can get. They pay, mostly without protest, what they are charged. And they mostly ignore certain critical questions about the quality and the cost of what they are sold: How fresh is it? How pure or clean is it, how free of dangerous chemicals? How far was it transported, and what did transportation add to the cost? How much did manufacturing or packaging or advertising add to the cost? When the food product has been manufactured or "processed" or "precooked," how has that affected its quality or price or nutritional value?

Most urban shoppers would tell you that food is produced on 4 farms. But most of them do not know what farms, or what kinds of farms, or where the farms are, or what knowledge or skills are involved in farming. They apparently have little doubt that farms will continue to produce, but they do not know how or over what obstacles. For them, then, food is pretty much an abstract idea—something they do not know or imagine—until it appears on the grocery shelf or on the table.

The specialization of production induces specialization of con- 5 sumption. Patrons of the entertainment industry, for example, entertain themselves less and less and have become more and more passively dependent on commercial suppliers. This is certainly true also of patrons of the food industry, who have tended more and more to be *mere* consumers—passive, uncritical, and dependent. Indeed, this sort of consumption may be said to be one of the chief goals of industrial production. The food industrialists have by now persuaded millions of consumers to prefer food that is already prepared. They will grow, deliver, and cook your food for you and (just like your mother) beg you to eat it. That they do not yet offer to insert it, prechewed, into your mouth is only because they have found no profitable way to do so. We may rest assured that they would be glad to find such a way. The ideal industrial food consumer would be strapped to a table with a tube running from the food factory directly into his or her stomach.

Perhaps I exaggerate, but not by much. The industrial eater is, in 6 fact, one who does not know that eating is an agricultural act, who no longer knows or imagines the connections between eating and the land, and who is therefore necessarily passive and uncritical—in short, a victim. When food, in the minds of eaters, is no longer associated with farming and with the land, then the eaters are suffering a kind of cultural amnesia that is misleading and dangerous. The current version of the "dream home" of the future involves "effortless" shopping from a list of available goods on a television monitor and heating precooked food by remote control. Of course, this implies, and depends on, a perfect ignorance of the history of the food that is consumed. It requires that the citizenry should give up their hereditary and sensible aversion to buying a pig in a poke. It wishes to make the selling of pigs in pokes an honorable and glamorous activity. The dreamer in this dream home will perforce know nothing about the kind or quality of this food, or where it came from, or how it was produced and prepared, or what ingredients, additives, and residues it contains—unless, that is, the dreamer undertakes a close and constant study of the food industry, in which case he or she might as well wake up and play an active and responsible part in the economy of food.

There is, then, a politics of food that, like any politics, involves our 7 freedom. We still (sometimes) remember that we cannot be free if our minds and voices are controlled by someone else. But we have neglected to understand that we cannot be free if our food and its sources are controlled by someone else. The condition of the passive consumer of food is not a democratic condition. One reason to eat responsibly is to live free.

But if there is a food politics, there are also a food esthetics and a 8 food ethics, neither of which is dissociated from politics. Like industrial sex, industrial eating has become a degraded, poor, and paltry thing. Our kitchens and other eating places more and more resemble filling stations, as our homes more and more resemble motels. "Life is not very interesting," we seem to have decided. "Let its satisfactions be minimal, perfunctory, and fast." We hurry through our meals to go to work and hurry through our work in order to "recreate" ourselves in the evenings and on weekends and vacations. And then we hurry, with the greatest possible speed and noise and violence, through our recreation—for what? To eat the billionth hamburger at some fast-food joint hellbent on increasing the "quality" of our life? And all this is carried out in a remarkable obliviousness to the causes and effects, the possibilities and the purposes, of the life of the body in this world.

One will find this obliviousness represented in virgin purity in the 9 advertisement of the food industry, in which food wears as much makeup as the actors. If one gained one's whole knowledge of food from these advertisements (as some presumably do), one would not know that the various edibles were ever living creatures, or that they all come from the soil, or that they were produced by work. The passive American consumer, sitting down to a meal of pre-prepared or fast food, confronts a platter covered with inert, anonymous substances that have been processed, dyed, breaded, sauced, gravied, ground, pulped, strained, blended, prettified, and sanitized beyond resemblance to any part of any creature that ever lived. The products of nature and agriculture have been made, to all appearances, the products of industry. Both eater and eaten are thus in exile from biological reality. And the result is a kind of solitude, unprecedented in human experience, in which the eater may think of eating as, first, a purely commercial transaction between him and a supplier and then as a purely appetitive transaction between him and his food.

And this peculiar specialization of the act of eating is, again, of 10 obvious benefit to the food industry, which has good reasons to obscure the connection between food and farming. It would not do for the consumer to know that the hamburger she is eating came from a steer who spent much of his life standing deep in his own excrement in a feedlot, helping to pollute the local streams, or that the calf that yielded the veal cutlet on her plate spent its life in a box in which it did not have room to turn around. And, though her sympathy for the slaw might be less tender, she should not be encouraged to meditate on the hygienic and biological implications of mile-square fields of cabbage, for vegetables grown in huge monocultures are dependent on toxic chemicals—just as animals in close confinement are dependent on antibiotics and other drugs.

The consumer, that is to say, must be kept from discovering that, in 11 the food industry—as in any other industry—the overriding concerns are not quality and heath, but volume and price. For decades now the entire industrial food economy, from the large farms and feedlots to the chains of supermarkets and fast-food restaurants, has been obsessed with volume. It has relentlessly increased scale in order to increase volume in order (presumably) to reduce costs. But as scale increases, diversity declines; as diversity declines, so does health; as health declines, the dependence on drugs and chemicals necessarily increases. As capital replaces labor, it does so by substituting machines, drugs, and chemicals for human workers and for the natural health and fertility of the soil. The food is produced by any means or any shortcut that will increase profits. And the business of the cosmeticians of advertising is to persuade the consumer that food so produced is good, tasty, healthful, and a guarantee of marital fidelity and long life.

It is possible, then, to be liberated from the husbandry and wifery 12 of the old household food economy. But one can be thus liberated only by entering a trap (unless one sees ignorance and helplessness as the signs of privilege, as many people apparently do). The trap is the ideal of industrialism: a walled city surrounded by valves that let merchandise in but no consciousness out. How does one escape this trap? Only voluntarily, the same way that one went in: by restoring one's consciousness of what is involved in eating; by reclaiming responsibility for one's own part in the food economy. One might begin with the illuminating principle of Sir Albert Howard's *The Soil and Health*, that we should understand "the whole problem of health in soil, plant, animal, and man as one great subject." Eaters, that is, must understand that eating takes place inescapably in the world, that it is inescapably an agricultural act, and that how we eat determines, to a considerable extent, how the world is used. This is a simple way of describing a relationship that is inexpressibly complex. To eat responsibly is to understand and enact, so far as one can, this complex relationship. What can one do? Here is a list, probably not definitive:

1. Participate in food production to the extent that you can. If you 13 have a yard or even just a porch box or a pot in a sunny window, grow something to eat in it. Make a little compost of your kitchen scraps and use it for fertilizer. Only by growing some food for yourself can you become acquainted with the beautiful energy cycle that revolves from soil to seed to flower to fruit to food to offal to decay, and around again. You will be fully responsible for any food that you grow for yourself, and you will know all about it. You will appreciate it fully, having known it all its life.

2. Prepare your own food. This means reviving in your own mind 14 and life the arts of kitchen and household. This should enable you to eat more cheaply, and it will give you a measure of "quality control": you will have some reliable knowledge of what has been added to the food you eat.

3. Learn the origins of the food you buy and buy the food that is 15 **produced closest to your home.** The idea that every locality should be, as much as possible, the source of its own food makes several kinds of sense. The locally produced food supply is the most secure, the freshest, and the easiest for local consumers to know about and to influence.

4. Whenever possible, deal directly with a local farmer, gardener, 16 **or orchardist.** All the reasons listed for the previous suggestion apply here. In addition, by such dealing you eliminate the whole pack of merchants, transporters, processors, packagers, and advertisers who thrive at the expense of both producers and consumers.

5. Learn, in self-defense, as much as you can of the economy and 17 **technology of industrial food production.** What is added to food that is not food, and what do you pay for these additions?

6. Learn what is involved in the *best* farming and gardening. 18

7. Learn as much as you can, by direct observation and experi- 19 **ence if possible, of the life histories of the food species.**

The last suggestion seems particularly important to me. Many peo- 20 ple are now as much estranged from the lives of domestic plants and animals (except for flowers and dogs and cats) as they are from the lives of the wild ones. This is regrettable, for these domestic creatures are in diverse ways attractive; there is much pleasure in knowing them. And farming, animal husbandry, horticulture, and gardening, at their best, are complex and comely arts; there is much pleasure in knowing them too.

It follows that there is great *dis*pleasure in knowing about a food 21 economy that degrades and abuses those arts and those plants and animals and the soil from which they come. For anyone who does know something of the modern history of food, eating away from home can be a chore. My own inclination is to eat seafood instead of red meat or poultry when I am traveling. Though I am by no means a vegetarian, I dislike the thought that some animal has been made miserable in order to feed me. If I am going to eat meat, I want it to be from an animal that has lived a pleasant, uncrowded life outdoors, on bountiful pasture, with good water nearby and trees for shade. And I am getting almost as fussy about food plants. I like to eat vegetables and fruits that I know have lived happily and healthily in good soil, not the products of the huge, bechemicaled factory-fields that I have seen, for example, in the Central Valley of California. The industrial farm is said to have been patterned on the factory production line. In practice, it looks more like a concentration camp.

The pleasure of eating should be an *extensive* pleasure, not that of the mere gourmet. People who know the garden in which their vegetables have grown and know that the garden is healthy will remember the beauty of the growing plants, perhaps in the dewy first light of morning when gardens are at their best. Such a memory involves itself with the food and is one of the pleasures of eating. The knowledge of the good health of the garden relieves and frees and comforts the eater. The same goes for eating meat. The thought of the good pasture and of the calf contentedly grazing flavors the steak. Some, I know, will think it bloodthirsty or worse to eat a fellow creature you have known all its life. On the contrary, I think it means that you eat with understanding and with gratitude. A significant part of the pleasure of eating is in one's accurate consciousness of the lives and the world from which food comes. The pleasure of eating, then, may be the best available standard of our health. And this pleasure, I think, is pretty fully available to the urban consumer who will make the necessary effort.

I mentioned earlier the politics, esthetics, and ethics of food. But to speak of the pleasure of eating is to go beyond those categories. Eating with the fullest pleasure—pleasure, that is, that does not depend on ignorance—is perhaps the profoundest enactment of our connection with the world. In this pleasure we experience and celebrate our dependence and our gratitude, for we are living from mystery, from creatures we did not make and powers we cannot comprehend. When I think of the meaning of food, I always remember these lines by the poet William Carlos Williams, which seem to me merely honest:

> There is nothing to eat,
>   seek it where you will,
>   but the body of the Lord.
> The blessed plants
>   and the sea, yield it
>   to the imagination
> intact.

Responding to Reading

1. What does Berry mean when he says that "eating is an agricultural act" (3)? Do you think he wants readers to take this statement seriously? Explain.
2. Berry assumes that most of his readers are urban shoppers who know only that food comes from the supermarket. What does he do to educate these readers? Is he able to provide enough information to acquaint them with the practicalities of food production? What else could he have done?
3. What suggestions does Berry give to readers to help them eat responsibly? How does he believe these suggestions will help readers escape the "trap [of] the ideal of industrialism" (12)? Can you offer any additional suggestions?

DEATH IN THE RAIN FORESTS

Shawn Carlson

Shawn Carlson is a physicist at Lawrence Berkeley Laboratories and a frequent contributor to the Humanist *magazine's "Science and Society" column and to* Scientific American. *In the following 1992 essay from the* Humanist, *Carlson argues that while tropical rain forests are unquestionably at serious risk, some ecologists and conservationists are exaggerating the potential loss of species and resorting to "scare tactics," which, he believes, may well backfire and "risk the credibility of the whole cause of rainforest conservation."*

Close your eyes and think of paradise. What do you see? Lush 1 warm tropical forests, perhaps? Exotic birds and a plethora of strange creatures busily going about the business of survival? For me, nothing could come closer to paradise than a rain forest—a place of fantastic diversity, unfathomably rich in color and form.

Unfortunately, there is one particularly efficient primate going 2 about its business in the rain forests as well. If the relentless industry of *Homo sapiens* proceeds unabated, it will ultimately devour these forests, forever eradicating at least half of all life on Earth. Fortunately, the situation is not as bleak as some people insist. All the vital signs suggest that the world's rain forests are in serious—but *not* critical—condition.

Surprisingly, these lavish forests grow in what biologists call *wet* 3 *deserts*—extremely poor soil whose nutrients are quickly leached away by over 40 inches of rain each year. This perpetual soaking leaves behind those minerals which do not dissolve in water and which, unhappily for the flora, cannot be absorbed by plant roots. Only about 0.1 percent of the nutrients released by the decaying matter on the forest floor ever feeds the next generation of vegetation. Furthermore, the struggle for sunlight favors the development of a network of high branches with broad expanses of large leaves to catch every morsel of the sun's nourishment. The branches of neighboring trees grow together into a thick canopy of leaves which absorbs rain water like green blotting paper and then slowly releases it to keep the air saturated with moisture. These canopies provide rich habitats for millions of organisms (mostly insects), which have evolved in such a way that they spend their entire lives in the tree tops and are therefore almost never seen by humans.

It is not surprising then that most of the rain forests' inhabitants 4 have never been described by science. Just how many species do these forests harbor? Nobody knows—not even to within a factor of ten. Any estimate of biodiversity must be based upon surveys of areas which are small enough for biologists to personally scrutinize. To estimate the total number, the species count in these areas must somehow be extrapolated to the entire rain forest. Unfortunately, we have no model, no mathematical formula, which relates the number of species to rain-forest area. Still, assessing the damage now being wreaked on the forests requires some estimate to be made.

Although the species-area formula is not known for rain forests, it 5 is well known for so-called islands—relatively small and isolated habitats. In this context, an "island" can be a conventional island—an outcropping of land in an ocean—but it can also be a mountaintop above the timber line or an oasis surrounded by desert. On an island, the total number of species scales roughly as the fourth root of the island's area. Thus, if two islands had the same environment but one was 16 times larger than the other, the larger island would be roughly twice as species-rich as the smaller one. To estimate how many species make a particular island their home, a biologist could simply count all the species in some small but representative piece of the island and then extrapolate to the whole. Even if the species started out evenly distributed throughout the island, the destruction of habitat would put pressures on the surviving organisms. Put simply, any given area can only support so many species, and, if there are too many, competition for resources will drive some of them into extinction. But while the island model predicts that every acre cleared contributes to extinctions, keep in mind that a fourth-root dependence is very slow. The island model predicts that annihilating 50 percent of a habitat extinguishes only 16 percent of its inhabitants. If 99 percent of the island is destroyed, 32 percent of the species should still survive in the 1 percent remaining.

Since there are no good models for rain forests, most people use the 6 island model to estimate both rain-forest biodiversity and extinction rates. But since rain forests are not very much like islands, the island model can give only the crudest estimates for the rain forests' problems.

Just how badly does the island model do? Islands can be rather 7
sparse in species, but rain forests absolutely *brim* with biodiversity. It is
not uncommon, for example, for a single leguminous tree in Peru to be
home to more than 40 species of ants representing more than 25 genera.
That's comparable to the total ant diversity found in the whole of
Brittany! Most islands just don't compare.

Also, rain forests are usually *much* bigger than islands. They occupy 8
gaping swaths of South America, Africa, and Indonesia and cover over
60 countries. Biologists do try to break up the rain forests into a number
of smaller microclimates and use the island model to estimate the total
number of species of each. Even so, the survey areas must be scaled to
regions that are sometimes *millions* of times larger. In fact, the island
model almost certainly fails for these huge extrapolations because,
while new ecological niches (the engines which drive biodiversity) are
easy to create on small islands, they are not so easily created in huge
forests. A small island contains comparatively few niches. Adding area
to an island adds lots of new niches and therefore enhances biodiversity,
but adding area to a large forest tends only to duplicate the niches that
are already available. And, according to University of Maryland
rain-forest expert Patrick Kangas, this is what the rain-forest data actually show. In a recent issue of *Science*, he said, "There's a finite number
of species within any community type. As you continue to move out,
the number levels off." In other words, the number of species in a rain
forest rises with area, but only to a point. And that's good news because
it means that *any large rain forest should be able to withstand at least some
clearing without any loss of species.*

And there's more good news. In the only available study on refor- 9
estation, J. P. Lanly showed in 1982 that over half of all virgin rain forest
cleared turned not into wasteland but into second-generation forests.
These new forests usually support less-diverse ecosystems than the virgin forests, but they do provide a buffer of support in which some endangered species can find safe haven. Furthermore, nearly 6 percent of the
rain forests—about 1.8 million hectares—are in protected parks, and
more land is being added all the time. Much of this land has been carefully chosen to protect both rare species and overall biodiversity. Also,
several million rain-forest hectares are inaccessible to people or impractical for human use. These areas are not likely to be disturbed soon.

But all this good news isn't what some conservationists want you to 10
hear. Don't get me wrong: there are many good reasons to be opposed
to cutting down the rain forests, and I am absolutely against any
destruction of virgin woodlands. I have emphasized the positives simply because conservationists often downplay scientific uncertainties
and manipulate the numbers to make things look far *worse* than they
actually are.

The island-model estimates of the number of rain-forest organisms   11
vary greatly, running from 5 million to 100 million species. (By contrast,
the total number of species which have been described by science,
including microscopic organisms, is less than 1.4 million.) Clearly, the
uncertainties in these calculations are huge.

Just how many species are becoming extinct each year is even more   12
uncertain. Even the experts disagree on how much of the forests we are
devouring annually. The numbers I've found so far from "official"
sources range from 0.5 percent to 1.8 percent forest cover lost each year.
Some environmentalists—such as E. O. Wilson of Harvard University—
estimate that we are "easily" losing 100,000 species every year. Others
use the above deforestation rates to argue that the number is between
6,250 and 22,500. But even these guesses are likely to be too high,
because they assume a species-area curve that we know *over-estimates*
rainforest biodiversity. What's more, to obtain these frightening rates,
one must apply the island model in the most naive way—with no
account of forest regeneration, the pattern of clearing, animal migration,
or a host of other critical details. While it is true that continued clearing
must at some point drive species to extinction, we simply don't know at
what point that is. In some countries, the damage is so great that it is
hard to imagine that some extinctions are not taking place; but in others, where large sections of forest remain intact, the extinction rates may
be closer to zero.

Television ads targeted to elicit your financial support for one envi-   13
ronmental group or another usually present the high extinction-rate
numbers combined with footage of exotic animals and discussions of
the cancer cures that might lie hidden in the plant species we are
destroying. These ads create the impression that plants and higher animals are taking the brunt of the disaster, but that's all smoke and mirrors. Almost all of the rain forests' biodiversity lies within their bugs,
and so even the island model predicts that the vast majority of species
being extinguished are not plants that could cure cancer but *insects*. As
unpopular as this may be to say, nature is so bug-abundant (more than
600,000 species of beetles have already been described and there are
likely to be many more out there) that losing a few percent of these is
not likely to cause an ecological collapse. However, resorting to scare
tactics in our attempts to save the rain forests could wind up being eco-
logically disastrous.

In his masterful book *The Mismeasure of Man*, Stephen Jay Gould[1]   14
documents just how badly biology has been misused by some scientists
to prop up the prevailing prejudices of the day. Although Gould focuses
on nineteenth-century biology, it would be folly to presume that no
modern scientist perpetrates similar abuses.

---

[1] A professor of biology at Harvard, Gould (b. 1941) is also a popular science writer. [Eds.]

Perhaps the field most abused these days is ecology, which some- 15
times seems to me more like a religious movement than a scientific discipline. Any "heretic" who dares stray from the most apocalyptic
interpretations of the data risks the professional scorn of Mother
Nature's self-appointed, doctoral-wielding apostolates. Several biologists who criticized the high species-extinction estimates have been
snubbed at professional conferences and vilified in print. A. E. Lugo,
project leader for the Institute of Tropical Forestry in Puerto Rico,
reports that, after giving a speech at the Smithsonian Institution in
which he criticized the high extinction rates usually quoted, a prominent conservationist verbally assaulted him in the cafeteria. Paul
Ehrlich, the well-known Stanford biologist who is perhaps the new
enviro-religion's foremost spokesperson, has even declared that we
must all undergo a "quasi-religious transformation" aimed at creating a
"revolution in attitudes toward other people, population growth, the
purpose of human life, and the intrinsic value of organic diversity" if
humanity is to survive.

This kind of rhetoric really frightens me. Why? Because the rain 16
forests *are* mortally imperiled. More than half the virgin forests have
already been cleared and many areas have already been devastated.
Stopping the destruction will require us to be very careful about our
facts. Alarmist statistics, dire predictions that don't come true, and
petty self-righteousness risk the credibility of the whole cause of
rain-forest conservation. Without credibility, there is no persuasion,
and, without persuasion, there is absolutely no hope for us to save the
forests.

We cannot save the rain forests without addressing the problems of 17
their 100 million human inhabitants. It's pretty tough to sell hungry parents on the idea that the next acre of virgin forest they want to clear has
a greater right to exist than their own families, and professional conservationists know this. That's why most programs to save the rain forests
have the primary goal of improving agricultural productivity to reduce
the need for further forest-clearing. Modern land-management techniques—the use of fertilizers to replenish the nutrients leached from the
soil, tractors to break up the earth, careful crop rotation, and the judi-
cious use of pesticides to maintain soil viability and reduce destruction
from pests—could greatly reduce the need to clear virgin forests.
Wastelands produced by logging can often be replanted with fast-
growing native trees of high lumber value to provide loggers with a
source of timber which can be more profitably harvested than virgin
forests. Although only about 13 percent of the cultivated land is currently being managed to produce a sustainable yield, several comprehensive plans—like the United Nations' Tropical Forestry Action
Plan—are now being implemented to slow the destruction. International strategies to reverse the rampant destruction of the world's rain

forests are in place. We must now find the political will to implement them.

Thus, everything is not gloom and doom. The forces of social cor- 18
rosion—poverty, governmental corruption, and foreign debt—are still hard at work conspiring to rid the world of our most biologically boun-tiful treasures, but there is plenty of reason for hope. What may be most dangerous and perhaps most difficult to overcome is our own tendency toward extremism. The winds of irrationality lash the public debate and make impossible the clear-headed discussion of the reasoned and prac-ticable steps we must take to save the rain forests. We must choose data over dogma if the rain forests are to stand a chance.

Responding to Reading

1. Carlson says that most researchers use an "island model" of how much damage is being done to the rain forests. Then, in paragraph 6, he suggests that because "rain forests are not very much like islands, the island model can give only the crudest estimates for the rain forests' problems." What is his point? How does this information support his overall argument?

2. Is the tone of this essay optimistic or pessimistic? Do you think a conserva-tionist would agree with Carlson's assessment of the severity of the prob-lem? Do *you* agree?

3. What does Carlson mean when he says, "We must choose data over dogma if the rain forests are to stand a chance" (18)? Would activists succeed in raising money for their causes if they followed Carlson's advice?

IS A TREE WORTH A LIFE?

Sally Thane Christensen

A native of Missoula, Montana, and a federal attorney who represents the U.S. Forest Service, Sally Thane Christensen (1954–   ) contributed the following essay to Newsweek *magazine's "My Turn" column in 1991. "My Turn" provides a forum in which readers offer their personal perspectives on a variety of social, cultural, political, and ethical issues. (Another "My Turn" column appears in Chapter 8, p. 617.) In her column, Christensen, who suffers from ovarian cancer, describes the potential cancer-fighting sub-stance provided by the bark of the Pacific yew tree and argues that it is wrong for environmentalists to block harvesting of the tree out of a misplaced con-cern that it may be endangered.*

For most of the last decade, federal timberlands in the West have 1
been held hostage in a bitter fight between environmental groups and

the timber industry. The environmentalists want to save the forests and their wildlife occupants. The timber industry wants to cut trees and provide jobs in a depressed economy. Caught in the middle is the United States Forest Service, which must balance the conflicting concepts of sustained yield and multiple use of national forest land.

The latest pawn in this environmental chess match is the Pacific 2 yew tree, a scrubby conifer found from southern Alaska to central California and in Washington, Oregon, Idaho and Montana. Historically the yew has not been harvested for value but often has been treated as logging slash and wasted. Not any longer. An extract of the bark of the Pacific yew known as taxol has been found to have cancer-fighting properties, particularly with ovarian cancer. As many as 30 percent of those treated with taxol have shown significant response. Some researchers call taxol the most significant new cancer drug to emerge in 15 years.

For the first time, the environmental debate over the use of a nat- 3 ural resource involves more than a question of the priority of the resource versus economic considerations. At stake is the value of a species of tree and the habitat it provides for wildlife as opposed to the value of the greatest of all natural resources, human life.

When I was first diagnosed three years ago, no one had an inkling 4 that I would become caught in the center of what may become the most significant environmental debate of my generation. Although as early as 1979 researchers had discovered that taxol killed cancer in a unique way, imprisoning malignant cells in a cage of scaffoldlike rods called microtubules, lab tests on animals were inconclusive. By 1985, however, a woman with terminal ovarian cancer was treated with taxol and had a dramatic response. Six years later, the once lowly yew tree is at the threshold of a controversy that challenges the fundamental precepts of even the most entrenched environmentalist.

It takes about three 100-year-old Pacific yew trees, or roughly 60 5 pounds of bark, to produce enough taxol to treat one patient. When the bark is removed, the tree dies. Environmental groups like the Oregon Natural Resources Council and the Audubon Society are concerned that the Pacific yew as a species may be decimated by the demand for taxol. But this year alone, 12,000 women will die from ovarian cancer. Breast cancer will kill 45,000 women. Is preservation of the Pacific yew worth the price?

It is sublimely ironic that my fate hinges so directly on the Pacific 6 yew. As a federal attorney representing the Forest Service, I have witnessed the environmental movement in the West from its embryonic stages. I have seen such diverse groups as the National Wildlife Federation and the Sierra Club challenge the Forest Service's ability to sell and harvest its trees. Win or lose, the forests are often locked up during the lengthy legal process.

The viability of the national forests does not rise or fall with the 7
Pacific yew. But, unfortunately for cancer victims, the tree is most abundant on national-forest lands which are subject to environmental review
by the public. Already challenges to the federal harvest of the yew have
begun. In Montana, the Save the Yaak Committee has protested the
Kootenai National Forest's intention to harvest yew trees and make them
available for experimental use. The committee contends that the yew
may be endangered by overharvesting.

I have news for the Save the Yaak Committee. I am endangered, too. 8
I've had four major abdominal surgeries in two years. I've had the conventional chemotherapy for ovarian cancer, and it didn't work. Though
I was in remission for almost a year, last August my cancer returned
with a vengeance. Taxol may be my last hope.

Because of the scarcity of supply, taxol is not commercially avail- 9
able. It is available only in clinical trials at a number of institutions.
Bristol-Myers, working with the National Cancer Institute in Bethesda,
Md., is asking the Forest Service to provide 750,000 pounds of bark for
clinical studies this year.

The ultimate irony of my story is that I am one of the lucky ones. 10
This May I was accepted by the National Cancer Institute for one of its
clinical trials. On May 8 I was infused with my first treatment of taxol.
Hospitalized in intensive care at NCI, I watched the precious, clear fluid
drip into my veins and prayed for it to kill the cancer that has ravaged
my body. I thought about the thousands of women who will die of cancer this year, who will not have my opportunity.

Every effort should be made to ensure that the yew tree is made 11
available for the continued research and development of taxol.
Environmental groups, the timber industry and the Forest Service must
recognize that the most important value of the Pacific yew is as a treatment for cancer. At the same time, its harvest can be managed in a way
that allows for the production of taxol without endangering the continued survival of the yew tree.

The yew may be prime habitat for spotted owls. It may be estheti- 12
cally appealing. But certainly its most critical property is its ability to
treat a fatal disease. Given a choice between trees or people, people
must prevail. No resource can be more valuable or more important than
a human life. Ask my husband. Ask my two sons. Ask me.

Responding to Reading

1. Christensen points out that before taxol, the Pacific yew tree had not been
   of much value. In what way does this information support environmentalist arguments that endangered habitats and species should be preserved?

2. Christensen makes a compelling case in favor of harvesting the Pacific yew. What would be the short-term and long-term effects of her proposal? Do you think she overstates her case?

3. Christensen ends her essay by appealing to her readers' emotions: "No resource can be more valuable or more important than a human life. Ask my husband. Ask my two sons. Ask me" (12). What does she gain by ending with this appeal? Would another, less emotional, conclusion have been more effective?

IN THE BELLY OF THE BEAST

Barbara Kingsolver

In the following essay from her collection High Tide in Tucson: Essays from Now and Never *(1995), novelist Barbara Kingsolver (see p. 64) describes a visit to a decommissioned nuclear missile silo near Tucson, Arizona. The experience ultimately leads her to reflect on "our great American capacity for denying objective reality in favor of defense mythology."*

The Titans, in the stories of the ancient Greeks, were unearthly 1 giants with heroic strength who ruled the universe from the dawn of time. Their parents were heaven and earth, and their children were the gods. These children squabbled and started a horrific, fiery war to take over ruling the universe.

A more modern legend goes this way: The Titans were giant mis- 2 siles with atomic warheads. The Pentagon set them in neat circles around chosen American cities, and there they kept us safe and free for twenty-two years.

In the 1980s they were decommissioned. But one of the mummified 3 giants, at least, was enshrined for public inspection. A Titan silo—a hole in the ground where an atomic bomb waited all its life to be launched— is now a missile museum just south of Tucson. When I first heard of it I was dismayed, then curious. What could a person possibly learn from driving down the interstate on a sunny afternoon and descending into the ground to peruse the technology of nuclear warfare?

Eventually I went. And now I know. 4

The Titan who sleeps in his sleek, deep burrow is surrounded with 5 ugliness. The museum compound, enclosed by an unkind-looking fence, is set against a lifeless backdrop of mine tailings. The grounds are gravel flatlands. The front office is blank except for a glass display case of souvenirs: plastic hard hats, model missile kits for the kids, a

Titan-missile golf shirt. I bought my ticket and was ushered with a few dozen others into a carpeted auditorium. The walls bore mementoes of this silo's years of active duty, including a missile-shaped silver trophy for special achievement at a Strategic Air Command combat competition. The lights dimmed and a gargly voice rose up against high-drama music as the film projector stuttered, then found its stride and began our orientation. A ring of Titan II missiles, we were told, encircled Tucson from 1962 until 1984. The Titan II was "conceived" in 1960 and hammered together in very short order with the help of General Motors, General Electric, Martin Marietta, and other contractors. The launch sites are below ground—"safely protected from a nuclear blast." The missile stands 103 feet tall, 10 feet in diameter, and weighs 150 tons. A fatherly-sounding narrator informed us, "Titan II can be up and out of its silo in less than a minute, hurling its payload at speeds of over 15,000 miles per hour nearly halfway around the world. This ICBM[1] waits quietly underground, its retaliatory potential available on a moment's notice."

The film went on to describe the typical day of a missile crew, and 6 the many tasks required to keep a Titan in a state of constant readiness. Finally we were told sternly, "Little remains to remind people that for 22 years a select group of men stood guard 24 hours a day, seven days a week, protecting the rights and freedom we enjoy in these United States." Day and night the vigilant crew monitored calls from their command post, "Waiting . . ." (a theatrical pause) "for a message that never came."

We filed out of the auditorium and stood in the hostile light of the 7 gravel compound. Dave, our volunteer guide, explained about reinforced antennas that could go on transmitting during an attack (nuclear war disturbs radio transmissions, among other things). One small, cone-shaped antenna sat out in the open where anyone could trip over it. Dave told us a joke: they used to tell the rookies to watch out, this was the warhead. My mind roamed. What sort of person would volunteer to be a bomb-museum docent?[2] The answer: he used to be a commander here. Now, semiretired, he trained cruise-missile operators.

It was still inconceivable that a missile stood erect under our feet, 8 but there was its lid, an enormous concrete door on sliding tracks. Grate-covered holes in the ground bore a stenciled warning: TOXIC VAPORS. During accidents or miscalculations, deadly fuel would escape through these vents. I wondered if the folks living in the retirement community just downhill, with the excruciatingly ironic name of Green Valley, ever knew about this. Dave pointed to a government-issue

---

[1] Intercontinental ballistic missile. [Eds.]
[2] Lecturer. [Eds.]

weathervane, explaining that it would predict which way the poisonous gases would blow. What a relief.

We waited by the silo entry port while a Boy Scout troop emerged. 9 I scanned the little boys' faces for signs of what I might be in for. Astonishment? Boredom? Our group then descended the cool stairwell into the silo. Just like a real missile crew, we put on hard hats to protect ourselves from low-hanging conduits and sharp edges. Signs warned us to watch for rattlesnakes. The hazards of snakes and bumped heads struck me as nearly comic against the steel-reinforced backdrop of potential holocaust. Or, put another way, being protected against these lesser hazards made the larger one seem improbable.

A series of blast doors, each thicker than my body, were all propped 10 open to let us pass. In the old days, you would have had to wait for security clearance at every door in turn before it would admit you and then heave shut, locking behind you. If you turned out to be an unauthorized intruder, Dave explained, you'd get a quick tour of the complex with your face very near the gravel.

Some forty steps down in the silo's bowels, we entered the "No 11 Lone Zone," where at least two people stood guard at all times. This was the control room. Compared with my expectations, undoubtedly influenced by Hollywood, it seemed unsophisticated. The Titan control room was run on cathode-ray tubes and transistor technology. For all the world, it had the look of those fifties spaceship movies, where men in crewcuts and skinny ties dash around trying to figure out what went wrong. No modern computers here, no special effects. The Titan system was built, Dave said, with "we-need-it-now technology." I tried to get my mind around the notion of slapping together some little old thing that could blow up a city.

Dave was already moving on, showing us the chair where the mis- 12 sile commander sat. It looks exactly like a La-z-boy recliner. The commander and one designated enlisted man would have the responsibility of simultaneously turning two keys and engaging the missile, if that call came through. All of us stared mutely at the little holes where those keys would go in.

A changeable wooden sign—similar to the ones the Forest Service 13 used to warn that the fire danger today is MEDIUM—hung above the controls to announce the day's STRATEGIC FORCES READINESS CONDITION. You might suppose it went to ultimate-red-alert (or whatever it's called) only a few times in history. Not since the Cuban missile crisis,[3] maybe. You would be wrong. Our guide explained that red-alerts come up all the time, sometimes triggered by a false blip on a radar, and sometimes (unbeknownst to crew members) as a test, checking their

---

[3] A major 1962 Cold War confrontation between the United States and the Soviet Union. [Eds.]

mental steadiness. Are they truly sane enough to turn that key and strike up nuclear holocaust? For twenty-two years, every activity and every dollar spent here was aimed toward that exact end, and no other.

"But only the President can issue that order," Dave said. I believe he   14
meant this to be reassuring.

We walked deeper into the artificially lit cave of the silo, down a   15
long green catwalk suspended from above. The entire control chamber hangs on springs like huge shock absorbers. No matter what rocked and raged above, the men here would not be jostled.

On the catwalk we passed an eyewash facility, an outfit resembling   16
a space suit, and a shower in case of mishaps involving toxic missile-fuel vapors. At its terminus the catwalk circled the immense cylindrical hole where the missile stood. We peered through a window into the shaft. Sure enough it was in there, hulking like a huge, dumb killer dog waiting for orders.

This particular missile, of course, is impotent. It has been relieved of   17
its nuclear warhead. Now that the Titans have been decommissioned, they're being used as launch missiles for satellites. A man in our group piped up, "Wasn't it a Titan that blew up a few weeks ago, when they were trying to launch a weather satellite?"

Dave said yes, it was, and he made an interesting face. No one pur-   18
sued this line of thought, although questions certainly hammered against the roof of my mouth. "What if it'd been headed out of here carrying a payload of death and destruction, Dave, for keeping Tucson safe and free? What then?

Like compliant children on a field trip, all of us silently examined a   19
metal hatch opening into the missile shaft, through which service mechanics would gain access to the missile itself. A sign on the hatch reminds mechanics not to use their walkie-talkies while inside. I asked what would happen if they did, and Dave said it would totally screw up the missile's guidance system. Again, I felt strangely inhibited from asking very obvious questions: What does this mean, to "totally screw up the missile's guidance system"? That the bomb might then land, for example, on Seattle?

The Pentagon has never discussed it, but the Titan missiles sur-   20
rounding Tucson were decommissioned, ostensibly, because of techni-cal obsolescence. This announcement came in 1980, almost a decade before the fall of the Berlin Wall; it had nothing to do with letting down the nation's nuclear guard. Make no mistake about this: in 1994 the U.S. sank $11.9 billion into the production and maintenance of nuclear mis-siles, submarines, and warheads. A separately allocated $2.8 billion was spent on the so-called Star Wars weapons research system. The U.S. government document providing budget authority for fiscal year 1996 states, "Although nuclear forces no longer play as prominent a role in

our defense capability as they once did, they remain an important part of our overall defense posture." It's hard to see exactly how these forces are on the wane, as the same document goes on to project outlays of roughly $10 billion for the nuclear war enterprise again the following year, and more than $9 billion every year after that, right on through the end of the century. In Nevada, New Mexico, Utah, Texas, the Great Plains, and many places we aren't allowed to know about, real live atomic bombs stand ready. Our leaders are hard-pressed to pretend some foreign power might invade us, but we are investing furiously in the tools of invasion.

The Pentagon was forced to decommission the Titans because, in 21 plain English, the Titans may have presented one of the most stupendous hazards to the U.S. public we've ever had visited upon us. In the 1960s a group of civilian physicists at the University of Arizona worked out that an explosion at any one of the silos surrounding Tucson would set up a chain reaction among the other Titans that would instantly cremate the city. I learned about this in the late seventies, through one of the scientists who authored the extremely unpopular Titan report. I had months of bad dreams. It was not the first or last time I was floored by our great American capacity for denying objective reality in favor of defense mythology. When I was a child in grade school we had "duck and cover" drills, fully trusting that leaping into a ditch and throwing an Orlon sweater over our heads would save us from nuclear fallout. The Extension Service produced cheerful illustrated pamphlets for our mothers, showing exactly how to stash away in the basement enough canned goods to see the family through the inhospitable aftermath of nuclear war. Now we can pass these pamphlets around at parties, or see the quaint documentary *Atomic Café,* and laugh at the antique charm of such naïveté. And still we go on living in towns surrounded by nuclear choke chains. It is our persistent willingness to believe in ludicrous safety measures that is probably going to kill us.

I tried to exorcise my nightmares in a poem about the Titans, which 22 began:

> When God was a child
> and the vampire fled from the sign of the cross,
> belief was possible.
> Survival was this simple.
> But the savior clutched in the pocket   5
> encouraged vampires to prosper
> in the forest.
>
> The mistake
> was to carry the cross,
> the rabbit's foot,   10
> the spare tire,

St. Christopher who presides
over the wrecks:
steel cauliflowers
proliferating in junkyard gardens.   15
And finally
to believe in the fallout shelter.

Now we are left in cities ringed with giants.

Responding to Reading

1. Kingsolver begins her essay with the ancient Greek legend of the Titans.
   She then says, "A more modern legend goes this way: The Titans were giant
   missiles with atomic warheads" (2). Why does she refer to the story of the
   Titan missile as a "legend"? What point does she hope to make? Do you
   agree with her?
2. Throughout her essay, Kingsolver mixes the subjective narrative of her tour
   with an objective discussion of American arms policy. What does she hope
   to accomplish with each of these perspectives? Do they work well together?
3. Kingsolver ends her essay with a poem. What are the strengths and weaknesses of this ending? What other concluding strategy could she have used?

FOCUS: WHO OWNS THE LAND?

GROWING UP GAME

Brenda Peterson

Brenda Peterson (1950–   ) grew up in the Pacific Northwest and the South, received her B.A. from the University of California at Davis, and then moved to New York City, where she became a staff writer for the New Yorker *magazine. She was later the fiction editor for* Rocky Mountain Magazine *and taught at Arizona State University at Tempe. She has published several novels, including* Becoming the Enemy *(1988) and* Duck and Cover *(1991), as well as the collection* Living by Water: Essays on Life, Land, and Spirit *(1991). Her most recent book is* Sister Stories: Taking the Journey Together *(1996). Currently a freelance editor and environmental writer, she lives on Puget Sound in Seattle, Washington. In the following essay, Peterson writes about how, throughout her childhood, she ate game shot by her father and how this experience led her to regard eating "as a conscious act."*

When I went off to college, my father gave me, as part of my tuition, 1
fifty pounds of moose meat. In 1969, eating moose meat at the
University of California was a contradiction in terms. Hippies didn't
hunt. I lived in a rambling Victorian house that boasted sweeping circular staircases, built-in lofts, and a landlady who dreamed of opening
her own health food restaurant. I told my housemates that my moose
meat in its nondescript white butcher paper was from a side of beef my
father had bought. The carnivores in the house helped me finish off
such suppers as sweet-and-sour moose meatballs, mooseburgers (gar-
nished with the obligatory avocado and sprouts), and mooseghetti. The
same dinner guests who remarked upon the lean sweetness of the meat
would have recoiled if I'd told them the not-so-simple truth: that I grew
up on game, and the moose they were eating had been brought down,
with one shot through his magnificent heart, by my father—a man who
had hunted all his life and all of mine.

One of my earliest memories is of crawling across the vast continent 2
of crinkled linoleum in our Forest Service cabin kitchen down splintered back steps, through wildflowers growing wheat-high. I was
eye-level with grasshoppers who scolded me on my first solo trip outside. I made it to the shed, a cool and comfortingly square shelter that
held phantasmagoric metal parts; they smelled good, like dirt and
grease. I had played a long time in this shed before some maternal

shriek made me lift up on my haunches to listen to those urgent, possessive sounds that were my name. Rearing up, my head bumped into something hanging in the dark; gleaming white, it felt sleek and cold against my cheek. Its smell was dense and musty and not unlike the slabs of my grandmother's great arms after her cool, evening sponge baths. In that shed I looked up and saw the flensed body of a doe; it swung gently, slapping my face. I felt then as I do even now when eating game: horror and awe and kinship.

Growing up those first years on a Plumas National Forest station 3 high in the Sierra Nevada near Oregon was somewhat like belonging to a white tribe. The men hiked off every day into their forest and the women stayed behind in the circle of official cabins, breeding. So far away from a store, we ate venison and squirrel, rattlesnake and duck. My first rattle, in fact, was from a diamondback rattler my father killed as we watched, by snatching it up with a stick and winding it, whiplike, around a redwood sapling. Rattlesnake tastes just like chicken, but has many fragile bones to slither one's way through. We also ate rainbow trout, rabbit, and geese galore. The game was accompanied by such daily garden dainties as fried okra, mustard greens, corn fritters, wilted lettuce (our favorite because of that rare, blackened bacon), new potatoes and peas, stewed tomatoes, barbecued butter beans.

I was four before I ever had a beef hamburger, and I remember 4 being disappointed by its fatty, nothing taste and the way it fell apart at the seams whenever my teeth sank into it. Smoked pork shoulder came much later, in the South; and I was twenty-one, living in New York City, before I ever tasted leg of lamb. I approached that glazed rack of meat with a certain guilty self-consciousness, as if I unfairly stalked those sweet-tempered white creatures myself. But how would I explain my squeamishness to those urban sophisticates? How explain that I was shy with mutton when I had been bred on wild things?

Part of it, I suspect, had to do with the belief I'd also been bred 5 on: we become the spirit and body of animals we eat. As a child eating venison, I liked to think of myself as lean and lovely just like the deer. I would never be caught dead just grazing while some man who wasn't even a skillful hunter crept up and conked me over the head. If someone wanted to hunt me, he must be wily and outwitting. He must earn me.

My father had also taught us as children that animals were our 6 brothers and sisters under their skin. They died so that we might live. And of this sacrifice we must be mindful. "God make us grateful for what we are about to receive," took on new meaning when we imagined the animal's surrender to our own appetites. We also used all the animal, so that an elk became elk steaks, stew, salami, and sausage. His head and horns went on the wall to watch us more earnestly than any baby-sitter, and every Christmas Eve we had a ceremony of making our own moccasins for the new year out of whatever Father had tanned. "Nothing wasted," my father would always say, or, as we munched on sausage cookies made from moosemeat or venison, "Think about who you're eating." We thought of ourselves as intricately linked to the food chain. We knew, for example, that a forest fire meant, at the end of the line, we'd suffer too. We'd have buck stew instead of venison steak, and the meat would be stringy, withered-tasting, because in the animal kingdom, as it seemed with humans, only the meanest and leanest and orneriest survived losing their forests.

Once when I was in my early teens, I went along on a hunting trip 7
as the "main cook and bottle-washer," though I don't remember any bottles; none of these hunters drank alcohol. There was something else coursing through their veins as they rose long before dawn and disappeared, returning to my little camp most often dragging a doe or pheasant or rabbit. We ate innumerable cornmeal-fried fish, had rabbit stew seasoned only with blood and black pepper.

This hunting trip was the first time I remember eating game as a 8
conscious act. My father and Buddy Earl shot a big doe and she lay with me in the back of the tarp-draped station wagon all the way home. It was not the smell I minded, it was the glazed great, dark eyes and the way that head flopped around crazily on what I knew was once a graceful neck. I found myself petting this doe, murmuring all those graces we'd been taught long ago as children. Thank you for the sacrifice, thank you for letting us be like you so that we can grow up strong as game. But there was an uneasiness in me that night as I bounced along in the back of the car with the deer.

What was uneasy is still uneasy—perhaps it always will be. It's not 9
easy when one really starts thinking about all this: the eating game, the food chain, the sacrifice of one for the other. It's never easy when one begins to think about one's most basic actions, like eating. Like becoming what one eats: lean and lovely and mortal.

Why should it be that the purchase of meat at a butcher shop is 10
somehow more righteous than eating something wild? Perhaps it has to do with our collective unconscious that sees the animal bred for slaughter as doomed. But that wild doe or moose might make it without the hunter. Perhaps on this primitive level of archetype and unconscious knowing we even believe that what's wild lives forever.

My father once told this story around a hunting campfire. His own 11
father, who raised cattle during the Great Depression on a dirt farm in the Ozarks, once fell on such hard times that he had to butcher the pet lamb for supper. My father, bred on game or their own hogs all his life, took one look at the family pet on that meat platter and pushed his plate away. His siblings followed suit. To hear my grandfather tell it, it was the funniest thing he'd ever seen. "They just couldn't eat Bo-Peep," Grandfather said. And to hear my father tell it years later around that

campfire, it was funny, but I saw for the first time his sadness. And I realized that eating had become a conscious act for him that day at the dinner table when Bo-Peep offered herself up.

Now when someone offers me game, I will eat it with all the qualms   12 and memories and reverence with which I grew up eating it. And I think I will always have this feeling of horror and awe and kinship. And something else—full knowledge of what I do, what I become.

Responding to Reading

1. What is Peterson's purpose in writing this essay? To tell people about her childhood? To explore issues about which she feels uncomfortable? To convince people not to eat meat? Something else? Explain.
2. In paragraph 7, Peterson tells about a hunting trip that she went on with her father. What is the purpose of this anecdote? In what way does it reinforce the main point of her essay?
3. In paragraph 2, Peterson tells about the "horror and awe and kinship" she feels whenever she eats game. She uses this phrase again in her conclusion. What does she mean by this phrase? How do you think Barbara Ehrenreich (p. 707) would respond to it?

OUR ANIMAL RITES

Anna Quindlen

Journalist and novelist Anna Quindlen (1953–) was born in Philadelphia, where she received what she calls "a liberal Catholic education." She attended college at Barnard and started her career as a reporter at Time *magazine in 1977. She moved to the* New York Times *in the early 1980s, where she contributed to the newspaper's "Hers" column (1985–1986) and eventually wrote the widely syndicated personal opinion columns "Life in the 30's" (1986–1988) and "Public and Private" (1990–1994); some of these columns have been collected in the books* Living Out Loud *(1988) and* Thinking Out Loud *(1993). In 1992, she won a Pulitzer Prize for journalism for her "Public and Private" columns. The success of Quindlen's two first novels—*Object Lessons *(1991) and* One True Thing *(1994)—led her to retire from the* Times *and concentrate on fiction-writing. Quindlen's newest book is a novel,* Black and Blue *(1998). She also published a children's book,* Happily Ever After, *in 1995. Of her nonfiction she has said, "Whenever my response to an important subject is rational and completely cerebral, I know there is something wrong with it. I have always been governed by my gut." In the following 1990 "Public and Private" column, Quindlen looks at the relationship between humans and the wild animals whose territory we are overtaking.*

The bear had the adenoidal breathing of an elderly man with a pas- 1
sion for cigars and a tendency toward emphysema. My first thought,
when I saw him contemplating me through tiny eyes from a rise just
beyond the back porch, was that he looked remarkably bearlike, like a
close-up shot from a public television nature program.

I screamed. With heavy tread—pad, pad, pad, harrumph, har- 2
rumph—the bear went off into the night, perhaps to search for garbage
cans inexpertly closed and apiaries[1] badly lighted. I sat on the porch,
shaking. Everyone asks, "Was he big?" My answer is, "Compared to
what?"

What I leave out when I tell the story is my conviction that the bear 3
is still watching. At night I imagine he is staring down from the hillside
into the lighted porch, as though he had a mezzanine seat for a performance on which the curtain had already gone up. "A nice female, but
not very furry," I imagine him thinking, "I see the cubs have gone to the
den for the night."

Sometimes I suspect I think this because the peace and quiet of the 4
country have made me go mad, and if only I could hear a car alarm, an
ambulance siren, the sound of a boom box playing "The Power" and its
owner arguing with his girlfriend over whether or not he was flirting
with Denise at the party, all that would drive the bear clear out of my
head.

Sometimes I think it is because instead of feeling that the bear is 5
trespassing on my property, in my heart I believe that I am trespassing
on his.

That feeling is not apparent to city people, although there is some- 6
thing about the sight of a man cleaning up after a sheepdog with a sheet
of newspaper that suggests a kind of horrible atonement. The city is a
place built by the people, for the people. There we say people are acting
like animals when they do things with guns and bats and knives that
your ordinary bear would never dream of doing. There we condescend
to our animals, with grooming parlors and cat carriers, using them to
salve our loneliness and prepare us for parenthood.

All you who lost interest in the dog after the baby was born, you 7
know who you are.

But out where the darkness has depth, where there are no street 8
lights and the stars leap out of the sky, condescension, a feeling of
supremacy, what the animal-rights types call speciesism, is impossible.
Oh, hunters try it, and it is pathetic to consider the firepower they
require to bring down one fair-sized deer. They get three bear days in
the autumn, and afterward there is at least one picture in the paper of a

---

[1] Bee farms. [Eds.]

couple of smiling guys in hats surrounding the carcass of an animal that looks, though dead, more dignified than they do.

Each spring, after the denning and the long, cold drowse, we wait 9 to see if the bear that lives on the hill above our house beat the bullets. We discover his triumph through signs: a pile of bear dung on the lawn, impossible to assign to any other animal unless mastodons still roam the earth. A garbage box overturned into the swamp, the cole slaw container licked clean. Symmetrical scratch marks five feet up on a tree.

They own this land. Once, long ago, someone put a house on it. 10 That was when we were tentative interlopers, when we put a farm-house here and a barn there. And then we went nuts, built garden condos with pools and office complexes with parking garages and developments with names that always included the words Park, Acres, or Hills. You can't stop progress, especially if it's traveling 65 miles an hour. You notice that more this time of year, when the possums stiffen by the side of the road.

Sometimes the animals fight back. I was tickled by the people who 11 bought a house with a pond and paid a good bit of money for a little dock from which to swim. It did not take long for them to discover that the snapping turtles were opposed to the addition to their ecosystem of humans wearing sunscreen. An exterminator was sent for. The pond was dredged. A guest got bit. The turtles won.

I've read that deer use the same trails all their lives. Someone comes 12 along and puts a neo-Colonial house in the middle of their deer paths, and the deer will use the paths anyway, with a few detours. If you watch, you can see that it is the deer that belong and the house which does not. The bats, the groundhogs, the weasels, the toads—a hundred years from now, while our family will likely be scattered, their descendants might be in this same spot. Somewhere out there the bear is watching, picking his nits and his teeth, breathing his raggedy bear breath, and if he could talk, maybe he'd say, "I wonder when they're going back where they belong."

Responding to Reading

1. Do you think that human beings are guilty of "speciesism" (8)?
2. Is Quindlen romanticizing nature? Do you think she attributes more insight and dignity to animals than they actually possess or deserve? Explain.
3. Quindlen spends much of her essay discussing a bear that she encountered near her house. Are her sentiments about the bear in this essay similar to or different from those expressed by William Stafford about the deer in "Traveling Through the Dark" (p. 709)?

THE MYTH OF MAN AS HUNTER

Barbara Ehrenreich

*An unabashed "feminist, populist, socialist, and secular humanist,"
Barbara Ehrenreich (1941–   ) was born in Butte, Montana, to a family of
self-avowed "free-thinkers" and "fourth- or fifth-generation atheists." Now a
resident of Long Island, she holds a Ph.D. from Rockefeller University and is
one of the country's most controversial social critics, offering a decidedly liberal perspective on many political and economic issues. Her books of social
criticism include* Fear of Falling: The Inner Life of the Middle Class
(1989), The Worst Years of Our Lives: Irreverent Notes on a Decade of
Greed *(1990),* The Snarling Citizen *(1995), and* Blood Rites: The
Origins and History of the Passions of War *(1997).* She is also the author
of a novel, Kipper's Game *(1993).* She is a featured essayist for Time *magazine, where the following piece originally appeared in 1993. In it,
Ehrenreich suggests that while early humans may have successfully made the
transition from prey to predators, we are still prey to many enemies, including others of our own species.*

It must seem odd to the duck and deer populations that Americans 1
have paid more than $255 million this summer for the experience of
being prey. In *Jurassic Park* we had the supreme thrill of being hunted
for food by creatures far larger, faster, and—counting teeth and claws—
better armed than we are. With the raptors closing in, we saw how vulnerable the human body is—no claws, no exoskeleton, no blinding
poison sprays. Take away our guns and high-voltage fences and we are,
from a typical predator perspective, tasty mounds of unwrapped meat.

If the experience resonates to the most ancient layers of our brains, 2
it's probably because we spent our first million years or so not just hunting and gathering, but being hunted and gathered. *T. Rex* had been gone
for 60 million years when our progenitors came along, but there were
saber-toothed tigers, lions, cougars, leopards, bears, wolves and wild
boars waiting at the edge of every human settlement and campground.

The myth of "man the hunter" has flatteringly obscured our true 3
prehistory as prey. According to the myth, "man" climbed down from
the trees one day, strode out into the savanna with a sharpened stick in
his hand and started slaughtering the local ungulates.[1] After that, supposedly, the only violence prehumans had to worry about was from
other stick-wielding bipeds like themselves. Thus some punctured aus-
tralopithecine skulls found in Africa were at first chalked up to "intentional armed assault"—until someone pointed out that the punctures
precisely fit the tooth gap of the leopard.

---

[1] Hooved animals. [Eds.]

Humans didn't even invent effective action-at-a-distance weapons 4
until a mere 40,000 or so years ago. Only with these new tools, like the
bow and arrow and the spear thrower, could our ancestors begin to
mimic the speed and sharpness of a big cat's claws. Even so, predator
animals remained a major threat. As late as the 7th century B.C., a stele[2]
erected by the Assyrian King Assurbanipal recounts the ferocity of the
lions and tigers after torrential rains had flushed them out of their lairs;
the great King, of course, stamped out the beasts.

Our collective memory of the war against the predator beasts is pre- 5
served in myth and fairy tale. Typically, a mythical hero starts out by
taking on the carnivorous monster that is ravaging the land: Perseus
saves Andromeda from becoming a sea monster's snack. Theseus con-
quers the Minotaur who likes to munch on Athenian youth. Beowulf
destroys the loathsome night-feeding Grendel. Heracles takes on a
whole zoo of horrors: lions, hydras, boars. In European fairy tales it's
the wolves you have to watch out for—if the cannibal witches don't get
you first.

No doubt the greatest single leap in human prehistory was the one 6
we made from being helpless prey to becoming formidable predators of
other living creatures, including, eventually, the ones with claws and
fangs. This is the theme that is acted out over and over, obsessively, in
the initiation rites of tribal cultures. In the drama of initiation, the young
(usually men) are first humiliated and sometimes tortured, only to be
"reborn" as hunters and warriors. Very often the initial torment
includes the threat of being eaten by costumed humans or actual beasts.
Orokaiva children in Papua New Guinea are told they will be devoured
like pigs; among Indians of the Pacific Northwest, the initiates were kid-
napped or menaced by wolves; young Norwegian men, at least in the
sagas, had to tackle bears single-handedly.

As a species, we've been fabulously successful at predation. We 7
enslaved the wild ungulates, turning them into our cattle and sheep,
pushing them into ever narrower habitats. We tamed some of the
wolves and big cats, trivializing them as household pets. We can dine
on shark or alligator fillets if we want, and the only bears we're likely
to know are the ones whose name is teddy. In fact, horror movies
wouldn't be much fun if real monsters lurked outside our theaters. We
can enjoy screaming at the alien or the raptor or the blob because we
know, historically speaking, it was our side that won.

But the defeat of the animal predators was not a clear-cut victory 8
for us. With the big land carnivores out of the way, humans decided
that the only worthwhile enemy was others like themselves—"enemy"
individuals or tribes or nations or ethnic groups. The criminal stalking

---

[2] Upright slab with an inscribed or sculptured surface. [Eds.]

his victim, the soldiers roaring into battle, are enacting an archaic drama in which the other player was originally nonhuman, either something to eat or be eaten by. For millenniums now, the earth's scariest predator has been ourselves.

In our arrogance, we have tended to forget that our own most for- 9 midable enemies may still be of the nonhuman kind. Instead of hungry tigers or fresh-cloned dinosaurs, we face equally deadly microscopic life forms. It will take a whole new set of skills and attitudes to defeat HIV or the TB bacterium—not the raging charge on the field of battle, but the cunning ambush of the lab.

And then there are all the nonliving enemies—Pinatubo,[3] Andrew,[4] 10 the murderously bloated Mississippi—to remind us that the earth has not passively accepted our dominion over it. We will go down, locked in incestuous combat with our own kind, while the earth quakes, the meteors hit and the viruses mindlessly duplicate in our living organs. Or we will take another great leap like the one our protohuman ancestors took so long ago when the threat was still from predator beasts: We will marshal all our skills and resources, our tools and talents, and face the enemy without.

Responding to Reading

1. How do Ehrenreich's arguments relate to the sport of hunting—for example, for duck or deer—as we know it today? What position do you think she would take on recreational hunting?
2. Ehrenreich asserts that the idea of man as hunter is not accurate. How does she support her position? If, as she claims, the concept of man as hunter is inaccurate, why do you think it has endured?
3. How are Brenda Peterson's (p. 701), Anna Quindlen's (p. 704), and Barbara Ehrenreich's ideas about the relationship between human beings and animals alike? How are they different? For example, do they agree that animals have certain rights? Do they believe people should hunt?

TRAVELING THROUGH THE DARK

William Stafford

William Stafford (1914–1993), a plain-talking poet of the western United States, was born in Hutchinson, Kansas, and earned an undergraduate degree from the University of Kansas and a doctorate from the University of Iowa. Although his poems hint at moral judgments, Stafford

---

[3] A volcano. [Eds.]
[4] A hurricane. [Eds.]

generally kept apart from trends and politics, following his own impulses. He once said that writing is like fishing in that the writer must be willing to fail. Some of his many collections of verse are Allegiances *(1970),* The Design of the Oriole *(1977), and* An Oregon Message *(1987). From* Stories That Could Be True *(1960) comes his poem "Traveling through the Dark," about an encounter between nature and technology.*

Traveling through the dark I found a deer
dead on the edge of the Wilson River road.
It is usually best to roll them into the canyon:
that road is narrow; to swerve might make more dead.

By glow of the tail-light I stumbled back of the car   5
and stood by the heap, a doe, a recent killing;
she had stiffened already, almost cold.
I dragged her off; she was large in the belly.

My fingers touching her side brought me the reason—
her side was warm; her fawn lay there waiting,   10
alive, still, never to be born.
Beside that mountain road I hesitated.

The car aimed ahead its lowered parking lights;
under the hood purred the steady engine.
I stood in the glare of the warm exhaust turning red;   15
around our group I could hear the wilderness listen.

I thought hard for us all—my only swerving—
then pushed her over the edge into the river.

Responding to Reading

1. In line 3, the speaker says, "It is usually best to roll them into the canyon." What information does this statement give you? Does it make it easier or more difficult to explain the speaker's initial hesitation? To understand his final action?
2. How does each of the following statements reveal the speaker's view of nature?
   • "Beside that mountain road I hesitated" (12)
   • "I could hear the wilderness listen" (16)
   • "I thought hard for us all" (17)
3. After hesitating, the speaker in this poem pushes the pregnant deer into the river. Why does he hesitate? Does he feel any of the "horror and awe and kinship" that Peterson (p. 000) speaks about in her essay? If so, why does he act the way he does?

Widening the Focus

- Jane Goodall , "A Plea for the Chimps" (p. 610)
- Annie Dillard, " The Deer at Providencia"(p. 720)
- Claire McCarthy, "Dog Lab"(p. 774)

WRITING

Earth in the Balance

1. In recent years, the Mediterranean fruit fly has damaged fruit in California and Florida. In an effort to stop the damage, both states have aggressively sprayed malathion, an insecticide with relatively low toxicity to plants and animals. At the present time, however, these efforts have not ended the infestation. Write an essay in which you discuss how Rachel Carson and Barbara Ehrenreich would address this problem.

2. Al Gore and Rachel Carson discuss ways in which the environment can be preserved. Write an essay in which you discuss how a specific change in government policy, social behavior, or industrial policy could improve the environment.

3. Reread one of the essays in this chapter. Then, write a letter to its author in which you argue against his or her position. Make sure you address the specific points the author makes in his or her essay, and support your position with references to your own observations and experiences.

4. Both Wendell Berry in "The Pleasures of Eating" and Brenda Peterson in "Growing Up Game" deal with the subject of eating. In what ways do these writers see the act of eating as having important social and political consequences? Compare their sentiments with those expressed by Annie Dillard in "The Deer at Provedencia" in Chapter 10 (p. 720).

5. What responsibility do you believe each individual has for doing his or her part to save the planet? Consider what in particular is worth saving in the natural world and what forces you see as working to destroy it. In your answer, refer to two of the following essays: "The Obligation to Endure" by Rachel Carson, "Recycling: No Panacea" by William Rathje and Cullen Murphy, and "Death in the Rain Forests" by Shawn Carlson.

6. In "Our Animal Rites," Anna Quindlen makes an effort to confront an animal on its own terms. Ultimately she fails, describing the bear in human terms and imagining what the bear would say if it could talk. Write an essay in which you discuss some of the writers in this chapter who are objective about animals in their natural settings and some who are not. What are the strengths and weaknesses of each approach?

7. A number of writers in this chapter suggest what individuals can do to improve the environment. Focus on two who seem to take different positions—Shawn Carlson and Sally Thane Christensen, for example—and compare their proposals. What are the strengths and

weaknesses of each writer's suggestions? Which writer presents the more feasible plan?

8. Write an essay in which you affirm (or deny) a person's right to hunt. Refer to two or three of the essays in the "Focus" section of this chapter to help you support your position. In addition, make sure you address the major arguments against your position.

9. Chief Seattle says that one day the whites will "suffocate in [their] own waste" (5). Write a letter from Al Gore to Chief Seattle in which you agree or disagree with this statement. Be specific, and refer to both essays.

10. In "Is a Tree Worth a Life?" Sally Thane Christensen says, "Given a choice between trees or people, people must prevail" (12). In "Our Animal Rites," Anna Quindlen says that human beings are interlopers on land owned by animals. With whom do you agree? Could both be right? Write an essay in which you consider whether the welfare of plants or animals should ever take precedence over the welfare of human beings. Support your points with references to Christensen's and Quindlen's essays as well as to any other essay in this chapter or elsewhere in this text.

10

MAKING CHOICES

Student Voices

"Making choices can be a very difficult thing to do, especially for a child or young adult. When adults make decisions, they have to think about what's best for them. When kids make decisions, they have to decide what's best for them and what will make their parents happy and proud—although it should be just what makes them happy. But when you're a kid or young adult, you want to make everyone else happy first. When you make the wrong choice, you are miserable. So making choices at this stage in life can be the most difficult thing you can do."

—*Kurt Banfi*

"Deciding whether to immigrate to the United States was the most complicated problem I have ever had. On one side of the scale was twenty years of life in a known and understood society with a pretty much predictable future; on the other, an unknown country with a different lifestyle, traditions, and language but offering a slim chance to make my life meaningful and to change my life through my abilities. I guess I just took a chance, which I have never regretted."

—*Gennadiy Levit*

"In my job, it seems as if no day is complete unless a difficult choice arises. As the budget officer for the Student Programming Association, I am constantly faced with decisions about who to hire for a concert, lecture, or comedy event. Most recently, a vote was taken on whether or not to hire an alternative rock group to perform. Two factors went through my mind during the meeting: the cost, and whether students would come and enjoy the event. Given the popularity of the group, I thought having students come out and enjoy the event outweighed the cost involved. I voted in favor of the concert. The show went off very well, but the number of students who attended was below what we expected. Still, I was glad to have been able to make that type of decision."

—*Michael Karam*

"Currently my daily habits are fairly regular and well established. The only choices that I make on a daily basis are what to wear and what to have for dinner. One of my more pressing choices is, 'Should I get a newer, more reliable car, or should I save my money?'"

—*Robert Barr*

"Until recently I lived a very sheltered life, thanks to my parents. All my choices and decisions were handled by them until I moved away to school. Now, most of the choices I make on a day-to-day basis deal with priorities in my life. For example, as a student athlete my first choice comes at 5 in the morning: whether or not to get out of my warm bed and head down to the gym for swimming practice. If I take the easy way out and stay in bed, I will have many consequences to deal with. Other choices involve deciding whether to go to class or not, whether to drink at a party, and whether to say 'No' to going out."

—*Natalie Chepelevich*

"Part of being responsible for our actions is knowing what our choices are and living with our decisions. Choosing to hit the snooze alarm can send shock waves through the rest of your life."

—*Matt Steigerwalt*

——————— PREPARING TO READ AND WRITE ———————

As Robert Frost suggests in his poem "The Road Not Taken" (p. 718), making choices is fundamental to our lives. The ability—and, in fact, the need—to make complex decisions is part of what makes us human. On a practical level, we choose friends, mates, careers, and places to live. On a more theoretical level, we struggle to make the moral and ethical choices that people have struggled with for thousands of years.

Many times, complex questions have no easy answers; occasionally, they have no answers at all. For example, should we stand up to authority even if our stand puts us at risk? Should we help less fortunate individuals if such help threatens our own social or economic position? Should we act to save an endangered species if that action may put people out of work? Should we tell the truth even if the truth may hurt us—or hurt someone else? Which road should we take, the easy one or the hard one?

Most of the time, the choice we (and the writers whose works appear in this chapter) face is the same: to act or not to act. To make a decision, we must understand both the long- and short-term consequences of acting in a particular way or of choosing not to act. We must struggle with the possibility of compromise, and with the possibility of making a morally or ethically objectionable decision. And, perhaps most important, we must learn to take responsibility for our decisions.

As you read and prepare to write about the selections in this chapter, you may consider the following questions:

- On what specific choice or choices does the selection focus? Is the decision to be made moral? Ethical? Political?

- Does the writer introduce a *dilemma*, a choice between two equally problematic alternatives?

- Does the choice the writer presents apply only to one specific situation or case, or does it also have a wider application?

- Is the writer emotionally involved with the issue he or she is discussing? Does this involvement (or lack of involvement) make the selection more or less convincing?

- What social, political, or religious ideas influence the writer? How can you tell? Are these ideas similar to or different from your own views?

- Does the decision under discussion cause the writer to examine his or her own values? The values of others? The values of the society at large? Does the selection lead you to examine your own values?

- Does the writer offer a solution? Do you find it reasonable?

- What choice or choices do you believe should be made? Why?

- Which writers' views seem most alike? Which seem most different?

TWO PERSPECTIVES
ON MAKING CHOICES

*The following poems consider the issues of personal choice and respon-
sibility and how their effects on individuals and on the larger world make "all
the difference." "The Road Not Taken" is one of the best-known works of
Robert Frost (1874–1963), most widely read and beloved of twentieth-
century American poets, whose language is familiar and accessible—though
not simple—and whose poems are often rich in symbols and allusions. The
speaker of this poem grapples in very concrete terms with the whole notion of
personal choice and what it entails. Poet Linda Pastan (b. 1932) won the*
Mademoiselle *poetry award as a senior at Radcliffe (the runner-up that
year was Sylvia Plath), but she gave up writing when she married in 1953
and did not resume her writing until her children entered school. The winner of numerous prizes, Pastan often focuses in her work on the complexity
of domestic life, using intense imagery to bring a sense of mystery to everyday matters. Her collections include* Waiting for My Life *(1981),* PM/AM:
New and Selected Poems *(1983), and* An Early Afterlife *(1995).
"Ethics," from* Waiting for My Life, *raises an ethical question that the
speaker suggests cannot really be resolved.*

THE ROAD NOT TAKEN

Robert Frost

Two roads diverged in a yellow wood,
And sorry I could not travel both
And be one traveller, long I stood
And looked down one as far as I could
To where it bent in the undergrowth;   5

Then took the other, as just as fair,
And having perhaps the better claim,
Because it was grassy and wanted wear;
Though as for that the passing there
Had worn them really about the same,   10

And both that morning equally lay
In leaves no step had trodden black.
Oh, I kept the first for another day!
Yet knowing how way leads on to way,
I doubted if I should ever come back.   15

I shall be telling this with a sigh
Somewhere ages and ages hence:
Two roads diverged in a wood, and I—
I took the one less travelled by,
And that has made all the difference.   20

ETHICS

Linda Pastan

In ethics class so many years ago
our teacher asked this question every fall:
if there were a fire in a museum
which would you save, a Rembrandt painting
or an old woman who hadn't many   5
years left anyhow? Restless on hard chairs
caring little for pictures or old age
we'd opt one year for life, the next for art
and always half-heartedly. Sometimes
the woman borrowed my grandmother's face   10
leaving her usual kitchen to wander
some drafty, half imagined museum.
One year, feeling clever, I replied
why not let the woman decide herself?
Linda, the teacher would report, eschews   15
the burdens of responsibility.
This fall in a real museum I stand
before a real Rembrandt, old woman,
or nearly so, myself. The colors
within this frame are darker than autumn,   20
darker even than winter—the browns of earth,
though earth's most radiant elements burn
through the canvas. I know now that woman
and painting and season are almost one
and all beyond saving by children.   25

Responding to Reading

1. What is the difference between the two paths Frost's speaker considers? Why does he make the choice he does?
2. Is "The Road Not Taken" simply about two paths in the wood, or does it suggest more? What makes you think so? To what larger choices might the speaker be alluding?

3. What does the speaker mean by "That has made all the difference" (20)? What choice might "make all the difference" for the speaker in Pastan's "Ethics"?
4. What choice actually confronts Pastan's speaker? What answer do you think the teacher expects the students to give?
5. Do you agree with the teacher in Pastan's poem that refusing to choose means avoiding responsibility? Does Frost's speaker have the option not to choose?
6. When Pastan's speaker says that "woman/and painting and season are almost one" (23–24), what does she mean? Does she imply that the teacher's question really has no answer? That the children who would "opt one year for life, the next for art" (8) are right?

THE DEER AT PROVIDENCIA

Annie Dillard

Known as a naturalist and essayist, Annie Dillard (1945–   ) won the Pulitzer Prize in 1974 for her first book, Pilgrim at Tinker Creek, *a non-fiction work in which she records her explorations in the Roanoke Valley of Virginia. Dillard calls herself a "stalker" of nature and its mysteries, and she delights in both the wonders and terrors it inspires. She contributes to periodicals, such as* Harper's *and the* Atlantic Monthly, *and has also written* Teaching a Stone to Talk *(1982),* An American Childhood *(1987),* The Writing Life *(1989),* The Living *(1992), and* Mornings like This: Found Poems *(1995). In "The Deer at Providencia," first published in 1982, Dillard moves the setting away from familiar territory to Ecuador. Her critically observant eye is at work as she describes a captured deer, whose "skin looked virtually hairless, . . . almost translucent, like a membrane." Then, Dillard deftly turns to a consideration of the paradoxical nature of suffering.*

There were four of us North Americans in the jungle, in the Ecuadoran jungle on the banks of the Napo River in the Amazon watershed. The other three North Americans were metropolitan men. We stayed in tents in one riverside village, and visited others. At the village called Providencia we saw a sight which moved us, and which shocked the men.

The first thing we saw when we climbed the riverbank to the village of Providencia was the deer. It was roped to a tree on the grass clearing near the thatch shelter where we would eat lunch.

The deer was small, about the size of a whitetail fawn, but apparently full-grown. It had a rope around its neck and three feet caught in the rope. Someone said that the dogs had caught it that morning and the villagers were going to cook and eat it that night.

This clearing lay at the edge of the little thatched-hut village. We could see the villagers going about their business, scattering feed corn for hens about their houses, and wandering down paths to the river to bathe. The village headman was our host; he stood beside us as we watched the deer struggle. Several village boys were interested in the deer; they formed part of the circle we made around it in the clearing. So also did four businessmen from Quito[1] who were attempting to guide us around the jungle. Few of the very different people standing in this circle had a common language. We watched the deer, and no one said much.

The deer lay on its side at the rope's very end, so the rope lacked slack to let it rest its head in the dust. It was "pretty," delicate of bone like all deer, and thin-skinned for the tropics. Its skin looked virtually hairless, in fact, and almost translucent, like a membrane. Its neck was no thicker than my wrist; it was rubbed open on the rope, and gashed. Trying to paw itself free of the rope, the deer had scratched its own neck with its hooves. The raw underside of its neck showed red stripes and some bruises bleeding inside the muscles. Now three of its feet were hooked in the rope under its jaw. It could not stand, of course, on one leg, so it could not move to slacken the rope and ease the pull on its throat and enable it to rest its head.

Repeatedly the deer paused, motionless, its eyes veiled, with only its rib cage in motion, and its breaths the only sound. Then, after I would think, "It has given up; now it will die," it would heave. The rope twanged; the tree leaves clattered; the deer's free foot beat the ground. We stepped back and held our breaths. It thrashed, kicking, but only one leg moved; the other three legs tightened inside the rope's loop. Its hip jerked; its spine shook. Its eyes rolled; its tongue, thick with spittle, pushed in and out. Then it would rest again. We watched this for fifteen minutes.

Once three young native boys charged in, released its trapped legs, and jumped back to the circle of people. But instantly the deer scratched up its neck with its hooves and snared its forelegs in the rope again. It was easy to imagine a third and then a fourth leg soon stuck, like Brer Rabbit and the Tar Baby.[2]

We watched the deer from the circle, and then we drifted on to lunch. Our palm-roofed shelter stood on a grassy promontory from which we could see the deer tied to the tree, pigs and hens walking

---

[1] Capital of Ecuador. [Eds.]

[2] Characters created by Southern writer Joel Chandler Harris.

under village houses, and black-and-white cattle standing in the river. There was even a breeze.

Lunch, which was the second and better lunch we had that day, was 9 hot and fried. There was a big fish called *doncella,* a kind of catfish, dipped whole in corn flour and beaten egg, then deep fried. With our fingers we pulled soft fragments of it from its sides to our plates, and ate; it was delicate fish-flesh, fresh and mild. Someone found the roe, and I ate of that too—it was fat and stronger, like egg yolk, naturally enough, and warm.

There was also a stew of meat in shreds with rice and pale brown 10 gravy. I had asked what kind of deer it was tied to the tree; Pepe had answered in Spanish, *"Gama."* Now they told us this was *gama* too, stewed. I suspect the word means merely game or venison. At any rate, I heard that the village dogs had cornered another deer just yesterday, and it was this deer which we were now eating in full sight of the whole article. It was good. I was surprised at its tenderness. But it is a fact that high levels of lactic acid, which builds up in muscle tissues during exertion, tenderizes.

After the fish and meat we ate bananas fried in chunks and served 11 on a tray; they were sweet and full of flavor. I felt terrific. My shirt was wet and cool from swimming; I had had a night's sleep, two decent walks, three meals, and a swim—everything tasted good. From time to time each one of us, separately, would look beyond our shaded roof to the sunny spot where the deer was still convulsing in the dust. Our meal completed, we walked around the deer and back to the boats.

That night I learned that while we were watching the deer, the oth- 12 ers were watching me.

We four North Americans grew close in the jungle in a way that was 13 not the usual artificial intimacy of travelers. We liked each other. We stayed up all that night talking, murmuring, as though we rocked on hammocks slung above time. The others were from big cities: New York, Washington, Boston. They all said that I had no expression on my face when I was watching the deer—or at any rate, not the expression they expected.

They had looked to see how I, the only woman, and the youngest, 14 was taking the sight of the deer's struggles. I looked detached, apparently, or hard, or calm, or focused, still. I don't know. I was thinking. I remember feeling very old and energetic. I could say like Thoreau that I have traveled widely in Roanoke, Virginia.[3] I have thought a great deal about carnivorousness; I eat meat. These things are not issues; they are mysteries.

---

[3] In *Walden,* Henry David Thoreau (see p. 731) says, "I have traveled a good deal in Concord." [Eds.]

Gentlemen of the city, what surprises you? That there is suffering 15 here, or that I know it?

We lay in the tent and talked, "If it had been my wife," one man 16 said with special vigor, amazed, "she wouldn't have cared *what* was going on; she would have dropped *everything* right at that moment and gone in the village from here to there to there, she would not have *stopped* until that animal was out of its suffering one way or another. She couldn't *bear* to see a creature in agony like that."

I nodded. 17

Now I am home. When I wake I comb my hair before the mirror 18 above my dresser. Every morning for the past two years I have seen in that mirror, beside my sleep-softened face, the blackened face of a burnt man. It is a wire-service photograph clipped from a newspaper and taped to my mirror. The caption reads: "Alan McDonald in Miami hospital bed." All you can see in the photograph is a smudged triangle of face from his eyelids to his lower lip; the rest is bandages. You cannot see the expression in his eyes; the bandages shade them.

The story, headed MAN BURNED FOR SECOND TIME, begins: 19

"Why does God hate me?" Alan McDonald asked from his hospital bed.

"When the gunpowder went off, I couldn't believe it," he said. "I just couldn't believe it. I said, 'No, God couldn't do this to me again.'"

He was in a burn ward in Miami, in serious condition. I do not even 20 know if he lived. I wrote him a letter at the time, cringing.

He had been burned before, thirteen years previously, by flaming 21 gasoline. For years he had been having his body restored and his face remade in dozens of operations. He had been a boy, and then a burnt boy. He had already been stunned by what could happen, by how life could veer.

Once I read that people who survive bad burns tend to go crazy; 22 they have a very high suicide rate. Medicine cannot ease their pain; drugs just leak away, soaking the sheets, because there is no skin to hold them in. The people just lie there and weep. Later they kill themselves. They had not known, before they were burned, that the world included such suffering, that life could permit them personally such pain.

This time a bowl of gunpowder had exploded on McDonald. 23

"I didn't realize what had happened at first," he recounted. "And then I heard that sound from 13 years ago. I was burning. I rolled to put the fire out and I thought, 'Oh God, not again.'

"If my friend hadn't been there, I would have jumped into a canal with a rock around my neck."

His wife concludes the piece, "Man, it just isn't fair."   24

I read the whole clipping again every morning. This is the Big Time 25
here, every minute of it. Will someone please explain to Alan McDonald
in his dignity, to the deer at Providencia in his dignity, what is going on?
And mail me the carbon.

When we walked by the deer at Providencia for the last time, I said 26
to Pepe, with a pitying glance at the deer, *"Pobrecito"*—"poor little
thing." But I was trying out Spanish. I knew at the time it was a ridiculous thing to say.

Responding to Reading

1. Could Dillard have done anything to free the deer? Why do you think she
    chose to do nothing? Does she regret her decision not to act? Do you think
    she *should* regret it?
2. In paragraph 14 , Dillard says, "I have thought a great deal about carnivo-
    rousness; I eat meat. These things are not issues; they are mysteries." What
    does she mean? Do you find this statement to be a satisfactory explanation
    of her ability to enjoy deer meat while she watches the trapped deer "con-
    vulsing in the dust" (11)? Why or why not?
3. What connection does Dillard see between Alan McDonald and the deer at
    Providencia? Do you see this as a reasonable association, or do you believe
    Dillard has exploited (or even invented) a connection?

SHOOTING AN ELEPHANT

George Orwell

This detailed account of a cruel incident with an elephant in Burma is
George Orwell's (see also p. 724) most powerful criticism of imperialism and
the impossible position of British police officers—himself among them—in
the colonies. Orwell says about the incident, "It was perfectly clear to me
what I ought to do," but then he thinks of "the watchful yellow faces behind,"
and he realizes that his choice is not so simple.

In Moulmein, in lower Burma, I was hated by large numbers of 1
people—the only time in my life that I have been important enough for
this to happen to me. I was sub-divisional police officer of the town,
and in an aimless, petty kind of way anti-European feeling was very
bitter. No one had the guts to raise a riot, but if a European woman
went through the bazaars alone somebody would probably spit betel

juice over her dress. As a police officer I was an obvious target and was baited whenever it seemed safe to do so. When a nimble Burman tripped me up on the football field and the referee (another Burman) looked the other way, the crowd yelled with hideous laughter. This happened more than once. In the end the sneering yellow faces of young men that met me everywhere, the insults hooted after me when I was at a safe distance, got badly on my nerves. The young Buddhist priests were the worst of all. There were several thousands of them in the town and none of them seemed to have anything to do except stand on street corners and jeer at Europeans.

All this was perplexing and upsetting. For at that time I had already 2 made up my mind that imperialism was an evil thing and the sooner I chucked up my job and got out of it the better. Theoretically—and secretly, of course—I was all for the Burmese and all against their oppressors, the British. As for the job I was doing, I hated it more bitterly than I can perhaps make clear. In a job like that you see the dirty work of Empire at close quarters. The wretched prisoners huddling in the stinking cages of the lock-ups, the grey, cowed faces of the long-term convicts, the scarred buttocks of the men who had been flogged with bamboos—all these oppressed me with an intolerable sense of guilt. But I could get nothing into perspective. I was young and ill-educated and I had had to think out my problems in the utter silence that is imposed on every Englishman in the East. I did not even know that the British Empire is dying, still less did I know that it is a great deal better than the younger empires that are going to supplant it.[1] All I knew was that I was stuck between my hatred of the empire I served and my rage against the evil-spirited little beasts who tried to make my job impossible. With one part of my mind I thought of the British Raj[2] as an unbreakable tyranny, as something clamped down, in *saecula saeculorum*,[3] upon the will of prostrate peoples; with another part I thought that the greatest joy in the world would be to drive a bayonet into a Buddhist priest's guts. Feelings like these are the normal by-products of imperialism; ask any Anglo-Indian official, if you can catch him off duty.

One day something happened which in a roundabout way was 3 enlightening. It was a tiny incident in itself, but it gave me a better glimpse than I had had before of the real nature of imperialism—the real motives for which despotic governments act. Early one morning the sub-inspector at a police station the other end of the town rang me up on the phone and said that an elephant was ravaging the bazaar. Would I please come and do something about it? I did not know what I could

---

[1] This essay was written in 1936, three years before the start of World War II; Stalin and Hitler were in power. [Eds.]
[2] Sovereignty. [Eds.]
[3] From time immemorial. [Eds.]

do, but I wanted to see what was happening and I got on to a pony and started out. I took my rifle, an old .44 Winchester and much too small to kill an elephant, but I thought the noise might be useful *in terrorem*. Various Burmans stopped me on the way and told me about the elephant's doings. It was not, of course, a wild elephant, but a tame one which had gone "must." It had been chained up, as tame elephants always are when their attack of "must"[4] is due, but on the previous night it had broken its chain and escaped. Its mahout,[5] the only person who could manage it when it was in that state, had set out in pursuit, but had taken the wrong direction and was now twelve hours' journey away, and in the morning the elephant had suddenly reappeared in the town. The Burmese population had no weapons and were quite helpless against it. It had already destroyed somebody's bamboo hut, killed a cow, and raided some fruit-stalls and devoured the stock; also it had met the municipal rubbish van and, when the driver jumped out and took to his heels, had turned the van over and inflicted violences upon it.

The Burmese sub-inspector and some Indian constables were wait-   4
ing for me in the quarter where the elephant had been seen. It was a very poor quarter, a labyrinth of squalid bamboo huts, thatched with palm-leaf, winding all over a steep hillside. I remember that it was a cloudy, stuffy morning at the beginning of the rains. We began questioning the people as to where the elephant had gone and, as usual, failed to get any definite information. That is invariably the case in the East; a story always sounds clear enough at a distance, but the nearer you get to the scene of events the vaguer it becomes. Some of the people said that the elephant had gone in one direction, some said that he had gone in another, some professed not even to have heard of any elephant. I had almost made up my mind that the whole story was a pack of lies, when we heard yells a little distance away. There was a loud, scandalized cry of "Go away, child! Go away this instant!" and an old woman with a switch in her hand came round the corner of a hut, violently shooing away a crowd of naked children. Some more women followed, clicking their tongues and exclaiming; evidently there was something that the children ought not to have seen. I rounded the hut and saw a man's dead body sprawling in the mud. He was an Indian, a black Dravidian coolie,[6] almost naked, and he could not have been dead many minutes. The people said that the elephant had come suddenly upon him round the corner of the hut, caught him with its trunk, put its foot on his back, and ground him into the earth. This was the rainy season and the ground was soft, and his face had scored a trench a foot

---

[4] Frenzy. [Eds.]
[5] Keeper. [Eds.]
[6] An unskilled laborer. [Eds.]

deep and a couple of yards long. He was lying on his belly with arms crucified and head sharply twisted to one side. His face was coated with mud, the eyes wide open, the teeth bared and grinning with an expression of unendurable agony. (Never tell me, by the way, that the dead look peaceful. Most of the corpses I have seen looked devilish.) The friction of the great beast's foot had stripped the skin from his back as neatly as one skins a rabbit. As soon as I saw the dead man I sent an orderly to a friend's house nearby to borrow an elephant rifle. I had already sent back the pony, not wanting it to go mad with fright and throw me if it smelt the elephant.

The orderly came back in a few minutes with a rifle and five car- 5 tridges, and meanwhile some Burmans had arrived and told us that the elephant was in the paddy fields below, only a few hundred yards away. As I started forward practically the whole population of the quarter flocked out of the houses and followed me. They had seen the rifle and were all shouting excitedly that I was going to shoot the elephant. They had not shown much interest in the elephant when he was merely ravaging their homes, but it was different now that he was going to be shot. It was a bit of fun to them, as it would be to an English crowd; besides they wanted the meat. It made me vaguely uneasy. I had no intention of shooting the elephant—I had merely sent for the rifle to defend myself if necessary—and it is always unnerving to have a crowd following you. I marched down the hill, looking and feeling a fool, with the rifle over my shoulder and an ever-growing army of people jostling at my heels. At the bottom, when you got away from the huts, there was a metalled road and beyond that a miry waste of paddy fields a thousand yards across, not yet ploughed but soggy from the first rains and dotted with coarse grass. The elephant was standing eight yards from the road, his left side towards us. He took not the slightest notice of the crowd's approach. He was tearing up bunches of grass, beating them against his knees to clean them and stuffing them into his mouth.

I had halted on the road. As soon as I saw the elephant I knew with 6 perfect certainty that I ought not to shoot him. It is a serious matter to shoot a working elephant—it is comparable to destroying a huge and costly piece of machinery—and obviously one ought not to do it if it can possibly be avoided. And at that distance, peacefully eating, the elephant looked no more dangerous than a cow. I thought then and I think now that his attack of "must" was already passing off; in which case he would merely wander harmlessly about until the mahout came back and caught him. Moreover, I did not in the least want to shoot him. I decided that I would watch him for a little while to make sure that he did not turn savage again, and then go home.

But at that moment I glanced round at the crowd that had followed 7 me. It was an immense crowd, two thousand at the least and growing every minute. It blocked the road for a long distance on either side. I looked at the sea of yellow faces above the garish clothes—faces all happy and excited over this bit of fun, all certain that the elephant was going to be shot. They were watching me as they would watch a conjurer about to perform a trick. They did not like me, but with the magical rifle in my hands I was momentarily worth watching. And suddenly I realized that I should have to shoot the elephant after all. The people expected it of me and I had got to do it; I could feel their two thousand wills pressing me forward, irresistibly. And it was at this moment, as I stood there with the rifle in my hands, that I first grasped the hollowness, the futility of the white man's dominion in the East. Here was I, the white man with his gun, standing in front of the unarmed native crowd—seemingly the leading actor of the piece; but in reality I was only an absurd puppet pushed to and fro by the will of those yellow faces behind. I perceived in this moment that when the white man turns tyrant it is his own freedom that he destroys. He becomes a sort of hollow, posing dummy, the conventionalized figure of a sahib.[7] For it is the condition of his rule that he shall spend his life in trying to impress the "natives," and so in every crisis he has got to do what the "natives" expect of him. He wears a mask, and his face grows to fit it. I had got to shoot the elephant. I had committed myself to doing it when I sent for the rifle. A sahib has got to act like a sahib; he has got to appear resolute, to know his own mind and do definite things. To come all that way, rifle in hand, with two thousand people marching at my heels, and then to trail feebly away, having done nothing—no, that was impossible. The crowd would laugh at me. And my whole life, every white man's life in the East, was one long struggle not to be laughed at.

But I did not want to shoot the elephant. I watched him beating his 8 bunch of grass against his knees, with that preoccupied grand-motherly air that elephants have. It seemed to me that it would be murder to shoot him. At that age I was not squeamish about killing animals, but I had never shot an elephant and never wanted to. (Somehow it always seems worse to kill a *large* animal.) Besides, there was the beast's owner to be considered. Alive, the elephant was worth at least a hundred pounds; dead, he would only be worth the value of his tusks, five pounds, possibly. But I had got to act quickly. I turned to some experienced looking Burmans who had been there when we arrived, and asked them how the elephant had been behaving. They all said the same thing: he took no notice of you if you left him alone, but he might charge if you went too close to him.

It was perfectly clear to me what I ought to do. I ought to walk up 9 to within, say, twenty-five yards of the elephant and test his behavior. If he charged, I could shoot; if he took no notice of me, it would be safe to leave him until the mahout came back. But also I knew that I was going

---

[7] Term used by natives of colonial India when referring to a European of rank. [Eds.]

to do no such thing. I was a poor shot with a rifle and the ground was soft mud into which one would sink at every step. If the elephant charged and I missed him, I should have about as much chance as a toad under a steam-roller. But even then I was not thinking particularly of my own skin, only of the watchful yellow faces behind. For at that moment, with the crowd watching me, I was not afraid in the ordinary sense, as I would have been if I had been alone. A white man mustn't be frightened in front of "natives"; and so, in general, he isn't frightened. The sole thought in my mind was that if anything went wrong those two thousand Burmans would see me pursued, caught, trampled on, and reduced to a grinning corpse like that Indian up the hill. And if that happened it was quite probable that some of them would laugh. That would never do. There was only one alternative. I shoved the cartridges into the magazine and lay down on the road to get a better aim.

The crowd grew very still, and a deep, low, happy sigh, as of people 10 who see the theatre curtain go up at last, breathed from innumerable throats. They were going to have their bit of fun after all. The rifle was a beautiful German thing with cross-hair sights. I did not then know that in shooting an elephant one would shoot to cut an imaginary bar running from ear-hole to ear-hole. I ought, therefore, as the elephant was sideways on, to have aimed straight at his ear-hole; actually I aimed several inches in front of this, thinking the brain would be further forward.

When I pulled the trigger I did not hear the bang or feel the kick— 11 one never does when a shot goes home—but I heard the devilish roar of glee that went up from the crowd. In that instant, in too short a time, one would have thought, even for the bullet to get there, a mysterious, terrible change had come over the elephant. He neither stirred nor fell, but every line of his body had altered. He looked suddenly stricken, shrunken, immensely old, as though the frightful impact of the bullet had paralysed him without knocking him down. At last, after what seemed a long time—it might have been five seconds, I dare say—he sagged flabbily to his knees. His mouth slobbered. An enormous senility seemed to have settled upon him. One could have imagined him thousands of years old. I fired again into the same spot. At the second shot he did not collapse but climbed with desperate slowness to his feet and stood weakly upright, with legs sagging and head dropping. I fired a third time. That was the shot that did for him. You could see the agony of it jolt his whole body and knock the last remnant of strength from his legs. But in falling he seemed for a moment to rise, for as his hind legs collapsed beneath him he seemed to tower upward like a huge rock toppling, his trunk reaching skywards like a tree. He trumpeted, for the first and only time. And then down he came, his belly towards me, with a crash that seemed to shake the ground even where I lay.

I got up. The Burmans were already racing past me across the mud. 12 It was obvious that the elephant would never rise again, but he was not dead. He was breathing very rhythmically with long rattling gasps, his great mound of a side painfully rising and falling. His mouth was wide open—I could see far down into caverns of pale pink throat. I waited a long time for him to die, but his breathing did not weaken. Finally I fired my two remaining shots into the spot where I thought his heart must be. The thick blood welled out of him like red velvet, but still he did not die. His body did not even jerk when the shots hit him, the tortured breathing continued without a pause. He was dying, very slowly and in great agony, but in some world remote from me where not even a bullet could damage him further. I felt that I had got to put an end to that dreadful noise. It seemed dreadful to see the great beast lying there, powerless to move and yet powerless to die, and not even to be able to finish him. I sent back for my small rifle and poured shot after shot into his heart and down his throat. They seemed to make no impression. The tortured gasps continued as steadily as the ticking of a clock.

In the end I could not stand it any longer and went away. I heard 13 later that it took him half an hour to die. Burmans were bringing dahs[8] and baskets even before I left, and I was told they had stripped his body almost to the bones by the afternoon.

Afterwards, of course, there were endless discussions about the 14 shooting of the elephant. The owner was furious, but he was only an Indian and could do nothing. Besides, legally I had done the right thing, for a mad elephant has to be killed, like a mad dog, if its owner fails to control it. Among the Europeans opinion was divided. The older men said I was right, the younger men said it was a damn shame to shoot an elephant for killing a coolie, because an elephant was worth more than any damn Coringhee coolie. And afterwards I was very glad that the coolie had been killed; it put me legally in the right and it gave me a sufficient pretext for shooting the elephant. I often wondered whether any of the others grasped that I had done it solely to avoid looking a fool.

Responding to Reading

1. The central focus of this essay is Orwell's struggle to decide how to control the elephant. Do you think he really has a choice? Explain.
2. What would you have done in Orwell's place? Why?
3. Orwell says that his encounter with the elephant, although "a tiny incident in itself," gave him an understanding of "the real nature of imperialism—the real motives for which despotic governments act" (3). In light of this statement, is his purpose in this essay to explore something about himself or something about the nature of British colonialism—or both?

---

[8] Large knives. [Eds.]

CIVIL DISOBEDIENCE

Henry David Thoreau

American essayist, journalist, and intellectual Henry David Thoreau (1817–1862) was a social rebel who loved nature and solitude. A follower of transcendentalism, a philosophic and literary movement that flourished in New England, he contributed to the Dial, *a publication that gave voice to the movement's romantic, idealistic, and individualistic beliefs. For three years, Thoreau lived in a cabin near Walden Pond in Concord, Massachusetts; his experiences there are recorded in his most famous book,* Walden *(1854). He left Walden, however, because, according to him, he had "several more lives to live and could not spare any more for that one." A canoe excursion in 1839 resulted in the chronicle* A Week on the Concord and Merrimack Rivers, *and other experiences produced books about Maine and Cape Cod. The following impassioned and eloquent defense of civil disobedience, published in 1849, has influenced such leaders as Gandhi and Martin Luther King, Jr.*

I heartily accept the motto,—"That government is best which 1 governs least;" and I should like to see it acted up to more rapidly and systematically. Carried out, it finally amounts to this, which also I believe,—"That government is best which governs not at all"; and when men are prepared for it, that will be the kind of government which they will have. Government is at best but an expedient; but most governments are usually, and all governments are sometimes, inexpedient. The objections which have been brought against a standing army, and they are many and weighty, and deserve to prevail, may also at last be brought against a standing government. The standing army is only an arm of the standing government. The government itself, which is only the mode which the people have chosen to execute their will, is equally liable to be abused and perverted before the people can act through it. Witness the present Mexican war,[1] the work of comparatively a few individuals using the standing government as their tool; for, in the outset, the people would not have consented to this measure.

This American Government,—what is it but a tradition, though a 2 recent one, endeavoring to transmit itself unimpaired to posterity, but each instant losing some of its integrity? It has not the vitality and force of a single living man; for a single man can bend it to his will. It is a sort of wooden gun to the people themselves. But it is not the less necessary for this; for the people must have some complicated machinery or other,

---

[1] In December 1845, the United States annexed Texas, an act leading to a war between the U.S. and Mexico (1846–1848). Thoreau opposed this war, thinking it served the interests of slaveholders, who believed that the land won from Mexico would be slave territory. In protest, he refused to pay the Massachusetts poll tax and was arrested for his act of civil disobedience. [Eds.]

and hear its din, to satisfy that idea of government which they have. Governments show thus how successfully men can be imposed on, even impose on themselves, for their own advantage. It is excellent, we must all allow. Yet this government never of itself furthered any enterprise, but by the alacrity with which it got out of its way. *It* does not keep the country free. *It* does not settle the West. *It* does not educate. The character inherent in the American people has done all that has been accomplished; and it would have done somewhat more, if the government had not sometimes got in its way. For government is an expedient by which men would fain succeed in letting one another alone; and, as has been said, when it is most expedient, the governed are most let alone by it. Trade and commerce, if they were not made of India-rubber, would never manage to bounce over the obstacles which legislators are continually putting in their way; and, if one were to judge these men wholly by the effects of their actions and not partly by their intentions, they would deserve to be classed and punished with those mischievous persons who put obstructions on the railroads.

But, to speak practically and as a citizen, unlike those who call 3 themselves no-government men, I ask for, not at once no government, but *at once* a better government. Let every man make known what kind of government would command his respect, and that will be one step toward obtaining it.

After all, the practical reason why, when the power is once in the 4 hands of the people, a majority are permitted, and for a long period continue, to rule is not because they are most likely to be in the right, nor because this seems fairest to the minority, but because they are physically the strongest. But a government in which the majority rule in all cases cannot be based on justice, even as far as men understand it. Can there not be a government in which majorities do not virtually decide right and wrong, but conscience?—in which majorities decide only those questions to which the rule of expediency is applicable? Must the citizen ever for a moment, or in the least degree, resign his conscience to the legislator? Why has every man a conscience, then? I think that we should be men first, and subjects afterward. It is not desirable to cultivate a respect for the law, so much as for the right. The only obligation which I have a right to assume is to do at any time what I think right. It is truly enough said, that a corporation has no conscience; but a corporation of conscientious men is a corporation *with* a conscience. Law never made men a whit more just; and, by means of their respect for it, even the well-disposed are daily made the agents of injustice. A common and natural result of any undue respect for law is, that you may see a file of soldiers, colonel, captain, corporal, privates, powder-monkeys, and all, marching in admirable order over hill and dale to the wars, against their wills, ay, against their common sense and consciences, which makes it very steep marching indeed, and produces a palpitation of the heart. They have no doubt that it is a damnable business in which they are concerned; they are all peaceably inclined. Now, what are they? Men at all? or small movable forts and magazines, at the service of some unscrupulous man in power? Visit the Navy-Yard, and behold a marine, such a man as an American government can make, or such as it can make a man with its black arts,—a mere shadow and reminiscence of humanity, a man laid out alive and standing, and already, as one may say, buried under arms with funeral accompaniments, though it may be,—

"Not a drum was heard, not a funeral note,
As his corse to the rampart we hurried;
Not a soldier discharged his farewell shot
O'er the grave where our hero we buried."[2]

The mass of men serve the state thus, not as men mainly, but as 5 machines, with their bodies. They are the standing army, and the militia, jailers, constables, posse comitatus, etc. In most cases there is no free exercise whatever of the judgment or of the moral sense; but they put themselves on a level with wood and earth and stones; and wooden men can perhaps be manufactured that will serve the purpose as well. Such command no more respect than men of straw or a lump of dirt. They have the same sort of worth only as horses and dogs. Yet such as these even are commonly esteemed good citizens. Others—as most legislators, politicians, lawyers, ministers, and office-holders—serve the state chiefly with their heads; and, as they rarely make any moral distinctions, they are as likely to serve the Devil, without *intending* it, as God. A very few, as heroes, patriots, martyrs, reformers in the great sense, and *men*, serve the state with their consciences also, and so necessarily resist it for the most part; and they are commonly treated as enemies by it. A wise man will only be useful as a man, and will not submit to be "clay," and "stop a hole to keep the wind away,"[3] but leave that office to his dust at least:—

"I am too high-born to be propertied,
To be a secondary at control,
Or useful serving-man and instrument
To any sovereign state throughout the world."[4]

He who gives himself entirely to his fellow-men appears to them 6 useless and selfish; but he who gives himself partially to them is pronounced a benefactor and philanthropist.

---

[2] From "The Burial of Sir John Moore at Corunna," by Irish poet Charles Wolfe (1791–1823). [Eds.]
[3] From *Hamlet* (act V, scene i) by William Shakespeare. [Eds.]
[4] From *King John* (act V, scene ii) by William Shakespeare. [Eds.]

How does it become a man to behave toward this American gov- 7
ernment to-day? I answer, that he cannot without disgrace be associated
with it. I cannot for an instant recognize that political organization as *my*
government which is the *slave's* government also.

All men recognize the right of revolution; that is, the right to refuse 8
allegiance to, and to resist, the government, when its tyranny or its inef-
ficiency are great and unendurable. But almost all say that such is not
the case now. But such was the case, they think, in the Revolution of '75.
If one were to tell me that this was a bad government because it taxed
certain foreign commodities brought to its ports, it is most probable that
I should not make an ado about it, for I can do without them. All
machines have their friction; and possibly this does enough good to
counterbalance the evil. At any rate, it is a great evil to make a stir about
it. But when the friction comes to have its machine, and oppression and
robbery are organized, I say, let us not have such a machine any longer.
In other words, when a sixth of the population of a nation which has
undertaken to be the refuge of liberty are slaves, and a whole country is
unjustly overrun and conquered by a foreign army, and subjected to
military law, I think that it is not too soon for honest men to rebel and
revolutionize. What makes this duty the more urgent is the fact that the
country so overrun is not our own, but ours is the invading army.

Paley,[5] a common authority with many on moral questions, in his 9
chapter on the "Duty of Submission to Civil Government," resolves all
civil obligation into expediency; and he proceeds to say, "that so long as
the interest of the whole society requires it, that is, so long as the established government cannot be resisted or changed without public incon-
veniency, it is the will of God that the established government be
obeyed, and no longer. . . . This principle being admitted, the justice of
every particular case of resistance is reduced to a computation of the
quantity of the danger and grievance on the one side, and of the probability and expense of redressing it on the other." Of this, he says, every
man shall judge for himself. But Paley appears never to have contemplated those cases to which the rule of expediency does not apply, in
which a people, as well as an individual, must do justice, cost what it
may. If I have unjustly wrested a plank from a drowning man, I must
restore it to him though I drown myself. This, according to Paley, would
be inconvenient. But he that would save his life, in such a case, shall lose
it. This people must cease to hold slaves, and to make war on Mexico,
though it cost them their existence as a people.

In their practice, nations agree with Paley; but does any one think 10
that Massachusetts does exactly what is right at the present crisis?

---

[5] William Paley (1743–1805), English clergyman and philosopher. [Eds.]

"A drab of state, a cloth-o'-silver slut,
To have her train borne up, and her soul trail in the dirt."[6]

Practically speaking, the opponents to a reform in Massachusetts   11
are not a hundred thousand politicians at the South, but a hundred
thousand merchants and farmers here, who are more interested in commerce and agriculture than they are in humanity, and are not prepared
to do justice to the slave and to Mexico, *cost what it may.* I quarrel not
with far-off foes, but with those who, near at home, coöperate with, and
do the bidding of, those far away, and without whom the latter would
be harmless. We are accustomed to say, that the mass of men are unprepared; but improvement is slow, because the few are not materially
wiser or better than the many. It is not so important that many should
be as good as you, as that there be some absolute goodness somewhere;
for that will leaven the whole lump. There are thousands who are *in
opinion* opposed to slavery and to the war, who yet in effect do nothing
to put an end to them; who, esteeming themselves children of
Washington and Franklin, sit down with their hands in their pockets,
and say that they know not what to do, and do nothing; who even postpone the question of freedom to the question of free-trade, and quietly
read the prices-current along with the latest advices from Mexico, after
dinner, and, it may be, fall asleep over them both. What is the price-
current of an honest man and patriot to-day? They hesitate, and they
regret, and sometimes they petition; but they do nothing in earnest and
with effect. They will wait, well disposed, for others to remedy the evil,
that they may no longer have it to regret. At most, they give only a
cheap vote, and a feeble countenance and Godspeed, to the right, as it
goes by them. There are nine hundred and ninety-nine patrons of virtue
to one virtuous man. But it is easier to deal with the real possessor of a
thing than with the temporary guardian of it.

All voting is a sort of gaming, like checkers or backgammon, with a   12
slight moral tinge to it, a playing with right and wrong, with moral
questions; and betting naturally accompanies it. The character of the
voters is not staked. I cast my vote, perchance, as I think right; but I am
not vitally concerned that that right should prevail. I am willing to leave
it to the majority. Its obligation, therefore, never exceeds that of expediency. Even voting *for the right* is *doing* nothing for it. It is only expressing to men feebly your desire that it should prevail. A wise man will not
leave the right to the mercy of chance, nor wish it to prevail through the
power of the majority. There is but little virtue in the action of masses of
men. When the majority shall at length vote for the abolition of slavery,
it will be because they are indifferent to slavery, or because there is but
little slavery left to be abolished by their vote. *They* will then be the only

---

[6] From act IV, scene iv, of Cyril Tourneur's *The Revenger's Tragedy* (1607). [Eds.]

slaves. Only *his* vote can hasten the abolition of slavery who asserts his own freedom by his vote.

I hear of a convention to be held at Baltimore, or elsewhere, for the selection of a candidate for the Presidency, made up chiefly of editors, and men who are politicians by profession; but I think, what is it to any independent, intelligent, and respectable man what decision they may come to? Shall we not have the advantage of his wisdom and honesty, nevertheless? Can we not count upon some independent votes? Are there not many individuals in the country who do not attend conventions? But no: I find that the respectable man, so called, has immediately drifted from his position, and despairs of his country, when his country has more reason to despair of him. He forthwith adopts one of the candidates thus selected as the only *available* one, thus proving that he is himself *available* for any purposes of the demagogue. His vote is of no more worth than that of any unprincipled foreigner or hireling native, who may have been bought. O for a man who is a *man*, and, as my neighbor says, has a bone in his back which you cannot pass your hand through! Our statistics are at fault: the population has been returned too large. How many *men* are there to a square thousand miles in this country? Hardly one. Does not America offer any inducement for men to settle here? The American has dwindled into an Odd Fellow,—one who may be known by the development of his organ of gregariousness, and a manifest lack of intellect and cheerful self-reliance; whose first and chief concern, on coming into the world, is to see that Almshouses[7] are in good repair; and, before yet he has lawfully donned the virile garb, to collect a fund for the support of the widows and orphans that may be; who, in short, ventures to live only by the aid of the Mutual Insurance company, which has promised to bury him decently.

It is not a man's duty, as a matter of course, to devote himself to the eradication of any, even the most enormous wrong; he may still properly have other concerns to engage him; but it is his duty, at least, to wash his hands of it, and, if he gives it no thought longer, not to give it practically his support. If I devote myself to other pursuits and contemplations, I must first see, at least, that I do not pursue them sitting upon another man's shoulders. I must get off him first, that he may pursue his contemplations too. See what gross inconsistency is tolerated. I have heard some of my townsmen say, "I should like to have them order me out to help put down an insurrection of the slaves, or to march to Mexico—see if I would go;" and yet these very men have each, directly by their allegiance, and so indirectly, at least, by their money, furnished a substitute. The soldier is applauded who refuses to serve in an unjust war by those who do not refuse to sustain the unjust

13

14

---

[7] Poorhouses; county homes that provided for the needy. [Eds.]

government which makes the war; is applauded by those whose own act and authority he disregards and sets at naught; as if the state were penitent to that degree that it hired one to scourge it while it sinned, but not to that degree that it left off sinning for a moment. Thus, under the name of Order and Civil Government, we are all made at last to pay homage to and support our own meanness. After the first blush of sin comes its indifference; and from immoral it becomes, as it were, *un*moral, and not quite unnecessary to that life which we have made.

The broadest and most prevalent error requires the most disinter- 15
ested virtue to sustain it. The slight reproach to which the virtue of patriotism is commonly liable, the noble are most likely to incur. Those who, while they disapprove of the character and measures of a government, yield to it their allegiance and support are undoubtedly its most conscientious supporters, and so frequently the most serious obstacles to reform. Some are petitioning the state to dissolve the Union, to disregard the requisitions of the President. Why do they not dissolve it themselves,—the union between themselves and the state,—and refuse to pay their quota into its treasury? Do not they stand in the same relation to the state that the state does to the Union? And have not the same reasons prevented the state from resisting the Union which have prevented them from resisting the state?

How can a man be satisfied to entertain an opinion merely, and 16
enjoy *it?* Is there any enjoyment in it, if his opinion is that he is aggrieved? If you are cheated out of a single dollar by your neighbor, you do not rest satisfied with knowing that you are cheated, or with saying that you are cheated, or even with petitioning him to pay you your due; but you take effectual steps at once to obtain the full amount, and see that you are never cheated again. Action from principle, the perception and the performance of right, changes things and relations; it is essentially revolutionary, and does not consist wholly with anything which was. It not only divides states and churches, it divides families; ay, it divides the *individual*, separating the diabolical in him from the divine.

Unjust laws exist: shall we be content to obey them, or shall we 17
endeavor to amend them, and obey them until we have succeeded, or shall we transgress them at once? Men generally, under such a government as this, think that they ought to wait until they have persuaded the majority to alter them. They think that, if they should resist, the remedy would be worse than the evil. But it is the fault of the government itself that the remedy *is* worse than the evil. *It* makes it worse. Why is it not more apt to anticipate and provide for reform? Why does it not cherish its wise minority? Why does it cry and resist before it is hurt? Why does it not encourage its citizens to be on the alert to point out its faults, and *do* better than it would have them? Why does it always crucify Christ, and excommunicate Copernicus and Luther, and pronounce Washington and Franklin rebels?

One would think, that a deliberate and practical denial of its author- 18
ity was the only offense never contemplated by government; else, why
has it not assigned its definite, its suitable and proportionate penalty? If
a man who has no property refuses but once to earn nine shillings for
the state, he is put in prison for a period unlimited by any law that I
know, and determined only by the discretion of those who placed him
there; but if he should steal ninety times nine shillings from the state, he
is soon permitted to go at large again.

If the injustice is part of the necessary friction of the machine of gov- 19
ernment, let it go, let it go: perchance it will wear smooth,—certainly the
machine will wear out. If the injustice has a spring, or a pulley, or a rope,
or a crank, exclusively for itself, then perhaps you may consider
whether the remedy will not be worse than the evil; but if it is of such a
nature that it requires you to be the agent of injustice to another, then, I
say, break the law. Let your life be a counter friction to stop the machine.
What I have to do is to see, at any rate, that I do not lend myself to the
wrong which I condemn.

As for adopting the ways which the state has provided for remedy- 20
ing the evil, I know not of such ways. They take too much time, and a
man's life will be gone. I have other affairs to attend to. I came into this
world, not chiefly to make this a good place to live in, but to live in it,
be it good or bad. A man has not everything to do, but something; and
because he cannot do *everything*, it is not necessary that he should do
something wrong. It is not my business to be petitioning the Governor or
the Legislature any more than it is theirs to petition me; and if they
should not hear my petition, what should I do then? But in this case the
state has provided no way: its very Constitution is the evil. This may
seem to be harsh and stubborn and unconciliatory; but it is to treat with
the utmost kindness and consideration the only spirit that can appreciate or deserve it. So is all change for the better, like birth and death,
which convulse the body.

I do not hesitate to say, that those who call themselves Abolitionists 21
should at once effectually withdraw their support, both in person and
property, from the government of Massachusetts, and not wait till they
constitute a majority of one, before they suffer the right to prevail
through them. I think that it is enough if they have God on their side,
without waiting for that other one. Moreover, any man more right than
his neighbors constitutes a majority of one already.

I meet this American government, or its representative, the state 22
government, directly, and face to face, once a year—no more—in the person of its tax-gatherer; this is the only mode in which a man situated as
I am necessarily meets it; and it then says distinctly, Recognize me; and
the simplest, the most effectual, and, in the present posture of affairs,
the indispensablest mode of treating with it on this head, of expressing
your little satisfaction with and love for it, is to deny it then. My civil

neighbor, the tax-gatherer, is the very man I have to deal with,—for it is, after all, with men and not with parchment that I quarrel,—and he has voluntarily chosen to be an agent of the government. How shall he ever know well what he is and does as an officer of the government, or as a man, until he is obliged to consider whether he shall treat me, his neighbor, for whom he has respect, as a neighbor and well-disposed man, or as a maniac and disturber of the peace, and see if he can get over this obstruction to his neighborliness without a ruder and more impetuous thought or speech corresponding with his action. I know this well, that if one thousand; if one hundred, if ten men whom I could name;—if ten *honest* men only,—say if *one* HONEST man, in this State of Massachusetts, *ceasing to hold slaves,* were actually to withdraw from this copartnership, and be locked up in the county jail therefor, it would be the abolition of slavery in America. For it matters not how small the beginning may seem to be: what is once well done is done forever. But we love better to talk about it: that we say is our mission. Reform keeps many scores of newspapers in its service, but not one man. If my esteemed neighbor, the State's ambassador, who will devote his days to the settlement of the question of human rights in the Council Chamber, instead of being threatened with the prisons of Carolina, were to sit down the prisoner of Massachusetts, that State which is so anxious to foist the sin of slavery upon her sister,—though at present she can discover only an act of inhospitality to be the ground of a quarrel with her,—the Legislature would not wholly waive the subject the following winter.

Under a government which imprisons any unjustly, the true place for a just man is also a prison. The proper place to-day, the only place which Massachusetts has provided for her freer and less desponding spirits, is in her prisons, to be put out and locked out of the State by her own act, as they have already put themselves out by their principles. It is there that the fugitive slave, and the Mexican prisoner on parole, and the Indian come to plead the wrongs of his race should find them; on that separate, but more free and honorable ground, where the State places those who are not *with* her, but *against* her,—the only house in a slave State in which a free man can abide with honor. If any think that their influence would be lost there, and their voices no longer afflict the ear of the State, that they would not be as an enemy within its walls, they do not know by how much truth is stronger than error, nor how much more eloquently and effectively he can combat injustice who has experienced a little in his own person. Cast your whole vote, not a strip of paper merely, but your whole influence. A minority is powerless while it conforms to the majority; it is not even a minority then; but it is irresistible when it clogs by its whole weight. If the alternative is to keep all just men in prison, or give up war and slavery, the State will not hesitate which to choose. If a thousand men were not to pay their tax-bills this year, that would not be a violent and bloody measure, as it would

be to pay them, and enable the State to commit violence and shed innocent blood. This is, in fact, the definition of a peaceable revolution, if any
such is possible. If the tax-gatherer, or any other public officer, asks me,
as one has done, "But what shall I do?" my answer is, "If you really
wish to do anything, resign your office." When the subject has refused
allegiance, and the officer has resigned his office, then the revolution is
accomplished. But even suppose blood should flow. Is there not a sort
of blood shed when the conscience is wounded? Through this wound a
man's real manhood and immortality flow out, and he bleeds to an
everlasting death. I see this blood flowing now.

I have contemplated the imprisonment of the offender, rather than 24
the seizure of his goods,—though both will serve the same purpose,—
because they who assert the purest right, and consequently are most
dangerous to a corrupt State, commonly have not spent much time in
accumulating property. To such the State renders comparatively small
service, and a slight tax is wont to appear exorbitant, particularly if they
are obliged to earn it by special labor with their hands. If there were one
who lived wholly without the use of money, the State itself would hesitate to demand it of him. But the rich man—not to make any invidious
comparison—is always sold to the institution which makes him rich.
Absolutely speaking, the more money, the less virtue; for money comes
between a man and his objects, and obtains them for him; and it
was certainly no great virtue to obtain it. It puts to rest many questions
which he would otherwise be taxed to answer; while the only new question which it puts is the hard but superfluous one, how to spend it. Thus
his moral ground is taken from under his feet. The opportunities of living are diminished in proportion as what are called the "means" are
increased. The best thing a man can do for his culture when he is rich is
to endeavor to carry out those schemes which he entertained when he
was poor. Christ answered the Herodians according to their condition.
"Show me the tribute-money," said he;—and one took a penny out of
his pocket;—if you use money which has the image of Caesar on it,
which he has made current and valuable, that is, *if you are men of the
State*, and gladly enjoy the advantages of Caesar's government, then
pay him back some of his own when he demands it. "Render therefore
to Caesar that which is Caesar's, and to God those things which are
God's,"—leaving them no wiser than before as to which was which; for
they did not wish to know.

When I converse with the freest of my neighbors, I perceive that, 25
whatever they may say about the magnitude and seriousness of the question, and their regard for the public tranquility, the long and the short
of the matter is, that they cannot spare the protection of the existing
government, and they dread the consequences to their property and
families of disobedience to it. For my own part, I should not like to
think that I ever rely on the protection of the State. But, if I deny the

authority of the State when it presents its tax-bill, it will soon take and waste all my property, and so harass me and my children without end. This is hard. This makes it impossible for a man to live honestly, and at the same time comfortably, in outward respects. It will not be worth the while to accumulate property; that would be sure to go again. You must hire or squat somewhere, and raise but a small crop, and eat that soon. You must live within yourself, and depend upon yourself always tucked up and ready for a start, and not have many affairs. A man may grow rich in Turkey even, if he will be in all respects a good subject of the Turkish government. Confucius said: "If a state is governed by the principles of reason, poverty and misery are subjects of shame; if a state is not governed by the principles of reason, riches and honors are the subjects of shame." No: until I want the protection of Massachusetts to be extended to me in some distant Southern port, where my liberty is endangered, or until I am bent solely on building up an estate at home by peaceful enterprise, I can afford to refuse allegiance to Massachusetts, and her right to my property and life. It costs me less in every sense to incur the penalty of disobedience to the State than it would to obey. I should feel as if I were worth less in that case.

Some years ago, the State met me in behalf of the Church, and commended me to pay a certain sum toward the support of a clergyman whose preaching my father attended, but never I myself. "Pay," it said, "or be locked up in the jail." I declined to pay. But, unfortunately, another man saw fit to pay it. I did not see why the schoolmaster should be taxed to support the priest, and not the priest the schoolmaster; for I was not the State's schoolmaster, but I supported myself by voluntary subscription. I did not see why the lyceum should not present its tax-bill, and have the State to back its demand, as well as the Church. However, at the request of the selectmen, I condescended to make some such statement as this in writing:—"Know all men by these presents, that I, Henry Thoreau, do not wish to be regarded as a member of any incorporated society which I have not joined." This I gave to the town clerk; and he has it. The State, having thus learned that I did not wish to be regarded as a member of that church, has never made a like demand on me since; though it said that it must adhere to its original presumption that time. If I had known how to name them, I should have then signed off in detail from all the societies which I never signed on to; but I did not know where to find a complete list. 26

I have paid no poll-tax for six years. I was put into a jail once on this account, for one night; and, as I stood considering the walls of solid stone, two or three feet thick, the door of wood and iron, a foot thick, and the iron grating which strained the light, I could not help being struck with the foolishness of that institution which treated me as if I were mere flesh and blood and bones, to be locked up. I wondered that it should have concluded at length that this was the best use it could put 27 me to, and had never thought to avail itself of my services in some way. I say that, if there was a wall of stone between me and my townsmen, there was a still more difficult one to climb or break through before they could get to be as free as I was. I did not for a moment feel confined, and the walls seemed a great waste of stone and mortar. I felt as if I alone of all my townsmen had paid my tax. They plainly did not know how to treat me, but behaved like persons who are underbred. In every threat and in every compliment there was a blunder; for they thought that my chief desire was to stand the other side of that stone wall. I could not but smile to see how industriously they locked the door on my meditations, which followed them out again without let or hindrance, and *they* were really all that was dangerous. As they could not reach me, they had resolved to punish my body; just as boys, if they cannot come at some person against whom they have a spite, will abuse his dog. I saw that the State was half-witted, that it was timid as a lone woman with her silver spoons, and that it did not know its friends from its foes, and I lost all my remaining respect for it, and pitied it.

Thus the State never intentionally confronts a man's sense, intellec- 28 tual or moral, but only his body, his senses. It is not armed with superior wit or honesty, but with superior physical strength. I was not born to be forced. I will breathe after my own fashion. Let us see who is the strongest. What force has a multitude? They only can force me who obey a higher law than I. They force me to become like themselves. I do not hear of *men* being *forced* to live this way or that by masses of men. What sort of life were that to live? When I meet a government which says to me, "Your money or your life," why should I be in haste to give it my money? It may be in a great strait, and not know what to do: I cannot help that. It must help itself; do as I do. It is not worth the while to snivel about it. I am not responsible for the successful working of the machinery of society. I am not the son of the engineer. I perceive that, when an acorn and a chestnut fall side by side, the one does not remain inert to make way for the other, but both obey their own laws, and spring and grow and flourish as best they can, till one, perchance, overshadows and destroys the other. If a plant cannot live according to its nature, it dies; and so a man.

The night in prison was novel and interesting enough. The prison- 29 ers in their shirt-sleeves were enjoying a chat and the evening air in the doorway, when I entered. But the jailer said, "Come, boys, it is time to lock up;" and so they dispersed, and I heard the sound of their steps returning into the hollow apartments. My room-mate was introduced to me by the jailer as "a first-rate fellow and a clever man." When the door was locked, he showed me where to hang my hat, and how he managed matters there. The rooms were whitewashed once a month; and this one, at least, was the whitest, most simply furnished, and probably the neatest apartment in the town. He naturally wanted to know where I came from, and what brought me there; and, when I had told him, I asked him in my turn how he came there, presuming him to be an honest man, of course; and, as the world goes, I believe he was. "Why," said he, "they accuse me of burning a barn; but I never did it." As near as I could discover, he had probably gone to bed in a barn when drunk, and smoked his pipe there; and so a barn was burnt. He had the reputation of being a clever man, had been there some three months waiting for his trial to come on, and would have to wait as much longer; but he was quite domesticated and contented, since he got his board for nothing, and thought that he was well treated.

He occupied one window, and I the other; and I saw that if one   30 stayed there long, his principal business would be to look out the window. I had soon read all tracts that were left there, and examined where former prisoners had broken out, and where a grate had been sawed off, and heard the history of the various occupants of that room; for I found that even here there was a history and a gossip which never circulated beyond the walls of the jail. Probably this is the only house in the town where verses are composed, which are afterward printed in a circular form, but not published. I was shown quite a long list of verses which were composed by some young men who had been detected in an attempt to escape, who avenged themselves by signing them.

I pumped my fellow-prisoner as dry as I could, for fear I should   31 never see him again; but at length he showed me which was my bed, and left me to blow out the lamp.

It was like traveling into a far country, such as I had never expected   32 to behold, to lie there for one night. It seemed to me that I never had heard the town-clock strike before, nor the evening sounds of the village; for we slept with the windows open, which were inside the grating. It was to see my native village in the light of the Middle Ages, and our Concord was turned into a Rhine stream, and visions of knights and castles passed before me. They were the voices of old burghers that I heard in the streets. I was an involuntary spectator and auditor of whatever was done and said in the kitchen of the adjacent village-inn,—a wholly new and rare experience to me. It was a closer view of my native town. I was fairly inside of it. I never had seen its institutions before. This is one of its peculiar institutions; for it is a shire town.[8] I began to comprehend what its inhabitants were about.

In the morning, our breakfasts were put through the hole in the   33 door, in small oblong-square tin pans, made to fit, and holding a pint of chocolate, with brown bread, and an iron spoon. When they called for the vessels again, I was green enough to return what bread I had left; but my comrade seized it, and said that I should lay that up for lunch

---

[8] County seat. [Eds.]

or dinner. Soon after he was let out to work at haying in a neighboring field, whither he went every day, and would not be back till noon; so he bade me good-day, saying that he doubted if he should see me again.

When I came out of prison,—for some one interfered, and paid that 34 tax,—I did not perceive that great changes had taken place on the common, such as he observed who went in a youth and emerged a tottering and gray-headed man; and yet a change had to my eyes come over the scene,—the town, and State, and country,—greater than any that mere time could effect. I saw yet more distinctly the State in which I lived. I saw to what extent the people among whom I lived could be trusted as good neighbors and friends; that their friendship was for summer weather only; that they did not greatly propose to do right; that they were a distinct race from me by their prejudices and superstitions, as the Chinamen and Malays are; that in their sacrifices to humanity they ran no risks, not even to their property; that after all they were not so noble but they treated the thief as he had treated them, and hoped, by a certain outward observance and a few prayers, and by walking in a particular straight though useless path from time to time, to save their souls. This may be to judge my neighbors harshly; for I believe that many of them are not aware that they have such an institution as the jail in their village.

It was formerly the custom in our village; when a poor debtor came 35 out of jail, for his acquaintances to salute him, looking through their fingers, which were crossed to represent the grating of a jail window, "How do ye do?" My neighbors did not thus salute me, but first looked at me, and then at one another, as if I had returned from a long journey. I was put into jail as I was going to the shoemaker's to get a shoe which was mended. When I was let out the next morning, I proceeded to finish my errand, and, having put on my mended shoe, joined a huckleberry party, who were impatient to put themselves under my conduct; and in half an hour,—for the horse was soon tackled,—was in the midst of a huckleberry field, on one of our highest hills, two miles off, and then the State was nowhere to be seen.

This is the whole history of "My Prisons."   36

I have never declined paying the highway tax, because I am as 37 desirous of being a good neighbor as I am of being a bad subject; and as for supporting schools, I am doing my part to educate my fellow-countrymen now. It is for no particular item in the tax-bill that I refuse to pay it. I simply wish to refuse allegiance to the State, to withdraw and stand aloof from it effectually. I do not care to trace the course of my dollar, if I could, till it buys a man or a musket to shoot one with,—the dollar is innocent,—but I am concerned to trace the effects of my allegiance. In fact, I quietly declare war with the State, after my fashion, though I will still make what use and get what advantage of her I can, as is usual in such cases.

If others pay the tax which is demanded of me, from a sympathy 38
with the State, they do but what they have already done in their own
case, or rather they abet injustice to a greater extent than the State
requires. If they pay the tax from a mistaken interest in the individual
taxed, to save his property, or prevent his going to jail, it is because they
have not considered wisely how far they let their private feelings interfere with the public good.

This, then, is my position at present. But one cannot be too much on 39
his guard in such a case, lest his action be biased by obstinacy or an
undue regard for the opinions of men. Let him see that he does only
what belongs to himself and to the hour.

I think sometimes, Why, this people mean well, they are only igno- 40
rant; they would do better if they knew how: why give your neighbors
this pain to treat you as they are not inclined to? But I think again, This
is no reason why I should do as they do, or permit others to suffer much
greater pain of a different kind. Again, I sometimes say to myself, When
many millions of men, without heat, without ill will, without personal
feeling of any kind, demand of you a few shillings only, without the
possibility, such is their constitution, of retracting or altering their
present demand, and without the possibility, on your side, of appeal to
any other millions, why expose yourself to this overwhelming brute
force? You do not resist cold and hunger, the winds and the waves, thus
obstinately; you quietly submit to a thousand similar necessities. You do
not put your head into the fire. But just in proportion as I regard this as
not wholly a brute force, but partly a human force, and consider that I
have relations to those millions as to so many millions of men, and not
of mere brute or inanimate things, I see that appeal is possible, first and
instantaneously, from them to the Maker of them, and, secondly, from
them to themselves. But if I put my head deliberately into the fire, there
is no appeal to fire or to the Maker of fire, and I have only myself to
blame. If I could convince myself that I have any right to be satisfied
with men as they are, and to treat them accordingly, and not accordingly,
in some respects, to my requisitions and expectations of what they and
I ought to be, then, like a good Mussulman[9] and fatalist, I should
endeavor to be satisfied with things as they are, and say it is the will of
God. And, above all, there is this difference between resisting this and a
purely brute or natural force that I can resist this with some effect; but I
cannot expect, like Orpheus,[10] to change the nature of the rocks and
trees and beasts.

I do not wish to quarrel with any man or nation. I do not wish to 41
split hairs, to make the fine distinctions, or set myself up as better than

---

[9] Muslim. [Eds.]

[10] Legendary Greek poet and musician who played the lyre so beautifully that wild beasts were
transfixed by his music and rocks and trees moved. [Eds.]

my neighbors. I seek rather, I may say, even an excuse for conforming to
the laws of the land. I am but too ready to conform to them. Indeed, I
have reason to suspect myself on this head; and each year, as the tax-
gatherer comes round, I find myself disposed to review the acts and
position of the general and State governments, and the spirit of the people, to discover a pretext for conformity.

> "We must affect our country as our parents,
> And if at any time we alienate
> Our love or industry from doing it honor,
> We must respect effects and teach the soul
> Matter of conscience and religion,
> And not desire of rule or benefit."[11]

I believe that the State will soon be able to take all my work of this   42
sort out of my hands, and then I shall be no better a patriot than my
fellow-countrymen. Seen from a lower point of view, the Constitution,
with all its faults, is very good; the law and the courts are very
respectable; even this State and this American government are, in many
respects, very admirable, and rare things, to be thankful for, such as a
great many have described them; but seen from a point of view a little
higher, they are what I have described them; seen from a higher still,
and the highest, who shall say what they are, or that they are worth
looking at or thinking of at all?

However, the government does not concern me much, and I shall   43
bestow the fewest possible thoughts on it. It is not many moments that
I live under a government, even in this world. If a man is thought-free,
fancy-free, imagination-free, that which *is not* never for a long time
appearing *to be* to him, unwise rulers or reformers cannot fatally interrupt him.

I know that most men think differently from myself; but those   44
whose lives are by profession devoted to the study of these or kindred
subjects content me as little as any. Statesmen and legislators, standing
so completely within the institution, never distinctly and nakedly
behold it. They speak of moving society, but have no resting-place without it. They may be men of a certain experience and discrimination, and
have no doubt invented ingenious and even useful systems, for which
we sincerely thank them; but all their wit and usefulness lie within certain not very wide limits. They are wont to forget that the world is not
governed by policy and expediency. Webster[12] never goes behind government, and so cannot speak with authority about it. His words are
wisdom to those legislators who contemplate no essential reform in the

---

[11] From *The Battle of Alcazar* (1594), a play by George Peele (1558?–1597?). [Eds.]

[12] Daniel Webster (1782–1852), legendary American orator, lawyer, and statesman. [Eds.]

existing government; but for thinkers, and those who legislate for all time, he never once glances at the subject. I know of those whose serene and wise speculations on this theme would soon reveal the limits of his mind's range and hospitality. Yet, compared with the cheap professions of most reformers, and the still cheaper wisdom and eloquence of politicians in general, his are almost the only sensible and valuable words, and we thank Heaven for him. Comparatively, he is always strong, original, and, above all, practical. Still, his quality is not wisdom, but prudence. The lawyer's truth is not Truth, but consistency or a consistent expediency. Truth is always in harmony with herself, and is not concerned chiefly to reveal the justice that may consist with wrong-doing. He well deserves to be called, as he has been called, the Defender of the Constitution. There are really no blows to be given to him but defensive ones. He is not a leader, but a follower. His leaders are the men of '87.[13] "I have never made an effort," he says, "and never propose to make an effort; I have never countenanced an effort, and never mean to countenance an effort, to disturb the arrangement as originally made, by which the various States came into the Union." Still thinking of the sanction which the Constitution gives to slavery, he says, "Because it was a part of the original compact,—let it stand." Notwithstanding his special acuteness and ability, he is unable to take a fact out of its merely political relations, and behold it as it lies absolutely to be disposed of by the intellect,—what, for instance, it behooves a man to do here in America to-day with regard to slavery,— but ventures, or is driven, to make some such desperate answer as the following, while professing to speak absolutely, and as a private man,—from which what new and singular code of social duties might be inferred? "The manner," says he, "in which the governments of those States where slavery exists are to regulate it is for their own consideration, under their responsibility to their constituents, to the general laws of propriety, humanity, and justice, and to God. Associations formed elsewhere, springing from a feeling of humanity, or any other cause, have nothing whatever to do with it. They have never received any encouragement from me, and they never will."

They who know of no purer sources of truth, who have traced up 45 its stream no higher, stand, and wisely stand, by the Bible and the Constitution, and drink at it there with reverence and humility; but they who behold where it comes trickling into this lake or that pool, gird up their loins once more, and continue their pilgrimage toward its fountain-head.

No man with a genius for legislation has appeared in America. 46 They are rare in the history of the world. There are orators, politicians,

---

[13] The 1787 framers of the Constitution. [Eds.]

and eloquent men, by the thousand; but the speaker has not yet opened his mouth to speak who is capable of settling the much-vexed questions of the day. We love eloquence for its own sake, and not for any truth which it may utter, or any heroism it may inspire. Our legislators have not yet learned the comparative value of free-trade and of freedom, of union, and of rectitude, to a nation. They have no genius or talent for comparatively humble questions of taxation and finance, commerce and manufacturers and agriculture. If we were left solely to the wordy wit of legislators in Congress for our guidance, uncorrected by the seasonable experience and the effectual complaints of the people, America would not long retain her rank among the nations. For eighteen hundred years, though perchance I have no right to say it, the New Testament has been written; yet where is the legislator who has wisdom and practical talent enough to avail himself of the light which it sheds on the science of legislation?

The authority of government, even such as I am willing to submit 47 to,—for I will cheerfully obey those who know and can do better than I, and in many things even those who neither know nor can do so well,— is still an impure one: to be strictly just, it must have the sanction and consent of the governed. It can have no pure right over my person and property but what I concede to it. The progress from an absolute to a limited monarchy, from a limited monarchy to a democracy, is a progress toward a true respect for the individual. Even the Chinese philosopher was wise enough to regard the individual as the basis of the empire. Is a democracy, such as we know it, the last improvement possible in government? Is it not possible to take a further step towards recognizing and organizing the rights of man? There will never be a really free and enlightened State until the State comes to recognize the individual as a higher and independent power, from which all its own power and authority are derived, and treats him accordingly. I please myself with imagining a State at last which can afford to be just to all men, and to treat the individual with respect as a neighbor; which even would not think it inconsistent with its own repose if a few were to live aloof from it, not meddling with it, nor embraced by it, who fulfilled all the duties of neighbors and fellow-men. A State which bore this kind of fruit, and suffered it to drop off as fast as it ripened, would prepare the way for a still more perfect and glorious State, which also I have imagined, but not yet anywhere seen.

Responding to Reading

1. What moral or political choice does each of the following statements by Thoreau imply?
   - "'That government is best which governs least'" (1).
   - "All men recognize the right of revolution" (8).

- "All voting is a sort of gaming, like checkers or backgammon" (12).
- "Under a government which imprisons any unjustly, the true place for a just man is also a prison" (23).
- "I did not see why the schoolmaster should be taxed to support the priest, and not the priest the schoolmaster" (26).

2. Do you believe civil disobedience is ever necessary? If so, under what circumstances?
3. Do you see any advantages in conforming to a law, however unjust, rather than disobeying it? Explain.

LETTER FROM BIRMINGHAM JAIL

Martin Luther King, Jr.

One of the greatest civil rights leaders and orators of this century (see also p. 431), Martin Luther King, Jr. (1929–1968), was also a Baptist minister and winner of the 1964 Nobel Peace Prize. He was born in Atlanta, Georgia, and earned degrees from four institutions. Influenced by Thoreau and Gandhi, King altered the spirit of African-American protest in the United States by advocating nonviolent civil disobedience to achieve racial equality. King's books include Letter from Birmingham Jail *(1963) and* Where Do We Go from Here: Chaos or Community? *(1967). King was assassinated on April 4, 1968. The following letter, written in 1963, is his eloquent and impassioned response to a public statement by eight fellow clergymen in Birmingham, Alabama, who appealed to the citizenry of the city to "observe the principles of law and order and common sense" rather than join in the principled protests that King was leading.*

MY DEAR FELLOW CLERGYMEN:[1]   1

While confined here in the Birmingham city jail, I came across your recent statement calling my present activities "unwise and untimely." Seldom do I pause to answer criticism of my work and ideas. If I sought to answer all the criticisms that cross my desk, my secretaries would have little time for anything other than such correspondence in the course of the day, and I would have no time for constructive work. But since I feel that you are men of genuine good will and that your

---

[1] This response to a published statement by eight fellow clergymen from Alabama (Bishop C. C. J. Carpenter, Bishop Joseph A. Durick, Rabbi Milton L. Grafman, Bishop Paul Hardin, Bishop Holan B. Harmon, the Reverend George M. Murray, the Reverend Edward V. Ramage and the Reverend Earl Stallings) was composed under somewhat constricting circumstances. Begun on the margins of the newspaper in which the statement appeared while I was in jail, the letter was continued on scraps of writing paper supplied by a friendly Negro trusty, and concluded on a pad my attorneys were eventually permitted to leave me. Although the text remains in substance unaltered, I have indulged in the author's prerogative of polishing it for publication.

criticisms are sincerely set forth, I want to try to answer your statement in what I hope will be patient and reasonable terms.

I think I should indicate that I am here in Birmingham, since you have been influenced by the view which argues against "outsiders coming in." I have the honor of serving as president of the Southern Christian Leadership Conference, an organization operating in every southern state, with headquarters in Atlanta, Georgia. We have some eighty-five affiliated organizations across the South, and one of them is the Alabama Christian Movement for Human Rights. Frequently we share staff, educational, and financial resources with our affiliates. Several months ago the affiliate here in Birmingham asked us to be on call to engage in a nonviolent direct-action program if such were deemed necessary. We readily consented, and when the hour came we lived up to our promise. So I, along with several members of my staff, am here because I was invited here. I am here because I have organizational ties here.

But more basically, I am in Birmingham because injustice is here. Just as the prophets of the eighth century B.C. left their villages and carried their "thus saith the Lord" far beyond the boundaries of their home towns, and just as the Apostle Paul left his village of Tarsus and carried the gospel of Jesus Christ to the far corners of the Greco-Roman world, so am I compelled to carry the gospel of freedom beyond my own home town. Like Paul, I must constantly respond to the Macedonian call for aid.

Moreover, I am cognizant of the interrelatedness of all communities and states. I cannot sit idly by in Atlanta and not be concerned about what happens in Birmingham. Injustice anywhere is a threat to justice everywhere. We are caught in an inescapable network of mutuality, tied in a single garment of destiny. Whatever affects one directly, affects all indirectly. Never again can we afford to live with the narrow, provincial "outside agitator" idea. Anyone who lives inside the United States can never be considered an outsider anywhere within its bounds.

You deplore the demonstrations taking place in Birmingham. But your statement, I am sorry to say, fails to express a similar concern for the conditions that brought about the demonstrations. I am sure that none of you would want to rest content with the superficial kind of social analysis that deals merely with effects and does not grapple with underlying causes. It is unfortunate that demonstrations are taking place in Birmingham, but it is even more unfortunate that the city's white power structure left the Negro community with no alternative.

In any nonviolent campaign there are four basic steps: collection of the facts to determine whether injustices exist; negotiation; self-purification; and direct action. We have gone through all these steps in Birmingham. There can be no gainsaying the fact that racial injustice engulfs this community. Birmingham is probably the most thoroughly segregated city in the United States. Its ugly record of brutality is widely known. Negroes have experienced grossly unjust treatment in the courts. There have been more unsolved bombings of Negro homes and churches in Birmingham than in any other city in the nation. These are the hard, brutal facts of the case. On the basis of these conditions, Negro leaders sought to negotiate with the city fathers. But the latter consistently refused to engage in good-faith negotiation.

Then, last September, came the opportunity to talk with leaders of 7
Birmingham's economic community. In the course of the negotiations, certain promises were made by the merchants—for example, to remove the stores' humiliating racial signs. On the basis of these promises, the Reverend Fred Shuttlesworth and the leaders of the Alabama Christian Movement for Human Rights agreed to a moratorium on all demonstrations. As the weeks and months went by, we realized that we were the victims of a broken promise. A few signs, briefly removed, returned; the others remained.

As in so many past experiences, our hopes had been blasted, and 8
the shadow of deep disappointment settled upon us. We had no alternative except to prepare for direct action, whereby we would present our very bodies as a means of laying our case before the conscience of the local and the national community. Mindful of the difficulties involved, we decided to undertake a process of self-purification. We began a series of workshops on nonviolence, and we repeatedly asked ourselves: "Are you able to accept blows without retaliating?" "Are you able to endure the ordeal of jail?" We decided to schedule our direct-action program for the Easter season, realizing that except for Christmas, this is the main shopping period of the year. Knowing that a strong economic-withdrawal program would be the by-product of direct action, we felt that this would be the best time to bring pressure to bear on the merchants for the needed change.

Then it occurred to us that Birmingham's mayoral election was 9
coming up in March, and we speedily decided to postpone action until after election day. When we discovered that the Commissioner of Public Safety, Eugene "Bull" Connor,[2] had piled up enough votes to be in the run-off, we decided again to postpone action until the day after the run-off so that the demonstrations could not be used to cloud the issues. Like many others, we wanted to see Mr. Connor defeated, and to this end we endured postponement after postponement. Having aided in this community need, we felt that our direct-action program could be delayed no longer.

You may well ask, "Why direct action? Why sit-ins, marches, and so 10
forth? Isn't negotiation a better path?" You are quite right in calling for

---

[2] An ardent segregationist, Connor ordered police officers to use police dogs and fire hoses to break up civil rights demonstrations. (Conner lost his bid for mayor.)

negotiation. Indeed, this is the very purpose of direct action. Nonviolent direct action seeks to create such a crisis and foster such a tension that a community which has constantly refused to negotiate is forced to confront the issue. It seeks so to dramatize the issue that it can no longer be ignored. My citing the creation of tension as part of the work of the nonviolent-resister may sound rather shocking. But I must confess that I am not afraid of the word "tension." I have earnestly opposed violent tension, but there is a type of constructive, nonviolent tension which is necessary for growth. Just as Socrates felt that it was necessary to create a tension in the mind so that individuals could rise from the bondage of myths and half-truths to the unfettered realm of creative analysis and objective appraisal, so must we see the need for nonviolent gadflies to create the kind of tension in society that will help men rise from the dark depths of prejudice and racism to the majestic heights of understanding and brotherhood.

The purpose of our direct-action program is to create a situation so   11
crisis-packed that it will inevitably open the door to negotiation. I therefore concur with you in your call for negotiation. Too long has our beloved Southland been bogged down in a tragic effort to live in monologue rather than dialogue.

One of the basic points in your statement is that the action that I and   12
my associates have taken in Birmingham is untimely. Some have asked: "Why didn't you give the new city administration time to act?" The only answer that I can give to this query is that the new Birmingham administration must be prodded about as much as the outgoing one, before it will act. We are sadly mistaken if we feel that the election of Albert Boutwell as mayor will bring the millennium to Birmingham. While Mr. Boutwell is a much more gentle person than Mr. Connor, they are both segregationists, dedicated to maintenance of the status quo. I have hoped that Mr. Boutwell will be reasonable enough to see the futility of massive resistance to desegregation. But he will not see this without pressure from devotees of civil rights. My friends, I must say to you that we have not made a single gain in civil rights without determined legal and nonviolent pressure. Lamentably, it is an historical fact that privileged groups seldom give up their privileges voluntarily. Individuals may see the moral light and voluntarily give up their unjust posture; but, as Reinhold Niebuhr[3] has reminded us, groups tend to be more immoral than individuals.

We know through painful experience that freedom is never volun-   13
tarily given by the oppressor; it must be demanded by the oppressed. Frankly, I have yet to engage in a direct-action campaign that was "well timed" in the view of those who have not suffered unduly from

---

[3] American religious and social thinker (1892–1971). [Eds.]

the disease of segregation. For years now I have heard the word "Wait!" It rings in the ear of every Negro with piercing familiarity. This "Wait" has almost always meant "Never." We must come to see, with one of our distinguished jurists, that "justice too long delayed is justice denied."[4]

We have waited for more than 340 years for our constitutional and   14 God-given rights. The nations of Asia and Africa are moving with jet-like speed toward gaining political independence, but we still creep at horse-and-buggy pace toward gaining a cup of coffee at a lunch counter. Perhaps it is easy for those who have never felt the stinging darts of segregation to say, "Wait." But when you have seen vicious mobs lynch your mothers and fathers at will and drown your sisters and brothers at whim; when you have seen hate-filled policemen curse, kick, and even kill your black brothers and sisters; when you see the vast majority of your twenty million Negro brothers smothering in an airtight cage of poverty in the midst of an affluent society; when you suddenly find your tongue twisted and your speech stammering as you seek to explain to your six-year-old daughter why she can't go to the public amusement park that has just been advertised on television, and see tears welling up in her eyes when she is told that Funtown is closed to colored children, and see ominous clouds of inferiority beginning to form in her little mental sky, and see her beginning to distort her personality by developing an unconscious bitterness toward white people; when you have to concoct an answer for a five-year-old son who is asking, "Daddy, why do white people treat colored people so mean?"; when you take a cross-country drive and find it necessary to sleep night after night in the uncomfortable corners of your automobile because no motel will accept you; when you are humiliated day in and day out by nagging signs reading "white" and "colored"; when your first name becomes "nigger," your middle name becomes "boy" (however old you are) and your last name becomes "John," and your wife and mother are never given the respected title "Mrs."; when you are harried by day and haunted by night by the fact that you are a Negro, living constantly at tiptoe stance, never quite knowing what to expect next, and are plagued with inner fears and outer resentments; when you are forever fighting a degenerating sense of "nobodiness"—then you will understand why we find it difficult to wait. There comes a time when the cup of endurance runs over, and men are no longer willing to be plunged into the abyss of despair. I hope, sirs, you can understand our legitimate and unavoidable impatience.

You express a great deal of anxiety over our willingness to break   15 laws. This is certainly a legitimate concern. Since we so diligently urge

---

[4] Attributed to British statesman William Ewart Gladstone (1809–1898), a stalwart of the Liberal Party who also said, "You cannot fight the future. Time is on our side." [Eds.]

people to obey the Supreme Court's decision of 1954 outlawing segregation in the public schools, at first glance it may seem rather paradoxical for us consciously to break laws. One may well ask: "How can you advocate breaking some laws and obeying others?" The answer lies in the fact that there are two types of laws: just and unjust. I would be the first to advocate obeying just laws. One has not only a legal but a moral responsibility to obey just laws. Conversely, one has a moral responsibility to disobey unjust laws. I would agree with St. Augustine[5] that "an unjust law is no law at all."

Now, what is the difference between the two? How does one deter-   16
mine whether a law is just or unjust? A just law is a man-made code that squares with the moral law or the law of God. An unjust law is a code this is out of harmony with the moral law. To put it in the terms of St. Thomas Aquinas:[6] An unjust law is a human law that is not rooted in eternal law and natural law. Any law that uplifts human personality is just. Any law that degrades human personality is unjust. All segregation statutes are unjust because segregation distorts the soul and damages the personality. It gives the segregator a false sense of superiority and the segregated a false sense of inferiority. Segregation, to use the terminology of the Jewish philosopher Martin Buber,[7] substitutes an "I-it" relationship for an "I-thou" relationship and ends up relegating persons to the status of things. Hence segregation is not only politically, economically, and sociologically unsound, it is morally wrong and sinful. Paul Tillich[8] has said that sin is separation. Is not segregation an existential expression of man's tragic separation, his awful estrangement, his terrible sinfulness? Thus it is that I can urge men to obey the 1954 decision of the Supreme Court, for it is morally right; and I can urge them to disobey segregation ordinances, for they are morally wrong.

Let us consider a more concrete example of just and unjust laws. An   17
unjust law is a code that a numerical or power majority group compels a minority group to obey but does not make binding on itself. This is *difference* made legal. By the same token, a just law is a code that a majority compels a minority to follow and that it is willing to follow itself. This is *sameness* made legal.

Let me give another explanation. A law is unjust if it is inflicted on   18
a minority that, as a result of being denied the right to vote, had no part in enacting or devising the law. Who can say that the legislature of Alabama which set up that state's segregation laws was democratically elected? Throughout Alabama all sorts of devious methods are used to

---

[5] Italian-born missionary and theologian (?–c.604) [Eds.]
[6] Italian philosopher and theologian (1225–1274). [Eds.]
[7] Austrian existentialist philosopher and Judaic scholar (1878–1965). [Eds.]
[8] American philosopher and theologian (1886–1965). [Eds.]

prevent Negroes from becoming registered voters, and there are some counties in which, even though Negroes constitute a majority of the population, not a single Negro is registered. Can any law enacted under such circumstances be considered democratically structured?

Sometimes a law is just on its face and unjust in its application. For instance, I have been arrested on a charge of parading without a permit. Now, there is nothing wrong in having an ordinance which requires a permit for a parade. But such an ordinance becomes unjust when it is used to maintain segregation and to deny citizens the First-Amendment privilege of peaceful assembly and protest. 19

I hope you are able to see the distinction I am trying to point out. In no sense do I advocate evading or defying the law, as would the rabid segregationist. That would lead to anarchy. One who breaks an unjust law must do so openly, lovingly, and with a willingness to accept the penalty. I submit that an individual who breaks a law that conscience tells him is unjust, and who willingly accepts the penalty of imprisonment in order to arouse the conscience of the community over its injustice, is in reality expressing the highest respect for law. 20

Of course, there is nothing new about this kind of civil disobedience. It was evidenced sublimely in the refusal of Shadrach, Meshach, and Abednego to obey the laws of Nebuchadnezzar, on the ground that a higher moral law was at stake.[9] It was practiced superbly by the early Christians, who were willing to face hungry lions and the excruciating pain of chopping blocks rather than submit to certain unjust laws of the Roman Empire. To a degree, academic freedom is a reality today because Socrates practiced civil disobedience.[10] In our own nation, the Boston Tea Party represented a massive act of civil disobedience. 21

We should never forget that everything Adolf Hitler did in Germany was "legal" and everything the Hungarian freedom fighters[11] did in Hungary was "illegal." It was "illegal" to aid and comfort a Jew in Hitler's Germany. Even so, I am sure that, had I lived in Germany at the time, I would have aided and comforted my Jewish brothers. If today I lived in a Communist country where certain principles dear to the Christian faith are suppressed, I would openly advocate disobeying that country's anti-religious laws. 22

---

[9] In the book of Daniel, Nebuchadnezzar commanded the people to worship a golden statue or be thrown into a furnace of blazing fire. When Shadrach, Meshach, and Abednego refused to worship any god but their own, they were bound and thrown into a blazing furnace, but the fire had no effect on them. Their escape led Nebuchadnezzar to make a decree forbidding blasphemy against their god. [Eds.]

[10] The ancient Greek philosopher Socrates was tried by the Athenians for corrupting their youth through his use of questions to teach. When he refused to change his methods of teaching, he was condemned to death. [Eds.]

[11] The Hungarian anti-Communist uprising of 1956 was quickly crushed by the Russian army. [Eds.]

I must make two honest confessions to you, my Christian and 23
Jewish brothers. First, I must confess that over the past few years I have
been gravely disappointed with the white moderate. I have almost
reached the regrettable conclusion that the Negro's great stumbling
block in his stride toward freedom is not the White Citizen's Counciler
or the Ku Klux Klanner, but the white moderate, who is more devoted
to "order" than to justice; who prefers a negative peace which is the
absence of tension to a positive peace which is the presence of justice;
who constantly says, "I agree with you in the goal you seek, but I cannot agree with your methods of direct action"; who paternalistically
believes he can set the timetable for another man's freedom; who lives
by a mythical concept of time and who constantly advises the Negro to
wait for a "more convenient season." Shallow understanding from people of good will is more frustrating than absolute misunderstanding
from people of ill will. Lukewarm acceptance is much more bewildering than outright rejection.

I had hoped that the white moderate would understand that law 24
and order exist for the purpose of establishing justice and that when
they fail in this purpose they become the dangerously structured dams
that block the flow of social progress. I had hoped that the white moderate would understand that the present tension in the South is a necessary phase of the transition from an obnoxious negative peace, in
which the Negro passively accepted his unjust plight, to a substantive
and positive peace, in which all men will respect the dignity and worth
of human personality. Actually, we who engage in nonviolent direct
action are not the creators of tension. We merely bring to the surface the
hidden tension that is already alive. We bring it out in the open, where
it can be seen and dealt with. Like a boil that can never be cured so long
as it is covered up but must be opened with all its ugliness to the natural medicines of air and light, injustice must be exposed, with all the
tension its exposure creates, to the light of human conscience and the air
of national opinion, before it can be cured.

In your statement you assert that our actions, even though peaceful, 25
must be condemned because they precipitate violence. But is this a logical assertion? Isn't this like condemning a robbed man because his possession of money precipitated the evil act of robbery? Isn't this like
condemning Socrates because his unswerving commitment to truth and
his philosophical inquiries precipitated the act by the misguided populace in which they made him drink hemlock? Isn't this like condemning
Jesus because his unique God-consciousness and never-ceasing devotion to God's will precipitated the evil act of crucifixion? We must come
to see that, as the federal courts have consistently affirmed, it is wrong
to urge an individual to cease his efforts to gain his basic constitutional
rights because the quest may precipitate violence. Society must protect
the robbed and punish the robber.

I had also hoped that the white moderate would reject the myth   26
concerning time in relation to the struggle for freedom. I have just
received a letter from a white brother in Texas. He writes: "All
Christians know that the colored people will receive equal rights eventually, but it is possible that you are in too great a religious hurry. It has
taken Christianity almost two thousand years to accomplish what it
has. The teachings of Christ take time to come to earth." Such an attitude stems from a tragic misconception of time, from the strangely irrational notion that there is something in the very flow of time that will
inevitably cure all ills. Actually, time itself is neutral; it can be used either
destructively or constructively. More and more I feel that the people
of ill will have used time much more effectively than have the people of
good will. We will have to repent in this generation not merely for the
hateful words and actions of the bad people, but for the appalling
silence of the good people. Human progress never rolls in on wheels of
inevitability; it comes through the tireless efforts of men willing to be
co-workers with God, and without this hard work, time itself becomes
an ally of the forces of social stagnation. We must use time creatively, in
the knowledge that the time is always ripe to do right. Now is the time
to make real the promise of democracy and transform our pending
national elegy into a creative psalm of brotherhood. Now is the time to
lift our national policy from the quicksand of racial injustice to the solid
rock of human dignity.

You speak of our activity in Birmingham as extreme. At first I was   27
rather disappointed that fellow clergymen would see my nonviolent
efforts as those of an extremist. I began thinking about the fact that
I stand in the middle of two opposing forces in the Negro community. One is a force of complacency, made up in part of Negroes who, as
a result of long years of oppression, are so drained of self-respect and a
sense of "somebodiness" that they have adjusted to segregation; and in
part of a few middle-class Negroes who, because of a degree of academic and economic security and because in some ways they profit by
segregation, have become insensitive to the problems of the masses. The
other force is one of bitterness and hatred, and it comes perilously close
to advocating violence. It is expressed in the various black nationalist
groups that are springing up across the nation, the largest and
best-known being Elijah Muhammad's Muslim movement. Nourished
by the Negro's frustration over the continued existence of racial discrimination, this movement is made up of people who have lost faith in
America, who have absolutely repudiated Christianity, and who have
concluded that the white man is an incorrigible "devil."

I have tried to stand between these two forces, saying that we need   28
emulate neither the "do-nothingism" of the complacent nor the hatred
and despair of the black nationalist. For there is the more excellent way
of love and nonviolent protest. I am grateful to God that, through the

influence of the Negro church, the way of nonviolence became an integral part of our struggle.

If this philosophy had not emerged, by now many streets of the 29 South would, I am convinced, be flowing with blood. And I am further convinced that if our white brothers dismiss as "rabblerousers" and "outside agitators" those of us who employ nonviolent direct action, and if they refuse to support our nonviolent efforts, millions of Negroes will, out of frustration and despair, seek solace and security in black-nationalist ideologies—a development that would inevitably lead to a frightening racial nightmare.

Oppressed people cannot remain oppressed forever. The yearning 30 for freedom eventually manifests itself, and that is what has happened to the American Negro. Something within has reminded him of his birthright of freedom, and something without has reminded him that it can be gained. Consciously or unconsciously, he has been caught up by the *Zeitgeist*,[12] and with his black brothers of Africa and his brown and yellow brothers of Asia, South America, and the Caribbean, the United States Negro is moving with a sense of great urgency toward the promised land of racial justice. If one recognizes this vital urge that has engulfed the Negro community, one should readily understand why public demonstrations are taking place. The Negro has many pent-up resentments and latent frustrations, and he must release them. So let him march; let him make prayer pilgrimages to the city hall; let him go on freedom rides—and try to understand why he must do so. If his repressed emotions are not released in nonviolent ways, they will seek expression through violence; this is not a threat but a fact of history. So I have not said to my people, "Get rid of your discontent." Rather, I have tried to say that this normal and healthy discontent can be channeled into the creative outlet of nonviolent direct action. And now this approach is being termed extremist.

But though I was initially disappointed at being categorized as an 31 extremist, as I continued to think about the matter I gradually gained a measure of satisfaction from the label. Was not Jesus an extremist for love: "Love your enemies, bless them that curse you, do good to them that hate you, and pray for them which despitefully use you, and persecute you." Was not Amos an extremist for justice: "Let justice roll down like waters and righteousness like an ever-flowing stream." Was not Paul an extremist for the Christian gospel: "I bear in my body the marks of the Lord Jesus." Was not Martin Luther an extremist: "Here I stand; I cannot do otherwise, so help me God." And John Bunyan: "I will stay in jail to the end of my days before I make a butchery of my conscience." And Abraham Lincoln: "This nation cannot survive half

---

[12] The spirit of the times. [Eds.]

slave and half free." And Thomas Jefferson: "We hold these truths to be self-evident, that all men are created equal. . . ." So the question is not whether we will be extremists, but what kind of extremists we will be. Will we be extremists for hate or for love? Will we be extremists for the preservation of injustice or for the extension of justice? In that dramatic scene on Calvary's hill three men were crucified. We must never forget that all three were crucified for the same thing—the crime of extremism. Two were extremists for immorality, and thus fell below their environment. The other, Jesus Christ, was an extremist for love, truth, and goodness, and thereby rose above his environment. Perhaps the South, the nation, and the world are in dire need of creative extremists.

I had hoped that the white moderate would see this need. Perhaps   32 I was too optimistic; perhaps I expected too much. I suppose I should have realized that few members of the oppressor race can understand the deep groans and passionate yearnings of the oppressed race, and still fewer have the vision to see that injustice must be rooted out by strong, persistent, and determined action. I am thankful, however, that some of our white brothers in the South have grasped the meaning of this social revolution and committed themselves to it. They are still all too few in quantity, but they are big in quality. Some—such as Ralph McGill, Lillian Smith, Harry Golden, James McBridge Dabbs, Ann Braden, and Sarah Patton Boyle—have written about our struggle in eloquent and prophetic terms. Others have marched with us down nameless streets of the South. They have languished in filthy, roach-infested jails, suffering the abuse and brutality of policemen who view them as "dirty nigger-lovers." Unlike so many of their moderate brothers and sisters, they have recognized the urgency of the moment and sensed the need for powerful "action" antidotes to combat the disease of segregation.

Let me take note of my other major disappointment. I have been so   33 greatly disappointed with the white church and its leadership. Of course, there are some notable exceptions. I am not unmindful of the fact that each of you has taken some significant stands on this issue. I commend you, Reverend Stallings, for your Christian stand on this past Sunday, in welcoming Negroes to your worship service on a nonsegregated basis. I commend the Catholic leaders of this state for integrating Spring Hill College several years ago.

But despite these notable exceptions, I must honestly reiterate that   34 I have been disappointed with the church. I do not say this as one of those negative critics who can always find something wrong with the church. I say this as a minister of the gospel, who loves the church; who was nurtured in its bosom; who has been sustained by its spiritual blessings and who will remain true to it as long as the cord of life shall lengthen.

When I was suddenly catapulted into the leadership of the bus 35
protest in Montgomery, Alabama, a few years ago, I felt we would be
supported by the white church. I felt that the white ministers, priests,
and rabbis of the South would be among our strongest allies. Instead,
some have been outright opponents, refusing to understand the freedom movement and misrepresenting its leaders; all too many others
have been more cautious than courageous and have remained silent
behind the anesthetizing security of stained glass windows.

In spite of my shattered dreams, I came to Birmingham with the 36
hope that the white religious leadership of this community would see
the justice of our cause and, with deep moral concern, would serve as
the channel through which our just grievances could reach the power
structure. I had hoped that each of you would understand. But again I
have been disappointed.

I have heard numerous southern religious leaders admonish their 37
worshipers to comply with a desegregation decision because it is the
law, but I have longed to hear white ministers declare: "Follow this
decree because integration is morally right and because the Negro is
your brother." In the midst of blatant injustices inflicted upon the
Negro, I have watched white churchmen stand on the sideline and
mouth pious irrelevancies and sanctimonious trivialities. In the midst of
a mighty struggle to rid our nation of racial and economic injustice, I
have heard many ministers say: "Those are social issues, with which the
gospel has no real concern." And I have watched many churches commit themselves to a completely otherworldly religion which makes a
strange, un-Biblical distinction between body and soul, between the
sacred and the secular.

I have traveled the length and breadth of Alabama, Mississippi, and 38
all the other southern states. On sweltering summer days and crisp
autumn mornings I have looked at the South's beautiful churches with
their lofty spires pointing heavenward. I have beheld the impressive
outlines of her massive religious-education buildings. Over and over I
have found myself asking: "What kind of people worship here? Who is
their God? Where were their voices when the lips of Governor Barnett[13]
dripped with words of interposition and nullification? Where were they
when Governor Wallace[14] gave a clarion call for defiance and hatred?
Where were their voices of support when bruised and weary Negro
men and women decided to rise from the dark dungeons of complacency to the bright hills of creative protest?"

---

[13] Ross Barnett, segregationist governor of Mississippi, best known for his resistance to the integration of the University of Mississippi in 1962. [Eds.]
[14] George Wallace, segregationist governor of Alabama, best known for standing in the doorway of
a University of Alabama building to block the entrance of two black students who were trying to
register. [Eds.]

Yes, these questions are still in my mind. In deep disappointment I 39
have wept over the laxity of the church. But be assured that my tears
have been tears of love. There can be no deep disappointment where
there is not deep love. Yes, I love the church. How could I do otherwise?
I am in the rather unique position of being the son, the grandson, and
the great-grandson of preachers. Yes, I see the church as the body of
Christ. But, oh! How we have blemished and scarred that body through
social neglect and through fear of being nonconformists.

There was a time when the church was very powerful—in the time 40
when the early Christians rejoiced at being deemed worthy to suffer for
what they believed. In those days the church was not merely a thermometer that recorded the ideas and principles of popular opinion; it
was a thermostat that transformed the mores of society. Whenever the
early Christians entered a town, the people in power became disturbed
and immediately sought to convict the Christians for being "disturbers
of the peace" and "outside agitators." But the Christians pressed on, in
the conviction that they were "a colony of heaven," called to obey God
rather than man. Small in number, they were big in commitment. They
were too God-intoxicated to be "astronomically intimidated." By their
effort and example they brought an end to such ancient evils as infanti-
cide and gladiatorial contests.

Things are different now. So often the contemporary church is a 41
weak, ineffectual voice with an uncertain sound. So often it is an
archdefender to the status quo. Far from being disturbed by the presence of the church, the power structure of the average community is
consoled by the church's silent—and often even vocal—sanction of
things as they are.

But the judgment of God is upon the church as never before. If 42
today's church does not recapture the sacrificial spirit of the early
church, it will lose its authenticity, forfeit the loyalty of millions, and be
dismissed as an irrelevant social club with no meaning for the twentieth
century. Every day I meet young people whose disappointment with
the church has turned into outright disgust.

Perhaps I have once again been too optimistic. Is organized reli- 43
gion too inextricably bound to the status quo to save our nation and the
world? Perhaps I must turn my faith to the inner spiritual church,
the church within the church, as the true *ekklesia*[15] and the hope of the
world. But again I am thankful to God that some noble souls from
the ranks of organized religion have broken loose from the paralyzing
chains of conformity and joined us as active partners in the struggle for
freedom. They have left their secure congregations and walked the
streets of Albany, Georgia, with us. They have gone down the highways of the South on tortuous rides for freedom. Yes, they have gone

---

[15] The Greek word for the early Christian church. [Eds.]

to jail with us. Some have been dismissed from their churches, have lost the support of their bishops and fellow ministers. But they have acted in the faith that right defeated is stronger than evil triumphant. Their witness has been the spiritual salt that has preserved the true meaning of the gospel in these troubled times. They have carved a tunnel of hope through the dark mountain of disappointment.

I hope the church as a whole will meet the challenge of this decisive 44 hour. But even if the church does not come to the aid of justice, I have no despair about the future. I have no fear about the outcome of our struggle in Birmingham, even if our motives are at present misunderstood. We will reach the goal of freedom in Birmingham and all over the nation, because the goal of America is freedom. Abused and scorned though we may be, our destiny is tied up with America's destiny. Before the pilgrims landed at Plymouth, we were here. Before the pen of Jefferson etched the majestic words of the Declaration of Independence across the pages of history, we were here. For more than two centuries our forebears labored in this country without wages; they made cotton king; they built the homes of their masters while suffering gross injustice and shameful humiliation—and yet out of a bottomless vitality they continued to thrive and develop. If the inexpressible cruelties of slavery could not stop us, the opposition we now face will surely fail. We will win our freedom because the sacred heritage of our nation and the eternal will of God are embodied in our echoing demands.

Before closing I feel impelled to mention one other point in your 45 statement that has troubled me profoundly. You warmly commended the Birmingham police force for keeping "order" and "preventing violence." I doubt that you would have so warmly commended the police force if you had seen its dogs sinking their teeth into unarmed, nonviolent Negroes. I doubt that you would so quickly commend the policemen if you were to observe their ugly and inhumane treatment of Negroes here in the city jail; if you were to watch them push and curse old Negro women and young Negro girls; if you were to see them slap and kick old Negro men and young boys; if you were to observe them, as they did on two occasions, refuse to give us food because we wanted to sing our grace together. I cannot join you in your praise of the Birmingham police department.

It is true that the police have exercised a degree of discipline in han- 46 dling the demonstrators. In this sense they have conducted themselves rather "nonviolently" in public. But for what purpose? To preserve the evil system of segregation. Over the past few years I have consistently preached that nonviolence demands that the means we use must be as pure as the ends we seek. I have tried to make clear that it is wrong to use immoral means to attain moral ends. But now I must affirm that it is just as wrong, or perhaps even more so, to use moral means to preserve immoral ends. Perhaps Mr. Connor and his policemen have been rather nonviolent in public, as was Chief Pritchett in Albany, Georgia, but they have used the moral means of nonviolence to maintain the immoral end of racial injustice. As T. S. Eliot[16] has said, "The last temptation is the greatest treason: To do the right deed for the wrong reason."

I wish you had commended the Negro sit-inners and demonstra- 47
tors of Birmingham for their sublime courage, their willingness to suffer, and their amazing discipline in the midst of great provocation. One day the South will recognize its real heroes. They will be the James Merediths,[17] with the noble sense of purpose that enables them to face jeering and hostile mobs, and with the agonizing loneliness that characterizes the life of the pioneer. They will be old, oppressed, battered Negro women, symbolized in a seventy-two-year-old woman in Montgomery, Alabama, who rose up with a sense of dignity and with her people decided not to ride segregated buses, and who responded with ungrammatical profundity to one who inquired about her weariness: "My feets is tired, but my soul is at rest." They will be the young high school and college students, the young ministers of the gospel and a host of their elders, courageously and nonviolently sitting in at lunch counters and willingly going to jail for conscience' sake. One day the South will know that when these disinherited children of God sat down at lunch counters, they were in reality standing up for what is best in the American dream and for the most sacred values in our Judaeo-Christian heritage, thereby bringing our nation back to those great wells of democracy which were dug deep by the founding fathers in their formulation of the Constitution and the Declaration of Independence.

Never before have I written so long a letter. I'm afraid it is much too 48
long to take your precious time. I can assure you that it would have been much shorter if I had been writing from a comfortable desk, but what else can one do when he is alone in a narrow jail cell, other than write long letters, think long thoughts, and pray long prayers?

If I have said anything in this letter that overstates the truth and 49
indicates an unreasonable impatience, I beg you to forgive me. If I have said anything that understates the truth and indicates my having a patience that allows me to settle for anything less than brotherhood, I beg God to forgive me.

I hope this letter finds you strong in the faith. I also hope that cir- 50
cumstances will soon make it possible for me to meet each of you, not as an integrationist or a civil-rights leader but as a fellow clergyman and a Christian brother. Let us all hope that the dark clouds of racial prejudice will soon pass away and the deep fog of misunderstanding will be lifted from our fear-drenched communities, and in some not too distant

---

[16] 1888–1965 American-born British poet, winner of the 1948 Nobel Prize for literature.

[17] First African-American to enroll at the University of Mississippi after federal troops were brought in to control demonstrators protesting his enrollment. [Eds.]

tomorrow the radiant stars of love and brotherhood will shine over our great nation with all their scintillating beauty.

Yours for the cause of Peace and Brotherhood,
MARTIN LUTHER KING, JR.

Responding to Reading

1. What decision do the clergy members King addresses believe he should rethink? Do you believe King would have been justified in arguing that he had no other alternative than to protest? Would you accept this argument?
2. In paragraph 30, King says, "Oppressed people cannot remain oppressed forever." Do you think world events of the last few years confirm or contradict this statement? Explain.
3. Throughout this letter, King uses elaborate diction and a variety of rhetorical devices: he addresses his audience directly; makes frequent use of balance and parallelism, understatement, and metaphor; and makes many historical and religious allusions. What effect do you think King intended these rhetorical devices to have on the letter's original audience of clergy-members? What is their effect on you? That is, do you find they enhance his argument, or do you think they just get in the way?

LIFEBOAT ETHICS: THE CASE AGAINST "AID" THAT HARMS

Garrett Hardin

Biologist Garrett Hardin (1915–) writes on moral and ethical issues in his field. His books include Filters against Folly: How to Survive Despite Economists, Ecologists, and the Merely Eloquent *(1985),* Living within Limits: How Global Population Growth Threatens Widespread Social Disorder *(1992), and* The Immigration Dilemma: Avoiding the Tragedy of the Commons *(1994). He often takes unpopular positions on subjects such as ecology and the scarcity of resources, and he is a fierce advocate of population limits. He has said, "Population is not a global problem. It is produced in each bedroom, a very local activity. So population control needs to be local." In this essay, which originally appeared in 1974 in* Psychology Today, *Hardin uses the metaphor of the wealthy nations of the world as lifeboats to illustrate the rights of both the needy and the rich in the problem of distributing the world's food. (Note that some of the world conditions on which Hardin bases his arguments have changed in the years since his essay was written.)*

Environmentalists use the metaphor of the earth as a "spaceship" in   1
trying to persuade countries, industries and people to stop wasting and
polluting our natural resources. Since we all share life on this planet,
they argue, no single person or institution has the right to destroy,
waste, or use more than a fair share of its resources.

But does everyone on earth have an equal right to an equal share of   2
its resources? The spaceship metaphor can be dangerous when used by
misguided idealists to justify suicidal policies for sharing our resources
through uncontrolled immigration and foreign aid. In their enthusiastic
but unrealistic generosity, they confuse the ethics of a spaceship with
those of a lifeboat.

A true spaceship would have to be under the control of a captain,   3
since no ship could possibly survive if its course were determined by
committee. Spaceship Earth certainly has no captain; the United
Nations is merely a toothless tiger, with little power to enforce any policy upon its bickering members.

If we divide the world crudely into rich nations and poor nations,   4
two thirds of them are desperately poor, and only one third comparatively rich, with the United States the wealthiest of all. Metaphorically
each rich nation can be seen as a lifeboat full of comparatively rich people. In the ocean outside each lifeboat swim the poor of the world, who
would like to get in, or at least to share some of the wealth. What should
the lifeboat passengers do?

First, we must recognize the limited capacity of any lifeboat. For   5
example, a nation's land has a limited capacity to support a population
and as the (current energy crisis) has shown us, in some ways we have
already exceeded the carrying capacity of our land.

So here we sit, say 50 people in our lifeboat. To be generous let us   6
assume it has room for 10 more, making a total capacity of 60. Suppose
the 50 of us in the lifeboat see 100 others swimming in the water outside,
begging for admission to our boat or for handouts. We have several
options: we may be tempted to try to live by the Christian ideal of being
"our brother's keeper," or by the Marxist ideal of "to each according to
his needs." Since the needs of all in the water are the same, and since
they can all be seen as "our brothers," we could take them all into our
boat, making a total of 150 in a boat designed for 60. The boat swamps,
everyone drowns. Complete justice, complete catastrophe.

Since the boat has an unused excess capacity of 10 more passen-   7
gers, we could admit just 10 more to it. But which 10 do we let in? How
do we choose? Do we pick the best 10, the neediest 10, "first come, first
served"? And what do we say to the 90 we exclude? If we do let an
extra 10 into our lifeboat, we will have lost our "safety factor," an engineering principle of critical importance. For example, if we don't leave
room for excess capacity as a safety factor in our country's agriculture,

a new plant disease or a bad change in the weather could have disastrous consequences.

Suppose we decide to preserve our small safety factor and admit no 8 more to the lifeboat. Our survival is then possible although we shall have to be constantly on guard against boarding parties.

While this last solution clearly offers the only means of our survival, 9 it is morally abhorrent to many people. Some say they feel guilty about their good luck. My reply is simple: "Get out and yield your place to others." This may solve the problem of the guilt-ridden person's conscience, but it does not change the ethics of the lifeboat. The needy person to whom the guilt-ridden person yields his place will not himself feel guilty about his good luck. If he did, he would not climb aboard. The net result of conscience-stricken people giving up their unjustly held seats is the elimination of that sort of conscience from the lifeboat.

This is the basic metaphor within which we must work out our 10 solutions. Let us now enrich the image, step by step, with substantive additions from the real world, a world that must solve real and pressing problems of overpopulation and hunger.

The harsh ethics of the lifeboat become even harsher when we con- 11 sider the reproductive differences between the rich nations and the poor nations. The people inside the lifeboats are doubling in numbers every 87 years: those swimming around outside are doubling on the average, every 35 years, more than twice as fast as the rich. And since the world's resources are dwindling, the difference in prosperity between the rich and the poor can only increase.

As of 1973, the U.S. had a population of 210 million people, who 12 were increasing by 0.8 percent per year. Outside our lifeboat, let us imagine another 210 million people (say the combined populations of Colombia, Ecuador, Venezuela, Morocco, Pakistan, Thailand and the Philippines), who are increasing at a rate of 3.3 percent per year. Put differently, the doubling time for this aggregate population is 21 years, compared to 87 years for the U.S.

Now suppose the U.S. agreed to pool its resources with those seven 13 countries, with everyone receiving an equal share. Initially the ratio of Americans to non-Americans in this model would be one-to-one but consider what the ratio would be after 87 years, by which time the Americans would have doubled to a population of 420 million. By then, doubling every 21 years, the other group would have swollen to 354 billion. Each American would have to share the available resources with more than eight people.

But, one could argue, this discussion assumes that current popula- 14 tion trends will continue, and they may not. Quite so. Most likely the rate of population increase will decline much faster in the U.S. than it will in the other countries, and there does not seem to be much we can do about it. In sharing with "each according to his needs," we must recognize that needs are determined by population size, which is determined by the rate of reproduction, which at present is regarded as a sovereign right of every nation, poor or not. This being so, the philanthropic load created by the sharing ethic of the spaceship can only increase.

The fundamental error of spaceship ethics, and the sharing it 15 requires, is that it leads to what I call "the tragedy of the commons." Under a system of private property, the men who own property recognize their responsibility to care for it, for if they don't they will eventually suffer. A farmer, for instance, will allow no more cattle in a pasture than its carrying capacity justifies. If he overloads it, erosion sets in, weeds take over, and he loses the use of the pasture.

If a pasture becomes a commons open to all, the right of each to use 16 it may not be matched by a corresponding responsibility to protect it. Asking everyone to use it with discretion will hardly do, for the considerate herdsman who refrains from overloading the commons suffers more than a selfish one who says his needs are greater. If everyone would restrain himself all would be well; but it takes only one less than everyone to ruin a system of voluntary restraint. In a crowded world of less than perfect human beings, mutual ruin is inevitable if there are no controls. This is the tragedy of the commons.

One of the major tasks of education today should be the creation of 17 such an acute awareness of the dangers of the commons that people will recognize its many varieties. For example, the air and water have become polluted because they are treated as commons. Further growth in the population or per-capita conversion of natural resources into pollutants will only make the problem worse. The same holds true for the fish of the oceans. Fishing fleets have nearly disappeared in many parts of the world; technological improvements in the art of fishing are hastening the day of complete ruin. Only the replacement of the system of the commons with a responsible system of control will save the land, air, water and oceanic fisheries.

In recent years there has been a push to create a new commons 18 called a World Food Bank, an international depository of food reserves to which nations would contribute according to their abilities and from which they would draw according to their needs. This humanitarian proposal has received support from many liberal international groups, and from such prominent citizens as Margaret Mead, U.N. Secretary General Kurt Waldheim, and Senators Edward Kennedy and George McGovern.

A world food bank appeals powerfully to our humanitarian 19 impulses. But before we rush ahead with such a plan, let us recognize where the greatest political push comes from, lest we be disillusioned later. Our experience with the "Food for Peace program," or Public Law 480, gives us the answer. This program moved billions of dollars worth of U.S. surplus grain to food-short, population-long countries during the past two decades. But when P.L. 480 first became law, a headline in the business magazine *Forbes* revealed the real power behind it: "Feeding the World's Hungry Millions: How It Will Mean Billions for U.S. Business."

And indeed it did. In the years 1960 to 1970, U.S. taxpayers spent a 20 total of $7.9 billion on the Food for Peace program. Between 1948 and 1970, they also paid an additional $50 billion for other economic-aid programs, some of which went for food and food-producing machinery and technology. Though all U.S. taxpayers were forced to contribute to the cost of P.L. 480, certain special interest groups gained handsomely under the program. Farmers did not have to contribute the grain; the Government, or rather the taxpayers, bought it from them at full market prices. The increased demand raised prices of farm products generally. The manufacturers of farm machinery, fertilizers and pesticides benefited by the farmers' extra efforts to grow more food. Grain elevators profited from storing the surplus until it could be shipped. Railroads made money hauling it to ports, and shipping lines profited from carrying it overseas. The implementation of P.L. 480 required the creation of a vast Government bureaucracy, which then acquired its own vested interest in continuing the program regardless of its merits.

Those who proposed and defended the Food for Peace program in 21 public rarely mentioned its importance to any of these special interests. The public emphasis was always on its humanitarian effects. The combination of silent selfish interests and highly vocal humanitarian apologists made a powerful and successful lobby for extracting money from taxpayers. We can expect the same lobby to push now for the creation of a World Food Bank.

However great the potential benefit to selfish interests, it should not 22 be a decisive argument against a truly humanitarian program. We must ask if such a program would actually do more good than harm, not only momentarily but also in the long run. Those who propose the food bank usually refer to a current "emergency" or "crisis" in terms of world food supply. But what is an emergency? Although they may be infrequent and sudden, everyone knows that emergencies will occur from time to time. A well-run family, company, organization or country prepares for the likelihood of accidents and emergencies. It expects them, it budgets for them, it saves for them.

What happens if some organizations or countries budget for acci- 23 dents and others do not? If each country is solely responsible for its own well-being, poorly managed ones will suffer. But they can learn from experience. They may mend their ways, and learn to budget for infrequent but certain emergencies. For example, the weather varies from year to year, and periodic crop failures are certain. A wise and competent government saves out of the production of the good years in anticipation of bad years to come. Joseph taught this policy to Pharoah in Egypt more than 2,000 years ago. Yet the great majority of the governments in the world today do not follow such a policy. They lack either the wisdom or the competence, or both. Should those nations that do manage to put something aside be forced to come to the rescue each time an emergency occurs among the poor nations?

"But it isn't their fault!" Some kind-hearted liberals argue, "How   24 can we blame the poor people who are caught in an emergency? Why must they suffer for the sins of their governments?" The concept of blame is simply not relevant here. The real question is, what are the operational consequences of establishing a world food bank? If it is open to every country every time a need develops, slovenly rulers will not be motivated to take Joseph's advice. Someone will always come to their aid. Some countries will deposit food in the world food bank, and others will withdraw it. There will be almost no overlap. As a result of such solutions to food shortage emergencies, the poor countries will not learn to mend their ways, and will suffer progressively greater emergencies as their populations grow.

On the average, poor countries undergo a 2.5 percent increase in   25 population each year; rich countries, about 0.8 percent. Only rich countries have anything in the way of food reserves set aside, and even they do not have as much as they should. Poor countries have none. If poor countries received no food from the outside, the rate of their population growth would be periodically checked by crop failures and famines. But if they can always draw on a world food bank in time of need, their population can continue to grow unchecked, and so will their "need" for aid. In the short run, a world food bank may diminish that need, but in the long run it actually increases the need without limit.

Without some system of worldwide food sharing, the proportion of   26 people in the rich and poor nations might eventually stabilize. The overpopulated poor countries would decrease in numbers, while the rich countries that had room for more people would increase. But with a well-meaning system of sharing, such as a world food bank, the growth differential between the rich and the poor countries will not only persist, it will increase. Because of the higher rate of population growth in the poor countries of the world, 88 percent of today's children are born poor, and only 12 percent rich. Year by year the ratio becomes worse, as the fast-reproducing poor outnumber the slow-reproducing rich.

A world food bank is thus a commons in disguise. People will have   27 more motivation to draw from it than to add to any common store. The less provident and less able will multiply at the expense of the abler and more provident, bringing eventual ruin upon all who share in the commons. Besides, any system of "sharing" that amounts to foreign aid from the rich nations to the poor nations will carry the taint of charity, which will contribute little to the world peace so devoutly desired by those who support the idea of a world food bank.

As past U.S. foreign-aid programs have amply and depressingly 28 demonstrated, international charity frequently inspires mistrust and antagonism rather than gratitude on the part of the recipient nation.

The modern approach to foreign aid stresses the export of technol- 29 ogy and advice, rather than money and food. As an ancient Chinese proverb goes: "Give a man a fish and he will eat for a day; teach him how to fish and he will eat for the rest of his days." Acting on this advice, the Rockefeller and Ford Foundations have financed a number of programs for improving agriculture in the hungry nations. Known as the "Green Revolution," these programs have led to the development of "miracle rice" and "miracle wheat," new strains that offer bigger harvests and greater resistance to crop damage. Norman Borlaug, the Nobel Prize winning agronomist who, supported by the Rockefeller Foundation, developed "miracle wheat," is one of the most prominent advocates of a world food bank.

Whether or not the Green Revolution can increase food production 30 as much as its champions claim is a debatable but possibly irrelevant point. Those who support this well-intended humanitarian effort should first consider some of the fundamentals of human ecology. Ironically, one man who did was the late Alan Gregg, a vice president of the Rockefeller Foundation. Two decades ago he expressed strong doubts about the wisdom of such attempts to increase food production. He likened the growth and spread of humanity over the surface of the earth to the spread of cancer in the human body, remarking that "cancerous growths demand food, but, as far as I know, they have never been cured by getting it."

Every human born constitutes a draft on all aspects of the environ- 31 ment: food, air, water, forests, beaches, wildlife, scenery and solitude. Food can, perhaps, be significantly increased to meet a growing demand. But what about clean beaches, unspoiled forests, and solitude? If we satisfy a growing population's need for food, we necessarily decrease its per capita supply of the other resources needed by men.

India, for example, now has a population of 600 million, which 32 increases by 15 million each year. This population already puts a huge load on a relatively impoverished environment. The country's forests are now only a small fraction of what they were three centuries ago, and floods and erosion continually destroy the insufficient farmland that remains. Every one of the 15 million new lives added to India's population puts an additional burden on the environment, and increases the economic and social costs of crowding. However human-itarian our intent, every Indian life saved through medical or nutri-tional assistance from abroad diminishes the quality of life for those who remain, and for subsequent generations. If rich countries make it possible, through foreign aid, for 600 million Indians to swell to 1.2 bil-lion in a mere 28 years, as their current growth rate threatens, will future generations of Indians thank us for hastening the destruction of their environment? Will our good intentions be sufficient excuse for the consequences of our actions?

My final example of a commons in action is one for which the pub- 33 lic has the least desire for rational discussion—immigration. Anyone who publicly questions the wisdom of current U.S. immigration policy is promptly charged with bigotry, prejudice, ethnocentrism, chauvin-ism, isolationism or selfishness. Rather than encounter such accusa-tions, one would rather talk about other matters, leaving immigration policy to wallow in the crosscurrents of special interests that take no account of the good of the whole, or the interests of posterity.

Perhaps we still feel guilty about things we said in the past. Two 34 generations ago the popular press frequently referred to Dagos, Wops, Polacks, Chinks and Krauts, in articles about how America was being "overrun" by foreigners of supposedly inferior genetic stock. But because the implied inferiority of foreigners was used then as justifica-tion for keeping them out, people now assume that restrictive policies could only be based on such misguided notions. There are other grounds.

Just consider the numbers involved. Our Government acknowl- 35 edges a net inflow of 400,000 immigrants a year. While we have no hard data on the extent of illegal entries, educated guesses put the figure at about 600,000 a year. Since the natural increase (excess of births over deaths) of the resident population now runs about 1.7 million per year, the yearly gain from immigration amounts to at least 19 percent of the total annual increase, and may be as much as 37 percent if we include the estimate for illegal immigrants. Considering the growing use of birth-control devices, the potential effect of educational campaigns by such organizations as Planned Parenthood Federation of America and Zero Population Growth, and the influence of inflation and the housing shortage, the fertility rate of American women may decline so much that immigration could account for all the yearly increase in population. Should we not at least ask if that is what we want?

For the sake of those who worry about whether the "quality" of the 36 average immigrant compares favorably with the quality of the average resident, let us assume that immigrants and nativeborn citizens are of exactly equal quality, however one defines that term. We will focus here only on quantity; and since our conclusions will depend on nothing else, all charges of bigotry and chauvinism become irrelevant.

World food banks *move food to the people*, hastening the exhaustion   37
of the environment of the poor countries. Unrestricted immigration, on
the other hand, *moves people to the food*, thus speeding up the destruction
of the environment of the rich countries. We can easily understand why
poor people should want to make this latter transfer, but why should
rich hosts encourage it?

As is the case of foreign-aid programs, immigration receives sup-   38
port from selfish interests and humanitarian impulses. The primary
selfish interest in unimpeded immigration is the desire of employers for
cheap labor, particularly in industries and trades that offer degrading
work. In the past, one wave of foreigners after another was brought into
the U.S. to work at wretched jobs for wretched wages. In recent years
the Cubans, Puerto Ricans and Mexicans have had this dubious honor.
The interests of the employers of cheap labor mesh well with the guilty
silence of the country's liberal intelligentsia. White Anglo-Saxon
Protestants are particularly reluctant to call for a closing of the doors to
immigration for fear of being called bigots.

But not all countries have such reluctant leadership. Most educated   39
Hawaiians, for example, are keenly aware of the limits of their environment, particularly in terms of population growth. There is only so much
room on the islands, and the islanders know it. To Hawaiians, immigrants from the other 49 states present as great a threat as those from
other nations. At a recent meeting of Hawaiian government officials in
Honolulu, I had the ironic delight of hearing a speaker, who like most
of his audience was of Japanese ancestry, ask how the country might
practically and constitutionally close its door to further immigration.
One member of the audience countered: "How can we shut the doors
now? We have many friends and relatives in Japan that we'd like to
bring here some day so that they can enjoy Hawaii too." The Japanese-
American speaker smiled sympathetically and answered: "Yes, but we
have children now, and someday we'll have grandchildren too. We can
bring more people here from Japan only by giving away some of the
land that we hope to pass on to our grandchildren some day. What right
do we have to do that?"

At this point, I can hear U.S. liberals asking: "How can you justify   40
slamming the door once you're inside? You say that immigrants should
be kept out. But aren't we all immigrants, or the descendants of immigrants? If we insist on staying, must we not admit all others?" Our craving for intellectual order leads us to seek and prefer symmetrical rules
and morals: a single rule for me and everybody else; the same rule yesterday, today and tomorrow. Justice, we feel, should not change with
time and place.

We Americans of non-Indian ancestry can look upon ourselves as   41
the descendants of thieves who are guilty morally, if not legally, of

stealing this land from its Indian owners. Should we then give back the land to the now living American descendants of those Indians? However morally or logically sound this proposal may be, I, for one, am unwilling to live by it and I know no one else who is. Besides, the logical consequence would be absurd. Suppose that, intoxicated with a sense of pure justice, we should decide to turn our land over to the Indians. Since all our other wealth has also been derived from the land, wouldn't we be morally obliged to give that back to the Indians too?

Clearly, the concept of pure justice produces an infinite regression to absurdity. Centuries ago, wise men invented statutes of limitations to justify the rejection of such pure justice, in the interest of preventing continual disorder. The law zealously defends property rights. Drawing a line after an arbitrary time has elapsed may be unjust, but the alternatives are worse. 42

We are all the descendants of thieves, and the world's resources are inequitably distributed. But we must begin the journey to tomorrow from the point where we are today. We cannot remake the past. We cannot safely divide the wealth equitably among all peoples so long as people reproduce at different rates. To do so would guarantee that our grandchildren, and everyone else's grandchildren, would have only a ruined world to inhabit. 43

To be generous with one's own possessions is quite different from being generous with those of posterity. We should call this point to the attention of those who, from a commendable love of justice and equality, would institute a system of the commons, either in the form of a world food bank, or of unrestricted immigration. We must convince them if we wish to save at least some parts of the world from environmental ruin. 44

Responding to Reading

1. Hardin presents his problem as one that has no comfortable solution. One alternative, welcoming all who wish to come into the lifeboat, is "complete justice, complete catastrophe" (6); the other, retaining the crucial "safety factor," is both "the only means of our survival" and "morally abhorrent to many people" (8–9). Does Hardin see these two alternatives as ethically and practically unacceptable? Do you? Is it really an either/or situation, or are there some solutions he ignores?
2. Does Hardin's use of the lifeboat metaphor clarify his arguments and present the problem he describes more in vivid terms? Or do you find it simplistic, distracting, or irrelevant?
3. In paragraph 2, Hardin asks, "But does everyone on earth have an equal right to an equal share of its resources?" That is, are some people more—or less—deserving than others? How would you answer this question?

DOG LAB

Claire McCarthy

A pediatrician at an inner-city clinic in Boston, Claire McCarthy graduated from Harvard Medical School and worked as a resident at Boston's Children's Hospital. During her medical training, she kept extensive journals to "help her understand the dramatic changes she was witnessing herself and the overwhelming events she was participating in at the hospital each day." These provided the basis of her book Learning How the Heart Beats: The Making of a Pediatrician *(1995), which physician and writer Richard Selzer (see p. 589) has called a "moving personal rendition of the anguish and the joy of one doctor's becoming."* McCarthy has also written articles for the *Boston Globe Magazine. In the following chapter from* Learning How the Heart Beats, *McCarthy recalls a controversial lab lesson in which students studied the cardiovascular system of a sedated living dog, a lesson culminating in the cutting open of the dog's chest and the dog's ultimate death.*

When I finished college and started medical school, the learning 1
changed fundamentally. Whereas in college I had been learning mostly
for learning's sake, learning in order to know something, in medical
school I was learning in order to *do* something, do the thing I wanted to
do with my life. It was exhilarating and at the same time a little scary.
My study now carried responsibility.

The most important course in the first year besides Anatomy was 2
Physiology, the study of the functions and processes of the human
body. It was the most fascinating subject I had ever studied. I found the
intricacies of the way the body works endlessly intriguing and ingenious: the way the nervous system is designed to differentiate a sharp
touch from a soft one; the way muscles move and work together to
throw a ball; the wisdom of the kidneys, which filter the blood and let
pass out only waste products and extra fluid, keeping everything else
carefully within. It was magical to me that each organ and system
worked so beautifully and in perfect concert with the rest of the body.

The importance of Physiology didn't lie just in the fact that it was 3
fascinating, however. The other courses I was taking that semester, like
Histology and Biochemistry, were fascinating, too. But because
Physiology was the study of how the body actually works, it seemed
the most pertinent to becoming a physician. The other courses were
more abstract. Physiology was practical, and I felt that my ability to
master Physiology would be a measure of my ability to be a doctor.

When the second-year students talked about Physiology, they 4 always mentioned "dog lab." They mentioned it briefly but significantly, sharing knowing looks. I gathered that it involved cutting dogs open and that it was controversial, but that was all I knew. I didn't pursue it, I didn't ask questions. That fall I was living day to day, lecture to lecture, test to test. My life was organized around putting as much information into my brain as possible, and I didn't pay much attention to anything else.

I would get up around six, make coffee, and eat my bowl of cereal 5 while I sat at my desk. There was nowhere else to sit in my dormitory room, and if I was going to sit at my desk, I figured I might as well study, so I always studied as I ate. I had a small refrigerator and a hot plate so that I could fix myself meals. After breakfast it was off to a morning of lectures, back to the room at lunchtime for a yogurt or soup and more studying, then afternoon lectures and labs. Before dinner I usually went for a run or a swim; although it was necessary for my sanity and my health, I always felt guilty that I wasn't studying instead. I ate dinner at my desk or with other medical students at the cafeteria in Beth Israel Hospital. We sat among the doctors, staff, and patients, eating our food quickly. Although we would try to talk about movies, current affairs, or other "nonmedical" topics, sooner or later we usually ended up talking about medicine; it was fast becoming our whole life. After dinner it was off to the eerie quiet of the library, where I sat surrounded by my textbooks and notes until I got tired or frustrated, which was usually around ten-thirty. Then I'd go back to the dorm, maybe chat with the other students on my floor, maybe watch television, probably study some more, and then fall asleep so that I could start the routine all over again the next morning.

My life had never been so consuming. Sometimes I felt like a true 6 student in the best sense of the word, wonderfully absorbed in learning; other times I felt like an automaton. I was probably a combination of the two. It bothered me sometimes that this process of teaching me to take care of people was making me live a very study-centered, self-centered life. However, it didn't seem as though I had a choice.

One day at the beginning of a physiology lecture the instructor 7 announced that we would be having a laboratory exercise to study the cardiovascular system, and that dogs would be used. The room was quickly quiet; this was the infamous "dog lab." The point of the exercise, he explained, was to study the heart and blood vessels in vivo,[1] to learn the effects of different conditions and chemicals by seeing them rather than just by reading about them. The dogs would be sedated and the changes in their heart rates, respiratory rates, and blood pressure

---

[1] Latin phrase for "in the living being." [Eds.]

would be monitored with each experiment. As the last part of the exercise the sleeping dogs' chests would be cut open so we could actually watch the hearts and lungs in action, and then the dogs would be killed, humanely. We would be divided up into teams of four, and each team would work with a teaching assistant. Because so many teaching assistants were required, the class would be divided in half, and the lab would be held on two days.

The amphitheater buzzed.   8

The lab was optional, the instructor told us. We would not be 9
marked off in any way if we chose not to attend. He leaned against the side of the podium and said that the way he saw it there was a spectrum of morality when it came to animal experimentation. The spectrum, he said, went from mice or rats to species like horses or apes, and we had to decide at which species we would draw our lines. He hoped, though, that we would choose to attend. It was an excellent learning opportunity, and he thought we ought to take advantage of it. Then he walked behind the podium and started the day's lecture.

It was all anyone could talk about: should we do dog lab or shouldn't 10
we? We discussed it endlessly.

There were two main camps. One was the "excellent learning 11
opportunity" camp, which insisted that dog lab was the kind of science we came to medical school to do and that learning about the cardiovascular system on a living animal would make it more understandable and would therefore make us better doctors.

Countering them was the "importance of a life" camp. The extreme 12
members of this camp insisted that it was always wrong to murder an animal for experimentation. The more moderate members argued that perhaps animal experimentation was useful in certain kinds of medical research, but that dog lab was purely an exercise for our education and didn't warrant the killing of a dog. We could learn the material in other ways, they said.

On and on the arguments went, with people saying the same things 13
over and over again in every conceivable way. There was something very important about this decision. Maybe it was because we were just beginning to figure out how to define ourselves as physicians—were we scientists, eager for knowledge, or were we defenders of life? The dog lab seemed to pit one against the other. Maybe it was because we thought that our lives as physicians were going to be filled with ethical decisions, and this was our first since entering medical school. It was very important that we do the right thing, but the right thing seemed variable and unclear.

I was quiet during these discussions. I didn't want to kill a dog, but 14
I certainly wanted to take advantage of every learning opportunity offered me. And despite the fact that the course instructor had said our

grades wouldn't be affected if we didn't attend the lab, I wasn't sure I believed him, and I didn't want to take any chances. Even if he didn't incorporate the lab report into our grades, I was worried that there would be some reference to it in the final exam, some sneaky way that he would bring it up. Doing well had become so important that I was afraid to trust anyone; doing well had become more important than anything.

I found myself waiting to see what other people would decide. I 15 was ashamed not to be taking a stand, but I was stuck in a way I'd never been before. I didn't like the idea of doing the lab; it felt wrong. Yet for some reason I was embarrassed that I felt that way, and the lab seemed so important. The more I thought about it, the more confused I became.

Although initially the students had appeared divided more or less 16 evenly between the camps, as the lab day drew nearer the majority chose to participate. The discussions didn't stop, but they were fewer and quieter. The issue seemed to become more private.

I was assigned to the second lab day. My indecision was becoming 17 a decision since I hadn't crossed my name off the list. I can still change my mind, I told myself. I'm not on a team yet, nobody's counting on me to show up. One of my classmates asked me to join his group. I hedged.

The day before group lists had to be handed in, the course instruc- 18 tor made an announcement. It was brief and almost offhand: he said that if any of us wished to help anesthetize the dogs for the lab, we were welcome to do so. He told us where to go and when to be there for each lab day. I wrote the information down.

Somehow, this was what I needed. I made my decision. I would do 19 the lab, but I would go help anesthetize the dogs first.

Helping with the anesthesia, I thought, would be taking full respon- 20 sibility for what I was doing, something that was very important to me. I was going to *face* what I was doing, see the dogs awake with their tails wagging instead of meeting them asleep and sort of pretending they weren't real. I also thought it might make me feel better to know that the dogs were treated well as they were anesthetized and to be there, help- ing to do it gently. Maybe in part I thought of it as my penance.

The day of the first lab came. Around five o'clock I went down to 21 the Friday afternoon "happy hour" in the dormitory living room to talk to the students as they came back. They came back singly or in pairs, quiet, looking dazed. They threw down their coats and backpacks and made their way to the beer and soda without talking to anyone. Some, once they had a cup in their hands, seemed to relax and join in conver- sations; others took their cups and sat alone on the couches. They all looked tired, worn out.

"Well?" I asked several of them. "What was it like?"   22

Most shrugged and said little. A few said that it was interesting and 23
that they'd learned a lot, but they said it without any enthusiasm. Every
one of them said it was hard. I thought I heard someone say that their
dog had turned out to be pregnant. Nobody seemed happy.

The morning of my lab was gray and dreary. I overslept, which I 24
hardly ever do. I got dressed quickly and went across the street to the
back entrance of the lab building. It was quiet and still and a little dark.
The streets were empty except for an occasional cab. I found the open
door and went in.

There was only one other student waiting there, a blond-haired 25
woman named Elise. I didn't know her well. We had friends in common, but we'd never really talked. She was sweet and soft-spoken; she
wore old jeans and plaid flannel shirts and hung out with the activist
crowd. She had always intimidated me. I felt as though I weren't political enough when I was around her. I was actually a little surprised that
she was doing the lab at all, as many of her friends had chosen not to.

We greeted each other awkwardly, nodding hello and taking our 26
places leaning against the wall. Within a few minutes one of the teaching assistants came in, said good morning, pulled out some keys, and
let us into a room down the hall. Two more teaching assistants followed
shortly.

The teaching assistants let the dogs out of cages, and they ran 27
around the room. They were small dogs; I think they were beagles. They
seemed happy to be out of their cages, and one of them, white with
brown spots, came over to me with his tail wagging. I leaned over to pet
him, and he licked my hand, looking up at me eagerly. I stood up again
quickly.

The teaching assistant who had let us in, a short man with tousled 28
brown hair and thick glasses, explained that the dogs were to be given
intramuscular injections of a sedative that would put them to sleep.
During the lab they would be given additional doses intravenously as
well as other medications to stop them from feeling pain. We could
help, he said, by holding the dogs while they got their injections. Elise
and I nodded.

So we held the dogs, and they got their injections. After a few min- 29
utes they started to stumble, and we helped them to the floor. I remember that Elise petted one of the dogs as he fell asleep and that she cried.
I didn't cry, but I wanted to.

When we were finished, I went back to my room. I sat at my desk, 30
drank my coffee, and read over the lab instructions again. I kept thinking about the dogs running around, about the little white one with the
brown spots, and I felt sick. I stared at the instructions without really
reading them, looking at my watch every couple of minutes. At five

minutes before eight I picked up the papers, put them in my backpack with my books, and left.

The lab was held in a big open room with white walls and lots of windows. The dogs were laid out on separate tables lined up across the room; they were on their backs, tied down. They were all asleep, but some of them moved slightly, and it chilled me.

We walked in slowly and solemnly, putting our coats and back-packs on the rack along the wall and going over to our assigned tables. I started to look for the dog who had licked my hand, but I stopped myself. I didn't want to know where he was.

Our dog was brown and black, with soft floppy ears. His eyes were shut. He looked familiar. We took our places, two on each side of the table, laid out our lab manuals, and began.

The lab took all day. We cut through the dog's skin to find an artery and vein, into which we placed catheters. We injected different drugs and chemicals and watched what happened to the dog's heart rate and blood pressure, carefully recording the results. At the end of the day, when we were done with the experiments, we cut open the dog's chest. We cut through his sternum and pulled open his rib cage. His heart and lungs lay in front of us. The heart was a fist-size muscle that squeezed itself as it beat, pushing blood out. The lungs were white and solid and glistening under the pleura that covered them. The instructor pointed out different blood vessels, like the aorta and the superior vena cava. He showed us the stellate ganglion, which really did look like a star. I think we used the electrical paddles of a defibrillator and shocked the dog's heart into ventricular fibrillation, watching it shiver like Jell-O in front of us. I think that's how we killed them—or maybe it was with a lethal dose of one of the drugs. I'm not sure. It's some-thing I guess I don't want to remember.

Dan was the anesthesiologist, the person assigned to making sure that the dog stayed asleep throughout the entire procedure. Every once in a while Dan would get caught up in the experiment and the dog would start to stir. I would nudge Dan, and he would quickly give more medication. The dog never actually woke up, but every time he moved even the slightest bit, every time I had to think about him being a real dog who was never going to wag his tail or lick anyone's hand again because of us, I got so upset that I couldn't concentrate. In fact, I had trouble concentrating on the lab in general. I kept staring at the dog.

As soon as we were finished, or maybe a couple of minutes before, I left. I grabbed my coat and backpack and ran down the stairs out into the dusk of the late afternoon. It was drizzling, and the medical school looked brown and gray. I walked quickly toward the street.

I was disappointed in the lab and disappointed in myself for doing it. I knew now that doing the lab was wrong. Maybe not wrong for everyone—it was clearly a complicated and individual choice—but wrong for me. The knowledge I had gained wasn't worth the life of a dog to me. I felt very sad.

The drizzle was becoming rain. I slowed down; even though it was 38 cold, the rain felt good. A couple of people walking past me put up their umbrellas. I let the rain fall on me. I wanted to get wet.

From the moment you enter the field of medicine as a medical stu- 39 dent, you have an awareness that you have entered something bigger and more important than you are. Doctors are different from other people, we are told implicitly, if not explicitly. Medicine is a way of life, with its own values and guidelines for daily living. They aren't bad values; they include things like the importance of hard work, the pursuit of knowledge, and the preservation of life—at least human life. There's room for individuality and variation, but that's something I realized later, much later. When I started medical school I felt that not only did I have to learn information and skills, I had to become a certain kind of person, too. It was very important to me to learn to do the thing that a doctor would do in a given situation. Since the course instructor, who represented Harvard Medical School to me, had recommended that we do the lab, I figured that a doctor would do it. That wasn't the only reason I went ahead with the lab, but it was a big reason.

The rain started to come down harder and felt less pleasant. I 40 walked more quickly, across Longwood Avenue into Vanderbilt Hall. I could hear familiar voices coming from the living room, but I didn't feel like talking to anyone. I ducked into the stairwell.

I got to my room, locked the door behind me, took off my coat, and 41 lay down on my bed. The rain beat against my window. It was the time I usually went running, but the thought of going back out in the rain didn't appeal to me at all. I was suddenly very tired.

As I lay there I thought about the course instructor's discussion of 42 the spectrum of morality and drawing lines. Maybe it's not a matter of deciding which animals I feel comfortable killing, I thought. Maybe it's about drawing different kinds of lines: drawing the lines to define how much of myself I will allow to change. I was proud of being a true student, even if it did mean becoming a little like an automaton. But I still needed to be the person I was before; I needed to be able to make some decisions without worrying about what a doctor would do.

I got up off the bed, opened a can of soup, and put it in a pan on the 43 hot plate to warm. I got some bread and cheese out of the refrigerator, sat down at my desk, and opened my Biochemistry text.

Suddenly I stopped. I closed the text, reached over, and turned on 44 the television, which sat on a little plastic table near the desk. There would be time to study later. I was going to watch television, read a newspaper, and call some friends I hadn't called since starting medical school. It was time to make some changes, some changes back.

Responding to Reading

1. Summarize the two main schools of thought about whether or not to participate in "dog lab." Do the students really have a choice? Explain.
2. Why does McCarthy decide to help anesthesize the dogs? Does her decision make sense to you?
3. Does McCarthy believe that the knowledge she has gained is worth the sacrifice of the dog? Do you agree with her? Do you think her experience in "dog lab" changed her? Do you think it will make her a better doctor? Explain.

DIRTY NEEDLE

Nicholas Jenkins

A writer with a particular interest in the arts, Nicholas Jenkins was an associate editor with the monthly periodical ARTnews *until 1993. Currently Jenkins is a freelancer based in New York City. In the following opinion essay, originally published in the* New Yorker *magazine in December 1994, Jenkins argues that proponents of the death penalty are hypocritical when they promote lethal injection as a "humane" form of execution; he believes they should "drop the cant about decency and concern" so the public can face the stark fact that "execution is still a killing, a legal homicide."*

Conscience argues against its ethos, statistics confirm its racial bias, skepticism revolts from its finality, and economics warns of its costs, yet the death penalty, like some unkillable movie gorgon, keeps coming. To slow its progress, opponents call its social effectiveness a myth. Proponents, although they usually don't come out and say so, know that the mythical, phantasmal aspects of the death penalty are precisely what account for its persistence.

Part of the myth—the symmetrical-justice part—is obvious, even to the convicted. Robert Lowell,[1] imprisoned in 1943 as a conscientious objector, found himself in Manhattan's West Street Jail alongside Louis (Lepke) Buchalter, the boss of Murder, Inc., who was awaiting electrocution. The prospect of the chair, Lowell wrote in a poem, shimmered before the enfeebled gangster like a mysterious gateway back to the violent highs of his youth, "an oasis in his air/of lost connections." For sizable segments of the electorate, too, capital punishment is a mirage

---

[1] American poet (1917–1977). [Eds.]

promising a return to a more "connected" world—a dream solution to a nightmare of social despair.

In order to survive, the death penalty must adapt to other fantasies 3 as well, prominent among them the wish to kill without making a show of it and without assuming the guilt that comes with inflicting pain. The search for mechanisms that execute cleanly and, by prevailing standards, humanely, which has been going on ever since drawing-and-quartering[2] gave way to the guillotine, continually forces death-penalty enthusiasts to compromise their (demonstrably false) deterrence argument by finding venues that are ever more private and methods that seem ever less overtly cruel.

New York has a special niche in this history. Slightly more than a 4 century ago, the state's governor appointed a panel—popularly known as the Death Commission—to provide him with an acceptable alternative to hanging. (Among the options rejected at the time was lethal injection.) The commission recommended the application of electric current as the most rapid and painless method available. Electricity, the symbol of modern civilization, would dispatch that civilization's irredeemably corrupted elements like a light bulb banishing darkness. The world's first electrocution took place at Auburn State Prison on August 6, 1890. William Kemmler was the convict. In the days before the execution, newspapers hailed the new method as "euthanasia by electricity." (After seeing Kemmler convulsed in the chair, after smelling his burning flesh, and noticing the "purplish foam" that spilled from his mouth, witnesses were less certain.) The man who pulled the switch, Edwin F. Davis, New York's first state electrician, was accounted a gentle soul, dutiful but concerned for the creatures in his care. Davis's hobby was beekeeping—a pastime in which, as a hooded intruder pillaging the hive and suffering the stings of the enraged bee-citizens, he could act out a vivid rite of identification with his prisoners.

What could be just barely presented as humane a century ago—and 5 still survives as a method of execution in twelve states—is now widely felt to be repugnant, obsolete, barbarous. To do to animals what is routinely done to people can even be criminal: in California, Cynthia McFadden, of ABC News, reported not long ago, prosecutions are under way against chinchilla ranchers who electrocute their animals. The American Veterinary Medical Association's guidelines for animal euthanasia sternly specify that for a creature to be killed humanely it must be rendered unconscious before it is jolted.

As electrocution has lost favor, lethal injection has gained ground. 6 (It is now lawful in twenty-seven states—more than two-thirds of those that execute.) This method, drawing on the iconography of doctorly

---

[2] Medieval form of execution. The victim, still alive, was first hanged and then split down the middle with a sword and chopped into four pieces. [Eds.]

efficiency, kindness, and discretion, conforms to a national habit of med-icalizing everything from laziness to incest. The lethal injection got its biggest public boost from the pioneer of high-tech, clean-war solutions to the nation's military needs. In 1973, when he was governor of California, Ronald Reagan likened executing a criminal with an injec-tion to the best way of dealing with a doomed horse: "You call the vet-erinarian and the vet gives it a shot and the horse goes to sleep—that's it." Just as external enemies would be fought with lasers and "surgical" strikes, so, under the dispensation of the needle, the internal enemy could be made to glide away as smoothly as King Arthur in his barge, drifting into the mist.[3]

The fact is that lethal injections aren't uncomplicated or foolproof. 7 In roughly one out of four cases, there are likely to be difficulties in locating a vein for the catheter through which a sedative, a paralytic agent, and a heart-stopping chemical must flow into the prisoner's body. When the probing fails, it can be necessary to perform a venous cutdown—a bloody procedure—to make a viable opening. (In 1985, in Texas, it took forty minutes of gurney time to pierce a vein in Stephen Peter Morin's body.) If the catheter misses a vein and instead penetrates subcutaneous tissue—always a possibility, since, despite the aura of medical ceremony surrounding lethal injections, doctors are forbidden to perform them—the sedative may wear off and the prisoner awaken while he or she is suffocating. In addition, just as the length of the drop was always a chancy calculation for the hangman, correct doses are dif-ficult to assess for convicts with serious alcohol or drug histories.

The fantasy that electrocution and, now, injection are steps toward 8 decency remains a powerful one. But what casts this humanitarianism in a different light and reveals the true object of its solicitude is some of the smaller procedures preceding an execution. In the states that elec-trocute, a prisoner may be invited (or forced) to put on a diaper before leaving the condemned cell for the last time. Muscle spasms mean that convicts usually defecate and urinate while they are in the all-powerful grip of the electric current. This sanitary etiquette has little to do with the needs of the prisoner and much to do with the sensibilities of those who carry out and witness the execution. Even more grotesque morally (because it involves an active denial of what is taking place) is the prac-tice during execution by injection of swabbing the prisoner's forearm, as if to insure that the puncture wound won't become infected. It is hard to avoid the conclusion that an important part of the evolving technology of execution is driven by a need to find a process that seems bland enough to allow the death penalty itself to persist. The methods

---

[3] In the medieval English legends, the noble Arthur, fatally wounded in battle, sails for the island of Avalon, never to return. [Eds.]

of execution have as much to do with a wish not to trouble our own tender consciences as with a desire not to cause pain to someone else.

Nobody yet knows whether it is to be back to the electric chair or in 9 with the needle in New York. But, with Governor-elect Pataki[4] and the legislature preparing to reintroduce executions, it's a good time to drop the cant about decency and concern. However advanced the aesthetics of state death, an execution is still a killing, a legal homicide. That fact ought to be faced in all its starkness, not wrapped in a veil of morally neutral, medico-technical mystification. If history is a guide, the lethal injection will look as sickening a hundred years from now as the electric chair does today. Decency will not be served until everyone has come to understand that the only good death-penalty statute is a repealed one.

Responding to Reading

1. What does Jenkins mean when he calls the death penalty "a dream solution to a nightmare of social despair" (2)? What, according to Jenkins, is wrong with this "dream solution"?
2. Does your own position on the death penalty differ from Jenkins's? What do you see as the advantages and disadvantages of the death penalty?
3. Much of Jenkins's discussion describes the search for a humane method of execution. Why do you think people look so hard for a humane method? Do you think it is possible for an execution to be humane, or do you see this as a contradiction in terms? Explain your reasoning.

THE PERILS OF OBEDIENCE

Stanley Milgram

Social psychologist Stanley Milgram (1932–1984) is best known for experiments that study aggression and human conformity, especially obedience. He has said that "it is only the person dwelling in isolation who is not forced to respond, with defiance or submission, to the commands of others." Milgram uses Nazi Germany as a tragic example of submission to obedience. The following selection is from his book Obedience to Authority (1974). *In this essay, Milgram's descriptions of some of his experiments on obedience raise perplexing moral questions.*

---

[4] In 1994, conservative George Pataki defeated Mario Cuomo, a staunch opponent of capital punishment, for the New York governorship. [Eds.]

Obedience is as basic an element in the structure of social life as one 1
can point to. Some system of authority is a requirement of all communal living, and it is only the person dwelling in isolation who is not
forced to respond, with defiance or submission, to the commands of
others. For many people, obedience is a deeply ingrained behavior tendency, indeed a potent impulse overriding training in ethics, sympathy,
and moral conduct.

The dilemma inherent in submission to authority is ancient, as old 2
as the story of Abraham,[1] and the question of whether one should obey
when commands conflict with conscience has been argued by Plato,
dramatized in *Antigone*,[2] and treated to philosophic analysis in almost
every historical epoch. Conservative philosophers argue that the very
fabric of society is threatened by disobedience, while humanists stress
the primacy of the individual conscience.

The legal and philosophic aspects of obedience are of enormous 3
import, but they say very little about how most people behave in concrete situations. I set up a simple experiment at Yale University to test
how much pain an ordinary citizen would inflict on another person
simply because he was ordered to by an experimental scientist. Stark
authority was pitted against the subjects' strongest moral imperatives
against hurting others, and, with the subjects' ears ringing with the
screams of the victims, authority won more often than not. The extreme
willingness of adults to go to almost any lengths on the command of an
authority constitutes the chief finding of the study and the fact most
urgently demanding explanation.

In the basic experimental design, two people come to a psychology 4
laboratory to take part in a study of memory and learning. One of them
is designated as a "teacher" and the other a "learner." The experimenter
explains that the study is concerned with the effects of punishment on
learning. The learner is conducted into a room, seated in a kind of
miniature electric chair; his arms are strapped to prevent excessive
movement, and an electrode is attached to his wrist. He is told that he
will be read lists of simple word pairs, and that he will then be tested on
his ability to remember the second word of a pair when he hears the first
one again. Whenever he makes an error, he will receive electric shocks
of increasing intensity.

The real focus of the experiment is the teacher. After watching the 5
learner being strapped into place, he is seated before an impressive
shock generator. The instrument panel consists of thirty lever switches

---

[1] Abraham, commanded by God to sacrifice his son Isaac, is ready to do so until an angel stops him.
[Eds.]

[2] In Plato's *Apology*, the philosopher Socrates provokes and accepts the sentence of death rather
than act against his conscience; the heroine of Sophocles' *Antigone* risks a death sentence in order to
give her brother a proper burial. [Eds.]

set in a horizontal line. Each switch is clearly labeled with a voltage designation ranging from 15 to 450 volts. The following designations are clearly indicated for groups of four switches, going from left to right: Slight Shock, Moderate Shock, Strong Shock, Very Strong Shock, Intense Shock, Extreme Intensity Shock, Danger: Severe Shock. (Two switches after this last designation are simply marked XXX.)

When a switch is depressed, a pilot light corresponding to each 6 switch is illuminated in bright red; an electric buzzing is heard; a blue light, labeled "voltage energizer," flashes; the dial on the voltage meter swings to the right; and various relay clicks sound off.

The upper left-hand corner of the generator is labeled SHOCK GEN- 7 ERATOR, TYPE ZLB, DYSON INSTRUMENT COMPANY, WALTHAM, MASS. OUTPUT 15 VOLTS–450 VOLTS.

Each subject is given a sample 45-volt shock from the generator 8 before his run as teacher, and the jolt strengthens his belief in the authenticity of the machine.

The teacher is a genuinely naïve subject who has come to the labo- 9 ratory for the experiment. The learner, or victim, is actually an actor who receives no shock at all. The point of the experiment is to see how far a person will proceed in a concrete and measurable situation in which he is ordered to inflict increasing pain on a protesting victim.

Conflict arises when the man receiving the shock begins to show 10 that he is experiencing discomfort. At 75 volts, he grunts; at 120 volts, he complains loudly; at 150, he demands to be released from the experiment. As the voltage increases, his protests become more vehement and emotional. At 285 volts, his response can be described only as an agonized scream. Soon thereafter, he makes no sound at all.

For the teacher, the situation quickly becomes one of gripping 11 tension. It is not a game for him; conflict is intense and obvious. The manifest suffering of the learner presses him to quit; but each time he hesitates to administer a shock, the experimenter orders him to continue. To extricate himself from this plight, the subject must make a clear break with authority.[3]

The subject, Gretchen Brandt,[4] is an attractive thirty-one-year-old 12 medical technician who works at the Yale Medical School. She had emigrated from Germany five years before.

On several occasions when the learner complains, she turns to the 13 experimenter coolly and inquires, "Shall I continue"? She promptly returns to her task when the experimenter asks her to do so. At the

---

[3] The ethical problems of carrying out an experiment of this sort are too complex to be dealt with here, but they receive extended treatment in the book from which this article is adapted. [The book is *Obedience to Authority* (New York: Harper & Row, 1974)—Eds.]

[4] Names of subjects described in this piece have been changed.

administration of 210 volts, she turns to the experimenter, remarking firmly, "Well, I'm sorry, I don't think we should continue."

> EXPERIMENTER: The experiment requires that you go on until he has learned all the word pairs correctly.
> BRANDT: He has a heart condition, I'm sorry. He told you that before.
> EXPERIMENTER: The shocks may be painful but they are not dangerous.
> BRANDT: Well, I'm sorry, I think when shocks continue like this, they are dangerous. You ask him if he wants to get out. It's his free will.
> EXPERIMENTER: It is absolutely essential that we continue . . .
> BRANDT: I'd like you to ask him. We came here of our free will. If he wants to continue I'll go ahead. He told you he had a heart condition. I'm sorry. I don't want to be responsible for anything happening to him. I wouldn't like it for me either.
> EXPERIMENTER: You have no other choice.
> BRANDT: I think we are here on our own free will. I don't want to be responsible if anything happens to him. Please understand that.

She refuses to go further and the experiment is terminated. 14

The woman is firm and resolute throughout. She indicates in the 15 interview that she was in no way tense or nervous, and this corresponds to her controlled appearance during the experiment. She feels that the last shock she administered to the learner was extremely painful and reiterates that she "did not want to be responsible for any harm to him."

The woman's straightforward, courteous behavior in the experi- 16 ment, lack of tension, and total control of her own action seem to make disobedience a simple and rational deed. Her behavior is the very embodiment of what I envisioned would be true for almost all subjects.

Before the experiments, I sought predictions about the outcome 17 from various kinds of people—psychiatrists, college sophomores, middle-class adults, graduate students and faculty in the behavioral sciences. With remarkable similarity, they predicted that virtually all subjects would refuse to obey the experimenter. The psychiatrists specifically predicted that most subjects would not go beyond 150 volts, when the victim makes his first explicit demand to be freed. They expected that only 4 percent would reach 300 volts, and that only a pathological fringe of about one in a thousand would administer the highest shock on the board.

These predictions were unequivocally wrong. Of the forty subjects 18 in the first experiment, twenty-five obeyed the orders of the experimenter to the end, punishing the victim until they reached the most potent shock available on the generator. After 450 volts were administered three times, the experimenter called a halt to the sessions. Many obedient subjects then heaved sighs of relief, mopped their brows, rubbed their fingers over their eyes, or nervously fumbled cigarettes. Others displayed only minimal signs of tension from beginning to end.

When the very first experiments were carried out, Yale undergrad- 19
uates were used as subjects, and about 60 percent of them were fully
obedient. A colleague of mine immediately dismissed these findings as
having no relevance to "ordinary" people, asserting that Yale undergraduates are a highly aggressive, competitive bunch who step on each
other's necks on the slightest provocation. He assured me that when
"ordinary" people were tested, the results would be quite different. As
we moved from the pilot studies to the regular experimental series, people drawn from every stratum of New Haven life came to be employed
in the experiment: professionals, white-collar workers, unemployed
persons, and industrial workers. *The experimental outcome was the same as
we had observed among the students.*

Moreover, when the experiments were repeated in Princeton, 20
Munich, Rome, South Africa, and Australia, the level of obedience was
invariably somewhat *higher* than found in the investigation reported in
this article. Thus one scientist in Munich found 85 percent of his subjects
obedient.

Fred Prozi's reactions, if more dramatic than most, illuminate the 21
conflicts experienced by others in less visible form. About fifty years old
and unemployed at the time of the experiment, he has a good-natured,
if slightly dissolute, appearance, and he strikes people as a rather ordinary fellow. He begins the session calmly but becomes tense as it proceeds. After delivering the 180-volt shock, he pivots around in his chair
and, shaking his head, addresses the experimenter in agitated tones:

PROZI: I can't stand it. I'm not going to kill that man in there. You hear
him hollering?
EXPERIMENTER: As I told you before, the shocks may be painful, but . . .
PROZI: But he's hollering. He can't stand it. What's going to happen to
him?
EXPERIMENTER (his voice is patient, matter-of-fact): The experiment
requires that you continue, Teacher.
PROZI: Aaah, but, unh, I'm not going to get that man sick in there—
know what I mean?
EXPERIMENTER: Whether the learner likes it or not, we must go on,
through all the word pairs.
PROZI: I refuse to take the responsibility. He's in there hollering!
EXPERIMENTER: It's absolutely essential that you continue, Prozi.
PROZI (indicating the unused questions): There's too many left here, I
mean, Jeez, if he gets them wrong, there's too many of them left. I
mean, who's going to take the responsibility if anything happens to
that gentleman?
EXPERIMENTER: I'm responsible for anything that happens to him.
Continue, please.
PROZI: All right. (Consults list of words.) The next one's "Slow—walk,
truck, dance, music." Answer, please. (A buzzing sound indicates the

learner has signaled his answer.) Wrong. A hundred and ninety-five volts. "Dance." (Zzumph!)

LEARNER (yelling): Let me out of here! My heart's bothering me! (Teacher looks at experimenter.)

EXPERIMENTER: Continue, please.

LEARNER (screaming): Let me out of here! You have no right to keep me here! Let me out of here, my heart's bothering me, let me out!

PROZI (shakes head, pats the table nervously): You see, he's hollering. Hear that? Gee, I don't know.

EXPERIMENTER: The experiment requires . . .

PROZI (interrupting): I know it does, sir, but I mean—hunh! He don't know what he's getting in for. He's up to 195 volts! (Experiment continues, through 210 volts, 225 volts, 240 volts, 255 volts, 270 volts, at which point Prozi, with evident relief, runs out of word-pair questions.)

EXPERIMENTER: You'll have to go back to the beginning of that page and go through them again until he's learned them all correctly.

PROZI: Aw, no. I'm not going to kill that man. You mean I've got to keep going up with the scale? No sir. He's hollering in there. I'm not going to give him 450 volts.

EXPERIMENTER: The experiment requires that you go on.

LEARNER: Ohhh. I absolutely refuse to answer anymore. (Shouting urgently now.) Let me out of here! You can't hold me here! Get me out. Get-me-out-of-here!

EXPERIMENTER: Continue. The next word is "Green," please.

PROZI: "Green—grass, hat, ink, apple." (Nothing happens. No answering buzz. Just gloomy silence.)

PROZI: I don't think he is going to answer.

EXPERIMENTER: If the learner doesn't answer in a reasonable time, about four or five seconds, consider the answer wrong. And follow the same procedures you have been doing for wrong answers. Say, "Wrong," tell him the number of volts, give him the punishment, read him the correct answer. Continue, please.

PROZI: "Green—grass, hat, ink, apple." Answer, please. (More silence. Subject just sits there.)

EXPERIMENTER: Go on with the procedure, please.

PROZI: Three hundred and fifteen volts. The answer is "ink." (Zzumph!)

LEARNER: Ohh. Oooohh.

PROZI (relieved to hear response): Next one . . .

LEARNER: I absolutely refuse to answer.

PROZI: You got to. You get a shock if you don't answer. (Experiment continues with learner refusing to answer, and, finally, failing even to grunt or groan. At 375 volts, the subject stands up.)

PROZI: I think something's happening to that fellow in there. I don't get no answer. He was hollering at less voltage. Can't you check in and see if he's all right, please?

EXPERIMENTER (with same detached calm): Not once we've started. Please continue, Teacher.

PROZI (sits down, sighs deeply): "Cool—day, shade, water, paint." Answer, please. Are you all right in there? Are you all right?

EXPERIMENTER: Please continue, Teacher. Continue, please. (Subject pushes lever. Zzumph!)

PROZI (swiveling around in his chair): Something's happened to that man in there. (Swiveling back.) Next one. "Low—dollar, necklace, moon, paint." (Turning around again.) Something's happened to that man in there. You better check in on him, sir. He won't answer or nothing.

EXPERIMENTER: Continue. Go on, please.

PROZI: You accept all responsibility?

EXPERIMENTER: The responsibility is mine. Correct. Please go on. (Subject returns to his list, starts running through words as rapidly as he can read them, works through to 450 volts.)

PROZI: That's that.

EXPERIMENTER: Continue using the 450 switch for each wrong answer. Continue, please.

PROZI: But I don't get anything!

EXPERIMENTER: Please continue. The next word is "white."

PROZI: Don't you think you should look in on him, please?

EXPERIMENTER: Not once we've started the experiment.

PROZI: What if he's dead in there? (Gestures toward the room with the electric chair.) I mean, he told me he can't stand the shock, sir. I don't mean to be rude, but I think you should look in on him. All you have to do is look in on him. All you have to do is look in the door. I don't get no answer, no noise. Something might have happened to the gentleman in there, sir.

EXPERIMENTER: We must continue. Go on, please.

PROZI: You mean keep giving him what? Four-hundred-fifty volts, what he's got now?

EXPERIMENTER: That's correct. Continue. The next word is "white."

PROZI (now at a furious pace): "White—cloud, horse, rock, house." Answer, please. The answer is "horse." Four hundred and fifty volts. (Zzumph!) Next word, "Bag—paint, music, clown, girl." The answer is "paint." Four hundred and fifty volts. (Zzumph!) Next word is "Short—sentence, movie . . ."

EXPERIMENTER: Excuse me, Teacher. We'll have to discontinue the experiment.

Morris Braverman, another subject, is a thirty-nine-year-old social 22 worker. He looks older than his years because of his bald head and serious demeanor. His brow is furrowed, as if all the world's burdens were carried on his face. He appears intelligent and concerned.

When the learner refuses to answer and the experimenter instructs 23 Braverman to treat the absence of an answer as equivalent to a wrong answer, he takes his instruction to heart. Before administering 300 volts he asserts officiously to the victim, "Mr. Wallace, your silence has to be considered as a wrong answer." Then he administers the shock. He offers halfheartedly to change places with the learner, then asks the experimenter. "Do I have to follow these instructions literally?" He is satisfied with the experimenter's answer that he does. His very refined and authoritative manner of speaking is increasingly broken up by wheezing laughter.

The experimenter's notes on Mr. Braverman at the last few shocks 24 are:

Almost breaking up now each time gives shock. Rubbing face to hide 25 *laughter.*

Squinting, trying to hide face with hand, still laughing. 26

Cannot control his laughter at this point no matter what he does. 27

Clenching fist, pushing it onto table. 28

In an interview after the session, Mr. Braverman summarizes the 29 experiment with impressive fluency and intelligence. He feels the experiment may have been designed also to "test the effects on the teacher of being in an essentially sadistic role, as well as the reactions of a student to a learning situation that was authoritative and punitive." When asked how painful the last few shocks administered to the learner were, he indicates that the most extreme category on the scale is not adequate (it read EXTREMELY PAINFUL) and places his mark at the edge of the scale with an arrow carrying it beyond the scale.

It is almost impossible to convey the greatly relaxed, sedate quality 30 of his conversation in the interview. In the most relaxed terms, he speaks about his severe inner tension.

EXPERIMENTER: At what point were you most tense or nervous?
MR. BRAVERMAN: Well, when he first began to cry out in pain, and I realized this was hurting him. This got worse when he just blocked and refused to answer. There was I. I'm a nice person, I think, hurting somebody, and caught up in what seemed a mad situation . . . and in the interest of science, one goes through with it.

When the interviewer pursues the general question of tension, Mr. 31 Braverman spontaneously mentions his laughter.

"My reactions were awfully peculiar. I don't know if you were 32 watching me, but my reactions were giggly, and trying to stifle laughter. This isn't the way I usually am. This was a sheer reaction to a totally impossible situation. And my reaction was to the situation of having to hurt somebody. And being totally helpless and caught up in a set of circumstances where I just couldn't deviate and I couldn't try to help. This is what got me."

Mr. Braverman, like all subjects, was told the actual nature and pur- 33 pose of the experiment, and a year later he affirmed in a questionnaire that he had learned something of personal importance: "What appalled me was that I could possess this capacity for obedience and compliance to a central idea, i.e., the value of a memory experiment, even after it became clear that continued adherence to this value was at the expense of violation of another value, i.e., don't hurt someone who is helpless and not hurting you. As my wife said, 'You can call yourself Eichmann.[5] I hope I deal more effectively with any future conflicts of values I encounter."

One theoretical interpretation of this behavior holds that all people 34 harbor deeply aggressive instincts continually pressing for expression, and that the experiment provides institutional justification for the release of these impulses. According to this view, if a person is placed in a situation in which he has complete power over another individual, whom he may punish as much as he likes, all that is sadistic and bestial in man comes to the fore. The impulse to shock the victim is seen to flow from the potent aggressive tendencies, which are part of the motivational life of the individual, and the experiment, because it provides social legitimacy, simply opens the door to their expression.

It becomes vital, therefore, to compare the subject's performance 35 when he is under orders and when he is allowed to choose the shock level.

The procedure was identical to our standard experiment, except that 36 the teacher was told that he was free to select any shock level on any of the trials. (The experimenter took pains to point out that the teacher could use the highest levels on the generator, the lowest, any in between, or any combination of levels.) Each subject proceeded for thirty critical trials. The learner's protests were coordinated to standard shock levels, his first grunt coming at 75 volts, his first vehement protest at 150 volts.

The average shock used during the thirty critical trials was less than 37 60 volts—lower than the point at which the victim showed the first signs of discomfort. Three of the forty subjects did not go beyond the very lowest level on the board, twenty-eight went no higher than 75 volts, and thirty-eight did not go beyond the first loud protest at 150 volts. Two subjects provided the exception, administering up to 325 and 450 volts, but the overall result was that the great majority of people delivered very low, usually painless, shocks when the choice was explicitly up to them.

This condition of the experiment undermines another commonly 38 offered explanation of the subjects' behavior—that those who shocked the victim at the most severe levels came only from the sadistic fringe of society. If one considers that almost two-thirds of the participants fall into the category of "obedient" subjects, and that they represented ordinary people drawn from working, managerial, and professional classes, the argument becomes very shaky. Indeed, it is highly reminiscent of the

[5] Nazi officer, executed in 1962, who engineered the mass extermination of Jews. Many concentration camp officials defended themselves afterward by saying they were "just following orders." [Eds.]

issue that arose in connection with Hannah Arendt's 1963 book, *Eichmann in Jerusalem.* Arendt contended that the prosecution's effort to depict Eichmann as a sadistic monster was fundamentally wrong, that he came closer to being an uninspired bureaucrat who simply sat at his desk and did his job. For asserting her views, Arendt became the object of considerable scorn, even calumny. Somehow, it was felt that the monstrous deeds carried out by Eichmann required a brutal, twisted personality, evil incarnate. After witnessing hundreds of ordinary persons submit to the authority in our own experiments, I must conclude that Arendt's conception of the banality of evil comes closer to the truth than one might dare imagine. The ordinary person who shocked the victim did so out of a sense of obligation—an impression of his duties as a subject—and not from any peculiarly aggressive tendencies.

This is, perhaps, the most fundamental lesson of our study: ordi- 39
nary people, simply doing their jobs, and without any particular hostility on their part, can become agents in a terrible destructive process. Moreover, even when the destructive effects of their work become patently clear, and they are asked to carry out actions incompatible with fundamental standards of morality, relatively few people have the resources needed to resist authority.

Many of the people were in some sense against what they did to the 40
learner, and many protested even while they obeyed. Some were totally convinced of the wrongness of their actions but could not bring themselves to make an open break with authority. They often derived satisfaction from their thoughts and felt that—within themselves, at least—they had been on the side of the angels. They tried to reduce strain by obeying the experimenter but "only slightly" encouraging the learner, touching the generator switches gingerly. When interviewed, such a subject would stress that he had "asserted my humanity" by administering the briefest shock possible. Handling the conflict in this manner was easier than defiance.

The situation is constructed so that there is no way the subject can 41
stop shocking the learner without violating the experimenter's definitions of his own competence. The subject fears that he will appear arrogant, untoward, and rude if he breaks off. Although these inhibiting emotions appear small in scope alongside the violence being done to the learner, they suffuse the mind and feelings of the subject, who is miserable at the prospect of having to repudiate the authority to his face. (When the experiment was altered so that the experimenter gave his instructions by telephone instead of in person, only a third as many people were fully obedient through 450 volts.) It is a curious thing that a measure of compassion on the part of the subject—an unwillingness to "hurt" the experimenter's feelings—is part of those binding forces inhibiting his disobedience. The withdrawal of such deference may be as painful to the subject as to the authority he defies.

The subjects do not derive satisfaction from inflicting pain, but they   42
often like the feeling they get from pleasing the experimenter. They are
proud of doing a good job, obeying the experimenter under difficult circumstances. While the subjects administered only mild shocks on their
own initiative, one experimental variation showed that, under orders,
30 percent of them were willing to deliver 450 volts even when they had
to forcibly push the learner's hand down on the electrode.

Bruno Batta is a thirty-seven-year-old welder who took part in the   43
variation requiring the use of force. He was born in New Haven, his
parents in Italy. He has a rough-hewn face that conveys a conspicuous
lack of alertness. He has some difficulty in mastering the experimental
procedure and needs to be corrected by the experimenter several times.
He shows appreciation for the help and willingness to do what is
required. After the 150-volt level, Batta has to force the learner's hand
down on the shock plate, since the learner himself refuses to touch it.

When the learner first complains, Mr. Batta pays no attention to   44
him. His face remains impassive, as if to dissociate himself from the
learner's disruptive behavior. When the experimenter instructs him to
force the learner's hand down, he adopts a rigid, mechanical procedure.
He tests the generator switch. When it fails to function he immediately
forces the learner's hand onto the shock plate. All the while he maintains the same rigid mask. The learner, seated alongside him, begs him
to stop, but with robotic impassivity he continues the procedure.

What is extraordinary is his apparent total indifference to the learner;   45
he hardly takes cognizance of him as a human being. Meanwhile, he
relates to the experimenter in a submissive and courteous fashion.

At the 330-volt level, the learner refuses not only to touch the shock   46
plate but also to provide any answers. Annoyed, Batta turns to him, and
chastises him: "You better answer and get it over with. We can't stay
here all night." These are the only words he directs to the learner in the
course of an hour. Never again does he speak to him. The scene is brutal and depressing, his hard, impassive face showing total indifference
as he subdues the screaming learner and gives him shocks. He seems to
derive no pleasure from the act itself, only quiet satisfaction at doing his
job properly.

When he administers 450 volts, he turns to the experimenter and   47
asks, "Where do we go from here, Professor?" His tone is deferential
and expresses his willingness to be a cooperative subject, in contrast to
the learner's obstinacy.

At the end of the session he tells the experimenter how honored he   48
has been to help him, and in a moment of contrition, remarks, "Sir, sorry
it couldn't have been a full experiment."

He has done his honest best. It is only the deficient behavior of the   49
learner that has denied the experimenter full satisfaction.

The essence of obedience is that a person comes to view himself as 50
the instrument for carrying out another person's wishes, and he therefore no longer regards himself as responsible for his actions. Once this
critical shift of viewpoint has occurred, all of the essential features of
obedience follow. The most far-reaching consequence is that the person
feels responsible to the authority directing him but feels no responsibility *for* the content of the actions that the authority prescribes. Morality
does not disappear—it acquires a radically different focus: the subordinate person feels shame or pride depending on how adequately he has
performed the actions called for by authority.

Language provides numerous terms to pinpoint this type of moral- 51
ity: *loyalty, duty, discipline* all are terms heavily saturated with moral
meaning and refer to the degree to which a person fulfills his obligations to authority. They refer not to the "goodness" of the person per se
but to the adequacy with which a subordinate fulfills his socially
defined role. The most frequent defense of the individual who has performed a heinous act under command of authority is that he has simply
done his duty. In asserting this defense, the individual is not introducing an alibi concocted for the moment but is reporting honestly on the
psychological attitude induced by submission to authority.

For a person to feel responsible for his actions, he must sense that 52
the behavior has flowed from "the self." In the situation we have studied, subjects have precisely the opposite view of their actions—namely,
they see them as originating in the motives of some other person.
Subjects in the experiment frequently said, "If it were up to me, I would
not have administered shocks to the learner."

Once authority has been isolated as the cause of the subject's behav- 53
ior, it is legitimate to inquire into the necessary elements of authority
and how it must be perceived in order to gain his compliance. We conducted some investigations into the kinds of changes that would cause
the experimenter to lose his power and to be disobeyed by the subject.
Some of the variations revealed that:

> *The experimenter's physical presence has a marked impact on his*   54
> *authority.* As cited earlier, obedience dropped off sharply when orders
> were given by telephone. The experimenter could often induce a dis-
> obedient subject to go on by returning to the laboratory.

> *Conflicting authority severely paralyzes action.* When two experi-   55
> menters of equal status, both seated at the command desk, gave
> incompatible orders, no shocks were delivered past the point of their
> disagreement.

> *The rebellious action of others severely undermines authority.* In one   56
> variation, three teachers (two actors and a real subject) administered

a test and shocks. When the two actors disobeyed the experimenter and refused to go beyond a certain shock level, thirty-six of forty subjects joined their disobedient peers and refused as well.

Although the experimenter's authority was fragile in some 57 respects, it is also true that he had almost none of the tools used in ordinary command structures. For example, the experimenter did not threaten the subjects with punishment—such as loss of income, community ostracism, or jail—for failure to obey. Neither could he offer incentives. Indeed, we should expect the experimenter's authority to be much less than that of someone like a general, since the experimenter has no power to enforce his imperatives, and since participation in a psychological experiment scarcely evokes the sense of urgency and dedication found in warfare. Despite these limitations, he still managed to command a dismaying degree of obedience.

I will cite one final variation of the experiment that depicts a 58 dilemma that is more common in everyday life. The subject was not ordered to pull the lever that shocked the victim, but merely to perform a subsidiary task (administering the word-pair test) while another person administered the shock. In this situation, thirty-seven of forty adults continued to the highest level of the shock generator. Predictably, they excused their behavior by saying that the responsibility belonged to the man who actually pulled the switch. This may illustrate a dangerously typical arrangement in a complex society: it is easy to ignore responsibility when one is only an intermediate link in a chain of action.

The problem of obedience is not wholly psychological. The form 59 and shape of society and the way it is developing have much to do with it. There was a time, perhaps, when people were able to give a fully human response to any situation because they were fully absorbed in it as human beings. But as soon as there was a division of labor things changed. Beyond a certain point, the breaking up of society into people carrying out narrow and very special jobs takes away from the human quality of work and life. A person does not get to see the whole situation but only a small part of it, and is thus unable to act without some kind of overall direction. He yields to authority but in doing so is alienated from his own actions.

Even Eichmann was sickened when he toured the concentration 60 camps, but he had only to sit at a desk and shuffle papers. At the same time the man in the camp who actually dropped Cyclon-b into the gas chambers was able to justify *his* behavior on the ground that he was only following orders from above. Thus there is a fragmentation of the total human act; no one is confronted with the consequences of his decision to carry out the evil act. The person who assumes responsibility has evaporated. Perhaps this is the most common characteristic of socially organized evil in modern society.

Responding to Reading

1. What is the "dilemma inherent in submission to authority" (2)? How do Milgram's experiments illustrate this dilemma? Why do you suppose virtually no one predicted that the subjects would continue to obey the orders of the experimenter?

2. Do you see the subjects as ordinary people—cooperative, obedient, and eager to please—or as weak individuals, too timid to defy authority? Explain.

3. In paragraph 51, Milgram says, "The most frequent defense of the individual who has performed a heinous act under command of authority is that he has simply done his duty." In your opinion, can such a defense ever excuse a "heinous act"? If so, under what circumstances?

THE RULES OF THE GAME

Carl Sagan

An astronomer, biologist, physicist, and popular science writer, Carl Sagan (1934–1996) was born in New York City and educated at the University of Chicago. A professor at Cornell, he lectured widely at other universities on subjects ranging from the birth of the cosmos to the threat of the nuclear arms race. His many books, which did much to educate average readers about a variety of scientific matters, include The Cosmic Connection *(1973);* The Dragons of Eden *(1977), winner of the Pulitzer Prize;* Cosmos *(1980), which provided the basis for a widely watched PBS television series that Sagan cowrote and narrated;* A Path Where No Man Thought: Nuclear Winter and the End of the Arms Race *(1989); and* Pale Blue Dot *(1994). He was also instrumental in developing NASA's Mariner, Viking, and Voyager interplanetary missions. The winner of many awards for his academic work, his television documentary, and his humanitarian achievements, Sagan, according to one critic, "sends out an exuberant message: science is not only vital for humanity's future well-being, but it is rousing good fun as well." His posthumously published* Billions and Billions: Thoughts on Life and Death at the Brink of the Millennium *(1997) was written as Sagan was undergoing ultimately unsuccessful treatment for cancer. In the following essay from that book, he explores the various moral codes people may choose to live by.*

Everything morally right derives from one of four sources: it concerns either full perception or intelligent development of what is true; or the preservation of organized society, where every man is rendered

his due and all obligations are faithfully discharged; or the greatness
and strength of a noble, invincible spirit; or order and moderation in
everything said and done, whereby is temperance and self-control.
—Cicero, *De Officiis*, I, 5 (45–44 B.C.)

I remember the end of a long ago perfect day in 1939—a day that power- 1
fully influenced my thinking, a day when my parents introduced me to the
wonders of the New York World's Fair. It was late, well past my bedtime. Safely
perched on my father's shoulders, holding onto his ears, my mother reassur-
ingly at my side, I turned to see the great Trylon and Perisphere, the architec-
tural icons of the Fair, illuminated in shimmering blue pastels. We were
abandoning the future, the "World of Tomorrow,"for the BMT subway train.
As we paused to rearrange our possessions, my father got to talking with a
small, tired man carrying a tray around his neck. He was selling pencils. My
father reached into the crumpled brown paper bag that held the remains of our
lunches, withdrew an apple, and handed it to the pencil man. I let out a loud
wail. I disliked apples then, and had refused this one both at lunch and at din-
ner. But I had, nevertheless, a proprietary interest in it. It was my apple, and
my father had just given it away to a funny-looking stranger—who, to com-
pound my anguish, was now glaring unsympathetically in my direction.

Although my father was a person of nearly limitless patience and tender- 2
ness, I could see he was disappointed in me. He swept me up and hugged me
tight to him.

"He's a poor stiff, out of work," he said to me, too quietly for the man to 3
hear. "He hasn't eaten all day. We have enough. We can give him an apple."

I reconsidered, stifled my sobs, took another wistful glance at the World of 4
Tomorrow, and gratefully fell asleep in his arms.

Moral codes that seek to regulate human behavior have been with 5
us not only since the dawn of civilization but also among our precivi-
lized, and highly social, hunter-gatherer ancestors. And even earlier.
Different societies have different codes. Many cultures say one thing
and do another. In a few fortunate societies, an inspired lawgiver lays
down a set of rules to live by (and more often than not claims to have
been instructed by a god—without which few would follow the prescriptions). For example, the codes of Ashoka (India), Hammurabi
(Babylon), Lycurgus (Sparta), and Solon (Athens), which once held
sway over mighty civilizations, are today largely defunct. Perhaps they
misjudged human nature and asked too much of us. Perhaps experience
from one epoch or culture is not wholly applicable to another.

Surprisingly, there are today efforts—tentative but emerging—to 6
approach the matter scientifically; i.e., experimentally.

In our everyday lives as in the momentous relations of nations, we 7
must decide: What does it mean to do the right thing? Should we help
a needy stranger? How do we deal with an enemy? Should we ever take

advantage of someone who treats us kindly? If hurt by a friend, or helped by an enemy, should we reciprocate in kind; or does the totality of past behavior outweigh any recent departures from the norm?

Examples: Your sister-in-law ignores your snub and invites you 8 over for Christmas dinner; should you accept? Shattering a four-year-long worldwide voluntary moratorium, China resumes nuclear weapons testing; should we? How much should we give to charity? Serbian soldiers systematically rape Bosnian women; should Bosnian soldiers systematically rape Serbian women? After centuries of oppression, the Nationalist Party leader F. W. de Klerk[1] makes overtures to the African National Congress; should Nelson Mandela and the ANC have reciprocated? A coworker makes you look bad in front of the boss; should you try to get even? Should we cheat on our income tax returns? If we can get away with it? If an oil company supports a symphony orchestra or sponsors a refined TV drama, ought we to ignore its pollution of the environment? Should we be kind to aged relatives, even if they drive us nuts? Should you cheat at cards? Or on a larger scale? Should we kill killers?

In making such decisions, we're concerned not only with doing 9 right but also with what works—what makes us and the rest of society happier and more secure. There's a tension between what we call ethical and what we call pragmatic. If, even in the long run, ethical behavior were self-defeating, eventually we would not call it ethical, but foolish. (We might even claim to respect it in principle, but ignore it in practice.) Bearing in mind the variety and complexity of human behavior, are there any simple rules—whether we call them ethical or pragmatic—that actually work?

How do we decide what to do? Our responses are partly deter- 10 mined by our perceived self-interest. We reciprocate in kind or act contrary because we hope it will accomplish what we want. Nations assemble or blow up nuclear weapons so other countries won't trifle with them. We return good for evil because we know that we can thereby sometimes touch people's sense of justice, or shame them into being nice. But sometimes we're not motivated selfishly. Some people seem just naturally kind. We may accept aggravation from aged parents or from children, because we love them and want them to be happy, even if it's at some cost to us. Sometimes we're tough with our children and cause them a little unhappiness, because we want to mold their characters and believe that the long-term results will bring them more happiness than the short-term pain.

Cases are different. Peoples and nations are different. Knowing how 11 to negotiate this labyrinth is part of wisdom. But bearing in mind the

---

[1] Of South Africa. [Eds.]

variety and complexity of human behavior, are there some simple rules, whether we call them ethical or pragmatic, that actually work? Or maybe we should avoid trying to think it through and just do what feels right. But even then how do we *determine* what "feels right"?

The most admired standard of behavior, in the West at least, is the 12
Golden Rule, attributed to Jesus of Nazareth. Everyone knows its formulation in the first-century Gospel of St. Matthew: **Do unto others as you would have them do unto you.** Almost no one follows it. When the Chinese philosopher Kung-Tzi (known as Confucius in the West) was asked in the fifth century B.C. his opinion of the Golden Rule (by then already well-known), of repaying evil with kindness, he replied, "Then with what will you repay kindness?" Shall the poor woman who envies her neighbor's wealth give what little she has to the rich? Shall the masochist inflict pain on his neighbor? The Golden Rule takes no account of human differences. Are we really capable, after our cheek has been slapped, of turning the other cheek so it too can be slapped? With a heartless adversary, isn't this just a guarantee of more suffering?

The Silver Rule is different: **Do not do unto others what you would** 13
not have them do unto you. It also can be found worldwide, including, a generation before Jesus, in the writings of Rabbi Hillel. The most inspiring twentieth-century exemplars of the Silver Rule were Mohandas Gandhi and Martin Luther King, Jr. They counseled oppressed peoples not to repay violence with violence, but not to be compliant and obedient either. Nonviolent civil disobedience was what they advocated—putting your body on the line, showing, by your willingness to be punished in defying an unjust law, the justice of your cause. They aimed at melting the hearts of their oppressors (and those who had not yet made up their minds).

King paid tribute to Gandhi as the first person in history to convert 14
the Golden or Silver Rules into an effective instrument of social change. And Gandhi made it clear where his approach came from: "I learnt the lesson on nonviolence from my wife, when I tried to bend her to my will. Her determined resistance to my will on the one hand, and her quiet submission to the suffering my stupidity involved on the other, ultimately made me ashamed of myself and cured me of my stupidity in thinking that I was born to rule over her."

Nonviolent civil disobedience has worked notable political change 15
in this century—in prying India loose from British rule and stimulating the end of classic colonialism worldwide, and in providing some civil rights for African-Americans—although the threat of violence by others, however disavowed by Gandhi and King, may have also helped. The African National Congress (ANC) grew up in the Gandhian tradition. But by the 1950s it was clear that nonviolent noncooperation was making no progress whatever with the ruling white Nationalist Party.

So in 1961 Nelson Mandela and his colleagues formed the military wing of the ANC, the *Umkhonto we Sizwe*, the Spear of the Nation, on the quite un-Gandhian grounds that the only thing whites understand is force.

Even Gandhi had trouble reconciling the rule of nonviolence with [16] the necessities of defense against those with less lofty rules of conduct: "I have not the qualifications for teaching my philosophy of life. I have barely qualifications for practicing the philosophy I believe. I am but a poor struggling soul yearning to be . . . wholly truthful and wholly non-violent in thought, word and deed, but ever failing to reach the ideal."

"Repay kindness with kindness," said Confucius, "but evil with [17] justice." This might be called the Brass or Brazen Rule: **Do unto others as they do unto you.** It's the *lex talionis*, "an eye for an eye, and a tooth for a tooth," *plus* "one good turn deserves another." In actual human (and chimpanzee) behavior it's a familiar standard. "If the enemy inclines toward peace, do thou also incline toward peace," President Bill Clinton quoted from the Qur'an[2] at the Israeli-Palestinian peace accords. Without having to appeal to anyone's better nature, we institute a kind of operant conditioning,[3] rewarding them when they're nice to us and punishing them when they're not. We're not pushovers but we're not unforgiving either. It sounds promising. Or is it true that "two wrongs don't make a right"?

Of baser coinage is the Iron Rule: **Do unto others as you like, [18] before they do it unto you.** It is sometimes formulated as "He who has the gold makes the rules," underscoring not just its departure from, but its contempt for the Golden Rule. This is the secret maxim of many, if they can get away with it, and often the unspoken precept of the powerful.

Finally, I should mention two other rules, found throughout the liv- [19] ing world. They explain a great deal: One is **Suck up to those above you, and abuse those below.** This is the motto of bullies and the norm in many nonhuman primate societies. It's really the Golden Rule for superiors, the Iron Rule for inferiors. Since there is no known alloy of gold and iron, we'll call it the Tin Rule for its flexibility. The other common rule is **Give precedence in all things to close relatives, and do as you like to others.** This Nepotism Rule is known to evolutionary biologists as "kin selection."

Despite its apparent practicality, there's a fatal flaw in the Brazen [20] Rule: unending vendetta. It hardly matters who starts the violence. Violence begets violence, and each side has reason to hate the other. "There is no way to peace," A. J. Muste said. "Peace *is* the way." But peace is hard and violence is easy. Even if almost everyone is for end-ing the vendetta, a single act of retribution can stir it up again: A dead

[2] The Koran, or sacred book of Islam. [Eds.]
[3] A process of behavioral modification. [Eds.]

relative's sobbing widow and grieving children are before us. Old men and women recall atrocities from their childhoods. The reasonable part of us tries to keep the peace, but the passionate part of us cries out for vengeance. Extremists in the two warring factions can count on one another. They are allied against the rest of us, contemptuous of appeals to understanding and loving-kindness. A few hotheads can force-march a legion of more prudent and rational people to brutality and war.

Many in the West have been so mesmerized by the appalling 21 accords with Adolf Hitler in Munich in 1938 that they are unable to distinguish cooperation and appeasement. Rather than having to judge each gesture and approach on its own merits, we merely decide that the opponent is thoroughly evil, that all his concessions are offered in bad faith, and that force is the only thing he understands. Perhaps for Hitler this was the right judgment. But in general it is not the right judgment, as much as I wish that the invasion of the Rhineland had been forcibly opposed. It consolidates hostility on both sides and makes conflict much more likely. In a world with nuclear weapons, uncompromising hostility carries special and very dire dangers.

Breaking out of a long series of reprisals is, I claim, very hard. There 22 are ethnic groups who have weakened themselves to the point of extinction because they had no machinery to escape from this cycle, the Kaingáng of the Brazilian highlands, for example. The warring nationalities in the former Yugoslavia, in Rwanda, and elsewhere may provide further examples. The Brazen Rule seems too unforgiving. The Iron Rule promotes the advantage of a ruthless and powerful few against the interests of everybody else. The Golden and Silver Rules seem too complacent. They systematically fail to punish cruelty and exploitation. They hope to coax people from evil to good by showing that kindness is possible. But there are sociopaths who do not much care about the feelings of others, and it is hard to imagine a Hitler or a Stalin being shamed into redemption by good example. Is there a rule between the Golden and the Silver on the one hand and the Brazen, Iron, and Tin on the other which works better than any of them alone?

With so many different rules, how can you tell which to use, which 23 will work? More than one rule may be operating even in the same person or nation. Are we doomed just to guess about this, or to rely on intuition, or just to parrot what we've been taught? Let's try to put aside, just for the moment, whatever rules we've been taught, and those we feel passionately—perhaps from a deeply rooted sense of justice—*must* be right.

Suppose we seek not to confirm or deny what we've been taught, 24 but to find out what really works. Is there a way to *test* competing codes of ethics? Granting that the real world may be much more complicated than any simulation, can we explore the matter scientifically?

We're used to playing games in which somebody wins and some- 25
body loses. Every point made by our opponent puts us that much further behind. "Win-lose" games seem natural, and many people are
hard-pressed to think of a game that isn't win-lose. In win-lose games,
the losses just balance the wins. That's why they're called "zero-sum"
games. There's no ambiguity about your opponent's intentions: Within
the rules of the game, he will do anything he can to defeat you.

Many children are aghast the first time they really come face to face 26
with the "lose" side of win-lose games. On the verge of bankruptcy in
Monopoly, they plead for special dispensation (forgoing rents, for
example), and when this is not forthcoming may, in tears, denounce the
game as heartless and unfeeling—which of course it is. (I've seen the
board overturned, hotels and "Chance" cards and metal icons spilled
onto the floor in spitting anger and humiliation—and not only by children.) Within the rules of Monopoly, there's no way for players to cooperate so that all benefit. That's not how the game is designed. The same
is true for boxing, football, hockey, basketball, baseball, lacrosse, tennis,
racquetball, chess, all Olympic events, yacht and car racing, pinochle,
potsie, and partisan politics. In none of these games is there an opportunity to practice the Golden or Silver Rules, or even the Brazen. There
is room only for the Rules of Iron and Tin. If we revere the Golden Rule,
why is it so rare in the games we teach our children?

After a million years of intermittently warring tribes we readily 27
enough think in zero-sum mode, and treat every interaction as a contest or conflict. Nuclear war, though (and many conventional wars),
economic depression, and assaults on the global environment are all
"lose-lose" propositions. Such vital human concerns as love, friendship, parenthood, music, art, and the pursuit of knowledge are "win-
win" propositions. Our vision is dangerously narrow if all we know is
win-lose.

The scientific field that deals with such matters is called game theory, 28
used in military tactics and strategy, trade policy, corporate competition,
limiting environmental pollution, and plans for nuclear war. The para-
digmatic game is the Prisoner's Dilemma. It is very much non-zero-sum.
Win-win, win-lose, and lose-lose outcomes are all possible. "Sacred"
books carry few useful insights into strategy here. It is a wholly pragmatic game.

Imagine that you and a friend are arrested for committing a serious 29
crime. For the purpose of the game, it doesn't matter whether either,
neither, or both of you did it. What matters is that the police say they
think you did. Before the two of you have any chance to compare stories or plan strategy, you are taken to separate interrogation cells. There,
oblivious of your Miranda rights ("You have the right to remain
silent . . ."), they try to make you confess. They tell you, as police sometimes do, that your friend has confessed and implicated you. (Some

friend!) The police might be telling the truth. Or they might be lying. You're permitted only to plead innocent or guilty. If you're willing to say anything, what's your best tack to minimize punishment?

Here are the possible outcomes: 30

If you deny committing the crime and (unknown to you) your 31 friend also denies it, the case might be hard to prove. In the plea bargain, both your sentences will be very light.

If you confess and your friend does likewise, then the effort the State 32 had to expend to solve the crime was small. In exchange you both may be given a fairly light sentence, although not as light as if you both had asserted your innocence.

But if you plead innocent and your friend confesses, the state will 33 ask for the maximum sentence for you and minimal punishment (maybe none) for your friend. Uh-oh. You're very vulnerable to a kind of double cross, what game theorists call "defection." So's he.

So if you and your friend "cooperate" with one another—both 34 pleading innocent (or both pleading guilty)—you both escape the worst. Should you play it safe and guarantee a middle range of punishment by confessing? Then, if your friend pleads innocent while you plead guilty, well, too bad for him, and you might get off scot-free.

When you think it through, you realize that whatever your friend 35 does you're better off defecting than cooperating. Maddeningly, the same holds true for your friend. But if you both defect, you're both worse off than if you had both cooperated. This is the Prisoner's Dilemma.

Now consider a repeated Prisoner's Dilemma, in which the two 36 players go through a sequence of such games. At the end of each they figure out from their punishment how the other must have pled. They gain experience about each other's strategy (and character). Will they learn to cooperate game after game, both always denying that they committed any crime? Even if the reward for finking on the other is large?

You might try cooperating or defecting, depending on how the 37 previous game or games have gone. If you cooperate overmuch, the other player may exploit your good nature. If you defect overmuch, your friend is likely to defect often, and this is bad for both of you. You know your defection pattern is data being fed to the other player. What is the right mix of cooperation and defection? How to behave then becomes, like any other question in Nature, a subject to be investigated experimentally.

This matter has been explored in a continuing round-robin com- 38 puter tournament by the University of Michigan sociologist Robert Axelrod in his remarkable book *The Evolution of Cooperation*. Various codes of behavior confront one another and at the end we see who wins (who gets the lightest cumulative prison term). The simplest strategy might be to cooperate all the time, no matter how much advantage is taken of you, or never to cooperate, no matter what benefits might accrue from cooperation. These are the Golden Rule and the Iron Rule. They always lose, the one from a superfluity of kindness, the other from an overabundance of ruthlessness. Strategies slow to punish defection lose—in part because they send a signal that noncooperation can win. The Golden Rule is not only an unsuccessful strategy; it is also dangerous for other players, who may succeed in the short term only to be mowed down by exploiters in the long term.

Should you defect at first, but if your opponent cooperates even once, cooperate in all future games? Should you cooperate at first, but if your opponent defects even once, defect in all future games? These strategies also lose. Unlike sports, you cannot rely on your opponent to be always out to get you.

The most effective strategy in many such tournaments is called "Tit-for-Tat." It's very simple: You start out cooperating, and in each subsequent round simply do what your opponent did last time. You punish defections, but once your partner cooperates, you're willing to let bygones be bygones. At first, it seems to garner only mediocre success. But as time goes on the other strategies defeat themselves, from too much kindness or cruelty, and this middle way pulls ahead. Except for always being nice on the first move, Tit-for-Tat is identical to the Brazen Rule. It promptly (in the very next game) rewards cooperation and punishes defection, and has the great virtue that it makes your strategy absolutely clear to your opponent. (Strategic ambiguity can be lethal.)

TABLE OF PROPOSED RULES TO LIVE BY

The Golden Rule	Do unto others as you would have them do unto you.
The Silver Rule	Do not do unto others what you would not have them do unto you.
The Brazen (Brass) Rule	Do unto others as they do unto you.
The Iron Rule	Do unto others as you like, before they do it unto you.
The Tit-for-Tat Rule	Cooperate with others first, then do unto them as they do unto you.

Once there get to be several players employing Tit-for-Tat, they rise 41
in the standings together. To succeed, Tit-for-Tat strategists must find
others who are willing to reciprocate, with whom they can cooperate.
After the first tournament in which the Brazen Rule unexpectedly won,
some experts thought the strategy too forgiving. Next tournament, they
tried to exploit it by defecting more often. They always lost. Even experienced strategists tended to underestimate the power of forgiveness
and reconciliation. Tit-for-Tat involves an interesting mix of proclivities:
initial friendliness, willingness to forgive, and fearless retaliation. The
superiority of the Tit-for-Tat Rule in such tournaments has been
recounted by Axelrod.

Something like it can be found throughout the animal kingdom and 42
has been well-studied in our closest relatives, the chimps. Described
and named "reciprocal altruism" by the biologist Robert Trivers, animals may do favors for others in expectation of having the favors
returned—not every time, but often enough to be useful. This is hardly
an invariable moral strategy, but it is not uncommon either. So there is
no need to debate the antiquity of the Golden, Silver, and Brazen Rules,
or Tit-for-Tat, and the priority of the moral prescriptives in the Book of
Leviticus. Ethical rules of this sort were not originally invented by some
enlightened human lawgiver. They go deep into our evolutionary past.
They were with our ancestral line from a time before we were human.

The Prisoner's Dilemma is a very simple game. Real life is consid- 43
erably more complex. If he gives our apple to the pencil man, is my
father more likely to get an apple back? Not from the pencil man; we'll
never see him again. But might widespread acts of charity improve the
economy and give my father a raise? Or do we give the apple for emotional, not economic rewards? Also, unlike the players in an ideal
Prisoner's Dilemma game, human beings and nations come to their
interactions with predispositions, both hereditary and cultural.

But the central lessons in a not very prolonged round-robin of 44
Prisoner's Dilemma are about strategic clarity; about the self-defeating
nature of envy; about the importance of long-term over short-term
goals; about the dangers of both tyranny and patsydom; and especially
about approaching the whole issue of rules to live by as an experimental question. Game theory also suggests that a broad knowledge of history is a key survival tool.

Responding to Reading

1. Sagan begins his essay with a story about what he calls "a day that powerfully influenced my thinking" (1). Exactly how do you suppose this experience affected him? How is the anecdote related to his discussion of moral
   codes?

2. Do you believe it is possible to devise a set of rules that can determine what is morally right in any given situation? Does Sagan? Do you think the moral questions Sagan asks in paragraph 7 and elsewhere can have definite answers that will work in all situations? Explain.

3. In what sense is the Prisoner's Dilemma a model for behavior in our society? How is "real life" different from this game? What lessons about moral codes does Sagan believe we can learn from the Prisoner's Dilemma?

FOCUS: ARE ALL IDEAS CREATED EQUAL?

EQUAL TIME FOR NONSENSE

Lawrence Krauss

Born in New York City, Lawrence Krauss (1954–) received a bachelor of science degree from Carleton University in Ottawa, Canada, and a Ph.D. in physics from the Massachusetts Institute of Technology. A professor of physics at Case Western Reserve, Krauss has written more than 125 articles for both scientific journals and popular magazines such as Scientific American *and* Nature. *He has also published several books, including* The Fifth Essence: The Search for Dark Matter in the Universe *(1989),* Fear of Physics: A Guide for the Perplexed *(1993), and* The Physics of Star Trek *(1995), an examination of the television series. Krauss has, he has said, "a strong interest in the connection between science and culture. In my writing I strive to bridge the enormous gap between the two that seems to exist in our society." In the following essay, published on the op-ed page of the* New York Times *in 1996, he argues that "nonsense masquerading as truth" ultimately imperils our democratic society.*

Four months ago, when his Presidential campaign still seemed 1 viable, Patrick Buchanan appeared on a national television program and argued in favor of creationism. This, by itself, is not so remarkable, given some of Mr. Buchanan's other views.

What seemed more significant, however, was that the same national 2 media that questioned other Buchanan campaign planks like trade protectionism and limits on immigration did not produce a major article or editorial proclaiming the candidate's views on evolution to be simple nonsense.

Why is this the case? Could it be that the fallacies inherent in a strict 3 creationist viewpoint are so self-evident that they were deemed not to deserve comment? I think not. Indeed, when a serious candidate for the highest office of the most powerful nation on earth holds such views you would think that this commentary would automatically become "newsworthy."

Rather, what seems to have taken hold is a growing hesitancy among 4 both journalists and scholars to state openly that some viewpoints are not subject to debate: they are simply wrong. They might point out flaws, but journalists also feel great pressure to report on both sides of a "debate."

Part of the reason is that few journalists naturally feel comfortable enough on scientific matters to make pronouncements. But there is another good reason for such hesitancy. In a truly democratic society, one might argue, everything is open to debate. Who has the authority to deem certain ideas incorrect or flawed? Indeed, appeal to authority is as much an anathema to scientists as it is to many on the academic left who worry about the authority of the "scientific establishment."

What is so wonderful about scientific truth, however, is that the authority which determines whether there can be debate or not does not reside in some fraternity of scientists; nor is it divine. The authority rests with experiment.

It is perhaps the most immutable but most widely misunderstood property of modern science: a proposition can never be proved to be absolutely true. There can always be some experiment lurking around the corner to require alteration of any model of reality. What is unequivocal, however, is falseness. A theory whose predictions fail the test of experiment is always wrong, period, end of story. The earth isn't flat, because you can travel around it, period, end of story.

This misunderstanding is at the heart of much scholarly debate in recent months, including the amusing hoax that a New York University physicist, Alan Sokal, played at the expense of the editors of the journal Social Text. The postmodernist journal published a bogus article that Professor Sokal had written as a satire of some social science criticism of the nature of scientific knowledge. It was aimed at those in the humanities who study the social context of science, but who, he argued, could not discern empirically falsifiable models from meaningless nonsense. The editors, on the other hand, argued that publication was based in part on their notion that the community of scholars depends on the goodwill of the participants—namely they had assumed Professor Sokal had something to say. They too have a point.

The great paranormal debunker and magician, the Amazing Randi, has shown time and again that earnest researchers can be duped by those who would have been willing to answer "yes" to the question "are you lying?" but who were never asked. We must always be skeptical. Being skeptical, however, does not get in the way of the search for objective truths. It merely assists in the uncovering of falsehoods.

Another popular misunderstanding of the nature of truth and falsehood in modern science involves the speculative ideas which often appear at the frontiers of research. For example, the science writer John Horgan has argued that such speculations are unrelated to the real world around us. But notions such as "superstrings" and "baby universes" are not akin to arguments about the number of angels on the head of a pin, much as they may bear a superficial resemblance.

They are merely the most recent straw men in a longstanding effort to get at the truth. They would not be taken seriously by anyone were it not for the belief that these notions, when properly understood, might in principle one day lead to either direct or indirect predictions which may be falsified by future experiments or else which may or may not explain existing data. The debate among physicists about the viability of these ideas is simply a debate among those who think the notions will be testable and those who suspect they won't.

No physicist I know has ever suggested that unprovable specula- 12 tion will shine on its own merits, whether or not it can be taken literally, or that it is progress to come up with a theory which cannot be proved false. Mr. Horgan is absolutely correct to suggest that this approach is impotent. But his error is to confuse this process with what physicists actually do, and thereby demean the notion of scientific truth.

This whole issue might make for simply an amusing academic 13 debate were it not for the potentially grave consequences for society at large. If we are unwilling, unilaterally, to brand scientific nonsense as just that, regardless of whose sensibilities might be offended—religious or otherwise—then the whole notion of truth itself becomes blurred.

The need to present both sides of an issue is only necessary when 14 there are two sides. When empirically verifiable falsehoods become instead subjects for debate, then nonsense associated with international conspiracy theories, holocaust denials and popular demagogues like Louis Farrakhan or Pat Robertson cannot effectively be rooted out.

When nonsense which can be empirically falsified is presented 15 under a creationist guise as critical thinking, a controversy is created in our schools where none should exist. When the empirically falsifiable supposition that someone was not present at a murder when his DNA is found mixed with the blood of victims at the crime scene is not recognized as nonsense, murderers can go home free.

Nonsense masquerading as truth has been with us as long as 16 records can date. But the increasingly blatant nature of the nonsense uttered with impunity in public discourse is chilling. Our democratic society is imperiled as much by this as any other single threat, regardless of whether the origins of the nonsense are religious fanaticism, simple ignorance or personal gain.

Perhaps the greatest single legacy our scientific heritage can bestow 17 on us is a well-defined procedure for exposing nonsense. We would all be wise to heed the advice passed on by Arthur Hays Sulzberger, the publisher of The New York Times from 1935 to 1961: "I believe in an open mind, but not so open that your brains fall out."

Responding to Reading

1. In paragraph 4, Krauss identifies "a growing hesitancy among both journalists and scholars to state openly that some viewpoints are not subject to

debate: they are simply wrong." Do you agree that some ideas are "simply wrong"? If so, what ideas would you place in this category?

2. Do you agree, at least in theory, with the statement "In a truly democratic society . . . everything is open to debate" (5)? Do you think Deborah Lipstadt (p. 811) would agree? Why or why not?

3. According to Kraus, what are the dangers in our tolerance for "scientific nonsense" (13)? Can you give examples of some specific cases in which our willingness to see "empirically verifiable falsehoods" as "subjects for debate" (14) has had negative results?

DENYING THE HOLOCAUST

Deborah Lipstadt

Deborah Lipstadt (1947–   ) was born in New York City and attended Hebrew University of Jerusalem, City College in New York, and Brandeis University, where she received her Ph.D. She has been teaching the history of religion and Jewish studies since 1974 and currently holds an endowed chair in modern Jewish and Holocaust studies at Emory University in Atlanta. Her books include Jewish Reflections on Death *(1975),* The Zionist Career of Louis Lipsky *(1982),* Beyond Belief: The American Press and the Coming of the Holocaust *(1986), and* Denying the Holocaust: The Growing Assault on Truth and Memory *(1993). In this book she argues that Holocaust deniers are not presenting an "other side" of history; rather they are "extreme antisemites" whose aim is "to confuse the matter by making it appear as if they are engaged in genuine scholarly effort when, of course, they are not." The following chapter from* Denying the Holocaust *focuses specifically on Lipstadt's argument that by accepting advertisements in which Holocaust deniers outline their claims, college newspapers can inadvertently add legitimacy to those claims.*

This is not a public stagecoach that has to take everyone who buys a ticket.

—Benjamin Franklin

In the early 1990s American college campuses became loci of intensive activity by a small group of Holocaust deniers. Relying on creative tactics and assisted by a fuzzy kind of reasoning often evident in academic circles, the deniers achieved millions of dollars of free publicity and significantly furthered their cause. Their strategy was profoundly simple. Bradley Smith, a Californian who has been involved in a variety of Holocaust denial activities since the early 1980s, attempted to place a full-page ad claiming that the Holocaust was a hoax in college newspapers throughout the United States. The ad was published by papers at some of the more prestigious institutions of higher learning in the United States.

Entitled "The Holocaust Story: How Much Is False? The Case for 2 Open Debate," the ad provoked a fierce debate on many of the campuses approached by Smith. His strategy was quite straightforward: He generally called a paper's advertising department to ascertain the charge for publication of a full-page ad and then submitted camera-ready copy and a certified check in the proper amount. On occasion he inquired in advance whether a paper would be willing to run this particular ad. Even when he was rejected, the attempt to place the ad won him significant media attention. Campus newspapers began to use his name in headlines without identifying him, assuming readers would know who he was. Articles, letters, and op-ed pieces defended Holocaust denial's right to make its "views" known. But not all the results were necessarily what Smith would have wanted. On some campuses there was a backlash against him and Holocaust denial. Courses on the Holocaust that had languished on the back burner for an extended period materialized in the next semester's offerings. Campus administrators admitted that the ad constituted the final push necessary to move these courses from the planning stage to the schedule books. Professors from a wide variety of disciplines included discussion of the Holocaust in their courses. Movies, speakers, photographic exhibits and other presentations relating to the Holocaust were brought to campus. Students participated in rallies, teach-ins, and protests.

This response prompted some observers to argue that the contro- 3 versy had a positive impact. Students had become increasingly aware not only of the Holocaust but of the contemporary attempt to subvert history and spread antisemitism. While this may be a relatively accurate analysis of the immediate outcome of Smith's endeavor, there is another more sobering and pessimistic aspect to the matter. Analysis of the students', faculty's, and administration's responses reveals both a susceptibility to the worst form of historical revisionism and a failure to fully understand the implications of Holocaust denial, even among those who vigorously condemned it. . . .

The ad Smith began to circulate in the spring of 1991 contained the 4 deniers' familiar litany of claims. It declared the gas chambers a fraud, photographs doctored, eyewitness reports "ludicrously unreliable," the Nuremberg trials a sham, and camp internees well fed until Allied bombings destroyed the German infrastructure in the most "barbarous form of warfare in Europe since the Mongol invasions," preventing food from being delivered and causing the inmates to starve. According to Smith the notion of a Nazi attempt to destroy the Jews was the product of Allied efforts to produce "anti-German hate propaganda." Today that same propaganda was used by powerful forces to "scape-goat old enemies," "seek vengeance rather than reconciliation," and pursue a "not-so-secret political agenda."

He repeated the familiar protest that his sole objective was to [5] uncover the truth through an open debate on the Holocaust—debate that had been suppressed by a powerful but secret group on campus as part of their larger political agenda. "Let's ask these people—what makes such behavior a social good? Who benefits?"

The ad contended that denial was forcing "mainline Holocaust his- [6] torians" to admit the "more blatant examples" of Holocaust falsehoods. It was the deniers who had forced them to revise the "orthodox" Holocaust story. They had had to admit that the number of Jews killed at Auschwitz was far smaller than originally claimed, and had been made to confess that the Nazis did not use Jewish cadavers for the production of soap. It is correct that in recent years newly revealed documentation has allowed scholars to assess more precisely the number of Jews thought to have been murdered at Auschwitz.[1] It is also accurate that scholars have long written that despite wartime rumors to the contrary, the Nazis apparently did not use Jewish cadavers for soap. There has been a wide array of other "revelations" by Holocaust historians, all part of the attempt to uncover the full details of one of the most horrifying acts of human destruction. Smith suggested to his readers that scholars and others who work in this field, all of whom vigorously repudiate Holocaust denial, have been compelled to admit the truth of deniers' claims: "We are told that it is 'anti-Jewish' to question orthodox assertions about German criminality. Yet we find that it is Jews themselves like Mayer, Bauer, Hier, Hilberg, Lipstadt and others who beginning [sic] to challenge the establishment Holocaust story." This notion—that deniers have exposed the truth and mainline historians are scrambling to admit it—remains a linchpin of the deniers' strategy. It has two objectives: to make it appear that Jewish scholars are responding to the pressure of the deniers' findings and to create the impression that Holocaust deniers' "questions" are themselves part of a continuum of respectable scholarship. If establishment scholars, particularly those who are Jews, can question previously accepted truths, why is it wrong when Bradley Smith does the same?

Though much of the ad consisted of familiar rhetoric, Smith added [7] a new twist that had a particular resonance on American college campuses. Since the 1980s the concept of "political correctness" has been a source of academic conflict. Conservative political groups have accused the "liberal establishment" of labeling certain topics politically incorrect

---

[1] The memorial stone at Auschwitz lists the number of victims of the camp as 4 million. Research now indicates that the number of people who died in the Auschwitz/Birkenau gas chambers was between 1.5 and 2 million, of whom 85 to 90 percent were Jews.

and therefore ineligible for inclusion in the curriculum. Smith framed his well-worn denial arguments within this rhetoric, arguing that Holocaust revisionism could not be addressed on campus because "America's thought police" had declared it out of bounds. "The politically correct line on the Holocaust story is, simply, it happened. You don't debate 'it.'" Unlike all other topics students were free to explore, the Holocaust story was off limits. The consequences, he charged, were antithetical to everything for which the university stood. "Ideology replaces free inquiry, intimidation represses open debate, and . . . the ideals of the university itself are exchanged for intellectual taboos." While most students who had to decide whether the ad should be published did not overtly succumb to CODOH's use of the political correctness argument, many proved prone to it, sometimes less than consciously—a susceptibility evident in their justifications for running the ad. Among the first universities to accept the ad were Northwestern, the University of Michigan, Duke, Cornell, Ohio State, and Washington University.[2]

At the University of Michigan the saga of the ad had a strange twist. 8 Smith mailed camera-ready copy directly to the *Michigan Daily*. According to the paper's business manager, the ad "slipped through without being read." When it appeared the business staff was appalled to learn what they had allowed to happen. On the following day they placed a six-column ad in the paper apologizing for running Smith's ad and acknowledging that its publication had been a mistake. They declared it a "sorrowful learning experience for the staff." The manager told the *Detroit Free Press*, "We make mistakes like any organization."

The story might well have ended here—an example of faulty mon- 9 itoring by a segment of the staff of the *Michigan Daily*—but the issue became more complicated when, despite the fact that those responsible for running the ad acknowledged doing so as a mistake, the editorial board attempted to transform a blunder into a matter of principle. They recast a snafu as an expression of freedom of speech. On the same day that the advertising staff published its apology, the front page carried an editorial explaining that, though the editors found the ad "offensive and inaccurate," they could not condone the censorship of "unpopular views from our pages merely because they are offensive or because we disagree with them." Editor in chief Andrew Gottesman acknowledged that had the decision been in his hands, he would have printed the ad. He argued that rejecting it constituted censorship, which the editorial board found unacceptable.

---

[2] The papers discussed in this chapter function as private newspapers. The courts have broadly defined their editorial discretion to accept or reject ads. In situations of "state action," where a state university administration controls the newspaper's content, the courts may prohibit content-based rejection of the ads. *Discretion of Student Editors to Accept or Reject Holocaust Revisionist Advertisements* (ADL Legal Affairs Dept., Feb. 1992).

The following day a campus rally attacked both Holocaust denial [10] and the paper's editorial policies. Stung by student and faculty condemnations and afraid that its editorial was being interpreted as an endorsement of CODOH, the editorial board devoted the next issue's lead editorial to the topic. Condemning Holocaust denial as "absurd" and "founded on historical fiction and anti-Jewish bigotry," they dismissed it as irrational, illogical, and ahistorical propaganda. The editors accurately assessed the ad as lacking intellectual merit. Nonetheless, they continued to support its publication. Their powerful condemnation of Holocaust denial in general and Smith's ad in particular appeared under a banner quoting Supreme Court Justice Hugo Black's opinion on free speech: "My view is, without deviation, without exception, without any ifs, buts, or whereases, that freedom of speech means that you shall not do something to people either for the views they have or the views they express or the words they speak or write."

The strange set of circumstances at Michigan—snatching a consti- [11] tutional principle from the jaws of a mistake—was further complicated by the entry of the university's president, James Duderstadt, into the debate. In a letter to the *Daily* he declared the ad the work of "a warped crank" and proclaimed that denying the Holocaust was to "deny our human potential for evil and to invite its resurgence." But he, too, defended the paper's decision, which was more of a nondecision, to run the ad. The president asserted that the *Daily* had a long history of editorial freedom that had to be protected even when "we disagree either with particular opinions, decisions, or actions." Most disturbing was Duderstadt's elevation of Smith's prejudices to the level of opinions.

There was no doubt about the message the editors and the presi- [12] dent were trying to convey: As absurd, illogical, and bigoted as the ad may be, First Amendment guarantees were paramount. The dictates of the American Constitution compelled the *Daily* to publish. None of those involved seemed to have considered precisely what the First Amendment said: "Congress shall make no law . . . abridging the freedom of speech or of the press." Those who argued that free speech guarantees acceptance of the ad ignored the fact that the First Amendment prevents *government* from interfering in any fashion with an individual's or group's right to publish the most outlandish argument. The *New York Times* made this point in an editorial when it adamantly repudiated the notion that this was a First Amendment question: "Government may not censor Mr. Smith and his fellow 'Holocaust revisionists,' no matter how intellectually barren their claims."

To call rejection of the ad censorship was to ignore the fact that, [13] unlike the government, whose actions are limited by the First Amendment, these papers do not have a monopoly of force. If the government denies someone the right to publish, they have no other option to publish in this country. But if a paper rejects someone's column, ad, or letter, there are always other publications. The First Amendment does not guarantee access to a private publication. It is designed to serve as a shield to protect individuals and institutions from government interference in their affairs. It is not a sword by which every person who makes an outlandish statement or notorious claim can invoke a Constitutional right to be published.[3] Nor did the *Michigan Daily* seem to notice how Justice Black, whom they quoted, framed it: "you shall not do something to people. . . ." No one was advocating "doing" anything to Smith.

One of the most ardent advocates of the free-speech argument was   14 the *Duke Chronicle*. In an editorial column the editor in chief, Ann Heimberger, justified the paper's decision by acknowledging that while the paper knew it could reject the ad, it "chose" to accept it as an expression of the paper's desire to "support the advertiser's rights." The editorial board believed that it was not the paper's responsibility to protect "readers from disturbing ideas," but to "disseminate them."

Echoing his Michigan colleague, Duke University president Keith   15 Brodie repeated the free-speech defense in a statement that, though it contained a strong refutation of the ad, was more vigorous in its support of the *Chronicle's* publication of the ad. To have "suppressed" the ad, he argued, would have violated the university's commitment to free speech and contradicted its "long tradition of supporting First Amendment rights."

When the *Cornell Daily Sun* ran the ad, the editors justified the deci-   16 sion in an editorial statement warning that "page twenty will shock most readers" but proclaimed that it was not the paper's role to "unjustly censor advertisers' viewpoints." Echoing their colleagues on many of the other campuses that printed the ad, the editors declared that they decided to print it because the "First Amendment right to free expression must be extended to those with unpopular or offensive ideas." Neeraj Khemlani, the editor in chief of the *Daily Sun*, said his role was not to "protect" readers. Cornell president Frank H. T. Rhodes joined his colleagues at Duke and Michigan in defending the paper's decision.

The University of Montana's paper, the *Montana Kaimin*, also used   17 the First Amendment to defend its publication of the ad. The editor contended that it was not the paper's place to "decide for the campus community what they should see." The University of Georgia's paper, the *Red and Black*, expressed the hope that publishing the ad would affirm America's unique commitment to "allowing every opinion to be heard, no matter how objectionable, how outright offensive, how clearly wrong that opinion may be." After the ad appeared the paper's editor

---

[3] In 1931, in *Near v. Minnesota*, the Supreme Court struck down a state attempt to gag a paper's freedom to publish "malicious, scandalous or defamatory" material. Fred W. Friendly, *Minnesota Rag* (New York, 1981).

defended the decision by describing it as "a business decision," arguing that "if the business department is set up to take ads, they darn well better take ads." Given the juxtaposition of these two explanations, there was, as Mark Silk, an editorial writer for the *Atlanta Constitution*, pointed out, something dubious about "this high-minded claim."

After an extensive debate Washington University's *Student Life* 18 decided to run the ad. When the ad appeared in the paper, Sam Moyn, the opinion editor, was responsible for conveying to the university community the reasoning behind the staff's "controversial action." The editors, he wrote, conceived of this as a free-speech issue: "The abridgment of Mr. Smith's rights endangers our own." The *St. Louis Post Dispatch* defended the students' actions. Declaring the ad "offensive, provocative and wrong," it praised the student newspaper's courage to print it and stated that its actions strengthened the cause of freedom of speech. The University of Arizona also depicted its actions as protecting the First Amendment. The editor in chief, Beth Silver, proclaimed that the mission of student newspapers is "to uphold the First Amendment and run things that are obviously going to be controversial and take the heat for it." This attitude—we have to do what is right irrespective of the costs—was voiced by a number of papers. Ironically, it echoed a theme frequently voiced by the deniers themselves: We will tell the truth, the consequences notwithstanding.

At Ohio State University the decision-making process was com- 19 plex. The *Lantern's* advertising policy is in the hands of a publications committee comprising faculty, students, editorial board members, and the paper's business manager. University policy requires committee approval before acceptance of an ad designating a religious group. The committee voiced five to four to reject CODOH's submission. But the story did not end there. Enjoined by the committee's decision from running the ad, the *Lantern's* editor, Samantha G. Haney, used her editorial powers to run it as an op-ed piece, explaining that the paper had an "obligation" to do so. This decision gave Smith added legitimacy and saved him the $1,134 it would have cost to place a full-page ad in the paper.

A lengthy editorial explaining the *Lantern's* decision condemned 20 Bradley Smith and his cohorts as "racists, pure and simple" and the ad as "little more than a commercial for hatred." Nonetheless the newspaper had to publish it because it could not only "run things that were harmless to everyone." Haney and her staff rejected the suggestion that they turn to the Ohio State History Department to "pick apart" the ad fact by fact. That, they explained, might suggest that the ad had some "relevancy" and some "substance," which they were convinced it did not. Given that one of the rationales the *Lantern* offered for publishing the article was that "truth will always outshine any lie," its refusal to ask professional historians to elucidate how the ad convoluted historical fact seemed self-defeating. It seemed to reflect an understandable reluctance to accord denial legitimacy. There is no better example of the fragility of reason than the conclusion by these editorial boards that it was their obligation to run an ad or an op-ed column that, according to their *own* evaluation, was totally lacking in relevance or substance.

In contrast to the position adopted by James Duderstadt at the 21 University of Michigan, Ohio State's president, Gordon Gee, attacked the decision to give Smith space in the newspaper, declaring the deniers' arguments "pernicious" and "cleverly disguised" propaganda that enhanced prejudice and distorted history.

When this issue was being debated at Ohio State, a CBS reporter 22 came to that campus to film a segment on Holocaust denial for a network show on hatred and extremism in the United States. Alerted in advance to the pending controversy, the cameras were conveniently present when the editor received a call from Smith congratulating her for running the ad and standing up for the principles of free speech and free press. When Haney hung up, the television reporter, who was standing nearby, asked how she felt. She turned and somewhat plaintively observed that she thought she had been had.

Not all the papers subscribed to the First Amendment argument; 23 indeed, some explicitly rejected it. The University of Tennessee's *Daily Beacon* dismissed the idea that not running the ad harmed the deniers' interests: It was not "censorship or even damaging." Pennsylvania State University's *Daily Collegian*, which had been one of the first to receive an ad from Smith, denied that the issue was one of free speech. After seeing student leaders and numerous individuals on campus inundated with material by deniers, the paper reasoned that those behind the ad had sufficient funds to propagate their conspiracy theory of Jewish control without being granted space in the paper.

In an eloquent editorial the *Harvard Crimson* repudiated Smith's 24 claim to a free-speech right to publish his ad. To give CODOH a forum so that it could "promulgate malicious falsehoods" under the guise of open debate constituted an "abdication" of the paper's editorial responsibility. The University of Chicago *Maroon* agreed that while the deniers "may express their views," it had "no obligation at any time to print their offensive hatred."

The argument that not publishing the ad constituted censorship 25 was not only a misinterpretation of the First Amendment but disingenuous. The editorial boards that reached this decision ignored the fact that they all had policies that prevented them from running racist, sexist, prejudicial, or religiously offensive ads. (Some of the papers in question even refuse cigarette ads.) How could they square their "principled" stand for absolute freedom of speech with policies that prevented them from publishing a range of ads and articles? Why was Bradley Smith entitled to constitutional protection while an ad for an

X-rated movie, *Playboy*, the KKK, or Marlboros was not? Recognizing this inconsistency, some of the boards tried to reconcile these two seemingly contradictory positions by adopting a stance that drew them even further into the deniers' trap. They argued that Holocaust denial was not antisemitic and therefore not offensive. The *Cornell Daily Sun* editorial board determined that the "ad does not directly contain racist statements about Jewish people." Valerie Nicolette, the *Sun's* managing editor, told the *Chronicle of Higher Education* that the editors had evaluated the ad based on their standards of "obscenity and racism" and decided that it passed. When a group of Jewish students at Duke met with the editorial board of the *Duke Chronicle* to protest the running of the ad, they were told that the paper's policy was not to run any ad that was "racist or contained ethnic slurs" but that this ad did not fall into that category.

Andrew Gottesman, who vigorously argued that he could not condone "censorship" of Smith's advertisement and whose *Michigan Daily* published its ringing denunciation of Holocaust denial under Justice Hugo Black's interpretation of the First Amendment, admitted that there were ads he would not run in the paper. This ad, however, did not deserve to be "banned from the marketplace of ideas, like others might be." Among those he would ban were a Ku Klux Klan announcement of lynching or a beer ad with a woman holding a beer bottle between her breasts. For Gottesman keeping such sexist and racist ads out of the paper would not constitute censorship; keeping Smith's out would. When Washington University's *Student Life* published the ad, an editorial explained that it did so in the interest of preventing "freedom of ideas from disappearing from its newspapers." Yet the same paper includes the following policy statement on its advertising rate card: "*Student Life* reserves the right to edit or reject any advertisement which does not comply with the policies or judgment of the newspaper."

The claim that the rejection of the ad constituted censorship also revealed the failure of editorial staffs and, in certain cases, university presidents to think carefully about what their papers did regularly: pick and choose between subjects they covered and those they did not, columns they ran and those they rejected, and ads that met their standards and those that did not. The *Daily Tar Heel*, the paper of the University of North Carolina, proclaimed that as soon as an editor "takes the first dangerous step and decides that an ad should not run because of its content, that editor begins the plunge down a slippery slope toward the abolition of free speech." What the *Tar Heel* failed to note was that newspapers continuously make such choices. As Tom Teepen, the editor of the *Atlanta Constitution's* editorial page, observed, "Running a newspaper is mainly about making decisions, not about ducking them." In fact the *Duke Chronicle*, whose editor had wondered how newspapers founded on the principles of free speech and free press could "deny those rights to anyone," had earlier rejected an insert for *Playboy* and an ad attacking a fraternity.

While some papers justified their decision by arguing that the ad   28
was not antisemitic and others leaned on the censorship argument, an even more disconcerting rationale was offered by many papers. They argued that however ugly or repellent Smith's "ideas," they had a certain intellectual legitimacy. Consequently it was the papers' responsibility to present these views to readers for their consideration. Those editors who made this argument fell prey to denial's attempt to present itself as part of the normal range of historical interpretation. That they had been deceived was evident in the way they described the contents of the ad. The editor in chief of the *Cornell Daily Sun* described the ad as containing "offensive *ideas*." The *Sun* argued that it was not the paper's role to "unjustly censor advertisers' *viewpoints*," however "unpopular or offensive." In a similar vein the *University of Washington Daily* defended giving Smith op-ed space because the paper must constitute a "forum for diverse *opinions* and *ideas*." Ironically, six weeks earlier, when it rejected the ad, it had described Smith's assertions as "so obviously false as to be unworthy of serious debate." The paper insisted that the op-ed column it eventually published was different because it was Smith's "opinion" and did not contain the "blatant falsehoods" of the ad. In the column Smith asserted that for more than twelve years he has been unable to find "one bit of hard evidence" to prove that there was a plan to "exterminate" the Jews, and that the gas-chamber "stories" were "allegations" unsupported by "documentation or physical evidence."

The *Michigan Daily* engaged in the same reasoning. It would not   29
censor "unpopular *views*" simply because readers might disagree with them. In a show of consistency, two weeks after Smith's ad appeared, the *Daily* supported the decision by Prodigy, the computer bulletin board, to allow subscribers to post Holocaust denial material. Prodigy, they contended, was similar to a newspaper, and like a newspaper it must be a *"forum for ideas."* In another suggestion that Smith's views were worthy of debate, the editor in chief of the *Montana Kaimin* argued that "this man's *opinions*, no matter how ridiculous they may be, need to be heard out there." According to the editor in chief of Washington University's *Student Life*, the board voted to run the ad because "we didn't feel comfortable censoring offensive *ideas*."

The *Ohio State Lantern*'s explanation of why it let Smith have his   30
"public say" despite the fact that it condemned Smith and CODOH as "racist, pure and simple," was more disturbing than the decision itself. The *Lantern* argued that it was "repulsive to think that the quality, or total lack thereof, of any idea or opinion has any bearing on whether it should be heard." It is breathtaking that students at a major university could declare repulsive the making of a decision based on the "quality" of ideas. One assumes that their entire education is geared toward the

exploration of ideas with a certain lasting quality. This kind of reasoning essentially contravenes all that an institution of higher learning is supposed to profess.

The editors of Washington University's *Student Life* demonstrated a   31 similar disturbing inconsistency. They dismissed Smith's claim to be engaged in a quest for the truth, describing him as someone who "cloaks hate in the garb of intellectual detachment." They believed that Smith was posing as a "truth seeker crushed by a conspiratorial society." Given their evaluation of Smith, his tactics, and the way conspiracy theorists have captured the imagination of much of American society, what followed was particularly disconcerting. Notwithstanding all their misgivings, the editors decided that they must give "Mr. Smith the benefit of the doubt if we mean to preserve our own rights." In an assertion typical of the confused reasoning that student papers nationwide displayed on this issue, the *Student Life* editors acknowledged that they could have suppressed Smith's views "if we attributed motives to him that contradict his statements. But we cannot in good conscience tell Mr. Smith that we 'know' him and his true intentions." Was not the fact that he was denying a historical fact about whose existence there is no debate among any reputable scholars indicative of something significant? The editorial board had concluded that "if we refused Mr. Smith's advertisement, we could censor anyone based on ulterior motives that we perceive them to harbor." At what point would the board feel it was appropriate to make a decision based on the objective merits of the information contained in the ad?

In this instance what the paper considered to be ulterior motives is   32 what scholars call coming to a conclusion based on a wide variety of facts, including historical data. In giving Smith the "benefit of the doubt," the editors fell prey to the notion that this was a rational debate. They ignored the fact that the ad contained claims that completely contravened a massive body of fact. They transformed what the *Harvard Crimson* described as "vicious propaganda" into iconoclasm.

The most controversial interpretation about precisely what this ad   33 represented was expressed by the *Duke Chronicle*. In a column justifying the paper's decision to run the ad, Ann Heimberger contended that "Revisionists are . . . reinterpreting history, a practice that occurs constantly, especially on a college campus." In a private meeting with Jewish student leaders on the Duke campus, the editors reiterated this argument. The students were told that the ad was neither racist nor antisemitic but was part of an ongoing "scholarly debate." The Duke editorial board viewed the advertisement more as "a political argument than as an ethnic attack." In editorials, articles, and interviews, those at the helm of the *Duke Chronicle* repeatedly referred to Holocaust denial as "radical, unpopular *views*," and "disturbing *ideas*" and argued that the ad was not a "slur" but an "*opinion.*" By doing so they not only clung to their First Amendment defense, they gave the ad historical and intellectual legitimacy. . . .

There were, of course, those college newspapers that had no problem evaluating the ad's intellectual value. The *Harvard Crimson* repudiated the idea that the ad was a "controversial argument based on questionable facts." In one of the most unequivocal evaluations of the ad, the *Crimson* declared it "vicious propaganda based on utter bullshit that has been discredited time and time again." More than "moronic and false," it was an attempt to "propagate hatred against Jews." The editorial board of the University of Pennsylvania's *Daily Pennsylvanian* argued that "running an ad with factual errors that fostered hate" was not in the best interests of the paper.

The *MIT Tech* simply decided that it would not accept an ad that it knew "did not tell the truth." For the *Brown Daily Herald* the ad was "a pack of vicious, antisemitic lies" parading as "history and scholarship." The *Daily Nexus*, the publication of the University of California at Santa Barbara, refused the ad because of its "blatant distortions of truth and its offensive nature." The paper described receiving the ad itself and the more than one thousand dollars to print it as "chilling." The *Dartmouth Review*, no stranger to controversy, also rejected the ad. It acknowledged that by so doing it was denying "someone a forum through which to speak to the paper's readership" but explained that it had a "bond of trust" with the public, which expected it to abide by "standards of accuracy and decency." Accepting an ad "motivated by hatred and informed by total disregard to the truth" would be to violate that trust. The *Chicago Maroon* saw no reason why it should run an ad whose "only objective is to offend and incite hatred." The *Yale Daily News* "simply" let Smith know that it found the ad "offensive."

Some of the papers that ran the ad did so on the basis of what may be called the light-of-day defense, a corollary of the free-speech argument: In the light of day truth always prevails over lies. Neeraj Khemlani of the *Cornell Sun* believed that by running the ad he had done the Jewish people a favor—reminding them that there were a "lot of people out to get [them]," which was something they needed to know. This attitude is reminiscent of the concept of "saving" the Jews (or women, African Americans, or any other potentially vulnerable group) despite themselves. Michael Gaviser, business manager of the *Daily Pennsylvanian*, decided to run the ad because of his belief that Smith was a "dangerous neo-Nazi" of whom the public had to be aware. (His decision was reversed by the editorial board.)

This assault on the ivory tower of academe illustrated how Holocaust denial can permeate that segment of the population that should be most immune to it. It was naive to believe that the "light of day" can dispel lies, especially when they play on familiar stereotypes. Victims of racism, sexism, antisemitism, and a host of other prejudices know of light's limited ability to discredit falsehood. Light is barely an antidote when people are unable, as was often the case in this investigation, to differentiate between reasoned arguments and blatant falsehoods. Most sobering was the failure of many of these student leaders and opinion makers to recognize Holocaust denial for what it was. This was particularly evident among those who argued that the ad contained ideas, however odious, worthy of discussion. This failure suggests that correctly cast and properly camouflaged, Holocaust denial has a good chance of finding a foothold among coming generations.

This chapter ends where it began. Given the fact that even the [38] papers that printed the ad dismissed Smith's claims in the most derogatory of terms—absurd, irrational, racist, and a commercial for hatred—one might argue that the entire affair had a positive outcome. Rarely did the ad appear without an editorial or article castigating Holocaust denial. Students were alerted to a clear and present danger that can easily take root in their midst. Courses on the Holocaust increased in number. One could argue that all this is proof that CODOH's attempt to make Holocaust denial credible backfired.

My assessment is far more pessimistic. It is probably the one issue [39] about which I find myself in agreement with Bradley Smith. Many students read both the ad and the editorials condemning it. Some, including those who read neither but knew of the issue, may have walked away from the controversy convinced that there are two sides to this debate: the "revisionists" and the "establishment historians." They may know that there is tremendous controversy about the former. They may not be convinced that the two sides are of equal validity. They may even know that the deniers keep questionable company. But nonetheless they assume there *is* an "other side." That is the most frightening aspect of this entire matter.

Responding to Reading

1. Do you believe the college newspapers Lipstadt discusses had a responsibility to publish the ad that called the Holocaust a hoax, or do you believe they had the right (or even the responsibility) *not* to publish it? Explain your position. Do you see any possibility of compromise—for example, publishing the ad along with a detailed opposing viewpoint?

2. Holocaust scholar Raul Hilberg has criticized Lipstadt for writing her book, arguing that it gives the Holocaust deniers valuable publicity. Do you think this criticism of Lipstadt is valid? How would Lawrence Krauss (p. 808) respond to this objection?

3. Regardless of the legal definition of *free speech*, do you believe that all viewpoints should be allowed to reach an audience? Or do you think some ideas

are so inaccurate, morally repugnant, or dangerous that they do not deserve to be heard? What specific views, if any, do you believe should *not* be aired?

Widening the Focus

- Dinesh D'Souza, "Sins of Admission" (p. 472)
- Deborah Tannen, "The Triumph of the Yell" (p. 276)
- Wendy Kaminer, "Testifying: Television" (p. 332)
- Barbara Grizutti Harrison, "Getting Away with Murder" (p. 531)

WRITING

Making Choices

1. What moral and ethical rules govern your behavior? Considering the rules Carl Sagan discusses in "The Rules of the Game" as well as the ethical guidelines set forth by several other writers in this chapter, define and explain your own personal moral code.

2. The question of whether or not to act to end another's suffering—possibly at one's own expense—is explored, implicitly or explicitly, in both "The Deer at Providencia" by Annie Dillard and "Shooting an Elephant" by George Orwell. What are your own feelings about this issue? You may also consider ideas explored in the essays by Lawrence J. Schneiderman, Jack Kevorkian, or Stephen L. Carter in Chapter 8.

3. Henry David Thoreau says, "Unjust laws exist: shall we be content to obey them, or shall we endeavor to amend them, and obey them until we have succeeded, or shall we transgress them at once?" (17). Choose a law or practice that you consider unjust, and write an essay in which you tell why you believe it should be disobeyed. Use ideas from Thoreau's essay to support your points.

4. Is all life equally valuable? Explain your position on this issue, considering the ideas raised by Garrett Hardin and by Anna Mae Halgrim Seaver in Chapter 8.

5. Stanley Milgram believes that his study illustrates Hannah Arendt's controversial theory, showing that "ordinary people, simply doing their jobs, and without any particular hostility on their part, can become agents in a terrible destructive process" (39). Cite examples from your own experience to support his conclusion.

6. Martin Luther King Jr., Milgram, and Thoreau all consider the difficulties of resisting majority rule, standing up to authority, and protesting against established rules and laws. Did you ever submit to authority even though you thought you should not have? Write an essay in which you describe your experience. What were the consequences of your act? (Or, describe a time when you stood up to authority. What motivated you? Was your resistance successful? Would you do the same thing again?) Be sure you draw a conclusion from your experience, and state this conclusion as your thesis.

7. What do you believe we gain and lose by using animals in scientific research? Do you believe this practice should be continued? If so, with which animals? Under what circumstances? If not, why not? What alternative do you propose? Reread Claire McCarthy's "Dog Lab" and Annie Dillard's "The Deer at Providencia" before you begin your essay.

8. The writers represented in this chapter present some pessimistic scenarios. For example, Hardin sees an overpopulated, underfed world, and King sees a world corrupted by prejudice. What world problems are you most pessimistic about? Why? What do you believe must be done to solve these problems?

9. Which of the two roads identified in Robert Frost's "The Road Not Taken" have you chosen? In what sense has that choice "made all the difference"?

10. How free should speech on your campus be? After reading Deborah Lipstadt's "Denying the Holocaust," write an editorial for your school newspaper in which you discuss the kinds of statements that should be censored and explain why. If you believe no ideas should be censored, support that position. In planning your essay, you may also consider ideas raised by Lawrence Krauss in "Equal Time for Nonsense."

Credits

Index of Authors and Titles